KU-241-416

HUMAN RIGHTS AND CRIMINAL JUSTICE

First Edition

by

Ben Emmerson Q.C.
of the Middle Temple, Barrister
and
Andrew Ashworth Q.C. (Hon.)
Vinerian Professor of English Law
University of Oxford

EDITORIAL ASSISTANT
Natasha Tahta
of Inner Temple, Barrister

LONDON
SWEET & MAXWELL
2001

Published in 2001 by
Sweet & Maxwell Limited of
100 Avenue Road, Swiss Cottage, London NW3 3PF
(*http://www.sweetandmaxwell.co.uk*)
Typeset by Interactive Sciences Ltd, Gloucester
Printed and bound in Great Britain by MPG Books Ltd, Bodmin, Cornwall

No natural forests were destroyed to make this product;
only farmed timber was used and replanted.

ISBN 0421 639 105

A catalogue record for this book
is available from the British Library

All right reserved, Crown Copyright legislation is reproduced under the
terms of Crown Copyright Policy Guidance issued by HMSO.

No part of this publication may be reproduced or transmitted, in any
form or by any means, electronic, mechanical, photocopying, recording or otherwise,
or stored in any retrieval system of any nature without the written permission of the
copyright holder and the publisher, application for which shall be made to the
publisher.

Learning Resources
Centre

1220481 1

©
Ben Emmerson Q.C. & Andrew Ashworth Q.C.
2001

FOREWORD

The aim of this book is to examine in detail the impact of European human rights law on the criminal justice system in England and Wales. Its origins lie in the work carried out by the authors for the Judicial Studies Board and the Law Commission in the period prior to the coming into force of the Human Rights Act 1998. The Act has now been in operation for nine months. It is still too early to draw firm conclusions about the emerging body of domestic human rights law. Nonetheless, it is possible to identify some important themes in the decisions of the English and Scottish courts. The House of Lords and the Privy Council have fashioned a domestic response to the concept of proportionality. They have established a reasonably clear standard of constitutional review, emphasising that the courts must apply the searching scrutiny required under the Convention, whilst allowing for a "discretionary area of judgment" in assessing the choices which Parliament has made on issues of social and moral policy. So far as the right to a fair trial is concerned, they have adopted the Strasbourg approach of assessing the fairness of the proceedings as a whole, whilst recognising the important principle that a breach of Article 6 will, almost inevitably, result in the quashing of a criminal conviction as "unsafe". They have considered the implications of the presumption of innocence in Article 6(2) for statutory reverse onus offences, and they have attempted to make sense of the confusing jurisprudence on the protection against self-incrimination. They have grappled (and continue to grapple) with the concept of retrospectivity under the Human Rights Act 1998, and with the weight to be attached to Strasbourg decisions which do not fit easily with English legal traditions. They have started to explore the creative potential of section 3 of the Act, recognising that it will sometimes be "possible" to adopt a strained or artificial construction of primary legislation, or to imply additional safeguards into an Act, in order to massage it into compliance with Convention rights. They have begun to redraw the boundaries between "civil", "administrative" and "criminal" proceedings for the purposes of Article 6 and they have conducted a limited exploration of the relationship between the breach of a constitutional right and the exclusion of evidence obtained as a result. Not everyone will agree with the judges' assessments of these issues. But the policy reasons which underpin their decisions are at least open to public scrutiny.

We have endeavoured to state the law as at July 5, 2001. We would like to express our thanks to Natasha Tahta, Adrian Marshall-Williams and Joanne Sawyer who assisted in the research and editing, to Tim Owen Q.C., Anthony Jennings Q.C., Danny Friedan and Keir Starmer, with whom we have discussed a number of the issues in the book and, above all, to Anne Shamash who has offered invaluable support throughout the process in her own inimitable way.

CONTENTS

PART ONE

CONTENTS

PART TWO

CONTENTS

APPENDICES

INDEX

TABLE OF U.K. CASES

TABLE OF U.K. STATUTES

[xli]

TABLE OF STATUTORY INSTRUMENTS

TABLE OF RULES

TABLE OF ECHR AND E.U. CASES

[lxi]

[lxv]

Part One

CHAPTER 1

THE EUROPEAN CONVENTION ON HUMAN RIGHTS

A. INTRODUCTION

The European Convention for the Protection of Human Rights and Fundamental **1–01**
Freedoms[1] is an international treaty adopted by the Member States of the Council
of Europe and opened for signature in November 1950. The Convention was
ratified by the United Kingdom in March 1951, and entered into force in
September 1953. A state's obligations are defined by the Convention itself, read
together with those optional Protocols which the state has chosen to ratify[2] but
subject to any reservations[3] or derogations[4] which have been notified to the
Secretary General of the Council of Europe.

Any person, non-governmental organisation or group of individuals situated **1–02**
within the jurisdiction of a contracting state has a right of individual petition to
the European Court of Human Rights under Article 34 of the Convention. This
extends to legal as well as natural persons, and is not confined to those with a
lawful right to be present in the territory of the state concerned.[5] Before submitting a petition the applicant must first exhaust any effective or potentially
effective domestic remedies.[6] The petition must be filed within six months of the
date of the violation, or the date of the final domestic remedy touching on the
subject matter of the complaint.[7]

A decision of the Court is final and binding.[8] Although the Court does not have **1–03**
jurisdiction to quash the decisions of a national authority, or to overturn a
criminal conviction, its judgments are more than merely declaratory in nature.
Under Article 41 of the Convention the Court has power to award "just satisfaction" to the victim of a violation in the form of compensation for pecuniary and
non-pecuniary loss, and to make a full award of costs. More importantly, the
contracting states are under an obligation to "abide by the decision of the Court
in any case to which they are parties".[9] This obligation is enforceable by the

---

[1] Cmnd. 8969.
[2] The United Kingdom has ratified Protocol 1, containing the right to property (Art. 1), the right to
education (Art. 2), and the duty to hold free elections (Art. 3); and Protocol 6 containing the
permanent abolition of the death penalty. The Government has indicated its intention to sign, ratify
and incorporate Protocol 7 containing safeguards relating to the expulsion of aliens (Art. 1), a right
of appeal in criminal cases (Art. 2), a right to compensation for miscarriages of justice (Art. 3), the
prohibition on double jeopardy (Art. 4), and the right to equality between spouses (Art. 5).
[3] See para. 1–161 below.
[4] See para. 1–164 below.
[5] *D. v. United Kingdom* (1997) 24 E.H.R.R. 423.
[6] Article 35(1).
[7] Article 35(1).
[8] Article 46(1).
[9] Formerly Art. 53.

Committee of Ministers of the Council of Europe which has the task of "supervising the execution" of the Court's judgments.[10]

B. ORIGINS AND INFLUENCE[11]

I. *The Universal Declaration of Human Rights*

1–04   In the immediate aftermath of the Second World War the international community entered a phase of intense diplomatic activity aimed at establishing intergovernmental structures which could prevent a recurrence of the atrocities of the previous decade and, at the same time, forge new political alliances for the postwar era. On June 26, 1945 the United Nations Charter was signed in San Francisco. A Human Rights Commission was established by the United Nations to begin work on proposals for an International Bill of Rights. The early results looked promising. The Universal Declaration of Human Rights was adopted by the General Assembly of the United Nations on December 10, 1948. Shortly afterwards, however, attempts to create a legally enforceable system of international human rights protection within the United Nations ran into the buffer of diplomatic procrastination. The two United Nations covenants[12] defining the rights outlined in the Universal Declaration, and establishing international machinery for their enforcement, were not concluded until December 1966 and did not come into force for a further 10 years.

II. *The Council of Europe*

1–05   In Europe meanwhile the movement for greater political integration was gathering momentum. Unofficial European movements sprang up in a number of western European countries.[13] In 1948 these organisations united, at the Congress of Europe in the Hague, to form the European Movement which was to act as a permanent but unofficial organisation to promote European unity. The Congress passed a number of resolutions around which the Council of Europe was subsequently constructed. Its international juridical section, which included Sir David Maxwell-Fyfe,[14] set about producing a draft human rights convention which would stand as a condition of entry to the new unified Europe.

1–06   Intergovernmental action soon followed. In January 1949 the governments of the United Kingdom, France and the three Benelux countries convened a diplomatic

---

[10] In the exercise of their powers under Art. 46(2). See para. 1–159 below; and see generally Adam Tomkins, "The Committee of Ministers; Its roles under the European Convention on Human Rights" [1995] E.H.R.L.R. 49. Note however that the Committee of Ministers' role under Art. 32 of the Convention has been abolished by Protocol 11.

[11] For a comprehensive overview of the history of the Convention see Lester and Pannick (eds), *Human Rights Law and Practice* (Butterworths, 1999) Chapter 1. See also Marston, "The United Kingdom's Part in the Preparation of the European Convention on Human Rights 1950" (1993) 42 I.C.L.Q. 796; Anthony Lester "Fundamental Rights: the United Kingdom Isolated?" (1984) P.L. 46; *Collected Edition of the Travaux Préparatoires of the European Convention on Human Rights.*

[12] The International Covenant on Civil and Political Rights, and the International Covenant on Economic, Social and Cultural Rights.

[13] The principal organisations were the United Europe Movement in Britain; the Economic League for European Cooperation; the French Council for United Europe; the European Union of Federalists; *Nouvelles Équipes Internationales*; and the Socialist Movement for the United States of Europe.

[14] Later Home Secretary and Lord Chancellor Kilmuir.

conference attended by 10 European countries. Germany, which had not yet regained its sovereignty, was excluded. The conference was given the task of drafting a treaty for the establishment of a Council of Europe. In so doing, the 10 governments went a long way towards carrying out the proposals made at the Hague Congress.

The Statute of the Council of Europe was signed in London on May 5, 1949. The **1–07** preamble declared that the contracting states were "reaffirming their devotion to the spiritual and moral values which are the common heritage of their peoples and the true source of individual freedom, political liberty, and the rule of law, principles which form the basis of all genuine democracy". This broad aspiration was reinforced by Article 3 of the Statute which provided that every member state "must accept the principles of the rule of law and of the enjoyment by all persons within its jurisdiction of human rights and fundamental freedoms".

The organs of the Council of Europe included an executive branch, the Commit- **1–08** tee of Ministers, which was made up of the Foreign Minister of each member state or their deputy; and a Parliamentary Assembly (originally known as the Consultative Assembly) consisting of elected members of the national parliaments. One of the Council of Europe's first tasks was to draft a legally binding human rights convention. The Committee of Ministers was asked by the Parliamentary Assembly to draw up a draft convention which would, for the most part, contain more specific defintions of the rights set out in the Universal Declaration of Human Rights, and which would establish a European Court of Human Rights for the purpose of ensuring collective enforcement.

III. *The European Convention on Human Rights*

The European Convention on Human Rights broke new ground in international **1–09** law in three important respects. First, it adopted a principle of collective enforcement of human rights. The signatory states recognised that the most effective way to prevent human rights abuses by public officials was to require states to submit to a form of external scrutiny which encroached on their national sovereignty. The responsibility for protecting human rights was no longer to rest with each state, but was to be a shared responsibility of the international community. Whereas international conventions had hitherto been regarded as reciprocal arrangements between nation states, the European Convention on Human Rights created "a network of mutual, bilateral undertakings, objective obligations which, in the words of the preamble, benefit from a 'collective enforcement' ".[15] In international law, these obligations bind all three branches of government—the Executive, the Legislature and the Judiciary.[16]

---

[15] *Ireland v. United Kingdom* (1979–80) 2 E.H.R.R. 25, para. 239; See also *Austria v. Italy* (1961) 4 Y.B. 116 at 138: "The obligations undertaken by the High Contracting Parties in the Convention are essentially of an objective character, being designed rather to protect the fundamental rights of individual human beings from infringement by any of the High Contracting Parties than to create subjective and reciprocal rights for the High Contracting Parties."
[16] The position in national law is different: The Human Rights Act 1998 does not bind the Legislature so that it will, in some instances, remain possible for an individual's Convention rights to breached by incompatible primary legislation, without an effective remedy being available in the national courts.

1–10   The second important departure from traditional international law was the inclusion of a right of individual petition—a recognition that individuals could have rights enforceable on the international plane. The right of individual petition lies at the heart of the Convention system, and has played a decisive role in its success. It has enabled individuals to seek remedies for human rights violations against the public authorities of their own states across a wide range of issues, and irrespective of whether the violation occurred through governmental or Executive action, through decisions of the elected legislature, or through rulings of the national courts.

1–11   The third important feature of the Convention system was the establishment of supervisory machinery to interpret, apply and enforce the Convention: the European Commission of Human Rights whose function was to determine the admissibility of a complaint, to establish the facts, and to express a non-binding opinion on the merits; the European Court of Human Rights, an independent and public judicial institution with one judge from each member state, whose function was to give a final and binding judgment and, if appropriate, to award just satisfaction in favour of the complainant; and the Committee of Ministers which had the dual functions of supervising the execution of Court judgments, and determining the merits of any complaint which was not considered suitable for reference to the Court.

1–12   Despite these innovative features the Convention was an international treaty, and like any international treaty, it contained the maximum acceptable to the state willing to go least far. That state was the United Kingdom. British diplomats lobbied hard for the right of individual petition to be made optional, and for the jurisdiction of the Commission to be conditional upon regular renewal. Their efforts were successful and the Convention enforcement machinery was weakened as a result. We are often reminded that the United Kingdom was the first state to ratify the Convention, in March 1951. But it is perhaps equally important to remember that the British government did not accept the right of individual petition until January 1966.[17]

IV. *The influence of the Convention*

1–13   The Convention came into force on September 23, 1953, but the Court did not begin functioning until 1959. In the first 15 years of its operation the Court heard an average of one case a year. In some years, it met only once and then only because it was required to do so under the Rules of Court for its plenary administrative session.[18] Since then however, the Court's caseload has grown steadily, due partly to an increasing awareness of its existence among the citizens and lawyers of the member states, and partly to the enlargement of the Council of Europe itself.

---

[17] For a fascinating account of the ministerial and diplomatic negotiations behind this process, see Lord Lester of Herne Hill Q.C., "UK Acceptance of the Strasbourg Jurisdiction: What Really Went On in Whitehall in 1966" [1998] P.L. 327.

[18] Rolv Ryssdall, "The Coming of Age of the European Convention on Human Rights" [1996] E.H.R.L.R. 18 at 20.

The decisions of the European Commission and Court of Human Rights have **1–14** produced a body of caselaw which extends its influence far beyond the parties to the individual case. Whilst a given judgment is only binding on the state concerned, other Convention states will look to the judgment for guidance as to the compatibility of their own domestic law with the requirements of the Convention.[19] In this way, the Convention has become "a constitutional instrument of European public order in the field of human rights".[20] As the former President of the Court has put it, the Convention is now "the single most important legal and political common denominator of the states of Europe in its widest geographical sense".[21]

The influence of the Convention is not however confined to European legal **1–15** systems. It was used as the basis for the human rights chapters in many of the independence constitutions adopted in Commonwealth Africa and the Commonwealth Caribbean. This was partly because British lawyers had played a central role in the drafting of the Convention, and partly because the United Kingdom had extended its obligations under the Convention to its dependent territories in 1953. The Convention was therefore an obvious source of inspiration for the Commonwealth constitutions. Commonwealth courts have come to accept the importance of interpreting equivalent constitutional guarantees in the light of their history and sources and, "whererever applicable, pronouncements on provisions similar to [constitutional human rights provisions] either by national courts or by international institutions".[22] Given that the text of many of these constitutional human rights guarantees is the same or very similar to the Convention, it is hardly surprising that the judgments of the European Court of Human Rights have been cited with approval by the constitutional courts of Canada, New Zealand, South Africa, Hong Kong, India, Zimbabwe and Mauritius, amongst others, and have served as a useful source of guidance for the Privy Council in exercising its constitutional jurisdiction. This cross-fertilization of jurisprudence reflects not only the close relationship of the various texts, but also the universality of the underlying concepts and values.

On the international plane, the European Convention was the model for the **1–16** American Convention on Human Rights, which came into force in 1978, and served as one of the principal reference texts for those drafting the African Convention on Human and Peoples' Rights. The caselaw of the European Court of Human Rights has been extensively relied upon by the institutions established under both of these regional mechanisms. References to Convention caselaw are also to be found in the decisions of the United Nations treaty bodies, including the decisions of the Human Rights Committee on individual applications under the Optional Protocol to the International Covenant on Civil and Political Rights,

---

[19] An example is the Court's judgment in *Brogan v. United Kingdom* (1989) 11 E.H.R.R. 117, following which the Netherlands introduced legislation restricting the time which may elapse between a suspect's arrest and first production in court.

[20] *Chrysostomos, Papachrysostomou and Loizidou v. Turkey* (1991) 68 D.R. 216 at 242.

[21] Rolv Ryssdall, "The Coming of Age of the European Convention on Human Rights" [1996] E.H.R.L.R. 18.

[22] *Pointu and Others v. The Minister of Education and Anor.* (1996) S.C.J. 359, Supreme Court of Mauritius. See generally Vinod Boolel, "The Influence of the European Convention on the Constitutional Law of Mauritius" [1996] E.H.R.L.R. 159.

and in the decisions of the International Criminal Tribunal for the Former Yugoslavia and Rwanda.

1–17 Finally, it should be recalled that the Court itself has given the Convention a measure of extra-territorial effect by holding that decisions to extradite[23] or deport[24] individuals to non-Convention countries where they risk treatment in violation of their Convention rights may engage the responsibility of the expelling state; and by holding that states are obliged to refuse their co-operation in criminal matters where an individual's conviction has resulted from a flagrant denial of justice in a non-Convention state.[25–26]

C. PROCEDURE

I. *Institutional reform*

1–18 By the early 1990's the Convention system had become a victim of its own success. Between 1988 and 1994 the number of applications registered by the Commission trebled from just over 1,000 each year to a little under 3,000. In the first 15 years of its operation, the Court considered an average of one case a year. By 1995 that figure had grown to more than 60 cases a year. The Court took until 1985 to deliver its first 100 judgments. In the 10 years which followed, it delivered 550.

1–19 The growing number of cases meant that it already took an average of five years between the initial lodging of an application by the Commission, and the final determination of a case by the Court or the Committee of Ministers. The two-tier procedure also gave rise to a considerable duplication of effort and expense. With the admission of new member states the position was set to worsen. By the early 1990's it was becoming clear that the machinery would break down under the strain if it was not substantially overhauled. At the same time there was an increasing recognition that the role of the Committee of Ministers, a political body, in adjudicating on certain Convention complaints was anomalous. There was now a general agreement that the system of protection under the Convention should become fully judicial.

1–20 Negotiations began for the adoption of a new Protocol to the Convention which would have the twin objectives of simplifying the structure with a view to shortening the length of proceedings and strengthening the judicial character of the system. These negotiations reached their conclusion when Protocol 11 was opened for signature by the member states on May 11, 1994. Protocol 11 abolished the European Commission of Human Rights and provided for the establishment of a single full-time Court to replace the previous two-tier system. It also abolished the role of the Committee of Ministers in adjudicating on complaints, confining its functions to the supervision of states' compliance with the judgments of the Court.

---

[23] *Soering v. United Kingdom* (1989) 11 E.H.R.R. 439.
[24] *D v. United Kingdom* (1997) 24 E.H.R.R. 423.
[25–26] *Drozd and Janousek v. France and Spain* (1992) 14 E.H.R.R. 745.

Protocol 11 entered into force on November 1, 1998. Whether the new machinery **1–21** will succeed in shortening proceedings in Strasbourg remains to be seen. The new Court inherited a backlog of 6,000 cases. With the disappearance of the Commission in November 1999, there were more than 16,000 cases awaiting determination.

II. *The procedure prior to November 1998*

The former procedure is of more than merely historical interest. Under section **1–22** 2(1) of the Human Rights Act 1998 a domestic court or tribunal determining any question which has arisen in connection with a Convention right is required to take into account not only judgments of the Court but also decisions of the Commission under former Article 26 and 27(2) of the Convention,[27] Commission opinions given in a report adopted under former Article 31, and decisions of the Committee of Ministers under Article 46.[28]

Prior to the coming into force of Protocol 11, it was for the Commission to **1–23** ascertain the facts of the case, and to determine the admissiblity of the application under former Articles 26 and 27. Article 26 embodied the requirement for the prior exhaustion of effective or potentially effective domestic remedies and the requirement that a complaint be introduced within six months of the date of the violation or the conclusion of the last domestic remedy touching on the subject matter of the complaint.[29] Article 27 required the Commission to reject as inadmissible any complaint which was anonymous, which was substantially the same as a complaint previously considered by the Commission or "another procedure of international investigation or settlement", or which the Commission considered to be (a) incompatible with the Convention, (b) manifestly ill-founded or (c) an abuse of the right of petition.[30] Proceedings before the Commission were strictly confidential and Commission hearings took place in private.

Once a case had been declared admissible, the Commission was required to put **1–24** itself at the disposal of the parties with a view to securing a friendly settlement pursuant to former Article 28(1)(b).[31] In the absence of a friendly settlement, the Commission was required to express its opinion on the merits of the complaint in a report adopted under former Article 31. Thereafter, the case could be referred to the Court for a final and binding judgment, either by the Commission or by the government, but not by the applicant.[32] This had to be done within a period of

---

[27] Under Protocol 11 the admissibility criteria which were formerly set out in Arts 26 and 27(2) of the Convention are now embodied in Art. 35(1) and (3).
[28] The references in s.2(1) are apt to confuse since s.2(1)(b) and (c) refer to the *former* Arts 26, 27(2) and 31 of the Convention relating to the functions of the Commission, whereas s.2(1)(c) refers to the function of the Committee of Ministers under Art. 46 of the Convention *as amended by Protocol 11*. Note however that s.21(3) of the 1998 Act provides that for this purpose the reference to Art. 46 is to be taken as including a reference to Arts 32 and 54 of the Convention immediately prior to its amendment (*i.e.* it includes "judicial" decisions of the Committee of Ministers under the old procedure).
[29] These requirements are now to be found in Art. 35(1), see paras 1–46 to 1–70 below.
[30] These admissibility criteria are now contained in Art. 35(2) and (3) and are, of course, determined by the Court; see paras 1–71 to 1–96 below.
[31] This function is now performed by the Court pursuant to Art. 38(1)(b), see para. 1–107 below.
[32] Former Arts 44 and 48.

three months from the adoption of the Commission's report on the case.[33] Protocol 9, which permitted individuals to refer a case from the Commission to the Court was never signed or ratified by the United Kingdom. The Court could only examine those complaints which had been declared admissible by the Commission.

1–25   If neither the Commission, nor the government referred the case to the Court, it was referred for decision by the Committee of Ministers under former Article 32(1). The execution of court judgments was supervised by the Committee of Ministers in the exercise of their powers under former Article 54.[34] Under Protocol 11, the Committee of Ministers' enforcement functions are now to be found in Article 46(2).

1–26   Accordingly, under section 2(1) of the Human Rights Act 1998 domestic courts are required to have regard to (i) Court judgments and (under the new procedure) Court admissibility decisions, (ii) Commission admissibility decisions, (iii) Commission decisions on the merits of a complaint, and (iv) Committee of Ministers' decisions supervising the execution of Court judgments and adjudicating on the merits of a complaint which was not referred to the Court.[35]

III. *The procedure under Protocol 11*

1–27   Protocol 11 to the Convention, which entered into force on November 1, 1998, provides for the establishment of a single full time Court to replace the previous two-tier system. The procedure to be followed in proceedings before the Court is set out in Protocol 11 itself, and in the Rules of Court. The Court has a power to issue practice directions[36] and may depart from the prescribed procedure in a particular case, after first consulting the parties.[37]

1–28   The Court sits in Committees (of three judges), in Chambers (of seven judges) and, exceptionally, in a Grand Chamber (of 17 judges).[38] The President of the European Court of Human Rights is Mr Wildhaber (Switzerland). The Court is divided into four chambers pursuant to Article 27 of the Convention. Mrs Palm (Sweden) is President of the First Chamber; Mr Rozakis (Greece) is President of the Second Chamber; Sir Nicholas Bratza (United Kingdom) is President of the Third Chamber; and Mr Pelonpaa (Finland) is President of the Fourth Chamber. The national judge sits *ex officio* in any case brought against the state in respect of which he was elected,[39] but may not preside in any such case.[40]

---

[33] Former Art. 47.
[34] see para. 1–159 below.
[35] Section 21(3) of the Human Rights Act 1998 provides that the reference in s.2(1)(d) to Art. 46 includes a reference to Arts. 32 and 54 of the Convention immediately prior to its amendment by Protocol 11.
[36] Rules of Court, Rule 32.
[37] Rule 31.
[38] Article 27(1).
[39] Article 27(2).
[40] Rule 13.

Institution of proceedings

An individual application must be submitted in writing and signed by the **1–29**
applicant or his or her representative.[41] Unless the President of the Chamber
decides otherwise, an application must be made on the application form provided
by the Registry.[42] The application must set out the name, date of birth, nationality, sex, occupation and address of the applicant[43]; the name, occupation and
address of his or her representative, if any[44]; the name of the respondent state[45];
a succinct statement of the facts and of the alleged violation of the Convention
and relevant argument[46]; a succinct statement of the applicant's compliance with
the admissibility criteria[47]; and a statement of the object of the application,
including any claims for just satisfaction which the applicant may wish to make
under Article 41.[48] It must accompanied by copies of any documents, including
judgments of the domestic courts, which are relevant.[49]

Legal Representation and Legal Aid

There is no requirement that an applicant must be legally represented for the **1–30**
purposes of the initial submission of an application.[50] However, representation is
mandatory for any oral hearing, and for any written proceedings which take place
after a case has been declared admissible, unless the President of the Chamber
decides otherwise.[51] The applicant's representative must generally be an advocate who is (a) authorised to practice in one of the contracting states *and* (b)
resident in the territory of one of the contracting states.[52] If the applicant wishes
to be represented by someone who does not fulfil these criteria then the specific
approval of the President must be obtained.[53] Either way, a signed power of
attorney or authority to act must be supplied to the Registry.[54] In exceptional
cases, the President may direct the applicant to seek alternative representation if
he considers that the circumstances or conduct of the advocate warrant this
course.[55]

Legal aid is not available for the initial preparation or submission of an applica- **1–31**
tion. However, once an application has been communicated to the respondent
government, the President of the Chamber may grant Council of Europe legal aid
to the applicant for all subsequent stages in the proceedings,[56] if it is necessary
for the proper conduct of the case, and the applicant has insufficient means to

---

[41] Rule 45(1).
[42] Rule 47(1).
[43] Rule 47(1)(a).
[44] Rule 47(1)(b).
[45] Rule 47(1)(c).
[46] Rule 47(1)(d) and (e).
[47] Rule 47(1)(f).
[48] Rule 47(1)(g).
[49] Rule 47(1)(h).
[50] Rule 36(1).
[51] Rule 36(3). If the President gives the applicant leave to present his or her own case, this may be
made subject to a requirement that the applicant be assisted by an advocate or other approved
representative.
[52] Rule 36(4)(a).
[53] Rule 36(4)(a).
[54] Rule 45(3).
[55] Rule 36(4)(c). Such a direction may be made at any stage of the proceedings.
[56] Rule 91.

meet all or part of the costs entailed.[57] Any case which has been communicated to the respondent government will, almost by definition, satisfy the first of these requirements. As to the second requirement, an application for legal aid must be accompanied by a form declaring the applicant's capital, income, and financial obligations, duly certified (where appropriate) by the relevant domestic authorities.[58] The relevant domestic authority in the United Kingdom is the Department of Social Security. The Court does not, however, apply the national threshold for eligibility, and may be willing to grant legal aid where the applicant's means would not qualify on domestic scales.[59] The decision to grant or refuse legal aid is to be made by the President[60] after the government has been afforded an opportunity to submit any comments in writing.[61] The Registrar will then fix the rate of fees and expenses to be paid in accordance with the scales currently in force.[62]

1–32   Council of Europe legal aid encompasses legal fees and any other costs or expenses necessarily incurred in pursuing the application.[63–64] The rates are not generous compared with the scale of fees charged by lawyers in the United Kingdom. However, the professional rules of both branches of the legal profession allow conditional fee agreements to be made in respect of litigation in Strasbourg. In the event of a finding of a violation, the Court will generally award costs in favour of the applicant on an equitable basis.[65] Any sums already paid in legal aid will be deducted from the Court's award of costs.[66]

Interim Measures

1–33   Under Rule 39[67] the Chamber or, in an urgent case, its President may indicate to the respondent government any interim measures which it considers should be adopted in the interests of the parties or of the proper conduct of the proceedings before it.[68] Such an indication may be given either at the request of the applicant, or by the Court of its own motion. The procedure is designed primarily to ensure that once the Court is seized of a complaint, the respondent state does not take steps which would deprive any subsequent finding of a violation of its practical effect.

1–34   An application for interim relief must be made promptly, and must be accompanied by a statement of the facts, and an outline of the applicant's complaint

---

[57] Rule 92.

[58] Rule 93.

[59] The Court recognises that the costs of pursuing a claim to Strasbourg are likely to be prohibitive for a person of modest means, and that where a serious human rights claim is in issue, it is in the public interest to enable it to be heard: Karen Reid, *A Practitioner's Guide to the European Convention on Human Rights* (Sweet & Maxwell, 1998). The income of spouses or family members will only be taken into account if their level of means is significant and the person concerned can reasonably be expected to contribute.

[60] Rule 93(3).

[61] Rule 93(2).

[62] Rule 95.

[63–64] Rule 94(2).

[65] See para. 1–147 below.

[66] This is standard procedure for all successful legally aided applications.

[67] Formerly, rule 36.

[68] Rule 39(1).

under the Convention. Rule 39 may not be invoked if the applicant is still in the process of exhausting a potentially effective domestic remedy, unless the remedy is incapable of having suspensive effect. Subject to these requirements, an application can be dealt with very speedily indeed, and sometimes within a matter of hours.[69] A Rule 39 indication will usually be made for a limited but renewable period. If the Court declines to give such an indication, it may nevertheless take urgent steps to communicate the complaint to the government concerned, and may expedite the hearing of the application.[70]

The Court will only grant interim relief if it considers that there is a real risk of **1–35** irreparable harm to the applicant, and there is "good reason to believe" that a violation will eventually be found.[71] Interim measures have generally been confined to expulsion cases (deportation or extradition), where it is alleged that the applicant will be killed or will suffer ill-treatment in breach of Articles 2 or 3 of the Convention. In *Soering v. United Kingdom*[72] the applicant complained that his extradition to the United States to face trial for murder would expose him to prolonged detention on "death row" in breach of Article 3. The President indicated to the government that "it was desirable, in the interests of the parties and the proper conduct of the proceedings, not to extradite the applicant to the United States until the Court had an opportunity to examine the application". It is not however always necessary for the applicant to establish a risk of intentional ill-treatment. Serious health risks may sometimes suffice. In *Poku v. United Kingdom*[73] a request was made in respect the proposed deportation of a woman who was in the late stages of a difficult pregnancy and who had a history of miscarriages. Likewise, in *D v. United Kingdom*[74] a request for suspension was made in respect of an applicant who was suffering from AIDS, and who alleged that he would be deprived of treatment if he were deported to St Kitts.

The Court has generally been unwilling to grant interim relief in relation to **1–36** detention or fair trial issues. There are, however, exceptions. In *Llijkov v. Bulgaria*[75] a request was made concerning measures to protect the health of a prisoner on hunger strike. And in *Ocalan v. Turkey*[76] the Court took the unusual course of requesting assurances that the leader of the Kurdish separatist movement (PKK) would receive adequate facilities to ensure that his trial for alleged terrorist offences was fair.[77]

Where a Rule 39 indication has been given, the Chamber will notify the **1–37** Committee of Ministers[78] and may request information from the respondent

---

[69] For a thorough explanation of the procedure, and a precedent letter of application, see Clements, Mole and Simmons, *European Human Rights: Taking a Case under the Convention* (Sweet & Maxwell, 1999), pp 59–62 and pp 343–345.
[70] Rule 40; see para. 1–43 below.
[71] *Cruz Varas v. Sweden* (1992) 14 E.H.R.R. 1 at para. 103.
[72] (1989) 11 E.H.R.R. 439.
[73] (1996) Application No. 26985/95.
[74] (1997) 24 E.H.R.R. 243.
[75] (1997) Application No. 33977/96.
[76] Unreported, 1999.
[77] It was doubtless significant in this case that the applicant faced the death penalty if convicted.
[78] Rule 39(2).

state.[79] Such an indication is not, however, binding on the government concerned.[80] The Court relies on the goodwill and co-operation of the contracting states.[81] Although states have almost invariably complied with such requests, the Court has held that this does not give rise to an enforceable expectation of compliance. In *Cruz Varas v. Sweden*[82] the applicant was expelled to Chile, despite a Rule 39 indication requesting suspension of the deportation order. The applicant argued that the action of the Swedish authorities was an interference with the right of individual petition, in breach of Article 34.[83] He submitted that the history of state compliance with requests for interim measures had acquired the status of a settled practice which affected the interpretation of the Convention. The Court, by a narrow majority, held that subsequent practice "cannot create new rights and obligations which were not included in the Convention at the outset". Compliance with a Rule 39 indication lay at the discretion of the contracting state. The Court nevertheless pointed out that a state which fails to comply with such a request "knowingly assumes the risk of being found in breach of Article 3". Accordingly, "where the state has had its attention drawn in this way to the dangers of prejudicing the outcome of the issue . . . any such finding would have to be seen as aggravated by the failure to comply with the indication".[84]

1–38   There have been a number of unsuccessful attempts to create a legally enforceable system of interim relief within the Council of Europe.[85] When Protocol 11 was adopted there was considerable debate as to whether the *Cruz Varas* principle should be overturned. In the end, however, there was insufficient consensus on the point to achieve an amendment to the Convention.

Preliminary Consideration

1–39   Once a case is registered, a judge rapporteur will be assigned to it by the relevant Chamber[86] and will prepare a confidential report on the case summarising the facts and issues, and making a provisional proposal on the admissibility and, if appropriate the merits of the complaint.[87] The rapporteur may refer the case to a Committee which may, by unanimous vote, declare a case inadmissible or strike it off the list if it considers that further examination of the application is

---

[79] Rule 39(3).
[80] This is to be contrasted with the position under other international treaties: see, for example, Art. 63 of the American Convention on Human Rights. In *Thomas and Hilaire v. Baptiste* [1999] 3 W.L.R. 249 the Privy Council held that it would be in breach of the due process clause in the Constitution of Trinidad and Tobago to execute an individual whilst his complaint was still under consideration by the Inter-American Commission and Court of Human Rights. This was despite the fact that the state had repudiated the Convention after the applications had been introduced.
[81] *Cruz Varas v. Sweden* (1992) 14 E.H.R.R. 1 at para. 100.
[82] (1992) 14 E.H.R.R. 1.
[83] See paras 90–104. The judgment refers to Art. 25(1) which provided, in part, that "The High Contracting Parties . . . undertake not to hinder in any way the effective exercise" of the right of individual petition. Under the amendments effected by Protocol 11, this provision is now to be found in Art. 34.
[84] *Cruz Varas (supra)* at para. 103.
[85] See, for example, Consultative Assembly Recommendation 623(1971) calling on the Committee of Ministers to draft an additional protocol to the Convention providing for a power to make binding orders for interim relief.
[86] Rule 49(1).
[87] Rule 49(3) and (4).

unnecessary.[88] The decision of a Committee is final[89] and must be supported by reasons,[90] although the reasons given in Committee decisions tend to be brief and formulaic in character.

Unless the Committee is unanimous in its decision to declare a case inadmissible **1–40** or to strike it off the list, it will be referred to a full Chamber which will decide on the admissibility and merits of the application.[91] Decisions on admissibility and merits will be taken separately, unless the Chamber, in exceptional circumstances, decides otherwise.[92] In its deliberations on the case the Chamber must take account of the report which has been submitted by the Judge Rapporteur.[93] The Chamber may, at that stage, either declare the application inadmissible or decide to invesigate it further.[94]

Written pleadings

If the Chamber does not declare an application inadmissible, it will communicate **1–41** it to the respondent state, and request the government's written observations on the admissibility and merits of the case.[95] The Chamber will generally invite the applicant to submit written observations in reply, and may invite further written pleadings from the parties, if necessary.[96] It is for the President to fix the time limit for each stage of the proceedings.[97] The time limits laid down must be strictly adhered to.[98] Any pleadings or other documents filed outside the time limit will be excluded from the case file unless the President, in the exercise of his discretion, decides otherwise.[99]

Joinder and simultaneous examination

The Chamber may, either at the request of the parties or of its own motion, order **1–42** the joinder of two or more applications.[1] Alternatively, the President may, after consulting the parties, order that applications which have been assigned to the same Chamber should be examined simultaneously.[2]

Expedition

The examination of a complaint under the Convention can take several years. In **1–43** cases of urgency, however, the President may authorise the Registrar to inform a

---

[88] Article 28.
[89] Article 28.
[90] Article 45(1).
[91] Article 29(3).
[92] Article 29(3).
[93] Article 54(1).
[94] Rule 54(2).
[95] Rule 54(3)(b).
[96] Rule 54(3)(c).
[97] Rule 54(5).
[98] Rule 38(1). For the purpose of determining whether a time limit has been complied with, the relevant date is the date of certified dispatch. If there is no certified date of dispatch, the relevant date is the date of receipt.
[99] Rule 38(1).
[1] Rule 43(1).
[2] Rule 43(2).

contracting state of the introduction of an application, and a summary of its objects.[3] This procedure is available whether or not the Court has made a request for interim measures pursuant to Rule 39.[4] Whilst cases will ordinarily be dealt with in the order in which they become ready for examination, the Court has a specific power to prioritise particular applications—in effect an order for expedition.[5] In *Soering v. United Kingdom*[6] the applicant's complaint concerning his proposed extradition was determined by the Court in just under a year; and in *X v. France*[7] a complaint made by an applicant who was dying of AIDS was resolved in 13 months.

Admissibility[8]

1–44 The criteria for determining the admissibility of a complaint are set out in Article 35:

(a) Under Article 35(1) the Court may only deal with an application after all domestic remedies have been exhausted, "according to the generally recognised rules of international law",[9] and within a period of six months from the date on which the final decision was taken in the national system.[10]

(b) Under Article 35(2) the Court may not deal with any application which is anonymous[11] or which is substantially the same as a matter which has already been examined by the Court[12] or which has already been submitted to "another procedure of international investigation or settlement".

(c) Finally, Article 35(3) requires the Court to declare inadmissible any individual application which it considers to be (a) incompatible with the provisions of the Convention,[13] (b) manifestly ill-founded,[14] or (c) an abuse of the right of petition.[15]

1–45 Before taking its decision on admissibility the Chamber may decide, either at the request of the parties or of its own motion, to hold an oral hearing. If this occurs then unless the Chamber, in exceptional circumstances, decides otherwise, the parties will be asked to address both the admissibility and the merits of the

---

[3] Rule 40.
[4] Rule 40 provides that the urgent notification procedure is "without prejudice to the taking of any other procedural steps".
[5] Rule 41.
[6] (1989) 11 E.H.R.R. 439.
[7] (1992) 14 E.H.R.R. 483.
[8] See generally Leo Zwart, *The Admissibility of Human Rights Petitions* (Martinus Nijhoff, 1994).
[9] See para. 1–46 below.
[10] See para. 1–65 below.
[11] See para. 1–71 below.
[12] See para. 1–73 below.
[13] See paras 1–74 to 1–94 below.
[14] See para. 1–95 below.
[15] See para. 1–98 below.

application at a single hearing.[16] Any decision to declare a complaint inadmissible (with or without a hearing) is final,[17] and must be supported by reasons.[18]

Exhaustion of domestic remedies

The first admissibility requirement in Article 35(1) is that the applicant must have 1–46
exhausted all domestic remedies before pursuing a complaint in Strasbourg. The
Court has frequently stated that the primary responsibility for ensuring compliance with the standards laid down in the Convention lies with the national
authorities.[19] In accordance with the general principles of international law,
member states must have the opportunity to redress any violation of Convention
rights within the domestic legal system.[20] The European Court becomes involved
"only through contentious proceedings and once all domestic remedies have
been exhausted".[21] The requirement to exhaust domestic remedies also enables
the national courts to make any necessary findings of fact. Although such
findings are not binding on the European Court of Human Rights, they will only
be disturbed if the national court has drawn an unfair or arbitrary conclusion from
the evidence before it.[22]

In determining whether the applicant has taken the necessary steps in the 1–47
domestic legal system, Article 35(1) must be applied with "some degree of
flexibility and without excessive formalism".[23] The applicant is under an obligation to make "normal use" of those remedies which are "likely to be effective
and adequate".[24] He is not required to pursue remedies which, though available
in theory, would be incapable in practice of providing any effective redress for
the complaint concerned.[25] An *ex post facto* remedy in damages will not necessarily be sufficient.[26] In certain situations national law must afford a means of
preventing a violation if a remedy is to be regarded as effective.[27] By the same

---

[16] Rule 54(4). For the procedure to be followed at an oral hearing, see para. 1–115 below.
[17] *Campbell and Fell v. United Kingdom* (1984) 7 E.H.R.R. 165 at para. 65.
[18] Article 45(1) and Rule 56(1). If the case has been declared inadmissible by a Chamber then the decision must state whether it was taken unanimously or by a majority: Rule 56(1). There is, however, no provision for dissenting opinions to be appended to an inadmissibility decision. Art. 45(2) and Rule 74(2), which make provision for dissenting opinions, apply only to a judgment on the merits of a complaint.
[19] See, amongst numerous other authorities, *Akdivar v. Turkey* (1997) 23 E.H.R.R. 143.
[20] *DeWilde Ooms and Versyp v. Belgium* (1979–80) 1 E.H.R.R. 373 at para. 50.
[21] *Handyside v. United Kingdom* (1979–80) 1 E.H.R.R. 737 at para. 48.
[22] *Klaas v. Germany* (1994) 18 E.H.R.R. 305 at 338 paras 24–31; *Edwards v. United Kingdom* (1993) 15 E.H.R.R. 417 at para. 34; *Van Mechelen v. Netherlands* (1998) 25 E.H.R.R. 647 at para. 50; *Barbera, Messegue and Jabardo v. Spain* (1989) 11 E.H.R.R. 360.
[23] *Van Oosterwijk v. Belgium* (1981) 3 E.H.R.R. 557 at paras 30–41; *Guzzardi v. Italy* (1981) 3 E.H.R.R. 333 para. 72; *Cf. Cardot v. France* (1991) 13 E.H.R.R. 583.
[24] *Donnelly v. United Kingdom* (1972) 4 D.R. 4 at para. 72.
[25] *Stogmuller v. Austria* (1979–80) 1 E.H.R.R. 155 at para. 11; *Vernillo v. France* (1991) 13 E.H.R.R. 880 at para. 27; *Lawless v. United Kingdom* (1958) 2 Y.B. 308 at 326.
[26] *X v. United Kingdom* (1977) 10 D.R. 5 (applicant complaining about conditions of detention in a mental hospital not required to bring civil action in damages); *X v. France* (1988) 56 D.R. 62 (in the context of a claim of excessive detention on remand, an action for damages is not a remedy requiring exhaustion).
[27] *M v. France* (1984) 41 D.R. 103 (in the context of threatened expulsion in breach of Art. 3, appeal without suspensive effect cannot be regarded as effective).

token, where national law does provide a procedure for preventing a violation, the applicant will generally be expected to make use of it.[28]

1–48   Difficult issues arise where the merits of any domestic remedy are dubious. The Court exerts pressure on potential applicants to make use of any national procedure which "does not clearly lack any prospect of success".[29] But in many cases, there may be room for differences of opinion as to whether an untried remedy is likely to succeed. The mere fact that there may be doubts about the prospects of success is not sufficient to absolve the applicant from the requirement to exhaust domestic remedies.[30] Where national case law is unclear, contradictory or in the process of ongoing interpretation, the domestic courts must, in general, be afforded the opportunity to clarify or develop the law.[31] Similarly, where new legislation is introduced, it may be necessary for the applicant to test its application before the national courts before pursuing a complaint in Strasbourg.[32]

1–49   There is however a competing imperative to pursue any complaint within the six month time limit. For this purpose time begins to run from the date of the violation, or from the conclusion of the last potentially effective domestic remedy, whichever is the latest. Time spent pursuing remedies which could not, on any view, have been effective, can result in an application being declared inadmissible for failure to observe the six month time limit.[33] Considerable care is therefore required in determining whether a particular remedy should be pursued.

1–50   In cases of uncertainty, the Court's approach is as follows: Where previous or subsequent litigation before the national courts has raised the same point without success, this will usually be sufficient to establish that the remedy was ineffective.[34] If the applicant can show that there is settled legal opinion to the effect that the remedy would be not succeed, there is no obligation to make use of it.[35] The Court may willing to accept the written opinion of senior counsel that the remedy in question would be bound to fail.[36] But if the advice subsequently turns out to be wrong, the applicant will not be able to rely upon the fact of having obtained advice in order to excuse non-exhaustion. In *K, F and P v. United Kingdom*[37] counsel's advice was held not to absolve the applicants from an obligation to apply for leave to appeal to the House of Lords, especially since the Court of Appeal had given leave is a similar case soon afterwards.

---

[28] *Cardot v. France* (1991) 13 E.H.R.R. 853 at para. 34.

[29] *DeWilde Ooms and Versyp v. Belgium* (1979–80) 1 E.H.R.R. 373.

[30] *Donnelly v. United Kingdom* (1972) 4 D.R. 4 at para. 72.

[31] *Whiteside v. United Kingdom* (1994) 76–A D.R. 80; *Spencer v. United Kingdom* [1998] E.H.R.L.R. 348.

[32] This has obvious implications for the Human Rights Act 1998, some of which are considered below.

[33] *X v. Switzerland* (1980) 22 D.R. 232; *Temple v. United Kingdom* (1985) 42 D.R. 171; *X v. Ireland* (1981) 26 D.R. 242; *H v. United Kingdom* (1983) 33 D.R. 247.

[34] *Campbell v. United Kingdom* 14 D.R. 186.

[35] *DeWilde Ooms and Versyp v. Belgium* (1979–80) 1 E.H.R.R. 373 at para. 50.

[36] *McFeely v. United Kingdom* (1980) 20 D.R. 44 at 71–76; *H v. United Kingdom* (1983) 33 D.R. 247.

[37] (1984) 40 D.R. 298 at 300.

It is not always necessary for the applicant to have pleaded a violation of the   **1–51**
Convention in specific terms before the national courts.[38] In general, the Court
adopts a substantive rather than a formal approach. It is the *substance* of the
applicant's Convention complaint which must previously have been put before
the relevant national authority.[39] But where the Convention is incorporated into
national law, it may be incumbent on the applicant to go further, and to show that
the relevant Convention provisions have been invoked directly in the domestic
courts,[40] particularly if this is the only means by which the point can be
ventilated.[41] In *Van Oosterwijk v. Belgium*[42] the Court explained its approach in
these terms:

> "Undoubtedly, in domestic proceedings the Convention as a general rule furnishes a
> supplementary ground of argument, to be prayed in aid if judged suitable for achieving
> an objective which is in principle rendered possible by other legal arguments ... In
> certain circumstances it may nonetheless happen that express reliance on the Conven-
> tion before the national authorities constitutes the sole appropriate manner of raising
> before those authorities first, as is required by [Article 35(1)] an issue intended, if need
> be, to be brought subsequently before the European review bodies."[43]

The burden of proving the existence of an effective remedy lies on the state.[44]   **1–52**
However once the existence of such a remedy has been raised, it is for the
applicant to establish why the remedy was unavailable or inadequate in the
circumstances[45]; or to identify other, exceptional, considerations which are said
to absolve him from the requirement to exhaust those remedies which exist.

In determining whether a remedy was genuinely liable to be effective, the Court   **1–53**
will require a close correlation between the applicant's complaint and the remedy
relied upon by the government. In *T and V v. United Kingdom*[46] two juvenile
applicants complained that their trial in an adult Crown Court, was in breach of
Articles 3 and 6 of the Convention since they had been unable to participate
effectively in the proceedings, due to their immaturity and emotional vulnerability, and the public nature of their trial. The government raised the plea of non-
exhaustion, arguing that the applicants' trial lawyers had failed to apply for a stay
of the criminal proceedings in the Crown Court. Although there was no authority
which directly supported the existence of a jurisdiction to stay in these circumstances, the government pointed to the decision of the Privy Council in *Kunnath
v. The State*[47] in support of the argument that English common law required a

---

[38] *Arrowsmith v. United Kingdom* (1978) 8 D.R. 123.
[39] *Gasus Dossier-und Fordertechnick GmbH v. Netherlands* (1995) 20 E.H.R.R. 360; *Castells v. Spain* (1992) 14 E.H.R.R. 445.
[40] *Cardot v. France* (1991) 13 E.H.R.R. 853.
[41] See generally Kruger, "The Practicalities of a Bill of Rights" [1997] E.H.R.L.R. 353.
[42] (1981) 3 E.H.R.R. 557 at para. 33.
[43] This is a principle which is likely to arise in connection with claims which can only be brought under section 7(1)(a) of the Human Rights Act 1998.
[44] *T and V v. United Kingdom* (2000) 30 E.H.R.R. 121, Judgment December 16, 1999 at para. 57; *DeWilde Ooms and Versyp v. Belgium* (1979–80) 1 E.H.R.R. 373 at para. 60; *DeWeer v. Belgium* (1979–80) 2 E.H.R.R. 439 at para 26; *Guincho v. Portugal* (1982) 29 D.R. 129 at 140.
[45] *Donnelly v. United Kingdom* (1972) 4 D.R. 4 at para. 64; *Akdivar v. Turkey* (1997) 23 E.H.R.R. 143 at para. 68.
[46] (2000) 30 E.H.R.R. 121.
[47] [1993] W.L.R. 1315.

criminal defendant to be able to understand and participate in the proceedings. In *Kunnath*, the Privy Council had said;

> "It is an essential principle of the criminal law that a trial for an indictable offence should be conducted in the presence of the defendant. The basis of this principle is not simply that there should be corporeal presence, but that the defendant, by reason of his presence, should be able to understand the proceedings and decide what witnesses he wishes to call, whether or not to give evidence and if so, upon what matters relevant to the case against him."

1–54   *Kunnath* however, concerned the absence of an interpreter. In the Court's view, the government had failed to establish that a similar principle would have been applied to an application to stay the proceedings on grounds of the defendants' immaturity and emotional disturbance. The Court subjected the government's claim that the remedy would have been effective to a very close scrutiny before rejecting it[48]:

> "The Court observes that in the *Kunnath* case the Privy Council was concerned with the very different situation of an accused person who was unable to participate in the criminal proceedings against him because they were conducted in a language which he did not understand. It notes the well-established rule of English criminal law that, in order to obtain a stay of proceedings, a defendant suffering from a disability such as mental illness must establish before a jury that he is 'unfit to plead', that is that he lacks the intellectual capacity to understand the plea of guilty or not guilty, to instruct his solicitors and to follow the evidence. In addition, English law attributes criminal responsibility to children between the ages of ten and fourteen, subject, at the time of the applicant's trial, to the proviso that the prosecution had to prove beyond reasonable doubt that, at the time of the alleged offence, the child understood that his behaviour was wrong as distinct from merely naughty. Finally, it is the rule that children over the age of ten accused or murder, manslaughter and other serious crimes are tried in public in the Crown Court. It is not suggested that the applicant's immaturity and level of emotional disturbance were sufficient to satisfy the test of unfitness to plead. Further, the prosecution were able to rebut the *doli incapax* presumption in respect of the applicant. However, the government have not referred the Court to any example of a case where an accused under a disability falling short of that required to establish unfitness to plead has been able to obtain a stay of criminal proceedings on the grounds that he was incapable of fully participating in them, or where a child charged with murder or another serious offence has been able to obtain a stay on the basis that the trial in public in the Crown Court would cause him detriment or suffering. In these circumstances, the Court does not consider that the government have discharged the burden upon them of proving the availability to the applicant of a remedy capable of providing redress in respect of his Convention complaints and offering reasonable prospects of success."

1–55   The applicant must be able to demonstrate that national time limits[49] and procedural requirements have been complied with,[50] unless they are manifestly unreasonable. In *Cardot v. France*[51] the Court summarised the position in this way:

---

[48] See the *T and V* (2000) 30 E.H.R.R. 121 at para. 59–61.
[49] *W v. Germany* (1986) 48 D.R. 102.
[50] *Cunningham v. United Kingdom* 43 D.R. 171; *T v. Switzerland* (1991) 72 D.R. 263.
[51] (1991) 13 E.H.R.R. 853 at para. 34.

"Admittedly, Article 26 must be applied with some degree of flexibility and without excessive formalism, but it does not require merely that applications should be made to the appropriate domestic courts and that use should be made of remedies designed to challenge decisions already given. It normally requires also that the complaints intended to be made subsequently at Strasbourg have been made to those same courts, at least in substance and in compliance with the formal requirements and time limits laid down in domestic law, and, further, that any procedural means which might prevent a breach of the Convention should have been used."

In exceptional circumstances the Court will absolve an applicant from the requirement to exhaust available remedies, where there are compelling reasons for doing so. In *Akdivar v. Turkey*[52] the Court held that; **1–56**

"One such reason may be constituted by the national authorities remaining totally passive in the face of serious allegations of misconduct or infliction of harm by state agents, for example where they have failed to undertake investigations or offer assistance. In such circumstances it can be said that the burden of proof shifts once again, so that it becomes incumbent on the respondent government to show what it has done in response to the scale and seriousness of the matters complained of."

In practice, however, it is rare for the Court to make an exception. The absence of legal aid is not generally regarded as a sufficient reason for failure to make use of remedies which are available,[53] although the position may be otherwise where the applicant could not reasonably be expected to conduct litigation without legal representation.[54] In an early case, the Commission suggested that the fact that the applicant was a patient in a psychiatric hospital did not relieve him of the responsibility to institute proceedings.[55] On the other hand, where there is more than one remedy available to an applicant it may be sufficient to show that a reasonable choice has been made.[56]

In order to be "effective", the remedy need not necessarily be judicial. The applicant must also make use of any administrative remedies available, providing they are realistically capable of affording effective redress.[57] However, the Court will scrutinise administrative remedies with particular care to determine their availability and effectiveness in practice. An administrative remedy will only be effective if the authority in question has jurisdiction to give a binding ruling on the complaint. Purely advisory powers are insufficient.[58] The fact that an administrative remedy is discretionary will not necessarily result in it being regarded as ineffective,[59] although it is a factor pointing in that direction.[60] **1–57**

---

[52] (1997) 23 E.H.R.R. 143; See also *Aksoy v. Turkey* (1997) 23 E.H.R.R. 553.
[53] *Van Oosterwijk v. Belgium* (1981) 3 E.H.R.R. 557.
[54] *Cf. Airey v. Ireland* (1979–80) 2 E.H.R.R. 305; *Granger v. United Kingdom* (1990) 12 E.H.R.R. 469.
[55] *X v. United Kingdom* (1977) 10 D.R. 5.
[56] *Yagci and Sargin v. Turkey* (1995) 20 E.H.R.R. 505 at paras 41–43; *Cremieux v. France* (1989) 59 D.R. 67 at 80. The selection of the appropriate remedy is primarily a matter for the applicant: *Airey v. Ireland* (1979–80) 2 E.H.R.R. 305 at para. 23.
[57] *McFeely v. United Kingdom* (1980) 20 D.R. 44 at 72.
[58] *Agee v. United Kingdom* (1976) 7 D.R. 164.
[59] *X v. United Kingdom* (1977) 10 D.R. 5.
[60] *Byloos v. Belgium* (1990) 66 D.R. 238; *X v. Denmark* (1981) 27 D.R. 50.

1–58   The power to award an *ex gratia* payment is not an effective remedy requiring exhaustion.[61] Neither is an applicant obliged to make use of exceptional administrative procedures which fall outside the normal legal remedies available. Thus, a criminal defendant is not obliged to petition the Criminal Cases Review Commission (CCRC) for a reference to the Court of Appeal under section 9 of the Criminal Appeal Act 1995 before pursuing a complaint in Strasbourg.[62] Once an appeal has been finally dismissed the applicant's conviction and sentence will acquire the quality of *res judicata*[63] and the ordinary appellate process is then at an end. In *Rowe and Davis v. United Kingdom*[64] the CCRC referred the applicants' convictions back to the Court of Appeal after the European Commission of Human Rights had declared their complaints under Article 6 admissible, but before the case had been argued before the Court. The Court nevertheless proceeded to determine the merits of the applicants' complaint before their appeal against conviction had been heard by the Court of Appeal.

1–59   Where administrative remedies are involved, the Court will be astute to detect any conflict of interest or lack of independence. In *Khan v. United Kingdom*[65] the Court held that the system of police complaints established under the Police and Criminal Evidence Act 1984 does not meet the requisite standards of independence needed to constitute sufficient protection against the abuse of authority and thus provide an effective remedy. In reaching this important conclusion, the Court attached particular significance to the limited powers of the Police Complaints Authority; to the function of the Home Secretary in appointing, remunerating and dismissing members of the PCA; and to the role played by the Chief Constable of the force under investigation.

1–60   In *Silver v. United Kingdom*[66] the Court drew a distinction between challenges directed to the validity of a Ministerial or Departmental order or policy, and challenges directed to a specific measure of implementation. In the former case, executive remedies are unlikely to be regarded as effective since they involve an appeal to the body which adopted the policy in the first place. But where the applicant complains that a policy, acceptable in itself, has been wrongly implemented, there will be an onus on him to petition the relevant authorities for redress. In the context of the prison disciplinary rule at issue in *Silver*, the Court said:

> "As for the Home Secretary, if there were a complaint to him as to the validity of an Order or Instruction under which a measure of control . . . had been carried out, he could not be considered to have a sufficiently independent standpoint to satisfy the requirements of Article 13. As the author of the directives in question, he would in reality be judge in his own cause. The position, however, would be otherwise if the complainant alleged that the measure of control resulted from a misapplication of one of those directives. The Court is satisfied that in such cases a petition to the Home

---

[61] *Temple v. United Kingdom* (1985) 42 D.R. 171.
[62] See, by anology, *X v. Ireland* (1981) 26 D.R. 242; *X v. Denmark* (1981) 27 D.R. 50; *KS and KS v. Switzerland* (1994) 76–A D.R. 70.
[63] A conviction will be *res judicata* when an appeal against conviction is finally dismissed or the relevant time limit has expired. An appeal out of time will not meet the requirements of Art. 35(1) unless the Court has extended time, and proceeded to hear the appeal.
[64] (2000) 30 E.H.R.R. 1.
[65] [2000] Crim. L.R. 684, *The Times*, May 23, 2000.
[66] (1983) 5 E.H.R.R. 347.

Secretary would in general be effective to secure compliance with the directive, if the complaint was well-founded."

The Court will consider the effectiveness of domestic remedies by reference to **1–61** the state of national law at the time of its admissibility decision, rather than the date of introduction of the complaint.[67] If, therefore, domestic law has developed so as to afford a remedy which was not previously available then this will provide a ground for declaring the complaint inadmissible, providing of course that the applicant's complaint remained within the national time limits when the change in the law took effect.[68]

Applying these principles to criminal cases in the United Kingdom it is possible **1–62** to draw a number of conclusions. As a general rule, a criminal defendant will be expected to pursue any available avenue of appeal, and to raise the substance of any Convention arguments before the appeal court. Thus, in *Edwards v. United Kingdom*,[69] the Court considered that non-disclosure of relevant evidence at the time of the applicant's trial was in breach of Article 6. However, in the Court's view, the violation had been remedied by the disclosure of the evidence prior to the hearing of the appeal, since the Court of Appeal had able to assess the impact of the evidence on the safety of the conviction. Insofar as the applicant sought to challenge the non-disclosure of evidence on grounds of public interest immunity, the Court considered that his failure to make an application to the Court of Appeal for production of the document was fatal to his complaint.[70]

For the purposes of determining the availability of an effective domestic remedy **1–63** it will be important to distinguish between cases in which the ordinary appeals process concluded prior to the coming into force of the Human Rights Act 1998,[71] and those in which the appeals process concluded thereafter. Prior to the 1998 Act, the powers of the domestic courts to grant a remedy for the violation of a Convention right were limited. If legislation was ambiguous,[72] or if the common law was developing or uncertain,[73] then this might well impose an obligation on the applicant to invoke Convention arguments before the national courts.[74] But if the domestic courts had no power to grant a remedy then the applicant would not be expected to appeal. In *ADT v. United Kingdom*,[75] for example, the applicant successfully challenged his summary conviction for gross indecency without having appealed to the Crown Court, and without having first pursued an application for judicial review or an appeal by way of Case Stated. The government did not seek to argue that the applicant's failure to appeal could

---

[67] *Luberti v. Italy* (1981) 27 D.R. 181.
[68] *Campbell and Fell v. United Kingdom* (1985) 7 E.H.R.R. 165; *Ringeisen v. Austria* (1979–80) 1 E.H.R.R. 455 at paras 89–93.
[69] (1993) 15 E.H.R.R. 417.
[70] Para. 38.
[71] On October 2, 2000.
[72] *Garland v. British Rail* [1983] 2 A.C. 751; *R. v. Secretary of State for the Home Department ex parte Brind* [1991] A.C. 696.
[73] *Attorney General v. Guardian Newspapers Ltd (No.2)* [1990] 1 A.C. 109 (*per* Lord Goff at 283); *Derbyshire County Council v. Times Newspapers* [1993] A.C. 534; *R. v. Chief Metropolitan Stipendiary Magistrate ex parte Choudhury* [1991] 1 Q.B. 429.
[74] *Spencer v. United Kingdom* [1998] E.H.R.L.R. 348.
[75] *The Times*, August 8, 2000; Judgment July 31, 2000.

be characterised as non-exhaustion since his conviction was based on an unambiguous provision of primary legislation, and the domestic courts had no power to afford a remedy for this legislative violation.

1–64   Where criminal proceedings have concluded after October 2, 2000, the position is more difficult. In summary, the position is as follows:

> (a) If the alleged violation involves a rule of practice, or a principle of the common law, then it will almost certainly be incumbent on the applicant to invoke Convention arguments in the domestic courts. This is because under the Human Rights Act, Convention rights will take precedence over any pre-existing rule of this kind.[76]

> (b) Where a provision of primary legislation is involved, the applicant will in general be expected to argue for a new construction which is compatible with Convention rights in accordance with section 3 of the 1998 Act.[77] This will be the case even if there is prior appellate authority on the point.[78]

> (c) The most difficult problems will arise where there appears to be no "possible" construction which would be compatible with Convention rights. Is a declaration of incompatibility under sections 4 and 5 of the new Act to be regarded as an effective remedy, requiring exhaustion, despite the fact that it does not affect the validity, operation or continuing enforcement of the legislation, and despite the fact that it is not binding on the parties to the proceedings in which it is made? The safest course is to assume that the applicant is under an obligation to seek a declaration of incompatibility since this will trigger the power to make a remedial order in section 10 and Schedule 2 of the Human Rights Act. Whilst a prospective amendment to the offending legislation would not, in itself, provide an effective remedy, Schedule 2 enables the responsible Minister to make a retrospective amendment, and to grant supplementary or consequential relief to the individual.[79]

> (d) Particular care is required when determining whether judicial review should be pursued:

>> (i) If the applicant's complaint relates to a failure to follow procedural rules, or an error of law, then judicial review is capable of providing an effective remedy. However, in *G v. United Kingdom*[80] the Commission held that the possibility of applying for judicial review of a refusal of legal aid in a criminal case could not be regarded as effective on the facts. Moreover, the practical availability of judicial review as a means of challenging an error of law in the course of a criminal prosecution has been severely circumscribed by the House of Lords' decision in *R v. Director of Public Prosecutions ex parte Kebilene*.[81]

---

[76] See para. 3–29 below.
[77] See para. 3–31 below.
[78] See para. 3–32 below.
[79] See paras 3–38 to 3–39 below.
[80] (1988) 56 D.R. 199.
[81] (1999) 3 W.L.R. 972.

(ii) As to challenges which are directed to the merits of a decision, the Court has held that judicial review is an effective remedy where the applicant alleges that a decision to extradite or deport him would involve a serious risk of treatment contrary to Articles 2 or 3.[82] This is because the domestic courts adopted a test of "anxious scrutiny" which coincides with the tests adopted by the Court. However, where a violation of Article 8 was in issue[83] judicial review was held to be ineffective. In *Smith and Grady v. United Kingdom*[84] the Court held that the irrationality threshold applied when the court is considering a challenge to the merits of an administrative decision " . . . was placed so high that it effectively excluded any consideration by the domestic courts of the question of whether the interference with the applicants' rights answered a pressing social need or was proportionate to the . . . aims pursued, principles which lie at the heart of the Court's analysis of complaints under Article 8 of the Convention."[85] In the light of this decision, the Administrative Court is of course required to adopt a more intrusive threshold for a judicial review directed to the merits of a decision under the Human Rights Act. Assuming that the test applied in the domestic courts coincides with the approach of the European Court of Human Rights under Article 8, there will be a corresponding onus on the applicant to seek judicial review.

(e) The Court has in the past been prepared to accept that appeal to the House of Lords is an exceptional remedy, available only where a case involves a point of law of general public importance.[86] As such, an applicant has only been required to apply for leave to appeal to the House of Lords where there is a realistic prospect that leave would be granted on the facts.[87] The Human Rights Act has broadened the scope of constitutional complaints which satisfy the requirements for the grant of leave. Potential applicants would therefore be well advised to apply for leave to appeal to the House of Lords in any case where it is considered likely that an application to Strasbourg will be made.

(f) In order to minimise the risk of falling foul of the six months rule in cases where the merits are doubtful, an applicant should consider lodging a protective application to Strasbourg. There is no express provision in the rules for this procedure, but the Registry is usually prepared to open a file on a complaint whilst domestic remedies are in the process of exhaustion (providing of course that they have been exhausted by the time the Court rules on admissibility). In that way, the applicant is protected both from an argument that the complaint is inadmissible for non-exhaustion, and from

---

[82] *Soering v. United Kingdom* (1989) 11 E.H.R.R. 439; *Vilvarajah v. United Kingdom* (1992) 14 E.H.R.R. 248; *D v. United Kingdom* (1997) 24 E.H.R.R. 423.
[83] And presumably also a violation of Arts 9 to 11 and Art. 14.
[84] (2000) 29 E.H.R.R. 493.
[85] This was despite the fact that the Court of Appeal had taken account of the human rights context, and had held that the more substantial the interference with human rights, the more the court would require by way of justification before it was satisfied that decision was reasonable.
[86] See generally Reid, *A Practitioners Guide to the European Convention of Human Rights* (Sweet & Maxwell, 1998), p. 22.
[87] *McGonnell v. United Kingdom* (2000) 30 E.H.R.R. 289 (concerning a similar right of appeal from the Royal Court of Guernsey to the Privy Council).

an argument that it was introduced outside the six month time limit. If this course is to be adopted, the applicant must submit a detailed letter of introduction, accompanied by the appropriate forms, and explaining that further remedies are being pursued in the national courts. The applicant should then maintain contact with the Registry. An application cannot be kept dormant indefinitely and may have to be re-introduced.[88]

(g) The final point relates to the rule that compliance with Article 35(1) is to be determined according to the remedies available at the time when the Court makes its ruling on the admissibility of the application. Under section 22(4) of the Human Rights Act a criminal defendant is entitled to invoke Convention rights retrospectively in certain circumstances.[89] It follows that even if there was no remedy available at the time the application was introduced, this may not necessarily be the position when the Court comes to rule on the admissibility of the complaint.

The six months rule

1–65   The second limb of Article 35(1) provides that the Court may only consider an application which has been introduced within six months "from the date on which the final decision was taken". Where there are effective or potentially effective domestic remedies for the violation, time begins to run from the day after the final decision in the process of exhaustion. If the national court or tribunal gives its ruling in public, then the date of judgment is generally taken to be the date on which the ruling is given. If the ruling is not given in public, then time runs from the date on which the applicant or his lawyer first received formal written notification.[90] Where the reasons for the national court's ruling are relevant to the application to Strasbourg, then the relevant date will be the date on which the applicant or his lawyer received the text of the court's reasoned judgment.[91]

1–66   Where the applicant has made an unsuccessful attempt to invoke a national remedy which was obviously ineffective (either because it had no prospect of success or because it was exceptional or discretionary in character[92]) time will run from the date he should have been aware of the situation.[93]

1–67   In a case in which there is no potentially effective domestic remedy available, time generally runs from the date of the act or omission in issue. There are three principal exceptions to this rule:

---

[88] Reid, *A Practitioners Guide to the European Convention of Human Rights* (Sweet & Maxwell, 1998), p. 20.
[89] See para. 3–04 below. See however *R. v. Lambert* (2001) UKHL 37, July 5, 2001, discussed at paras 3–09 and 17–06 below.
[90] *X v. France* (1983) 32 D.R. 266; *K, C and M v. Netherlands* (1995) 80–A D.R. 87 at 88; *Cf. Aarts v. Netherlands* (1991) 70 D.R. 208 (Delay by lawyer in communicating the ruling to the applicant did not suspend the time limit: The relevant date was the date upon which the lawyer was informed).
[91] *P v. Switzerland* (1984) 36 D.R. 20; *Worm v. Austria* (1998) 25 E.H.R.R. 454.
[92] See, for example, *X v. Ireland* (1981) 26 D.R. 242, where the rejection of the applicant's petition to the Attorney General for a certificate of appeal to the Supreme Court on a point of law of exceptional public importance was held not to have extended the time limit under the Convention.
[93] *X v. Switzerland* (1980) 22 D.R. 232; *Temple v. United Kingdom* (1985) 42 D.R. 171; *X v. Ireland* (1981) 26 D.R. 242; *H v. United Kingdom* (1983) 33 D.R. 247; *Lacin v. Turkey* (1995) 81–A D.R. 76 at 81.

(a) The six month time limit will not apply where the applicant's complaint relates to a state of affairs which is continuing when the Court examines the admissibility of the application, or to a provision of domestic law which is said, by its very existence, to violate the applicant's Convention rights. In *McFeely v. United Kingdom*,[94] where the applicant complained about repeated punishments for persistent refusal to obey prison rules, the Commission held that time would only start to run "after this state of affairs had ceased to exist". Similarly, in *Norris v. Ireland*,[95] where the applicant complained that the offence of gross indecency, by its very existence, interfered with his rights under Article 8, there could be no question of the complaint being out of time.

(b) Where the action complained of is authorised under an administrative measure extending over a period of time, the six months period will run from the last date on which the measure caused prejudice to the applicant's Convention rights. In *Christians Against Racism and Fascism v. United Kingdom*[96] the applicant organisation complained about an order under section 3 of the Public Order Act 1936, banning processions within the Metropolitan Police district for two months. Time was held to run from the date of a procession which the applicant had planned to hold, rather than from the date on which the order had been made.

(c) Where the applicant was initially unaware of the violation, time runs from the date of knowledge. In *Hilton v. United Kingdom*[97] the applicant was a journalist who discovered that she may have been the subject of MI5 security vetting procedures nine years earlier, when she was rejected for an appointment at the BBC. Time was held to run from the date of this discovery.

In relation to criminal proceedings, the relevant date will usually be the conclu- **1–68** sion of any appeal.[98] Where a criminal prosecution involves multiple charges, and the applicant's conviction for one offence is affirmed before the remaining charges have been finally determined, time runs (in relation to the first offence) from the date on which the first conviction was affirmed, rather than from the conclusion of the proceedings as a whole.[99]

The date of introduction will, as a general rule, be considered to be the date of **1–69** the first communication from the applicant setting out, even summarily, the object of the application.[1] The communication relied upon must, as a minimum, identify the applicant and particularise the complaint in sufficient detail to enable the Court to comprehend the violation alleged.[2] The relevant date is the date of posting or transmission shown on the documents, rather than the date of receipt.[3]

---

[94] (1980) 20 D.R. 44 at 76.
[95] (1991) 13 E.H.R.R. 186.
[96] (1980) 21 D.R. 138.
[97] (1988) 57 D.R. 108.
[98] As to the obligation to seek leave to appeal to the House of Lords, see para. 1–64(e) above.
[99] *N v. Germany* (1982) 31 D.R. 154.
[1] Rule 47(5).
[2] *Khan v. United Kingdom* (1995) 21 E.H.R.R. CD 67 (a letter setting out the applicant's name and the fact that his complaint related to "an immigration matter" held to be insufficient).
[3] It is nevertheless a sensible precaution to establish that the communication has actually been received in the Registry by the prescribed date.

Telephone communication is not sufficient,[4] save perhaps in cases of extreme urgency and importance.[5]

1–70 The Court has a discretion to direct that a different date should be treated as the date of introduction where there are good reasons for doing so.[6] However, it is a discretion which is rarely exercised in the applicant's favour. Neither a lack of knowledge of the applicable law,[7] nor an applicant's illness or mental incapacity[8] has been held to be sufficient justification for departing from the strict requirements of Article 35(1).

Anonymity and Confidentiality

1–71 In accordance with Article 35(2)(a), the Court may not consider an anonymous application.[9] All written applications submitted under Article 34 must adequately identify the applicant for the benefit of the Court and the respondent government.[10] Applicants who do not wish their identity to be disclosed *to the public* must submit a statement of the reasons which are said to justify a departure from the normal rule of public access to information in proceedings before the Court.[11] An order preserving anonymity will only be made in "exceptional and duly justified cases".[12] For a recent example of a criminal case in which the Court has granted anonymity see *ADT v. United Kingdom*.[13]

1–72 All pleadings and other documents deposited with the Registry, apart from those filed for the purposes of friendly settlement negotiations, are available for inspection by the public.[14] Either party may, however, apply to the President for an order that the pleadings or documents, or any part of them, should remain confidential. Such an order may be made in the interest of morals, public order or national security, where the interests of juveniles or the protection of the private life of the parties so require, or to the extent strictly necessary in the opinion of the President in special circumstances where publicity would prejudice the interests of justice.[15] Any such application must be supported by reasoned argument and must specify which of the documents or pleadings it relates to.[16] In addition, the President may make a confidentiality order of his or her own motion.[17]

---

[4] *Rosemary West v. United Kingdom* (1997) 91–A D.R. 85.
[5] In *West, supra* n. 4, the Commission was prepared to assume that there might be very exceptional circumstances in which an oral application would suffice, but held that it would require an overriding reason why it was not possible to submit an application in writing, coupled with an express and unequivocal statement on the part of the applicant and his lawyer that they were seeking formally to introduce an application by this means.
[6] Rule 47(5).
[7] *Bozano v. Italy* (1984) 39 D.R. 147.
[8] *X v. Austria* (1975) 2 D.R. 87 at 88; *K v. Ireland* (1984) 38 D.R. 158 at 160.
[9] Article 35(2)(a).
[10] Rule 47(1)(a).
[11] Rule 47(3).
[12] Rule 47(3).
[13] *The Times*, August 8, 2000; judgment July 31, 2000.
[14] Article 40(2).
[15] Rule 33(2) and (3).
[16] Rule 33(4).
[17] Rule 33(3).

Substantially the same

Article 35(2)(b) provides that the Court may not consider an application which **1–73** is substantially the same as a matter that has already been examined by the Court or has already been submitted to another procedure of international investigation or settlement and which contains no relevant new information. Where an application has already been determined in Strasbourg, the Court may only reconsider it if there are fresh factual considerations. A complaint may, however, be re-submitted if it was initially rejected for non-exhaustion of domestic remedies and the applicant has since complied with the requirements of Article 35(1). Similarly, in *W v. Germany*[18] the Commission held that where a previous application concerning delay in domestic proceedings had been rejected, the continuation of those proceedings constitutes a new fact allowing a re-examination of the complaint. However, new grounds of argument based on the same facts will not suffice.[19]

So far as criminal cases in the United Kingdom are concerned, there are no other relevant international procedures available.

Application incompatible with the Convention

The first limb of Article 35(3) provides that the Court may not consider any **1–74** application which is incompatible with the Convention. There are four grounds of incompatibility:

(a) Incompatibility *ratione temporis*. A complaint will be incompatible with the Convention if the events to which it relates occurred before the Convention came into force, or before it was ratified by the state against which the complaint is made.

(b) Incompatibility *ratione loci*. An application will be incompatible if it relates to events occurring outside the territory of the contracting state and where there is no link with any authority within the jurisdiction.[20]

(c) Incompatibility *ratione personae*. An application will be incompatible if it is directed towards a state which is not a party to the Convention; if it is a complaint against an individual or a body for which the state is not responsible[21]; or if the applicant lacks standing[22] or is unable to show that he is a victim of the violation alleged.[23]

(d) Incompatibility *ratione materiae*. An application will be declared inadmissible if it asserts a right which is not protected by the Convention, or if the complaint(s) made fall outside the scope of the particular right(s) invoked.

Territorial application

The protection afforded by the Convention extends to any person within the **1–75** jurisdiction of the contracting state,[24] or of any overseas territory for whose

---

[18] (1986) 48 D.R. 102.
[19] *X v. United Kingdom* (1981) 25 D.R. 147.
[20] See para. 1–75 below.
[21] See para. 1–76 below.
[22] See para. 1–80 below.
[23] See para. 1–84 below.
[24] Article 1.

international relations that state is responsible under Article 56. Where a state exercises *de facto* control over another state's territory,[25] or where agents of a contracting state detain an individual abroad,[26] any person affected by the action may bring a complaint against the state concerned. Moreover, authorised agents of a state, such as its diplomatic and consular authorities, and its armed forces, not only remain subject to the state's jurisdiction abroad, but bring any other persons or property over which they have authority within the state's jurisdiction.[27]

State responsibility

1–76   The applicant's complaint must be directed towards a person for whom or a body for which the state is responsible. The Commission and the Court have, in the past, left open the question whether the state is responsible for certain public bodies such as the BBC[28] British Rail[29] and the Bar Council Professional Conduct Committee.[30] This issue is brought into sharp focus by section 6 of the Human Rights Act 1998 which provides that the legal duty to act compatibly with Convention rights applies to any "public authority", a term which is defined so as to include "any person, certain of whose functions are functions of a public nature".[31] It is important, however, to recall that the Convention can impose positive obligations on the state to protect a private individual from a violation of his Convention rights by another private individual.[32] Accordingly, the fact that the "proximate cause" of a violation was the act or omission of a private individual is not necessarily decisive.[33]

1–77   A further issue which may arise under the rubric of state responsibility is the question of vicarious liability for unauthorised acts of government servants. The Commission has explained the Convention approach as follows[34];

> "[T]he responsibility of a state under the Convention may arise for acts of all its organs and servants. As in connection with international law generally, the acts of persons acting in an official capacity are imputed to the state. In particular, the obligations of a Contracting Party under the Convention can be violated by a person exercising an

---

[25] *Loizidou v. Turkey* (1997) 23 E.H.R.R. 513.
[26] *Reinette v. France* (1989) 63 D.R. 189.
[27] *Mrs W v. Ireland* (1983) 32 D.R. 211 at para. 14. Note however, that taking part in the activities of the European Union or the Council of Europe in not, in itself, sufficient: *Confederation Francais Democratique du Travail v. the European Communities and their Member States* (1978) 13 D.R. 231.
[28] *Hilton v. United Kingdom* (1988) 57 D.R. 108 at 117–118.
[29] *Young, James and Webster v. United Kingdom* (1982) 4 E.H.R.R. 38 at paras 48–49.
[30] *X v. United Kingdom* (1978) 15 D.R. 242.
[31] See s.6(3)(b). See paras 3–22 to 3–27. Note, however, that where a private body is brought within the extended definition of a "public authority" by virtue of s.6(3)(b) the duty to act compatibly does not apply to any act or omission which is private in nature: s.6(5).
[32] See para. 2–59 below.
[33] Thus, in *Young, James and Webster v. United Kingdom* (1982) 4 E.H.R.R. 38 at para. 49 the Court held that although the "proximate cause" of the applicants' complaint was an agreement between British Rail and the railway unions, "it was the domestic law in force at the relevant time that made lawful the treatment of which the applicants complained". Accordingly the state's responsibility would be engaged for the failure to secure the applicant's rights "in the enactment of domestic legislation". It was this finding which made it unnecessary to consider whether "the state might also be responsible on the ground that it should be regarded as employer or that British Rail was under its control".
[34] *Wille v. Liechtenstein* (1997) 24 E.H.R.R. CD 45.

official function vested in him, even where his acts are outside or against instructions."

Thus, in *A v. France*[35] the Court held that the state was liable for the unauthorised   **1–78**
acts of a police officer who had made a recording of a telephone conversation
without the necessary authorisation and in breach of French law. Similarly, in
Cyprus v. Turkey[36] the Commission held the state responsible for acts of rape by
Turkish soldiers on the ground that it had "not been shown that the Turkish
authorities took adequate measures to prevent this happening or that they generally took any disciplinary measures following such incidents". And in *Ireland
v. United Kingdom*[37] the Court was dismissive of the Government's argument
that it could not be held liable for unlawful ill-treatment of detainees:

> "It is inconceivable that the higher authorities of a state should be, or at least should be
> entitled to be, unaware of the existence of such a practice. Furthermore, under the
> Convention those authorities are strictly liable for the conduct of their subordinates;
> they are under a duty to impose their will on subordinates and cannot shelter behind
> their inability to ensure that [detainees' rights are] respected."

This approach has the potential to bring about a significant change to the   **1–79**
principles of vicarious liability in human rights cases. Compare the cases of
Makanjuola v. Metropolitan Police Commissioner[38] with *Aydin v. Turkey*.[39] In
Makanjuola the plaintiff alleged that she had been indecently assaulted by a
police officer who had first offered to suppress a report on an immigration
offence in return for sex. Henry J. held that the Commissioner was not vicariously liable under section 48 of the Police Act 1964 since the officer had not
been acting in the performance or purported performance of his functions. In
Aydin, by contrast, the applicant alleged that she had been raped whilst in police
custody. The Court noted that "rape leaves deep psychological scars on the
victim which do not respond to the passage of time as quickly as other forms of
physical and mental violence",[40] and had no difficulty at all in ascribing responsibility to the state.

Standing

The Court may receive applications from any legal or natural person, non-   **1–80**
governmental organisation or group of individuals, claiming to be a victim of a
violation of the Convention.[41] There is no requirement that the complainant must
be a citizen of the respondent state, or of any Council of Europe member state.[42]
It is sufficient if the complainant is *either* physically[43] *or* legally within the

---

[35] (1994) 17 E.H.R.R. 462.
[36] (1982) 4 E.H.R.R. 482.
[37] (1979–80) 2 E.H.R.R. 25.
[38] *The Times* August 8, 1989.
[39] (1998) 25 E.H.R.R. 251.
[40] Para. 83.
[41] Article 34.
[42] See, for example, *Ahmed v. Austria* (1997) 24 E.H.R.R. 278; *D v. United Kingdom* (1997) 24
E.H.R.R. 423.
[43] In *D v. United Kingdom* (1997) 24 E.H.R.R. at para. 48 the Court held that it was unnecessary for
the applicant to have entered the United Kingdom "in the technical sense" (*i.e.* lawfully) since he was
physically present.

jurisdiction. An applicant need not have legal capacity under domestic law: a complaint can be introduced by a child[44] or a person who is mentally incapacitated,[45] whether or not there is a parent or competent adult willing to act on their behalf.

1–81   An individual may submit a complaint through a duly authorised representative. Parents may represent their children unless there is a conflict of interest or the parent lacks the necessary standing to act on the child's behalf.[46] Custodial parents and legal guardians apart, the Court will generally require either a signed letter of authority stating that the applicant wishes the representative to act, or some other evidence of the representative's authority.[47] Next of kin may introduce an application on behalf of an individual who has died[48]; and may continue a complaint where the applicant dies during the course of the proceedings, providing the next of kin has a sufficient interest in the case.[49]

1–82   The right of individual petition extends to corporate bodies,[50] to non-governmental organisations[51] and to groups of individuals, including political parties[52] and trade unions.[53] Complaints may not, however, be brought by local or central government bodies,[54] or by other public authorities.[55] Where a complaint is brought by an organisation with the necessary standing, it must be signed by those competent to represent the organisation.[56] If the organisation or group has

---

[44] *SP, DP, and T v. United Kingdom* (1996) 22 E.H.R.R. CD 148.

[45] *X and Y v. Netherlands* (1986) 8 E.H.R.R. 235.

[46] See *Hokkanen v. Finland* (1995) 19 E.H.R.R. 139, where the father lacked standing to represent his child under domestic law.

[47] In *SP, DP, and T v. United Kingdom* (1996) 22 E.H.R.R. CD 148 the children's legal representative was held sufficient, despite the inability of the children to give instructions. In *Z v. United Kingdom* Application No. 28945/95 the Official Solicitor, acting on behalf of children abused by their parents, was held sufficient.

[48] *McCann v. United Kingdom* (1996) 21 E.H.R.R. 97; *Osman v. United Kingdom* (1999) 1 F.L.R. 198. In this situation the complaint is brought in the name of the next of kin rather than that of the deceased.

[49] *X v. United Kingdom* (1982) 4 E.H.R.R. 188; *Laskey, Jaggard and Brown v. United Kingdom* (1997) 24 E.H.R.R. 39; *X v. France* (1992) 14 E.H.R.R. 483.

[50] *Air Canada v. United Kingdom* (1995) 20 E.H.R.R. 150: *Autotronic AG v. Switzerland* (1990) 12 E.H.R.R. 485; *National and Provincial Building Society v. United Kingdom* (1998) 25 E.H.R.R. 127. In exceptional cases, the Court may be willing to pierce the corporate veil and allow individual shareholders to bring a complaint in respect of an administrative act directed against the company: *Neves E Silva v. Portugal* (1989) 13 E.H.R.R. 576; *Agrotexim and others v. Greece* (1996) 21 E.H.R.R. 250.

[51] *Association X v. United Kingdom* (1978) 14 D.R. 31.

[52] *Liberal Party v. United Kingdom* (1980) 21 D.R. 211. The Commission held that a political party, as "a gathering of people with a common interest", can be considered as a non-governmental organisation or group of individuals.

[53] *CCSU v. United Kingdom* (1987) 50 D.R. 228; *Cf. Ahmed v. United Kingdom* (1995) 20 E.H.R.R. CD 72.

[54] *Rothenthurm Commune v. Switzerland* (1988) 59 D.R. 251; *Ayuntamiento de M. v. Spain* (1991) 68 D.R. 209.

[55] In *BBC v. United Kingdom* (1996) 84A D.R. 129 the Commission left open the question whether the BBC had standing to bring a complaint under the Convention. *Cf. Hilton v. United Kingdom* (1988) 57 D.R. 108 where the Commission left open the question whether the state could be held responsible for the acts of the BBC which were alleged to have breached the applicant's Convention rights.

[56] Rule 45(2).

no clearly defined legal structure then the application should be signed by all of those on whose behalf it is submitted.

Unincorporated bodies can act on behalf of their members providing they **1–83** identify those members who are "directly affected" by the measure in question, and establish their authority to represent them.[57] In certain circumstances an unincorporated association may itself claim to be a victim of a violation. In *Christians Against Racism and Fascism v. United Kingdom*,[58] for example, the applicant association was entitled to claim victim status in respect of an order under section 3 of the Public Order Act 1936 banning a planned procession.

Victim status

In order to qualify as a "victim", within the meaning of Article 34, it is generally **1–84** necessary to establish that the applicant has been directly affected by the measure in issue. The Convention does not permit a class action.[59] Nor does it entitle an individual or organisation to claim in the abstract that a law is incompatible with the Convention.[60]

It does not necessarily follow that an applicant must have suffered a specific **1–85** detriment.[61] The Court has held that in certain situations the concept of a victim may include a person who runs the risk of being directly affected by a law, even in the absence of measure applying it to him or her. In *Norris v. Ireland*[62] the applicant was found to be a victim of a law criminalising consensual homosexual activity in private, although he had not been prosecuted, and the risk of prosecution was "minimal". The very existence of the law in question affected the applicant since he was forced to choose between refraining from sexual activity on the one hand and breaking the law on the other. The same reasoning was applied by the Commission in *Sutherland v. United Kingdom*,[63] in connection with a complaint that the age of consent for lawful homosexual activity was in breach of Articles 8 and 14 of the Convention. The applicant in that case was found to be a victim despite the fact that the domestic authorities had never shown any interest at all in his sexual activities. Similarly, in *Bowman v. United Kingdom*[64] the applicant alleged that her prosecution for incurring unauthorised expenditure during an election was in breach of the right to freedom of expression in Article 10. Although she had been acquitted of the charge the Court held that she was nevertheless a victim of the alleged violation. The acquittal was on technical grounds (the summons had been issued outside the statutory time limit) and the fact that she had been prosecuted was an indication that unless she modified her behaviour during future elections she was liable to prosecuted

---

[57] A failure to identify the members on whose behalf the complaint is made may result in the application being rejected as anonymous.
[58] (1980) 21 D.R. 138.
[59] *Lindsay v. United Kingdom* (1997) 23 E.H.R.R. CD 199.
[60] *X v. Austria* (1976) 7 D.R. 87.
[61] *Eckle v. Germany* (1983) 5 E.H.R.R. 1 at para. 66.
[62] (1991) 13 E.H.R.R. 186 at para. 31.
[63] (1997) 24 E.H.R.R. CD 22.
[64] (1998) 26 E.H.R.R. 1.

again, and possibly convicted and punished. This was sufficient to establish that she was directly affected by the very existence of the law in question.[65]

1–86   The important point to note about this group of cases is that the finding of a violation was based not on a potential future breach, but on the state of affairs existing at the time of the complaint. In each case the provisions of domestic law were alleged, by their mere existence, to have a direct effect on the applicants, and therefore to have violated their Convention rights to privacy and freedom of expression respectively.

1–87   In the context of Article 3 however the Court has been prepared to go further, and has accepted that a potential future violation may be sufficient in itself to satisfy the victim requirement. This approach was first signalled in *Campbell and Cosans v. United Kingdom*,[66] a corporal punishment case, where the Court observed *obiter* that "a *mere threat* of conduct prohibited by Article 3 may itself conflict with that provision", provided the threat was sufficiently real and immediate. As an example, the Court suggested that to threaten an individual with torture might constitute "at least" inhuman treatment. This approach was taken to its logical conclusion in the landmark decision of *Soering v. United Kingdom*.[67] The applicant in that case complained that the decision to extradite him to face trial in the United States would involve a breach of Article 3 of the Convention since he would, if convicted, be liable be detained under intolerable conditions on death row. Despite the inherent uncertainty in the situation—and, in particular, the possibility of an acquittal—the Court held that the applicant could claim to be a "victim" of the potential violation. In the Court's view, the gravity of the harm to which he was potentially exposed justified a relaxation of the "victim" requirement[68]:

> "It is not normally for the Convention institutions to pronounce on the existence or otherwise of potential violations of the Convention. However, where an applicant complains that a decision to extradite him would, if implemented, be contrary to Article 3 by reason of its foreseeable consequences in the requesting country, a departure from this principle is necessary, in view of the serious and irreparable nature of the alleged suffering risked, in order to ensure the effectiveness of the safeguard provided by that Article."

1–88   The Court established the fundamental principle that a decision to extradite a fugitive offender will give rise to an issue under Article 3, and hence engage the responsibility of the contracting state, if there are "substantial grounds for believing" that the person concerned faces a "real risk" of being subjected to torture or inhuman or degrading treatment or punishment in the requesting

---

[65] The Court's approach in *Bowman* is consistent with *Times Newspapers Ltd v. United Kingdom* (1990) 65 D.R. 307 in which the Commission observed that a publisher might be a victim of a violation of Art. 10, arising from real uncertainty in the law of defamation, even though no defamation proceedings had been brought against any of its newspapers. *Cf. Leigh, Guardian Newspapers and Observer Ltd v. United Kingdom* (1984) 38 D.R. 75, where the Commission held that the applicants could not claim to be victims in relation to a decision of the House of Lords establishing potential liability in contempt, simply on the basis that on some future date, in unknown circumstances, they may be prosecuted.
[66] (1982) 4 E.H.R.R. 293 at para. 26.
[67] (1989) 11 E.H.R.R. 439.
[68] At para. 90.

country. In *D v. United Kingdom*[69] the Court applied the same approach to a decision to deport a convicted drug trafficker after the expiry of his sentence.[70]

The Court has also given an extended meaning to the term "victim" in the   **1-89**
context of secret surveillance and other intelligence-gathering measures. A relaxation of the "victim" requirement is necessary in this area to ensure that the right of individual petition is effective. The applicable principles are considered in Chapter 7 below.[71]

In certain circumstances an individual may claim to be an "indirect victim" for   **1-90**
the purposes of Article 34. This will usually arise where the applicant has suffered as a result of a violation of the Convention rights of another and the primary victim is unable to pursue a complaint. Thus, in *McCann v. United Kingdom*[72] the relatives of three members of an IRA active service unit killed by British soldiers in Gibraltar were held to be indirect victims of a violation of the right to life in Article 2. Similarly, in *Osman v. United Kingdom*,[73] which concerned an alleged failure by the police to prevent a homicidal attack, the Court assumed that the wife of the deceased could claim to be an indirect victim.

The Court has held, on a number of occasions, that it is not necessary for an   **1-91**
applicant to show that the measure in question has caused specific prejudice or damage[74] (damage being relevant primarily to the assessment of just satisfaction under Article 41). Thus, in *Artico v. Italy*,[75] the Court held that where a criminal defendant could establish that his legal representation failed to meet the standards imposed by Article 6(3)(c), it was unnecessary, and arguably impossible, for him to prove that effective representation would have secured his acquittal. Similarly, in *Benham v. United Kingdom*[76] the Court found a violation of Article 6(3)(c) arising from the absence of legal aid for committal proceedings in the Magistrates Court, but awarded the applicant no compensation "in view of the impossibility of speculating as to whether the magistrates would have made the order for [the applicant's] detention had he been represented at the hearing before them".

On the other hand, an individual may fail to qualify as a victim if adequate   **1-92**
redress has been afforded in the national legal system. Thus, the Commission has held that an applicant who complains that his conviction was obtained in breach of the due process guarantees in Article 6, will cease to be a victim if he has been

---

[69] (1997) 24 E.H.R.R. 423.
[70] This was despite the fact that the risk of inhuman treatment identified in that case arose not from the threatened acts of the authorities in the state concerned, but from the absence of adequate medical facilities.
[71] At paras 7–05 to 7–06.
[72] (1996) 21 E.H.R.R. 97.
[73] (1999) 1 F.L.R. 198.
[74] *Eckle v. Germany* (1983) 5 E.H.R.R. 1 at para. 66.
[75] (1981) 3 E.H.R.R. 1 at para. 35.
[76] (1996) 22 E.H.R.R. 293 at para. 68; See also *Perks and Others v. United Kingdom* (2000) 30 E.H.R.R. 33.

acquitted,[77] if his conviction has been quashed,[78] or if the procedural defect has been fully remedied on appeal.[79]

1–93   In *Eckle v. Germany*[80] the criminal proceedings against the applicants were found to have exceeded the reasonable time guarantee in Article 6(1). The domestic courts had reduced the sentence imposed on the applicants and discontinued subsequent proceedings. On the facts, this was held not to have deprived the applicants of their status as victims. However, the Court went on to say that the position may be different where the national courts have acknowledged the breach of the Convention and have adequately reduced a criminal sentence with the express intention of providing appropriate redress for the violation.

1–94   The question whether the domestic courts have provided adequate redress will in the end depend upon the nature of the violation alleged. Where, for example, the applicant's complaint relates to the substance of the criminal law,[81] rather than any specific measure which has been taken against him, it will often be difficult for the prosecution to argue that an acquittal or a successful appeal has remedied the violation.[82] As we have seen, the Court did not consider that the acquittal of the applicant in *Bowman v. United Kingdom*[83] deprived her of her status as a victim in the context of a complaint that the existence of a particular criminal offence violated her right to freedom of expression.

Manifestly ill-founded

1–95   The second limb of Article 35(3) requires the Court to declare inadmissible any application which is manifestly ill-founded. This has been interpreted as a test of *prima facie* arguability. In principle it applies to cases where the evidence submitted fails to substantiate the complaint; where the facts do not disclose an interference with a protected right; where the interference is plainly justified; or where the applicant has ceased to be a victim. In practice however, the Court has used this ground of inadmissibility as a means of controlling its caseload, and has often conducted a quite detailed examination of the merits of a complaint before declaring it to be "manifestly" ill-founded.

Abuse of the right of petition

1–96   The third limb of Article 35(3) requires the Court to declare inadmissible any complaint which constitutes an abuse of the right of petition. It may be applied in cases of forgery or misrepresentation; vexatious or repeated applications; offensive or provocative language[84]; or deliberate breach of the Court's rulings. A refusal to enter into friendly settlement negotiations will not constitute an

---

[77] *X v. Austria* (1974) 1 D.R. 44 at 45.
[78] *Reed v. United Kingdom* (1979) 19 D.R. 113 at 142 (quashing of an adjudication by a prison Board of Visitors).
[79] See *Edwards v. United Kingdom* (1993) 15 E.H.R.R. 417. *Cf. Rowe and Davis v. United Kingdom* (2000) 30 E.H.R.R. 1; *Condron and Condron v. United Kingdom* [2000] Crim.L.R. 677.
[80] (1983) 5 E.H.R.R. 1 at paras 66 to 70.
[81] See para. 1–85 above and Chapter 8 below.
[82] Unless the court in question is able under the Human Rights Act to remove the incompatibility by construction: see para. 3–34 below.
[83] (1998) 26 E.H.R.R. 1.
[84] *Stamoulakatos v. United Kingdom* (1997) 23 E.H.R.R. CD 113.

abuse of the right of petition.[85] Nor is an application abusive merely because it has a political motivation[86]; or because it is brought by a criminal defendant who has absconded from custody.[87]

Estoppel

The Rules of Court specifically provide that a respondent state must raise any **1–97** inadmissibility arguments in its written or oral observations prior to the Court's decision on admissibility, unless it is impracticable to do so.[88] This reflects the long-established practice of the former Court.[89] In *DeWilde, Ooms Versyp v. Belgium (No.1)*[90] the respondent government was estopped from raising preliminary objections to admissibility which had not been argued before the Commission. The Court explained that:

"It is in fact the usual practice in international and national courts that objections to admissibility should as a general rule be raised *in limine litis*. This, if not always mandatory, is at least a requirement of the proper administration of justice and of legal stability... [I]t results clearly from the general economy of the Convention that objections to jurisdiction and admissibility must, in principle, be raised first before the Commission to the extent that their character and the circumstances permit."

Likewise, in *Artico v. Italy*,[91] the Court emphasised that "the structure of the machinery of protection established by... the Convention is designed to ensure that the course of the proceedings is logical and orderly". In the Court's view "the spirit of the Convention requires that respondent States should normally raise their preliminary objections at the stage of the initial examination of admissibility, failing which they will be estopped".

Moreover, any admissibility objection must be clearly and explicitly pleaded.[92] If **1–98** an argument has been raised prior to a ruling on admissibility that the applicant is not a "victim" within the meaning of Article 34, it is not open to the government to resurrect the same argument at a later stage in the form of a plea of non-exhaustion.[93] Similarly, if the government has relied on one remedy in support of a plea of non-exhaustion at the admissibility stage, it may be estopped from invoking a different remedy thereafter.[94] In *Aydin v. Turkey*,[95] a case involving an allegation of rape in custody, the government was estopped from

---

[85] *Andronicou and Constantinou v. Cyprus* (1997) 25 E.H.R.R. 491.
[86] *Akdivar v. Turkey* (1997) 23 E.H.R.R. 143; *Cf. McFeely v. United Kingdom* (1980) 20 D.R. 44; *McQuiston v. United Kingdom* (1986) 46 D.R. 182 (An application motivated by the desire for publicity or propaganda may be abusive if it is not supported by any facts or if it is outside the scope of the Convention).
[87] *Van der Tang v. Spain* (1996) 22 E.H.R.R. 363.
[88] Rule 55. For a recent application of this principle see *Baskay and Okcuoglu v. Turkey* (Application Nos 23536/94 and 24408/94) Judgment of July 8, 1999, paras 68–70.
[89] *De Wilde, Ooms and Versyp v. Belgium* (1979–80) 1 E.H.R.R. 373; *Artico v. Italy* (1981) 3 E.H.R.R. 1; *Bozano v. France* (1986) 9 E.H.R.R. 297.
[90] (1979–80) 1 E.H.R.R. 373 at paras 53–54.
[91] (1981) 3 E.H.R.R. 1 at para. 27.
[92] *Foti v. Italy* (1983) 5 E.H.R.R. 313 at para. 47: "vague assertions" of non-exhaustion of domestic remedies found insufficient.
[93] *Pine Valley Developments v. Ireland* (1992) 14 E.H.R.R. 319 at para. 45.
[94] *Tomassi v. France* (1993) 15 E.H.R.R. 1 at para. 106.
[95] (1998) 25 E.H.R.R. 251 at para. 60.

arguing non-exhaustion and abuse of the right of individual petition since it had failed to assert these arguments clearly before the Commission.

1–99   The Court may however declare a case inadmissible at any stage of the proceedings.[96] There are three principal situations in which the Court will be prepared to consider admissibility objections at the merits stage of its deliberations. The first is where the objection was raised at the appropriate time, but was wrongly rejected.[97] Although the existing decisions in this category concern Commission rulings on the admissibility of a complaint, there is no reason in principle why the same point could not arise under Protocol 11 (where a Chamber has rejected an admissibility objection which is then re-argued before the Grand Chamber, either on a relinquishment[98] or on a referral[99]).

1–100   The second situation is where there has been a development in national law clarifying the existence of a domestic remedy which appeared doubtful when the admissibility of the application was initially considered. *Campbell and Fell v. United Kingdom*[1] is an example. At the time of the Commission's decision on the admissibility of the applicants' complaints, there was binding Divisional Court authority excluding the possibility of judicial review.[2] This was subsequently reversed by the Court of Appeal.[3] In the Court's view the government could not have been expected to raise the plea of non-exhaustion prior to the decision of the Court of Appeal, and accordingly no estoppel arose.[4]

1–101   The third situation is where the scope of the applicant's complaint has broadened since the admissibility decision so as to generate new admissibility objections not previously open to the government. In *Bonisch v. Austria*[5] the application, which alleged a breach of Article 6(1), was declared admissible by the Commission. In his memorial to the Court however, the applicant argued that in addition to the pleaded violation of Article 6(1), the complaint disclosed a breach of the presumption of innocence in Article 6(2). The Court held that it had jurisdiction to consider the new argument since it had "an evident connection" with the complaints which the applicant had raised before the Commission. However, the fresh complaint would be subject to any admissibility objections which could have been taken at the appropriate stage.[6]

1–102   Finally, it should be noted that it is not open to a contracting state to rely on an objection to admissibility which is inconsistent with a submission made on its

---

[96] Article 35(4).
[97] *Van Oosterwijk v. Belgium* (1981) 3 E.H.R.R. 557 paras. 30–34; *Cardot v. France* (1991) 13 E.H.R.R. 853 at paras 32–36; *Bahaddar v. Netherlands* (1998) 26 E.H.R.R. 278.
[98] See para. 1–114 below.
[99] See para. 1–149 below.
[1] (1985) 7 E.H.R.R. 165.
[2] *R v. Hull Prison Board of Visitors ex parte St Germain and others* [1978] 2 All E.R. 198.
[3] [1979] Q.B. 425.
[4] In the case of the first applicant, however, the Court considered that it would be unjust to reject the complaint for non-exhaustion since he had allowed the time limit for judicial review to expire in reliance in the Commission's decision: para. 63.
[5] (1987) 9 E.H.R.R. 191.
[6] In the event the Court did not consider it necessary to rule on the alleged violation of Art. 6(2).

behalf before the national courts. Thus, for example, it is not open to a government to argue that an applicant has failed to exhaust domestic remedies when it has argued in the domestic proceedings that such remedies are unavailable.[7]

Post admissibility procedures

Once a case has been declared admissible the Chamber will have the functions **1–103** of examining the merits of the application and placing itself at the disposal of the parties with a view to reaching a friendly settlement.[8] The Chamber may carry out fact-finding investigations anywhere in the territory of the Convention states, and may hold an oral hearing. At any point prior to the delivery of a judgment on the merits, the Chamber may decide to relinquish jurisdiction in favour of a Grand Chamber. If the Chamber decides to retain jurisdiction it will deliver a judgment on the merits of the complaint and on the applicant's claim for just satisfaction.

Factual investigations

Article 38(1)(a) provides that the Court may undertake an investigation to clarify **1–104** the facts of a case, and if it does so, the respondent state must "furnish all necessary facilities". Whilst the seat of the Court is at Strasbourg, the rules expressly permit the Court to perform any of its functions elsewhere in the Council of Europe, and enable the Court to delegate its investigative functions to individual judges.[9]

The Chamber may obtain any evidence which it considers capable of providing **1–105** clarification of the facts of the case.[10] It may request the parties to furnish documents, or hear any witness, including an expert witness, whose testimony or statements seem likely to assist[11]; it may depute an individual judge or a delegation of judges to conduct an inquiry, carry out an on the spot investigation, or take evidence in any manner[12]; it may appoint an independent expert to assist a delegation[13]; and it may ask any person or institution to obtain information, express an opinion or make a report on any specific point.[14]

Where a fact-finding delegation is appointed, the head of the delegation presides **1–106** over any hearing and the delegation has jurisdiction to exercise any power conferred on a Chamber under the Convention or the Rules of Court.[15] The President of the Court may request the assistance of the government of any contracting state in making the necessary arrangements for on the spot investigations, or for the service of summonses to procure evidence or attendance of witnesses situated in the state's territory.[16]

---

[7] *Pine Valley Developments v. Ireland* (1992) 14 E.H.R.R. 319; *Kolompar v. Belgium* (1993) 16 E.H.R.R. 197.
[8] Articles 38 and 39.
[9] Rule 19(1) and (2).
[10] Rule 42(1).
[11] Rule 42(1).
[12] Rule 42(2).
[13] Rule 42(2).
[14] Rule 42(3).
[15] Rule 63(2).
[16] Rule 37(2) and (3).

Friendly settlement

1–107   Once an application has been declared admissible the Registrar will contact the parties with a view to securing a friendly settlement "on the basis of respect for human rights as defined in the Convention and its protocols".[17] The Chamber may take any steps that appear appropriate to facilitate such a settlement.[18] Each party's proposals will be communicated to the opposing party and, in exceptional cases, the Registry may convene a meeting to discuss the proposals. The friendly settlement procedure is confidential.[19] Any position may be adopted by either party without prejudice to the arguments they have advanced or may advance in the proceedings.[20] Thus, no written or oral communication, or concession made in the course of friendly settlement negotiations may be referred to or relied on in the contentious proceedings.[21]

1–108   Prior to the introduction of Protocol 11 it was common for the Commission to communicate its provisional view of the merits of a complaint to the parties in confidence, with a view to promoting a friendly settlement. The Explanatory Report to Protocol 11 appears to assume that the Court will follow the same practice.[22] Such a procedure does not, however, sit comfortably with the Court's function of delivering a final and binding judgment on the merits of a case, and the Court has not been enthusiastic about disclosing the state of its deliberations to the parties before it has reached a final decision.

1–109   Any settlement reached between the parties must be approved by the Chamber, to ensure that it has been reached on the basis of "respect for human rights".[23] If the Court approves a settlement then the application will be struck off the Court's list.[24] The Court will then issue a decision containing a brief statement of the facts and the solution reached.[25]

1–110   Most friendly settlements consist of monetary compensation together with the payment of the applicant's reasonable legal costs.[26] Sometimes, however, a government may agree to introduce changes to rules of practice or delegated legislation as part of the settlement.[27] It is rare for states to agree to amend or introduce primary legislation since it will usually be impossible for the government to guarantee that any proposal will be approved by the legislature. Where

---

[17] Article 38(1)(b) and Rule 62(1).

[18] Rule 62(1).

[19] Article 38(2).

[20] Rule 62(2). A refusal to enter into friendly settlement negotiations cannot be characterised as an abuse of the right of petition: *Andronicou and Constantinou v. Cyprus* (1998) 25 E.H.R.R. 491.

[21] Rule 62(2).

[22] (1994) 17 E.H.R.R. 514 at 529, para. 78.

[23] Rule 62(3). In principle, the Court may reject a settlement reached between the parties. This is only likely to occur in practice if the complaint disclosed a pattern of violations, and the government had no plans to amend the relevant provisions of domestic law.

[24] Article 39, Rule 62(3).

[25] Article 39.

[26] It is always preferable to include a figure for costs as part of the agreed settlement approved by the Court since there is no method of taxation in the friendly settlement procedure once the case has been struck off the list.

[27] In *Faulkner v. United Kingdom, The Times*, January 11, 2000 the government agreed, as part of the friendly settlement approved by the Court, to introduce a system of civil legal aid for Guernsey.

an amendment to primary legislation is the only way to prevent further violations, the government will sometimes agree to introduce draft legislation into Parliament, and ask the Court to adjourn its consideration of the case pending the outcome.[28]

Withdrawal

Once a complaint has been registered, it is for the Court to decide whether or not **1–111** the case should proceed to a final judgment on the merits. The applicant is not free to withdraw at will. The Court may strike off its list any complaint which the applicant does not intend to pursue, or which has been resolved.[29] However, the Court must continue with its examination of the case if "respect for human rights as defined in the Convention and the protocols thereto so requires".[30] This reflects the fact that many applications have implications for the public order of the Council of Europe, so that the significance of a case may not be confined to the vindication of the rights of the individual applicant.

In *Tyrer v. United Kingdom*[31] the applicant had been sentenced to judicial **1–112** corporal punishment on the Isle of Man following his conviction for an offence of assault. The punishment had been carried out six years earlier, when the applicant was aged 15. Whilst the complaint was being considered by the Commission, the applicant indicated that he wished to withdraw. The Commission refused to accede to his request on the ground that "the case raised questions of a general character affecting the observance of the Convention which necessitated a further examination of the issued involved". The applicant took no further part in the proceedings. When the case came before the Court, the government applied to strike it out of the list in view of the applicant's position and in view of the fact that legislation had been adopted by the Manx Parliament to abolish corporal punishment for assault. The Court held that it could only strike a case from the list if there had been "a friendly settlement, arrangement or other fact of a kind to provide a solution to the matter". In the Court's view, the applicant's request to withdraw unilaterally did not constitute a friendly settlement or a solution to the matter. Nether did the Court consider the proposal to amend the law constituted a solution:

> "There is no certainty as to whether or when the proposal will become law and, even if adopted, it cannot erase a punishment already inflicted. What is more, the proposed legislation does not go to the substance of the issue before the Court, namely whether judicial corporal punishment as inflicted on the applicant in accordance with Manx legislation is contrary to the Convention."

By contrast in *Z v. United Kingdom*[32] the Commission permitted the withdrawal **1–113** of an application which had been introduced by the Official Solicitor on behalf of a child. The complaint alleged that the failure of social services to protect the child and her four siblings from parental abuse was in breach of Article 3. The

---

[28] This course was adopted following the Commission's decision in *Sutherland v. United Kingdom* (1997) 24 E.H.R.R. CD 22.
[29] Article 37(1).
[30] Article 37(1).
[31] (1979–80) 2 E.H.R.R. 1.
[32] Application No. 29392/95.

child had since been adopted, and her adoptive parents had expressed an intention to withdraw. In reaching the conclusion that the child should cease to be an applicant, the Commission "had regard to the expressed wishes of the adoptive parents who, in the normal course of events, would be the appropriate representatives of D, and to the fact that the important Convention issues in the case would be examined in respect of the remaining applicants".[33]

Relinquishment to a Grand Chamber

1–114   Where a case raises a serious question concerning the interpretation of the Convention, or where the judgment of the Chamber may be inconsistent with a previous judgment of the Court, the Chamber may, at any time before it has rendered its judgment, relinquish the case to a Grand Chamber, unless one of the parties to the case objects.[34] If the Chamber proposes to adopt this course, the Registrar will notify the parties, who will have one month within which to file a "duly reasoned" objection.[35] The Chamber need not give reasons for its decision to relinquish jurisdiction.[36] A Grand Chamber dealing with a case which has been relinquished prior to judgment by the Chamber will include the national judge elected in respect of the state against which the case has been brought,[37] the President and Vice Presidents of the Court, and the Presidents of the four Chambers.

Oral hearings

1–115   There is no absolute entitlement to an oral hearing, but the Explanatory Report to Protocol 11[38] creates a strong presumption in favour of an oral stage to the proceedings.[39] As we have seen, a Chamber may decide to hold such a hearing before declaring a case admissible. Where the Chamber has declared the case admissible on the written pleadings alone, an oral hearing is generally to be held at the merits stage, if either party requests one.[40] However the Chamber may, *exceptionally*, decide to dispense with an oral hearing altogether.[41]

1–116   Where a hearing is held, the Court may ask the parties to address specific issues in their oral pleadings. The President will decide the order and duration of the

---

[33] Para. 23.

[34] Article 30.

[35] Rule 72(2). Under Rule 72(2), an objection which is not "duly reasoned" will be considered invalid by the Chamber. There is no indication in the Convention or the Rules as to what reasons need to be advanced. This gives rise to a potential conflict between the Rules and the Explanatory Report to Protocol 11 (1994) 17 E.H.R.R. 514. Paras 46 and 79 of the Explanatory Report suggest that the reason why relinquishment has been made subject to the approval of the parties is to ensure that they are not otherwise deprived of their right to a re-hearing under Art. 43. However, Rule 72 suggests that once the Chamber has decided to relinquish jurisdiction the parties must advance adequate reasons for their objection.

[36] Rule 71(2).

[37] Article 27(2). The national judge may not however preside: Rule 13.

[38] (1994) 17 E.H.R.R. 514.

[39] Para. 44 provides that "The procedure will be written and oral, unless otherwise decided by the Court after consultation with the parties". Para. 45 provides "The parties will present their submissions by means of a written procedure. Oral procedure will consist of a hearing at which the applicant . . . and the respondent state will have the right to speak.".

[40] Rule 59(2).

[41] Rule 59(2). The Court has construed its powers to dispense with an oral hearing flexibly, enabling it to decide straightforward cases—which would previously have been referred to the Committee of Ministers—without an oral hearing at any stage.

parties' submissions.[42] In a typical case, the applicant will begin, and will be afforded 30 minutes to address the principal issues in the case. The government will respond for a similar period. The members of the Court may then put further questions to the parties' representatives.[43] The parties will then be given a further 15 minutes in which to answer the judges' questions and respond to the submissions of the opposing party. Exceptionally, the Court may summon witnesses to give evidence on oath,[44] who may then be examined by the judges and the parties.[45]

Evidence and burden of proof

There are no formal rules for the admissibility of evidence under the Convention. **1–117** Parties may submit any relevant documentary material, whether or not it complies with the formalities of domestic law governing admissibility, and there is no restriction on the admission of hearsay evidence. It is extremely rare for the Court to hear evidence on oath,[46] although provision is made for this in the Rules of Court.[47]

At the admissibility stage, the government bears the burden of proving the **1–118** existence and availability of effective remedies in the national legal system in support of plea of non-exhaustion.[48] Once the existence of such a remedy has been raised it is for the applicant to show why it was unavailable or inadequate in the circumstances.[49]

The Court does not apply formalised rules for the burden and standard of proof, **1–119** when it comes to consider the merits of a complaint. Instead, it will base its assessment on an examination of "all the material before it, whether originating from the Commission, the Parties or other sources" and, if necessary, material obtained by the Court of its own motion.[50] The Court's approach to the evidence is determined by the nature of the violation and the issues in dispute between the parties.

In general, it is for the applicant make out a *prima facie* case that there has been **1–120** an interference with a protected right,[51] and to raise at least an arguable basis for an eventual finding of violation. In the absence of any evidence on a disputed issue of fact, the Court will tend to accord the benefit of the doubt to the government, unless the nature of the breach is such as to create a presumption in

---

[42] Rule 63(1).
[43] Rule 68.
[44] Rules 65 to 69.
[45] Rule 68.
[46] In recent years the Court has taken oral evidence in a number of cases alleging serious violations against Turkey. There is, however, no recent example in which the Court has taken oral evidence in a case involving the United Kingdom.
[47] Rules 65–69.
[48] See para. 1–52 above.
[49] *Donnelly v. United Kingdom* (1972) 4 D.R. 4 at para. 64; *Akdivar v. Turkey* (1997) 23 E.H.R.R. 143 at para. 68.
[50] *Ireland v. United Kingdom* (1979–80) 2 E.H.R.R. 25 at para. 160. The Court has since held that this approach is applicable in individual applications as well as inter-state cases: *Artico v. Italy* (1981) 3 E.H.R.R. 1 at para. 30.
[51] *Artico v. Italy* (1981) 3 E.H.R.R. 1 at para. 30.

the applicant's favour.[52] In *Goddi v. Italy*[53] for example, the applicant complained that he had not been produced for the hearing of his appeal. He maintained that he had notified the prison authorities of the date of the hearing. The government contested this allegation, but neither party adduced any evidence in support of its position. The Court held that in these circumstances it was unable to resolve the dispute, and it was not therefore prepared to find that the Italian authorities were at fault. However, where the applicant has submitted evidence in support of a complaint it is not enough for the government to express reservations about that evidence. The state is under a positive duty to provide the Court with any relevant information which is in its possession, or to which it could gain access.[54]

1–121 The Court will start from an assumption that the domestic authorities have acted impartially,[55] in good faith[56] and in accordance with domestic law.[57] It will generally rely on findings of fact which have been reached by the domestic courts, unless they have drawn arbitrary conclusions from the evidence before them.[58] This is especially true in cases which depend on the credibility of witnesses.[59] As the Commission observed in *Stewart v. United Kingdom*[60] "the national judge, unlike the Commission, has had the benefit of listening to the witnesses at first hand and assessing the credibility and probative value of their testimony".

1–122 If an interference is established or admitted, the burden will shift to the government to advance "relevant and sufficient reasons" to justify it.[61] The government is expected to adduce evidence in support of any justification which it advances.[62] The standard of justification required depends on the nature of the

---

[52] See paras 1–125 and 5–37 below.

[53] (1984) 6 E.H.R.R. 457.

[54] *Artico v. Italy* (1981) 3 E.H.R.R. 1 at para. 30.

[55] *LeCompte, Van Leuren and DeMeyer v. Belgium* (1982) 4 E.H.R.R. 1 at para. 58.

[56] *Kraska v. Switzerland* (1994) 18 E.H.R.R. 188.

[57] See *Esbester v. United Kingdom* (1993) 18 E.H.R.R. CD 72 at 76, where the Commission found that the compilation of intelligence information about the applicant under the Security Services Act 1989 was compatible with Art. 8 because of the statutory safeguards and "the absence of any evidence or indication that the system is not functioning as required by domestic law".

[58] *Klaas v. Germany* (1994) 18 E.H.R.R. 305 at paras 29–31; *Edwards v. United Kingdom* (1993) 15 E.H.R.R. 417 at para. 34; *Van Mechelen v. Netherlands* (1998) 25 E.H.R.R. 647 at para. 50; *Barbera, Messegue and Jabardo v. Spain* (1989) 11 E.H.R.R. 360; *Kostovski v. Netherlands* (1990) 12 E.H.R.R. 434 at para. 39; *Monnell and Morris v. United Kingdom* (1987) 10 E.H.R.R. 205 at paras 49 and 69.

[59] *Murray and ors v. United Kingdom* (1995) 19 E.H.R.R. 193 at paras 57–63; *Klaas v. Germany* (1993) 18 E.H.R.R. 305 at 338 paras 30–31.

[60] (1984) 39 D.R. 162 at 168.

[61] See, for example, *Buckley v. United Kingdom* (1997) 23 E.H.R.R. 101 at para. 77. In the context of alleged discrimination contrary to Art. 14 the Court has held that the burden is on the applicant to demonstrate a difference in treatment on grounds of "status" between himself and another person who is in a relevantly similar position: *Selcuk and Asker v. Turkey* (1998) 26 E.H.R.R. 477 at para. 102. If this burden is discharged then it is for the government to establish an "objective and reasonable justification" for the difference: *Darby v. Sweden* (1991) 13 E.H.R.R. 774 at para. 31; *Marckx v. Belgium* (1979–80) 2 E.H.R.R. 330 at para. 32.

[62] *Autotronic AG v. Switzerland* (1990) 12 E.H.R.R. 485 at paras 60–63. See also *Smith and Grady v. United Kingdom* (2000) 29 E.H.R.R. 493 at para. 99, where the Court referred to "the lack of concrete evidence" to substantiate the justification for excluding homosexuals from the armed forces; *Kokkinakis v. Greece* (1994) 17 E.H.R.R. 397 where the Court found a violation of Art. 9 on the ground that the government had adduced no evidence that the applicant was guilty of attempting to convert others to his faith "by improper means".

violation. In *Dudgeon v. United Kingdom*,[63] for example, the Court held that the government must demonstrate "particularly serious reasons" to justify an inter-ference with a person's private sexual activity. Similarly, the Court has held that "very weighty reasons" are required to justify a difference in treatment based on gender, race or other "suspect categories" of discrimination.[64] Where an inter-ference with the right to freedom of expression is in issue, the justification must be "convincingly established".[65]

The burden of justifying an arrest or detention always rests on the government.[66] **1–123** In *Fox, Campbell and Hartley v. United Kingdom*[67] the government found itself unable to discharge this burden since the evidence upon which it sought to rely involved matters of national security which it was unable to disclose. The Court was not prepared to rely on a bare assertion that the arrest was justified:

> "The Court must be enabled to ascertain whether the essence of the safeguard afforded by Article 5(1)(c) has been secured. Consequently the respondent government has to furnish at least some facts or information capable of satisfying the Court that the arrested person was reasonably suspected of having committed the alleged offence."[68]

The limited information supplied by the government did not meet the minimum **1–124** standard set by Article 5(3)(c) for judging the reasonbleness of a suspicion relied upon to justify the arrest of an individual. There had therefore been a violation of Article 5. However, four years later, in *Murray v. United Kingdom*,[69] the Court was "prepared to attach some credence" to the government's assertion that the applicants' arrests were justified by confidential information. Whilst such an assertion could never be sufficient in itself,[70] the Court went to considerable lengths in *Murray* to identify other objective evidence which was capable of justifying the applicants' arrests.

Where it is alleged that state agents have inflicted inhuman and degrading **1–125** treatment, the Court has observed that "heightened vigilance" is required.[71] In *Ireland v. United Kingdom*[72] the Court held that a violation of Article 3 requires proof beyond reasonable doubt, but went on to say that "such proof may follow from the coexistence of sufficiently strong, clear and concordant inferences or of *similar unrebutted presumptions of fact*".[73] One such presumption of fact arises where an applicant has sustained injuries whilst in police custody.[74]

---

[63] (1982) 4 E.H.R.R. 149.
[64] *Karlheinz and Schmidt v. Germany* (1994) 18 E.H.R.R. 513 at para. 24; *East African Asians Case* (1981) 3 E.H.R.R. 76.
[65] *Barthold v. Germany* (1985) 7 E.H.R.R. 383 at para. 58.
[66] *Zamir v. United Kingdom* (1983) 40 D.R. 42.
[67] (1991) 13 E.H.R.R. 157.
[68] Para. 34.
[69] (1995) 19 E.H.R.R. 193 at para. 59.
[70] See para. 60.
[71] *Ribitsch v. Austria* (1996) 21 E.H.R.R. 573 at para. 32.
[72] (1979–80) 2 E.H.R.R. 25.
[73] At para. 161.
[74] See para. 6–37 below.

Judgment on the merits

1–126 In the absence of a friendly settlement or relinquishment, the Chamber will deliver a judgment on the merits of the application. Whether it is sitting as a Chamber or a Grand Chamber, the Court deliberates in private and its deliberations are secret.[75] The Registrar may be present but may not take part in the deliberations.[76] The Court's judgments are expressed in the form of a single collegiate ruling, which may be accompanied by separate opinions in which individual judges express concurring or dissenting views.[77] Article 45(2) provides that "if a judgment does not represent, in whole or in part, the unanimous opinion of the judges, any judge shall be entitled to deliver a separate opinion".[78] This represents a compromise between the usual common law approach, under which each member of the court is required to state his or her decision, however briefly, and the approach adopted by the European Court of Justice and some constitutional courts[79] where a single judgment is delivered with no scope for elaboration or dissent by individual judges.

1–127 The content of the judgment is prescribed by the Convention and the Rules of Court. Article 45(1) simply requires that "reasons shall be given for judgments, as well as for decisions declaring a case admissible or inadmissible". Rule 74 is more specific. It provides that the judgment must set out the names of the judges; the date of the adoption of the judgment; a description of the parties; the names of the agents, advocates or advisers of the parties; an account of the procedure followed; the facts of the case; a summary of the submissions of the parties; the reasons in point of law; the operative provisions of the Convention; the decision, if any, in respect of costs; the number of judges constituting the majority; and, where appropriate, a statement of which language text is to be regarded as authentic.[80]

1–128 The Court's decisions are reached by voting on specific resolutions,[81] following discussion between the judges about the precise form of words to be used. Under this process of collegiate decision-making the judges adopt the formulation which the greatest number are able to agree upon. The Court's judgments rarely display the depth of judicial analysis which common lawyers are accustomed to expect. Important principles are often reduced to a set formula which is repeated, more or less verbatim, in one judgment after another.

1–129 This economy of reasoning sometimes means that major questions of interpretation can be left open. Moreover, the Court has in the past been inclined to

---

[75] Rule 22(1).

[76] Rule 22(2).

[77] Any decision of the Chamber must state whether it was taken unanimously or by a majority and must be accompanied by reasons: Rule 56(1).

[78] See also Rule 74(2) which provides that "any judge who has taken part in the consideration of a case shall be entitled to annex to the judgment either a separate opinion, concurring or dissenting from that judgment, or a bare statement of dissent".

[79] Article 34(4)(5) of the Irish Constitution, for example, expressly provides that where the Supreme Court is called upon to determine the constitutional validitiy of a law, the court is to nominate one of its number to give the judgment and no other opinion, dissenting or concurring, is to be delivered.

[80] Court judgments are normally given in either English or French, but the Court may direct that a particular judgment should be given in both official languages: Rule 57(1).

[81] Rule 23(1). The resolution must be formulated in precise terms (Rule 23(4)). Abstentions are not permitted (Rule 23(2). In the event of a tie the President has the casting vote (Rule 23(1)).

decide cases on the narrowest possible ground. If it has found a violation of one provision of the Convention, it will often decline to rule on another alleged violation arising out of the same complaint. In *Campbell and Fell v. United Kingdom*,[82] for example, the Court found that the absence of a right to consult privately with a legal representative constituted a breach of Article 6. Having reached this conclusion the Court considered it unnecessary to go on to consider whether it was also in breach of Article 8. Similarly, in *Malone v. United Kingdom*[83] the Court found that the absence of legal regulation for the interception of telecommunications was in breach of Article 8, and declined to consider whether the applicant had also been the victim of a violation of Article 13.

Just satisfaction

Article 41 of the Convention provides that "if the Court finds that there has been a violation of the Convention . . . and the internal law of the High Contracting Party concerned allows only partial reparation to be made, the Court shall, if necessary, afford just satisfaction to the injured party".[84] The Court does not have jurisdiction under Article 41 to quash a criminal conviction,[85] or to issue any order requiring the national authorities to take particular steps to remedy a violation.[86] It is confined to the award of monetary compensation and costs. Moreover, the Court's powers under Article 41 are discretionary.[87] Just satisfaction cannot be claimed as of right.

1–130

Awards under Article 41 may encompass:

1–131

(a) pecuniary loss suffered as a result of the violation including, if appropriate, loss of earnings and a sum equivalent to any penalty imposed by the national courts;

(b) non-pecuniary loss, *i.e.* compensation for physical injury, suffering and distress caused by the violation; and

(c) legal costs and expenses incurred in attempting to forestall or secure redress for the violation, both through the domestic legal system and under the Convention.

The Court will include interest on compensation where this is necessary to avoid unfair diminution in its value.[88]

Any claim for just satisfaction must be set out in the applicant's written observations on the merits of the complaint or, if no such observations have been filed, in a special document filed no later than two months after the decision declaring

1–132

---

[82] (1985) 7 E.H.R.R. 165.
[83] (1985) 7 E.H.R.R. 14.
[84] Prior to Protocol 11, this power was set out (in identical terms) in Article 50 of the Convention.
[85] *Schmautzer v. Austria* (1996) 21 E.H.R.R. 511 at paras 43–44.
[86] See, for example, *Ireland v. United Kingdom* (1979–80) 2 E.H.R.R. 25, an inter-state case in which the Court rejected a request made by the Irish government that criminal prosecutions should be brought against those responsible for ill-treatment in custody.
[87] *Sunday Times v. United Kingdom* (Unreported) November 6, 1980.
[88] See, for example, *Stran Greek Refineries v. Greece* (1994) 19 E.H.R.R. 293 at 331 paras 82–83.

the case admissible.[89] The claim should be itemised in detail, and accompanied by all relevant supporting documents.[90] The Court may include its ruling on just satisfaction in the judgment on the merits of the complaint.[91] However if the issue in not "ready for decision" the Court will reserve it, and fix the subsequent procedure. The parties may, at this stage, negotiate a settlement and, providing the Court considers the settlement to be "equitable", it will strike the case out of the list.

1–133   An award of compensation may be reduced, or even refused altogether, if the applicant's own conduct has contributed to the loss suffered. In *Johnson v. United Kingdom*[92] the Court reduced the compensation awarded for excessive detention in a psychiatric hospital on the ground that the applicant had adopted a "negative attitude towards his rehabilitation" and had refused to co-operate with plans to find him suitable accommodation in the community. And in *McCann, Savage and Farell v. United Kingdom*[93] the Court refused to award any compensation for a violation of the right to life "having regard to the fact that the three terrorist suspects who were killed had been intending to plant a bomb on Gibraltar". On the other hand, the fact that the applicant has serious criminal convictions is not, in itself, a ground to reducing an award.[94]

(i) Pecuniary loss

1–134   Where causation is established, the Court is generally prepared to award any pecuniary losses which the applicant is able to substantiate. In *Allenet de Ribemont v. France*[95] the applicant was awarded compensation for damage to his business opportunities as a result of statements by public officials which breached the presumption of innocence in Article 6(2). In *Baggetta v. Italy*[96] the Court awarded compensation for the financial repurcussions of criminal proceedings which had failed to conclude within a reasonable time. And in *Lingens v. Austria*[97] the applicant was awarded a sum equivalent to the fine and costs which had been awarded against him in proceedings for criminal defamation, together with a sum to represent a loss of profits.

(ii) Non-pecuniary loss

1–135   The assessment of non-pecuniary loss is inherently uncertain. The Court rarely gives detailed reasons for its awards, usually confining itself to a statement that the assessment has been made "on an equitable basis". Whilst it is possible to identify certain general principles, the Court's application of those principles to particular cases has been inconsistent and unpredictable.

---

[89] Rule 60(1).
[90] Rule 60(2).
[91] Rule 75(1).
[92] (1999) 27 E.H.R.R. 296.
[93] (1996) 21 E.H.R.R. 97 at para. 219.
[94] In *Weeks v. United Kingdom* (1991) 13 E.H.R.R. 435, for example, the applicant who was serving a life sentence for armed robbery and firearms offences, was awarded a substantial sum in damages for a breach of Art. 5(4) (see (1988) 10 E.H.R.R. 293).
[95] (1995) 20 E.H.R.R. 557.
[96] (1988) 10 E.H.R.R. 325.
[97] (1986) 8 E.H.R.R. 407.

The primary purpose of any award of just satisfaction is to put the applicant into **1–136** the position that he would have been in if the violation had not occurred.[98] It follows that exemplary damages (which are intended to punish and deter "oppressive, arbitrary and unconstitutional action by servants of the government"[99]) are not awarded under Article 41.[1]

The Court does not recognise a separate category of aggravated damages. **1–137** Nevertheless it frequently makes an award for non-pecuniary loss in respect of anxiety, distress and injury to feelings. Thus, awards have been made for feelings of "frustration and helplessness" arising from an inability to argue for early release[2]; and for "confusion and neglect" caused by ineffective legal representation.[3] When awarding compensation for injury to feelings the Court does not always require specific evidence in support.

Where the applicant has suffered a specific detriment as a result of the violation, **1–138** the Court has usually been willing to make an award for non-pecuniary loss. In *Tomasi v. France*[4] the applicant was awarded more than FF 700,000 in respect of assaults in police custody,[5] and delay in the conduct of criminal proceedings.[6] And in *Quinn v. France*[7] the Court awarded the applicant FF10,000 for 11 hours wrongful detention with no aggravating features.

It is not always necessary to prove any tangible or physical harm. In *S v.* **1–139** *Switzerland*[8] the applicant was awarded Sfr 2,500 for interference with his right to communicate with his lawyer in confidence whilst he was in detention. Other examples include *Z v. Finland*[9] where an award of 200,000 FIM was made in respect of the disclosure of confidential medical information about a witness in court proceedings; *Funke v. France*[10] where an award of FF 50,000 was made for

---

[98] *Piersack v. Belgium* (1984) 7 E.H.R.R. 251 at para. 12; Van Dijk and Van Hoof, *Theory and Practice of the European Convention on Human Rights* (Kluwer, 1998), p. 250.
[99] *Rookes v. Barnard* [1964] A.C. 1129.
[1] See *Campbell v. United Kingdom* (1993) 15 E.H.R.R. 137 at paras 68–70 where the Court rejected a claim for £3,000 advanced on the ground that such an award might "discourage the Government from interfering with prisoners' correspondence". Note, however, that in certain cases the Court has made an award which comes close to an award of exemplary damages. In *Teixeira de Castro v. Portugal* (1999) 28 E.H.R.R. 101 the Court awarded the applicant a significant sum under the heading of non-pecuniary loss following his prosecution for an offence of drug dealing committed as a result of police entrapment. *Cf. Fose v. Minister of Safety and Security* (1997) 2 B.H.R.C. 434 at 466–468 where the South African Constitutional Court held that exemplary damages were outside the scope of "appropriate relief", as that term is used in the Interim Constitution, since they amounted to the anomalous imposition of a penalty in civil proceedings which would be paid out of public funds, and would constitute a windfall to the victim.
[2] *Weeks v. United Kingdom* (1991) 13 E.H.R.R. 435.
[3] *Artico v. Italy* (1981) 3 E.H.R.R. 1.
[4] (1993) 15 E.H.R.R. 1.
[5] See also *Ribitsch v. Austria* (1996) 21 E.H.R.R. 573 (applicant awarded £6,287 in relation to assaults in police custody); *Aksoy v. Turkey* (1997) 23 E.H.R.R. 553 (£25,040 awarded in respect of serious ill-treatment in custody over a period of 14 days); *Aydin v. Turkey* (1998) 25 E.H.R.R. 251 (£25,000 for rape and assault in custody, together with failure to carry out an effective investigation).
[6] This was in addition to compensation which the applicant had received for excessive detention on remand in domestic proceedings.
[7] (1996) 21 E.H.R.R. 529.
[8] (1992) 14 E.H.R.R. 670.
[9] (1998) 25 E.H.R.R. 371.
[10] (1993) 16 E.H.R.R. 297.

an unlawful search and for subsequent infringements of the protection against self-incrimination; and *Halford v. United Kingdom*[11] where the applicant was awarded £10,000 for unlawful interception of her private office telephone. If, however, the applicant's challenge relates to the very existence of law, rather than a specific measure applying it to him the Court will often conclude that the finding of the violation is sufficient just satisfaction.[12]

1–140   The Court is generally reluctant to award compensation if there is a tenuous causal link between the violation and the loss claimed.[13] Particular problems of causation will arise where the Court has found a violation of one of the procedural provisions of Article 5 or Article 6, and the applicant claims compensation for the consequences of a conviction. The Court's approach can be illustrated by reference to three types of complaint: applications alleging a lack of independence or impartiality in the tribunal; applications involving the admission of evidence in breach of Article 6; and applications based upon the absence of effective legal representation.

1–141   Where the applicant's complaint relates to the structural independence or impartiality of a tribunal, the Court is usually unwilling to speculate as to whether the outcome of the domestic proceedings would have been different if they had conformed to the procedural requirements of Article 6.[14] Thus, in *Findlay v. United Kingdom*[15] the Court declined to award compensation where the applicant had been convicted by a Court Martial which was found to be procedurally unfair in its constitution. The Court took a similar approach in *Hauschildt v. Denmark*[16] (where the applicant complained that some of the judges who tried him had made previous adverse rulings at a preliminary stage of the criminal proceedings); in *Holm v. Sweden*[17] (where the jury included five members who were connected with one of the parties); and in *Remli v. France*[18] (where there was evidence of race bias within the jury which had not been properly investigated).

1–142   In cases concerning the admission of evidence in breach of Article 6 there is a marked inconsistency of approach. In *Delta v. France*[19] the Court awarded a substantial sum where the applicant's conviction was based on hearsay evidence admitted in breach of Article 6. The Court expressly declined to speculate as to whether the applicant would have been acquitted if the evidence had been excluded, stating simply that it was "not unreasonable" to regard the applicant as having suffered a real loss of opportunity. In *Windisch v. Austria*[20] the Court found a clear causal link between the admission of the evidence of anonymous witnesses in breach of Article 6, and the applicant's detention in custody as a result of his conviction. In the Court's view the applicant was entitled to compensation for the loss of his liberty since this was "the direct consequence of

---

[11] (1997) 24 E.H.R.R. 371.
[12] *Norris v. Ireland* (1991) 13 E.H.R.R. 186; *Bowman v. United Kingdom* (1998) 26 E.H.R.R. 1 at para. 51.
[13] See, for example, *Saunders v. United Kingdom* (1997) 23 E.H.R.R. 313.
[14] *Vacher v. France* (1997) 24 E.H.R.R. 482; *Schmautzer v. Austria* (1995) 21 E.H.R.R. 417.
[15] (1997) 24 E.H.R.R. 221.
[16] (1990) 12 E.H.R.R. 266 at paras 55–58.
[17] (1994) 18 E.H.R.R. 79 at paras 35–36.
[18] (1996) 22 E.H.R.R. 253.
[19] (1993) 16 E.H.R.R. 574.
[20] (1991) 13 E.H.R.R. 281 at para. 35.

the establishment of his guilt, which was effected in a manner that did not comply with Article 6". Similarly, in *Teixeira de Castro v. Portugal*[21] the applicant was awarded compensation where the Court found that evidence obtained by entrapment had been admitted in breach of Article 6.

However, in *Saunders v. United Kingdom*[22] the Court refused to award com-   1–143
pensation in respect of a violation of Article 6 arising from the admission of compulsory questioning evidence. The Court was apparently concerned that such an award might be interpreted as casting doubts on the correctness of the applicant's conviction:

> "[The Court] cannot speculate as to the question whether the outcome of the trial would
> have been any different had use not been made of the transcripts by the prosecution and,
> like the Commission, underlines that the finding of a breach of the Convention is not
> to be taken to carry any implications as regards that question. It therefore considers that
> no causal connection has been established between the losses claimed by the applicant
> and the Court's finding of a violation."

Similar inconsistencies are apparent where the procedural violation consists of   1–144
the absence of effective legal representation. In *Artico v. Italy*[23] the Court accepted that it was unnecessary for an applicant to prove prejudice in order to establish a violation of Article 6(3)(c). This would, in the Court's view, be "asking the impossible" since it could never be proved conclusively that effective legal representation would have secured the applicant's acquittal. The Court went on to award the applicant a substantial sum for "confusion and neglect" caused by ineffective legal representation.[24] Similarly in *Goddi v. Italy*[25] the Court awarded compensation on the ground that the applicant's domestic appeal had been dismissed in the absence of his lawyer,[26] observing that; "[T]he outcome might *possibly* have been different if Mr Goddi had had the benefit of a practical and effective defence. In the present case such a loss of real opportunities warrants the award of just satisfaction."[27]

In other cases, however, the Court has held that in order to receive any compensa-   1–145
tion at all an applicant must prove that legal representation would have had a decisive effect on the outcome of the domestic proceedings. In *Benham v. United Kingdom*[28] the applicant was sentenced to 30 days imprisonment for failure to pay the Community Charge, under a procedure for which there was no legal aid available. The Court found a violation of Article 6(3)(c), but declined to speculate "as to whether the magistrates would have made the order for B's detention had he been represented at the hearing before them". Accordingly, he was awarded no compensation for the breach.[29]

---

[21] (1999) 28 E.H.R.R. 101.
[22] (1997) 23 E.H.R.R. 313 at paras 83–89.
[23] (1981) 3 E.H.R.R. 1 at para. 35.
[24] *Artico v. Italy* (1981) 3 E.H.R.R. 1.
[25] (1984) 6 E.H.R.R. 457.
[26] The applicant was also absent, although this was not central to the Court's decision.
[27] Our emphasis.
[28] (1996) 22 E.H.R.R. 293.
[29] This was despite an earlier High Court ruling that there was insufficient evidence to justify the magistrates' decision.

1–146   This ruling was challenged in *Perks and others v. United Kingdom*[30] a series of linked applications raising similar issues. In the *Perks* judgment the Court adopted the same general approach as in *Benham*. However one of the applicants—a man who suffered from serious mental and physical handicaps— was singled out for an award of compensation. This was primarily due to a concession by the government that a reasonably competent solicitor would have drawn the man's disabilities to the attention of the magistrates.[31]

Costs

1–147   Where the Court has found a violation of the Convention, it will generally make an award of costs in favour of the successful applicant. Such an award is made "on an equitable basis", taking account of the violations alleged and found. If the applicant has succeeded on one alleged violation but failed on another, the Court may award only part of his legal costs.[32] Moreover, the scale of fees charged by lawyers in the United Kingdom is higher than in many other parts of the Council of Europe, and the Court has, on occasions, made significant deductions from the fee claims submitted by applicants from this country. Any sums already paid in legal aid will be deducted from the Court's award of costs.[33]

1–148   The circumstances in which an award of costs can be made against an unsuccessful applicant are very limited.[34] The applicant can never be required to pay the government's legal costs or any costs associated with the preparation of the government's case. However, an unsuccessful applicant can, exceptionally, be required to pay the costs of securing the attendance of witnesses or obtaining evidence *which has been requested by the Court on his or her behalf.* The general rule is that the party who requested that the evidence be obtained should bear the costs, unless the court directs otherwise.[35] If the applicant is successful then the witness costs will of course generally be recoverable from the government as part of the applicant's bill of costs. But if the applicant is unsuccessful then he may be left to pay the costs of the witness concerned. However, the Court has discretion to direct that the costs be borne by the Council of Europe.[36]

Subsequent referral to the Grand Chamber

1–149   Within three months of the judgment of a Chamber, either party can request a re-hearing before a Grand Chamber under Article 43(1). During that period, the

---

[30] (2000) 30 E.H.R.R. 33.

[31] The Divisional Court had expressly found that it was "unlikely" that the magistrates would have sent the applicant to prison if they had understood the extent of his handicaps.

[32] See, for example, *Benham v. United Kingdom* (1996) 22 E.H.R.R. 293; *Mats Jacobsson v. Sweden* (1991) 13 E.H.R.R. 79. This is not, however, an invariable practice: see *Osman v. United Kingdom* (2000) 29 E.H.R.R. 245; *Eckle v. Germany* (1983) 5 E.H.R.R. 1; *Sunday Times v. United Kingdom (No. 2)* (1979–80) 2 E.H.R.R. 317; *Perks v. United Kingdom* (2000) 30 E.H.R.R. 33.

[33] This is standard procedure for all successful legally aided applications.

[34] This corresponds with the practice adopted by the Privy Council and the Supreme Court of South Africa, where a principle has been recognised that courts should exercise special caution before making an award of costs against a party invoking the protection of the courts for his or her constitutional human rights. Judicial protection and vindication of human rights is a matter of public rather than purely individual concern and it would therefore be contrary to the public interest if substantial costs awards were to act as a deterrent to the vindication of individual rights. See para. 3–55 below.

[35] Rules 42(5) and 65(3).

[36] Rule 42(5) and 65(3).

judgment of the Chamber will not become final. Such a request will be considered by a panel of five judges appointed by the Grand Chamber. The panel will grant the request "if the case raises a serious question affecting the interpretation or application of the Convention . . . or a serious issue of general importance".[37] The request must specify the issue or issues which are said to satisfy these requirements.[38] No new evidence or argument may be put forward at this stage: the panel is confined to a consideration of the existing case file.[39] The panel is not required to give reasons for a refusal to refer a case to the Grand Chamber.[40]

If the panel grants the request for a referral, the Grand Chamber will decide the **1–150** case by means of a judgment.[41] A further oral hearing is possible, but the Grand Chamber is likely, in most cases, to rely upon the verbatim record of the hearing before the Chamber. The composition of the Grand Chamber is basically the same on a referral as on a relinquishment.[42] However, the Grand Chamber may not include any judge who sat in the Chamber which rendered the judgment, apart from the President of that Chamber, and the national judge of the respondent state.[43]

The risk that this procedure will unduly complicate or prolong proceedings is **1–151** offset by the power of the Chamber to relinquish jurisdiction before delivering its judgment. Although the parties have the right to submit a "duly reasoned" objection to prior relinquishment,[44] any party who has made such an objection is likely to encounter serious difficulty in obtaining a subsequent referral of the case to the Grand Chamber.

Third party interventions

Article 36(2) and Rule 61, together provide that the President of a Chamber may, **1–152** in the interests of the proper administration of justice, invite or grant leave to any person[45] who is not a party to the proceedings to make submissions or take part in the proceedings.[46] Any request for leave to intervene must be "duly reasoned" and submitted within a reasonable time after the written procedure has been fixed.[47] Leave will generally be confined to the submission of written comments, but the President may, in exceptional cases, grant leave to take part in an oral hearing.[48] Any written submissions (known as *amicus curiae* briefs) will be

---

[37] Article 43(2).
[38] Rule 73(1).
[39] Rule 73(2).
[40] Rule 73(2).
[41] Article 43(3).
[42] See para. 1–114 above.
[43] Article 27(3).
[44] See para. 1–114 above.
[45] The Explanatory Report to Protocol 11 (1994) 17 E.H.R.R. 514 at 529, para. 91 explains that this may be a legal or natural person.
[46] Where the applicant is a national of another contracting state, that state may intervene as of right. In *Soering v. United Kingdom* (1989) 11 E.H.R.R. 439 the applicant was a German citizen whose extradition was sought from the United Kingdom to the United States. Germany intervened in the application arguing that it was prepared to try the applicant in Germany, where the death penalty did not apply.
[47] Rule 61(3).
[48] Rule 61(3). In *T and V v. United Kingdom* [2001] 1 All E.R. 737 the mother and father of a child who had been murdered by the applicants was granted leave to make written and oral submissions on the role of the victim in the sentencing process.

communicated to the parties who will be given an opportunity to file observations in reply.[49]

1–153 The Court will consider the expertise of the intervenor and the extent to which an *amicus* brief could provide information or evidence which would not otherwise be available to the Court. The President will usually specify the ambit of the intervention in detail, and will often prescribe its length. The grant of leave will usually be made conditional on a concise written submission which conforms to the terms set by the President.

1–154 *Amicus* interventions will typically be received from non-governmental organisations offering a perspective on the issues which supplements the arguments put forward by the parties. They are expected to be non-partisan, and to refrain from commenting on the merits of the individual application. The Court is, however, generally receptive to accurate and reliable interventions on relevant national, international or comparative law, and will often receive submissions on wider factual issues which may be relevant to the Court's assessment of a case.

1–155 In *Malone v. United Kingdom*,[50] the Post Office Engineering Union was granted leave to file a memorial in connection with a complaint about telephone interception. In *Soering v. United Kingdom*[51] Amnesty International was permitted to intervene to give evidence about the "death row phenomenon" in the United States. More recent examples include *Chahal v. United Kingdom*[52] where Liberty and others intervened in relation to the system of adjudication of immigration appeals involving questions of national security; *Murray v. United Kingdom*[53] where Amnesty International, Liberty and others intervened in a case which concerned the drawing of adverse inferences from a suspect's failure to testify; *Khan v. United Kingdom*[54] where Justice and Liberty filed a joint brief setting out the comparative law position on the exclusion of unlawfully obtained evidence; *T and V v. United Kingdom*[55] where the Court gave leave to Justice to intervene on the international standards governing the treatment of juvenile offenders, and to the parents of a child murdered by the applicants who wished to make submissions on the role of the victim in the criminal justice system; and *Sheffield and Horsham v. United Kingdom*[56] where Liberty filed a comparative analysis of the legal and medical implications of transsexualism.

1–156 This aspect of the Court's procedure has already begun to have a significant influence on the approach of the appellate courts in the United Kingdom where important issues are raised under the Human Rights Act. Even before the Act was passed the House of Lords had permitted a number of *amicus* interventions in

---

[49] Rule 61(5).
[50] (1988) 7 E.H.R.R. 14.
[51] (1989) 11 E.H.R.R. 439.
[52] (1997) 23 E.H.R.R. 413.
[53] (1996) 22 E.H.R.R. 29.
[54] (1995) 21 E.H.R.R. CD 67.
[55] (2000) 30 E.H.R.R. 121.
[56] (1999) 27 E.H.R.R. 163.

criminal cases,[57] and the Lord Chancellor has suggested that the courts will be more willing to accept such assistance in the future.[58]

Advisory Opinions

The Court has a very limited jurisdiction to give advisory opinions on legal **1–157** questions concerning the interpretation of the Convention and its protocols.[59] An advisory opinion may only be given at the request of the Committee of Ministers,[60] and may not deal with "any question relating to the content or scope of the rights or freedoms defined [in the Convention]", or with any other question which the Court or the Committee of Ministers might have to consider in the course of adjudicating on a Convention complaint.[61]

Interpretation, revision and rectification

Any party may, within 12 months of the delivery of the Court's judgment, apply **1–158** to the Registrar, requesting an interpretation of the judgment.[62] The Court may also consider an application from either party for the revision of a judgment if a fact is discovered which could have had a decisive influence on the Court's judgment, and which could not reasonably have been known to the party relying on it at the time of the judgment.[63] Any application for revision must be made within six months of the original judgment. The Court has a general discretion to rectify clerical errors and obvious mistakes in admissibility decisions or judgments, within one month of the decision in question.[64]

Execution of court judgments

Under Article 46(1) state parties undertake "to abide by the final judgment of the **1–159** Court in any case to which they are parties". The judgment is to be "transmitted to the Committee of Ministers, which shall supervise its execution".[65] Thus, it is the Committee of Ministers which oversees action taken by governments in response to a finding of a violation. The primary focus of the Committee of Ministers' role is to ensure that the appropriate remedies are put into effect by the state concerned. In some cases this will mean no more than the payment of compensation and costs to the applicant by way of just satisfaction.[66] In other cases however the judgment may require legislative, constitutional, administrative or regulatory amendment.[67] The Committee of Ministers' functions

---

[57] For example in *R v. Sultan Khan* [1997] A.C. 558 Liberty was permitted to intervene; and in *R v. Secretary of State ex parte Venables and Thompson* [1998] A.C. 407 Justice was given leave. More recently in *R v. Bow Street Stipendiary Magistrate ex parte Pinochet Ugarte* [2000] 1 A.C. 147 the House of Lords permitted Amnesty International to intervene in an extradition case with major international law implications.

[58] See para. 3–44 below.

[59] Article 47.

[60] Article 47(1).

[61] Article 47(2). The procedure for obtaining an advisory opinion is set out in Rules 82–90.

[62] Rule 79.

[63] Rule 80.

[64] Rule 81.

[65] Article 46(2).

[66] For an account of this function see Robertson and Merrils, *Human Rights in Europe* (3rd ed., 1993), pp 341–341.

[67] In a survey of 162 resolutions adopted by the Committee of Ministers up to 1992, 74 required some kind of legislative or administrative change: See Adam Tomkins, "The Committee of Ministers; Its roles under the European Convention on Human Rights" [1995] E.H.R.L.R. 49 at 58.

under Article 46 generally involve a dialogue with the government concerned as to the nature and extent of the remedy required.[68] The applicant may also make representations, if the Committee of Ministers considers this necessary.[69]

1–160 In an extreme case of non-compliance the Committee of Ministers has the power to take enforcement action against the state concerned. Article 3 of the Statute of the Council of Europe provides that every member state "must accept the principles of the rule of law and of the enjoyment by all persons within its jurisdiction of human rights and fundamental freedoms". If the Committee of Ministers considers that a state has seriously violated this obligation it may take action under Article 8 of the Statute to suspend the state concerned and request that it withdraw from the Council of Europe.[70] In the unlikely event of a refusal to withdraw, the Committee of Ministers may expel the state concerned.[71]

D. RESERVATIONS AND DEROGATIONS

Reservations

1–161 Article 57 of the Convention provides that any state may, when signing the Convention or when depositing its instrument of ratification, make a reservation in respect of any particular provision of the Convention, to the extent that any law then in force in its territory is not in conformity with the provision. Any reservation must relate to the law of the contracting state, rather than to actions taken by its officials.

1–162 A reservation must be specific in its terms: Article 57(1) provides that "reservations of a general character will not be permitted". Moreover, it must contain a brief statement of the law concerned.[72] In *Gradinger v. Austria*[73] the Court held that Austria's reservation to Article 4 of Protocol 7, which prohibits double jeopardy in criminal cases, was invalid. The reservation did not set out clearly the laws in respect of which it applied, and was insufficiently specific in its terms.[74] In *Weber v. Switzerland*[75] the Court reached a similar conclusion in relation to a Swiss reservation designed to exclude from Article 6 any criminal charges "which, in accordance with the Cantonal legislation, are heard before an administrative authority".

1–163 The United Kingdom's only reservation is in respect of Article 2 of Protocol 1 (the right to education) and is outside the scope of this work. Under the Human

---

[68] In three Swiss cases, for example, the Committee of Ministers considered that it was sufficient for the government to publicise the Court's judgment to enable the relevant authorities to take account of it in similar cases in future: *Minelli v. Switzerland* Resolution DH(83)10; *Zimmerman and Steiner v. Switzerland* Resolution DH(83)17; *Schoenenberger v. Switzerland* D.H.(89)12.

[69] Note to Rule 2(a) of the Rules adopted by the Committee of Ministers for the application of former Art. 54.

[70] Greece withdrew from the Council of Europe and renounced the Convention in 1969, following proceedings by the Committee of Ministers under Art. 8 of the Statute of Council of Europe. It was readmitted in 1974 following the restoration of democracy.

[71] Article 8 of the Statute of Council of Europe.

[72] Article 57(2).

[73] Judgment October 23, 1995.

[74] See also *Chorherr v. Austria* Judgment September 24, 1998 at para. 20.

[75] (1990) 12 E.H.R.R. 508.

Rights Act 1998, this reservation, and any future reservation, must be designated by an order of the Secretary of State in order to have effect in domestic law.[76–77]

Derogations

Article 15(1) provides that;   **1–164**

> "In time of war or other public emergency threatening the life of the nation any High Contracting Party may take measures derogating from its obligations under this Convention to the extent strictly required by the exigencies of the situation, provided that such measures are not inconsistent with its other obligations under international law."

Certain rights are, however, are of such high importance that no derogation is   **1–165**
permitted, even in times of national emergency.[78] This applies to the right to life in Article 2 (save to the extent that a death is the result of a lawful act of war); the prohibition on torture and inhuman and degrading treatment in Article 3; the prohibition on slavery and servitude in Article 4(1)[79]; and the prohibition on the retrospective application of the criminal law in Article 7.

The United Kingdom's only derogation applies to Article 5(3). It was entered in **1–166**
response to the judgment in *Brogan v. United Kingdom*[80] where the Court held that detention for four days and six hours under the Prevention of Terrorism (Temporary Provisions) Act 1984 was incompatible with the requirement that a detained person should be brought promptly before a judge or judicial officer following arrest. The derogation preserved the power of the Secretary of State to extend the period of detention of persons suspected of terrorism in connection with Northern Ireland for a total of up to seven days. The Human Rights Act 1998 retains the derogation[81] but places a time limit of five years on its operation[82] subject to renewal by order of the Secretary of State.[83]

The compatibility of the United Kingdom derogation with the terms of Article 15 **1–167**
was tested in *Brannigan and McBride v. United Kingdom*.[84] The Court held that it falls to each contracting state, in the first instance, to determine whether there exists a public emergency threatening the life of the nation and, if so, to decide on the measures necessary to overcome the emergency. Despite the language of strict necessity in Article 15(1), states were to be afforded a wide margin of appreciation.[85] The Court held that in determining whether the state had exceeded this margin, it had to give "appropriate weight to such relevant factors as the nature of the rights affected by the derogation, the circumstances leading to, and the duration of, the emergency situation". The Court was in no doubt that there was a national emergency in the United Kingdom at the time when the

---

[76–77] Section 15. Note that whilst a designated derogation must be renewed at periodic intervals (s.16), the same does not apply to reservations.
[78] Article 15(2).
[79] But not the prohibition on forced or compulsory labour in Art. 4(2).
[80] (1989) 11 E.H.R.R. 117.
[81] Section 14(1)(a). The text of the derogation is set out at Sched. 3 Part. I.
[82] Section 16.
[83] See para. 3–13 below.
[84] (1994) 17 E.H.R.R. 539.
[85] Para. 43.

derogation was entered, this being the relevant moment for the application of Article 15.[86] As to the extent of the measures taken the Court observed[87]:

> "Having regard to the nature of the terrorist threat in Northern Ireland, the limited scope of the derogation and the reasons advanced in support of it, as well as the existence of basic safeguards against abuse, the Court takes the view that the Government has not exceeded its margin of appreciation in considering that the derogation was strictly required by the exigencies of the situation."

---

[86] The Court held that it was not necessary to consider whether the emergency still existed "since a decision to withdraw a derogation is, in principle, a matter within the discretion of the State" (para. 47).

[87] Para. 66.

CHAPTER 2

PRINCIPLES OF INTERPRETATION

A. INTRODUCTION

I. *The Vienna Convention on the Law of Treaties*

The interpretation of the Convention is governed by the principles enunciated in   **2–01**
Articles 31 to 33 of the Vienna Convention on the Law of Treaties (May 23,
1969).[1] The "general rule" in Article 31 of the Vienna Convention is that a treaty
"shall be interpreted in good faith in accordance with the ordinary meaning to be
given to the terms of the treaty in their context and in the light of its object and
purpose".[2] The context includes the preamble to the treaty and any other
agreements which the parties have entered into which may be relevant to the
interpretation of the treaty.[3] Whilst the "ordinary meaning" of words is to be
adopted where this is consistent with the object and purpose of the Convention,
a "special meaning" is to be given to a term if it established that the parties so
intended.[4] Recourse may be had to supplementary means of interpretation,
including the *travaux préparatoires*, only where the meaning is otherwise ambiguous, obscure or absurd.[5] The English and French texts of the Convention are to
be treated as equally authentic[6] and are presumed to have the same meaning.[7] In
cases of divergence between the English and French versions, the meaning which
best reconciles the two texts, having regard to the object and purpose of the
treaty, is to prevail.[8] In *Golder v. United Kingdom*[9] the Court observed that:

> "In the way in which it is presented in the "general rule" in Article 31 of the Vienna
> Convention, the process of interpretation is a unity, a single combined operation; this
> rule, closely integrated, places on the same footing the various elements enumerated in
> the four paragraphs of the Article".

---

[1] Article 4 of the Vienna Convention provides that the Vienna Convention does not have retrospective
effect. It does not therefore strictly apply to to the European Convention on Human Rights (which
was concluded in 1950). Nevertheless, in *Golder v. United Kingdom* (1979–80) 1 E.H.R.R. 525 paras
29–30 the Court accepted that the Vienna Convention provided the appropriate international law
guidance for the determination of the scope and content of the European Convention. The Vienna
Convention has been described as "not so much an innovation but rather a codification of previous
practice" F. Matscher, "Methods of Interpretation of the Convention", in R. St. J. Macdonald, F.
Matscher & H. Petzold, *The European System for the Protection of Human Rights* (Martinus Nijhoff,
1993), p. 65.
[2] See Art. 31(1), Vienna Convention.
[3] Article 31(2) and (3).
[4] Article 31(4). This is the basis for the European Court of Human Rights adoption of an autonomous
approach to the construction of certain Convention terms: see paras 2–43 to 2–45 below.
[5] Article 32.
[6] Article 33(1). The last paragraph of the ECHR provides in terms that the French and English
language versions are equally authentic.
[7] Article 33(3).
[8] Article 33(4).
[9] (1979–80) 1 E.H.R.R. 525 paras 29–30.

2–02   This approach to interpretation leaves the Court a wide degree of latitude as to which of the elements of the "general rule" should be emphasised in a particular case. The Court will usually begin with a textual analysis, including (if necessary) a comparison between the English and French texts. However, the Court has sometimes been willing to interpret a provision in a way which is inconsistent with the "ordinary meaning" of the words, where this is necessary in order to give effect to the object and purpose of the Convention.[10]

II. *Object and purpose*

2–03   The principal object and purpose of the Convention is the protection of individual rights from infringement by the contracting states.[11] The Convention seeks to achieve this objective through the maintenance and promotion of "the ideals and values of a democratic society".[12] The Convention is "a constitutional instrument of European public order in the field of human rights".[13] It cannot therefore be interpreted merely as a reciprocal agreement between the contracting states. Rather, it creates "a network of mutual, bilateral undertakings, objective obligations which, in the words of the preamble, benefit from a 'collective enforcement'."[14]

2–04   Particularly important features of a democratic society, in the context of criminal cases, are "pluarlism, tolerance and broadmindedness"[15] and the "rule of law".[16] The Court has emphasised that the protection of the right to life (in Article 2 of the Convention), and the prohibition on torture and inhuman and degrading treatment (in Article 3) together enshrine "one of the basic values of the democratic societies making up the Council of Europe".[17] Democratic values also involve a recognition of the importance of the rights of the defence in criminal proceedings since the right to a fair trial "holds a prominent place in a democratic society".[18] The requirement in Article 6(1) for an "independent and impartial" tribunal encompasses the principle of separation of powers in a democracy, and guarantees the independence of the courts from the executive,[19]

---

[10] Frequently, this technique is adopted in a manner designed to achieve more effective protection of human rights. On rare occasions, however, the Court has adopted a similar approach in order to restrict Convention rights: see, for example, *Pretto v. Italy* (1984) 6 E.H.R.R. 182 at para. 26.

[11] *Austria v. Italy* (1961) 4 Y.B. 116 at 138; *Ireland v. United Kingdom* (1979–80) 2 E.H.R.R. 25 at para. 239.

[12] *Kjeldsen and others v. Denmark* (1979–80) 1 E.H.R.R. 711 at para. 53. These principles are reflected in the preamble to the Convention which speaks in terms of the "maintenance and further realisation of human rights and fundamental freedoms" on the basis of "an effective political democracy", and the primacy of "the rule of law".

[13] *Chrysostomos, Papachrysostomou and Loizidou v. Turkey* (1991) 68 D.R. 216 at 242.

[14] *Ireland v. United Kingdom* (1979–80) 2 E.H.R.R. 25 at para. 239; *Austria v. Italy* (1961) 4 Y.B. 116 at 138; *Chrysostomos, Papachrysostomou and Loizidou v. Turkey* (1991) 68 D.R. 216 at 242.

[15] *Handyside v. United Kingdom* (1979–80) 1 E.H.R.R. 737 at para. 49; *Dudgeon v. United Kingdom* (1981) 4 E.H.R.R. 149 at para. 53.

[16] *Golder v. United Kingdom* (1979–80) 1 E.H.R.R. 525 at para. 34; *Klass v. Germany* (1979–80) 2 E.H.R.R. 214 at para. 55; *Iatrides v. Greece* Judgment March 25, 1999 para. 62.

[17] *McCann, Savage and Farrell v. United Kingdom* (1996) 21 E.H.R.R. 97 at para. 147 citing *Soering v. United Kingdom* (1989) 11 E.H.R.R. 439 at para. 88.

[18] *DeCubber v. Belgium* (1985) 7 E.H.R.R. 236 at para. 30; *Colozza v. Italy* (1985) 7 E.H.R.R. 516 at para. 32; *Soering v. United Kingdom* (1989) 11 E.H.R.R. 439 at para. 113; *Van Mechelen v. Netherlands* (1998) 25 E.H.R.R. 647 at para. 58.

[19] *McGonnell v. United Kingdom* (2000) 30 E.H.R.R. 289.

the parties,[20] and the legislature.[21] Freedom of expression is "one of the essential foundations of a democratic society"[22] and access by the media to the courts is of particular importance in ensuring a fair and public trial[23] and in maintaining public confidence in the courts.[24]

It is important to distinguish between "democratic values" and the protection of majority sentiment. The duty to protect inalienable rights sometimes requires the Court to set standards, even where these do not meet with majority approval.[25] The Convention exists, at least in part, to protect the rights of unpopular groups and individuals. If the democratic process were always sufficient there would be no necessity for a code of legally enforceable minimum rights. The Court has therefore been careful to emphasise that "although the interests of the individual must on occasion be subordinated to those of a group, democracy does not simply mean that the views of the majority must always prevail: a balance must be achieved which ensures the fair and proper treatment of minorities and avoids any abuse of a dominant position".[26] Thus, the Court has consistently held that degrading forms of punishment cannot be justified on the ground that they have been in use for a long time or meet with general approval.[27] In *Tyrer v. United Kingdom*[28] the Court held that judicial corporal punishment was in breach of Article 3, despite the fact that a majority of the population of the Isle of Man favoured its retention. As the Court pointed out, "it might well be that one of the reasons why they view the penalty as an effective deterrent is precisely the element of degradation which it involves". Similarly, in *Handyside v. United Kingdom*[29] the Court held that the right to freedom of expression extends to information and ideas that "offend, shock or disturb society or a section of it"; and in *Dudgeon v. United Kingdom*[30] the Court found that criminal offences prohibiting consensual homosexual activity in private were in breach of Article 8, despite the "strength of the view that it would be seriously damaging to the moral fabric of Northern Ireland" if such conduct were to be decriminalised.

2–05

References to the object and purpose of the Convention are not to be dismissed as mere statements of aspiration. Together they form the core guiding principles to the Convention's interpretation and application. In *Wemhoff v. Germany*[31] the Court observed that it is "necessary to seek the interpretation that is most

2–06

---

[20] *Campbell and Fell v. United Kingdom* (1985) 7 E.H.R.R. 165 at para. 78.
[21] *Crociani and others v. Italy* (1980) 22 D.R. 147; *Demicoli v. Malta* (1992) 14 E.H.R.R. 47 Op. Comm. para. 40.
[22] *Handyside v. United Kingdom* (1979–80) 1 E.H.R.R. 737 at para. 49; *Sunday Times v. United Kingdom (No. 1)* (1979–80) 2 E.H.R.R. 245 at para. 65; *Lingens v. Austria* (1986) 8 E.H.R.R. 407 at paras 41–42.
[23] *Axen v. Germany* (1984) 6 E.H.R.R. 195 at para. 25.
[24] *Hodgson, Woolf Productions and the NUJ v. United Kingdom* (1988) 10 E.H.R.R. 503; *Worm v. Austria* (1998) 25 E.H.R.R. 454 at para. 50.
[25] In *Inze v. Austria* (1988) 10 E.H.R.R. 394 at para. 44 the Court considered that support amongst the local population for measures discriminating against illegitimate children merely reflected "the traditional outlook".
[26] *Young, James and Webster v. United Kingdom* (1981) 4 E.H.R.R. 38 at para. 63.
[27] *Tyrer v. United Kingdom* (1978) 2 E.H.R.R. 1; *Campbell and Cosans v. United Kingdom* (1988) 4 E.H.R.R. 1 at para. 29.
[28] (1978) 2 E.H.R.R. 1 at para. 31.
[29] (1979–80) 1 E.H.R.R. 737.
[30] (1981) 4 E.H.R.R. 149.
[31] (1979–80) 1 E.H.R.R. 55 at para. 8.

appropriate in order to realise the aim and achieve the objective of the treaty, and not that which would restrict to the greatest degree possible the obligations undertaken by the parties". Similarly, in *Golder v. United Kingdom*[32] the Court said that it would be "a mistake" to see the reference to the rule of law in the Preamble to the Convention as a "merely . . . rhetorical reference, devoid of significance for those interpreting the Convention". And in *Soering v. United Kingdom*[33] the Court observed that;

> "In interpreting the Convention, regard must be had to its special character as a treaty for the collective enforcement of human rights and fundamental freedoms. Thus, the object and purpose of the Convention as an instrument for the protection of individual human beings require that its provisions be interpreted and applied so as to make its safeguards practical and effective."

B. THE COURT'S INTERPRETATIVE TECHNIQUES

2–07   In order to give effect to the object and purpose of the Convention, the Court has developed a series of interpretative techniques that differ significantly from the common law approach to legal reasoning. The remainder of this Chapter examines the principal themes that emerge from the Court's caselaw.

I. *Practical and Effective Interpretation*

2–08   It is a general principle governing the interpretation of a law-making treaty[34] that "particular provisions are to be interpreted so as to give them their fullest weight and effect consistent with the normal sense of the words, and with other parts of the text, and in such a way that reason and a meaning can be attributed to every part of the text".[35] Applying this principle the Court has rejected a formalistic approach, holding that the Convention "is intended to guarantee not rights that are theoretical and illusory but rights that are practical and effective".[36]

2–09   The Convention is thus concerned with the substance of an individual's position rather than its formal classification, and courts may need to "look behind appearances and examine the realities of the procedure in question".[37] One consequence of this approach is that compliance by the state with the letter of a

---

[32] (1979–80) 1 E.H.R.R. 525 at para. 34.

[33] (1989) 11 E.H.R.R. 439 at para. 87.

[34] International law distinguishes between law-making treaties (*traités-loi*) and contractual treaties (*traités-contrats*). In a law-making treaty, such as the European Convention on Human Rights, the intention of the contracting parties is not simply to establish reciprocal undertakings, but to create objective rights with corresponding legal liabilities.

[35] G.G. Fitzmaurice, *The Law and Procedure of the International Court of Justice*, (Grotius, Cambridge, 42–9 1986), p. 345, cited in J.G. Merrils, *The Development of International Law by the European Court of Human Rights* (2nd ed., Manchester, 1993), p. 77. See also Jacobs and White *The European Convention on Human Rights* (2nd ed., Oxford), p. 35.

[36] *Marckx v. Belgium* (1979–80) 2 E.H.R.R. 330 at para. 31; *Airey v. Ireland* (1979–80) 2 E.H.R.R. 305 at para. 24; *Artico v. Italy* (1981) 3 E.H.R.R. 1 at para. 33; *Soering v. United Kingdom* (1989) 11 E.H.R.R. 439 at para. 87.

[37] See, amongst numerous other authorities, *Deweer v. Belgium* (1979–80) 2 E.H.R.R. 439 at para. 44; *Adolf v. Austria* (1982) 4 E.H.R.R. 315 at para. 30; *Welch v. United Kingdom* (1995) 20 E.H.R.R. 247 at para. 27.

Convention obligation will not necessarily be sufficient, if the protection afforded in practice has been substantially undermined. In *Artico v. Italy*,[38] where the legal aid lawyer appointed to represent the applicant was shown to have been ineffective, the Court found a violation of Article 6(3)(c). Noting that this provision guaranteed legal "assistance" rather than simply the "nomination" of a lawyer, the Court pointed out that:

> "[M]ere nomination does not ensure effective assistance, since the lawyer appointed may die, fall seriously ill, be prevented for a protracted period from acting, or shirk his duties. If they are notified of the situation, the authorities must either replace him or cause him to fulfil his obligations."[39]

Moreover, the Court held that it was not necessary for the applicant to establish that the shortcomings in legal representation had caused actual prejudice to his case. This would be "asking the impossible" since it could never be proved that effective representation would have secured the acquittal of an accused. The Court considered that an interpretation which introduced this requirement into Article 6(3)(c) "would deprive it in large measure of its substance".[40] In *Campbell and Fell v. United Kingdom*[41] the Court held that Article 6(3)(c) implied not merely effective representation at the hearing itself, but an adequate opportunity for prior consultation.

Minelli v. Switzerland[42] provides another example of practical and effective **2–10** interpretation. In that case the Court was called upon to determine whether the presumption of innocence in Article 6(2) applied to an application for an award of costs to an acquitted defendant. The government argued that the right to be presumed innocent applied only to the determination of a criminal charge, and not to proceedings subsequent to an acquittal. The Court disagreed, holding that Article 6(2) "governs criminal proceedings in their entirety, irrespective of the outcome of the prosecution, and not solely the examination of the merits of the charge". The presumption of innocence would therefore be violated by a judicial pronouncement after acquittal reflecting an opinion that the accused was, in reality, guilty of the offence.

One of the most important illustrations of the effectiveness principle is the **2–11** Court's recognition of the Convention's extra-territorial effect. In its landmark decision in *Soering v. United Kingdom*[43] the Court held that a decision to extradite an individual to a non-Convention state where there were substantial grounds for believing that he would be exposed to inhuman or degrading treatment contrary to Article 3 would engage the responsibility of the state from which extradition was sought. The Court held that a decision to surrender an individual in such circumstances "would hardly be compatible with the underlying values of the Convention, that 'common heritage of political traditions,

---

[38] (1981) 3 E.H.R.R. 1 at para. 33.
[39] See also *Goddi v. Italy* (1984) 6 E.H.R.R. 457 at para. 31 where the state was found in violation of Art. 6(3)(c) since the lawyer appointed to represent the applicant was unable properly to represent his client, who had absconded. The Court held that in order to ensure effective legal assistance, the trial should have been adjourned.
[40] Para. 35.
[41] (1985) 7 E.H.R.R. 165 at para. 99.
[42] (1983) 5 E.H.R.R. 554. See also *Leutscher v. Netherlands* (1996) 24 E.H.R.R. 181.
[43] (1989) 11 E.H.R.R. 439.

ideals, freedom and the rule of law' to which the Preamble refers".[44] While an obligation to refuse co-operation was "not explicitly referred to in the brief and general wording of Article 3", a decision to surrender an individual to face such treatment "would plainly be contrary to the spirit and intendment of the Article". There was therefore an "inherent obligation not to extradite".[45] This principle has since been extended to a decision to deport a convicted drug trafficker after the expiry of his sentence.[46]

2–12   More recently, in *Aydin v. Turkey*[47] the Court held that where an individual made an allegation of torture or inhuman or degrading treatment, the state was under an obligation to carry out "a thorough and effective investigation capable of leading to the identification and punishment of those responsible, and including effective access for the complainant to the investigatory procedure".

II. *Rights to be broadly construed/restrictions to be narrowly interpreted*

2–13   The effectiveness principle has led the Court to hold that provisions of the Convention conferring rights are to be broadly and purposively construed, whilst those establishing exceptions and limitations must be restrictively interpreted. The application of this principle is most apparent in relation to the qualified rights in Articles 8 to 11. In its interpretation of these provisions the Court has consistently maintained that a generous construction is appropriate in determining the scope of the protected right set out in the first paragraph of each article.[48] In *Niemetz v. Germany*,[49] for example, the Court held that the concepts of a person's home and private life in Article 8, included business premises and activities on the ground that "it would be too restrictive to limit the notion [of private life] to an 'inner circle' in which an individual may live his own personal life as he chooses". Similarly, in *Kokkinakis v. Greece*[50] the right to freedom of thought, conscience and religion in Article 9 was held to apply not only to recognised religious or ethical value systems but also to the conscientious beliefs of "atheists, agnostics, sceptics and the unconcerned".

2–14   However, when the Court turns to assess the purported justification for an interference with the protected right (under the second paragraph of each of these Articles) it has generally adopted the strictly conservative approach exemplified in *Klass v. Germany*[51]:

> "The cardinal issue arising under Article 8 in the present case is whether the interference . . . is justified by the terms of paragraph 2 of the Article. This paragraph, since

---

[44] Para. 88.
[45] *Soering* at para. 88.
[46] *D v. United Kingdom* (1997) 24 E.H.R.R. 423.
[47] (1998) 25 E.H.R.R. 251 at para. 103.
[48] A possible exception to this is *Laskey and ors v. United Kingdom* (1997) 24 E.H.R.R. 39, where the court doubted whether organised group sadomasochism was fully within the notion of private life.
[49] (1993) 16 E.H.R.R. 97 at paras 29 to 30.
[50] (1994) 17 E.H.R.R. 397.
[51] (1979–80) 2 E.H.R.R. 214 at para. 42.

it provides for an exception to a right guaranteed by the Convention, is to be narrowly interpreted."

Applying this approach, the Court held that powers of secret surveillance "are tolerable under the Convention only insofar as strictly necessary for safeguarding the democratic institutions". Likewise, when determining whether an inteference with freedom of expression under Article 10(1) is justified by reference to the public interests identified in Article 10(2), the Court has held that it is "faced not with a choice between two conflicting principles but with the principle of freedom of expression that is subject to a number of exceptions which must be narrowly interpreted".[52]

Whilst the application of this principle is most clearly seen in relation to Articles 8 to 11, it has in fact been applied to all Convention rights.[53] Thus, the right to life in Article 2 has been held to encompass both deliberate and unintentional loss of life.[54] Its provisions must be strictly construed and any deprivation of life must be subjected to the "most careful scrutiny".[55] In the context of the right to personal liberty in Article 5, the Court has held that the exceptions set out in paragraph 5(1)(a) to (f) provide an "exhaustive defintion" of the circumstances in which a person may be deprived of his or her liberty and are to be given a narrow interpretation.[56] A wide interpretation "would entail consequences incompatible with the notion of the rule of law from which the whole Convention draws its inspiration".[57] In *Cuilla v. Italy*[58] the Court applied this approach in holding that the arrest and detention of a suspect pending an order for "preventive measures" fell outside the permitted exceptions in Article 5(1), despite the acknowledged importance of the fight against organised crime in Italy. **2–15**

The right to a fair trial in Article 6 is also to be given a broad construction[59] since a restrictive interpretation "would not be consonant with the object and purpose of the provision".[60] Any restriction on the rights of the defence is to be scrutinised with special care, and departures from a truly adversarial procedure are to be kept to the minimum possible. In the leading case of *Van Mechelin v. Netherlands*[61] the Court observed that: "Having regard to the place that the right to a fair administration of justice holds in a democratic society, any measures restricting the rights of the defence should be strictly necessary. If a less restrictive measure can suffice then that measure should be applied." **2–16**

---

[52] *Sunday Times v. United Kingdom* (1979–80) 2 E.H.R.R. 245 at para. 65.
[53] The prohibition on forced or compulsory labour in Art. 4(2) is a possible exception. The Court has held that the categories established in Art. 4(3) are not limitations on the right in Art. 4(2). Rather, they delimit the content of that right and therefore aid its interpretation: *Schmidt v. Germany* (1994) 18 E.H.R.R. 513; *Van der Mussele v. Belgium* (1984) 6 E.H.R.R. 163. It would seem to follow that Art. 4(2) does not necessarily prohibit all forms of compulsory labour which are outside the examples set out in Art. 4(3).
[54] *Stewart v. United Kingdom* (1985) 7 E.H.R.R. 453.
[55] *McCann, Savage and Farrell v. United Kingdom* (1996) 21 E.H.R.R. 97 at paras 147–150.
[56] *Winterwerp v. Netherlands* (1979–80) 2 E.H.R.R. 387 at para. 37.
[57] *Engel v. Netherlands* (1979–80) 1 E.H.R.R. 647 at para. 69.
[58] (1991) 13 E.H.R.R. 346 at para. 41.
[59] *Moreira de Azvedo v. Portugal* (1992) 13 E.H.R.R. 731 at para. 66; *Delcourt v. Belgium* (1979–80) 1 E.H.R.R. 355.
[60] *De Cubber v. Belgium* (1985) 7 E.H.R.R. 236 at para. 30.
[61] (1998) 25 E.H.R.R. 647 at para. 59.

III. *Permissible limitations must not impair the essence of a Convention right*

2–17　　Another aspect of the doctrine of practical and effective interpretation is the principle that limitations and conditions imposed on the exercise of a Convention right must not impair its very existence or deprive it of its effectiveness.[62] In *Fox, Campbell and Hartley v. United Kingdom*[63] the government argued that a power of detention which was exercisable on the ground of "genuine suspicion" was sufficient to meet the requirements of Article 5(1)(c) which permits arrest or detention on "*reasonable* suspicion" of the commission of an offence. The Court held that the difficulties associated with policing terrorist crime, including the need to protect informers, "cannot justify stretching the notion of 'reasonableness' to the point where the essence of the right secured by Article 5(1)(c) is impaired". In *Golder v. United Kingdom*[64] the government sought to argue that Article 8, which protects (amongst other things) the right to respect for a person's correspondence, applied only to state interference with existing correspondence rights, and did not therefore restrict the state's right to control or prohibit correspondence to and from prisoners. Not surprisingly, the Court rejected this argument, holding that "it would be placing an undue and formalistic restriction on the concept of interference with correspondence not to regard it as covering the case of correspondence which has not yet taken place, only because the competent authority, with power to enforce its ruling, has ruled that it will not be allowed".

IV. *Evolutive interpretation*

2–18　　The Convention has been described as a "living instrument which must be interpreted in the light of present day conditions".[65] It calls for an evolutive and dynamic approach to its interpretation rather than a static and historical one. The concepts used in the Convention are therefore to be understood in the context of the democratic societies of modern Europe, and not according to the conceptions of 50 years ago when the Convention was drafted.[66] As Lord Hope pointed out in *R. v. Director of Public Prosecutions ex parte Kebilene*[67] "the Convention should be seen as an expression of fundamental principles rather than as a set of mere rules".

2–19　　Whilst evolutive interpretation has an important role to play in ensuring that rights remain relevant, a court applying the Convention cannot, through the process of interpretation, create wholly new obligations which the contracting parties have not undertaken. Thus, in *Soering v. United Kingdom*[68] the Court

---

[62] *Mathieu-Mohin and Clerfayt v. Belgium* (1988) 10 E.H.R.R. 1 at para. 52; *Ashingdane v. United Kingdom* (1985) 7 E.H.R.R. 528 at para. 57. *Winterwerp v. Netherlands* (1979–80) 2 E.H.R.R. 387 at para. 60; *Lithgow v. United Kingdom* (1986) 8 E.H.R.R. 329 at para. 194; *Philis v. Greece* (1991) 13 E.H.R.R. 741 at para. 59.
[63] (1991) 13 E.H.R.R. 157 at para. 32.
[64] (1979–80) 1 E.H.R.R. 525.
[65] *Tyrer v. United Kingdom* (1979–80) 2 E.H.R.R. 1 at para. 31; *Airey v. Ireland* (1979–80) 2 E.H.R.R. 305 at para. 26.
[66] It is for this reason that the *travaux préparatoires* are of only marginal relevance in the interpretation of the Convention.
[67] [1999] 3 W.L.R. 972.
[68] (1989) 11 E.H.R.R. 439.

rejected the submission of Amnesty International that "evolving standards in Western Europe regarding the death penalty required that the death penalty should now be considered as an inhuman and degrading punishment within the meaning of Article 3". The Court observed that Article 3 could not have been intended by the drafters of the Convention to include a general prohibition on the death penalty since the death penalty was expressly permitted by Article 2. Noting that the death penalty in peacetime had in fact been abolished by all contracting states, the Court observed;

> "Subsequent practice in national penal policy, in the form of a generalised abolition of capital punishment, could be taken as establishing the agreement of the Contracting States to abrogate the exception provided for under Article 2(1) and hence remove a textual limit on the scope for evolutive interpretation of Article 3. However, Protocol No. 6, as a subsequent written agreement, shows that the intention of the Contracting Parties as recently as 1983 was to adopt the normal method of amendment of the text in order to introduce a new obligation to abolish capital punishment in time of peace and, what is more, to do so by an optional instrument allowing each State to choose the moment when to undertake such an engagement. In these conditions, notwithstanding the special character of the Convention, Article 3 cannot be interpreted as generally prohibiting the death penalty."

Similarly, in *Cruz Varas v. Sweden*[69] the Court held that in the absence of a specific provision in the Convention enabling the Court to make a legally binding order for interim relief, a failure by a state to comply with a request for interim measures could not be regarded as an interference with the right of individual petition. Despite the history of almost invariable compliance with such requests, the Court could not "create new rights and obligations which were not included in the Convention at the outset".   **2–20**

Evolutive interpretation thus requires the Court to strike a careful balance, which recognises that it is not the task of the interpreter to change the content of a norm established in the Convention, whilst at the same time acknowledging that if the content of a norm "has undergone a change in social reality, the interpreter must take account of this".[70] As a former President of the Court has put it[71]:   **2–21**

> "Human rights treaties must be interpreted in an objective and dynamic manner, by taking into account social conditions and developments; the ideas and conditions prevailing at the time when the treaties were drafted retain hardly any continuing validity. Nevertheless, treaty interpretation must not amount to treaty revision. Interpretation must therefore respect the text of the treaty concerned."

The court must, in the end, make a judgment as to whether a new social or legal standard has achieved sufficiently wide acceptance to affect the interpretation and application of the Convention. In making this judgment a consideration of comparative law and practice within Europe and elsewhere may be relevant, as may other international agreements which the contracting parties (or the majority of them) have concluded.

---

[69] (1992) 14 E.H.R.R. 1 see paras 1–33 to 1–38 above.
[70] Sereni *Diritto Internazionale* 1 (1956), p. 182 cited in F. Matscher, "Methods of Interpretation of the Convention" in R. St. J. Macdonald, F. Matscher and H. Petzold, *The European System for the Protection of Human Rights* (Martinus Nijhoff, 1993), p. 70.
[71] R. Bernhardt, *The European Dimension: Studies in Honour of Gérard J. Wiarda* (Koln, 1988), p. 65 at p. 71.

2–22   Many Convention concepts are obviously rooted in the current legal and social standards of the contracting states. The requirements of the "protection of morals", for example, or the question of whether an interference with a Convention right is "necessary in a democratic society" can only be judged according to contemporary standards, and the Court has been particularly willing to adopt an evolutive approach to such questions. Thus, in *Dudgeon v. United Kingdom*[72] the Court observed that:

> "As compared with an era when [the legislation] was enacted there in now a better understanding and, in consequence, an increased tolerance of homosexual behaviour to the extent that it is no longer considered to be necessary or appropriate to treat homosexual practices [between consenting adults in private] as in themselves a matter to which the sanctions of the criminal law should be applied. The Court cannot overlook the marked changes which have occurred in this regard in the domestic law of the member states."

2–23   *Dudgeon* was concerned with the position of male homosexuals over the age of 21. It took a further 15 years before the Convention organs came to accept that the same principle should apply to those aged over 16. In *Sutherland v. United Kingdom*[73] the Commission overturned its previous caselaw,[74] holding that the potential application of the offence of gross indecency to consensual sexual activity between 16 and 17 year old males was in breach of Articles 8 and 14. In coming to the conclusion that a differential age of consent for homosexuals could no longer be justified, the Commission referred to "major changes" which had occurred in professional opinion on the need to protect young male homosexuals and the desirability of an equal age of consent. The Commission considered that it was "opportune to reconsider its earlier case law in the light of these modern developments and, more especially, in the light of the weight of current medical opinion that to reduce the age of consent to 16 might have positively beneficial effects on the sexual health of young homosexual men without any corresponding harmful consequences".

2–24   This requirement for a dynamic interpretation is not however confined to the qualified rights in Articles 8 to 11. It applies generally, and governs the interpretation of all aspects of the Convention. In *Tyrer v. United Kingdom*[75] the Court held that judicial birching was in breach of Article 3, saying that it "could not but be influenced by the developments and commonly accepted standards in the penal policy of the member states of the Council of Europe". In the Court's view it was the standards which were currently prevalent which were decisive of the issue, and not those which were prevalent when the Convention was adopted: Article 3 embodied the *concept* of inhuman and degrading punishment and not the particular *conception* which may have been held in 1950.

2–25   Similarly in *Winterwerp v. Netherlands*[76] the Court found that the term "person of unsound mind" in Article 5(1)(e) was;

---

[72] (1982) 4 E.H.R.R. 149 at para. 60.
[73] (1997) 24 E.H.R.R. CD 22.
[74] *X v. United Kingdom* (1980) 19 D.R. 66.
[75] (1979–80) 2 E.H.R.R. 1 at para. 31.
[76] (1982) 4 E.H.R.R. 228.

"[A] term whose meaning is continually evolving as research in psychiatry progresses, an increasing flexibility in treatment is developing, and society's attitude to mental illness changes, in particular so that greater understanding of the problems of mental patients is becoming more widespread."

And in *Borgers v. Belgium*[77–78] the Court held that the requirements of a fair trial in Article 6 had undergone a "considerable evolution" in the Court's caselaw, particularly as regards the importance attached to the appearance of fairness, and the increased sensitivity of the public to the fair administration of justice.

The inevitable consequence of this approach is that the strict doctrine of prece- **2–26** dent does not apply to decisions of the European Court and Commission of Human Rights. Older Convention caselaw must be approached with this principle in mind. Where there is some evidence that standards may be in transition, the Court may be willing to reconsider its own decisions at relatively frequent intervals, and sometimes even calls for a particular situation to be kept under review. In *Rees v. United Kingdom*,[79] for example, the Court rejected a complaint under Article 8 brought by a transsexual who had been denied the right to a change of legal status. Nevertheless the Court said that it was "conscious of the seriousness of the problems affecting these persons and the distress they suffer", and continued; "The Convention has always to be interpreted in the light of current circumstances. The need for appropriate legal measures should therefore be kept under review, having regard particularly to the scientific and societal developments". In the subsequent cases of *Cossey v. United Kingdom*[80] and *Sheffield and Horsham v. United Kingdom*[81] the Court adhered to its earlier decision in *Rees*, but by a diminishing majority in each case. In the *Sheffield* case, the finding of no violation was by a majority of only 11 to nine, and the Court openly criticised the United Kingdom for its failure to carry out a review of the need to maintain the existing arrangements. Whilst voting with the majority "after much hesitation" the British judge, Sir John Freeland, suggested that further inaction by the United Kingdom "could well tilt the balance in the other direction".

The Court's evolutive approach to interpretation does not, however, mean that **2–27** the parties can simply ignore a previous decision of the Court which has been reached after hearing full argument. Whilst the strict doctrine of precedent has no place in Strasbourg, there is, in practice, a heavy onus on an applicant seeking to persuade the Court to depart from a recent decision. In *Wynne v. United Kingdom*,[82] a case concerning the rights of a mandatory life sentence prisoner, the Court suggested that it would require "cogent reasons" to depart from the conclusion that it had reached on the nature of the mandatory life sentence three years earlier in *Thynne, Wilson and Gunnell v. United Kingdom*.[83]

77–78 (1993) 15 E.H.R.R. 92.
79 (1987) 9 E.H.R.R. 56.
80 (1991) 13 E.H.R.R. 622.
81 (1999) 27 E.H.R.R. 163.
82 (1995) 19 E.H.R.R. 333 at para. 36.
83 (1991) 13 E.H.R.R. 666.

V. *Practice in other jurisdictions*

2–28   The Court has observed that the main purpose of the Convention is "to lay down certain international standards to be observed by the Contracting States in their relations with persons under their jurisdiction".[84] Thus, the Court has consistently held that the existence of a "generally shared approach" in other contracting states is relevant to the application of the Convention[85] although "absolute uniformity" is not required.[86] The Court has no systematic means of establishing the comparative law position on a particular issue, even within the Council of Europe. It relies on the collective experience of the judges of the Court, on the research of the parties, and on any *amicus* interventions[87] for its information.

2–29   As we have seen, the Court was heavily influenced by commonly accepted European standards in *Tyrer v. United Kingdom*[88] and *Dudgeon v. United Kingdom*.[89] On the other hand, when considering the length of a criminal sentence the Commission has held that "the mere fact that an offence is punished more severely in one country than in another does not suffice to establish that the punishment is inhuman or degrading".[90] And in *T and V v. United Kingdom*[91] the Court referred to the absence of a European consensus on the age of criminal responsibility in concluding that the prosecution of two boys for a murder committed when they were 10 was compatible with Article 3 of the Convention.

2–30   When called upon to determine whether an interference with freedom of expression is justified under the protection of morals exception in Article 10(2), the Court has often stressed that "it is not possible to find in the legal and social orders of the contracting states a uniform Europen conception of morals".[92] Thus, in *Handyside v. United Kingdom*,[93] the Court attached little significance to the fact that the book to which the applicant's conviction related had been distributed elsewhere in Europe without attracting prosecution. Similarly, in *Wingrove v. United Kingdom*[94] where the applicant's complaint under Article 10 related to the English offence of blasphemy, the Court observed that;

> "[T]here is no uniform European conception of the requirements of 'the protection of the rights of others' in relation to attacks on their religious convictions. What is likely

---

[84] *Belgian Linguistics Case (No. 1)* (1979–80) 1 E.H.R.R. 241 at 250 para. [e].
[85] *Marckx v. Belgium* (1979–80) 2 E.H.R.R. 330 para. 41; *Tyrer v. United Kingdom* (1979–80) 2 E.H.R.R. 1 para. 31; *Dudgeon v. United Kingdom* (1982) 4 E.H.R.R. 149 para. 60; *X, Y and Z v. United Kingdom* (1997) 24 E.H.R.R. 143 para. 52.
[86] *Sunday Times v. United Kingdom (No. 1)* (1979–80) 2 E.H.R.R. 245 para. 61; *Muller v. Switzerland* (1991) 13 E.H.R.R. 212 para. 35; *Wingrove v. United Kingdom* (1996) 24 E.H.R.R. 1 para. 58; *F v. Switzerland* (1988) 10 E.H.R.R. 411 para. 33. *Monnell and Morris v. United Kingdom* (1987) 10 E.H.R.R. 205 para. 47.
[87] See para. 1–152 above.
[88] (1978) 2 E.H.R.R. 1.
[89] (1982) 4 E.H.R.R. 149.
[90] *C v. Germany* (1986) 46 D.R. 176.
[91] (2000) 30 E.H.R.R. 121, paras 73–74.
[92] *Muller v. Switzerland* (1991) 13 E.H.R.R. 212 para. 35; *Handyside v. United Kingdom* (1979–80) 1 E.H.R.R. 737.
[93] (1979–80) 1 E.H.R.R. 737.
[94] (1997) 24 E.H.R.R. 1 at para. 58.

to cause substantial offence to persons of a particular religious persuasion will vary significantly from time to time and from place to place, especially in an era characterised by an ever growing array of faiths and denominations."

The Court's reference to comparative practice in *Monnell and Morris v. United* 2–31
Kingdom[95] was unusual. The applicants complained that a "loss of time" order under section 29(1) of the Criminal Appeal Act 1968[96] was in violation of Article 5. In concluding that such an order was compatible with Article 5(1)(a) the Court noted that:

"[U]nder the law of many of the Convention countries detention pending a criminal appeal is treated as detention on remand and a convicted person does not start to serve his or her sentence until the conviction has become final. In such systems, the appellate court itself determines the sentence and, in some of them, exercises a discretion in deciding whether or to what extent detention pending appeal shall be deducted from the sentence."

Finally, it should be borne in mind that the Court's consideration of comparative 2–32
practice is not necessarily confined to European jurisdictions. In *Chahal v. United Kingdom*[97] the Court relied on the practice adopted in Canada for resolving national security cases as illustrating that "there are techniques which can be employed which both accommodate legitimate security concerns ... and yet afford the individual a substantial measure of procedural justice".

VI. *Ordinary meaning*

In interpreting a provision of the Convention, the Court will seek to ascertain the 2–33
ordinary meaning of a word insofar as this accords with the context of the provision and the object and purpose of the Convention.[98] In detemining the ordinary meaning of a term, regard should be had to the French and English texts of the Convention, both of which are equally authentic.[99] On occasions, the Court has resorted to dictionary definitions. In *Luedicke, Belkacem and Koc v. Germany*[1] the Court was concerned with the meaning of Article 6(3)(e) of the Convention, which provides that an accused person is to be provided with "the free assistance of an interpreter". The German government argued that when viewed in its context this provision allowed for the costs of an interpreter to be reclaimed from a convicted defendant. The Court held that "the ordinary meaning of the terms '*gratuiment*' and 'free' in Article 6(3)(c) of the Convention [was] not contradicted by the context of the sub-paragraph, and [was] confirmed by the object and purpose of Article 6". These terms denoted "neither a conditional remission, nor a temporary exemption, nor a suspension, but a once and for all exemption or exoneration".

---

[95] (1988) 10 E.H.R.R. 205 at para. 47.
[96] Under s.29(1) the Court of Appeal may, if it considers that an appeal is without merit, direct that time served between the imposition of the sentence and the disposal of the appeal should not count towards the accused person's sentence. As to the circumstances in which such an order may be made see *Practice Direction (Crime: Sentence: Loss of Time)* [1980] 1 W.L.R. 270.
[97] (1997) 23 E.H.R.R. 413 at para. 131.
[98] *Johnson v. Ireland* (1987) 9 E.H.R.R. 203 at para. 51. *Luedicke, Belkacem and Koc v. Germany* (1979–80) 2 E.H.R.R. 149 at para. 40.
[99] *Luedicke, Belkacem and Koc v. Germany* (1979–80) 2 E.H.R.R. 149 at para. 40.
[1] (1979–80) 2 E.H.R.R. 149 at para. 40.

2–34 In the event of a conflict between the ordinary meaning of a provision and the clear object and purpose of the Convention, the latter will generally prevail. In *Wemhoff v. Germany*[2] the Court was called upon to interpret Article 5(3), which provides that an accused is "entitled to trial within a reasonable time *or* to release pending trial". As the Court observed, a "purely grammatical" construction would leave the authorities with a choice between two obligations—that of conducting the proceedings within a reasonable time, or that of releasing an accused pending trial. The Court was;

> " . . . quite certain that such an interpretation would not conform to the intention of the High Contracting Parties. It is inconceivable that they should have intended to permit their judicial authorities, at the price of release of the accused, to protract proceedings beyond a reasonable time."

As a result, Article 5(3) is to be read as if the word "or" is replaced by the word "and".

2–35 A similar approach is evident in relation to Article 6(3)(c), which provides that the accused has the right "to defend himself in person *or* through legal assistance of his own choosing *or*, if he has not sufficient means to pay for legal assistance, to be given it free when the interests of justice so require". Here again, the wording of the English text of Article 6(3)(c) suggests that the right to free legal representation is an alternative to the right of an accused person to represent himself. However, in *Pakelli v. Germany*[3] the Court preferred to follow the French text, which links the rights contained in Article 6(3)(c) by the word "*et*", on the basis that this would result in a more faithful reflection of the underlying aims of Article 6. Accordingly, the Court held that Article 6(3)(c) guarantees three related but independent rights:

> "Having regard to the object and purpose of this Article, which is designed to secure effective protection of the rights of the defence . . . a person charged with a criminal offence who does not wish to defend himself in person must be able to have recourse to legal assistance of his own choosing; if he does not have sufficient means to pay for such assistance, he is entitled under the Convention to be given it free when the interests of justice so require."[4]

2–36 A second issue which arose in the *Wemhoff*[5] case was whether the period to be considered in connection with the right to "trial within a reasonable time" in Article 5(3) came to an end when the accused was first produced before the trial court, or continued until the trial court's judgment was delivered. The Court noted that the English text permitted either interpretation, but the use of the word

---

[2] (1979–80) 1 E.H.R.R. 55 at paras 4–5.
[3] (1984) 6 E.H.R.R. 1.
[4] At para. 31. Note, however, that in *X v. Austria* (Application No. 1242/61) the Commission observed that;
> "While [Article 6(3)(c)] guarantees the right to an accused person that proceedings against him will not take place without an adequate representation of the case for the defence, [it] does not give an accused person the right to decide for himself in what manner his defence should be assured . . . the decision as to which of the two alternatives should be chosen, namely the applicant's right to defend himself in person or to be represented by a lawyer of his own choosing, or in certain circumstances one appointed by the court, rests with the competent authorities concerned."
[5] (1979–80) 1 E.H.R.R. 55.

"*jugée*" in the French text allowed for only one meaning, namely that the period to be considered continued until the judgment terminating the trial:

> "Thus confronted with two versions of a treaty which are equally authentic but not exactly the same, the Court must, following established international law precedents, interpret them in a way that will reconcile them as far as possible. Given that it is a law-making treaty it is also necessary to seek the interpretation that is most appropriate in order to realise the aim and achieve the object of the treaty, not that which would restrict to the greatest degree possible the obligations undertaken by the Parties. It is impossible to see why the protection against unduly long detention on remand, which Article 5 seeks to ensure for persons suspected of offences, should not continue up to the delivery of judgment rather than cease at the moment the trial opens."[6]

A similar problem arose in *Brogan v. United Kingdom*[7] in connection with the **2–37** permissible interval between a person's arrest and first appearance in court. There, the Court was faced with a difference between the word "promptly" in the English text of Article 5(3) and the word "*aussitot*" in the French text (which literally means immediately). The Court held that "the use in the French text of the word '*aussitot*', with its constraining connotation of immediacy, confirm[ed] that the degree of flexibility attaching to the notion of 'promptness' [was] limited". As a result, a delay of four days and six hours was found to exceed the time permitted under Article 5(3).

In the *Belgian Linguistics Case (No.2)*[8] the Court was concerned with the scope **2–38** of the prohibition on discrimination in Article 14. The English text guarantees the delivery of Convention rights "without discrimination", whereas the French text uses the much stricter term "*sans distinction aucune*". The Court considered that "one would reach absurd results were one to give Article 14 an interpretation as wide as that which the French version seems to imply".

A final example is provided by the case of *Jespers v. Belgium*[9] where the **2–39** Commission observed, in connection with Article 6(3)(c), that;

> " . . . the word 'facilities' (French 'facilités') is qualified by the adjective 'adequate' (French 'nécessaire'). Despite the slight difference in meaning between the adjective in the French text and the one in the English text it is clear that the facilities which must be granted to the accused are restricted to those which assist or may assist him in the preparation of his defence."

Where one language version uses a particular word or phrase throughout the **2–40** Convention, whilst the other version includes slight differences, the likelihood is that the differences have no significance. The French text, for example, uses the term "*prévues par la loi*" throughout Articles 8 to 11, as well as in Article 1 of Protocol 1. The English text, on the other hand, uses the term "in accordance with the law" in Article 8, "prescribed by law" in Articles 9 to 11 and "provided

---

[6] Note that the right to the determination of a criminal charge within a reasonable time in Art. 6(1) of the Convention has been interpreted as including the time taken for the final determination of any appeal: *Neumeister v. Austria (No. 1)* (1979–80) 1 E.H.R.R. 91 at para. 19; *Wemhoff v. Germany* (1979–80) 1 E.H.R.R. 55; *Konig v. Germany (No. 1)* (1979–80) 2 E.H.R.R. 170 at para. 98; *Eckle v. Germany* (1983) 5 E.H.R.R. 1 at para. 76.

[7] (1989) 11 E.H.R.R. 117 at para. 59.

[8] (1979–80) 1 E.H.R.R. 252 at 284, para. 10.

[9] (1981) 27 D.R. 61 at para. 57.

for by law" in Article 1 of Protocol 1. The Court has attached no significance to the different versions of the English text.[10]

VII. *Travaux Préparatoires*

2–41 Recourse to *travaux préparatoires*[11] is classed as a supplementary means of interpretation under Article 32 of the Vienna Convention on the Law of Treaties. It may be deployed only in order to confirm the meaning of a provision as established in accordance with Article 31,[12] or where the application of the principles in Article 31 leaves the meaning ambiguous, obscure or absurd. This restriction is especially appropriate to the European Convention on Human Rights, in view of the Court's evolutive approach to interpretation.[13] Whilst the *travaux préparatoires* may have a certain relevance in determining the object and purpose of the Convention, they cannot be used as a primary aid to the construction of particular provisions. Thus, in *Lawless v. Ireland*[14] the Court observed that:

"Having ascertained that the text of Article 5 paragraphs (1)(c) and (3) is sufficiently clear in itself, [and] having also found that the meaning of this text is in keeping with the purpose of the Convention, the Court cannot, having regard to a generally recognised principle regarding the interpretation of international treaties, resort to the preparatory work."

2–42 The Court has sometimes referred to the *travaux préparatoires* in order to confirm an interpretation which it had already reached by other means.[15] But it has been perfectly prepared to adopt a construction which appears to conflict with the *travaux préparatoires* if it considers this is necessary to ensure that Convention rights are given practical effect in a modern context.[16]

VIII. *Autonomous terms*

2–43 Many of the terms used in the Convention, and especially those concerned with due process rights, refer directly to established concepts in domestic law. As we have seen, Article 31 of the Vienna Convention envisages the possibility of a "special meaning" being given to particular terms used in a treaty, where this is necessary to achieve the purpose of the measure in question. Under the European

---

[10] *Sunday Times v. United Kingdom (No. 1)* (1979–80) 2 E.H.R.R. 245 at para. 48. (The Court referred, in this connection, to Art. 33(4) of the Vienna Convention.)

[11] See *Collected Edition of the Travaux Préparatiores of the European Convention on Human Rights*.

[12] See para. 2–01 above.

[13] See paras 2–18 to 2–27 above.

[14] (1979–80) 1 E.H.R.R. 15 at para. 14.

[15] *James v. United Kingdom* (1986) 8 E.H.R.R. 123; *Belgian Linguistic Case (No. 2)* (1979–80) 1 E.H.R.R. 252; *Johnston v. Ireland* (1987) 9 E.H.R.R. 203; *Marckx v. Belgium* (1979–80) 2 E.H.R.R. 330.

[16] *Golder v. United Kingdom* (1979–80) 1 E.H.R.R. 525; *Campbell and Cosans v. United Kingdom* (1982) 4 E.H.R.R. 293; *Young, James and Webster v. United Kingdom* (1982) 4 E.H.R.R. 38; *Sigurjonsson v. Iceland* (1993) 16 E.H.R.R. 462.

Convention on Human Rights, this process is known as "autonomous interpretation".

There are two principal reasons why the Court interprets Convention terms   2–44
"autonomously". First, where a particular term does not have an identical scope
in the national legal systems of the contracting states, such an approach is
necessary to ensure uniformity of the Convention's application.[17] More importantly, autonomous interpretation is necessary in order to prevent contracting
states from evading their obligations by classifying procedures in national law so
as to deprive an individual of his Convention rights. To take an extreme example,
an autonomous approach to the term "persons of unsound mind" in Article
5(1)(e) is necessary to prevent a state from classifying dissidents as mentally
unbalanced, and then relying on that classification in order to detain them in a
closed institution. Thus, in its interpretation of Article 5(1)(e) the Court requires
a close correlation between the legal and medical definitions of unsoundness of
mind, and has held that a person may only be detained on the basis of objective
medical expertise.[18]

The process of autonomous interpretation has significant implications for the   2–45
criminal law. The very concept of "criminal" proceedings has been autonomously defined so as to include certain types of proceeding which would be
classified as civil, disciplinary or administrative proceedings in national law.[19]
An autonomous approach has also been taken to the meaning of the term
"charge" in Article 6(1)[20]; to the term "witness" in Article 6(3)(d)[21]; and to the
term "penalty" in Article 7.[22–23]

IX. *Implied rights*

In order to ensure that the protection afforded by the Convention is practical and   2–46
effective the Court has, on occasions, been prepared to imply rights into the
Convention which are absent from its text. We have already seen how, in the
context of extradition, the Court has implied into Article 3 of the Convention an
obligation on contracting states to refuse co-operation where a fugitive's extradition might expose him to inhuman or degrading treatment. In *Soering v. United
Kingdom*[24] the Court emphasised the importance of other international agreements as an aid to the interpretation of Convention rights. Referring to the United
Nations Convention Against Torture and Other Cruel, Inhuman or Degrading
Treatment or Punishment (1984), the Court observed[25]; "The fact that a specialised treaty should spell out in detail a specific obligation attaching to the

---

[17] Jacobs and White refer to a similar approach adopted by the Court of Justice of the European
Communities to the meaning of terms in both the E.C. Treaty and the Brussels Convention on Civil
Jurisdiction and the Enforcement of Judgments: Sir Francis Jacobs and Robin White, *The European
Convention on Human Rights* (2nd ed., Oxford, 1996) pp 28–29.
[18] *Winterwerp v. Netherlands* (1979–80) 2 E.H.R.R. 387 at paras 36–38.
[19] *Engel v. Netherlands* (1979–80) 1 E.H.R.R. 647 at para. 678. This subject is considered in detail
in Chapter 4 below.
[20] See, *e.g., Adolf v. Austria* (1982) 4 E.H.R.R. 315 at para. 30; *Eckle v. Germany* (1983) 5 E.H.R.R.
1 at para. 73; *Deweer v. Belgium* (1980) 2 E.H.R.R. 439 at para. 46. See Chapter 4 below.
[21] See, *e.g., Kostovski v. Netherlands* (1990) 12 E.H.R.R. 434. See para. 15–113 below.
[22–23] See *Welch v. United Kingdom* (1995) 20 E.H.R.R. 247 at para. 27. See para. 16–74 below.
[24] *Soering v. United Kingdom* (1989) 11 E.H.R.R. 439.
[25] At para. 87.

prohibition of torture does not mean that an essentially similar obligation is not already inherent in the general terms of Article 3 of the European Convention." More recently, in *Aydin v. Turkey*[26] the Court relied on the United Nations Torture Convention in order to imply into Article 13 of the Convention a duty on the state to carry out a prompt and impartial investigation into allegations of serious ill-treatment in custody.

2–47 The right to a fair trial, in Article 6, has been given a particularly open-textured interpretation, allowing scope for a range of rights to be read into its text by implication. The Court has held that the rights accorded to criminal defendants by Article 6(2) and 6(3) are "specific aspects of the general principle stated in paragraph 1" and are therefore to be regarded as a "non-exhaustive list" of minimum rights which form "constituent elements, amongst others, of the notion of a fair trial in criminal proceedings".[27] The relationship between the right to a fair trial in Article 6(1) and the specific rights set out in Article 6(2) and (3) has been described as "that of the general to the particular".[28] As the Commission put it in *Jespers v. Belgium*[29]:

> "Article 6 does not define the notion of a fair trial in criminal cases. Paragraph 3 of that Article lists certain specific rights which constitute essential elements of that general notion. The term 'minimum' [in Article 6(3)] clearly shows that the list of rights in paragraph 3 is not exhaustive and that a trial could well not fulfil the general conditions of a fair trial even if the minimum rights guaranteed by paragraph 3 were respected."

2–48 This approach has enabled the Court and Commission to imply into Article 6 a right of access by the accused to the unused evidence in the possession of the prosecution.[30] In *Edwards v. United Kingdom*[31] the Court held that "it is a requirement of fairness under Article 6(1) . . . that the prosecution authorities disclose to the defence all material evidence for or against the accused". It has also enabled the Court to develop strong protection for legal professional privilege.[32] Thus, in *S v. Switzerland*[33] the Court invoked Article 8(2)(d) of the American Convention on Human Rights, and Article 93 of the Standard Minimum Rules for the Treatment of Prisoners[34] in order to imply into Article 6 the right to consult with a solicitor privately and free from state supervision.

2–49 The cases of *Funke v. France*[35] and *Saunders v. United Kingdom*[36] provide further examples of this process. Article 14(2)(g) of the International Covenant on Civil and Political Rights expressly provides that an accused person has the right "not to be compelled to testify against himself or to confess guilt". That

---

[26] (1998) 25 E.H.R.R. 251 at para. 103.
[27] *Deweer v. Belgium* (1979–80) 2 E.H.R.R. 439 at para. 56.
[28] *Jespers v. Belgium* (1981) 27 D.R. 61 at para. 54.
[29] (1981) 27 D.R. 61 at para. 54.
[30] *Jespers v. Belgium* (1981) 27 D.R. 61 at para. 56.
[31] (1993) 15 E.H.R.R. 417 at para. 36.
[32] As to legal professional privilege generally, see paras 14–14 to 14–24 below.
[33] (1992) 14 E.H.R.R. 670 at para. 48.
[34] Annexed to Resolution (73) 5 of the Committee of Ministers.
[35] (1993) 16 E.H.R.R. 297.
[36] (1997) 23 E.H.R.R. 313.

right was not however included in the text of Article 6 of the European Convention. Despite this omission, the Court in *Funke* held that a person charged with a criminal offence within the meaning of Article 6 had the right to remain silent and not to contribute to incriminating himself.[37] Three years later, in *Saunders* the Court explained its approach in more detail:

> "The Court recalls that, although not specifically mentioned in Article 6 of the Convention, the right to silence and the right not to incriminate oneself, are generally recognised international standards which lie at the heart of the notion of a fair procedure under Article 6. Their rationale lies, *inter alia*, in the protection of the accused against improper compulsion by the authorities, thereby contributing to the avoidance of miscarriages of justice and to the fulfilment of the aims of Article 6."

Similarly, in *T and V v. United Kingdom*[38] the Court relied in part on the United   **2–50**
Nations Convention on the Rights of the Child, and the Standard Minimum Rules for the Administration of Juvenile Justice (the Beijing Rules) to conclude that the procedures for trying juveniles charged with serious crime should be adapted so as to enable the defendant to participate fully and effectively in the trial process. In that case the Court found a violation of Article 6 where two juvenile defendants charged with murder had been tried in public in an adult Crown Court, and their names and photographs had been released to the press. Here again, it was perhaps significant that Article 14(4) of the International Covenant on Civil and Political Rights specifically requires that the procedure for juvenile trial be adapted to take account of the defendant's age and the desirability of promoting rehabilitation. Far from pointing towards a deliberate omission in Article 6, the existence of relevant international instruments, which had been widely ratified, enabled the Court to conclude that a specially adapted procedure was a generally recognised international standard for the fair trial of juveniles. This, of course, is entirely in accordance with the evolutive approach to interpretation outlined above.

It does not follow that any right contained in a comparable international instru-   **2–51**
ment will necessarily be implied into the Convention. As one commentator has observed, a tribunal charged with interpreting the Convention has to strike a careful balance[39]:

> "Although implied terms are unavoidable if the interpretation of agreements is to produce sensible results, how far the interpreter may go in this direction is always likely to be controversial. Interpreting a treaty is one thing, rewriting it another, and if excessive caution is likely to produce decisions with no regard for the purpose of the agreement, excessive zeal turns the judge into a legislator, abusing his authority as interpreter to impose on the parties an agreement they never made."

An example of a situation in which the Commission was not prepared to read into   **2–52**
the Convention a right expressly contained in the International Covenant is the protection of an accused against double jeopardy. Article 14(7) of the International Covenant expressly provides that; "No one shall be liable to be tried or punished again for an offence for which he has already been finally convicted or

---

[37] Para. 44.
[38] (2000) 30 E.H.R.R. 121.
[39] J.G. Merrils, *The Development of International Law by the European Court of Human Rights* (2nd ed., Manchester, 1993), p. 85.

acquitted in accordance with the law and penal procedure of each country". In its early caselaw the Commission left open the question whether this principle could be implied into the right to a fair trial in Article 6.[40] However, in 1983, in *S v. Germany*[41] the Commission held that "the Convention system guarantees neither expressly nor by implication the principle of *ne bis in idem*". If such a principle was to be included within the Convention then it would require legislative action by the contracting states. Shortly after this decision, on November 22, 1984, Protocol 7 to the Convention was opened for signature, which made express provision for double jeopardy along lines very similar to Article 14(7) of the Covenant.

X. *Positive obligations*

2–53   The principal purpose of the Convention is the protection of individual rights from infringement by the contracting states. In general, this object is achieved by the imposition of negative obligations on the state and its officials, requiring them to refrain from interference with the rights in question. However, the Court has recognised that in order to secure truly effective protection, certain rights must be read as imposing obligations on the state to take positive action. These are known as "positive obligations", and they derive, at least in part, from the overarching duty on the contracting states in Article 1 of the Convention to "*secure* to everyone within their jurisdiction" the rights and freedoms set out in the Convention.[42]

2–54   Some positive obligations are inherent in the text of the Convention itself. Article 2, for example, provides that the right to life "shall be protected by law". This imposes an express obligation on the state, as a minimum, to "secure the right to life by putting in place effective criminal law provisions to deter the commission of offences against the person, backed up by law enforcement machinery for the prevention, suppression and sanctioning of breaches of such provisions".[43] Similarly, Article 6 imposes an express obligation on the state to establish courts which operate within a reasonable time,[44] interpreters[45] and legal aid in criminal proceedings.[46]

2–55   A second form of positive obligation arises where the state has some pastoral responsibility for the individual which has been delegated to a private body. In *Costello-Roberts v. United Kingdom*,[47] for example, the Court held that the state would be liable for abusive corporal punishment, amounting to inhuman or degrading treatment, not only in state schools but also in private schools. In the

---

[40] See, for example, *X v. Austria* (1970) 35 CD 151.
[41] (1983) 39 D.R. 43.
[42] The recognition of positive obligations is carried over into the Human Rights Act, not only by the duty to "have regard" to Convention jurisprudence in s.2 of the Act, but also by s.6(6) which expressly provides that the Act's provisions are to apply not only to positive actions by public authorities, but also to "a failure to act" (see para. 3–22 below).
[43] *Osman v. United Kingdom* (2000) 29 E.H.R.R. 245.
[44] Article 6(1).
[45] Article 6(3)(e).
[46] Article 6(3)(c).
[47] (1995) 19 E.H.R.R. 112 at para. 27.

Court's view, the state could not "absolve itself from responsibility . . . by delegating its obligations to private bodies or individuals".[48]

The principle of positive obligations, however, extends considerably further than **2–56** this. The Court has become increasingly willing in recent years to imply positive obligations into Convention rights which are expressed in purely negative terms. Thus, in relation to Article 8, the Court has held that[49]:

> "[T]he object of the Article is 'essentially' that of protecting the individual against arbitary interference by public authorities. Nevertheless, it does not merely compel the state to abstain from such interference: in addition to this primarily negative undertaking, there may be positive obligations inherent in an effective 'respect'."

In determining whether or not a positive obligation exists, "the Court will have **2–57** regard to the fair balance that has to be struck between the general interest of the community and the competing public interests of the individual, or individuals, concerned".[50] In striking this balance, the legitimate aims set out in the second paragraphs of Articles 8 to 11 may have a "certain relevance".[51]

The Court has recognised that effective protection may require states to take **2–58** legislative or administrative action to prevent one private individual from violating the Convention rights of another.[52] In *Plattform Artze fur das Leben v. Austria*[53] the Court held that the right to freedom of assembly in Article 11 of the Convention imposed obligations on the police to protect a peaceful demonstration from disruption by violent counter-demonstrators:

> "Genuine, effective freedom of peaceful assembly cannot . . . be reduced to a mere duty on the part of the state not to interfere: a purely negative conception would not be compatible with the object and purpose of Article 11. Like Article 8, Article 11 sometimes requires positive measures to be taken, even in the sphere of relations between individuals."

The "positive obligations" doctrine has significant implications for the rights of **2–59** victims of crime. The Court has held that the state is under a duty to adopt an adequate system of law to deter and punish individuals guilty of violating the Convention rights of others,[54] and that any available defences must not be cast in terms so wide as to undermine the effectiveness of the criminal sanction.[55] Where the right to life and the right to be protected from inhuman and degrading treatment are concerned, the police[56] and other relevant public bodies[57] are now

---

[48] This principle too is carried over into the Human Rights Act by s.6(3)(c) which provides that the Act's provisions bind "any person, certain of whose functions are of a public nature" See Chapter 3 para. 3–25 below.
[49] *Marckx v. Belgium* (1979–80) 2 E.H.R.R. 330 at para. 31.
[50] *McGinley and Egan v. United Kingdom* (1999) 27 E.H.R.R. 1; *Rees v. United Kingdom* (1987) 9 E.H.R.R. 56 para. 37.
[51] *Rees v. United Kingdom* (1987) 9 E.H.R.R. 56 at para. 37.
[52] See generally Clapham, *Human Rights in the Private Sphere* (Clarendon, 1993).
[53] (1991) 13 E.H.R.R. 204 at para. 32.
[54] *X and Y v. Netherlands* (1985) 8 E.H.R.R. 235: *Osman v. United Kingdom* (2000) 29 E.H.R.R. 245, para. 115.
[55] *A v. United Kingdom* (1999) 27 E.H.R.R. 611.
[56] *Mrs W v. United Kingdom* (1983) 32 D.R. 190; *Mrs W v. Ireland* (1983) 32 D.R. 211; *Osman v. United Kingdom*, Judgment of October 28, 1998.
[57] *Z and others v. United Kingdom* Application No. 29392/95 Judgment May 10, 2001 (concerning the liability of social services under Art. 3 for failure to take an abused child into care).

recognised as being under a positive operational obligation to take reasonable measures to prevent a criminal violation of an individual's rights under Articles 2 and 3; and (where such violations have occurred) to carry out an effective and independent investigation[58] which is capable of leading to the identification and prosecution of the offender.[59] Whilst the issue has not been finally resolved in Strasbourg, it seems likely that the prosecuting authorities are under a corresponding duty to prosecute in appropriate cases.[60] Where a crime involves a serious violation of the victim's Convention rights, the adoption of adequate criminal laws and their effective enforcement through investigation and prosecution must now be seen as constituent parts of the state's positive obligation to "secure" the Convention rights of victims and potential victims. These issues are considered in more detail in Chapter 18 below. The positive obligations principle may also have implications for the rights of those convicted of notorious crimes. In *Venables and Thompson v. News Group Newspapers and ors*[60a] the President of the Family Division held that Article 2 imposed a positive obligation on the Court to grant an injunction protecting the identity of an offender who was at serious risk of life-threatening attack.

XI. *Implied limitations*

2–60   Just as the Court has been willing to imply rights into the text of the Convention where this is necessary to render its protection practical and effective so it has, on occasion, recognised that certain rights carry with them implied limitations which are not spelt out in the text. The extent of these limitations is not subject to any general formula[61] and depends very much upon the context, and especially upon the nature of the right in question. As always, the guiding principle is that limitations must not undermine the effective protection of the right concerned.

2–61   The areas in which the Court has been most willing to accept the existence of implied limitations is where the right itself has been implied by the Court into the text of the Convention, or where it involves the recognition of a positive obligation on the state. In the civil law context, for example, the Court has recognised that Article 6 includes a right of access to court for the resolution of a dispute concerning a civil right or obligation.[62] However, in *Ashingdane v. United Kingdom*[63] the Court held that this right is not absolute and may be subject to limitations since by its very nature it calls for regulation by the state "which may vary in time and place according to the needs and resources of the community and of individuals". The Court went on, however, to hold that any

---

[58] *McCann, Savage and Farrell v. United Kingdom* (1996) 21 E.H.R.R. 97 at para. 161.

[59] *Aydin v. Turkey* (1998) 25 E.H.R.R. 251 at paras 103–109.

[60] *Aydin v. Turkey* (1998) 25 E.H.R.R. 251 at para. 103 (the investigation must be capable to leading to the "*punishment*" of the offender); *Osman v. United Kingdom* (2000) 29 E.H.R.R. 245, para. 115 (The state must establish effective machinery for the "*sanctioning*" of criminal violations of the right to life). See also the decision of the Inter-American Court of Human Rights in *Velaquez-Rodriguez v. Honduras* (1989) 28 I.L.M. 291.

[60a] January 8, 2001.

[61] *Deweer v. Belgium* (1979–80) 2 E.H.R.R. 439 at para. 49: "[I]t is not the Court's function . . . to elaborate a general theory of such limitations".

[62] *Golder v. United Kingdom* (1979–80) 1 E.H.R.R. 525; *Ashingdane v. United Kingdom* (1985) 7 E.H.R.R. 528; *Fayed v. United Kingdom* (1994) 18 E.H.R.R. 393.

[63] (1985) 7 E.H.R.R. 528 at para. 57.

such restrictions must not reduce the individual's access to court in such a way as to impair the essence of the right. Furthermore, the Court said, "a limitation will not be compatible with Article 6(1) if it does not pursue a legitimate aim, and if there is not a reasonable relationship of proportionality between the means employed and the aim sought to be achieved".[64]

A similar principle has been applied in relation to criminal proceedings. Under   2–62
Article 6(1) a person charged with a criminal offence has, in principle, the right to a determination by a court. This does not, however, prevent the prosecution from withdrawing an indictment or abandoning a criminal charge without a ruling from a court, even though the consequence of such action is to deprive the accused of a formal acquittal.[65] As the Court observed in *Deweer v. Belgium*[66];

> "The 'right to a court', which is a constituent element of the right to a fair trial, is no more absolute in criminal than in civil matters. It is subject to implied limitations, two examples of which are . . . [a] decision not to prosecute and [an] order for discontinuance of the proceedings".

In *Murray v. United Kingdom*,[67] another case concerned with implied rights, the   2–63
Court held that the right to remain silent under police questioning, and the privilege against self-incrimination were not "absolute in the sense that the exercise by the accused of the right to silence cannot under any circumstances be used against him at trial".[68] Whether the drawing of adverse inferences from an accused's silence infringed Article 6 was to be determined in the light of the conditions upon which an inference may be drawn, the weight attached to it, and the degree of compulsion inherent in the situation.[69] A similar limitation was recognised by the Court in *Rowe and Davis v United Kingdom*[70] in the context of the implied right to disclosure of unused material. The Court held that whilst Article 6 generally requires the prosecution to disclose to the defence all material evidence for or against the accused, considerations of national security or the protection of vulnerable witnesses could, in certain circumstances, justify an exception to this rule (providing there were adequate procedural safeguards in place to protect the rights of the accused).

In *Osman v. United Kingdom*[71] the Court held that Article 2 imposed a positive   2–64
obligation on the police to take reasonable steps to prevent a foreseeable homicidal attack. The Court was, however, careful to emphasise that this obligation had to be "interpreted in a way which does not impose an impossible or disproportionate burden on the authorities".[72] Moreover, it could not be interpreted in a manner inconsistent with the rights of the suspect in view of the;

> "need to ensure that the police exercise their powers to control and prevent crime in a manner which fully respects the due process and other guarantees which legitimately

---

[64] *ibid.*
[65] *X, Y and Z v. Austria* (1980) 19 D.R. 213 at 217–218.
[66] (1979–80) 2 E.H.R.R. 439 at para. 49.
[67] (1996) 22 E.H.R.R. 29.
[68] At paras 46–47.
[69] At para. 47.
[70] (2000) 30 E.H.R.R. 1.
[71] (2000) 29 E.H.R.R. 245.
[72] Para. 116.

place restraints on the scope of their action to investigate crime and bring offenders to justice, including the guarantees contained in Articles 5 and 8 of the Convention".

2–65 The Court has, for obvious reasons, been cautious in implying limitations into express Convention rights. Nevertheless, where the right concerned is framed in general terms, without detailed or exhaustive definition, the Court has held that there may be "room for implied limitations".[73] As we have seen, the right to a fair trial in criminal cases is not exhaustively defined in Article 6(1),[74] and the specific rights contained in Articles 6(2) and 6(3) are regarded as "constituent elements" of the general notion of a fair trial.[75] Whilst this allows the Court to imply additional fair trial guarantees into Article 6(1), it also enables it to adopt a substantive rather than formalistic approach to breaches of Articles 6(2) and (3). Thus, in *Croissant v. Germany*[76] the Court held that the right of an accused to defend himself in person, which is expressly guaranteed by Article 6(3)(c) does not prevent the national authorities from imposing reasonable restrictions on the right to appear without a lawyer in a complex case; and the right to counsel of choice has been held not to apply to a defendant whose representation is funded by legal aid.[77] Similarly, the right of an accused in Article 6(3)(d) "to examine or have examined witnesses against him" does not amount to an absolute bar on the admission of documentary hearsay.[78] In keeping with its approach to the interpretation of Article 6(1) the Court will examine the importance of the disputed hearsay in the context of the prosecution case as a whole,[79] and will take account of any safeguards imposed by domestic law.[80]

2–66 In *Pretto v. Italy*[81] the Court took the unusual course of invoking the object and purpose of the Convention in order to restrict the rights of the accused, albeit in a matter of formality rather than substance. The Court held that the apparently unqualified requirement in Article 6(1) for a public pronouncement of judgment did not apply to a court of cassation (or, presumably, to any appellate court). It was sufficient to meet the requirement of public "pronouncement" if the judgment was lodged in the Court registry where it would be available for inspection by the public. As the Court observed[82]:

> "[M]any member states of the Council of Europe have a long-standing tradition of recourse to other means, besides reading out aloud, for making public the decisions of all or some of their courts, and especially of their courts of cassation, for example deposit in a registry accessible to the public. The authors of the Convention cannot have overlooked that fact . . . The Court therefore does not feel bound to adopt a literal interpretation. It considers that in each case the form of publicity to be given to the 'judgment' under the domestic law of the respondent state must be assessed in the light of the special features of the proceedings in question and by reference to the object and purpose of the Convention."

---

[73] *Mathieu-Mohin and Clerfayt v. Belgium* (1988) 10 E.H.R.R. 1 at para. 52.
[74] *Jespers v. Belgium* (1981) 27 D.R. 61 at para. 56.
[75] *Deweer v. Belgium* (1979–80) 2 E.H.R.R. 439 at para. 56.
[76] (1993) 16 E.H.R.R. 135.
[77] *X v. United Kingdom* (1983) 5 E.H.R.R. 273.
[78] See Chapter 15, para. 15–08 below.
[79] See, for example, *Unterpertinger v. Austria* (1991) 13 E.H.R.R. 175.
[80] *Trivedi v. United Kingdom* (1997) 89A D.R. 136.
[81] (1984) 6 E.H.R.R. 182.
[82] Para. 26.

The Court's recent caselaw has accorded increasing recognition to the rights of victims and witnesses in the criminal justice system. This can, of course, bring with it corresponding limitations on the due process rights of the accused. In *Doorson v. Netherlands*[83] the Court held that in appropriate cases the interests of the defence must be "balanced against those of witnesses or victims called upon to testify". Whilst noting that Article 6 does not expressly require the interests of witnesses to be taken into account, the Court pointed out that in certain situations, and especially where there is a serious risk of reprisals, the rights of the victim or witness under other provisions of the Convention[84] may be imperilled if protective measures are not taken. **2–67**

There is one area in which the Court has not been prepared to countenance implied limitations, and that is where the right in question is both defined and subject to express qualification. This arises in relation to the qualified rights in Articles 8 to 11, which lay down in detail the conditions under which the state may interfere with the protected right in issue. The Court has held that where the Convention itself spells out the permissible qualifications on a right, there is no justification for further implied limitations. Thus, in *Golder v. United Kingdom*,[85] in the context of an alleged interference with the right to correspondence in Article 8, the Court held that: **2–68**

> "The restrictive formulation used at Article 8(2) ('There shall be no interference . . . except such as . . . ') leaves no room for the concept of implied limitations. In this regard, the legal status of the right to respect for correspondence, which is defined by Article 8 with some precision, provides a clear contrast to that of the right [of access] to a court."

XII. *Waiver of Convention rights*

The Court has held that "the nature of some of the rights safeguarded by the Convention is such as to exclude a waiver of the entitlement to exercise them, but the same cannot be said of certain other rights".[86] The limits of doctrine of waiver have never been fully spelt out by the Court. The guiding principle however is that any waiver "must be made in an unequivocal manner, and must not run counter to an important public interest".[87] **2–69**

Not surprisingly, the Court has been very reluctant to accept that a person can waive the right to personal liberty in Article 5. Thus, in *De Wilde, Ooms and Versyp v. Belgium*[88] the Court observed that; **2–70**

---

[83] (1996) 23 E.H.R.R. 330 at para. 70.
[84] The Court referred to Arts 2, 3, 5 and 8.
[85] (1979–80) 1 E.H.R.R. 525 at para. 44.
[86] *Albert and LeCompte v. Belgium* (1983) 5 E.H.R.R. 533 at para. 35.
[87] *Schuler-Zraggen v. Switzerland* (1993) 16 E.H.R.R. 405 at para. 58; *Hakansson and Sturesson v. Sweden* (1991) 13 E.H.R.R. 1 at para. 66; *Colozza v. Italy* (1985) 7 E.H.R.R. 516 at para. 28. In *Van der Mussele v. Belgium* (1984) 6 E.H.R.R. 25 the Court held that the fact that a barrister had voluntarily entered the legal profession did not mean that he had waived his right to complain about an obligation inherent in the professional rules to perform free representation It was, however, a significant factor in assessing whether he had been required to perform forced or compulsory labour in breach of Art. 4(2).
[88] (1979–80) 1 E.H.R.R. 373 at para. 65.

"... the right to personal liberty is too important in a 'democratic society' within the meaning of the Convention for a person to lose the benefit of the protection of the Convention for the single reason that he gives himself up to be taken into detention. Detention might violate Article 5 even although the person concerned might have agreed to it. When the matter is one which concerns the *ordre public* within the Council of Europe, a scrupulous supervision by the organs of the Convention of all measures capable of violating the rights and freedoms which it guarantees is necessary in every case."

Similarly in *Amuur v. France*[89] the Court held that an asylum seeker who was detained in an airport transit area could not be taken to have waived his rights under Article 5 simply because it was possible for him voluntarily to leave the country in which he was seeking refuge.

2–71 So far as Article 6 is concerned, the position is more complex. The Court's approach depends on the aspect of the right which is in issue. In *Pfeifer and Plankl v. Austria*[90] the Court doubted whether it would ever be possible for a defendant to waive the fundamental right in Article 6(1) to a tribunal which was independent and impartial. In the Court's view "such a right is of essential importance, and its exercise cannot depend on the parties alone". Accordingly, a failure to object to two judges who had been involved in the investigation of an offence was held not to amount to a waiver.[91]

2–72 The Court has held that it is open to an accused person to waive the right to a trial altogether, provided any "settlement" of criminal proceedings is express and unequivocal, and that it is freely entered into.[92] Implied waiver of the right to a hearing in one's presence is more problematic. In a number of cases the Court has stated that a defendant who fails to attend for his trial, after having been given effective notice of it, will only be taken to have forfeited the right to a hearing in his presence if the waiver is clear and unequivocal.[93] The difficulty, of course, lies in determining when a failure to appear amounts to a deliberate and unequivocal waiver. The Court has attempted to resolve this problem by holding that the state may proceed in the absence of an accused where it has acted diligently but unsuccessfully to secure his attendance, providing the accused is able to obtain "a fresh determination of the merits of the charge" when he later learns of the proceedings.[94]

2–73 The right to a hearing in public can also be waived. In *Albert and LeCompte v. Belgium*[95] the Court held that this aspect of Article 6 may "yield in certain circumstances to the will of the person concerned". In the Court's view "neither the letter nor the spirit of Article 6(1) would prevent [an applicant] from waiving, of his own free will and in an unequivocal manner ... the entitlement to have his

---

[89] (1996) 22 E.H.R.R. 533 at para. 48.
[90] (1992) 14 E.H.R.R. 692 at paras 38–39.
[91] See also *Obserchlick v. Austria (No.1)* (1995) 19 E.H.R.R. 389.
[92] *Deweer v. Belgium* (1979–80) 2 E.H.R.R. 439 (concerning the "settlement" of criminal proceedings). As to the implications of this decision for the reduction of a sentence following a plea of guilty, see paras 16–64 and 16–65 below.
[93] *Colozza v. Italy* (1985) 7 E.H.R.R. 516; *Brozicek v. Italy* (1990) 12 E.H.R.R. 371 at paras 43–46.
[94] *Colozza v. Italy* (1985) 7 E.H.R.R. 516 at para. 29.
[95] (1983) 5 E.H.R.R. 533 at para. 35.

case heard in public." The Court has been prepared to accept that an implied waiver is possible in this context. In *Hakansson and Sturesson v. Sweden*[96] the Court held that the failure of the applicants to apply for an oral hearing of their appeal (which was possible under Swedish legislation) amounted to an unequivocal waiver of the right to a public hearing. The position will of course be otherwise if there is no provision for such a hearing in domestic law, or if there is little prospect of securing one.[97] Equally, it is plain that an accused can waive the right to be represented by a lawyer.[98]

XIII. *Convention to be read as a whole*

Article 31 of the Vienna Convention on the Law of Treaties[99] requires that provisions of a treaty should be construed in their context. The Court has interpreted this to mean that "the Convention and its Protocols must be read as a whole; consequently a matter dealt with mainly by one of their provisions may also, in some of its aspects, be subject to other provisions thereof".[1]   2–74

The fact that the subject-matter of a complaint is addressed directly in an optional protocol which the state concerned has not ratified will not necessarily be decisive, since the issue may also be covered by a provision of the Convention itself.[2] In *Guzzardi v. Italy*[3] the Court held that a suspected Mafia member was deprived of his liberty within the meaning of Article 5 when he was made the subject of a compulsory residence order confining him to a small island where his movements were closely monitored by officials. This was despite the fact that freedom of movement, a more apposite right in the circumstances, was expressly guaranteed by Article 2 of Protocol 4 which Italy had not ratified.   2–75

In *Ekbatani v. Sweden*[4] the government relied on the adoption of Protocol 7, to argue that "only the fundamental guarantees of Article 6 applied in appeal proceedings" and that these did not include the right to an oral hearing on appeal. The Court noted that the Explanatory Report to Protocol 7 emphasised that "the Protocol cannot be interpreted as prejudicing the rights guaranteed by the Convention"[5] and drew attention to the provisions of Article 53 of the Convention.[6] The Court concluded that there was "no warrant for the view that the addition of this Protocol was intended to limit, at the appellate level, the guarantees contained in Article 6 of the Convention".[7]   2–76

It does not follow however that the existence of an unratified protocol is irrelevant. In *Soering v. United Kingdom*[8] the Court treated the adoption of   2–77

---

[96] (1991) 13 E.H.R.R. 1 at para. 67.
[97] *H v. Belgium* (1988) 10 E.H.R.R. 339.
[98] *Melin v. France* (1994) 17 E.H.R.R. 1 at para. 25.
[99] See para. 2–01 above.
[1] *Abdulaziz, Cabales and Balkandali v. United Kingdom* (1985) 7 E.H.R.R. 471 at para. 60.
[2] In *Abdulaziz, Cabales and Balkandali* the Court rejected the Government's argument that immigration matters were governed solely by Protocol 4 which the United Kingdom had not ratified.
[3] (1981) 3 E.H.R.R. 333.
[4] (1991) 13 E.H.R.R. 504.
[5] Explanatory Report para. 43.
[6] The Court in fact referred to Art. 60, which was the predecessor to Art. 53 prior to Protocol 11.
[7] At para. 26.
[8] (1989) 11 E.H.R.R. 439.

Protocol 6 as determinative of the issue of whether it was possible, through the technique of evolutive interpretation, to hold that the death penalty was *per se* in breach of Article 3. The Court considered that by including an optional protocol prohibiting the death penalty, the contracting parties had signalled their intention "to adopt the normal method of amendment of the text in order to introduce a new obligation".[9] Accordingly, the virtual abolition of the death penalty throughout the Council of Europe could not justify an evolutive interpretation of Article 3, so as to amount to prohibition on the death penalty altogether.

XIV. *The lex specialis principle*

2–78   The Court sometimes refers to a provision of the Convention as the *lex specialis* for a particular complaint.[10] This principle holds that if there is an article of the Convention which is specifically aimed at the subject-matter of the application, then that provision will generally be applied in preference to a more general provision, since it more closely reflects the intentions of the contracting parties.

XV. *The Rule of Law*

2–79   The preamble to the Convention refers to the "rule of law" as an integral part of the "common heritage" of the contracting states.[11] The Court has held that this is one of the "fundamental principles of a democratic society"[12] and should be treated as a guiding principle in the interpretation of the Convention.[13] In *Silver v. United Kingdom*[14] the Court held that respect for the rule of law implied "that an interference by the authorities with an individual's rights should be subject to effective control. This is especially so where . . . the law bestows on the executive wide discretionary powers." In *Klass v. Germany*,[15] the Court held that where intrusive surveillance was in issue such control should normally be assured by the judiciary, since "judicial control offer[s] the best guarantees of independence, impartiality and a proper procedure". However a review carried out by a body which is truly independent of the executive may suffice in some circumstances, even if it is not strictly judicial in character, providing the body concerned is "vested with sufficient powers and competence to exercise an effective and continuous control".[16]

XVI. *The principle of legal certainty*

2–80   A number of Convention rights contain an express requirement that state action must be "lawful", "prescribed by law" or "in accordance with the law".

---

[9] See para. 2–19 above.

[10] This principle pulls in the opposite direction to the requirement to read the Convention as a whole, and the Court has applied it selectively.

[11] The "rule of law" is also referred to in the preamble to the Statute of the Council of Europe, and in Art. 3 of the Statute, which provides that "every Member of the Council of Europe must accept the principle of the rule of law . . . ".

[12] *Iatrides v. Greece* Judgment March 25, 1999, para. 62.

[13] *Golder v. United Kingdom* (1979–80) 1 E.H.R.R. 525 at para. 34.

[14] (1983) 5 E.H.R.R. 347 at para. 90.

[15] (1979–80) 2 E.H.R.R. 214 at para. 55.

[16] *Klass* at para. 56. This qualification does not, of course, apply to Arts 5 and 6.

Whenever such a reference appears in the text, it is to be interpreted as a semi-autonomous concept, involving a mixed Convention and domestic law interpretation. First, the act in question must have a legal basis in national law. Statute law, secondary legislation, applicable rules of European Community law,[17] ascertainable common law,[18] and even rules of professional bodies[19] may be sufficient. However, non-statutory guidance to the executive is unlikely to be sufficient since it will not usually have the force of law.[20]

In addition the law itself must meet certain "quality of law" requirements. It   2–81
must be *publicly accessible* so as to enable citizens to ascertain the applicable legal rules in advance; and it must be sufficiently *precise* for the individual to be able to regulate his conduct in accordance with the law. More generally, the Court has recognised that the principle of legal certainty distinguishes government based upon the rule of law from government characterised by excessive executive or judicial discretion, which carries with it the potential for arbitrary interference with individual rights.[21] A law which confers a discretion must, as a minimum, give an adequate indication of the scope of the discretion.[22]

The principle of legal certainty has been interpreted as requiring that a citizen   2–82
must be able to foresee, to a degree that is reasonable in the circumstances, the consequences that a given action may entail.[23] This does not mean that the individual must be able to predict the legal consequences of his actions with absolute certainty. As the Court has observed:

> "[E]xperience shows this to be unattainable . . . Whilst certainty is highly desireable, it may bring in its train excessive rigidity and the law must always be able to keep pace with changing circumstances. Accordingly, many laws are inevitably couched in terms which, to a greater or lesser extent, are vague and whose interpretation and application are questions of practice".[24]

In judging whether a legal rule satisfies the requirements of certainty and foreseeability, the Court will approach the question on the assumption that the applicant could have obtained appropriate legal advice.[25] The fact that a statutory provision is capable of more than one construction does not necessarily involve a breach of the principle of legal certainty.[26] Nor does the fact that a common law

---

[17] *Groppera Radio AG v. Switzerland* (1990) 12 E.H.R.R. 321.
[18] *Sunday Times v. United Kingdom (No. 1)* (1979–80) 2 E.H.R.R. 245 at paras 46–53.
[19] *Barthold v. Germany* (1985) 7 E.H.R.R. 383 at para. 46.
[20] *Khan v. United Kingdom* [2000] Crim.L.R. 684 (concerning Home Office guidance on intrusive surveillance).
[21] *Amuur v. France* (1996) 22 E.H.R.R. 533 at para. 50.
[22] *Silver v. United Kingdom* (1983) 5 E.H.R.R. 347. In certain instances the requirement for legal certainty may imply the need for procedural safeguards. Thus, in *Hentrich v. France* (1994) 18 E.H.R.R. 440 at para. 42 the Court found a violation of Art. 1 of Protocol 1 where the revenue authorities operated a pre-emptive procedure where they believed there to be a sale at an undervalue. The procedure was found to be in breach because it "operated arbitrarily and selectively, and was scarcely foreseeable, *and it was not attended by basic procedural guarantees*".
[23] *Sunday Times v. United Kingdom (No. 1)* (1979–80) 2 E.H.R.R. 245 at para. 49.
[24] *Sunday Times v. United Kingdom (No. 1)* (1979–80) 2 E.H.R.R. 245 at para. 49.
[25] *Sunday Times v. United Kingdom (No. 1)* (1979–80) 2 E.H.R.R. 245 at para. 49; *Cantoni v. France* Judgment November 15, 1996.
[26] *Castells v. Spain* (1992) 14 E.H.R.R. 445; *Vogt v. Germany* (1996) 21 E.H.R.R. 205.

offence may be susceptible to change over time, providing any development is reasonably foreseeable and consistent with the essence of the offence.[27]

2–83   The application of this principle in criminal cases can be illustrated by reference to Articles 5 and 7 of the Convention and by reference to the qualified rights in Articles 8 to 11. Article 5(1), for instance, requires that any deprivation of liberty must be "lawful" and carried out "in accordance with a procedure prescribed by law". The Court has held that the requirement embodied in these terms "refers essentially to national law and lays down the obligation to conform to the substantive and procedural rules of national law".[28] In addition, however, a detention must be "in keeping with the purpose of Article 5, namely to protect the individual from arbitrariness".[29] In *Amuur v. France*[30] the Court pointed out that this latter requirement reflects the principle of respect for the rule of law which runs throughout the Convention:

> "In laying down that any deprivation of liberty must be effected 'in accordance with a procedure prescribed by law', Article 5(1) primarily requires any arrest or detention to have a legal basis in domestic law. However, these words do not merely refer back to domestic law; like the expressions 'in accordance with the law' and 'prescribed by law' in the second paragraphs of Articles 8 to 11, they also relate to the quality of the law, requiring it to be compatible with the rule of law, a concept inherent in all the Articles of the Convention. In order to ascertain whether a deprivation of liberty has complied with the principle of compatibility with domestic law, it therefore falls to the Court to assess not only the legislation in force in the field under consideration, but also the quality of the other legal rules applicable to the persons concerned. Quality in this sense implies that where a national law authorises deprivation of liberty... it must be sufficiently accessible and precise, in order to avoid all risk of arbitrariness."

2–84   In *Zamir v. United Kingdom*[31] the Commission recognised that even in the context of a deprivation of liberty, some flexibility in the law is permissible:

> "While particular decisions of the courts may be seen as unexpected within the legal community, it does not follow that the legal rule in question was not sufficiently certain... The Commission's approach must be to examine whether the margin of uncertainty that surrounds legal rules in this field of law, exceeds acceptable boundaries."

2–85   In relation to the substantive criminal law, the requirement for legal certainty is embodied in Article 7. On its face Article 7 constitutes no more than a guarantee against the retrospective application of the criminal law. However, consistent with its short title in the Convention ("*no punishment without law*") the Court has held that Article 7 is to be broadly construed. Thus, Article 7 has been held to embody the principle that the criminal law must not be extensively construed to an accused's disadvantage, and that criminal offences must be clearly defined

---

[27] See Chapter 10.

[28] *Amuur v. France* (1996) 22 E.H.R.R. 533 at para. 50; *Tsirilis and Koyloumpas v. Greece* (1998) 25 E.H.R.R. 440 at para. 42; *Benham v. United Kingdom* (1996) 22 E.H.R.R. 293 at para. 40; *Quinn v. France* (1996) 21 E.H.R.R. 529 at para. 47; *Winterwerp v. Netherlands* (1979–80) 2 E.H.R.R. 387 at para. 37.

[29] *Amuur v. France* (1996) 22 E.H.R.R. 533 at para. 50; *Quinn v. France* (1996) 21 E.H.R.R. 529 at para. 47.

[30] (1996) 22 E.H.R.R. 533 at para. 50.

[31] (1983) 40 D.R. 42 at para. 91.

in law.[32] Accordingly, Article 7 prohibits the extension of a statutory or common law offence so as to encompass conduct which would not previously have been regarded as a crime.[33] However, in *SW and CR v. United Kingdom*[34] the Court emphasised that this principle does not prohibit the development of the criminal law through judicial decisions.

Each of the qualified rights in Articles 8 to 11 of the Convention stipulate the conditions on which an interference by the state with the right concerned will be permissible. The first condition which must be satisfied is that the measure taken was "prescribed by law" or "in accordance with law". There is no significance to be attached to the minor differences between the terminology employed in these provisions.[35] In each case, the Convention requires that the measure in question has "some basis in domestic law"[36] and that the domestic law must satisfy the "quality of law" requirements discussed above.   **2–86**

In *McLeod v. United Kingdom*[37] the Court was concerned with the police power   **2–87** of entry without warrant into a person's home to deal with or prevent a breach of the peace. The applicant argued that the common law power of entry was insufficiently clear to meet the quality of law requirement in Article 8. The common law power had been preserved (without elaboration or clarification) by section 17(6) of the Police and Criminal Evidence Act 1984. Having reviewed the domestic authorities on the issue, the Court concluded that the power was "defined with sufficient precision for the foreseeability criterion to be satisfied".

Two recent cases illustrate the operation of this principle in relation to the powers   **2–88** of the English courts to make bindover orders. In *Steel and others v. United Kingdom*[38] the applicants complained that the law governing bindovers for breach of the peace was inconsistent, and in particular that the domestic caselaw contained contradictory statements of principle. However, a number of these apparent conflicts had been resolved in a series of decisions in the Divisional Court. Having regard to these developments, the Court observed that:

> "[T]he concept of breach of the peace has been clarified by the English courts over the last two decades, to the extent that it is now sufficiently established that a breach of the peace is committed only when an individual causes harm, or appears likely to cause harm, to persons or property, or acts in a manner the natural consequence of which would be to provoke others to violence. It is also clear that a person may be arrested for causing a breach of the peace or where it is reasonably apprehended that he or she is likely to cause a breach of the peace. Accordingly, the Court considers that the relevant legal rules provided sufficient guidance and were formulated with the degree of precision required by the Convention."

---

[32] *Kokkinakis v. Greece* (1994) 17 E.H.R.R. 397 at para. 52.
[33] In *Harman v. United Kingdom* (1984) 38 D.R. 53 the Commission declared admissible an application in which it was claimed that the domestic courts had created a wholly new category of contempt. The case eventually settled without a judgment from the Court.
[34] (1996) 21 E.H.R.R. 363 at paras 36 (SW) and 34 (CR).
[35] *Sunday Times v. United Kingdom* (1979–80) 2 E.H.R.R. 245 at para. 48.
[36] *Silver v. United Kingdom* (1983) 5 E.H.R.R. 347 at para. 86.
[37] (1998) 27 E.H.R.R. 493.
[38] (1999) 28 E.H.R.R. 603; [1998] Crim. L.R. 893.

2–89   In *Hashman and Harrup v. United Kingdom*,[39] by contrast, the Court held that the power of a court to bind an individual over to be of good behaviour (that is not to act *contra bonos mores*) was insufficiently defined to enable the affected individual to identify the sort of behaviour which would be likely to breach the order. The Court reiterated the principle that "a norm cannot be regarded as a 'law' unless it is formulated with sufficient precision to enable the citizen to regulate his conduct". The level of precision required depended "to a considerable extent on the content of the instrument in question, the field it is designed to cover, and the number and status of those to whom it is addressed". The most precise definition of conduct *contra bonos mores* was that provided by Glidewell L.J. in *Hughes v. Holley*,[40] namely behaviour which is "wrong rather than right in the judgment of the majority of contemporary fellow citizens". In the Court's view, conduct falling within this definition was "not described at all, but merely expressed to be "wrong" in the opinion of the majority". This formulation lacked sufficient objectivity to amount to a legal rule. Accordingly, the exercise of the power by the Crown Court was found to be in violation of Article 10.

2–90   The distinction between these two cases lies not only in the legal definition of the prohibited conduct, but also in the nature of the conduct proved against the applicants in each case. In *Steel* the complainants had been convicted of a breach of the peace, and so might reasonably foresee what conduct was said to be unacceptable. The complainants in *Hashman*, on the other hand, had committed no offence, and had no objective standard against which to judge whether their future conduct would be regarded as "wrong rather than right".

2–91   The term "in accordance with law" in Article 8(2) has a special meaning in the context of powers of secret surveillance.[41] In *Malone v. United Kingdom*[42] the Court accepted that the requirement of foreseeability cannot mean that an individual must be able to predict with certainty whether or not the authorities are likely to intercept his communications in any given situation. However, domestic law must indicate "with reasonable clarity" the circumstances and conditions under which such surveillance can occur.[43] Domestic procedures permitting intrusive surveillance must be based on a framework of positive rules—with the force of law—for regulating the operation of the system,[44] and must include adequate and effective safeguards against abuse.[45]

XVII. *Necessary in a democratic society*

2–92   The second condition for any interference with the rights protected in Articles 8 to 11 is that it must be "necessary in a democratic society" in pursuit of one or more of the legitimate aims prescribed in the second paragraph of each Article. These aims vary according to the right in issue, but typically include the interests of national security, public safety, or the economic well-being of the country; the

---

[39] (2000) 30 E.H.R.R. 241.
[40] [1988] 86 Cr. App. R. 130.
[41] See Chapter 7 below.
[42] (1984) 7 E.H.R.R. 14.
[43] *Malone v. United Kingdom* (1984) 7 E.H.R.R. 14.
[44] *Kruslin v. France* (1990) 12 E.H.R.R. 547; *Kopp v. Switzerland* (1999) 27 E.H.R.R. 91.
[45] *Klass v. Germany* (1979–80) 2 E.H.R.R. 214 at para. 55.

prevention of disorder or crime; the protection of health or morals; and the protection of the rights and freedoms of others.

The Court has, over the years, used a number of different formulations for **2–93** determining whether an interference was "necessary in a democratic society" in the sense in which that expression is used in Articles 8 to 11. In *Sunday Times v. United Kingdom*[46] the Court held that "whilst the adjective 'necessary' is not synonymous with 'indispensible', neither does it have the flexibility of such expressions as 'admissible', 'ordinary', 'useful', 'reasonable' or 'desireable'; rather it implies a 'pressing social need'". In applying the "pressing social need" test, subsequent cases have emphasised that;

> " . . . it is for the Court to make the final determination as to whether the inteference in issue corresponds to such a need, whether it is 'proportionate to the legitimate aim pursued', and whether the reasons given by the national authorities to justify it are 'relevant and sufficient'".[47]

In recent years it has become the settled practice of the Court, when faced with **2–94** an alleged violation of Articles 8 to 11, to consider the question in two distinct stages. First, the Court will inquire whether the measure in question pursued one of the stated legitimate aims. More often than not, this turns out to be uncontroversial. Secondly the Court will inquire whether there is a "reasonable relationship of proportionality" between the means employed and the aim sought to be achieved. It is on the issue of proportionality that most alleged violations of Articles 8 to 11 ultimately turn.[48]

The concept of "necessity" has a stricter connotation where it arises elsewhere **2–95** in the Convention. In the context of alleged violations of the right to life, the Court has held that the use of the term "absolutely necessary" in Article 2(2) indicates that "a stricter and more compelling test of necessity must be employed from that normally applicable when determining whether state action is 'necessary in a democratic society' under paragraph 2 of Articles 8 to 11 of the Convention".[49] Any force used by the state "must be *strictly* proportionate to the achievement of the aims" set out in Article 2(2).[50] This approach probably owes more to the importance of the right at stake than to the precise terminology employed in the text of Article 2.

The Court has taken a similar approach to the prohibition on torture and inhuman **2–96** or degrading treatment or punishment. The text of Article 3 makes no explicit reference to the requirement of "necessity". Nevertheless, in *Ribitsch v. Austria*[51] the Court emphasised that "in respect of a person deprived of his liberty, any recourse to physical force which has not been made *strictly necessary* by his own

---

[46] (1979–80) 2 E.H.R.R. 245 at para. 59; see also *Handyside v. United Kingdom* (1979–80) 1 E.H.R.R. 737 at para. 48.
[47] *Barthold v. Germany* (1985) 7 E.H.R.R. 383 at para. 55. See, to similar effect, *Sunday Times v. United Kingdom (No. 1)* (1979–80) 2 E.H.R.R. 245 at para. 59; *Olsson v. Sweden* (1989) 11 E.H.R.R. 259.
[48] As to the Court's approach to the concept of proportionality, see paras 2–99 to 2–112 below.
[49] *McCann and ors v. United Kingdom* (1996) 21 E.H.R.R. 97 at para. 149; *Andronicou and Constantinou v. Cyprus* (1998) 25 E.H.R.R. 491 at para. 171.
[50] *ibid.*
[51] (1996) 21 E.H.R.R. 573 at para. 38.

conduct diminishes human dignity and is in principle an infringement of the right set forth in Article 3 of the Convention."

2–97   Article 6(1) permits the exclusion of the press and the public "to the extent *strictly necessary* in the opinion of the Court in special circumstances where publicity would prejudice the interests of justice"—a textual restriction which does not apply to the other grounds for exclusion permitted by Article 6(1). In *Handyside v. United Kingdom*,[52] the Court suggested that the language of this exception pointed to a restrictive approach. In practice, however, the Court has eschewed a mechanistic application of the text, and has applied the exception in a realistic manner which takes account of the nature of the proceedings in issue. In the context of prison disciplinary proceedings a proportionality test similar to that applicable under Articles 8 to 11 has been applied. In *Campbell and Fell v. United Kingdom*[53] the Court held that a requirement to permit public access to proceedings heard inside a prison[54] "would impose a disproportionate burden on the authorities of the state". However, in *Diennet v. France*,[55] where proceedings before a medical disciplinary tribunal were in issue, the Court held that the exclusion of the public was in breach of Article 6; "While the need to protect professional confidentiality and the private lives of patients may justify holding proceedings in camera, such an occurrence must be *strictly required* by the circumstances."

Another application of the strict necessity principle in the context of Article 6 is to be found in the case of *Van Mechelen v. Netherlands*.[56] In that case the Court established the important principle that any measures which restrict the rights of the defence in a criminal case should be "strictly necessary" such that if a less restrictive measure could suffice then that measure should be adopted.

2–98   Finally it should be noted that Article 15 permits derogations in times of public emergency "to the extent *strictly required* by the exigencies of the situation". Despite the wording of this provision, the Court has recognised that the national authorities enjoy a margin of appreciation in assessing whether such an emergency exists and, if so, what measures are necessary to deal with it.[57]

XVIII. *Proportionality*

2–99   Although the principle of proportionality is not mentioned in the text of the Convention itself, it has become a dominant theme in the Court's caselaw.[58] The Court has held that proportionality is "inherent in the whole of the Convention".[59] However, it arises in a number of different contexts with subtly different

---

[52] (1979–80) 1 E.H.R.R. 737 at para. 48.

[53] (1985) 7 E.H.R.R. 165 at para. 87.

[54] Or to require the accused to prisoner to be transported from the prison to a public court in every case.

[55] (1996) 21 E.H.R.R. 554. See also *Albert and Le Compte v. Belgium* (1983) 5 E.H.R.R. 533; *H v. Belgium* (1988) 10 E.H.R.R. 339.

[56] (1998) 25 E.H.R.R. 647 at para. 59.

[57] *Ireland v. United Kingdom* (1979–80) 1 E.H.R.R. 15 at para. 28; *Brannigan and McBride v. United Kingdom* (1994) 17 E.H.R.R. 539 at para. 43.

[58] See generally, Essien, "The Principle of Proportionality in the Caselaw of the European Court of Human Rights" in R. St. J. Macdonald, F. Matscher and H. Petzold, *The European System for the Protection of Human Rights* (Martinus Nijhoff, 1993).

[59] *Sporrong and Lonroth v. Sweden* (1983) 5 E.H.R.R. 35 at para. 69; *Soering v. United Kingdom* (1989) 11 E.H.R.R. 439 at para. 89.

meanings. Proportionality, in the classic sense, is the technique by which the Court determines whether an interference with one of the qualified rights protected in Articles 8 to 11 is necessary in a democratic society.[60] But it is also central to the determination of whether there is an unjustified difference in treatment in breach of Article 14[61]; it is the Court's principal yardstick for testing the limits of implied rights, such as the right of access to court[62]; and it is the means by which the Court determines whether a positive obligation should be imposed on a contracting state in any given situation.[63]

In these contexts, proportionality involves two closely related concepts. First, it implies that there must be a rational connection between the public policy objective which a particular measure pursues, and the means which the state has employed to achieve that objective.[64] Secondly, it involves the striking of a fair balance between the demands of the general interest of the community, and the requirements of the protection of an individual's fundamental rights.[65] On either formulation, the Court must in the end determine whether a measure of interference which is aimed at promoting a legitimate public policy is either unacceptably broad in its application, or has imposed an excessive or unreasonable burden on certain individuals.[66] Accordingly, even where it is clear that there is a legitimate reason for restricting the exercise of a Convention right, the authorities must show that the measures actually applied to the applicant did not go beyond what was necessary to achieve that objective. **2–100**

The burden of establishing proportionality lies on the government.[67] The Court will sometimes formulate the question by asking whether the state has demonstrated "relevant and sufficient" reasons for a restriction or interference. In *Jersild v. Denmark*[68] the Court explained that it would; **2–101**

" . . . look at the interference complained of in the light of the case as a whole and determine whether the reasons adduced by the national authorities to justify it are relevant and sufficient and whether the means employed were proportionate to the legitimate aim pursued."

Thus, in *Goodwin v. United Kingdom*[69] an order for the disclosure of a journalist's source of information for a story was held to be disproportionate because it was not supported by "relevant and sufficient reasons"; and in

---

[60] See para. 2–94 above.
[61] *Belgian Linguistic Case (No. 2)* (1979–80) 1 E.H.R.R. 252.
[62] *Ashingdane v. United Kingdom* (1985) 7 E.H.R.R. 528 at para. 57; and see paras 2–61 to 2–62 above.
[63] *McGinley and Egan v. United Kingdom* (1999) 27 E.H.R.R. 1; *Rees v. United Kingdom* (1987) 9 E.H.R.R. 56 para. 37 and see para. 2–53 above.
[64] *James v. United Kingdom* (1986) 8 E.H.R.R. 123 at para. 50.
[65] *Sporrong and Lonroth v. Sweden* (1983) 5 E.H.R.R. 35 at para. 69; *Soering v. United Kingdom* (1989) 11 E.H.R.R. 439 at para. 89.
[66] See, for example, *Sporrong and Lonroth v. Sweden* (1983) 5 E.H.R.R. 35 at para. 73.
[67] *Smith and Grady v. United Kingdom* (2000) 29 E.H.R.R. 493 at para. 99; *Kokkinakis v. Greece* (1994) 17 E.H.R.R. 397; *Autotronic AG v. Switzerland* (1990) 12 E.H.R.R. 585 at paras 60–63; *Vereinigung Demokratisher Soldaten Osterreichs and Gubi v. Austria* (1995) 20 E.H.R.R. 56; *Buckley v. United Kingdom* (1997) 23 E.H.R.R. 101 at para. 77.
[68] (1995) 19 E.H.R.R. 1 at para. 31.
[69] (1996) 22 E.H.R.R. 123.

Dudgeon v. United Kingdom[70] the government's justification was described as relevant "but not sufficient to justify the maintenance in force of the impugned legislation".

2–102   The standard of justification required depends on a range of factors including the nature of the right in issue, the extent of the interference, the importance of the public policy justification which is relied upon, and the context in which the interference has occurred. The Court has identified certain qualified rights as deserving of special protection. Thus, the state must demonstrate "particularly serious reasons" to justify an interference with an intimate aspect of private life[71]; any justification for an interference with the right to freedom of expression must be "convincingly established"[72]; measures which obstruct correspondence with a lawyer,[73] or intrude on legal professional privilege[74] require particularly compelling justification[75]; and the Court will require "very weighty reasons" to justify a difference in treatment on grounds of sex, race or other "suspect categories".[76]

2–103   The extent of the interference will obviously be another highly material factor. A measure which reduces or restricts a right "in such a way or to such an extent that the very essence of the right is impaired" will, almost by definition, constitute a disproportionate interference.[77] In *Smith and Grady v. United Kingdom*[78] the Court referred to the "exceptionally intrusive character" of disciplinary investigations which had been carried out into the applicants' sexual orientation. In general, however, a criminal prosecution involves a more substantial interference than a measure applied in civil proceedings and will therefore require a weightier justification. Where it is alleged that criminal proceedings have interfered with one of the rights protected by Articles 8 to 11,[79] the Court will look to the combination of the prosecution, the conviction and the sentence to determine whether the measure taken was proportionate. In *Laskey v. United Kingdom*[80] the Court attached importance in its assessment of proportionality to the fact that the applicants' sentences for sadomasochistic assault had been reduced by the Court of Appeal. Similarly, in *Hoare v. United Kingdom*,[81] a case concerning the distribution of obscene videotapes, the Commission considered that the sole issue of proportionality was the length of the prison sentence imposed. Non-custodial measures will of course vary greatly in gravity. In *Handyside v. United Kingdom*[82] an allegedly obscene book distributed by the applicant was confiscated,

---

[70] (1982) 4 E.H.R.R. 149 at para. 61.
[71] *Dudgeon v. United Kingdom* (1982) 4 E.H.R.R. 149.
[72] *Barthold v. Germany* (1985) 7 E.H.R.R. 383 at para. 58; *Autotronic AG v. Switzerland* (1990) 12 E.H.R.R. 585 at para. 61.
[73] *Golder v. United Kingdom* (1979–80) 1 E.H.R.R. 524 paras 41–45.
[74] *Silver v. United Kingdom* (1983) 5 E.H.R.R. 347; *Campbell v. United Kingdom* (1993) 15 E.H.R.R. 137.
[75] *Niemietz v. Germany* (1993) 16 E.H.R.R. 97 at para. 37 (search of lawyer's office).
[76] *Karlheinz and Schmidt v. Germany* (1994) 18 E.H.R.R. 513 at para. 24. See para. 2–138 below.
[77] *Rees v. United Kingdom* (1987) 9 E.H.R.R. 56 at para. 50; *Golder v. United Kingdom* (1979–80) 1 E.H.R.R. 525: *cf. Fox, Campbell and Hartley v. United Kingdom* (1991) 13 E.H.R.R. 157 at para. 32. And see para. 2–99 above.
[78] (2000) 29 E.H.R.R. 493 at para. 90.
[79] See generally Chapter 8 below.
[80] (1997) 24 E.H.R.R. 39 at para. 49.
[81] [1997] E.H.R.L.R. 678.
[82] (1979–80) 1 E.H.R.R. 737.

but could have been reprinted with the offending passages removed. In *Muller v. Switzerland*,[83] on the other hand, the Court considered that an order for the forfeiture of an original oil painting raised particularly serious concerns.[84]

As a means of testing proportionality, the Court will often inquire whether **2–104** the state could have achieved the same objective by other means, less harmful to the rights of the individual. Thus, in *Campbell v. United Kingdom*[85] a blanket rule permitting the opening of prisoners' mail was found to breach Article 8. The government's argument that the interference was necessary to establish that letters did not contain prohibited material was rejected on the ground that these concerns could have been met by opening correspondence in the presence of the prisoner without actually reading it. Where the state has amended its law since the interference occurred, in a way which provides more effective protection for Convention rights, this may be some evidence that the previous regime was disproportionate.[86]

If an interference involves the exercise of a discretionary power, the principle of **2–105** proportionality may impose requirements of procedural fairness. In the context of Article 8, the Court has said:

"Whenever discretion capable of interfering with the enjoyment of a Convention right such as the one in issue in the present case is conferred on national authorities, the procedural safeguards available to the individual will be especially material in determining whether the respondent state has, when fixing the regulatory framework, remained within its margin of appreciation. Indeed, it is settled case law that, whilst Article 8 contains no explicit procedural requirements, the decision-making process leading to measures of interference must be fair and such as to afford due respect to the interests safeguarded to the individual by Article 8."[87]

Similarly, where powers of intrusive surveillance are in issue, the Court has observed that the existence of independent safeguards against abuse is part of the "compromise between the requirements for defending democratic society and individual rights".[88]

The strength of the public policy in issue will often be decisive. In *Leander v.* **2–106** *Sweden*,[89] where national security considerations were invoked, the Court was prepared to accord the state a wide margin of appreciation. Particularly difficult issues can arise where the Court is required to balance competing Convention rights. In some cases, for example, the right to freedom of expression can come into conflict with the right to a fair trial.[90] In *Worm v. Austria*[91] the Court was concerned with the prosecution of a journalist for publishing an article about

---

[83] (1991) 13 E.H.R.R. 212 at para. 43.
[84] In the end, however, the Court rejected the applicant's complaint on the ground that he could have applied to the Cantonal Court for the return of the painting and had failed to do so.
[85] (1993) 15 E.H.R.R. 137.
[86] *Inze v. Austria* (1988) 10 E.H.R.R. 394 at para. 44.
[87] *Buckley v. United Kingdom* (1997) 23 E.H.R.R. 101 at para. 76.
[88] *Klass v. Germany* (1979–80) 2 E.H.R.R. 214.
[89] (1987) 9 E.H.R.R. 433 at para. 59.
[90] See, for example, *Sunday Times v. United Kingdom (No. 1)* (1979–80) 2 E.H.R.R. 245; *Allenet de Ribemont v. France* (1995) 20 E.H.R.R. 557; *Worm v. Austria* (1998) 25 E.H.R.R. 454.
[91] (1998) 25 E.H.R.R. 454 at paras 50–59.

Hannes Androsch, the former Austrian Vice Chancellor. The article was published while Mr. Androsch was facing criminal proceedings for tax evasion and stated that he was guilty of the offence with which he was charged. The applicant was convicted of having exercised prohibited influence on criminal proceedings. In considering the proportionality of the measure, the Court observed that:

> "There is a general recognition that the courts cannot operate in a vacuum. Whilst the courts are the forum for the determination of a person's guilt or innocence on a criminal charge, this does not mean that there can be no prior or contemporaneous discussion on the subject-matter of criminal trials elsewhere, be it in specialised journals, in the general press or amongst the public at large. Provided that it does not overstep the bounds imposed in the interests of the proper administration of justice, reporting, including comment, on court proceedings contributes to their publicity and is thus perfectly consonant with the requirement under Article 6(1) of the Convention that hearings be in public . . . However, public figures are entitled to the enjoyment of the guarantees of a fair trial set out in Article 6, which in criminal proceedings include the right to an impartial tribunal, on the same basis as every other person. This must be borne in mind by journalists when commenting on pending criminal proceedings since the limits of permissible comment may not extend to statements which are likely to prejudice, whether intentionally or not, the chances of a person receiving a fair trial or to undermine the confidence of the public in the role of the courts in the administration of criminal justice."

2–107   In *Bowman v. United Kingdom*[92] the Court was concerned with a criminal prosecution for incurring unauthorised election expenditure. The Court noted that "free elections and freedom of expression, particularly freedom of political debate, together form the bedrock of any democratic system". Nonetheless, the Court observed,

> "in certain circumstances the two rights may come into conflict, and it may be considered necessary, in the period preceding or during an election, to place certain restrictions, of a type which would not usually be acceptable, on freedom of expression, in order to secure the 'free expression of the opinion of the people in the choice of the legislature'."

2–108   The principle of proportionality has a more limited role to play in relation to those rights that are unqualified on their face. The Court has used the language of proportionality in a variety of contexts, often with very different connotations. In *McCann and others v. United Kingdom*,[93] for instance, the Court held that when considering whether the use of lethal force was justified under Article 2 a test of *strict* proportionality should be applied. In *Soering v. United Kingdom*[94] the Court suggested that a sentence which was "wholly unjustified or grossly disproportionate" to the gravity of the crime could, in principle, amount to inhuman and degrading treatment in breach of Article 3. In *Van der Mussele v. Belgium*[95] the Court held that a requirement to provide legal services free of charge, as a condition of entry to the legal profession, could only amount to

---

[92] (1998) 26 E.H.R.R. 1 at para. 42–43.
[93] (1996) 21 E.H.R.R. 97 at para. 149; See also *Andronicou and Constantinou v. Cyprus* (1998) 25 E.H.R.R. 491 at para. 171.
[94] (1989) 11 E.H.R.R. 439 at para. 104 (Conditions on death row in the United States found to violate Art. 3).
[95] (1984) 6 E.H.R.R. 25 at para. 37.

forced labour (within the meaning of Article 4) "if the service imposed a burden which was so excessive or disproportionate to the advantages attached to the future exercise of that profession that the service could not be treated as having been voluntarily accepted". Finally, in *Deweer v. Belgium*[96] the Court found a violation of Article 6 where the applicant had been offered the choice between paying a relatively modest fine by way of a "compromise" or facing extended criminal proceedings during which his business would have remained closed by administrative order. Whilst such a procedure would not necessarily violate Article 6, the Court found that the applicant had been deprived of his right to a fair trial since there was a "flagrant disproportion" between the two alternatives facing him. These cases illustrate the shades of meaning which have been attached to the Convention concept of proportionality and serve as a warning against treating it as if it were a term of art.

The principle of proportionality is an important feature of constitutional review   **2–109**
in all jurisdictions that have a Bill of Rights (although the terminology used is not always exactly the same). The common law constitutional courts have adopted a rather more analytical approach to the application of this principle than has the European Court of Human Rights. In *R. v. Oakes*[97] the Canadian Supreme Court applied a two stage test for determining whether an interference with a constitutional right is "demonstrably justified in a free and democratic society".[98] First, the objective which the measure is designed to achieve must be of sufficient importance to warrant overriding a constitutionally protected right or interest. This is the equivalent of the "legitimate aim" stage of the Strasbourg analysis. Secondly, the measure chosen to achieve the objective must be "proportional". In determining this latter question, the Supreme Court established three guiding principles:

(a) The measure adopted must be carefully designed to achieve the objective in question; it must not be arbitrary, unfair or based on irrational considerations;

(b) The limitation or interference should impair as little as possible the right or freedom in question; and

(c) Even if an objective is of sufficient importance, and the first two elements of the proportionality test are satisfied, it is still possible that, because of the severity of the deleterious effects of a measure on individuals or groups, the measure will not be justified by the purposes it is intended to serve.[99]

The Canadian Supreme Court has also emphasised that the proportionality principle must be "applied flexibly, so as to achieve a proper balance between

---

[96] (1979–80) 2 E.H.R.R. 439 at para. 51.
[97] [1986] 1 S.C.R. 103; (1986) 26 D.L.R. (4th) 200.
[98] Under s.1 of the Canadian Charter of Rights and Freedoms 1982.
[99] See also *RJR-MacDonald Inc v. Attorney-General of Canada* [1995] 3 S.C. 199 at para. 60; *R. v. Edwards Books and Art Ltd* [1986] 2 S.C.R. 713.

individual rights and community needs"[1] and that the burden of proving justification always rests squarely on the state.[2]

2–110   A very similar approach has been endorsed by the Privy Council. In *De Freitas v. Permanent Secretary of Ministry of Agriculture, Fisheries, Lands and Housing*[3] Lord Clyde approved a three stage test for determining whether a measure was "arbitrary or excessive" within the meaning of the Constitution of Antigua. The court should ask itself whether;

> "(i) the legislative objective is sufficiently important to justify limiting a fundamental right; (ii) the legislative measures designed to meet the objective are rationally connected to it; and (iii) the means used to impair the right or freedom are no more than is necessary to accomplish that objective."[3a]

In *Thomas and Hillaire v. Baptiste*[4] the Privy Council held that time limits imposed by Trinidad for exhausting rights of petition to the United Nations Human Rights Committee in a death penalty case were "disproportionate because they curtailed the prisoners rights further than was necessary to deal with the mischief created by the delays in the international appellate processes".

2–111   In *S v. Makwanyane and Another*[5] the South African Constitutional Court approached the issue in this way:

> "The limitation of constitutional rights for a purpose that is reasonable and necessary in a democratic society involves the weighing up of competing values, and ultimately an assessment based on proportionality . . . The fact that different rights have different implications for democracy . . . means that there is no absolute standard which can be laid down for determining reasonableness and necessity. Principles can be established, but the application of those principles to particular circumstances can only be done on a case by case basis. This is inherent in the requirement of proportionality, which calls for a balancing of different interests. In the balancing process, the relevant considerations will include the nature of the right that is limited, and its importance to an open and democratic society based on freedom and equality; the purpose for which the right is limited and the importance of that purpose to such a society; the extent of the limitation, its efficacy, and particularly where the limitation has to be necessary, whether the desired ends could reasonably be achieved through other means less damaging to the right in question."

2–112   In *Coetzee v. The Government of the Republic of South Africa*[6] Sachs J. put it more simply;

> "The more profound the interest being protected, and the graver the violation, the more stringent the scrutiny; at the end of the day, the court must decide whether, bearing in mind the nature and intensity of the interest to be protected, and the degree to which, and the manner in which it is infringed, the limitation is permissible."

---

[1] *Ross v. New Brunswick School District No. 15* [1996] 1 S.C.R. 825 at 872.
[2] *Andrews v. Law Society of British Columbia* (1989) 56 D.L.R. (4th) 1 at 21.
[3] (1999) 1 A.C. 69.
[3a] This formulation was expressly endorsed by Lord Steyn in *R v. A*, (judgment May 17, 2000; 2000 (UKHL) 25 at para. 38). It was, he said, unnecessary to "reinvent the wheel".
[4] [1999] 3 W.L.R. 249.
[5] 1995 B.C.L.R. 665 (CC) at 708D-G, *per* Chaskalson P. (cited with approval in *Coetzee v. The Government of the Republic of South Africa* [1995] 4 L.R.C. 220 at 239–40).
[6] [1995] 4 L.R.C. 220 at 239–40.

XIX. *Subsidiarity*

The concept of subsidiarity was recognised by the European Court of Human **2–113** Rights many years before it assumed its present importance in the European Community law context. It has been defined as the principle that "a central authority should have a subsidiary function, performing only those tasks which cannot be performed effectively at a more immediate or local level".[7] The concept of subsidiarity reflects three basic features of the Convention system.

(a) First, the list of rights and freedoms set out in the Convention is not exhaustive, so that contracting states are free to provide better protection under their own law or by any other international agreement. This principle finds expression in Article 53 which states that nothing in the Convention "shall be construed as limiting or derogating from any of the human rights and fundamental freedoms which may be ensured under the laws of any High Contracting Party or under any other agreement to which it is a Party".[8]

(b) Secondly, the Convention does not impose uniform rules. It lays down standards of conduct, and leaves the choice of implementation to the contracting states. The Court has held that it cannot assume the responsibility for prescribing national standards in detail since that would be to;

" ... lose sight of the subsidiary nature of the international machinery of collective enforcement established by the Convention. The national authorities remain free to choose between the measures which they consider appropriate in those matters governed by the Convention. Review by the Court concerns only the conformity of those measures with the requirements of the Convention."[9]

(c) Thirdly, the Court has repeatedly stressed that the national authorities are generally in a better position than the supervisory bodies in Strasbourg to strike the right balance between the competing interests of the community and the protection of the fundamental rights of the individual. This principle is reflected in Article 1 which obliges states to secure Convention rights to everyone within their jurisdiction; by Article 13, which requires an effective remedy before a national authority for any arguable breach of a Convention right; and by Article 35(1) which provides that an applicant must first exhaust any effective or potentially effective domestic remedy before introducing a complaint under the Convention.[10] It is also reflected in the so-called "fourth instance" and "margin of appreciation" doctrines.

XX. *Fourth instance doctrine*

The Court has held that it is not its function to substitute its own judgment for **2–114** that of the national courts, or to act as a fourth instance appeal.[11] Its role is

---

[7] *New Shorter Oxford English Dictionary*, p. 3123.
[8] This principle is also enshrined in the Human Rights Act 1998, s.11, see para. 3–21 below.
[9] *Belgian Linguistics Case (No. 2)* (1979–80) 1 E.H.R.R. 252 at para. 10.
[10] See para. 1–46 above.
[11] *Edwards v. United Kingdom* (1992) 15 E.H.R.R. 417 at para. 34.

confined to ensuring that the contracting states have complied with their obligations under the Convention. This is the source of the twin principles that the
assessment of domestic law is primarily for the national courts[12]; and that the
Court will not interfere with the findings of fact made by the domestic courts,
unless they have drawn arbitrary conclusions from the evidence before them.[13]

XXI. *Margin of appreciation*

2–115 The margin of appreciation is a doctrine of restrained review at the international
level, which reflects the primary role that the national authorities, including the
courts, are intended to perform in human rights protection. According to a former
judge of the Court it is simply the term used to describe "the amount of latitude
left to national authorities once the appropriate level of review has been decided
by the Court".[14] The concept incorporates a degree of discretion into the Court's
assessment, particularly where difficult issues of social, moral or economic
policy are involved, on which there is no clear European consensus. In *James and
others v. United Kingdom*[15] the Court explained that:

> "Because of their direct knowledge of their society and its needs, the national author-
> ities are in principle better placed than the international judge to appreciate what is 'in
> the public interest'. Under the system of protection established by the Convention, it is
> thus for the national authorities to make the initial assessment both of the existence of
> a problem of public concern . . . and of the remedial action to be taken . . . Here, as in
> the other fields to which the safeguards of the Convention extend, the national author-
> ities accordingly enjoy a certain margin of appreciation."

2–116 There is no universal formula for determining when and how the margin of
appreciation should be applied,[16] although the Court has given reasons for its
application in particular contexts. The width of the discretion left to the contracting states will vary, according to such factors as the nature of the Convention
right in issue, the importance of that right for the individual, the nature of the

---

[12] *Winterwerp v. Netherlands* (1979–80) 2 E.H.R.R. 387 at para. 37; *Wassink v. Netherlands* (1990)
Series A No. 185–A at para. 24; *Bozano v. France* (1987) 9 E.H.R.R. 297 at para. 58; *Van der Leer
v. Netherlands* (1990) 12 E.H.R.R. 567; *Benham v. United Kingdom* (1996) 22 E.H.R.R. 293;
Loukanov v. Bulgaria (1997) 24 E.H.R.R. 121.
[13] *Klaas v. Germany* (1994) 18 E.H.R.R. 305 at paras 29–31; *Edwards v. United Kingdom* (1992) 15
E.H.R.R. 417 at para. 34; *Van Mechelen v. Netherlands* (1998) 25 E.H.R.R. 647 at para. 50; *Barbera,
Messegue and Jabardo v. Spain* (1990) 11 E.H.R.R. 360; *Kostovski v. Netherlands* (1990) 12
E.H.R.R. 434 at para. 39; *Monnell and Morris v. United Kingdom* (1988) 10 E.H.R.R. 205 at paras
49 and 69.
[14] R. St. J. Macdonald *Methods of Interpretation of the Convention* in MacDonald, Matscher and
Petzold (eds) *The European System for the Protection of Human Rights* (Martinus Nijhoff, 1993). See
also Paul Mahoney *Judicial Activism and Judicial Self Restraint in the European Court of Human
Rights: Two Sides of the Same Coin* [1990] H.R.L.J. 57; Nicholas Lavender, "The Problem of the
Margin of Appreciation" [1997] E.H.R.L.R. 380.
[15] (1986) 8 E.H.R.R. 123 at para. 46.
[16] Two former judges of the Court have suggested that the margin of appreciation is simply incapable
of definition, since it is wholly dependent on the context of a particular case: R. Bernhardt, "Thoughts
on the Interpretation of Human Rights Treaties", in Matscher and Petzold (eds) *Protecting Human
Rights: The European Dimension* (1988); R. St. J. Macdonald, "Methods of Interpretation of the
Convention" in R. St. J. Macdonald, F. Matscher and H. Petzold, *The European Systems for the
Protection of Human Rights* (Martinus Nijhoff, 1993).

activity involved in the case,[17] the extent of the interference,[18] and the nature of the state's justification.[19] In practice this means that the intensity of the Court's review can range from extreme deference on issues such as social and economic policy,[20] and national security,[21] to hard edged review in cases involving criminal procedure,[22] intimate aspects of private life,[23] or political debate on matters of public interest.[24] Where there is a clear European consensus on a particular issue, the Court will generally be unwilling to accord the state a significant margin of appreciation.[25]

The Court has consistently emphasised that the margin of appreciation goes **2–117** "hand in hand"[26] with European supervision, and that it can never supplant the Court's primary duty to assess the proportionality of a measure. Even at its widest, therefore, the margin of appreciation;

> " . . . does not mean that the [Court's] supervision is limited to ascertaining whether the respondent state has exercised its discretion reasonably, carefully and in good faith; what the Court has to do is to look at the interference complained of in the light of the case as a whole and determine whether it was 'proportionate to the legitimate aim pursued' and whether the reasons adduced by the national authorities to justify it are 'relevant and sufficient'."[27]

The complex interplay between the various factors involved makes it difficult to **2–118** identify hard and fast principles governing the application of the margin of appreciation to particular rights or particular grounds of interference.[28] The essence of the Court's task is to assess the extent to which the proportionality balance would be more appropriately performed at the national level in any given case. This is an issue of jurisdictional policy, which ultimately depends on the nature of the issues in dispute between the parties.

---

[17] *Buckley v. United Kingdom* (1997) 23 E.H.R.R. 101 at para. 129; *Rasmussen v. Denmark* (1985) 7 E.H.R.R. 352 at para. 40.
[18] *Dudgeon v. United Kingdom* (1982) 4 E.H.R.R. 149.
[19] *Sunday Times v. United Kingdom (No. 1)* (1979–80) 2 E.H.R.R. 245 at para. 59.
[20] *Buckley v. United Kingdom* (1997) 23 E.H.R.R. 101; *Powell and Rayner v. United Kingdom* (1990) 12 E.H.R.R. 355; *James and others v. United Kingdom* (1986) 8 E.H.R.R. 123 at para. 46.
[21] *Leander v. Sweden* (1987) 9 E.H.R.R. 433.
[22] *Borgers v. Belgium* (1993) 15 E.H.R.R. 92; See also the comments in *Sunday Times (No. 1) v. United Kingdom* (1979–80) 2 E.H.R.R. 245 at para. 59.
[23] *Dudgeon v. United Kingdom* (1981) 4 E.H.R.R. 149.
[24] *Barthold v. Germany* (1985) 7 E.H.R.R. 383; *Bowman v. United Kingdom* (1998) 26 E.H.R.R. 1; *cf. Wingrove v. United Kingdom* (1996) 24 E.H.R.R. 1.
[25] *Rasmussen v. Denmark* (1985) 7 E.H.R.R. 352 at para. 40; *Sunday Times v. United Kingdom (No. 1)* (1979–80) 2 E.H.R.R. 245 at para. 59. See also paras 2–28 above.
[26] *Handyside v. United Kingdom* (1979–80) 1 E.H.R.R. 737 at para. 49.
[27] *Vogt v. Germany* (1996) 21 E.H.R.R. 205 at para. 52(iii); *Sunday Times v. United Kingdom (No. 1)* (1979–80) 2 E.H.R.R. 245 at para. 59; *Dudgeon v. United Kingdom* (1982) 4 E.H.R.R. 149 at para. 59.
[28] The apparent lack of consistency in the Court's caselaw has attracted serious criticism. R St. J. Macdonald has identified a "disappointing lack of clarity" ("Methods of Interpretation of the Convention" in R. St. J. MacDonald, F. Matscher and H. Petzold, *The European System for the Protection of Human Rights* (Martinus Nijhoff, 1993). See also Lord Lester of Herne Hill Q.C.: "The concept of the 'margin of appreciation' has become as slippery and elusive as an eel. Again and again the Court now appears to use the margin of appreciation as a substitute for coherent legal analysis of the issues at stake." ("The European Convention on Human Rights in the New Architecture of Europe" in *Proceedings of the 9 International Colloquy on the European Convention on Human Rights* (Council of Europe, 1996)).

2–119 Thus, where the protection of morals exception in Article 10(2) is relied upon to restrict the right to freedom of expression, the Court has generally been inclined to allow a relatively wide margin of appreciation. In *Handyside v. United Kingdom*,[29] a case concerning the distribution of allegedly obscene material, the Court explained that:

> "[I]t is not possible to find in the domestic law of the various contracting states a uniform European conception of morals. The view taken by their respective laws of the requirements of morals varies from time to time and from place to place. By reason of their direct and continuous contact with the vital forces of their countries, state authorities are in principle in a better position than the international judge to give an opinion on the exact content of those requirements of morals as well as on the "necessity" of a "restriction" or "penalty" intended to meet them . . . Nevertheless, Article 10(2) does not give contracting states an unlimited power of appreciation. The Court, which . . . is responsible for ensuring observance of those states' engagements, is empowered to give the final ruling on whether a "restriction" or "penalty" is reconcilable with freedom of expression as protected by Article 10. The domestic margin of appreciation thus goes hand in hand with a European supervision."

2–120 Similarly, in *Wingrove v. United Kingdom*[30] the Court allowed a broad margin of appreciation in the context of restrictions on the right to freedom of expression said to be justified in order to protect the rights of others to respect for their religious convictions. The British Board of Film Classification had refused a certificate to a videotape on the ground that it was blasphemous. In finding no violation the Court observed:

> "Whereas there is little scope under Article 10(2) of the Convention for restrictions on political speech or on debate of questions of public interest, a wider margin of appreciation is generally available to the Contracting States when regulating freedom of expression in relation to matters liable to offend intimate personal convictions within the sphere of morals or, especially, religion. Moreover, as in the field of morals, and perhaps to an even greater degree, there is no uniform European conception of the requirements of 'the protection of the rights of others' in relation to attacks on their religious convictions. What is likely to cause substantial offence to persons of a particular religious persuasion will vary significantly from time to time and from place to place, especially in an era characterised by an ever growing array of faiths and denominations. By reason of their direct and continuous contact with the vital forces of their countries, State authorities are in principle in a better position than the international judge to give an opinion on the exact content of these requirements with regard to the rights of others as well as on the 'necessity' of a 'restriction' intended to protect from such material those whose deepest feelings and convictions would be seriously offended."

2–121 However, where the right to freedom of expression is restricted in order to maintain the authority and impartiality of the judiciary, the Court has held that the margin of appreciation should be narrower. This is because the notion of the authority of the judiciary is the subject of a broad level of agreement among the parties to the Convention, and is a more objective concept than the protection of morals or religious convictions. In *Sunday Times v. United Kingdom (No. 1)*[31] the Court observed that:

---

[29] (1979–80) 1 E.H.R.R. 737 at paras 48–89.
[30] (1997) 24 E.H.R.R. 1 at para. 58.
[31] (1979–80) 2 E.H.R.R. 245.

"The domestic law and practice of the contracting states reveal a fairly substantial measure of common ground in this area. This is reflected in a number of provisions of the Convention, including Article 6, which have no equivalent as far as 'morals' are concerned. Accordingly, here a more extensive European supervision corresponds to a less discretionary power of appreciation.".[32]

In *Dudgeon v. United Kingdom*,[33] the government relied on the Court's *Handy-* **2–122** *side* judgment to argue that a wide margin of appreciation was appropriate whenever the protection of morals was in issue. But, as the Court pointed out, this was to ignore the difference in the extent of the interference between a criminal prosecution for private sexual activity on the one hand, and the public distribution of allegedly obscene material on the other. Whilst the public policy justification for a restriction was an important factor in determining the intensity of review, it was not necessarily decisive. The scope of the margin of appreciation would be determined not only by "the nature of the aim of the restriction", but also by "the nature of the activities involved".[34] Since the applicant's activities involved a "most intimate aspect of private life" the state's margin of appreciation was narrow, and the government would have to demonstrate "particularly serious reasons before interferences on the part of the public authorities can be legitimate for the purposes of Article 8(2)".[35]

Since the margin of appreciation has been developed as a means of delineating **2–123** the supervisory functions of an international court, it has no direct application to cases brought under the Human Rights Act 1998. As we have seen, there are two principal strands of reasoning which underlie the European Court's approach. The first is that the function of an international court is different from that of a national court; and the second is that in certain cases there may be a lack of European consensus on a particular point. Both rationales are inextricably bound up with the institutional position of the European Court of Human Rights. As a former President of the Court has explained, the Strasbourg margin of appreciation is a direct function of the principle of subsidiarity.[36]

At the insitutional level, the margin of appreciation doctrine sets the European **2–124** Court's standard of review and (together with the 'fourth instance' doctrine) distinguishes constitutional challenge (or *cassation*) from an appeal on fact and/ or law. The European Court of Human Rights is a court of constitutional review, which depends on inter-governmental co-operation and support for its mandate. Like any reviewing court it is reluctant to substitute its own opinion for that of the body under review. It is no part of the European Court's function to set finely calibrated standards within the national legal system. That is the function of the domestic authorities.

More importantly, the Strasbourg margin of appreciation applies to the response **2–125** of the national authorities as a whole, *including the courts*. When applied to decisions of the national courts, its rationale is that those courts are better placed

---

[32] Para. 59; see also *Worm v. Austria* (1997) 25 E.H.R.R. 454.
[33] (1982) 4 E.H.R.R. 149.
[34] Para. 52.
[35] Para. 52; see also *Smith and Grady v. United Kingdom* (2000) 29 E.H.R.R. 493.
[36] Rolv Ryssdall, "The Coming of Age of the European Convention on Human Rights" [1996] E.H.R.L.R. 18 at 24.

to carry out the necessary assessment because they are more closely in touch with local conditions. The European Court's self-denying ordinance presupposes that the national courts will have scrutinised a case, with the benefit of local knowledge, before it is brought to Strasbourg; and that in doing so they will have made a primary, rather than a secondary, judgment of the proportionality of any interference with Convention rights.

2–126 Once the different functions of the national and the international court have been identified, it becomes obvious that the Strasbourg margin of appreciation cannot be applied by the national court. Under section 6 of the Human Rights Act 1998 the domestic courts, as public authorities, are bound by the duty to act compatibly with Convention rights, unless they are prevented from doing so by primary legislation which cannot be interpreted compatibly with Convention rights.[37] The Strasbourg margin of appreciation only becomes relevant to this process if the decision of the national court comes to be re-examined by the European Court of Human Rights. If the national courts were to apply the Strasbourg margin of appreciation directly to decisions of the legislature or the executive, within their own legal system, an element of "double counting" would creep in, and an important part of the rationale for the European Court's approach would disappear. As Sir John Laws has pointed out:

> "The margin of appreciation doctrine, as it has been developed in Strasbourg, will necessarily be inapt to the administration of the Convention in the domestic courts for the very reason that they are domestic; they will not be subject to an objective inhibition generated by any cultural distance between themselves and the state organs whose decisions are impleaded before them".[38]

2–127 This is not, however, to say that the Court's jurisprudence on the margin of appreciation is irrelevant to cases brought under the Human Rights Act. It could hardly be irrelevant since it circumscribes the Court's review of the proportionality of a measure. The national courts will need to be aware of the Strasbourg caselaw on the margin of appreciation, if only to ensure that they do not adopt a less intrusive standard of scrutiny. Moreover, the Act itself provides that the Court's caselaw is to be taken into account by a national court when considering any question which has arisen in connection with a Convention right.[39] In *R. v. Stratford Justices ex parte Imbert* Buxton L.J. attempted the square the circle thus[40]:

> "The application of the doctrine of the margin of appreciation would appear to be solely a matter for the Strasbourg Court. By appealing to the doctrine that court recognises that the detailed content of at least some Convention obligations is more appropriately determined in the light of national conditions ... The English judge cannot therefore himself apply or have recourse to the doctrine of the margin of appreciation as implemented by the Strasbourg Court. He must, however, recognise the impact of that

---

[37] Human Rights Act 1998, ss.3 and 6, see paras 3–22 to 3–33 below. As the Lord Chancellor pointed out during the debates on the Act: "The courts will often be faced with cases that involve factors perhaps specific to the United Kingdom which distinguish them from cases considered by [the Strasbourg Court]". January 19, 1998 484 (H.L.) 1270 at 1271.

[38] Sir John Laws, "The Limitations of Human Rights" [1998] P.L. 254 at 258.

[39] Section 2, see para. 3–17 below. Note that the obligation on the national courts is to take the Convention caselaw into account. They are not bound to follow the Strasbourg approach in every respect.

[40] [1999] 2 Cr.App.R. 276.

doctrine upon the Strasbourg Court's analysis of the meaning and implications of the broad terms of the Convention provisions: which is the obvious source of guidance as to those provisions, and a source that in any event the English court will be obliged, once section 2(1)(a) of the 1998 Act has come into force, to take into account."

How then are the national courts to fix the appropriate standard of review under the Human Rights Act? The answer lies in the nature of constitutional review. The Human Rights Act does not require the national courts to take the place of the primary decision-maker whenever an executive or legislative decision infringes human rights. The recognition that other public bodies are often better placed than the courts to carry out the necessary assessment is a universal feature of constitutional review, in Europe and elsewhere. At the constitutional level, the relative specialist knowledge of the body under review on the one hand, and the court on the other, will always be a relevant factor. The level of scrutiny will depend upon the court's conception of the separation of powers principle, and the respective responsibilities of the judiciary vis-á-vis the other two branches of government. At one end of the spectrum the court is usually the arbiter of what is procedurally fair in a criminal trial, and this points to a thorough and searching scrutiny in criminal cases.[41] At the other end of the spectrum, the legislature has not only the relevant expertise but also the necessary democratic mandate to make decisions in the field of public finance. **2–128**

The Canadian Supreme Court has adopted a sliding scale of constitutional review, which preserves the most intrusive standard of scrutiny for criminal cases. In *RJR-MacDonald Inc v. Attorney-General of Canada*[42] La Forest J. commented: **2–129**

> "Courts are specialists in the protection of liberty and the interpretation of legislation and are, accordingly, well placed to subject criminal justice legislation to careful scrutiny. However, courts are not specialists in the realm of policy-making, nor should they be. This is a role properly assigned to the elected representatives of the people, who have at their disposal the necessary institutional resources to enable them to compile and assess social science evidence, to mediate between competing social interests and to reach out and protect vulnerable groups."[43]

Similarly, in *Libman v. Attorney-General of Quebec*[44] the Supreme Court pointed out that; **2–130**

> " . . . in the social, economic and political spheres, where the legislature must reconcile competing interests in choosing one policy among several that might be acceptable, the courts must accord great deference to the legislature's choice because it is in the best

---

[41] Even in the criminal context, however, a degree of deference to the legislature will sometimes be appropriate. The Privy Council has observed that;
"In order to maintain the balance between the individual and the society as a whole, rigid and inflexible standards should not be imposed on the legislature's attempts to resolve the difficult and intransigent problems with which society is faced when seeking to deal with serious crime. It must be remembered that questions of policy remain primarily the responsibility of the legislature." (*per* Lord Woolf in *Attorney-General of Hong Kong v. Lee Kwong-kut* [1993] A.C. 951 at 975C-D.)
[42] [1995] 3 S.C.R. 199 at 279 and 331–332.
[43] See also *Irwin Toy Ltd. v. Attorney-General of Quebec* [1989] 1 S.C.R. 927 at 993–994; *McKinney v. University of Guelph* [1990] 3 S.C.R. 229 at 304–305; *Stoffman v. Vancouver General Hospital* [1990] 3 S.C.R. 483 at 521.
[44] (1997) 3 B.H.R.C. 269 at 289E-F.

position to make such a choice. On the other hand, the courts will judge the legislature's choices more harshly in areas where the government plays the role of the 'singular antagonist of the individual'—primarily in criminal matters—owing to their expertise in these areas."

2–131   The application of this principle under the Human Rights Act does not mean "stripping" the Strasbourg margin of appreciation of its international dimension, since this would be virtually impossible to do. Rather, it requires the courts to ascertain their own scale of national constitutional review. To quote Sir John Laws again: "[I]t is necessary to distinguish the idea of a margin of appreciation, which is apt for an international court reviewing a national decision, from the different idea of a discretion left to elected authorities on democratic grounds."[45]

It has been suggested[46] that the factors which should influence this scale include the importance of the right at stake; the seriousness of the interference with that right; the relative specialist knowledge of the body under review; the democratic mandate of that body; whether the interference aims to promote competing rights of others; whether the applicant comes from a particularly vulnerable group; and whether the context is one in which there is a discernable European standard.

2–132   The existence of a variable standard of constitutional review under the Human Rights Act, which is distinct from the Strasbourg margin of appreciation was recognised by the House of Lords in *R. v. Director of Public Prosecutions ex parte Kebilene and others*[47] where Lord Hope observed that;

> "[The doctrine of the margin of appreciation] is an integral part of the supervisory jurisdiction which is exercised over state conduct by the international court. By conceding a margin of appreciation to each national system, the Court has recognised that the Convention, as a living system, does not need to be applied uniformly by all states but may vary in its application according to local needs and conditions. This technique is not available to the national courts when they are considering Convention issues within their own countries. But in the hands of the national courts also the Convention should be seen as an expression of fundamental principles rather than as a set of mere rules. The questions which the courts will have to decide in the application of these principles will involve questions of balance between competing interests and issues of proportionality. In this area difficult choices may have to be made by the executive or the legislature between the rights of the individual and the needs of society. In some circumstances it will be appropriate for the courts to recognise that there is an area of judgment within which the judiciary will defer, on democratic grounds, to the considered opinion of the elected body or person whose act or decision is said to be incompatible with the Convention . . . It will be easier for such an area of judgment to be recognised where the Convention itself requires a balance to be struck, much less so where the right is stated in terms which are unqualified. It will be easier for it to be recognised where the issues involve questions of social or economic policy, much less

---

[45] Sir John Laws, "Wednesbury" in *The Golden Metwand and the Crooked Cord: Essays in Public Law in Honour of Sir Willliam Wade QC* (1998), p. 201.
[46] Singh, Hunt and Demetriou, "Is there a Role for the Margin of Appreciation in National Law after the Human Rights Act?" [1999] E.H.R.L.R. 15.
[47] [1999] 3 W.L.R. 972.

so where the rights are of high constitutional importance or are of a kind where the courts are especially well placed to assess the need for protection."

The difficulty of assessory the "discretionary area of judgment" to be accorded **2–133** to Parliament came into sharp focus in *R. v. Lambert and ors.*[48] In that case, the Court of Appeal held that the provisions of section 5(4), 28(2) and 28(3) of the Misuse of Drugs Act 1971 (specific "knowledge" defences available on a charge of possession of drugs) were compatible with the presumption of innocence in Article 6(2). Lord Woolf C.J. held that as a matter of principle a balance must be struck between the demands of the general interest of the community and the protection of the fundamental rights of the individual. He observed that the burden of proof imposed by the Act had been deliberately cast on the accused by Parliament, for policy reasons which it considered justified. Since 1971 that justification had increased. Although the method selected by the legislature had been "roundly criticised" the Court did not consider that Parliament's chosen course violated Article 6. The House of Lords reached the opposite conclusion, by a majority of 4:1 holding that Parliament's true intention could be met through the imposition of a purely evidential burden of proof.[48a] The Court of Appeal again emphasised the importance of deferring to the legislature in *R. v. Benjafield and ors*[49] when considering the assumptions made under the confiscation provisions of the Drug Trafficking Act 1994 and the Criminal Justice Act 1988. Applying Lord Hope's formulation in *Kebilene*, the Court of Appeal considered that it was incontrovertible that the legislation addressed a serious social problem and Parliament had sought to offset the interference with the presumption of innocence by providing a number of safeguards to the defendant. Shortly after *Benjafield* was decided, the Privy Council reached the same conclusion (albeit by a slightly different route) in relation to confiscation legislation in Scotland. In *McIntosh v. Lord Advocate,*[50] Lord Bingham held that the Proceeds of Crime (Scotland) Act 1995 struck a fair balance between the competing interests at stake, adding that the statutory scheme was "approved by a democratically elected Parliament and should not be at all readily rejected".

The relative expertise of the courts *via-a-vis* the legislature was invoked by the **2–133a** Privy Council in *Brown v. Stott*[51] in holding that the provisions of section 172(2) of the Road Traffic Act 1978 were compatible with the protection against self-incrimination in Article 6(1). The Board distinguished the decision in *Saunders v. United Kingdom*[52] noting that Parliament was at least as well placed as the judiciary to assess the balance between the safety of road users and the rights of the accused. Lord Steyn explained that:

"On this aspect the legislature was in as good a position as the court to assess the gravity of the problem and the public interest in addressing it. It really then boils down to the question whether, in adopting the procedure enshrined in section 172(2), rather than a reverse burden technique, it took more drastic action than was justified. While

---

[48] [2001] 2 W.L.R. 211.
[48a] *R. v. Lambert* [2001] UKHL 37.
[49] Judgment December 21, 2000.
[50] Judgment February 5, 2001.
[51] [2001] 2 W.L.R. 817. For a disussion, see para. 15–89 below.
[52] (1997) 23 E.H.R.R. 313.

this is ultimately a question for the court, it is not unreasonable to regard both techniques as permissible in the field of the driving of vehicles."

2–133b   In *R. v. A*,[53] however, a majority[54] of the House of Lords identified the limits to this approach when considering whether a statutory restriction on the cross-examination of a rape complainant was compatible with Article 6. The restriction had been imposed by Parliament to redress the "twin myths" that a woman who is sexually active is either promiscuous or untruthful or both. As Lord Steyn put it:

> "Clearly the House must give weight to the decision of Parliament that the mischief encapsulated by the twin myths must be corrected. On the other hand, when the question arises whether in the criminal statute in question Parliament has adopted a legislative scheme which makes an excessive inroad into the right to a fair trial the court is qualified to make its own judgment and must do so".

2–134   Finally, it is important to point out that even in Strasbourg, where the broader international margin of appreciation is applicable, the Court's standard of deference allows considerably fewer "degrees of latitude"[55] to the state than the *Wednesbury*[56] standard of review. We have already seen that the Strasbourg margin of appreciation is not confined to "ascertaining whether the respondent state has exercised its discretion reasonably, carefully and in good faith".[57] More significantly, the irrationality threshold has led to the condemnation of judicial review as an ineffective remedy by the European Court of Human Rights. This was despite the fact that the Court of Appeal had recognised a heightened level of scrutiny for judicial review in human rights cases.[58] In *Smith and Grady v. United Kingdom*,[59] the challenge to the Ministry of Defence ban on homosexuals serving in the armed forces, the Court observed that the *Wednesbury* threshold;

> " . . . was placed so high that it effectively excluded any consideration by the domestic courts of the question of whether the interference with the applicants' rights answered a pressing social need or was proportionate to the national security and public order aims pursued, principles which lie at the heart of the Court's analysis of complaints under Article 8 of the Convention."

2–134a   The reconciliation of these principles with the standard adopted by the Administrative Court on judicial review was considered in *R. (Mahmood) v Secretary*

---

[53] Judgment May 17, 2001; [2001] UKHL 25. See para. 15–136 below.
[54] Lord Hope held that the provision in issue fell within the ambit of policy in which the courts should defer on democratic grounds to the considered opinion of the legislature: "I think that, if any doubt remains on this matter, it raises the further question whether Parliament acted within its discretionary area of judgment when it was choosing the point of balance indicated by [the relevant provision]. The area is one where Parliament was better equipped than the judges are to decide where the balance lay. The judges are well able to assess the extent to which the restrictions will inhibit questioning or the leading of evidence. But it seems to me that in this highly sensitive and carefully researched field, an assessment of the prejudice to the wider interests of the community if the restrictions were not to take that form was more appropriate for Parliament."
[55] See Neill L.J. in *Rantzen v. Mirror Group Newspapers (1986) Ltd* [1994] Q.B. 670.
[56] *Associated Provincial Picture Houses Ltd v. Wednesbury Corporation* [1948] 1 K.B. 223.
[57] *Vogt v. Germany* (1996) 21 E.H.R.R. 205 at para. 52(iii), see para. 2–117 above.
[58] *R. v. Ministry of Defence ex parte Smith* [1996] Q.B. 517.
[59] (2000) 29 E.H.R.R. 493 at para. 138.

of State for the Home Department.[60] Lord Phillips M.R. held that under the 1998 Act, the courts should anxiously scrutinise Executive decisions which interfere with human rights. In a case concerning an alleged violation of Articles 8 to 11, this would involve asking the question whether, judged by an objective standard, the decision maker could reasonably have concluded that the interference was necessary to achieve one or more legitimate aims recognised by the Convention. As Laws L.J. put it in the same case, the 1998 Act "does not authorise the judges to stand in the shoes of Parliament's delegates, who are decision makers given their responsibilities by the democratic arm of the state". That would require the judges to "usurp those functions of government which are controlled and distributed by powers whose authority is derived from the ballot box". It followed that there must be "a principled distance" between the court's adjudication and the Executive's decision, which would be based on the merits of the case. *Mahmood* was considered in the House of Lords in *R. v. Secretary of State for the Home Department ex parte Daly.*[61] Lord Steyn observed that the test laid down in *Mahmood* was "couched in language reminiscent of the traditional *Wednesbury* ground of review". After citing with approval the test for proportionality laid down in *de Freitas v. Permanent Secretary of Ministry of Agriculture, Fisheries, Lands and Housing*[62] he continued:

> "The starting point is that there is an overlap between the traditional grounds of review and the approach of proportionality. Most cases would be decided in the same way whichever approach is adopted. But the intensity of review is somewhat greater under the proportionality approach. Making due allowance for important structural differences between various convention rights, which I do not propose to discuss, a few generalisations are perhaps permissible. I would mention three concrete differences without suggesting that my statement is exhaustive. First, the doctrine of proportionality may require the reviewing court to assess the balance which the decision maker has struck, not merely whether it is within the range of rational or reasonable decisions. Secondly, the proportionality test may go further than the traditional grounds of review inasmuch as it may require attention to be directed to the relative weight accorded to interests and considerations. Thirdly, even the heightened scrutiny test developed in *R. v. Ministry of Defence, ex p. Smith*[63] is not necessarily appropriate to the protection of human rights . . . [T]he intensity of the review, in similar cases, is guaranteed by the twin requirements that the limitation of the right was necessary in a democratic society, in the sense of meeting a pressing social need, and the question whether the interference was really proportionate to the legitimate aim being pursued. The differences in approach between the traditional grounds of review and the proportionality approach may therefore sometimes yield different results. It is therefore important that cases involving convention rights must be analysed in the correct way. This does not mean that there has been a shift to merits review. On the contrary, as Professor Jowell[64] has pointed out the respective roles of judges and administrators are fundamentally distinct and will remain so. To this extent the general tenor of the observations in *Mahmood* are correct. And Laws L.J. rightly emphasises in *Mahmood* 'that the intensity of review in a public law case will depend on the subject matter in hand'. That is so even in cases involving Convention rights. In law context is everything."

---

[60] [2001] 1 W.L.R. 840.
[61] [2001] UKHL 26.
[62] [1999] 1 A.C. 69; see para. 2–110 above.
[63] [1996] Q.B. 517 at 554.
[64] "Beyond the Rule of Law: Towards Constitutional Judicial Review" [2000] P.L. 671 at 681.

C. SPECIFIC PROVISIONS

I. *Non-discrimination*

2–135 Article 14 provides that;

> "The enjoyment of the rights set forth in this Convention shall be secured without discrimination on any ground such as sex, race, colour, language, religion, political or other opinion, national or social origin, association with a national minority, property, birth or other status."

The Convention differs from other international instruments in that its anti-discrimintation provision may only be invoked *in conjunction* with a substantive Convention right.[65] There is, however, no requirement for an applicant to show that there has been a violation of the substantive Convention right concerned. As the Court observed in the *Belgian Linguistic Case (No. 2)*[66];

> "While it is true that this guarantee has no independent existence in the sense that under the terms of Article 14 it relates solely to 'rights and freedoms set forth in the Convention', a measure which in itself is in conformity with the requirements of the Article enshrining the right or freedom in question may however infringe this Article when read in conjunction with Article 14 for the reason that it is of a discriminatory nature."

Thus, providing the complaint falls within the broad ambit of a Convention right, it is sufficient that there has been a failure to afford equal treatment in the delivery of that right.[67] It is "as though Article 14 formed an integral part of each of the provisions laying down the specific rights and freedoms".[68]

2–136 Article 14 is a general prohibition on unequal treatment on grounds of "status", which guarantees equality before the law. To that extent, it affords a broader range of protection than domestic anti-discrimination legislation. The term "other status" has been held to include sexual orientation,[69] transsexuality,[70] illegitimacy,[71] professional status,[72] and even pension status.[73]

2–137 The Court's structured approach requires two questions to be posed.[74] First, the Court will inquire whether there has been a difference in treatment between two persons who are in a "relevantly similar"[75] position, on grounds of the victim's

---

[65] *cf.* Art. 26 of the International Covenant on Civil and Political Rights.
[66] (1979–80) 1 E.H.R.R. 252 at para. 9.
[67] *Rasmussen v. Denmark* (1985) 7 E.H.R.R. 352. This point is well illustrated by *RM v. United Kingdom* (1994) 77A D.R. 98, where the Commission accepted that discrimination in sentencing could, in principle, amount to a breach of Art. 5 in conjunction with Art. 14. *Cf. Botta v. Italy* (1998) 26 E.H.R.R. 241 (right of disabled person to access to a holiday beach did not fall within the ambit of Art. 8, so Art. 14 inapplicable).
[68] *RM v. United Kingdom* (1994) 77A D.R. 98 at 105.
[69] *Sutherland v. United Kingdom* (1997) 24 E.H.R.R. CD 22.
[70] *Sheffield and Horsham v. United Kingdom* (1999) 27 E.H.R.R. 163.
[71] *Marckx v. Belgium* (1979–80) 2 E.H.R.R. 330.
[72] *Van der Muselle v. Belgium* (1984) 6 E.H.R.R. 163.
[73] *Szrabjer and Clarke v. United Kingdom* [1998] E.H.R.L.R. 230.
[74] *Belgian Linguistic Case (No. 2)* (1979–80) 1 E.H.R.R. 252.
[75] *National and Provincial Building Society v. United Kingdom* (1998) 25 E.H.R.R. 127 at para. 88.

"status".[76] The burden of proving this lies on the applicant.[77] If this burden is discharged, the Court must go on to determine whether the difference which has been identified has an "objective and reasonable" justification.[78] Here, the burden lies on the state.[79] The Court's assessment involves the familiar process of asking whether there is a legitimate aim for the difference in treatment, and whether there is "a reasonable relationship of proportionality between the means employed and the aim sought to be realised".[80] This requires the Court to "strike a fair balance between the protection of the interests of the community and respect for the rights and freedoms safeguarded by the Convention".[81] In determining whether a difference in treatment satisfies the proportionality test the Court will allow the state a certain margin of appreciation, and will have regard to comparative European practice[82] and any relevant international standards.[83]

Certain forms of discrimination are regarded as particularly serious. Very weighty reasons would have to be advanced to justify a difference in treatment on any one of these grounds. The Court has identified gender,[84] illegitimacy,[85] nationality,[86] race[87] and sexual orientation[88] as falling within these "suspect categories", and has held that in a serious case, discrimination on certain of these grounds could amount to inhuman and degrading treatment contrary to Article 3.[89] Positive discrimination will not violate Article 14 if it has an objective and reasonable justification, since "certain legal inequalities tend only to correct factual inequalities".[90]

2-138

---

[76] For examples of case which failed at this hurdle, see *Stubbings and others v. United Kingdom* (1997) 23 E.H.R.R. 213 where the Court described the comparison between negligently and intentionally inflicted injury (for the purposes of different limitation periods) as "artificial"; and *Van der Muselle v. Belgium* (1984) 6 E.H.R.R. 163 where a trainee barrister's claim that he was treated differently from trainees in other professions was rejected on the ground that there were fundamental differences between the various professions.

[77] See the Court's approach in *Selcuk and Asker v. Turkey* (1998) 26 E.H.R.R. 477 at para. 102 and *Mentes v. Turkey* (1998) 26 E.H.R.R. 595 at para. 96.

[78] *Belgian Linguistic Case (No. 2)* (1979–80) 1 E.H.R.R. 252 at para. 9.

[79] *Darby v. Sweden* (1991) 13 E.H.R.R. 774 at para. 31 (where the state failed to put forward any substantive justification); *Marckx v. Belgium* (1979–80) 2 E.H.R.R. 330 at para. 32 (where the Court rejected a generalised assertion unsupported by evidence).

[80] *Belgian Linguistic Case (No. 2)* (1979–80) 1 E.H.R.R. 252 at para. 10; *Darby v. Sweden* (1991) 13 E.H.R.R. 774 at para. 31.

[81] *Belgian Linguistic Case (No. 2)* (1979–80) 1 E.H.R.R. 252 at para. 9.

[82] *Rasmussen v. Denmark* (1985) 7 E.H.R.R. 352.

[83] *Inze v. Austria* (1988) 10 E.H.R.R. 394.

[84] *Karlheinz and Schmidt v. Germany* (1994) 18 E.H.R.R. 513 at para. 24; *Van Raalte v. Netherlands* (1997) 24 E.H.R.R. 503 at para. 42; *Abdulaziz, Cabales and Balkandali v. United Kingdom* (1985) 7 E.H.R.R. 471; *Burghartz v. Switzerland* (1994) 18 E.H.R.R. 101; *Schuler-Zraggen v. Switzerland* (1993) 16 E.H.R.R. 405.

[85] *Inze v. Austria* (1988) 10 E.H.R.R. 394.

[86] *Gaygusuz v. Austria* (1997) 23 E.H.R.R. 364.

[87] *East African Asians Case* (1981) 3 E.H.R.R. 76.

[88] *Sutherland v. United Kingdom* (1997) 24 E.H.R.R. CD 22; *Smith and Grady v. United Kingdom* (2000) 29 E.H.R.R. 493 at para. 121.

[89] *East African Asians Case* (1981) 3 E.H.R.R. 76; *Smith and Grady v. United Kingdom* (2000) 29 E.H.R.R. 493 at para. 121.

[90] *Belgian Linguistic Case (No. 2)* (1979–80) 1 E.H.R.R. 252; See also *DG and DW v. United Kingdom* (1986) 49 D.R. 181—tax advantage for married women had "an objective and reasonable justification in the aim of providing positive discrimination" to encourage married women back to work.

2–139   The principle of equal treatment is enshrined in all comparable constitutional instruments,[91] and has been recognised by the Privy Council as a fundamental principle of constitutional adjudication. In *Matadeen v. Pointu*[92] Lord Hoffman observed that the requirement to treat like cases alike and unlike cases differently was a "general axiom of rational behaviour".

II. *Abuse of rights*

2–140   Article 17 provides that;

> "Nothing in this Convention may be interpreted as implying for any State, group or person any right to engage in any activity or perform any act aimed at the destruction of any of the rights and freedoms set forth herein or at their limitation to a greater extent than is provided for in the Convention."

2–141   The aim of this provision is to prevent the state, or any individual within its jurisdiction, from invoking a Convention right in order to perform acts which are *aimed* at undermining the Convention rights of others. It is therefore directed towards two very different situations. The first is where the state seeks to rely on a Convention right in order to justify an interference or restriction with another Convention right. In this situation, Article 17 provides that the limitations[93] contained within the articles creating substantive rights are exhaustive: the state cannot derive from one provision of the Convention a justification for implying greater restrictions into another Convention right.

2–142   Insofar as it applies to individuals, however, Article 17 has been interpreted restrictively by the Court. In particular, the Court has held that it cannot be relied upon to deprive those who are charged with serious crime of the due process guarantees afforded by Articles 5 to 7 of the Convention.[94] In *Lawless v. Ireland (No.3)*,[95] a case involving internment for alleged terrorism, the Court observed that:

> " . . . the purpose of Article 17, in so far as it refers to groups or individuals, is to make it impossible for them to derive from the Convention a right to engage in any activity, or perform any act aimed at destroying any of the rights and freedoms set forth in the Convention. Therefore no person may be able to take advantage of the provisions of the Convention to perform acts aimed at destroying the aforesaid rights and freedoms. This provision, which is negative in scope, cannot be construed *a contrario* as depriving a physical person of the fundamental individual rights guaraneed by Articles 5 and 6 of the Convention. In the present case [the applicant] has not relied on the Convention in order to justify or perform acts contrary to the rights and freedoms recognised therein but has complained of having been deprived of the guarantees granted in Articles 5 and 6 of the Convention."

---

[91] See, for example, Canadian Charter of Rights and Freedoms, s. 15; New Zealand Bill of Rights Act, ss.19 and 20; South African Constitution, s. 8.

[92] [1998] 3 W.L.R. 18 at 26F.

[93] As to implied limitations see para. 2–60 above.

[94] Neither can the gravity of an alleged offence ever justify treatment in breach of Art. 3: *Ribitsch v. Austria* (1995) 21 E.H.R.R. 573.

[95] (1979–80) 1 E.H.R.R. 15 at para. 7.

The potential conflict which the Court foreshadowed in *Lawless* eventually **2–143** materialised in *SW and CR v. United Kingdom*,[96] a case concerning the retrospective removal of the marital rape exemption by the House of Lords.[97] In a concurring opinion in the Commission, the Irish member argued that the House of Lords' decision would have amounted to a breach of Article 7 were it not for the fact that the applicant had violated his wife's right to respect for her physical and moral integrity, a component of the concept of private life recognised by Article 8. Relying on Article 17 she said that the applicant was;

> " . . . indisputably seeking to rely on Article 7 to justify the act of forcing his wife to have sexual intercourse with him . . . an act aimed at destroying her right to bodily integrity. However, Article 17 precludes him from deriving from the Convention justification for his conduct or a finding that the United Kingdom authorities infringed his fundamental rights by punishing such conduct after a fair trial."

The flaw in this reasoning is that the applicant was not in reality relying on Article 7 to assert a right to engage in criminal activity. He was asserting a right to be tried, convicted and sentenced for alleged criminal activity in accordance with the Convention's guarantees. The construction adopted by the Irish member of the Commission would mean that any defendant charged with a serious offence against the person would unable to rely on the due process guarantees of the Convention. The Court rightly declined to adopt this analysis.[98]

Article 17 may nevertheless be relevant in the criminal context where the **2–144** assertion of the Convention right *in itself* involves an attack on the rights of others. In *Glimmerveen and Haagenback v. Netherlands*,[99] for example, the Commission relied on Article 17 to hold that speech which was intended to incite race hatred was outside the protection of Article 10 altogether, because of its potential to undermine the rights of the targeted minority. In subsequent cases, however, the Commission and the Court have reached the same conclusion without reference to Article 17, holding simply that prosecutions for race hate speech are necessary in a democratic society within the meaning of Article 10(2).[1]

III. *Convention not to prejudice existing rights*

Article 53 provides; **2–145**

> "Nothing in this Convention shall be construed as limiting or derogating from any of the human rights and fundamental freedoms which may be ensured under the laws of any High Contracting Party or under any other agreement to which it is a Party."

---

[96] (1996) 21 E.H.R.R. 363. See further, para. 10–27 below.
[97] *R. v. R.* [1992] A.C. 559.
[98] Note, however, that the Court referred to the "essentially debasing character of rape" in concluding that the decision of the House of Lords was not "at variance with the object and purpose of Article 7". In the Court's view, "the abandonment of the unacceptable idea of a husband being immune against prosecution for rape of his wife was in conformity not only with a civilised concept of marriage but also, and above all, with the fundamental objectives of the Convention, the very essence of which is respect for human dignity and human freedom" (para. 44/42).
[99] (1979) 18 D.R. 187.
[1] *Kuhnen v. Germany* (1988) 56 D.R. 205; *Jersild v. Denmark* (1995) 19 E.H.R.R. 1. See para. 8–33 below.

2–146   The object of Article 53 is to make it clear that the list of rights and freedoms set out in the Convention is not exhaustive, and that states are free to provide more extensive human rights protection either in their national law, or through other international agreements. This principle is reflected in section 11 of the Human Rights Act 1998. As the Lord Chancellor explained in the course of the debates on the Act: "Convention rights are, as it were, a floor of rights; and if there are different or superior rights or freedoms conferred by or under any law having effect in the United Kingdom, this is a Bill which only gives and does not take away."[2]

---

[2] November 18, H.L. col. 510.

CHAPTER 3

THE HUMAN RIGHTS ACT 1998

A. INTRODUCTION

The Human Rights Act 1998 gives "further effect"[1] in domestic law to the rights **3–01** and freedoms guaranteed under the European Convention on Human Rights. The White Paper *Rights Brought Home* explained that the legislation was intended to enable people in the United Kingdom to enforce their Convention rights directly in the British courts, without having to incur the expense and endure the delay of taking a case to the European Court of Human Rights in Strasbourg.[2] Under the Act it is unlawful for any public authority, including a court or tribunal at any level, to act in a manner which is incompatible with a Convention right, unless required to do so by the terms of primary legislation which cannot be interpreted in a manner which is compatible with the Convention.[3] Convention rights thus take precedence over rules of common law or equity,[4] and over most (but not all) subordinate legislation.[5] Primary legislation must be read and given effect in a manner which is compatible with Convention rights, "so far as it is possible to do so".[6] If it is impossible to resolve a conflict between a Convention right and a provision of primary legislation by construction, the legislation remains valid, operative and enforceable,[7] but the higher courts may grant a formal "declaration of incompatibility",[8] drawing the position to the attention of Parliament, and enabling the relevant Minister to amend the legislation by order if there are "compelling reasons to do so".[9] In this way, the Act enables the courts to afford considerable protection for fundamental rights, whilst maintaining the principle of Parliamentary sovereignty.

A person who claims that a public authority has acted (or proposes to act) in a **3–02** way which is made unlawful under the Act may bring proceedings in an appropriate court or tribunal,[10] or may rely on a Convention right in any legal proceedings,[11] providing he is or would be a "victim" of the unlawful act for the

---

[1] This terminology is intended to reflect the fact that prior to the Human Rights Act 1998 the courts of the United Kingdom already had recourse to the Convention in a variety of circumstances: H.L. Debs, col. 478 (November 18, 1997). For a useful summary of the pre-Act position see Beloff and Mountfield, "Unconventional Behaviour? Judicial Uses of the European Convention in England and Wales" [1996] E.H.R.L.R. 467.

[2] *Rights Brought Home*, Cmnd. 3782, (1997), p. 1.

[3] Section 6: see para. 3–22 below.

[4] See para. 3–29 below.

[5] See para. 3–34 below.

[6] Section 3(1): see para. 3–31 below.

[7] Section 3(2)(b).

[8] Sections 4 and 5: see para. 3–35 below.

[9] Section 10: see para. 3–38 below.

[10] Section 7(1)(a): see para. 3–41 below.

[11] Section 7(1)(b): see para. 3–42 below.

purposes of Article 34 of the Convention.[12] Where a court finds that a public authority has acted (or proposes to act) in such a manner, it may grant such relief or remedy, or make such order, within its powers, as it considers "just and appropriate".[13] In determining any question which arises under the Act in connection with a Convention right, all courts and tribunals must take into account any relevant judgment of the European Court of Human Rights, opinion of the European Commission of Human Rights, or decision of the Committee of Ministers of the Council of Europe.[14]

B. INTERPRETATION

3–03 Constitutional human rights legislation is "*sui generis*, calling for principles of interpretation of its own, suitable to its character".[15] Respect must be paid to the language which has been used and to the traditions and usages which have given meaning to the language.[16] The guiding principle is that an enactment giving effect to fundamental rights has a "special character" which calls a broad and purposive approach to construction.[17] It requires "a generous interpretation avoiding what has been called 'the austerity of tabulated legalism', suitable to give to individuals the full measure of the fundamental rights and freedoms referred to".[18] The court should look to "the substance and reality of what was involved and should not be over-concerned with what are no more than technicalities".[19] The moral and political values underpinning the legislation must be taken into account.[20] Where appropriate, courts should be willing to look to comparative caselaw since "[e]very system of law stands to benefit by an awareness of the answers given by other courts and tribunals to similar problems".[21] Decisions on the interpretation of constitutional human rights provisions in other jurisdictions are, however, of persuasive rather than binding authority.[22]

C. RETROSPECTIVE APPLICATION IN CRIMINAL PROCEEDINGS

3–04 The operative provisions of the Human Rights Act came into force on October 2, 2000.[23] However, the Act has a partially retrospective application, which has

---

[12] Section 7(1),7(3) and 7(7): see para. 3–43 below.
[13] Section 8(1): see para. 3–46 below.
[14] Section 2: see para. 3–17 below.
[15] *Ministry of Home Affairs v. Fisher* [1980] A.C. 319 at 329C-E P.C.
[16] *ibid*. at 329E-F
[17] *Ministry of Transport v. Noort* [1992] 3 N.Z.L.R. 260 at 271, 276–278; *R. v. DPP ex parte Kebilene and ors* [1999] 3 W.L.R. 972 at 988 H.L., *per* Lord Hope.
[18] *ibid*. at 328G-H; *Attorney-General of Gambia v. Momodou Jobe* [1984] A.C. 689 at 700H (P.C.); *Attorney-General of Hong Kong v. Lee Kwong-kut* [1993] A.C. 951 at 966B-E (P.C.); *Vasquez and O'Neil v. R.* [1994] 1 W.L.R. 1304 at 1313B *et seq*. (P.C.); *Flicklinger v. Crown Colony of Hong Kong* [1991] 1 N.Z.L.R. 439 at 440.
[19] *Huntley v. Attorney-General for Jamaica* [1995] 2 A.C. 1 at 12G-H, (P.C.)
[20] *Matadeen v. Pointu and ors* [1999] 1 A.C. 98 *per* Lord Hoffman.
[21] *R. v. Khan (Sultan)* [1997] A.C. 558, (H.L.) *per* Lord Nicholls at 583C. See also *Reynolds v. Times Newspapers* [1999] 3 W.L.R. 1010.
[22] *Attorney-General of Hong Kong v. Lee Kwong-kut* [1993] A.C. 951 at 966G (P.C.)
[23] The Human Rights Act 1998 (Commencement No. 2) Order 2000 (S.I. 2000 No. 1851).

important implications for criminal proceedings. The general rule is that a complainant may not commence proceedings under section 7(1)(a) of the Act,[24] or rely on Convention rights in accordance with section 7(1)(b)[25] unless the act or omission complained of occurred after October 2, 2000.[26] However, where the proceedings have been brought by or at the instigation of a public authority,[27] and the individual wishes to invoke his Convention rights as part of a defence to those proceedings, the position is different. By virtue of section 22(4) a person may rely on his Convention rights in the course of proceedings initiated by a public authority "whenever the act in question took place".

The effect of section 22(4) was first considered in *R. v. DPP ex parte Kebilene*   **3–05**
and others.[28] The case concerned a challenge to the compatibility of reverse onus offences under sections 16A and 16B of the Prevention of Terrorism (Temporary Provisions) Act 1989 with the presumption of innocence in Article 6(2) of the Convention. Relying on section 22(4), the applicants sought judicial review of the decision to prosecute,[29] arguing that any conviction in the proceedings was liable to rendered retrospectively unlawful when the remaining provisions of the Act came into force. In the Divisional Court, Lord Bingham C.J. agreed[30]:

> "If, at the time of the appeal hearing, the central provisions of the 1998 Act had been brought into force, the applicants would on appeal be entitled to rely on sections 7(1)(b) and 22(4) of the Act and the convictions (on the hypothesis of inconsistency between section 16A and the Convention) would in all probability have to be quashed, at some not inconsiderable cost to the public purse."

Before the House of Lords, it was argued on behalf of the DPP that section 22(4)   **3–06**
did not apply to an appeal against conviction since proceedings in the Court of Appeal (Criminal Division) were instituted by the individual appellant and not by a public authority. The effect of this construction would have been to permit defendants to invoke Convention rights retrospectively at trial, but not on appeal. Lord Steyn rejected this submission. It was, he observed, "an argument of some technicality"[31]: "The language of the statute does not compel its adoption and a construction which treats the trial and the appeal as parts of one process is more in keeping with the purpose of the Convention and the Act of 1998."

On this construction, an appellant in proceedings which were initially instituted by   **3–07**
a public authority could rely on his Convention rights on appeal, notwithstanding that the first instance proceedings were determined prior to October 2, 2000. Thus, in *R. v. Lambert and ors*[32] Lord Woolf C.J. accepted that in light of section 22(4) it was incumbent on the Court of Appeal (Criminal Division) to approach

---

[24] See para. 3–41 below.
[25] See para. 3–42 below.
[26] Sections 7(1) and 22(4).
[27] It is open to doubt whether s.22(4) can apply to a private prosecution.
[28] [1999] 3 W.L.R. 175 (D.C.); [1999] 3 W.L.R. 972 (H.L.)
[29] In giving his consent to the prosecution, the DPP had concluded that there was no incompatibility, and the applicants sought a declaration that his understanding was wrong.
[30] [1999] 3 W.L.R. 175 at 187 C.
[31] [1999] 3 W.L.R. 972 at 982.
[32] [2001] 2 W.L.R. 211.

the safety of a conviction as if the Act had been in force at the time of the trial.[33] It did not, however, follow that non-compliance with the Convention before the Act came into force would be regarded as a ground for extending time for appealing.

3–08   The issue was considered in detail in *R. v. Benjafield and ors.*[34] Lord Woolf reiterated that it would not usually be appropriate to grant leave to appeal out of time where the grounds of appeal are based on post-trial changes in the law, including the enactment of the Human Rights Act. Where, however, the appeal involved a point of general public interest it might be appropriate to depart from the normal practice. In *Benjafield*, the Crown argued that section 22(4) did not permit the Court of Appeal to apply the interpretative obligation in section 3 of the Act retrospectively. Lord Woolf pointed out that the "vast majority" of criminal proceedings were within section 22(4). Whilst the argument advanced by the Crown was different from that advanced in *Kebilene*, the result was the same:

> "In our judgment, where the original proceedings are brought by or at the instigation of a public authority, as is the case with a prosecution, an appeal by the defendant is part of the proceedings to which section 22(4) applies. There cannot be a different position on an appeal from that of the trial so far as the issue of retrospectivity of the Human Rights Act is concerned. Any other construction would mean that in criminal cases, the Court of Appeal could not give the required protection to the individual (who would clearly be a victim of any unlawful act) so that there would be a need for an otherwise unnecessary but time-consuming and expensive trip to Strasbourg. In addition, otherwise section 7(1)(b) will apply where appeal is by a public authority, but not when the appeal is made by the defendant. In cases where primary legislation has not required the trial court to make a decision which is incompatible with a Convention right, there is no difficulty. The Appeal Court will be able to apply the Convention and determine whether any relief should result. But if the decision below was based on a provision of primary legislation, section 6(2)(a) will apply . . . This means that the prosecution and the court below, if unable to apply the approach required by section 3(1), would have been unable to decide differently, so that section 6(1) and consequently section 7 could not apply to them. But section 6(1) does not apply to the Court of Appeal, and section 7(1) covers not only a past, but a proposed act. It would, in those circumstances, be curious if the Court were unable to apply section 3(1). Then, if satisfied that there was an incompatibility, the Court would be unable to remedy it by applying a compatible construction of the relevant provision. Furthermore, and equally importantly, the Court would be unable to give the guidance needed for future application of the relevant provisions. This is not the position, and section 3(1) has retrospective effect if section 22(4) and section 7(1)(b) apply."

3–08a   The implications of this approach for cases referred to the Court of Appeal by the Criminal Cases Review Commission (CCRC) under section 9 of the Criminal Appeal Act 1995 were considered in *R. v. Kansal.*[35] Rose L.J. pointed out that there was no statutory limit of time on a reference back. Combined with the retrospective application of the Human Rights Act, this had two consequences:

---

[33] The Court had "reservations as to whether Parliament coud have intended such a result" but accepted that it was the correct interpretation where an appellant alleged a breach of the right to a fair trial in Article 6.

[34] Judgment December 21, 2000.

[35] Judgment May 24, 2001 (CA).

"(i) the CCRC, subject to the proper exercise of the discretion conferred by section 9 of the Criminal Appeal Act, can refer to this Court a conviction following a trial whenever it took place; (ii) this Court, once such a reference has been made, has no option, however old the case, but to declare the conviction unsafe if that is the result either of the admission of evidence obtained in breach of Article 6 or of a change in the common law, which is deemed always to have been that which it is authoritatively declared to be."

The appeal in that case was based upon the admission at trial of answers obtained as a result of compulsory questioning in a manner incompatible with the European Court's judgment in *Saunders v. United Kingdom*.[36] The appellant's trial had taken place five years before the judgment in *Saunders* was delivered. The Court quashed the appellant's conviction "with no enthusiasm whatever", noting that the reference back procedure had effectively deprived the Court of any discretion to refuse leave where an appeal is based on a subsequent change in the law:

"For over 20 years this Court has adopted a pragmatic approach, confirmed by successive Lord Chief Justices, whereby a refusal to extend time to apply for leave to appeal has filtered out those seeking to take advantage of a change in the law since they were convicted. This, in our judgment, reflects the public interest that there be finality in litigation and it is an approach which has also helped this Court to concentrate its limited resources on determining more meritorious appeals arising from more recent convictions. Subject to the outcome of further consideration of the breadth of the CCRC's discretion, it appears that Parliament, consciously or unconsciously, has completely emasculated that approach. If so, the consequential prospective workload for the CCRC and for this Court is alarming. If this is what Parliament intended, so be it. If not, the sooner the matter is addressed, by Parliament or by the House of Lords on appeal from this Court, the better."

Rose L.J.'s call for a reconsideration of these difficult issues was answered by the **3–09** House of Lords in *R. v. Lambert*.[37] By a 4 to 1 majority,[38] their Lordships held that neither section 22(4), nor section 6 of the Human Rights Act permitted an appellant to rely on his Convention rights on appeal in order to challenge a decision of a trial court made prior to October 2, 2000, where the judicial

---

[36] (1997) 23 E.H.R.R. 313.

[37] [2001] UKHL 37, July 5, 2001. As to the implications of this decision for the Court of Appeal, see para. 17–06 below.

[38] Lord Steyn dissented on this issue. In his view the House of Lords, as a public authority, was bound to act compatibly with Article 6. For an appellate court to uphold a conviction after October 2, 2000 which had been obtained in breach of Article 6 prior to that date would be to act incompatibly and therefore unlawfully. This did not involve retrospectivity. Section 6 regulated the powers of the Court for the present and for the future. There was no legitimate basis for restricting the plain words of the section. The construction of the majority would frustrate the intention of the Act, and would lead to a continuing residue of non-compliant decisions of public authorities kept indefinitely in effect by their own antiquity.

decision in question was lawful at the time it was made.[39] Lord Hope, however, drew a distinction between challenges directed to the act of the trial court, and challenges directed to decisions of the prosecutor. Despite concurring with the majority on this issue, he held that the Act would nevertheless operate retrospectively on appeal where the appellant relied on an alleged breach of his Convention rights by the prosecuting authority.

D. THE CONVENTION RIGHTS

I. *The rights incorporated*

3–10   Section 1(1) of the Act identifies the rights to which the Act gives domestic effect[40] namely the right to life (Article 2); the prohibition of torture (Article 3); the prohibition of slavery and forced labour (Article 4); the right to liberty and security (Article 5); the right to a fair trial (Article 6); the principle of no punishment without law (Article 7); the right to respect for private and family life (Article 8); the right to freedom of thought, conscience and religion (Article 9); the right to freedom of expression (Article 10); the right to freedom of assembly and association (Article 11); the right to marry and found a family (Article 12); the prohibition of discrimination (Article 14); the protection of property (Article 1 of Protocol 1); the right to education (Article 2 of Protocol 1); the right to free elections (Article 3 of Protocol 1); and the abolition of the death penalty in peacetime (Articles 1 and 2 of Protocol 6). The text of these rights is set out in Schedule 1 to the Act.

II. *The omission of Articles 1 and 13*

3–11   Articles 1 and 13 of the Convention are not included in the list of scheduled rights. Article 1 enshrines the obligation on contracting states to "secure to everyone within their jurisdiction" the rights and freedoms set out in the Convention. The Government's reason for omitting Article 1 was explained by the Lord Chancellor during debates. It was, he said, unnecessary for this obligation to be specifically incorporated because the Human Rights Act itself "gives effect to Article 1 by securing to people in the United Kingdom the rights and freedoms of the Convention".[41] Its sister provision Article 13, which guarantees the right to an effective remedy before a national authority for any arguable violation of

---

[39] The case concerned a reverse onus clause in the Misuse of Drugs Act 1971 which, construed according to conventional cannons of construction, was held to be incompatible with the presumption of innocence in Article 6(2). The majority of the House of Lords held that when read with the benefit of the interpretative obligation in section 3, the relevant provision should, henceforth, be construed as imposing a purely evidential burden on the accused. The appellant could not, however, take the benefit of this ruling since section 22(4) did not apply to a challenge brought on appeal to a decision of a court or tribunal (in this case, the decision to direct the jury on the appropriate burden of proof) made before sections 3 and 6 of the Act came into force.

[40] The rights incorporated are those set out in Sched. 1: see s.1(3).

[41] H.L. Debs, col 475 (November 18, 1998).

a Convention right, was omitted for essentially the same reason.[42] This does not mean, however, that Articles 1 and 13 are irrelevant to the national courts' functions under the Human Rights Act. On the contrary, since the Human Rights Act is intended to give effect to Articles 1 and 13, national courts and tribunals are entitled to take these provisions into account when exercising the discretionary power to grant "just and appropriate" remedies under section 8 of the Act.[43] Moreover the Government made it clear on a number of occasions during the course of the Parliamentary debates that the obligation in section 2(1) of the Act (which requires national to take account of relevant Convention jurisprudence) was intended to include jurisprudence under Article 13.[44]

III. *The relevance of Articles 16 to 18*

Section 1(1) provides that the rights incorporated by the Act are to be read in conjunction with Articles 16 to 18 of the Convention. Article 16 relates to restrictions on the political activity of aliens. Article 17 provides that the rights contained in the Convention are not to be interpreted as implying for any state, group or person the right to engage in activity which is aimed at the destruction of the Convention rights of others, or their limitation to a greater extent than is provided for in the Convention.[45] Article 18 provides that the limitations permitted under the Convention to the rights guaranteed, may not be applied for any purpose other than the purpose for which they were prescribed. **3–12**

IV. *Derogations*

The Convention rights take effect in domestic law subject to any "designated derogation".[46] Article 15 of the Convention permits contracting states to derogate from their obligations under the Convention in times of war or "other public emergency threatening the life of the nation"; providing the derogation is "strictly required by the exigencies of the situation",[47] and is consistent with the state's other obligations under international law.[48] The United Kingdom's only **3–13**

---

[42] As the Lord Chancellor explained during debates, the Human Rights Act "gives effect to Art. 13 by establishing a scheme under which Convention rights can be raised before our domestic courts": H.L. Debs, col. 475 (November 18, 1997).

[43] It is a long established principle of interpretation that particular weight will be attached to Convention caselaw when the court is considering legislation which has been enacted in order to bring domestic law into line with the requirements of the Convention: *R. v. Secretary of State for the Home Department ex parte Norney* (1995) 7 Admin. L.R. 861.

[44] During the Committee stage in the House of Commons, the Home Secretary acknowledged that "[T]he courts must take account of the large body of Convention jurisprudence when considering remedies . . . Obviously, in doing so, they are bound to take judicial notice of Art. 13, without being specifically bound by it": H.C. Debs, col. 981 (May 20, 1998). Similarly, the Lord Chancellor observed that "[T]he courts may have regard to Article 13. In particular, they may wish to do so when considering the very ample provisions of [section] 8(1).": H.L. Debs, col. 477 (November 18, 1997). He went on to say: "One always has in mind *Pepper v. Hart* when one is asked questions of that kind" (*ibid.*). See *Pepper v. Hart* [1993] A.C. 593.

[45] See para. 2–140 above.

[46] Section 1(2).

[47] Article 15(1).

[48] Article 15(1). Note however that no derogation is permitted from Art. 2 (save in respect of deaths resulting from lawful acts of war), Art. 3, Art. 4(1) or Art. 7: Art. 15(2).

derogation applies to Article 5(3). It was entered in response to the judgment in *Brogan v. United Kingdom*[49] where the Court held that detention for four days and six hours under the Prevention of Terrorism (Temporary Provisions) Act 1984 was incompatible with the requirement that a detained person should be brought promptly before a judge or judicial officer. The derogation preserved the power of the Secretary of State to extend the period of detention of persons suspected of terrorism in connection with Northern Ireland for a total of up to seven days.[50] The Human Rights Act 1998 expressly retains the derogation to Article 5(3)[51] but places a time limit of five years on its operation[52] subject to renewal by order of the Secretary of State.[53] In addition, the Secretary of State may, by order, designate any future derogation (or proposed derogation[54]) from the Convention or its protocols.[55] Such an order must be approved by affirmative resolution of both Houses of Parliament within a period of 40 days, failing which it will cease to have effect.[56] Once approved a designation order remains in effect for a period of five years after it was made[57] unless, prior to its expiry, it is extended by order of the Secretary of State.[58]

V. *Reservations*

3–14   The Convention rights also take effect subject to any "designated reservation".[59] Article 57 of the Convention permits a state to enter a reservation at the time of signature or ratification of the Convention or a protocol, where a particular provision in its domestic law is considered to be incompatible with the obligations it is undertaking. Reservations must be specific, and must contain a brief statement of the law to which they relate.[60] The United Kingdom has entered a reservation to Article 2 of Protocol 1, (the right of parents to ensure that their children are educated in conformity with their own religious and philosophical convictions). Referring to certain provisions of the Education Acts, the reservation states that this obligation is accepted "only in so far as it is compatible with the provision of efficient instruction and training, and the avoidance of unreasonable public expense".[61] The Human Rights Act gives domestic effect to this

---

[49] (1989) 11 E.H.R.R. 117.
[50] The derogation was subsequently held to be compatible with Art. 15: *Brannigan and McBride v. United Kingdom* (1994) 17 E.H.R.R. 539.
[51] HRA 1998, s.14(1)(a). The text of the derogation is set out in the Human Rights Act 1998, Sched. 3.
[52] HRA 1998, s.16(1)(a).
[53] Section 16(2): At any time prior to its expiry, the Secretary of State may, by order, extend the period of the designation for a further five years. Such an order may be made by statutory instrument (s.20(1)) but must be laid before Parliament (s.20(3)).
[54] Section 14(6).
[55] Section 14(1)(b).
[56] Section 16 (3) and (5). Note, however, that the lapsing of a designation order under s.16(3) does not affect anything done in reliance on the order during the interim period: s.16(4)(a). Nor does it prevent the Secretary of State from making a fresh designation order: s.16(4)(b).
[57] Section 16(1)(b).
[58] Section 16(2).
[59] Section 1(2).
[60] Article 57(1) and (2).
[61] For the full text of the reservation see Human Rights Act 1998 Sched. 3, Part II.

reservation[62] and invests the Secretary of State with power to designate any reservation which the United Kingdom may enter in the future.[63] Any designated reservation is subject to five yearly review by the appropriate Minister,[64] the result of which must be reported to Parliament.[65] There is, however, no requirement for periodic renewal or Parliamentary approval.[66]

VI. *Protocols*

The rights incorporated by the Act may be amended by order of the Secretary of   **3–15** State to reflect the effect in relation to the United Kingdom of any protocol which has been ratified, or signed with a view to ratification.[67] This enables the Act to keep pace with any additional obligations which the United Kingdom may undertake in the future. Such an order may be made by statutory instrument,[68] but must be laid before, and approved by, both Houses of Parliament.[69] No such order may be made so as to come into force before the protocol to which it relates is in force in relation to the United Kingdom.[70] The protocols which confer additional substantive rights are;

(a) *Protocol 1*. This guarantees the protection of property,[71] the right to education,[72] and the right to free elections.[73] The United Kingdom has signed and ratified Protocol 1, and the rights which it enshrines are incorporated into domestic law by section 1(1) of the Human Rights Act.

(b) *Protocol 4*. This guarantees the prohibition on imprisonment for debt,[74] the right to freedom of movement,[75] the prohibition on expulsion of nationals,[76] and the prohibition on the collective expulsion of aliens.[77] The United Kingdom signed Protocol 4 in 1963 but has never ratified it, and according to the White Paper *Rights Brought Home*, the Government has no intention of ratifying Protocol 4 at present.[78]

---

[62] Section 15(1)(a) and Sched. 3, Part II.
[63] Section 15(1)(b). A state cannot enter a reservation after ratifying the Convention or protocol to which it relates. Accordingly, the power under s.15(1)(b) will arise in practice only in relation to any additional protocols which the United Kingdom may ratify, or if it should partially withdraw (or amend) the reservation to Art. 2 of Protocol 1.
[64] Section 17(1) and (2).
[65] Section 17(3).
[66] *cf.* the position in relation to designated derogations.
[67] Section 1(4) and (5).
[68] Section 20(1).
[69] Section 20(4).
[70] Section 1(6).
[71] Article 1.
[72] Article 2.
[73] Article 3.
[74] Article 1.
[75] Article 2.
[76] Article 3.
[77] Article 4.
[78] *Rights Brought Home*, Cmnd. 3782, (1997), para. 4.11.

3–16   (c) *Protocol 6.* This provides for the abolition of the death penalty in peace-time.[79] The United Kingdom ratified Protocol 6 on January 27, 1999, following a successful backbench amendment to the Human Rights Act incorporating Articles 1 and 2 of Protocol 6 into section 1(1).[80] The Home Office Minister in the House of Lords, Lord Williams of Mostyn Q.C. explained during the debates that the amendment makes it "impossible for Parliament to reintroduce the death penalty in future, except for acts committed in time of war, or imminent threat of war, without denouncing the Convention itself".[81]

(d) *Protocol 7.* This guarantees the right of an alien not to be expelled without due process of law,[82] the right of appeal against a conviction and sentence in criminal proceedings,[83] the right to compensation for a miscarriage of justice,[84] the protection against double jeopardy in criminal cases,[85] and the right to equality between spouses.[86] The Government has confirmed the United Kingdom's intention to sign, ratify and incorporate Protocol 7 once certain legislative changes, relating to the property rights of spouses, have been made.[87]

(e) *Protocol 12.* The Council of Europe has recently concluded a new protocol to the Convention which is intended to supplement Article 14 by guaranteeing a free-standing right to be protected against discrimination in the delivery of any right guaranteed under national law.

VII. *Relevance of the Strasbourg jurisprudence*

3–17   Section 2(1) provides that when determining a question which has arisen in connection with a Convention right, courts and tribunals must take into account the decisions of the Strasbourg institutions, whenever made or given,[88] so far as, in the opinion of the court or tribunal, they are relevant to the proceedings in which the question has arisen. This applies to judgments, decisions, declarations and advisory opinions of the European Court of Human Rights[89]; opinions of the former[90] Commission on Human Rights concerning the merits of a complaint,[91] or its admissibility[92]; and rulings of the Committee of Ministers concerning the

---

[79] The death penalty was abolished for murder by the Murder (Abolition of Death Penalty) Act 1965; for treason and piracy by the Crime and Disorder Act 1998, s.36. Any liability to the death penalty under the Army Act 1955, the Air Force Act 1955 and the Naval Discipline Act 1957 is abolished by s.21(5) of the Human Rights Act 1998, and replaced with a liability to imprisonment for life.
[80] H.C. Debs, cols 987—1013 (May 20, 1998). The amendment was moved by Kevin MacNamara M.P.
[81] H.L. Debs, col. 2084 (October 29, 1998)
[82] Article 1.
[83] Article 2.
[84] Article 3.
[85] Article 4.
[86] Article 5.
[87] *Rights Brought Home* Cmnd. 3782, (1997), para. 4.15.
[88] The inclusion of the words "whenever made or given" is intended to make it clear that the obligation applies to future decisions as well as past ones: H.C. Debs, col. 405 (June 3, 1998).
[89] Section 2(1)(a).
[90] The European Commission on Human Rights was abolished by Protocol 11.
[91] Section 2(1)(b).
[92] Section 2(1)(c).

merits of a complaint or the supervision of a Court judgment.[93] Section 2(2) provides that evidence of any such decision is to be given in accordance with the relevant Rules of Court.

Under section 2(1) the courts are obliged to take the Convention caselaw into account, but they are not bound to follow it. As the Lord Chancellor explained during the debates the domestic courts "may depart from existing Strasbourg decisions, and on occasion it might well be appropriate to do so, and it is possible they might give a successful lead to Strasbourg".[94] There are a number of factors which may affect the weight to be attached to a particular decision. A decision of a Chamber obviously carries less weight than a decision of the Grand Chamber; Commission decisions are less authoritative than decisions of the Court; admissibility decisions (of the Commission or the new Court) are less persuasive than binding judgments on the merits of a complaint; decisions relating to states with very different legal traditions may be of limited assistance[95–99]; the "living instrument" principle[1] means that older caselaw may no longer be a sure guide to the requirements of the Convention[2]; and decisions which are expressly based on the "margin of appreciation" doctrine are unlikely to give a reliable indication of the approach to be taken by a national court.[3] **3–18**

There is no doubt that domestic courts are free in appropriate cases to adopt a higher standard than the Strasbourg caselaw demands.[4] It is less clear that they are free to adopt a lower standard. The United Kingdom remains bound by the **3–19**

---

[93] Section 2(1)(d). The references to the Articles of the Convention in s.2(1) are apt to confuse since s.2(1)(b) and (c) refer to the *former* Arts 26, 27(2) and 31 of the Convention (relating to the functions of the Commission prior to the abolition of the Commission under Protocol 11); whereas s.2(1)(d) refers to the function of the Committee of Ministers in supervising court judgments under Art. 46 *as amended* by Protocol 11. However, s.21(3) of the Act provides that for the purposes of s.2(1)(d) the reference to Art. 46 is to be taken to include a reference to former Arts 32 and 54. Former Art. 32 was the provision under which the Committee of Ministers had jurisdiction to determine the merits of a complaint which was not referred to the Court. This jurisdiction was abolished by Protocol 11. Former Art. 54 conferred on the Committee of Ministers the responsibility for supervising the execution of court judgments, and is now to be found in Art. 46.

[94] H.L. Debs, col. 514 (November 18, 1997).

[95–99] Note, however, that during the Committee stage the Lord Chancellor made it clear that s.2 was intended to require courts to take account of Strasbourg decisions irrespective of the identity of the respondent state: H.L. Debs, col. 513 (November 18, 1997).

[1] See para. 2–18 above.

[2] A point made by the Lord Chancellor in debate: H.L. Debs, cols 1270–1271 (January 19, 1998).

[3] See, for example, the observations of Lord Hope in *R. v. DPP ex parte Kebilene and ors* [1999] 3 W.L.R. 972 (H.L.) See also para. 2–115 to 2–134 above.

[4] Sir Nicholas Bratza, the British judge on the Court has observed that
"since the Convention provides a floor not a ceiling for rights throughout the Council of Europe, it is perfectly possible that the courts of this country will provide greater protection for human rights under the Act than is strictly required by case law emanating from Strasbourg . . . [I]t is thus possible that the courts of this country will disregard some of the more controversial case law of the Convention organs": Bratza, "Implications of the Human Rights Act 1998 for Commercial Practice" [2000] E.H.R.L.R. 1 at 4.
See also *Fitzpatrick v. Sterling Housing Corporation* [2001] 1 A.C. 27 where the House of Lords, in defining the term "family" to include homosexual couples, departed from the more restrictive Convention caselaw on the point. Note, however, that in *Re Al-Fauwaz* [2000] All E.R. (D) 2052 Buxton L.J. observed that "it will only be very rarely that a national court feels able to rule on the meaning and reach of an article of the ECHR in terms different from those adopted, on the identical question, by one of the Convention organs".

supervisory jurisdiction of the European Court of Human Rights, and an unsuccessful litigant retains the right of individual petition under Article 34 of the Convention. A national court which departed from recent Convention jurisprudence, so as to adopt a lower standard of protection, would be acting contrary to the stated purpose of the Human Rights Act, which is to enable litigants to enforce their Convention rights without having to bring proceedings in Strasbourg.

VIII. *Freedom of expression and freedom of religion*

3–20   Section 12 of the Human Rights Act makes specific provision for cases involving freedom of expression. It does not, however, apply to a criminal court and is accordingly outside the scope of this work.[5] A criminal court is, nevertheless, a public authority under section 6 of the Act and is therefore obliged to act compatibly with Article 10, unless it is bound by the terms of primary legislation to do otherwise.[6] Section 13 provides that if a court's[7] determination of any question arising under the Act might affect the exercise by a religious[8] organisation[9] of the Convention right to freedom of thought, conscience and religion,[10] the court must have "particular regard" to the importance of that right.[11]

IX. *Saving for existing rights*

3–21   Section 11 provides that a person's reliance on a Convention right does not restrict any other right or freedom conferred on him by or under any law having effect in any part of the United Kingdom.[12] Nor does it restrict his right to make any claim or bring any proceedings which he could make or bring apart from the Human Rights Act, sections 7 to 9.[13] Section 11 gives domestic effect to Article 53 of the Convention, which provides; "Nothing in this Convention shall be construed as limiting or derogating from any of the human rights and fundamental freedoms which may be ensured under the laws of any High Contracting Party or under any other agreement to which it is a Party."

During the Parliamentary debates on section 11 the Lord Chancellor explained that "Convention rights are, as it were, a floor of rights; and if there are different or superior rights or freedoms conferred by or under any law having effect in the United Kingdom, this is a Bill which only gives and does not take away".[14] The Human Rights Act cannot therefore be used to restrict rights which are directly enforceable in domestic law. Nor does it limit the extent to which litigants can

---

[5] See s.12(5). Section 12 itself does not therefore apply to decisions concerning reporting restrictions in criminal proceedings.

[6] See the comments of the Home Secretary H.C. Debs, col. 540 (July 2, 1998).

[7] The term "court" includes a tribunal: s.13(2).

[8] The Act provides no definition of religion, and there is some uncertainty in the Strasbourg caselaw about the boundaries of this term: see, for example, *Chappell v. United Kingdom* (1987) 53 D.R. 241 (druidism); *Church of Scientology v. Sweden* (1979) 16 D.R. 68.

[9] This extends to the organisation itself, or its members collectively: s.13(1).

[10] As to Art. 9 see para. 8–16 below.

[11] Section 13(1).

[12] Section 11(1).

[13] Section 11(2). As to ss.7 to 9, see paras 3–40 to 3–53 below.

[14] H.L. Debs, col. 510 (November 18, 1997).

invoke other international human rights instruments under the existing common law principles.[15]

E. APPLICATION TO PUBLIC AUTHORITIES

I. *The duty to act compatibly*

The guiding principle of the Human Rights Act is to be found in section 6(1). **3–22** This provides that it is "unlawful for a public authority to act in a manner which is incompatible with a Convention right" unless required to do so by the terms of primary legislation which cannot be interpreted compatibly with the Convention.[16] An "act", for this purpose, includes a failure to act, but does not include a failure to legislate or make a remedial order.[17] Section 6(1) does not, however, apply to an act if, as the result of one or more provisions of primary legislation, the authority could not have acted differently[18]; or in the case of one or more provisions of, or made under, primary legislation which cannot be read or given effect in a way which is compatible with the Convention rights,[19] the authority was acting so as to give effect to or enforce those provisions.[20] This ensures that

---

[15] In the absence of statutory incorporation, an international instrument does not form part of the law of England and Wales: *Chundawadra v. Immigration Appeal Tribunal* [1988] Imm. A.R. 161; *Pan Amercian World Airways Inc. v. Department of Trade* [1976] 1 Lloyd's Reports 257. However, there is a presumption that Parliament does not intend to legislate in breach of the Crown's international obligations, and accordingly, it has long been established that an international treaty may be used to resolve an ambiguity in a statutory provision: *Waddington v. Miah* [1974] 1 W.L.R. 683 (H.L.); *Garland v. British Rail* [1983] A.C. 751, (H.L.); *Re M and H (Minors)* [1990] 1 A.C. 686 (H.L.) (*per* Lord Brandon at 721G); *R. v. Secretary of State for the Home Department ex parte Brind* [1991] 1 A.C. 696. Particular weight will be attached to an international treaty obligation where the court is considering legislation which has been enacted in order to bring domestic law into line with the requirements thereof: *R. v. Secretary of State for the Home Department ex parte Norney* (1995) 7 Admin. L.R. 861. An international human rights treaty which binds the United Kingdom may also be used as an aid to the development of the common law: see *Attorney-General v. Guardian Newspapers Ltd (No.2)* [1990] 1 A.C. 109, (H.L.) (*per* Lord Goff at 283); *Derbyshire County Council v. Times Newspapers* [1992] Q.B. 770 (C.A.) (*per* Butler-Sloss L.J. at 830); and *R. v. Chief Metropolitan Stipendiary Magistrate ex parte Choudhury* [1991] 1 Q.B. 429 (D.C.) (*per* Watkins L.J. at 449). In *Rantzen v. Mirror Group Newspapers (1986) Ltd.* [1994] Q.B. 670 the Court of Appeal went further, and held that the European Convention on Human Rights, though unincorporated, could be deployed when a court is considering how to exercise a judicial discretion: see also *R. v. Secretary of State for the Environment ex parte NALGO* (1992) 5 Admin L.R. 785 (C.A.); *R. v. Khan (Sultan)* [1996] 3 W.L.R. 162 (H.L.) (*per* Lord Slynn at 165 and Lord Nicholls at 176). For a useful summary of the domestic courts' approach to the European Convention on Human Rights, prior to its incorporation, see Beloff and Mountfield, "Unconventional Behaviour? Judicial Uses of the European Convention in England and Wales" [1996] E.H.R.L.R. 467.

[16] See s.6(2). As to the obligation to interpret primary legislation compatibly with Convention rights, see s.3(1) and para. 3–31 below.

[17] Section 6(6). Section 6 thus preserves Parliamentary sovereignty and insulates the executive from challenge in relation to the introduction of legislation. As to remedial orders, see para. 3–38 below.

[18] Section 6(2)(a).

[19] As to the duty to interpret primary legislation compatibly with Convention rights, see s.3(1) and para. 3–31 below.

[20] Section 6(2)(b).

section 6 cannot be used as a means of mounting a collateral challenge to primary legislation which is irreconcilable with a Convention right.

II. *Scope of the obligation imposed on public authorities*

3–23   Where the body in question is plainly a public authority, such as the police, the Commissioners for Customs and Excise, or the Crown Prosecution Service, the duty in section 6(1) applies to all its activities, irrespective of whether function in issue is public or private in nature. As the Lord Chancellor explained during the course of the Parliamentary debates[21];

> "[Section 6(1)] refers to a 'public authority' without defining the term. In many cases it will be obvious to the courts that they will be dealing with a public authority. In respect of government departments, for example, or police officers, or prison officers, or immigration officers, or local authorities, there can be no doubt that the body in question is a public authority. Any clear case of that kind comes under [section 6(1)]; and it is then unlawful for the authority to act in a way which is incompatible with one or more of the Convention rights. There is no exemption for private acts such as is conferred by [section 6(5)] for [hybrid bodies]."

3–24   A public authority will be liable even where the alleged violation arises from an act or omission of one of its employees which is beyond the scope of their authority. The Home Secretary made it clear in debate that the definition of public authority was intended to correspond with the notion of state responsibility under the Convention,[22] a notion which extends to the acts of subordinates, even where they have exceeded their mandate, or acted in defiance of express instructions.[23] Thus, the Commission has explained that "the obligations of a Contracting Party under the Convention can be violated by a person exercising an official function vested in him, even where his acts are outside or against instructions".[24]

III. *Hybrid bodies*

3–25   The term "public authority" in section 6(1) is deemed by section 6(3)(b) to include "any person certain of whose functions are of a public nature". This provision does not, however, apply where the act which is the subject of challenge is "private" rather than "public" in nature.[25] Thus, when hybrid bodies are under consideration "the focus should be on their functions and not on their

---

[21] H.L. Debs, col. 811 (November 24, 1997).
[22] "The principle of bringing rights home suggested that liability in domestic proceedings should lie with bodies in respect of whose actions the United Kingdom Government was answerable in Strasbourg . . . As a minimum, we must accept what Strasbourg has developed and is developing": H.C. Debs, cols 406–408 (June 17, 1998).
[23] *Ireland v. United Kingdom* (1979–80) 2 E.H.R.R 25 at para. 159; *A v. France* (1994) 17 E.H.R.R. 462; *Cyprus v. Turkey* (1982) 4 E.H.R.R. 482; *Aydin v. Turkey* (1998) 25 E.H.R.R. 251. *Cf. Makanjuola v. Commissioner of Police for the Metropolis, The Times*, August 8, 1989. These decisions are discussed at para. 1–79 above.
[24] *Wille v. Lichtenstein* (1997) 24 E.H.R.R. CD 45.
[25] Section 6(5). De Smith, Woolf and Jowell suggest that a body is exercising a public function for the purposes of judicial review "when it seeks to achieve some collective benefit for the public, or a section of the public and is accepted by the public or that section of the public as having authority to do so": *Judicial Review of Administrative Action* (5th ed., 1995) para. 3–024.

nature as an authority".[26] During the Parliamentary debates the Lord Chancellor explained[27] that section 6(3)(b) was intended:

> ". . . to include bodies which are not manifestly public authorities, but some of whose functions only are functions of a public nature. It is relevant to cases where the courts are not sure whether they are looking at a public authority in the full-blooded . . . sense with regard to those bodies which fall into the grey area between public and private. The Bill reflects the decision to include as 'public authorities' bodies which have some public functions and some private functions."

Similarly, the Home Secretary explained[28] that the government;   3–26

> ". . . wanted a realistic and modern definition of the state so as to provide a correspondingly wide protection against the abuse of human rights. Accordingly, liability under the Bill would go beyond the narrow category of central and local government and the police—the organisations that represent a minimalist view of what constitutes the state."

This extended definition of "public authority" corresponds with the Strasbourg caselaw on state responsibility.[29] It is a fundamental principle of the Strasbourg jurisprudence that a state cannot escape liability under the Convention by delegating its essentially public functions to private bodies. In *Costello-Roberts v. United Kingdom*,[30] for example, the Court held that the United Kingdom would be liable under Article 3 for corporal punishment notwithstanding that it was inflicted in a private school. Examples of hybrid bodies falling within section 6(1) would thus include professional regulatory bodies such as the Law Society and the Bar Council, and a privatised company carrying out statutory functions[31] such as a private security company carrying out functions in relation to the management of a private prison or court security, (although not when providing security for commercial premises).[32]

---

[26] H.L. Debs, col. 797 (November 24, 1997), The Lord Chancellor. See also the Home Secretary at H.C. Debs col. 433 (June 17, 1998), "As we are dealing with public functions and with an evolving situation, we believe that the test must relate to the substance and nature of the act, not to the form and legal personality." The government's aim was "to provide as much protection as possible to those who claim that their rights have been infringed": H.L. Debs, col. 582 (November 3, 1997), the Lord Chancellor.

[27] H.L. Debs, col. 811 (November 24, 1997).

[28] H.C. Debs, cols 406–408 (June 17, 1998).

[29] See the Lord Chancellor at H.L. Debs, cols 1231–1232 (November 3, 1997), where he observed that s.6(3)(b) "reflects the arrangements for taking cases to the Convention institutions in Strasbourg". Similarly, the Home Secretary explained during the debates that

"Under the Convention the government are answerable in Strasbourg for any acts or omissions of the state about which an individual has complaint under the Convention. The government has a direct responsibility for core bodies, such as central government and the police, but they also have responsibility for other public authorities, insofar as the actions of such authorities impinge on private individuals. The [Human Rights Act] had to have a definition that went at least as wide and took account of the fact that, over the past 20 years, an increasingly large number of private bodies, such companies or charities, have come to exercise public functions that were previously exercised by public authorities. . . it was not practicable to list all the bodies to which the [Human Rights Act's] provisions should apply. Nor would it have been wise to do so . . . [Section 6] therefore adopts a non-exhaustive definition of a public authority.": H.C. Debs, col. 775 (February 16, 1998).

[30] (1995) 19 E.H.R.R. 112.

[31] *Rights Brought Home* Cmnd. 3782, (1997), para. 2.2. See also *DPP v. Manners* [1978] A.C. 43 (H.L.).

[32] H.L. Debs, col. 811 (November 24, 1997) the Lord Chancellor.

IV. *Parliament is not bound by section 6(1)*

3–27 The term "public authority" in section 6(1) does not include either House of Parliament (other than the House of Lords, sitting in its judicial capacity) or a person exercising functions in connection with proceedings in Parliament.[33] The Act thus prevents an individual from seeking to challenge incompatible primary legislation by alleging that Parliament has acted unlawfully in passing it. There is a complementary provision prohibiting potential challenges arising from a failure to legislate. Section 6(6) provides that a failure to introduce in, or lay before, Parliament a proposal for legislation, or to make any primary legislation or remedial order is excluded from the duty imposed by section 6(1).[34]

V. *The position of the courts*

3–28 The term "public authority" in section 6(1) includes a court or tribunal.[35] This ensures not only that the Convention rights afford an independent ground upon which to challenge the acts of external public authorities before an appropriate court or tribunal, but that the courts and tribunals themselves, as public authorities, are obliged to ensure that their own decisions are consistent with Convention rights (unless they are required to act otherwise by the terms of primary legislation, which cannot be interpreted compatibly[36]).

VI. *Rules of common law*

3–29 The inclusion of the courts within the definition of a "public authority" for the purposes of section 6(1) has important implications for the common law. Whilst the Act contains specific provisions insulating incompatible primary legislation from judicial override, there is no such saving for incompatible rules of common law. Pre-existing common law rules which infringe Convention rights must therefore give way to the statutory duty imposed on the courts by section 6(1). This will apply to private prosecutions as well as proceedings brought by a prosecuting authority. As the Lord Chancellor explained in debate[37]:

> "We ... believe that it is right as a matter of principle for the courts to have the duty of acting compatibly with the Convention not only in cases involving other public authorities but also in developing the common law in deciding cases between individuals. Why should they not? In preparing this Bill, we have taken the view that it is the other course, that of excluding Convention considerations altogether from cases between individuals which would have to be justified. The courts already bring the Convention to bear and I have no doubt that they will continue to do so in developing the common law."

3–30 This approach is consistent with the Convention jurisprudence on "positive obligations"[38] and state responsibility.[39] Under the former principle, a state can

---

[33] Section 6(3) and (4). *Cf. R. v. Parliamentary Commissioner for Standards ex parte Al Fayed* [1998] 1 W.L.R 669.
[34] As to the position where an applicant alleges a breach of a Convention right on the ground that an interference is unregulated by statute, see para. 3–36 below.
[35] Section 6(3)(a).
[36] As to the duty of compatible construction under s.3(1) see para. 3–31 below.
[37] H.L. Debs, col. 783 (November 24, 1997).
[38] See para. 2–53 above.
[39] See para. 1–76 above.

be held liable in Strasbourg when its substantive law (including its common law) fails to afford adequate protection against a violation of an individual's Convention rights by another private individual.[40] Under the latter principle, the state is answerable under the Convention for all its institutions, including the courts. Accordingly, a judicial decision which interferes with Convention rights will give rise to state liability, even where it was made in purely private litigation.[41] This principle was applied in a criminal context in *Venables and Thompson v. News Group Newspapers and ors*[41a] where the President of the Family Division held that Article 2 imposed a positive obligation on the Court to grant an injunction against the private news media, in order to protect the identity of the two juveniles convicted of the murder of James Bulger, since there was compelling evidence that if their identities were revealed in the press, their lives would be put at serious risk. Although the defendants were not public authorities, the Court was under an obligation to develop its equitable jurisdiction to grant injunctions in order to meet the requirements of the Convention.

F. APPLICATION TO LEGISLATION

I. *The new approach to statutory interpretation*

By section 3(1) primary and subordinate legislation[42] must[43] be read and given **3-31** effect in a way which is compatible with the Convention rights so far as it possible[44] to do so. This obligation applies to past and future legislation.[45] As the White Paper *Rights Brought Home* made clear[46] section 3(1);

". . . goes far beyond the present rule which enables the courts to take the Convention into account in resolving any ambiguity in a legislative provision. The courts will be required to interpret legislation so as to uphold the Convention rights unless the

---

[40] See *X and Y v. Netherlands* (1988) 8 E.H.R.R. 235 (absence of a criminal offence prohibiting sexual abuse of mentally handicapped teenager found to violate Art. 8); *A v. United Kingdom* (1997) 27 E.H.R.R. 611 (common law offence of assault afforded insufficient protection to a child against a violation of Art. 3 in view of the breadth of the defence of lawful correction); *Young, James and Webster v. United Kingdom* (1982) 4 E.H.R.R. 38 (closed shop legislation in breach of Art. 11).
[41] An obvious example is *Tolstoy v. United Kingdom* (1995) 20 E.H.R.R. 442, where the United Kingdom was held responsible for an excessive award of damages in libel proceedings, which was held to violate Art. 10.
[41a] January 8, 2001.
[42] The terms "primary legislation" and "subordinate legislation" are defined by s.21(1).
[43] The word "must" in s.3(1) makes it clear that the new approach to interpretation is mandatory. It follows that the court is under a duty to consider the obligation of compatible construction in every case, before considering the lawfulness of a public authority's action under s.6 (see para. 3–22 above), or—where it has power to do so—the grant of a declaration of incompatibility under s.4 (see para. 3–35 below).
[44] For discussion on the meaning of the term "possible" see Lord Lester of Herne Hill Q.C., "The Art of the Possible: Interpreting Statutes under the Human Rights Act" [1998] E.H.R.L.R. 665; Lord Irvine of Lairg, "The Development of Human Rights in Britain under an Incorporated Convention on Human Rights" [1998] Public Law 221; Lord Irvine of Lairg, "Activism and Restraint: Human Rights and the Interpretative Process" [1999] E.H.R.L.R. 350.
[45] Section 3(2)(a).
[46] *Rights Brought Home*, Cmnd. 3782, (1997) para. 2.7.

legislation itself is so clearly incompatible with the Convention that it is impossible to do so."

3–32 The process of statutory interpretation is no longer dominated by a search for the intention of Parliament. Instead, the courts' first duty is to adopt any possible construction which is compatible with Convention rights.[47] Section 3(1) requires the courts to strive for compatibility,[48] if necessary by reading down over-broad legislation or reading necessary safeguards into an Act.[49] The courts are not mandated to "contort" words "to produce implausible or incredible meanings".[50] However they may be required to give a meaning to a statutory provision which it would not ordinarily bear,[51] to imply words into a section[52] or to interpret general words as being subject to implied exceptions.[53] Only "in the last

---

[47] Writing extra-judicially Lord Steyn has explained that
"Traditionally, the search has been for the one true meaning of a statute. Now the search will be for a possible meaning that would prevent the need for a declaration of incompatibility. The questions will be: (1) What meanings are the words capable of yielding? (2) And, critically, can the words be made to yield a sense consistent with the Convention rights? In practical effect, there will be a rebuttable presumption in favour of an interpretation consistent with Convention rights. Given the inherent ambiguity of language the presumption is likely to be a strong one." "Incorporation and Devolution: A Few Reflections on the Changing Scene" [1998] E.H.R.L.R. 153 at 155.
As Lord Cooke of Thorndon explained during the second reading debate in the House of Lords, s.3(1) "will require a very different approach to interpretation from that to which the United Kingdom courts are accustomed. Traditionally, the search has been for the true meaning: now it will be for a possible meaning that would prevent the making of a declaration of incompatibility". H.L. Debs, col. 1272 (November 3, 1997).
[48] During the Parliamentary debates the Government successfully resisted an amendment, which would have replaced the word "possible" with the word "reasonable", on the ground that this would unduly restrict the courts' powers of construction: H.L. Debs, cols 533–536 (November 18, 1997); H.C. Debs, cols 415 and 421 (June 3, 1998).
[49] cf. Attorney-General of Gambia v. Momodou Jobe [1984] A.C. 689 at 700H P.C.; Flicklinger v. Crown Colony of Hong Kong [1991] 1 N.Z.L.R. 439 at 440; Ministry of Transport v. Noort [1992] 3 N.Z.L.R. 260.
[50] See the comments of the Home Secretary during the Committee stage of the Bill in the House of Commons: H.C. Debs, col. 422 (June 3, 1998). The Lord Chancellor has observed that "the Act, while significantly changing the nature of the interpretative process, does not confer on the courts a licence to construe legislation in a way which is so radical and strained that that it arrogates to the judges the power completely to rewrite existing law": Lord Irvine of Lairg, "Activism and Restraint: Human Rights and the Interpretative Process" [1999] E.H.R.L.R. 350 at 367.
[51] In R. v. DPP ex parte Kebilene and ors [1999] 3 W.L.R. 972 Lord Cooke of Thorndon described s.3(1) as "a strong adjuration" which permits a court to depart from "the natural and ordinary meaning" of a statutory provision. Since it conveys "a rather more powerful message" than its counterpart in the New Zealand Bill of Rights Act 1990, it was "distinctly possible", within the meaning of s.3(1), to read the word "prove" in a criminal statute as imposing no more than an evidential burden (a construction which had been rejected in New Zealand: see R. v. Phillips [1991] 3 N.Z.L.R. 175). Cf. Webb v. EMO Air Cargo (U.K.) Ltd. (No. 2) [1995] 1 W.L.R. 1454 (H.L.)
[52] The Lord Chancellor has cited Lister v. Forth Dry Dock & Engineering Co Ltd [1990] 1 A.C. 546 (H.L.) as an example of the sort of implication which might be permitted by s.3(1): "The Development of Human Rights in Britain under an Incorporated Convention on Human Rights" [1998] Public Law 221. See also Pickstone v. Freemans plc [1989] 1 A.C. 66 at 112D (H.L.). More radical approaches are sometimes permissible under Commonwealth Constitutions, see Vasquez and O'Neil v. R [1994] 1 W.L.R. 1304 at 1314D-G.
[53] In R. v. Secretary of State for the Home Department ex parte Simms and anor. [1999] 3 W.L.R. 328 at 341–2 Lord Hoffman equated the duty imposed by s.3(1) with the "principle of legality" under which a court will presume that primary or subordinate legislation expressed in general terms is to be read "subject to the basic rights of the individual". See also R. v. Secretary of State for the Home Department ex parte Pierson [1998] A.C. 539 at 573G–575D, 587C–590A.

resort"[54] should a court conclude that a compatible construction is impossible.[55] The obligation in section 3(1) applies to all courts and tribunals.[56] Lower courts are thus no longer bound by a previous construction[57] which has been given to existing legislation by a higher court if, in the opinion of the inferior court, this construction would lead to a result which is incompatible with a Convention right.

An early illustration of the new approach to interpretation was the decision in *R.* **3–32a** *v. Offen and ors*,[58] which Lord Woolf C.J. described as "a good example of how the 1998 Act can have a beneficial effect on the administration of justice, without defeating the policy which Parliament was seeking to implement". The case concerned section 2 of the Crime (Sentences) Act 1997 (now section 109 of the Powers of the Criminal Courts (Sentencing) Act 2000) which provides for the imposition of an automatic life sentence following conviction for a second serious offence. The section obliges the court to impose such a sentence where the relevant qualifying offence is proved, regardless of whether the offender would otherwise have qualified for a discretionary life sentence. This is subject to a proviso that the court need not impose a life sentence where the circumstances are exceptional. Concerns had been voiced from an early stage that section 2 could lead to the imposition of a life sentence where the offender posed no serious risk to the public. In *Offen* the appellants argued that to impose a life sentence on grounds of assumed dangerousness when it was clear that the defendant was not in fact dangerous would result in arbitrary deprivation of liberty, and thus breach Article 5. Lord Woolf C.J. agreed, and held that applying section 3 it was "possible" to read the expression "exceptional circumstances" so as to prevent such a result:

"The question of whether circumstances are appropriately to be regarded as exceptional must surely be influenced by the context in which the question is being asked. The policy and intention of Parliament was to protect the public against a person who had committed two serious offences. It therefore can be assumed the section was not intended to apply to someone in relation to whom it was established there would be no need for protection in the future. In other words, if the facts showed the statutory assumption was misplaced, then this, in the statutory context was not the normal

---

[54] See the observations of the Lord Chancellor during Committee stage in the House of Lords (H.L. Debs, col. 535 (November 18, 1997)) and the Home Secretary during Committee stage in the House of Commons (H.C. Debs cols 415 and 421 (June 3, 1998)). The Home Secretary voiced the Government's belief that "in almost all cases the courts will be able to interpret legislation compatibly with the Convention" (H.C. Debs, col. 780 (February 16, 1998).

[55] Section 3(1) nevertheless requires a balance to be struck.:
"If the courts were to adopt a very narrow view of this duty of consistent construction, their ability interpretatively to guarantee Convention rights would be severely curtailed. Instead of reading municipal law in a way which gave effect to individuals' rights, the courts would tend to discover irreconcileable conflicts between United Kingdom law and the Convention. In contrast, a judiciary which took an extremely radical view of its interpretative duty would be likely to stretch legislative language, beyond breaking point, if necessary, in order to effect judicial vindication of Convention rights . . . Both of these approaches would be wrong. The constitutional theory on which the Human Rights Act rests is one of balance." Lord Irvine of Lairg, "Activism and Restraint: Human Rights and the Interpretative Process" [1999] E.H.R.L.R. 350 at 367.

[56] Indeed, the duty in s.3(1) extends to the executive and any person or body with responsibility for interpreting or implementing legislation.

[57] *i.e.* a construction reached without the benefit of s.3(1).

[58] [2001] 1 W.L.R. 253.

situation and in consequence, for the purposes of the section, the position was exceptional."

3–32b   In *Donogue v. Poplar Housing and Regeneration Community Association Ltd.*[59] Lord Woolf C.J. observed that it was "difficult to overestimate the importance of section 3":

> "It applies to legislation both before and after the HRA came into force. Subject to the section not requiring the court to go beyond that which is possible, it is mandatory in its terms. In the case of legislation pre-dating the HRA where the legislation would otherwise conflict with the Convention, section 3 requires the court to now interpret legislation in a manner which it would not have done before the HRA came into force. When the court interprets legislation usually, its primary task is to identify the intention of Parliament. Now, when section 3 applies, the courts have to adjust their traditional role in relation to interpretation so as to give effect to the direction contained in section 3. It is as though the legislation which pre-dates the HRA and conflicts with the Convention has to be treated as being subsequently amended to incorporate the language of section 3".

As a matter of priority the court should first construe the section according to ordinary cannons of construction. If the result was compatible with Convention rights then section 3 had no role to play. It was important to recall that section 3 does not entitle the court to legislate. Its task is one of interpretation. If, in order to achieve compliance, it was necessary radically to alter the effect of the legislation, then this would be an indication that more than interpretation was involved.

3–32c   In *R v. A*,[60] Lord Steyn, with whom the majority of the House of Lords agreed, described the obligation imposed by section 3 in these terms:

> "[T]he interpretative obligation under section of the 1998 Act is a strong one. It applies even if there is no ambiguity in the language in the sense of language being capable of two different meanings. It is an emphatic adjuration by the legislature . . . The draftsman of the Act had before him the slightly weaker model in section 6 of the New Zealand Bill of Rights Act 1990 but preferred stronger language. Parliament specifically rejected the legislative model of requiring a reasonable interpretation. Section 3 places a duty on the court to strive to find a possible interpretation compatible with Convention rights. Under ordinary methods of interpretation a court may depart from the language of the statute to avoid absurd consequences: section 3 goes much further. Undoubtedly, a court must always look for a contextual and purposive interpretation: section 3 is more radical in its effect. It is a general principle of the interpretation of legal instruments that the text is the primary source of interpretation: other sources are subordinate to it. Section 3 qualifies this general principle because it requires a court to find an interpretation compatible with Convention rights if it is possible to do so . . . In accordance with the will of Parliament as reflected in section 3 it will sometimes be necessary to adopt an interpretation which linguistically may appear strained. The techniques to be used will not only involve the reading down of express language in a statute but also the implication of provisions. A declaration of incompatibility is a measure of last resort. It must be avoided unless it is plainly impossible to do so".

Applying this approach, Lord Steyn held that section 3 required courts to "subordinate the niceties of the language" of the statutory restriction to broader

---

[59] [2001] EWCA Civ 595.
[60] [2001] 2 W.L.R. 1546, Judgment May 17, 2001. See para. 15–136 below.

considerations of relevance judged by logical and common sense criteria. This was achieved by implying into the section a judicial discretion to permit the admission of evidence which was necessary to secure a fair trial within the meaning of Article 6.[61]

II. *Legislation enacted after the Human Rights Act*

A Minister of the Crown responsible for new legislation introduced in either **3–33** House of Parliament must, before second reading,[62] make a statement in writing to the effect that in his view the Bill is compatible with the Convention rights.[63] If the Minister is unable to make such a statement,[64] he must inform Parliament that despite the potential incompatibility, the government nevertheless wishes to proceed with the Bill.[65] In *R v. A*[66] Lord Hope emphasised that a section 19 statement of compatibility could not, in any way, bind the courts: "These statements may serve a useful purpose in Parliament. They may also be seen as part of the parliamentary history, indicating that it was not Parliament's intention to cut across a Convention right . . . No doubt they are based on the best advice that is available. But they are no more than expressions of opinion by the Minister. They are not binding on the court, nor do they have any persuasive authority".

III. *Incompatible legislation*

The courts have no power to strike down or disapply a provision in primary **3–34** legislation which cannot be interpreted compatibly under section 3(1). Section 3(2)(b) provides that the duty of construction imposed by section 3(1) "does not affect the validity, continuing operation, or enforcement of any incompatible primary legislation".[67] The position of incompatible subordinate legislation is more complex. If (disregarding the possibility of revocation) the parent statute

---

[61] Lord Hope dissented on this issue, saying that he would find it "very difficult" to accept so substantial an implication by way of interpretation: "[T]he rule is only a rule of interpretation. It does not entitle the judges to act as legislators". For an equally far-reaching application of section 3 see *R. v. Lambert* [2001] UKHL 37 where the House of Lords held that a provision requiring the accused to *prove* an issue of fact could be read as imposing a purely evidential burden of proof.

[62] The statement should be included alongside the Explanatory and Financial Memorandum: *Rights Brought Home*, Cmnd. 3782, (1997) para. 3.3. The obligation to make a s.19 statement prior to second reading ensures that the implications of such a statement can be subject to effective Parliamentary scrutiny.

[63] Section 19(1)(a). Section 19 came into force on November 24, 1998: Human Rights Act 1998 (Commencement) Order 1998 S.I. 1998 No. 2882. The government has undertaken to justify the inclusion of a statement of compatibility if the issue is raised in debate: See the answer of Lord Williams of Mostyn Q.C. H.L. Debs, col. 186 (December 17, 1998).

[64] This may be either because the Bill is plainly incompatible, or because its compatibility is uncertain.

[65] Section 19(1)(b). The decision to make (or not to make) a statement of incompatibility is outside the control of the courts: Section 6(3)(b) provides that "a person exercising functions in connection with proceedings in Parliament" is not a public authority for the purposes of the Act. See also *Mangawaro Enterprises Ltd. v. Attorney-General* [1994] 2 N.Z.L.R. 451 (equivalent provision in the New Zealand Bill of Rights Act 1990 held non-justiciable).

[66] [2001] 2 W.L.R. 1546, Judgment May 17, 2001. See para. 15–136 below.

[67] Note, however, that the higher courts have power to grant a declaration of incompatibility: see para. 3–35 below.

prevents the removal of the incompatibility, then the courts must give effect to the incompatible subordinate legislation.[68] But where (as is often the case) the enabling provision is framed in general terms (and assuming it is impossible to read or give effect to the subordinate legislation in a manner which is compatible with Convention rights), the courts may then set a provision in subordinate legislation aside (either by striking it down, or by simply disapplying it).[69]

IV. *Declarations of incompatibility*

3–35 Where it is impossible[70] to interpret primary legislation compatibly with Convention rights, the higher courts,[71] may[72] grant a formal declaration of incompatibility under section 4(2). This power also applies to subordinate legislation in respect of which primary legislation prevents the removal of an incompatibility.[73] Section 4 is thus central to the constitutional balance which the Act strikes between Parliamentary sovereignty and the judicial protection of human rights. A declaration of incompatibility enables the courts to bring incompatible legislation to the attention of Parliament, and triggers the power to take remedial action in response.[74] It does not, however, affect the validity, continuing operation, or enforcement of the legislation.[75] Nor is it binding on the parties to the proceedings in which it was made.[76] It follows that a declaration of incompatibility in the Court of Appeal (Criminal Division) will not, of itself, afford a ground for quashing a criminal conviction, or reducing the sentence which would otherwise be appropriate. The effect of such a declaration in the course of a criminal appeal is considered in Chapter 17 below.[77]

---

[68] Section 3(2)(c).

[69] As regards prior subordinate legislation, this result follows from the provisions of s.3(2)(c) read in conjunction with s.3(1). As regards future subordinate legislation, the Minister making the legislation will be acting unlawfully (within the meaning of s.6(1)), and thus *ultra vires*, if he enacts a provision which is incompatible with a Convention right, unless he is required to do so by the terms of primary legislation which cannot be interpreted in any other way. Note that in *R. v. Lord Chancellor ex parte Witham* [1998] 2 W.L.R. 849 Laws L.J. adopted a similar approach to the common law right of access to court, holding invalid so much of the Supreme Court Fees (Amendment) Order 1996 as withdrew exemption from court fees for those on income support, and also withdrew the discretion to remit fees in cases of exceptional hardship.

[70] Within the meaning of s.3(1): see para. 3–31 above.

[71] Section 4(5) defines the courts with power to make a declaration of incompatibility. They are the House of Lords, the Privy Council, the Courts-Martial Appeal Court, the Court of Appeal, the High Court and, in Scotland, the High Court of Justiciary (sitting otherwise than as a trial court) and the Court of Session.

[72] The power is discretionary, but the courts will normally be expected to make such an order where legislation has been found to be incompatible, and it has not been possible to remove the incompatibility by construction. The Lord Chancellor suggested during the debates that the only circumstances in which a court might, in the exercise of its discretion, decline to make such a declaration would be where there is an alternative statutory appeal which the court considers ought to be utilised, or where there is another procedure which the court thinks an applicant should exhaust before a declaration is granted: See H.L. Debs, col. 546 (November 18, 1997).

[73] Section 4(3) and (4).

[74] See para. 3–38 below.

[75] Section 4(6)(a).

[76] Section 4(6)(b).

[77] At paras 17–38 to 17–43. Under paragraph 2(aa) of the Criminal Appeal Rules 1968 (as amended) an appellant in criminal proceedings must include within his grounds of appeal written notice of any application for a declaration of incompatibility or of any issue which may lead the court to make such a declaration.

During the Parliamentary debates, an amendment was tabled which would have **3–36** enabled courts to grant a declaration of incompatibility in cases where the applicant's complaint related to the *absence* of legislation governing an interference with a Convention right.[78] The Lord Chancellor explained that such a provision was unnecessary since the individual concerned would be able to invoke his Convention rights in accordance with section 7 of the Act. The absence of legislation would mean that there was no legislative warrant for the interference, and "there is nothing to stop the courts providing a remedy" in such a case.[79]

V. *Right of Crown to intervene*

Where a court is considering whether to make a declaration of incompatibility, **3–37** the Crown is entitled to notice in accordance with the Rules of Court.[80] Once notified, the relevant Minister,[81] or a person nominated by him, is entitled as of right to be joined as a party to the proceedings.[82] This right can be exercised by giving notice of an intention to be joined,[83] at any stage of the proceedings.[84] In criminal cases[85] a Minister who has been joined as a party may, with leave,[86] appeal to the House of Lords against any declaration of incompatibility made in the proceedings.[87] The interests of the Crown will not always be adequately represented by the prosecution in a criminal case, and in certain circumstances it will be appropriate for the responsible Minister to be separately represented.[88]

VI. *Remedial orders*

The government has indicated that a declaration of incompatibility will "almost **3–38** certainly" prompt legislative change,[89] either by way of amending primary

---

[78] H.L. Debs, cols 814–815 (November 24, 1997).

[79] These comments relate to those situations in which an interference with a Convention right is required under the Strasbourg jurisprudence to be authorised by statute (see, for example, *Khan v. United Kingdom, The Times*, May 23, 2000). In such a situation the courts would be able to provide a remedy because the complaint would be directed to the interference itself, rather than to the failure to legislate as such. Note, however, that a challenge directed to the legislature or the executive arising out of a failure to legislate is expressly excluded from the duty to act compatibly with Convention rights: s.6(6).

[80] Section 5(1). As to the procedure to be followed for giving notice to the relevant Minister see the Criminal Appeal (Amendment) Rules 2000 (S.I. 2000 No. 2056).

[81] In Scotland, the right to intervene applies to a member of the Scottish Executive (s.5(1)(b)). In Northern Ireland it applied to a Northern Ireland Minister (s.5(1)(c)), or a Northern Ireland department (s.5(1)(d)).

[82] Section 5(2).

[83] Section 5(2).

[84] Section 5(3).

[85] There is no need for specific provision in civil proceedings since any person joined as a party to civil proceedings is entitled to exercise rights of appeal open to any other party.

[86] "Leave" means leave granted by the court making the declaration of incompatibility or by the House of Lords: s.5(5).

[87] Section 5(4). The scope of any such appeal is confined to the grant of a declaration of incompatibility. Note: This provision does not apply to Scotland since there is no right of appeal to the House of Lords in relation to criminal proceedings in Scotland.

[88] *R. v. A* [2001] 2 W.L.R. 1546 (HL). The procedural issue is reported as *R. v. A (Joinder of Appropriate Minister)* [2001] 1 W.L.R. 789.

[89] *Rights Brought Home* Cmnd. 3782, (1997), para. 2.9. See also the remarks of the Lord Chancellor during debate: H.L. Debs, col. 1230 (November 3, 1997).

legislation, or under section 10 of the Act.[90] Section 10 confers a power on the relevant Minister of the Crown to amend incompatible primary legislation by remedial order. This power arises in three situations[91]:

(i) Where a provision of primary legislation has been the subject of a declaration of incompatibility under section 4, and all parties to the proceedings have either exercised or abandoned any rights of appeal, or the time limit for appealing has expired[92];

(ii) Where it appears to a Minister of the Crown or Her Majesty in Council[93] that, having regard to a finding of the European Court of Human Rights made after October 2, 2000, in proceedings against the United Kingdom, a provision of legislation is incompatible with an existing obligation under the Convention[94];

(iii) In the case of incompatible subordinate legislation, where a Minister of the Crown considers that it is necessary to amend the parent legislation.[95]

3–39   In each case, if the Minister considers that there are "compelling reasons" for doing so,[96] he may by order make such amendments to the primary legislation as he considers necessary to remove the incompatibility.[97] A remedial order may contain "such incidental, supplemental, consequential or transitional provision" as the Minister "considers appropriate"[98]; may be made retrospective[99]; may make provision for the delegation of specific functions[1]; and may make different provision for different cases.[2] The relevant Minister must lay before Parliament a document containing a draft of the proposed order, an account of the incompatibility it is seeking to remove,[3] and an explanation for proceeding under section 10, rather than by way of primary legislation.[4] He must then allow a period of 60 days to enable representations[5] to be made.[6] Following this consultation period,

---

[90] Note, however, that a failure to introduce legislation or to make a remedial order following a declaration of incompatibility cannot be challenged in the courts: see s.6(6).
[91] Section 10 also applies where a provision of subordinate legislation has been quashed, or declared invalid, by reason of its incompatibility with Convention rights, and the relevant Minister intends to proceed under the power conferred to take remedial action in urgent cases under Sched. 2 para. 2(b).
[92] Section 10(1)(a).
[93] If the legislation in question is an Order in Council, the power to make a remedial order is exerciseable by Her Majesty in Council: s.10(5).
[94] Section 10(1)(b).
[95] Section 10(3).
[96] If there are no such compelling reasons, the Minister will be expected to proceed by way of amending primary legislation.
[97] Section 10(2).
[98] Sched. 2, para. 1(1)(a).
[99] Sched. 2, para. 1(1)(b). Note, however, that in order to avoid a violation of Art. 7 of the Convention, no person is to be guilty of an offence solely as a result of the retrospective effect of a remedial order: Sched. 2, para. 1(4).
[1] Sched. 2, para 1(1)(c).
[2] Sched. 2, para 1(1)(d).
[3] As to the information required, see Sched. 2, para. 5.
[4] Sched. 2, para. 3(1). As to the information required, see Sched. 2, para. 5.
[5] "Representations" means representations about a remedial order (or proposed remedial order) made to the person making (or proposing to make) it and includes any relevant Parliamentary report or resolution: Sched. 2, para. 5.
[6] Sched. 2, para. 3(1)(b).

the draft must be formally laid before Parliament, together with a summary of any representations the Minister has received, and any amendments he has made in the light of those representations.[7] After a further interval of 60 days, the draft must be put to both Houses of Parliament for approval by affirmative resolution.[8] In urgent cases, the Minister may make a remedial order without the approval of Parliament.[9] In that event, the order must be laid before Parliament after it has been made,[10] together with the required information,[11] and must be approved within 120 days of the day on which it was made.[12] If, during the period of 60 days after the making of the order, representations have been made to the Minister, a summary of those representations must be laid before Parliament, together with the details of any changes the Minister considers appropriate in the light of the representations received.[13]

G. Claims and Remedies

The procedural philosophy behind the Human Rights Act is that litigants should,   **3–40** wherever possible, use existing claims and remedies for enforcing Convention rights in the national courts. The White Paper *Rights Brought Home* explained that Convention arguments would normally arise in proceedings taken against individuals or already open to them, but that if none were available, it would be possible for a complainant to bring proceedings on Convention grounds alone.[14] This is reflected in sections 7 to 9 of the Act.

I. *Free-standing claims*

By section 7(1)(a) a person who claims that a public authority[15] has acted (or   **3–41** proposes to act) in a way which is made unlawful by section 6[16] may bring proceedings against that authority[17] in the appropriate court or tribunal.[18] This ensures that an individual is able to bring a claim alleging breach of a Convention right where there is no existing remedy available which is capable of adaptation. The expression "appropriate court or tribunal" is defined by the Civil Procedure (Amendment No. 4) Rules 2000 (S.I. 2000 No. 2092),[18a] which make amendments to the CPR. CPR Rule 7.11 provides that a claim under section 7(1)(a) may

---

[7] Sched. 2, paras 2(a) and 3(2).
[8] Sched. 2, para. 2(a).
[9] Sched. 2, para. 2(b).
[10] Sched. 2, para. 4(1).
[11] As to the information required, see Sched. 2, para. 5.
[12] Sched. 2, para. 4(4). If the order has not been so approved, it ceases to have effect. Para. 4(4) makes it clear, however, that this does not affect the lawfulness of anything previously done under the order.
[13] Sched. 2, para. 4(2). If, in the light of representations, the Minister considers it appropriate to make changes to the order, then he must make a further order and lay it before Parliament in the ordinary way: Sched. 2, para. 4(3).
[14] *Rights Brought Home*, Cmnd. 3782, (1997), para. 2.3.
[15] As to the meaning of "public authority", see s.6(3) and paras 3–22 to 3–30 above.
[16] See para. 3–22 above.
[17] The term "proceedings against a public authority" in s.7(1)(a) includes a counter-claim or similar proceeding: s.7(2).
[18] Section 7(1)(a).
[18a] Made under s.7(2), (9) and (10).

be brought either in the County Court or in the High Court (subject to normal jurisdictional limits) unless it is a claim in respect of a judicial act, in which case it must be commenced in the High Court.

Proceedings under section 7(1)(a) must be brought within one year of the act complained of,[19] unless the court, in its discretion, considers that a longer period would be equitable, having regard to all the circumstances.[20] This is, however, subject to any rule imposing a stricter time limit in relation to the procedure in question.[21] Where, therefore, the proceedings are brought by way of judicial review, the time limit remains three months.

II. *Reliance on Convention rights*

3–42   By section 7(1)(b) a person who claims that a public authority[22] has acted (or proposes to act) in a way which is made unlawful by section 6[23] may rely on a Convention right in any legal proceedings. The term "legal proceedings" includes proceedings brought by or at the instigation of a public authority,[24] and an appeal against the decision of a court or tribunal.[25] The Act adopts a deliberately broad and inclusive definition of "legal proceedings" so as to ensure that Convention arguments can be raised in all litigation, and at every level.[26]

III. *The "victim" requirement*

3–43   An individual may only bring proceedings under section 7(1)(a), or rely on his Convention rights in other proceedings under section 7(1)(b), if he is (or would be) a "victim" of the unlawful act[27] for the purposes of Article 34 of the Convention.[28] Under Article 34 the European Court of Human Rights has held that an applicant must have been directly affected by the measure in question.[29] However, this concept includes cases where the mere existence of a law is alleged to interfere with the exercise of a Convention right[30]; where there is a real threat of a future violation[31]; or where the victim is "indirect".[32] Special rules apply to cases involving secret surveillance, where it may be impossible for the individual to prove that the surveillance has occurred.[33]

---

[19] Section 7(5)(a).

[20] Section 7(1)(b).

[21] Section 7(5).

[22] As to the meaning of "public authority", see s.6(3) and paras 3–23 to 3–28 above.

[23] See para. 3–22 above.

[24] Section 7(6)(a).

[25] Section 7(6)(b). The reference to appeals ensures that Convention arguments can be raised for the first time on appeal against a decision of a court or tribunal where the applicant alleges the decision itself to be incompatible with a Convention right.

[26] This includes a collateral challenge to action taken by a public authority: *Boddington v. British Transport Police* [1998] 2 All E.R. 203. During debates the Home Office Minister Mike O'Brien M.P. confirmed that private prosecutions were included since the definition in s.7(6) was non-exhaustive: H.C. Debs, col. 1057 (June 24, 1998).

[27] "Unlawful act" means an act made unlawful by s.6(1): s.6(6). As to s.6(1) see para. 3–22 above.

[28] Section 7(1), 7(3) and 7(7).

[29] See generally para. 1–88 above.

[30] See para. 1–89 above.

[31] See para. 1–91 above.

[32] See para. 1–94 above

[33] See para. 1–93 above.

If the Convention right is invoked in judicial review proceedings, the applicant **3–44** is to be taken to have "sufficient interest" only if he is, or would be, a "victim" of the unlawful act relied on.[34] In recent years the courts have adopted a more liberal approach to the "sufficient interest" test in judicial review proceedings, holding (for example) that responsible public interest organisations have standing to bring representative challenges where they are qualified to do so, and there is no obvious alternative challenger.[35] Although organisations which meet the "sufficient interest" test continue to have standing for the purposes of judicial review generally, they are not entitled to invoke the provisions of the Human Rights Act on behalf of the public (or a section of the public). Such organisations may nevertheless invoke the Act where it is their own rights as an organisation (or those of their members collectively) which are at stake.[36] And as the Lord Chancellor explained during the Parliamentary debates, they will have an important role to play in assisting and providing representation for individual victims, and in filing *amicus curiae* briefs.[37] Even before the Act was passed the House of Lords had permitted public interest organisations to file *amicus* briefs in a number of important criminal cases.[38] Moreover, since the Act preserves existing human rights,[39] such organisations may continue to invoke the Convention in accordance with the common law principles applicable before the Act came into force.[40]

IV. *Remedies*

In the context of criminal proceedings, section 7(1)(a) may be relevant where the **3–45** Magistrates Court or Crown Court has found that a public authority acted incompatibly with the defendant's Convention rights, and he then seeks damages for the breach. In this situation, the individual will be expected to pursue separate civil proceedings.[41] Usually, however the vehicle for invoking Convention rights in criminal proceedings is likely to be section 7(1)(b). This raises the question of the remedies which a criminal court is able to grant.

Section 8(1) provides that where a court finds that a public authority has acted (or **3–46** proposes to act) in a manner which is made unlawful by section 6, it may grant such relief or remedy, or make such order, *within its powers*, as it considers just and appropriate. The White Paper *Rights Brought Home* suggested that the

---

[34] Section 7(3). Similar provision is made in relation to petitions for judicial review in Scotland by s.7(4).
[35] See for example *R. v. Secretary of State for Social Services ex parte CPAG* [1990] 2 Q.B. 540; *R. v. Secretary of State for the Environment ex parte EOC* [1994] 2 W.L.R. 409; *R. v. Her Majesty's Inspectorate of Pollution ex parte Greenpeace (No.2)* [1994] 4 All E.R. 329; *R. v. Secretary of State for Foreign Affairs ex parte World Development Movement* [1995] 1 W.L.R. 386; *R. v. Secretary of State for Social Security ex parte JCWI* [1997] 1 W.L.R. 275.
[36] See, for example, *Christians Against Racism and Fascism v. United Kingdom* (1980) 21 D.R. 138; *Open Door Counselling and Dublin Well Woman v. Ireland* (1993) 15 E.H.R.R. 244.
[37] H.L. Debs, col. 810 (February 5, 1998). For an example see the intervention by Justice in *Brown v. Stott* [2000] 2 W.L.R. 211.
[38] *R. v. Sultan Khan* [1997] A.C. 558 (Liberty); *R. v. Secretary of State for the Home Department ex parte Venables and Thompson* [1998] A.C. 407 (Justice); *R. v. Bow Street Stipendiary Magistrate ex parte Pinochet Ugarte* [1999] 2 W.L.R. 1015 (Amnesty and others).
[39] See s.11 and para. 3–21 above.
[40] See para. 3–21 above.
[41] See para. 3–48 below.

remedy appropriate in any case would depend "on a proper balance being struck between the rights of the individual and the public interest".[42] In exercising this jurisdiction, the courts may have regard to the obligation under Article 13 of the Convention to provide an effective remedy (notwithstanding that Article 13 is omitted from the list of incorporated rights). This is because the Act itself is intended to give effect to the United Kingdom's obligations under Article 13, and because the courts are required by section 2(1) to have regard to Convention jurisprudence under Article 13.[43] As the Lord Chancellor explained during the Parliamentary debates it is difficult to "conceive of any state of affairs in which an English court, having held an act to be unlawful because of its infringement of a Convention right, would under [section] 8(1) be disabled from giving an effective remedy".[44-45]

3–47 In criminal proceedings the courts have power under section 8 to quash an indictment, to stay the proceedings as an abuse of process, to allow a submission of no case to answer, to exclude evidence, or even to reflect the breach in the sentence which is imposed. The Court of Appeal (Criminal Division) has power to quash a conviction where the offence itself breaches a Convention right, or where there has been a breach of Article 6 in the course of the trial.[46]

V. *Damages*

3–48 Damages may only be awarded by a court which has power to award damages, or to order the payment of compensation, in civil proceedings.[47] Damages may not therefore be awarded by a criminal court.[48]

3–49 An award of damages is only to be made where it necessary to afford "just satisfaction" to the person in whose favour it is made.[49] In determining whether a monetary award is necessary, the court must have regard to all the circumstances including any other remedy or relief granted, or order made, in relation to the act in question (by that or any other court),[50] and the consequences of any decision (of that or any other court) in respect of that act.[51] If, therefore, a criminal court has excluded evidence or stayed criminal proceedings, or the Court of Appeal has quashed the applicant's conviction, this will be highly

---

[42] *Rights Brought Home*, Cmnd. 3782, (1997), para. 2.6.
[43] See para. 3–11 above.
[44-45] H.L. Debs, col. 479 (November 18, 1997). See also the approach of the New Zealand Court of Appeal in *Simpson v. Attorney-General* [1994] 3 N.Z.L.R. 667.
[46] As to the difference between the "fairness" of proceedings, and the "safety" of a conviction for the purposes of the Criminal Appeal Act 1968, as amended, see *Condron and Condron v. United Kingdom The Times*, May 9, 2000. This issue is considered in detail in Chapter 17 below.
[47] Section 8(2).
[48] During debates the Lord Chancellor explained that
  "it is not the Bill's aim that, for example, the Crown Court should be able to make an award of damages where it finds, during the course of a trial, that a violation of a person's Convention rights has occurred. We believe that it is appropriate for an individual who considers that his rights have been infringed in such a case to pursue any matter of damages through the civil courts where this type of issue is normally dealt with": H.L. Debs, col. 855 (November 24, 1997).
[49] Section 8(3).
[50] Section 8(3)(a).
[51] Section 8(3)(b).

material in determining whether and to what extent an award of damages is necessary.

In determining whether to make an award of damages against a public author- **3-50** ity,[52] and in fixing the amount of any such award, the court should take into account the principles[53] applied by the European Court of Human Rights under Article 41 of the Convention.[54] The government's intention was that "people will be able to receive compensation from a domestic court equivalent to what they would have received in Strasbourg".[55]

VI. *Judicial acts*

Where the complaint concerns a judicial act,[56] proceedings must be brought by **3-51** way of appeal[57] or judicial review,[58] or in such other forum as may be prescribed by rules.[59] The amendments to the CPR provide that a claim under section 7(1)(a) in respect of a judicial act must be commenced in the High Court.

The Act does not affect any rule of law which prevents a court from being subject **3-52** to judicial review.[60] Accordingly, the prohibition on judicial review of a matter arising out of trial on indictment, which is reflected in section 29(3) of the Supreme Court Act 1981,[61] continues to apply. Moreover, in the absence of bad faith or other exceptional circumstances, there is a strong presumption against judicial review of a decision to prosecute in criminal proceedings.[62]

Damages may not be awarded in respect of a judicial act done in good faith[63] **3-53** save to the extent required by Article 5(5) of the Convention.[64] Article 5(5) provides that any person whose arrest or detention was unlawful must have an

---

[52] A public authority against which damages are awarded is to be treated for the purposes of the Civil Liability (Contribution) Act 1978 as liable in respect of damage suffered by the person to whom the award is made: s.8(5)(b). Accordingly, the normal principles of contribution apply to persons who are jointly and severally liable. Similar provision is made for Scotland by s.8(5)(a).

[53] The paucity of reasoning in the Court's rulings under Art. 41 makes it difficult to identify a coherent set of principles capable of being applied by the national courts.

[54] Section 8(4).

[55] *Rights Brought Home*, Cmnd. 3782, (1997), para. 2.6. See also H.L. Debs, col. 1232 (November 3, 1997).

[56] Section 9(5) provides that term "judicial act" means a judicial act of a court and includes an act done on the instructions, or on behalf, of a judge; and the term "judge" includes a member of a tribunal, a justice of the peace and a clerk or other officer entitled to exercise the jurisdiction of a court.

[57] Section 9(1)(a).

[58] Section 9(1)(b).

[59] Section 9(1)(c).

[60] Section 9(2).

[61] As to the principles governing the application of s.29(3) see *In re Smalley* [1985] A.C. 622 (H.L.); *In re Sampson* [1987] 1 W.L.R. 194 (H.L.); *In re Ashton* [1994] 1 A.C. 9 (H.L.); *R. v. Manchester Crown Court ex parte DPP* [1993] 1 W.L.R. 1524 (H.L.).

[62] *R. v. DPP ex parte Kebilene and ors* [1999] 3 W.L.R. 972 (H.L.).

[63] Where a judicial act is done in bad faith, s.9(3) does not apply. As to the immunity of judges see *Sirros v. Moore* [1975] 1 Q.B. 118. As to the liability of magistrates for acts in the performance of their judicial functions, see Justices of the Peace Act 1997 ss.51 and 52 (a magistrate may is only liable for acts done in excess of jurisdiction and in bad faith).

[64] Section 9(3).

enforceable right to compensation. Where a person has been imprisoned unlawfully by order of a court,[65] the United Kingdom is thus obliged under the Convention to afford a right to compensation, irrespective of fault.[66] In order to meet this obligation, whilst preserving the immunity of judges and magistrates from personal liability for judicial acts, any such award is to be made against the Crown.[67] Under CPR Rule 19.4A(3) a claim for damages in respect of a judicial act must be set out in the statement of case or appeal notice. An award of damages in respect of a judicial act may only be made after the "appropriate person", if not already a party, has been joined.[68] The Lord Chancellor, as the "appropriate person" will be notified of the claim when it is made, and has 21 days (or such other period as the Court directs) in which to indicate whether he wishes to be joined at the outset, either to contest the substance of the claim, or to make representations on the quantum of damages.[69] Thereafter, he may be joined by the court at any time prior to the making of the award.[70] Where a claim is made under section 7 of the Act in respect of a judicial act which is alleged to have infringed the claimant's rights under Article 5 of the Convention, and that claim is based upon a finding by another court or tribunal that the claimant's Convention rights have been infringed, the court hearing the claim may proceed on the basis of the finding of the first court or tribunal, but is not bound to do so. Instead, it may reach its own conclusion in the light of that finding and of the evidence heard in the earlier proceedings.[71]

H. MISCELLANEOUS PROVISIONS

I. Commencement

3–54 A number of the Act's procedural provisions came into force when it received the Royal Assent on November 9, 1998.[72] Section 19, which makes provision for Ministerial statements of compatibility, came into force on November 24, 1998.[73] The remaining provisions came into force on October 2, 2000.[74]

II. Costs

3–55 The presumption that costs follow the event may not always be appropriate in litigation under the Human Rights Act. The Privy Council has recognised that

---

[65] As to the circumstances in which an error by a Magistrates Court will deprive the court of its jurisdiction to imprison see *Re McC* [1985] A.C. 528 (H.L.); *R. v. Manchester City Magistrates Justices ex parte Davies* [1989] Q.B. 631.

[66] As to the application of Art. 5(1) and (5) in these circumstances see *Benham v. United Kingdom* (1996) 22 E.H.R.R. 293; *Poole v. United Kingdom* (1998) Application No. 28190/95; *Johnson v. United Kingdom* (1998) Application No. 28455/95; *Denson v. United Kingdom* (1998) Application No. 25286/94: *Perks and ors v. United Kingdom,* (2000) 30 E.H.R.R. 33.

[67] Section 9(4).

[68] Section 9(4).

[69] CPR Rule 19.4A(3) and (4).

[70] CPR Rule 19.4A(4).

[71] CPR Rule 33.9(1) and (2).

[72] Section 22(1): the provisions concerned were s.18 (appointment of judges to the European Court of Human Rights), s.20 (supplemental provisions and rule-making powers), s.21(5) (abolition of the death penalty in the armed forces) and s.22 (the commencement provisions).

[73] Human Rights Act 1998 (Commencement) Order 1998 S.I. 1998 No. 2882.

[74] The Human Rights Act 1998 (Commencement No. 2) Order 2000 (S.I. 2000 No. 1851).

where the substance of a challenge involves important questions affecting fundamental rights, an award of costs against an unsuccessful applicant may be inappropriate since "*bona fide* resort to rights under the constitution ought not to be discouraged".[75] A similar approach has been taken by the Constitutional Court of South Africa. In *Motsepe v. IRC*[76] Ackerman J. observed that:

> " . . . one should be cautious in awarding costs against litigants who seek to enforce their constitutional rights against the state, particularly where the constitutionality of a statutory provision is attacked, lest such orders have an unduly inhibiting or "chilling" effect on other potential litigants in this category. This cautious approach cannot, however, be allowed to develop into an inflexible rule so that litigants are induced into believing that they are free to challenge the constitutionality of statutory provisions in this court, no matter how spurious the grounds for doing so may be."

III. *The Act does not create criminal offences*

Nothing in the Human Rights Act creates a criminal offence.[77] It does not **3–56** necessarily follow that the Act is irrelevant to the scope of offences which already exist.[78]

---

[75] *Ahnee and ors v. DPP* (March 17, 1999) [1999] 2 A.C. 294.
[76] (1997) (6) B.C.L.R. 692 at 705 para. 30.
[77] Section 7(8).
[78] See, for example, *A v. United Kingdom* (1999) 27 E.H.R.R. 611.

Part Two

CHAPTER 4

THE DEFINITION OF A CRIMINAL CHARGE

A. INTRODUCTION

The most stringent of the Convention's due process guarantees are reserved for **4–01** those charged with a criminal offence. Whilst the right to a fair trial in Article 6(1) applies to civil as well as to criminal proceedings, its requirements are more extensive where the determination of a "criminal charge" is in issue.[1] In addition, there are a number of important due process rights which are expressly confined to criminal defendants: the presumption of innocence in Article 6(2); the "minimum rights" spelt out in Article 6(3); the requirement for legal certainty in the definition of an offence, the principle of restrictive interpretation, and the prohibition on retrospective offences and penalties in Article 7; the right of appeal in Article 2 of Protocol 4; and the prohibition on double jeopardy in Article 4 of that Protocol.[2] In order to determine whether an applicant can rely on any of these rights, it is necessary to have a clear understanding of what constitutes a criminal charge for the purposes of the Convention.[3]

B. CRIMINAL PROCEEDINGS

I. *General Principles*

The Court has held that an autonomous definition of the term "criminal" is **4–02** necessary in order to prevent contracting states from undermining the Convention's due process guarantees by reclassifying an offence as a disciplinary, administrative, regulatory, or civil penalty.[4] Adopting a realistic and substantive approach, the Court will look behind the national classification, and inquire whether a proceeding which involves the determination of an accusation is "by

---

[1] Note, however, that in *Albert and LeCompte v. Belgium* (1983) 5 E.H.R.R. 533 the Court held that where professional disciplinary proceedings have serious consequences for the individual, rights analagous to those set out in Arts 6(2) and 6(3) will be implied into Art. 6(1): see para. 4–32 below.

[2] Although the United Kingdom has not yet ratified Protocol 7, the Government has signalled its intention to sign, ratify, and incorporate Protocol 7 as soon as practicable: *Rights Brought Home*, Cmnd. 3782. (1997) paras 4.15–4.16.

[3] The "criminal charge" jurisprudence also has implications for Art. 5(1): see para. 4–40 below.

[4] For discussion, see Stavros, *The Guarantees for Accused Persons under Art. 6 of the European Convention on Human Rights* (Martinus Nijhoff, 1993), pp 1–39. D.J. Harris, M. O'Boyle and C. Warbrick, *The Law of the European Convention on Human Rights* (Butterworths, 1995), pp 166–173. For the common law perspective on the definition of crime see Glanville Williams *The Definition of Crime* in *Current Legal Problems* (1995) at p. 107; G. Hughes, "The Concept of Crime, An American View" (1959) Crim. L.R. 239 *et seq.*; Seton Pollock, "The distinguishing Mark of Crime" (1929) 22 M.L.R. 4895. For the origins of the true crime/regulatory distinction in English law, see *Sherras v. DeRutzen* [1895] 1 Q.B. 918.

its nature 'criminal' from the point of view of the Convention", or has exposed the person concerned to a sanction which "belongs in general to the 'criminal' sphere".[5] In the leading case of *Engel v. Netherlands*[6] the Court explained its reasoning as follows:

> "The Convention without any doubt allows the States, in the performance of their function as the guardians of the public interest, to maintain or establish a disctinction between criminal law and disciplinary law, and to draw the dividing line, but only subject to certain conditions . . . If the Contracting States were able, at their discretion, to classify an offence as disciplinary instead of criminal, or to prosecute the author of a 'mixed' offence on the disciplinary rather than on the criminal plane, the operation of the fundamental clauses of Articles 6 and 7 would be subordinated to their sovereign will. A latitude extending thus far might lead to results incompatible with the purpose and object of the Convention. The Court thus has jurisdiction . . . to satisfy itself that the disciplinary does not improperly encroach upon the criminal".

The Court has since emphasised that there is nothing to prevent a state from decriminalising certain conduct, and prosecuting it instead as an administrative or regulatory offence, provided that in doing so it does not deprive the accused of the due process rights guaranteed by the Convention.[7]

II. *The Engel Criteria*

4–03   In *Engel* the Court established three criteria for determining whether proceedings are "criminal" from the point of view of the Convention, namely (a) the domestic classification, (b) the nature of the offence, and (c) the severity of the potential penalty which the person concerned risks incurring.[8] The Court's subsequent caselaw establishes that these criteria are to be assessed independently and that most importance is to be attached to the third.

4–04   The first criterion—domestic classification—"is of relative weight and serves only as a starting point".[9] If domestic law classifies an offence as criminal, then this will be decisive,[10] even if the penalty imposed is relatively slight.[11] But if the domestic law classifies the offence as civil, disciplinary, or administrative then the Court will look behind the national classification and examine the substantive

---

[5] *Lutz v. Germany* (1988) 10 E.H.R.R. 182 at para. 55; *Garyfallou AEBE v. Greece* (1999) 28 E.H.R.R. 344 at para. 33; *Lauko v. Slovakia* Judgment September 2, 1998 at para. 57.
[6] (1979–80) 1 E.H.R.R. 647 at para. 81.
[7] *Ozturk v. Turkey* (1984) 6 E.H.R.R. 409 at para. 49.
[8] *Engel v. Netherlands* (1979–80) 1 E.H.R.R. 647 at para. 82; *Benham v. United Kingdom* (1996) 22 E.H.R.R. 293 at para. 56; *Garyfallou AEBE v. Greece* (1999) 28 E.H.R.R. 344 at para. 32; *Lauko v. Slovakia* Judgment September 2, 1998 at para. 56.
[9] *Benham v. United Kingdom* (1996) 22 E.H.R.R. 293 at para. 56; *Engel v. Netherlands* (1979–80) 1 E.H.R.R. 647 at para. 82; *Weber v. Switzerland* (1990) 12 E.H.R.R. 508 at para. 31; *Demicoli v. Malta* (1992) 14 E.H.R.R. 47 at para. 33; *Ozturk v. Turkey* (1984) 6 E.H.R.R. 409 at para. 52; *Campbell and Fell v. United Kingdom* (1985) 7 E.H.R.R. 165 at para. 71.
[10] *Engel v. Netherlands* (1979–80) 1 E.H.R.R. 647 at para. 82.
[11] As the Court put it in *Ozturk v. Germany* (1984) 6 E.H.R.R. 409 at para. 54: "The relative lack of seriousness of the penalty at stake cannot divest an offence of its inherently criminal character".

reality of the procedure in question.[12] As the Court said in *Engel*, "the autonomy of the concept of 'criminal' operates, as it were, one way only".[13]

The second criterion—the nature of the offence—"carries more weight".[14] Here, **4–05** the Court will examine whether the legal rule in question is addressed exclusively to a specific group, or is of a generally binding character[15]; whether the proceedings are instituted by a public body with statutory powers of enforcement[16]; whether there is a punitive or deterrent element to the process[17]; whether the imposition of any penalty is dependent upon a finding of culpability[18]; and how comparable procedures are classified in other Council of Europe member states.[19] The fact that an offence does not give rise to a criminal record may be relevant,[20] but is unlikely to be decisive, since it is usually a reflection of the domestic classification.[21]

The third criterion—the severity of the penalty—will often be decisive, partic- **4–06** ularly if the potential penalties include imprisonment. In *Engel* the Court held that a deprivation of liberty liable to imposed as a punishment is, in general, a penalty that belongs to the "criminal" sphere, unless by its "nature, duration or manner of execution, [it] cannot be appreciably detrimental".[22] Significant finan-

---

[12] See, for example, *Campbell and Fell v. United Kingdom* (1985) 7 E.H.R.R. 165 where the Court defined prison disciplinary proceedings as "criminal" despite settled domestic authority to the effect that they were not a "criminal cause or matter" for the purposes of judicial review and appeal; and *Benham v. United Kingdom* (1996) 22 E.H.R.R. 293 at para. 56 where the same approach was taken in relation to proceedings for commitment to prison for non-payment of the community charge, despite the dicta of Henry J. in *R. v. Highbury Corner Magistrates Court ex parte Watkins* [1992] R.A. 300 to the effect that such proceedings were "plainly legal proceedings other than criminal proceedings".

[13] *Engel v. Netherlands* (1979–80) 1 E.H.R.R. 647 at para. 81.

[14] *Benham v. United Kingdom* (1996) 22 E.H.R.R. 293 at para. 56; *Ozturk v. Germany* (1984) 6 E.H.R.R. 409 at para. 52; *Campbell and Fell v. United Kingdom* (1985) 7 E.H.R.R. 165 at para. 71.

[15] See, for example *Bendenoun v. France* (1994) 18 E.H.R.R. 54 at para. 47; *Weber v. Switzerland* (1990) 12 E.H.R.R. 508 at para. 33; *Demicoli v. Malta* (1992) 14 E.H.R.R. 47 at para. 32; In *Benham v. United Kingdom* (1996) 22 E.H.R.R. 293 at para. 56 the Court attached importance to the fact that the obligation to pay the Community Charge, and the procedure for its enforcement, was of general application to all citizens. Similarly in *Campbell and Fell v. United Kingdom* (1985) 7 E.H.R.R. 165 at para. 71 the Court noted that the illegality of some acts which constituted offences against prison discipline "may not turn on the fact that they were committed in prison; certain conduct which constitutes an offence under the Rules may also amount to an offence under the criminal law".

[16] See *Benham v. United Kingdom* (1996) 22 E.H.R.R. 293 at para. 56.

[17] *Ozturk v. Germany* (1984) 6 E.H.R.R. 409 at para. 53; *Bendenoun v. France* (1994) 18 E.H.R.R. 54 at para. 47; *Benham v. United Kingdom* (1996) 22 E.H.R.R. 293 at para. 56.

[18] *Benham v. United Kingdom* (1996) 22 E.H.R.R. 293 at para. 56.

[19] *Ozturk v. Germany* (1984) 6 E.H.R.R. 409 at para. 53.

[20] *Ravnsborg v. Sweden* (1994) 18 E.H.R.R. 38.

[21] *Benham v. United Kingdom* (1996) 22 E.H.R.R. 293; *Campbell and Fell v. United Kingdom* (1985) 7 E.H.R.R. 165; *Lauko v. Slovakia* Judgment September 2, 1998. *Cf. Ravnsborg v. Sweden* (1994) 18 E.H.R.R. 38; and *Pierre-Bloch v. France* (1998) 26 E.H.R.R. 202 where the fact that a finding of guilt was not recorded as a criminal conviction was held to confirm the Court's view that the proceedings were not criminal in character.

[22] *Engel v. Netherlands* (1979–80) 1 E.H.R.R. 647 at para. 82; See also *Benham v. United Kingdom* (1996) 22 E.H.R.R. 293 (Op. Comm) at para. 67, where the Commission noted the Magistrates' power to imprison a person for up to 30 days for non-payment of the community charge, and said that "this alone would be sufficiently important to warrant classifying the 'offence' with which the applicant was charged as a criminal one under the Convention".

cial penalties may be sufficient, particularly if they are enforceable by imprisonment in default.[23] Even a minor financial penalty will suffice where it has a clearly deterrent and punitive purpose.[24] In each case, it is the potential penalty, rather than the actual penalty imposed which is decisive.[25]

4–07   The Court has emphasised in a number of cases that the second and third criteria are alternative, and not necessarily cumulative.[26] For proceedings to be defined as 'criminal' it suffices *either* that the offence in question is 'criminal' in nature *or* that the penalty belongs to the 'criminal sphere'.[27] A cumulative approach may, however, be adopted where a separate analysis of the criteria does not make it possible to reach a clear conclusion as to the existence of a criminal charge.[28]

III. *"Administrative" offences*

4–08   A number of the member states of the Council of Europe have maintained a discrete category of "administrative" offences, which are subject to a separate enforcement regime, falling outside the ordinary criminal justice system. The leading case in this field is *Ozturk v. Germany*[29] which involved the imposition of a fine for a minor road traffic offence. The offence in question had been decriminalised, and the power to impose a fine transferred to the administrative authorities. The first of the *Engel* criteria thus supported the government's argument that the criminal guarantees of Article 6 were inapplicable. However, the Court considered that the offence was criminal in nature.[30] Offences which give rise to deterrent penalties, typically including a fine or imprisonment, would usually come within the ambit of the criminal law. The Court noted that in the vast majority of contracting states, conduct of the kind alleged against the

---

[23] *Bendenoun v. France* (1994) 18 E.H.R.R. 54 at para. 47. But this is not necessarily the case: *Ravnsborg v. Sweden* (1994) 18 E.H.R.R. 38. Note also that in *Welch v. United Kingdom* (1995) 20 E.H.R.R. 247 a confiscation order under the Drug Trafficking Offences Act 1985 was held to be a "criminal penalty" for the purposes of Art. 7, partly because it was enforceable by imprisonment in default.

[24] *Schmautzer v. Austria* (1995) 21 E.H.R.R. 511; *Pfarrmeier v. Austria* (1996) 22 E.H.R.R. 175; *Umlauft v. Austria* (1996) 22 E.H.R.R. 76; *Lauko v. Slovakia* Judgment September 2, 1998.

[25] See *Engel v. Netherlands* (1979–80) 1 E.H.R.R. 647 para. 85 where the Court emphasised that "the final outcome of the appeal cannot diminish the importance of what was initially at stake"; and *Demicoli v. Malta* (1992) 14 E.H.R.R. 47 at para. 34 where the Court considered that it was the potential rather than the actual penalty which determined the importance of what was at stake for the accused.

[26] See, for example, *Lutz v. Germany* (1987) 10 E.H.R.R. 182 at para. 55; *Garyfallou AEBE v. Greece* (1999) 28 E.H.R.R. 344 at para. 33.

[27] Thus, where an offence is plainly criminal in character, the relative lack of seriousness of the penalty actually imposed cannot deprive it of its inherently criminal character: *Ozturk v. Germany* (1984) 6 E.H.R.R. 409 at para. 54; *Lutz v. Germany* (1987) 10 E.H.R.R. 182 at para. 55; *Lauko v. Slovakia* Judgment September 2, 1998 at para. 57. Equally, the nature and severity of the penalty can be sufficient in itself to define an offence as criminal: *Engel v. Netherlands* (1979–80) 1 E.H.R.R. 647 paras 82–85; *Benham v. United Kingdom* (1996) 22 E.H.R.R. 293 (Op. Comm) at para. 67; *Demicoli v. Malta* (1992) 14 E.H.R.R. 47 at para. 34.

[28] *Bendenoun v. France* (1994) 18 E.H.R.R. 54 para. 47; *Garyfallou AEBE v. Greece* (1999) 28 E.H.R.R. 344 at para. 34; *Lauko v. Slovakia* Judgment September 2, 1998 at para. 57. See also *Campbell and Fell v. United Kingdom* (1985) 7 E.H.R.R. 165 at para. 73.

[29] (1984) 6 E.H.R.R. 409.

[30] Para. 53.

applicant would be treated as an ordinary criminal offence. Although the domestic legislation undoubtedly had the object of decriminalisation, its principal effect was to alter the procedural rules and the applicable penalties. The essence of the offence itself had "undergone no change in content". It was a rule of law directed towards all road users proscribing certain conduct and imposing a sanction for its breach. The penalty was intended to be punitive and deterrent in its effect. In the Court's view the general character of the rule, and the purpose of the penalty were sufficient to show that the offence was, in terms of Article 6 of the Convention, criminal in nature. The fact that it was of a minor character, and was unlikely to involve damage to the accused's reputation was irrelevent, since there was "nothing to suggest that the criminal offence referred to in the Convention necessarily implies a certain degree of seriousness."[31] The "relative lack of seriousness of the penalty at stake" could not, in the Court's view "divest an offence of its inherently criminal character". The Court therefore found it unnecessary to apply the third of the *Engel* criteria.

The substantive right at issue in *Ozturk* was the guarantee of free interpretation 4–09 in Article 6(3)(e). In *Lutz v. Germany*,[32] however, the Court reached a similar conclusion in relation to the presumption of innocence in Article 6(2). *Lutz* concerned a regulatory road traffic offence punishable by a fine and disqualification from driving for a period up the three months. The proceedings against the applicant had been discontinued, but he had been refused his costs on the ground that the acquittal was technical in character. The Court held that since the proceedings were, in substance, criminal, he was entitled to invoke the protection of Article 6(2).[33]

The Court has taken a similar approach in relation to minor motoring offences 4–10 under Austrian and French administrative law.[34] In *Schmautzer v. Austria*,[35] the applicant was stopped by police for failing to wear a seat-belt when driving. He received an order from the local police authority, obliging him to pay a fine. Under the relevant legislation there was a right to appeal, but no right to an adversarial trial. The European Court held that although in Austrian law the procedure fell entirely within the administrative sphere, it should be treated as criminal for the purposes of the Convention. Austrian law referred ambiguously to "administrative *offences*", and the fine imposed on the applicant was accompanied by an order for his committal to prison in the event of his defaulting on payment.[36] In *Gradinger v. Austria*[37] the Court applied the same autonomous approach to the definition of a criminal offence in Article 4 of Protocol 7 (the prohibition on double jeopardy). This was despite the fact that Austria had lodged a reservation when it ratified Protocol 7, with the specific object of

---

[31] Para. 53.
[32] (1987) 10 E.H.R.R. 182.
[33] On the facts, however, the Court found no breach.
[34] *Schmautzer v. Austria* (1995) 21 E.H.R.R. 511; *Pfarrmeier v. Austria* (1996) 22 E.H.R.R. 175; *Umlauft v. Austria* (1996) 22 E.H.R.R. 76.
[35] (1995) 21 E.H.R.R. 511.
[36] *ibid.*, at para. 28.
[37] Judgment October 23, 1995; See also *Olivera v. Switzerland* (1999) 28 E.H.R.R. 289 where the Court assumed the applicability of Art. 4 of Protocol 7 in respect of a minor motoring offence prosecuted administratively.

preserving the administrative/criminal distinction.[38] A similar result was reached in *Malige v. France*,[39] a case concerning the administrative imposition of penalty points on the applicant's driving licence for exceeding the speed limit. Since the sanction could result in the loss of the applicant's driving licence, it had a deterrent and punitive purpose sufficient to identify it as a criminal charge.

4–11   In *Lauko v. Slovakia*,[40] the applicant was fined by a local admistrative office for a "minor offence" of causing a nuisance. He complained to the Slovakian Constitutional Court that there had been no judicial hearing of the allegation, but his complaint was dismissed on the ground that the offence was insufficiently serious to justify examination by a court. The European Court held that the proceedings were criminal in nature because of the generally applicable character of the legal rule in issue, and because of the punitive purpose behind the fine imposed. Reiterating that the second and third of the *Engel* criteria were to be independently assessed, so that the relative lack of seriousness of the offence and its penalty could not deprive the charge of its essentially criminal character,[41] the Court held that the applicant was entitled to the benefit of a fair procedure, including the right to appeal the penalty to a judicial tribunal.

IV. *Tax and customs penalties*

4–12   In *Bendenoun v. France*[42] the applicant was prosecuted and fined by the French customs and tax authorities for various customs, exchange control and tax offences. He alleged that the non-disclosure of relevant evidence was in breach of Article 6(1). The Court observed that the contracting states must be free to empower their revenue authorities to impose penal surcharges in cases of bad faith, providing the taxpayer is able to bring any such decision before a court that affords the safeguards of Article 6. It rejected, however, the argument of the French government that such proceedings should be classified as falling outside the criminal sphere for the purposes of the Convention. In the Court's view there were four factors which pointed to the opposite conclusion. First, the offence belonged to a general tax code, applying to all citizens. Secondly, the surcharge was intended primarily as a punishment rather than as a measure of pecuniary compensation. Thirdly, the object of the power to impose a surcharge was both deterrent and punitive. And fourthly, the amount of the surcharge was substantial (a total of FF992,932) and it was enforceable by imprisonment in default. Whilst none of these factors would have been sufficient on its own to categorise the proceedings as criminal, their cumulative effect rendered the criminal guarantees of Article 6 applicable.

4–13   Similarly, in *JJ v. Netherlands*[43] a fiscal penalty was imposed on the applicant for non-payment of income tax. During the course of the applicant's appeal to the Supreme Court, the Advocate General submitted an advisory opinion which was

---

[38] The Court held that the terms of the Austrian reservation were insufficiently specific to meet the requirements of Art. 57: See para. 1–162 above.
[39] Judgment September 23, 1998.
[40] Judgment September 2, 1998.
[41] See para. 54.
[42] (1994) 18 E.H.R.R. 54.
[43] (1999) 28 E.H.R.R. 168.

made available to the Court, but not to the applicant. The European Court held that the penalty constituted a criminal sanction, and accordingly that the applicant was entitled to a fully adversarial procedure which respected his rights under Article 6(1).[44] In view of the fact that he had not been afforded the opportunity to comment on the Advocate General's submissions, the proceedings had violated the applicant's right to a fair trial.[45] In *AP, MP, and TP v. Switzerland*[46] the Court held that measures taken against the heirs of the deceased in respect of the latter's evasion of tax amounted to a criminal charge. This was despite the fact that it was the guilt of the deceased, rather than the heirs, which had to be demonstrated.[47]

The leading case in this field is now *Garyfallou AEBE v. Greece*,[48] in which the **4–14** Greek Deputy Minister of Commerce had used a statutory power to order the applicant to pay a large fine for breaching import regulations. The Court held that the sanctions available were sufficiently severe in themselves to justify classifying the proceedings as criminal, such that it was unnecessary to consider separately whether the offence was criminal in nature:

> "[The company] risked a maximum fine equal to the value of the imported goods, that is, nearly three times the amount actually fined. In the event of non-payment, national law provided for the seizure of the applicant company's assets and, more importantly for the purposes of the Court's examination, the detention of its directors for up to one year."[49]

In *Georgio v. United Kingdom*[50] the Court held that penalty assessments in **4–14a** respect of VAT, and appeals therefrom were criminal proceedings. This principle was applied in *King v. Walden (Inspector of Taxes)*[51] where Jacobs J. held that the system of imposition of penalties for fraudulent or negligent delivery of incorrect income tax returns was likewise criminal for the purposes of Article 6. It was a system designed to punish defaulting taxpayers. The amount of the fine was potentially very substantial and on appeal the burden of proof lay on the Crown. Whilst the proceedings at issue had been protracted there was, on the facts, no breach of the right to trial within a reasonable time. However, it was highly desirable that such appeals should, in future, be distinguished from other determinations and appeals, and should be put on a "fast track". By contrast in *Goldsmith v. Commissioners of Customs and Excise*[52] the Divisional Court held that proceedings for the condemnation of goods forfeited by Customs and Excise under section 139 of and Schedule 3 to the Customs and Excise Management Act 1979 were not criminal proceedings for the purposes of the presumption of innocence in Article 6(2). The relevant provisions of the Excise Duties (Personal Reliefs) Order 1992 (as amended) provided that a certain quantity of specified goods should be presumed to have been imported for private purposes. If the

---

[44] Para. 37.
[45] Paras 41 to 43.
[46] (1998) 26 E.H.R.R. 541.
[47] Proceedings had to be issued against the heirs because under Swiss law the deceased's estate had no legal personality.
[48] (1999) 28 E.H.R.R. 344.
[49] (1999) 28 E.H.R.R. 344 at para. 34.
[50] Application No. 40042/98 [2001] S.T.C. 80.
[51] *The Times*, June 12, 2001.
[52] *The Times*, June 12, 2001.

amount actually imported exceeded that quantity, the Order created a presumption that the goods had been imported for commercial purposes, and placed the burden on the importer to prove otherwise. In the Court's view, the relevant considerations were that the legislation defined the proceedings as civil in nature; none of the usual consequences of a criminal conviction followed from condemnation and forfeiture proceedings; there was no conviction or finding of guilt; and the person concerned was not subject to any other penalty, apart from the forfeiture and loss of the goods. However, even if the proceedings had been classified as criminal, the reverse burden of proof was proportionate, reasonable and justifiable.

V. *Forfeiture orders made against third parties*

4–15   In *Allgemeine Gold- und Silberscheideanstalt v. United Kingdom*[53] the applicant company was the owner of a quantity of Krugerrands which had been illegally imported into the United Kingdom without the company's knowledge. The dealers responsible for the importation were prosecuted by customs and convicted, and the coins were thereafter declared forfeit under the Customs Act 1952. The company brought an unsuccessful action against the Customs and Excise Commissioners for the return of the coins. Before the European Court of Human Rights it was argued that the proceedings were in violation of the presumption of innocence in Article 6(2). The Court rejected the submission:

> "The fact that measures consequential upon an act for which third parties were prosecuted affected in an adverse manner the property rights of AGOSI cannot of itself lead to the conclusion that, during the course of the procedures complained of, any "criminal charge", for the purposes of Article 6 could be considered as having been brought against the applicant company."

4–16   The same reasoning was applied in *Air Canada v. United Kingdom*[54] in which an aircraft was seized following the discovery that it was carrying a consignment of cannabis resin, and returned on payment of a £50,000 penalty. There was no requirement for a judicial finding of guilt or negligence on the part of the company. Although in one sense the procedure was intended to act as a deterrent, by encouraging airline companies to adopt more stringent security measures, it could not be characterised as the determination of a criminal charge. The forfeiture was a process *in rem*; it was consequent on the criminal activity of a third party rather than the applicant company; and there was no threat of criminal proceedings against the company if it chose not to pay the penalty.[55]

VI. *Criminal Confiscation Orders*

4–16a   In *McIntosh v. Lord Advocate*[56] the High Court of Justiciary in Scotland held, by a majority, that the presumption of innocence in Article 6(2) applied to confiscation orders made under the Proceeds of Crime (Scotland) Act 1995 and the Drug

---

[53] (1987) 9 E.H.R.R. 1 at 17–18.
[54] (1995) 20 E.H.R.R. 150.
[55] *cf. Deweer v. Belgium* ((1979–80) 2 E.H.R.R. 439) where the applicant was obliged to pay a sum of money under constraint of the provisional closure of his business in order to avoid criminal proceedings from being brought against him.
[56] Judgment October 13, 2000.

Trafficking Offences Act 1994. In the opinion of the majority, a person against whom confiscation proceedings were brought was "charged with a criminal offence" for the purposes of Article 6. Drug trafficking was, on any view, criminal conduct, even if it was not the subject of a criminal charge in domestic law terms. Accordingly, the imposition of a sanction which is referable to such conduct amounted in substance to the determination of a criminal charge (albeit one which was not proved on the indictment). In *R. v. Benjafield and ors*[57] the same point was argued before the English Court of Appeal in connection with the provisions of the Drug Trafficking Act 1994 and the Criminal Justice Act 1988 (as amended by the Proceeds of Crime Act 1995). Following the approach in *McIntosh* Lord Woolf C.J. accepted that Article 6(2) applied to the confiscation proceedings, notwithstanding that the person against whom the proceedings were brought had, by definition, been convicted of a qualifying criminal offence (or offences). He reasoned that:

"The confiscation order is made in criminal proceedings. It is accepted by all the parties that it is penal. It must therefore be regarded for the purposes of Article 6(1) as at least part of the determination of a criminal charge since there is no other option for which Article 6(1) provides. The fact that a defendant who does not comply with a confiscation order, which may not be based on criminal conduct proved at the trial, may be ordered to serve a substantial consecutive sentence in default underlines that fact. A defendant threatened with consequences of this nature would be expected to be entitled to protection equivalent to that provided by Article 6(2) even if that paragraph did not exist, under Article 6(1)."

Shortly after the Court of Appeal's decision in *Benjafield* the Privy Council heard, and allowed, the prosecutor's appeal in *McIntosh*.[58] Lord Bingham rejected the argument that Article 6(2) applied to confiscation proceedings. Although the sentencing court was making an assumption that the defendant had engaged in other criminal conduct, that person was never formally charged or notified of a criminal charge relating to those offences, and "[t]he process involves no inquiry into the commission of drug trafficking offences". Unless the Strasbourg jurisprudence pointed to different result (which in his view, it did not), Lord Bingham was not prepared to "conclude that a person against whom application for a confiscation order is made is, by virtue of that application, a person charged with a criminal offence". The difficulty with this analysis is that a convicted defendant is undoubtedly a person charged with a criminal offence for the purpose of the other guarantees of Article 6, which are applicable both at the sentencing stage and during any appeal against conviction or sentence. The alternative route to the same conclusion would have been to hold that the presumption of innocence ceases to apply once a person has been proved guilty. This, indeed, seems to be the basis of Lord Hope's approach, when he said that the defence argument:

" . . . overlooks the fact that the procedure on which the prosecutor is now engaged assumes that the accused has already been convicted of the offence with which he was charged . . . Article 6(2) provides that everyone charged with a criminal offence shall be presumed innocent *until proved guilty according to law*. That stage is now passed. The court is concerned only with confiscation of the kind which the law prescribes where the

---

[57] Judgment December 21, 2000.
[58] Judgment February 5, 2001.

conviction is for a drug trafficking offence. The respondent is not now being charged with another offence, nor is he at risk in these proceedings of being sentenced again for the offence of which he has been convicted."

This approach was subsequently followed by the European Court of Human Rights in *Phillips v. United Kingdom.*[58a]

VII. *Competition law penalties*

4–17   In *Societe Stenuit v. France*[59] a fine of FF50,000 imposed by the French Minister of Economy and Finance, following a finding by the Competition Commission, was held to constitute a "criminal charge". It was the potential level of the penalties at stake (5 per cent of annual turnover for a firm, and FF5,000,000 for other contraventions) which identified them as deterrent in their effect. However, in *Krone-Verlag GmbH and Mediaprint Anzeigen GmbH & Co KG v. Austria*[60] the imposition of a fine for failing to obey an injunction, ordered in the course of civil proceedings for unfair competition, was held not to involve a criminal charge. The Commission emphasised that the fine and the injunction were sanctions which belonged to civil procedural law.[61] Although the potential penalties involved were not negligible this was not in itself sufficient to lead to the conclusion that the proceedings were criminal.

VIII. *Regulatory offences*

4–18   It is difficult to generalise about the impact of the "criminal charge" jurisprudence on the regulatory process in the United Kingdom.[62] There are, however, certain conclusions that can be drawn from the Strasbourg caselaw. The conduct of an investigation by inspectors appointed under the Companies Act 1985 does not, in itself, attract the protections of Article 6 since it cannot lead directly to an adjudication, and is not inherently criminal in character.[63] The same principle would presumably apply to an oral examination undertaken by a court under section 236 of the Insolvency Act 1986 or to the investigatory powers of the

---

[58a] Judgment July 5, 2001.

[59] (1992) 14 E.H.R.R. 509. The case was settled before the Court.

[60] (1997) 23 E.H.R.R. CD 152.

[61] The Commission drew an analogy with Art. 5(1) which distinguishes between imprisonment following conviction for a criminal offence (Art. 5(1)(a)) and imprisonment "for non-compliance with a lawful order of a court or in order to secure the fulfilment of any obligation prescribed by law" (Art. 5(1)(b)). Detention ordered by an "enforcement court" for non-compliance with an injunction issued in unfair competition proceedings would, in the Commission's view, fall to be considered under Art. 5(1)(b) rather than Art. 5(1)(a). Based on this somewhat circular reasoning, the Commission therefore concluded that the fine involved the determination of a civil right or obligation rather than a criminal charge.

[62] See generally Paul Davies, *Self-Incrimination, Fair Trials, and the Pursuit of Corporate and Financial Wrongdoing* in *The Impact of the Human Rights Bill on English Law* (Clarendon, 1998); George Staple, *Financial Services and the Human Rights Act* in *The Human Rights Act and the Criminal Justice and Regulatory Process* (Hart, 1999).

[63] *Fayed v. United Kingdom* (1994) 18 E.H.R.R. 393; *Saunders v. United Kingdom* (1997) 23 E.H.R.R. 313.

regulatory authorities. The position is different, of course, if criminal proceedings are brought following such an investigation.[64]

Regulatory offences which can result only in disqualification are unlikely to be **4–19** regarded as criminal. The legal rules in issue are not of general application, and the penalty of disqualification is not one which usually belongs to the criminal law. Thus, in *X v. United Kingdom*,[65] where the Secretary of State had objected to the applicant's appointment as Chief Executive of an insurance company on the ground that he was not a "fit and proper person", as required by the Insurance Companies Act 1982, the Commission assumed that the proceedings were civil in nature. A similar conclusion was reached in *APB v. United Kingdom*[66] in connection with the proceedings of IMRO (the insurance regulator). And in *Wilson v. United Kingdom*[67] the Commission declared inadmissible an application arguing that the exercise of the power to disqualify a director under section 6 of the Company Director's Disqualification Act 1986 rendered proceedings criminal:

> "In the present case, the proceedings were classified as civil in domestic law, the disqualification of directors is a matter which is regulatory rather than criminal, and the penalty is neither a fine nor a prison sentence, but rather a prohibition on acting as a company director without the leave of the court. None of these criteria indicates that the applicant was charged with a 'criminal offence'."

IX. *Enforcement proceedings*

The Commission has held that the imposition of a fine for refusing to obey an **4–20** injunction issued in civil proceedings does not involve a criminal charge.[68] However, proceedings resulting in imprisonment for non-payment of criminal fines or disobedience to a court order to pay local government taxes are likely to be regarded as criminal proceedings. In *Benham v. United Kingdom*,[69] the applicant had been committed to prison for failure to comply with a Magistrates Court order to pay the community charge (a "liability order"). Among the breaches of the Convention he alleged was a failure to provide legal aid for committal proceedings, as required by Article 6(3)(c). In order to bring his case within this provision he needed to establish that he had been "charged with a criminal offence." In English law it was plain that he had not: the proceedings for recovery of unpaid community charge were civil in nature.[70] However, the Court went on to consider the substance of the matter,[71] noting that the obligation to pay the community charge applied to all adults; that the enforcement proceedings were "brought by a public authority"; and that they had "punitive elements", since committal to prison was only possible after a finding of "wilful refusal to pay or culpable neglect". The sanction for disobedience was a "relatively

---

[64] *Saunders v. United Kingdom* (1997) 23 E.H.R.R. 313.
[65] Application No. 28530/95 January 18, 1998.
[66] Application No. 30552/96 January 15, 1998.
[67] (1998) 26 E.H.R.R. CD 195.
[68] *Krone-Verlag GmbH and Mediaprint Anzeigen GmbH & Co KG v. Austria* (1997) 23 E.H.R.R. CD 152.
[69] (1996) 22 E.H.R.R. 293.
[70] See *R. v. Highbury Corner Magistrates Court ex parte Watkins* [1992] R.A. 300 *per* Henry J.
[71] At paras 55–56.

severe" maximum penalty of three months' imprisonment, (and an actual penalty of 30 days). The Court therefore concluded that the applicant had been charged with a criminal offence, and that the failure to provide a system of legal aid was in breach of Article 6(3)(c).

X. *Contempt*

4–21   The Court has not so far been called upon to determine the classification of contempt proceedings in the United Kingdom.[72] In *Weber v. Switzerland*[73] the applicant journalist was fined in summary proceedings for having revealed during a press conference the existence of a confidential judicial investigation to which he was a party. He complained that the summary proceedings[74] had deprived him of the right to an adversarial hearing and, in particular, that he had been afforded no opportunity to challenge the witnesses against him. The fact that the relevant provisions of domestic law used the word *"peine"* (punishment), was considered by the Court to be relevant, but not decisive. As to the nature of the offence, the Court drew a distinction between sanctions for the disclosure of confidential information imposed on judges, lawyers and "those closely associated with the functioning of the courts", on the one hand, and similar sanctions imposed on a party to litigation, on the other. In the former case, the sanction would be classified as a disciplinary measure taken against the person concerned on account of their membership of a particular profession.[75] But parties to litigation "only take part in the proceedings as people subject to the jurisdiction of the courts, and . . . therefore do not come within the disciplinary sphere of the judicial system". Since the relevant offence potentially affected the whole population it was to be regarded as criminal. The potential penalty (a substantial fine, enforceable by imprisonment in default) pointed in the same direction.[76]

4–22   The Court drew a similar distinction between criminal and disciplinary powers in *Demicoli v. Malta*,[77] a case concerning contempt of Parliament. The applicant was the editor of a political magazine which published an article criticising two Members of Parliament for their performance during a debate. The House of Representatives instituted proceedings against him for contempt (categorised as breach of privilege). At the conclusion of the proceedings, the applicant was found guilty and fined, and his appeal to the Constitutional Court was dismissed. Although the domestic classification was uncertain,[78] the Court considered that the offence was criminal in substance. The Court drew a distinction, similar to that drawn in *Weber,* between the powers of a legislature to regulate its own

---

[72] In *Harman v. United Kingdom* (1984) 38 D.R. 53 the Commission declared admissible a complaint that the applicant's conviction for contempt, arising from the unauthorised disclosure of documents which had previously been read in open court, was in breach of Art. 7. The case subsequently settled.
[73] (1990) 12 E.H.R.R. 508.
[74] The proceedings were conducted in writing by the President of the Criminal Cassation Division of the Cantonal Court.
[75] As to wasted costs orders, see para. 4–25 below.
[76] Switzerland had lodged a reservation to Art. 6 designed to exclude any criminal charges "which, in accordance with the Cantonal legislation, are heard before an administrative authority". The Court, however, found the reservation to be invalid since it did not append a statement of the laws concerned, as required by Art. 57 (former Art. 64).
[77] (1992) 14 E.H.R.R. 47.
[78] See para. 32.

proceedings by disciplining Members for breach of privilege within the precincts of the House, on the one hand, and an extended jurisdiction to punish non-members for acts occurring elsewhere, on the other. Whilst the former might be categorised as disciplinary proceedings, the latter were properly regarded as criminal:

> "Mr Demicoli was not a Member of the House. In the Court's view, the proceedings taken against him in the present case for an act of this sort done outside the House are to be distinguished from other types of breach of privilege proceedings which may be said to be disciplinary in nature in that they relate to the internal regulation and orderly functioning of the House. [The relevant Ordinance] potentially affects the whole population since it applies whether the alleged offender is a Member of the House or not, and irrespective of where in Malta the publication of the defamatory libel takes place. For the offence thereby defined the Ordinance provides for the imposition of a penal sanction and not a civil claim for damages. From this point of view, therefore the particular breach of privilege is akin to a criminal offence."[79]

This classification was confirmed by the severity of the potential penalty which **4–23** could have been imposed on the applicant (imprisonment for up to 60 days and a fine of up to 500 Maltese liri). Since the proceedings were criminal for the purpose of the Convention the House of Representatives could not be regarded as an independent judicial tribunal because it was, in effect, judge in its own cause.[80]

In *Ravnsborg v. Sweden*,[81] by contrast, the Court attached little significance to the **4–24** fact that an applicant, who had been prosecuted for contempt of court, was a litigant rather than a professional participant in the judicial process. The applicant had been fined summarily for including in documents submitted to a court certain insulting statements about public officials. There were a number of factors suggesting that the jurisdiction to impose such fines belonged to the criminal law,[82] but there were also a number of factors pointing in the opposite direction.[83] The Court considered that the formal classification under domestic law was "open to different interpretations". In assessing the substantive nature of the offence, the Court attached importance to the fact that the charge applied only to statements made by a person participating in the proceedings. More importantly, it was for the court conducting the proceedings in which the statement was made to examine whether an offence had been committed;

> "In this respect the situation is different from those at issue in the cases of *Weber* and *Demicoli* . . . Rules enabling a court to sanction disorderly conduct in proceedings before it are a common feature of the legal systems of the Contracting States. Such rules and sanctions derive from the indispensable power of a court to ensure the proper and

---

[79] See para. 32.
[80] The two Members allegedly defamed participated in the proceedings throughout.
[81] (1994) 18 E.H.R.R. 38.
[82] The code of judicial procedure referred to the fines as "*straff*" (punishment); the power to impose fines was to be found in a section of the code entitled "On the procedure in criminal cases"; academic opinion regarded the jurisdiction as criminal; and a fine could, in certain circumstances, be converted into a term of imprisonment.
[83] The Court examined the allegation of its own motion, without the involvement of a prosecutor; the relevant provisions dealt only with offences against the good order of court proceedings, whilst improper behaviour of a more serious character was prosecuted as an ordinary criminal offence; and unlike an ordinary criminal fine in Swedish law, the amount was not calculated by reference to the defendant's means.

orderly functioning of its own proceedings. Measures ordered by courts under such rules are more akin to the exercise of disciplinary powers than to the imposition of a punishment for commission of a criminal offence."[84]

As to the severity of the sanction, the Court held that neither the maximum penalty (Skr 1,000), nor the "theoretical possibility" of a term of imprisonment rendered the sanction a criminal one".[85]

XI. *Wasted costs orders*[86]

4–25 In *B v. United Kingdom*[87] the Commission considered that a wasted costs order made against a solicitor in criminal proceedings involved neither the determination of a criminal charge nor the determination of civil rights and obligations. The Commission considered that the proceedings consisted essentially of an investigation of the applicant solicitor's conduct of the defence case, in the exercise of judicial control over the proper administration of justice, with a view to preventing avoidable delay in criminal proceedings. Moreover, the maximum amount of the sanction was the equivalent of the costs thrown away. Accordingly, neither the nature of the proceedings, nor the severity of the potential penalty justified the classification of the proceedings as the determination of a criminal charge.

XII. *Tribunals of Inquiry*

4–26 In *Goodman International and anor. v. Ireland*[88] the applicants were a beef processsing company and its chief executive whose activities were investigated by a Tribunal of Inquiry set up by Parliament to examine alleged illegalities in the industry. The Tribunal had powers to compel witnesses to give evidence, and to make an award of costs against the applicants. In concluding that the proceedings could not involve the determination of a criminal charge, the Commission noted that the Tribunal's functions were limited to inquiring into the allegations, stating its conclusions and, if appropriate, making recommendations for the future. It had not applied the criminal standard of proof,[89] and its power to award costs could not be said to approach the standard required to identify the proceedings as criminal. Moreover, the tribunal had been at pains to emphasise that it would not interfere with the administration of criminal justice and that if there was a danger of this occurring, it would cease its investigation.

XIII. *Offences against military discipline*

4–27 In *Engel v. Netherlands*[90] the Court was concerned with a number of different offences against military discipline. Certain of the offences were specific to the armed forces, whilst others "also lent themselves to criminal proceedings" under

---

[84] Para. 34.
[85] Para. 35.
[86] As to professional disciplinary proceedings, see para. 4–32 below.
[87] (1984) 38 D.R. 213.
[88] (1993) 16 E.H.R.R. CD 26.
[89] There is a certain circularity in the Commission's reasoning on this point.
[90] (1979–80) 1 E.H.R.R. 647.

national law.[91] Applying the first and second of the criteria it had adopted, the Court considered that "the choice of disciplinary action was justified".[92] When it came to analysing the third criterion, however, the Court distinguished between the applicants, according to the level of penalty which the military tribunal had power to impose. The four penalties under consideration were "light arrest",[93] "aggravated arrest",[94] "strict arrest"[95] and "committal to a disciplinary unit".[96] In the Court's view neither "light arrest" not "aggravated arrest" constituted a deprivation of liberty and were insufficiently serious to render the proceedings "criminal" for the purposes of Article 6.[97]

Whilst "strict arrest" could in principle amount to a deprivation of liberty, the maximum period which could have been imposed on the facts was two days. In the context of military discipline, this was held to be "of too short a duration to belong to the 'criminal' law".[98] Three of the applicants, however, were liable to be committed to a disciplinary unit for periods of up to three and four months respectively. In the Court's view the charges against these applicants "did indeed come within the 'criminal' sphere since their aim was the imposition of serious punishments involving deprivation of liberty".[99] The fact that one of these three applicants was eventually sentenced only to 12 days aggravated arrest could not affect the classification of the proceedings against him, since the penalty actually imposed "cannot diminish the importance of what was initially at stake".[1]   **4–28**

The applicant in *Findlay v. United Kingdom*[2] was a soldier who had developed   **4–29** post traumatic stress disorder as a result of his experiences during the Falklands war. After a bout of heavy drinking he held members of his own unit at gunpoint, and threatened to kill himself and others. The applicant pleaded guilty before a court-martial to three charges of common assault (a civilian offence), two charges of conduct to the prejudice of good order and discipline (a purely military offence), and two charges of threatening to kill (a civilian offence). Notwithstanding his medical condition the applicant was sentenced to two years' imprisonment, reduction in rank and dismissal from the army. In the Court's

---

[91] Para. 84.
[92] Para. 84.
[93] See para 61: "Although confined during off duty hours to their dwellings or to military buildings or premises . . . servicemen subjected to [light arrest] are not locked up and continue to perform their duties . . . .They remain, more or less, within the ordinary framework of their army life."
[94] See para. 62: "Aggravated arrest differs from light arrest on one point alone: in off-duty hours soldiers serve the arrest in a specially designated place which they may not leave in order to visit the canteen, cinema or recreation rooms, but they are not kept under lock and key."
[95] See para. 63: "Strict arrest . . . differed from light arrest and aggravated arrest in that non-commissioned officers and ordinary servicemen served it by day and by night locked in a cell and were accordingly excluded from the performance of their normal duties."
[96] See para. 64: "Committal to a disciplinary unit . . . represented the most severe penalty under military disciplinary law in the Netherlands. Privates condemned to this penalty following disciplinary proceedings were not separated from those so sentenced by way of supplementary punishment under the criminal law, and during a month or more they were not entitled to leave the establishment. The committal lasted for a period of three to six months; this was considerably longer than the duration of the other penalties, including strict arrest which could be imposed for one to 14 days."
[97] Para. 85.
[98] Para. 85.
[99] Para. 85.
[1] Para. 85.
[2] (1997) 24 E.H.R.R. 221.

view, Article 6(1) was "clearly applicable to the court-martial proceedings, since they involved the determination of Mr Findlay's sentence following his plea of guilty to criminal charges".[3]

XIV. *Offences against prison discipline*

4–30   In a number of early cases the Commission held that prison disciplinary proceedings were outside the scope of Article 6 altogether.[4] However, in *Campbell and Fell v. United Kingdom*[5] the Court reversed the Commission's caselaw, holding that certain prison disciplinary offences were sufficiently serious to attract the criminal due process guarantees of Article 6. Campbell was charged with mutiny, incitement to mutiny, and doing gross personal violence to a prison officer. He was convicted by a Board of Visitors, and sentenced to 570 days loss of remission and 91 days loss of privileges. There was no doubt that the offences were regarded as disciplinary rather than criminal in national law.[6] The Court considered that some offences within prison were characteristic of a disciplinary system,[7] whilst others belonged simultaneously to the criminal and the disciplinary sphere. The Court emphasised the close connection between the offences which Campbell was convicted of, and the equivalent offences in the ordinary criminal law, as tending to show that the disciplinary charges at issue constituted criminal proceedings for the purpose of Article 6. In the Court's view;

> " . . . these factors, whilst not of themselves sufficient to lead to the conclusion that the offences with which the applicant was charged have to be regarded as "criminal" for Convention purposes, do give them a certain colouring which does not entirely coincide with that of a purely disciplinary matter."

4–31   Turning to the third criterion, the Court noted that the maximum penalty that could have been imposed was the forfeiture of all remission of sentence available to the applicant at the time of the Board's decision (just under three years). Relying on the settled caselaw of the Commission,[8] the government argued that loss of remission did not constitute loss of liberty, as that term was used in *Engel*. The Court accepted that loss of remission was not, strictly speaking, to be

---

[3] The government did not dispute the applicability of the "criminal" provisions of Art. 6.

[4] *X v. United Kingdom* (1976) 2 Digest 241; *X v. Switzerland* (1977) 11 D.R. 216; *X v. United Kingdom* (1977) 2 Digest 243; *X v. Germany* (1977) 2 Digest 243; Application No. 7794/77 (1980) 2 Digest 247.

[5] (1985) 7 E.H.R.R. 165.

[6] Para. 70.

[7] Such as the offence of making a false allegation against a prison officer at issue in *Kiss v. United Kingdom* (1976) 7 D.R. 55; or the offences of failure to wear prison uniform or to work, described in *McFeely v. United Kingdom* (1980) 20 D.R. 44 at para. 95 as "clearly disciplinary in nature".

[8] *X v. United Kingdom* (1976) 2 Digest 241; *X v. Switzerland* (1977) 11 D.R. 216; *X v. United Kingdom* (1977) 2 Digest 243; *X v. Germany* (1977) 2 Digest 243; Application No. 7794/77 (1980) 2 Digest 247. The approach of the Commission in these early cases is illustrated by the decision in *Kiss v. United Kingdom* (1976) 7 D.R. 55 at para. 2. where it was held that:
> "Loss of remission does not constitute deprivation of liberty. A prisoner, unlike a person doing military service, is deprived of his liberty for the whole of his sentence, and remission of that sentence for good behaviour is mere privilege, and loss of that remission does not alter the original basis for detention."

categorised as a loss of liberty,[9] but nevertheless held that it could amount to a criminal penalty where the consequences for the individual were sufficiently severe[10]:

> "The Court, for its part, does not find that the distinction between privilege and right is of great assistance to it for the present purposes; what is more important is that the practice of granting remission—whereby a prisoner will be set free on the estimated date for release given to him as the outset of his sentence, unless remission has been forfeited in disciplinary proceedings—creates in him a legitimate expectation that he will recover his liberty before the end of his term of imprisonment . . . By causing detention to continue for substantially longer than would otherwise have been the case, the sanction came close to, even if it did not technically constitute, deprivation of liberty, and the object and purpose of the Convention require that the imposition of a measure of such gravity should be accompanied by the guarantees of Article 6."

In *Greenfield v. Secretary of State for the Home Department*[11] Latham L.J. held that a charge of drug abuse against a serving prisoner was a disciplinary proceeding and not a criminal charge, and as such did not attract the protection of Article 6. Thus a serving prisoner in such a situation had no right to a fair and public hearing by an independent tribunal.

XV. *Professional disciplinary proceedings*

The Court's approach to professional disciplinary proceedings is less clear cut. In **4–32** *Albert and LeCompte v. Belgium*,[12] the applicant doctors faced disciplinary proceedings before the Belgian *Ordre des Médecins*. One was charged with issuing false medical certificates (an offence which also had implications under the criminal law), and the other with bringing the *Ordre* into disrepute (a purely disciplinary matter). Dr Albert argued that the proceedings were criminal in character. The Court considered it unnecessary to decide the point,[13] holding that even if the proceedings were classified as civil for the purposes of Article 6, they had sufficiently serious consequences to attract due process guarantees analagous to those set out in Articles 6(2) and 6(3). In the Court's view the civil and criminal aspects of Article 6 were not necessarily mutually exclusive,[14] and:
" . . . the principles set out in paragraph 2 and in the provisions of paragraph 3 invoked by Dr. Albert . . . are applicable, *mutatis mutandis*, to disciplinary

---

[9] Note that the legal basis for detention following loss of remission has been changed by the Crime (Sentences) Act 1997 which replaced the system of discretionary remission with a statutory entitlement to release after serving one half or two thirds of the sentence (depending on the length of the overall term): *R. v. Governor of Brockhill Prison ex parte Evans (No.2)* [1999] 2 W.L.R. 103. Instead of withdrawing remission, disciplinary sanctions now involve the imposition of "additional days".
[10] Para. 72. It does not, of course, follow that any disciplinary measure within the prison system involves the determination of a criminal charge: *X v. United Kingdom* (1979) 20 D.R. 202 (classification of a prisoner as Category A not the determination of a criminal charge); *Galloway v. United Kingdom* [1999] E.H.R.L.R. 119 (mandatory drug testing in prisons not criminal).
[11] *The Times*, March 6, 2001.
[12] (1983) 5 E.H.R.R. 533.
[13] See para. 30.
[14] See para. 30.

proceedings subject to paragraph 1 in the same way as in the case of a person charged with a criminal offence".[15]

A similar approach has since been taken to the disciplinary proceedings of other professions regulated by law in the public interest, including lawyers[16] and architects.[17]

XVI. *Disciplinary proceedings against civil servants*

4–33 Whether disciplinary proceeding against civil servants involve the determination of a "criminal charge" depends on the classification of the act in domestic law, the nature of the offence and the potential punishment for the act in question.[18] Article 6(1) is not applicable to disciplinary proceedings following a criminal conviction when the disciplinary court limits itself to establishing that the commission of the criminal offence also constitutes a disciplinary offence and imposes a sanction provided for by disciplinary law.[19] Disciplinary proceedings brought against a police officer for failure to account for property received have been held not to amount to a "criminal charge", notwithstanding that the potential penalty was dismissal.[20]

XVII. *Election offences*

4–34 In *Bowman v. United Kingdom*,[21] where the applicant was prosecuted under the Representation of the People Act 1983 for incurring unauthorised election expenditure, there could be no dispute that the proceedings were criminal in nature, since they were so classified under domestic law.[22] However that is not necessarily the position, particularly where the penalty is imposed on a Parliamentarian. In *Pierre-Bloch v. France*[23] the applicant was disqualified from standing in elections for the National Assembly, and fined for exceeding permitted election expenditure. Since the amount of the fine was equivalent to the excess expense incurred, the Court found that he was not subject to a "criminal charge":

> "[T]he obligation to pay relates to the amount by which the Constitutional Council has found the ceiling to have been exceeded. This would appear to show that it is in the nature of a payment to the community of the sum of which the candidate in question

---

[15] Para. 39. See also para. 30 where the Court observed that the principles enshrined in Art. 6(2) and 6(3)(a), (b) and (c) "are, for the present purposes, already contained in the notion of a fair trial as embodied in paragraph 1". See also *Diennet v. France* (1996) 21 E.H.R.R. 554 at para. 28. *Cf. Wickramsinghe v. United Kingdom* Application No. 31503/96 December 8, 1997 (proceedings before the GMC civil in nature).

[16] *H v. Belgium* (1988) 10 E.H.R.R. 339; *Ginikanwa v. United Kingdom* (1988) 55 D.R. 251.

[17] *Guchez v. Belgium* (1984) 40 D.R. 100.

[18] *Leiningen-Westerburg v. Austria* No. 26601/95 88–A D.R. 85 citing *Ravnsborg v. Sweden* (1994) 18 E.H.R.R. 38 (paras 30–35).

[19] *Kremzow v. Austria* No. 16417/90 67 D.R. 307 at 309.

[20] *X v. United Kingdom* No. 8496/79 21 D.R. 168. See also *Sygounis, Kotsis and others v. Greece* No. 18598/91 78–A D.R. 71 (breach of police duty). Nor were such disciplinary proceedings found to be determinative of any "civil right or obligation".

[21] (1998) 26 E.H.R.R. 1.

[22] The applicant complained of a violation of Art. 10. However, it is clear that the criminal guarantees of Art. 6 were equally applicable to the proceedings, on the first of the *Engel* criteria.

[23] (1998) 26 E.H.R.R. 202.

improperly took advantage to seek the votes of his fellow citizens, and that it too forms part of the measures designed to ensure the proper conduct of parliamentary elections and in particular, equality of the candidates ... [A]part from the fact that the amount payable is neither determined according to a fixed scale nor set in advance, several features differentiate this obligation to pay from criminal fines in the strict sense: no entry is made in the criminal record, the rules that consecutive sentences are not imposed in respect of multiple offences does not apply, and imprisonment is not available to sanction failure to pay ... [T]he obligation to pay the Treasury a sum equal to the amount of the excess cannot be construed as a fine."

XVIII. *Measures adopted for the prevention of disorder or crime*

In *Raimondo v. Italy*[24] the Court held that the imposition of a special supervision order in conjunction with criminal proceedings did not amount to a criminal sanction, since it was designed to prevent rather than to punish the commission of offences. The Commission adopted a similar approach in *Ibbotson v. United Kingdom*[25] where the registration requirements of the Sex Offenders Act 1997 were found not to constitute a criminal penalty[26] since they were predominantly preventative rather than punitive in character. Similary, in *B. v. Chief Constable of Avon and Somerset Constabulary*[27] Lord Bingham C.J. concluded that proceedings to obtain a sex offender order under section 2 of the Crime and Disorder Act 1998 were not criminal in character.   **4–35**

XIX. *Breach of the peace*

Proceedings in England and Wales whereby a defendant may be bound over to keep the peace[28] or to be "of good behaviour"[29] involve the determination of a criminal charge for the purposes of Article 6. In *Steel and others v. United Kingdom*[30] the Court explained that: **4–36**

"Breach of the peace is not classed as a criminal offence under English law. However, the Court observes that the duty to keep the police is in the nature of a public duty; the police have powers to arrest any person who has breached the peace or whom they reasonably fear will breach the peace; and the magistrates may commit to prison any person who refuses to be bound over not to breach the peace where there is evidence beyond reasonable doubt that his or her conduct caused or was likely to cause a breach of the peace and that he or she would otherwise cause a breach of the peace in the future. Bearing in mind the nature of the proceedings and the penalty at stake, the Court considers that breach of the peace must be regarded as an 'offence' within the meaning of Article 5(1)(c)."

---

[24] (1994) 18 E.H.R.R. 237.
[25] [1999] Crim. L.R. 153.
[26] The complaint was brought under Art. 7 and concerned the retrospective nature of the registration requirement imposed by the 1997 Act. However, the criteria for determining whether a measure constitutes a criminal "penalty" for the purposes of Art. 7 are directly analogous to the criteria established in *Engel* for the interpretation of the term "criminal charge" in Art. 6(1): *Welch v. United Kingdom* (1995) 20 E.H.R.R. 247.
[27] [2001] 1 W.L.R. 340.
[28] *Steel and ors v. United Kingdom* (1999) 28 E.H.R.R. 603 (paras 48–49 in context of Art. 5).
[29] *Hashman and Harrap v. United Kingdom, The Times*, December 1, 1999.
[30] (1999) 28 E.H.R.R. 603 (para. 48).

XX. *Antisocial Behaviour Orders*

4–37   Section 1 of the Crime and Disorder Act 1998 enables a magistrates' court to make an order prohibiting a defendant from certain forms of behaviour for a minimum of two years, as a result of proceedings that are classified as civil in domestic law. Section 1(10) then creates a strict liability offence of violating the prohibition in the order, without reasonable excuse, and provides a penalty of up to six months' imprisonment in summary proceedings, and up to five years on indictment. Moreover, section 1(11) prevents a court from granting a conditional discharge for this offence of breach. No doubt any proceedings under section 1(10) are criminal in nature, and legal representation would have to be provided before any sentence of imprisonment was imposed.[31] The more difficult question is whether the proceedings that result in the imposition of an anti-social behaviour order in the first place are themselves criminal proceedings.

4–38   On the one hand, there is an analogy with cases like *Krone-Verlag GmbH and Mediaprint Anzeigen GmbH & Co KG v. Austria*,[32] involving civil injunctions. It might be thought that the order, though made by a criminal court, is no different in substance from a civil injunction. On the other hand there is an argument for treating the proceedings as a whole (including the "civil" stage at which the magistrates decide upon and frame the order) as criminal.[33] In terms of the criteria set out in *Benham* the proceedings are "brought by a public authority", they involve the application of a law applicable to society in general, and the bridge between the making of the order and the undoubtedly severe maximum penalties does not require a separate finding of "wilful refusal" or "culpable neglect": Simple non-compliance is sufficient (unless the defendant proves "reasonable excuse").

4–39   The foundation for the strict liability offence is laid by the earlier proceedings in the magistrates' court, which have only the civil standard of proof and do not provide for full legal aid. The Government's aim was to avoid granting to defendants the rights guaranteed by Article 6.[34] In *R. v. Manchester Crown Court ex parte McCann and ors*[35] the Court of Appeal considered that this aim had been successfully carried into effect. The Master of the Rolls held that proceedings for obtaining anti-social behaviour orders were civil and not criminal and that they were accordingly outside the protection of Article 6(2) and (3). Lord Phillips accepted that the consequences of such an order may be severe but pointed out that many orders in civil proceedings had severe consequences. The Court had to have regard not only to the consequences of the measure but to the purpose it was intended to serve. The purpose of an anti-social behaviour order was the restraint of those whose conduct founded a reasonable belief that a measure of restraint was necessary to protect members of the public. The position was thus directly

---

[31] Section 21 Powers of Criminal Courts Act 1973, as applied (for example) in *Wilson* (1995) 16 Cr. App. R.(S) 997.

[32] (1997) 23 E.H.R.R. CD 152.

[33] The same conclusion is reached, on somewhat different reasoning, by R.C.A. White, "Anti-social behaviour orders under section 1 of the Crime and Disorder Act 1998" (1999) 24 E.L. Rev. 55, at 59.

[34] The intention to avoid the normal procedural protections is apparent from the Labour Party's documents, *A Quiet Life* (1995) and *Protecting our Communities* (1996), which form the background for s.1 of the 1998 Act.

[35] *The Times*, March 9, 2001.

analogous to that of a sex offender order imposed under section 2 of the Crime and Disorder Act 1998, which had been held to be civil in character for the purposes of Article 6.[36] Although the standard of proof to be applied was the civil standard, that was a flexible standard to be applied with greater or lesser strictness according to the seriousness of what had to be proved.

XXI. *Issues arising under Article 5*

There is a degree of confusion in the Convention caselaw as to the effect of the   **4–40** "criminal charge" jurisprudence on the classification of detention under Article 5(1). So far as disciplinary offences are concerned, the Court has held that the "conviction" referred to in Article 5(1)(a) may be either a criminal or a disciplinary conviction.[37] The more difficult question is whether the fact that proceedings fall within Article 5(1)(b) (detention for non compliance with court orders or legal obligations) necessarily means that they are not "criminal" proceedings for the purposes of Article 6.[38] We have seen that in *Krone-Verlag GmbH and Mediaprint Anzeigen GmbH & Co KG v. Austria*[39] the Commission assumed that this was so.[40] However, this approach is hard to reconcile with the Court's earlier decision in *Benham v. United Kingdom*[41] where the applicant's detention was held to be justified under Article 5(1)(b),[42] despite the conclusion that it resulted from the determination of a criminal charge, for the purposes of Article 6. It follows from *Benham* that the categories of detention in Article 5(1) are not necessarily mutually exclusive, and that the Commission's reasoning in *Krone-Verlag* is open to doubt.

XXII. *Comparative law position*

The classification of offences is not an area in which there is a clear international   **4–41** or comparative consensus. It has been suggested that an autonomous approach to the definition of criminal proceedings is appropriate under Article 14 of the International Covenant on Civil and Political Rights.[43] On the other hand it appears that Article 8 of the American Convention on Human Rights is intended to apply only to offences of a certain level of gravity.[44]

Section 35 of the South African Constitution, which enshrines the right to a fair   **4–42** trial in criminal proceedings, has been held not to apply to statutory powers of

---

[36] *B. v. Chief Constable of Avon and Somerset Constabulary* [2001] 1 W.L.R. 340.

[37] *Engel v. Netherlands* (1979–80) 1 E.H.R.R. 647 at para. 68.

[38] Art. 5(1)(a) permits lawful detention after "conviction by a competent court", whilst Art. 5(1)(b) permits detention for disobedience to a lawful order of a court, or in order to secure the fulfilment of an obligation prescribed by law.

[39] (1997) 23 E.H.R.R. CD 152.

[40] See para. 4–17 above.

[41] (1996) 22 E.H.R.R. 293.

[42] Para. 39.

[43] Nowak, *UN Covenant on Civil and Political Rights* (Engel, 1993), p. 243. Certain states have included regulatory offences and fiscal penalties in their reports on Art. 14.

[44] Article 8 of the American Convention applies to "an accusation of a criminal nature". However, the *travaux préparatoires* indicate that the drafters intended to exclude minor offences, designated as "*faltas*" in the majority of Latin American systems: Burgenthal and Norris, *Human Rights, the Inter-American System* (Oceana, 1982), p. 250.

compulsory questioning during a fraud inquiry,[45] or to professional disciplinary proceedings.[46] These decisions are broadly consistent with the approach taken in Strasbourg. A more restrictive approach is evident in Ireland[47] and New Zealand.[48]

4–43　　Section 11 of the Canadian Charter applies only to persons charged with a criminal offence. In the leading case of *Wrigglesworth*[49] Wilson J., for a unanimous Supreme Court held that:

> "The rights guaranteed by section 11 of the Charter are available to persons prosecuted by the state for public offences involving punitive sanctions, *i.e.* criminal, quasi-criminal and regulatory offences, either federally or provincially enacted . . . It cannot seriously be contended that just because a minor traffic offence leads to a very slight consequence, perhaps only a small fine, that offence does not fall within section 11."

4–44　　An offence would therefore attract the protection of section 11 either if it was "criminal" by its "very nature" or if it would lead to "true penal consequences". As to the former criterion, the Supreme Court distinguished between offences of "a public nature, intended to promote public order and welfare within a particular sphere of activity", which were criminal by their very nature, and "private, domestic or disciplinary matters which are regulatory, protective or corrective and which are primarily intended to maintain discipline, professional integrity and professional standards or to regulate conduct within a limited, private, sphere of activity". As to the relevance of the penalty imposed, a disciplinary offence would fall to be classified as "criminal" for the purposes of section 11 if it involved a punitive measure of sufficient severity, such as a fine or imprisonment.[50] In terms which echo the Strasbourg jurisprudence, the Canadian Supreme Court has held that "[t]he characterisation of certain offences and statutory schemes as "regulatory" or "criminal", although a useful factor, is not the last word for the purposes of Charter analysis"[51]; and in *Wholesale Travel Group*

---

[45] *Park Ross v. The Director, Office for Serious Economic Offences* (1995) 2 B.C.L.R. 198 (applying s.25 of the Interim Constitution, the predecessor to s.35). The answers to such questions could not be used in any subsequent criminal proceedings: *cf. Saunders v. United Kingdom* (1997) 23 E.H.R.R. 313.

[46] *Myburgh v. Voorsitter van die Schoemanpark Ontspanningsklub Dissiplinere Verhoor* (1995) 9 B.C.L.R. 1145; *Cuppan v. Cape Display Supply Chain Services* (1995) 5 B.C.L.R. 598 (both concerning s.25 of the Interim Constitution).

[47] *The State (Murray) v. McRann* [1976] I.R. 133 (prison disciplinary proceedings); *Keady v. Guarda Commissioner* [1992] 2 I.R. 197 (police disciplinary proceedings).

[48] See generally Butler "Regulatory Offences and the Bill of Rights" in Hushcroft and Rishworth (eds) *Rights and Freedoms: The New Zealand Bill of Rights Act 1990 and the Human Rights Act 1993* (Brookers, 1995).

[49] (1987) 60 C.R. (3d) 193 (SCC).

[50] Applying these principles, the Canadian courts have held that s.11 rights would inapplicable to proceedings to determine fitness to obtain or maintain a licence, and to administrative proceedings to protect the public in accordance with the police of a statute (*R. v. Wrigglesworth* (1987) 60 C.R. (3d) 193 (SCC) at 210–211); police disciplinary proceedings which could lead to dismissal (*Trimm v. Durham Regional Police Force* (1987) 37 C.C.C. (3d) 120 (SCC); *Burnham v. Ackroyd* (1987) 37 C.C.C. (3d) 118 (SCC); *Trumbley v. Metropolitan Police Force* (1987) 37 C.C.C. (3d) 120 (SCC); to professional disciplinary proceedings of doctors (*Fang v. College of Physicians and Surgeons of Alberta* [1986] 2 W.W.R. 380 (Alta CA) or lawyers (*Belhumeur v. Discipline Committee of Quebec Bar Association* (1983) 34 C.R. (3d) 279 (Que SC)). As to prison disciplinary proceedings, the Supreme Court has held that a charge resulting in five days solitary confinement and a restricted diet was insufficiently serious to qualify for s.11 protection: *Shubley* (1990) 74 C.R. (3d) 1 (SCC).

[51] *Baron v. Canada* (1993) 99 D.L.R. (4th) 350 at 370.

Ltd[52] La Forest J., for the Ontario Court of Appeal, said that "what is ultimately important are not labels (though these are undoubtedly useful), but the values at stake in the particular context".

C. CHARGE

I. *Autonomous Interpretation*

The criminal guarantees of Article 6 apply only once the individual concerned 4–45 has been "charged" with a criminal offence. In *Adolf v. Austria*[53] the Court observed that;

"The prominent place held in a democratic society by the right to a fair trial favours a 'substantive' rather than a 'formal' conception of the 'charge' referred to by Article 6; it impels the Court to look behind the appearances and examine the realities of the procedure in question in order to determine whether there has been a 'charge' within the meaning of Article 6."

Accordingly, the term "charge" has been given an autonomous Convention 4–46 interpretation, and is defined as: "[T]he official notification given to an individual by the competent authority of an allegation that he has committed a criminal offence, a definition that also corresponds to the test whether the situation of the [suspect] has been substantially affected."[54]

Thus, there must be some formal notification of the accusation, but a "charge" 4–47 can be constituted by any official act that carries such an implication.[55] This may be the date of formal charge by the police,[56] but in a case where the charge is delayed, or subsequent charges are added, it may be the date of the arrest,[57] "the date when the preliminary investigations were opened",[58] or the date on which the defendant becomes aware that he is being "seriously investigated" and that "immediate consideration" is being given to the possibility of a prosecution.[59] The Court and Commission have thus held Article 6 to be applicable from the date on which an order was made for the closure of the applicant's business premises pending payment of a penalty as an alternative to prosecution,[60] the date on which the applicant was informed that his Parliamentary immunity had been lifted,[61] and the date of an order for the production of evidence or the freezing of a bank account in the course of an investigation.[62]

---

[52] (1989) 73 C.R. (3d) 320.
[53] (1982) 4 E.H.R.R. 313 at para. 30.
[54] *Eckle v. FRG* (1983) 5 E.H.R.R. 1 at para. 73; *Deweer v. Belgium* (1979–80) 2 E.H.R.R. 439 at para. 46.
[55] *Corigliano v. Italy* (1983) 5 E.H.R.R. 334.
[56] *Ewing v. United Kingdom* (1988) 10 E.H.R.R. 141.
[57] *Foti v. Italy* (1983) 5 E.H.R.R. 313 at para. 52.
[58] *Foti v. Italy* (1983) 5 E.H.R.R. 313 at para. 52.
[59] *X v. United Kingdom* (1979) 14 D.R. 26; *X v. United Kingdom* (1978) 17 D.R. 122.
[60] *Deweer v. Belgium* (1979–80) 2 E.H.R.R. 439.
[61] *Frau v. Italy* (1991) Series A No. 195–E.
[62] *Funke v. France* (1993) 16 E.H.R.R. 297.

4-48   In certain circumstances a person may be "charged" within the meaning of
Article 6 even before a decision to prosecute has been taken.[63] In *X v. United
Kingdom*[64] the applicant was convicted of burglary and handling in October 1973
and sentenced to four years imprisonment. At the time of his conviction, he was
suspected of having procured arms and explosives for use in Northern Ireland
although there was insufficient evidence to prosecute him. Six months later, a
witness came forward, and in October 1974 a decision was taken to prosecute the
applicant on conspiracy charges. The indictment was issued in December of that
year. The government argued that the applicant was not "charged" for the
purposes of Article 6 until the indictment was preferred since, prior that time, his
situation was unaffected (given that he was already serving a sentence of
imprisonment). The Commission disagreed, holding that Article 6 was applicable
from the moment the applicant was convicted on the first indictment:

> "In the Commission's opinion . . . the applicant's position was substantially affected as
> soon as the suspicion against him was seriously investigated and the prosecution case
> compiled. For it was from this moment onwards that uncertainty and anxiety as to his
> future began and he needed to consider and prepare his defence . . . [T]he commence-
> ment of the prospective conspiracy proceedings can be considered to be the end of the
> [first] Crown Court trial . . . immediate consideration having been given, and sub-
> sequent action taken, by the DPP as to the viability of further charges."

4-49   The question whether Article 6 is applicable during the early stages of an
investigation appears to depend, at least in part, on the nature and powers of the
authority conducting the investigation. In *Funke v. France*[65] customs officers
searched the applicant's home for evidence of his involvement in certain
exchange control offences. When they were unable to find the documents they
brought criminal proceedings against the applicant for the compulsory disclosure
of bank statements relating to accounts which the applicant held with a number
of foreign banks. The Court held Article 6 to be applicable, given the criminal
character of the investigation. However in *Saunders v. United Kingdom*[66] Article
6 was held inapplicable to investigations conducted by DTI Inspectors appointed
under the Companies Act 1985 since they were "essentially investigative in
nature" and "did not adjudicate in form or in substance". The Court noted that
the purpose of the DTI investigation was to ascertain facts which might subsequently be used by *other* competent authorities—prosecuting, regulatory, disciplinary or even legislative.[67]

4-50   Providing the applicant has been "charged" in the extended sense described
above, the guarantees of Article 6 will apply even if he is not finally brought to
trial. In *Allenet de Ribemont v. France*,[68] the applicant was arrested for the
murder of a French M.P. on December 29, 1976. On the same day, the French

---

[63] A mere hearsay allegation to the police is not, however, sufficient to engage Art. 6: *R. v. HM
Advocate*, 2000 J.C. 368 (High Court of Justiciary in Scotland).
[64] (1978) 14 D.R. 26.
[65] (1993) 16 E.H.R.R. 297.
[66] (1997) 23 E.H.R.R. 313 at para. 67.
[67] See also *R. v. Hertfordshire County Council ex parte Green Environmental Industries Ltd and anor.*
[2000] 2 W.L.R. 373 (H.L.) in which Lord Hoffman held that the protection against self-incrimination
in Article 6 was inapplicable to an investigation under the Environmental Protection Act 1990, since
the investigation "did not form part, even a preliminary part, of any criminal proceedings" and did
"not therefore touch the principle which prohibits interrogation of a person charged or accused".
[68] (1995) 20 E.H.R.R. 557.

Interior Minister and two senior police officers gave a press conference in which they made comments suggesting that he was guilty of the offence for which he had been arrested. The applicant was charged on January 14, 1977, but released on bail two and a half months later. The proceedings were eventually discontinued without a trial in March 1980. The Court held that the applicant had been "charged" with a criminal offence for the purposes of Article 6 from the moment of his arrest, and that the remarks made during the press conference infringed the presumption of innocence in Article 6(2).

Where multiple offences are jointly tried, Article 6 will be applicable from the earliest date on which the defendant can be said to have been "charged". In *Ewing v. United Kingdom*,[69] the applicant had been arrested in connection with dishonesty offences on December 5, 1979. He was charged with those offences on the same day, and subsequently released on bail. He was then re-arrested and charged with further related offences on March 13, 1980. He appeared in different Magistrates Courts on several occasions, and was subject to three separate committals, all arising out of the same sequence of events. In February 1991 the charges were amalgamated into a single indictment, and the applicant was thereafter tried and convicted. He complained of the length of the proceedings. The government argued that for the purposes of the reasonable time guarantee in Article 6 the proceedings began when the amalgamated indictment was signed. Perhaps unsurprisingly, the Commission rejected this view, and held that the proceedings had to be considered as a whole and that Article 6 was accordingly applicable with effect from December 5, 1979.

4–51

In *Callaghan and others v. United Kingdom*[70] the Commission held that Article 6 applied to proceedings on appeal following a reference under section 17 of the Criminal Appeal Act 1968 (prior to its amendment by the Criminal Appeal Act 1995[71]). The case arose out of the first (unsuccessful) appeal by the six men convicted of the Birmingham pub bombings. Although the charge against the applicants had been finally determined, and their convictions had the quality of *res judicata*, the reference back had the effect of reopening the proceedings such that the applicants were, once again, "charged" with a criminal offence:

4–52

"The Commission notes that in this case the criminal proceedings had long been completed and that the reference procedure was not a normal step. Nonetheless the proceedings on the Secretary of State's reference had all the features of an appeal against conviction, and could have resulted in the applicants being found not guilty or, as in fact happened, the convictions being upheld. They must therefore . . . be regarded as having the effect of determining, or redetermining, the charges against the applicants."

II. *Comparative Law Position*

The decisions of the Canadian and New Zealand courts afford less flexibility to the notion of a criminal charge. In *Kalanj*[72] the Canadian Supreme Court held, by

4–53

---

[69] (1988) 10 E.H.R.R. 141.
[70] (1989) 60 D.R. 296.
[71] Sections 9 to 13 of the 1995 Act now govern the powers of reference back to the Court of Appeal or (in the case of a summary conviction) the Crown Court by the Criminal Cases Review Commission.
[72] (1989) 70 C.R. (3d) 260 (SCC).

a majority of three to two[73] that a person is charged with a criminal offence for the purposes of section 11 of the Charter only when an information is sworn to a justice alleging an offence, or an indictment is laid.[74] The minority view, which was closer to the tests laid down in the Convention jurisprudence, was that the section should apply when the impact of the criminal justice system was felt by the accused through the service of a summons, notice of appearance or an arrest, with or without a warrant. Similarly the High Court of New Zealand has held that the term "charged" in the New Zealand Bill of Rights Act applies to "an intermediate step in the prosecutorial process", between arrest and appearance in court, "when the prosecuting authority formally advises an arrested person that he is to be prosecuted and gives him particulars of the charges he will face."[75]

---

[73] This has since been confirmed as the position of the full Court: *Morin* (1992) 12 C.R. (4th) 1 (SCR).

[74] Note, however, that in *Heit* (1984) 11 C.C.C. (3d) 97 (Sask CA) the Court suggested that the service of a traffic ticket which had not been sworn in court was sufficient to engage s.11.

[75] *Gibbons* [1997] 2 N.Z.L.R. 585, *per* Goddard J. at 595.

CHAPTER 5

RIGHTS RELATING TO ARREST AND DETENTION IN POLICE CUSTODY

A. INTRODUCTION

The core provision governing powers of arrest and detention is Article 5, which **5–01**
protects the liberty and security of the person and occupies an important position
in the Convention system.[1] The Court has consistently emphasised that it is one
of the fundamental principles of a democratic society that the state must strictly
adhere to the rule of law when interfering with the right to personal liberty.[2] The
underlying aim of Article 5 is "to ensure that no one should be dispossessed of
[their] liberty in an arbitrary fashion".[3] In this chapter we examine the requirements of legality prescribed by Article 5(1), the power of arrest on reasonable
suspicion, the power of arrest or detention for breach of a court order or to secure
compliance with a legal obligation, the right to be informed of the reasons for an
arrest, the information to be provided at the time of charge, the right to be
produced promptly before a court after arrest, and the right to have the legality
of a detention reviewed by a court in *habeas corpus* proceedings. Finally, we
consider the Convention approach to allegations of ill-treatment in police custody
under Article 3.

B. DEPRIVATION OF LIBERTY

I. *The Strasbourg Caselaw*

Article 5 contemplates individual liberty "in its classic sense, that is to say the **5–02**
physical liberty of the person".[4] It is concerned with the *deprivation* of liberty
and not with mere *restrictions* on freedom of movement.[5] The distinction is not
always easy to identify since the difference is "merely one of degree or intensity,
and not one of nature or substance".[6] In determining whether the level of

---

[1] *Brogan v. United Kingdom* (1989) 11 E.H.R.R. 117, para. 58; *De Wilde, Ooms and Versyp v.
Belgium* (1979–80) 1 E.H.R.R. 373, para. 65.
[2] *Brogan v. United Kingdom* (1989) 11 E.H.R.R. 117, para. 58; *Engel v. Netherlands* (1979–80) 1
E.H.R.R. 647, para. 69.
[3] *Engel v. Netherlands* (1979–80) 1 E.H.R.R. 647, para. 58; *Winterwerp v. Netherlands* (1979–80) 2
E.H.R.R. 387, para. 37; *Guzzardi v. Italy* (1981) 3 E.H.R.R. 333, para. 92; *Bozano v. France* (1987)
9 E.H.R.R. 297, para. 54; *Van Droogenbroeck v. Belgium* (1982) 4 E.H.R.R. 443, para. 40; *Weeks v.
United Kingdom* (1988) 10 E.H.R.R. 293, para. 49.
[4] *Engel v. Netherlands* (1979–80) 1 E.H.R.R. 647, para. 58.
[5] *Engel v. Netherlands* (1979–80) 1 E.H.R.R. 647, para. 58; *Guzzardi v. Italy* (1981) 3 E.H.R.R. 333,
para. 92; *Raimondo v. Italy* (1994) 18 E.H.R.R. 237, para. 39. Lesser restrictions on freedom of
movement are governed by Art. 2 of the fourth protocol, to which the United Kingdom is not a
party.
[6] *Guzzardi v. Italy* (1981) 3 E.H.R.R. 333, para. 93; *Ashingdane v. United Kingdom* (1985) 7 E.H.R.R.
528, para. 41.

restraint involved amounts to a detention, regard should be had to "a whole range of criteria such as the type, duration, effects and manner of implementation of the measure in question".[7] Thus, the Court has held that a person detained in a mental hospital under a compulsory detention order could rely on Article 5 even though he was kept in an open ward for part of the time and could leave the hospital unaccompanied on occasions.[8] On the other hand, a patient who, whilst remaining subject to a detention order, was provisionally released, was no longer deprived of her liberty.[9] In *X v. Switzerland*[10] the Commission held that a disciplinary order confining a prisoner to his cell did not lead to an additional deprivation of liberty,[11] whereas in *Campbell and Fell v. United Kingdom*[12] an order for the forfeiture of remission was held to have imposed an additional period of detention. In *Engel v. Netherlands*[13] the Court held that "strict arrest" imposed on soldiers for disciplinary offences amounted to a deprivation of liberty despite the different standards which apply to military personnel.

5–03   In this country, claims that a person was merely "helping the police with their inquiries" should be scrutinised with care. This anomalous category of quasi-detention is preserved by the Police and Criminal Evidence Act 1984,[14] but should it be regarded as amounting to a deprivation of liberty for the purposes of Article 5? There is no clear answer in the Convention caselaw, and the applicability of Article 5 in this context would appear to depend on the facts of the individual case. As a general proposition it can be said that Article 5 will not apply where the individual consents to the restriction, providing the consent is clearly established and unequivocal. But the fact that a person initially agreed to enter a custodial institution does not prevent him from relying on Article 5 if he subsequently wishes to leave.[15] In 1989, in the case of *Nielsen v. Denmark*,[16] the Court held that where the detention of a child was in issue, consent of the parent or guardian might be sufficient, even if the detention was contrary to the child's wishes. The Court, however, noted that parental rights were not absolute and that it was incumbent on the State to provide safeguards against abuse.[17]

5–04   The duration of the detention is not necessarily decisive[18]: Article 5 has been held to apply to detention for the purposes of carrying out a compulsory blood

---

[7] *Guzzardi v. Italy* (1981) 3 E.H.R.R. 333, para. 92; *Ashingdane v. United Kingdom* (1985) 7 E.H.R.R. 528, para. 41; *Engel v. Netherlands* (1976) 1 E.H.R.R. 647, paras 58–59.

[8] *Ashingdane v. United Kingdom* (1985) 7 E.H.R.R. 528, para. 42.

[9] *W v. Sweden* 59 D.R. 158 (1988).

[10] Application 7754/77 (1977) 11 D.R. 216, para. 2.

[11] *cf. R. v. Deputy Governor of Parkhurst Prison ex parte Hague* [1992] 1 A.C. 58 where the House of Lords came to the same conclusion in relation to the tort of false imprisonment.

[12] (1985) 7 E.H.R.R. 165, para. 72.

[13] (1979–80) 1 E.H.R.R. 647, para. 63.

[14] The powers of the police in England and Wales to question a suspect without arrest are governed by the Police and Criminal Evidence Act 1984, s.29 *et seq.* and para. 3.15 of the Code of Practice on Detention, Treatment and Questioning (Code C).

[15] *De Wilde, Ooms and Versyp v. Belgium* (1979–80) 1 E.H.R.R. 373, para. 65. See also *Amuur v. France* (1996) 22 E.H.R.R. 533, para. 48.

[16] (1989) 11 E.H.R.R. 175.

[17] The U.N. Convention on the Rights of the Child (1989) affords the child the right to be consulted over decisions affecting its future and provides express protection against arbitrary deprivation of liberty.

[18] *X and Y v. Sweden* (1976) 7 D.R. 123 (detention for one hour prior to deportation).

test,[19] or during the course of a journey in a moving vehicle,[20] or an aircraft.[21] In the past, the Commission has attached considerable (and perhaps undue) importance to the intention of the authorities. Thus, in *X v. Germany*,[22] the Commission held that a 10 year old girl who was questioned at a police station for two hours without being arrested, locked into a cell or formally detained was not deprived of her liberty for the purposes of Article 5. Together with another pupil, the applicant had been taken to the police station in the course of an investigation into thefts of stationery from other children, despite the fact that she was below the age of criminal responsibility. Somewhat unconvincingly the Commission observed that: " . . . in the present case the police action was not aimed at depriving the children of their liberty but simply to obtain information from them about how they obtained possession of the objects found on them and about thefts which had occurred previously at the school."

This formulation appears to turn entirely on the intentions of the police, a view **5–05** reinforced by the Commission's statement that it was "regrettable that the children may not have been able to understand the police action and may have felt that they were deprived of their liberty". This is surely an unsatisfactory (or at the very least an incomplete) test. It gives the appearance of depriving a person who is being interrogated by the police of the minimum rights guaranteed by Article 5, even where they are led to believe that they are being detained against their will.

II. *Comparative Approaches*

In Canada the Ontario Court of Appeal has held that whether or not a person who **5–06** has not been formally arrested is "detained" depends not solely on whether he or she believed that this was the case but more widely on a number of situational criteria.[23] These criteria were approved by the New Zealand High Court in *M*,[24] where it was held that the defendant had been detained when he had formed the belief, reasonably founded on police conduct, that he was not free to leave. The Chief Justice of New Zealand adopted the same approach in *P*:

"Arrest is defined as a communication or manifestation by the police of an intention to apprehend and to hold the person concerned in the exercise of authority to do so; or, as long as the conduct of the arrester, seen to be acting or purporting to act under legal authority, has made it plain that the subject had been deprived of the liberty to go where he pleased."[25]

C. THE "LEGALITY" REQUIREMENTS OF ARTICLE 5(1)

Article 5(1) provides that everyone has the right to liberty and security of the **5–07** person, and that no one is to be deprived of their liberty save in the circumstances prescribed in Article 5(1)(a) to (f). The list of exceptions set out in Article 5(1)

---

[19] Application 8278/78 *X v. Austria* (1979) 18 D.R. 154.
[20] *Bozano v. France* (1987) 9 E.H.R.R. 297.
[21] *X and Y v. Sweden* (1976) 7 D.R. 123.
[22] Application 8819/79 (1981) 24 D.R. 158 at 161.
[23] *Moran* (1987) 36 C.C.C. (3d) 225.
[24] [1995] 1 N.Z.L.R. 242.
[25] *P* [1996] 3 N.Z.L.R. 132 at 136.

thus provides an exhaustive[26] definition of the circumstances in which a person may be lawfully deprived of his liberty and is to be given a narrow construction.[27] In addition to falling within sub-paragraphs (a)–(f),[28] any detention must be: (i) 'lawful' and (ii) carried out "in accordance with a procedure prescribed by law".[29] These terms refer to conformity with national law and procedure and it is therefore "in the first place for the national authorities, notably the courts, to interpret and apply domestic law".[30]

5–08   Nevertheless, it remains the function of the European Court of Human Rights to determine whether Article 5 has been violated, and the Court therefore has the ultimate power to interpret and apply national law.[31] The scope of the Court's task in this connection "is subject to limits inherent in the logic of the European system of protection",[32] so that on the international level[33] a certain margin of appreciation will be afforded to the decisions of the domestic courts.[34] However, a detention which is unlawful under domestic law will be *a fortiori* in breach of Article 5.[35]

5–09   For a detention to comply with Article 5, it must conform to the general principles contained in the Convention.[36] Thus the Court has held that; "[An] arrested or detained person is entitled to a review of the 'lawfulness' of his detention in the light not only of the requirements of domestic law, but also of the text of the Convention, the general principles embodied therein, and the aim of the restrictions permitted by Article 5(1)".[37]

5–10   The term "lawful" implies that the domestic law on which the detention is based must itself be "accessible and precise".[38] In *Steel and others v. United King-*

---

[26] *Ireland v. United Kingdom* (1979–80) 2 E.H.R.R. 25, para. 194.
[27] *Guzzardi v. Italy* (1981) 3 E.H.R.R. 333, paras 98 and 100; *Winterwerp v. Netherlands* (1979–80) 2 E.H.R.R. 387, para. 37; *Quinn v. France* (1996) 21 E.H.R.R. 529, para. 42.
[28] The grounds enumerated in sub-paras (a)–(f) are not mutually exclusive: *McVeigh, O'Neill and Evans v. United Kingdom* (1981) 25 D.R. 15.
[29] *Winterwerp v. Netherlands* (1979–80) 2 E.H.R.R. 387, para. 39.
[30] *Bozano v. France* (1987) 9 E.H.R.R. 297, para. 58; *Winterwerp v. Netherlands* (1979–80) 2 E.H.R.R. 387; *Wassink v. Netherlands* (1990) Series A/185–A, para. 24; *Benham v. United Kingdom* (1996) 22 E.H.R.R. 293, para. 41.
[31] *Bozano v. France* (1987) 9 E.H.R.R. 297, para. 58; *Benham v. United Kingdom* (1996) 22 E.H.R.R. 293, para. 41.
[32] *Bozano v. France* (1987) 9 E.H.R.R. 297, para. 58.
[33] As to the relevance of the "margin of appreciation" doctrine before the national courts see paras 2–123 to 2–134 above.
[34] *Weeks v. United Kingdom* (1988) 10 E.H.R.R. 293, para. 50; *Winterwerp v. Netherlands* (1979–80) 2 E.H.R.R. 387, para. 40.
[35] *Benham v. United Kingdom* (1996) 22 E.H.R.R. 293; *cf. Poole v. United Kingdom* (1998) Application No. 28190/95; *Johnson v. United Kingdom* (1998) Application No. 28455/95; *Denson v. United Kingdom* (1998) Application No. 25286/94. See also *Steel and ors v. United Kingdom* (1999) 28 E.H.R.R. 603, where the Court, in determining the compatibility of the applicants' detention, distinguished between them by applying the relevant test under national law.
[36] *Winterwerp v. Netherlands* (1979–80) 2 E.H.R.R. 387, para. 37; *Herczegfalvy v. Austria* (1993) 15 E.H.R.R. 437, para. 63; *Bozano v. France* (1987) 9 E.H.R.R. 297, para. 54; *Weeks v. United Kingdom* (1988) 10 E.H.R.R. 293, para. 42. The "general principles" contained in the Convention include the "rule of law": *Engel v. Netherlands* (1989) 11 E.H.R.R. 117, para. 69; *Brogan v. United Kingdom* (1989) 11 E.H.R.R. 117, para. 58.
[37] *E v. Norway* (1994) 17 E.H.R.R. 30, para. 49.
[38] Application 9174/80 *Zamir v. United Kingdom* (1983) 40 D.R. 42; *Sunday Times (No. 1) v. United Kingdom* (1979–80) 2 E.H.R.R. 245, para. 49; *Amuur v. France* (1996) 22 E.H.R.R. 533, para. 50.

dom,[39] a case concerning arrest and detention for breach of the peace, the Court held that given the importance of personal liberty, it is essential that national law governing detention be sufficiently precise to allow the citizen—if need be, with appropriate advice—to foresee, to a degree that is reasonable in the circumstances, the consequences which a given action of his may entail. In the Court's view the concept of breach of the peace had been clarified by judicial decision such that the applicable rules provided sufficient guidance, and were formulated with the degree of precision required by the Convention.[40]

Article 5 has been held to prohibit deprivation of liberty which is "arbitrary" in   **5–11**
its motivation or effect.[41] A detention will be arbitrary if it is not in keeping with the purpose of the restrictions permissible under Article 5(1) or with Article 5 generally.[42] Detention which is ostensibly for the purpose of deportation but which is in reality a disguised illegal extradition is arbitrary.[43] Even if properly motivated, a detention may be arbitrary if it is disproportionate to the attainment of its purpose.[44] Thus, for example, imprisonment imposed on grounds of dangerousness by reference to characteristics which are susceptible to change with the passage of time will become arbitrary if those characteristics are no longer present.[45] On the other hand, the fact that time spent in custody abroad is not taken into account in computing the length of a prison sentence does not render the additional period of detention arbitrary.[46] Nor does the fact that detention results from a "loss of time" order by the Court of Appeal Criminal Division under section 29(1) of the Criminal Appeal Act 1968.[47]

These principles were encapsulated by Lord Hope in *R. v. Governor of HMP*   **5–12**
Brockhill ex parte Evans (No.2)[48]:

> "The jurisprudence of the European Court of Human Rights indicates that there are various aspects to Article 5(1) which must be satisfied in order to show that the detention is lawful for the purposes of the article. The first question is whether the detention is lawful under domestic law. Any detention which is unlawful in domestic

---

[39] (1999) 28 E.H.R.R. 603.
[40] *cf. Hashman and Harrap v. United Kingdom, The Times,* December 1, 1999, where the Court reached the opposite conclusion in relation to an order to be bound over to be "of good behaviour".
[41] *Winterwerp v. Netherlands* (1979–80) 2 E.H.R.R. 387, paras 37–39; *Van Droogenbroeck v. Belgium* (1982) 4 E.H.R.R. 443, para. 48; *Weeks v. United Kingdom* (1988) 10 E.H.R.R. 293, para. 49; *Bozano v. France* (1987) 9 E.H.R.R. 297, para. 54; *Ashingdane v. United Kingdom* (1985) 7 E.H.R.R. 528, para. 44. Cf. *Ong Ah Chuan v. Public Prosecutor* [1981] A.C. 648, (P.C.).
[42] *Winterwerp v. Netherlands* (1979–80) 2 E.H.R.R. 387, para. 39; *Bouamar v. Belgium* (1988) 11 E.H.R.R. 1, para. 50; *Weeks v. United Kingdom* (1987) 10 E.H.R.R. 293, para. 42; *Ashingdane v. United Kingdom* (1985) 7 E.H.R.R. 528, para. 44.
[43] *Bozano v. France* (1987) 9 E.H.R.R. 297.
[44] *Winterwerp v. Netherlands* (1979–80) 2 E.H.R.R. 387 para. 39; *Van Droogenbroeck v. Belgium* (1982) 4 E.H.R.R. 443. *Bouamar v. Belgium* (1989) 11 E.H.R.R. 1, para. 53.
[45] *Van Droogenbroeck v. Belgium* (1982) 4 E.H.R.R. 443; *Weeks v. United Kingdom* (1988) 10 E.H.R.R. 293; *Thynne, Wilson and Gunnell v. United Kingdom* (1991) 13 E.H.R.R. 666; *Abed Hussain v. United Kingdom* (1996) 22 E.H.R.R. 1.
[46] *C v. United Kingdom* (1985) 43 D.R. 177.
[47] *Monnell and Morris v. United Kingdom* (1988) 10 E.H.R.R. 205. Under the Criminal Appeals Act 1968, s.29(1) the Court of Appeal may, if it considers that an appeal is without merit, direct that time served between the imposition of the sentence and the disposal of the appeal should not count towards the accused person's sentence. As to the circumstances in which such an order may be made see *Practice Direction (Crime: Sentence: Loss of Time)* [1980] 1 W.L.R. 270.
[48] [2000] 3 W.L.R. 843.

law will automatically be unlawful under Article 5(1)... The second question is whether, assuming that the detention is lawful under domestic law, it nevertheless complies with the general requirements of the Convention. These are based on the principle that any restriction on human rights must be prescribed by law... They include the requirements that the domestic law must be sufficiently accessible to the individual and that it must be sufficiently precise to enable the individual to foresee the consequences of the restriction... The third question is whether, again assuming that the detention is lawful under domestic law, it is nevertheless open to criticism on the ground that it is arbitrary because, for example, it was resorted to in bad faith or was not proportionate."

D. ARREST ON REASONABLE SUSPICION AND RELATED GROUNDS

I. General

5–13   Article 5(1)(c) authorises lawful arrest or detention for the purpose of bringing a person before the competent legal authority on reasonable suspicion of having committed a criminal offence, or when it is reasonably considered necessary to prevent him committing an offence or fleeing having done so. It has to be read in conjunction with Article 5(3) which provides additional protection for persons arrested in these circumstances.[49]

II. Criminal Offences

5–14   Article 5(1)(c) is confined to criminal offences[50] within the extended Convention definition of that term.[51] The term "offence" means a criminal or disciplinary[52] offence which is "concrete and specified".[53] Article 5(1)(c) is not therefore capable of authorising a general power of preventative detention since this would lead to "conclusions repugnant to the fundamental principles of the Convention".[54] In *Brogan v. United Kingdom*[55] the applicants were detained for questioning in connection with alleged involvement in "acts of terrorism". The Court held that although an "act of terrorism" (which was defined as "the use of violence for political ends"[56]) was not a criminal offence in itself under domestic law, it was "well in keeping with the idea of an offence" for the purposes of Article 5(1)(c), particularly since the applicants had been questioned about specific offences immediately after their arrests. In *Steel and others v. United Kingdom*[57] the Court held that breach of the peace fell to be regarded as an

---

[49] *Ciulla v. Italy* (1989) 13 E.H.R.R. 346, para. 38; *Lawless v. Ireland (No. 3)* (1979–80) 1 E.H.R.R. 15, para. 14. On Art. 5(3), see para. 5–28.
[50] *Ciulla v. Italy* (1991) 13 E.H.R.R. 346, para. 38, where the Court held that detention of the applicant in order to bring him before a competent legal authority in connection with a compulsory residence order did not fall within Art. 5(1)(c).
[51] *Steel and ors v. United Kingdom* (1999) 28 E.H.R.R. 603. As to the meaning of "criminal" proceedings for the purposes of Art. 6, Chapter 4 above.
[52] *De Jong, Baljet and Van Den Brink v. Netherlands* (1986) 8 E.H.R.R. 20.
[53] *Guzzardi v. Italy* (1981) 3 E.H.R.R. 333, para. 102.
[54] *Lawless v. Ireland (No. 3)* (1979–80) 1 E.H.R.R. 15, para. 14.
[55] (1989) 11 E.H.R.R. 117, para. 51. *cf. Ireland v. United Kingdom* (1979–80) 2 E.H.R.R. 25, para. 196.
[56] See the Prevention of Terrorism (Temporary Provisions) Act 1984, s.14.
[57] (1999) 28 E.H.R.R. 603 (para. 48).

offence for the purposes of Article 5(1)(c).[58] The relevant test under domestic law was found to be sufficiently precise to meet the requirement of legal certainty implicit in Article 5.[59] The determination of the applicants' complaints therefore depended upon compliance with national law. The arrests of two of the applicants were found to comply with national law, but in the case of the remaining three applicants the Court found a breach of Article 5(1)(c).

III. *Competent Legal Authority*

The requirement that detention must have been effected for the purpose of   **5–15** bringing a person before the competent legal authority is not confined to arrest on reasonable suspicion. It applies to all three grounds of detention in Article 5(1)(c).[60] Thus, in *Lawless v. Ireland*[61] the Court held that the internment of a suspected terrorist could not be justified under Article 5(1)(c) on the ground that it was necessary to prevent him committing an offence, since the detention was not effected for the purpose of initiating a criminal prosecution. The term "competent legal authority" has the same meaning as the term "judge or other officer authorised by law to exercise judicial power" in Article 5(3).[62] The competent legal authority in England and Wales is a Magistrates' Court.

IV. *Reasonable Suspicion*

In order for an arrest on reasonable suspicion to be justified under Article 5(1)(c)   **5–16** it is not necessary to establish either that an offence has been committed or that the person detained has committed it.[63] Neither is it necessary that the person detained should ultimately have been charged or taken before a court. As the Court observed in *Murray v. United Kingdom*,[64] the object of detention for questioning is to further a criminal investigation by confirming or discounting suspicions which provide the grounds for detention. However the requirement that the suspicion must be based on reasonable grounds "forms an essential part of the safeguard against arbitrary arrest and detention".[65] The fact that a suspicion is honestly held is insufficient.[66] The words "reasonable suspicion" mean the existence of facts or information which would satisfy an objective observer that the person concerned may have committed the offence.[67] This substantially accords with the test formulated by the Privy Council in *Shaaban Bin Hussein v. Chang Fook Kam*[68]:

> "The circumstances of the case must be such that a reasonable man acting without passion or prejudice would fairly have suspected the person of having committed the

---

[58] See para. 4–36 above.
[59] Para. 55. See further, para. 2–28 above.
[60] *Lawless v. Ireland (No. 1)* (1979–80) 1 E.H.R.R. 15, para. 14; *De Jong, Baljet and Van Den Brink v. Netherlands* (1986) 8 E.H.R.R. 20, paras 43 and 44.
[61] (1979–80) 1 E.H.R.R. 15, paras 14 and 15.
[62] *Schiesser v. Switzerland* (1979–80) 2 E.H.R.R. 417, para. 29.
[63] *X v. Austria* (1989) 11 E.H.R.R. 112.
[64] (1995) 19 E.H.R.R. 193, para. 55.
[65] *Fox, Campbell and Hartley v. United Kingdom* (1991) 13 E.H.R.R. 157, para. 32.
[66] *Fox, Campbell and Hartley v. United Kingdom* (1991) 13 E.H.R.R. 157, para. 32.
[67] *Fox, Campbell and Hartley v. United Kingdom* (1991) 13 E.H.R.R. 157, para. 32. Cf. *Hussein v. Kam* [1970] A.C. 942 at 946.
[68] [1970] A.C. 942.

offence . . . suspicion in its ordinary meaning is a state of conjecture or surmise where proof is lacking: 'I suspect but I cannot prove.' Suspicion arises at or near the starting point of an investigation of which the obtaining of *prima facie* proof is at the end."[69]

5–17 What may be regarded as reasonable will depend on all the circumstances. Even in relation to offences with national security implications however, the state must be in a position to provide evidence which is capable of satisfying a court that the arrested person was reasonably suspected of having committed the offence.[70] In *Fox, Campbell and Hartley v. United Kingdom*[71] the Court had to consider a power of arrest under section 11 of the Northern Ireland (Emergency Provision) Act 1978, which provides that a constable may arrest "any person whom he suspects of being a terrorist". The power of arrest conferred by section 11 did not therefore include an objective test of "reasonableness" and could be satisfied by an honest belief.[72] The applicants argued that their detention in consequence of the exercise of this power of arrest violated Article 5(1)(c). The government declined to furnish all the evidence on which the suspicion was based, on the ground that the material and its sources were sensitive. The Court recognised that "terrorist crime falls into a special category", because the police often have to respond to an apparently urgent threat to life and limb, and stated that "Article 5(1)(c) of the Convention should not be applied in such a manner as to put disproportionate difficulties in the way" of state responses to terrorism.[73] But, despite this general affirmation, the Court went on to hold that "the exigencies of dealing with terrorist crime cannot justify stretching the notion of 'reasonableness' to the point where the essence of the safeguard in Article 5(1)(c) is impaired". Accordingly, the Court must be enabled to decide whether that safeguard had been secured in the particular case.[74] Since the necessary evidence was not adduced, the Court found a violation of Article 5(1)(c).[75]

E. ARREST OR DETENTION FOR BREACH OF A COURT ORDER

5–18 The first limb of Article 5(1)(b) provides for detention where the applicant has failed to comply with an injunction or other court order. The order must have been made by a court of competent jurisdiction,[76] it must be sufficiently precise to meet the Convention test of legal certainty,[77] and it must be capable of enforcement. Article 5(1)(b) has been held to permit detention for failure to pay

---

[69] *Per* Lord Devlin at 948.

[70] *Fox, Campbell and Hartley v. United Kingdom* (1991) 13 E.H.R.R. 157, para. 34. *Cf. Murray v. United Kingdom* (1995) 19 E.H.R.R. 193, paras 56, 61–63.

[71] (1990) 13 E.H.R.R. 157, at para. 32. See also *Murray v. United Kingdom* (1995) 19 E.H.R.R. 193, at paras 56 and 61–2.

[72] *McKee v. Chief Constable for Northern Ireland* [1984] 1 W.L.R. 1358.

[73] (1991) 13 E.H.R.R. 157, at paras 32, 34.

[74] *ibid.*, paras 32 and 34.

[75] Note, however, that in *Murray v. United Kingdom* (1995) 19 E.H.R.R. 193 the Court went to considerable lengths to find that this requirement was met.

[76] A warning by the Chief of Police does not constitute an order of a court for the purposes of Art. 5(1)(b): *Guzzardi v. Italy* (1981) 3 E.H.R.R. 333, para. 101.

[77] *Steel and ors v. United Kingdom* (1999) 28 E.H.R.R. 603 (paras 71 to 78).

a fine,[78] for refusal to undergo a blood test[79] or medical examination[80] ordered by a court; and for failure to observe a residence restriction.[81] In *Steel and others v. United Kingdom*[82] the Court considered that the applicants' detention for refusing to be bound over to keep the peace fell within Article 5(1)(b) since it was imposed as a result of their refusal to comply with the court's order. As to the terms of the order, the Court observed that;

> " . . . the orders were expressed in rather vague and general terms; the expression 'to be of good behaviour' was particularly imprecise and offered little guidance to the person bound over as to the type of conduct which would amount to a breach of the order. However, in each applicant's case the binding over order was imposed after a finding that she had committed a breach of the peace. Having considered all the circumstances, the Court is satisfied that, given the context, it was sufficiently clear that the applicants were being requested to agree to refrain from causing further, similar, breaches of the peace during the ensuing 12 months."

The Court reached the opposite conclusion in *Hashman and Harrap v. United*   **5–19** *Kingdom*[83] in which a bind over order imposed on two hunt saboteurs, requiring them to be "of good behaviour" (not to act *"contra bonos mores"*) was held to be too vague to qualify as law, and failed to provide any objective criteria against which their past and future actions could be judged.

F. DETENTION TO SECURE COMPLIANCE WITH A LEGAL OBLIGATION

The second limb of Article 5(1)(b) provides for a person's arrest or detention "in   **5–20** order to secure the fulfilment of any obligation prescribed by law". In general, the obligation must be one which is "already incumbent on the person concerned".[84] However, in *McVeigh, O'Neill and Evans v. United Kingdom*[85] the Commission held that in certain "limited circumstances of a pressing nature" a coercive power of detention may be permissible where it is necessary to secure fulfilment of a specific obligation at the time when it arises.[86] This principle may only be invoked where there is an immediate necessity for the fulfilment of the obligation, and where there is no reasonably practicable alternative means available for securing compliance.[87] Assuming these criteria are satisfied, the importance and urgency of the obligation must nevertheless be balanced against the individual's right to liberty and the length of the period of the detention. In *McVeigh* the Commission held that there was no breach of Article 5(1) where persons entering the United Kingdom were required to submit to "further

---

[78] Application 6289/73 *Airey v. Ireland* (1977) 8 D.R. 42.
[79] Application 8275/78 *X v. Austria* (1979) 18 D.R. 154.
[80] Application 6659/74 *X v. Federal Republic of Germany* (1975) 3 D.R. 92.
[81] Application 8916/80 *Freda v. Italy* (1980) 21 D.R. 250.
[82] (1999) 28 E.H.R.R. 603 (paras 71 to 78).
[83] *The Times*, December 1, 1999. The case concerned a complaint under Art. 10, but the applicable test for "lawfulness" is the same under Art. 5.
[84] *Ciulla v. Italy* (1991) 13 E.H.R.R. 346, para. 36; *Guzzardi v. Italy* (1981) 3 E.H.R.R. 333, para. 101. Imprisonment for a failure to fulfil a contractual obligation is not a violation of Art. 5(1) since it is separately protected under Art. 1 of Protocol 4 to which the United Kingdom is not a party.
[85] (1983) 5 E.H.R.R. 71.
[86] (1983) 5 E.H.R.R. 71, paras 175 and 190–191.
[87] (1983) 5 E.H.R.R. 71, para. 191.

examination" at the point of entry pursuant to the Prevention of Terrorism (Supplemental Temporary Provisions) Order 1976.[88] The applicants were detained for that purpose and released after 45 hours, having been questioned, searched, photographed and fingerprinted but not charged with any offence. In finding no violation the Commission attached importance to the fact that the obligation applied only on entering and leaving the United Kingdom and in order to verify the particular matters referred to in the legislation.[89] The same principle would presumably apply to other powers of temporary detention exercisable by the police without reasonable suspicion, such as the power to detain for the purpose of verifying ownership of a vehicle or the power to establish a road-block. It might also be expected to apply to the burgeoning police "stop and search" powers under statutory provisions such as section 60 of the Criminal Justice and Public Order Act 1994,[90] section 8 of the Knives Act 1997, and sections 25–27 of the Crime and Disorder Act 1998.

G. The Right to be Given Reasons for Arrest

5–21   Article 5(2) requires that anyone arrested or detained should be "informed promptly, in a language which he understands, of the reasons for his arrest and of any charge against him". This principle is closely followed by section 28 of the Police and Criminal Evidence Act 1984, which imposes a duty to give reasons for an arrest as soon as practicable, and makes this a condition precedent to a lawful detention.[91] The primary purpose of the obligation is to enable the detained person to apply to a court to challenge the lawfulness of the detention in accordance with Article 5(4).[92] Where a person has been arrested in connection with a criminal offence, Article 5(2) is also intended to enable him to deny the offence at the earliest opportunity.[93]

5–22   The detained person must be told "in simple, non-technical language that he can understand, the essential legal and factual grounds for his arrest".[94] The extent of the information required will depend on the circumstances.[95] Mere reference to the applicable statutory provision is generally insufficient.[96] Where the reason for the arrest is suspicion of involvement in a particular offence, the detainee must be informed of the facts which are the foundation of the decision to detain, and in particular he should be asked whether he admits or denies the allegation.[97]

---

[88] S.I. 1976 No. 465.

[89] *Cf. Ireland v. United Kingdom* (1979–80) 2 E.H.R.R. 25.

[90] Which caters for stop and search in reasonable anticipation of violence.

[91] In making the lawfulness of an arrest dependent upon the provision of reasons s. 28 embodies the common law rule in *Christie v. Leachinsky* [1947] A.C. 573.

[92] *Fox, Campbell and Hartley v. United Kingdom* (1991) 13 E.H.R.R. 157, para. 40. *Cf. Christie v. Leachinsky* [1947] A.C. 573; the Police and Criminal Evidence Act 1984, s. 28. On Art. 5(4), see paras 5–33 to 5–35.

[93] *X v. Germany* (1978) 16 D.R. 111 at 114.

[94] *Fox, Campbell and Hartley v. United Kingdom* (1991) 13 E.H.R.R. 157, para. 40. *Cf. Christie v. Leachinsky* [1947] A.C. 573; the Police and Criminal Evidence Act 1984, s.28.

[95] *Fox, Campbell and Hartley v. United Kingdom* (1991) 13 E.H.R.R. 157, para. 40.

[96] *Ireland v. United Kingdom* (1979–80) 2 E.H.R.R. 25, para. 198; *Fox, Campbell and Hartley v. United Kingdom* (1991) 13 E.H.R.R. 157, para. 41; *Murray v. United Kingdom* (1995) 19 E.H.R.R. 193, para. 76.

[97] *X v. Germany* (1978) 16 D.R. 111, para. 114.

It will not always be necessary to inform a detained person of every charge which may later be brought, providing the information supplied is sufficient to justify the arrest.[98] Once a person has been charged, however, there is an additional entitlement under Article 6(3)(a) to be informed in detail of the nature and cause of the accusation against him.[99]

It is not always necessary for the relevant information to be given at the very   **5–23** moment of the arrest, provided it is given within a sufficient period following the arrest.[1] In a number of cases the Court and Commission have held that the obligation in Article 5(2) will be met if the information is provided during the course of questioning following an initial arrest.[2] In *Fox, Campbell and Hartley v. United Kingdom*[3] the Court held that the offences in relation to which the applicants were being questioned by the police must have come to their attention through the questions being asked of them, even though they were not directly informed of the reasons for their arrest. The court further held that the period of several hours during which the reasons for the arrest emerged from the police questioning "cannot be regarded as falling outside the constraints of time imposed by the notion of promptness in Article 5(2)".[4] In *Delcourt v. Belgium*[5] an arrest warrant was issued in Dutch in respect of a French speaking detainee. The Commission found no violation because the subsequent questioning, in which the reasons for the arrest became apparent, was conducted in French.

H. INFORMATION TO BE PROVIDED AT THE MOMENT OF CHARGE

Article 6(3)(a) provides that an accused person should be informed promptly, in   **5–24** a language he understands and in detail, of the nature and cause of the accusation against him. What is the scope of this obligation? Article 6(3) applies when a person is "charged with a criminal offence". As we have seen,[6] the term "charge" has an autonomous meaning under the Convention. The Court in *Eckle v. Germany*[7] held that a person may be "charged" within the meaning of Article 6:

> " . . . on a date prior to the case coming before the trial court, such as the date of arrest, the date when the person concerned was officially notified that he would be prosecuted or the date when preliminary investigations were opened. 'Charge' for the purposes of

---

[98] Application 4220/69 *X v. United Kingdom* (1971) 14 Y.B. 250 at 278; *McVeigh, O'Neill and Evans v. United Kingdom* (1983) 5 E.H.R.R. 71, para. 210.
[99] See para. 5–24.
[1] *Fox, Campbell and Hartley v. United Kingdom* (1991) 13 E.H.R.R. 157, para. 40. *Cf. Van der Leer v. Netherlands* (1990) 12 E.H.R.R. 567 where a delay of 10 days was held to violate Art. 5(2) in the context of detention of a mental patient.
[2] *Fox, Campbell and Hartley v. United Kingdom* (1991) 13 E.H.R.R. 157, para. 41; *Murray v. United Kingdom* (1995) 19 E.H.R.R. 193, para. 77.
[3] (1990) 13 E.H.R.R. 157.
[4] *ibid.*, at para. 42.
[5] (1967) 10 Y.B. 238 at 270–272.
[6] See para. 4–45 above.
[7] (1983) 5 E.H.R.R. 1.

Article 6(1), may be defined as 'the official notification given to an individual by the competent authority of an allegation that he has committed a criminal offence.' "[8]

5–25   This decision concerned the concept of delay in Article 6(1) rather than the information to be provided at the time of arrest (Article 5(3)) or "charge" (Article 6(3)(a)). The tests ought to be similar, but it is fair to say that the Court in *Eckle* was not dealing with the kind of problem that may arise under Article 6(3)(a). Whilst it therefore provides authority for the suggestion that an arrest may amount to a "charge" for the purposes of determining whether or not Article 6 is applicable, the proposition that the two events are indistinguishable seems counter-intuitive in the present context, particularly in view of the fact that the Convention makes separate provision for the information to be provided at the moment of "arrest" and "charge". This conclusion draws some support from the ruling of the High Court of New Zealand, albeit in the slightly different context of the New Zealand Bill of Rights Act, that the term "charged" refers to "an intermediate step in the prosecutorial process", between arrest and appearance in court, "when the prosecuting authority formally advises an arrested person that he is to be prosecuted and gives him particulars of the charges he will face."[9]

5–26   The requirement that an accused person be informed "in a language he understands" was held to have been violated in *Brozicek v. Italy*,[10] where the Italian authorities brushed aside the applicant's protest that he did not understand the documents sent to him in Italian. Turning to the level of detail to be given to the accused about the charges, the *Brozicek* decision interpreted Article 6(3)(a) somewhat restrictively. The documents in that case: "sufficiently listed the offences of which he was accused, stated the place and date thereof, referred to the relevant Articles of the Criminal Code and mentioned the name of the victim."[11]

5–27   The information provided under English law by the issuing of a summons or the proffering of a charge will almost always be sufficient to meet the limited requirements of Article 6(3)(a). However, there may be circumstances in which greater detail is required. For example, in the Canadian case of *Lucas*[12] the information gave the date and place of the offence, but merely alleged the operating of an overweight vehicle contrary to a certain Act. In fact there were regulations made under that Act which set out eight different ways in which the offence might be committed, and the Supreme Court of Nova Scotia held that the accused had not been adequately "informed of the specific offence", as required by the Canadian Charter. He should have been informed which of the eight forms of the offence was to be relied upon by the prosecution.[13]

---

[8] *ibid.*, at para. 73, quoting from *Deweer v. Belgium* (1979–80) 2 E.H.R.R. 439, at para. 46.

[9] *Gibbons* [1997] 2 N.Z.L.R. 585, *per* Goddard J. at 595.

[10] (1990) 12 E.H.R.R. 371.

[11] *ibid.*, at para. 42. See also *X v. Belgium* (1977) 9 D.R. 169.

[12] (1983) 6 C.C.C. (3d) 147.

[13] A question might be raised about the wording of some indictments alleging complicity, in which, taking advantage of the Accessories and Abettors Act 1861, the prosecution charges a person with an offence without specifying whether he is alleged to be the principal or an accessory. It is well established in English law that the prosecution may then proceed on either basis (see the discussion in *Giannetto* [1997] 1 Cr. App. R. 1), but in at least one case the House of Lords has recognised that it is desirable for the prosecution to be as precise as possible (see *Maxwell v. DPP for Northern Ireland* [1979] 1 W.L.R. 1350). The thrust of Art. 6(3)(a) might suggest that precision should be the rule here.

I. DETENTION IN POLICE CUSTODY

Article 5(3) provides that every person who has been arrested or detained in **5–28** accordance with Article 5(1)(c) must be brought promptly before a judge or other judicial officer, and is entitled to trial within a reasonable time or to release pending trial. It applies only to criminal offences.[14] The twin aims of this provision are (a) to limit the period of detention by the police before a detainee's first production in court and (b) to establish a *prima facie* right to bail. The right to bail is considered in detail in chapter 13 below. This section is concerned with the permissible length of detention prior to an accused person's first appearance in court.

The requirements of Article 5(3) are to be construed in the light of the object and **5–29** purpose of Article 5 which is "the protection of the individual against arbitrary interferences by the state with his right to liberty"[15] and in the context of the importance attached to Article 5 within the Convention legal order.[16] The term "judge or other officer authorised by law" has the same meaning as the term "competent legal authority" in Article 5(1)(c).[17]

In the case of a person arrested by the police this will be a magistrates' court. **5–30** However, the detention of service personnel pending a court martial by order of the commanding officer does not meet the requirements of Article 5(3).[18] The tribunal must be independent of the investigating and prosecuting authorities,[19] and it must be impartial in the sense of being free from actual bias and from the appearance of bias.[20] It must also be empowered to make a legally binding decision ordering release.[21] In addition:

> " . . . under Article 5(3) there is both a procedural and a substantive requirement. The procedural requirement places the 'officer' under the obligation of himself hearing the individual brought before him; the substantive requirement imposes on him the obligations of reviewing the circumstances militating for or against detention, of deciding, by reference to legal criteria, whether there are reasons to justify detention and of ordering release if there are no such reasons".[22]

The state is obliged to take the initiative for a detained person to be brought **5–31** before an appropriate tribunal. In *McGoff v. Sweden*[23] the Commission held that

---

[14] *De Wilde, Ooms and Versyp v. Netherlands* (1979–80) 1 E.H.R.R. 373 para. 71.
[15] *Brogan v. United Kingdom* (1989) 11 E.H.R.R. 117, para. 58.
[16] *Brogan v. United Kingdom* (1989) 11 E.H.R.R. 117, para. 58.
[17] *Lawless v. Ireland (No. 3)* (1979–80) 1 E.H.R.R. 15, paras 13–14; *Ireland v. United Kingdom* (1979–80) 2 E.H.R.R. 25, para. 199; *Schiesser v. Switzerland* (1979–80) 2 E.H.R.R. 417, para. 29. On Art. 5(1)(c), see para. 5–16.
[18] *Hood v. United Kingdom* (2000) 29 E.H.R.R. 365; *Jordan v. United Kingdom, The Times*, March 17, 2000.
[19] *De Jong, Baljet and Van Den Brink v. Netherlands* (1986) 8 E.H.R.R. 20, para. 49; *Schiesser v. Switzerland* (1979–80) 2 E.H.R.R. 417, paras 29 and 30.
[20] *Huber v. Switzerland* (1990) Series A/188, para. 43. *Cf.* the Court's interpretation of the impartiality requirement in Art. 6(1) (see paras 14–67 to 14–80 below).
[21] *Ireland v. United Kingdom* (1979–80) 2 E.H.R.R. 25, para. 199.
[22] *Schiesser v. Switzerland* (1979–80) 2 E.H.R.R. 417, para. 31.
[23] (1982) 31 D.R. 72.

Article 5(3) imposes an "unconditional obligation" on the State to bring the accused "automatically and promptly" before a court.[24]

5-32 In the context of Article 5(3) the Court has observed that "the degree of flexibility attached to the notion of 'promptness' is limited".[25] Whilst allowance will be made for the special features of each case, the Court has held that the significance attached to those features can never be taken to the point "of effectively negativing the state's obligation to ensure a prompt release or a prompt appearance before a judicial authority".[26] Although the Court and Commission have refrained from setting abstract time limits, it seems certain that the general regime established by the Police and Criminal Evidence Act 1984, ss 41–46 would be found to comply with Article 5(3). By contrast in *Brincat v. Italy*[27] the Court held that detention for four days without being brought before a judicial officer was not "prompt" within the meaning of Article 5(3). Similarly, detention for four days and six hours under the Prevention of Terrorism (Temporary Provisions) Act 1976 was found to breach Article 5(3) in *Brogan v. United Kingdom.*[28] Even accepting the considerable margin of appreciation allowed to states in the sphere of prevention of terrorism, the Court held that detention of this length without being brought before a court ran counter to the principle of "judicial control of interferences by the executive with the individual's right to liberty."[29] Following this decision the British government entered a derogation from Article 5(3), retaining the power of extended detention. A subsequent challenge to the derogation was defeated in *Brannigan and McBride v. United Kingdom,*[30] where the Court held the derogation to be compatible with the requirements of Article 15. This remains the United Kingdom's only designated derogation, and is expressly incorporated into domestic law by section 14(1)(a) and Schedule 3 to the Human Rights Act 1998. Section 16(1)(a) of the Act places a time limit of five years on its operation, subject to renewal by the Secretary of State under section 16(2).

J. HABEAS CORPUS

5-33 Article 5(4) provides that everyone who is deprived of his liberty is entitled to take proceedings by which the lawfulness of his detention can be decided speedily by a court and his release ordered if his detention is not lawful.[31] This guarantees the right to *habeas corpus* in order to challenge the legality of

---

[24] This decision does not appear to have been cited in *Olotu v. Home Office* [1997] 1 W.L.R. 328 where Lord Bingham C.J. held that detention following the expiry of custody time limits did not involve a breach of Art. 5(3) because the relevant legislation placed the onus on the defendant to make an application for bail.

[25] Note that the French text uses the word "aussitôt" which connotes a greater degree of immediacy: *Brogan v. United Kingdom* (1989) 11 E.H.R.R. 117 paras 58–59. See also *Koster v. Netherlands* (1992) 14 E.H.R.R. 396, para. 24.

[26] *Brogan v. United Kingdom* (1989) 11 E.H.R.R. 117, para. 59; *Koster v. Netherlands* (1992) 14 E.H.R.R. 396, para. 24.

[27] (1993) 16 E.H.R.R. 591.

[28] (1989) 11 E.H.R.R. 117.

[29] *ibid.*, at para. 58.

[30] (1994) 17 E.H.R.R. 539.

[31] The term "lawfulness" in Art. 5(4) has the same meaning as the term "lawful" in Art. 5(1): *Brogan v. United Kingdom* (1989) 1 E.H.R.R. 117, para. 65.

executive detention. On any Article 5(4) review, the burden of proving the lawfulness of the detention rests with the state,[32] a principle which is fully observed in domestic *habeas corpus* proceedings. Thus, in *Brogan v. United Kingdom*[33] the Court found that *habeas corpus* would have been an adequate procedure for challenging detention under Article 5(1)(c).

In the context of criminal proceedings, the right to challenge the legality of 5–34 detention arises automatically on first appearance in court, when the accused has the right to apply for bail.[34] To that extent, the requirements of Article 5(4) intersect with the right to prompt production, and the right to bail in Article 5(3). As we have seen, the rights guaranteed by Article 5(3) are automatic, whereas Article 5(4) affords a right for the detained person to *initiate proceedings* to challenge the legality of a detention. In the context of arrest and detention in police custody, the principal relevance of Article 5(4) is that it guarantees the right of the accused to challenge the legality of his detention by the police prior to his first production in court. Although such applications are rare, the High Court will hear a *habeas corpus* application relating to a person in police custody as a matter of urgency where it is alleged that the police have no legal right to detain (or to continue the detention of) a suspect.

Under Article 5(4), the application for release must be determined "speedily".[35] 5–35 In *Sanchez-Reisse v. Switzerland*[36] the Court emphasised that the term "speed-ily" cannot be defined in the abstract. As with the "reasonable time" stipulations in Article 5(3) and Article 6(1) it must be determined in the light of the circumstances of the individual case. Relevant considerations include the dili-gence shown by the authorities, any delay caused by the detained person, and any other factors causing delay that do not engage the state's responsibility.[37] The speed with which a *habeas corpus* application is generally heard in the High Court undoubtedly meets the standards set by Article 5(4).[38]

K. ILL-TREATMENT IN CUSTODY

The admission in criminal proceedings of evidence obtained by ill-treatment in 5–36 breach of Article 3 will violate Article 6.[39] It is a settled principle of Article 3 jurisprudence that "where an individual is taken into police custody in good

---

[32] Application 9174/80 *Zamir v. United Kingdom* (1983) 40 D.R. 42, para. 58. The Court of Appeal made a declaration of incompatibility under section 4 of the Human Rights Act 1998 in *R. v. Mental Health Review Tribunal, North and East London Region and anor, The Times,* April 2, 2001, holding that sections 72 and 73 of the Mental Health Act 1983 were incompatible with Article 5 as they imposed the burden of proof on the patient to satisfy the tribunal that he was no longer suffering from a mental disorder warranting detention.

[33] (1989) 11 E.H.R.R. 117, para. 65.

[34] See Chapter 13 below.

[35] The requirement of "promptness" in Art. 5(3) connotes a greater degree of urgency than the term "speedily" in Art. 5(4): *E v. Norway* (1994) 17 E.H.R.R. 30, para. 64.

[36] (1987) 9 E.H.R.R. 71, para. 55.

[37] *Sanchez-Reisse v. Switzerland* (1987) 9 E.H.R.R. 71, para. 56.

[38] Periods of four days and 16 days have been held acceptable (*Egue v. France* (1988) 57 D.R. 47 at 71; *Christenet v. Switzerland* (1979) 17 D.R. 25 at 57), whereas delays of 31 days and 46 days have been held to violate Art. 5(4) (*Sanchez-Reisse v. Switzerland* (1987) 9 E.H.R.R. 71).

[39] *Austria v. Italy* (1963) 6 Y.B. 740 at 748.

health, but is found to be injured at the time of release, it is incumbent on the state to provide a plausible explanation as to the causing of the injury".[40] In *Tomasi v. France*[41] the applicant, a terrorist suspect, alleged that he had been slapped, kicked, punched, and ill-treated in other ways, over a two day period whilst he was being questioned in a police station. He adduced medical evidence establishing that he was injured at the time of his release. In the absence of any explanation from the government, the Court presumed the necessary causal connection, and found a violation of Article 3. This was despite the findings of the French courts that the officers concerned had no case to answer.[42] Similarly, in *Ribitsch v. Austria*[43] the Court endorsed the Commission's statement that "it was for the Government to produce evidence establishing facts which cast doubt on the account of events given by the victim, particularly if this account was supported by medical certificates".[44] On the facts of that case, the Court considered that the government had "not satisfactorily established that the applicant's injuries were caused otherwise than . . . by the treatment he underwent while in police custody". The fact that the alleged perpetrator had been acquitted in criminal proceedings was not sufficient.[45]

5–37   In *Selmouni v. France*[46] the Court held that "in respect of a person deprived of his liberty, recourse to physical force which has not been made strictly necessary by his own conduct diminishes human dignity and is in principle an infringement of the right set forth in Article 3". Altering the boundaries of the treatment prohibited by Article 3, the Court held that the standards of treatment of those detained in custody had evolved, and that certain acts which would in the past have been classified as "inhuman and degrading treatment" should now be regarded as deserving the special stigma attached to the term "torture". In the Court's view, "the increasingly high standard being required in the area of the protection of human rights and fundamental liberties correspondingly and inevitably requires greater firmness in assessing breaches of the fundamental values of democratic societies." On the facts, the applicant had been subjected to serious assaults over a number of days in police custody. He had been struck several times, dragged along a corridor by his hair, made to run the gauntlet of a number of officers trying to trip him up, made to kneel, urinated upon and threatened with

---

[40] *Aksoy v. Turkey* (1996) 23 E.H.R.R. 553 at para. 61.

[41] (1993) 15 E.H.R.R. 1 at paras 104–116.

[42] *Tomasi* was distinguished in *Klaas v. Germany* (1994) 18 E.H.R.R. 305 at paras 26–31 where the applicant's injuries were allegedly sustained *during the course of an arrest*. The applicant and the police officers involved gave conflicting accounts as to how the applicant's injuries had been sustained. The medical evidence was, in the Court's view, consistent with both accounts, and the Court was not prepared to depart from the findings of the national courts in the absence of "cogent evidence". In the light of the Court's subsequent judgment in *Ribitsch v. Austria* (1996) 21 E.H.R.R. 573, *Klaas* must now be regarded as confined to cases where injuries are sustained at the time of initial detention.

[43] (1996) 21 E.H.R.R. 573.

[44] Para. 31.

[45] See *Ribitsch* at para. 34, where the Court emphasised that an "acquittal in criminal proceedings by a court bound by the principle of the presumption of innocence does not absolve [the state] from its responsibility under the Convention". The judgment in *Ribitsch* draws a clear distinction between the standard of proof required for a criminal conviction and the standard adopted by the Court under Art. 3. This distinction is not easy to reconcile with the standard of proof beyond reasonable doubt referred to in *Ireland v. United Kingdom* (1979–80) 2 E.H.R.R. 25 at para. 161.

[46] (2000) 29 E.H.R.R. 403 at para. 99.

a blowtorch and a syringe. This was sufficient to amount to torture within the meaning of Article 3.

L. ACCESS TO LEGAL ADVICE IN POLICE CUSTODY

Section 58 of the Police and Criminal Evidence Act 1984 provides that a detained   **5–38**
person may have access to independent legal advice on request, unless delayed access is authorised in accordance with the section. A breach of section 58 may be a ground for exclusion of evidence under sections 76 or 78.[47] The relevant Convention standard is generally flexible enough to permit the restrictions established in section 58. The right of access to a solicitor has been implied by the Commission and the Court into Article 6(3), since it is "fundamental to the preparation of [an accused person's] defence".[48] However in *Bonzi v. Switzerland*[49] the Commission observed that "in the absence of any explicit provision [in the Convention] it cannot be maintained that the right to confer with one's counsel and exchange confidential instructions or information with him is subject to no restriction whatsoever".[50] The Court has explicitly rejected the argument that the right to legal representation in Article 6(3)(c) only becomes relevant at the trial: although it forms part of the "fair trial" requirements, it "may also be relevant before a case is sent for trial if and in so far as the fairness of the trial is likely to be prejudiced by an initial failure to comply with them."[51] In *Imbroscia v. Switzerland*, however, the Court held that the failure of the police and public prosecutor to notify the defence lawyers of the interrogations (with the result that the applicant was questioned in their absence) was remedied when the defence lawyer did attend the final interview, and made no objection to the record of the previous interviews.[52]

Against this general background, there are two potential areas of difficulty which   **5–39**
deserve particular mention. The first concerns delay in access to a solicitor in the context of sections 34 to 37 of the Criminal Justice and Public Order Act 1994 (CJPOA) which permit juries to draw adverse inferences from a defendant's failure to answer questions in the police station, and/or failure to testify at trial. In *Murray v. United Kingdom*[53] the Court held that where domestic legislation permits the drawing of adverse inferences from a decision not to answer questions in interview, the right of access to a solicitor in the police station is "of paramount importance"[54] such that a substantial delay on any ground will breach the right to a fair trial. In view of the adverse inference provisions of the Criminal Evidence (Northern Ireland) Order 1988, a delay in granting access to legal advice was held to amount to a breach of Article 6, even though it was carried out lawfully: "[E]ven a lawfully exercised power of restriction is capable of

---

[47] *R. v. Samuel* [1988] Q.B. 615; *R. v. Silcott and ors*, *The Times*, December 9, 1991; *R. v. Alladice* (1988) 87 Cr. App. R. 380 and *R. v. Absolam* (1989) 88 Cr. App. R. 332.
[48] *Bonzi v. Switzerland* (1978) 12 D.R. 185 at 190.
[49] (1978) 12 D.R. 185.
[50] *ibid.*, at 190.
[51] *Imbroscia v. Switzerland* (1994) 17 E.H.R.R. 441 at para. 36.
[52] *ibid.*; *cf.* the vigorous dissenting judgment of Judge Pettiti.
[53] (1996) 22 E.H.R.R. 29.
[54] *ibid.*, para. 66.

depriving an accused, in certain circumstances, of a fair procedure."[55] The Court held that:

> "[T]he concept of fairness enshrined in Article 6 requires that the accused has the benefit of the assistance of a lawyer . . . at the initial stage of police interrogation. To deny access to a lawyer for the first 48 hours of police questioning, in a situation where the rights of the defence may well be irretrievably prejudiced, is—whatever the justification for such denial—incompatible with the rights of the accused under Article 6."[56]

5–40   That view has now been accepted by the government, as recent legislation demonstrates.[57] It was also used as a plank in the reasoning of the Court of Appeal decision in *Aspinall*,[58] where a schizophrenic defendant had been interviewed without the presence of an "appropriate adult" and after such a long delay in obtaining a duty solicitor that he agreed to be interviewed without legal advice. The Court of Appeal relied on *Murray* in concluding that the trial judge should have excluded the interview under his section 78 discretion.

5–41   *Murray* must be taken to have overruled earlier decisions on this point. In *G v. United Kingdom*[59] the applicant had been refused access to a lawyer until he confessed, and the Commission left open the question whether Article 6(3)(c) guaranteed access to a lawyer at the pre-charge stage. This is surely inconsistent with, and displaced by, *Murray*. In *Di Stefano v. United Kingdom*[60] the applicant's lawyer was present when he was charged and when his home and the lawyer's office were searched by police. He then spent over two days in custody, during which the police refused to allow him to see his lawyer. The lawyer made a bail application on his behalf, and there were many consultations during the lengthy period before his trial. The Commission noted that an accused person's right to communicate freely with a lawyer "cannot be said to be insusceptible of restriction," and that the general principle of fairness under Article 6 should be the guiding criterion. The comparatively short period during which the applicant was prevented from seeing his solicitor, after charge, was held not to violate either Article 6(3)(b) (preparation of defence) or Article 6(3)(c) (right to legal assistance).

5–42   The second area of difficulty concerns the facilities which are available for private telephone consultations in the police station. In *S v. Switzerland*[61] the Court held that Article 6(3)(c) should be interpreted so as to guarantee confidentiality of communications between a detained person and his lawyer. Eavesdropping or interception by a third person (here, the government) was held to violate "one of the basic requirements of a fair trial in a democratic society".[62] There are

---

[55] *ibid.*, para. 65.
[56] *ibid.*, para. 66.
[57] The right is recognised in the Criminal Justice (Terrorism and Conspiracy) Act 1998, and the Youth Justice and Criminal Evidence Act 1999.
[58] [1999] Crim. L.R. 741.
[59] (1984) 35 D.R. 75.
[60] (1989) 60 D.R. 182.
[61] (1992) 14 E.H.R.R. 670.
[62] *ibid.*, at para. 48.

other occasions on which the Court has emphasised the principle of the confidentiality of lawyer-client communications.[63] This principle has the potential to raise significant practical problems since very few police stations in England and Wales are equipped with facilities to enable a detained person to consult a solicitor privately over the telephone. Telephone consultations are usually required to take place in the presence of the custody officer, who is then in a position to hear at least part of the conversation.

Finally, brief reference should be made to *Schonenberger and Durmaz v. Switzer-*   **5–43**
land[64] where the Court emphasised the importance of enabling a person in police custody to consult a lawyer of his (or in this case his family's) choice. Whilst the second applicant was in police custody for drugs offences his wife instructed a lawyer (the first applicant) to represent her husband. The lawyer wrote a letter addressed to the suspect and sent it to the public prosecutor's office, asking that it be forwarded to his client. The letter contained forms of authority and also gave certain basic advice on the right to remain silent. Having read the letter the public prosecutor refused to pass it on, on the ground that it might impede the inquiry. In seeking to resist a finding that there had been a violation of the right to legal professional privilege in Article 6[65] the Swiss government argued that privilege did not attach since the lawyer had not been formally instructed by the suspect. The Court rejected this argument, noting that the lawyer had been instructed by the suspect's wife, and had subsequently made attempts to contact his client. In the Court's view, these contacts "amounted to preliminary steps intended to enable the second applicant to have the benefit of the assistance of a defence lawyer of his choice and, thereby, to exercise a right enshrined in another fundamental provision of the Convention, namely Article 6".

---

[63] *E.g. Niemietz v. Germany* (1993) 16 E.H.R.R. 97, at para. 37: "where a lawyer in involved, an encroachment on professional secrecy may have repercussions on the proper administration of justice and hence on the rights guaranteed by Article 6 of the Convention." See also *Kopp v. Switzerland* [1998] E.H.R.L.R. 508.
[64] (1989) 11 E.H.R.R. 202.
[65] See generally para. 14–14 *et seq.* below.

CHAPTER 6

ENTRY, SEARCH AND SEIZURE

A. INTRODUCTION

I. *The Common Law Principle*

In *Entick v. Carrington*[1] Lord Camden C.J. laid down the fundamental principle   **6–01** that the executive cannot enter private premises without judicial or statutory authority;

> "No man can set his foot upon my ground without my licence, but he is liable to an action, though the damage is nothing . . . If he admits the fact, he is bound to show by way of justification, that some positive law has empowered or excused him. The justification is submitted to the judges, who are to look into the books and if such a justification can be maintained by the text of the statute law, or by the principles of the common law. If no such excuse can be found or produced, the silence of the books is an authority against the defendant . . . Papers are the owner's goods and chattels . . . and so far from enduring a seizure . . . they will hardly bear an inspection; and though the eye cannot by the laws of England be guilty of trespass, yet where private papers are removed and carried away, the secret nature of those goods will be an aggravation of the trespass and demand more considerable damages in that respect. Where is the written law that gives any magistrate such a power? I can safely answer, there is none; and therefore it is too much for us without such authority to pronounce a practice legal, which would be subversive of all the comforts of society."

Accordingly, an entry and search carried out pursuant to an executive warrant   **6–02** was held to be unlawful. The common law thus protects the principle, reflected in Article 8 of the Convention, that any interference with the right to respect for private life, home and correspondence, must be prescribed by law. This does not, however, exhaust the requirements of Article 8 and there are numerous statutory, and certain common law powers of entry which must be exercised in conformity with the Human Rights Act.

II. *The Police and Criminal Evidence Act 1984*

The Police and Criminal Evidence Act 1984 (PACE), Part II, consolidated many   **6–03** but not all[2] of the statutory powers of entry, search and seizure in English law.

---

[1] [1765] 19 State Trials 1029.
[2] The police powers of entry not repealed by PACE include the warrant powers in the Obscene Publications Act 1959, s.3, the Theft Act 1968, s.26, and the Misuse of Drugs Act 1971, s.23. There are, in addition, numerous statutory powers of entry, search and seizure conferred on other public officials, including the Inland Revenue Commissioners, Customs and Excise officials and officers of central and local government: see generally Stone, *Entry, Search and Seizure* (3rd ed., 1997). Section 9(2) of PACE provides that any Act under which a search of premises for the purposes of a criminal investigation could be authorised by the issue of a search warrant shall cease to have effect insofar as it relates to authorisation of searches for items subject to legal professional privilege, excluded material or special material.

Section 8 governs the power of a justice of the peace to issue a search warrant where there are reasonable grounds for believing that a serious arrestable offence has been committed, and that there is relevant evidence on the premises to be searched which is likely to be of substantial value to the investigation. The power does not apply[3] to items subject to legal professional privilege,[4] excluded material (confidential personal records, medical samples, or journalistic material held in confidence),[5] or to "special procedure" material.[6] A search warrant is only to be granted under section 8 if it is impracticable to communicate with the person entitled to grant entry to the premises or access to the evidence, if entry would not be granted without a warrant, or if the purpose of the search would be frustrated or seriously impeded if police were unable to obtain immediate access.[7]

6–04 Section 9 and Schedule 1 provide a "special procedure" for obtaining access to excluded and special procedure material, either by means of a production order, or by means of a warrant. Such an application is to be made to a circuit judge.[8] So far as production orders are concerned, Schedule 1 provides two sets of "access conditions" which must be met as a precondition to the grant of an order.[9] The first set of access conditions applies to special procedure material other than excluded material, and consists of three requirements. First, there must be reasonable grounds for believing that a serious arrestable offence has been committed, that there is special procedure material on the premises,[10] and that the material consists of relevant evidence[11] which is likely to be of substantial value to the investigation.[12] Secondly, other methods of obtaining the material must have been tried without success or otherwise be bound to fail.[13] Thirdly, the judge must consider that the making of an order would be in the public interest, having regard to the benefit likely to accrue to the investigation if the material is obtained, and the circumstances in which it is held.[14] The second set of access conditions applies to special procedure *or excluded material*, and requires that the conditions for the grant of a warrant are otherwise met.[15] When either set of conditions is fulfilled, the judge may make an order requiring the person in

---

[3] Section 8(1)(d). See also *R. v. Guildhall Magistrates ex parte Primlaks Holdings* [1990] 1 Q.B. 261.
[4] As to the meaning of legal professional privilege see s.10. See also para. 6–14 below.
[5] As to the meaning of excluded material see s.11.
[6] Special procedure material is defined by s.12 to be (a) journalistic material, other than material held in confidence, and (b) material held by a person a person who created or acquired it in the course of a trade, business, profession, occupation or office and which is held subject to an express or implied undertaking to hold it in confidence, or subject to a statutory restriction on its disclosure.
[7] Section 8(3).
[8] Such an application may be heard in chambers: *R. v. Central Criminal Court ex parte DPP*, *The Times*, April 1, 1998.
[9] The judge may not make an order unless he is personally satisfied that the access conditions are met: *R. v. Lewes Crown Court ex parte Hill* 93 Cr. App. R. 60.
[10] The applicant must set out a description of all the material sought: *R. v. Central Criminal Court ex parte Adegbesan* 84 Cr. App. R. 219. There is a duty of full disclosure: *R. v. Acton Crown Court ex parte Layton* [1993] Crim. L.R. 458.
[11] This means "anything that would be admissible in evidence at a trial for the offence": s.8(4).
[12] Sched. 1 para. 2(a).
[13] Sched. 1 para 2(b).
[14] Sched. 1 para. 2(c).
[15] Sched. 1 para. 3.

possession of the material to produce it or give access to it,[16] which is enforce-able through proceedings for contempt of court.[17] The power to make a production order is discretionary. In *R. v. Central Criminal Court ex parte The Guardian, The Observer and Martin Bright*,[18] Judge L.J. held that in exercising this discretion, the judge should take account of fundamental rights, including the right to privacy, the right to freedom of expression and the protection against self-incrimination;

> "This provision, as it seems to me, is the final safeguard against an oppressive order, and in an appropriate case, provides the judge with the opportunity to reflect on and take account of matters which are not expressly referred to in the set of relevant access conditions and, where they arise, to reflect on all the circumstances including, where appropriate, what can, without exaggeration, be described as fundamental principles . . . [I]n my judgment the judge must take account of an apparent disproportion between what might possibly be gained by the production of the material and the offence to which it is said to relate, and . . . in the case of journalistic material, to the potential stifling of public debate, and . . . to the risk of imposing an obligation requiring the individual to whom the order is directed to incriminate himself".[19]

This is an important principle suggesting as it does[20] that the exercise of judicial   **6–05** discretion prior to the authorisation of a power of entry, search and seizure, provides an opportunity for judicial consideration of the compatibility of such an entry with Convention rights.[21] In certain circumstances a judge may, instead of making a production order, issue a warrant.[22] A warrant is only to be issued under section 9 and Schedule 1 where (a) it is impracticable to communicate with the person entitled to give entry to the premises or access to the material,[23] (b) the service of a production order notice would seriously prejudice the investigation,[24] or (c) the search is necessary to prevent a person from disclosing information in breach of a statutory obligation.[25]

Sections 15 and 16 provide additional safeguards governing the grant and   **6–06** execution of search warrants, whether issued under PACE or other legislation, and are to be read in conjunction with the detailed guidance set out in Code B (Code of Practice for the Searching of Premises by Police Officers). The application must state the ground on which, and the legislation under which, it is made; and must specify the premises to be searched, and—so far as practicable—the

---

[16] Sched. 1 para. 4.
[17] Sched. 1 para. 15.
[18] [2001] 1 W.L.R. 662.
[19] See also *R. v. Bristol Crown Court ex parte Bristol Press and Picture Agency Ltd* [1987] 85 Cr. App. R. 190.
[20] Judge L.J. was careful to emphasise that the decision applied only to s.9 and Sched. 1, but the principle would appear equally applicable to the power of a justice to grant or refuse a search warrant.
[21] *cf. Baron v Canada* [1993] 1 S.C.R. 416 where the Canadian Supreme Court held that the authorisation of a warrant must leave scope for judicial discretion if fundamental rights are to be respected.
[22] Sched. 1 para. 12.
[23] Sched. 1 para. 14(a) and (b).
[24] Sched. 1 para. 14(d).
[25] Sched. 1 para. 14(c).

articles sought.[26] This information is to be included in the warrant, together with the name of the officer making the application.[27] A warrant which is too widely drawn, or which includes privileged material is liable to be quashed.[28] The application is to be made *ex parte*, supported by an information in writing,[29] but the officer making it is to be available to give evidence on oath.[30] A warrant may authorise entry only on one occasion.[31] It authorises entry by any police constable together with any other person named or identified in the warrant.[32] Entry must take place within one month of the issue of the warrant,[33] and must be at a reasonable hour unless this would frustrate the purpose of the search.[34] Where the occupier or any other person is present the officer carrying out the search must identify himself, and provide the person concerned with a copy of the warrant.[35] If no one is present a copy of the warrant is to be left in a prominent place on the premises.[36] The constable executing the warrant is required to endorse it with a record of the items found and seized,[37] and to return it to the issuing court,[38] which is to retain the warrant for a period of 12 months, during which time it is available for inspection by the occupier of the premises to which it relates.[39] One of the most important safeguards is that contained in section 16 (8) which provides that "[a] search under a warrant may only be a search to the extent required for the purpose for which the warrant was issued"—in effect a requirement that the warrant be executed in a manner proportionate to its objective. Code B provides that:

> "Premises may be searched only to the extent necessary to achieve the object of the search, having regard to the size and nature of whatever is sought. A search under warrant may not continue under the authority of that warrant once all the things specified in it have been found, or the officer in charge of the search is satisfied that they are not on the premises[40] . . . Searches must be conducted with due consideration for the property and privacy of the occupier of the premises searched with no more disturbance than necessary . . . "[41]

6–07 Sections 17 and 18 of PACE set out the powers of police officers to enter private premises other than in pursuance of a warrant to search for evidence. Section 17 governs the power of entry for the purposes of executing an arrest warrant or a

---

[26] Section 15(2). See generally, *R. v. Central Criminal Court ex parte AJD Holdings* [1992] Crim. L.R. 669; *R. v. Reading Justices ex parte South West Meat Ltd* [1992] Crim. L.R. 672. See also *R. v. Maidstone Crown Court ex parte Waitt* [1988] Crim. L.R. 384; *R. v. Leeds Crown Court ex parte Switalski* [1991] C.O.D. 199
[27] Section 15(6).
[28] *R. v. Southampton Crown Court ex parte J and P* [1993] Crim. L.R. 962.
[29] Section 15(3).
[30] Section 15(4). As to the relevance of claims to public interest immunity in connection with the information provided, see *Taylor v. Anderton, The Times*, October 16, 1986.
[31] Section 15(5).
[32] Section 16(1) and (2).
[33] Section 16(3).
[34] Section 16(4).
[35] Section 16(5) and (6).
[36] Section 16(7).
[37] Section 16(9).
[38] Section 16(10). If the warrant has not been executed within the required time, it is to be returned to the issuing court on its expiry: *ibid.*
[39] Section 16(11) and (12).
[40] Para. B.5.9.
[41] Para. B.5.10.

warrant of commitment[42]; for the purposes of arresting a person for an arrestable offence[43] and certain specified non-arrestable offences[44]; for the purpose of recapturing persons unlawfully at large[45]; or for the purpose of saving life or limb or preventing serious damage to property.[46] Where the object of the entry is to effect an arrest, the power may only be exercised if,[47] and to the extent that,[48] there are reasonable grounds for believing that the person sought is on the premises. The power of search conferred by section 17 is "only a power to search to the extent that is reasonably required for the purpose for which the power of entry is exercised".[49] Apart from the power of entry to deal with or prevent a breach of the peace,[50] all common law powers of entry without warrant are abolished.[51]

Section 18 provides a statutory power of entry and search following arrest for an **6–08** arrestable offence. The power may be exercised where there are reasonable grounds for suspecting that there is, on premises occupied or controlled by the person under arrest, evidence (other than items subject to legal privilege) which relates to the offence for which he is under arrest or to another, connected or similar, arrestable offence.[52] A search under section 18 requires the written authorisation of an officer of the rank of inspector or above,[53] unless the accused's presence is required (in which case an inspector or above must be informed as soon as practicable).[54] The power of search may only be exercised "to the extent that is reasonably required for the purposes of discovering [the] evidence".[55] Any item which is evidence of an arrestable offence may be seized and retained.[56] Sections 19 to 21 make further provision for the seizure of evidence.

B. THE CONVENTION APPROACH

I. *General*

The Convention differs from other constitutional instruments in failing to make **6–09** specific provision against unlawful entry, search and seizure. These issues are,

---

[42] Section 17(1)(a).
[43] Section 17(1)(b).
[44] Section 17(1)(c).
[45] Section 17(1)(ca), (cb) and (d).
[46] Section 17(1)(e).
[47] Section 17(2)(a).
[48] Section 17(2)(b) imposes further limitations where the property to be searched is a dwelling.
[49] Section 17(4).
[50] Section 17(6).
[51] Section 17(5).
[52] Section 18(1).
[53] Section 18(4). Section 18(7) provides that the authorising officer must record the grounds for the search and the nature of the evidence sought in writing. As to the effect of a breach of this provision see *Krohn v. DPP* [1997] C.O.D. 345. Section 18(8) provides that where the person concerned is in police custody this information is to be included in the custody record. A failure to comply does not however necessarily render the evidence so obtained inadmissible: *R. v. Wright* [1994] Crim. L.R. 55.
[54] Section 18(5).
[55] Section 18(3).
[56] Section 18(2).

however, addressed in the Court's caselaw under Article 8. In general, it can be said that any entry onto private premises will amount to an interference with the rights guaranteed by Article 8(1). This applies not only to a person's home, but also to business premises.[57] Such an interference must therefore meet the requirements of Article 8(2). Any entry or search must be "in accordance with the law" and proportionate to one of the legitimate aims there set out—typically the prevention of crime. This implies that the law must be accessible and foreseeable; it must afford adequate safeguards against abuse; there must be no other, less intrusive method, of obtaining the relevant evidence; and a power of search must be exercised in practice in a manner which is proportionate. Prior judicial authorisation is not necessarily indispensible, but in the absence of such authorisation the Court will closely scrutinise the safeguards in place in domestic law to prevent disproportionate interference with privacy rights,[58] paying particular attention to the manner in which the power has been exercised in practice.[59]

6–10 As we have seen, the framework established by the Police and Criminal Evidence Act 1984 broadly reflects the requirements of Article 8, at least so far as the warrant and production order procedures are concerned. The Act affords a statutory basis for entry into private premises; requires prior judicial authorisation where practicable; confines powers of entry to arrestable offences; requires that less intrusive methods should either have failed or be impracticable; affords added protection for confidential, journalistic and privileged material; and embodies the principle that searches may only be made to the extent reasonably required for the purpose. The powers of police officers and others to enter and search premises without a warrant are less secure in Convention terms.[60] But the important point in either case is that it is the *exercise* of those powers on a particular set of facts, and not merely the legislation itself, which must be examined for compatibility with the Convention. As the Strasbourg caselaw has shown, the powers conferred by PACE are capable of being exercised in a manner which amounts to a disproportionate interference with privacy rights.

II. *Powers of Entry*

6–11 Section 17(6) of PACE expressly preserves the common law power of entry to deal with or prevent a breach of the peace. The leading authority on the exercise of this power is *Thomas v. Sawkins*.[61] In *McLeod v. United Kingdom*[62] police officers had relied on this power in order to enter the applicant's home in her absence, so as to assist her former husband to remove property. The officers (wrongly) believed that the husband was entitled to remove the property in question under a court order made in the course of acrimonious matrimonial proceedings. The husband and his solicitor had asked the police to accompany them in order to prevent trouble occurring. The applicant complained that her right to respect for her private life and home under Article 8 had been violated. In the Court's view the officers' actions were "in accordance with the law", the

---

[57] *Niemietz v. Germany* (1993) 16 E.H.R.R. 97 at para. 29.
[58] *Camenzind v. Switzerland* (1999) 28 E.H.R.R. 458.
[59] *McLeod v. United Kingdom* (1999) 27 E.H.R.R. 493.
[60] See the principle cited in *Camenzind v. Switzerland* (1999) 28 E.H.R.R. 458 at para. 45.
[61] [1935] K.B. 249.
[62] (1999) 27 E.H.R.R. 493.

power of entry to prevent a breach of the peace being defined with sufficient precision to meet the Convention standard of legal certainty.[63] As to the justification for the entry, the Court accepted that the prevention of disorder was a legitimate aim in this context, but held that the officers' actions were not "necessary in a democratic society". The Court concluded that the officers ought to have checked the court order themselves rather than taking the former husband's word for it. Had they done so, they would have realised that the applicant was not obliged to surrender the property at that time. Moreover, the officers ought to have realised that no breach of the peace was likely (only the applicant's elderly mother being in the house when the entry occurred).[64] In finding a violation of Article 8 on the facts, the Court emphasised that the power of entry to prevent a breach of the peace must, in the same way as the power of arrest to prevent a breach of the peace be regarded as an incursion into a citizen's private life and liberty which requires careful justification.

III. *Search and Seizure*

The leading decision on search and seizure is *Funke v. France*,[65] where customs officials had searched the applicant's house and had seized documents as part of an inquiry into exchange-control offences. The French government conceded that the applicant's Article 8 right had been interfered with. The Court held that the search pursued the legitimate aim of protecting "the economic well-being of the country", but emphasised that the exceptions in Article 8(2) should be interpreted narrowly and that, although judicial authorisation of search warrants was not a requirement of Article 8, "the relevant legislation and practice must afford adequate and effective safeguards against abuse." In the Court's view, the French customs law in force at that time failed to satisfy this standard. The powers of the customs officers were unduly wide since "they had exclusive competence to assess the expediency, number, length and scale of inspections". Moreover, "the restrictions and conditions provided for in law . . . appear[ed] too lax and full of loopholes for the interferences with the applicant's right to have been strictly proportionate to the legitimate aim pursued."[66] With these strong words the Court found that the search was not "necessary in a democratic society" and constituted a violation of Article 8.   **6-12**

The Court pursued a similarly strong approach in *Niemietz v. Germany*,[67] where the German police had searched a lawyer's offices, under a court warrant, in order to find evidence of the whereabouts of one of the lawyer's clients. The German government argued that the case did not engage Article 8 at all, on the ground that a person's professional activities do not fall within the notion of "private life." The Court dismissed this argument, holding that most people's business or professional lives are so intimately connected with their private lives that they should equally be protected from arbitrary interference.[68] The Court   **6-13**

---

[63] This finding corresponds with the Court's finding in *Steel v. United Kingdom* (1999) 28 E.H.R.R. 603.
[64] *McLeod* judgment, para. 57.
[65] (1993) 16 E.H.R.R. 297.
[66] *ibid.*, paras 55–57.
[67] (1993) 16 E.H.R.R. 97.
[68] *ibid.*, paras 27–33.

accepted that the interference was in accordance with German law and had the aim of preventing crime. But it nevertheless held that the search was disproportionate because the warrant was drawn in broad and unspecific terms (it referred to 'documents' without any limitation) and because German law failed to provide any extra safeguards for searches of lawyers' offices where issues of professional confidentiality could be involved.[69] Moreover, the search had been carried out without the presence of an independent observer, and had been more extensive than was necessary for its stated purpose.

6–14   In *R. v. Chesterfield Justices and anor., ex parte Bramley*[70] the Divisional Court applied the principles laid down in *Niemietz* in considering the scope of a police officer's powers to seize and examine material which may be subject to legal professional privilege when executing a search warrant issued under section 8(1) of the Police and Criminal Evidence Act 1984. Under section 8(1) a magistrate may only issue a warrant if he has reasonable grounds for believing that the material on the premises does not consist of or include material subject to legal professional privilege. The Court held that where the officer applying for a warrant makes no reference to privilege, the magistrate is required to ask whether the material sought included privileged material. If, having made inquiries on the point, the magistrate had reasonable grounds to believe that material sought included privileged material then the terms of the warrant must be redefined. Once the warrant had been issued, it was unnecessary for the police officer executing it to be independently satisfied that there were no reasonable grounds for believing that privileged material was included within the material sought. That qualification in section 8(1) is directed to the state of mind of the magistrate not that of the officer executing the warrant. However, where the officer in fact has reasonable grounds for believing that material to be seized is covered by privilege, he has no power to seize it. Moreover, the Court held that an officer was not entitled to remove material for sifting outside the premises covered by the warrant. If he removed items which, on examination, turned out to be outside the scope of the warrant then the 1984 Act afforded no defence to a claim in trespass. As Kennedy L.J. explained:

> "To put the matter in terms which would meet the requirements of the Convention, it seems to me that if in a democratic society it is necessary for the prevention of crime to invade privacy to a greater extent than is spelt out in the 1984 Act, then the limits of the invasion must be spelt out in the statute or in some regulations or code made thereunder, and there must be a convenient forum available for dealing with disputes. Meanwhile, in order to defend the right to privacy, I see no escape from the proposition that the words of the statute should be strictly applied."

Statutory authority for the practice of removal for sifting was subsequently given in the Criminal Justice and Police Act 2001.

6–15   The Court has been especially cautious in considering searches conducted under executive warrant. In *Camezind v. Switzerland*[71] the applicant was suspected of contravening telecommunications legislation by using an unauthorised cordless

---

[69] *ibid.*, para. 37; see also *Kopp v. Switzerland* [1998] E.H.R.L.R. 508. *Cf.* the "special procedure" under Sched. 1 of PACE.
[70] [2000] 1 All E.R. 411.
[71] (1999) 28 E.H.R.R. 458.

telephone. Under the relevant legislation the area director of the Post and Telecommunications Authority had power to issue a search warrant. The Court held that where a search took place without prior judicial authorisation, it was necessary to be "particularly vigilant" to ensure that the power was subject to very strict limits:

> "The Contracting States may consider it necessary to resort to measures such as searches of residential premises and seizures in order to obtain physical evidence of certain offences. The Court will assess whether the reasons adduced to justify such measures were relevant and sufficient and whether the aforementioned proportionality principle has been adhered to. As regards the latter point, the Court must first ensure that the relevant legislation and practice afford individuals 'adequate and effective safeguards against abuse'; notwithstanding the margin of appreciation which the Court recognises the Contracting States have in this sphere, it must be particularly vigilant where, as in the present case, the authorities are empowered under national law to order and effect searches without a judicial warrant. If individuals are to be protected from arbitrary interference by the authorities with the rights guaranteed under Article 8, a legal framework and very strict limits on such powers are called for. Secondly, the Court must consider the particular circumstances of each case in order to determine whether, in the concrete case, the interference in question was proportionate to the aim pursued."

The safeguards in place in *Camezind* were similar to those imposed by sections **6–16** 15 and 16 of PACE and Code B in respect of judicial warrants in England and Wales. The Court found these to be sufficient to meet the requirements of Article 8. In particular, the Court noted that a warrant could only be issued by officials of a certain level of seniority, and could only be executed by officials who had been specially trained for the purpose. Searches of dwellings had to take place at a reasonable time "except in important cases or where there is imminent danger". The person executing the search was required to produce evidence of identity, to inform the occupier of the purpose of the search, to permit the occupier to be present, to make a record of the search and to provide a copy of the record to the occupier. As to the facts, the applicant had been permitted to consult a lawyer and to read the file against him before the search began; the search had involved only one official and was confined to an examination of electrical equipment in the house. Having regard to the limited scope of the search, and the safeguards in place, the Court found no violation of Article 8.

C. Comparative Approaches

Decisions from other jurisdictions may assist in developing the principles on **6–17** search and seizure under the Human Rights Act. Just as the European Court in *Funke* stated that the procedures for authorisation need not be judicial, so the Supreme Court of Canada has taken a similar view under the Charter. In *Hunter v. Southam Inc*[72] the Supreme Court held that there must be a fair and independent procedure for prior authorisation of any search of premises. The authorisation need not be judicial, but it must be made by someone capable of acting judicially and independently, weighing the conflicting interests of law enforcement and individual liberty in an impartial way. This would rule out anyone connected with

---

[72] [1984] 2 S.C.R. 145.

the investigatory or prosecutorial functions. In *Baron v. Canada*[73] the Supreme Court made the further point that the process of authorisation must leave some discretion to the judge or other authorising person. A Canadian tax statute which provided that a judge "shall issue a warrant", if satisfied that there were reasonable grounds to believe that an offence under the statute had been committed, was therefore struck down as inconsistent with section 8 of the Charter.

6–18　　Both these decisions make it clear that authorisation should only be given after consideration of the rights of the person whose premises are to be searched, as well as the claims of the law enforcement agency. This point was elaborated in *Television New Zealand v. Attorney-General*,[74] where the New Zealand Court of Appeal stated that, before issuing a search warrant in respect of the premises of a media organisation, courts must (i) avoid, so far as possible, impairing the dissemination of news; (ii) only issue a warrant which might result in the "drying up" of confidential sources of information if this is "truly essential in the interests of justice"; and (iii) not grant a warrant unless the films to be seized are likely to have a direct and important place in any subsequent court case.[75] These three Commonwealth decisions demonstrate the need to give proper weight to the rights of the subject, including the right to freedom of expression and the right to privacy, when considering the grant of a search warrant.

---

[73] [1993] 1 S.C.R. 416.
[74] [1995] 2 N.Z.L.R. 641.
[75] *Per* Cooke P., at 648, on the last point following Lord Denning M.R. in *Senior v. Holdsworth* [1976] Q.B. 23, at 34–35.

CHAPTER 7

INTRUSIVE SURVEILLANCE

A. GENERAL PRINCIPLES

The decisions of the European Court and Commission of Human Rights establish **7–01**
a number of important principles governing the use of secret surveillance. The
exercise of such powers constitutes an "interference" with the right guaranteed
by Article 8,[1] and is tolerable in a democratic society only in so far as strictly
necessary for safeguarding democratic institutions. But in order to counter threats
of espionage, terrorism or serious crime, secret surveillance can, in principle, be
justified under Article 8(2).[2] Although states enjoy a certain latitude in deciding
the conditions under which a system of surveillance can be operated, they do not
enjoy an unlimited discretion to subject citizens to such forms of investigation.
Since secret surveillance "can undermine or even destroy democracy on the
ground of defending it", there must be adequate and effective safeguards against
abuse.[3] Whilst it is desirable that the machinery of supervision should be in the
hands of a judge, this is not a requirement either of Article 8 or of Article 13.
Supervisory bodies will be capable of providing an adequate and effective
safeguard providing they enjoy sufficient independence to give an objective
ruling.[4]

The expression "in accordance with the law" is not limited to an examination of **7–02**
whether a particular measure was permitted under domestic law. If covert
surveillance is conducted in breach of domestic law it will inevitably violate
Article 8. In addition, however, the law governing the exercise of such powers
must be "accessible and precise".[5] This expression has a special meaning when
applied to secret surveillance or telecommunications interception. It does not
entitle citizens to know in advance when the authorities are likely to observe or
intercept their communications and thereby enable them to adapt their conduct.
Nevertheless, the law must give an adequate indication of the circumstances in
which, and the conditions under which, authorities are empowered to resort to
"this secret and potentially dangerous interference with the right to respect for
private life and correspondence".[6] An unpublished non-statutory directive from
a Department of State which is not legally binding is incapable of satisfying this
requirement.[7] It is not necessary that the framework of safeguards should be
provided entirely by statute. If, however, the common law is relied upon then it

---

[1] *Klass v. Germany* (1979–80) 2 E.H.R.R. 214; *Malone v. United Kingdom* (1985) 7 E.H.R.R. 14;
Huvig v. France (1990) 12 E.H.R.R. 528.
[2] *Klass v. Germany* (1979–80) 2 E.H.R.R. 214.
[3] *Klass v. Germany* (1979–80) 2 E.H.R.R. 214.
[4] *Klass v. Germany* (1979–80) 2 E.H.R.R. 214.
[5] *Malone v. United Kingdom* (1985) 7 E.H.R.R. 14.
[6] *Huvig v. France* (1990) 12 E.H.R.R. 528; *Kruslin v. France* (1990) 12 E.H.R.R. 547.
[7] *Hewitt and Harman v. United Kingdom* (1992) 14 E.H.R.R. 657; *Khan v. United Kingdom* [2000]
Crim. L.R. 684.

must be sufficiently clear and unambiguous to enable a citizen to know the precise extent of his legal entitlements without the necessity for extrapolation.[8] The rules must define with clarity the categories of citizens liable to be the subject of such techniques, the offences which might give rise to such an order, the permitted duration of the surveillance, and the circumstances in which recordings are to be destroyed.[9] An exhaustive definition is not always necessary. It is sufficient for the law adequately to identify the types of activity which may fall within the scope of the power.[10] However, a constitutional provision which merely states that communications are to be private "unless the court decides otherwise" fails to indicate with sufficient certainty the extent of the authorities' discretion or the manner in which it is to be exercised.[11]

7–03   For the purposes of Article 8, it is unnecessary to establish that the contents of the conversation intercepted concerned matters of privacy.[12] However, special safeguards are required where covert surveillance may intrude upon legal professional privilege. In *Kopp v. Switzerland*[13] the Court emphasised the importance of protecting "a lawyer's work under instructions from a party to proceedings", and described it as "astonishing" that domestic law entrusted the authorisation of intrusive surveillance "in the sensitive area of the confidential relations between a lawyer and his clients" to an official "without supervision by an independent judge".

7–04   The Court has given an extended meaning to the term "victim" in this context. A relaxation of the "victim" requirement is necessary to ensure that the right of individual petition is effective. This is because it will usually be impossible for the individual to establish conclusively that he has been the subject of such measures. The Court has drawn a distinction here between complaints directed towards the existence of a regime which is alleged to fall short of the requirements of the Convention, and complaints concerning specific instances of unlawful activity by the state. In the former situation the Court has sometimes been prepared, in effect, to examine the impugned provisions of domestic law on their face; whereas in the latter situation it has generally required the applicant to show a "reasonable likelihood" that he has been the subject of unlawful surveillance.

7–05   Thus, in *Klass v. Germany*[14] the applicants' complaint concerned the absence of legal safeguards governing intrusive surveillance in Germany. There was however, no evidence to suggest that any of the applicants had been the subject of such surveillance (indeed, there was evidence to the contrary). The Court held that an applicant who seeks to challenge the compatibility of a regime authorising secret intelligence or surveillance techniques is not required to establish "any concrete measure specifically affecting him" since he will, by definition, be

---

[8] *Huvig v. France* (1990) 12 E.H.R.R. 528.
[9] *Huvig v. France* (1990) 12 E.H.R.R. 528; *Kruslin v. France* (1990) 12 E.H.R.R. 547; *Valenzuela Contreras v. Spain* (1999) 28 E.H.R.R. 483.
[10] In *Hewitt and Harman v. United Kingdom* (1992) 14 E.H.R.R. 657 the Commission considered that it was unnecessary for legislation to define the term "interests of national security".
[11] *Valenzuela Contreras v. Spain* (1999) 28 E.H.R.R. 483.
[12] *A v. France* (1994) 17 E.H.R.R. 462.
[13] (1999) 27 E.H.R.R. 91 at para. 74.
[14] (1979–80) 2 E.H.R.R. 214 .

unaware of what has occurred. In order to ensure that the right of individual petition was effective in relation to such a complaint, any person who was potentially affected by secret surveillance could claim to be a "victim". This was held to include any user or potential user of the post or telecommunications systems;

> "[A]n individual may, under certain conditions, claim to be the victim of a violation occasioned by the mere existence of secret measures or of legislation permitting secret measures, without having to allege that such measures were in fact applied to him. The relevant conditions are to be determined in each case according to the Convention right or rights alleged to have been infringed, the secret character of the measures objected to, and the connection between the applicant and those measures."

The Court adopted the same analysis in *Malone v. United Kingdom*,[15] holding that "the existence in England and Wales of laws and practices which permit and establish a system for effecting secret surveillance of communications amounted in itself to an 'interference' ".

In *Halford v. United Kingdom*,[16] by contrast, the Court applied a more restrictive **7–06** approach. There the applicant's complaint was not that the *regime* established by Interception of Communications Act 1985 was incompatible with Article 8,[17] but that her calls had been unlawfully intercepted, outside the Act's provisions. In this situation, the Court held, it was necessary for the applicant to establish a "reasonable likelihood" that the alleged interception had in fact occurred. Similarly, in *Hilton v. United Kingdom*,[18] the Commission applied the "reasonable likelihood" test in determining whether a journalist could claim to be a victim of a violation of Article 8 arising out of the alleged retention of personal information on a security service file.

Where an invasion of privacy through secret surveillance infringes Article 8, it **7–07** is immaterial that the complainant is not the primary victim of the invasion, providing the he has also been affected by it.[19] For the purposes of Article 8 therefore, it is irrelevant that the telephone or premises which are subject to surveillance did not belong to the victim.[20] In *Lambert v. France*[21] the Court observed that any other conclusion; " . . . could lead to decisions whereby a large number of people are deprived of the protection of the law, namely all those who have conversations on a telephone line other than their own. That would in practice render the protective machinery largely devoid of substance."

Where surveillance has (or may have) occurred unlawfully, domestic law must **7–08** provide an effective remedy before a national authority, whether or not the surveillance has resulted in a criminal prosecution.[22] Such an authority need not

---

[15] (1984) 7 E.H.R.R. 14 at para. 63.
[16] (1997) 24 E.H.R.R. 523 at paras 48 and 57.
[17] The 1985 Act had previously been found by the Commission to be compatible with the requirements of Article 8: *Christie v. United Kingdom* (1994) 78A D.R. 119.
[18] (1986) 57 D.R. 108 at 118.
[19] *Kruslin v. France* (1990) 12 E.H.R.R. 547.
[20] *Khan v. United Kingdom* [2000] Crim. L.R. 684.
[21] [1999] E.H.R.L.R. 123.
[22] See generally Art. 13 of the Convention. For a case in which a violation of Art. 13 was found on this basis, see *Khan v. United Kingdom* [2000] Crim. L.R. 684.

necessarily be judicial, and the nature of the remedy may be determined by the sensitivity of the information.[23]

7–09   The redress has to be as effective as it can be having regard to the restricted scope for recourse inherent in any system of secret surveillance.[24] However, it is not necessarily a requirement of a fair trial in Article 6 that evidence obtained in breach of Article 8 be excluded. The Court will examine the nature of the breach and the importance of the disputed evidence in the context of the proceedings as a whole. This issue is considered in detail in Chapter 15.[25]

B. APPLICATION TO THE UNITED KINGDOM

7–10   Powers of covert surveillance in the United Kingdom have led to a number of adverse rulings in Strasbourg. The United Kingdom's response has been piece-meal and essentially reactive. The Interception of Communications Act 1985, the Security Service Acts 1989 and 1996, the Intelligence Services Act 1994 and the Police Act 1997 were all introduced to redress or to forestall violations of Article 8. The Regulation of Investigatory Powers Act 2000 (RIPA), the latest piece of legislation designed to bring domestic law into line with the Convention, goes a long way towards meeting this country's obligations, and is to be welcomed. However Parliament has once again missed the opportunity to create a single unified regime providing consistent and coherent protection of privacy. Instead, RIPA will sit alongside the Police Act and the Intelligence Services Act, creating a number of different and overlapping procedures for authorisation, thereby adding to the complexity of legal regulation in this area, rather than reducing it. In this section, we outline the evolution of the Court's caselaw in relation to the United Kingdom and the legislative measures taken in response.

7–11   We begin with the position prior to the Interception of Communications Act 1985. In *Malone v. United Kingdom*[26] the Court held that the system under which telephone and mail interception was, at that time, conducted under a warrant issued by the Secretary of State, with no statutory framework, afforded insufficient legal protection to satisfy the requirements of Article 8. The Court held that:

> "[I]n its present state the law in England and Wales governing interception of communications for police purposes is somewhat obscure and open to differing interpretations . . . Detailed procedures concerning interception of communications on behalf of the police in England and Wales do exist. What is more, published statistics show the efficacy of those procedures in keeping the number of warrants granted relatively low, especially when compared with the rising number of indictable crimes committed and telephones installed. The public have been made aware of the applicable arrangements and principles through publication of the Birkett report and the White Paper and through statements by the responsible Ministers in Parliament. Nonetheless, on the evidence before the Court, it cannot be said with any reasonable certainty what elements of the powers to intercept are incorporated in legal rules and what elements

---

[23] *Klass v. Germany* (1979–80) 2 E.H.R.R. 214 at para. 67.
[24] *ibid.*, at para. 69.
[25] See paras 15–08 *et seq.* below.
[26] (1985) 7 E.H.R.R. 14.

remain within the discretion of the executive. In view of the attendant obscurity and uncertainty as to the state of the law in this essential respect, the Court cannot but reach a similar conclusion to that of the Commission [namely that Article 8 had been violated]. In the opinion of the Court, the law of England and Wales does not indicate with reasonable clarity the scope and manner of exercise of the relevant discretion conferred on the public authorities. To that extent the minimum degree of legal protection to which citizens are entitled under the rule of law in a democratic society is lacking."

The 1985 Act was a direct response to this ruling. It established a statutory **7–12** framework including a requirement for the prior issue of a warrant by the Secretary of State, and subsequent review by a Commissioner, acting as an independent tribunal. In passing the 1985 Act, Parliament endeavoured to limit the use to which the product of a telephone intercept would be put, and thus by extension, to protect rights of privacy. The Home Office White Paper[27] which preceded the 1985 Act, stated that; "The Bill will provide for controls over the use of intercepted material. By making such material generally inadmissible in legal proceedings it will ensure that interception can be used only as an aspect of investigation, not prosecution."[28]

However, secret surveillance of private property through the use of bugging **7–13** devices remained entirely unregulated by statute until the Security Service Act 1989.[29] Such surveillance is of course as much an intrusion on privacy as a telephone interception. Indeed, it frequently involves a greater intrusion since access is often gained to private property in order to "plant" a device. Prior to the 1989 Act, however, the Security Service had no statutory mandate for their activities in this respect. In *Hewitt and Harman v. United Kingdom*[30] the Commission concluded that the absence of a legislative framework had led to a violation of the applicants' rights under Article 8. Based on an affidavit of a former MI5 agent Cathy Massiter, the applicants alleged that personal information about them had been compiled by MI5 because of their positions as the General Secretary and Legal Officer of the National Council for Civil Liberties (now Liberty). The information derived in part from telephone and mail intercepts directed towards other people, and was retained because of their alleged left wing sympathies. Assuming the allegations to be correct, the Commission held that such activities required clear legal authority, which was absent:

> "The Commission notes that the activities of the Security Service are governed by a Directive of the Home Secretary to the Director-General of the Security Service dated 24 September 1952. Although the Directive is published, it is not claimed by the Government that it has the force of law or that its contents constitute legally enforceable rules concerning the operation of the Security Service. Nor does the Directive provide a framework which indicates with the requisite degree of certainty the scope and manner of the exercise of discretion by the authorities in the carrying out of secret surveillance activities. The Commission finds that in these circumstances the interference with the applicants' right to respect for private life was not 'in accordance with the law' ".

---

[27] *The Interception of Communications in the United Kingdom* Cmnd. 9438.
[28] Confirmed by the House of Lords in *R. v. Preston (Stephen)* [1994] 2 A.C. 130 *per* Lord Mustill at 147.
[29] See now the Intelligence Services Act 1994, as amended by the Security Service Act 1996.
[30] (1992) 14 E.H.R.R. 657.

7–14 Following this decision, the 1989 Act was passed to place MI5 onto a statutory footing, and to provide a system of prior authorisation for intrusive surveillance. Under the Act an application for a warrant to enable the Security Services (MI5) to interfere with property or wireless telegraphy was to be made to the Secretary of State, and was subject to scrutiny by a Tribunal and Commissioner. This procedure was extended to encompass the Intelligence Services (MI6) and GCHQ by the Intelligence Servces Act 1994.[31] In *Esbester v. United Kingdom*[32] the Commission held that the new framework was sufficient to meet the requirements of Article 8:

> "In the absence of any evidence or indication that the system is not functioning as required by domestic law, the Commission finds that the framework of safeguards achieves a compromise between the requirements of defending a democratic society and the rights of the individual, which is compatible with the provisions of the Convention."

7–15 Subsequent challenges to the scope of the legislation were equally unsuccessful. In *Hewitt and Harman v. United Kingdom (No.2)*[33] the Commission dismissed as manifestly ill-founded a complaint that the term "national security" in the 1989 Act was unduly vague:

> "The principles [in Article 8(2)] do not necessarily require a comprehensive definition of the notion of "the interests of national security" . . . the Commission considers that in the present case the law is formulated with sufficient precision to enable the applicants to anticipate the role of the Security Service."

And in *Christie v. United Kingdom*[34] the Commission reached a similar conclusion in relation to the term "economic well-being of the country" (in both the 1985 and the 1989 Acts):

> "It is compatible with the requirements of foreseeability that terms which are on their face general and unlimited are explained by administrative or executive statements and instructions, since it is the provision of sufficiently precise guidance to enable individuals to regulate their conduct, rather than the source of that guidance, which is of relevance."

7–16 By 1989 therefore the United Kingdom had adopted acceptable legislation governing interception of mail and telecommunications, and the conduct of intrusive surveillance by the Security Service. However, other forms of intrusive surveillance conducted by the *police* were not covered by either Act. Although bugging devices had been used routinely in major police investigations for many years, they had been subject only to non-statutory guidelines issued by the Home Office.[35] According to Home Office statistics in 1995 (the year the Interception

---

[31] Section 5(3) of the 1994 Act originally prohibited the grant of a warrant in respect of criminal investigations which did not involve an element of national security where the action to be taken related to property in the British Isles. This prohibition was lifted so far as the Security Services were concerned by s.2 of the Security Services Act 1996.
[32] (1993) 18 E.H.R.R. CD 72.
[33] Application No. 20317/92, September 1, 1993.
[34] (1994) 78–A D.R. 119 at 134.
[35] The Guidelines on the Use of Equipment in Police Surveillance Operations (December 19, 1984, Dep. NS 1579).

of Communications Act was passed) there were approximately 2,100 authorisations by chief officers of intrusive surveillance operations in the United Kingdom
undertaken by the police and customs.[36] This figure included 1,300 authorisations by police officers in England and Wales. Despite the prevalence of the
practice, one former Home Secretary said during a Parliamentary debate in 1997
that he had no knowledge of the scale of intrusive surveillance by the police
during his term of office.[37]

The inadequacy of the Home Office guidelines as a system of supervising secret   **7–17**
surveillance was brought into focus by the House of Lords' decision in *R. v.
Khan*.[38] The defendant in that case was charged with importation of heroin.
Acting on the authority of a chief constable, police officers placed a listening
device in a house in which he was staying and recorded a series of highly
incriminating conversations. At his trial the defendant argued that the tapes had
been obtained in consequence of an act of criminal damage and/or trespass. In
upholding the applicant's conviction, the Court of Appeal observed that;

> "There are, in the United Kingdom, no statutory provisions which govern the use by the
> police of secret listening devices on private property. This is to be contrasted with the
> position in relation to the interception of public telephone calls or postal communica-
> tions . . . It is also to be contrasted with the controls on the use of surveillance devices
> by the security service, laid down in the Security Service Act 1989 . . . The Home
> Office guidelines, and other documents to which we have been referred, certainly
> prescribe criteria and procedures limiting such use. However, although not a legal rule,
> 'an Englishman's home is his castle' is a tenet jealously held and widely respected. It
> is, in our view, at least worthy of consideration as to whether the circumstances in
> which bugging a private home by the police can be justified should be the subject of
> statutory control. It may be thought that such control is, by analogy with the 1985 Act,
> just as desirable for bugging devices as for telephone tapping."

In the House of Lords, Lord Nolan similarly observed that;   **7–18**

> "The sole cause of this case coming to your Lordships' House is the lack of a statutory
> system regulating the use of surveillance devices by the police. The absence of such a
> system seems astonishing, the more so in view of the statutory framework which has
> governed the use of such devices by the Security Service since 1989, and the inter-
> ception of communications by the police as well as by other agencies since 1985."

When the case was considered in Strasbourg, the absence of a statutory regime   **7–19**
for the use of covert listening devices by the police was held to be conclusive of
the alleged violation of Article 8. In *Khan v. United Kingdom*[39] the Court held
that the Home Office guidelines were neither legally binding nor publicly
accessible and the interference was therefore inadequately regulated by law.
Moreover, the Court held that there was no effective remedy for the violation, as
required by Article 13 of the Convention. In the absence of a statutory scheme
there was no procedure for determining complaints. The discretion to exclude
evidence under section 78 of the Police and Criminal Evidence Act 1984 was
held to be inadequate because, prior to the enactment of the Human Rights Act

---

[36] H.C. Debs, col. 512 (January 21, 1997).
[37] Lord Callaghan H.L. Debs, col. 401 (January 20, 1997).
[38] [1997] A.C. 558.
[39] [2000] Crim. L.R. 684.

1998, the national courts did not have jurisdiction under section 78 to determine the substance of the applicant's complaint, nor did they have power to grant appropriate relief for the violation. Significantly, the Court also held that the system for investigating complaints against the police established in Part IX of the 1984 Act failed to meet the standards of independence necessary to constitute sufficient protection against abuse of authority, and thus to provide an effective remedy within the meaning of Article 13.[40]

7–20   The journey of *Khan's* case through the courts was thus the immediate catalyst for Part III of the Police Act 1997. As originally drafted the Police Bill was plainly inadequate to meet the requirements of Article 8. In stark contrast to the previous legislation dealing with covert surveillance, the original proposals contained no requirement for prior independent authorisation. The decision was to reside with the authorising police officer alone. Following extensive political pressure in the House of Lords and in the media, amendments to the Bill were passed which require certain types of surveillance to have the prior approval of an independent Commissioner, who has the rank of a High Court judge or above. The scope of Part III of the Act extends only to "entry on or interference with property or wireless telegraphy".[41] It does not therefore regulate other forms of covert surveillance which require no physical entry onto property, such as the use of long distance microphones. Initial authorisation may be given by an authoris- ing officer, who must hold the rank of chief officer or above,[42] and may cover "the taking of such action, in respect of such property . . . as the authorising officer may specify".[43] This surprisingly broad formulation appears to impose no limits on the action which could be authorised. However, if the property to be entered is a dwelling, a hotel bedroom or an office then the authorisation will not take effect unless it has the prior approval of a Commissioner.[44] The same procedure applies if the surveillance is liable to reveal information subject to legal professional privilege, confidential personal information, or confidential journalistic material.[45] The Commissioner's prior approval is not, however, required if the authorising officer believes the case is urgent.[46]

7–21   Authorisation and approval is only to be given where the action to be taken is likely to be of substantial value in the prevention or detection of serious crime, and its purpose cannot be achieved by other means.[47] A crime is "serious" for this purpose if it would be likely to result in a sentence of three years imprison- ment or more, or if it involves violence, results in substantial financial gain, or is "conduct by a large number of persons in pursuit of a common purpose".[48] This wording follows that of the Interception of Communications Act 1985 and the Intelligence Services Act 1994. However, as Lord Browne-Wilkinson pointed

---

[40] See also *Govell v. United Kingdom* [1999] E.H.R.L.R. 121, since affirmed by the Committee of Ministers (Resolution DH (98) 212.
[41] Section 92.
[42] Section 93.
[43] Section 93(1).
[44] Section 97(2)(a).
[45] Section 97(2)(b).
[46] Section 97(3).
[47] Section 93(2).
[48] Section 93(4).

out during debates on the Bill,[49] the definition is wide enough to encompass many organised protest groups:

> "Suppose Mr A is one of a large number of protestors against making a new road; for example the Newbury bypass. The form of the protest, as in all these cases, is likely to involve the commission of a crime; for example criminal damage to property or obstruction of the police. Such crime will, to some eyes surprisingly, constitute a serious crime within the meaning of the Bill, because it is a large number of persons acting together".

It remains open to question whether the regime established by the 1997 Act **7–22** complies with Article 8 in all respects. As to the legal framework, it is at least arguable that the absence of a general requirement for prior independent authorisation may, in certain cases, lead to a violation of the Convention. The Court's approach in *Lambert v. France*[50] might suggest that confining the requirement for independent authorisation to the bugging of a person's home or office, or to specified categories of sensitive information, is inadequate. Moreover, the provisions permitting the use of listening device in a lawyer's office without prior approval in cases of urgency are difficult to reconcile with the strong statements of principle in *Kopp v. Switzerland*.[51] As to the ground for authorisation, it must be open to doubt whether that the Strasbourg Court would consider the use of intrusive surveillance powers against political protesters, in the circumstances envisaged by Lord Browne-Wilkinson, to be a proportionate response to the prevention of crime or disorder.

These issues aside, the 1997 Act left a number of gaping holes in the statutory **7–23** regime. In particular:

(a) A range of intrusive surveillance devices were already available to the police which did not require either the interception of a telephone call or an entry onto property. Prior to the Regulation of Investigatory Powers Act 2000, these techniques were not covered by legislation and lacked any system of authorisation or independent scrutiny. Their use was accordingly unlawful in Article 8 terms.

(b) In the case of portable telephones used in the home, the House of Lords had held that the interception of radio signals passing between the handset and the base unit were outside the scheme of the Interception of Communications Act 1985 since the radio signal does not form part of a public telecommunications system.[52] The consequence of this ruling was that the interception of calls received on a portable handset was unregulated by statute, in a manner incompatible with Article 8.

(c) Eavesdropping on private telephone lines which took place within the premises of the person listening to the call was not covered by the 1985 Act. In *Halford v. United Kingdom*[53] the Court found a violation of Article

---

[49] H.L. Debs, cols 811–812 (November 11, 1996).
[50] [1999] E.H.R.L.R. 123.
[51] (1999) 27 E.H.R.R. 91 at para. 74, see para. 7–03 above.
[52] *R v. Effick* [1995] 1 A.C. 309. This principle does not apply to mobile telephones: H.C. Debs, cols 158–159 (March 11, 1997).
[53] (1997) 24 E.H.R.R. 523.

8 where the alleged interception was by a chief constable of the private office telephone of a senior police officer.

The Regulation of Investigatory Powers Act 2000 is intended to redress these shortcomings. A detailed analysis of the Act's provisions is outside the scope of this work.[54] In summary, however:

(a) Part I governs the interception of communications. It repeals the Interception of Communications Act 1985 and replaces it with a framework encompassing interception of communications on public and private networks. Under section 1(1) it is an offence for a person intentionally and without lawful authority to intercept any communication in the course of its transmission by a public postal service or public telecommunications system. Section 1(2) creates a similar offence in connection with unauthorised interceptions on a private telecommunications system.[55] This is subject to section 1(6) which provides that it is not an offence to intercept a communication in the course of its transmission on a private telecommunications system if the interception is conducted by or on behalf of a person who has a right to control the operation or the use of the system. In these circumstances however, the interception is made actionably tortious under section 1(3) if it is carried out without lawful authority. The Act makes provision for certain forms of interception to be conducted without warrant (including interceptions carried out with the consent of both parties; interceptions carried out as part of directed surveillance in accordance with Part II of the Act; and interceptions for the purpose of monitoring telephone calls to or from prisoners or patients in high security psychiatric institutions). Where the interception falls outside the prescribed categories, the Secretary of State may issue a warrant providing it is necessary in the interests of national security, for the purpose of preventing or detecting serious crime, for the purpose of safeguarding the economic well-being of the United Kingdom or for the purpose of giving effect to an international mutual assistance agreement.[56] Mirroring the requirements of Article 8, section 5(2) provides that the Secretary of State may only issue a warrant where he believes that the conduct authorised is proportionate to what is sought to be achieved by that contract. Generally, no evidence can be adduced, question asked, assertion or disclosure made or other thing done in, for the purposes of, or in connection with any legal proceedings, which is likely to reveal the existence of or application for an interception warrant[57] or the commission of an offence under section 1 by any public official. This is subject to exceptions similar to those set out in section 9(3) and (4) of the Interception of Communications Act 1985. Section 18(7)(a) specifically provides that the prohibition on disclosure does not operate to prevent disclosure to a prosecutor for the purpose of enabling him "to determine what is required of him by his duty to secure the fairness of the prosecution". This must be read in conjunction with

---

[54] For a critical assessment of the Act see the articles by Akdeniz, Taylor and Walker [2001] Crim. L.R. 73 and by Mirfield [2001] Crim. L.R. 91.

[55] A private telecommunications system is one which is attached, directly or indirectly to a public telecommunications system: section 2(1).

[56] Section 5(3).

[57] Section 17. This is subject to the provisions of section 18.

section 18(7)(b), (8) and (9) which together provide that a judge may order the prosecution to disclose the material to the court alone (presumably in the course of a public interest immunity hearing) but only where the "exceptional circumstances of the case make the disclosure essential in the interests of justice". Where the judge makes such an order he may, after having considered the material, direct the prosecutor to make any admission of fact which he considers essential in the interests of justice, but may not order the prosecutor to disclose the material itself, or facts relating to the circumstances in which it was obtained. Mirfield has argued[58] that this procedure fails to secure equality of arms between the parties and sits uneasily with the Court's judgment in *Rowe and Davis v. United Kingdom*.[59] In addition, Part I establishes a regulatory structure for access to and handling of "communications data".[60] Under sections 22 and 23 a "designated person" may serve a notice requiring the production of such data on grounds which mirror the grounds on which the Secretary of State may grant an interception warrant. There are, however, no statutory restrictions on the disclosure in criminal proceedings or use in evidence of communications data.

(b) Part II of the Act introduces regulatory procedures for many other forms of surveillance, by technology or by human beings, which have hitherto had no statutory basis. It is intended to regulate covert surveillance which does not involve a physical entry onto property and which is therefore outside the existing statutory authorisation powers in the Police Act 1997 and the Intelligence Services Act 1994 (the relevant provisions of which remain in force). Part II governs surveillance by the police, the National Criminal Intelligence Service, the National Crime Squad, Customs and Excise, the Security and Intelligence Services, GCHQ, government departments and other specified public authorities that carry out investigations. Section 24 defines three forms of surveillance:

(i) *Directed surveillance* consists of covert (but non-intrusive) monitoring, observing or listening for the purposes of a specific investigation that is likely to reveal private information, including details of a person's private life. Surveillance is covert if, and only if, it is carried out in a manner that is calculated to ensure that persons who are subject to the surveillance are unaware that it is taking place.

(ii) *Intrusive surveillance* is covert surveillance carried out in relation to anything taking place on residential premises[61] or in any private vehicle, whether carried out by a person or a device. Where a device is used which is located outside the premises, it must be capable of providing information of the same quality and detail as might be

---

[58] [2001] Crim. L.R. 91.

[59] (2000) 30 E.H.R.R. 1.

[60] "Communications data" is defined to include the address or other information attached to a communication, any information (other than the contents of the communication) which records the use of postal or telecommunications systems, and any other information which is held the provider of post or telecommunications service about users of that service: section 21. It thus includes what used to be known as "metering" information of the kind in issue in *Malone v. United Kingdom* (1984) 7 E.H.R.R. 14.

[61] The exclusion of business premises does not appear to cater for premises where there is a reasonable expectation of privacy, such as the business premises at issue in *Neimeitz v. Germany* (1992) 16 E.H.R.R. 97.

expected from an internally placed device in order to qualify as intrusive. It does not therefore include unaided visual observation from an external observation post. Electronic tracking devices are expressly excluded.

(iii) *Covert human intelligence sources* are persons who establish or maintain a personal or other relationship with a person for the covert purpose of using such a relationship to obtain information or to provide access to any information to another person, or who covertly discloses information obtained by the use of such a relationship. The Act requires that where a source is used for this purpose, there must at all times be an office holder who is responsible for day to day dealings with the source and for their welfare and security (a designated handler); another office holder who has general oversight of the use made of the source (a designated controller); and a person who at all times is responsible for maintaining a record of the use made of the source.[62] Where a source is used to make a telephone conversation which is recorded with the consent of the source, the resulting surveillance is to be treated as directed surveillance and is not subject to the controls of Part I of the Act.

The authorisation procedure depends upon the category of surveillance in issue:

(i) *Directed and covert surveillance* may be authorised by an officer of the relevant agency holding a rank equivalent to Superintendent or above, unless the case is urgent when it may be authorised by an officer of the rank of Inspector or above. The authorisation may be given only where it is necessary on one of the specified grounds and where the action to be authorised is proportionate to the end sought to be achieved. The statutory grounds are national security, the prevention or detection of serious crime, the protection of the economic well-being of the United Kingdom, the interests of public safety, the protection of health, the assessment or collection of any tax or levy due to any government department, or for any other purpose which the Secretary of State may order. The Code of Practice issued under the Act affords additional protection for material subject to legal professional privilege, confidential journalistic material and confidential personal information. The Act contains detailed provision as to the information to be included within an application, and provides that the authorisation must be given in writing unless the case is urgent. Written authorisations continue to have effect for three months and are renewable. Urgent authorisations lapse after 72 hours. Where covert human intelligence sources are used, the authorising officer should not grant an authorisation unless he is satisfied that there are arrangements in place for ensuring at all times that there is a person with responsibility for maintaining a record of the use made of the source.

---

[62] Section 28(5). Records revealing the source's identity will not in general be disclosed.

(ii) *Intrusive surveillance* is subject to an authorisation procedure similar to that established under Part III of the Police Act 1997. Authorisation may only be given on grounds of national security, the prevention or detection of serious crime or the economic well-being of the United Kingdom. As with directed surveillance, authorisation is subject to the requirements of necessity and proportionality, including a mandatory consideration of whether the information could reasonably be obtained by other, less intrusive, means. Under section 30 an authorisation may be given by the Secretary of State and any listed "senior authorising officer" who holds the rank of Chief Constable or equivalent. However, where the application is made on behalf of the police, the case is urgent, and it is not reasonably practicable to obtain authorisation from a senior authorising officer, the authorisation may be granted by a deputy. Once authorisation has been given, a Surveillance Commissioner must be notified as soon as reasonably practicable. In general, the authorisation does not take effect until the Commissioner has granted prior approval. In urgent cases, the authorisation may take effect without prior approval, but the senior authorising officer must then notify the Commissioner as soon as reasonably practicable setting out the reason for proceeding without prior approval. The Commissioner may quash any authorisation if he believes the statutory criteria have not been met or have since ceased to apply. A relevant senior officer has the right to appeal the decision of a Commissioner to the Chief Surveillance Commissioner.

There are no statutory restrictions on the disclosure in criminal proceedings of information obtained under Part II, nor on its use in evidence.

(c) Part III provides new and potentially far-reaching powers for official access to electronic data protected by encryption and includes an authorisation procedure for requiring access to decrypted information, and the production of encryption keys.

(d) Part IV establishes the machinery for scrutinising the investigatory powers conferred by the Act. It makes provision for the creation of three new commissioners—the Interception of Communications Commissioner (to replace the existing Commissioner under section 8 of the Interception of Communications Act 1985), the Intelligence Services Commissioner (to replace the existing Commissioners under section 4 of the Security Service Act 1989 and section 8 of the Intelligence Services Act 1994) and an Investigatory Powers Commissioner for Northern Ireland. The Commissioners established by Part III of the Police Act 1997 are given additional functions. Section 65 establishes a single Regulation of Investigatory Powers Tribunal to replace the existing tribunals under the Security Services Act, the Intelligence Services Act and the Police Act. The Tribunal has jurisdiction to determine;

(i) any action under section 7(1)(a) of the Human Rights Act 1998 in relation to an act or omission of the intelligence services or any public authority concerning the use of powers under the Regulation of Investigatory Powers Act or any other entry on or interference

[217]

with property or wireless telegraphy which is alleged to be incompatible with a Convention right;

(ii) any complaint concerning the use of powers under the Regulation of Investigatory Powers Act or any other entry on or interference with wireless telegraphy which is alleged to have been carried out by the intelligence services or by another public authority under a warrant, authorisation, authority or permission granted under the Act, or where the circumstances are alleged to be such that it would not have been appropriate for the conduct to take place without authorisation, or without proper consideration having been given to whether authorisation should have been sought;

(iii) any complaint alleging that the complainant has suffered detriment as the result of any prohibition under section 17 on the disclosure or use of intercepted material in court proceedings.

Subject to a one year time limit, the Tribunal must investigate whether the person against whom the complaint is made has engaged in any such conduct; investigate the authority (if any) for the conduct; and determine the complaint by reference to judicial review principles. In considering a complaint under the Human Rights Act 1998 the Tribunal must apply the same principles as a court would apply on an application for judicial review. The Tribunal may award compensation or make any other order, including the quashing or cancellation of a warrant or authorisation, and an order for the destruction of records of information obtained as a result of the surveillance in issue. The Tribunal is required to give notice to the complainant indicating either that a determination has been made in his favour, in which case it must provide a summary of the determination including any findings of fact, or that no determination has been made in his favour. The Tribunal's procedure is set out in the Investigatory Powers Tribunal Rules 2000.[63]

7–24 Finally, mention should be made in this context of the powers of a Trustee in Bankruptcy to intercept correspondence in the course of proceedings connected with the enforcement of a criminal confiscation order. In *Foxley v. United Kingdom*[64] a Receiver was appointed under section 80(2) of the Criminal Justice Act 1988 to enforce a confiscation order made following the applicant's conviction for offences of corruption arising out of his employment with the Ministry of Defence. The same individual was appointed as Trustee in Bankruptcy in parallel civil proceedings brought by the Ministry. An order for re-direction of the applicant's mail was made under section 371 of the Insolvency Act 1986 in favour of the Trustee in Bankruptcy. During the currency of the order letters passing between the applicant and his legal advisers were opened, and copies retained. The Court observed that it could "see no justification for this procedure" and considered that "the action taken was not in keeping with the principles of confidentiality and professional privilege attaching to relations between a lawyer and his client". Accordingly, the opening and copying of these letters amounted to a disproportionate interference. In addition, certain packages had been opened after the order had expired, due to an administrative oversight. Here, the position was even more straightforward. The Trustee in Bankruptcy

---

[63] S.I. 2000 No. 2665.
[64] 8 B.H.R.C. 571.

must have known the terms of the order she had applied for. Since that order had expired, there was no legal basis for the interference.

C. UNDERCOVER OPERATIONS AND ARTICLE 8

The implications of Article 6 for the admission of evidence obtained from **7–25** undercover police officers and participant informants in considered in Chapter 15. It is important, however, to recall that such operations may also have implications for the right to privacy in Article 8, particularly where a partipant informer is "wired" to record conversations in furtherance of an offence. The nearest that the Court has come to considering this situation is the decision in *Ludi v. Switzerland*.[65] In that case the applicant's telephone had been lawfully tapped pursuant to a judicial warrant. Senior police officers then authorised an undercover agent to pose as a potential purchaser of cocaine and the applicant offered to sell the drugs to him. During the course of the transaction various conversations were recorded, which were relied upon in the subsequent criminal prosecution for offences connected with drug trafficking. The Commission considered that whilst the telephone tap itself was compatible with Article 8, the use of an undercover officer to initiate conversations required separate consideration:

> "Mere surveillance of telephone conversations is an essentially passive official listening in on conversations which the authorities are powerless to influence. Involvement of an undercover officer altered the nature of the operation, as the words intercepted resulted wholly or in part from the relationship which the officer established with the suspect, a relationship based on the suspect's misapprehension, which was induced and maintained, as to the officer's identity and motives. By means of this subterfuge the officer gained entry into the suspect's private life."

The Commission held that the use of an undercover officer required a clear legal **7–26** framework analogous to that applicable to intrusive surveillance. Since the relevant legislation provided no independent safeguards for the suspect, his Article 8 rights had been violated. The Court, however, disagreed. In the Court's view, having regard to the applicant's involvement in serious drugs offences, the use of the undercover officer, either alone or in combination with a lawful telephone tap, was compatible with Article 8. In somewhat shaky reasoning, the Court held that since the applicant must have been aware that he was engaging in a criminal act punishable under Swiss anti-drugs legislation, he was knowingly running the risk of encountering an undercover police officer whose task it would be to expose him. He could not therefore claim that his right to privacy had been violated.

Ludi was followed by the Commission in *Speckman v. United Kingdom*.[66] The **7–27** applicant had been convicted of exporting electrical components to Iraq in breach of export controls, although her conviction was subsequently quashed on appeal. The prosecution case was that she had conspired to fabricate end user certificates so as to conceal the potential military use of the components. She alleged that the

---

[65] (1993) 15 E.H.R.R. 173.
[66] Application No. 27007/95.

contract had been prompted by an officer of United States customs, acting as an agent provocateur. In rejecting her complaint under Article 8, the Commission observed that:

> "[T]he actions of [the U.S. customs official] and the customs authorities took place in the context of a business deal for the purchase of 85 capacitators, 40 of which were believed to be intended for use in a nuclear weapon. The Commission is therefore of the view that, assuming the responsibilities of the [United Kingdom] were involved (which the Commission has not in the circumstances found it necessary to determine) the activities of [the U.S. customs official] or the authorities did not in any event affect private life within the meaning of Article 8."

7-28   As a statement of general principle the Court's decision in *Ludi* is very difficult to reconcile with its previous and subsequent case law on intrusive surveillance, where it has consistently held that a suspect's involvement in criminal activity does not relieve the authorities of their obligations under Article 8. In *A v. France*,[67] for example, the Court found a violation of Article 8 where a police officer, at the suggestion of a third party and with his consent, recorded a conversation between that person and the applicant. The Court roundly rejected the argument that Article 8 was inapplicable in view of the fact that one of the parties to the call was consenting, and the conversation had concerned the commission of a criminal offence. Applying the principles established in cases like *Klass* and *Malone* it seems clear that where an encounter between an undercover officer and a suspect is tape recorded, the use of the equipment should require an adequate legal framework, with necessary safeguards against abuse.[68]

7-29   In the United States there are conflicting decisions on the point. The leading Supreme Court case of *United States v. White*[69] held that the element of consent by the participant renders such surveillance constitutional, whereas there are several state appellate decisions going the other way. The leading decision in the Supreme Court of Canada comes down in favour of the latter view. In *Duarte*[70] the Court held that a sub-section of the Canadian Criminal Code, which purports to exempt from regulation those communications where either the originator or recipient consents, violates the provision against "unreasonable search or seizure" in section 8 of the Canadian Charter. The reasoning behind the decision in *United States v. White* was that participant recording was no different from participant recollection: the participant would be able to testify to a recollection of what was said, and the recording merely improves the accuracy of that recollection. In *Duarte* the Canadian Supreme Court, through La Forest J., regarded this reasoning as unpersuasive. The idea of regulating electronic surveillance is to protect citizens "from a risk of a different order", that of:

> " . . . allowing the state, in its unfettered discretion, to record and transmit our words. The reason for this protection is that if the state were free, at its sole discretion, to make permanent electronic recordings of our private communications, there would be no meaningful residuum to our right to live our lives free from surveillance . . . This is not

---

[67] (1994) 17 E.H.R.R. 462.
[68] Note however the approach of the Commission under Art. 6 where one party to the conversation was an undercover MI5 officer: *Smith v. United Kingdom* [1997] E.H.R.L.R. 277.
[69] 401 U.S. 745 (1971).
[70] [1990] 1 S.C.R. 30.

to deny that it is of vital importance that law enforcement agencies be able to employ electronic surveillance in their investigation of crime . . . But, for the reasons I have touched on, it is unacceptable in a free society that the agencies of the state be free to use this technology at their sole discretion."[71]

The essence of the Supreme Court's reasoning in *Duarte* is that, if one of the participants to a conversation consents to recording it, that should not deprive the other party of her or his right to privacy, and that therefore the rules for authorising such surreptitious recording or surveillance ought to apply.[72]

The logic of this position is reflected in Part II of the Regulation of Investigatory **7–30** Powers Act 2000, which provides a statutory framework governing the use of covert human intelligence sources.[73] The Act provides a system for authorising the use of undercover officers and participant informers, subject to the requirement that it be necessary for one of the stated aims, and proportionate to the aim which it seeks to achieve. Where a source consents to the recording of a telephone conversation with a suspect, this is to be treated as directed surveillance rather than interception of communication subject to the safeguards of Part I. Whilst the absence of judicial or independent supervision in these circumstances is an undoubted weakness, there are at least statutory criteria and safeguards, including a requirement for records to be made of the use of a source, and a right of complaint to the Regulation of Investigatory Powers Tribunal, on grounds which include incompatibility with Convention rights.

---

[71] *ibid.*, at 44.
[72] The New Zealand Court of Appeal in *A* [1994] 1 N.Z.L.R. 429 accepted the reasoning in *Duarte* to the extent of holding that participant recording constitutes a "search and seizure", and then held that in deciding whether the intrusion was unreasonable a court should consider *inter alia* the seriousness of the crime under investigation. *Cf.* also *Barlow* (1995) 14 C.R.N.Z. 9.
[73] See para. 7–23(b) above.

CHAPTER 8

THE SUBSTANTIVE CRIMINAL LAW

A. INTRODUCTION

As a general proposition it can be said that "the Convention leaves states free to **8–01** designate as criminal an act or omission not constituting the normal exercise of one of the rights that it protects".[1] There are, however, a number of qualifications to this principle. The first is that the state may not define as "criminal" any conduct which constitutes an unjustified interference with the right to privacy, the right to freedom of expression or the right to peaceful assembly and association. This principle is the subject of the present chapter. In addition, where an individual is prosecuted for a criminal[2] offence, he is entitled to the protection of Articles 6 and 7 of the Convention. These rights have implications for the elements of an offence as defined in domestic law, which are discussed in Chapters 9 and 10 below. The third main qualification is that there are certain situations in which the state is under a *positive obligation* to create an enforceable criminal offence, or to restrict available defences, so as to protect the Convention rights of victims of crime.[3] The extent of this obligation is considered in Chapter 18.

B. THE RIGHT TO PRIVATE LIFE

Article 8 of the Convention has important implications for the anomalous and **8–02** anachronistic collection of statutory sexual offences in English law. In *R. v. Savage*[4] Lord Ackner described the Sexual Offences Act 1956 as "a rag-bag of offences brought together from a variety of sources with no attempt, as the draftsman frankly acknowledged, to introduce consistency as to substance or as to form".[5] The Indecency with Children Act 1960 has been described as "an appendix to the 1956 Act",[6] and the same might be said of the Sexual Offences Act 1967. The law on sexual offences was reviewed by the Wolfenden Committee in 1957[7] (focussing on homosexual offences and prostitution), and by the

---

[1] *Engel v. Netherlands* (1979–80) 1 E.H.R.R. 647 at para. 81.
[2] As to the meaning of a "criminal charge" for the purposes of the Convention, see Chapter 4 above.
[3] As to positive obligations generally see para. 2–53 above.
[4] *R. v. Savage; R. v. Parmenter* [1992] 1 A.C. 699 at 752, *per* Lord Ackner quoting Professor Smith Q.C., approved in *B v. DPP* [2000] 1 All E.R. 833.
[5] In *B v. DPP* [2000] 1 All E.R. 833 at 843 Lord Steyn traced the history of the offences in the 1956. Many of them originated in legislation passed in the 19th century, and some dated back to medieval times.
[6] *B v. DPP* [2000] 1 All E.R. 833 at 843, *per* Lord Steyn.
[7] Report of the Committee on Homosexual Offences and Prostitution, Cmnd. 247

Criminal Law Revision Committee in 1985.[8] A number of the recommendations made in those reviews have been left unimplemented, and the law is in urgent need of reform. The Home Office has recently carried out a review of the legislation in this area, and made proposals to bring it into line with the requirements of the Convention.[9]

I. *General Principles*

8–03   The European Court of Human Rights has frequently held that "sexual orientation and activity concern an intimate aspect of private life".[10] Accordingly, "particularly serious reasons"[11] are required to justify a criminal prosecution relating to consensual sexual activity in private. It is well established that not only a criminal prosecution but even the threat of prosecution[12] may be sufficient to constitute an interference with the rights guaranteed by Article 8. The central question in each case will therefore be whether the prosecution, conviction and sentence, taken individually or together, are proportionate to one of the legitimate aims prescribed in Article 8(2).

II. *Homosexual Offences*

8–04   One of the earliest criminal cases under Article 8 concerned the offences of buggery[13] and gross indecency[14] in Northern Ireland. In contrast to the laws elsewhere in the United Kingdom, the relevant legislation allowed no exception for the acts of consenting adults in private. In *Dudgeon v. United Kingdom*[15] the Court held that the Northern Ireland legislation could not be said to be "necessary in a democratic society" because there was no evidence of a "pressing social need"[16] to use the criminal law in order to prohibit consensual homosexual activity in private. The application of criminal sanctions was disproportionate to any legitimate aim which was sought to be achieved. In the Court's view, such justifications as there were for retaining the law in force were outweighed by the detrimental effect it could have on the life of a person of homosexual orientation. Although members of the public who regarded homosexuality as immoral might be shocked, offended or disturbed by the commission of homosexual acts in private, that could not, in itself, justify the application of penal sanctions when

---

[8] Cmnd. 9213, (1985).
[9] *Setting the Boundaries: Reforming the Law on Sex Offences* (July 27, 2000).
[10] *e.g. Laskey v. United Kingdom* (1997) 24 E.H.R.R. 39, para. 36.
[11] *Dudgeon v. United Kingdom* (1982) 4 E.H.R.R. 149.
[12] *Norris v. Ireland* (1991) 13 E.H.R.R. 186.
[13] Under ss.61 and 62 of the Offences Against the Person Act 1861.
[14] Under s.11 of the Criminal Law Amendment Act 1885.
[15] (1982) 4 E.H.R.R. 149.
[16] The term "necessary" in Art. 8(2) implies the existence of a pressing social need: see *Dudgeon* at para. 51: "'[N]ecessary,' in this context, does not have the flexibility of such expressions as 'useful', 'reasonable', or 'desirable', but implies the existence of a 'pressing social need' for the interference in question."
     For the origin of the 'pressing social need' test see *Handyside v. United Kingdom* (1979–80) 1 E.H.R.R. 737 at para. 48.

both participants were consenting adults.[17] The Court's judgment recognised that there are gradations of "private life" and that sexual orientation, as one its most intimate aspects, should be given special protection.[18]

In seeking to justify the legislation the government cited the strength of feeling **8-05** in Northern Ireland on the issue, arguing that there was a strongly held view that the abolition of the offence "would be seriously damaging to the moral fabric" of society.[19] The Court was forthright in its rejection of this argument:

> "The Convention right affected by the impugned legislation protects an essentially private manifestation of the human personality. As compared with the era when the legislation was enacted, there is now a better understanding, and in consequence an increased tolerance, of homosexual behaviour to the extent that in the great majority of the member states of the Council of Europe it is no longer considered to be necessary or appropriate to treat homosexual practices of the kind now in question as in themselves a matter to which the sanctions of the criminal law should be applied; the Court cannot overlook the marked changes which have occurred in this regard in the domestic law of the member states."

The Court went on to point out that in Northern Ireland itself, the authorities had **8-06** refrained from enforcing the legislation where both participants were over 21 and capable of valid consent. There was no evidence that this had been injurious to moral standards.

As to the applicant's standing to challenge the legislation, the Court held that the **8-07** "very existence of this legislation continuously and directly affects his private life: either he respects the law and refrains from prohibited sexual acts to which he is disposed . . . or he commits such acts and thereby becomes liable to criminal prosecution".[20] *Dudgeon* was followed in *Norris v. Ireland*.[21] In *Norris*, the Irish government directly challenged the applicant's status as a "victim",[22] arguing that he had never been prosecuted for the offence in question, and there had been no prosecutions in Ireland for many years, except where minors were involved, or where the acts occurred in public or without consent. The Court accepted that the risk of prosecution was "minimal" but pointed out that there was no stated policy on the part of the prosecuting authorities to refrain from enforcing the law. Whilst the offence remained on the statute book there was a possibility that it could be applied in the future if there was a change of policy. In the Court's view, the applicant ran the risk of being prosecuted, however slight that risk might be, and could therefore claim "victim" status under the Convention.[23]

---

[17] At para. 60.
[18] *cf.* the much more restrictive approach of the U.S. Supreme Court in *Bowers v. Hardwick* 478 U.S. 186 (1986) and subsequent decisions, discussed extensively by Wintemute, *Sexual Orientation and Human Rights*, (Clarendon) Chapter 2.
[19] At para. 46.
[20] At para. 41.
[21] (1991) 13 E.H.R.R. 186.
[22] See para. 1–84 above.
[23] A similar conclusion was reached in *Modinos v. Cyprus* (1993) 16 E.H.R.R. 485 where the Court rejected an argument that the law in question was invalid (as being in conflict with the constitution) and thus inapplicable, noting that there was a statement to the contrary in the caselaw of the Supreme Court of Cyprus.

III. *Age of Consent*

8–08   Whilst the age of consent for sexual relations is, in principle, a matter which falls within the state's margin of appreciation[24] the Commission has held that different ages of consent for heterosexual and homosexual offences can no longer be justified.[25] In *Sutherland v. United Kingdom*[26] the applicant successfully relied upon Article 8, in conjunction with Article 14, in order to challenge the offence of gross indecency under section 13 of the Sexual Offences Act 1956, as amended by section 1 of the Sexual Offences Act 1967. As presently defined, the offence applies to any sexual activity between men, other then consenting adults in private. The applicant, who was aged 17, argued that the definition of "adult" (requiring both participants to be over 18) amounted to an unjustified difference in treatment when compared with the position of heterosexuals (for whom the age of consent is 16).

8–09   The government advanced two arguments in favour of the differential. First, it was submitted that young men with an unsettled sexual orientation should be protected from activities which "might cause them later to repent"; and secondly, it was submitted that society was justified in indicating its disapproval of homosexuality and its preference for a heterosexual lifestyle. The Commission rejected both arguments, overturning its earlier case-law on the point.[27] As to the first argument, current medical opinion suggested that sexual orientation was fixed by the age of 16, and the Commission considered that the risk posed by predatory older men was just as serious whether the victim was male or female. Moreover, the "weight of current medical opinion" was to the effect that a reduction in the age of homosexual consent to 16 might have "positively beneficial effects on the sexual health of young homosexual men, without any corresponding harmful consequences". As to the second point, the Commission held that society's supposed right to express its disapproval did not afford an objective and reasonable justification for the difference in treatment. The decriminalisation of consensual homosexual activity for 16 and 17 year olds would not imply approval of it, and a fear that some sectors of the population might draw misguided conclusions from reform of the legislation was not a ground for keeping it in force. More generally, the Commission held that where there was a difference of treatment in the application of the criminal law on the grounds of a person's sexual orientation, the margin of appreciation was a "relatively narrow" one.[28]

---

[24] *Dudgeon v. United Kingdom* (1982) 4 E.H.R.R. 149, para. 62.

[25] A similar approach has been taken in Canada. In *Halem v. Minister of Employment and Immigration* (1995) 27 C.R.R. (2d) 23 (Federal Court, Trial Division), a provision in the Criminal Code which fixed the age of consent for anal intercourse at 18 (whereas the age for other sexual activity was 14) was declared unconstitutional for being in breach of the equal protection clause of the Charter.

[26] (1997) 24 E.H.R.R. CD 22.

[27] Notably *X v. United Kingdom* (1980) 19 D.R. 66, where a very similar application failed, at a time when the interpretation of Art. 8 was little developed; *cf.* also *Johnson v. United Kingdom* (1986) 47 D.R. 72. The Commission appears to have upheld the differential ages in Austrian law: see Wintemute, *Sexual Orientation and Human Rights* (1997), vii and pp 108–109 on the unreported decision in *Zukrigl v. Austria*. The Belgian Court of Cassation, considering Arts 8 and 14, has upheld the age difference in Belgian law as being necessary in the interests of *ordre public*: F. Tulkens, "Belgium", in M. Delmas-Marty (ed.), *The European Convention for the Protection of Human Rights* (1992), p. 112.

[28] Following the Commission's ruling the government indicated that it did not intend to contest the case before the Court, and undertook to introduce legislation to equalise the age of consent.

IV. *The Public/Private Divide*

A further challenge to section 1 of the 1967 Act, aimed at the term "private", was **8–10** upheld by the Court in *ADT v. United Kingdom*.[29] The applicant was convicted of gross indecency after police found a videotape depicting sexual acts between a group of middle aged men (including the applicant) which had been filmed in the bedroom of the applicant's home.[30] Section 11(2) of the 1967 Act provides that an act shall not be treated as having occurred in "private" if more than two persons were present at the time. The offence applies only to male homosexual acts, and not to heterosexual or lesbian sexual acts. The applicant accordingly alleged a violation of Article 8 alone and in conjunction with Article 14, arguments that had been unsuccessful before the Commission, some 20 years ago.[31]

The Government argued that the offences had not occurred in "private", either **8–11** for the purposes of the domestic law or for the purposes of Article 8, in view of the fact that a number of men were involved, and the sessions had been videotaped. The Court rejected this view, holding that:

"The sole element in the present case which could give rise to any doubt about whether the applicant's private life was involved is the video recording of the activities. No evidence has been put before the Court to indicate that there was any actual likelihood of the contents of the tapes being rendered public, deliberately or inadvertently. In particular, the applicant's conviction related not to any offence involving the making or distribution of the tapes, but solely to the acts themselves. The Court finds it most unlikely that the applicant, who had gone to some lengths not to reveal his sexual orientation, and who has repeated his desire for anonymity before the Court, would knowingly be involved in any such publication ... The Court thus considers that the applicant has been the victim of an interference with his right to respect for his private life both as regards the existence of legislation prohibiting consensual sexual acts between more than two men in private, and as regards the conviction for gross indecency ... The Court can agree with the Government that, at some point, sexual activities can be carried out in such a manner that State interference may be justified, either as not amounting to an interference with the right to respect for private life, or as being justified for the protection, for example, of health or morals. The facts of the present case, however, do not indicate any such circumstances. The applicant was involved in sexual activities with a restricted number of friends in circumstances in which it was most unlikely that others would become aware of what was going on ... The activities were therefore genuinely "private", and the approach of the Court must be to adopt the same narrow margin of appreciation as it found applicable in other cases involving intimate aspects of private life."

V. *Sadomasochist "Assaults"*

None of the cases so far considered involved any element of violence. This was **8–12** regarded as a major distinguishing feature when the Court came to decide on the

---

[29] *The Times*, August 8, 2000; Judgment July 31, 2000.
[30] There was no element of sadomasochism involved in these offences: *cf. Laskey v. United Kingdom* (1997) 24 E.H.R.R. 39.
[31] *X v. United Kingdom* (1980) 19 D.R. 66, and also *Johnson v. United Kingdom* (1986) 47 D.R. 72, discussed by Wintemute, *Sexual Orientation and Human Rights*, pp 102–103.

Article 8 challenge in *Laskey and others v. United Kingdom*,[32] the "Operation Spanner" case. The applicants had been charged with assaults arising out of consensual sadomasochistic activity involving the infliction of minor physical injuries to one another's genitals. They pleaded guilty after the trial judge ruled that they could not rely on the consent of their "victims" as a defence to the charge, and were sentenced to terms of imprisonment. The issue of consent was appealed to the House of Lords which ruled, by a three to two majority, that consent was no defence.[33] In Strasbourg the applicants argued that their convictions represented an unjustified intrusion into their right to respect for their private lives.

8–13   The Court unanimously concluded that the state was entitled to regulate, through the operation of the criminal law, activities which involved the infliction of physical harm, whether the injuries occurred in the context of sexual activity or otherwise. In the Court's view the English law on this point fell within the margin of appreciation left to member states in such matters, and none of the strong phrases used by the Court in *Dudgeon* and the subsequent decisions on consensual sexual offences are to be found in the judgment.[34] Instead, the Court held that the prosecution pursued the legitimate aim of the protection of health,[35] and possibly also of the protection of morals.[36] It was, in the first instance, for the domestic authorities, including the courts, to determine the level of physical harm which should be tolerated in situations where the victim consented. The Court noted that the injuries sustained were not insignificant, and that the factors at stake included public health considerations and the general deterrent effect of the criminal law. Accordingly, the Court rejected the applicants' arguments that their behaviour formed part of their private morality which it was not the state's business to regulate. Having regard to the fact that the Court of Appeal had reduced the sentences originally imposed by the trial judge, the prosecution and conviction was not disproportionate to the legitimate aim(s) of the protection of health and/or morals.

8–14   The emphasis which the Court placed in *Laskey* on the severity of the injuries inflicted drove it to distinguish the English Court of Appeal decision in *Wilson*[37] on tenuous grounds. In *Wilson* the Court of Appeal held that a defence of consent was available to the defendant, who had branded his initials on to his wife's buttocks. Consensual activity between husband and wife, in the privacy of the matrimonial home, was held not to be a proper subject for criminal prosecution. The applicants in *Laskey* argued that if this were true for heterosexual sadomasochism, it must be equally true for homosexuals. In an unconvincing response, the Court held that there was no evidence of a difference in the treatment of homosexuals, because it was the "extreme nature of the practices involved" in *Laskey* that distinguished it, rather than the sexual orientation of the participants.

---

[32] (1997) 24 E.H.R.R. 39.
[33] *R. v. Brown* [1994] 1 A.C. 212.
[34] *cf.* the critique by L. Moran, "*Laskey v. United Kingdom*: Learning the Limits of Privacy" (1998) 61 M.L.R. 77.
[35] See para. 50.
[36] See para. 51; for general discussion of the "public morals" exception to Arts 8–11, see R. Koering-Joulin, "Public Morals", in M. Delmas-Marty (ed.), *The European Convention for the Protection of Human Rights: International Protection versus National Restrictions* (1992).
[37] [1996] 2 Cr. App. R. 241.

The facts of *Wilson* were "not at all comparable in seriousness" with those in *Laskey*,[38] even though they amounted to assault occasionally actual bodily harm.

VI. *Heterosexual Buggery*

One of the more bizarre decisions of the Commission arose out of the criminal- **8–15**
isation of anal intercourse between heterosexuals. In *PL v. Ireland*[39] the applicant
complained that he was convicted as a result of consensual buggery with his
partner. The Commission drew an extraordinary distinction between homosexuals who found their activities barred by the criminal law, and the applicant
in the present case who did not claim that his sexual orientation made him
"disposed to" consensual buggery. There were other points relevant to the
decision, but the Commission's reasoning seems to fit very awkwardly with other
Strasbourg jurisprudence.

C. FREEDOM OF THOUGHT, CONSCIENCE AND RELIGION

I. *General Principles*

Article 9(1) accords unqualified protection to freedom of thought, conscience and **8–16**
religion. It also protects the right to *manifest* one's religion or belief "in worship,
teaching, practice or observance". This latter right (of manifestation) may be
subject to limitations if the conditions in Article 9(2) are fulfilled. So far as
organised religions in the United Kingdom are concerned, the protection of
Article 9 is emphasised by section 13 of the Human Rights Act 1998.[40]

II. *Religious exemptions*

The Court and Commission have been generally unwilling to accept that individ- **8–17**
uals can claim exemption from particular provisions of the criminal law on the
grounds of their personal or religious beliefs. Thus, the Commission held that
the protection of health criterion in Article 9(2) justified both the requirement of
the criminal law that a sikh motorcyclist should wear a crash helmet,[41] and the
prosecution of a farmer who had refused, on religious grounds, to participate in
a compulsory vaccination scheme for farm animals.[42] In *Seven Individuals v.
Sweden*[43] the Commission held that a Swedish law which criminalised parental
chastisement of children was compatible with Article 9, despite the parents'
claim that their religious convictions required such measures. The protection of
children from inhuman and degrading treatment under Article 3 was plainly a
legitimate objective, within the meaning of Article 9(2), for restricting corporal
punishment despite any suggested religious objections.

---

[38] (1997) 24 E.H.R.R. 39 at para. 47.
[39] [1998] E.H.R.L.R. 232.
[40] See para. 3–20 above.
[41] *X v. United Kingdom* (1978) 14 D.R. 234.
[42] *X v. Netherland* 5 Y.B. 278.
[43] (1982) 29 D.R. 104 at 114.

8–18   A similar reluctance to permit exceptions on religious grounds was evident in *Pendragon v. United Kingdom*.[44] A prohibition order under the Public Order Act 1986 had been made to prevent all trespassory asssemblies within a radius of four miles of Stonehenge for the four days of the summer solstice. The applicant claimed that his prosecution for breaching the prohibition notice (he was actually acquitted) violated his Convention rights. The Commission, by a majority, declared the application inadmissible and held that the limitation on the rights in Articles 9 and 11 was necessary "for the prevention of disorder," taking account of the disturbances which had occurred in the Stonehenge area in previous years.

III. *Prosecution for Religious Activity*

8–19   Prosecutions which directly involve religious activity have been more favourably received. In *Kokkinakis v. Greece*[45] the Court held that the prosecution of a Jehovah's witness for "proselytism" was in breach of Article 9.[46] The law limited the applicant's right to "manifest his religion or belief . . . in practice," and the limitation was not proportionate to the protection of the rights and freedoms of others. The Court distinguished "true evangelism" (which was the essential mission of the Christian religions) from "improper proselytism" (which was defined as an attempt to convert others by offering material or social benefits or taking advantage of the need, distress or incapacity of others).[47] The applicant, a Jehovah's Witness, had been persistent but had not acted improperly. He had done nothing more than attempt to persuade an adherent of another Christian religion of the virtues of his faith.

IV. *Ethical and Moral Values*

8–20   Greater difficulty has been encountered when dealing with the manifestation of non-religious moral convictions. Article 9(1) is not confined to recognised religions: it expressly mentions freedom of conscience and belief, and the Court has held that these freedoms are also; " . . . a precious asset for atheists, agnostics, sceptics and the unconcerned. The pluralism indissociable from a democratic society, which has been dearly won over the centuries, depends on it."[48]

8–21   In *Arrowsmith v. United Kingdom*[49] the Commission accepted that pacifism fell within the ambit of the right to freedom of thought and conscience. The applicant, who had distributed leaflets to soldiers urging them to go absent or refuse to serve in Northern Ireland, was prosecuted for incitement to disaffection. The Commission, however, held that the prosecution did not violate Article 9 since the applicant's actions did not amount to the "practice" of her pacifist beliefs.[50] The word "practice" in Article 9(1) did "not cover every act which is motivated

---

[44] [1999] E.H.R.L.R. 223; see also *Chappell v. United Kingdom* (1987) 53 D.R. 241, where it was first accepted that Druidism qualifies as a religion for these purposes.
[45] (1994) 17 E.H.R.R. 397.
[46] *ibid.*, paras 49–50.
[47] *ibid.*, para. 48.
[48] In *Kokkinakis v. Greece* (1994) 17 E.H.R.R. 397 at para. 31.
[49] (1978) 19 D.R. 5 at para. 69.
[50] *ibid.*, at para. 75.

or influenced by a religion or belief".[51] The Commission drew a slender and unconvincing distinction between the applicant's conduct on the one hand, and "public declarations proclaiming generally the idea of pacifism and urging the acceptance of a commitment to non-violence", on the other.

D. FREEDOM OF EXPRESSION

Criminal offences committed through the medium of speech, publication or **8-22** broadcasting amount to an interference with the right to freedom of expression.[52] The information or ideas protected by Article 10 may be ones that "offend, shock or disturb the State or any sector of the population"[53] and in this context the phrase "necessary in a democratic society" in Article 10(2) assumes a society characterised by "pluralism, tolerance and broad-mindedness."[54] Thus, where Article 10 rights are engaged, the reasons for any criminal penalty must be "convincingly established."[55]

I. *Obscenity Offences*

The Convention caselaw establishes clearly that potentially obscene material is **8-23** within the scope of Article 10, and that the compatibility of prosecution of such material is to be determined primarily by the likely audience. To that extent the Convention standard echoes the test in section 1 of the Obscene Publications Act 1959 Act that the material must be likely to deprave and corrupt "persons who are likely, having regard to all relevant circumstances, to read, see or hear the matter contained in [it]."

One of the earliest criminal cases under Article 10 was *Handyside v. United* **8-24** *Kingdom*.[56] The applicant was prosecuted under the Obscene Publications Acts 1959 and 1964 for having obscene books in his possession for gain. He had acquired the distribution rights for a publication called *The Little Red School-book*, an anti-authoritarian publication aimed at adolescents aged between 12 and 18, which contained a factually accurate—but explicit—section on sexual activity. The book was marketed so as to appear as if it were a schoolbook. The applicant was convicted by Lambeth magistrates' court and fined £100. The Court also ordered the forfeiture and destruction of his remaining stock. The applicant's appeal to Inner London Quarter Sessions was dismissed. In Strasbourg he complained that his conviction was in breach of Article 10. The Court concluded that the prosecution amounted to an interference with the applicant's freedom of expression, contrary to Article 10(1). Turning to Article 10(2), the Court found that the interference was adequately "prescribed by law," and held that the legislation pursued the legitimate aim of the protection of morals. Noting that it was in the first place for the national authorities, including the courts, to

---

[51] *ibid.*, at para. 71.
[52] See generally E. Barendt, *Freedom of Speech* (1985).
[53] *Handyside v. United Kingdom* (1979–80) 1 E.H.R.R. 737, para. 40
[54] *Handyside v. United Kingdom* (1979–80) 1 E.H.R.R. 737, para. 49.
[55] *Otto-Preminger Institut v. Austria* (1995) 19 E.H.R.R. 34 at para. 50; *Jersild v. Denmark* (1995) 19 E.H.R.R. 1 at para. 37.
[56] (1979–80) 1 E.H.R.R. 737.

determine the extent of the protection of morals required, the Court went on to establish the following important statement of principle:

"Freedom of expression constitutes one of the essential foundations of a [democratic] society, one of the basic conditions necessary for its progress and for the development of every man. Subject to paragraph 2 of Article 10, it is applicable not only to information and ideas that are favourably received, or regarded as inoffensive, but also to those that offend, shock, or disturb the state or any sector of the population. Such are the demands of that pluralism, tolerance and broadmindedness without which there is no 'democratic society'."[57]

8–25   Nevertheless, the Court concluded that having regard to the potential audience and the subject-matter of the book it was within the state's margin of appreciation to take criminal proceedings. It may be doubted whether the Court would take the same approach to such a publication today.

8–26   In *X and Y v. Switzerland*[58] the Commission held that a prosecution for selling obscene videos did not breach Article 10 because the case concerned a chain of video shops which were open to the general public. The Commission held that a "conviction for renting or selling the video films...would correspond to a pressing social need and would be proportionate to the legitimate aim pursued within the meaning of the Convention organs' case-law." In *Scherer v. Switzerland*,[59] by contrast, the Court found that a conviction for publication of an obscene film did violate Article 10 because the films had only been shown at a cinema to which public access was restricted. The applicant ran a sex shop in Zurich for homosexuals, behind which was a small projection room used for showing video films of an explicit sexual nature. Applying the *Handyside* principle the Court held that the right to freedom of expression encompassed the publication of allegedly obscene material. The interference was prescribed by law (under Article 204 of the Swiss Criminal Code), and pursued the legitimate aim of protecting morals within the meaning of Article 10(2). The question was whether it was "necessary in a democratic society." The Court considered that it was of particular relevance that the obscene material was not displayed to the general public. It was very unlikely that the projection room would be visited by persons who were unaware of the nature of the films shown, and there was control in the shop ensuring that minors could not gain access. In the opinion of the Court, the case did not concern the protection of the morals of Swiss society in general since no adult or child would be confronted with the films unintentionally or against his will. Where this is so, the Court held that there would have to be "particularly compelling reasons" justifying the interference. Since no such reasons had been shown, the Court held that the prosecution had amounted to a violation of Article 10.[60]

8–27   The application in *X Co v. United Kingdom*[61] related to the seizure of magazines under the Obscene Publications Act. The editor and publisher argued that the magazines were for export, so that the Article 10(2) justification of protecting the morals of United Kingdom citizens did not apply. To this the Commission replied

---

[57] At para. 49.
[58] 16564/90 April 8, 1991, (unreported).
[59] (1994) 18 E.H.R.R. 276 at paras 59–67.
[60] *ibid.*, at paras 59–67.
[61] (1983) 32 D.R. 231.

that "the protection of morals" can extend to a state's interest in the diffusion of immoral publications from its territory. The applicant company also argued that the seizure of the magazines amounted to an unjustified deprivation of possessions and a violation of Article 1 of Protocol 1. The Commission found, however, that a measure that is "necessary" for one of the reasons stated in Article 10(2) satisfies the test of "public interest" for permitting deprivations of possessions in Article 1 of Protocol 1. The application was therefore declared inadmissible.

In *Hoare v. United Kingdom*[62] the applicant was engaged in the publication and   **8–28** distribution of pornographic videotapes by post. The tapes depicted anal intercourse, bondage and the consumption of faeces. The applicant advertised in the *Sunday Sport* newspaper, and those responding to the advert would be sent a brochure describing the contents of the videos. The tapes would then be distributed on request. The applicant was charged with six counts of publishing obscene articles contrary to section 2(1) of the 1959 Act. He was convicted and sentenced to 30 months imprisonment. The applicant contended that the videos could not deprave or corrupt since only those who shared his interests would have purchased them from the brochure. He invited the Commission to have regard to the more liberal standards towards pornography applied in some Member States of the Council of Europe. In rejecting the application as manifestly ill-founded, the Commission again relied upon the protection of morals exception in Article 10(2). In the Commission's view, the sole question arising under the proportionality test was whether the sentence imposed was necessary. Although the Commission noted the precautions which the applicant had taken to prevent the tapes falling into the wrong hands, it nevertheless considered that there was no certainty that only the intended purchasers would have access to the material.

In considering analogous issues under the Charter, the Canadian courts have   **8–29** tended to focus on the inherent nature of the material, and the attitude of society generally to material in a certain category, rather than the likely audience for the particular publication. In *Butler*[63] the Supreme Court was concerned with material depicting a variety of sexual and violent activities. The relevant section of the Canadian Criminal Code, provided that "any publication a dominant characteristic of which is the undue exploitation of sex, or of sex and any one or more of . . . crime, horror, cruelty and violence, shall be deemed to be obscene." The question for the Supreme Court of Canada was whether this offence infringed the right to free expression in section 2(b) of the Charter. The Court held that it did, but that the infringement was saved by section 1 of the Charter as being "a reasonable limit demonstrably justified in a free and democratic society". In the leading judgment, Sopinka J. held that, in a matter on which individual opinions differed considerably, judges should strive to ascertain the community view:

> "The courts must determine as best they can what the community would tolerate others being exposed to on the basis of the degree of harm that may flow from such exposure. Harm in this context means that it predisposes persons to act in an anti-social manner as, for example, the physical or mental mistreatment of women by men, or what is perhaps debatable, the reverse. Anti-social conduct for this purpose is conduct which society formally recognizes as incompatible with its proper functioning. The stronger the inference of a risk of harm the lesser the likelihood of tolerance. The inference may

---

[62] [1997] E.H.R.L.R. 678.
[63] [1992] 1 S.C.R. 452.

be drawn from the material itself or from the material and other evidence . . . In making this determination with respect to the three categories of pornography . . . the portrayal of sex coupled with violence will almost always constitute undue exploitation of sex. Explicit sex which is degrading or dehumanizing may be undue if the risk of harm is substantial. Finally, explicit sex that is not violent and neither degrading nor dehumanizing is generally tolerated in our society and will not qualify as undue exploitation unless it employs children in its production. If material is not obscene under this framework, it does not become so by reason of the person to whom it is or may be shown or exposed nor by reason of the place or manner in which it is shown."

II. *Artistic Expression*

8–30   Artistic expression has generally been afforded less stringent protection than political and journalistic speech.[64] In *Muller v. Switzerland*[65] the applicant was a serious artist exhibiting at an exhibition to celebrate the 500th anniversary of Fribourg's entry into the Swiss Federation. He produced a series of large paintings, one of which included graphic depictions of sexual activity including homosexuality and bestiality. The paintings were displayed in a public exhibition with no warnings about their content. They were seen by a young girl visiting the exhibition with her father, who informed the public prosecutor. The applicant was convicted of publishing obscene items and fined. The paintings were confiscated, and not returned until almost eight years later.

8–31   In concluding that there had been no violation of Article 10, the Court placed considerable emphasis on the manner in which the paintings had been exhibited—in a gallery which sought to attract the public at large; which did not warn visitors about the content of the exhibition; and which permitted admission without age restriction. The Court held that the conviction was justified for the protection of public morals and the rights of others. It was within the state's margin of appreciation to conclude that the conviction was a proportionate means of achieving that aim. Whilst conceptions of sexual morality had changed in recent years, the Swiss courts were not unreasonable in finding the paintings grossly offensive to persons of ordinary sensitivity and in imposing a fine.[66] However, the confiscation of an original work of art (as opposed to a reproduction) raised a rather different issue since the artist lost the opportunity of showing his work in places where the demands of the protection of morals were less strict. In the end the Court found that the confiscation did not violate Article 10 since the applicant could have applied for the return of the painting sooner than he did. Nevertheless, it is implicit in the decision that an order for the destruction of an original work of art or its permanent confiscation would require a particularly compelling justification.

---

[64] See generally D.J. Harris, M. O'Boyle and C. Warbrick, *The Law of the European Convention on Human Rights* (1995), pp 377–386; Paul Mahoney, "Universality versus Subsidiarity in Strasbourg Free Speech Cases" [1997] E.H.R.L.R. 364; and Lord Lester of Herne Hill, "Universality versus Subsidiarity: a Reply" [1998] E.H.R.L.R. 73.
[65] (1991) 13 E.H.R.R. 212.
[66] On the relatively restrictive Swiss law, see S. Trechsel, "Switzerland", in M. Delmas-Marty (ed.), *The European Convention for the Protection of Human Rights* (1992) at pp 254–256.

III. *Race Hate Speech and Holocaust Denial*[67]

Section 18 of the Public Order Act 1986 creates the offence of incitement to   **8–32**
racial hatred which is committed where a person uses abusive or insulting words,
or displays abusive or insulting written material, which is likely to stir up racial
hatred, providing the words have been spoken or the material displayed with that
intention. Sections 19 to 22 apply the same principle to the publication or
distribution of written material, to the public performance of plays, to the
distribution, showing or playing of visual images or sounds, and to television
broadcasts. Possession of such material with a view to its publication or broadcast is also an offence.[68] "Racial hatred" means hatred against a group of persons
in Great Britain defined by reference to colour, race, nationality (including
citizenship) or ethnic or national origins.[69]

Applying Article 17 of the Convention[70] the Commission has, in the past, held   **8–33**
that speech which is intended to incite race hatred is outside the protection of
Article 10 altogether, because of its potential to undermine public order and the
rights of the targeted minority.[71] In its later decisions, the Commission tended to
reach the same conclusion via a slightly different route, accepting that such
speech could, in principle, fall within Article 10(1), but referring to Article 17 as
a factor relevant to the proportionality test in Article 10(2).[72] Thus, the Commission has found no violation of Article 10 where the applicant was prosecuted for
membership of a neo-fascist organisation,[73] or where prison authorities refused to
deliver to a prisoner publications encouraging anti-semitism and racism.[74]

However, the scope of the criminal law prohibiting the publication of race hate   **8–34**
speech must not extend beyond that which is strictly necessary and proportionate.
In *Jersild v. Denmark*[75] the applicant was a journalist convicted of aiding and
abetting the dissemination of racial insults. He had produced a short documentary
in which a television presenter interviewed three Danish youths about their
avowedly racist views. The programme included extreme and offensive expressions of racism which were broadcast without any comment or disclaimer. The
applicant had solicited the contributions and had edited the film so as to give
prominence to the most extreme expressions of view. Nevertheless, it was
common ground that the programme consisted of good faith reporting of current
affairs and that the journalist did not intend to promote racist attitudes. The
youths were convicted of making racist statements and the journalist of aiding
and abetting them. The Court was quite clear that the convictions of the youths
themselves were justified: "There can be no doubt that the remarks in respect of

---

[67] See generally Cooper and Marshall Williams, "Hate Speech, Holocaust Denial and International
Human Rights Law" [1999] E.H.R.L.R. 593.
[68] Section 23.
[69] Section 17.
[70] See para. 2–140 above.
[71] *Glimmerveen and Hagenback v. Netherlands* (1979) 18 D.R. 187.
[72] *Kunen v. Germany* (1982) 29 D.R. 194; *H, W, P and K v. Austria* (1989) 62 D.R. 216; *Marais v.
France* (1996) 86A D.R. 184. But see the approach of the Court in *Lehideux and Isorni v. France*
(1998) 5 B.H.R.C. 540.
[73] *X v. Italy* (1976) 5 D.R. 83.
[74] *Lowes v. United Kingdom* (1988) 59 D.R. 244.
[75] (1995) 19 E.H.R.R. 1.

which the [neo-nazis] were convicted were more than insulting to members of the targeted groups and did not enjoy the protection of Article 10."[76]

8–35   But the Court nevertheless held that the conviction of the journalist was not proportionate to the interest of protecting the rights of the minorities against whom the racism was directed.[77] News reports based on interviews constituted one of the most important means by which the press was able to perform its vital role of "public watchdog".[78] Although the Court declared the importance of combating racism in all its manifestations, it held that the punishment of a journalist for disseminating the statements of others in an interview would seriously hamper press freedom and "should not be envisaged unless there are particularly strong reasons for doing so."[79] As to the absence of an express disclaimer, the Court concluded that the form of the programme was essentially a matter of journalistic freedom.

8–36   In *Lehideux and Isorni v. France*[80] the applicants were prosecuted for publishing a newspaper advertisement allegedly apologising for the war crimes of Marshall Petain. They represented two organisations that were campaigning for a review of the Petain trial, and the advertisement stated in terms that it was not seeking to excuse or minimise the atrocities of the Nazi regime. The Court observed that statements which sought to deny clearly established historical facts, such as the Holocaust, would be removed from the protection of Article 10 altogether, by the operation of Article 17. On the facts, however, the applicants statements did not fall into this category, and the prosecution was therefore a breach of Article 10. These principles were applied by the Court in *Witzsch v. Germany*[81] where the applicant had been convicted of an offence of disparaging the memory of the dead in connection with protests about the introduction of Holocaust denial legislation in Germany. Following *Lehideux and Isorni* the Court held that;

> " . . . the public interest in the prevention of crime and disorder due to disparaging statements regarding the Holocaust, and the requirements of protecting the interests of the victims of the Nazi regime, outweigh, in a democratic society the applicant's freedom to impart views denying the existence of the gas chambers and mass murder therein."

8–37   This emphasis on denial of established historical facts is echoed in the international and comparative caselaw. The United Nations Human Rights Committee has adopted a similar approach in relation to the right to freedom of expression in Article 19 of the International Covenant on Civil and Political Rights. In *Faurisson v. France*[82] the applicant had been the subject of a private prosecution under French Gayssot Act 1990 (which creates a criminal offence of contesting the existence of the crimes against humanity tried at Nuremberg). In a magazine interview he had asserted a personal belief that there were no gas chambers for the extermination of Jews in the Nazi concentration camps. The Human Rights

---

[76] *ibid.*, para. 35.
[77] *ibid.*, para. 37.
[78] *ibid.*, para. 35; see generally on the role of the press, *Observer and Guardian Newspapers v. United Kingdom* (1992) 14 E.H.R.R. 153.
[79] *Jersild*, para. 35.
[80] (1998) 5 B.H.R.C. 540.
[81] Judgment April 20, 1999.
[82] Communication No. 550/1993, U.N. Doc. C.C.P.R./C/58/D/550/1993 (1996).

Committee held that the prosecution was a valid restriction on free expression, within the meaning of Article 19, because the statements were such as to raise or reinforce anti-semitic sentiment, and their suppression served the purpose of respecting the right of the Jewish community to live free from an atmosphere of fear.

Similarly, the German Constitutional Court has referred to the Basic Law to **8–38** uphold the use of provisions in the Penal Code which criminalise Holocaust denial. In one case,[83] the police had banned a neo-Nazi meeting on the ground that, since a revisionist historian who denied the holocaust was due to speak, criminal offences were likely to be committed. The organisers of the meeting challenged the order as a restriction on the constitutional right of freedom of speech. The Constitutional Court held that, although the Basic Law protects expressions of opinion (even if they are untrue or irrational), it does not protect the utterance of "demonstrably untrue statements of fact". To hold that such speech is protected would violate the right of Jewish people to their personality and their human dignity, both of which are protected by the Basic Law.

The jurisprudence of the United States Supreme Court on these matters is **8–39** extensive and detailed.[84] In *Beauharnais v. Illinois*,[85] the Supreme Court held that a statute criminalising group defamation did not infringe the First Amendment right of free speech. Later decisions seem to have placed greater emphasis on the First Amendment right, without actually overruling *Beauharnais*.[86] However, the matter is still attracting vigorous debate, and there is a formidable lobby in favour of interpreting the First Amendment so as to permit states to curb hate speech.[87]

The Canadian Supreme Court, for its part, has accepted that such restrictions are **8–40** compatible with the free speech guarantee in the Charter. The point arose for consideration in *Keegstra*,[88] which concerned a schoolteacher who had communicated anti-semitic statements to his pupils. He was convicted of wilfully promoting hatred against an identifiable group, contrary to the Criminal Code, and argued that the offence contravened the Charter. The Supreme Court unanimously held, in the first place, that the offence is an infringement of the right to freedom of expression secured by section 2(b) of the Charter. That freedom should be upheld whatever the content of the expression: the only possible exception would be expressions communicated in a violent way. The Court specifically declined to treat hate propaganda as analogous to violence, but nevertheless went on to hold, by a four to three majority, that the offence

---

[83] (1994) 90 B.Verf.G.E. 241.
[84] D.P. Kommers and J.E. Finn, *American Constitutional Law* (1998), p. 463, and the treatise by K. Greenawalt, *Speech, Crime and the Uses of Language* (1989).
[85] 343 U.S. 250 (1952).
[86] Of the many Supreme Court decisions, see, *e.g. Cohen v. California* 403 U.S. 15 (1971). Much discussed is the *Skokie* case, in which a local ordinance regulating assemblies in an area fraught with racial tension was struck down as unconstitutional: *Collin v. Smith* (1978) F. 2d 1197.
[87] For a thoughtful comparative analysis, see I. Hare, "Legislating against Hate—the Legal Response to Bias Crimes" (1997) 17 Oxford J.L.S. 415. See further J.B. Jacobs and K. Potter, *Hate Crimes: Criminal Law and Identity Politics* (1998), discussed in relation to the new racially aggravated offences under the Crime and Disorder Act 1998 by F. Brennan, "Racially Motivated Crime: the Response of the Criminal Justice System" [1999] Crim. L.R. 17.
[88] [1990] 3 S.C.R. 697.

amounted to a "reasonable limit" on freedom of expression, and was therefore saved by section 1 of the Charter. The offence sent out a strong message of disapprobation to those who threatened the values of a multicultural society. This reasoning was strengthened by reference to section 27 of the Charter, which requires its provisions to be interpreted "in a manner consistent with the preservation and enhancement of the multi-cultural heritage of Canada".[89]

IV. Blasphemy

8–41 Blasphemy and blasphemous libel are indictable offences at common law.[90] Blasphemy is the publication of material which is "contemptuous, reviling, scurrilous or ludicrous" in relation to the objects of veneration of the Christian religion or of the Church of England.[91] It is not blasphemous to speak or publish opinions hostile to the Church or to deny the existence of God, providing the expression of opinion is couched in "decent and temperate language."[92] Prosecutions for blasphemy are nowadays very rare in this country,[93] the most recent being in 1977.[94]

8–42 Although many European states have repealed blasphemy laws altogether, the Commission has held that prohibition of blasphemy through the criminal law is not in violation of Article 10.[95] This view has been endorsed by the Court, which has shown a particular sensitivity to the religious concerns of certain sections of the community. In *Otto-Preminger-Institut v. Austria*[96] the applicant institute announced the public showing of a satirical film which contained provocative and offensive portrayals of the objects of veneration of the Roman Catholic religion (the Eucharist was ridiculed, God the Father was portrayed as senile and impotent, the Virgin Mary was portrayed as a wanton woman with sexual interest in the devil, and Christ as mentally impaired). The film was based on a 19th century play which had been performed without censorship elsewhere. Before the first showing the public prosecutor instituted criminal proceedings against the manager and a judicial order was made for the seizure and forfeiture of the film. The Court accepted that the seizure was prescribed by law. Since Article 9 of the Convention protects the peaceful enjoyment of religious freedom it followed—in the Court's opinion—that the interference pursued the legitimate aim of protecting the rights of others. Although believers must tolerate and accept the denial of their beliefs by other people, and even the propagation of doctrines hostile to their faith, the manner in which such denial or opposition takes place could engage the responsibility of the state to take positive action. Respect for the religious beliefs of others could legitimately be thought to have been violated by

---

[89] For a detailed analysis of the Canadian and European authorities, together with those under the ICPPR, see D. McGoldrick and T. O'Donnell, "Hate-speech laws: consistency with national and international human rights law." (1998) 18 Legal Studies 453.
[90] See generally *Archbold* (1998) 27–1 to 27–6.
[91] Stephen, *Digest of the Criminal Law* (9th ed.,) approved by Lord Scarman in *Whitehouse v. Gay News* [1979] A.C. 617 at 665–666.
[92] *ibid.*
[93] As the Court noted in *Wingrove v. United Kingdom* (1997) 24 E.H.R.R. 1 at para. 57.
[94] *Whitehouse v. Gay News Ltd* [1979] A.C. 617.
[95] *X Ltd and Y v. United Kingdom* (1982) 28 D.R. 77.
[96] (1995) 19 E.H.R.R. 34; see the note by D. Pannick, "Religious Feelings and the European Court" [1995] P.L. 7.

"provocative portrayals of objects of religious veneration," which may be regarded as "malicious violation of the spirit of tolerance which must also be a feature of a democratic society."[97]

The Court went on to emphasise that those exercising freedom of expression also **8–43** undertake duties and responsibilities, amongst which was an obligation to avoid as far as possible expressions that are gratuitously offensive to others, and thus an infringement of their rights, and which do not contribute to any form of public debate. Since there was no discernible consensus throughout Europe on the significance of religion in society it was impossible to define comprehensively the interferences with anti-religious speech which might be permissible. In this instance, the fact that the applicant organisation had restricted admission by way of an age limit and an admission fee was not considered sufficient. The widely advertised nature of the film meant that its proposed screening must be considered sufficiently "public" to cause offence.[98] In the Court's opinion, the Austrian authorities had acted to ensure religious peace and to prevent people feeling that their religion was being subjected to unwarranted attacks with the acquiescence of the state. The interference was accordingly proportionate to the legitimate aim which it pursued.

The Court's judgment in the *Otto Preminger Institut* case demonstrates the **8–44** important relationship between Article 10 and Article 9 on these matters, holding that states have a "responsibility to ensure the peaceful enjoyment of the right guaranteed under Article 9 to the holders of those beliefs and doctrines" and also referring to "members of a religious majority or minority."[99] This approach may be thought to sit awkwardly with the limitation of the English law of blasphemy to the Christian faith, which is surely discriminatory since it fails to accord equal protection to minority faiths, and gives cause to doubt the earlier ruling of the Commission in *Choudhury v. United Kingdom*[1] that this restriction on the English offence does not violate Article 9.

Article 10 formed the basis of the challenge in *Wingrove v. United Kingdom*,[2] **8–45** where the British Board of Film Classification (BBFC) had denied a classification certificate to a short video film concerning St. Teresa of Avila, a 16th century nun who experienced powerful ecstatic visions of Christ. The work depicted a youthful nun having erotic fantasies involving sexual arousal with the crucified figure of Christ. The refusal to issue a classification certificate was based not upon the sexual imagery as such, but upon the view of the BBFC that the film infringed the criminal law of blasphemy. The Court held that there was no violation of Article 10 since the decision did not exceed the national authorities' margin of appreciation—a margin wider "within the sphere of morals or, especially, religion" than on matters such as political speech:

> "[B]lasphemy legislation is still in force in various European countries. It is true that the application of these laws has become increasingly rare and that several states have

---

[97] (1995) 19 E.H.R.R. 34 at para. 47.
[98] *ibid.*, at para. 54.
[99] *ibid.*, at para. 47.
[1] (1991) 12 H.R.L.J. 172. For the English proceedings, see *R. v. Chief Metropolitan Stipendiary Magistrate ex parte Choudhury* [1991] 1 Q.B. 429.
[2] (1997) 24 E.H.R.R. 1.

recently repealed them altogether... Strong arguments have been advanced in favour of the abolition of blasphemy laws, for example that such laws may discriminate against different faiths or denominations ... or that legal mechanisms are inadequate to deal with matters of faith or individual belief ... However, the fact remains that there is as yet not sufficient common ground in the legal and social orders of the Member States of the Council of Europe to conclude that a system whereby a State can impose restrictions on the propagation of material on the basis that it is blasphemous is, in itself, unnecessary in a democratic society and thus incompatible with the Convention."[3]

8–46 This rather pusillanimous reasoning demonstrates the difficulties felt by the Court on this subject. In principle it should be for the government to establish that there is a "pressing social need" to justify the censorship of a video film, according to the usual interpretation of Article 10(2), whereas the double negatives in the Court's reasoning betray unease and hesitation.[4] Although the Court placed considerable emphasis on the margin of appreciation allowed to states in these matters, it did at least point to "the breadth and open-endedness of the notion of blasphemy, and the risks of arbitrary or excessive interferences with freedom of expression under the guise of action taken against allegedly blasphemous material."[5] This leaves open the possibility of challenges under Article 10 against an over-restrictive or discriminatory use of blasphemy law in the future.

V. *Defamatory Libel*

8–47 Defamatory libel is a common law offence punishable with up to two years imprisonment and/or a fine.[6] The offence may be committed through any publication of defamatory material in permanent form. The libel must be of a serious character,[7] and the offence is triable only on indictment. It is not necessary for the prosecution to prove either an intention to defame or knowledge that the information published is false.[8] However, it is necessary to prove that the defendant was aware of the allegedly libelous statement and not merely of the publication in which it appears.[9] Nevertheless if a defendant who was unaware of the presence of the libel was in such a position that he ought to have known of it, then the onus is on the defence to prove that he was not negligent.[10] A prosecution against the publisher, proprietor or editor of a newspaper requires leave,[11] and if the subject-matter involves a play then the consent of the Attorney-General is required.[12] Under the Human Rights Act, the caselaw under Article 10 should be the guiding principle in the grant or refusal of leave or consent, as well as in the scope of the offence itself and the potential defences available. In *Gleaves v. Deakin*[13] Lord Diplock considered the offence to be altogether incompatible with Article 10:

[3] *ibid.*, para. 57.
[4] See the forceful criticism of the decision by S. Gandhi and J. James, "The English Law of Blasphemy and the European Convention on Human Rights" [1998] 4 E.H.R.L.R. 430.
[5] (1997) 24 E.H.R.R. 1 at para. 58.
[6] Libel Act 1843, ss.4–5.
[7] *Gleaves v. Deakin* [1980] A.C. 477 H.L.; *Desmond v. Thorne* [1983] 1 W.L.R. 163 Q.B.D.
[8] If the defendant was not aware of the falsity of the information published, the maximum sentence is one year's imprisonment and/or a fine: Libel Act 1843, s.5.
[9] *Vitzelly v. Mudie's Select Library Ltd* [1900] 2 Q.B. 170.
[10] *ibid.*
[11] Law of Libel Amendment Act 1888, s.8.
[12] Theatres Act 1968, s.8.
[13] [1980] A.C. 477 (H.L.).

"[T]he truth of the defamatory statement is not in itself a defence to a charge of defamatory libel under our criminal law . . . No onus lies on the prosecution to show that the defamatory matter was of a kind that it is necessary in a democratic society to suppress or penalise in order to protect the public interest. On the contrary, even though no public interest can be shown to be injuriously affected by imparting to others accurate information about seriously discreditable conduct of an individual, the publisher of the information must be convicted unless he himself can prove to the satisfaction of a jury that the publication of it was for the public benefit. That is to turn Article 10 of the Convention on its head."

Prosecutions for criminal defamation are not uncommon in other Council of **8–48** Europe member states. Such prosecutions will be compatible with Article 10 only insofar as they relate to untruthful and seriously damaging allegations of fact. In *Lingens and Leitgens v. Austria*[14] the applicants were prosecuted for libel following the publication of an article which alleged that a politician had lied in a public speech. The Commission held that such a prosecution had the legitimate aim of protecting the reputations of others. A distinction had to be drawn "between the necessity of the legal regulations as such, and the necessity of their application in the particular case." In view of "the fundamental importance [of free expression] in the field of political discussion" the Commission considered it to be "of the utmost importance that these restrictive regulations should only be applied where it is really necessary in the particular case".[15] Politicians, in particular, must be prepared to accept even harsh criticisms of their public activities and statements. Such criticism could not be characterised as defamatory unless it threw considerable doubt on their character and integrity. However, since the article had presented as established fact the untruthful allegation that the politician had lied, a criminal prosecution was justified.

This conclusion is to be contrasted with the decision of the Court in a later case **8–49** brought by the same applicant in respect of another prosecution for criminal defamation. In *Lingens v. Austria*[16] the applicant wrote articles accusing the Austrian Chancellor of protecting former members of the Nazi S.S. for political reasons. He was convicted, fined and ordered to print the court's judgment in a subsequent issue of his magazine. The European Court of Human Rights emphasised the need to distinguish between assertions of fact and value judgments.[17] The offending passages in the articles were, in the Court's view, essentially expressions of opinion. It was therefore impossible to expect the applicant to prove their truth. In finding a violation of Article 10, the Court emphasised that it was incumbent on the press to impart information and ideas on political issues, and accordingly that the limits of acceptable criticism are wider as regards politicians than for private individuals.

In *Oberschlick v. Austria*[18] the applicant was the editor of a journal called *Forum*. **8–50** He printed the text of a speech given by a politician which had glorified all those who fought in the Second World War and argued that it was wrong to distinguish between "good" and "bad" soldiers. The speech was criticised in an article written by the applicant entitled "Idiot rather than Nazi." The article denounced

---

[14] *Lingens and Leitgens v. Austria* (1982) 4 E.H.R.R. 373 at 393.
[15] *ibid.*, at para. 10c.
[16] (1986) 8 E.H.R.R. 407.
[17] *ibid.*, at para. 40.
[18] [1997] E.H.R.L.R. 676.

the politician as a fool on the ground that he had suggested in the speech that those who did not fight in the war could not lay claim to democratic freedoms. The applicant was prosecuted for defamation and fined 200 Austrian schillings (with 10 days imprisonment in default). The domestic courts held that the word "idiot" was incapable of amounting to objective criticism. The Austrian Court of Appeal did not consider that Article 10 extended to the protection of defamatory speech aimed at politicians since this would lead to the general debasement of political debate. The European Court disagreed: the article had to be looked at in context, taking account of all the circumstances of the case and in particular of the extreme views expressed by the politician in his speech. Article 10 protected not only the substance of ideas but also the form in which they were conveyed. The limits of acceptable criticism were wider with regard to a politician acting in his public capacity than in relation to a private individual. The article, although polemical, was not a gratuitous attack on the politician because the author provided a rational basis for his criticism. Accordingly, the conviction and sentence had violated the applicant's rights under Article 10.

8–51   In *Thorgeir Thorgeirson v. Iceland*[19] the applicant was prosecuted for two articles he had published in a national newspaper alleging a pattern of brutality by unspecified members of the Rekjavíc police force. The Court held that the role of the press as a public watchdog was not confined to political discussion, but extended to other matters of public concern. The principal purpose of the articles was, in the court's view, not to damage the reputation of the police, but to press for an independent investigation of allegations which had been made by others. In concluding that the defamation conviction violated Article 10 the Court emphasised that one of the instances of police brutality referred to was capable of proof. As to the broader picture, the articles had made it clear that the author was reporting allegations which had emanated from others and which had affected public opinion about the police. No police officers had been named, and the report emphasised that such brutality was the exception rather than the rule. In short, the articles had been prepared and presented responsibly and in good faith.

VI. *Defamation of judges*

8–52   In this country it is still a common law contempt of court to publish matter so defamatory of a judge or court as to be likely to interfere with the due administration of justice by seriously lowering the authority of the judge or the court.[20] The offence, known as "scandalising the court," is so infrequently used that it has been described as "virtually obsolescent."[21] Moreover, the restrictions which have been imposed on the scope of the offence are such that it almost certainly complies with the requirements of Article 10. The authorities establish that it is only in a clear case that this branch of the contempt jurisdiction may be exercised

---

[19] (1992) 14 E.H.R.R. 842.
[20] *R. v. Gray* [1990] 2 Q.B. 36; *R. v. Editor of the New Statesman* (1928) 44 T.L.R. 301; see further *Arlidge, Eady and Smith on Contempt* (1999), paras 5–205 to 5–269.
[21] *Per* Lord Diplock in *Secretary of State for Defence v. Guardian Newspapers* [1985] A.C. 339 at 347.

since any citizen must be free to criticise a decision of a court, even in an outspoken manner.[22]

Prosecutions for defamation of the judiciary do occur in a number of other **8–53** Convention countries. In *Barford v. Denmark*[23] the applicant journalist was prosecuted for defamation of two lay judges. He wrote an article suggesting that they "did their duty" in the course of litigation over which they were presiding by voting for the local authority by which both of them were employed. The article criticised the structural impartiality of having a case decided by a panel of judges including two employees of one of the litigants, and the personal integrity of the two individuals. The Court held that the prosecution was proportionate to the legitimate aim of protecting the reputations of others, and the authority and impartiality of the judiciary. The conviction had been based on the personal attacks which had been made on the judges, and not upon the structural unfairness of the tribunal (which would have been a legitimate subject of free public debate).[24]

VII. *Speech Attacking the State*

Turning to speech which is intended to undermine the state or its authorities, **8–54** there are a number of statutory offences involving incitement to disaffection in the armed forces[25] or the police,[26] as well as the common law offence of seditious libel. The latter consists of the publication of words intended or tending to bring into hatred or contempt or to excite disaffection against the monarch, the government, Parliament or the administration of justice.[27] The offence requires proof of an intention to incite violence against constituted authority.[28] Lawful criticism which involves pointing out errors or defects in government with a view to encouraging change by lawful means is not seditious libel.[29]

Where such offences are involved the Strasbourg institutions require convincing **8–55** evidence of a threat to national security or to the prevention of disorder. They will, however, take account of the context in which the speech has occurred. In *Engel v. Netherlands*[30] the applicants were servicemen convicted of disciplinary offences following the publication and distribution of a journal which had been prohibited as being inconsistent with military discipline. The Court held that the term "disorder" in Article 10(2) encompassed not only public order, but the order required by membership of a specified group, such as the military. Since the publication had been in direct contravention of an order from a senior officer,

---

[22] *Ambard v. AG for Trinidad and Tobago* [1936] A.C. 322; *McCleod v. St. Aubyn* [1989] A.C. 549; *R. v. Metropolitan Police Commissioner ex parte Blackburn* [1968] 2 Q.B. 150.
[23] (1991) 13 E.H.R.R. 493.
[24] *cf. Schopfer v. Switzerland* [1998] E.H.R.L.R. 646, where the Court held that there had been no breach of Art. 10 when a lawyer was fined by his professional body for alleging that local judges knew of irregularities in their area and had been acting for years in flagrant disregard of human rights.
[25] Under the Incitement to Disaffection Act 1934, s.1 *et seq.*
[26] See for example the Police Act 1997, s.43.
[27] Stephen's *Digest of Criminal Law* (9th ed.,), Art. 114.
[28] *R. v. Metropolitan Stipendiary Magistrate ex parte Choudhury* [1991] Q.B. 429 at 453.
[29] *R. v. Burns* (1886) 16 Cox. 355.
[30] (1979–80) 1 E.H.R.R. 647.

the prosecution was based upon the legitimate requirement of preventing service-men from undermining military discipline. More controversially, this principle has been extended to civilian defendants. In *Arrowsmith v. United Kingdom*[31] the Commission rejected a complaint that a prosecution for incitement to disaffection amounted to a breach of Article 10. The applicant had distributed leaflets to soldiers advising them of ways to avoid serving in Northern Ireland. The Commission considered that the promotion of disaffection amongst soldiers could amount to a threat to national security, and accordingly that the restriction pursued a legitimate aim within Article 10(2). A prosecution was necessary because the applicant had expressed an intention to continue with the distribution.

8–56   On the other hand in *Grigoriades v. Greece*[32] the Court found a breach of Article 10 where the applicant was convicted of an offence of insulting the army, and imprisoned. During his period of military service the applicant had written a letter critical of the army to his commanding officer. The Court held that the conviction was in breach of the right to freedom of expression. The letter, though it was expressed in harsh terms, addressed problems facing conscripts in general and did not insult any individual. It was sent only to the commanding officer and not to the press or other conscripts, so its potential to undermine army discipline was insignificant. In view of the penalty imposed, the conviction was neither "necessary in a democratic society" for the prevention of disorder in the army, nor proportionate to a legitimate aim.

8–57   Violations of Article 10 have been found in some of the cases arising out of the Kurdish conflict in Turkey, where the government has used an offence under the anti-terrorist legislation to prosecute people who have written articles critical of the government's approach.[33] However in *Surek v. Turkey*[34] the Court found that Article 10 had not been violated. The applicant, the owner of a Turkish news journal, published two articles critical of the Turkish government's handling of the Kurdish situation. He was convicted under the anti-terrorism legislation of disseminating propaganda against the indivisibility of the state and provoking enmity and hatred among the people. The Court accepted that the right to freedom of expression was engaged, and held that the preservation of national security could only justify proportionate interference with the Article 10 right. However, the line is crossed when political polemics support unlawful violence, and the articles here could be taken as supporting the armed struggle and thereby encouraging further violence.

VIII. *Disclosure of Official Secrets*

8–58   The Court and Commission have accepted that where the disclosure of state secrets is damaging to national security, and is not justified by an overriding public interest, the imposition of sanctions in respect of that disclosure is unlikely

---

[31] (1978) 19 D.&R. 5.
[32] (1999) 27 E.H.R.R. 464.
[33] See *Zana v. Turkey* (1997) 27 E.H.R.R. 667 and the cases discussed at [1998] E.H.R.L.R. 645.
[34] [1999] E.H.R.L.R. 636. *Cf.* the series of cases decided on the same day and discussed at [1999] E.H.R.L.R. 637–639.

to constitute a violation of Article 10.[35] In *Hadjianastassiou v. Greece*[36] the applicant was an airforce officer in charge of a project to design and produce guided missiles, who complained that his conviction for "disclosing military information of minor importance" constituted a violation of Article 10. He had sold information from his work to a private company. He argued that the disclosure could not be regarded as damaging to national security since it was a routine technical study based entirely on his own documentation. The Court considered that the disclosure of a state's interest in a given weapons system and the corresponding technical knowledge could give an indication as to the state's progress in the manufacture of the weapon and that consequently it was capable of causing considerable damage to national security. Having regard to the "duties and responsibilities" incumbent on members of the armed forces and the obligation of confidentiality on the applicant, his conviction and suspended sentence did not constitute a violation of Article 10. The court's judgment in *Hadjianastassiou* played an important part in the reasoning of Moses J. in *R. v. Shalyer*,[37] where he held that the absence of a public interest defence to charges under sections 1(1) and 4(1) of the Official Secrets Act 1989 was compatible with Article 10. The judge rejected the submission of the Crown that national courts should apply the same broad margin of appreciation as would be applied in Strasbourg. Nevertheless, the national court had to approach the issue of compatibility by recognising that a number of choices were open to the legislature to preserve official secrecy. Applying the standards of the Convention, it was incumbent on the national court anxiously to scrutinise the justification advanced for the imposition of criminal sanctions and to require substantial justification within the limits imposed by Article 10. But it was not for the court to substitute its own view for that of the legislature. The court could only conclude that the legislation was incompatible with Article 10 if the legislative technique which had been adopted fell outside the range of responses reasonably open to Parliament. Under the relevant provisions of the 1989 Act it is an offence for a member or former member of the security or intelligence services, to disclose without lawful authority information which is in his possession by virtue of his position as such. There is no requirement for the Crown to prove that the information is damaging to the national interest,[38] and it is no defence for the accused to show that the disclosure was made in the public interest. Moses J. held that there were two factors which, in combination, provided a substantial and compelling justification for prohibiting a former member of the services from raising in his defence the argument that disclosure to the press was necessary in the public interest. First, to permit such a defence would require the Crown to adduce evidence to establish the damage caused, and to rebut the claim that disclosure was necessary in the public interest. This would involve an adversarial examination of the very category of information which the legislation was designed to protect, and would create a substantial risk that the information disclosed in the course of the

---

[35] *Vereniging Weekend Bluf! v. Netherlands* (1995) 20 E.H.R.R. 189. The Court has generally been prepared to recognise a wide margin of appreciation where measures taken to safeguard national security are at stake: *Leander v. Sweden* (1987) 9 E.H.R.R. 433.

[36] (1992) 16 E.H.R.R. 219.

[37] Unreported, May 14, 2001 (T2000 1009).

[38] Where the disclosure is made by someone who is not a former member of the services, the offence is only made out if the disclosure is damaging. Accordingly, it is an offence for a member or former member of the services to disclose information notwithstanding that the disclosure of the same information would not be an offence if the disclosure was made by another person.

criminal proceedings would be as damaging or more damaging to national security than the original disclosure. Since the defence could put the point in issue simply by assertion, the disclosure of sensitive information in the course of the trial (and the resulting damage to national security) could occur even where the claim to public interest turned out, on examination, to be spurious. Secondly, the 1989 Act did not impose a blanket ban on disclosure of wrong-doing within the services. A former member of the services is entitled to make disclosure to a Crown servant for the purposes of his functions as such. "Crown servants" are defined for this purpose,[39] to include a Minister of the Crown, civil servants, and police officers. Accordingly, it is no offence to disclose information to any one of those persons for the purposes of their functions as such. Moreover, by section 7(3) and (5) a former officer may seek official authorisation from an authorised Crown servant to make disclosure to others (including the media). In *Shayler*, the Crown accepted that a refusal to give authorisation would be amenable to judicial review. It followed that an officer or former officer who had a valid claim that disclosure was necessary in the public interest would be able, in the last resort, to have that claim tested by a court *before* the disclosure was made. Given the inevitable risk that disclosure may be damaging to national security, it was plainly preferable for the individual's assessment of the public interest to be capable of being tested in advance. Following October 2000 the Administrative Court would be required to apply the provisions of the Human Rights Act 1998, so that if a refusal of authorisation was, on the facts, incompat-ible with Article 10 the court would have power to quash it on that ground. This provided a vital safeguard. Whilst it was theoretically possible to conceive of circumstances in which all the specified Crown servants might wrongly seek to suppress information which it was in the public interest to disclose, it was going too far to suggest that the courts considering the matter on judicial review would collude with such an approach:

"Section 7(3) and section 12 provide a forum for debate as to whether disclosure is necessary in the public interest. Those sections provide a mechanism for meeting the concerns of one who seeks to make disclosure. Should no action take place in the face of a well-founded claim to make disclosure in the public interest, the court can be the final arbiter."

Accordingly, the Act enabled the public interest to be tested by a court before the potentially damaging disclosure was made, rather than afterwards by way of a public interest defence available in criminal proceedings.

IX. *Free Speech and Public Order*

8–59   In *Steel v. United Kingdom*[40] five applicants claimed that their arrests for breach of the peace violated their rights of freedom of expression. All of them were involved in protests, and in the cases of the first two applicants the protests took the form of physically obstructing the activities of others. The Court, citing

---

[39] See section 12, and the orders made thereunder.
[40] (1999) 28 E.H.R.R. 603; See also *McLeod v. United Kingdom*, (1999) 27 E.H.R.R. 493 a decision of the Court on the same day which also concerns the use of "breach of the peace" powers.

Chorherr v. Austria,[41] held that their conduct nonetheless constituted an expression of opinion within Article 10. In respect of two of the applicants, who had caused physical obstructions, the Court held that their arrest, conviction and subsequent imprisonment was a proportionate response in order to avert the danger of disorder and violence.[42] However, in relation to the other three applicants, who were merely distributing leaflets and holding a placard, the Court held that they were exercising their freedom of expression and (unanimously) that their arrest was a disproportionate response, which violated Article 10.

A similar issue arose in *Hashman and Harrup v. United Kingdom,*[43] where the **8–60** applicants were hunt saboteurs who had blown a horn, and shouted at hounds during a fox-hunt. They were bound over to keep the peace by magistrates, and the Crown Court upheld the binding over on the ground that their conduct, although not involving either violence or the likelihood of a breach of the peace, was *"contra bonos mores."* The Court held that this amounted to a breach of Article 10. In the light of *Steel,* there was no doubt that the applicants' acts were forms of expression within Article 10(1). The more difficult question was whether the interference with their right was "prescribed by law", as required by Article 10(2). On this point the Court distinguished *Steel.* In *Steel* the Court had held that the concept of breach of the peace was sufficiently certain to fulfil the "quality of law" test required by the Court.[44] Here, by contrast, the concept of behaviour *contra bonos mores* was not defined with sufficient clarity to enable citizens to regulate their conduct, and there was therefore a risk of arbitrary interference with the applicants' Article 10 rights. It is noteworthy that the Law Commission had reached the same conclusion in its inquiry into the subject.[45]

Less encouraging is the majority decision of the Court in *Janowski v. Poland.*[46] **8–61** The applicant had been convicted of the offence of insulting civil servants. He was a journalist who witnessed two municipal guards directing stall holders to move their stalls to another place. Believing that they were acting unlawfully he intervened, eventually calling them "oafish" and "dumb". Overturning a finding of the Commission that Article 10 had been infringed, the Court observed that the applicants' remarks did not form part of an open discussion of matters of public concern, and that his conviction was based on the insults, rather than his criticisms of the officers' unlawful conduct. Whilst public servants should generally expect criticism of their actions, it could not be said that civil servants such as these municipal guards laid themselves open to the same degree of scrutiny as politicians. In the end the fact that the applicant had insulted the guards in front of a group of bystanders was held sufficient to justify his prosecution. In a strong dissenting opinion Sir Nicholas Bratza observed that there were good grounds for considering the guards' actions to be unlawful;

---

[41] (1994) 17 E.H.R.R. 358 cited at para. 92 of *Steel.*
[42] The first applicant was held on arrest for 44 hours and then imprisoned for 28 days when she refused to be bound over to keep the peace. Four judges dissented from the finding that this was "not disproportionate" and held that her Art. 10 right had been violated, two of them going so far as to describe the length of custody as "manifestly extreme."
[43] *The Times,* December 1, 1999.
[44] See paras 2–81 to 2–90 above.
[45] *Binding Over,* Law Com. No. 222, (1994), paras 4.34 and 5.7.
[46] (2000) 29 E.H.R.R. 705.

"The applicant was, in these circumstances, amply justified in exercising his freedom of expression in remonstrating with [them]. The fact that, in the course of doing so, he used two insulting words which evidently reflected his sense of frustration with the attitude of the guards, could not in my view justify his prosecution . . . [E]ven though the language used by the applicant may be considered exaggerated, it did not amount to a deliberate and gratuitous personal attack."

8–62   The relevance of Article 10 in a public order context was considered by the Divisional Court in *Redmond-Bate v. DPP*.[47] The defendant and two others were Christian fundamentalists and were preaching from the steps of a cathedral. When some members of the crowd began to show hostility towards what they were saying, the police arrested the defendant for breach of the peace, and she was subsequently convicted of obstructing a police officer in the execution of his duty. The Divisional Court quashed the conviction, on an appeal by way of case stated, and placed considerable emphasis on the defendants' rights under Article 9, 10 and 11 of the Convention in doing so. Two points emerge from the decision. First, Sedley L.J. explicitly recognised that the right to freedom of expression extends to opinions that are controversial: "free speech includes not only the inoffensive but the irritating, the contentious, the heretical, the unwelcome and the provocative, provided it does not tend to provoke violence."[48] Secondly, the Divisional Court confirmed the principle in *Beatty v. Gillbanks*[49] by holding that if the threat to the police does not come from the defendants themselves but from hecklers, the police ought to arrest the hecklers and not the defendants. Both of them have a right to freedom of expression, of course, but the threat to public order comes from the heckler (unless the original speaker makes statements likely to provoke violence). This is a principle which the Strasbourg Court itself has articulated in the context of Article 11.[50]

X. *Election offences*

8–63   In *Bowman v. United Kingdom*[51] the defendant, a pro-Life campaigner, had distributed leaflets during an election campaign setting out the candidates' voting record on abortion. She was prosecuted under section 75 of the Representation of the People Act 1983 for an offence of incurring unauthorised expenditure. The Court held that the prosecution was a disproportionate interference with her right to freedom of expression. It accepted that the legislation pursued a legitimate aim, namely to control expenditure of individual candidates so as ensure, as far as possible, that they are on an equal financial footing. However, the Court found that the statutory restriction of expenditure to £5 in the weeks preceding an election was disproportionate to this aim. It was "particularly important in the period preceding an election that opinions and information of all kinds are permitted to circulate freely", and the applicant was therefore entitled to disseminate factually accurate information to the local electorate "during the crucial period when their minds were focussed on their choice of representative".

---

[47] [1999] Crim. L.R. 998.
[48] [1999] Crim. L.R. 998 at 1000; *cf.* the similar statements in *Handyside v. United Kingdom*, para. 8–24 above.
[49] (1882) 9 Q.B.D. 308.
[50] *Plattform "Artze fur das Leben" v. Austria* (1991) 13 E.H.R.R. 204 at para. 32.
[51] (1998) 26 E.H.R.R. 1, noted at [1998] Public Law 592.

E. FREEDOM OF ASSEMBLY

I. *General principles*

The Convention protects the right to organise and to participate in peaceful **8–64**
public demonstrations[52] and marches.[53] The right extends to meetings which
cause obstruction of public thoroughfares,[54] and to private meetings,[55] provided
they are planned to be peaceful. The focus here is on the intention of the
organisers. Thus, the Commission has held that:

" . . . the right to freedom of peaceful assembly is secured to everyone who has the
intention of organising a peaceful demonstration . . . [T]he possibility of violent
counter-demonstrations, or the possibility of extremists with violent intentions . . .
joining the demonstration cannot as such take away that right."[56]

A peaceful demonstration will be protected by Article 11(1) even if it is unlaw- **8–65**
ful. Thus, for example, in *G v. Federal Republic of Germany*[57] the Commission
held that a non-violent unlawful sit-in which blocked the entrance to American
barracks in Germany constituted "peaceful assembly", attracting the protection
of Article 11.[58] The longer a demonstration goes on, however, the more likely it
is that an interference will be justified under Article 11(2), particularly if it causes
serious disruption to others. In *Friedl v. Austria*[59] the applicant had organised a
sit-in in a busy underpass in Vienna to publicise the plight of the homeless. The
sit-in obstructed passers-by, and numerous complaints were made to the authorities. About 50 people were initially involved, and the demonstration continued
for a week until the police dispersed it. The Commission concluded that the
decision to disperse, after such a long period of time, fell squarely within the
state's margin of appreciation.

Requirements to notify the authorities or to seek prior permission will not **8–66**
generally constitute an interference with the right to peaceful assembly.[60] The
Court has, however, held that *ex post facto* criminal or disciplinary sanctions do
amount to an interference. In *Ezelin v. France*[61] a lawyer had carried a placard
during a demonstration against the judicial system. His own conduct was peaceful, but when others began to hurl abuse and daub graffiti he failed to leave. The
European Court held that his Article 11 rights had been violated despite the

---

[52] *Rassemblement Jurassien and Unite Jurassienne v. Switzerland* (1979) 17 D.R. 93 at 119.
[53] *Christians against Racism and Fascism v. United Kingdom* (1980) 21 D.R. 138 at 148.
[54] *Rassemblement Jurassien* (above) at 119.
[55] *ibid.*, although there is no elaboration of what constitutes a "private meeting" for this purpose.
[56] *Christians against Racism and Fascism v. United Kingdom* (1980) 21 D.R. 138, emphasis
added.
[57] (1989) 60 D.R. 256 at 263.
[58] In the event, the applicant's arrest and conviction were justified under Art. 11(2) since the protest
had caused "more obstruction than would normally arise from the exercise of the right to peaceful
assembly".
[59] Application No. 15225/89 (unreported) (Admissibility). A different aspect of the case was declared
admissible under Art. 8, and the Court's judgment is at (1996) 21 E.H.R.R. 83.
[60] *Rassemblement Jurassien*, (1979) 17 D.R. 93 at 119. Obviously, if permission is refused then this
will amount to an interference.
[61] (1992) 14 E.H.R.R. 362.

comparatively light the penalty subsequently imposed on him (a professional reprimand for "breach of discretion" as a lawyer).

8–67 The Court has held that there is some measure of positive obligation on the state to protect those exercising their right of peaceful assembly from violent disturbance by counter-demonstrators. In *Plattform "Artze fur das Leben" v. Austria*[62] the Court explained that "genuine, effective freedom of peaceful assembly cannot be reduced to a mere duty on the part of the State not to interfere", and that "Article 11 sometimes requires positive measures to be taken." If both demonstrations are peaceful, and thus entitled to protection, then the authorities must balance their rights. But if one demonstration is aimed at the disruption of the activities of another, then the authorities come under an obligation to protect those exercising the right of peaceful assembly. The threat of violence from an opposing demonstration does not of itself justify interference with a peaceful demonstration[63]:

> "A demonstration may annoy or give offence to person opposed to the ideas or claims that it is seeking to promote. The participants must, however, be able to hold the demonstrations without having to fear that they will be subjected to physical violence by their opponents; such a fear would be liable to deter associations or other groups supporting common ideas or interests from openly expressing their opinions on highly controversial issues affecting the community. In a democracy, the right to counter-demonstrate cannot extend to inhibiting the right to demonstrate."

8–68 In the public order context, the principle of fair balance between competing interests is easier to state than it is to apply.[64] In *Chorrer v. Austria*,[65] the applicant held up banners at a military ceremony as a protest against the arms trade. Certain members of the crowd became agitated and threatened him with physical violence. The police asked him to desist and when he refused, he was arrested and subsequently fined. The Court found no violation, considering that the applicant's protest had been antagonistic. Given the occasion, there were no reasonable alternative means available to preserve public order, and the applicant's arrest was accordingly justified.

II. *Offences under the Public Order Act 1986 and Criminal Justice and Public Order Act 1994*[66]

8–69 In England and Wales the carrying out of public demonstrations is regulated primarily by Part II of the Public Order Act 1986, as amended by the Criminal Justice and Public Order Act 1994. Section 11 of the 1986 Act creates a duty of advance notification to the police. Sections 12 and 14 create police powers to impose conditions on processions and assemblies. Sections 13 and 14 (as amended) create powers to prohibit processions and trespassory assemblies, and to stop persons proceeding to trespassory assemblies. The Act creates a number

---

[62] (1991) 13 E.H.R.R. 204 at para. 32.
[63] (1991) 13 E.H.R.R. 204 at para. 32.
[64] See, however, *Redmond-Bate v. DPP* [1999] Crim. L.R. 998, (considered at para. 8–62 above) where the Divisional Court struck the balance firmly in favour of free expression.
[65] (1994) 17 E.H.R.R. 358.
[66] See generally B. Fitzpatrick and N. Taylor, "Trespassers might be Prosecuted: the European Convention and Restrictions on the Right to Assemble" [1998] E.H.R.L.R. 292.

of summary offences of organising and participating in a prohibited demonstration.

Whilst the requirements for notice and the dependent offences appear on their **8–70** face to be compatible with Article 11 as interpreted, the issuance of a ban on assemblies in a particular area raises more difficult issues. In *Christians against Racism and Fascism v. United Kingdom*[67] the Commission held that two separate bans imposed under the Public Order Act 1936 on all marches in a particular area were justified under Article 11(2). The bans were justified on the ground that there was evidence of mounting tension in the area, and the police expected disorder to occur. The Commission pointed to the limited duration of the ban and its comparatively small geographical scope. Although it was drawn so as to encompass all processions in London, it had been aimed primarily at marches organised by the National Front and was supported by evidence that such marches had frequently degenerated into violence in the past.[68] In the light of the principles subsequently stated by the Court in *Plattform "Artze fur das Leben"*,[69] it is at least open to question whether the case would be decided in the same way today.

The application of Article 11 to the provisions of the Public Order Act 1986 arose **8–71** in *Rai, Allmond and "Negotiate Now" v. United Kingdom*,[70] where the Secretary of State had used a statutory power to make regulations requiring permission for all demonstrations in Trafalgar Square, and had announced and adopted a policy of refusing permission for all demonstrations relating to Northern Ireland that were not "uncontroversial". The Commission held that this restriction could be brought within Article 11(2), since its purpose was to prevent an outbreak of violence. One interesting aspect in this application was that the Secretary of State had reminded the applicants that permission was likely to be granted for a demonstration in Hyde Park.[71]

In *Pendragon v. United Kingdom*[72] an order under section 14A of the Public **8–72** Order Act 1986 (as amended) had been made prohibiting all trespassory assemblies of 20 or more people within a four-mile radius of Stonehenge for a four-day period creating what was, in effect, an exclusion zone. The applicant was arrested and prosecuted for his part in breaching the order. He was acquitted, but alleged that his rights under Articles 9, 10 and 11 had been violated. The Commission declared the application inadmissible, noting that there had been disorder in previous years, which was capable of justifying the prohibition. Moreover, it remained possible for the applicant to exercise his right to freedom of religion by

---

[67] (1980) 21 D.R. 138.
[68] The Commission in *Rassemblement Jurassien v. Switzerland* (1979) 17 D.R. 93 had earlier upheld a temporary local ban on demonstrations in a particular town in a Swiss canton, insisting that such bans should be "proportionate" but also stating that the margin of appreciation in this field is "fairly broad" when there is a foreseeable danger to public safety which requires prompt decisions.
[69] See para. 8–67 above.
[70] (1995) 81 D.R. 146.
[71] The applicants sought to argue, albeit unsuccessfully, that if there was thought to be no danger to public safety from a meeting in Hyde Park it could not be said that a meeting in Trafalgar Square would be more liable to violence.
[72] [1999] E.H.R.L.R. 223; the Commission had earlier held in *Chappell v. United Kingdom* (1988) 10 E.H.R.R. 510, that a ban on assemblies at Stonehenge was necessary for "the prevention of disorder or crime, or for the protection of the rights and freedoms of others."

proceeding in a group of less than 20. These decisions clearly establish that it will be easier for the authorities to justify restrictions if there is a reasonably-founded fear of violence, but it is noticeable that both in *Pendragon,* and in *Rai, Allmond and "Negotiate Now"* alternative means of exercising Convention rights were available.

8–73 The Criminal Justice and Public Order Act 1994 amended the 1986 Act, and introduced further offences. The offence of aggravated trespass, contrary to section 68 of the 1994 Act, penalises persons who trespass on land and do acts intended, *inter alia*, to obstruct or disrupt an activity being lawfully conducted by others on that land. In the light of the Commission's decision in *G v. Federal Republic of Germany*, discussed above,[73] it seems clear that a peaceful (albeit illegal) demonstration which is intended only to disrupt, and not to intimidate, constitutes an exercise of the Article 11(1) right to peaceful assembly.[74] This may give rise to difficult questions as to the applicability of Article 11 to private property.[75]

8–74 The 1994 Act also introduced various offences connected with trespassory assemblies, (inserting sections 14A, B and C into the Public Order Act 1986).[76] In *DPP v. Jones*[77] the defendant and others had been charged under section 14B(2) with holding a trespassory assembly in defiance of an order prohibiting such assemblies at Stonehenge. They were convicted in the magistrates' court but the Crown Court upheld their submission of no case to answer, on the ground that the demonstration had been peaceful and had not obstructed the highway. The prosecutor's appeal by way of case stated was allowed, the Divisional Court holding that the offence was committed even if the demonstration was peaceful and did not cause an obstruction. However, the House of Lords allowed the appeal and held that the defendants should not have been convicted of taking part in a trespassory assembly. The right to use a public highway was not restricted to passing and re-passing, but extended to a range of other activities such as taking photographs, handing out leaflets, collecting for charity, playing games on the pavement, or having a picnic, so long as the activity does not create a nuisance or an obstruction. This is an important decision in its own right, as a development of the common law, but it also chimes well with Articles 10 and 11 of the Convention. It moves towards the idea of the protection of the individual's rights as the court's starting point, whilst leaving room for the authorities to justify interference with the right on appropriate grounds.

III. *A right to assemble on private property?*

8–75 One question that is not yet fully resolved is whether the right of assembly conferred by Article 11 extends to meetings held on private premises. This may be important in any consideration of whether the offence of aggravated trespass

---

[73] See para. 8–65 above.
[74] See also *Ezelin v. France* (1992) 14 E.H.R.R. 362.
[75] See para. 8–75 below.
[76] As amended by ss.70 and 71 of the Criminal Justice and Public Order Act 1994.
[77] [1999] 2 A.C. 240.

(discussed above) is compatible with Article 11. The question was ventilated in *Anderson v. United Kingdom*,[78] where the applicants had been excluded from a shopping centre by a letter from the owners alleging misconduct and disorderly behaviour. The lease granted to the owners of the shopping centre by the local authority required them to allow the public access to the centre during shopping hours. The applicants alleged that their Article 11 rights had been violated. The Commission declared the application inadmissible, not on the ground that the premises were private, but on the ground that the right to peaceful assembly and freedom of association relates to gatherings of individuals "in order to attain various ends," and does not apply to people assembling for merely social purposes. The Commission appeared to consider that freedom of assembly in the Convention is confined to political purposes. This seems to be an unusually narrow reading of Article 11, and is more restrictive than the English law stated by the House of Lords in *DPP v. Jones*.[79] It is one thing to accord special protection to the right to demonstrate on matters of public concern, but it is surely quite another thing to hold that there is no right at all to assemble for social purposes.[80]

Several common law jurisdictions have come to recognise that the law of trespass is subject a right of reasonable access to quasi-public spaces. Under this principle owners of large private areas which are generally accessible to the public may only exclude particular individuals on grounds which are objectively reasonable. In the United States, the principle was first established in the context of "company towns",[81] but has since developed to include shopping precincts and other quasi-public spaces.[82] A similar approach has been taken by the Supreme Court of Canada.[83]   **8–76**

F. Other Issues

This Chapter has been concerned primarily with the rights guaranteed under Articles 8 to 11 of the Convention. Issues may occasionally arise under other substantive guarantees. In *Family H v. United Kingdom*,[84] for example, the applicants were convicted of failing to comply with an order requiring them to send their children to state school or provide evidence of their education at home.   **8–77**

---

[78] [1998] E.H.R.L.R. 218. For a comprehensive discussion of *Anderson* and the international and comparative law on the subject, see Kevin Gray and Susan Gray, "Civil Rights, Civil Wrongs and Quasi-Public Space" [1999] E.H.R.L.R. 46.

[79] See para. 8–74 above.

[80] The application in *Anderson* was also brought under Art. 14. The applicants were black and alleged that the exclusion was discriminatory, but the Commission found no evidence of this.

[81] *Marsh v. Alabama* 326 U.S. 501; 90 L. Ed. 265 (1946).

[82] *Amalgamated Food Employees Union Local 590 v. Logan Valley Plaza* 391 U.S. 308 at 319–320; 20 L. Ed. 2d. 603 at 612–613 (1968); *New Jersey Coalition Against War in the Middle East v. JMB Realty Corporation* 650 A2d 757 (1994) at 777.

[83] See, for example, *The Queen in Right of Canada v. Committee for the Commonwealth of Canada* (1991) 77 D.L.R. (4th) 385 at 393D-H.

[84] (1984) 337 D.R. 105.

They had elected to educate their children at home because of learning difficulties. The family complained that the prosecution infringed their right to education under Article 2 of the First Protocol. The Commission rejected the complaint, holding that since the state is entitled to establish a system of compulsory state education, it did not breach Article 2 of the First Protocol by requiring parents to co-operate in an assessment of their children's educational standards.

CHAPTER 9

THE BURDEN AND STANDARD OF PROOF

A. INTRODUCTION

The principles established in the Convention caselaw have to accommodate **9–01** criminal procedure systems as diverse as the former soviet legal systems of Central and Eastern Europe, continental legal systems and common law systems, with an emphasis on jury trial. It is inevitable that any constitutional standards which are applicable to so many different legal traditions will be insufficiently detailed to afford a comprehensive guide to the application of the Convention in the United Kingdom criminal law. In some areas of criminal procedure more useful and detailed guidance is to be found in the caselaw of other common law jurisdictions with a comparable Bill of Rights. The burden and standard of proof in criminal proceedings is one such area.

B. REVERSE ONUS PROVISIONS

I. *Introduction*

The starting point in any analysis of reverse onus provisions in England and **9–02** Wales[1] is the well-known statement of Viscount Sankey L.C. in *Woolmington v. DPP*[2] that "throughout the web of the English criminal law one golden thread is always to be seen, that is that it is the duty of the prosecution to prove the prisoner's guilt." This principle is reflected in Article 6(2) of the Convention which enshrines the presumption of innocence in criminal proceedings.[3] The only common law exception to the *Woolmington* principle is the defence of insanity.[4] There are, however, numerous statutory provisions which impose a burden of some kind on the accused in the course of a criminal trial. As Lord Hope observed in *R v. DPP ex parte Kebilene and others*[5];

> "[I]t has always been open to Parliament by way of a statutory exception to transfer the onus of proof as to some matter arising in a criminal case from the prosecution to the

---

[1] As to the position in Scotland, see *Slater v. HM Advocate* 1928 J.C. 94 at 105.
[2] [1935] A.C. 462 at 481.
[3] Article 6(2) is an aspect of the defendant's right to a fair trial so that an infringement of the presumption of innocence *a fortiori* renders a trial unfair within the meaning of Art. 6. In *Deweer v. Belgium* (1979–80) 2 E.H.R.R. 439 at para. 56 the European Court of Human Rights observed that the rights contained in Art. 6(2) and 6(3) " . . . represent specific applications of the general principle stated in paragraph 1 of the Article. The presumption of innocence embodied in paragraph 2 and the various rights of which a non-exhaustive list appears in paragraph 3 . . . are constituent elements, amongst others, of the notion of a fair trial in criminal proceedings.".
[4] See para. 11–09 below.
[5] [1999] 3 W.L.R. 972 (H.L.).

accused . . . [U]ntil now, under the doctrine of sovereignty, the only check on Parliament's freedom to legislate in this area has been political. All that will now change with the coming into force of the Human Rights Act 1998 . . . [T]he change will affect the past as well as the future. Unlike the constitutions of many of the countries within the Commonwealth which protect pre-existing legislation from challenge under their human rights provisions, the 1998 Act will apply to all legislation, whatever its date, in the past as well as in the future."

9–03   The extent to which a statutory burden of proof imposed on the accused encroaches on the presumption of innocence will depend on the legislative technique which has been adopted.[6] It is possible to identify three broad categories of reverse onus clause—persuasive (or ultimate) burdens, evidential burdens, and "special defences". A "persuasive" burden of proof requires the accused to prove, on a balance of probabilities, an ultimate fact necessary to the determination of guilt or innocence. Such a presumption may relate to an essential element (of greater or lesser importance) making up either the *actus reus* or the *mens rea* of the offence; and may be either mandatory[7] or discretionary[8] in its operation. Where a mandatory persuasive burden of proof is placed on the accused, it is possible for a conviction to be returned, even where the tribunal of fact entertains a reasonable doubt as to his guilt.[9] Such provisions require close scrutiny, in order to determine their compatibility with Article 6(2).

9–04   An "evidential" burden, by contrast, requires only that the accused must adduce sufficient evidence to raise an issue before it has to be determined by the tribunal of fact. Once the accused has adduced evidence sufficient to raise the issue, the burden of proving (or disproving) that issue rests on the prosecution. In the final assessment of guilt, the burden on the accused is thus no more than a burden to raise a reasonable doubt as to guilt. The imposition of an evidential burden on the accused is not incompatible with the presumption of innocence.[10]

9–05   A "special defence" arises where a statute prohibits the doing of an act save where it is done with a licence or permission, or subject to an exemption or proviso. In *R. v. Edwards*[11] Lawton L.J. said;

---

[6] See generally Glanville Williams, *The Proof of Guilt*, (3rd ed., Stevens, 1963), pp 183–186.

[7] Where a presumption operating against the accused is mandatory, the trier of fact has no discretion as to whether or not to apply the presumption, and it may therefore be possible to judge its compatibility with the presumption of innocence on the face of the statute, without reference to the facts of an individual case. In *R. v. DPP ex parte Kebilene and ors* [1999] 3 W.L.R. 972 Lord Hope said "I can see no reason why, in a clear case, where the facts of the case are of no importance, a decision that a provision is incompatible [with Article 6(2)] should not be capable of being taken at a very early stage". Similarly, the U.S. Supreme Court has held that where a mandatory reverse onus clause is in issue, the question of its constitutional compatibility is "logically divorced" from the facts of the case, so that the issue falls to be determined "facially" (*i.e.* on a consideration of the statute on its face): *County Court of Ulster County v. Allen* 442 U.S. 140 (1979).

[8] A discretionary presumption of guilt may breach the presumption of innocence, depending upon whether or not the tribunal of fact relies on the presumption in order to convict the accused. Accordingly, it will usually be necessary to consider the facts of a case before reaching a conclusion as to whether the presumption of innocence has been violated.

[9] This will occur where the accused adduces evidence which is sufficient to raise a reasonable doubt on the issue, but fails to discharge the burden of proof on the balance of probabilities.

[10] See *R. v. DPP ex parte Kebilene and ors* [1999] 3 W.L.R. 972 *per* Lord Hope (see below at para. 9–43). The same conclusion has been reached in Canada and South Africa: see paras 9–25 and 9–30 below.

[11] [1975] Q.B. 27 (C.A.).

"[O]ver the centuries the common law, as a result of experience and the need to ensure that justice is done both to the community and to defendants, has evolved an exception to the fundamental rule of our criminal law that the prosecution must prove every element of the offence charged. This exception, like so much else in the common law, was hammered out on the anvil of pleading. It is limited to offences arising under enactments which prohibit the doing of an act save in specified circumstances or with the licence or permission of specified authorities. Whenever the prosecution seeks to rely on this exception, the court must construe the enactment under which the charge is laid. If the true construction is that the enactment prohibits the doing of acts, subject to provisos, exemptions and the like, then the prosecution can rely upon the exception."[12]

Edwards was approved in *R. v. Hunt*,[13] where the House of Lords held that it was **9–06** not a pre-requisite that the statute should specifically provide for the burden to rest on the defendant. Exceptions could be express or implied, and the relevant proviso did not need to appear in the section creating the offence. Where a linguistic construction did not clearly indicate on whom the burden should lie, the court could have regard to other considerations to determine the intention of Parliament, such as the mischief at which the offence was aimed, and practical considerations such as who is likely to be best able to discharge the burden. The distinguishing feature of a special defence is that the accused knows, at the time when he commits the act in question, that his conduct amounts to a criminal offence unless he can bring himself within the licence or permission requirements specified in the Act.[14] A special defence may breach the presumption of innocence,[15] but is less likely to do so than a persuasive burden on an important essential element of the offence.[16]

In *Hunt* Lord Griffiths emphasised that the *Edwards* exception applied only to **9–07** statutory offences prohibiting the doing of an act without a licence or permission, and optimistically suggested that "the occasions upon which a statute will be construed as imposing a burden of proof upon a defendant which do not fall within this formulation are likely to be exceedingly rare".[17] There are, however, a number of English statutes which expressly impose an ultimate burden on the accused.[18] Under the Human Rights Act 1998 it is for the courts to determine whether such provisions are compatible with Article 6(2). In particular, they will have to ascertain whether the statute in question can and should be read as imposing no more than an evidential burden, in accordance with the new principle of statutory construction in section 3(1) of the 1998 Act.[19] If not, the question of a declaration of incompatibility will arise.[20]

---

[12] A similar rule was introduced for summary proceedings by Magistrates' Courts Act 1980, s.101. This provides that wherever a statute creates a defence, exception, or proviso it must be proved by the defendant (on a balance of probabilities).

[13] [1987] A.C. 352.

[14] *Attorney-General for Hong Kong v. Lee Kwong-kut and anor.* [1993] A.C. 951 (P.C.) *per* Lord Woolf at 962C–E; 964E–G.

[15] *R. v. DPP ex parte Kebilene and ors* [1999] 3 W.L.R. 972, *per* Lord Hope, see para. 9–44 below.

[16] See, for example, *R. v. Schwartz* (1988) 55 D.L.R. (4th) 1 (SCC).

[17] *R. v. Hunt (Richard)* [1987] A.C. 352 at 375 (cited with approval in *Attorney-General for Hong Kong v. Lee Kwong-kut and anor.* [1993] A.C. 951 P.C., *per* Lord Woolf at 961H–962G).

[18] See para. 9–55 below.

[19] See para. 3–31 above.

[20] See para. 3–35 above.

9–08   In considering these issues, the national courts will derive only limited assistance from the Strasbourg caselaw. The European Court of Human Rights has adopted vague and general formulae on this issue, which raise more questions than they answer.[21] But Article 6(2) has direct parallels in all the major constitutional human rights provisions in other common law jurisdictions, and the courts in those jurisdictions have had to grapple with issues very similar to those which arise under the Human Rights Act. The decisions of the Canadian and South African courts in particular will afford a useful source of guidance.

II. *The Strasbourg Caselaw*

9–09   The European Court of Human Rights has held that, whilst Article 6(2) does not automatically prohibit all presumptions of fact or law, neither does it regard such presumptions "with indifference". Rules which transfer the burden to the defence to disprove specific facts or matters must be confined "within reasonable limits" which respect the rights of the defence, and ensure that the prosecution bear the overall burden of proving the defendant's guilt. As the Court has observed[22]:

> "Presumptions of fact or of law operate in every legal system. Clearly the Convention does not prohibit such presumptions in principle. It does, however, require the Contracting States to remain within certain limits in this respect as regards the criminal law . . . Article 6(2) does not therefore regard presumptions of fact or of law provided for in the criminal law with indifference. It requires States to confine them within reasonable limits which take into account the importance of what is at stake and maintain the rights of the defence."

9–10   In *X v. United Kingdom*[23] the Commission upheld the rebuttable presumption that a man who was proved to be living with, or controlling a prostitute was knowingly living off immoral earnings. The Commission nevertheless observed that a presumption of law or fact; " . . . could, if widely or unreasonably worded, have the same effect as a presumption of guilt. It is not, therefore, sufficient to examine only the form in which the presumption is drafted. It is necessary to examine the substance and effect."

9–11   In *Lingens and another v. Austria*[24] the Commission was concerned with a "special defence"[25] under the Austrian penal code. The relevant section provided that it was an offence to publish defamatory material, unless the accused was able to prove the truth of the statement. The Commission considered that this offence did not violate Article 6(2) since all the essential elements of the offence of publishing a defamatory statement had to be proved by the prosecution. In the Commission's view the prosecution retained the overall burden of proving guilt, and "the mutual position of the parties to the criminal proceedings [was] exactly the same as in all other criminal proceedings."

---

[21] See para. 9–09 below.
[22] *Salabiaku v. France* (1991) 13 E.H.R.R. 379.
[23] Application No. 5124/71 (1975) 42 C.D. 135.
[24] (1982) 4 E.H.R.R. 373.
[25] See para. 9–05 above.

The leading case on this issue is *Salabiaku v. France*.[26] The applicant challenged   **9–12**
a rule under the French Customs Code whereby an accused who was proved to
have physically imported a consignment of prohibited drugs was presumed to
have known that the drugs were in his possession, and therefore to be guilty of
an offence of importation. The applicant had been acquitted of the criminal
offence of knowingly importing drugs, but had been convicted of a strict liability
"customs offence" of importing goods in breach of the Customs Code, which
carried a much lighter maximum penalty (three months imprisonment). The
Court held that the presumption of knowledge did not violate Article 6(2) since
the prosecution bore the burden of proving the *actus reus* of the offence, and it
was a defence for the accused to prove that he was unaware of the contents of the
consignment. Moreover, the accused could avoid liability by proving *force
majeure*, and the domestic courts had in fact found that he knew the drugs were
in his possession (although not strictly required to do so). In the Court's view
therefore the trial court had not been entirely deprived of "any genuine power of
assessment."[27] Indeed, the *Salabiaku* case may be best regarded as involving a
strict liability offence rather than an offence which reverses the onus of proof on
mens rea.[28]

Salabiaku was followed in *Pham Hoang v. France*,[29] a case on very similar facts.   **9–13**
The Court emphasised that it was not its function to consider whether the
legislative presumptions in issue were compatible with Article 6(2). Its task was
to examine the facts of the case in order to determine whether the legislation had
been applied in a manner consistent with the presumption of innocence.[30] The
Court noted that the Paris Court of Appeal had made no express reference to the
presumptions in its judgment, but had taken account of "a cumulation of facts"
and had; " . . . duly weighed the evidence before it, assessed it carefully and
based its findings of guilt on it. It refrained from any automatic reliance on the
presumptions . . . and did not apply them in a manner incompatible with Article
6(1) and (2) of the Convention."[31]

The Court's approach in *Salabiaku* and *Pham Hoang* demonstrates the difficulty   **9–14**
of applying the Strasbourg jurisprudence directly in the national courts. The
European Court of Human Rights has the luxury of a retrospective review of the
domestic proceedings as a whole, and can examine *ex post facto* whether any
presumption was in fact applied in a manner which failed to respect the rights of
the defence. A national court, on the other hand, has to determine the issue on the
case arising before it. In particular, it has to determine whether any particular
burden of proof should be treated as evidential or persuasive in character. As the
Commission's decision in *Hardy v. Ireland*[32] shows, this question can be far from
straightforward.

---

[26] (1991) 13 E.H.R.R. 379.
[27] A similar principle might apply to offences of strict liability in English law that have a "due
diligence" exception, allowing a defendant to avoid liability by proving that reasonable precautions
were taken. For examples and discussion, see M. Wasik, "Shifting the Burden of Strict Liability"
[1982] Crim. L.R. 567.
[28] See para. 9–60 below.
[29] (1993) 16 E.H.R.R. 53.
[30] At para. 33.
[31] At para. 36.
[32] Application No. 23456/94 (unreported).

9–15   *Hardy* concerned a statutory explosives offence which provided that:

> "Any person who makes or knowingly has in his possession or under his control any explosive substance, under such circumstances as to give rise to a reasonable suspicion that he is not making it or does not have it in his possession or under his control for a lawful object, shall, unless he can show that he made it or had it in his possession or under his control for a lawful object, be . . . liable to penal servitude for a term not exceeding 14 years."

9–16   An identical provision in England and Wales (section 4 of the Explosive Substances Act 1883) has been held to impose a persuasive burden on the accused to prove a lawful object on the balance of probabilities.[33] In Ireland however the provision had been interpreted as imposing a merely evidential burden on the accused to raise a doubt as to whether he had the explosive in his possession for a lawful object.[34] In finding that the Irish provision was compatible with Article 6(2), the Commission attached particular importance to the principle that it was for the Crown to prove the guilt of the accused on each element of the offence to the requisite standard of proof, and that the burden on the accused was merely evidential:

> "The Commission further notes that, in the context of the constitutional challenge, the High Court and the Supreme Court emphasised that under Irish criminal law the persuasive burden of proof (that is, beyond all reasonable doubt) remains on the State and where an evidential burden of proof is transferred to the accused (as in section 4 of the 1883 Act) it is in a "saving or excusatory context" and the maximum obligation on the accused in such circumstances is merely to raise a doubt of substance in relation to the prosecution's case."

9–17   In *Bates v. United Kingdom*,[35] the applicant was convicted of an offence under the Dangerous Dogs Act 1991, which places on the defendant the burden of proving that a dog is not a member of the specified breed.[36] The Commission found no violation of Article 6(2). The applicant was found to have admitted that the dog was a member of the specified breed, and he had the opportunity to adduce evidence to disprove the presumption.

III. *Canada*

9–18   In Canada the Supreme Court has taken a much stronger line. The equivalent guarantee under the Canadian Charter of Rights and Freedoms is section 11(d), which provides: "Any person charged with an offence has the right . . . (d) to be presumed innocent until proven guilty according to law in a fair and public hearing by an independent and impartial tribunal." Section 1 provides that the Charter rights are subject to "such reasonable limits prescribed by law as can be demonstrably justified in a free and democratic society". This has led the

---

[33] *R. v. Berry (No.3)* [1985] A.C. 246; *R. v. Fegan* [1972] N.I. 80; In *R. v. DPP ex parte Kebilene and ors* [1999] 3 W.L.R. 972 (H.L.) Lord Hope identified the English provision as imposing a persuasive burden of proof, coupled with a mandatory presumption of guilt if it is not discharged, and falling outside the category of "special defences" identified in *Edwards*, see para. 9–43 below.

[34] *Hardy v. Ireland* (Irish Supreme Court, March 18, 1993).

[35] [1996] E.H.R.L.R. 312.

[36] The dog is presumed to be a member of the breed "unless the contrary is shown by the accused."

Supreme Court to adopt a two stage test to the application of section 11(d), asking first whether a reverse onus clause infringes the presumption of innocence protected by that provision, and if it does, going on to consider whether the interference is justified under section 1. The Canadian Supreme Court has emphasised the need to "keep sections 1 and 11(d) . . . analytically distinct".[37] However, despite the fact that the process of reasoning is different from some of the other constitutional jurisdictions, the result is often the same.[38]

Applying these provisions, the Canadian Supreme Court has held that the **9–19** minimum requirement of section 11(d) is that the state must prove the guilt of the accused beyond a reasonable doubt. Thus, section 11(d) requires that the prosecution should bear the ultimate burden of proving each of the important essential elements of an offence. A provision requiring the accused to disprove an essential element on the balance of probabilities is incompatible with section 11(d) since it would be possible for a conviction to occur despite the existence of a reasonable doubt.[39] In such a situation, the state must advance a convincing justification under section 1 of the Charter if the provision in issue is to escape constitutional condemnation.

The facts of the leading case of *Oakes*[40] bear a passing resemblance to those of **9–20** *Salabiaku*.[41] Oakes was found in possession of eight grammes of cannabis in the form of hashish oil. He was charged with possession for the purpose of trafficking, and the prosecution relied on a statutory presumption in the Narcotic Control Act that a person found in possession of a narcotic is presumed to be trafficking unless he establishes to the contrary. The Supreme Court held unanimously that this provision violated Article 11(d) of the Charter, in that it required the accused to prove his innocence, albeit on a balance of probabilities, in relation to an important element of the offence. Dickson C.J., for the Court, stated the guiding principle in these terms:

> "In general one must, I think, conclude that a provision which requires an accused to disprove on a balance of probabilities the existence of a presumed fact, which is an important element of the offence in question, violates the presumption of innocence . . . If an accused bears the burden of disproving on a balance of probabilities an essential element of an offence, it would be possible for a conviction to occur despite the existence of a reasonable doubt. This would arise if the accused adduced sufficient evidence to raise a reasonable doubt as to his or her innocence but did not convince the jury on a balance of probabilities that the presumed fact was untrue."

The Supreme Court went on to consider whether, under section 1, the presump- **9–21** tion was "demonstrably justified in a democratic society". This required the Court to examine whether the objectives of the Narcotic Control Act were sufficiently important to justify overriding a constitutionally protected right. In order to meet this test, the Court held that the measure in issue (a) had to be

---

[37] *R. v. Oakes* 26 D.L.R. (4th) 200 at 223.
[38] *Attorney-General for Hong Kong v. Lee Kwong-kut and anor.* [1993] A.C. 951 (P.C.), *per* Lord Woolf at 971H.
[39] *R. v. Oakes* 26 D.L.R. (4th) 200; [1986] 1 S.C.R. 103. For applications of this principle see *R. v. Driscoll* (1987) 60 C.R. (3d) 88 (Alta CA); *R. v. Ireco Canada II Inc.* (1988) 65 C.R. (3d) 160 (Ont. CA); *R. v. Shisler* (1990) 53 C.C.C. (3d) 531 (Ont. CA).
[40] 26 D.L.R. (4th) 200; [1986] 1 S.C.R. 103.
[41] See para. 9–12 above.

carefully designed to achieve its objective and rationally connected to that objective, (b) had to impair the protected right to the minimum degree, and (c) had to be proportionate to the importance of the objective (so that the greater the incursions into a constitutionally protected right, the more persuasive the state's justification would have to be). The presumption of drug trafficking failed to satisfy this test, because there was insufficient rational connection between the possession of a small amount of drugs and engagement in trafficking.

9–22 In subsequent decisions the Canadian Supreme Court has held that a statutory provision which requires the accused to prove a matter which is *not* an essential element of the offence may also be *prima facie* inconsistent with section 11(d). In *R. v. Whyte*[42] the Court explained;

> "[T]he distinction between elements of the offence and other aspects of the charge is irrelevant to the s.11(d) inquiry. The real concern is not whether the accused must disprove an element or prove an excuse, but that an accused may be convicted while a reasonable doubt exists. When that possibility exists, there is a breach of the presumption of innocence. The exact characterisation of a factor as an essential element, a collateral factor, an excuse, or a defence should not affect the analysis of the presumption of innocence. It is the final effect of a provision on the verdict that is decisive. If an accused is required to prove some fact on the balance of probabilities to avoid conviction, the provision violates the presumption of innocence because it permits a conviction in spite of a reasonable doubt in the mind of the trier of fact as to the guilt of the accused."

9–23 However, a presumption will be easier to justify under section 1, if it relates not to an essential element of the offence, but to an exemption, proviso, excuse or the like. Thus, in *Whyte* the Court upheld a presumption that a person found impaired in the driving seat of a vehicle had "care or control" so as to be guilty of an offence, unless he proved by way of defence that he did not intend to set the vehicle in motion. And in *Keegstra*[43] the Court upheld a provision to the effect that a person who wilfully promotes hatred against an identifiable group is guilty of an offence unless the accused establishes by way of defence that the statements are true.

9–24 Statutory offences which require the accused to prove the existence of a certificate or licence, have been held to be consistent with section 11(d). In *R. v. Schwartz*[44] a provision requiring the accused to prove that he was the holder of a firearms certificate was held not to reverse the burden of proof. Under such a provision;

> "[The accused was] not required to prove or disprove any element of the offence or for that matter, anything related to the offence . . . Although the accused must establish that he falls within the exemption, there is no danger that he could be convicted . . . despite the existence of a reasonable doubt as to guilt, because the production of the certificate resolves all doubts in favour of the accused and in the absence of the certificate no defence is possible once possession has been shown. In such a case, where the only relevant evidence is the certificate itself, it cannot be said that the accused could adduce evidence sufficient to raise doubt without at the same time establishing conclusively

---

[42] 64 C.R. (3d) 123 (SCC) at 134–135 [1998] 2 S.C.R. 3.
[43] (1990) 1 C.R. (4th) 129 (SCC) [1990] 3 S.C.R. 697.
[44] (1988) 55 D.L.R. (4th) 1 (SCC).

that the certificate had been issued. The theory behind any licencing system is that when an issue arises as to the possession of the licence, it is the accused who is in the best position to resolve the issue."

The Canadian Supreme Court has thus achieved a result in *Schwartz* which is equivalent to the "special defence" rule in *Edwards* and *Hunt*.[45]

On several occasions the Supreme Court has held that reverse onus offences **9–25** could be saved from constitutional invalidation by reading them as imposing a purely evidential burden. The case of *Downey*[46] has facts similar to those in *X v. United Kingdom*.[47] The charge was living on the earnings of prostitution and the Canadian Criminal Code included a provision to the effect that evidence that a person "lives with or is habitually in the company of prostitutes" would be proof, "in the absence of evidence to the contrary", of living on the earnings of prostitution. By a majority of four to three the Canadian Supreme Court upheld the statutory presumption. Although it violated section 11(d) it could be saved by section 1 as a "reasonable limit" on the presumption of innocence, because it amounted merely to placing an evidential burden on the defendant in respect of an element that would be otherwise difficult to prove. That point was reinforced in *Laba*,[48] where a reverse onus provision was held not to satisfy the *Oakes* proportionality test because it imposed on defendants a burden of proving ownership on the balance of probabilities. The Court held that the provision could take effect as imposing a mere evidential burden on the accused.

The Canadian decisions embody a far more searching and principled examination **9–26** of the issues than is to be found in the Convention jurisprudence. Nonetheless, there is sufficient similarity in the criteria to be applied—"reasonable limit" in section 1 of the Canadian Charter, and "reasonable limits" read into Article 6(2) of Convention by the Court in *Salabiaku*—to suggest that arguments from Canada might be of some interest to English courts, as they have been to the Privy Council.[49] Overall, the Canadian decisions support an approach to "reasonable limits" test in *Salabiaku* that encourages courts to read statutes as placing merely an evidential burden on the accused wherever possible.

IV. *South Africa*

In the relatively short time since the present Constitution came into effect,[50] the **9–27** Constitutional Court of South Africa has developed a substantial body of case law on the compatibility of statutory reverse onus clauses with the constitutional presumption of innocence. The equivalent provision to Article 6(2) of the Convention is section 25(3)(c) of the Constitution which provides: "Every accused person shall have the right to a fair trial, which shall include the right . . . (c) to be presumed innocent . . . during plea proceedings or trial . . . ". Like the Canadian Charter, the South African Constitution contains a general savings

---

[45] See para. 9–05 above.
[46] [1992] 2 S.C.R. 10.
[47] See para. 9–10 above.
[48] [1994] 3 S.C.R. 965.
[49] See *Attorney-General for Hong Kong v. Lee Kwong-Kut* [1993] A.C. 951, discussed below, at para. 9–38.
[50] On April 27, 1994.

clause (section 33(1)).[51] Applying these provisions, the South African Constitutional Court has followed the approach of the Canadian Supreme Court in holding that statutes which require the accused to disprove an important essential element of an offence on the balance of probabilities are in breach of the presumption of innocence, since they permit the conviction of an accused despite the existence of a reasonable doubt as to his guilt.

9–28   In *State v. Mbatha*[52] the Constitutional Court was concerned with a statutory presumption which provided that the accused was deemed to be in possession of any firearm which was found at premises in which he was present, or of which he was the occupier "until the contrary is proved". In the Court's view, this presumption was in breach of section 25(3)(c) and was not saved by section 33(1). Giving the judgment of the Court, Langa J. said[53]:

> "The effect of the provision is to relieve the prosecution of the burden of proof with regard to an essential element of the offence. It requires that the presumed fact must be disproved by the accused on a balance of probabilities . . . [A] presumption of this nature is in breach of the presumption of innocence since it could result in the conviction of an accused person despite the existence of a reasonable doubt as to his or her guilt. No legal system can guarantee that no innocent person can ever be convicted. Indeed, the provision of corrective action by way of appeal and review procedures is an acknowledgement of the ever present possibility of judicial fallibility. Yet it is one thing for the law to acknowledge the possibility of wrongly but honestly convicting the innocent and then to provide appropriate measures to reduce the possibility of this happening as far as is practicable; it is another for the law itself to heighten the possibility of a miscarriage of justice by compelling the trial court to convict where it entertains real doubts as to culpability and then to prevent the reviewing court from altering the conviction even if it shares in the doubts."

9–29   As to the justification for the presumption, Langa J. observed:

> "The issue before us . . . is not simply whether there is a pressing social need to combat crimes of violence—there clearly is—but also whether the instrument to be used in meeting this need is itself fashioned in accordance with specifications permitted by the Constitution . . . The presumption of innocence is clearly of vital importance in the establishment and maintenance of an open and democratic society based on freedom and equality. If, in particular cases, what is effectively a presumption of guilt is to be substituted for the presumption of innocence, the justification for doing so must be established clearly and convincingly. It was argued that without the presumption it would be almost impossible for the prosecution to prove both the mental and physical elements of possession . . . There will no doubt be cases in which it will be difficult to prove that a particular person against whom the presumption would have operated, was in fact in possession of the prohibited article. If that person was in fact guilty, the absence of the presumption might enable him or her to escape conviction. But this is inevitably a consequence of the presumption of innocence; this must be weighed against

---

[51] Section 33(1) is in the following terms:
"The rights entrenched in this Chapter may be limited by law of general application, provided that such limitation—(a) shall be permissible only to the extent that it is—(i) reasonable; and (ii) justifiable in an open and democratic society based on freedom and equality; and (b) shall not negate the essential content of the right in question and . . . shall . . . also be necessary."
[52] [1996] 2 L.R.C. 208.
[53] See 215G to 222D.

the danger that innocent people may be convicted if the presumption were to apply. In that process the rights of innocent persons must be given precedence."

Following the Canadian Supreme Court, Langa J. suggested that an evidential **9–30** burden would meet many of the concerns which were said to justify the provision, without necessarily infringing the presumption of innocence:

> "I am not persuaded that the presumption, as it stands, satisfies the requirements of reasonableness and justifiability. I am fortified in this conclusion by the fact that it has also not been demonstrated that its objective, that is facilitating the conviction of offenders, could not reasonably have been achieved by other means, less damaging to constitutionally entrenched rights. Although the choice of appropriate measures necessary to address the need is that of the legislature, it has not been shown that an evidentiary burden, for example would not be as effective ... [B]y requiring the accused to provide evidence sufficient to raise a reasonable doubt, such a provision would be of assistance to the prosecution whilst at the same time being less invasive of section 25(3) rights."

In *State v. Bhulwana*,[54] the Constitutional Court struck down a statutory offence **9–31** which provided that where it was proved that an accused had been found in possession of "dagga" exceeding 115g "it shall be presumed, until the contrary is proved, that the accused dealt in such dagga". O'Regan J., giving the judgment of the unanimous Court, held that[55]:

> "The effect of the provision is that once the state has proved that the accused was found in possession of an amount of dagga in excess of 115g, the accused will, on a balance of probabilities, have to show that such possession did not constitute dealing as defined in the Act. Even if the accused raises a reasonable doubt as to whether he or she was dealing in the drug, but fails to show it on a balance of probabilities, he or she must nevertheless be convicted. The effect of imposing the legal burden on the accused may therefore result in a conviction for dealing despite the existence of a reasonable doubt as to his or her guilt."

In *Scagell and Others v. Attorney General and Others*,[56] the same conclusion was **9–32** reached, for the same reasons, in relation to reverse onus clauses in two offences connected with illegal gambling contrary to the Gambling Act 1965. Similarly, in *State v. Coetzee and Others*,[57] the Constitutional Court struck down two reverse onus clauses under the Criminal Procedure Act 1977. The first provided that if it was proved in a criminal proceeding that a false representation had been made by an accused, the accused was deemed, unless the contrary was proved, to have made the representation knowing it to be false. The second provided that a director or servant of a corporate body was guilty of an offence committed by that body unless it was proved that the person took no part in the commission of the offence and could not have prevented it. Both clauses were struck down on the ground that they were capable of permitting the conviction of an accused

---

[54] [1996] 1 L.R.C. 194.
[55] At 199H to 200A.
[56] [1997] 4 L.R.C. 98.
[57] [1997] 2 L.R.C. 593.

Learning Resources
Centre

despite the existence of a reasonable doubt as to his guilt. In *Coetzee*[58] Langa J. observed:

"In a number of cases decided by this court, we have emphasised the importance of the rights entrenched in section 25(3)(c) of the Constitution, which include the right to be presumed innocent, in an open and democratic society based on freedom and equality . . . Underlying the decisions in those cases is the recognition that a consequence of the value system introduced by the Constitution is that the freedom of the individual may not lightly be taken away. Presumptions which expose an accused person to the real risk of being convicted despite the existence of a reasonable doubt as to his or her guilt are not consistent with what is clearly a fundamental value in our criminal justice system."

V. *New Zealand*

9–33   The development of the New Zealand caselaw in this field has been inhibited by the restrictive effect which the courts have given to the interpretation provision in the New Zealand Bill of Rights Act 1990. Section 6 of that Act provides that "[w]henever an enactment can be given a meaning that is consistent with the rights and freedoms contained in this Bill of Rights, that meaning shall be preferred to any other meaning". The New Zealand Court of Appeal has interpreted this provision to mean that;

"[if] a particular statutory provision, properly interpreted, is inconsistent with the full enjoyment of such a right or freedom, the statutory provision must be given effect and the right or freedom will remain only to the extent that it too can be given effect to".[59]

9–34   In *R. v. Phillips*[60] a challenge to a presumption of possession in a narcotics offence failed on the ground that the wording of the relevant provision, which required the accused to "prove" certain facts, could not be interpreted as imposing a merely evidential burden, and it was therefore unnecessary for the Court to rule on its compatibility with the presumption of innocence. This decision can provide no assistance to courts in England and Wales in their application of the Human Rights Act. In *R. v. DPP ex parte Kebilene and others*.[61] Lord Cooke of Thordon, the former President of the New Zealand Court of Appeal, accepted that the construction argument which had been rejected in *Phillips* could succeed under section 3(1) of the Human Rights Act 1998. Section 3(1) requires courts to construe legislation compatibly with Convention rights so far as it is *possible* to do so. That was, he said, a "strong adjuration"; "[S]ection 6 of the New Zealand Bill of Rights Act 1990 is in terms different from section 3(1) of the Human Rights Act 1998. The United Kingdom subsection, read as a whole, conveys, I think, a rather more powerful message."

---

[58] At 604E-G.
[59] *Noort v. MOT; Curran v. Police* [1992] 3 N.Z.L.R. 260.
[60] [1991] 3 N.Z.L.R. 175.
[61] [1999] 3 W.L.R. 972.

VI. *The United States Supreme Court*

The United States Supreme Court has held that the due process clause in the US **9–35**
Constitution imposes limits on the power of Congress or that of a State legislature to "make the proof of one fact or group of facts evidence of the existence
of the ultimate fact on which guilt is predicated" In *Tot v. United States*[62] the test
adopted by the Supreme Court for the constitutionality of such a provision was
that there must be "a rational connection between the facts proved and the fact
presumed". This basic standard has, however, developed over time into something resembling a proportionality test.

In *Leary v. United States*[63] Harlan J., giving the opinion of the Supreme Court, **9–36**
held that "a criminal statutory presumption must be regarded as 'irrational' or
'arbitrary' and hence unconstitutional, unless it can at least be said with substantial assurance that the presumed fact is more likely than not to flow from the
proved fact on which it is made to depend". Ten years later, in *County Court of
Ulster County v. Allen*[64] the Supreme Court distinguished between the approach
appropriate to a discretionary (or permissive) presumption, on the one hand, and
the approach appropriate to a mandatory presumption on the other. The "more
likely than not" standard adopted in *Leary* was confined to cases where the
presumption was "permissive". A permissive presumption was one which
"allows, but does not require, the trier of fact to infer the elemental fact from
proof by the prosecutor of the basic one, and which places no burden of any kind
on the defendant". In that situation, "the basic fact may constitute *prima facie*
evidence of the elemental fact", but the presumption "leaves the trier of fact free
to credit or reject the inference". But a mandatory presumption was "a far more
troublesome evidentiary device". Where a mandatory presumption was in issue,
"the presumption must be rejected unless the evidence necessary to invoke the
inference is sufficient for a rational jury to find the inferred fact beyond a
reasonable doubt". In considering the constitutionality of a statutory criminal
presumption there was thus a fundamental distinction;

> " . . . between a permissive presumption on which the prosecution is entitled to rely as
> one not necessarily sufficient part of its proof and a mandatory presumption which the
> jury must accept even if it is the sole evidence of an element of the offence . . . In the
> latter situation, since the prosecution bears the burden of establishing guilt, it may not
> rest its case entirely on a presumption unless the fact proved is sufficient to support the
> inference of guilt beyond reasonable doubt."

The Court drew a further distinction between mandatory and discretionary **9–37**
provisions concerning the manner in which a constitutional challenge of this sort
should be determined. The constitutionality of a mandatory provision could be
determined without reference to the facts of an individual case:

> "To the extent that the trier of fact is forced to abide by the presumption, and may not
> reject it based on an independent evaluation of the particular facts presented by the
> State, the analysis of presumption's constitutional validity is logically divorced from
> those facts and based on the presumption's accuracy in the run of cases".

---

[62] 319 U.S. 463 (1943) at 467 *per* Roberts J.
[63] 395 U.S. 6 23 (1969) L. Ed 2nd 57 at 36–37.
[64] 442 U.S. 140 (1979).

However, where a discretionary or permissive presumption is in issue, the Supreme Court would require "the party challenging it to demonstrate its invalidity *as applied to him*". This would depend upon an examination of the record of the court of trial.

VII. *The Approach of The Privy Council*

9–38   In *Attorney-General for Hong Kong v. Lee Kwong-kut*[65] the Privy Council held that a reverse onus provision in Hong Kong violated the presumption of innocence in Article 11(1) of the Bill of Rights Ordinance 1991, (which is in virtually identical terms to Article 6(2) of the Convention). Lord Woolf, delivering the opinion of the Board, said that the starting point for any court in determining whether a reverse onus provision respected the presumption of innocence was to identify the essential elements of the criminal liability which the offence imposed[66]: "In deciding what are the essential ingredients, the language of the relevant statutory provision will be important. However, what will be decisive will be the substance and reality of the language creating the offence rather than its form".[67]

9–39   Once the elements of the offence have been identified, the Court should then go on to apply the principle which lies at the heart of the decision, namely that it is impermissible for a statute to put the burden upon the defence to disprove an important essential element in the offence. Referring to *Salabiaku*, and the decisions of the Canadian Supreme Court, Lord Woolf pointed out that the presumption of innocence had been applied with an implicit degree of flexibility[68]:

> "This implicit flexibility allows a balance to be drawn between the interest of the person charged and the state. There are situations where it is clearly sensible and reasonable that deviations should be allowed from the strict application of the principle that the prosecution must prove the defendant's guilt beyond reasonable doubt. Take an obvious example in the case of an offence involving the performance of some act without a licence. Common sense dictates that the prosecution should not be required to shoulder the virtually impossible task of establishing that a defendant has not a licence when it is a matter of comparative simplicity for a defendant to establish that he has a licence ... Some exceptions will be justifiable, others will not. Whether they are justifiable will in the end depend upon whether it remains primarily the responsibility of the prosecution to prove the guilt of the accused to the required standard and whether the exception is reasonably imposed, notwithstanding the importance of maintaining the principle which article 11(1) enshrines. The less significant the departure from the

---

[65] [1993] A.C. 951.
[66] At 969H to 970A.
[67] For further references to the importance of considering the substance of the elements of the offence, rather than the form of the words used to create it, see 968E ("... and if it is also remembered that it is the substance rather than the letter of the language of the statute which is important ... "); 972E ("... by examining the substance of the statutory provision ... "); 973B ("... their Lordships regard the answer as being relatively straightforward once the substance of the offences has been identified ... "); 973B-C ("... the substantive effect of the statutory provision is to place the onus on the defence to establish that he can give an explanation as to his innocent possession of the property ... "); 973D ("... the substance of the offence is contained in section 25(1) ... ").
[68] At 969C to 970B.

normal principle, the simpler it will be to justify an exception. If the prosecution retains responsibility for proving the essential ingredients of the offence, the less likely it is that an exception will be regarded as unacceptable ... If the exception requires certain matters to be presumed until the contrary is shown, then it will be difficult to justify that presumption unless, as was pointed out by the United States Supreme Court in *Leary v. United States* (1969) 23 L. Ed. 2d. 82, 'it can at least be said with substantial assurance that the presumed fact is more likely than not to flow from the proved fact on which it is made to depend' ".

On the first of the two appeals before the Board, the offence was that of **9–40** possessing cash that is reasonably suspected of being stolen, and the Privy Council confirmed the ruling of the Hong Kong Court of Appeal that this was inconsistent with the presumption of innocence:

"[T]he substantive effect of the statutory provision is to place the onus on the defence to establish that he can give an explanation as to his possession of the property. That is the most significant element of the offence. It reduces the burden on the prosecution to proving possession by the defendant and facts from which a reasonable suspicion can be inferred that the property has been stolen or obtained unlawfully, matters which are likely to be a formality in the majority of cases."[69]

On the second appeal, the offence required the prosecution to prove the defendant's involvement in dealing with another's drug trafficking proceeds, and the existence of reasonable grounds for believing that the other party was a drug trafficker, leaving the accused to prove one or more defences on a balance of probabilities. The Privy Council held that this provision was justifiable.

VIII. *The House of Lords Judgment in* Kebilene

The application of Article 6(2) to statutory reverse onus provisions in England **9–41** and Wales arose for consideration by the House of Lords before the Human Rights Act came into force, in *R. v. DPP ex parte Kebilene and others*.[70] The applicants had applied for judicial review of the decision to prosecute them for offences under section 16A and 16B of the Prevention of Terrorism (Temporary Provisions) Act 1989. In giving and maintaining his consent to the prosecution, the DPP had obtained counsel's advice to the effect that the provisions were not incompatible with Article 6(2). The applicants challenged that conclusion, and the Divisional Court granted a declaration that the DPP had erred and that his decision was therefore unlawful. This ruling was overturned by the House of Lords on jurisdictional grounds. Lord Steyn, with whom the other members of the House of Lords agreed, held that in the absence of bad faith or other exceptional circumstances the Divisional Court should not entertain an application for judicial review of a decision to prosecute. The issue should be determined in the criminal trial and appeals process. Satellite litigation in criminal proceedings was to be discouraged.

---

[69] *ibid.*, at 973.
[70] [1999] 3 W.L.R. 972 (H.L.)

9–42 In view of this conclusion, it was unnecessary for the House of Lords to rule on the merits of the issue. Lord Hope nevertheless went on to consider the caselaw from Strasbourg and the common law jurisdictions where constitutional challenge is possible, and distilled a number of general principles which should govern such challenges in the United Kingdom. In doing so he said that the issue was "so important to a consideration of the impact of Article 6(2) of the Convention upon so many of the statutory provisions which are to be found in our criminal law that the opportunity ought to be taken to set out and review the competing arguments on this issue."

9–43 Lord Hope held that the first stage in any inquiry as to whether a statutory reverse onus provision is vulnerable to challenge under Article 6(2) is to identify the nature of the provision which is said to transfer a burden of proof. Some provisions would be more objectionable than others. A merely evidential burden, requiring the accused to do no more than raise a reasonable doubt on the issue to which it related, would not breach the presumption of innocence. Such provisions; " . . . take their place alongside the common law evidential presumptions which have built up in the light of experience. They are a necessary part of preserving the balance of fairness between the accused and the prosecutor in matters of evidence."

9–44 However, a statute which imposed a persuasive burden, requiring the accused to prove, on a balance of probabilities, a fact which is essential to his guilt or innocence, required further examination. The Court should determine whether the legislative technique which had been adopted was mandatory or discretionary, and whether it related to an essential element of the offence, or merely to an exemption or proviso. A mandatory presumption of guilt on an important essential element of an offence would be inconsistent with the presumption of innocence. So far as "special defences"[71] were concerned, these "may or may not violate the presumption of innocence, depending on the circumstances".

9–45 It did not necessarily follow, however, that a provision which was incompatible with the presumption of innocence would be found to violate Article 6(2). The Convention caselaw showed that although Article 6(2) is framed in absolute terms, it was not regarded in Strasbourg as imposing an absolute prohibition on reverse onus clauses. In each case, the question would be whether the presumption was confined within reasonable limits. In determining that issue a court might usefully consider three questions. (1) What do the prosecution have prove in order to transfer the onus to the defence? (2) Does the burden imposed on the accused relate to something which is likely to be difficult for him to prove, or does it relate to something which is likely to be within his knowledge or to which he has ready access? (3) What is the nature of the threat faced by society which the provision is designed to combat?

9–46 The third of these questions might be taken to imply that the courts should more readily accept that a reverse onus of proof is compatible with Article 6(2) where the offence is particularly serious. If that was the intention, then it is difficult to

---

[71] See para. 9–05 above.

reconcile either with the Strasbourg caselaw[72] or with the decisions of the common law constitutional courts.[73]

It is precisely when an accused person is charged with an offence which excites   **9–47** public outrage that he is most in need of the right to a fair trial. It may be, however, that Lord Hope's third question should be read as referring not to the *gravity* of the threat to society which is posed by a particular offence, but to the *nature* of that threat. On the authority of the common law constitutional deci- sions, this would require the prosecution to advance a convincing and logical explanation for the reverse onus, in the context of the particular offence at issue. Mere reference to the seriousness of the crime would not suffice. The prosecution would be required to demonstrate that the reversal of the burden of proof was rationally connected to a clear policy justification, and that it was proportionate, in the sense that the objective in question could not be met by the imposition of a purely evidential burden. If applied with the rigour that is evident in Canada and South Africa, this test would provide effective protection tempered by a necessary degree of flexibility.

This reading of Lord Hope's three questions is also consistent with his comments   **9–48** about the existence of a "discretionary area of judgment" for the legislature in such matters.[74] In some circumstances, he said, it would be appropriate for the courts to recognise that there is an area of judgment within which the judiciary will defer on democratic grounds to the considered opinion of the elected body or person whose act or decision is said to be incompatible with the Convention. It would be easier for the courts to recognise such a discretionary area of judgment where the Convention itself required a balance to be struck, or where questions of social or economic policy were involved; much less so where the Convention right in issue is stated in terms which are unqualified, is of high

---

[72] The European Court and Commission have consistently maintained that the same standards of fairness must apply to all types of offence. In *Saunders v. United Kingdom* (1997) 23 E.H.R.R. 313 at 329, para. 70, for example, the Commission observed that

"It cannot be compatible with the spirit of the Convention that varying degrees of fairness apply to different categories of accused in criminal trials . . . [Article 6] must apply as equally to alleged company fraudsters as to those accused of other types of fraud, rape, murder or terrorist offences. Further, there can be no legitimate aim in depriving someone of the guarantees necessary in securing a fair trial."

See, to the same effect, the decision of the Court at 340, para. 75. Similarly in *Teixeira de Castro v. Portugal* (1999) 28 E.H.R.R. 101 (para. 36) the Court held that

"[w]hile the rise in organised crime undoubtedly requires that appropriate measures be taken, the right to a fair administration of justice nevertheless holds such a prominent place that it cannot be sacrificed for the sake of expedience. The general requirements of fairness embodied in Article 6 apply to proceedings concerning all types of criminal offence, from the most straightforward to the most complex."

See also, in the context of terrorism, *Heaney and McGuinness v. Ireland*, Judgment of December 21, 2000.

See also *Kostovski v. Netherlands* (1990) 12 E.H.R.R. 434 (para. 44).

[73] In *State v. Mbatha* [1996] 2 L.R.C. 208 the South African Constitutional Court held that a "real and pressing social concern" about the upsurge of violent gun-related crime in that country could not justify a provision reversing the onus of proof on possession. As Langa J., pointed out, it is the evidence, including the circumstantial evidence, which determines whether the prosecution can prove the necessary intent to the criminal standard. More generally, in *State v. Zuma* [1995] 1 L.R.C. 145 at 155 (approving *Attorney-General v. Maogi* (1982) (2) B.L.R. 124 at 184) the Court observed that "Constitutional rights conferred without express limitation should not be cut down so by reading implicit restrictions into them so as to bring them into line with the common law".

[74] [1999] 3 W.L.R. 972 at 993.

constitutional importance, or raises questions which the court is especially well-placed to determine. Lord Hope's formulation finds strong echoes in the Canadian caselaw, where the Supreme Court has emphasised that the legislature's choices would be judged most harshly in criminal matters, owing to the courts' special expertise in this field.[75]

9–49   The provisions which were the subject of challenge in *Kebilene* involved, on any view, a substantial incursion into the presumption of innocence. They created a reverse onus on the two most important essential elements of the offence. Section 16A provides;

> "(1) A person is guilty of an offence if he has any article in his possession in circumstances giving rise to a reasonable suspicion that the article is in his possession for a purpose connected with the commission, preparation or instigation of acts of terrorism to which this section applies.
>
> (3) It is a defence for a person charged with an offence under this section to prove that at the time of the alleged offence the article in question was not in his possession for such a purpose as is mentioned in subsection (1) above.
>
> (4) Where a person is charged with an offence under this section and it is proved that at the time of the alleged offence (a) he and that article were both present in any premises; or (b) the article was in premises of which he was the occupier or which he habitually used otherwise than as a member of the public, the court may accept the fact proved as sufficient evidence of his possessing that article unless it is further proved that he did not at that time know of its presence in the premises in question, or if he did know, that he had no control over it."

Thus, section 16A(1) and (3) create a *mandatory* reverse onus on the issue of terrorist intent; and section 16A(4) creates a *discretionary* reverse onus on the issue of possession. Construed without the benefit of section 3(1) of the Human Rights Act 1998, both provisions would be taken to require proof by the accused on the balance of probabilities.

9–50   In the Divisional Court Lord Bingham C.J. considered that this involved a "blatant and obvious" violation of Article 6(2)[76]:

> "The gravamen of the offence charged by section 16A is the possession of articles, in themselves innocent, for terrorist purposes. The crucial ingredients of the offence are, in reality possession (the *actus reus*) and the terrorist purpose (the *mens rea*). But neither of these crucial ingredients need be proved by the prosecution to the criminal standard to secure a conviction ... A defendant who chooses not to give or call evidence may be convicted by virtue of the presumptions against him and on reasonable suspicion falling short of proof ... Under section 16A a defendant could be convicted even if the jury entertained a reasonable doubt whether he knew that the items were in his premises and whether he had the items for a terrorist purpose."

9–51   Laws L.J. gave a concurring judgment in which he pointed out that the mischief which the offence was aimed at must be regarded as a terrorist intent since "otherwise the policy of the statute must be taken to mean that a man is rightly

---

[75] *RJR-MacDonald Inc v. Attorney-General of Canada* [1995] 3 S.C.R. 199 at 279 and 331–332; *Libman v. Attorney-General of Quebec* (1997) 3 B.H.R.C. 269 at 289E-F. See paras 2–129 to 2–130 above.
[76] [1999] 3 W.L.R. 175 at 190.

to be exposed to a prison sentence of up to 10 years upon a reasonable suspicion only". That being so, the section "requires the defendant to disprove the offence's principal element".[77] The Crown's plea was not, in truth, a plea for a fair balance. It was an argument that Article 6(2) should be disapplied; and that would be "an affront to the rule of law". The Court was unanimous in concluding that the issue was sufficiently clear that it could be judged on the face of the statute, without the necessity for a consideration of the evidence in the particular case.

In view of their ruling on the jurisdictional issue, it was not necessary for the **9–52** House of Lords to decide the point. Lord Steyn, with whom Lord Slynn agreed, regarded the issue as "arguable" and "entirely open". Lord Cooke, however, was more forthright:

> "My Lords, I see great force in the Divisional Court's view that on the natural and ordinary interpretation there is repugnancy . . . at best it is doubtful whether Article 6(2) can be watered down to an extent that would leave section 16A unscathed. The judgment of the Privy Council delivered by Lord Woolf in *Attorney-General of Hong Kong v. Lee Kwong-kut* [1993] A.C. 951 strongly suggests that it cannot."

Lord Hobhouse thought the question was less clear than the Divisional Court believed it to be; "Surprising though it may seem to those trained in the common law and the English traditions of statutory construction, there is clearly room for some doubt as to the outcome, were the defendants to seek to challenge their convictions in Strasbourg."

Lord Hope was equally cautious. He "parted company" with the Divisional **9–53** Court on the question whether a finding of incompatibility was inevitable. Having regard to the specific nature of the provisions he considered that the issue could only be determined in the light of the evidence adduced at trial[78]:

> "A sound judgment as to whether the burden which he has to discharge is an unreasonable one is unlikely to be possible until the facts are known. It is not immediately obvious that it would be imposing an unreasonable burden on an accused who was in possession of articles from which an inference of involvement in terrorism could be drawn to provide an explanation for his possession of them which would displace that inference. Account would have to be taken of the nature of the incriminating circumstances and the facilities which were available to the accused to obtain the necessary evidence. It would be one thing if there was good reason to think that the accused had easy access to the facts, quite another if access to them was very difficult."

In reaching the conclusion that section 16A was not necessarily incompatible on **9–54** its face, Lord Hope analysed it thus:

> "What subsection (1) requires is *prima facie* proof, not mere suspicion. The prosecution must lead evidence which is sufficient to prove beyond reasonable doubt (a) that the accused had the article in his possession and (b) that it was in his possesion in circumstances giving rise to a reasonable suspicion that it was in his possesion for a purpose connected with terrorism . . . It should not be thought that proof to this standard will be a formality."

---

[77] [1999] 3 W.L.R. 175 at 201.
[78] *cf.* the approach of the United States Supreme Court to "facial" challenges relating to mandatory reverse onus offences, summarised at para. 9–37 above.

This conclusion sits uneasily with Lord Woolf's reference to such proof, in the context of the similarly-worded offence in *Lee Kwong-kut*, as being a formality in the majority of cases.[79]

IX. *Dealing with Incompatible Burdens of Proof*

9–55   Lord Hope's judgment in *Kebilene* recites an agreed list of statutory indictable offences which impose a persuasive burden of proof on the accused, coupled with a mandatory presumption of guilt if it is not discharged, and which do not fall within the "special defence" exception identified in *Edwards*.[80] One of these provisions arose for consideration in *R v. Attorney-General, ex parte Rockall*.[81] The Attorney-General had given his consent to prosecutions of the defendant for two offences of corruption and one offence of conspiracy to corrupt, and the applicant sought judicial review of those decisions, relying on the Divisional Court judgment in *Kebilene*. Before the Divisional Court hearing however, the Attorney-General elected to proceed only on the conspiracy count. This made it straightforward for the Court to refuse the application, since the offence of conspiracy under the Criminal Law Act 1977 requires the prosecution to prove fault, irrespective of the fault requirements of the substantive offence. However, if the substantive corruption charges had been preferred,[82] the trial court would have been bound, under section 3(1) of the Human Rights Act, to read them compatibly with Article 6(2), so far as it is possible to do so.

9–56   The key question is whether it is *possible*, within the meaning of section 3(1) to read the word "prove", where it relates to an onus on the accused, as imposing no more than an evidential burden. The basis for such a construction was explained, as long ago as 1988, by Professor Glanville Williams, in an article entitled, "The Logic of Exceptions".[83] Many statutory reverse onus offences are cast in terms which provide that once the prosecution "prove" fact A, fact B is to be presumed unless the defence "prove" fact C. Despite the fact that such a provision uses the word "prove" to apply both to the prosecution's burden, and to that of the defence, the courts interpret the obligation differently according to where the burden lies. If it is the prosecution which must "prove" a fact, then this requires proof beyond reasonable doubt. If it is the defence, then proof on the balance of probabilities is required. Thus the courts give two different meanings to the same word, even where it appears in the same subsection. Having swallowed this "camel", argues Professor Williams, why should the courts "strain at the remaining gnat"? The word "prove", when it applies to the

---

[79] See para. 9–40 above.
[80] See para. 9–05 above. The offences are Prevention of Corruption Act 1916, s.2; the Sexual Offences Act 1956, s.30(2); the Obscene Publications Act 1959, s.2(5), the Obscene Publications Act 1964, s.1(3); the Misuse of Drugs Act 1971, s.28; the Public Order Act 1986, ss.18(4), 19(2), 20(2), 21(3), 22(3)–(5), and 23(3); the Criminal Justice Act 1988, s.93D(6); the Prevention of Terrorism (Temporary Provisions) Act 1989, ss.10(2)–(3), 11(2), 16A(3), 16B(1) and 17(3)(a) and (3A)(a); the Official Secrets Act 1989, ss.1(5), 2(3), 3(4), and 4(4)–(5), and the Drug Trafficking Act 1994, ss.53(6) and 58(2)(a). The list is non-exhaustive and Lord Hope added the Explosive Substances Act 1883, s.4(1).
[81] [2000] 1 W.L.R. 882.
[82] Section 2 of the Prevention of Corruption Act 1916 enacts that, once the prosecution establish that any money or gift has been given to or received by a public official, it shall be deemed to have been given or received corruptly unless the contrary is proved.
[83] [1988] Camb. L.J. 261 at 264–265.

defence, could be interpreted as requiring the accused to adduce sufficient evidence to raise a reasonable doubt in the mind of the court.

This question was considered by some of their Lordships in *Kebeline*. Lords   **9–57**
Steyn and Slynn regarded it as "a respectable argument which is reinforced by the disfavour with which reverse legal burden provisions have been regarded by the Privy Council . . . and leading judgments in other countries". Lord Cooke's view was that it was

> " . . . *distinctly possible* that [section 3(1)] may require section 16A . . . to be interpreted as imposing on the defendant an evidential, but not a persuasive (or ultimate), burden of proof. I agree that such is not the natural and ordinary meaning of s.16A(3). Yet for evidence that it is a *possible* meaning one can hardly ask for more than the opinion of Professor Glanville Williams.[84]"

As a postscript to the *Kebilene* case, it is interesting to see how the judge   **9–58**
approached the issue when the case returned to the Crown Court. Even without the benefit of section 3(1), which was still not in force at the time, he concluded that the section could be read as imposing an evidential burden[85]:

> "The words 'prove' and 'proof' in our law have different shades of meaning, depending on the context. Here there are two ways of interpreting the word 'prove' and I think it right to choose the one which means 'produce evidence to neutralise a *prima facie* presumption against them', in other words imposing on them . . . an evidential burden leaving the overall burden of proving their guilt so that the jury are sure of it on the prosecution."

The logic of this approach was given statutory effect when section 16A was re-enacted as section 57 of the Terrorism Act 2001. Section 57, which is in identical terms to its predecessor, is now subject to section 118(2). That subsection provides that if the accused "adduces sufficient evidence to raise an issue with respect to" the existence or absence of a terrorist intent, the jury "shall assume that the defence is satisfied unless the prosecution proves beyond reasonable doubt" that the defence is not made out. The new Act thus imposes a purely evidential burden on the accused.

There will, of course, be many borderline cases. Take, for example, the burden   **9–59**
of proof in the offence of assisting another to retain the benefit of criminal conduct, contrary to section 93A of the Criminal Justice Act 1988. The prohibited conduct consists of facilitating the retention or control of the proceeds of another's crime, and the fault is "knowing or suspecting" that the other has been engaged in criminal conduct. Section 93A(4) provides that "it is a defence to prove that he did not know or suspect that the arrangement related to any person's proceeds of criminal conduct." The prosecution must therefore prove one element of fault, the "knowing or suspecting", but it is for the defence to disprove another component of the fault, namely an actual awareness that the arrangement related to the proceeds of crime.[86] It seems plain that the prosecution does not have to prove all the ingredients of the offence, since one element of fault is for the defendant to disprove. On the other hand, one might reply that,

---

[84] In "The Logic of Exceptions" [1988] Camb. L.J. 261.
[85] His Honour Judge Pownall Q.C., Central Criminal Court, February 14, 2000.
[86] *Colle* (1992) 95 Cr. App. R. 67, *Butt* [1999] Crim. L.R. 414.

once the prosecution have proved that the defendant knew or suspected that the other person had been engaged in criminal conduct, there are grounds for presuming his awareness that the proceeds of crime were involved.[87] What is clear from the authorities is that where it is possible to do so courts should treat mandatory provisions as imposing no more than an evidential burden. If the approach which finally prevailed in *Kebilene* is followed in other cases, there should be fewer statutes which are interpreted as placing an ultimate burden of proof on the accused.

X. The decision in Lambert

9–59a   In *R. v. Lambert and Ali*[88] the Court of Appeal held that neither the provisions of section 2(2) of the Homicide Act 1957 (the defence of diminished responsibility) nor the provisions of sections 28(2) and 28(3) of the Misuse of Drugs Act 1971 (specific "knowledge" defences available on a charge of possession of drugs) were incompatible with the presumption of innocence in Article 6(2). Lord Woolf C.J. held that where the court was called upon to assess the compatibility of a reverse onus rule with the presumption of innocence, a balance must be struck between the demands of the general interest of the community and the protection of the fundamental rights of the individual. Since proof of diminished responsibility was pre-eminently a matter for defence evidence (and since proof of the contrary was extremely difficult for the prosecution) the Court had no hesitation in holding that section 2 of the 1957 Act was compatible with Article 6(2). The nub of the problem under the Misuse of Drugs Act was that a person who is proved to be in physical possession of a controlled drug is guilty of an offence unless he proves, on the balance of probabilities, that he did not know the substance was in his possession or that he did not know it was a controlled drug. Lord Woolf held that section 28(2) and (3) were compatible with Article 6(2). The House of Lords disagreed.[89] There was an objective justification for some interference with the burden of proof in drugs cases. But, in enacting sections 28(2) and (3), Parliament had recognised that it would be wrong to expose a person to conviction for an offence carrying a maximum sentence of life imprisonment if he did not, in fact, have the requisite knowledge. It was immaterial whether the issue of knowledge was characterised as an essential element of the offence, or as a defence. The important point was its impact on the issues before the jury. Read according to orthodox cannons of construction the provisions imposed a persuasive or legal burden on the accused. This meant that an accused could be convicted if he succeeded in raising a reasonable doubt on the issue, but failed to discharge the burden of proof on the balance of probabilities. That was imcompatible with Article 6(2). Applying section 3 of the Human Rights Act, the proper balance could be achieved by reading the provisions as imposing an evidential burden only. Their Lordships adopted the approach of Glanville Williams, discussed in paragraph 9–56 above, holding that the word "prove" should be interpreted to mean "adduces sufficient evidence to raise the issue".

---

[87] This derives some support from Lord Woolf's decision on the second charge in *Lee Kwong-kut* [1993] A.C. 951 at 973D-H.
[88] *The Times*, September 5, 2000. At the time of writing, the case is pending before the House of Lords.
[89] *R. v. Lambert* [2001] UKHL 37, July 5, 2001.

Once this hurdle was overcome, it would then be for the prosecution to prove guilty knowledge on the ordinary criminal standard.

XI. *Strict liability offences*

It is important to distinguish strict liability offences (where criminal liability **9–60** consists of the *actus reus* alone) from offences with a reverse onus of proof on *mens rea*.[90] In *Sweet v. Parsley*[91] Lord Reid observed that:

" . . . there has for centuries been a presumption that Parliament did not intend to make criminals of persons who were in no way blameworthy in what they did. That means that, whenever a section is silent as to *mens rea*, there is a presumption that, in order to give effect to the will of Parliament, we must read in words appropriate to require *mens rea* . . . it is firmly established by a host of authorities that *mens rea* is an essential ingredient of every offence unless some reason can be found for holding that that is not necessary".

The strength of this presumption was recently reaffirmed by the House of Lords **9–61** in *B v. DPP*.[92] For a statute to be construed as creating a strict liability offence, it would either have to say so in express terms, or by a "truly necessary"[93] implication. It would not be sufficient that the section was designed to combat a grave social evil,[94] nor that the context suggested that the imposition of strict liability was a reasonable reading. As Lord Hutton explained[95]: "[T]he test is not whether it is a reasonable implication that the statute rules out *mens rea* as a constituent part of the crime—the test is whether it is a *necessary* implication."

The interplay between the approach of the House of Lords in *B v. DPP* and **9–62** section 3(1) of the Human Rights Act is complex. If the courts are to imply a *mens rea* requirement whenever this is not excluded expressly or by necessary implication, then the issue will arise as to where the burden of proof should lie. In light of the principles discussed in the preceding section, the courts may be

---

[90] As to the importance of looking to the substance of the offence in determining its essential elements see para. 9–38 above. See also the analysis of Lord Bingham C.J. and Laws L.J. in *R. v. DPP ex parte Kebilene and ors* [1999] 3 W.L.R. 175.

[91] [1970] A.C. 132 at 148–149.

[92] [2000] 1 All E.R. 833.

[93] *Per* Lord Steyn at 845.

[94] *Per* Lord Steyn at 846.

[95] *Per* Lord Hutton at 855. In *R. v. K, The Times*, November 7, 2000 the Court of Appeal held that it was no defence to a charge of indecent assault on a girl under 16, contrary to section 14 of the Sexual Offences Act 1956, that the accused believed the girl to be over 16. Applying *B v. DPP* the Court held that the *mens rea* for the offence was an intention to commit the assault, and that Parliament had, by necessary implication, excluded a defence of honest but mistaken belief as to the girl's age. Moreover, the Court held that this reading was not incompatible with Article 6(2). Parliament, in 1956, considered the balance between the demands of the general interest of the community and the protection of the fundamental rights of the individual required that girls under the age of 16 should be protected by making it an offence for a person to touch them in circumstances which were indecent. The rights of the defence were maintained in that it was still for the prosecution to prove that the complainant was under 16 years of age and that there had been a deliberate touching of that girl in circumstances which made the touching indecent. In striking the balance in that way Parliament had not been acting unfairly or unreasonably although the Court expressed the hope that Parliament might look again at this area of the law in the near future.

required, in the light of section 3(1), to impose the burden on the prosecution. Such a reading will plainly be *possible*, since the section will, by definition be silent on the matter. The offence in issue in *B v. DPP* was incitement of a child under 14 to perform an act of gross indecency contrary to section 1(1) of the Indecency with Children Act 1960. The appellant was a 15 year old boy who had repeatedly asked a 13 year old girl to perform oral sex on him, and the question was whether the fact that the boy believed the girl to be over 14 amounted to a defence. The House of Lords, overruling *R v. Prince*,[96] held it did, and further held that since *mens rea* was an element of the offence, it was for the prosecution to prove, on the ordinary criminal standard, that the defendant knew the child was under 14.

9–63   There are, nonetheless, numerous statutory provisions which expressly create offences with no *mens rea*. In this situation, the decision in *B v. DPP* is of no direct assistance. How then should the court approach the construction of such a statute under the Human Rights Act? The starting point, once again, is Article 6(2). A strict liability offence is more likely be compatible with Article 6(2) precisely because a conviction for such an offence does not involve a finding that the defendant had a guilty state of mind. Since *mens rea* is not an element of the offence, there is no reversal of the burden of proof. The prosecution bears the burden of proving all the essential elements of the offence (*i.e.* those which make up the *actus reus*).

9–64   Thus the European Court of Human Rights has held that strict liability offences are generally compatible with Article 6(2), provided the prosecution retains the burden of proving the commission of the offence. In *Salabiaku v. France*[97] the Court observed that; " . . . the contracting states may, *under certain conditions*, penalise a simple or objective fact as such, irrespective of whether it results from criminal intent or from negligence."[98]

9–65   The Court did not spell out what these "conditions" might be. One factor of obvious importance is the penalty for the offence. Since conviction for a strict liability offence does not depend on a guilty state of mind, the penalties tend to be correspondingly lower. In *Salabiaku* the applicant had been acquitted of the more serious "criminal" offence of importation, which required proof of intent, but convicted of a strict liability "customs offence" carrying a maximum penalty of six months imprisonment. We have seen that in *Kebilene* Laws L.J. regarded with some alarm the prospect that a statute might impose a maximum sentence of 10 years imprisonment for an offence with no *mens rea*,[99] and the Canadian Supreme Court has gone so far as to invalidate some strict liability offences that may lead to the imposition of imprisonment.[1] It is surely wrong that a person should be liable to imprisonment for an offence without proof of any fault on his

---

[96] [1874–80] All E.R. 881, (CCR).
[97] (1991) 13 E.H.R.R. 379.
[98] Emphasis added.
[99] See the passage cited at para. 9–51 above.
[1] See, for example, *References re Section 94(2) of Motor Vehicle Act (BC)* (1986) 48 C.R. (3d) 289.

or her part; it is even more objectionable when a substantial prison sentence is possible.[2]

C. THE STANDARD OF PROOF

It has rightly been pointed out that the *standard* of proof required in criminal **9–66**
proceedings is largely unexplored in the Convention jurisprudence.[3] Nevertheless, it is implicit in the reasoning of the Strasbourg institutions that proof
beyond reasonable doubt is necessary. The Court has emphasised on a number of
occasions that "any doubt should benefit the accused".[4] In rejecting an application as inadmissible the Commission in one case observed that "the judge, in
explaining that proof must be beyond reasonable doubt, also explained what was
meant by a 'reasonable doubt' and told the jury that they must acquit if they had
such a doubt".[5]

This assumption is also evident in other contexts. When considering whether **9–67**
state officials have deliberately tortured or inflicted inhuman and degrading
treatment on a person in custody the Court has held that Article 3 requires proof
beyond reasonable doubt, and has observed that "such proof may follow from the
coexistence of sufficiently strong, clear and concordant inferences".[6] And in
concluding that certain proceedings were not "criminal" within the autonomous
interpretation given to the term "criminal charge" in Article 6,[7] the Commission
has referred to the fact that a tribunal did not apply the criminal standard of proof
beyond reasonable doubt.[8]

In practice this issue is only likely to arise in proceedings which are not classified **9–68**
as criminal under domestic law, but which will fall to be so classified under
Article 6. Where the proceedings concern a criminal offence recognised as such
in domestic law, the criminal standard of proof beyond reasonable doubt will
obviously apply. Any possible doubts on this issue are removed by section 11 of
the Human Rights Act 1998 which provides that the Act does not restrict any
right or freedom which is currently guaranteed under national law, including the
common law.[9]

---

[2] *e.g.* the maximum of five years' imprisonment for the strict liability offence of failing to conform
to the terms of an anti-social behaviour order, contrary to s.1 of the Crime and Disorder Act
1998.
[3] Sir Richard Buxton, "The Human Rights Act and the Substantive Criminal Law" [2000] Crim. L.R.
331.
[4] *Barbera, Messegue, and Jabardo v. Spain* (1989) 11 E.H.R.R. 360 at para. 77. See also *Austria v.
Italy* (1963) Y.B. VI 740 at 784, where the Commission observed that under Art. 6(2) "the onus to
prove guilt falls on the prosecution and any doubt is to the benefit of the accused.".
[5] Application No. 5768/72 (1975) 2 Digest 388.
[6] *Ireland v. United Kingdom* (1979–80) 2 E.H.R.R. 25.
[7] See Chapter 4 above.
[8] *Goodman v. Ireland* (1993) 16 E.H.R.R. CD 26.
[9] See para. 3–21 above.

CHAPTER 10

RETROSPECTIVITY AND THE PRINCIPLE OF LEGAL CERTAINTY

A. INTRODUCTION

The principle of legal certainty runs throughout the Convention.[1] It plays an **10–01** important role in determining whether a detention is "lawful" for the purposes of Article 5,[2] and in the Court's assessment of whether an interference with one of the qualified rights in Article 8 to 11 is "prescribed by law" or "in accordance with the law".[3] So far as the substantive criminal law is concerned, the principle is embodied in Article 7(1) (*no punishment without law*) which provides that; "No one shall be held guilty of any criminal offence on account of any act or omission which did not constitute a criminal offence under national or international law at the time when it was committed . . . "

The first limb of Article 7(1) thus prohibits the retroactive application of criminal **10–02** offences so as to penalise conduct which was not criminal at the time when the relevant act or omission occurred. More generally, however, the Court has held that Article 7(1);

" . . . embodies . . . the principle that only the law can define a crime and prescribe a penalty (*nullum crimen, nulla poena sine lege*) and the principle that the criminal law must not be extensively construed to an accused's detriment, for example by analogy; it follows from this that an offence must be clearly defined in law."[4]

The Court has emphasised the close relationship between the principle of legal **10–03** certainty guaranteed by Article 7 and the general requirement, to be found in other provisions of the Convention, that an interference with an individual's fundamental rights must be governed by clear legal principles[5]: "When speaking of 'law' Article 7 alludes to the very same concept as that to which the Convention refers elsewhere when using the term, a concept which comprises written as well as unwritten law and implies qualitative requirements, notably those of accessibility and foreseeability"

Accordingly, for the purposes of the Convention; **10–04**

" . . . a norm cannot be regarded as "law" unless it is formulated with sufficient precision to enable the citizen to regulate his conduct: he must be able—if need be with

---

[1] See para. 2–80 above.
[2] See paras 2–83 and 5–07 to 5–12 above.
[3] See para. 2–86 above.
[4] *Kokkinakis v. Greece* (1994) 17 E.H.R.R. 397 at para. 52.
[5] *SW and CR v. United Kingdom* (1996) 21 E.H.R.R. 363 at paras 32 (SW) and 34 (CR). In *Sunday Times (No. 1) v. United Kingdom* (1979–80) 2 E.H.R.R. 245 the applicants challenged contempt of court proceedings on the grounds of lack of legal certainty under Art. 10, whilst in *Harman v. United Kingdom* (1984) 38 D.R. 53 a similar challenge was mounted by reference to Art. 7.

appropriate advice—to foresee, to a degree that is reasonable in the circumstances, the consequences which a given action may entail."[6]

10–05   There are thus two closely connected principles underlying Article 7. The first is that the substantive criminal law should be sufficiently accessible and precise to enable an individual to know in advance whether his conduct is criminal; and the second is that developments of the criminal law by the courts (whether through the interpretation of statutory offences, or the development of common law offences) must be kept within the bounds of what is reasonably foreseeable.

B.   CERTAINTY OF DEFINITION

I.   *At Common Law*

10–06   The principle that the criminal law must meet the requirements of reasonable certainty and accessibility is "deeply embedded" in English law.[7] Professor Glanville Williams has explained the principle as an aspect of the Dicean conception of the rule of law[8];

> "'Englishmen are ruled by the law, and by the law alone', wrote Dicey. 'A man may with us be punished for breach of law, but he can be punished for nothing else'. In its Latin dress of *Nullum crimen sine lege, Nulla Poena sine lege*—that there must be no crime or punishment except in accordance with fixed, predetermined law—this has been regarded by most thinkers a self-evident principle of justice ever since the French Revolution. The citizen must be able to ascertain beforehand how he stands with regard to the criminal law; otherwise to punish him for breach of that law is purposeless cruelty."

10–07   This constitutional requirement of foreseeability forms an important part of the rationale for the rule that criminal statutes are to be restrictively interpreted, and for the principle that any ambiguity is to be resolved in favour of the accused. It is also the basis for the maxim that ignorance of the law does not generally afford an excuse for criminal conduct. As Scott L.J. observed in *Blackpool Corporation v. Locker*[9]:

> "That maxim applies in legal theory just as much to written or to unwritten law, *i.e.* to statute law as much as to common law or equity. But the very justification for that basic maxim is that the whole of our law, written or unwritten, is accessible to the public—in the sense, of course, that at any rate, its legal advisers have access to it, at any moment, as of right."

A similar sentiment underlies Lord Diplock's observations in *Ong Ah Chuan v. Public Prosecutor of Singapore*,[10] where he said that it would be a misuse of language to describe as "law" a norm which did not conform to the fundamental rules of natural justice which are inherent in the common law.

---

[6] *Silver v. United Kingdom* (1983) 5 E.H.R.R. 347.
[7] See DeSmith, Woolf and Jowell, *Judicial Review of Administrative Action* (5th ed., 1995), para. 13–026.
[8] *Criminal Law: The General Part* (2nd ed., 1961) pp 575.
[9] [1948] 1 K.B. 349 at 361.
[10] [1981] A.C. 648 at 670F.

The principle of legal certainty in criminal legislation has figured prominently in **10–08**
public law challenges to the validity of byelaws enforceable by criminal prosecution.[11] In *Staden v. Tarjanyi*[12] Lord Lane C.J. explained that;

> " ... to be valid, a byelaw, carrying as this one does penalties for infringement, must
> be certain and clear in the sense that anyone engaged upon [an] otherwise lawful
> pursuit ... must know with reasonable certainty when he is breaking the law and when
> he is not breaking the law. That proposition scarcely needs demonstration or
> authority."

In this context, however, the threshold test for uncertainty has been set relatively **10–09**
high, and there is a presumption that an ambiguously worded byelaw "must, if
possible, be given such a meaning as to make it reasonable and valid, rather than
unreasonable and invalid".[13] Thus in *Fawcett Properties Ltd v. Buckingham
County Council*[14] Lord Denning held that a provision would only be void for
uncertainty "if it can be given no meaning, or no sensible or ascertainable
meaning, and not merely because it is ambiguous or leads to absurd results".[15]
The consequence, as Woolf J. pointed out in *R. v. Secretary of State for Trade and
Industry ex parte Ford*,[16] is that "uncertainty of language rarely creates the
necessary degree of invalidity to cause the courts to intervene".

It is important, however, to recall that the requirement for legal certainty takes **10–10**
colour from its context. Doubts as to the precise scope of a legal prohibition may
be sufficient to afford a defence in criminal proceedings where the conduct in
question falls within the penumbra of uncertainty surrounding a particular byelaw, without necessarily affording grounds for striking the byelaw down in its
entirety. In *Bugg v. DPP*[17] the Divisional Court found byelaws prohibiting entry
onto military land to be insufficiently certain, and therefore "defective on their
face", since they failed to refer to any plan or boundary setting out the precise
limits of the area protected: "Byelaws such as are here under consideration which
create offences must clearly state what action is required in order to commit an
offence. A person who is subjected to the byelaw is, therefore, entitled to be
given the necessary details to enable him to avoid contravening the byelaw."

---

[11] As long ago as 1898 it was established that " ... a byelaw to be valid must, among other
conditions, have two properties—it must be certain, that is, it must contain adequate information as
to the duties of those who are to obey, and it must be reasonable": *Kruse v. Johnson* [1898] 2 Q.B.
91 *per* Mathew J. at 108. The rationale for this principle was explained by Diplock L.J. in *Mixnam's
Properties Ltd v. Chertsey Urban District Council* [1964] 1 Q.B. 214 at 238 as deriving from
Parliamentary intention: "[I]f the courts can declare subordinate legislation to be invalid for 'uncertainty' ... this must be because Parliament is presumed not to have intended to authorise the
subordinate legislation authority to make changes in the existing law which are uncertain."
[12] (1980) 78 L.G.R. 614 at 623. See also *Nash v. Findlay* (1901) 85 L.T. 682; *Scott v. Pilliner* [1904]
2 K.B. 855; *Leyton Urban District Council v. Chew* [1907] 2 K.B. 283; *Attorney-General v. Denby*
[1925] Ch. 596; *United Bill Posting Co Ltd v. Somerset County Council* (1926) 42 T.L.R. 537; *R. v.
Secretary of State for Trade and Industry ex parte Ford* (1984) 4 Tr. L. 150.
[13] *Fawcett Properties Ltd v. Buckingham County Council* [1961] A.C. 636 at 677.
[14] [1961] A.C. 636.
[15] *Fawcett* was in fact concerned with the validity of a planning condition, but Lord Denning
expressly equated the test with that to be applied to byelaws. The *Fawcett* test was expressly
approved as applying to byelaw offences by the Court of Appeal in *Percy v. Hall* [1997] Q.B.
924.
[16] (1984) 4 Tr. L. 150.
[17] [1993] Q.B. 473.

10–11   In *Percy v. Hall*,[18] however, the Court of Appeal declined to follow *Bugg*, holding that "however narrow or precise the line on a map, there will always be, literally, a borderline of uncertainty". This would not be sufficient to invalidate the byelaws so as to render them void and unenforceable even against those who deliberately trespassed within the centre of the protected area. But that did not mean that uncertainty as to the boundary would be irrelevant to criminal liability. As Simon Brown L.J. appeared to accept,[19] if there were genuine uncertainty as to whether or not a byelaw applies at a particular point on or around the boundary, then the benefit of the doubt should be given to the individual, and he should not be convicted of a byelaw offence.

II. *The Strasbourg Caselaw*

10–12   The European Court of Human Rights has also recognised the need for flexibility in this area,[20] emphasising that the test of legal certainty must take account not only of the wording of the relevant provision, but also of the courts' interpretation of it, and of other readily available guidance as to its meaning and application. In *Sunday Times v. United Kingdom (No. 1)*[21] the Court expressly recognised that absolute precision is unattainable, and observed that:

> " . . . whilst certainty is highly desirable, it may bring in its train excessive rigidity and the law must be able to keep pace with changing circumstances. Accordingly, many laws are couched in terms which, to a greater or lesser extent, are vague and whose interpretation and application are questions of practice."

Similarly, in *Kokkinakis v. Greece*[22] the Court held that the requirement for an offence to be clearly defined in law "is satisfied where the individual can know from the wording of the relevant provision *and, if need be, with the assistance of the courts' interpretation of it*, what acts and omissions will make him liable" (emphasis added).

10–13   Accordingly the Convention institutions have consistently looked to national caselaw defining or interpreting an offence in order to determine whether the margin of uncertainty surrounding the essential elements of criminal liability is so wide that it is liable to deprive the affected individual of the information necessary to regulate his conduct. Thus, in *Handyside v. United Kingdom*,[23] a case concerning the definition of obscenity in the Obscene Publications Acts 1959–1964, the Commission held that it was sufficient that the legislation provided a general description, which was then interpreted and applied by the courts. The Court has subsequently endorsed the view that the concepts such as obscenity[24] and blasphemy[25] are incapable of precise statutory definition. In the

---

[18] [1997] Q.B. 924.
[19] See counsel's submission at 936D, and Simon Brown L.J.'s response at 937H to 938B.
[20] Writing extra-judicially, Sir Richard Buxton has suggested that the Strasbourg caselaw "has disappointingly little to offer in practice" since "it is difficult to discern in the ECHR jurisprudence any general principle that the criminal law must be accessible and certain above a very modest level": R. Buxton, "The Human Rights Act and the Substantive Criminal Law" [2000] Crim. L.R. 331.
[21] (1979–80) 2 E.H.R.R. 245 at para. 59.
[22] (1994) 17 E.H.R.R. 397 at para. 52.
[23] (1974) 17 Y.B. 228. The Court's judgment is reported at (1979–80) 1 E.H.R.R. 737.
[24] *Muller v. Switzerland* (1991) 13 E.H.R.R. 212.
[25] *Wingrove v. United Kingdom* (1996) 24 E.H.R.R. 1.

Kokkinakis case, a statutory offence of "proselytism" was held to have been clarified by a body of settled national caselaw on the meaning of the provision.[26] In reaching this conclusion the Court reiterated that "the wording of many statutes is not absolutely precise", and that "the interpretation and application of such enactments depend on practice".

The relevance of external guidance was considered in *Ainsworth v. United*   **10–14** *Kingdom*.[27] The applicant challenged his conviction under section 69 of the Army Act 1955 for engaging "conduct to the prejudice of good order and military discipline". As a lieutenant in the Royal Marines he had failed to prevent the consumption of alcohol by under-age recruits, one of whom has died from alcohol poisoning. He contended that the terms of section 69 were insufficiently specific to enable him to know in advance that he was committing a criminal offence, and argued that there had been a "blind eye" policy of allowing the consumption of alcohol by under-age recruits. In concluding that the standard set by Article 7 had been met, the Commission considered that section 69 had to be read in the light of "detailed and precise" standing orders which spelt out the duties of a supervising officer. Moreover, the adoption of a "blind eye" policy by more senior officers could not be said to amount to an "implicit abrogation" of the offence.

On occasion, the Court has been prepared to accept general wording, even in the   **10–15** absence of judicial interpretation or external guidance as to its meaning. In *Grigoriades v. Greece*[28] the applicant challenged a Greek military offence of "insulting the armed forces", on the ground that it was not *lex certa* and was therefore in breach of Article 7. The Court held that, although "couched in broad terms", the offence met the required standard, since the ordinary meaning of the word "insult" (which was akin to the word "offend") was clear enough to encompass the applicant's conduct of writing a letter to a superior officer criticising the army.

An example of an "offence" which failed to meet the requisite standard, was the   **10–16** bindover order imposed in *Hashman and Harrup v. United Kingdom*[29] requiring the defendants to be "of good behaviour" (that is, not to act *contra bonos mores*). The Court considered that the conduct prohibited by such an order was "not described at all" and failed to afford any objective criteria by which the applicants' past or future actions could be judged. It was thus too vague to qualify as "law". However, as one commentator has pointed out[30]; " . . . it would have been extraordinary if any other conclusion had been reached, in view of the conclusion of the English Law Commission that to impose restrictions on the basis of that concept is contrary to elementary English notions of fair process."

III. *Comparative Approaches*

A similar flexibility is evident in most constitutional jurisdictions. However,   **10–17** criminal statutes can be (and have been) declared "void for vagueness" both in

---

[26] (1994) 17 E.H.R.R. 397 at paras 40–41 and 52.
[27] Application No. 35095/97, unreported.
[28] (1999) 27 E.H.R.R. 464.
[29] *The Times*, December 1, 1999.
[30] R. Buxton, "The Human Rights Act and the Substantive Criminal Law" [2000] Crim. L.R. 331.

the United States and in Canada if they fail to provide an "intelligible standard" for the application of the prohibition. In *Connally v. General Construction Co*[31] the United States Supreme Court[32] held that a law is void on its face if it is so vague that persons "of common intelligence must necessarily guess at its meaning and differ as to its application". This principle has been explained on the basis that a law which fails to define clearly the conduct it proscribes "may trap the innocent by not providing fair warning" and may in practical effect impermissibly delegate "basic policy matters to policemen, judges and juries for resolution on an ad hoc and subjective basis, with the attendant dangers of arbitrary and discriminatory application".[33] Nevertheless, the constitutional presumption of validity will often save an otherwise vague law, by restricting its application in practice. In *Grayned v. City of Rockford*[34] the Supreme Court was faced with an ordinance which provided that "no person on public or private grounds adjacent to any building in which a school [is] in session shall willfully make [any] noise or diversion which disturbs or tends to disturb the peace or good order of such school". The provision was held to be constitutionally valid, since state courts could be expected to apply it "to prohibit only actual or imminent interference" with the peace or good order of the school. Accordingly, it was clear what the ordinance prohibited.

10–18   A more searching standard seems to have been applied to criminal offences involving the right to free expression. In *Smith v. Goguen*[35] the Supreme Court invalidated a statute which prohibited the public mutilation, defacement or contemptuous treatment of the American flag. Recognising that use of the flag for adornment or to attract attention had become commonplace, the Court held that the legislation failed "to draw reasonably clear lines between the kinds of nonceremonial treatment that are criminal, and those that are not". Similarly, in *Stromberg v. California*[36] the Court declared unconstitutional a statutory provision which made it an offence to express "opposition to organised government" by displaying "any flag, badge, banner or device". Stressing the fundamental importance of the "opportunity of free political discussion", the Court observed that; "A statute which upon its face, and as authoritatively construed, is so vague and indefinite as to permit the punishment of the fair use of this opportunity is repugnant to the guarantee of liberty contained in the Fourteenth Amendment".

10–19   The Canadian Supreme Court has recognised a similar void for vagueness doctrine, grounded in the principles of fundamental justice guaranteed by section 7 of the Canadian Charter. In *Prosecution Reference*[37] the Court rejected a challenge alleging that offences of keeping a "common bawdy house" and soliciting for the purposes of prostitution, were unconstitutionally vague. Lamer J. referred to the leading United States decisions and continued:

---

[31] 269 U.S. 385 (1926) at 391.
[32] See generally, Amsterdam, "The Void-for-Vaguenss Doctrine in the Supreme Court" 109 U. Pa. L. Rev. 67 (1960).
[33] *Grayned v. City of Rockford* 408 U.S. 104 (1972).
[34] 408 U.S. 104 (1972).
[35] 415 U.S. 566 (1974).
[36] 283 U.S. 359 (1931).
[37] (1990) 77 C.R. (3d) 1 (S.C.C.).

"The principles expressed in these two citations are not new to our law. In fact they are based on the ancient Latin maxim *nullum crimen sine lege, nulla poena sine lege*—that there can be no crime or punishment unless it is in accordance with law that is certain, unambiguous and not retroactive. The rationale underlying this approach is clear. It is essential in a free and democratic society that citizens are able, as far as is possible, to foresee the consequences of their conduct in order that persons be given fair notice of what to avoid, and that the discretion of those entrusted with law enforcement is limited by clear and explicit legislative standards."

In words which find a strong echo in the Strasbourg jurisprudence, he said that   **10–20** the void for vagueness doctrine did not "require that a law be absolutely certain: no law can meet this standard". The doctrine was not to be applied to the "bare words" of a statutory provision, but rather to "the provision as interpreted and applied in judicial decisions". The test in each case was "whether the impugned sections of the Criminal Code can be or have been given sensible meanings by the courts". Put another way, the court should ask whether the statute was "so pervasively vague" that it permits a "standardless sweep".

The Canadian decisions were reviewed in *R. v. Nova Scotia Pharmaceutical*   **10–21** *Society*,[38] which concerned a statutory offence of conspiracy to lessen competition "unduly". Rejecting the challenge Gonthier J., for a unanimous Supreme Court, characterised the vagueness doctrine as being founded on the principles of fair notice to citizens and limitation of prosecution discretion, which were aspects of the rule of law. These principles had both a formal aspect (that citizens were presumed to know the law, such that ignorance of its requirements was no excuse) and a substantive aspect (that the citizen must in reality be able to ascertain whether particular conduct falls within the control of the law). A provision which was unintelligible gave insufficient guidance for legal debate (that is, for reaching a conclusion as to its meaning by reasoned analysis, applying legal criteria) and was therefore unconstitutionally vague. But the threshold for a finding of unintelligibility was a "relatively high" one. It could not be argued that a statute must provide sufficient guidance to predict the legal consequences of any given course of conduct in advance. All it could do was to enunciate the boundaries of risk with reasonable clarity.

The decisions in other constitutional jurisdictions are to broadly similar effect. In   **10–22** South Africa, a statutory offence of contempt in the face of the court has been held sufficiently clear and unambiguous,[39] as has a common law offence of fraud.[40] And in *Dharmarajen Sabapathee v. The State*,[41] Lord Hope, on behalf of the Privy Council, held that a statutory provision in Mauritius which criminalised the "trafficking" of drugs was sufficiently precise to enable citizens to understand those transactions which fell within, and those which fell outside, the ordinary meaning of the expression.

---

[38] (1992) 15 C.R. (4th) 1 (S.C.C.).
[39] *State v. Lavhengwa* (1996) 2 S.A.C.R. 453. The Court held that this issue had to be approached on the assumption that the statutory definition was directed at ordinary intelligent people who were capable of thinking for themselves.
[40] *State v. Friedman* (1996) 1 S.A.C.R. 181.
[41] *Privy Council Appeal No. 1 of 1999* (unreported).

IV. *Legal Certainty under the Human Rights Act*

10–23   It will be apparent from the discussion in the preceding paragraphs that the standard of certainty required under the Convention, and under comparable constitutional principles, is not a particularly exacting one. The essential elements of the offence must be intelligible, and capable of interpretation in a manner which is reasonably clear. So far as offences created by primary and subordinate legislation are concerned, the wording of the relevant provision must be considered in conjunction with any interpretative caselaw.

10–24   The common law principle of restrictive interpretation is now reinforced by the duty of compatible construction imposed by section 3 of the Human Rights Act (read in conjunction with Article 7). In the light of section 3, the circumstances in which it will be necessary to grant a declaration of incompatibility on grounds of vagueness will be few and far between. If the wording of primary or subordinate legislation is ambiguous, general, or objectionably vague, it will, almost by definition, be "possible", within the meaning of section 3, to adopt a narrow construction, limiting the scope of criminal liability so as to avoid the imposition of a penalty.[42] In the unlikely event that an offence created in primary legislation is truly unintelligible, or has no readily ascertainable meaning, it will be unenforceable on ordinary common law principles,[43] and a declaration of incompatibility would seem both unnecessary and inappropriate. The position of unintelligible byelaws is similar. Since the House of Lords decision in *Boddington v. British Transport Police*[44] it has been clear that challenges to the validity of subordinate legislation may be mounted by way of defence in criminal proceedings, irrespective of the nature of the challenge. This principle is reflected in section 7(1)(b) of the Human Rights Act 1998. As we have seen, the English courts have elaborated a theory of vagueness which resembles the Canadian authorities, and which has (on occasion) resulted in the striking down of certain byelaw offences. Where a byelaw is intelligible but ambiguous, or where its precise boundaries are uncertain, the benefit of the doubt may be given to the accused without impugning the validity of the byelaw itself. The potential impact of the Human Rights Act on this line of authority was considered, *obiter*, by Brooke L.J. in *Westminster City Council v. Blenheim Leisure (Restaurants) Ltd and others*.[45] The defendants had been charged with failing to "maintain good order" contrary to the City Council's Rules of Management for Places of Public Entertainment, by permitting prostitutes to offer sexual services for money. Brooke L.J. observed that the Council would "do well . . . to tighten up the language of [the relevant provision] if it wishes to be able to use it to prohibit

---

[42] *cf. Fawcett Properties Ltd v. Buckingham County Council* [1961] A.C. 636 at 662 where Lord Cohen said that the principle that "a man is not to be put in peril upon an uncertainty . . . involves that if a statutory provision is ambiguous, the court should adopt any reasonable interpretation which would avoid the penalty".

[43] See, for example, *Mixnam's Properties Ltd v. Chertsey Urban District Council* [1964] 1 Q.B. 214 at 238 where Lord Diplock drew a distinction between the power of courts to declare subordinate legislation invalid for uncertainty and the power to treat legislation as being *"unenforceable*, as in the case of a clause in a statute to which it is impossible to ascribe a meaning" (emphasis added). See also *Fawcett Properties Ltd v. Buckingham County Council* [1961] A.C. 636 at 662 where Lord Cohen recognised that a court could "strike a provision out of an Act on the ground of uncertainty" only where "it is impossible to resolve the ambiguity which it is said to contain".

[44] [1998] 2 All E.R. 203.

[45] (1999) 163 J.P. 401.

activities like these on licensed premises after the Human Rights Act 1998 comes into force". He continued:

> "The extension of the very vague concept of the maintenance of good order to the control of the activities of prostitutes may have passed muster in the days when English common law offences did not receive critical scrutiny from national judicial guardians of a rights-based jurisprudence, but those days will soon be over. English judges will then be applying a Human Rights Convention which has the effect of prescribing that a criminal offence must be clearly defined in law. I do not accept [the] submission that it is impossible to define the kind of conduct [the Council] desire[s] to prohibit with greater precision, or that it is satisfactory to leave it to individual magistrates to decide, assisted only be some fairly arcane case law, whether or not activities of the type of which the Council complains in this case amount to a breach of good order so as to render the licensees liable to criminal penalties."

C. JUDICIAL DEVELOPMENT OF THE ELEMENTS OF AN OFFENCE

In practical terms, it is unlikely that the courts will be faced with statutory **10–25** offences which are expressly retrospective,[46] but difficult problems can arise when the elements of an offence are developed by judicial decision. In *X Ltd and Y v. United Kingdom*[47] the Commission recognised that where an offence is created by the common law this "presents certain peculiarities for the very reason that it is, by definition, law developed by the courts". In determining whether such developments overstep the "margin of uncertainty"[48] the Commission suggested that Article 7;

> " . . . implies that constituent elements of an offence such as e.g. the particular form of culpability required for its completion may not be essentially changed, at least not to the detriment of the accused, by the case law of the courts. On the other hand it is not objectionable that the existing elements of the offence are clarified and adapted to new circumstances which can reasonably be brought under the original concept of the offence".

In that case the House of Lords had held that the common law offence of **10–26** blasphemous libel required only proof of an intention to publish, and not of an intention to blaspheme. In view of the absence of previous authority on the point, the Commission considered that the House of Lords ruling on the requisite *mens rea* for the offence was a clarification of the existing law, and not a change of the law to the applicant's detriment. In *Harman v. United Kingdom*,[49] by contrast, the Commission declared admissible a complaint that the applicant had been convicted of contempt of court for showing documents to a journalist, even though the documents had been read out in open court, when (so it was submitted) it was not reasonably foreseeable that this would be regarded as a contempt. Under the

---

[46] In *Waddington v. Miah* [1974] 1 W.L.R. 683 at 694 the House of Lords described as "hardly credible" the proposition that a Minister would propose or that Parliament would enact retrospective criminal legislation. Whilst this is undoubtedly true of legislation creating substantive offences, there are a number of examples of criminal statutes which impose retrospective penalties in breach of Art. 7: see, for example, *Welch v. United Kingdom* (1995) 20 E.H.R.R. 247.

[47] (1982) 28 D.R. 77 at para. 9.

[48] *Zamir v. United Kingdom* (1983) 40 D.R. 42 at para. 91.

[49] (1984) 38 D.R. 53; the friendly settlement of this case, in which the Government undertook to change the law, is reported at (1986) 46 D.R. 57.

Human Rights Act the courts may be called upon to determine whether certain common law offences have been extended in a way that breaches Article 7, or (more accurately) they may be constrained not to develop the law in that way.

10–27   The leading case on this issue is now *SW and CR v. United Kingdom*,[50] in which the Court held that the removal of the marital rape exemption by the House of Lords in *R. v. R.*[51] did not amount to a retrospective change in the elements of the offence. The Court emphasised that Article 7 does not prohibit the development of the criminal law through judicial decisions:

> "However clearly drafted a legal provision may be, in any system of law, including criminal law, there is an inevitable element of judicial interpretation. There will always be a need for elucidation of doubtful points and for adaptation to changing circumstances. Indeed, in the United Kingdom, as in the other Convention states, the progressive development of the criminal law through judicial law-making is a well entrenched and necessary part of legal tradition. Article 7 of the Convention cannot be read as outlawing the gradual clarification of the rules of criminal liability through judicial interpretation from case to case, providing the resultant development is consistent with the essence of the offence and could reasonably be foreseen."

10–28   Applying this dubiously elastic formulation, the Court unanimously found that the development of the law by the House of Lords "did no more than continue a perceptible line of case law development dismantling the immunity". There had been an evolution in the law creating a number of specific exceptions to the immunity, which "had reached a stage where judicial recognition of the absence of immunity had become a reasonably foreseeable development of the law".

10–29   The decision in *SW and CR* has been extensively criticised on the ground that the Court sacrificed an important constitutional principle in order to achieve a socially desirable result in the individual case.[52] It is certainly difficult to characterise such a significant development as a mere "clarification" of the law, given that an act which would previously have fallen outside the scope of the offence altogether was brought within it by the *ex post facto* removal of an established immunity which had until then defined the boundaries of criminal liability. It is far from clear that a hypothetical legal adviser would have understood the scope of the offence as the House of Lords subsequently declared it to be. Shortly before the issue arose in the courts, the Law Commission had expressed the view that the immunity was so well settled in English law that legislation would be required to remove it,[53] and a number of judges had considered themselves bound by the rule.[54]

10–30   It is clear that the Court's assessment of the issue in *SW and CR* was heavily influenced by the nature of the offence:

> "The essentially debasing character of rape is so manifest that the result of the decisions of the Court of Appeal and the House of Lords . . . cannot be said to be at variance with

---

[50] (1996) 21 E.H.R.R. 363.
[51] [1992] A.C. 599.
[52] See, for example, Craig Osborne, "Does the End Justify the Means? Retrospectivity, Article 7 and the Marital Rape Exemption" [1996] E.H.R.L.R. 406.
[53] Law Commission working paper No. 116 at para. 2.08.
[54] See, for example, *R. v. J.* [1991] 1 All E.R. 759.

the object and purpose of Article 7 of the Convention . . . What is more, the abandonment of the unacceptable idea of a husband being immune against prosecution for rape of his wife was in conformity not only with a civilised concept of marriage but also, and above all, with fundamental objectives of the Convention, the very essence of which is respect for human dignity and human freedom."

It is understandable that the Court should have been reluctant to allow a human   **10-31** rights instrument to be invoked by a convicted rapist, so as to exclude criminal liability on the basis of an anachronistic conception of the rights of women *vis-á-vis* their husbands. But the nature of the offence should surely have been irrelevant when the Court came to lay down principles governing so important a right as the protection against retrospectivity in the development of the criminal law by judicial decision. The Court's appeal to the object and purpose of the Convention is especially unconvincing in this context since many criminal offences involve a violation of the Convention rights of the victim. If the "essentially debasing" nature of the offence were properly to be regarded as a consideration affecting the principles of retrospectivity, Article 7 would apply differentially to different categories of crime, and would be deprived of much of its purpose. It is difficult to believe that the Court intended this result. The decision in *SW and CR* is perhaps best regarded as a salutory reminder that the European Court of Human Rights is as vulnerable as any other court to the accusation that hard cases make bad law. Sir Richard Buxton has argued that following *SW and CR*;

" . . . a 'criminal offence' under Article 7 can be an offence merely *in gremio*, provided that its appearance can be said to be foreseeable on the basis of a not very demanding standard of foresight. That adds nothing to the protection of the individual that is provided by English domestic principle, and indeed falls short of what English principle has always been thought to require."[55]

It is, however, worth considering whether, even after *SW and CR*, Article 7 may   **10-32** nonetheless be interpreted as placing some outer limits on judicial creativity. In *Shaw v. DPP*[56] the House of Lords notoriously created the offence of conspiracy to corrupt public morals, (whereas 10 years later in *Knuller v. DPP*[57] the House foreswore the use of this power in future[58]). In *Tan*,[59] the Court of Appeal proclaimed that "courts should not, or should at least be slow to create new offences". Where, as in that case, the prosecution is described as "novel", there may be a role for Article 7 to play. What is to happen if, for example, the Court of Appeal effectively narrows a defence so as to uphold the conviction of an accused? This was done in *Elbekkay*,[60] where the Court held that it was no defence for a man to argue that his impersonation of the victim's boyfriend (as distinct from a husband) was insufficient to negative the woman's apparent consent. This decision was all the more remarkable because section 142 of the Criminal Justice and Public Order Act 1994 had recently re-defined rape but had

---

[55] R. Buxton, "The Human Rights Act and the Substantive Criminal Law" [2000] Crim. L.R. 331.
[56] [1962] A.C. 220.
[57] [1973] A.C. 435.
[58] For discussion of the limits of judicial creativity, see A.T.H. Smith, "Judicial Lawmaking in the Criminal Law" (1984) 100 L.Q.R. 46.
[59] [1983] Q.B. 1053.
[60] [1995] Crim. L.R. 163, on which see J.C. Smith and B. Hogan, *Criminal Law* (8th ed., 1996), p.469.

repeated the reference to rape by impersonating a husband (without extending the reference to a partner or cohabitee), and because—as the Court acknowledged— there was no previous decision or statute which required it to reach the conclusion it did. It might be argued that this development of the law by the courts was not reasonably foreseeable. Whereas in the case of marital rape there had at least been a series of lesser decisions suggesting that the courts might be moving in the direction of restricting a husband's immunity for rape of his wife, there was nothing in the law prior to *Elbekkay* to serve warning that a change might be imminent. It is therefore suggested that there might be cases in which it can be argued that the expansion of an offence or the contraction of a defence would be contrary to Article 7, in the sense that the law has been developed "by analogy" in a way that is not foreseeable and which operates "to an accused's detriment."[61]

D. CRIMES UNDER INTERNATIONAL LAW

10–33   A conviction which results from the retrospective application of domestic law will not breach Article 7(1) if the conduct of the accused was a crime under international law at the time that it occurred.[62] Certain offences, such as war crimes, piracy, torture and genocide are treated as crimes of universal jurisdiction under public international law. A state may prosecute individuals for such offences, wherever committed, solely on the basis that it has custody of the alleged offender. The United Kingdom has given effect to this principle in a number of statutes,[63] which can therefore be retrospectively applied[64] without violating Article 7.

E. WAR CRIMES

10–34   Article 7(2) provides that the protection of Article 7(1); " . . . shall not prejudice the trial and punishment of any person for any act or omission which, at the time when it was committed, was criminal according to the general principles of law recognised by civilised nations."

The exception created by Article 7(2) was intended to allow the application of national and international legislation enacted during and after the Second World War to punish war crimes, treason and collaboration with the enemy.[65] The practical effect of Article 7(2) is simply to make it clear that the international law exception in Article 7(1) is not confined to treaty-based or customary international law, but extends to conduct regarded as criminal under "the general principles of law recognised by civilised nations".

---

[61] See the passage from *Kokkinakis v. Greece* (1994) 17 E.H.R.R. 397.

[62] Article 7(1) prohibits conviction or punishment for an act or omission which did not constitute a crime "under national *or international law*" at the time when it was committed.

[63] The War Crimes Act 1991, s.1 (offences of murder, manslaughter, or culpable homicide committed in German occupied territory during the Second World War to be triable in United Kingdom courts); the Criminal Justice Act 1988, s.134 (torture, wherever committed, to be triable in the United Kingdom); the Genocide Act 1969, s.1 (genocide, wherever committed, to be triable in the United Kingdom); the Geneva Conventions Act 1957, s.1 (grave breaches of the Geneva Conventions, wherever committed, to be triable in the United Kingdom).

[64] Providing the relevant rule of international law was in existence at the time of the offence.

[65] *X v. Belgium* (1957) 1 Y.B. 239.

CHAPTER 11

ISSUES OF CRIMINAL RESPONSIBILITY

A. The Age of Criminal Responsibility

The age of criminal responsibility in England and Wales is 10 years.[1] Below this   **11–01**
age, no child can be found guilty of a criminal offence. The age of 10 was
endorsed by the Home Affairs Select Committee in October 1993[2] and again by
Parliament in 1998.[3] It is, however, one of the lowest ages of criminal responsibility in the member states of the Council of Europe. In Spain, Belgium and
Luxembourg the age of criminal responsibility is 18. In Poland, Portugal
and Andorra it is 16. In Germany, Austria, Italy and in many of the Central and
Eastern states, it is 14, and in France it is 13. It is, however, fair to say that there
is not yet a clear European consensus on this issue, and that some countries have
set an even lower age than England and Wales. Scotland, for example, sets the
age of criminal responsibility at eight, and there are four countries in which it is
set at seven.[4]

Until 1998 a child in England and Wales was subject to the *doli incapax* rule,   **11–02**
which presumed that between the ages of 10 and 14 he was not criminally
responsible. That presumption could be rebutted by the prosecution proving
beyond reasonable doubt that at the time of the offence the child knew that the
act in question was wrong as distinct from merely naughty or childish mischief.[5]
However crude such a test may seem, it at least had the benefit of allowing for
the phased introduction of criminal responsibility, so as to take account of the
rapid development that occurs during the transition from childhood to early
adolescence, and of the huge variation in emotional maturity between children in
this group (even between children of the same chronological age). A child or
young person in this developmentally diverse age group would only be held
criminally responsible if he could be shown to have a real grasp of the difference
between right and wrong. The *doli incapax* presumption was abolished with
effect from September 20, 1998.[6]

Despite the absence of a settled international consensus on this issue, it is clear   **11–03**
that there is an emerging international trend towards raising the age of criminal
responsibility. Article 40(3)(a) of the United Nations Convention on the Rights
of the Child, the most widely ratified international convention in the world,
requires states to establish a minimum age below which children shall be

---

[1] Section 50 of the Children and Young Persons Act 1933 as amended by s.16(1) of the Children and
Young Persons Act 1963.
[2] *Juvenile Offenders*, Sixth Report of the Session (HMSO, 1992–3).
[3] See s.34 of the Crime and Disorder Act 1998 and para. 11–02 below.
[4] Cyprus, Ireland, Lictenstein and Switzerland.
[5] See generally *C (a minor) v. The Director of Public Prosecutions* [1996] A.C. 1.
[6] Section 34 of the Crime and Disorder Act 1998.

presumed not to have the capacity to infringe the criminal law.[7] The United Nations Standard Minimum Rules for the Administration of Juvenile Justice (the Beijing Rules) recommend[8] that those countries which recognise an age for criminal responsibility of juveniles should not fix that age "at too low an age level, bearing in mind the facts of emotional, mental and intellectual maturity".[9] The Commentary to this provision observes[10]:

> "The minimum age of criminal responsibility differs widely, owing to history and culture. The modern approach would be to consider whether a child can live up to the moral and psychological components of criminal responsibility; that is whether a child, by virtue of her or his individual discernment and understanding, can be held responsible for essentially antisocial behaviour.[11] If the age of criminal responsibility is fixed too low or if there is no age limit at all, the notion of criminal responsibility becomes meaningless. In general, there is a close relationship between the notion of criminal responsibility for delinquent or criminal behaviour and other social rights and responsibilities (such as marital status, civil majority etc.) Efforts should therefore be made to agree on a reasonable lowest age limit that is applicable."

This equiparation between criminal responsibility and civil capacity points towards an age much higher than 10. It is thus not surprising that the United Nations Committee on the Rights of the Child,[12] has recommended that "serious consideration be given to raising the age of criminal responsibility throughout the areas of the United Kingdom".[13]

11–04   These issues came up for consideration in *T and V v. United Kingdom*.[14] The applicants in that case were two juveniles charged with murder, who were 10 at the time of the offence, and 11 at the time of their trial. There was evidence that both of them were psychologically damaged, and that they were immature for their age. The *doli incapax* presumption was rebutted by evidence from their head teacher to the effect that the applicants, like any child over the age of about five, knew that it was seriously wrong to hit a younger child with a weapon. They were each convicted of murder and sentenced to be detained at Her Majesty's Pleasure. In their application to Strasbourg they alleged that the cumulative effect of the low age of criminal responsibility in England and Wales and their trial in public, in an adult Crown Court, and under intense media scrutiny, reached the level of severity necessary to constitute a violation of Article 3. The Court rejected the argument, after careful consideration. In doing so, it noted that the trend towards raising the age of criminal responsibility had not yet hardened into a European consensus[15];

> "The Court has considered first whether the attribution to the applicant of criminal responsibility in respect of acts committed when he was ten years old could, in itself,

---

[7] Although it does not state what that age should be.
[8] The Court has accepted that Beijing Rules are not binding in international law. The Preamble invites states to adopt the standards laid down but does not oblige them to do so.
[9] Rule 4.1.
[10] Commentary to Rule 4.1.
[11] *cf.* The *doli incapax* presumption.
[12] The treaty body established to monitor the implementation of the United Nations Convention on the Rights of the Child.
[13] U.N. doc. CRC/C/15/add. 34, February 15, 1995, para. 36. This recommendation was made prior to the abolition of the *doli incapax* presumption.
[14] (2000) 30 E.H.R.R. 121.
[15] At paras 72 to 74.

give rise to a violation of Article 3. In doing so, it has regard to the principle, wel
established in its caselaw that, since the Convention is a living instrument, it is
legitimate when deciding whether a certain measure is acceptable under one of its
provisions to take account of the standards prevailing amongst the member states of the
Council of Europe . . . In this connection the Court observes that, at the present time,
there is not yet a commonly accepted minimum age for the imposition of criminal
responsibility in Europe. While most of the Contracting States have adopted an age
limit which is higher than that in force in England and Wales, other States, such as
Cyprus, Ireland, Liechtenstein and Switzerland, attribute criminal responsibility from a
younger age . . . The Court does not consider that there is at this stage any clear
common standard amongst the member states of the Council of Europe as to the
minimum age of criminal responsibility. Even if England and Wales is among the few
European jurisdictions to retain a low age of criminal responsibility, the age of ten
cannot be said to be so young as to differ disproportionately from the age limit followed
by other European States. The Court concludes that the attribution of criminal responsibility to the applicant does not in itself give rise to a breach of Article 3 of the Convention."

There are a number of points to make about this decision. The first and most   **11–05**
obvious one is that the Court laid emphasis on the existence or otherwise of an
international consensus on the issue *at the present time.* The implication is that
a convergence of European standards on this issue, which may well be on the
horizon, could set a benchmark; and that the Court might then find a violation of
Article 3 if there were a disproportionate difference between the age adopted by
a particular state and the standard prevailing in the Council of Europe. It is
important in this context to recall that the decision in *T and V* related to a trial
which took place prior to the abolition of the *doli incapax* presumption. To the
extent that this rule mitigated the harshness of an indisputably low age of
criminal responsibility, the present position is, if anything, less likely to comply
with the emerging requirements of international human rights law.

The second point is that even in the absence of a European consensus, the low   **11–06**
age of criminal responsibility in England and Wales undoubtedly contributed to
the finding of a violation of Article 6 in *T and V.* The younger a state sets its age
of criminal responsibility, the greater will be its obligation to ensure that real
safeguards are put in place to promote the best interests of the child, to protect
him from unnecessary harassment, publicity, and distress, and to provide the best
possible conditions for rehabilitation. As the Court explained[16]; "[I]t is essential
that a child charged with an offence is dealt with in a manner which takes full
account of his age, level of maturity and intellectual and emotional capacities,
and that steps are taken to promote his ability to understand and participate in the
proceedings."

Although the Crown Court had made a number of modifications to the
procedure in *T and V,*[17] these were found insufficient in view of the applicants'
age and emotional vulnerability, to meet the requirements of Article 6.

The third point relates to the anomalous consequences of the present age of   **11–07**
criminal responsibility, as it applies to those charged with murder. The applicants

---

[16] Para. 86.
[17] The applicants were seated next to social workers in a specially raised dock so that they could see
the witnesses and the judge; their parents and lawyers were seated "within whispering distance"; the
hearing times were shortened to reflect the school day; and they were permitted to spend time with
their parents and social workers in a play area during adjournments.

in *T and V* argued before the Commission that the attribution of full criminal responsibility for murder to a child of 10 was incompatible with Article 14 in conjunction with Article 6. Their argument, in summary, was that a fixed age of 10 was arbitrary and disproportionate when the applicants' position was compared with that of a child just under 10, or an adult whose mental age was that of a 10 year old. Article 14 will, of course, only be violated where there is a difference in treatment between persons in a "relevantly similar" position which pursues no legitimate aim, or bears no reasonable relationship of proportionality to the aim which it pursues.[18] In *T and V* the underlying issue of proportionality fell to be considered in the context of the applicants' Article 6 complaint, and accordingly the Article 14 point was not pursued before the Court. It is nevertheless worth recalling the anomaly that a child of 10 whose mental age corresponds with his chronogical age will be held fully responsible for murder in England and Wales, whereas a child who is a few months younger cannot be held criminally responsible at all, and an adult with a mental age of 10 would, almost certainly, be able to rely on the defence of diminished responsibility so as to reduce the offence to one of manslaughter.[19] This perhaps gives some indication of just how far out of line domestic law on this issue has become.

11–08 In a strongly worded dissent on this point, five judges considered that the age of criminal responsibility was fixed so low as to violate Article 3:

> "As far as the age of criminal responsibility is concerned, we do not accept the conclusion of the Court that no clear tendency can be ascertained from the developments amongst European States and from international instruments. Only four Contracting States out of 41 are prepared to find criminal responsibility at an age as low as, or lower than, that applicable in England and Wales. We have no doubt that there is a general standard amongst the Member States of the Council of Europe under which there is a system of relative criminal responsibility beginning at the age of 13 or 14—with special court procedures for juveniles—and providing for full criminal responsibility at the age of 18 or above. Where children aged from 10 to about 13 or 14 have committed crimes, educational measures are imposed to try to integrate the young offender into society. Even if Rule 4 of the Beijing Rules does not specify a minimum age of criminal responsibility, the very warning that the age should not be fixed too low indicates that criminal responsibility and maturity are related concepts. It is clearly the view of the vast majority of the Contracting States that this kind of maturity is not present in children below the age of 13 or 14. In the present case we are struck by the paradox that, whereas the applicants were deemed to have sufficient discrimination to engage their criminal responsibility, a play area was made available for them to use during adjournments."

B. INSANITY

11–09 In Convention terms, the detention of persons found not guilty by reason of insanity falls to be considered under Article 5. The key provision is Article 5(1)(e), which permits "the lawful detention of . . . persons of unsound mind."

---

[18] See para. 2–135 above.
[19] Section 2 of the Homicide Act 1957 specifically refers to abnormality of mind arising from *inter alia* "arrested or retarded development of mind".

The guiding principles were first laid down in *Winterwerp v. Netherlands*,[20] where the Court had to consider a number of basic questions about the application of Article 5(1)(e). Three of the points made by the Court have potential implications for the insanity defence in English criminal law.

First, whilst the Court declined to lay down a definition of unsoundness of mind   **11–10**
and recognised that the meaning of the term is changing as psychiatry evolves,[21] it laid emphasis on the importance of a close correspondence between expert medical opinion and the definition of mental disorder used in the domestic law.[22] In this country a close correspondence does not exist on certain issues. Thus the courts have tried to draw a distinction between insanity and automatism by developing the notion that "diseases of the mind" which spring from "internal" causes should be classified as insanity whereas those that spring from "external" factors should be classified as automatism. Not only is this distinction unknown to, and probably rejected by, current medical opinion; it has also led to special verdicts of insanity in cases of epilepsy,[23] diabetes leading to hyperglycaemia,[24] and sleep-walking,[25] none of which would be regarded as forms of mental disorder by current psychiatric opinion.[26] There is therefore a strong argument for reforming the insanity verdict so as to avoid this wide divergence between medical opinion and the existing law, developed as it has been from the *M'Naghten* Rules of 1843.[27] The inadequacy of the *M'Naghten* Rules as the basis for a finding of insanity was recognised by the Royal Commission on Capital Punishment in 1953, by the Butler Committee on Mentally Abnormal Offenders in 1975, and in the Law Commission's draft Criminal Code in 1989. As Professor Mackay has observed,[28] "the manner in which the judiciary have interpreted 'disease of the mind' is largely governed by policy considerations, and has little or nothing to do with the practice of psychiatry".[29] In the absence of legislative reform, courts should at least refrain from depriving of his liberty a defendant who is acquitted on grounds of insanity in a case falling outside current psychiatric definitions. Committal to hospital in such cases could well violate the

---

[20] (1979–80) 2 E.H.R.R. 387. See also *Luberti v. Italy* (1984) 6 E.H.R.R. 440.
[21] At para. 37.
[22] At paras 37 to 39.
[23] *Sullivan* [1984] 1 A.C. 156.
[24] *Hennessy* [1989] 1 W.L.R. 287.
[25] *Burgess* [1991] 2 Q.B. 92.
[26] In this context it is worth noting that the Supreme Court of Canada has categorised sleepwalking as a form of non-insane automatism, on the basis that it is not a neurological, psychiatric or other illness. Although the court did not support the internal/external distinction, it pointed out that sleepwalking does not fall clearly on either side of the line: *Parks* (1993) 15 C.R. (4th) 289.
[27] See P.J. Sutherland and C.A. Gearty, "Insanity and the European Court of Human Rights" [1992] Crim. L.R. 418, for an elaboration of this and other relevant arguments.
[28] Professor R.D. Mackay, *Mental Condition Defences in the Criminal Law* (Oxford, 1995).
[29] Professor H.L.A. Hart explained the evolution of this conflict between law and psychiatry in *Punishment and Responsibility, Essays in the Philosophy of Law*: "This dispute raged throughout the nineteenth century and was certainly marked by some curious features. In James Fitzjames Simon's great *History of the Criminal Law* the dispute is vividly presented as one between doctors and lawyers. The doctors are pictured as accusing the lawyers of claiming to decide a medical or scientific issue about responsibility by out of date criteria when they limited legal inquiry to the question of knowledge. The lawyers replied that doctors, in seeking to give evidence about other matters, were attempting illicitly to thrust upon juries their views on what should excuse a man when charged with a crime; illicitly because responsibility is a question not of science but of law."

defendant's Article 5 rights.[30] In *Attorney General v. Prior,*[31] the Royal Court of Jersey declined to adopt the *M'Naghten* rules as the basis for the defence of insanity[32] holding that they were arguably inconsistent with Article 5:

> "It is true that the Convention jurisprudence is looking at the matter from the perspective of the lawfulness of detaining a person of unsound mind rather than from the perspective of exculpation from criminal liability by reason of insanity. But these are simply different ends of the same spectrum. If a person is excused from responsibility for a criminal act by his insanity, he is liable to be detained during Her Majesty's Pleasure.[33] That detention will be unlawful unless it complies with the requirements of the Convention."

11–11   A second point made by the Court in *Winterwerp* is that decisions on unsoundness of mind "call for objective medical expertise" and that a defendant deprived of liberty under Article 5(1)(e) should be "reliably shown to be 'of unsound mind' ". The Criminal Procedure (Insanity and Unfitness of Plead) Act 1991 has improved matters somewhat, in that section 1(1) prohibits a court from returning an insanity verdict "except on the written or oral evidence of two or more registered medical practitioners at least one of whom is duly approved." This brings English law closer to compliance with the requirements of Article 5, although the wording states only that the court should receive such evidence, not that it should follow it. It would be a bold course of reasoning to go further and argue that section 3(1) of the Human Rights Act 1998, read in conjunction with section 1 of the 1991 Act, opens the way for the courts to bring the substantive definition of the defence of insanity closer to current psychiatric opinion.[34]

11–12   A third point concerns cases in which committal to hospital follows automatically from a special verdict. Although the 1991 Act conferred on the courts a discretion in the disposal of most special verdict cases,[35] committal to hospital indefinitely remains mandatory where "the offence to which the special verdict [relates] is an offence the sentence for which is fixed by law." Until 1997 the only practical example of this was murder, for which, despite the availability of diminished responsibility, there remains a trickle of insanity verdicts.[36] Since 1997 there are also cases where a mandatory sentence of life imprisonment applies on a second conviction for a serious offence, under section 2 of the Crime (Sentences) Act 1997, unless the court finds "exceptional circumstances".[37] On the assumption that section 2 creates a "sentence fixed by law", and in the rare case where an insanity verdict is returned, the court is at least required to begin

---

[30] Since the Criminal Procedure (Insanity and Unfitness to Plead) Act 1991, the disposal decision has been at the discretion of the court in all cases in which the penalty is not mandatory: see further para. 11–12 below.

[31] Unreported, February 2001.

[32] Within the meaning of the Criminal Justice (Insane Persons) Jersey Law 1964.

[33] There is no equivalent in Jersey of the sentencing discretion afforded in England and Wales by the Criminal Procedure (Insanity and Unfitness to Plead) Act 1991.

[34] This bold course is examined by E. Baker, "Human Rights, *M'Naghten* and the 1991 Act" [1994] Crim. L.R. 84.

[35] For discussion, see S. White, "The Criminal Procedure (Insanity and Unfitness to Plead) Act 1991" [1992] Crim. L.R. 4.

[36] There were four insanity verdicts in murder cases in the five years 1992–96: R.D. Mackay and G. Kearns, "More Fact(s) about the Insanity Defence" [1999] Crim. L.R. 714.

[37] As to the meaning of exceptional circumstances in the context of the Human Rights Act 1998, s.3, see *R. v. Offen* [2001] 1 W.L.R. 253. See also paras 3–32a above and 16–39 below.

from the assumption that it is obliged by the 1991 Act to commit the defendant to hospital, without receiving medical advice on whether that course is necessary. The Court in *Winterwerp* held that, before a person is deprived of liberty, "the mental disorder must be of a kind or degree warranting compulsory confinement".[38] Mandatory committal to hospital leaves no opportunity for such a finding. Moreover, in cases where the special verdict is based on the "internal factors" doctrine (*e.g.*, epilepsy, hyperglycaemia, sleep-walking), it is highly unlikely that compulsory confinement would be necessary. This yields two possible conclusions. First, if the 1991 Act cannot be read compatibly with Article 5(1)(e) in cases where the sentence for the offence is fixed by law,[39] there may be grounds for the issue of a declaration of incompatibility under section 4 of the Human Rights Act 1998.[40] Secondly, even in cases where the court has a discretion as to disposal under the 1991 Act, it ought to be satisfied that the defendant's disorder is "of a kind or degree warranting compulsory confinement" before it makes such an order, if Article 5 is to be complied with.

One final point about the insanity defence concerns the burden of proof. The **11–13** general issues raised by Article 6(2) in the context of "reverse onus" provisions are considered in Chapter 9, but it is convenient at this point to mention the burden of proof where insanity is raised. In the leading case of *Woolmington v. DPP*,[41] insanity was identified as the only common law exception to the principle that the prosecution should prove guilt beyond reasonable doubt. In general, where a common law defence is in issue, the defendant bears no more than an evidential burden to raise the defence, and then the prosecution must disprove the defence beyond reasonable doubt. The imposition of a purely evidential burden does not infringe the presumption of innocence in Article 6(2) of the Convention.[42] But if insanity is the defence, the accused must go further than discharging an evidential burden, and must prove on a balance of probabilities that he or she comes within the *M'Naghten* Rules.

It may be thought that this would infringe the presumption of innocence, but **11–14** when the argument was put to the Commission in 1990, it declared the application inadmissible.[43] The current position may or may not be justifiable under Article 6(2), but the Commission's reasoning on the point was apparently a long way wide of the mark. It held that "requiring the defence to *present evidence* concerning the accused's mental health at the time of the offence" was compatible with the presumption of innocence. But this, of course, neglects the difference between the presentation of evidence, which may be equated with an evidential burden, and the ultimate burden proving insanity to the court on the balance of probabilities. The Commission went on to remark that "in English law the burden of proof remains with the prosecution to prove beyond reasonable

---

[38] In *Winterwerp* the Court expressed its full agreement with the view that "no one may be confined as a 'person of unsound mind' in the absence of medical evidence establishing that his mental state is such as to justify his compulsory hospitalisation", (1979–80) 2 E.H.R.R. 387, para. 39, quoting from para. 76 of the Commission's report.

[39] It may well be possible for the House of Lords to overrule previous decisions such as *Sullivan* [1984] 1 A.C. 156 and to alter the common law so as to align the definition of insanity with current psychiatric opinion.

[40] See para. 3–35 above.

[41] [1935] A.C. 462.

[42] *R. v. DPP ex parte Kebilene and ors* [1999] 3 W.L.R. 972 (H.L.) *per* Lord Hope.

[43] Application No. 15923/89 noted at (1990) 87 Law Society Gazette 31.

doubt that the accused did the act or made the omission charged". This may be true as a general principle, but it does not alter the fact that the defendant bears the burden of proving insanity. In an attempt to square this circle, the Commission characterised the existing rule as relating to the presumption of sanity, rather than the presumption of innocence. Once again, this a highly questionable distinction given that a person found insane, in the *M'Naghten* sense is, as a matter of English law, not guilty of any offence. The best jusitification for the Commission's conclusion lies in its observation that the burden imposed on the accused in insanity cases is neither arbitrary nor unreasonable. This is a point which has been taken up in some of the Canadian decisions.[44]

11–15   In Canada the reverse onus in insanity cases was challenged under the Charter in the leading case of *Chaulk*.[45] A majority of the Supreme Court found that the reverse onus provision was incompatible with the presumption of innocence declared by the Charter, but was saved by section 1 of the Charter as being a "reasonable limit" on the presumption of innocence which was "demonstrably justifiable" because the burden of the prosecution would otherwise be virtually impossible. The *Oakes* test of proportionality[46] was held to be fulfilled, and so the reverse onus survives.

11–16   Whilst there were other issues in the case,[47] it must be said that the majority's reasoning on this point fails to grapple with the practical or theoretical basis for distinguishing insanity from the other defences on the issue of burden of proof. There would appear to be no insurmountable obstacle to a rule which places a merely evidential burden on the accused. This would require the introduction by the defence of medical evidence sufficient, if left uncontradicted, to raise a reasonable doubt as to the sanity of the accused. It would then be for the prosecution to call evidence to disprove this. In *R. v. DPP ex parte Kebilene* Lord Hope pointed out that the courts had declined to impose a persuasive onus in cases of non-insane automatism, despite the conceptual proximity of the two defences. Lord Hope cited the words of Lord Devlin in *Hill v. Baxter*[48]: "As automatism is akin to insanity in law there would be a great practical advantage if the burden of proof was the same in both cases. But so far insanity is the only matter of defence in which, under the common law, the burden of proof has been held to be completely shifted."

11–17   One might equally ask the question the other way around—why should the law impose a persuasive burden in cases of insanity, when this has not been found necessary in cases of automatism? In the United States it seems that about half of the states place only an evidential burden on the defendant in insanity cases, whereas the other half go further and impose a legal burden of proof.[49] The

---

[44] For a wide-ranging examination of this topic, see T.H. Jones, "Insanity, Automatism and the Burden of Proof on the Accused" (1995) 111 L.Q.R. 475.

[45] [1990] 3 S.C.R. 1303.

[46] See para. 9–20 above.

[47] Notably the exploration of the view that the insanity defence is not a mere negation of *mens rea* or *actus reus* but relates to a basic precondition of all criminal responsibility, expounded in the judgment of McLachlin J.

[48] [1958] 1 Q.B. 277 at 285.

[49] S.H. Kadish and S.J. Schulhofer, *Criminal Law and its Processes* (6th ed., 1995), p. 936.

United States Supreme Court has, however, held that it is not contrary to the Constitution to place the legal or persuasive burden on the accused.[50]

C. DIMINISHED RESPONSIBILITY

Section 2 of the Homicide Act 1957 introduced the defence of diminished **11–18** responsibility, so as to reduce homicide from murder to manslaughter where the accused was suffering from such abnormality of mind (whether arising from a condition of arrested or retarded development of mind or any inherent causes or induced by disease or injury) as substantially impaired his mental responsibility. Section 2(2) provides that "it shall be for the defence to prove that the person charged is by virtue of this section not liable to be convicted of murder". The compatibility of this onus of proof was considered in *R. v. Lambert and Ali*.[51] The Court held that since proof of diminished responsibility was pre-eminently a matter for defence evidence, and since proof of the contrary was extremely difficult for the prosecution, section 2 of the 1957 Act was compatible with Article 6(2).

---

[50] *Patterson v. New York* 432 U.S. 197 (1977).
[51] [2001] 2 W.L.R. 211, para. 1118 (CA).

CHAPTER 12

DOUBLE JEOPARDY

A. Introduction

In its report on *Double Jeopardy and Prosecution Appeals*[1] the Law Commission **12–01** recommended that the Court of Appeal should have power to set aside an acquittal for murder and order a retrial where there is compelling new evidence of guilt and the Court is satisfied that it would be in the interests of justice to do so. The Law Commission concluded that the introduction of such a procedure would be compatible with the provisions of the Convention and, in particular, with Article 4 of Protocol 7. Article 4 provides:

"1. No one shall be liable to be tried or punished again in criminal proceedings under the jurisdiction of the same state for an offence for which he has already been finally acquitted or convicted in accordance with the law and penal procedure of that state.
    2. The provisions of the preceding paragraph shall not prevent the reopening of the case in accordance with the law and penal procedure of the state concerned, if there is evidence of new or newly discovered facts, or if there has been a fundamental defect in the previous proceedings, which could affect the outcome of the case.
    3. No derogation from this article shall be made under Article 15 of the Convention."

Protocol 7 was adopted so as to bring the Convention into line with the broader **12–02** range of rights protected under the International Covenant on Civil and Political Rights[2] (ICCPR). In its White Paper, *Rights Brought Home*,[3] the Government expressed its intention to sign, ratify and incorporate Protocol 7 once certain provisions of national law, outside the scope of the present work, have been amended. In order to understand the impact of Article 4 of Protocol 7 on domestic law, it is necessary to consider the practice of other Council of Europe Member states, the current approach in England and Wales, the approach taken under the ICCPR, and the caselaw under the Convention.

B. The Approach in Other Council of Europe Member States

All European states recognise the principle that once ordinary appellate remedies **12–03** have been exhausted, or the relevant time limit for appealing has expired, a conviction or acquittal is to be regarded as irrevocable, and acquires the quality of *res judicata*.[4] However many states permit a final decision to be reopened if fresh evidence becomes available which demonstrates that the original verdict

---

[1] Law Commission No. 267, January 24, 2001.
[2] See *Rights Brought Home*, Cmnd. 3782, paras 4.9 and 4.14. As to the ICCPR see above.
[3] Cmnd. 3782, (1997).
[4] See Explanatory Report to Protocol 7 of the Convention, CE Doc H (83) 3, para. 22.

was wrong or if there has been a fundamental defect in the original proceedings. Provisions which permit the reopening of a final conviction or acquittal generally require the involvement of an appellate court. Where the original verdict is set aside in accordance with such a procedure the appellate court may, in some states, order a retrial. The power of an appellate court to reopen criminal proceedings, and to order a retrial, is thus to be distinguished from the concept of double jeopardy as it is understood in common law systems. In many European jurisdictions, the prohibition on double jeopardy operates to prevent prosecuting authorities from commencing a fresh prosecution on their own initiative. It does not necessarily prevent an appellate court from overturning a final conviction or acquittal and ordering a retrial.

12–04   There is considerable variation between the practices adopted on this issue in the criminal procedure systems which make up the Council of Europe. In Italy, for example, once ordinary appellate remedies have been exhausted, a judgment becomes final and an acquitted or convicted person may not be tried again for the same offence, even if relevant new facts or evidence has become available.[5] In Finland, on the other hand, any criminal proceedings can be reopened if an acquittal has been obtained through fraud; and an acquittal in respect of an aggravated offence can be reopened if, within a year, fresh evidence becomes available which could have led to a conviction or a penalty which is substantially more severe than that which was actually imposed.[6]

12–05   Provisions permitting a final conviction or acquittal to be reopened are to be found in the criminal procedure systems of a number of Western European states.[7] In some states the rules apply in the same way whether it is the prosecution which is seeking to overturn a final acquittal, or the defence which is seeking to overturn a final conviction. In other states the right to apply to an appellate court to reopen a criminal verdict which has the force of *res judicata* is available only to the defence.

12–06   The absence of a European consensus on these procedural issues has inhibited the adoption of a uniform double jeopardy principle in international human rights law. However, a clear distinction is drawn in most states between the power of an appellate court to reopen proceedings and to order a retrial; and the prohibition on a second prosecution for the same offence, initiated by the prosecuting authorities without the involvement of an appellate court.

C. ENGLAND AND WALES

12–07   The position in England and Wales is a hybrid. The defence may seek to reopen criminal proceedings which have resulted in a final verdict of guilty, even where all ordinary remedies have been exhausted and the verdict has acquired the force of *res judicata*. This power is exercised through the jurisdiction of the Court of

---

[5] See generally Van Den Wyngaert, *Criminal Procedure Systems in the European Community* (Butterworths, 1993), p. 258.
[6] See Finland's Reservation to the ICCPR, para. 6, cited in Nowak, *CCPR Commentary* (Engel, 1993), p. 753.
[7] See generally Nowak pp 272–273.

Appeal to entertain an appeal out of time, and through the powers of the Criminal Cases Review Commission to refer a case back to the Court of Appeal. On such an appeal, the Court of Appeal may quash the conviction on the basis of fresh evidence, or a fundamental defect (such as material non-disclosure), subject always to the requirement that the new consideration is such as to render the conviction unsafe. In either case the Court of Appeal has, since 1988, had the power to order a retrial without infringing the prohibition on double jeopardy.

Sections 54 to 56 of the Criminal Procedure and Investigations Act 1996 **12–08** introduced a new procedure whereby the prosecution may apply to reopen an acquittal which has acquired the force of *res judicata*, if there is convincing evidence that the acquittal was tainted by intimidation of a witness or juror. Again, the consequence of such an order is that the accused may be retried without infringing the prohibition on double jeopardy. The procedure applies where a person has been acquitted of an offence and either the defendant or another person has been convicted of an administration of justice offence involving the intimidation of a juror or witness in the proceedings which led to the acquittal.[8] In those circumstances, if it appears to the court before which the latter was convicted that "there is a real possibility that, but for the interference or intimidation, the acquitted person would not have been acquitted" the court shall certify that it so appears.[9] The power is not, however, to be exercised if, because of the lapse of time, or for any other reason, it would be contrary to the interests of justice to take proceedings against the acquitted person for the offence of which he has been acquitted.[10] Where such a certification is issued, the prosecution may apply to the High Court for an order quashing the acquittal.[11] The High Court is required to quash the acquittal if, but only if, four conditions are satisfied:

(a) It appears to the High Court that it is *likely* that, but for the interference or intimidation, the acquitted person would not have been acquitted[12];

(b) It does not appear to the High Court that, because of the lapse of time or for any other reason, it would be contrary to the interests of justice to take proceedings against the acquitted person for the offence of which he has been acquitted[13];

(c) The acquitted person has been given a reasonable opportunity to make written representations to the Court[14]; and

(d) It appears to the Court that the conviction for the administration of justice offence will stand.[15]

The effect of an order quashing a conviction is that "proceedings may be taken against the acquitted person *for the offence of which he was acquitted*".[16] The

---

[8] Section 54(1).
[9] Section 54(2).
[10] Sections 54(2)(b) and 54(5).
[11] Section 54(3).
[12] Section 55(1).
[13] Section 55(2).
[14] Section 55(3).
[15] Section 55(4). The Court should not quash the conviction if, at the time the application is made, the time limit for appeal against conviction for the administration of justice offence has not expired, or an appeal is pending: s.55(6).
[16] Section 54(4).

Act does not permit the prosecution to bring proceedings for another offence based upon the same facts, even if that offence is less serious than the offence of which the accused was originally convicted.

12–09   In England and Wales there is, at present, no procedure permitting the prosecution to apply to an appellate court to reopen a final acquittal on fresh evidence grounds. The prosecution are thus prevented by the prohibition on double jeopardy from commencing a fresh prosecution for the same offence, since such a prosecution could only be brought on the initiative of the prosecutor alone, without the involvement of an appellate court. In those circumstances the accused is entitled to rely on the plea in bar of *autrefois acquit*.

D. ARTICLE 14 OF THE INTERNATIONAL COVENANT ON CIVIL AND POLITICAL RIGHTS

12–10   The drafting of ICCPR was carried out by the United Nations Human Rights Commission in parallel with the drafting of the Convention by the Council of Europe in the immediate aftermath of the Second World War. The two organisations worked closely together on the texts, and the Council of Europe relied in part on the drafts prepared by the Human Rights Commission.[17] The ICCPR was not however finally adopted by the General Assembly of the United Nations until 1966, and did not enter into force until 1976. The rights contained in the ICCPR are broadly similar in their content to those contained in the Convention, although there are a number of significant differences.

12–11   Article 14(7) of the ICCPR provides: "No one shall be liable to be tried or punished again for an offence for which he has already been finally convicted or acquitted in accordance with the law and penal procedure of each country."

Article 14 applies both to the reopening of a conviction and to the reopening of an acquittal. Read literally, it therefore prohibits even the power of an appellate court to quash a criminal conviction and to order a retrial if fresh evidence or a procedural defect is discovered after the ordinary appeals process has been concluded.

12–12   In the drafting process which led to the adoption of the ICCPR the Committee of Experts of the Council of Europe noted that in many European states it was permissible to reopen criminal proceedings which had acquired the force of *res judicata*, where there had been serious procedural flaws or fresh evidence had become available.[18] They considered such procedures to be arguably inconsistent with Article 14(7) and recommended that states which permitted the reopening of criminal proceedings should submit a formal reservation. Reservations were

---

[17] The interrelation between the ICCPR and the Convention is explained in Cohen-Jonathon, *La Convention Europeenne des Droits de L'Homme* (Paris, 1989), at p. 15ff.
[18] CE Doc H (70) 7, 40 f. para. 149.

submitted by Austria,[19] Denmark,[20] Finland,[21] Iceland,[22] the Netherlands,[23] Norway[24] and Sweden.[25]

In its General Comment on Article 14(7)[26] however, the United Nations Human **12–13** Rights Committee, the treaty body charged with implementing the ICCPR, expressed the view that the reopening of criminal proceedings "justified by exceptional circumstances", did not infringe the principle of double jeopardy (*ne bis in idem*), even in respect of those states which had not lodged a reservation. The Committee drew a distinction between the "resumption" of criminal proceedings, which it considered to be permitted by Article 14(7), and "retrial" which was expressly forbidden:

> "In considering state reports, differing views have often been expressed as to the scope of paragraph 7 of Article 14. Some states parties have even felt the need to make reservations in relation to procedures for the resumption of criminal cases. It seems to the Committee that most states parties make a clear distinction between a resumption of a trial justified by exceptional circumstances and a retrial prohibited pursuant to the principle of *ne bis in idem* as contained in paragraph 7. This understanding of the meaning of *ne bis in idem* may encourage states parties to reconsider their reservations to Article 14, paragraph 7."

The distinction between "resumption" and "retrial" is not one which has so far **12–14** been expressly recognised in the law of England and Wales.[27] However, as we have explained above, it is a distinction which is, in substance, reflected in the power of the Court of Appeal to order a retrial following an appeal brought out of time or on a reference by the Criminal Cases review Commission, and in the statutory provisions permitting the reopening of an acquittal tainted by intimidation.[28]

The dividing line between what is permitted by Article 14(7) and what is **12–15** forbidden thus rests primarily upon the involvement of an appellate court. Article 14(7) permits a state's prosecuting authorities to apply to "reopen" an acquittal, in exceptional circumstances, after it has the quality of *res judicata*; but it prevents the prosecuting authorities from bringing fresh criminal proceedings on

---

[19] Nowak pp 750–751, para. 4(c).
[20] Nowak p. 753, para. 2(b).
[21] Nowak pp 753–754, para. 6.
[22] Nowak pp 757–758, para. 4.
[23] Nowak p. 765.
[24] Nowak p. 765.
[25] Nowak p. 766.
[26] Gen C 13/21. Para 19, reproduced in Nowak pp 857–861.
[27] The distinction between resumption and retrial has been expressly rejected by the Inter-American Commission of Human Rights (IAC). Article 8(4) of the American Convention on Human Rights (ACHR) provides: "An accused person acquitted by a non-appealable judgment shall not be subjected to a new trial for the same cause". In the *Garcia Case* (Case No. 10.006 (Peru) 1994 Annual Report 71 at 102) the Commission observed that on a literal reading Art. 8(4) referred only to a "new trial" and did not therefore expressly prohibit the "reopening" of criminal proceedings. The Commission held however that the protection afforded by Art. 8(4) "implicitly includes those cases in which reopening a case has the effect of reviewing questions of fact and law which have come to have the authority of *res judicata*". The approach of the IAC may be explained by the fact that Art. 8(4) of the ACHR applies only in relation to acquittals, and not in relation to convictions.
[28] The Criminal Procedure and Investigations Act 1996, ss.54 to 56.

their own initiative. This distinction has taken firm root in European human rights law, and is now reflected in Article 4(2) of Protocol 7 to the European Convention.

E. ARTICLE 4 OF PROTOCOL 7

I. *General*

12–16   When the Convention was drafted in 1950, the original signatory states made no express reference to the prohibition on double jeopardy. In its early caselaw the Commission left open the question whether the principle could be implied into the right to a fair trial in Article 6.[29] However, in 1983, in *S v. Federal Republic of Germany*,[30] the Commission held that "the Convention guarantees neither expressly nor by implication the principle of *ne bis in idem*". Shortly after this decision, on November 22, 1984, Protocol 7 to the Convention was opened for signature. It entered into force, in respect of those states which had ratified it, on November 1, 1988.

12–17   Article 4(1) embodies the principle of double jeopardy as it applies to the unilateral action of a prosecuting authority, or private prosecutor. The Explanatory Report to Protocol 7[31] makes it clear that the words "under the jurisdiction of the same state" are intended to limit the operation of Article 4 to the national level.[32] Article 4(1) does not therefore prohibit successive prosecutions for the same offence in different countries,[33] and thus appears to be narrower than the domestic rules on double jeopardy which have been assumed to encompass a conviction before a foreign court.[34]

12–18   As to the degree of finality required before Article 4(1) can be invoked, the Explanatory Report states that "the principle established in this provision applies only after the person has been finally acquitted or convicted in accordance with the law and penal procedure of the state concerned".[35] A decision is to be regarded as final;

> "if, according to the traditional expression, it has acquired the force of *res judicata*. This is the case when it is irrevocable, that is to say when no further ordinary remedies are available or when the parties have exhausted such remedies or have permitted the time limit to expire without availing themselves of them".[36]

---

[29] See, for example, *X v. Austria* (1970) 35 C.D. 151.
[30] (1983) 39 D.R. 43.
[31] CE Doc H (83) 3.
[32] Explanatory Report at para. 27.
[33] The United Nations Human Rights Committee has adopted the same construction in relation to Art. 14(7) of the ICCPR: *AP v. Italy* (Application No. 204. 1986, para. 7.3).
[34] *R. v. Roche* (1775) 1 Leach 134; *R. v. Aughet* 13 Cr. App. R. 101; *R v. Lavercombe* [1988] Crim. L.R. 435; *R. v. Thomas* [1985] Q.B. 604. *Cf. R. v. Beedie* [1998] Q.B. 356, where the Court of Appeal held that the plea of *autrefois acquit* was confined to a prosecution for the same offence in law.
[35] Explanatory Report at para. 29.
[36] Explanatory Memorandum at para. 22, adopting the commentary on Art. 1(a) of the European Convention on the International Validity of Criminal Judgments (1970).

Article 4(2) permits a case to be "reopened", in accordance with the provisions   **12–19**
of domestic law, "if there is evidence of new or newly discovered facts", or if
there has been "a fundamental defect in the previous proceedings". In either case
the new consideration must be such as could have an affect on the outcome of the
case. It thus preserves the power of an appellate court to overturn an acquittal or
conviction outside the ordinary appeals process, and to order a retrial. So far as
the prosecution are concerned, this exceptional power may only be exercised on
the two grounds specified in Article 4(2). However, the Explanatory Report
makes clear that Article 4 imposes no limitation on the grounds upon which an
appellate court may reopen criminal proceedings to the benefit of the
defence.[37]

The exceptions permitted by Article 4(2) have their origins in the practice of   **12–20**
those European states which submitted reservations to Article 14(7) of the
ICCPR,[38] and in the approach taken by the United Nations Human Rights
Committee in its General Comment on Article 14.[39] In relation to acquittals, the
fundamental defect exception is now reflected in sections 54 to 56 of the
Criminal Procedure and Investigations Act 1996 (CPIA), which provide a means
of reopening an acquittal which is tainted by intimidation. However, there is at
present no parallel in the law of England and Wales for the fresh evidence
exception in relation to acquittals.

There is very little guidance in the Court's caselaw concerning the scope of the   **12–21**
fresh evidence exception in Article 4(2). There are however two limitations in the
wording of Article 4(2) itself. The evidence must be such as "could affect the
outcome of the case" and it must be evidence of "a new or newly discovered
fact". The first requirement is analogous to the condition in section 55(1) of the
CPIA in relation to tainted acquittals: the evidence must be such that it is *likely*
that if it has been presented to the trial court, the accused would not have been
acquitted. This obviously involves a requirement that the evidence must be
credible and relevant. But it also involves a requirement that the evidence must
be sufficiently probative of guilt to have a significant and substantial effect on the
outcome of the case.

Turning to the requirement for evidence of "new or newly discovered facts", this   **12–22**
requirement is not intended to confine the operation of Article 4(2) to wholly new
factual elements in the case. The Explanatory Memorandum makes it clear that
the term "new or newly discovered facts" includes "new means of proof relating
to previously existing facts".[40] However, in using the words "new or newly
discovered", Article 4(2) obviously contemplates evidence which was not available to the prosecuting authorities at the time of the trial. This caters for the
position where a new witness comes forward, or new scientific techniques
produce incriminating evidence which was not previously available. A further
possible consequence relates to changes in the rules governing the admissibility
of evidence. If the law were amended so as to render admissible evidence which

---

[37] Para. 31 states: "Furthermore, this article does not prevent a reopening of the proceedings in favour
of the convicted person and any other changing of the judgment to the benefit of the convicted
person".
[38] See para. 12–12 above.
[39] See para. 12–13 above.
[40] Explanatory Report at paras 30–31.

the prosecution had previously been unable to adduce, such evidence might be thought to constitute a "new means of proof relating to previously existing facts", in the words of the Explanatory Report. This would of course involve a retrospective application of the criminal law, but the Commission has in the past held that the retrospective application of an important precedent in the law of evidence was not in violation of Article 7.[41]

II. *The Strasbourg Caselaw*

12–23 The first case in which the European Court of Human Rights considered Article 4 of Protocol 7 was *Gradinger v. Austria*.[42] The applicant was convicted of a criminal offence of causing death by negligent driving, but acquitted of the aggravated form of the offence. The offence of which he was acquitted required proof that the amount of alcohol in his blood exceeded the prescribed limit at the time of the offence. It was not in dispute that the applicant had consumed alcohol on the day of the offence, but the court accepted medical evidence which placed his blood/alcohol level at the time of the collision beneath the prescribed limit. The local administrative authorities subsequently acquired a medical report which contradicted the evidence adduced by the applicant at his trial. On the basis of the new report the authorities imposed an administrative penalty (a fine) on the applicant for driving with excess alcohol.

12–24 The Court concluded that Article 4(1) was applicable in these circumstances. Although the second set of proceedings were classified as "administrative" for the purposes of national law, they fell to be categorised as criminal proceedings for the purpose of the Convention.[43] In determining whether Article 4(1) had been violated, the Court adopted a substantive rather than a formalistic approach to the double jeopardy principle. Although the elements of the two offences were different, and they pursued different aims, the blood/alcohol level required for the two offences was the same. Since both charges were "based on the same conduct" the Court concluded that there had been a violation of Article 4.

12–25 There is no discussion in the judgment of the effect of Article 4(2), and it seems clear that the Court did not consider it to be relevant. The imposition of the administrative penalty did not involve a "reopening" of the earlier proceedings because (a) there was no requirement for the authorities to seek a ruling from an appellate court overturning the acquittal, and (b) the subsequent proceedings involved a different charge. It appears that if, instead of imposing an administrative penalty for the less serious offence, the authorities had been able to apply to a court to reopen the applicant's acquittal for the aggravated criminal offence, this would have complied with the requirements of Article 4(2). This apparently anomalous result reflects the limits inherent in Article 4 itself.

12–26 In the subsequent case of *Oliveira v. Switzerland*[44] the Court recognised that successive prosecutions will not violate Article 4 if they relate to two separate

---

[41] *X v. United Kingdom* (1976) 3 D.R. 95.
[42] Judgment October 23, 1995, unreported.
[43] Applying the criteria laid down by the Court in *Engel v. Netherlands (No.1)* (1979–80) 1 E.H.R.R. 647 and *Ozturk v. Germany* (1984) 6 E.H.R.R. 409.
[44] Judgment July 30, 1998, unreported.

offences arising out of the same course of criminal conduct. The applicant was involved in a road traffic accident in which another motorist was seriously injured. As the result of an administrative error, her case was dealt with by the police magistrate, whose jurisdiction was limited to minor offences. The magistrate convicted the applicant of a minor offence of failing to control her vehicle, and imposed a fine of CHF 200. He had no jurisdiction to consider the more serious offence of negligently inflicting physical injury, and he failed to refer the case to the district attorney, as he was required to do under the relevant provisions of Swiss law. The district attorney's office subsequently issued a penal order fining the applicant CHF 2000 for the more serious offence of negligently injuring the other motorist. The applicant appealed against the order to the Zurich District Court and subsequently to the Zurich Court of Appeal. The conviction was upheld, but the fine was reduced, and the applicant was given credit for the fine imposed by the magistrate.

The applicant complained that she had been prosecuted twice in respect of the same offence. The Court rejected this complaint, holding that this was "a typical example of a single act constituting various offences". As the Court explained: **12–27**

> "The characteristic feature of this notion is that a single criminal act is split up into two separate offences, in this case the failure to control the vehicle and the negligent causing of physical injury. In such cases, the greater penalty will usually absorb the lesser one. There is nothing in that situation which infringes Article 4 of Protocol No. 7 since that provision prohibits people being tried twice for the same offence, whereas in cases concerning a single act constituting various offences, one criminal act constitutes two separate offences."

The Court observed that it would have been more consistent with the principles governing the proper administration of justice for sentence in respect of both offences to have been passed by the same court in a single set of proceedings. Nevertheless, the fact that this had not occurred was irrelevant to the issues arising under Article 4 since; " . . . that provision does not preclude separate offences, even if they are all part of a single criminal act, being tried by different courts, especially where, as in the present case, the penalties were not cumulative, the lesser being absorbed by the greater."   **12–28**

The decision in *Olivera* confirms the previous practice of the Commission which has consistently distinguished between successive prosecutions for the same offence, and prosecutions for multiple offences arising out the same facts. In *Palaoro v. Austria*,[45] for example, the Commission rejected as manifestly ill-founded a complaint brought under Article 4 by an applicant who had been convicted of two offences of exceeding the prescribed speed limit in the course of a single journey, since the two offences had been committed on separate sections of road. Similarly, in *Iskandarani v. Sweden*,[46] the Commission rejected a complaint under Article 4 where the applicant had previously been convicted of abducting his daughter, and was subsequently prosecuted for withholding the child from its legal custodian after the abduction had occurred. These were   **12–29**

---

[45] Application No. 16718/90, unreported.
[46] Application No. 23222/94, unreported.

separate offences arising out the same course of criminal conduct. Article 4 of Protocol 7 did not prohibit separate proceedings for such offences.

F. THE LAW COMMISSION PROPOSAL

12–30 In its report *Double Jeopardy and Prosecution Appeals*[47] the Law Commission recommended that the common law prohibition on double jeopardy—the rules of *autrefois acquit* and *autrefois convict*—should be put into statutory form. In principle the new statutory rule would apply not only to decisions of the national courts, but to foreign convictions or acquittals. However, the English court would be permitted to disregard a verdict delivered in a foreign jurisdiction if the judge was satisfied that it would be in the interests of justice to do so, having regard in particular to the independence and impartiality of the tribunal concerned. In the case of a conviction, the rule would apply even where the convicting court had imposed no sentence for the offence. It would also extend to offences which have been "taken into consideration" for the purposes of sentence, without a formal verdict having been recorded. The most far-reaching aspect of the proposal, however, was the recommendation of a fresh evidence exception in cases where there has been an acquittal for murder.

12–31 When the proposal was first put forward in the Law Commission's consultation paper on double jeopardy[48] it was to apply to all offences. The paradigm example of the mischief which the reform was intended to redress was the situation in which forensic techniques unavailable at the time of the original trial point conclusively to the guilt of an acquitted person. The responses from consultees revealed a deep division of opinion on the issue. A majority of individual judges who responded supported the new exception, but the Council of H.M. Circuit Judges was against it. A majority of individual practitioners who responded supported the change, but it was opposed by the Criminal Bar Association, the London Criminal Courts Solicitors Association and the Criminal Law Committee of the Law Society. The police and prosecuting authorities were in favour of change, the academic community against it. The public were equally divided. In the end, the Law Commission appears to have opted for a middle path—a pragmatic compromise between the two opposing views. Whilst recognising the strength of feeling against the proposed reform, it concluded that there was a case for treating murder as a special exception:

> "Murder, as the most serious form of homicide, is in a unique position and can as a matter of principle be separated off from all other offences . . . Confining the exception to murder would meet our requirement that its scope should be clear cut and notorious. By radically reducing the number of acquitted defendants to whom the exception could ever apply, it would also reduce the number who might be subject to a continuing fear of their acquittals being reopened. It is a striking fact, moreover, that all of the factual or near-factual concrete examples of cases in which it has been suggested that the new evidence exception could be used have been cases of murder."

12–32 This explanation is not convincing. Whilst it may be true that the crime of murder has a special place in the criminal law, it is difficult to justify treating a conviction

---

[47] Law Commission No. 267, January 24, 2001.
[48] CP 156.

for murder differently on the ground of the moral culpability of the offender. As the Law Commission itself recognised, "there is probably no offence in the criminal calendar that varies so widely both in character and in degree of moral guilt as that which falls within the legal definition of murder".[49] The anomalous result of the proposal is that where fresh evidence has become available there could be a second prosecution for murder in respect of a doctor convicted of mercy killing, or a person who used excessive force in the course of a pub brawl, but not in respect of a serial rapist or a habitual paedophile. This distinction is difficult to defend either in terms of the moral culpability of the offender or in terms of danger which the offender poses to the public.

At the root of the issue lies a debate about the relative weight to be attached to **12–33** the values of accuracy and finality in the criminal justice system. If the sole criterion for reform is to improve the accuracy of the trial process then there are powerful arguments against a rule which erects an insurmountable obstacle preventing an acquitted defendant from being brought to justice where overwhelming evidence of guilt has subsequently come to light. But accuracy is not the only value at stake[50] and there is a strong body of opinion in favour of a rule which ensures finality as a safeguard against oppression and unfair delay, and promotes probity and diligence in the investigation of crime. The balance to be struck between these opposing positions is surely a question of principle. It cannot be made to depend on the categorisation of a particular offence within the outdated framework of the law of homicide. Whilst the Law Commission's approach has the advantage of limiting the number of cases to which the new exception could apply, it fails to grapple with the underlying issues which have divided judicial, professional and public opinion on the subject. That said, however, the proposal is undoubtedly compatible with the limited requirements of Article 4 of Protocol 7.

Equally controversial was the Law Commission's proposal to give retrospective **12–34** effect to the change. The basis for this recommendation was explained in the report in these terms:

> "If the new exception were not retrospective, it could well be a number of years before it could be used. In deciding to recommend a new exception we have taken account of the fact that, in recent years, we have seen considerable advances in forensic science, particularly in DNA analysis. It is the possibility of bringing these new techniques to bear on materials from old cases that is likely to constitute a major source of cases said to fall within the new exception. If there were no retrospective effect, the potential advantage in being able to bring these new techniques to bear on materials from old cases would be lost . . . [A]rbitrary distinctions would be drawn between persons who happened to have been acquitted before and after the relevant date . . . [W]e do not believe that a person against whom there is compelling evidence of guilt should be protected by a mere accident of timing."

The Law Commission rightly concluded that if the new exception were to be **12–35** given retrospective effect, it would not breach Article 7[51]:

---

[49] Para. 4–34 citing the Report of the Committee on the Penalty for Homicide (1993), chaired by Lord Lane.
[50] Hence the principle that "a conviction may be unsafe even where there is no doubt about guilt but the trial process has been vitiated by serious unfairness or significant misdirection" *R. v. Davis, Rowe and Johnson* [2001] 1 Cr.App.R. 115. See generally para. 17–25 *et seq.* below.
[51] See generally para. 2–85 and Chapter 10 above.

"The objective of [Article 7] is to ensure that a person should be able to judge, at the time of engaging in particular conduct, whether or not it amounts to a crime. The article does not, however, prohibit retrospective changes in the rules of criminal procedure so as to remove a bar or obstacle to a prosecution. The requirements of Article 7 are, in our view, satisfied if the conduct in question constituted a crime at the time when the offence was committed: it is immaterial that the procedural rules in existence at the time of an acquittal or conviction prevented it from being reopened. Article 7 would not prevent the reopening of such an acquittal or conviction under provisions subsequently coming into force."

CHAPTER 13

BAIL

A. INTRODUCTION

The right to apply for bail pending trial is governed by Articles 5(3) and 5(4) of **13-01** the Convention, and by the presumption of innocence in Article 6(2). The compatibility of the Bail Act 1976 with the Convention caselaw under these provisions was considered in detail by the Law Commission, in a consultation paper published in November 1999.[1] The consultation paper recommended the amendment or repeal of a number of statutory provisions, the publication of detailed guidance on the application of others and, more generally, the provision of training for judges and magistrates on making and recording of bail decisions in a way which is compliant with Articles 5 and 6. The enactment of the New Zealand Bill of Rights Act led to similar calls for a tightening of remand procedures so as to give greater weight to the presumption of innocence,[2] and there have been a number of successful challenges to bail legislation under the Canadian Charter.[3] Following consultation the Law Commission adopted an altogether more cautious approach in its final report, *Bail and the Human Rights Act 1998*.[3a] In this Chapter we consider the Convention caselaw, and the decisions reached by the domestic courts under the 1998 Act, against the background of the criticisms made in the Law Commission's original consultation paper and its final recommendations.[3b]

B. GENERAL PRINCIPLES

Article 5(3) provides that every person who has been arrested or detained in **13-02** accordance with Article 5(1)(c) must be brought promptly before a judge or other judicial officer and is entitled to trial within a reasonable time or to release pending trial. The state is obliged to take the initiative for a detained person to be brought before an appropriate tribunal. In *McGoff v. Sweden*[4] the Commission held that Article 5(3) imposes an "unconditional obligation" on the state to bring the accused "automatically and promptly" before a court.[5] The term "judge or other officer authorised by law" has the same meaning as the term "competent

---

[1] Consultation Paper No. 157, *Bail and the Human Rights Act 1998*.
[2] See the discussion of the judgment in *Gillbanks v. Police* [1994] 3 N.Z.L.R. 61 by the New Zealand Court of Appeal in *Tonihi* [1995] 1 N.Z.L.R. 154.
[3] N. Padfield, "The Right to Bail: a Canadian Perspective" [1993] Crim. L.R. 510.
[3a] Law Commission No. 269, June 21, 2001.
[3b] For the Law Commission's revised position see Law Commission No. 269, June 21, 2001.
[4] (1982) 31 D.R. 72.
[5] This decision does not appear to have been cited in *Olotu v. Home Office* [1997] 1 W.L.R. 328 where Lord Bingham C.J. held that detention following the expiry of custody time limits did not involve a breach of Art. 5(3) because the relevant legislation placed the onus on the defendant to make an application for bail.

legal authority" in Article 5(1)(c).[6] The tribunal must be independent of the investigating and prosecuting authorities,[7] and it must be impartial in the sense of being free from actual bias and from the appearance of bias.[8] It must also be empowered to make a legally binding decision ordering release.[9] In addition;

" . . . under Article 5(3) there is both a procedural and a substantive requirement. The procedural requirement places the 'officer' under the obligation of himself hearing the individual brought before him; the substantive requirement imposes on him the obligations of reviewing the circumstances militating for or against detention, of deciding, by reference to legal criteria, whether there are reasons to justify detention and of ordering release if there are no such reasons".[10]

Whilst a criminal court, acting in accordance with the Bail Act 1976, will generally meet these structural requirements, the detention of service personnel pending a court martial by order of the commanding officer has been held to violate the independence and impartiality standard implicit in Article 5(3).[11]

13–03 The second limb of Article 5(3) expressly entitles an accused person "to trial within a reasonable time or to release pending trial". The use of the word "or" does not indicate that prompt trial is an alternative to release on bail.[12] As the Court explained in *Wemhoff v. Germany*[13]; "[S]uch an interpretation would not conform to the intention of the High Contracting Parties. It is inconceiveable that they should have intended to permit their judicial authorities, at the price of release of the accused, to protract proceedings beyond a reasonable time."

13–04 Accordingly, the Court has held that the proper construction of Article 5(3) is that a person charged with an offence must always be released pending trial unless the state can show that there are "relevant and sufficient" reasons to justify his continued detention.[14] Moreover, the state must show that detention in penal custody is required. Where an accused person is suffering from mental disorder, a therapeutic measure (such as supervision in the community or committal to a mental hospital) is more likely to comply with Article 5.[15]

13–05 Article 5(3) applies throughout the period from the arrest of an accused to his conviction or acquittal by the trial court, but not to detention pending appeal.[16]

---

[6] *Lawless v. Ireland (No. 3)* (1979–80) 1 E.H.R.R. 15, paras 13–14; *Ireland v. United Kingdom* (1979–80) 2 E.H.R.R. 25, para. 199; *Schiesser v. Switzerland* (1979–80) 2 E.H.R.R. 417, para. 29. On Art. 5(1)(c), see para. 5–13 above.
[7] *De Jong, Baljet and Van Den Brink v. Netherlands* (1986) 8 E.H.R.R. 20, para. 49; *Schiesser v. Switzerland* (1979–80) 2 E.H.R.R. 417, paras 29 and 30.
[8] *Huber v. Switzerland* (1990) Series A/188, para. 43. *Cf.* the Court's interpretation of the impartiality requirement in Art. 6(1) (see paras 14–67 *et seq.* below).
[9] *Ireland v. United Kingdom* (1979–80) 2 E.H.R.R. 25, para. 199.
[10] *Schiesser v. Switzerland* (1979–80) 2 E.H.R.R. 417, para. 31.
[11] *Hood v. United Kingdom, The Times*, March 11, 1999; *Jordan v. United Kingdom, The Times*, March 17, 2000.
[12] *Neumeister v. Austria (No. 1)* (1979–80) 1 E.H.R.R. 91, para. 4; *Wemhoff v. Germany* (1979–80) 1 E.H.R.R. 55, paras 4–5.
[13] (1979–80) 1 E.H.R.R. 55, para. 5.
[14] *Wemhoff v. Germany* (1979–80) 1 E.H.R.R. 55, para. 12; *Yagci and Sargin v. Turkey* (1995) 20 E.H.R.R. 505, para. 52.
[15] *Clooth v. Belgium* (1992) 14 E.H.R.R. 717 at para. 40.
[16] *Wemhoff v. Germany* (1979–80) 1 E.H.R.R. 55, paras 7–9; *B v. Austria* (1991) 13 E.H.R.R. 20, paras 36–40.

The procedural requirements imposed by Article 5(4) where a court is considering bail in criminal proceedings are discussed in detail below. In brief, the defence must be afforded adequate access to the evidence in the possession of the prosecution, and the procedure must ensure equality of arms and be "truly adversarial".[17] The court is obliged to pay due regard to the presumption of innocence[18] and must record the arguments for and against release in a reasoned ruling.[19]

C. GROUNDS FOR REFUSAL OF BAIL

I. *The Strasbourg Principles*

The European Court of Human Rights has recognised four principal grounds **13–06** upon which a national court may legitimately rely in refusing bail under Article 5(3). Whilst these reasons broadly coincide with certain of the grounds specified under the Bail Act 1976, it should not be assumed that the Human Rights Act will have no impact in this field. The Court has consistently stressed the need for concrete evidence in bail decisions, and the need to avoid abstract or generalised reasoning. As we shall see, the Law Commission's audit of bail law for compatibility with the Convention identified a number of areas of mismatch.

Risk that the accused will fail to appear for trial

The Court has held that a defendant may be remanded in custody pending trial, **13–07** consistently with Article 5(3), where there is well-founded fear that if released on bail he would fail to surrender. Refusal of bail on this ground requires "a whole set of circumstances . . . which give reason to suppose that the consequences and hazards of flight will seem to him to be a lesser evil than continued imprisonment".[20] Relevant considerations are those "relating to the character of the person involved, his morals, his home, his occupation, his assets, his family ties, and all kinds of links with the country in which he is being prosecuted".[21] The severity of the potential sentence, though important, is not an independent ground and cannot itself justify the refusal of bail.[22] The fact that it is possible for the accused to escape from the jurisdiction does not necessarily warrant the conclusion that he would abscond if released.[23] If the risk of absconding is the only justification for the detention, release of the accused pending trial should be ordered if it is possible to impose adequate and enforceable bail conditions. In *Wemhoff v. Germany*[24] the Court held that:

"[T]he concluding words of Article 5(3) of the Convention show that, when the only remaining reason for continued detention is the fear that the accused will abscond and

[17] *Lamy v. Belgium* (1989) 11 E.H.R.R. 529, para. 29.
[18] *Letellier v. France* (1992) 14 E.H.R.R. 83, para. 35.
[19] *Letellier v. France* (1992) 14 E.H.R.R. 83, para. 35; *Yagci and Sargin v. Turkey* (1995) 20 E.H.R.R. 505, para. 52.
[20] *Stögmüller v. Austria* (1979–80) 1 E.H.R.R. 155, para. 15.
[21] *Neumeister v. Austria (No. 1)* (1979–80) 1 E.H.R.R. 91, para. 10.
[22] *Neumeister v. Austria (No. 1)* (1979–80) 1 E.H.R.R. 91, para. 10; *Letellier v. France* (1992) 14 E.H.R.R. 83, para. 43.
[23] *Stogmuller v. Austria* (1979–80) 1 E.H.R.R. 155.
[24] (1979–80) 1 E.H.R.R. 55, para. 15.

thereby subsequently avoid appearing for his trial, his release pending trial must be ordered if it is possible to obtain from him guarantees that will ensure such appearance."

13–08 More controversially, the Court has held that the risk of a defendant absconding diminishes as the trial approaches, a view which some English judges may find difficult to accept. In *Neumeister v. Austria*[25] the Court explained its reasoning as follows:

> "The danger of flight necessarily decreases as the time spent in detention passes by, for the probability that the length of detention on remand will be deducted from the period of imprisonment which the person concerned may expect, if convicted, is likely to make the prospect seem less awesome to him and reduce his temptation to flee".

Interference with the course of justice

13–09 Bail may be refused under Article 5(3) where there is a well-founded risk that the accused, if released, would take action to prejudice the administration of justice.[26] The risk may involve interference with witnesses, warning other suspects, or the destruction of relevant evidence.[27] However, the Court has held that a generalised risk is insufficient. The risk must be identifiable and there must be evidence in support.[28] Further, the court must bear in mind that this risk will often diminish with time, once the investigation has concluded.[29] In *Letellier v. France,* for example, the Court accepted that "a genuine risk of pressure being brought on the witnesses may have existed initially", but took the view that this risk had "diminished and indeed disappeared with the passing of time."[30] In particular, if the accused has previously been on bail and there is no evidence that he or she interfered with the course of justice during that period, this will be a strong factor militating against a custodial remand on this ground.[31]

Prevention of further offences

13–10 The public interest in the prevention of crime may justify detention on remand where there are good reasons to believe that the accused, if released, would be likely to commit further offences.[32] However, the danger must be "a plausible one" and the appropriateness of a remand in custody on this ground must be considered "in the light of the circumstances of the case and, in particular, the

---

[25] *Neumeister v. Austria* (1979–80) 1 E.H.R.R. 91, para. 10.

[26] *Wemhoff v. Germany* (1979–80) 1 E.H.R.R. 55, para. 14.

[27] *Letellier v. France* (1992) 14 E.H.R.R. 83, para. 39; *Wemhoff v. Germany* (1979–80) 1 E.H.R.R. 55.

[28] *Clooth v. Belgium* (1992) 14 E.H.R.R. 717, para. 44; *Tomasi v. France* (1993) 15 E.H.R.R. 1, paras 84 and 91. This does not necessarily have to be evidence which would be admissable at trial: *R. v. Havering Magistrates Court, ex parte DPP* [2001] 1 W.L.R. 805.

[29] *Clooth v. Belgium* (1992) 14 E.H.R.R. 717, para. 43; *W v. Switzerland* (1994) 17 E.H.R.R. 60, para. 35; *Letellier v. France* (1992) 14 E.H.R.R. 83, para. 39.

[30] (1992) 14 E.H.R.R. 83, at para. 39; to same effect, *Clooth v. Belgium* (1992) 14 E.H.R.R. 717 at para. 43.

[31] *Ringeisen v. Austria (No.1)* (1979–80) 1 E.H.R.R. 455 at para. 106; after the accused had been on bail for five months, the Austrian court used this reason in support of a custodial remand, without referring to any particular evidence in support. The European Court commented that this "does not stand up to examination."

[32] *Matznetter v. Austria* (1979–80) 1 E.H.R.R. 198, para. 9; *Toth v. Austria* (1992) 14 E.H.R.R. 551, para. 70; *Clooth v. Belgium* (1992) 14 E.H.R.R. 717, para. 40.

past history and the personality of the person concerned".[33] A risk of further offences cannot be automatically assumed from the fact that the accused has a criminal record.[34] The court should consider whether any previous convictions are "comparable, either in nature or in the degree of seriousness to the charges preferred against [the accused]".[35] The Court has also emphasised that a risk of trivial offences is insufficient.[36] Where the mental condition of a person charged with murder is cited as a ground for refusal of bail, steps should be taken to provide him with the necessary psychiatric care whilst on remand.[37]

The preservation of public order[38]

Where the nature of the crime alleged and the likely public reaction to it are such   **13–11**
that the release of the accused may give rise to public disorder, then temporary detention on remand may be justified.[39] In *Letellier v. France*,[40] the Court emphasised that this ground was confined to exceptional offences which "by reason of their particular gravity and public reaction to them . . . may give rise to a social disturbance". The Court has held that a premeditated act of terrorism by an organisation which has caused death or serious injury may qualify as such a risk.[41] In *AI v. France*[42] the Court observed that there may be cases in which; " . . . the safety of a person under investigation requires his continued detention, for a time at least. However, this can only be so in exceptional circumstances having to do with the nature of the offences concerned, the conditions in which they were committed and the context in which they took place."

Detention on this ground may only continue for as long as the threat to public order remains.[43]

II. *Application to the Bail Act 1976*

Section 4 of the Bail Act 1976 provides that a person brought before a magis-   **13–12**
trates' court or a Crown Court charged with a criminal offence has a right to be released on bail, unless one of the grounds for refusing bail set out in Part 1 of Schedule 1 applies. There are eight such grounds listed in the schedule. The first three grounds, which are most commonly invoked, are contained in paragraph 2. This provides that a defendant need not be granted bail if the court is satisfied that there are substantial grounds for believing that if released on bail he would (a) fail to surrender to custody, (b) commit an offence whilst on bail, or (c)

---

[33] *Clooth v. Belgium* (1992) 14 E.H.R.R. 717, para. 40.
[34] *Muller v. France* 1997–II, para. 44.
[35] *Clooth v. Belgium* (1992) 14 E.H.R.R. 717, para. 40.
[36] *Matznetter v. Austria* (1979–80) 1 E.H.R.R. 198 at para. 9 On the facts, the Court referred to "the very prolonged continuation of reprehensible activities and the huge extent of the loss sustained by the victims".
[37] *Clooth v. Belgium* (1992) 14 E.H.R.R. 717, para. 40.
[38] It should be noted that a provision in the Canadian Criminal Code which allowed courts to refuse bail on the ground that it was "necessary in the public interest" was struck down as unduly vague and contrary to the Canadian Charter: *Morales* [1992] 3 S.C.R. 711. For an accessible discussion, see N. Padfield, "The Right to Bail: a Canadian Perspective" [1993] Crim. L.R. 510.
[39] *Letellier v. France* (1992) 14 E.H.R.R. 83, para. 51.
[40] (1992) 14 E.H.R.R. 83.
[41] *Tomasi v. France* (1993) 15 E.H.R.R. 1, para. 91.
[42] 1998–IV Judgment September 23, 1998, para. 108.
[43] *Letellier v. France* (1992) 14 E.H.R.R. 83, para. 51; *Tomasi v. France* (1993) 15 E.H.R.R. 1, para. 91.

interfere with witnesses or otherwise obstruct the course of justice. It is not necessary for the court to conclude that one of these consequences will occur, or even that it is more likely than not. The court merely has to be satisfied that there are *substantial grounds for believing* that one of them would occur.[44] In considering any objection under paragraph 2 the court is required to "have regard" to (a) the nature and seriousness of the offence and the probable sentence, (b) the character, antecedents, associations and community ties of the defendant, (c) the defendant's history of compliance with any bail conditions previously imposed on him, and (d) the strength of the evidence. A defendant may also be denied bail under the Act if he is charged with an indictable offence or either way offence and is already on bail for another offence[45]; where it is necessary that he be kept in custody for his own protection[46]; if he is already serving a sentence of imprisonment[47]; if there is insufficient time to obtain the information necessary to make a bail decision[48]; or if he has been arrested for a Bail Act Offence.[49] In addition, section 25(1) of the Criminal Justice and Public Order Act 1984, as amended, imposes a statutory restriction on the grant of bail in respect of certain serious offences, where the defendant has a relevant previous conviction.[50] In its initial review of bail law for compatibility with the Convention,[51] the Law Commission considered that a number of these exceptions required amendment, repeal or clarification.

Paragraph 2(b): Risk of further offences

13–13 The criteria for a refusal of bail under paragraphs 2(a) and (c) appear to correspond closely with the Strasbourg caselaw. Providing there is convincing evidence in support of the alleged risk, and the decision is adequately reasoned,[52] it is unlikely that a refusal of bail on either of these grounds will violate Article 5(3). However, the refusal of bail on the ground that there is a risk that the accused would commit further offences (paragraph 2(b)), requires more detailed consideration. As we have seen, the Court has laid particular emphasis on the seriousness of the anticipated crimes and the need for real grounds establishing the likelihood of their commission.[53] This contrasts with paragraph 2(b), which contains no requirement that the potential offence(s) must be serious. It is notable in this connection that a recent amendment to the Irish Constitution provides for pre-trial detention where reasonably necessary "to prevent the commission of a *serious* offence by that person".[54]

13–14 In considering the compatibility of paragraph 2(b) with the Strasbourg caselaw, the Law Commission suggested that a defendant's previous convictions would be relevant only where they were comparable to the offence which it is feared that

---

[44] *R. v. Nottingham Justices ex parte Davies* [1981] Q.B. 38.
[45] Bail Act 1976, Sched. 1, Part 1, para. 2A.
[46] Bail Act 1976, Sched. 1, Part 1, para. 3.
[47] Bail Act 1976, Sched. 1, Part 1, para. 4.
[48] Bail Act 1976, Sched. 1, Part 1, para. 5.
[49] Bail Act 1976, Sched. 1, Part 1, para. 6.
[50] See para. 13–18 below.
[51] Consultation Paper No. 157, *Bail and the Human Rights Act 1998*.
[52] See para. 13–29 below.
[53] *Matznetter v. Austria* (1979–80) 1 E.H.R.R. 198 (para. 44).
[54] For analysis and discussion, see U. ni Raifeartaigh, "Reconciling Bail Law with the Presumption of Innocence" (1997) 17 Oxford J.L.S. 1.

the defendant might commit. It recommended that guidance be issued to judges and magistrates emphasising that bail should only be refused on this ground, where the offence feared might properly be characterised as "serious", and was likely to attract a custodial sentence; where it could be shown that there is a *real risk* of the defendant committing the offence; and where detention was the appropriate measure in the light of that risk, and all the circumstances of the case. In its final report the Law Commission suggested specific guidance to this effect.

Defendant already on bail

Paragraph 2A[55] of Schedule 1, Part 1, provides that a defendant need not be   **13–15** granted bail if he is charged with an indictable or either way offence, and he was already on bail for another offence on the date of the commission of the offence for which he is before the court. The Law Commission rightly pointed out that this is not among the *grounds* recognised in the Strasbourg caselaw as "relevant and sufficient". Whilst the fact that a defendant was already on bail at the date of his arrest *may* give reason to believe that there is a likelihood that he will commit further offences if released, this is by no means a necessary inference in every case. As the Law Commission observed:

> "In the first place, the court cannot simply assume, for the purpose of the bail decision, that the defendant did commit the offence charged: it must bear in mind the presumption of innocence under Article 6(2). Secondly, where there are substantial grounds for believing that the defendant would commit an offence if given bail, the right to bail is excluded by paragraph 2(b) anyway. If the fact that the defendant was on bail at the time of the alleged offence did justify the belief that he or she would commit an offence if given bail again, paragraph 2A would add nothing to paragraph 2(b). It is redundant unless that fact does *not* justify that belief. But in that case it is hard to see what legitimate purpose paragraph 2A serves."

Accordingly, the Law Commission provisionally recommended that this exception be repealed, and included instead amongst the list of factors which a court should take into account in deciding whether there is a risk that the accused will commit further offences. In its final report, however, the Law Commission recommended that the issue be resolved by judicial training. Judges and magistrates should be given guidance that the factors listed in paragraph 2A do not, in themselves, amount to a ground for the refusal of bail. To base a refusal of bail on those factors alone would be a breach of Article 5. On the other hand, they could legitimately be relevant factors in a decision to withhold bail on the basis of another exception such as the risk of further offences.

The defendant's own protection

Under paragraph 3 of Schedule 1, Part 1, bail need not be granted if the court is   **13–16** satisfied that the defendant should be kept in custody for his own protection. As the Law Commission has observed, this ground "might be invoked where the defendant is at risk of self-harm, or of harm from criminal associates, or where public feeling is running high because of the nature of the alleged offence".[56] In

---

[55] Inserted by the Criminal Justice and Public Order Act 1994, s.26.
[56] Consultation Paper No. 157, *Bail and the Human Rights Act 1998*, para. 2.28.

the light of the Convention caselaw, the Law Commission concluded that guidance should be issued to judges and magistrates making it clear this exception could only be compatible with the Convention if there are exceptional circumstances relating to the nature of the offence or the conditions or context in which it is alleged to have been committed. In its final report the Law Commission suggested specific guidance on this issue. As to a decision to remand an accused person in custody to protect him against a risk of self-harm, the Law Commission considered that this would be compatible with Article 5 provided the court was satisfied that the risk was real and that a proper medical examination would take place promptly.

Defendant arrested for a Bail Act offence

13–17 Paragraph 6 of Schedule 1, Part 1, provides that bail need not be granted if the defendant has previously been granted bail in the same proceedings, and has been arrested under section 7 of the Act (which relates to failure to surrender, absconding or breaching a bail condition). The Law Commission provisionally considered this exception to be objectionable in several respects. First, it assumes that merely because the accused has breached his bail conditions in the past, he is likely to do so again in the future. Whilst past breaches may be relevant in an assessment of whether the accused is likely to comply with any conditions of bail which the court may wish to impose, it cannot be conclusive. It may be an *argument* in favour of denying bail, but it cannot, in itself, be a *ground* for detaining a person in custody. Secondly, the exception applies to a person who has been arrested under section 7 by a constable who has reasonable grounds to believe that the defendant will abscond or break a bail condition *in the future*, and to a person who has been arrested on reasonable suspicion of having breached a condition of bail. In other words, it is not even necessary to establish that the person concerned has failed to comply with the conditions previously imposed on him. The Law Commission provisionally concluded that a refusal of bail under Paragraph 6 is likely to infringe Article 5, and accordingly recommended its repeal. The correct approach to section 7 was subsequently considered in *R. v. Havering Magistrates Court ex parte DPP.*[56a] Latham L.J. held that Article 6 was inapplicable to the procedure whereby the magistrates court considers whether to remand an accused in custody following arrest for breach, or potential future breach, of a bail condition. Accordingly, neither the strict rules of evidence nor the criminal standard of proof applied, and there was no power to adjourn the hearing. The Court held, however, that in order to give effect to the requirements of Article 5, paragraph 6 of Part I and paragraph 5 of Part II of Schedule 1 to the 1976 Act, which on their face appear to entitle a court to deny bail simply on the basis that the defendant has been arrested under section 7(3), should be construed as providing that such an arrest was capable of being taken into account in determining whether or not any of the grounds for refusing bail existed. This appears to meet the thrust of the Law Commission's objections without the necessity for repeal or amendment. In its final report, the Law Commission modified its approach, recommending that Magistrates should receive guidance to the effect that a decision to remand an accused person in custody simply on the ground that he has breached a condition of bail would not be compatible with Article 5 "because that breach might, in the circumstances of the case, be no

---

[56a] [2001] 1 W.L.R. 805.

indication of a real risk" that he is likely to abscond, commit further offences or interfere with the course of justice.

Section 25(1) of the Criminal Justice and Public Order Act 1984

In *Caballero v. United Kingdom*[57] the European Commission of Human Rights **13–18** concluded that section 25(1) of the Criminal Justice and Public Order Act 1984 was in breach of Article 5(3). As enacted, the section imposed an absolute prohibition on the grant of bail on a charge of murder, attempted murder, manslaughter, rape or attempted rape where the accused had a prior conviction for such an offence. It deprived the court of any jurisdiction to consider the individual circumstances of the case or of the accused. As the Commission pointed out, it imposed an obligation to refuse bail even in the theoretical case of a person who was totally paralysed. In the Commission's view; "[T]he exclusion from the risk assessment of a consideration of all the particular circumstances and facts of each accused's case (other than the two facts contained in section 25) exposes, of itself, accused persons to an arbitrary deprivation of liberty."

The Government accepted the Commission's conclusion, and conceded the **13–19** alleged violation before the Court.[58] In consequence, section 25 was amended (by section 56 of the Crime and Disorder Act 1998), so as to restore an element of judicial discretion. It now provides that: "A person who in any proceedings has been charged with or convicted of an offence to which this section applies . . . shall be granted bail in those proceedings only if the court . . . considering the grant of bail is satisfied that there are *exceptional circumstances* which justify it."

The difficulty with this formulation is that there is no statutory definition of the term "exceptional circumstances". It is unclear what has to be established or by whom. Is it, for example, sufficient for the accused to establish that there is no (or very little) risk of absconding, of the commission of further offences, or of interference with the course of justice? Or is it necessary to go further than that?

In *Niklovka v. Bulgaria*[59] the Court found a violation of Article 5[60] where the **13–20** national courts applied a strong presumption in domestic law against the grant of bail, without addressing specific submissions put to them. It does not of course follow that any presumption against the grant of bail will be incompatible with Article 5.[61] As we have seen,[62] the Strasbourg Court has held that the imposition of a reverse onus of proof may be compatible with the presumption of innocence, even where it applies to the establishment of guilt. However, the vice of section 25 as amended lies not so much in the fact that it creates a presumption (or reverse onus), but in the fact that the exceptional circumstances exception is open

---

[57] Application No. 4465/70 October 31, 1998; [1999] Crim. L.R. 228.
[58] *The Times,* February 28, 2000.
[59] Judgment March 25, 1999.
[60] The applicant's complaint was brought under Art. 5(4) which also applies to bail proceedings.
[61] Canadian law imposes on the defendant the burden of "showing cause" that a custodial remand is not justified, where the charge is a serious drug offence or an offence committed whilst on bail for another offence. This reverse onus provision was held compatible with the Canadian Charter in *Perason* [1992] 3 S.C.R. 365.
[62] See Chapter 9 above.

to widely differing interpretations. At one extreme, it might be read as depriving the court of any real discretion to grant bail in all but the most unusual cases. At the other extreme it might be read as entitling a court to grant bail where, having taken account of the matters referred to in the section, the court would otherwise consider the grant of bail to be appropriate. The Law Commission tentatively concluded that the former view would be incompatible with Article 5, whilst the latter view would be difficult, if not impossible, to reconcile with the statutory language (even with the benefit of the interpretative obligation imposed by section 3 of the Human Rights Act). In the Law Commission's opinion, the correct view was that in order to comply with Article 5(3), section 25 must be read in a way which gives appropriate weight to the statutory criteria whilst retaining a true judicial discretion—in effect, a middle path. Applying this approach, the court might legitimately attach special weight to the factors identified in the section, and might even treat them as decisive in the balance it has to perform. But it should not treat them as conclusive for the grant of bail since that would, in substance, involve returning section 25 to its original form. Whilst it was possible for the section, as currently drafted, to be applied in a manner compatible with Article 5(3), the Law Commission provisionally concluded that without amendment or judicial guidance, it was liable to misunderstood as having dispensed with the need to take all relevant circumstances into account.

13–20a In the light of the Court of Appeal decision in *Offen*,[63] construing the term "exceptional circumstances" in section 109 of the Powers of the Criminal Courts (Sentencing) Act 2000, the Law Commission's initial assessment appears overcautious. If the *Offen* approach is adopted in the present context, the court should treat section 25 as establishing a presumption that a defendant with a qualifying conviction will commit further serious offences. If the facts disclose that this assumption is misplaced then, applying section 3 of the Human Rights Act 1998 to the words of section 25(1), the Parliamentary intention behind the provision is not met, and the situation can properly be regarded as "exceptional". In its final report, the Law Commission appears to have adopted this approach, recommending judicial guidance to the effect that the expression "exceptional circumstances" should be construed "so that it encompasses a defendant who, if released on bail, would not pose a real risk of committing a serious offence". This would meet Parliament's intention by ensuring that "decision-takers focus on the risk the defendant may pose to the public by re-offending".[64]

D. CONDITIONS OF BAIL

13–21 Article 5(3) expressly provides that "release may be conditioned by guarantees to appear for trial". The Court in *Wemhoff* implied that, wherever conditional bail would be a satisfactory solution, it is to be preferred to a custodial remand—a point particularly relevant where the risk of absconding is the primary reason for continued detention.[65] Permissible conditions of bail under Article 5(3) include

---

[63] [2001] 1 W.L.R. 253. See para. 2–32a above.
[64] Guidance to Bail Decision-Takers, para. 18.
[65] (1979–80) 1 E.H.R.R. 55 at para. 15.

a requirement to surrender travel documents and driving documents,[66] the imposition of a residence requirement,[67] and the provision of a sum of money as a surety or security.[68] Where a financial condition is imposed the figure must be assessed by reference not to the financial loss occasioned by the alleged offence[69] but by reference to the means of the accused, if it is a security, or of the person standing surety, and of the relationship between the two.[70] If the accused refuses to furnish the necessary information to enable an assessment to be made of his assets, it is permissible to establish a bail figure based on hypothetical assets.[71] Where a person is charged with a minor public order offence, the practice of imposing a bail condition prohibiting the defendant from attending a demonstration or a picket may raise issues under Articles 10 or 11.[72]

E. PROCEDURAL REQUIREMENTS

I. *General*

Article 5(4) of the Convention provides that everyone who is deprived of his liberty is entitled to take proceedings by which the lawfulness of his detention can be decided speedily by a court and his release ordered if his detention is not lawful.[73] This guarantees the right to *habeas corpus* in order to challenge the legality of executive detention. It also applies to other proceedings in which a court is called upon to determine whether a person should be detained, including a bail application in criminal proceedings. In this context therefore, Article 5(4) overlaps with the requirements of Article 5(3). The former entitles the individual to apply to a court for his release and imposes certain procedural requirements, including the right to make repeated applications, whilst the latter governs the circumstances in which a court may extend pre-trial detention. The procedural requirements for a bail application in England and Wales are accordingly to be derived from a consideration of Articles 5(3) and 5(4) together. Article 6 does not apply directly, although the Court has been prepared to imply analogous procedural protection under Article 5(3) and (4). The extent of the analogy was considered in *R. v. Havering Magistrates Court ex parte DPP*[74] where Latham L.J. observed:

13–22

> "[T]he Court has been prepared to borrow some of the general concepts of fairness in judicial proceedings from Article 6. But that does not mean that the process required for conformity with Article 5 must also be in conformity with Article 6. That would

---

[66] *Stögmüller v. Austria (No. 1)* (1979–80) 1 E.H.R.R. 155, para. 15; Application No. 10670/83 *Schmid v. Austria* (1985) 44 D.R. 195.
[67] Application No. 10670/83 *Schmid v. Austria* (1985) 44 D.R. 195.
[68] *Wemhoff v. Germany* (1979–80) 1 E.H.R.R. 55.
[69] *Can v. Austria* (1984) 4 E.H.R.R. 121 (para. 31 Op. Comm).
[70] *Neumeister v. Austria* (1979–80) 1 E.H.R.R. 91, para. 14; *Schertenleib v. Switzerland* (1980) 23 D.R. 137 at 196.
[71] *Bonnechaux v. Switzerland* (1979) 18 D.R. 100 at 144.
[72] By analogy with *Steel v. United Kingdom* (1999) 28 E.H.R.R. 603.
[73] The term "lawfulness" in Art. 5(4) has the same meaning as the term "lawful" in Art. 5(1): *Brogan v. United Kingdom* (1989) 11 E.H.R.R. 117, para. 65.
[74] [2001] 1 W.L.R. 805.

conflate the Convention's control over two separate sets of proceedings, which have different objects."

II. *A fully adversarial hearing*

13–23 The minimum requirements for a "court" are the same under Article 5(4) and Article 5(1)(a),[75] namely independence of the executive and the parties, impartiality,[76] and a power to give a legally binding judgment concerning a person's release. On any Article 5(4) review, the burden of proving the lawfulness of the detention rests with the state.[77] If the state provides a right of appeal against a refusal to order release, the appeal body must itself comply with the requirements of Article 5(4).[78] The European Court of Human Rights has held that Article 5(4) requires procedural guarantees appropriate to the kind of deprivation of liberty in question.[79] The "equality of arms" principle which has been inferred by the Court into Article 6, also applies to Article 5(4) review[80]: the procedure adopted must "ensure equal treatment" and be "truly adversarial".[81] The detained person must be told the reasons for his detention[82] and be given disclosure of all relevant evidence in the possession of the authorities.[83] He must also have adequate time to prepare an application for release.[84] In *Lamy v. Belgium*[85] the Court held that the requirements of Article 5(4) had not been fulfilled when: " . . . the investigating judge and crown counsel had had an opportunity to make their submissions

---

[75] See Chapter 5 above.

[76] In *K v. Austria* (1993) Series A/255–B the Commission ruled that the requirement for impartiality was not satisfied where a judge who imposed a fine later ruled upon a person's detention for failure to pay the fine.

[77] *Zamir v. United Kingdom* (1983) 40 D.R. 42, para. 58.

[78] See *Toth v. Austria* (1992) 14 E.H.R.R. 551, para. 84, where the Court held that although Art. 5(4) does not require states to establish a second level of jurisdiction for applications for release from detention, where a system of appeal is established it 'must in principle accord to the detainees the same guarantees on appeal as at first instance'; *Navarra v. France* (1994) 17 E.H.R.R. 594, para. 28.

[79] *Wassink v. Netherlands* (1990) Series A/185–A, para. 30. See also *Winterwerp v. Netherlands* (1979–80) 2 E.H.R.R. 387, para. 60 (the procedural guarantees required by Art. 5(4) are "not always" the same as those required by Art. 6(1) for criminal or civil litigation). *Cf. Lamy v. Belgium* (1979–80) 11 E.H.R.R. 529, para. 29 (the appraisal of the need for a remand in custody in a criminal case and the subsequent assessment of guilt are 'too closely linked' to permit a wholly different approach to the duty of prosecution disclosure); *De Wilde Ooms and Versyp v. Belgium* (1979–80) 1 E.H.R.R. 373, paras 78–79 (procedural guarantees appropriate to a criminal prosecution required in proceedings leading to the detention of vagrants).

[80] See, *e.g. Toth v. Austria* (1992) 14 E.H.R.R. 551, para. 84 (prosecutor present at an appeal on the question of detention while the applicant was not: violation of Art. 5(4)). There are suggestions in some of the early cases that the "equality of arms" guarantee does not apply in Art. 5(4) proceedings: *Neumeister v. Austria (No. 1)* (1979–80) 1 E.H.R.R. 91 at 132, paras 22–25; approved in *Matznetter v. Austria* (1979–80) 1 E.H.R.R. 198 at 228, para. 13. These decisions have not, however, been followed: see *Toth v. Austria* (1992) 14 E.H.R.R. 551, para. 84; *Lamy v. Belgium* (1989) 11 E.H.R.R. 529, para. 29; *Sanchez-Reisse v. Switzerland* (1987) 9 E.H.R.R. 71, paras 52–52.

[81] *Toth v. Austria* (1992) 14 E.H.R.R. 551, para. 84; *Lamy v. Belgium* (1989) 11 E.H.R.R. 529, para. 29.

[82] *X v. United Kingdom* (1982) 4 E.H.R.R. 188, para. 66.

[83] *Lamy v. Belgium* (1989) 11 E.H.R.R. 529, para. 29; *Weeks v. United Kingdom* (1988) 10 E.H.R.R. 293, para. 66. *Cf. Wassink v. Netherlands* (1990) Series A/185–A, para. 28.

[84] *Farmakopoulos v. Belgium* (1993) 16 E.H.R.R. 187.

[85] (1989) 11 E.H.R.R. 529.

in full knowledge of the contents of a substantial file, while the defence could only argue its case on the vaguest of charges made on an arrest warrant."[86]

More recently, in *Nikolava v. Bulgaria*,[87] the Court held that "equality of arms is **13–24** not ensured if counsel is denied access to those documents in the investigation file which are essential in order effectively to challenge the lawfulness of his client's detention." Procedural standards of this kind pose particular problems for the English system. At remand hearings in England and Wales, the defence often have very little on which to base their submissions, and are unlikely to have sight of the contents of the file on which the prosecutor's representations are based. The Law Commission has rightly pointed out that there is no legal requirement in English law for disclosure in bail hearings[88]: "Practice may vary, but we suspect that disclosure may not always be made as matter of course, particularly at the first hearing after the defendant's arrest. If bail is refused where disclosure has not been made, it may be arguable that the hearing is not sufficiently 'adversarial' to satisfy Article 5(4)."

The scope of the disclosure obligation imposed by Article 5(4) is plainly less extensive than the obligation of disclosure imposed by Article 6 in relation to the trial.[89] However, the test adopted in *Nikolova* suggests that the defence must, as a minimum, have access to the documents necessary to enable an effective bail application to be made.

The absence of a legal obligation of disclosure for the purposes of bail hearings **13–24a** has, to some extent, been remedied by *R. v. DPP ex parte Lee*[90] where the Divisional Court held that for a bail application to be effective in a complex case there must be some residual duty of disclosure.[91] The Attorney General's Guidelines on *Disclosure of Information in Criminal Proceedings*[92] now provide that:

"Prosecutors must always be alive to the need, in the interests of justice and fairness in the particular circumstances of any case, to make disclosure of material after the commencement of proceedings but before the prosecutor's duty arises under the Act. For instance, disclosure ought to be made of significant information that might affect a bail decision . . . "

The Law Commission's final report notes that the duty of disclosure does not require that the whole of the prosecution file be made available to the defence

---

[86] *ibid.*, para. 27.
[87] March 25, 1999, unreported.
[88] Consultation Paper No. 157, *Bail and the Human Rights Act 1998*, para. 11.19.
[89] In *Rowe and Davies v. United Kingdom* (2000) 30 E.H.R.R. 1, (Op. Comm.) at para. 71, the Commission observed that the disclosure requirements imposed by Art. 6 are "more extensive" than those imposed by Art. 5(4). As to the obligation of disclosure under Art. 6 see generally paras 14–87 *et seq.* below.
[90] [1999] 2 All E.R. 237.
[91] See also *Procurator Fiscal, Glasgow v. Burn and McQuilken* 2000 J.C. 403, where the High Court of Justiciary held that whilst a prosecutor should be in a position to explain the basis for any fears that the accused may interfere with witnesses, he was not required to disclose sensitive operational information. *Cf. Garcia Alva v. Germany*, Judgment February 13, 2001, where the European Court of Human Rights found a violation of Article 5(4) arising from a failure of the prosecutor to disclose relevant evidence on grounds of its sensitivity.
[92] November 29, 2000.

prior to a bail hearing. It is sufficient if disclosure is provided of the material the defendant needs in order to enjoy "equality of arms" with the prosecution.[93]

III. *Legal representation*

13–25   Article 5(4) requires the provision of legal assistance, whenever this is necessary to enable the detained person to make an effective application for release.[94] In *Woukam Moudefo v. France*[95] the Commission considered that legal assistance should be available prior to the hearing as well as during it. The onus is on the state to take the initiative to provide legal representation[96] and to provide legal aid where representation is necessary and the detained person has insufficient means to pay for it.[97] Article 5(4) generally requires that a detained person or his legal representative be permitted to participate in an oral hearing.[98]

IV. *Presence of the accused*

13–26   It is unclear from the Convention caselaw whether Article 5(4) entitles the accused to be present during a bail application. In a number of decisions the Court has suggested that a detained person is entitled to be present in person at any Article 5(4) review, even if he is legally represented.[99] However in *Sanchez-Reisse v. Switzerland*,[1] which concerned the refusal of bail in extradition proceedings, the Court suggested that a right to participate in person had "no basis in the actual text of Article 5(4)". Providing the applicant had a proper opportunity to challenge the decision to detain him, either personally or through a lawyer, this would be sufficient. It is likely, therefore, that the requirements of Article 5(4) will depend on the facts of the case. Where the accused could reasonably be expected to make a contribution to the hearing, or where there are other strong arguments for his attendance, the safest course is to assume that he is entitled under Article 5(4) to be present.

13–27   Under English law, a defendant has no express right to be present at a bail application. Section 122 of the Magistrates Court Act 1980 entitles magistrates to proceed in the absence of a defendant, provided he is legally represented. In

---

[93] Guidance to Bail Decision-Takers, para. 28.
[94] *Winterwerp v. Netherlands* (1979–80) 2 E.H.R.R. 387, para. 60; *Bouamar v. Belgium* (1988) 11 E.H.R.R. 1, para. 60; *Megyeri v. Germany* (1993) 15 E.H.R.R. 584, paras 23–25; *Woukam Moudefo v. France* (1988) 13 E.H.R.R. 549.
[95] (1988) 13 E.H.R.R. 549.
[96] *Megyeri v. Germany* (1993) 15 E.H.R.R. 584, para. 27; *Winterwerp v. Netherlands* (1979–80) 2 E.H.R.R. 387, para. 66.
[97] Application 9174/80 *Zamir v. United Kingdom* (1983) 40 D.R. 42 at 60.
[98] *Keus v. Netherlands* (1991) 13 E.H.R.R. 700, para. 27; *Farmakopoulos v. Belgium* (1992) 16 E.H.R.R. 187, (para. 46); *Winterwerp v. Netherlands* (1979–80) 2 E.H.R.R. 387, para. 60; *Bouamar v. Belgium* (1989) 11 E.H.R.R. 1, para. 60; *Cf. Sanchez-Reisse v. Switzerland* (1987) 9 E.H.R.R. 71, para. 51 (written proceedings held sufficient in a case under Art. 5(1)(f)).
[99] See, for example, *Winterwerp v. Netherlands* (1979–80) 2 E.H.R.R. 387, which concerned an applicant detained in a psychiatric institution, where the Court held that a decision to proceed in the absence of a legally represented applicant should be regarded as an exceptional measure, only to be adopted where the applicant is unable to attend. See also *Assenov v. Bulgaria* [1999] E.H.R.L.R. 225, where the Court found a violation of Art. 5(4) in relation to a hearing which had taken place *in camera* and at which the applicant had not been heard in person.
[1] (1987) 9 E.H.R.R. 71.

practice, however, magistrates generally treat an accused person as entitled to be present, unless he or his legal representative invite the court to proceed in his absence. The Law Commission has suggested that magistrates "would expect the procedure to be challenged by judicial review if they gave their decision in the defendant's absence against his or her wishes".[2] The position in the Crown Court and the High Court, however, is different. In most cases, bail applications take place in chambers, and the defendant is not produced. Given the importance of what is at stake, it is difficult to see the public interest justification for a routine practice of determining such applications in the absence of the accused.[3] The Law Commission's final report suggests that participation through a legal representative will generally be sufficient, although a court should not finally dispose of a bail application in the absence of the defendant "where the defendant's presence is essential to fair proceedings".[4]

V. *A hearing in public?*

In its early decisions the Court held that there was no requirement under Article   **13–28**
5(4) that bail proceedings must take place in public. In *Neumeister v. Austria*[5] the Court observed that "publicity in such matters is not . . . in the interest of accused persons as it is generally understood". However, this was before the Court had developed its current emphasis on a fully adversarial procedure. In later decisions, the Court has implied that Article 5(4) hearings should ordinarily take place in public.[6] Once again, there is a distinction to be drawn between the practice in the magistrates court, where such applications are always heard in public, and the practice in the Crown Court and the High Court, where bail applications are invariably heard in chambers, irrespective of the facts of the case. A national court certainly has a discretion to sit in private where this is necessary in the interests of justice (see, generally, Article 6(1)). However, it is doubtful whether the current practice in the Crown Court and the High Court is fully compatible with Article 5(4). It may well be that in most cases it will be in the interests of the accused for the proceedings to take place in chambers (as, for example, where it is necessary to discuss the accused's previous convictions). But any defence application for the proceedings to be heard in open court should be scrutinised with care. The Law Commission's final report recommends that if the defendant requests that a bail hearing take place in public, then it should be held in public unless there are good reasons for not doing so.[7]

---

[2] Consultation Paper No. 157, *Bail and the Human Rights Act 1998,* para. 11.14, n. 18.
[3] Section 57 of the Crime and Disorder Act 1998 provides that a defendant may be permitted to participate in certain hearings via live television link. There seems to be no reason in principle why such facilities should not be used for the purposes of a bail application in the Crown Court or in the High Court if there are genuine obstacles to arranging for the accused to be produced.
[4] Guidance to Bail Decision-Takers, para. 27.
[5] (1979–80) 1 E.H.R.R. 91 at 132, para. 23. *Cf. De Wilde Ooms and Versyp v. Belgium* (1979–80) 1 E.H.R.R. 373 at 409, para. 79, where the Court suggested that a requirement for a public hearing and public pronouncement of judgment were "judicial features" required by Art. 5(4).
[6] *Assenov v. Bulgaria* [1999] E.H.R.L.R. 225 where the Court held that the fact that a hearing was held in a closed court was one of several factors contributing to a breach of Art. 5(4). See also *Nikolova v. Bulgaria*, March 25, 1999, unreported.
[7] Guidance to Bail Decision-Takers, para. 28.

VI. *The duty to give a reasoned ruling*

13–29 The Convention caselaw under Article 5(3) and (4) imposes an obligation on a court considering bail to give reasons for its decision. In *Letellier v. France*,[8] the Court explained that, in considering an application for bail, domestic courts:

> " . . . must examine all the facts arguing for and against the existence of a genuine requirement of public interest justifying, with due regard to the principle of the presumption of innocence, a departure from the rule of respect for individual liberty and set them out in their decisions on the applications for release. It is essentially on the basis of the reasons given in these decisions and of the true facts mentioned by the applicant in his application for release and his appeals that the Court is called upon to decide whether or not there has been a violation of Article 5(3) of the Convention."

13–30 The Court has stated on a number of occasions that the reasoning of the domestic courts will be regarded as inadequate if it is "abstract" or "stereotyped".[9] In *Van der Tang v. Spain*[10] the Court found no breach of Article 5(3) where the applicant's detention in custody was justified on the facts, and he was aware of the reasons on which it was based. Nevertheless, the Court emphasised the need for adequate reasoning. In response to the applicant's contention that "the decisions refusing to grant conditional release contained very poor reasoning", the Court stated that "it would certainly have been desirable for the Spanish courts to have given more detailed reasoning as to the grounds of the applicant's detention."[11]

13–31 Any requirement of detailed reasoning for custodial remands would necessitate considerable change in the practice of the English courts, but such a requirement appears to be the inevitable consequence of a strict adherence to the presumptions of innocence and liberty, and the right to full procedural justice if an individual is to be deprived of their liberty before trial. In practical terms, this would require not only greater care by magistrates and their clerks in formulating reasons for custodial remands, but also improved preparation of files by the police and Crown Prosecution Service. Moreover, the principle of equality of arms, as we have seen, means that the defence ought to be informed of the arguments they have to meet and the evidence on which they are based. Section 5(3) of the Bail Act provides that where a court refuses bail to a person to whom the right to bail applies "the court shall, with a view to enabling him to consider making an application in the matter to another court, give reasons for withholding bail". Despite this provision, the Law Commission concluded that adequately reasoned rulings are rarely given[12]:

> "In practice . . . we understand that bail decisions are commonly recorded on forms which require only the ticking of boxes to indicate both the grounds on which bail is denied and the statutory reasons for that conclusion . . . Our view of the Strasbourg case law is that reasons recorded simply by repeating the statutory wording on a standard form are likely to be considered 'abstract' or 'stereotyped' . . . [T]he Strasbourg Court

---

[8] (1992) 14 E.H.R.R. 83 at para. 35.
[9] *Clooth v. Belgium* (1992) 14 E.H.R.R. 717, para. 44; *Yagci and Sargin v. Turkey* (1995) 20 E.H.R.R. 505, para. 52; *AI v. France* 1998–IV Judgment September 23, 1998, para. 108.
[10] (1996) 22 E.H.R.R. 363.
[11] *ibid.*, para. 60.
[12] Consultation Paper No. 157, *Bail and the Human Rights Act 1998*, paras 4.20 to 4.21.

assumes that the quality of the reasons given indicates the quality of the decision-making process recorded. As a result, any refusal of bail which is recorded in standard form is in danger of being held to violate Article 5."

Moreover, the Law Commission could see no good reason in principle why bail   **13–32**
decisions should not be subject to the administrative law principle that when a
duty to give reasons arises, those reasons must be "clear and adequate and deal
with the substantial issues in the case".[13] Accordingly, the Law Commission
proposed that magistrates and judges should be given training on how to
approach bail decisions in a manner compatible with Article 5, and how to record
their decisions in a manner which clearly indicates how the decision has been
reached. In particular, magistrates courts should be required to use forms which
encourage an explanation of their decision, rather than a mere recitation of the
statutory criteria. The Law Commission's final report emphasises the need for
judges and magistrates to make a note for the file recording the gist of the
arguments adduced by both sides, and the oral reasons given in open court for a
remand in custody. As to the method of recording a decision it states that
"standard forms should be completed accurately and should show that a decision
has been taken in a way that complies with the Convention".[14]

VII. *Practical obstacles*

It is worth recalling that the remedy required by Article 5(4) must be available   **13–33**
in practice as well as in theory. In *RMD v. Switzerland*,[15] a prisoner on remand
was moved from one prison to another and across a number of Swiss cantons.
Although there was a procedure in each canton through which he could challenge
the lawfulness of his detention, the procedure had to be re-started each time the
prisoner was transferred from one canton to another. The Court held that
although appropriate procedures were theoretically available, the procedural
obstacles involved in using them were so great that the remedy was not effective
in practice, and there had accordingly been a violation of Article 5(4).

VIII. *Periodic reconsideration of remand in custody*

In *Bezicheri v. Italy*,[16] the Court held that a person who is detained before trial   **13–34**
should have the opportunity to test the lawfulness of continued detention at
reasonable intervals. The Italian government had argued that in cases of pre-trial
detention the intervals need not be so frequent as, for example, where a mentally
disordered person is detained. The Court rejected this approach in clear terms:
"The nature of detention on remand calls for short intervals; there is an assumption in the Convention that detention on remand is to be of strictly limited
duration . . . because its *raison d'etre* is essentially related to the requirements of
an investigation which is to be conducted with expedition."[17]

---

[13] *R. v. Immigration Appeal Tribunal ex parte Jebunisha Kharvaleb Patel* [1996] Imm. A.R. 161 at 167.
[14] Guidance to Bail Decision-Takers, paras 25 and 26.
[15] (1999) 28 E.H.R.R. 225.
[16] (1990) 12 E.H.R.R. 210.
[17] *ibid.*, at para. 21.

In that case the accused had re-applied within a month, and the Court regarded that as a reasonable interval, taking account of the need for the judge to examine the evidence and the fact that the accused was deprived of his liberty.[18] Other decisions lay emphasis on the possibility that the strength of reasons for refusing bail may diminish over time, and also on the insufficiency of courts relying on stereotyped formulae for continued remands in custody.[19]

13–35   It is open to question whether English law fully meets this requirement. In *R. v. Nottingham Justices ex parte Davies*[20] the Divisional Court held that a person may only make a renewed application for bail if there has been a "material change of circumstances". The Criminal Justice Act 1988 inserted a new Part IIA into Schedule 1 to the Bail Act. Paragraph 2 provides that this requirement does not apply to the second application for bail: "At the first hearing after that at which the court decided not to grant the defendant bail he may support an application for bail with any argument as to fact or law that he desires (whether or not he has advanced that argument previously)."

13–36   However, paragraph 3 goes on to provide that at any *subsequent* hearing, "the court need not hear arguments as to fact or law which it has heard previously". In *R. v. Barking Justices ex parte Shankshaft*,[21] the Divisional Court held that where a new argument for bail was advanced by the defendant, the court should consider that new argument in addition to any arguments which had previously been advanced. Applying this principle to paragraph 3, it would appear that where the accused is able to advance a new argument, he is entitled to rely on arguments previously considered as well. The fact remains, however, that there is no entitlement under English law to periodic reconsideration of bail on the ground of the passage of time. If the defendant is unable to advance any fresh arguments of fact or law after the second hearing, the court is not obliged to entertain the application. This appears to be inconsistent with Article 5(4).

13–37   In light of the Strasbourg caselaw, the Law Commission considered that an accused should be able to re-apply for bail at 28 day intervals, without having to advance any fresh arguments[22]:

> "Article 5(4) requires that the defendant should be able to mount a legal challenge to the grounds for detention, and, after the lapse of a reasonable time, should be able to do so again—even, it would seem, if there has been no change of circumstances other than the lapse of time. Yet the [Bail] Act expressly says that, after the second hearing, the court need not hear arguments which it has already heard . . . [I]f there is no new argument, the court has a discretion not to hear any arguments at all. And if it does refuse to hear argument, we think it most unlikely that the hearing could be regarded as giving the defendant sufficient opportunity for challenge to satisfy Article 5(4) . . . Our provisional view is that where, after a remand in custody of 28 days, the defendant makes a further application for bail, and the court refuses to hear arguments that were

---

[18] The judge did not rule on the renewed bail application for over five months, and the Court held that to be a violation of Art. 5(3).
[19] See *Clooth v. Belgium* (1992) 14 E.H.R.R. 717 and *Mansur v. Turkey* (1995) 20 E.H.R.R. 535 at para. 55, for example. *Cf.* the domestic courts' approach in *W v. Switzerland* (1994) 17 E.H.R.R. 60, which was detailed and well-documented.
[20] [1981] Q.B. 38.
[21] (1983) 147 J.P. 399.
[22] Consultation Paper No. 157, *Bail and the Human Rights Act 1998*, paras 12.17 *et seq.*

put forward at the previous hearing, the Strasbourg Court might well find an infringement of the defendant's rights under Article 5(4). It follows that in these circumstances a magistrates' court should be willing to hear such arguments again."

In order to achieve this result without the need for legislative amendment, the Law Commission proposed that "courts should be given guidance to the effect that a lapse of 28 days since the last fully argued bail application should itself be treated as an argument which the court has not previously heard". The Law Commission's final report makes specific proposals for such guidance, noting in particular the possibility that time served on remand may have reduced the risk of the defendant absconding.[23]

F. CUSTODY TIME LIMITS

Where the court orders that a person should remain in custody pending trial there **13–38** will be a breach of Article 5(3) if the proceedings are not conducted with appropriate expedition.[24] The fact that an accused has been refused bail requires special diligence in the conduct of the proceedings[25] and entitles him to have his case treated as a priority by the prosecution and the court.[26] There is however no absolute limit to the permissible period of pre-trial detention; the reasonableness of the length of the proceedings depends on the facts of the case.[27] The requirement for expedition has to be balanced against the duty of the court to ascertain the facts and to allow both parties to present their case.[28]

The standard which the Court has imposed is not a particularly exacting one. In **13–39** *W v. Switzerland*[29] the Court (by a narrow majority) found no violation of Article 5(3) where an accused person had been detained for four years before his trial. The case was a particularly complex fraud, which required lengthy preparation and the Court held that there were valid reasons for refusing bail. Against this background, it seems certain that the regime established by the Prosecution of Offences Act 1985, and the Prosecution of Offences (Custody Time Limits) Regulations 1987[30] would be found to satisfy Article 5(3). The court's power to extend the time limit when satisfied that there is "good and sufficient cause for doing so" and that "the prosecution has acted with all due expedition" is also likely to comply with the Convention, especially if the court's discretion is exercised according to the guidance laid down by Lord Bingham C.J. in *R. v. Manchester Crown Court ex parte McDonald*,[31] where the Divisional Court

---

[23] Guidance to Bail Decision-Takers, para. 27. As to the Strasbourg approach to this question, see para. 13–08 above.

[24] The standard of diligence required is the same as under Art. 6(1): *Abdoella v. Netherlands* (1995) 20 E.H.R.R. 585, para. 24.

[25] *Clooth v. Belgium* (1992) 14 E.H.R.R. 717, para. 36; *Tomasi v. France* (1993) 15 E.H.R.R. 1, para. 84; *Herczegfalvy v. Austria* (1993) 15 E.H.R.R. 437, para. 71.

[26] *Wemhoff v. Germany* (1979–80) 1 E.H.R.R. 55, para. 17.

[27] *W v. Switzerland* (1994) 17 E.H.R.R. 60 (four years: no breach of Art. 5(3)); *Toth v. Austria* (1992) 14 E.H.R.R. 551 (two years and one month: violation of Art. 5(3); *Tomasi v. France* (1993) 15 E.H.R.R. 1 (five years and seven months: violation of Art. 5(3)).

[28] *Wemhoff v. Germany* (1979–80) 1 E.H.R.R. 55, para. 17.

[29] (1994) 17 E.H.R.R. 60.

[30] S.I. 1987 No. 299.

[31] [1999] 1 W.L.R. 841.

considered the Convention authorities. In *Wildman v. DPP*[32] the High Court held that the principles established in *R. v. Havering Magistrates Court ex parte DPP*[33] applied equally to applications to extend custody time limits. Thus, neither the strict rules of evidence, nor the requirement for formal disclosure[34] applied. The Court did, however, recognise that insofar as it may be necessary for a defendant to test any aspect of the application, the procedural means must be made available to enable him to do so. The House of Lords held in *R. v. Leeds Crown Court ex parte Wardle*,[35] by a 3–2 majority, that Regulation 4(4) of the Prosecution of Offences (Custody Time Limits) Regulations,[36] which state that each offence attracts its own custody time limit, is compatible with Article 5.

13–40   One might have assumed that if a defendant were to be detained in breach of the custody time limits, this would amount to a violation of Article 5(3), and thus to give rise to a right to compensation under Article 5(5). This issue arose for consideration in *Olotu v. Home Office*,[37] where the claimant had been detained beyond the expiry of the custody time limits. As the result of an oversight, her case had not been brought before the Crown Court. Lord Bingham C.J., for the Court of Appeal, held that the detention did not amount to a violation of Article 5(3) since expiry of the custody time limits did not entitle a defendant to be released, but merely to apply to the Crown Court for bail. Although the court would have been under an obligation to grant bail, the failure of the claimant's solicitor to apply for bail meant that the detention, though unlawful, did not give rise to a violation of Article 5(3). Nor, therefore, did it give rise to a right to compensation under Article 5(5). There are a number of difficulties with the reasoning in this decision. Lord Bingham accepted in terms that the claimant's detention was unlawful as a matter of domestic law. If that analysis is correct,[38] then it is difficult to see how the detention could have met the requirements of legality in Article 5(1) or (3). Moreover, the Court of Appeal does not appear to have been referred to *McGoff v. Sweden*[39] where the Commission held that Article 5(3) imposed an "unconditional" obligation on the state to bring the accused automatically before a court.

---

[32] *The Times*, February 8, 2001.
[33] [2001] 1 W.L.R. 805, see para. 13–17 above.
[34] Note, however, that paragraph 34 of the Attorney General's Guidelines on *Disclosure of Information in Criminal Proceedings* (November 29, 2000) provides that "disclosure ought to be made of significant information that might affect a bail decision".
[35] [2001] 2 W.L.R. 865.
[36] S.I. 1987 No. 299.
[37] [1997] 1 W.L.R. 328.
[38] It was of course open to the Court of Appeal to hold that the detention was lawful on the ground that until a bail application was made, the defendant was in lawful custody by order of the Crown Court. This is not, however, how the decision is expressed.
[39] (1982) 31 D.R. 72.

CHAPTER 14

ASPECTS OF CRIMINAL PROCEDURE

A. LEGAL REPRESENTATION AND RELATED MATTERS

I. *Introduction*

Article 6(3)(c) guarantees the right of a defendant in criminal proceedings "to **14–01** defend himself in person, or through legal assistance of his own choosing or, if he has not sufficient means to pay for legal assistance, to be given it free when the interests of justice so require". The purpose of this provision is to secure "equality of arms" so as "to place the accused in a position to put his case in such a way that he is not at a disadvantage *vis-à-vis* the prosecution."[1] We have already seen[2] that denial of access to a solicitor during police detention may violate Article 6(3)(c) in conjunction with Article 6(1), particularly if adverse inferences are subsequently drawn from a defendant's failure to answer questions in an interview.[3] In this section, we examine the right to legal representation more generally, including the imposition of mandatory representation requirements, issues surrounding the appointment and dismissal of counsel, the standard of representation and the adequacy of the time allowed for preparation of the defence case, legal professional privilege and the right to legal aid in criminal proceedings.

II. *Mandatory Representation*

Subject to the requirement to provide legal aid in appropriate cases[4] it is, in the **14–02** first place, for the national authorities to determine whether the accused should have the right to defend himself in person, or through a lawyer. In *X v. Austria*[5] the Commission observed that:

> "While [Article 6(3)(c)] guarantees to an accused person that proceedings against him will not take place without an adequate representation of the case for the defence, [it] does not give an accused person the right to decide for himself in what manner his defence should be assured . . . [T]he decision as to which of the two alternatives should be chosen, namely the applicant's right to defend himself in person or to be represented by a lawyer of his own choosing, or in certain circumstances one appointed by the court, rests with the competent authorities concerned."

---

[1] *X v. FRG* (1984) 8 E.H.R.R. 225; *Bonisch v. Austria* (1987) 9 E.H.R.R. 191.
[2] See para. 5–38 above.
[3] *Murray v. United Kingdom* (1996) 22 E.H.R.R. 29.
[4] See paras 14–25 *et seq.* below.
[5] Application No. 1242/61.

14–03 Thus, the Court has recognised that there may be circumstances in which domestic law might justifiably insist on legal representation.[6] In *Croissant v. Germany*[7] the applicant was charged in connection with his activities as the lawyer of various members of the Red Army Faction. The relevant German legislation required that he be legally represented at all stages of the proceedings. He was initially represented by two court-appointed lawyers of his own choosing. Because of the complexity of the case the court then appointed a third lawyer to whom the applicant objected on political grounds. In finding no violation of Article 6 the Court considered that a requirement for legal representation could not breach Article 6(3)(c): "The requirement that a defendant be assisted by counsel at all stages of the Regional Court's proceedings—which finds parallels in the legislation of other contracting states—cannot, in the Court's opinion, be deemed incompatible with the Convention."

14–04 Similarly in *Imbroscia v. Switzerland*[8] the Court held that a requirement of legal representation is in the first instance a question for the national authorities, the Court considering the matter in the light of the overall fairness of the trial. The Commission has expressed a similar view in relation to appeal proceedings.[9] Moreover, it is to be noted that mandatory professional defence in the case of serious offences was considered permissible by most members of the United Nations Human Rights Committee.[10]

14–05 It is against this background that domestic courts will have to evaluate statutory provisions requiring a defendant to be legally represented for the purposes of cross-examining a child victim of assault, cruelty or sexual abuse or an adult rape victim. Section 34A of the Criminal Justice Act 1988 prohibits a defendant in person from cross-examining any child witness who is alleged to be a victim of or witness to a sexual or violent offence.[11-12] Similar restrictions were introduced in relation to adult rape victims by the Youth Justice and Criminal Evidence Act 1999. Providing the accused has been given a proper opportunity to cross-examine through counsel,[13] we consider that it is unlikely that such a provision would be found to breach Article 6. Although some commentators have assumed that the prohibition might infringe defendants' rights under the Convention, this neglects the point that such rules are intended to strike a proper balance between the rights of the accused and those of the victim.[14] Indeed, it is arguable that obliging a victim to be cross-examined by the person alleged to have abused them has the potential to violate the Article 3 rights of the victim.[15]

---

[6] In Italy, for example, it seems that only legal representatives are able to attend appeal proceedings in the Court of Cassation: *Tripodi v. Italy* (1994) 18 E.H.R.R. 295 at para. 30. As to the practice of the European Court of Human Rights on this issue, see para. 1–30 above.

[7] (1993) 16 E.H.R.R. 135.

[8] (1994) 17 E.H.R.R. 441.

[9] *Philis v. Greece* (1990) 66 D.R. 260.

[10] U.N. Docs. CCPR/C/SR. 132 (May 16, 1994). Report on Jordan.

[11-12] Within the meaning of s.32(2) of that Act.

[13] The Youth Justice and Criminal Evidence Act 1999, makes provision for the appointment of a "special counsel", where this is necessary in the interests of justice, to conduct cross-examination of a complainant where the accused is unrepresented. As the role of "special counsel" in criminal proceedings generally, see para. 14–116 below.

[14] See *Doorson v. Netherlands* (1997) 23 E.H.R.R. 330.

[15] Such a complaint was made in *M v. United Kingdom* (Unreported) see para. 18–57 below.

III. *Choice of Representation*

In general, an accused's choice of lawyer should be respected,[16] and an appoint- **14–06**
ment made against the wishes of the accused will be "incompatible with the
notion of a fair trial . . . if it lacks relevant and sufficient justification".[17] Factors
to be taken into account include the basis of the accused's objection to the
appointment and the existence or absence of prejudice. Article 6(3)(c) does not
however guarantee the accused the right to choose a court-appointed lawyer, nor
to be consulted with regard to the choice of an official defence counsel.[18] This
principle has been held to apply to legally aided defendants in the United
Kingdom.[19] A lawyer may be excluded by the court for good reason.[20] Thus, in
X v. United Kingdom[21] the Commission found no violation of Article 6(3)(c)
where the Professional Conduct Committee of the Bar Council had ruled that it
would be improper for defence counsel to represent his father in a criminal trial.
The fact that an accused has failed to attend the hearing does not entitle the court
to proceed in the absence of his lawyer.[22]

The accused's right to representation by a lawyer can be undermined by a **14–07**
breakdown in the relationship between counsel and his client or by professional
embarrassment. How far does the court have to go in permitting the instruction
of alternative counsel in such circumstances? The problem of professional
embarrassment arose in *X v. United Kingdom*.[23] In the course of evidence given
on a *voir dire* the defendant departed from his instructions and admitted that
certain incriminating statements which he was alleged to have made were true.
Despite this, he wished defence counsel to continue to represent him on the basis
that the statements were untrue. Defence counsel withdrew. The judge took the
view that given the extent of the admissions which the defendant had made on the
voir dire, any fresh counsel appointed would be unavoidably embarrassed.
Accordingly, he declined to permit the appointment of new counsel and required
the defendant to continue unrepresented, albeit with the assistance of his solicitors. The Commission considered that "the trial judge offered the applicant every
assistance and advice in the presentation of his case,"[24] and took account of the
fact that the applicant's solicitors continued to act for him and were available to
advise and assist him during the trial; the fact that the defendant in person was
permitted the opportunity to cross-examine witnesses and call evidence; the fact
that the judge had offered the defendant the opportunity to make an unsworn
statement from the dock; the fact that the judge gave clear directions on the
burden and standard of proof; and the fact that the judge had directed an acquittal
on three of the counts. The Commission observed that:

---

[16] *Goddi v. Italy* (1984) 6 E.H.R.R. 457.
[17] *Croissant v. Germany* (1993) 16 E.H.R.R. 135 (para. 27).
[18] *X v. Germany* (1976) 6 D.R. 114.
[19] *X v. United Kingdom* (1983) 5 E.H.R.R. 273.
[20] *X v. United Kingdom* Application No. 6298/73, (1975) 2 Digest 831 (disrespect to the court);
Ensslin, Baader and Raspe v. Federal Republic of Germany (1978) 14 D.R. 64 (breach of professional
ethics).
[21] (1978) 15 D.R. 242 (paras 243–244).
[22] *Lala v. Netherlands* (1994) 18 E.H.R.R. 586.
[23] (1980) 21 D.R. 126.
[24] *ibid.*, at para. 16.

> "[A]n accused person cannot require counsel to disregard basic principles of his professional duty in the presentation of his defence. If such an insistence results in the accused having to conduct his own defence, any consequent 'inequality of arms' can only be attributable to his own behaviour . . . [S]uch was the nature, scope and specificity of the incriminating statements made by the applicant, [that] it was not unreasonable for the trial judge to have formed the opinion that fresh counsel could not continue to act on his behalf in a manner consistent with his professional duty not to mislead the court."[25]

14–08　In *Kamasinski v. Austria*[26] the applicant expressed to the judge on several occasions his dissatisfaction with his counsel, and eventually, as a result of a dispute in court, counsel asked the judge to discharge him from his function. The request was refused, and the applicant was convicted. The Court held that even though the trial could have been conducted differently, and even if counsel had sometimes acted in a way that the applicant thought contrary to his best interests, there had been no violation of Article 6(3)(c). There was no manifest failure to provide effective legal representation in this case.[27] In *Frerot v. France*[28] the applicant had dismissed his lawyer towards the end of a trial. The first replacement lawyer declined to act, so a second lawyer was assigned to him. That lawyer then applied for an adjournment but the French court, taking account of the procedural difficulties this would cause, refused the request. The Commission held that this did not amount to a violation of Article 6(3)(c), because the applicant had been advised and represented by the same counsel for all but the last day of the trial, and the late change did not render the trial unfair.

IV. *The Right to Effective Representation*

14–09　In order to meet the requirements of Article 6(3)(c), representation provided by the state must be effective. The state will not generally be responsible for shortcomings in the way a legal aid lawyer performs his duties,[29] but the relevant authorities may be required to intervene where the failure to provide effective representation is manifest and has been brought to their attention.[30] Thus in *Artico v. Italy*[31] the accused had been sentenced to custody for various fraud offences in his absence and without his knowledge. Wishing to appeal, he applied for legal aid and was assigned counsel. The lawyer declined to act, pleading ill-health and the onerous nature of the brief. The accused's various efforts to have a new lawyer appointed met with no success for some months, and by the time he succeeded his appeal had already been dismissed. The Court gave short shrift to the Italian government's argument that it had complied with Article 6 by appointing the first lawyer, holding that "the Convention is intended to guarantee not rights that are theoretical or illusory but rights that are practical and effective." In the Court's view, the authorities should have either compelled the lawyer to act or appointed a new one. Nor was it necessary for the applicant to establish that the result of the proceedings would have been different if he had

---

[25] *ibid.*, at paras 6–8.
[26] (1991) 13 E.H.R.R. 36.
[27] *cf. Pakelli v. Germany* (1984) 6 E.H.R.R. 1.
[28] (1996) 85–B D.R. 103.
[29] *Artico v. Italy* (1981) 3 E.H.R.R. 1, para. 36.
[30] *Artico v. Italy* (1981) 3 E.H.R.R. 1; *Kamasinki v. Austria* (1991) 13 E.H.R.R. 36, para. 65.
[31] (1981) 3 E.H.R.R. 1.

been effectively defended. Whilst the existence or absence of prejudice was relevant to extent of the remedy required by way of just satisfaction, it was not a pre-requisite for a finding that Article 6(3)(c) had been violated. The Court found a violation on a similar basis in *Daud v. Portugal*[32]:

> "The first appointed lawyer had not taken any steps before reporting sick and the second did not have the necessary time to study the file, visit the client and prepare the defence. The time between the notification of the replacement of the lawyer and the hearing was too short for a serious, complex case in which there had been no judicial investigation and which led to a heavy sentence."[33]

In those circumstances the state, or the court itself, ought to have ensured that the trial was adjourned until counsel had had adequate time for preparation.

Where counsel has been instructed so late as to leave insufficient time to master **14–10** the brief, the accused's right under Article 6(3)(b) to adequate time and facilities for the preparation of his defence may be violated. However, the Court is unlikely to find a violation on this ground unless an application has been made for an adjournment to enable the case to be prepared.[34] The adequacy of the time allowed will obviously depend upon the complexity of the case.[35] The defence lawyer must be appointed in sufficient time to enable the case to be properly prepared.[36] Where there is a change of legal representation, the newly-appointed lawyers must be permitted additional time to prepare.[37] Although it was formerly the practice of the Commission to examine a case to determine if the late appointment of the defence lawyer had actually prejudiced the accused,[38] the current emphasis in the Court's case-law is upon the necessity for criminal proceedings to have the appearance of fairness, and upon "the increased sensitivity of the public to the fair administration of justice."[39] The provision of legal assistance does not, however, require unlimited access by a defendant to a lawyer. It may be acceptable for the lawyer to limit the number of consultations so as to ensure that the legal aid budget is not exceeded.[40]

The approach of the Commission to the question of state responsibility was not **14–11** always consistent. In *F v. United Kingdom*[41] defence counsel had to withdraw the day before the trial, and the defendant met new counsel only on the morning of the trial. Although the trial was for attempted murder, and the new counsel declined to apply for an adjournment to ensure fuller preparation of the case, the Commission dismissed the application on the basis that the conduct of counsel

---

[32] [1998] E.H.R.L.R. 634.
[33] *ibid.*, at 635.
[34] *Murphy v. United Kingdom* (1972) 43 C.D. 1; 2 Digest 794.
[35] See generally *Albert and Le Compte v. Belgium* (1983) 5 E.H.R.R. 533 at para. 41.
[36] *X and Y v. Austria* (1978) 15 D.R. 160; *Perez Mahia v. Spain* (1987) 9 E.H.R.R. 145.
[37] *Goddi v. Italy* (1984) 6 E.H.R.R. 457.
[38] *X v. United Kingdom* (1970) 13 Y.B. 690; *Murphy v. United Kingdom* (1972) 43 C.D. 1.
[39] See, in another context, *Borgers v. Belgium* (1993) 15 E.H.R.R. 92 at para. 24.
[40] *M v. United Kingdom* (1984) 36 D.R. 155; see also the Canadian decision in *Munroe* (1990) 59 C.C.C. (3d) 446.
[41] (1992) 15 E.H.R.R. CD 32.

could not be attributed to the state.[42] In *Daud v. Portugal*,[43] however, new counsel was appointed only three days before the hearing of a complex drugs case, at the conclusion of which the applicant was sentenced to nine years' imprisonment. The Court found a breach of Article 6(3)(c). While respecting the independence of the Bar, the Court held that it was the state's duty to ensure that everyone received "the effective benefit of his right". On the facts of this case it should have been obvious to the authorities that the legal representation offered was inadequate.

14–11a The English authorities have traditionally assumed that shortcomings in legal representation must cross the threshold of "flagrant incompetence" before they are capable of amounting to a ground of appeal against conviction.[44] That approach appeared to be softening somewhat in *R. v. Clinton*[45] where the Court of Appeal observed that "it is probably less helpful to approach the problem via the somewhat semantic exercise of trying to assess the qualitative value of counsel's alleged ineptitude, but rather to seek to assess its effect on the trial and the verdict". However in *R. v. Donnelly*[46] the Court retreated to its former position, holding that the practice of criticising trial counsel on appeal without alleging flagrant incompetence should not be followed. This rather arid debate seems to have been put to rest by the Human Rights Act. In *R. v. Nangle*[47] the Court of Appeal observed that in view of the requirements of the Convention, flagrant incompetence may no longer be regarded as the appropriate measure of when the Court will quash a conviction for the alleged error of legal representatives: "What Article 6 requires in this context is that the hearing of the charges against the accused should be fair. If the conduct of the legal advisers has been such that this objective is not met, then this Court may be compelled to intervene."

14–12 In the New Zealand case of *Shaw*,[48] defence counsel informed the Crown of his unavailability on the trial date, but it was not until five days before the trial that the Crown sent a reply objecting to any alteration of the trial date. The judge refused an adjournment at the start of the trial, and the accused was left to conduct his own defence. He was found guilty and sentenced to six months' imprisonment. The Court of Appeal found that the defendant's right to legal representation had been violated, not least because counsel's understanding of the law and ability to cross-examine might have influenced the outcome of the trial.[49]

14–13 There is considerable North American jurisprudence on the provision of "effective assistance" by counsel. In the United States the test is whether counsel's

---

[42] See also the Court in *Kamasinski v. Austria* (1991) 13 E.H.R.R. 36 at para. 65: "It follows from the independence of the legal profession of the State that the conduct of the defence is essentially a matter between the defendant and his counsel, whether counsel be appointed under a legal aid scheme or be privately financed."
[43] [1998] E.H.R.L.R. 634.
[44] *R. v. Ensor* 89 Cr. App. R. 139 (CA) considering *R. v. Irwin* 85 Cr. App. R. 294 (CA) and *R. v. Gautam* [1988] Crim. L.R. 109 (CA).
[45] 97 Cr. App. R. 320; See also *R. v. Fergus* 98 Cr. App. R. 313.
[46] [1998] Crim. L.R. 131.
[47] Judgment November 1, 2000 (C.A.).
[48] [1992] N.Z.L.R. 652.
[49] Under the Strasbourg jurisprudence the requirement to show prejudice is considered as relevant only to the extent of the remedy required: See *Artico v. Italy* (1981) 3 E.H.R.R. 1 at para. 35.

performance fell below a reasonable standard, bearing in mind the Bar's standards of conduct.[50] A similar approach has been adopted in the Canadian cases,[51] where a two-stage test is now applied. The court should enquire (a) whether counsel's conduct showed a lack of competence; and (b) whether it is probable that, but for that lack of competence, the result of the proceedings would have been different.[52]

V. *Legal Professional Privilege*

The inviolability of legal professional privilege in English law was re-affirmed   **14-14** by the House of Lords in *R. v. Derby Magistrates' Court ex parte B*,[53] where Lord Taylor described it as "a fundamental human right protected by the European Convention". B was arrested for murder, and admitted in interview with the police that he was solely responsible. Shortly before his trial he retracted his confession and alleged that the murder had been committed by his step-father (A). B was acquitted, and the police thereupon arrested A and charged him with the murder. At committal proceedings against A, his counsel sought an order for the disclosure of statements made by B to his solicitor. B declined to waive privilege. The magistrate made the order, considering that B no longer had an interest in maintaining his privilege (since he could not be prosecuted for the murder a second time), and holding that the public interest in the acquittal of the innocent outweighed the public interest in protecting solicitor and client communications. The House of Lords overturned the magistrate's order, Lord Taylor explaining that it breached the "long established rule that a document protected by privilege continues to be protected so long as the privilege is not waived by the client: once privileged, always privileged":

> "[T]he privilege is the same whether the documents are sought for the purpose of civil or criminal proceedings, and whether by the prosecution or the defence, and . . . the refusal of the client to waive his privilege, for whatever reason, or for no reason, cannot be questioned or investigated by the court . . . [T]he privilege is that of the client, which he alone can waive, and . . . the court will not permit, let alone order, the attorney to reveal the confidential communications which have passed between him and his former client. His mouth is shut forever."

Having reviewed the English authorities, he continued;   **14-15**

> "The principle which runs through all these cases . . . is that a man must be able to consult his lawyer in confidence, since otherwise he might hold back half the truth. The client must be sure that what he tells his lawyer in confidence will never be revealed without his consent. Legal professional privilege is thus much more than an ordinary rule of evidence, limited in its application to the facts of a particular case. It is a fundamental condition on which the administration of justice as a whole rests . . . Nobody doubts that legal professional privilege could be modified, or even abrogated,

---

[50] *Strickland v. Washington* 466 U.S. 668 (1984).
[51] *E.g.* two cases from Ontario, *Silvini* (1991) 68 C.C.C. (3d) 251 and *Collier* (1992) 77 C.C.C. (3d) 570, and the Nova Scotia decision in *Schofield* (1996) 148 N.S.R. (2d) 175.
[52] See *McAuley* (1996) 150 N.S.R. (2d) 1 (counsel relied on submission of no case; no incompetence proved); *B (LC)* (1996) 46 C.R. (4th) 368 (counsel refused to visit defendant in prison; even if incompetent, not established that result would probably have been different.)
[53] [1996] A.C. 487.

by statute, subject always to the objection that legal professional privilege is a fundamental human right protected by the European Convention for the Protection of Human Rights and Fundamental Freedoms."

14–16   For its part, the European Court of Human Rights has recognised that a high degree of protection is to be afforded to the confidentiality of communications passing between a lawyer and his client. Breach of professional privilege can involve a violation of the right to privacy in Article 8, as well as having implications for the right to a fair trial in Article 6(1) and, in particular, for the right to effective legal representation in Article 6(3)(b). In *Schonenberger and Durmaz v. Switzerland*[54] the second applicant had been arrested for drugs offences. Whilst he was in police custody his wife instructed a lawyer, the first applicant, to represent her husband. Mr Schonenberger wrote a letter addressed to Mr Durmaz and sent it to the public prosecutor's office, asking that it be forwarded to his client. The letter contained forms of authority and also advised Mr Durmaz that he was not obliged to answer questions, that his answers could be used in evidence, and that it would be to his advantange to maintain his silence. The public prosecutor read the letter and decided to withhold it from Mr Durmaz on the ground that it might jeopardise the proper conduct of the investigation. The Court was in no doubt that this constituted a violation of Article 8:

> "[T]he Government relies in the first place on the contents of the letter in issue: according to the Government, it gave Mr Durmaz advice relating to pending criminal proceedings which was of such a nature as the jeopardise their proper conduct. The Court is not convinced by this argument. Mr Schonenberger sought to inform the second applicant of his right 'to refuse to make any statement', advising him that to exercise it would be to his 'advantage'. In that way, he was recommending that Mr Durmaz adopt a certain tactic, lawful in itself since, under the Swiss Federal Court's case law—whose equivalent may be found in other contracting states—it is open to an accused person to remain silent. Mr Schonenberger could also properly regard it as his duty, pending a meeting with Mr Durmaz, to advise him of his right and of the possible consequences of exercising it. In the Court's view, advice given in these terms was not capable of creating a danger of connivance between the sender of the letter and its recipient and did not pose a threat to the normal conduct of the prosecution."

14–17   Neither was the Court attracted by the argument that the communication did not attract privilege since Mr Schonenberger had not been formally instructed by Mr Durmaz. He had received instructions from Mrs Durmaz and had made attempts to contact his client. In the Court's view, these contacts "amounted to preliminary steps intended to enable the second applicant to have the benefit of the assistance of a defence lawyer of his choice and, thereby, to exercise a right enshrined in another fundamental provision of the Convention, namely Article 6".

14–18   The passing reference to Article 6 in *Schonenberger and Durmaz* was taken up in *S v. Switzerland*,[55] where the Court implied into Article 6(3)(c) the right of an accused person to consult with his lawyer in private, without the risk of infringements of privilege by the state. Although Article 6 makes no explicit reference to legal professional privilege, the Court noted that this right was guaranteed

---

[54] (1989) 11 E.H.R.R. 202.
[55] (1992) 14 E.H.R.R. 670, para. 48.

under the national law of a number of contracting states, and expressly enshrined in Article 8(2)(d) of the American Convention on Human Rights. The Court also attached importance to the fact that within the Council of Europe, an equivalent protection was recognised by Article 93 of the Standard Minimum Rules for the Treatment of Prisoners.[56] This provides that "interviews between [a] prisoner and his legal adviser may be within the sight, but not within the hearing, either direct or indirect, of a police or institution official". On the strength of these comparative and international standards, the Court concluded that;

> "[A]n accused's right to communicate with his advocate out of the hearing of a third person is one of the basic requirements of a fair trial in a democratic society and follows from Article 6(3)(c) of the Convention. If a lawyer were unable to confer with his client and receive confidential instructions from him without such surveillance, his assistance would lose much of its usefulness, whereas the Convention is intended to guarantee rights that are practical and effective."

As a result, the monitoring of the applicant's correspondence with his lawyer, and **14–19** the supervision of visits to him in custody, constituted a breach of Article 6(3)(c). The possibility that defence lawyers might co-ordinate their strategies could not justify such supervision since there was nothing unusual or unethical about such an approach. Neither was it necessary for the applicant to prove that he had been in any way prejudiced in the preparation of his case since "[a] violation of the Convention does not necessarily imply the existence of injury".

In *Campbell v. United Kingdom*[57] the Court emphasised that where correspon- **14–20** dence or communication with a lawyer was concerned, it was unnecessary to establish that the communication was directly concerned with pending or contemplated legal proceedings. Whilst this would obviously be relevant to any potential violation of Article 6, the nature of the lawyer/client relationship itself was a confidential one, such that any communication which was not unlawful was to be regarded as privileged, and thus protected by Article 8:

> "It is clearly in the general interest that any person who wishes to consult a lawyer should be free to do so under conditions which favour full and uninhibited discussion ... Admittedly, as the Government pointed out, the borderline between mail concerning contemplated litigation and that of a general nature is especially difficult to draw and correspondence with a lawyer may concern matters which have little or nothing to do with litigation. Nevertheless, the Court sees no reason to distinguish between the different categories of correspondence with a lawyers which, whatever their purpose, concern matters of a private and confidential character. In principle such letters are privileged under Article 8."

The close relationship between Article 6 and Article 8 was also emphasised in **14–21** *Niemietz v. Germany*[58] which concerned the execution of a search warrant at the offices of a lawyer in order to ascertain the whereabouts of a third party who was under investigation for a criminal offence. The Commission and the Court both held that the concept of "privacy" extended to a lawyer's dealings with his

---

[56] Annexed to Resolution (73) 5 of the Committee of Ministers.
[57] (1993) 15 E.H.R.R. 137, paras 46 to 48.
[58] (1993) 16 E.H.R.R. 97. See, however, *F v. United Kingdom* (1986) 47 D.R. 230 where the Commission found that the seizure of privileged documents did not violate Article 6 because the documents were not used at trial.

clients. After noting the principle of professional secrecy guaranteed under the German Federal Regulations for Lawyers, the Commission observed:

"These features of privacy are particularly strong as regards the lawyer's activities in his own law office. There he exercises domestic authority and general access by the public is excluded. Such privacy is a necessary basis for the lawyer-client relationship . . . The interference complained of affected the applicant in his position as a lawyer *i.e.* as an independent organ in the administration of justice and as independent counsel of his clients, with whom he must entertain a relationship of confidentiality, ensuring the secrecy of information received from his clients and documents relating thereto. Such are also the demands of the right to a fair trial and the effective use of defence rights as envisaged by Article 6(1) and (3) of the Convention in cases of representation by counsel."

14–22 In finding a violation of Article 8, the Court explained that:

"[T]he search impinged on professional secrecy to an extent that appears disproportionate in the circumstances; it has, in this connection, to be recalled that, where a lawyer is involved, an encroachment on professional secrecy may have repurcussions on the proper administration of justice and hence on the rights guaranteed by Article 6 of the Convention."

14–23 In *Foxley v. United Kingdom*[59] the Court treated Article 8 and Article 6 as effectively interchangeable where a violation of legal professional privilege was alleged. In that case, a Receiver and Trustee in Bankruptcy, appointed in the context of proceedings for the enforcement of a confiscation order under the Criminal Justice Act 1988, had obtained an order from the county court under the Insolvency Act 1986,[60] authorising the re-direction of the applicant's mail. The letters opened and copied included correspondence with the applicant's legal advisers. The Court found a violation of Article 8, observing that it could find "no justification" for the actions of the Receiver, which were contrary to "the principles of confidentiality and professional privilege attaching to relations between a lawyer and his client". It noted that the government had not sought to argue that "the privileged channel of communication was being abused". Nor were there "any other exceptional circumstances" justifying the intrusion. Having found a violation of Article 8, the Court held that it was unnecessary to examine the same complaint under Article 6 of the Convention.

14–24 As a matter of English law, legal professional privilege does not extend to communications made to a solicitor by his client for the purpose of being guided or helped in the commission of crime,[61] or to communications which are themselves in furtherance of a criminal enterprise.[62] This principle applies whether or not the solicitor is aware of his client's unlawful purpose.[63] It is implicit in the *Schonenberger and Durmaz, Campbell* and *Foxley* cases that abuse of a privileged relationship is capable of affording a ground for restricting the protection afforded to legal professional privilege. Nevertheless, the Court has emphasised

---

[59] 8 B.H.R.C. 571.
[60] Section 371.
[61] *R. v. Cox and Railton* (1884) 14 Q.B.D. 153; *R. v. Hayward* (1846) 2 C. & K. 234; *R. v. Smith (GJ)* 11 Cr. App. R. 229. See also *R. v. Snaresbrook Crown Court ex parte DPP* [1988] 1 Q.B. 532 at 537 and *R. v. Central Criminal Court ex parte Francis & Francis (a firm)* [1989] A.C. 346.
[62] *Bullivant v. Attorney-General for Victoria* [1901] A.C. 196 at 200.
[63] *Banque Keyser Ullman SA v. Skandia (UK) Insurance Co Ltd* [1986] 1 Lloyd's Rep. 336 (C.A.)

the need to ensure that the exception is narrowly and carefully defined, and that procedures are in place to ensure that any interference is kept within this limited category. Thus, in *Kopp v. Switzerland*[64] the Court held that even where it is alleged that the lawyer himself is involved in criminal activity, special safeguards are required to ensure that a proper distinction is drawn between "matters specifically connected with a lawyer's work under instructions from a party to proceedings and those relating to activity other than that of counsel". The applicant was a lawyer under investigation in connection with the disclosure of official secrets. The Court considered that the absence of independent judicial authorisation for the interception of the applicant's telephone calls was "astonishing", especially "in this sensitive area of the confidential relations between a lawyer and his clients, which directly concern the rights of the defence".

VI. *Legal aid in criminal cases*

The second limb of Article 6(3)(c) imposes a requirement to provide legal aid in **14–25** criminal cases. The wording of the English text appears to suggest that the right to free legal representation is an alternative to the right of an accused person to represent himself. This is not however how it has been interpreted by the Court. In *Pakelli v. Germany*[65] the Court held that Article 6(3)(c) guarantees three related but independent rights to a person charged with a criminal offence: First, the right to defend himself in person; secondly, the right to defend himself through legal assistance of his own choosing; and thirdly, on certain conditions being met, the right to free legal assistance and representation:

> "Having regard to the object and purpose of this Article, which is designed to secure effective protection of the rights of the defence ... a person charged with a criminal offence who does not wish to defend himself in person must be able to have recourse to legal assistance of his own choosing; if he does not have sufficient means to pay for such assistance, he is entitled under the Convention to be given it free when the interests of justice so require."

The "interests of justice" criterion will take account of the complexity of the **14–26** proceedings, the capacity of the individual to represent himself, and the severity of the potential sentence.[66] Legal aid is not necessarily required where the factual and legal issues in the case are straightforward, and there is no requirement for expert cross-examination.[67] On the other hand, the Court has rejected the argument that a violation of Article 6(3)(c) will only arise where the absence of legal assistance can be shown to have actually prejudiced the accused.[68]

Where the accused faces imprisonment, this will usually be sufficient in itself to **14–27** require the grant of legal aid.[69] However, the requirements of the Convention go

---

[64] (1999) 27 E.H.R.R. 91.
[65] (1984) 6 E.H.R.R. 1 at para. 31.
[66] *Quaranta v. Switzerland* (1991) Series A No. 205; *Granger v. United Kingdom* (1990) 12 E.H.R.R. 469.
[67] *X v. Norway* Application No. 8202/78, (unreported).
[68] *Artico v. Italy* (1981) 3 E.H.R.R. 1 at para. 34.
[69] *Benham v. United Kingdom* (1996) 22 E.H.R.R. 293; *Quaranta v. Switzerland* (1991) Series A No. 205. Note that s.21 of the Powers of Criminal Courts Act 1973 provides that before a court can impose a custodial sentence on a defendant who has never previously been sent to prison, that person must have been offered legal representation. See *Wilson* (1995) 16 Cr. App. R(S) 997.

further than this. In *Pham Hoang v. France*[70] the Court found a violation of Article 6 where the French courts had denied legal aid to the applicant, despite the fact that "the proceedings were clearly fraught with consequences" for him, because he had been convicted of importing drugs and was ordered to pay a substantial fine. This decision suggests the restriction of legal aid to cases where custody is a real possibility may not be honouring the "interests of justice" criterion in Article 6(3)(c).[71] Thus, where a Scottish magistrate peremptorily refused legal aid on the ground that it was not in the interests of justice to grant it in cases of breach of the peace and resisting arrest, the case proceeded to a friendly settlement.[72]

14–28   In practice, the European Court of Human Rights adopts a strict approach to the requirement to provide free legal assistance in criminal cases, which is illustrated by a series of cases against the United Kingdom. In *Granger v. United Kingdom*,[73] a Scottish case, the Court held that a refusal of legal aid for the applicant's appeal against a conviction for perjury violated Article 6(3)(c) taken together with Article 6(1). Legal aid had been refused on the ground that the appeal was without substance and had no reasonable prospect of success. The Court however held that the interests of justice criterion had to be assessed in the light of all the circumstances of the case. The applicant was serving a five year prison sentence so that there was no doubt about the importance of what was at stake for him. The Court of Appeal had been addressed at length by the Solicitor General who appeared for the Crown. One of the issues which arose was of considerable complexity, but the applicant was not in a position to understand the prepared statement he read out, or the opposing arguments. Nor could he reply to those arguments or answer questions from the bench.

14–29   At first sight the Court's decision in *Granger* may appear to turn on the complexity of the issues which arose in the appeal. However, in *Boner v. United Kingdom*[74] and *Maxwell v. United Kingdom*[75] the Court unanimously found a violation of Article 6(3)(c) despite concluding that the legal issues were straightforward. Under Scots law there was, at the time, no requirement for leave to appeal. But the decision as to whether legal aid should be granted lay with the Scottish Legal Aid Board which had to decide whether an applicant for legal aid had substantial grounds for appealing and whether it was in the interests of justice that he should be granted legal aid. The Board could therefore refuse legal aid on the ground that the appeal was unmeritorious. The European Court of Human Rights held that the interests of justice required free legal assistance. This was despite the fact that the legal issues in the case were not complex, no point of substance had arisen in the appeal, and prosecution counsel had not addressed the Court of Appeal. The Court held that in the absence of legal representation the applicants had been unable to address the court on the issues raised in the

---

[70] (1992) 16 E.H.R.R. 53.
[71] For evidence of this, see R. Young, "The Merits of Legal Aid in Magistrates' Courts" [1993] Crim. L.R. 336. However, the Strasbourg organs have been unwilling to intervene if there is no evidence that the magistrates applied the wrong test or applied the right test unfairly: see, *e.g.*, *Bell v. United Kingdom* (1989) 11 E.H.R.R. 83.
[72] *McDermitt v. United Kingdom* (1987) 52 D.R. 244.
[73] (1990) 12 E.H.R.R. 469 at paras 42–48.
[74] (1995) 19 E.H.R.R. 246.
[75] (1995) 19 E.H.R.R. 97.

appeal and thus had been deprived of the opportunity to defend themselves effectively.

It is now quite clear that the requirement for effective legal representation will be   **14–30**
mandatory not only in the higher courts but in all courts or tribunals where loss
of liberty may be at stake. In *Benham v. United Kingdom*,[76] the Court was called
upon to determine whether the "interests of justice" criterion in Article 6(3)(c)
was satisfied in Magistrates Court proceedings leading to imprisonment for non-
payment of the community charge. Under the applicable regulations there was no
right to full legal aid, but a debtor was entitled to Green Form advice and
assistance and, in the discretion of the Magistrates Court, to representation under
the ABWOR[77] scheme. The Government submitted that this level of provision
was adequate in the circumstances. In the Government's submission, the proceedings were intended to be straightforward and amounted, in effect, to a means
inquiry at which full legal representation was unnecessary. The Court disagreed:

> "[W]here deprivation of liberty is at stake, the interests of justice in principle call for
> legal representation. In this case B faced a maximum term of three months imprison-
> ment . . . Furthermore, the law which the magistrates had to apply was not straightfor-
> ward. The test for culpable negligence in particular was difficult to understand and
> operate, as was evidenced by the fact that, in the judgment of the Divisional Court, the
> magistrates' finding could not be supported on the evidence before them."

The Court went on to hold that the existing provision was inadequate since under   **14–31**
Article 6(3)(c) the applicant was entitled to representation at the hearing *as of
right*:

> "The Court has regard to the fact that there were two types of legal aid provision
> available to B. Under the Green Form scheme he was entitled to up to two hours advice
> and assistance from a solicitor prior to the hearing, but the scheme did not cover legal
> representation in court. Under the ABWOR scheme the magistrates could, at their
> discretion, have appointed a solicitor to represent him, if one had happened to be in
> court. However, B was not entitled as of right to be represented . . . In view of the
> severity of the penalty risked by B, and the complexity of the applicable law, the Court
> considers that the interests of justice demanded that, in order to receive a fair hearing,
> B ought to have benefitted from free legal representation during the proceedings before
> the magistrates."

Despite the Court's reference to the complexity of the domestic proceedings, it   **14–32**
is clear that the decisive criterion in *Benham* was the seriousness of what was at
stake for the applicant in terms of the potential penalty that the court could
impose. The approach of the United Nations Human Rights Committee under
Article 14 of the ICCPR appears to be broadly the same. In *OF v. Norway*[78] the
Committee held that a defendant who had been convicted of two minor motoring
offences which could only lead to a small fine had not shown that the interests

---

[76] (1996) 22 E.H.R.R. 293 at paras 61–64.
[77] Advice By Way Of Representation.
[78] Application No. 158/1983; See Nowak, *UN Covenant on Civil and Political Rights*, (Kluwer, 1993), p. 260.

of justice in the particular case required the assignment of a defence lawyer at the state's expense.[79]

14–32a In *Procurator Fiscal, Fort William v. McLean and anor*[80] the High Court of Justiciary held that a fixed fee for certain summary prosecutions was not incompatible with Article 6. The relevant regulation[81] provided for a flat fee of £550 for all work done in summary proceedings up to and including a diet at which a plea of guilty was made and accepted, or a plea in mitigation was made, and the first 30 minutes of any summary trial. The lawyer would receive the same fee regardless of the work done or of how essential or costly any outlays may have been. The defence argued that such a rigid system of payment, with no safeguard to allow for the actual requirements of a given case, imported a substantial risk that even an honourable solicitor acting in good faith might allow professional standards to fall below an acceptable minimum. The Court accepted that the system produced what could properly be called a conflict of interest since it was in the interests of the defence lawyer to keep outlays and work done to a minimum. However, on the facts, there was no actual prejudice to the defendants since there was no suggestion that their lawyers had omitted to do anything which was necessary for the presentation of their defence. The Court was not persuaded by the more general argument that all defendants were necessarily prejudiced by the regulations since they were at risk of receiving inadequate representation. The suggestion that a lawyer would betray his client's interests was unacceptably speculative. Whether the matter was approached in terms of "conflict of interest" or in terms of "equality of arms" there was no basis for holding that what might be the case in particular circumstances was inevitably the case in all circumstances.

B. Cautioning and Discontinuance

14–33 Neither the presumption of innocence in Article 6(2), nor the right of access to court implicit in Article 6(1), entitles an accused to insist that any criminal charge which has been brought be carried through to its conclusion in order to enable him to establish his innocence. In *X, Y and Z v. Austria*[82] the Commission held that Article 6(2) does not;

> " ... prevent the Public Prosecutor's Office from deciding not to prosecute or to withdraw the indictment and the judge from terminating the proceedings without a ruling. In other words Article 6(2) does not confer on the accused an absolute right that the charge brought against him should be determined by a court."[83]

The Commission noted that if the decision had involved any suggestion that the applicant was guilty this would be different.

---

[79] By contrast the Committee has held that it is "axiomatic" that free legal representation should be provided where the defendant is at risk of the death penalty: *Robinson v. Jamaica* Application No. 223/1987, and the cases cited at Nowak, p. 260 n. 140.
[80] *The Times*, August 11, 2000.
[81] Criminal Legal Aid (Fixed Payments) (Scotland) Regulations (S.I. 1999 No. 491), Regulation 4 and Schedule 1.
[82] (1980) 19 D.R. 213 at 217–218.
[83] *ibid.*, at 217.

Notwithstanding this general principle the Court has held that any compromise of   **14–34**
criminal proceedings (such as the administration of a caution or the acceptance
of a plea of guilty to a lesser offence) must be truly voluntary and free from
constraint. In the leading decision of *Deweer v. Belgium*[84] the applicant was a
butcher who was alleged to have been selling over-priced pork. The public
prosecutor issued an order requiring the provisional closure of the applicant's
business pending the conclusion of the criminal prosecution, or until the applicant paid a penalty of B. Fr. 10,000 by way of "settlement". The applicant opted
to pay the penalty under protest. In Strasbourg, he complained that the procedure
had denied him the right to a fair trial. The Court began by observing that "the
'right to a court', which is a constituent element of the right to a fair trial, is no
more absolute in criminal than in civil matters". It was subject to implied
limitations. Without wishing to elaborate a general theory of such limitations, the
Court pointed to a decision not to prosecute, and an order for discontinuance of
proceedings as being obvious examples. The Court held that by agreeing to pay
the penalty the applicant had waived his right to a trial. That did not, however,
exhaust the requirements of Article 6. The right to a fair trial was of such
importance that any compromise reached between the state and the accused had
to be free from constraint. In the present case the amount of the fine was minimal
when compared to the consequences of contesting the proceedings. Had the
applicant elected to proceed to trial, his business would have remained closed
throughout the period, and he would have been exposed to the risk of a far more
substantial penalty in the event of a conviction. In the Court's view, there was a
"flagrant disporportion" between the two alternatives facing the applicant. This
created a pressure so compelling that it was hardly surprising that he had yielded.
As a result the procedure was held to be "tainted by constraint" and to have
amounted to a breach of Article 6.

C. SEVERANCE

The principles of English law governing severance of defendants who are   **14–35**
properly joined in the same indictment are reasonably settled. The fact that
evidence which is admissible against one defendant may be inadmissible against
another is a relevant consideration, but is not in itself generally sufficient to
require the court to order separate trials since the risk of unfairness can be
countered by clear directions to the jury.[85] Similarly, the fact that the defence of
one accused inevitably involves an attack on a co-accused, whilst material to the
exercise of the discretion, is not decisive.[86]

The Strasbourg institutions have generally held that admissibility of evidence is   **14–36**
primarily a matter for domestic law.[87] Nevertheless, the admission of certain
types of evidence is capable of rendering the trial as a whole unfair.[88] Where
evidence inadmissible against one defendant is admitted against another in a joint

---

[84] (1979–80) 2 E.H.R.R. 439.
[85] See, *e.g. R. v. Lake* (1976) 64 Cr. App. R. 172 at 175 (C.A.).
[86] *R. v. Grondkowski and Malinowski* [1946] K.B. 369; *R. v. Miller* (1952) 36 Cr. App. R. 169.
[87] See generally Chapter 15 below.
[88] See, *e.g., Austria v. Italy* (1963) 6 Y.B. 740 at 784, and more recently *Teixeira de Castro v. Portugal*
(1999) 28 E.H.R.R. 101.

trial, the Commission appears to accept that a refusal to order severance *may* exceptionally raise an issue under Article 6 if the evidence which has been elicited puts the fairness of the trial in jeopardy. In one unreported decision[89] the applicant complained that evidence elicited during cross-examination of a co-defendant was prejudicial to his defence. He had not however applied for severance before or during the trial. In rejecting the complaint, the Commission observed that:

> " . . . in a trial, like the present, where four co-defendants are tried together, it is inevitable that some evidence elicited from or in relation to one of the defendants may be considered prejudicial to another defendant by his counsel. In the present case, however, the applicant does not appear to have applied to be tried separately from his co-defendants, and the Commission does not find that the evidence given by this co-defendant was such as to jeopardise the fairness of the applicant's trial."[90]

14–37 A challenge to the constitutionality of severance provisions under the South African Constitution failed in *State v. Shuma*.[91] The Court held that the existing provisions in the Criminal Procedure Act, which enabled severance at any point during the proceedings where this was in the interests of justice, struck a fair balance between the interests of the accused and those of the state. Erasmus J. observed that "courts should not readily declare well-established procedure offensive to the constitution". The issue had to be judged "in the real context of criminal trials in general and the facts of the particular case".

D. DELAY

I. *The Strasbourg Caselaw*

14–38 Article 6(1) guarantees a right to a hearing within a reasonable time in both civil and criminal cases. Its purpose is to protect all parties from excessive procedural delays.[92] In guaranteeing a trial within a reasonable time Article 6(1) underlines "the importance of rendering justice without delays which might jeopardise its effectiveness and credibility".[93] In criminal cases it serves the additional function of protecting individuals from "remaining too long in a state of uncertainty about their fate".[94] It is thus a guarantee of expedition in the conduct of the proceedings themselves. In determining what constitutes a "reasonable time" for the purposes of Article 6, regard must be had to the circumstances of each case including, in particular, the complexity of the factual or legal[95] issues raised by the case; the

---

[89] Application No. 10159/82, 2 Dig. Supp. 6.1.1.4.4.5, at 6.
[90] *ibid.*, at 7.
[91] [1994] 4 S.A. 583 E.
[92] *Stögmüller v. Austria* (1979–80) 1 E.H.R.R. 155.
[93] *H v. France* (1990) 12 E.H.R.R. 74.
[94] *Stögmüller v. Austria* (1979–80) 1 E.H.R.R. 155, para. 5.
[95] If a particular case will have important repercussions on the national case-law in a particular area, this may be a relevant consideration: *Katte Klitsche de la Grange v. Italy* (1994) 19 E.H.R.R. 368, para. 62.

conduct of the applicant and of the competent administrative and judicial authorities; and what is "at stake" for the applicant.[96]

States are obliged to organise their legal systems so as to allow the courts to **14-39** comply with the requirements of Article 6(1).[97] Thus, breaches of the Convention have been found in cases where excessive delays resulted from a long-term backlog of work in the court system coupled with the failure of the state to take remedial measures.[98] A lack of resources is unlikely to amount to a sufficient justification for delay in a trial,[99] particularly where the detention or continued detention of the defendant is at stake.[1]

In criminal cases, the reasonable time guarantee runs from the date of charge **14-40** until its final determination, including the exhaustion of all ordinary avenues of appeal.[2] A person is subject to a "charge" within the meaning of Article 6 when he is "officially notified" of the allegation, or "substantially affected" by the proceedings taken against him.[3] In a straightforward case this will usually be the date of charge by the police.[4] But in a case where the charge is delayed, it may be the date of a person's arrest,[5] or the date upon which the defendant becomes aware that "immediate consideration" is being given to the possibility of a prosecution.[6] In *IJL, GMR and AKP v. United Kingdom*[7] the applicants, who had been prosecuted for alleged involvement in a share support scheme during the Guinness takeover bid for Distillers, contended that time should be taken to run from the date upon which they had been called in for interview by Inspectors from the Department of Trade and Industry (DTI). The Court disagreed. Since the DTI investigation did not involve the determination of a criminal charge, time was held to run from the commencement of the criminal proceedings proper. In respect of the first two applicants, this meant the date of charge. In respect of the third it was the date of his arrest in the United States on an extradition warrant.

If an accused is not finally brought to trial, Article 6 ceases to apply as at the date **14-41** of discontinuance.[8] Where charges have been left to "lie on the file", Article 6 ceases to apply if the prosecution undertake not to proceed with them[9] or if it is

---

[96] *Zimmermann and Steiner v. Switzerland* (1984) 6 E.H.R.R. 17, para. 24.
[97] *Muti v. Italy* Judgment March 23, 1994 Series A No. 281–C (para. 15); *Süßmann v. Germany* (1998) 25 E.H.R.R. 64, paras 55–56.
[98] *Zimmermann and Steiner v. Switzerland* (1984) 6 E.H.R.R. 17, paras 27–32; *Guincho v. Portugal* (1985) 7 E.H.R.R. 223, paras 40–41.
[99] *Hentrich v. France* (1994) 18 E.H.R.R. 440, para. 61.
[1] *Mansur v. Turkey* (1995) 20 E.H.R.R. 535, para. 68; *Zana v. Turkey* (1999) 27 E.H.R.R. 667, para. 84.
[2] *Eckle v. Federal Republic of Germany* (1983) 5 E.H.R.R. 1, para. 76; *Neumeister v. Austria (No. 1)* (1979–80) 1 E.H.R.R. 91, para. 19.
[3] *Deweer v. Belgium* (1979–80) 2 E.H.R.R. 439, para. 46; *Eckle v. Federal Republic of Germany* (1983) 5 E.H.R.R. 1. As to the autonomous meaning of the term "charge" for the purposes of Art. 6(1), see Chapter 4 above.
[4] See for example *Ewing v. United Kingdom* (1988) 10 E.H.R.R. 141.
[5] *X v. United Kingdom* (1979) 17 D.R. 122.
[6] *X v. United Kingdom* (1978) 14 D.R. 26.
[7] [2001] Crim. L.R. 133.
[8] *Orchin v. United Kingdom* (1984) 6 E.H.R.R. 391 (entering of a *nolle prosequi*).
[9] *X v. United Kingdom* (1979) 17 D.R. 122.

the settled practice of the prosecuting authorities not to do so.[10] Thus in *L v. United Kingdom*[11] the applicant argued that, when a court ordered that five charges should "lie in the file" following a plea of guilty to a specimen charge of indecent assault, this deprived him of the right to trial within reasonable time on those counts. The Commission held that "the established practice in English law of not proceeding with other charges so long as the first conviction remains undisturbed, coupled with the judicial control over any further proceedings, means that in fact the accused is no longer faced with any criminal charges which require determination."[12] Where a case is referred back to the Court of Appeal by the Criminal Cases Review Commission time is taken to run from the date of the referral.[13] In order to ascertain whether the proceedings as a whole were determined within a reasonable time, the Court will aggregate the length of the first proceedings with the time taken to determine the appeal following the reference back, but will disregard the period in between.[14]

14–42   In order to establish a breach of Article 6(1) on the ground of excessive procedural delay, it is unnecessary to show that the accused has suffered prejudice in the preparation or presentation of his defence.[15] As Schiemann L.J. pointed out in *Weeks and Porter v. Magill*[16]; "The concept of reasonableness in this context is not limited by the effect of the delay on the reliability of any verdict produced after trial. Pursuant to the Convention there can be a remedy for the distress or other loss caused by delay even if there is an acquittal."

14–43   Factors to be taken into account include the complexity of the prosecution case, the conduct of the defendant,[17] and the conduct of the prosecuting authorities. A failure on the part of the defendant to co-operate with the judicial authorities is not necessarily to be held against him since Article 6 does not require active co-operation.[18] A more rigorous standard applies when the defendant is in custody.[19] Complexity may arise from the number of charges, from the difficulty of the legal issues involved, from the need to obtain evidence from abroad,[20] from the volume of evidence,[21] or from excusable delays in the obtaining of expert evidence.[22] Thus in *X v. United Kingdom*[23] certain fraud charges had been left outstanding for four years and eight months before the prosecution notified the applicant that it no longer intended to proceed with them. The Commission

---

[10] *X v. United Kingdom* (1983) 5 E.H.R.R. 508.
[11] (1990) 65 D.R. 325. The case was argued under Art. 5(3) (trial within reasonable time of arrest) but the issue is the same.
[12] *ibid.*, at para. 2.
[13] *IJL, GMR and AKP v. United Kingdom* [2001] Crim. L.R. 133.
[14] *ibid.*
[15] *Crummock (Scotland) Ltd v. HM Advocate*, 2000 J.C. 408. *Cf. Attorney-General's Reference No. 1 of 1990* [1992] Q.B. 630. The same approach has been taken by the Privy Council in relation to the right to trial within a reasonable time in Commonwealth Constitutional challenges: *Cf. Bell v. DPP* [1985] 1 A.C. 937; *DPP v. Tokai* [1996] A.C. 856.
[16] [2000] 2 W.L.R 1420 (C.A.).
[17] *cf.* the decision of the Privy Council in *Attorney-General of Hong Kong v. Cheung Wai-bun* [1993] 2 All E.R. 509.
[18] *Zana v. Turkey* (1999) 27 E.H.R.R. 667, para. 79.
[19] *Abdoella v. Netherlands* (1992) 20 E.H.R.R. 585, para. 24.
[20] *Neumeister v. Austria (No. 1)* (1979–80) 1 E.H.R.R. 91.
[21] *Wemhoff v. Germany* (1968) 1 E.H.R.R. 55.
[22] *Wemhoff v. Germany* (1979–80) 1 E.H.R.R. 55.
[23] (1979) 17 D.R. 122 at para. 73.

held that an application based on Article 6(1) was inadmissible, because the length of time was not "unreasonable" in view of the complexity of the issues and their dependence on other charges against the applicant which were themselves so complex that two trials took over six months in all.[24] Similarly, in *IJL, GMR and AKP v. United Kingdom*[25] the Court held that four and a half years to determine complex fraud charges (which included the determination of a reference back to the Court of Appeal) was not unreasonable:

"The Court observes that the criminal proceedings were of undoubted complexity. The applicants were each charged with multiple offences arising out of an alleged unlawful and highly complicated share support operation. The applicants' trial lasted 75 days during which the jury heard ten days of speeches by counsel and a five day summing up by the trial judge. The trial itself was prefaced by a lengthy trial on the *voir dire* in the course of which the applicants sought to have transcripts of their interviews with the Inspectors ruled inadmissible. As a further example of the case's complexity, it is to be observed that the Court of Appeal's second judgment delivered on 27 December 1995 ran to 113 pages, following a ten day hearing."

The state is not responsible for delays attributable to the defendant or his lawyers[26] and periods spent unlawfully at large are to be disregarded in determining the overall length of the proceedings.[27] The state is, however, responsible for delays attributable to the prosecution or the court. In *Orchin v. United Kingdom*[28] three years of delay (out of a total period of five years and three months during which the charges were outstanding) were attributed by the government to an administrative oversight. The Northern Ireland DPP had decided not to proceed with the charges, but failed to notify the applicant or to enter a *nolle prosequi* for another three years. The Commission held that it was "the sole responsibility of the prosecuting authorities to take steps to terminate proceedings reasonably promptly after they had decide not to proceed". Violations of the reasonable time guarantee have been found in relation to the dilatory transfer of cases between courts[29]; delay in determining whether the court has jurisdiction[30]; delay to enable an appeal court to deal with four appeals together[31]; delay between the proffering of an indictment and the commencement of a trial, and delay in the communication of judgment to the accused[32]; and excessive time taken for the hearing of appeals.[33]

II. *Article 6(1) and Abuse of Process*

It will be apparent from the preceding paragraphs that the right to trial within a reasonable time in Article 6(1) is a fundamentally different concept from the

---

[24] In *Boddaert v. Belgium* (1992) 3 H.R.C.D. 227 the Court held that six years and three months did not amount to an unreasonable time for the investigation and trial of a complex murder, in which there were other parallel proceedings.
[25] [2001] Crim. L.R. 133.
[26] *cf. König v. Federal Republic of Germany (No. 1)* (1979–80) 2 E.H.R.R. 170.
[27] *Girolani v. Italy* (1991) Series A No. 196–E.
[28] (1984) 6 E.H.R.R. 391.
[29] *Foti and ors v. Italy* (1983) 5 E.H.R.R. 313, para. 72.
[30] *Zana v. Turkey* (1999) 27 E.H.R.R. 667, para. 81.
[31] *Hentrich v. France* (1994) 18 E.H.R.R. 440, para. 61.
[32] *Eckle v. Federal Republic of Germany* (1983) 5 E.H.R.R. 1, para. 84.
[33] *Ferraro v. Italy* (1991) Series A No.197–A.

common law jurisdiction to stay a prosecution as an abuse of process on grounds of delay, as that jurisdiction has hitherto been understood in England and Wales. The absence of a requirement to show prejudice in order to establish a breach of Article 6(1)[34] is in direct conflict with the pre-Human Rights Act principle that a court should stay an indictment on grounds of delay only in exceptional circumstances, and only where the accused has been so prejudiced in the conduct of his defence that a fair trial is no longer possible.[35] In the absence of prejudice (in the narrow sense), domestic case law had, prior to the Human Rights Act, treated the hardship flowing from procedural delay as a factor in mitigation of sentence.[36] The time frame is accordingly different. Since the decisions on abuse of process have been concerned with the risk of prejudice to the defence, the jurisdiction has focussed upon the period between the commission of the offence and the start of the trial. As we have seen, Article 6(1) is concerned with the procedural delays between the moment that the defendant was first affected by the proceedings, and the final determination of any appeal.

14–46   Does it follow that under the Human Rights Act a court must stay a prosecution for abuse of process, even where the delay has caused no conceivable prejudice to the accused? The answer lies in section 8 of the Human Rights Act, which provides that where a court finds that an individual's Convention rights have been violated, it may grant any remedy which it considers to be just and appropriate. The South African Constitutional Court has held that whilst prejudice in the conduct of the defence is irrelevent in determining whether the accused has been the victim of a violation of the constitutional right to trial within a reasonable time, it may be relevant in determining the appropriate remedy. The Court has held that the "draconian step" of an absolute stay is only one possible remedy. A criminal court could, instead, exclude evidence, if appropriate, or effect a real, as opposed to a nominal, reduction in sentence to reflect the hardship caused by the constitutional breach.[37]

14–47   In *Weeks and Porter v. Magill*[38] Schiemann L.J. appears to have adopted a similar approach. The applicants sought to appeal against a decision of the Divisional Court upholding the imposition of a surcharge under the Local Government Finance Act on the ground that they had caused or contributed to a substantial loss to Westminster City Council through "wilful misconduct" (arising from the "homes for votes" controversy). It was submitted that the proceedings had exceeded a reasonable time, in breach of Article 6(1), and that the only effective remedy was to quash the auditor's certificate, whether or not the delay had resulted in erroneous conclusions on the part of the auditor or the Divisional Court. Schiemann L.J. disagreed;

> "I reject the submission that . . . the natural consequence of the lapse of a reasonable time is that there must be a quashing of any order made after the lapse of this period—in the context of the present case a setting aside of the order of the Divisional Court and a quashing of the certificate . . . The passage of time may have one or both of two results. First, it may cast doubt on the reliability of the conclusions reached by the

---

[34] See para. 14–42 above.
[35] *Attorney-General's Reference No. 1 of 1990* [1992] Q.B. 630.
[36] *R. v. Derby Crown Court ex parte Brooks* (1984) 80 Cr. App. R. 164 at 169.
[37] *Wild and anor v. Hoffert and ors* (1998) 6 B.C.L.R. 656; (1998) 25 S.A.C.R. 1 (CC).
[38] [2000] 2 W.L.R. 1420 (C.A.).

tribunal. Second, it may cause or aggravate financial, physical or psychological harm to one or more of the parties to litigation. In so far as the court considers that the reliability of the conclusions reached by the tribunal has been impaired by the tribunal's failure to give appropriate weight to the effects of the passage of time the court may treat this as a ground for quashing the judgment arrived at by the tribunal . . . However, in so far as the passage of time has resulted in other harm to litigants, the requirement of Article 13 of the Convention that everyone be given an effective remedy for a violation of his rights does not have as a logical or inevitable consequence that the decision of the tribunal be quashed. An award of damages may well be a more appropriate remedy for damage caused to a litigant by an unduly delayed trial. This is clearly so where the litigant has been acquitted or found not liable. While in the case of an unsuccessful litigant no doubt the quashing of the decision will be welcome it does not as such provide any relief which is commensurate with the loss which has been suffered."

He went on, however, to draw a distinction between delay as a ground for staying **14–48** proceedings prior to their conclusion, and delay as a ground for quashing a decision after the event:

"Questions as to the effect of delay may come before the court both before and after the decision of the tribunal. When they arise before the decision of the tribunal then it will often be appropriate to take into account both the danger of an unreliable verdict and the danger of other damage caused to the litigant by the delay. Both of these can be averted by a stay of proceedings and may be averted by an order for a speedy trial. However, when questions as to the effect of delay arise after the decision it seems to me that quashing is likely to be the appropriate remedy for delay resulting in unreliable conclusions by the tribunal whereas an award of damages is likely to be the appropriate remedy for delay resulting in damage to the litigants."

Many would question whether an award of damages is an appropriate remedy for **14–49** a criminal defendant whose conviction has been found safe on appeal. More importantly, Schiemann L.J.'s approach appears to suggest that a delay which breaches Article 6(1) might afford a ground for staying a prosecution in advance of the trial, even though it would not generally afford a ground for quashing the conviction. It is difficult to see why the remedies provided at trial and on appeal should be different. If delay would, in itself, justify a stay of the proceedings, then there would appear to be no good reason why the Court of Appeal should be inhibited from quashing a conviction on the same ground, when a stay has been wrongly refused by the trial judge.

The correct approach to this issue has not yet been finally resolved at appellate **14–49a** level. On the one hand the House of Lords has established the important principle that a breach of Article 6 will inevitably result in the quashing of a criminal conviction.[39] On the other hand, where unconstitutional delay is in issue, there are recent conflicting decisions of the Privy Council as to the appropriate remedy. In *Darmalingham v. The State*[40] the Privy Council held that the right to a trial within a reasonable time in the constitution of Mauritius (modelled on Article 6) was distinct from the right to a fair trial. Accordingly, a breach of that guarantee did not depend on proof of prejudice:

[39] *R. v. Forbes* [2001] 2 W.L.R. 1; *R. v. A* [2001] 2 W.L.R. 1546. See also *R. v. Togher and ors* [2001] Crim. L.R. 124 (CA).
[40] (2000) 2 Cr. App. R. 445 (PC).

"Hence, if a defendant is convicted after a fair hearing by a proper court, this is no answer to a complaint that there was a breach of the guarantee of a disposal within a reasonable time. And, even if his guilt is manifest, this factor cannot justify or excuse a breach of the guarantee of a disposal within a reasonable time. Moreover, the independence of the 'reasonable time' guarantee is relevant to its reach. It may, of course, be applicable where by reason of inordinate delay a defendant is prejudiced in the deployment of his defence. But its reach is wider. It may be applicable in any case where the delay has been inordinate and oppressive."

14–49b   As to remedy, their Lordships held that it would ordinarily be right to quash the conviction. This was despite a submission from the prosecutor that the case should have been remitted to the Supreme Court with a direction to impose a non-custodial sentence in recognition of the breach:

"The normal remedy for a failure of this particular guarantee, *viz.* the reasonable time guarantee, would be to quash the conviction. That is, of course, the remedy for a breach of the other two requirements of section 10(1) . . . Their Lordships do not wish to be overly prescriptive on this point. They do not suggest that there may not be circumstances in which it might arguably be appropriate to affirm the conviction but substitute a non-custodial sentence, e.g. in a case where there had been a plea of guilty or where the inexcuseable delay affected the convictions on some counts but not on others. But their Lordships are quite satisfied that the only disposal which will properly vindicate the constitutional rights of the appellant in the present case would be the quashing of the conviction."

14–49c   Soon afterwards, however, a differently constituted Board of the Privy Council delivered judgment in *Flowers v. The Queen*,[41] rejecting the principle that there was a presumption that unconstitutional delay should result in the quashing of a conviction. Lord Hutton held that in assessing the impact of delay it was necessary to have regard to (a) the length of the delay (b) the reason for the delay (c) whether or not the accused had asserted the right to a speedy trial in the course of the proceedings and (d) the extent of any prejudice. In assessing prejudice, the court should take account not only of evidential prejudice, but of (a) the need to prevent oppressive pre-trial detention (b) the need to minimise the anxiety and concern of the accused and (c) the need to limit the possibility that the presentation of the defence would be evidentially impaired. The right to trial within a reasonable time had to be balanced against the public interest in the conviction of the guilty. Although the delay had been "lengthy and regrettable" it did not afford grounds for quashing the conviction where the accused had been convicted on strong evidence of a serious murder in the course of a robbery. Lord Hutton distinguished *Darmalingham* on the ground that the appellant in that case did not pose a serious threat to society. On this latter point, the implicit suggestion that the remedy should depend on the gravity of the crime finds no reflection either in the Strasbourg principles or in the leading Commonwealth decisions.

14–50   So-called "systemic delay" has been recognised as a ground for constitutional challenge under the Canadian Charter and the New Zealand Bill of Rights Act. In *R v. B*[42] the New Zealand Court of Appeal criticised a delay of 23 months for largely institutional reasons (a backlog of cases to be heard) but stopped short of

---

[41] October 30, 2000.
[42] [1996] 1 N.Z.L.R. 385.

quashing the appellant's conviction. The leading Canadian decision is *Morin*,[43] where the Supreme Court set out a number of factors that have a bearing on whether a delay should be regarded as "unreasonable". The court should have regard to the length of the delay; any waiver of time periods by the defence; the reasons for the delay (including the inherent time requirements of the case, the actions of the accused, the actions of the Crown, and the limits on institutional resources); and the existence or absence of any resulting prejudice to the accused."[44] In relation to the requirement to show prejudice, it is to be noted that this concept has a wider ambit under most constitutional instruments than under the doctrine of abuse of process at common law. Thus in the leading United States case of *Barker v. Wingo*[45] Justice Powell recognised a broad conception of prejudice flowing from procedural delays. The object of the sixth Amendment right to a "speedy trial" was "(i) to prevent oppressive pre-trial incarceration; (ii) to minimize anxiety and concern of the accused; and (iii) to limit the possibility that the defence will be impaired." Similarly, in *Doggett v. United States*.[46] the Supreme Court observed that;

> "Between diligent prosecution and bad faith delay, official negligence in bringing an accused to trial occupies the middle ground. While not compelling relief in every case where bad faith delay would make relief virtually axiomatic, neither is negligence automatically tolerable simply because the accused cannot demonstrate exactly how it has prejudiced him."

This approach has been widely adopted in common law countries.[47] Thus the Canadian and the New Zealand courts have taken the view that the psychological effects of delay on a defendant may constitute a strong argument that the delay is unreasonable, even if a fair trial could still be held.[48]

E. PUBLICITY, FAIR TRIALS AND CONTEMPT

I. *General*

Adverse publicity concerning a criminal prosecution carries an inevitable risk of prejudice to the fair trial of the accused, particularly if the case is to be tried by a jury. English courts have responded to this risk by holding that prejudicial publicity may lead to the stay of a criminal prosecution on grounds of abuse of process where no fair trial is possible,[49] and may in certain instances lead to the

14–51

---

[43] (1992) 12 C.R. (4th) 1, followed by the New Zealand Court of Appeal in *Martin v. District Court at Tauranga* [1995] 2 N.Z.L.R. 419.
[44] (1992) 12 C.R. (4th) 1 at 12–13, *per* Sopinka J.
[45] 407 U.S. 514 (1972) at 532.
[46] (1992) 120 L. Ed. 2d. 520.
[47] *E.g.* by the Supreme Court of Zimbabwe in *Re Miambo* [1993] 2 L.R.C. 28.
[48] *cf. Askov.* [1990] 2 S.C.R. 1199, and *Martin v. District Court at Tauranga* [1995] 2 N.Z.L.R. 419. For an analysis of the English, Canadian and other authorities up to 1993, see A. Choo, *Abuse of Process and Judicial Stays of Criminal Proceedings* (1993).
[49] *R. v. Reade* October 15, 1993, Central Criminal Court (Garland J.) (prosecution for perjury arising out of the conviction of six men for the Birmingham pub bombings); *R. v. Magee and ors* January 24, 1997, Belmarsh Crown Court, (Kay J.) (escape from HMP Whitemoor).

quashing of a criminal conviction.[50] The publication of prejudicial matter may also render the publisher liable to prosecution under the Contempt of Court Act 1981.[51] If proceedings are *active* (in the sense that there has been an arrest, summons or the issue of an arrest warrant), it will be an offence to publish material which creates a substantial risk that the course of public justice will be seriously impeded or prejudiced.[52] In *Attorney General v. BBC*,[53] the BBC was held to be in contempt for broadcasting an inaccurate report of a trial that had just started. The Divisional Court held that there was a substantial risk of prejudice, despite the judge's ruling that it was unnecessary to discharge the jury (since the interests of the accused could be secured by a strong direction to ignore the broadcast). Under section 4(2) of the Contempt of Court Act 1981 a trial judge may order the postponement of contemporary reporting of court proceedings where this is necessary to avoid a substantial risk of prejudice to the administration of justice in those proceedings, or in any other proceeding pending or imminent. Moreover, statutory reporting restrictions are automatically imposed in respect of committal proceedings,[54] applications to dismiss a charge and preparatory hearings ordered in serious or complex fraud cases under the Criminal Justice Act 1987,[55] and in respect of preparatory hearings and pre-trial rulings under the Criminal Procedure and Investigations Act 1996.[56]

14–51a More generally, it is a settled principle of English criminal procedure that all evidence and argument must take place in public, with access being afforded to the press, unless a departure from the principle of open justice is strictly necessary. In *Attorney General v. Leveller Magazine*[57] Lord Diplock explained that:

> "As a general rule the English system of administering justice does require that it be done in public: *Scott v Scott* [1913] AC 417. If the way that courts behave cannot be hidden from the public ear and eye this provides a safeguard against judicial arbitrariness or idiosyncrasy and maintains the public confidence in the administration of justice. The application of this principle of open justice has two aspects: as respects proceedings in the court itself, it requires that they should be held in open court to which the press and public are admitted and that, in criminal cases at any rate, all evidence communicated to the court is communicated publicly. As respects the publication to a wider public of fair and accurate reports of proceedings that have taken place in court the principle requires that nothing should be done to discourage this."

---

[50] *R. v. McCann and ors* (1991) 92 Cr. App. R. 239; *R. v. Taylor and Taylor* (1994) 98 Cr. App. R. 361; *R. v. Wood* [1996] 1 Cr. App. R. 207. For discussion of these and other cases, see D. Corker and M. Levi, "Pre-Trial Publicity and its Treatment in English Courts" [1996] Crim. L.R. 622.
[51] The 1981 Act was, of course, passed following the decision of the European Court in *Sunday Times v. United Kingdom (No. 1)* (1979–80) 2 E.H.R.R. 245 that the common law of contempt violated Art. 10 on freedom of expression.
[52] Section 2(2) of the Contempt of Court Act 1981. For fuller discussion, see *Arlidge, Eady and Smith on Contempt* (1999), chapter 4.
[53] [1992] C.O.D. 264.
[54] See s.8(4) of the Magistrates Courts Act 1980.
[55] See s.11(12) of the Criminal Justice Act 1987.
[56] See ss.37, 41 and 42 of the Criminal Procedure and Investigations Act 1996. Where automatic reporting restrictions apply, there is no requirement for the judge to balance the risk of prejudice to the trial against the rights of the media to report the proceedings or the right of the public to receive such information. For a critique of these provisions by reference to the Convention, see Cram, "Automatic Reporting Restrictions in Criminal Proceedings and Art. 10 of the ECHR" [1998] E.H.R.L.R. 742.
[57] [1979] A.C. 440 at 454H–450H.

The importance of this principle was reaffirmed in *R. v. Legal Aid Board ex parte* **14–51b**
Kaim Todner (a firm).[58] Lord Woolf M.R. explained that the courts should be
especially vigilant when considering departures from the principle of open justice:

> "The need to be vigilant arises from the natural tendency for the general principle to be
> eroded and for exceptions to grow by accretion as the exceptions are applied by analogy
> to existing cases. This is the reason it is so important not to forget why proceedings are
> required to be subjected to the full glare of a public hearing. It is necessary because the
> public nature of the proceedings deters inappropriate behaviour on the part of the court.
> It also maintains the public's confidence in the administration of justice. It enables the
> public to know that justice is being administered impartially. It can result in evidence
> becoming available which would not become available if the proceedings were con-
> ducted behind closed doors or with one or more of the parties' or the witnesses' identity
> concealed. It makes uninformed and inaccurate comment about the proceedings less
> likely . . . Any interference with the public nature of court proceedings is therefore to be
> avoided unless justice requires it. However Parliament has recognised there are situa-
> tions where interference is necessary . . . In deciding whether to accede to an application
> for protection from disclosure of the proceedings it is appropriate to take into account
> the extent of the interference with the general rule which is involved. If the interference
> is for a limited period that is less objectionable than a restriction on disclosure which
> is permanent. If the restriction relates only to the identity of a witness or a party this is
> less objectionable than a restriction which involves proceedings being conducted in
> whole or in part behind closed doors."

In *Ex parte Guardian*[59] the Court of Appeal accepted that the first of the **14–51c**
principles in *Kain Todner* should be more broadly expressed, and that:

> "Open justice promotes the rule of law. Citizens of all ranks in a democracy must be
> subject to transparent legal restraint, especially those holding judicial or executive
> offices. Publicity, whether in the courts, the press, or both, is a powerful deterrent to
> abuse of power and improper behaviour."

Consistent with the Convention approach, the Court emphasised that whatever
order is made should be proportionate to the risk which the court considers to be
attendant upon disclosure and should be balanced against the rights of the press
and the public.[60]

From the perspective of the Convention, these issues involve a delicate interplay **14–52**
between the right to a fair trial in Article 6 (and especially the presumption of
innocence in Article 6(2)), and the right to freedom of expression in Article 10.
Article 6(1) generally requires that the hearing of criminal charges should take
place in public. The purpose of this guarantee is to protect litigants "against the
administration of justice in secret with no public scrutiny" and to maintain public
confidence.[61] The Court has held that access for the press is of particular
importance in this context, and that media reporting of criminal proceedings
plays an important part in the public administration of justice.[62] Nevertheless, the

---

[58] [1999] Q.B. 966 at 977 to 978.
[59] [1999] 1 W.L.R. 2130 at 2144, para. 25, and 2148, para. 39.
[60] At 2140, para. 5.
[61] *Pretto v. Italy* (1984) 6 E.H.R.R. 182, para. 21.
[62] *Axen v. Germany* (1984) 6 E.H.R.R. 195, para. 25; *Pretto v. Italy* (1984) 6 E.H.R.R. 182, para.
21.

right to a public hearing is subject to the express qualifications set out in the second sentence of Article 6(1). The press may be excluded from all or part of a trial in the interests of morals, public order or national security, where the interests of juveniles[63] or the protection of the private lives of the parties so require, or to the extent strictly necessary in the opinion of the court in special circumstances where publicity would prejudice the interests of justice. Article 10(2) contains a similar, though less specific, qualification, referring to the maintenance of "the authority and impartiality of the judiciary" as a legitimate aim for restricting freedom of expression. The two issues are closely inter-related, but it is necessary to identify the separate considerations that the Court has taken into account under Article 6 and Article 10 respectively.

II. *Pre-Trial Publicity and the Presumption of Innocence*

14–53   In *Allenet de Ribemont v. France*,[64] the French Interior Minister and a number of senior police officers held a press conference shortly after the applicant's arrest, in which they named him as one of the instigators of the murder of a French MP. Their statements were widely reported in France. The applicant was later charged but subsequently released without trial. The Court held that the making of the statements, which carried with it the clear implication that the applicant was guilty of the charge, violated the presumption of innocence in Article 6(2). In its judgment the Court laid down the following principles on pre-trial statements of this nature:

> "The presumption of innocence enshrined in paragraph 2 of Article 6 is one of the elements of a fair criminal trial that is required by paragraph 1 . . . The Court considers that the presumption of innocence may be infringed not only by a judge or court but also by other public authorities . . . Freedom of expression, guaranteed by Article 10 of the Convention, includes the freedom to receive and impart information. Article 6(2) cannot therefore prevent the authorities from informing the public about criminal investigations in progress, but it requires that they do so with all discretion and circumspection necessary if the presumption of innocence is to be respected.
>
> The Government maintained that [the Minister's] remarks came under the head of information about criminal proceedings in progress and were not such as to infringe the presumption of innocence, since they did not bind the courts . . . The Court notes that in the instant case some of the highest ranking officers in the French police referred to Mr Allenet de Ribemont, without any qualification or reservation, as one of the instigators of a murder, and thus an accomplice in that murder. This was clearly a declaration of the applicant's guilt which, firstly, encouraged the public to believe him guilty and, secondly, prejudged the assessment of the facts by the competent judicial authority. There has therefore been a breach of Article 6(2)".[65]

14–54   It has long been established that even without official statements of this kind, a "virulent press campaign against the accused" is capable of violating the right to

---

[63] In *T and V v. United Kingdom* (2000) 30 E.H.R.R. 121 the presence of the media during a trial of two juveniles, and an order made by the judge lifting reporting restrictions to permit the publication of their identities and their photographs was held to have contributed to a violation of Art. 6(1). The Court referred to the possibility that procedures such as publicity, which are generally considered to safeguard the rights of adults on trial, could have the opposite effect on young defendants, and may need to be abrogated in order to ensure their understanding and participation.
[64] (1995) 20 E.H.R.R. 557.
[65] *ibid.*, at paras 35–41.

a fair trial, particularly where the trial is to take place with a jury.[66] Nevertheless, the Commission will take account of the fact that some press comment on a trial involving a matter of public interest is inevitable.[67] As the Commission has observed[68]; "[T]he mass media and even the authorities responsible for crime policy cannot be expected to refrain from all statements, such as the mere existence of criminal proceedings or the fact that a suspicion exists. What is excluded however is a formal declaration that somebody is guilty."[69]

In one case the Commission went slightly further, holding that it would be unreasonable to require either the press or the authorities to refrain from referring to the dangerous character of an accused person when they are in possession of uncontested facts.[70]

A number of inadmissibility decisions illustrate the differing approaches of the Commission, according to the nature of the tribunal. In one unreported case[71] newspaper and television reports referred to the fact that the applicant had previously been tried for the same offence, and that the jury had been unable to agree. One of the reports incorrectly stated that the applicant had pleaded guilty at the first trial. At the end of the retrial the judge summoned the newspaper proprietors for contempt of court, and acknowledged that the reports might have prejudiced the trial. The judge had not given the jury specific warnings which would have drawn their attention to the contents of the reports but gave them a general warning to ignore any press statements they might have seen. The Commission considered that there was no appearance of a violation. In particular, it considered that the report of the fact that the jury at the first trial had been unable to agree was more likely to prejudice the prosecution than the defence. In *X v. Austria*[72] the Commission observed that: **14–55**

> "in certain cases, and in particular in cases where laymen participate as jurors in the proceedings, [the right to a fair trial] may be seriously impaired by a virulent press campaign against the accused, which so influences public opinion, and thereby the jurors, that the hearing can no longer be considered to be a 'fair hearing' within the meaning of Article 6 of the Convention."

A similar argument was raised in relation to the trial of Rosemary West, but the application foundered on procedural grounds.[73]

The Commission has often emphasised that where the hearing is to take place before judges the risk of prejudice is substantially reduced, and the latitude afforded to the press will be correspondingly greater. Where press reports of statements by the Public Prosecutor alleged that the applicant had committed offences other than those listed on the indictment, and the case was tried at first instance and on appeal by judges, the Commission considered that the judges were unlikely to be affected by the publicity[74]: **14–56**

---

66 *X v. Austria* (1963) 11 C.D. 31 at 43.
67 *X v. Norway* (1970) 35 C.D. 37 at 48.
68 Application No. 9433/81 (unreported), (1981) 2 Dig. 738.
69 *ibid.*, at 738.
70 *Ensslin, Baader and Raspe v. Germany* (1978) 14 D.R. 64.
71 Application No. 5768/72 Dec. 21.5.1975 (unreported), (1975) 2 Dig. 684.
72 Application No. 1476/62, (1963) 11 C.D. 31 at 43; 2 Dig. 696.
73 *West v. United Kingdom* [1998] E.H.R.L.R. 204.
74 Application No. 7748/76 Dec. 10.10.1977 (unreported), (1977) 2 Dig. 688.

"In the present case the Court of Appeal comprised no jurors who were likely to be influenced by such a campaign; neither the charge nor the conviction of the judges was founded upon the statements of an influenceable witness. Nothing, moreover, suggests that the judges hearing the case at first instance and on appeal, before whom the existence of the facts was scarcely challenged, might have been really influenced by a press campaign of this kind. The mere fact that they sentenced the applicant to the maximum term (6 months) does not permit the Commission to conclude that the Public Prosecutor's statements of which he complains led the judges to believe that the applicant had accorded more substantial advantages to Mr X than those recorded in the indictment."[75]

14–57   The same principle has been applied to the English Court of Appeal. In rejecting one complaint,[76] the Commission took account of the fact that the Court of Appeal sits without a jury, and had extensively examined the merits of the case and found the conviction to be safe. In the Commission's opinion, any risk of bias in the jury had been rectified by the hearing before the Court of Appeal,[77] which had paid specific regard to the publicity as a factor affecting the safety of the conviction. The Court of Appeal had concluded that "there was no real risk that the jury was influenced by the publicity," and that "the case for the Crown was so overwhelming that no jury could conceivably have returned any different verdicts." The Commission saw no reason to take a different view. Where the case has not achieved national coverage, the risk of unfairness caused by adverse publicity is sometimes dealt with by means of an order for change of venue. In *Austria v. Italy*[78] the Commission held that an application for a change of venue, on the grounds of legitimate suspicion of bias, could constitute a remedy which was effective and sufficient.

14–57a   The Convention caselaw on adverse publicity and jury bias[79] was extensively reviewed by Lord Hope for the Privy Council in *Montgomery and Coulter v. HM Advocate and anor.*[80] Under Scots law the test for staying a criminal prosecution on grounds of prejudicial media coverage, laid down in *Stuurman v. HM Advocate,*[81] was whether the continuation of the prosecution would be oppressive in the sense that the risk of prejudice was so grave that no direction by the trial judge could reasonably be expected to remove it. In judging that issue, the court was to take account of all the circumstances of the case, including the length of time since publication, the focusing effect of listening to evidence over a prolonged period, and the likely directions of the trial judge. Applied in that way, the test was "well-suited for use in the context of a complaint which is made under Article 6(1) of the Convention". In Lord Hope's view the *Stuurman* test fitted in well with the Strasbourg caselaw on jury bias[82] which took account of the adequacy of safeguards against a lack of impartiality. Article 6 did not require the issue of objective impartiality to be resolved with mathematical accuracy.

---

[75] *ibid.*, at 688.

[76] (1969) 30 C.D. 70 at 74–75; 2 Dig. 697.

[77] The Court has since taken a more robust view of the ability of the Court of Appeal to rectify unfairness arising at trial: see Chapter 17 below.

[78] (1961) 4 Y.B. 116; and see also *Jespers v. Belgium* (1980) 22 D.R. 100 at 126–127, where a failure to apply for a change of venue was held not to amount to non-exhaustion of domestic remedies, in view of the Commission's doubts that such an application would have succeeded.

[79] See para. 14–81 below.

[80] Judgment October 19, 2000.

[81] 1980 J.C. 111 at 122.

[82] See para. 14–81 below.

Rather, it called for "sufficient" guarantees and safeguards, and for the exclusion of any "legitimate doubt" of bias. However, there was one respect in which the approach under Scots law required modification. The concept of "oppression" had been held to involve a balancing exercise between the interests of the defendant in having a fair trial, and the public interest in ensuring that serious crime is prosecuted.[83] Lord Hope held that there was no scope for the concept of balance when the matter was approached from the standpoint of Article 6:

> "The right of an accused to a fair trial by an independent and impartial tribunal is unqualified. It is not to be subordinated to the public interest in the detection and suppression of crime. In this respect it might be said that the Convention right is superior to the common law right . . . [T]he only question to be addressed in terms of Article 6(1) of the Convention is the right of the accused to a fair trial. An assessment of the weight to be given to the public interest does not enter the exercise. Provided this point of principle is recognised, I see no reason why the *Stuurman* test should not continue to be used in this context. The logical justification for doing so is that it directs attention to the effectiveness of the principal measures . . . which the tribunal itself can provide. The likely effect of any warnings or directions given to the jury by the trial judge, in the light of the other circumstances of the trial, will in most cases be the critical issue."

III. *Freedom of Expression*

Section 12 of the Human Rights Act 1998 makes special provision for the rights   **14–58** of the media, restricting the making of *ex parte orders* and requiring the courts to pay particular regard to the importance of the Convention right to freedom of expression.[84] For reasons which are not entirely clear, criminal proceedings are excluded from the scope of the duty imposed by section 12.[85] A criminal court is, nevertheless, a public authority under section 6 of the Act and is therefore obliged to act compatibly with Article 10, unless it is bound by the terms of primary legislation to do otherwise.

Any restriction on the reporting of a criminal investigation, charge or prosecution   **14–59** will involve an interference with the right to freedom of expression in Article 10(1) of the Convention.[86] However, such restrictions will be justifiable under Article 10(2) where they are necessary and proportionate to ensure the fair trial of an accused. In *Sunday Times v. United Kingdom*[87] the Court observed that;

> "[I]nsofar as the law of contempt may serve to protect the rights of litigants, this purpose is already included in the phrase 'maintaining the authority and impartiality of the judiciary': the rights so protected are the rights of individuals in their capacity as litigants, that is as persons involved in the machinery of justice, and the authority of that machinery will not be maintained unless protection is afforded to all those involved in or having recourse to it."

The Court emphasised, however, that any given restriction must be strictly necessary on the particular facts of the case before the court:

---

[83] *X v. Sweeney* 1982 J.C. 70.
[84] See para. 3–20 above.
[85] See s.12(5).
[86] *Hodgson, Woolf Productions and the NUJ v. United Kingdom* (1988) 10 E.H.R.R. 503.
[87] (1980) 2 E.H.R.R. 245.

"[W]hilst the mass media must not overstep the bounds imposed in the interests of the proper administration of justice, it is incumbent on them to impart information and ideas concerning matters that come before the courts just as in other areas of public interest. Not only do the media have the task of imparting such information and ideas: the public also has a right to receive them ... The Court is faced not with a choice between two conflicting principles, but with a principle of freedom of expression that is subject to a number of exceptions which must be narrowly interpreted ... It is not sufficient that the interference involved belongs to that class of exceptions listed in Article 10(2) which has been invoked. Neither is it sufficient that the interference was imposed because its subject-matter fell within a particular category or was caught by a legal rule formulated in general or absolute terms. The Court has to be satisfied that the interference was necessary having regard to the facts and circumstances prevailing in the specific case before it."[88]

14–60   *Hodgson, Woolf Productions and the NUJ v. United Kingdom*[89] concerned a proposal to broadcast daily reconstructions of the trial of Clive Ponting for Official Secrets Act offences arising from the disclosure of information about the sinking of the *General Belgrano* during the Falklands war. Channel Four proposed to broadcast a programme entitled *Court Report* each day during the trial, which would take the form of studio readings from a transcript that had been carefully checked for accuracy and fairness. The trial judge made an order under section 4(2) of the Contempt of Court Act 1981, prohibiting the broadcast until the conclusion of the trial. Whilst he had no doubt that the broadcasters would make a sincere attempt present a balanced picture of the day's events, he held that if five hours of court proceedings were condensed into a 25 minute reading, it was inevitable that the programme would focus on certain parts of the evidence at the expense of other parts. As a result of the ruling, Channel Four altered the format of the programme, using newsreaders instead of actors, and presenting the broadcast as an extended news report.

14–61   The journalists and the production company complained that their rights under Article 10 had been violated. Notwithstanding the fact that Channel Four had been able to broadcast substantially the same information in a news format, the Commission was satisfied that there had been an intereference with the applicants' right to freedom of expression:

> "The Commission considers that the effect of the court order was to transform the television programme as initially devised by the applicants. It was no longer permissible for them to use actors to play the role of the participants in the trial and the transcript of the court proceedings had to be read by a newsreader. In the Commission's view, such an interference with the manner of conveying information to the public, as opposed to the content of the information, constitutes an interference with freedom of expression ... In reaching this view the Commission has attached particular importance to the role played by production and presentation techniques in the making of television programmes."

14–62   However, the restriction was held to be justified by the need to ensure the fairness of the *Ponting* trial. The Commission attached particular weight to the role of the trial judge in assessing the risk of prejudice:

---

[88] See also *R. v. Home Secretary ex parte Simms* [1999] 3 W.L.R. 328 at 336, where Lord Steyn emphasised that any interference with freedom of expression must be "measured in specifics".
[89] (1988) 10 E.H.R.R. 503.

"[T]he need to ensure a fair trial and to protect members of the jury from exposure to prejudicial influences corresponds to a 'pressing social need'. Such an interpretation is reflected in the importance attached in a democratic society to the right to a fair trial. Furthermore, where a trial judge is confronted, in the opening of a highly publicised and controversial trial, with a potentially prejudicial media report, great weight must be attached to his on-the-spot assessment of the dangers of prejudicing the jury and thereby harming the fairness of the trial ... It is true that there may have been other less objectionable courses open to the trial judge, short of prior restraint, such as instructing the jury not to watch the programme or watching it himself before taking the decision. However the Commission considers that where there is a real risk of prejudice the appropriate response, in the circumstances, is one which must lie, in principle, with the person responsible for ensuring the fairness of the trial, namely, the trial judge."

In *Atkinson, Crook and The Independent v. United Kingdom*[90] the applicants were **14–63** journalists and a national newspaper who complained that their Article 10 rights had been violated by a court's decision to exclude public and press from sentencing proceedings. The Commission declared the application inadmissible, holding that since Article 6(1) provides explicitly for the possibility of holding proceedings *in camera* it followed that Article 10 must, in appropriate circumstances, give way. The leading decision of the Court is *Worm v. Austria*,[91] in which the applicant was a journalist who had written an article asserting that Hannes Androsch, the former Austrian Vice Chancellor and Minister of Finance, was guilty of tax evasion. The article was published whilst the criminal proceedings were still in progress and the applicant was charged and convicted of an offence of "exercising a prohibited influence on criminal proceedings", a decision upheld by the Vienna Court of Appeal. The Court re-iterated that it was the task of journalists to impart such information, and that the public also had a right to receive it;

"There is general recognition of the fact that the courts cannot operate in a vacuum. Whilst the courts are the forum for the determination of a person's guilt or innocence on a criminal charge, this does not mean that there can be no prior or contemporaneous discussion of the subject-matter of criminal trials elsewhere, be it in specialised journals, in the general press or amongst the public at large. Provided that it does not overstep the bounds imposed in the interests of the proper administration of justice, reporting, including comment, on court proceedings contributes to their publicity and is thus perfectly consonant with requirement under Article 6(1) of the Convention that hearings be public."

This was all the more so when a public figure, and especially a former politician, **14–64** is involved since in that context "the limits of acceptable comment are wider."[92] The Court however emphasised that the limits of permissible comment did not extend to statements that were likely to prejudice a fair trial, even where public figures were involved. The objectionable feature of the article in question was that the assertion of Mr Androsch's guilt was made in such absolute terms that it conveyed the impression that the court could not do otherwise than convict him, and indeed it appeared to be intended to influence the outcome of the case.[93] The national courts had a margin of appreciation in determining whether it was

---

[90] (1990) 67 D.R. 244.
[91] (1998) 25 E.H.R.R. 454.
[92] *ibid.*, para. 50; *cf.* the discussion of the English law on court reporting in *Arlidge, Eady and Smith on Contempt* (1999), Chapter 7.
[93] Paras 52–53.

necessary to restrict the publication of such an article for the purpose of "maintaining the authority and impartiality of the judiciary". The breadth of that margin was circumscribed by the fact that there was a substantial measure of common ground on the issue in the member states of the Council of Europe. However, the Austrian courts were entitled to guard against the risk that the public would become "accustomed to the regular spectacle of pseudo-trials in the news media [which] might in the long run have nefarious consequences for the acceptance of the courts as the proper forum for the determination of a person's guilt or innocence". Insofar as the applicant was quoting the words of the prosecutor in opening the case against the accused, he should have indicated that the words were a quotation, rather than appearing to adopt them as a statement of his own. Accordingly the Court was satisfied that the reasons given by the Austrian courts were sufficient, and that the journalist's right to freedom of expression was not—in the manner in which it was exercised—so great as to outweigh the adverse consequences for the authority of the Austrian judicial system.[94]

14–65   There appears to be no settled international consensus as to the relative weight to be attached to the competing factors at stake when it is alleged that media coverage may prejudice a fair trial. One influential decision is that of the Supreme Court of Canada in *Re Dagenais and Canadian Broadcasting Corporation*.[95] The accused, members of a Catholic order who were being tried for various offences of sexual and physical abuse against boys at a training school, sought to prevent the CBC from screening a programme that gave a fictional account of physical and sexual abuse at a Catholic institution. A publication ban was made by the courts, but the Supreme Court held that this failed to provide sufficient protection for the right of freedom of expression. The existing law on publication bans was held to go too far in protecting the right of fair trial over the right to freedom of expression, when the Charter accorded equal status to the two rights. Such a ban would only be in accordance with the Charter if there was a substantial risk to the fairness of the trial, which could not be avoided by other means (such as an adjournment, a change of venue, or strong judicial direction to jury), and if the deleterious effects of a ban were clearly outweighed by its benefits for the administration of justice.

14–66   That approach was considered but not followed by the New Zealand Court of Appeal in *Gisborne Herald v. Solicitor General*.[96] In that case a local newspaper had published details of a man recently arrested for wounding a police officer, stating that he was on bail on other charges and setting out his previous convictions. The New Zealand courts held that the newspaper was guilty of contempt, particularly because in a small community it was unlikely that people would forget what had been written. The Court of Appeal adopted the view that, where freedom of expression and the right to a fair trial come into conflict, it would be appropriate to curtail temporarily the former right in order to secure the latter. The alternative methods of ensuring a fair trial mentioned in the Canadian case of *Dagenais* were not considered to be adequate to guard against prejudice at the trial.

---

[94] Para. 56.
[95] (1994) 94 C.C.C. (3d) 289.
[96] [1995] 3 N.Z.L.R. 563.

IV. Protection of the Identity of Offenders

In *Venables and Thompson v. News Group Newspapers and ors*,[97] the President   **14-66a**
of the Family Division held that the High Court had jurisdiction to grant a
lifelong injunction against the world where there was compelling evidence that
this was strictly necessary to protect the new identities to be given to the two
juveniles convicted of the murder of James Bulger. The claimants were due to be
released and there was clear evidence before the Court that attempts would be
made to identify them in the community, leading to potentially fatal reprisal
attacks. Whilst emphasising that the facts of the case were wholly exceptional,
Butler-Sloss L.J. held that there was a positive obligation[98] on the courts, under
Article 2 of the Convention, to take steps to prevent the dissemination of
information which could expose their lives to unnecessary risk.

F. THE RIGHT TO AN INDEPENDENT AND IMPARTIAL TRIBUNAL

I. General Principles

Article 6(1) guarantees the right to trial by an independent and impartial tribunal.   **14-67**
The concepts of independence and impartiality are closely linked, and it will
often be appropriate to consider them together.[99] A tribunal must be independent
of the executive, of the parties, and of the legislature.[1] In determining whether
this requirement is met, regard must be had to the manner of appointment of a
tribunal's members, their term of office, the existence of guarantees against
outside pressures, and the question whether the body presents an appearance of
independence.[2] It is doubtful whether the requirements of independence and
impartiality can be waived, in view of their importance for confidence in the
judicial system.[3] Thus, in *Bulut v. Austria*[4] the Court considered itself bound to
examine the impartiality of a tribunal, irrespective of an alleged waiver by the
applicant.[5]

Appointment by the executive or the legislature is permissible under Article 6,   **14-68**
provided the appointees are free from influence or pressure when carrying out

---

[97] January 8, 2001.
[98] As to positive obligations generally see para. 2–53 above.
[99] *Findlay v. United Kingdom* (1997) 24 E.H.R.R. 221, para. 73; *Incal v. Turkey* Judgment of June 9,
1998 (para. 65); *McGonnell v. United Kingdom* (2000) 30 E.H.R.R. 289.
[1] *Campbell and Fell v. United Kingdom* (1985) 7 E.H.R.R. 165, para. 78; *Crociani and ors v. Italy*
No. 8603/79 22 D.R. 147 (independence of Parliament) and *Demicoli v. Malta* (1992) 14 E.H.R.R.
47 (Comm. Rep. para. 40); *McGonnell v. United Kingdom* (2000) 30 E.H.R.R. 289.
[2] *Langborger v. Sweden* (1990) 12 E.H.R.R. 416 para. 32; *Campbell and Fell v. United Kingdom*
(1985) 7 E.H.R.R. 165, para. 78; *Findlay v. United Kingdom* (1997) 24 E.H.R.R. 22;. *Incal v. Turkey*
(2000) 29 E.H.R.R. 449; *Piersack v. Belgium* (1983) 5 E.H.R.R. 169, para. 27; *Delcourt v. Belgium*
(1979–80) 1 E.H.R.R. 355, para. 31; *Bryan v. United Kingdom* (1996) 21 E.H.R.R. 342, para. 37. As
to the requirement for an appearance of independence and impartiality, see para. 14–73 below.
[3] *Oberschlick v. Austria* (1995) 19 E.H.R.R. 389, para. 51 (waiver "in so far as it is permissible" must
be established in unequivocal manner).
[4] (1996) 24 E.H.R.R. 84, para. 30.
[5] The Government's argument in this regard was also rejected in *McGonnell v. United Kingdom*
(2000) 30 E.H.R.R. 289. *Cf.* the approach of the Court of Appeal to the question of waiver in *Locobail
(UK) Ltd v. Bayfield Properties Ltd and anor* [2000] 1 All E.R. 65 (para. 14–80 below).

their adjudicatory role.[6] In order to establish a lack of independence in the manner of appointment, it is necessary to show that the practice of appointment as a whole was unsatisfactory, or alternatively, that the establishment of the particular court, or the appointment of the particular judge (or jury member) gave rise to a risk of undue influence over the outcome of the case.[7] A relatively short term of office has been held acceptable for unpaid judicial appointments.[8] However, a renewable four year appointment for a judge who is a member of a national security court was considered "questionable".[9] In *Starrs and Chalmers v. Procurator Fiscal*,[10] the High Court of Justiciary in Scotland held the post of temporary sheriff to be incompatible with Article 6 since the appointment was for a fixed period of 12 months, and its renewal was within the unfettered discretion of the executive. The Court considered that security of tenure was the cornerstone of judicial independence, and that such independence could be threatened not only by interference, but also by a judge being influenced, consciously or unconciously, by his hopes and fears about possible treatment by the executive in the future. In Canada there have been several challenges under the equivalent section of the Charter against part-time judges and justices of the peace, but the leading decision of the Supreme Court upholds the existing system of appointment and training and discounts fears (particularly in relation to part-time judges) about conflicts of interest arising from their other professional duties.[11]

14–69   In *Campbell and Fell v. United Kingdom*,[12] a case concerning disciplinary adjudications under the former prison visitors regime, the Court held that members of a tribunal must as a very minimum, be protected against removal *during* their term of office:

> "[T]he irremovability of judges by the executive during their term of office must in general be considered as a corollary of their independence and thus included in the guarantees of Article 6(1). However, the absence of a formal recognition of this irremovability in the law does not in itself imply lack of independence provided that it is recognised in fact and that the other necessary guarantees are present."

14–70   Independence requires that each judge and tribunal member be free from outside pressure, whether from the executive, legislature, parties to the case or other members of the court or tribunal. Thus where a tribunal's members "include a person who is in a subordinate position, in terms of his duties and the organisation of his service, *vis à vis* one of the parties, litigants may entertain a legitimate doubt about that person's independence."[13] In *Findlay v. United Kingdom*[14] the Court found that there were objectively justified doubts as to the independence and impartiality of a court martial, where a "convening officer" was responsible for arranging the court martial, and for appointing the members of the court, the

---

[6] *Campbell and Fell v. United Kingdom* (1985) 7 E.H.R.R. 165, para. 79; *Crociani v. Italy* No. 8603/79 22 D.R. 147.
[7] *Zand v. Austria* (1978) 15 D.R. 70 at 81 (para. 78).
[8] *Campbell and Fell v. United Kingdom* (1984) 7 E.H.R.R. 165, para. 80 (*e.g.* a term of three years for prison visitors).
[9] *Incal v. Turkey* (2000) 29 E.H.R.R. 449.
[10] *The Times*, December 17, 1999, [2000] H.R.L.R. 191; 2000 S.L.T. 42.
[11] See *Quebec (AG) v. Lippe* (1991) 64 C.C.C. (3d) 513, and other authorities discussed by D. Stuart, *Charter Justice in Canadian Criminal Law* (2nd ed., 1996), pp 349–354.
[12] (1985) 7 E.H.R.R. 165, para. 80.
[13] *Sramek v. Austria* (1985) 7 E.H.R.R. 351.
[14] *Findlay v. United Kingdom* (1997) 24 E.H.R.R. 221, paras 73–77.

prosecuting and defending officers (who were all subordinate in rank, and fell within his chain of command). He also had the function of "confirming" the conviction and sentence imposed by the court.

The requirement for an impartial tribunal embodies the protection against actual   **14–71**
and presumed bias. The Court has adopted a dual test, examining first the evidence of actual bias, and then making an objective assessment of the circumstances alleged to give rise to a risk of bias.[15] In *Hauschildt v. Denmark*[16] the Court expressed the test in these terms:

"The existence of impartiality for the purpose of Article 6(1) must be determined according to a subjective test, that is on the basis of the personal conviction of a particular judge in a given case, and also according to an objective test, that is ascertaining whether the judge offered guarantees sufficient to exclude any legitimate doubt in this respect."[17]

The onus of establishing actual bias on the subjective test is a heavy one.[18] There   **14–72**
is a presumption that the court has acted impartially, which must be displaced by evidence to the contrary.[19] In applying the objective test, the question is whether a legitimate doubt as to the impartiality of the tribual can be "objectively justified".[20] The Court will inquire whether the tribunal offered guarantees sufficient to exclude such a doubt,[21] or whether there are "ascertainable facts" that may raise doubts as to a tribunal's impartiality.[22] In making an assessment of a tribunal's impartiality, "even appearances may be important".[23] Where there is legitimate doubt as to a judge's impartiality, he must withdraw from the case.[24]

An appearance of independence and impartiality is important because "what is at   **14–73**
stake is the confidence which the courts in a democratic society must inspire in the public".[25] The applicable test has been described in the following ways: whether the public is "reasonably entitled" to entertain doubts as to the independence or impartiality of the tribunal[26]; whether there are "legitimate grounds

---

[15] *Piersack v. Belgium* (1983) 5 E.H.R.R. 169, para. 30 applied in *Ferrantelli and Santangelo v. Italy* (1997) 23 E.H.R.R. 288, para. 56; *Bulut v. Austria* (1997) 24 E.H.R.R. 84, para. 31; *Thomann v. Switzerland* (1997) 24 E.H.R.R. 553, para. 30.
[16] (1990) 12 E.H.R.R. 266.
[17] *ibid.*, at para. 46.
[18] The test adopted by the Court is that the members of a tribunal must be "subjectively free of personal prejudice or bias": *Findlay v. United Kingdom* (1997) 24 E.H.R.R. 221, para. 73.
[19] *Hauschildt v. Denmark* (1989) 12 E.H.R.R. 266, para. 47; *Piersack v. Belgium* (1983) 5 E.H.R.R. 169, para. 30(a); *Thomann v. Switzerland* (1997) 24 E.H.R.R. 553, para. 31.
[20] *Hauschildt v. Denmark* (1990) 12 E.H.R.R. 266, para. 48; *Ferrantelli and Santangelo v. Italy* (1997) 23 E.H.R.R. 288, para. 58; *Incal v. Turkey* Judgment June 9, 1998 (para. 71); *Castillo Agar v. Spain* (2000) 30 E.H.R.R 827, para. 46.
[21] *Piersack v. Belgium* (1983) 5 E.H.R.R. 169, para. 30; *Incal v. Turkey* (2000) 29 E.H.R.R. 449, para. 65.
[22] See for example, *Hauschildt v. Denmark* (1990) 12 E.H.R.R. 266, para. 48.
[23] *Piersack v. Belgium* (1983) 5 E.H.R.R. 169, para. 30; *Sramek v. Austria* (1985) 7 E.H.R.R. 35, para. 42; *Findlay v. United Kingdom* (1997) 24 E.H.R.R. 221, para. 76.
[24] *Hauschildt v. Denmark* (1990) 12 E.H.R.R. 266, paras 46, 48; *Castillo Algar v. Spain* Judgment September 28, 1998, para. 45. As to the test to be applied in English law, see *Locobail (UK) Ltd v. Bayfield Properties Ltd and anor.* [2000] 1 All E.R. 65 (C.A.) (guidance on judicial impartiality).
[25] *Incal v. Turkey* (2000) 29 E.H.R.R. 449, para. 71; *Fey v. Austria* (1993) 16 E.H.R.R. 387, para. 30 (confidence of accused also essential in context of criminal trial).
[26] *Campbell and Fell v. United Kingdom* (1985) 7 E.H.R.R. 165, para. 81.

for fearing" that the tribunal is not independent or impartial[27]; whether "there are ascertainable facts that may raise doubts" as to independence or impartiality[28]; or whether such doubts can be "objectively justified".[29]

14–74   The fact that a trial judge or appeal judge has made pre-trial decisions in a case, including those concerning detention on remand, cannot in itself be held to justify fears as to the judge's impartiality, since:

> "[Q]uestions which the judge has to answer when taking such pre-trial decisions are not the same as those which are decisive for his final judgment. When taking a decision on detention on remand and other pre-trial decisions of this kind the judge summarily assesses the available data in order to ascertain whether *prima facie* the police have grounds for their suspicion; when giving judgment at the conclusion of the trial he must assess whether the evidence that has been produced and debated in court suffices for finding the accused guilty. Suspicion and formal finding of guilt are not to be treated as being the same."[30]

14–75   Where however, the issues determined at the pre-trial stage are closely related to those which arise at a final determination, the court's impartiality is capable of appearing open to doubt.[31] While it is not contrary to Article 6(1) for the same judge to take part in different proceedings against several persons accused of the same offence,[32] the position is otherwise where the judge has previously expressed views suggesting that he has formed an opinion as to the accused's guilt.[33]

14–76   There is no general rule resulting from the obligation to be impartial that a superior court which sets aside a decision of an inferior tribunal is bound to send the case back to a differently constituted bench.[34] The same principle applies where the first trial was held *in absentia* since:

> "[J]udges who retry in the defendant's presence a case that they have first had to try *in absentia* on the basis of the evidence that they had available to them at the time are in no way bound by their first decision. They undertake a fresh consideration of the whole case; all the issues raised by the case remain open and this time are examined in adversarial proceedings with the benefit of the more comprehensive information that may be obtained from the appearance of the defendant in person . . . [I]f a court had to alter its composition each time that it accepted an application for a retrial from a person who had been convicted in his absence, such person would be placed at an advantage in relation to defendants who appeared at the opening of their trial, because this would

---

[27] *Langborger v. Sweden* (1990) 12 E.H.R.R. 416, para. 35; *Procola v. Luxembourg* (1996) 22 E.H.R.R. 193, para. 45; *McGonnell v. United Kingdom* (2000) 30 E.H.R.R. 289.

[28] *Castillo Algar v. Spain* (2000) 30 E.H.R.R. 827.

[29] *Hauschildt v. Denmark* (1990) 12 E.H.R.R. 266, para. 48.

[30] *Hauschildt v. Denmark* (1990) 12 E.H.R.R. 266, para. 50. See also *Bulut v. Austria* (1997) 24 E.H.R.R. 84, paras 33–34 (role of judge in pre-trial proceedings restricted to questioning of two witnesses, but no assessment as to applicant's involvement in offence—no objective justification for lack of impartiality); *Sainte-Marie v. France* (1993) 16 E.H.R.R. 116, paras 32–34; *Fey v. Austria* (1993) 16 E.H.R.R. 387, paras 31–33; *Padovani v. Italy* Judgment February 26, 1993, para. 28; *Nortier v. Netherlands* (1994) 17 E.H.R.R. 273, paras 33–35.

[31] *Hauschildt v. Denmark* (1990) 12 E.H.R.R. 266, paras 51–52.

[32] *Ferrantelli and Santangelo v. Italy* (1997) 23 E.H.R.R. 288 (Comm. Rep.) para. 57.

[33] *Ferrantelli and Santangelo v. Italy* (1997) 23 E.H.R.R. 288, paras 59–60.

[34] *Thomann v. Switzerland* (1997) 24 E.H.R.R. 553, paras 33–36; *Ringeisen v. Austria (No. 1)* (1979–80) 1 E.H.R.R. 455, para. 97; *Diennet v. France* (1996) 21 E.H.R.R. 554, paras 37–38.

enable the former to obtain a second hearing of their case by different judges at the same level of jurisdiction."[35]

Where a trial judge was previously the head of the section of the public **14–77**
prosecutor's department which had investigated the applicant's case and commenced proceedings against him, the Court, not surprisingly, held that the "impartiality of the 'tribunal' which had to determine the merits . . . was capable of appearing open to doubt".[36] It was not necessary for the applicant to establish that the judge had been directly involved in the case:

> "In order that the courts inspire the confidence which is indispensable, account must also be taken of questions of internal organisation. If an individual, after holding in the public prosecutor's department an office whose nature is such that he may have to deal with a given matter in the course of his duties, subsequently sits in the same case as a judge, the public are entitled to fear that he does not offer sufficient guarantees of impartiality."[37]

However, the court considered that;   **14–78**

> "[I]t would be going too far . . . to maintain that former judicial officers in the public prosecutor's department were unable to sit on the bench in every case that had been examined initially by that department, even though they had never had to deal with the case themselves. So radical a solution, based on an inflexible and formalistic conception of the unity and indivisibility of the public prosecutor's department would erect a virtually impenetrable barrier between that department and the bench. It would lead to an upheaval in the judicial system of several Contracting States where transfers from one of those offices to the other are a frequent occurrence. Above all, the mere fact that a judge was once a member of the public prosecutor's department is not a reason for fearing that he lacks impartiality".[38]

Where a judge has a financial or personal interest in the case, a party is **14–79**
objectively justified in fearing lack of impartiality.[39] Any direct involvement in the passage of legislation or the enactment of executive rules is likely to be sufficient to cast doubt on the judicial impartiality of a person subsequently called upon to determine a dispute as to the existence of reasons for permitting a variation from the legislation or rules at issue. In *McGonnell v. United Kingdom*[40] the Bailiff of Guernsey, when sitting in his judicial capacity, was held not to be "independent" since he had performed a presiding role in the local legislature when it adopted the measure in dispute. In the light of the *McGonnell* decision, it is open to doubt whether the Lord Chancellor, or any senior judge, who has participated in Parliamentary debates on a Bill, can subsequently sit on an appeal in which the interpretation or application of the resulting legislation is in issue.

---

[35] *Thomann v. Switzerland* (1997) 24 E.H.R.R. 553 at 556–557 (paras 35–36).
[36] *Piersack v. Belgium* (1983) 5 E.H.R.R. 169 at 181, para. 31.
[37] *Piersack v. Belgium* (1983) 5 E.H.R.R. 169 at 180 (para. 30(d)).
[38] *Piersack v. Belgium* (1983) 5 E.H.R.R. 169 at 179 (para. 30(d)).
[39] See *Demicoli v. Malta* (1992) 14 E.H.R.R. 47 (paras 36–42) (members of the House of Representatives who were the subject of alleged offence of breach of parliamentary privilege were among those who sat in Judgment); *Langborger v. Sweden* (1990) 12 E.H.R.R. 416, para. 35 (lay members of tribunal adjudicating on deletion of clause in tenancy agreement were nominated by organisations having an interest in the clause's continued existence).
[40] (2000) 30 E.H.R.R. 289.

14–80 The test of judicial bias in domestic law has recently been revisited by the House of Lords and by the Court of Appeal. In *R. v. Bow Street Metropolitan Stipendiary Magistrate ex parte Pinochet Ugarte (No.2)*,[41] the House of Lords held that Lord Hoffman's connection with Amnesty International, which had intervened in the appeal, violated the principle that a person may not be a judge in his own cause. That principle goes wider than financial interests, and encompasses the promotion of a cause in which the judge is involved with one of the parties. Following the *Pinochet* ruling there was a sharp increase in the number of applications for recusal, and in *Locobail (UK) Ltd v. Bayfield Properties Ltd and another* the Court of Appeal gave guidance, in a series of linked appeals, on the approach to be adopted where it is alleged that a judge has a personal interest in the outcome of the proceedings.[42] Referring to Article 6, the Court of Appeal held that the right to a fair hearing by an impartial tribunal was fundamental. This pointed to a rule of automatic disqualification when a judge had a direct pecuniary or proprietary interest in the subject-matter of a proceeding, however small,[43] and where the matter at issue was concerned with the promotion of a cause and the judge is involved with one of the parties seeking to promote that cause.[44] In other cases, there was no rule of automatic disqualification. The question was whether a reasonable, objective and informed person, would on the correct facts, reasonably apprehend that the judge will not bring an impartial mind to bear on the adjudication of the case, that is a mind open to persuasion by the evidence and the submissions of counsel.[45] The religion, ethnic or national origin, gender, age, class, means or sexual orientation of a tribunal member could not conceivably form the basis of a sound objection. Nor could an objection generally be based on matters of social, educational, service or employment background or history, nor that of the tribunal member's family. Other factors which would generally be irrelevant were previous political associations, previous judicial decisions, extra-judicial comment, previous instructions to act for or against any party, solicitor or advocate engaged in the case, or membership of the same Inn of Court, circuit, local Law Society or chambers. By contrast a real danger of bias might arise from personal friendship or animosity between the tribunal member and any other person involved in the case, or a close acquaintance (especially where credibility is in issue). It would generally be appropriate for a tribunal member to recuse himself if, in a previous case, he had rejected the evidence of a witness in such outspoken terms as to throw doubt on his ability to approach that witness's evidence in subsequent proceedings with an open mind; if he had expressed views on any question at issue in the case in such strong and unbalanced terms as to throw doubt on his ability to try the case with an objective

---

[41] [2000] 1 A.C. 119; see also the High Court of Australia in *Webb v. R.* (1994) 181 C.L.R. 41, where the test was whether the judge's interests or affiliations would give rise to a suspicion, in a fair-minded and informed member of the public, that the judge might be biased.

[42] [2000] 1 All E.R. 65 (C.A.). As to police disciplinary proceedings, see *Regina (Bennion) v. Chief Constable of Merseyside Police, The Times*, June 12, 2001 (no breach of Article 6 where the Chief Constable adjudicated on disciplinary proceedings under Regulation 13(1) of the Police (Disciplinary) Regulations 1985, despite the fact that the officer being disciplined had brought a sex discrimination claim against the relevant force in which the chief constable was cited as defendant. The disciplinary function of a chief constable was to be distinguished from that of a judge.

[43] See *Dimes v. The Proprietors of the Grand Junction Canal* (1852) 3 H.L. Cas 759.

[44] *R. v. Bow Street Metropolitan Stipendiary Magistrate ex parte Pinochet Ugarte (No.2)* [1999] 2 W.L.R. 272.

[45] *R. v. Gough* [1993] A.C. 646; *President of the Republic of South Africa & ors v. South African Rugby Football Union & ors 1999* (7) B.C.L.R. (C.C.) 725.

mind; or if, for any reason, there were real grounds to doubt his ability to ignore extraneous considerations, prejudices and predilections, and bring an objective mind to bear on the issues. In any case of doubt, that doubt was to be resolved in favour of recusal. If an appropriate disclosure has been made to the parties, and no objection is taken, the party affected will be taken to have waived his right to complain (other than in cases requiring automatic disqualification).[46]

II. Jury Bias

The requirement of independence and impartiality applies equally to juries.[47]   **14–81**
Article 6(1) imposes an obligation on every court to check whether, as constituted, it is an "impartial tribunal" within the meaning of that provision when
there is an allegation of bias that does not immediately appear manifestly devoid
of merit.[48] The test applied in Strasbourg appears to coincide, in broad terms,
with the rule established by the House of Lords in *R. v. Gough*.[49] Prior to *Gough*
there was inconsistent domestic authority as to whether the test was one of actual
bias (which was the test applied to jurors) or appearance of bias (which was the
test applied to magistrates). The House of Lords ruled that the same test should
apply to both. The court should inquire into the circumstances, and then ask itself
whether there was "a real danger" of bias on the part of the relevant member of
the tribunal in the sense that he might unfairly regard with favour or disfavour the
case of one of the parties. Stating the test in terms of "real danger" rather than
"real likelihood" was intended to ensure that the court is thinking in terms of
possibility rather than probability.

The standard adopted in Strasbourg appears to have strengthened over the years,   **14–82**
consistent with the Court's emphasis on the increasing sensitivity of the public to
an appearance of fairness. In *X v. Norway*[50] the Commission declared inadmissible a complaint that a jury member was the godchild of an interested party.
Similarly, in *X v. Austria*[51] a complaint that the jury foreman was employed by
the organisation which owned the shop where a robbery had taken place was also
rejected by the Commission. But in *Holm v. Sweden*[52] the Court found a violation
of Article 6(1) where a number of jury members were also members of a political
party that owned a publishing company which was one of the defendants in the
case. In *Pullar v. United Kingdom*,[53] a Scottish case, the defendant discovered
after his conviction that one of the jurors who had tried him was an employee of
the principal prosecution witness, and was acquainted with another of the
prosecution witnesses. Surprisingly, the Court held, by five votes to four, that
there was no evidence of prejudice to the defence, and no violation of Article
6(1). The fact that the juror would have been discharged if the trial court had been

---

[46] This approach to waiver does not appear to sit comfortably with the approach of the European Court of Human Rights: see para. 14–67 above.
[47] *Pullar v. United Kingdom* (1996) 22 E.H.R.R. 391, para. 30.
[48] *Remli v. France* (1996) 22 E.H.R.R. 253, paras 46–48.
[49] [1993] A.C. 646; For analysis, see I. Bing, "Curing Bias in Criminal Trials," [1998] Crim. L.R. 148. In *Weeks and Porter v. Magill* [2000] 2 W.L.R. 1420 (C.A.) Schiemann L.J. observed that "[t]he Convention caselaw does not suggest that the test in *R. v. Gough* is either wrong or inadequate".
[50] (1970) 35 C.D. 37 at 49.
[51] (1978) 13 D.R. 38.
[52] (1994) 18 E.H.R.R. 79.
[53] (1996) 22 E.H.R.R. 391.

aware of the connection was not sufficient to provide "objective justification" for the applicant's fear of bias. The Court appeared to require a higher standard of proof to oblige the domestic courts to disturb a conviction on this ground than would be required for the discharge of a juror during the trial:

> "[I]t is by no means decisive that (as the High Court of Justiciary observed) the sheriff would probably have dismissed F. from the jury had he known about the connection between the latter and M. It is natural that a presiding judge should strive to ensure that the composition of the jury is beyond any reproach whatsoever, at a time when this is still possible, before or during the trial. However, once the trial is over and a verdict had been given, it became material whether F's continued presence on the jury constituted a defect grave enough to justify setting aside that verdict."[54]

14–83   After examining the circumstances, the Court held that the risk of bias was not objectively justified. The Court placed reliance upon the fact that the juror was a junior employee of the firm owned by the witness, that he had not worked on the project which formed the background to the accusations, and that he had been served with a redundancy notice three days before the trial began.

14–84   Where the risk of bias has been brought to the court's attention before or during the trial, the key question will usually be whether the judge took adequate steps to investigate the source of the potential bias, and to remedy the defect. In *Remli v. France*[55] one of the jurors in the Rhone Assize Court was overheard expressing racist attitudes towards the defendant, but the trial judge failed to conduct any examination of the allegation or take steps to remedy the situation. The Court held that this failure was sufficient in itself to give rise to a violation of Article 6:

> "Article 6(1) of the Convention imposes an obligation on every national court to check whether, as constituted, it is an 'impartial tribunal' within the meaning of that provision where, as in the instant case, this is disputed on a ground that does not immediately appear to be manifestly devoid of merit. In the instant case [the court] did not make any such check, thereby depriving [the applicant] of the possibility of remedying—if it proved necessary—a situation contrary to the requirements of the Convention. This finding (regard being had to the confidence which the courts must inspire in those subject to their jurisdiction) suffices for the Court to hold that there has been a breach of Article 6(1)."[56]

14–85   *Remli* is to be contrasted with *Gregory v. United Kingdom*,[57] where the Court found no violation of Article 6. During the trial of a defendant who was black, the judge received a note from one jury member indicating that at least one other member of the jury was "showing racial prejudice." The Court held that it was sufficient that the judge had investigated the matter, had consulted both counsel, and had then given the jury a clear direction to decide the case on the evidence, free from any prejudice. The fact that the judge had not considered it necessary to discharge the jury did not give rise to a violation of Article 6, because he had recognised the problem and had dealt with it in a satisfactory way. It was the French court's refusal to examine the matter at all that led to the finding of a

---

[54] *ibid.*, at para. 36.
[55] (1996) 22 E.H.R.R. 253.
[56] *ibid.*, at para. 48.
[57] (1998) 25 E.H.R.R. 577.

violation in *Remli*. The court had failed to offer guarantees sufficient to exclude any legitimate doubt about the juror's impartiality.

In *Miah v. United Kingdom*[58] a statement emanating from a member of the jury, **14-86** produced one year after the trial, alleged that some members had decided on the defendant's guilt at an early stage, and did so on the basis of racist assumptions. The Court of Appeal concluded that the statement "lacked substance". The Commission similarly held that there was "no convincing evidence of actual or subjective bias on the part of one or more jurors." In the Commission's view, the Court of Appeal's enquiries into the origins and content of the statement were adequate. However, in *Sander v. United Kingdom*[59] the Court found a violation of Article 6 where, during the trial of two Asian defendants, one member of the jury sent a note to the judge alleging that at least two other members of the jury were making racist jokes and remarks. On examination, there was evidence confirming that such remarks had been made, although the juror concerned dismissed them as a joke. The Court considered that this was sufficient to give rise to a legitimate doubt as to the impartiality of the jury. Such a doubt could not be dispelled by a direction from the judge to try the case on the evidence, or to put prejudice aside, however strongly the direction was worded. Accordingly, there had been a violation of Article 6.

These authorities were considered by the Court of Appeal in *R. v. Lewis*.[60] Three **14-86a** days after the appellant's conviction by unanimous verdict, the Crown Court received a letter from one of the jurors stating that the jury had not in fact been unanimous. The Court of Appeal declined to order that inquiries be made of the jury. Keene L.J. held that the principles established in *R. v. Millward*[61] remained valid, notwithstanding the coming into force of the Human Rights Act 1998.

G. DISCLOSURE AND PUBLIC INTEREST IMMUNITY

I. *Introduction*

Prior to 1996, the duty of disclosure in England and Wales was governed solely **14-87** by common law.[62] It was a broad duty which was capable of applying to any material "that has, or might have, some bearing on the offences charged."[63] In determining whether an item of evidence was *prima facie* discloseable the central criterion was "materiality". This was inclusively defined in *R. v. Keane*[64] as:

> "that which can be seen on a sensible appraisal by the prosecution (1) to be relevant or possibly relevant to an issue in the case; (2) to raise or possibly raise a new issue whose existence is not apparent from the evidence which the prosecution proposes to use; (3)

---

[58] (1998) 26 E.H.R.R. CD 199.
[59] *The Times*, May 12, 2000.
[60] *The Times*, April 26, 2001.
[61] [1999] 1 Cr. App. R. 61.
[62] *R. v. Ward* [1993] 1 W.L.R. 619; *R. v. Livingstone* [1993] Crim L.R. 597; *R. v. Saunders*, September 29, unreported, C.C.C. (Henry J.); *R. v. Keane* [1994] 1 W.L.R. 746.
[63] *R. v. Saunders*, *ibid*.
[64] [1994] 1 W.L.R. 746.

to hold out a real (as opposed to fanciful) prospect of providing a lead on evidence which goes to (1) or (2)."

14–88   The Criminal Procedure and Investigations Act 1996 (CPIA) created a statutory framework which has significantly restricted the prosecution duty of disclosure. Under the Act, primary disclosure (of material which, in the view of the police disclosure officer, might undermine the case for the prosecution) is automatic; but secondary disclosure (of material which might assist the accused's defence) is dependent upon the disclosure of a defence case statement by the accused.[65] It is open to doubt whether this regime fully meets the requirements of Article 6. In the sections which follow, we examine the general principles governing the duty of disclosure under Article 6, the issues arising under the CPIA, and the position in the magistrates court. After brief reference to the approach adopted in Canada, we consider the specific problem posed by *ex parte* public interest immunity hearings.

II. *The Strasbourg Caselaw*

14–89   The most extensive consideration of the impact of the equality of arms principle on the pre-trial disclosure of evidence is to be found in the decision of the Commission in *Jespers v. Belgium*,[66] a decision which is now 20 years old. The applicant was a Belgian judge who had been prosecuted and convicted for the attempted murder of his wife and other serious offences. He complained before the Commission that a "special folder" containing relevant evidence had been withheld from the defence. Although the Commission found no grounds for concluding that the folder contained material that would have assisted in the preparation of the defence, it nevertheless took the opportunity to consider and explain the scope of the disclosure obligation imposed by Article 6(1) and (3)(b). The Commission noted the disparity in resources between prosecution and defence, and elaborated the implications of the principle of "equality of arms" in these terms:

> "As regards the interpretation of the term 'facilities' [in Article 6(3)(b)], the Commission notes firstly that in any criminal proceedings brought by a state authority, the prosecution has at its disposal, to back the accusation, facilities deriving from its powers of investigation supported by judicial and police machinery with considerable technical resources and means of coercion. It is in order to establish equality, as far as possible, between the prosecution and defence that national legislation in most countries entrusts the preliminary investigation to a member of the judiciary or, if it entrusts the investigation to the public prosecutor's department, instructs the latter to gather evidence in favour of the accused as well as evidence against him. It is also, and above all, to establish that same equality that the 'rights of the defence' of which Article 6 paragraph (3) of the Convention gives a non-exhaustive list, have been instituted. The Commission has already had occasion to point out that the so called 'equality of arms' principle could be based not only on Article 6 paragraph (1) but also on Article 6 paragraph (3), especially sub-paragraph (b) . . . In particular, the Commission takes the view that the 'facilities' which everyone charged with a criminal offence should enjoy include the opportunity to acquaint himself, for the purpose of preparing his defence, with the results of investigations carried out throughout the proceedings. Furthermore, the

---

[65] For brief analysis, see J. Sprack, "The Duty of Disclosure" [1997] Crim. L.R. 308; for fuller discussion, see R. Leng and R. Taylor, *The Criminal Procedure and Investigations Act 1996*.
[66] (1981) 27 D.R. 61.

Commission has already recognised that although a right of access to the prosecution file is not expressly guaranteed by the Convention, such a right can be inferred from Article 6 paragraph 3(b) . . . It matters little moreover, by whom and when the investigations are ordered or under whose authority they are carried out . . . Any investigation [the prosecution] causes to be carried out in connection with criminal proceedings and the findings thereof consequently form part of the 'facilities' within the meaning of Article 6 paragraph 3(b) of the Convention . . . In short, Article 6 paragraph 3(b) recognises the right of the accused to have at his disposal, for the purposes of exonerating himself or of obtaining a reduction in his sentence, all relevant elements that have been or could be collected by the competent authorities. The Commission considers that, if the element in question is a document, access to that document is a necessary facility ('facilite necessaire') if . . . it concerns acts of which the defendant is accused, the credibility of testimony etc."[67]

In *Edwards v. United Kingdom*,[68] the applicant had been convicted of robbery, the evidence against him consisting primarily of admissions he was alleged to have made to the police. The applicant's case was that the admissions had been fabricated. Following an independent police inquiry, the case was referred back to the Court of Appeal by the Secretary of State under section 17(1)(a) of the Criminal Appeal Act 1968. The principal ground of appeal was that the conviction was rendered unsafe by non-disclosure of relevant evidence during the trial. Two areas of non-disclosure were relied upon. The first related to fingerprint evidence. During the course of the trial one of the officers to whom the applicant was alleged to have confessed gave evidence that no fingerprints had been found at the scene of the robbery. The police inquiry uncovered two fingerprints which had been found during the original investigation but had not been disclosed to the defence. The finger marks were attributable to a neighbour who was a frequent visitor to the house where the robbery took place. The applicant argued on appeal that the existence of the fingerprint evidence showed that the officer concerned had lied on this aspect of the case, which in turn cast doubt upon his credibility in relation to the disputed admissions. He did not however apply to the Court to exercise its powers to hear a fresh cross-examination of the officer on the basis of the new evidence. In addition, the elderly victim of the robbery had made witness statements in which she said that she had had a brief glimpse of the robber's face and thought that she would be able to identify him if she saw him again. She did not give evidence at the trial but her statements were read to the jury by consent. A police inquiry later discovered that during the investigation the victim had been shown an album of photographs which included the applicant, and had failed to pick him out. This information had not been disclosed to the defence. The Court of Appeal dismissed the appeal, concluding that the new evidence did not cast doubt on the safety of the conviction. **14–90**

In proceedings before the European Court of Human Rights, the failure of the prosecution to disclose the material evidence at trial was held to have given rise to a defect in the proceedings. However the Court attached considerable importance to the fact that the undisclosed evidence had been discovered by the time of the appeal hearing and the Court of Appeal had therefore been able to assess its impact on the safety of the conviction: **14–91**

---

[67] *Jespers v. Belgium* (1981) 27 D.R. 61 at 87–88.
[68] (1993) 15 E.H.R.R. 417, on which see S. Field and J. Young, "Disclosure, Appeals and Procedural Traditions" [1994] Crim. L.R. 264.

"The Court considers that it is a requirement of fairness under Article 6, indeed one which is recognised under English law, that the prosecution authorities disclose to the defence all material evidence for or against the accused and that the failure to do so in the present case gave rise to a defect in the trial proceedings. However, when this was discovered, the Secretary of State, following an independent police investigation, referred the case to the Court of Appeal, which examined the transcript of the trial including the applicant's alleged confession, and considered in detail the impact of the new evidence on the conviction. In the proceedings before the Court of Appeal the applicant was represented by senior and junior counsel who had every opportunity to seek to persuade the Court that the conviction should not stand in view of the evidence of non-disclosure. Admittedly, the police officers who had given evidence at the trial were not heard by the Court of Appeal. It was, nonetheless, open to counsel for the applicant to make an application to the Court—which they chose not to do—that the police officers be called as witnesses ... Having regard to the above, the Court concludes that the defects of the original trial were remedied by the subsequent procedure before the Court of Appeal. Moreover, there is no indication that the proceedings before the Court of Appeal were in any respect unfair."

14–92 In *Rowe and Davis v. United Kingdom*,[69] which is considered in detail below, the evidence which was the subject of the application had been withheld at trial *and on appeal*. The Court distinguished *Edwards* on the ground that there had been no opportunity for adversarial argument before the Court of Appeal. In *IJL, GMR and AKP v. United Kingdom*[70] the applicants relied on *Rowe and Davis* where the prosecution had wrongly withheld evidence at trial and on their first appeal to the Court of Appeal. However, by the time the case was considered in Strasbourg, the applicants' convictions had been referred back to the Court of Appeal by the Home Secretary (prior to the establishment of the Criminal Cases Review Commission). On the second appeal, the Court of Appeal considered the fresh evidence, and held that whilst it should have been disclosed at trial, the procedural irregularity had caused no prejudice to the accused since the jury's verdict would inevitably have been the same if disclosure had been given. In finding no violation of Article 6, the Court reverted to the analysis adopted in *Edwards*:

"[A]ll of the materials at issue were disclosed to the applicants before the start of the Court of Appeal proceedings. The applicants had a full opportunity to persuade the Court of Appeal that their convictions were unsafe on account of the prosecution's failure to disclose materials which may have assisted their defence. The Court of Appeal extensively reviewed the materials at issue and considered the possible prejudice which their non-disclosure may have had on the fairness of the trial ... In the Court's opinion, the particular defect identified by the Court of Appeal was remedied by the subsequent and extensive review of the issue conducted by the Court of Appeal in the reference proceedings ... The Court observes that the applicants' case is to be distinguished from the circumstances underlying the case of *Rowe and Davis v. the United Kingdom* in which the Court found that the prosecution's failure to lay evidence before the trial judge to permit him to rule on the question of disclosure deprived the latter applicants of a fair trial. It notes in this connection that, and in contrast to the position in the *Rowe and Davis* case, the present applicants had received all the materials which had not been disclosed to them by the stage of the second set of appeal proceedings and the Court of Appeal was able to consider the impact of the new

---

[69] (2000) 30 E.H.R.R. 1.
[70] [2001] Crim. L.R. 133.

material on the safety of the conviction in the light of detailed argument from their defence lawyers."

Bendenoun v. France[71] was an unusual case since three different sets of proceed-   **14–93**
ings had been brought against the applicant on account of his cross-border art dealings. The French customs authorities had used their powers to fine him, and he had been prosecuted in the criminal courts and imprisoned for tax evasion. The application to Strasbourg concerned administrative proceedings brought by the French tax authorities. The Court rejected the applicant's claim that the tax authorities had acted in breach of Article 6 by failing to disclose certain documents which should have been disclosed. This conclusion turned on two issues of fact. First, the undisclosed documents were not relied upon by the tax authorities in relation to the administrative proceedings, and the applicant had given no specific reasons for wishing to see them. And secondly, the applicant and his lawyers were aware of the content of most of the documents because they had been given access to the complete file in the proceedings before the criminal courts. The second point may well have coloured the Court's approach to the first, and so the implications of this case are uncertain.

In *Hardiman v. United Kingdom*[72] a rather different issue arose. The applicant   **14–94**
was jointly charged with murder. He and his co-accused sought to blame one another for the killing. The co-accused gave evidence implicating the applicant. After the applicant's conviction, his lawyers discovered the existence of prison psychiatric report on the co-accused which could have cast serious doubt on his credibility as a witness. The report was in the possession of the judge, the prosecution and the co-accused's defence team but had not been disclosed to the applicant or his lawyers. The Commission found no violation of Article 6 because of the special circumstances in which the report had come into existence. The co-accused was not cautioned before the interview with the psychiatrist, and did not have his solicitor present. Given the settled practice of not referring to such reports unless a medical issue arose in the trial, and given that the purpose of this practice was to protect the rights of defendants (by obtaining information about them as to their mental capacity), the refusal to disclose the material to a co-defendant was held not to be either unfair or arbitrary. The Commission's decision was heavily influenced by the need to guarantee the protection of one accused person's legal professional privilege, and the confidential relationship between the accused and the psychiatrist preparing the report.

In *Preston v. United Kingdom*[73] the applicants complained that telephone inter-   **14–95**
cept material obtained pursuant to a warrant issued under the Interception of Communications Act 1985 had not been disclosed to the defence. The Commission however dismissed the application as manifestly ill-founded on the ground that the material could not, in any event, be introduced into evidence due to the statutory prohibition on the use of such material under the 1985 Act. Moreover, the applicants had failed to show how the material could have assisted or harmed

---

[71] (1994) 18 E.H.R.R. 54.
[72] [1996] E.H.R.L.R. 425.
[73] [1997] E.H.R.L.R. 695.

the defence case.[74] The Court confirmed this approach in *Jasper v. United Kingdom*[75]:

> "[T]he applicant has alleged that his trial had been unfair because the product of a telephone intercept had been withheld from the defence without being placed before the trial judge. However, the Court notes that it is not established any such material existed at the time of the trial. Moreover, since under section 9 of the 1985 Act both the prosecution and the defence were prohibited from adducing any evidence which might tend to suggest that calls had been intercepted by the state authorities, the principle of equality of arms was respected. It would, further, have been open to the applicant himself to testify, or to call evidence from other sources, as to the fact and contents of the instructions he allegedly received by telephone the day before his arrest."

III. *The Criminal Procedure and Investigations Act 1996*

14–96 It is notable that there have been only a few successful applications in Strasbourg relating to the non-disclosure of evidence by the prosecution.[76] Moreover, it is clear that certain propositions have been stated without the kind of detailed exploration of arguments that is to be found in some of the English decisions on disclosure. It is important to appreciate the context in which those statements have been made. The notion of a case file as an open document has no parrallel in English criminal procedure. To some extent this arises from the difference between adversarial and inquisitorial systems of criminal justice. Thus, the Commission in *Jespers* observed that, in order to achieve equality of arms, "most countries" entrust the preliminary investigation to "a member of the judiciary or, if it entrusts the preliminary investigation to a member of the Public Prosecutor's Department, instructs the latter to gather evidence in favour of the accused as well as against him."[77] English criminal procedure fits neither of these descriptions. The important principle that the police should seek evidence for a defendant as well as evidence against him finds only a weak reflection in English practice,[78] and the idea of the police as trustees of the information they uncover has yet to establish itself as fundamental.[79]

---

[74] This observation shows again that the ultimate concern of the Strasbourg organs when reviewing conformity with Art. 6 is whether in fact the criminal process as a whole was fair in this case. For a similar holding, see the unusual case of *F v. United Kingdom* (1986) 47 D.R. 230, where the applicant had complained that the seizure, retention and examination of his defence documents by the police deprived him of a fair trial and prevented adequate preparation of his defence. In declaring the application manifestly ill-founded, the Commission attached particular importance to the fact that no information from the documents was used against the applicant during his trial.

[75] (2000) 30 E.H.R.R. 441.

[76] The Court did find a violation of Art. 6 due to non-disclosure in *Foucher v. France* (1997) 25 E.H.R.R. 36 and in *Rowe and Davis v. United Kindgdom* (2000) 30 E.H.R.R. 1. These decisions are considered in detail below.

[77] (1981) 27 D.R. 61 at 87.

[78] The Royal Commission on Criminal Justice argued that it is "important that the police should see it as their duty when conducting investigations to gather and consider all the relevant evidence, including any which may exonerate the suspect" (*Report*, Cmnd. 2263 (1993), p. 10). Some changes in investigation techniques have been noted in more recent times, but it is not clear how widespread they are. *Cf.* the Royal Commission's recommendations on disclosure, *ibid.*, pp 95–97. See also the observations of the Court of Appeal in *R. v. Fergus* 98 Cr. App. R. 313.

[79] *cf.* P. O'Connor, "Prosecution Disclosure: principle, practice and justice" [1992] Crim. L.R. 464.

With these caveats, it is possible to identify three main differences between the   **14–97**
domestic law embodied in the Criminal Procedure and Investigations Act 1996
and the statements of principle in the Strasbourg caselaw. First, the Act appears
to adopt a test of relevance which is narrower than Article 6. If the prosecutor
considers that the material will neither undermine the prosecution case, nor
advance the defence, then it need not be disclosed. This does not appear to
conform to the "common pool" principle, referred to in *Edwards* and the other
Strasbourg cases, under which the prosecution should disclose all of the evidence
in its possession, or to which it could gain access, including evidence which is
neutral or harmful to the defence. The Commission appears, for example, to have
assumed that the duty of disclosure extends to material which may undermine the
credibility of a defence witness.[80] This is a category of disclosure which the
House of Lords has expressly declined to recognise at common law,[81] holding
that the principle of fairness that lies at the heart of the duty of disclosure; " . . .
has to be seen in the context of the public interest in the detection and punishment
of crime. A defendant is entitled to a fair trial, but fairness does not require that
his witnesses should be immune from challenge as to their credibility."[82]

A similar point can be made about the principle, now well-settled in the Article   **14–98**
6 case law, that the prosecution must disclose not only material which is relevant
to guilt or innocence, but any material which may assist an accused in obtaining
a reduction in sentence.[83] This is an aspect of the disclosure obligation which has
not, thus far, been thoroughly explored in English law. Moreover, the Convention
duty of disclosure encompasses any material to which the prosecution or the
police could gain access,[84] a principle which points to a broad duty of third party
disclosure.[85]

The second area of potential incompatibility arises from the fact that the 1996   **14–99**
Act vests a very wide discretion in the prosecuting authorities to determine
relevance. At the stage of primary disclosure it is the police who take the decision
whether or not an item of evidence "might undermine the case for the prosecution against the accused." It may be argued that the absence of adequate
safeguards against abuse falls short of the requirements of Article 6.[86] The
fairness of the current regime depends on the judgment, diligence and honesty of
the disclosure officer and the impartiality of the CPS reviewing lawyer. In the
context of adversarial litigation, the potential for a serious conflict of interest is
obvious. The Convention caselaw suggests that where potentially relevant evidence may be withheld from the defence, there should a measure of scrutiny

---

[80] *Jespers v. Belgium* (1981) 27 D.R. 61.
[81] *R. v. Brown* [1997] 3 W.L.R. 447.
[82] *ibid., per* Lord Hope at 456. This principle is unaffected by the Attorney General's Guidelines on
Disclosure of Information in Criminal Proceedings (2000). See para. 14–105 below.
[83] *Jespers v. Belgium* (1981) 27 D.R. 61.
[84] See *Jespers v. Belgium* (1981) 27 D.R. 61.
[85] Note, however, that in *Z v. Finland* (1998) 25 E.H.R.R. 371 the Court recognised that the disclosure
of confidential medical information relating to a witness in criminal proceedings is protected by Art.
8.
[86] See the argument of S. Sharpe, "Art. 6 and the Disclosure of Evidence in Criminal Trials" [1999]
Crim. L.R. 273 at 280–281, relying on *Miailhe v. France (No.2)* (1997) 23 E.H.R.R. 491 at paras
43–44.

which is independent of the executive.[87] The involvement of independent prosecution counsel might be said to afford such a safeguard. However this is doubtful for a number of reasons. Surveys conducted during 1999 by the Law Society and the Criminal Bar Association suggest that prosecution counsel does not always view all of the unused material personally, particularly in less serious cases.[88] The DPP has publicly recognised that prosecutors have not always complied with their obligations.[89] From a Strasbourg perspective it may in any event be doubted whether prosecution counsel would be regarded as truly independent, and the extension of rights of audience to employed prosecutors adds a further tier of complexity to the problem.

14–100   Thirdly, the duty of disclosure under Article 6 of the Convention is not dependent upon disclosure of the defence case. The duty to serve a defence case statement may, in itself, be thought to sit uncomfortably with the Convention caselaw on freedom from self-incrimination.[90] Certainly, it is open to question whether such an obligation can be a precondition to the grant of other fair trial guarantees, such as the duty of disclosure.

14–101   In considering the application of the Human Rights Act 1998 to the duty of disclosure, there is an important distinction to be drawn between the function of the European Court of Human Rights, in applying Article 6, and the function of a national court. The European Court of Human Rights conducts a retrospective review of the whole of the criminal proceedings before the national courts in determining whether the proceedings, in their entirety, were fair. Thus, in *Edwards*, the Court held that non-disclosure of evidence at the time of the applicant's trial was in breach of Article 6, but went on to find that the breach had been remedied by the disclosure of the evidence prior to the hearing before the Court of Appeal. The position of the national courts under the Human Rights Act is different. They do not have the benefit of hindsight. Each successive stage of the criminal justice system is bound by the Act to apply the standards of the Convention directly to the case before it. In considering the compatibility of the present disclosure regime, it is therefore necessary to distinguish between complaints which are specific to the facts of a particular case, and complaints which relate to the *structure* of the existing regime.

14–102   As to cases in which the evidence in question has subsequently been disclosed, the position is relatively straightforward. The non-disclosure of evidence which is significantly helpful to the defence would, if a conviction resulted, involve a breach of Article 6. But it would also, in all probability, justify the quashing of a conviction under the current interpretation of section 2 of the Criminal Appeal Act. Insofar as there may be a gap between the standard of fairness required by

---

[87] *Rowe and Davis v. United Kingdom* (2000) 30 E.H.R.R. 1; *Jasper v. United Kingdom* (2000) 30 E.H.R.R. 441 Application No. 27052/95; *Fitt v. United Kingdom* (2000) 30 E.H.R.R. 1 Application No. 29777/96. See further para. 14–114 below.

[88] The surveys were published in a series of papers presented to the British Academy of Forensic Sciences on December 1, 1999 (see Med. Sci. Law (2000) Vol. 40. No. 2).

[89] At his first meeting with 42 newly appointed Chief Crown Prosecutors in May 1999 the DPP David Calvert-Smith Q.C. said there was proveable evidence that prosecutors were still not complying with the obligations imposed on them by the 1996 Act, and that as a result there was a risk of wrongful convictions. He subsequently commissioned a review by the CPS Inspectorate.

[90] See Chapter 15 below.

Article 6, and the test of "safety" in section 2,[91] it is clear that this gap has been narrowed considerably by the Human Rights Act.[92] The term "unsafe" in section 2, like any other statutory provision, has to be interpreted as far as possible in a manner which is compatible with the Convention.[93]

Where the complaint is directed to the scheme established by the 1996 Act, the position is more difficult. The correct means of challenge will depend on the nature of the complaint and the powers of the court before which the point is argued. The three broad heads of challenge suggested above lend themselves to different potential remedies.   **14–103**

The first point to note is that the 1996 Act will have to be read, so far as possible, to conform with the requirements of Article 6. This may require a court at any level to read into the Act safeguards which are absent from its face, providing it is *possible* to imply those safeguards consistently with the express wording of the legislation. Take, for example, the current test of relevance. It might be possible for a Crown Court to construe the duty of secondary disclosure more broadly, by treating all forms of evidence (even evidence which is neutral or damaging) as assisting the defence case (*e.g.*, by alerting the defence to possible pitfalls). This would undoubtedly be a strained construction, but it may nevertheless, be a *possible* one. If such a construction were possible then the point could be taken in the Crown Court. However where the nature of the challenge goes to the very heart of the statutory regime then it will, in all probability, be impossible to read the legislation compatibly. A challenge to the absence of independent safeguards, or to the requirement for the service of a defence case statement, might be thought to fall into this category. The defendant would be obliged to argue this challenge before the Court of Appeal, either on an appeal against a ruling made at a preparatory hearing, or on an appeal against conviction. The Court of Appeal of course has power to grant a declaration of incompatibility if it accepts that the challenge is well founded. Finally, it is important to recall that the Crown Court rules made under the Act take effect subject to Article 6 unless the provision about which complaint is made is one which derives from a provision of the parent legislation which cannot be construed compatibly under section 3 of the Human Rights Act.   **14–104**

IV. *The Attorney General's Guidelines (2000)*

Certain of the shortcomings of the 1996 Act have now been addressed in the Attorney General's *Guidelines on the Disclosure of Information in Criminal Proceedings*.[94] The foreword to the Guidelines notes that in the three years since the Act came into force "concerns have been expressed about the operation of the provisions by judges, prosecutors and defence practitioners". The new Guidelines are intended to improve the operation of the Act pending a review of the legislation itself, and acknowledge in terms that the guidance given in some areas   **14–105**

---

[91] See *Condron and Condron v. United Kingdom* [2000] Crim. L.R. 677.

[92] *R. v. Togher and ors* [2001] Crim. L.R. 124 (CA); *R. v. Forbes* [2001] 2 W.L.R. 1 (HL); *R. v. A* [2001] 2 W.L.R. 1546. For a discussion of the effect of a breach of Art. 6 on the "safety" of a conviction, see para. 17–25 below.

[93] Section 3 of the Human Rights Act 1998; see para. 3–31 above.

[94] November 29, 2000.

"goes beyond the requirements of the legislation where experience suggests that such guidance is desirable". The introduction refers directly to Article 6, observing that a fair trial is "the proper object and expectation of all participants in the trial process", that fair disclosure to the accused is "an inseparable part" of a fair trial, and that disclosure which fails to ensure timely preparation and presentation of the defence case "risks preventing a fair trial taking place".

14–106 In order to improve the existing arrangements, and bring them closer into line with the requirements of Article 6, the Guidelines establish a series of principles, among the most important of which are the following:

(a) An individual must not be appointed as disclosure officer, or continue in that role, if that is likely to result in a conflict of interest.[95]

(b) Where investigators have seized a large volume of material, but have decided not to examine it because it seems unlikely to be relevant, the existence of the material should be made known to the defence, and permission given for its inspection.[96]

(c) Prosecutors should review disclosure schedules for completeness and accuracy, and should take steps to make good any deficiencies.[97] If they conclude that a fair trial cannot take place because of a failure to disclose information which cannot or will not be remedied, the prosecution should be discontinued.[98]

(d) Prosecutors should not adduce evidence of a defence case statement, other than in the circumstances permitted by section 11 of the Act or to rebut alibi evidence.[99]

(e) The practice of "counsel to counsel" disclosure, where it occurs, should cease.[1]

(f) Where a Government department or other Crown body appears to be in possession of material which may be relevant to an issue in the case, reasonable steps should be taken to identify and consider the material.[2] Where it appears that a non-governmental third party is in possession of material which might be discloseable if it were in the possession of the prosecution, the prosecutor must take appropriate steps to seek access to the material.[3] If access is denied then the prosecutor should apply for a witness summons[4] if it considered that it is reasonable to seek production of the material.

---

[95] Para. 7. The example given, however, appears unduly narrow—"if the disclosure officer is the victim of the alleged crime which is the subject of criminal proceedings".
[96] Para. 9.
[97] Paras 14 to 17, and 23 to 24.
[98] Para. 21.
[99] Para. 18.
[1] Para. 26.
[2] Para. 29.
[3] Para. 30. The Guidelines emphasise that it will be especially important to seek access to third party material if it is likely to undermine the prosecution case or assist the defence.
[4] Assuming the conditions of section 2 of the Criminal Procedure (Attendance of Witnesses) Act 1965 or section 97 of the Magistrates Courts Act 1980 are met.

(g) The duty of primary disclosure should be treated as extending not only to material which directly contradicts a prosecution witness's version of events, but also to material which could be useful in cross-examination, or which could lead to the exclusion of evidence, the grant of a stay of the proceedings or a finding that a public authority has acted incompatibly with the rights of the accused under the Human Rights Act 1998.[5] Any material which relates to the defendant's mental or physical health, his intellectual capacity or any alleged ill-treatment whilst in custody should be treated as relevant to the reliability of a purported confession.[6]

(h) The duty of secondary disclosure should be treated as applying to certain categories of "linked" material which "relates to" a defence being put forward, whether or not it directly supports such a defence. The categories include[7] scientific findings which relate to the accused; records of all previous descriptions or identification procedures carried out, including any photographs taken of the accused at the time of his arrest; information concerning rewards received or requested by or promised to a prosecution witness; plans or video recordings of the scene of a crime; names of witnesses with relevant information who have not been interviewed; and records of any information provided by other individuals.

(i) The prosecution should serve on the defence all evidence upon which the Crown intends to rely in summary proceedings.[8]

(j) The prosecution should consider disclosing any material which is relevant to sentence, such as information which might mitigate the seriousness of the offence or assist the accused to lay blame in whole or in part on a co-accused or another person.[9]

V. *The Magistrates Court*

The European Court of Human Rights has held that the right of access to the **14–107** prosecution file applies even to minor offences. Thus in *Foucher v. France*[10] the applicant and his father had been charged with insulting behaviour towards persons entrusted with public service duties. The case was to be tried in the local police court, and they were to represent themselves. The public prosecutor refused them access to their files on the ground that a copy could not be supplied to a private individual, except through a lawyer. The Court held that this constituted a violation of Articles 6(1) and 6(3)(b). Although the decision turned chiefly on the point that defendants should not be denied access to documents simply because they are representing themselves, it also demonstrates that the general principles discussed above apply even at the lowest level of criminal courts.

This approach may be compared to the position in the magistrates court in **14–108** England and Wales. Where a defendant is charged with a summary only offence,

---

[5] Para. 36.
[6] Para. 38.
[7] Para. 40.
[8] Para. 43.
[9] Para. 44.
[10] (1998) 25 E.H.R.R. 234.

the Magistrates Court (Advance Information) Rules 1985 do not require the prosecution to disclose even the evidence upon which it intends to rely. In some areas the CPS were prepared to give voluntary disclosure, but in others they were not. In *R. v. Stratford Justices ex parte Imbert*,[11] the Divisional Court (*per* Buxton L.J. and Collins J.) held that advance disclosure in the magistrates court was not a requirement of the right to a fair trial, and expressed the view *obiter*, that their decision would be unaffected by the implementation of the Human Rights Act. As a statement of general principle this decision is perhaps a little surprising, and it may come to be reconsidered now that the Act is fully in force. The practical importance of this point is, however, substantially diminished by the Attorney General's *Guidelines on Disclosure of Information in Criminal Proceedings (2000)*,[12] which now provide that;

> "The prosecutor should, in addition to complying with the obligations under the CPIA, provide to the defence all evidence upon which the Crown proposes to rely in a summary trial. Such provision should allow the accused or their legal advisers sufficient time properly to consider the evidence before it is called. Exceptionally, statements may be withheld for the protection of witnesses or to avoid interference with the course of justice."

14–109 This change of practice was absolutely essential to ensure that the CPIA was workable in the magistrates court. Under the Act the defendant in the magistrates court has the right to 'primary' disclosure of evidence which might undermine the prosecution case.[13] But—in view of the absence of any right to advanced information—he did not have the right to see the statements of the witnesses whom the prosecution proposed to call. The right to secondary disclosure—that is, of material which may advance the defence case—is dependent upon the service by the defendant of a case statement setting out the matters upon which he takes issue with the prosecution witnesses, and the reasons he takes issue with them.[14] In the magistrates court the service of such a statement is voluntary, but the Crown's duty of secondary disclsoure is nevertheless contingent upon such a statement having been served.[15] It was obviously impossible for the defendant to take advantage of this opportunity—and thereby to avail himself of a fundamental protection—if he had not seen the prosecution evidence in the first place.

VI. *Canada*

14–110 In the leading Canadian case of *Stinchcombe*[16] Sopinka J., speaking for a unanimous Supreme Court, stated that: "[T]he fruits of the investigation which are in the possession of counsel for the Crown are not the property of the Crown for use in securing a conviction but the property of the public to be used to ensure that justice is done." He went on to hold that the overriding concern of the courts is to ensure that the accused can "make full answer and defence", which he

---

[11] [1999] 2 Cr.App.R. 276.
[12] November 29, 2000, at para. 42. See paras 14–105 to 14–106 above.
[13] Sections 1(1)(a) and 3(1)(a).
[14] Section 5(6).
[15] Sections 6 and 7.
[16] [1991] 3 S.C.R. 326.

described as "one of the pillars of criminal justice on which we heavily depend to ensure that the innocent are not convicted."[17]

Sopinka J. also delivered the judgment in the unanimous Supreme Court decision **14–111** in *Chaplin*.[18] He reiterated that the Crown's obligation is only to disclose relevant evidence, although one test of relevance is whether the material is "of some use to the defence." Where the existence of relevant information was established, "the Crown must justify non-disclosure by demonstrating either that the information sought is beyond its control, or that it is clearly irrelevant or privileged." Where, on the other hand, the Crown denies the existence of the material sought, "the defence must establish a basis which could enable the presiding judge to conclude that there is in existence further [identifiable] material which is potentially . . . useful to the accused in making full answer and defence." Once the defence overcome this threshold, designed to exclude "fishing expeditions and conjecture," the Crown once again bears the burden of justifying non-disclosure.

The leading Canadian case on third party disclosure is *O'Connor*.[19] The question **14–112** in that case was whether the defence should be granted an order to compel the complainants, prior to a trial for sexual offences some 25 years previously, to authorize their therapists and other counsellors to pass their reports to the Crown, and the Crown then to disclose them to the defence. The application was originally granted by a judge, but Crown counsel thought it unduly wide and delayed compliance. The trial judge then stayed the prosecution for abuse of process. On appeal the Supreme Court held by a five to three majority that the stay should not have been granted because the defendant's right to make full answer and defence had not been impaired on the facts. The Court went on to determine the appropriate procedure for dealing with applications for third party disclosure. The first stage places a threshold burden on the defence to satisfy the judge that the evidence will be relevant to the defendant's case.[20] The second stage requires the judge to examine the records to decide whether, and to what extent, they should be disclosed to the defence. Both L'Heureux-Dube J. and Lamer C.J.C., agreed, in their separate judgments, that in balancing the competing rights at stake the following factors should be considered:

> "(1) The extent to which the record is necessary for the accused to make full answer and defence; (2) the probative value of the record in question; (3) the nature and extent of the reasonable expectation of privacy vested in that record; (4) whether production of the record would be premised upon any discriminatory belief or bias; . . . and (5) the potential prejudice to the complainant's dignity, privacy or security of person that would be occasioned by production of the record in question."[21]

---

[17] *ibid.*, at 336.
[18] [1995] 1 S.C.R. 727.
[19] (1996) 103 C.C.C. (3d) 1; see also the decision in *A (LL) v. B (A)* [1995] 4 S.C.R. 536, handed down on the same day.
[20] The standard of the threshold, and the notion of relevance, are similar to those established in *Stinchcombe*.
[21] (1996) 103 C.C.C. (3d) 1 at para. 156 (L'Heureux-Dube J.) and at para. 31 (Lamer C.J.C.); at para. 32 Lamer C.J.C. declined to associate himself with other factors that L'Heureux-Dube J. regarded as relevant, such as the wider social interest in encouraging people to report sexual offences against them.

14–113 Although little is said about the weight to be assigned to these factors and how they should be balanced, the process is securely tied to the range of rights declared in the Charter. Similar reasoning, arising from Convention rights, might now be appropriate in this country. In *Z v. Finland*,[22] for example, the Court held that the lawful seizure of a third party's medical records and an order that her medical advisers give evidence in criminal proceedings did not violate Article 8, but that the threatened disclosure to the public of her identity and medical condition did constitute a violation.

VII. *Public Interest Immunity*

14–114 The Court in *Edwards*[23] specifically left open the question whether the rules of public interest immunity, as applied to criminal proceedings in England and Wales, conform to the requirements of Article 6. As Judge Pettiti explained in his dissenting opinion[24];

> "[T]he principle of public interest immunity . . . in English law allows the prosecution, in the public interest, not to disclose or communicate to the defence all the evidence in its possession and to reserve certain evidence . . . The Court made no express statement of its views on this point and its silence might be understood as approval of this principle, which is not the case. The Court had regard primarily to the failure by the defence to rely on this ground of appeal. To be sure, it is understandable that the plea of 'defence secrets' should be invoked at the stage of duly authorised telephone taps. But once there are criminal proceedings and an indictment, the whole of the evidence, favourable or unfavourable to the defendant, must be communicated to the defence in order to be the subject of adversarial argument in accordance with Article 6 of the Convention . . . Under the European Convention an old doctrine, such as that of 'public interest' must be revised in accordance with Article 6."[25]

14–115 The issue arose for consideration in *Rowe and Davis v. United Kingdom*.[26] The applicants had been convicted of a murder and a series of robberies committed in 1988. An important part of the evidence against them was given by three men, one of whom (as it subsequently turned out) was a police informer who had claimed and been paid a reward. The evidence relating to the role of the informer was withheld by the Crown, without reference to the judge, in accordance with guidelines on prosecution disclosure issued by the Attorney General in 1981.[27] On their appeal against conviction, the Court of Appeal established a procedure for judicial supervision of the decision to withhold evidence on grounds of public

---

[22] (1998) 25 E.H.R.R. 371. The Court recognised at para. 97, that the confidentiality of medical data might be trumped, in appropriate cases, by the importance of investigating and prosecuting crime.
[23] (1993) 15 E.H.R.R. 417.
[24] (1993) 15 E.H.R.R. 417 at 433.
[25] *ibid.*, at 433–435.
[26] (2000) 30 E.H.R.R. 1.
[27] (1982) 74 Cr. App. R. 302. As to the Guidelines issued in 2000 see para. 14–105 above. In its Opinion on the merits in *Rowe and Davis* ((2000) 30 E.H.R.R. 1 at 18 *et seq.*) the Commission held that the Attorney-General's guidelines (as they stood at that time) "include at least three [categories of sensitive material] where the interests of the State in maintaining confidentiality for the purposes of encouraging information to be given to the police would *prima facie* rarely if ever outweigh the interests of the accused in having access to information of possible help to the defence." The three categories mentioned were (e) information supplied by banks, etc; (f) evidence relating to serious allegations against, or convictions of, other persons; and (g) matters of private delicacy that might cause domestic strife.

interest immunity. In *R. v. Davis, Johnson and Rowe*[28] the Court held that it was not necessary in every case for the prosecution to give notice to the defence when it wished to claim public interest immunity, and outlined three different procedures to be adopted. The first procedure, which had generally to be followed, was for the prosecution to give notice to the defence that they were applying for a ruling by the court and indicate to the defence at least the category of the material which they held. The defence would then have the opportunity to make representations to the court. Secondly, however, where the disclosure of the category of the material in question would in effect reveal that which the prosecution contended should not be revealed, the prosecution should still notify the defence that an application to the court was to be made, but the category of material need not be disclosed and the application should be made *ex parte*. The third procedure would apply in an exceptional case where to reveal even the fact that an *ex parte* application was to be made would in effect be to reveal the nature of the evidence in question. In such a case, the prosecution should apply to the court *ex parte* without notice to the defence. Having laid down these procedural guidelines, the Court of Appeal then proceeded to view the material in issue in the case, and endorsed the decision of the Crown to withhold it.

The applicants argued in Strasbourg that the procedure adopted was in breach of   **14–116**
Article 6. Whilst accepting that it may be legitimate, in certain circumstances, to withhold relevant evidence on grounds of national security or the protection of vulnerable witnesses, they submitted that the *ex parte* procedure lacked the necessary safeguards to ensure that the rights of the accused were adequately protected. In the present case the evidence had been withheld at trial without judicial supervision. This amounted, in itself to a breach of Article 6. The resulting defect was not cured by the *ex parte* hearing before the Court of Appeal, which offered no procedural safeguards and which did not result in the disclosure of the evidence sought. The applicants argued that in order to counterbalance the exclusion of the accused from the procedure it was necessary to introduce an adversarial element, such as the appointment of an independent "special counsel" who could advance argument on behalf of the defence as to the relevance of the undisclosed evidence, test the strength of the claim to public interest immunity, and act as an independent safeguard against the risk of judicial error or bias. They pointed to four situations in which such a "special counsel" procedure had been introduced in English law as a means of safeguarding sensitive information whilst affording a party to litigation a measure of procedural justice.[29] Under these procedures an independent lawyer is appointed, subject to security vetting, to *represent the interests* of the accused. The "special counsel" is not, however, instructed by, nor directly accountable to the accused, and is under a duty to maintain the confidentiality of the proceedings.

The Court held that while Article 6 generally requires the prosecution to disclose   **14–117**
to the defence all material evidence for or against an accused, considerations of

[28] [1993] 1 W.L.R. 613.
[29] Following *Chahal v. United Kingdom* (1997) 23 E.H.R.R. 413, and *Tinnelly v. United Kingdom* (1999) 27 E.H.R.R. 249 a "special counsel" procedure had been introduced into immigration appeals and employment discrimination cases involving national security issues by the Special Immigration Appeals Commission Act 1997 and the Northern Ireland Act 1998. A similar proposal was before Parliament in relation to the interception of electronic communications, and the Youth Justice and Criminal Evidence Bill 1999 proposed the use of "special counsel" where an unrepresented accused was prohibited from cross-examining the complainant in a sexual offence.

national security or the protection of vulnerable witnesses may, in certain circumstances, justify an exception to this rule:

> "It is a fundamental aspect of the right to a fair trial that criminal proceedings, including the elements of such proceedings which relate to procedure, should be adversarial and that there should be equality of arms between the prosecution and the defence. The right to an adversarial trial means, in a criminal case, that both the prosecution and defence must be given the opportunity to have knowledge of and comment on the observations filed and the evidence adduced by the other party. In addition, Article 6(1) requires, as indeed does English law, that the prosecution authorities should disclose to the defence all material evidence in their possession for or against the accused. However, as the applicants recognised, the entitlement to disclosure of relevant evidence is not an absolute right. In any criminal proceedings there may be competing interests, such as national security or the need to protect witnesses at risk of reprisals or keep secret police methods of investigation of crime, which must be weighed against the rights of the accused. In some cases it may be necessary to withhold certain evidence from the defence so as to preserve the fundamental rights of another individual or to safeguard an important public interest."

14–118 However, the Court went on to apply the important principle that any departure from a system of open adversarial justice had to be "strictly necessary". The consequent handicap imposed on the defence required the adoption of compensating procedural safeguards;

> "[O]nly such measures restricting the rights of the defence which are strictly necessary are permissible under Article 6(1). Moreover, in order to ensure that the accused receives a fair trial, any difficulties caused to the defence by a limitation on its rights must be adequately counterbalanced by the procedures followed by the judicial authorities."

14–119 On the facts, the Court unanimously found a violation of Article 6. Since the prosecution had withheld relevant evidence on public interest immunity grounds, without first submitting it to the trial judge, the requirements of a fair procedure were not met. In contrast to the position in *Edwards*,[30] the resulting defect could not be cured by submitting the material to the Court of Appeal in the course of an appeal against conviction (unless, of course, the Court of Appeal ordered disclosure of the material):

> "During the applicants' trial at first instance the prosecution decided, without notifying the judge, to withhold certain relevant evidence on grounds of public interest. Such a procedure, whereby the prosecution itself attempts to assess the importance of concealed information to the defence and weigh this against the public interest in keeping the information secret, cannot comply with the above-mentioned requirements of Article 6(1) . . . It is true that at the commencement of the applicants' appeal prosecution counsel notified the defence that certain information had been withheld, without however revealing the nature of this material, and that on two separate occasions the Court of Appeal reviewed the undisclosed evidence and, in *ex parte* hearings with the benefit of submissions from the Crown but in the absence of the defence, decided in favour of non-disclosure. However, the Court does not consider that this procedure before the appeal court was sufficient to remedy the unfairness caused at the trial by the absence of any scrutiny of the withheld information by the trial judge. Unlike the latter, who saw the witnesses give their testimony and was fully versed in all the evidence and issues in the case, the judges in the Court of Appeal were dependent for their

---

[30] See para. 14–90 above.

understanding of the possible relevance of the undisclosed material on transcripts of the Crown Court hearings and on the account of the issues given to them by prosecuting counsel. In addition, the first instance judge would have been in a position to monitor the need for disclosure throughout the trial, assessing the importance of the undisclosed evidence at a stage when new issues were emerging, when it might have been possible through cross-examination seriously to undermine the credibility of key witnesses and when the defence case was still open to take a number of different directions or emphases. In contrast, the Court of Appeal was obliged to carry out its appraisal *ex post facto* and may even, to a certain extent, have unconsciously been influenced by the jury's verdict of guilty into underestimating the significance of the undisclosed evidence."

In *Atlan v. United Kingdom*[30a] the Court rejected an attempt to distinguish *Rowe and Davis*. The government argued that the applicants in that case were in a different position since they were unable to show that the evidence which had been the subject of an *ex parte* hearing before the Court of Appeal was relevant to the defence they had advanced at trial. The government also pointed out that the Court of Appeal had postponed its ruling on the application for disclosure until it had heard argument on the merits of the appeal, and that before dismissing the appeal it had made a number of factual assumptions in the applicants' favour. The Court, however, considered that there was a "strong suspicion" that the evidence was relevant, and noted that the applicants had asked for access to any undisclosed material at the time of their trial. The principle in *Rowe and Davis* meant that it was for the trial judge rather than the Court of Appeal to rule on the issue of public interest immunity. Moreover, the court considered that if the evidence had been put before the judge he may have summed the case up differently to the jury. **14–119a**

However, in two judgments handed down on the same day as *Rowe and Davis* (*Fitt v. United Kingdom*[31] and *Jasper v. United Kingdom*[32]) the Court held, by the narrowest of majorities (nine votes to eight), that there was no violation of Article 6 where the material in question had been submitted to the trial judge at an *ex parte* hearing of which the defence had been given notice. In each case, evidence had been withheld following a "type two" hearing under the guidelines issued by the Court of Appeal in *R. v. Davis, Johnson and Rowe*.[33] In *Jasper* the majority explained its conclusion as follows: **14–120**

"The Court is satisfied that the defence were kept informed and permitted to make submissions and participate in the above decision-making process as far as was possible without revealing to them the material which the prosecution sought to keep secret on public interest grounds. Whilst it is true that in a number of different contexts the United Kingdom has introduced, or is introducing, a "special counsel", the Court does not consider that such a procedure was necessary in the present case. The Court notes, in particular, that the material which was not disclosed in the present case formed no part of the prosecution case whatever, and was never put to the jury. This position must be contrasted with the circumstances addressed by the [legislation making provision for "special counsel"], where impugned decisions were based on material in the hands of the executive, material which was not seen by the supervising courts at all.

[30a] Judgment of June 19, 2001.
[31] (2000) 30 E.H.R.R. 1.
[32] (2000) 30 E.H.R.R. 441.
[33] [1993] 1 W.L.R. 613.

The fact that the need for disclosure was at all times under assessment by the trial judge provided a further, important safeguard in that it was his duty to monitor throughout the trial the fairness or otherwise of the evidence being withheld. It has not been suggested that the judge was not independent and impartial within the meaning of Article 6(1). He was fully versed in all the evidence and issues in the case and in a position to monitor the relevance to the defence of the withheld information both before and during the trial. Moreover it can be assumed—not least because the Court of Appeal confirmed that the transcript of the *ex parte* hearing showed that he had been 'very careful to ensure and to explore whether the material was relevant, or likely to be relevant to the defence which had been indicated to him'—that the judge applied the principles which had recently been clarified by the Court of Appeal, for example that in weighing the public interest in concealment against the interest of the accused in disclosure, great weight should be attached to the interests of justice, and that the judge should continue to assess the need for disclosure throughout the progress of the trial. The jurisprudence of the English Court of Appeal shows that the assessment which the trial judge must make fulfils the conditions which, according to the Court's caselaw, are essential for ensuring a fair trial in instances of non-disclosure of prosecution material. The domestic trial court in the present case thus applied standards which are in conformity with the relevant principles of a fair trial embodied in Article 6(1). Furthermore, during the appeal proceedings the Court of Appeal also considered whether or not the evidence should have been disclosed, providing an additional level of protection for the applicant's rights."

14–121   The minority, by contrast, considered that in the absence of "special counsel" the *ex parte* procedure had to be considered fundamentally unfair:

"We note that, although the defence in this case were notified that an *ex parte* application was to be made by the prosecution for material to be withheld on grounds of public interest immunity, they were not informed of the category of material which the prosecution sought to withhold, they were not—by definition—involved in the *ex parte* proceedings, and they were not informed of the reasons for the judge's subsequent decision that the material should not be disclosed. This procedure cannot, in our view, be said to respect the principles of adversarial proceedings and equality of arms, given that the prosecuting authorities were provided with access to the judge and were able to participate in the decision-making process in the absence of any representative of the defence. We do not accept that the opportunity given to the defence to outline their case before the trial judge took his decision on disclosure can affect the position, as the defence were unaware of the nature of the matters they needed to address. It was purely a matter of chance whether they made any relevant points.

The fact that the judge monitored the need for disclosure throughout the trial cannot remedy the unfairness created by the defence's absence from the *ex parte* proceedings. In our view, the requirements . . . that any difficulties caused to the defence by a limitation on defence rights must be sufficiently counterbalanced by the procedures followed by the judicial authorities, are not met by the mere fact that it was a judge who decided that the evidence be withheld . . . Our concern is that, in order to be able to fulfil his judicial functions as the judge in a fair trial, the judge should be informed by the opinions of both parties, not solely the prosecution. The proceedings before the Court of Appeal were, in our view, inadequate to remedy these defects, since, as at first instance, there was no possibility of making informed submissions to the court on behalf of the accused . . .

We accept that there may be circumstances in which material need not be disclosed to the defence, but we find that the way in which the United Kingdom courts dealt with the sensitive material in the present case was not satisfactory. It is not for this Court to prescribe specific procedures for domestic courts to follow, but we note that, in the light of two Convention cases, a "special counsel" system has been introduced in the United Kingdom where it is necessary to withhold evidence from one of the parties to litigation, and that other examples are likely to be introduced. These examples do not exactly match the circumstances of the present case, but we have no doubt that the practical problems raised by the Government can be solved ... [These procedures] show that legitimate concerns about confidentiality can be accommodated at the same time as according the individual a substantial measure of procedural justice."

The Court of Appeal has since held that the procedure for *ex parte* public interest **14–122** immunity applications is unaffected by the case law summarised above.[34] It may be doubted, however, whether the current procedure will always satisfy the requirements of Article 6. Where, for example, material has not been submitted to the trial judge (whether as a result of an oversight, or otherwise) it appears from the *Rowe and Davis* decision that the conduct of an *ex parte* procedure on appeal will not remedy the defect (at least if the Court of Appeal endorses the decision to withhold the material.[35]) More significantly, it is important to recall that the decisions in *Jasper* and *Fitt* related to the "type two" procedure, identified in *R. v. Davis, Johnson and Rowe*,[36] whereby the defence were informed of the fact of the application, and at least given an opportunity to make submissions to the judge. They have no direct bearing on the compatibility of the "type three" procedure. Given the narrowness of the majority in these two cases, it may at least be open to doubt whether a procedure under which the defence are unaware even of the fact that an application is to be made would survive challenge in Strasbourg.

H. THE PROTECTION OF VULNERABLE WITNESSES

I. *Introduction*

The protection of the identity of a police informant who does not give evidence **14–123** is one of the principal grounds for claiming public interest immunity. As we have seen,[37] the Court has held that the withholding of evidence which might expose such a witness to a risk of reprisals is not necessarily incompatible with Article 6. However, prosecuting authorities may also wish to protect the identity of witnesses who *are* called to give evidence. A variety of methods may be employed to achieve this, and the court's powers have been extended and re-structured by Part II of the Youth Justice and Criminal Evidence Act 1999. A witness may be permitted to give evidence anonymously (using a letter in place of his/her name); screens may be used to prevent the witness being seen by the defendant or the public; a witness may be allowed to give evidence by live link; permission may be given to use video-recorded examination or cross-examination; or the Court may be asked to sit *in camera*. The 1999 Act does not deal specifically with witness anonymity, but it provides new procedures for the approval of the other four methods of witness protection.

---

[34] *R. v. Davis, Rowe and Johnson (No. 2) Times*, April 24, 2000.
[35] See also *Atlan v. United Kingdom*, judgment of June 19, 2001, considered at para. 14–119a above. If the material is disclosed the principles established in *Edwards* (see para. 14–90 above) would presumably apply.
[36] [1993] 1 W.L.R. 613.
[37] See para. 14–117 above.

II. *Anonymity*

14–124 Applications for witness anonymity have long been made in blackmail cases, and have now become common in terrorist cases involving security service witnesses, in prosecutions involving child witnesses, and in cases involving serious or organised crime. The House of Lords has held that in rare and exceptional circumstances a judge may permit a witness to conceal his identity entirely from the accused.[38] In *R. v. Taylor (Gary)*[39] the Court of Appeal held that whether such circumstances exist was for the discretion of the trial judge. The following factors were held to be relevant to the exercise of the discretion:

(a) There must be real grounds for fear of the consequences if the identity of the witness were revealed. It might not be necessary for the witness himself to be fearful, or to be fearful for himself alone.

(b) The evidence must be sufficiently important to make it unfair for the Crown to proceed without it. A distinction can be drawn between cases where a witness's credit is in issue and cases where it is the witness's accuracy which is at stake.

(c) The Crown must satisfy the Court that the creditworthiness of the witness has been fully investigated and disclosed.

(d) The Court must be satisfied that there will be no undue prejudice to the accused.

(e) The Court should balance the need for the protection of the witness, including the extent of that protection, against the unfairness or appearance of unfairness to the accused.

14–125 In its early decisions the European Court of Human Rights adopted a stringent approach to such measures, relying exclusively on the rights of the accused under Article 6. Thus in *Kostovski v. Netherlands*[40] the Court drew attention to the different standards applicable in the investigation phase and the trial phase:

> "The Government stressed the fact that case law and practice in the Netherlands in the matter of anonymous evidence stemmed from an increase in the intimidation of witnesses and were based on a balancing of the interests of society, the accused and the witnesses . . . [T]he Court does not underestimate the importance of the struggle against organised crime. Yet the Government's line of argument, whilst not without force, is not decisive . . . [T]he right to a fair administration of justice holds so prominent a place in a democratic society that it cannot be sacrificed to expediency. The Convention does not preclude reliance, at the investigation stage, on sources such as anonymous informants. However, the subsequent use of anonymous statements to found a criminal conviction . . . is a different matter. It involved limitations on the rights of the defence which were irreconcilable with the guarantees contained in Article 6."[41]

---

[38] For the general rule, see *Scott v. Scott* [1913] A.C. 417, and *Attorney-General v. Leveller Magazine* [1979] A.C. 440. See the discussion in *Archbold* (1998), paras 8.69—8.71.

[39] [1995] Crim. L.R. 253; *The Times*, August 17, 1994. As to the need for that anonymity applications are scrutinised with care, see *R. v. Legal Aid Board ex parte Kaim Todner (a firm)* [1999] Q.B. 966. See also paras 14–51a to 14–51c above.

[40] (1990) 12 E.H.R.R. 434.

[41] *ibid.*, at para. 44.

The Court further observed that if the defence are deprived of information   **14–126**
necessary to challenge a witness's credibility, then this may amount to an
insurmountable obstacle to a fair trial:

> "If the defence is unaware of the identity of the person it seeks to question, it may be
> deprived of the very particulars enabling it to demonstrate that he or she is prejudiced,
> hostile or unreliable. Testimony or other declarations inculpating an accused may well
> be designedly untruthful, or simply erroneous and the defence will scarcely be able to
> bring this to light if it lacks the information permitting it to test the author's reliability
> or cast doubt on his credibility. The dangers inherent in such a situation are
> obvious."[42]

Likewise, in *Windisch v. Austria* the Court held that[43]: "[T]he defence was
confronted with an almost insurmountable handicap: it was deprived of the
necessary information permitting it to test the witnesses' reliability or cast doubt
on their credibility."

However, a change of approach was signalled in *Doorson v. Netherlands.*[44] The   **14–127**
Court began by noting that in certain circumstances, the disclosure of a witness's
identity could put his right to physical security, or even his life, at risk. Against
this background the Court considered it necessary to balance the interests of the
witness against the interests of the accused:

> "It is true that Article 6 does not explicitly require the interests of witnesses in general,
> and those of victims called upon to testify in particular, to be taken into consideration.
> However, their life, liberty or security of person may be at stake, as may interests
> coming generally within the ambit of Article 8 of the Convention . . . Contracting States
> should organise their criminal proceedings in such a way that those interests are not
> unjustifiably imperilled. Against this background, principles of fair trial also require
> that in appropriate cases the interests of the defence are balanced against those of
> witnesses or victims called upon to testify."[45]

In the *Doorson* case itself there was no evidence that any of the witnesses had   **14–128**
been threatened by the defendant. On the other hand there was evidence that drug
dealers in general often resorted to threats of or actual violence against persons
who testified against them. Moreover, one of the witnesses in the case had
suffered violence at the hands of a different drug dealer against whom he had
given evidence in the past. The Court held that these factors were sufficient to
justify maintaining anonymity, provided that there was an adequate system of
safeguards in place to ensure that the rights of the defence were respected:

> "The maintenance of the anonymity of the witnesses . . . presented the defence with
> difficulties which criminal proceedings should not normally involve. Nevertheless, no
> violation of Article 6(1) taken together with Article 6(3)(b) of the Convention will be
> found if it is established that the handicaps under which the defence laboured were
> sufficiently counterbalanced by the procedures followed by the judicial authorities."

The safeguards approved by the Court in *Doorson* were that the anonymous   **14–129**
witnesses had been questioned in the presence of counsel by an investigating

---

[42] *ibid.*, at para. 42.
[43] (1991) 13 E.H.R.R. 281 at para. 28.
[44] (1996) 22 E.H.R.R. 330.
[45] *ibid.*, at para. 70.

magistrate; the magistrate was aware of their identity; the magistrate noted in the official report the circumstances on the basis of which the court was able to draw conclusions as to the reliability of the evidence; counsel was able to ask the witnesses whatever questions he considered to be in the interests of the defence except those which might lead to the disclosure of their identity, and all questions had been answered. The Court emphasised that;

> "[E]ven when 'counterbalancing' procedures are found to compensate sufficiently the handicaps under which the defence labours, a conviction should not be based either solely or to a decisive extent on anonymous statements ... Furthermore, evidence obtained from witnesses under conditions in which the rights of the defence cannot be secured to the extent normally required by the Convention should be treated with extreme care."

On the facts the Court held that the trial had not been unfair when two prosecution witnesses remained anonymous and were questioned by the judge in the presence of both counsel (but not the accused).

14–130　In *Van Mechelen v. Netherlands*,[46] by contrast, the Court found a violation of Article 6 when 11 police officers gave evidence for the prosecution, remained anonymous, and were questioned by the judge whilst prosecution and defence counsel were kept in another room, with only a sound link to the judge's chambers. The Court began by distinguishing *Doorson* on the ground that the position of police officers is different from that of ordinary members of the public (since it is part of their duty to give evidence in court). Only exceptionally, when there was clear evidence of direct threats, would it be proper to grant anonymity in respect of professional witnesses of this kind. In the *Van Mechelen* case the defendants and their counsel were not only unaware of the identity of the witnesses, "but were also prevented from observing their demeanour under direct questioning, and thus from testing their reliability". In finding a violation of Article 6, the Court restated the principle established in *Doorson* that any measure restricting the rights of the defence must be "strictly necessary". The Court in *Van Mechelen* interpreted this to mean that "[i]f a less restrictive measure can suffice, then that measure should be adopted". On the facts, the Court considered that the government had failed to offer a satisfactory explanation as to why it was necessary to resort to such extreme limitations on the rights of the defence, or why less far-reaching measures had not been not considered.

14–131　The existing practice in England and Wales does not appear to conform fully with the criteria established by the Court in *Doorson* and *Van Mechelen*. In particular, the Strasbourg case-law appears to prohibit reliance on anonymous witnesses whose evidence is likely to be "decisive" to the outcome of the case. The equivalent domestic law rules point in the opposite direction: anonymity is only to be permitted where the evidence is sufficiently important to make it unfair to oblige the Crown to proceed without it.[47] A Home Office committee recently

---

[46] (1998) 25 E.H.R.R. 647.
[47] *Taylor (Gary)* [1995] Crim. L.R. 253.

considered the *Taylor* principles, without reference to the Convention, and pronounced them satisfactory.[48]

Some mention should be made in this context of the approach of the International   14-132
Criminal Tribunal for the former Yugoslavia (ICTY). The ICTY has sought to apply the Convention case law in the difficult context of trying war criminals. There are two significant points for present purposes. First, the ICTY has not chosen to adopt the Strasbourg approach which holds that convictions should not be based solely or to a decisive extent on the evidence of anonymous witnesses. Instead, it has followed the same course as the United Kingdom courts, holding that one of the criteria *in favour* of allowing anonymity is that the evidence must be of importance in proving the prosecution case. Secondly, the ICTY has not expressly adopted the principle in *Doorson* that evidence from an anonymous witness should be treated with "extreme care."

In the *Blaskic (Protective Measures)* decision[49] the Trial Chamber issued guide-   14-133
lines allowing witness anonymity under the following conditions:

> "First and foremost, there must be real fear for the safety of the witness or her or his family. Secondly, the testimony of the particular witness must be important to the Prosecutor's case. Thirdly, the Trial Chamber must be satisfied that there is no *prima facie* evidence that the witness is untrustworthy. Fourthly, the ineffectiveness or non-existence of a witness protection programme is another point that . . . has considerable bearing on any decision to grant anonymity . . . Finally, any measures taken should be strictly necessary. If a less restrictive measure can secure the desired protection, that measure should be applied."

In the *Tadic First Instance (Witness Protection)* decision the Trial Chamber made   14-134
three further points[50]:

> "Firstly, the Judges must be able to observe the demeanour of the witness, in order to assess the reliability of the testimony . . . Secondly, the Judges must be aware of the identity of the witness in order to test the reliability of the witness . . . Thirdly, the defence must be allowed ample opportunity to question the witness on issues unrelated to his or her identity or current whereabouts, such as how the witness was able to obtain the incriminating information, but still excluding information that would make the new name traceable. Finally, the identity of the witness must be released when there are no longer reasons to fear for the security of the witness."

The Chamber accepted that the general rule must be that, in the words of the   14-135
European Court in *Kostovski*, "in principle, all the evidence must be adduced in the presence of the accused at a public hearing with a view to adversarial argument." Having stated this general rule however, the Chamber went on to hold that:

> "The interest in the ability of the defendant to establish facts must be weighed against the interest in the anonymity of the witness. The balancing of these interests is inherent in the notion of a fair trial. A fair trial means not only fair treatment to the defendant

---

[48] Report of the Interdepartmental Working Group on the treatment of Vulnerable or Intimidated Witnesses in the Criminal Justice System, *Speaking Up for Justice* (Home Office, 1998), para. 8.32.
[49] U.N. Docs. IT–95–14–T (November 5, 1996).
[50] U.N. Docs. IT–94–1–T (August 10, 1995) at para. 71.

but also to the prosecution and to the witnesses . . . The European Court of Human Rights, when determining whether non-disclosure of the identity of a witness constitutes a violation of the principle of fair trial looks at all the circumstances of the case (see *Kostovski* paras 43, 45). The Court identifies any infringement of the rights of the accused and considers whether the infringement was necessary and appropriate in the circumstances of the case."[51]

14-136 Some of the language used by the Trial Chamber in these two cases will be familiar to British judges and lawyers. But it should be stressed that the ICTY's guidelines are not—and are not intended to be—a reflection of the Strasbourg case law applicable to criminal procedure at the national level. The correct test under Article 6 remains that established in the *Doorson/Van Mechelen* line of cases, and considerable caution should be exercised in drawing any analogies with the procedural rules of the ICTY. Writing extra-judicially, the former President of the ICTY, Professor Antonio Cassese, has emphasised that the guidelines were the product of the wholly exceptional conditions under which the Tribunal is obliged to carry out its duties[52]:

> "The Trial chamber [in *Tadic First Instance (Witness Protection)*] noted that only in exceptional circumstances may the Trial Chamber restrict the accused's right of cross-examination. In support of its findings that 'exceptional circumstances *par excellence*' exist in former Yugoslavia in view of the conflict which was then ongoing, the Trial Chamber cited Article 15 of the European Convention which allows for derogation in 'time of war or other public emergency threatening the life of the nation' . . . In the words of the Trial Chamber 'The fact that some derogation is allowed in cases of national emergency shows that the rights of the accused guaranteed under the principle of the right to a fair trial are not wholly without qualification . . .
>
> The Majority Opinion of the Trial Chamber was, of necessity, selective in its reliance on the *Kostovski* case. Indeed, it must be borne in mind that the finding of the majority in *Tadic First Instance (Witness Protection)* was that fair trial guarantees were not violated with anonymous witnesses, whereas the finding of the European Court in *Kostovski* was that such guarantees were violated. The majority of the trial chamber saw its task as providing guidelines to ensure fair trial based *inter alia* on the guidance provided by the case-law of the European Court of Human Rights, but only as subject to 'the unique object and purpose of the International Tribunal, particularly recognising its mandate to protect victims and witnesses'."

14-137 Section 2 of the Human Rights Act expressly requires domestic courts to have regard to the decisions of the European Court and Commission of Human Rights. Insofar as the standards adopted by ICTY offer weaker protection for the accused than those adopted by the European Court of Human Rights, it is submitted that the latter should prevail. However, as we have seen, the drift of the European Court's jurisprudence has been away from strict insistence on Article 6 rights and towards greater recognition of the rights of witnesses and victims.

III. *Screens*

14-138 In *R. v. X and others*[53] the Court of Appeal approved the erection of a screen in a courtroom to prevent young children from seeing, or being seen by, the

---

[51] *ibid.*, at paras 55–56.
[52] Cassese, "The International Criminal Tribunal for the Former Yugoslavia and Human Rights" [1997] E.H.R.L.R. 329.
[53] (1990) 91 Cr. App. R. 36.

defendants. The test in each case is whether the interests of justice require the use of screens in the sense that it would seriously inhibit the calling of relevant evidence if the appearance of the witness was to become known to the accused and/or the public. In practice it has become routine for security service officers giving evidence in terrorist trials to do so from behind screens.[54] The same is true of trials involving serious sexual offences, especially where the offence involves a child complainant. In *R. v. Cooper and Schaub*[55] the Court of Appeal held that the use of screens should generally be confined to cases involving child witnesses, and that in the case of an adult witness such a course should be adopted only in the most exceptional cases, because it could be prejudicial even if the judge gave an appropriate direction. The matter was held to be one for the discretion of the trial judge, however, and the use of a screen in this particular rape trial was held not to have been unreasonable. In *Foster,*[56] a differently constituted Court of Appeal took a distinctly more flexible approach and implied disagreement with *Cooper and Schaub*. The point of the trial judge's discretion is to ensure that justice is done, and where the judge decides that this requires the use of a screen, a proper judicial warning should remove the risk of prejudice. Section 23 of the Youth Justice and Criminal Evidence Act 1999 now provides for the screening of a witness from the accused, in cases where the witness falls into one of the special categories established by sections 16 and 17 of the Act.

In the European context the issue came up for consideration by the Commission   **14–139** in *X v. United Kingdom*.[57] The applicant was convicted of a murder of two soldiers in Northern Ireland during a Republican funeral. Parts of the incident had been captured on film and the Crown wished to conceal the identity of the journalists, cameramen and photographers who had witnessed the incident and taken the film. The case was tried by judge alone. The witnesses were shielded so that the accused, the press and the public were unable to see them, but they could be seen by the judge and by counsel. In rejecting the applicant's complaint, the Commission stressed that far from being decisive in the conviction, the evidence of the screened witnesses was neutral as to his guilt:

> "The Commission recalls the case-law of the European Court of Human Rights that in principle all evidence must be adduced in the presence of the accused at a public hearing with a view to adversarial argument, but this does not mean that a statement from a witness must always be made in court and in public if it is to be admitted in evidence. The defendant must be given an adequate and proper opportunity to challenge and question the witnesses against him. In the present case the witnesses whose identity was not disclosed to the public or the accused were present in court and could be seen by the judge and by the representatives of both prosecution and defence. The evidence itself concerned not the question of identification of the applicant (which evidence was given by police officers whose identity was not withheld), but merely the making of certain filmed and photographic evidence. It was accepted by the defence that the evidence did not implicate the applicant.

> Accordingly, given that the applicant was able, through his representatives who could see the witnesses, to put all questions he wished to the witnesses in question, and that

---

[54] See, *e.g.*, *O'hAdhmaill* (C.C.C., 1994, Rougier J.); *Friars and Jack* (C.C.C., 1995, Ebsworth J.); *McHugh et al.* (C.C.C., 1997, Smedley J.).
[55] [1994] Crim. L.R. 531; *The Times*, December 3, 1993.
[56] [1995] Crim. L.R. 333.
[57] (1992) 15 E.H.R.R. CD 113.

far from being the only item of evidence on which the trial court based its decision to convict, the evidence in question did not implicate the applicant at all, the Commission finds no indication that the decision to screen witnesses from the applicant interfered with his rights under either Article 6(1) or Article 6(3)(d) of the Convention.

Moreover, to the extent that the public was not able to see the screened witnesses, the Commission notes that the interference with the right to publicity was kept to a minimum by the fact that the public was not excluded from the proceedings, but could hear all the questions put to and answers given by those witnesses. The Commission finds that the screening was 'in the interests of . . . public order or national security' and 'to the extent strictly necessary in the opinion of the court in special circumstances where publicity would prejudice the interests of justice'.[58]

14–140 The Commission also held that a trial judge should be made aware of the names and addresses of the witnesses whose identities had been withheld. *X v. United Kingdom* does not of course establish that screening of witnesses in a terrorist case is always compatible with Article 6. The fact that the case was tried without a jury substantially reduced any risk of prejudice. Moreover, the Commission attached considerable weight to the fact that the evidence in issue was of a purely formal character. Where the screened witnesses are decisive to the case against an accused, different considerations—of the kind set out in *Van Mechelen v. Netherlands*,[59] should be borne in mind.

IV. *Hearings in camera*

14–141 The general principle of English criminal procedure is that all evidence must be given in public unless a departure from the general rule is strictly necessary.[60] However, section 25 of the Youth Justice and Criminal Evidence Act 1999 now provides that a court may make a "special measures direction", where a witness falls into one of the categories in sections 16 and 17 of the Act, requiring "the exclusion from the court, during the giving of the witness's evidence, of persons of any description specified in the direction." Section 25 only applies where the offence is a sexual one, or where there are reasonable grounds for believing that the witness has been or will be subject to intimidation. The 1999 Act also introduces further possibilities, such as the giving of evidence by live link or the use of video-recorded testimony, which may be used in appropriate cases so as to protect the rights of witnesses.

14–142 This is an area in which the Convention establishes no more than a minimum standard. The right to a public hearing "protects litigants against the administration of justice in private with no public scrutiny,"[61] and is intended to maintain public confidence in the administration of justice.[62] However, the terms of Article 6(1) are considerably broader and more permissive than the relevant principles of domestic law, providing that the press and public may be excluded "in the interests of morals, public order or national security in a democratic society, where the interests of juveniles or the protection of the private life of the parties

---

[58] *ibid.*
[59] (1998) 25 E.H.R.R. 647.
[60] See para. 14–15a above.
[61] *Pretto v. Italy* (1984) 6 E.H.R.R. 182 at para. 21.
[62] *Diennet v. France* (1996) 21 E.H.R.R. 554 at para. 31.

so require, or to the extent strictly necessary in the opinion of the court in special circumstances where publicity would prejudice the interests of justice." Applying these restrictions, the Commission has upheld the exclusion of the public from the trial of an accused for sexual offences against children.[63]

I. THE RIGHT TO A HEARING IN THE PRESENCE OF THE ACCUSED

It is the almost invariable practice in the Crown Court and magistrates courts for **14–143** the accused to be present throughout the proceedings. In *R. v. Lee Kun* Lord Reading C.J. explained that[64]:

> "There must be very exceptional circumstances to justify proceeding with the trial in the absence of the accused. The reason why the accused should be present at the trial is that he may hear the case against him and have the opportunity... of answering it. The presence of the accused means not merely that he must be physically in attendance, but also that he must be capable of understanding the proceedings."

More recently, both the Court of Appeal[65] and the House of Lords[66] have held **14–144** that in principle it is unacceptable for any part of the trial to take place *in camera* in the absence of the defendant. However, both the Crown Court and magistrates courts do have jurisdiction to continue with a trial in the absence of the accused, providing he has previously entered a plea.[67] The most common circumstances in which the discretion will be exercised are where the accused has absconded during the trial or created a disturbance, where he refuses to leave his cell to come into the dock,[68] or where he is absent through illness (though in the latter case the discretion is to be sparingly exercised, and should never be exercised if the defence could be prejudiced).[69] In *R. v. Hayward, Jones and Purvis*[70] the Court of Appeal emphasised that an accused person had a fundamental right to be present and represented, but could waive that right by absenting himself. The Court then set out the principles to be applied when a trial court is considering whether to proceed in the absence of the defendant.

The power to continue a trial in the absence of the accused must of course be **14–145** exercised in conformity with the Human Rights Act. The European Court of Human Rights has held that the right of an accused person to be present at the hearing of a criminal charge is fundamental to the fairness of the proceedings.[71] An individual may waive his right to be present by failing to attend, having been given effective notice.[72] Trial *in absentia* may also be permitted where the state has acted diligently, but unsuccessfully, to give an accused effective notice of the

---

[63] *X v. Austria* (1965) Application No. 1913/63; 2 Dig. 438.
[64] [1916] K.B. 337 at 341.
[65] *Agar* (1990) 90 Cr. App. R. 318 at 324.
[66] *Preston* [1994] 2 A.C. 130 at 171.
[67] For the authorities, see *Archbold* (2001) para. 3–197.
[68] *O'Boyle* (1991) 92 Cr. App. R. 202.
[69] *Howson* (1981) 74 Cr. App. R. 172 at 179.
[70] *The Times*, February 14, 2001.
[71] *Ekbatani v. Sweden* (1988) 13 E.H.R.R. 504 (para. 25).
[72] *C v. Italy* (1988) 56 D.R. 40 at 59–60.

hearing.[73] Where a court proceeds in the accused's absence, the hearing must be "attended by minimum safeguards commensurate to its importance".[74] In particular, the absent individual must be afforded effective legal representation.[75]

14–146   In *Colozza v. Italy*[76] the Court held that a defendant who absconds with the intention of evading justice has not waived his right to be present at the hearing, since the right to a fair trial is absolute and applies to an accused person who has absconded as much as it does to any other defendant who has not expressly waived the right to be present. Accordingly, the accused must be able to obtain "a fresh determination of the merits of the charge" when he later learns of the proceedings which took place in his absence.[77] This suggests that the fact that a trial has proceeded *in absentia* should, in itself, be a ground for quashing a conviction and ordering a retrial.[78]

14–147   Exceptionally, a court may proceed where the accused is absent through illness, provided the accused's interests are fully protected.[79] Thus where defendants went on hunger strike, the Commission held that there was no absolute right to be present in all circumstances. The point of Article 6(3)(c) was to ensure that the defence had the opportunity to present its arguments adequately, and this right had been secured because they were able to receive practically unlimited visits from their lawyers.[80]

14–148   The right to be present implies not merely physical presence, but the ability to hear and follow the proceedings,[81] to understand the evidence and argument, to instruct lawyers, and to give evidence.[82] The state is under an obligation to give the accused adequate notice of a hearing and, if he is in custody, to take steps to secure his attendance.[83]

---

[73] *Colozza v. Italy* (1985) 7 E.H.R.R. 516 (paras 28–29); *Rubinat v. Italy* (1985) 7 E.H.R.R. 512. This was not established in *FCB v. Italy* (1992) 14 E.H.R.R. 909.

[74] *Poitrimol v. France* (1994) 18 E.H.R.R. 130 (para. 31).

[75] *Lala v. Netherlands* (1994) 18 E.H.R.R. 586; *Pelladoah v. Netherlands* (1994) 19 E.H.R.R. 81; *Van Geyseghem v. Belgium* Judgment January 21, 1999.

[76] (1985) 7 E.H.R.R. 516 at para. 28. The issue was actually left open by the Court because the applicant in *Colozza* had not absconded but had simply left his last known address. The applicant in *Rubinat v. Italy*, a case that was originally joined with *Colozza*, had absconded deliberately, and had taken no part in proceedings. The Commission's finding of a violation in *Rubinat* was unanimous, because the Italian courts had refused to re-open the proceedings: (1985) 7 E.H.R.R. 512 at para. 13.

[77] *Colozza v. Italy* (1985) 7 E.H.R.R. 516 (paras 28–29); *Rubinat v. Italy* (1985) 7 E.H.R.R. 512.

[78] It should be noted that the Ontario Court of Appeal has taken a similar view to that of the English courts, holding in *Czuczman* (1986) 49 C.R. (3d) 385 that a defendant who absconds during the trial may be deemed to have waived the right to be present during the trial, a right stemming from s.7 of the Charter. This decision has been strongly criticised (see D. Stuart, *Charter Justice in Canadian Criminal Law* (2nd ed., 1996), p. 168) on the ground that it gives insufficient weight to the Charter right—a critique in line with the Strasbourg jurisprudence.

[79] *Ensslin, Baader and Raspe v. Federal Republic of Germany* (1978) 14 D.R. 64 at 115–116 (hunger strike (para. 22)).

[80] *Ensslin, Baader and Raspe v. Germany* (1978) 14 D.R. 64.

[81] *Standford v. United Kingdom* (1994) Series A No. 282–A (No violation where a defendant who was hard of hearing had failed to raise objection at the appropriate time).

[82] *T and V. v. United Kingdom* (2000) 30 E.H.R.R. 121.

[83] *Goddi v. Italy* (1984) 6 E.H.R.R. 457.

In *R. v. Preston*[84] the trial judge conducted a number of hearings *in camera*   **14–149**
concerning the products of telephone interceptions under the Interceptions of
Communications Act 1985. The hearings took place in the presence of counsel
but in the absence of the accused and their solicitors. The judge directed that
counsel must not inform the accused of what had occurred. The House of Lords
heavily criticised the procedure which the judge had adopted but dismissed the
appeal. The appellants brought a complaint to the Commission, alleging *inter
alia* that their exclusion from parts of the trial constituted a violation of Article
6. In rejecting the complaint the Commission noted that the applicants had been
excluded for 30 hours during a trial lasting three and a half months, and that they
were legally represented during their absence (although their counsel were
ordered not to divulge to them what was said).[85] The Commission was not
satisfied that the exclusion of the applicants was strictly necessary but found no
violation of Article 6, relying in particular on the fact that the hearings *in camera*
concerned matters of law, and the jury were not present.

The right of an absent appellant to be legally represented on appeal is considered   **14–150**
in detail in Chapter 17. In brief, however, the Court has held that:

> "The right of everyone charged with a criminal offence to be effectively defended by
> a lawyer is one of the basic features of a fair trial. An accused does not lose that right
> merely on account of not attending a court hearing. Even if the legislature had to be able
> to discourage unjustified absences, it may not penalise them by creating exceptions to
> the right to legal assistance."[86]

By refusing counsel leave to make submissions on the applicant's behalf, the
Court of Cassation had violated her right under Articles 6(1) and 6(3)(c).
Similarly, in *Omar v. France*[87] the Court held that a rule which required an
appellant in criminal proceedings to surrender to custody, in accordance with an
order made by a lower court, before he could be heard on appeal against the
decision, was incompatible with the right of access to court. In the light of this
decision, the Court of Appeal has held that it is no longer appropriate to treat as
ineffective an application for leave to appeal made on behalf of a defendant who
has absconded.[88]

J. TRIAL OF JUVENILES IN THE CROWN COURT

Section 24 of the Magistrates Courts Act 1980 provides that children and young   **14–151**
persons under 18 years must be tried summarily (usually in the Youth Court).
However this provision does not apply where the child is charged with murder,
manslaughter or an offence punishable, if committed by an adult, with 14 years
imprisonment or more. In *T and V v. United Kingdom*[89] the Court held that where
juveniles are tried in the Crown Court, Article 6 requires a specially adapted
procedure which promotes the welfare of the young defendant, adequately

---

[84] [1994] 2 A.C. 130.
[85] *Preston and ors v. United Kingdom* [1997] E.H.R.L.R. 695 at 698.
[86] *Van Geyseghem v. Belgium* Judgment January 21, 1999.
[87] (2000) 29 E.H.R.R. 210.
[88] *R. v. Charles, R. v. Tucker, The Times*, February 20, 2001.
[89] (2000) 30 E.H.R.R. 121.

respects his right to privacy, and enables him to understand and participate fully in the proceedings. The applicants were two children charged with murder, who were 10 at the time of the offence and 11 at the time of their trial. The trial, which was accompanied by massive national and international publicity, took place over a three week period. Throughout the proceedings, the arrival of the applicants at court was greeted by a hostile crowd. In the courtroom, the press benches and the public gallery were full. The proceedings were conducted with the formality of an adult criminal trial. The judge and counsel wore wigs and gowns. The procedure was, however, modified to a certain extent in view of the defendants' age. They were seated next to social workers in a specially raised dock. Their parents and lawyers were seated nearby. The hearing times were shortened to reflect the school day and a 10 minute interval was taken every hour. During adjournments the defendants were allowed to spend time with their parents and social workers in a play area. The judge made it clear that he would adjourn the trial if he was informed that either defendant was showing signs of tiredness or stress. Despite these modifications, the Court found that the procedure was in breach of Article 6:

> "The Court notes that Article 6, read as a whole, guarantees the right of an accused to participate effectively in his criminal trial. It has not until now been called upon to consider how this Article 6(1) guarantee applies to criminal proceedings against children, and in particular whether procedures which are generally considered to safeguard the rights of adults on trial, such as publicity, should be abrogated in respect of children in order to promote their understanding and participation . . . The Court [agrees] with the Commission that it is essential that a child charged with an offence is dealt with in a manner which takes full account of his age, level of maturity and intellectual and emotional capacities, and that steps are taken to promote his ability to understand and participate in the proceedings.
>
> It follows that in respect of a child charged with a grave offence attracting high levels of media and public interest, it would be necessary to conduct the hearing in such a way as to reduce as far as possible his or her feelings of intimidation and inhibition. In this connection it is noteworthy that in England and Wales children charged with less serious crimes are dealt with in the Youth Courts, from which the general public is excluded and in relation to which there are imposed automatic reporting restrictions on the media."

14–152   After referring to a number of international standards on juvenile justice, including the United Nations Convention on the Rights of the Child and the United Nations Standard Minimum Rules for the Administration of Juvenile Justice, the Court rejected the government's submission that public trial was necessary. The public interest in the open administration of justice could be satisfied, where appropriate, by a modified procedure providing for selected attendance rights and judicious reporting. As to the circumstances of the applicants' trial, the Court noted the steps which had been taken to adapt the procedure in court, but observed;

> "Nonetheless, the formality and ritual of the Crown Court must at times have seemed incomprehensible and intimidating for a child of 11, and there is evidence that certain of the modifications to the courtroom, in particular the raised dock which was designed to enable the defendants to see what was going on, had the effect of increasing the applicant's sense of discomfort during the trial, since he felt exposed to the scrutiny of the press and the public. The trial generated extremely high levels of press and public interest, both inside and outside the courtroom, to the extent that the judge in his

summing-up referred to the problems caused to witnesses by the blaze of publicity and asked the jury to take this into account when assessing their evidence."

The Court referred to psychiatric evidence suggesting that the applicant V. had **14–153** been extremely distressed throughout the trial and was unable to concentrate on the proceedings, or to instruct his lawyers, and concluded:

"In such circumstances the Court does not consider that it was sufficient for the purposes of Article 6(1) that the applicant was represented by skilled and experienced lawyers . . . .[A]lthough the applicant's legal representatives were seated, as the Government put it 'within whispering distance', it is highly unlikely that the applicant would have felt sufficiently uninhibited, in the tense courtroom and under public scrutiny, to have consulted with them during the trial or, indeed, that, given his immaturity and his disturbed emotional state, he would have been capable outside the courtroom of co-operating with his lawyers and giving them information for the purposes of his defence."

The Court accordingly found that the proceedings had violated Article 6(1). In **14–154** order to give effect to the judgment, the Lord Chief Justice issued the *Practice Direction (Crown Court: Young Defendants).*[90] The guiding principle is that the trial should not expose the young defendant to avoidable intimidation, humiliation or distress, and should be conducted with regard to his welfare. The trial should, where practicable, be held in a courtroom where all participants are on the same level. The young defendant should be permitted to sit with his family in a position which permits easy access to his lawyers. All participants should make efforts to use language appropriate to the defendant's age and understanding and the proceedings should be explained to him by the judge in terms he can understand. The timetable should take account of a young defendant's inability to concentrate for long periods, and it will often be appropriate to take frequent and regular breaks. Robes and wigs should not be worn, and there should be no visible police presence. Security staff should not be in uniform. The court should be prepared to restrict attendance to a small number of people, who will normally be those with an immediate and direct interest in the outcome of the trial. Subject to reporting restrictions, facilities should be made available for the trial to be reported but the judge may limit the number of press representatives who are in court. Moreover, as a general rule, it will be appropriate to make an order for severance so as to enable a young defendant to be tried separately from any adult co-accused.

K. SECURITY MEASURES

I. *Handcuffing*

Domestic law permits the handcuffing of an accused during trial only in excep- **14–155** tional circumstances. Unless there is a danger of escape or violence a defendant ought not to be restrained in the dock.[91] It is always for the court rather than the police or prison service to decide whether it is necessary for the accused to be handcuffed during any court appearance.[92]

---

[90] [2000] 1 W.L.R. 659.
[91] *Vratsides* [1988] Crim. L.R. 251 (C.A.).
[92] *Cambridgeshire Justices ex parte Peacock* (1992) 152 J.P. 895 (D.C.).

14–156   In the past, the Commission has held that the handcuffing of a defendant during a trial,[93] or a view of the *locus in quo*,[94] did not necessarily violate the presumption of innocence or the right to a fair trial generally, since handcuffing was "a measure of security which could not lead to any false conclusions on the part of the jury." However, this should probably be viewed as an area in which the case-law is developing in the light of what the Court has described as an "increased sensitivity" to the appearance of fairness.[95] It seems likely that *unnecessary* handcuffing of an accused in the presence of the jury could be sufficiently prejudicial to threaten the fairness of the trial. In a 1997 case the Commission held that unnecessary handcuffing of an arrested person was degrading treatment in breach of Article 3, in the sense that it diminished his human dignity when he appeared in public.[96] Although the Court disagreed with the Commission's conclusion that the handcuffing was sufficiently serious to constitute a violation of Article 3, it emphasised the need to ensure that such measures were only used where necessary:

> "As regards the kind of treatment in question in the present case, the Court is of the view that handcuffing does not normally give rise to an issue under Article 3 of the Convention where the measure has been imposed in connection with lawful arrest or detention and does not entail use of force, or public exposure, exceeding what is reasonably considered necessary in the circumstances. In this regard, it is of importance for instance whether there is reason to believe that the person concerned would resist arrest or abscond, cause injury or damage or suppress evidence."

II. *Other Exceptional Security Measures*

14–157   Certain trials require exceptional security measures. These may take the form of jury protection, the searching of those entering or leaving court, and even the presence of armed officers. Measures of this kind obviously have the potential to prejudice a defendant on trial in the eyes of the jury. Nevertheless they will not violate the right to a fair trial if they are justified by the nature of the offences or the history of the accused. In *Ensslin, Baader and Raspe v. FRG*[97] the Commission held that visible security measures in a terrorist trial were not in breach of Article 6:

> "The exceptional security measures surrounding the trial were admittedly such as to foster the public conviction that the applicants were criminals. These measures and the statements made by the authorities were, however, a response to the acts and declarations of the applicants and other members of the Red Army Faction and were not designed to create artificially a climate of opinion unfavourable to the accused."

14–158   The Commission in that case attached importance to the fact that the applicants were to be tried by professional judges rather than by a jury "which by its very nature is more easily influenced." However the Commission has adopted the same approach to a jury trial in England involving a terrorist offence:

---

[93] *Campbell v. United Kingdom* Application No. 12323/86.
[94] *X v. Austria* (1967) 24 C.D. 20 at 31; 2 Dig. 745.
[95] See, in another context, *Borgers v. Belgium* (1993) 15 E.H.R.R. 92 at para. 24.
[96] *Kaj Raninen v. Finland* (1998) 26 E.H.R.R. 563.
[97] (1978) 14 D.R. 64.

"It is undoubtedly the case that the trial was conducted in the midst of heavy security and substantial publicity. However, the Commission considers that this was inevitable in a trial of this kind arising from the 'Aldershot bombings' where seven people lost their lives. In itself, it cannot be a basis for holding that the trial was unfair. The Commission attaches importance in this context to the recognition by the trial judge of the dangers of prejudice and his direction to the jury at the beginning of the trial to 'search their consciences' to eliminate any possible prejudice."[98]

The Commission also noted that a co-defendant, who was subject to the same prejudice, was acquitted.

L. Other Issues

I. *Late Introduction of Evidence*

In *R. v. Francis*[99] the Court of Appeal held that there remains a discretion to permit the Crown to re-open their case, which may be exercised where the prosecution case was marked by a fundamental omission arising from a misunderstanding between counsel, and the only way of safeguarding the interests of justice was to re-open submissions or evidence.   **14–159**

The Commission has held that complaints of late introduction of evidence must be considered in the context of fairness of the trial as a whole, and not solely under the specific right in Article 6(3)(c) to be informed promptly and in detail of the nature and cause of the accusation.[1] Thus, in a case where the statements of two additional witnesses were served six days after the trial began, the Commission held that there was no violation of Article 6(3)(c) since "[t]he evidence of the two witnesses concerned did not change the nature and cause of the accusation already made against the applicant and which was supported by other evidence." Similarly, in *X v. United Kingdom* the Commission observed that[2]; "It is generally within the discretion of the competent domestic court to admit a witness if the court considers that the evidence he will give would be relevant to the matters in issue."   **14–160**

The Commission noted that the Court of Appeal had described the admission of evidence at this late stage in the proceedings to be a "rare exception", and accepted the view of the Court of Appeal that exceptional circumstances had arisen in the course of the trial which justified the trial judge's decision.

In recent years the Supreme Court of Canada has tightened its approach to the discretion to allow re-opening of the Crown case. In *P (MB)*[3] Lamer C.J., giving the majority judgment, held that a distinction should be drawn between two phases of the trial. If the Crown applies to re-open its case before the defence has started to answer it, the judge's discretion may be exercised favourably if there has been some oversight or inadvertent omission, so long as defence rights are   **14–161**

---

[98] Application No. 7542/76 (unpublished, 1978); 2 Dig. 689.
[99] (1990) 1 W.L.R. 1264.
[1] Application No. *7220/75* (unpublished, 1977); 2 Dig. 779.
[2] (1972) 45 C.D. 85 at 98; 2 Dig. 384.
[3] [1994] 1 S.C.R. 555, restricting the approach set out previously in *Robillard* [1978] 2 S.C.R. 728.

not prejudiced. But if the defence has started to give its evidence or, *a fortiori*, if it has closed its case:

" . . . it will only be in the narrowest of circumstances that the Crown will be permitted to re-open its case. Traditionally, an *ex improviso* limitation was said to apply to this stage of the proceeding; that is, the Crown was only allowed to re-open if some matter arose which no human ingenuity could have foreseen. At this late stage, the question of what 'justice' requires will be directed much more to protecting the interests of the accused than to serving the often wider societal interests represented by the Crown."

II. *Alternative Verdicts, Added Counts and Voluntary Bills*

14–162   The practice of leaving lesser alternative verdicts to the jury has been challenged unsuccessfully under Article 6(3)(a) (which provides that an accused person has the right to be informed promptly and in detail of the nature and cause of the accusation against him). In *X v. United Kingdom*[4] the applicant was charged on the indictment with wounding with intent contrary to section 18 of the Offences Against the Person Act 1861. He was convicted of the alternative charge of unlawful wounding contrary to section 20, a charge which had not been on the indictment. The applicant complained that he had not been informed "in detail" of the nature of the accusation against him. The Commission rejected the argument in fairly robust terms:

"Both charges related to the same matter. The charge of which the applicant was convicted was thus identical to that with which he was originally charged, save that the jury did not find proved the intent to do grievous bodily harm. There is furthermore no indication that the fact that the alternative charge was not included in the indictment hindered the applicant in any way in the preparation of his defence. It was less serious than the charge on the indictment and the applicant suffered no prejudice from the fact that it was not also included."

14–163   However, the prospect of an Article 6 challenge may be greater where counts are added to an indictment or where the voluntary bill procedure is used. In *R. v Osieh*[5] the Court of Appeal held that, if the prosecution wish to add counts to an existing indictment which are based on evidence not relied upon at committal, they may apply to the trial judge to do so. The defence would also be allowed to make representations on the matter, and the judge would then exercise discretion appropriately. The decision has attracted strong criticism, as lacking any authoritative foundation and contrary to established understanding of the law.[6] Whether it incorporates an adequate safeguard for the defendant's rights under Article 6(3)(a) is impossible to determine in the abstract. The Strasbourg Court would doubtless ask whether the defendant was disadvantaged to an extent which made the trial as a whole unfair. The fact that defence counsel must be given an opportunity to address the judge before the decision is taken, might be regarded as affording a sufficient safeguard in most cases.

14–164   But even that safeguard was missing where the former voluntary bill procedure was used. Section 2(2)(b) of the Administration of Justice (Miscellaneous Provisions) Act 1933 empowers a High Court judge to allow a count to be added to

---

[4] Application No. 6762/74 (unpublished, 1976); 2 Dig. 779.
[5] [1996] 1 W.L.R. 1260.
[6] J. C. Smith, "Adding Counts to an Indictment" [1996] Crim. L.R. 889; see also *Archbold* (2001), para. 1–149.

an indictment even though that count is not founded on the facts or evidence presented to the examining justices. Under the former procedure the application was generally made by the prosecutor on documentary material alone, with the defence being permitted to make written representations in exceptional circumstances.[7] Following the enactment of the Human Rights Act 1998, however, the *Practice Direction (Crime: Voluntary Bills)*[8] was issued, which makes improved provision for adversarial argument. The practice direction affirms that there is no legal requirement, either in the 1933 Act or in the Indictment Rules 1971 for the prosecution to notify the defence of an application for a voluntary bill, and no legal right for the accused to make representations, either orally or in writing. However, it goes on to note that with effect from July 1999 prosecutors are directed that they should, as a matter of good practice,[9] notify the defence of the application, serve on the defence a copy of the papers to be placed before the judge, and inform the defence that they may make submissions in writing within nine days of the service of the notice. Paragraph 6 states that the judge "may invite oral submissions from either party or accede to a request for an opportunity to make such oral submissions in order to make a sound and fair decision on the application". Any oral submissions are to be made on notice and *inter partes*. Whilst the practice direction stops short of acknowledging any legal entitlement to make oral or written representations, it does at least provide a mechanism whereby such representations may be made when they are necessary to ensure the fairness of the proceedings. As Farrell and Friedman have argued,[10] there is much in the Strasbourg jurisprudence to suggest that the former voluntary bills procedure was inadequate to safeguard defence rights. In *Bulut v. Austria,*[11] where the Court had to consider a procedure in Austrian law whereby the Attorney-General could submit observations to an appeal court without serving them on the defence (and therefore without any defence right of reply), a violation of Article 6 was found. The Court spoke in strong terms:

> "[T]he principle of the equality of arms does not depend on further, quantifiable unfairness flowing from a procedural inequality. It is a matter for the defence to assess whether a submission deserves a reaction. It is therefore unfair for the prosecution to make submissions to a court without the knowledge of the defence."[12]

A similar point was made by the Court in *Rowe and Davis v. United Kingdom.*[13] Providing the procedure envisaged by the 1999 Practice Direction is followed, it should be possible in most cases to ensure the equality of arms that Article 6 has been held to require.

---

[7] See the *Practice Direction (Crime: Voluntary Bills)* [1990] 1 W.L.R. 1633; *R. v. Raymond* (1980) 72 Cr.App.R. 151.

[8] *The Times*, August 5, 1999.

[9] The procedure laid down in the Practice Direction is to be followed unless there are good reasons for departing from it, in which case those reasons are to be recorded in the papers submitted to the judge.

[10] S. Farrell and D. Friedman, "Voluntary Bills of Indictment: the Administration of Justice or a Rubber Stamp?" [1998] Crim. L.R. 616.

[11] (1997) 24 E.H.R.R. 84.

[12] *Bulut v. Austria* (1997) 24 E.H.R.R. 84 at para. 46; for another assertion of the same principle, see *Van Orsoven v. Belgium* (1998) 26 E.H.R.R. 55.

[13] (2000) 30 E.H.R.R. 1 at para. 60, where the Court observed that it is "a fundamental aspect of the right to a fair trial that criminal proceedings, *including the elements of such proceedings which relate to procedure*, should be adversarial and that there should be equality of arms between the prosecution and the defence" (emphasis added).

III. *Duties of Prosecution Counsel*

14–165   The fairness of a trial may be imperiled where there has been improper conduct by prosecution counsel. The Commission has held that inflammatory conduct by the prosecution is not in itself a violation of the right to a fair trial, since Article 6 focuses primarily on the fairness of the tribunal.[14] Nevertheless, in the opinion of the Commission, such conduct could violate the right to a fair trial if it went uncorrected by the judge, or if there was any evidence that the bias of the prosecution had "communicated itself" to the judge and from him to the jury.[15]

IV. *Summing up*

14–166   Strong adverse comment by a trial judge on the facts of a case obviously has the potential to undermine the fairness of the trial. But this is another area in which the relevant domestic law standard[16] appears—on the face of it—to be stricter and more detailed than the test applied by the Commission under Article 6. It is important however to bear in mind that any application considered and rejected by the Commission on the merits has previously been rejected by the Court of Appeal. It is therefore difficult to draw any firm conclusions about the apparent difference of approach.

14–167   Under domestic law the proper test is not whether the judge usurped the jury's function, but whether the judicial comment was such as to make the summing up fundamentally unbalanced. If it was, a repetition of the standard direction that the facts are for the jury, and that an expression of opinion by the judge is to be ignored if the jury disagree with it, would not remedy the unfairness.[17] Whilst strong—and sometimes very strong—comment may be permissible, a judge should never give an express indication of disbelief of the evidence of a partic-ular witness, let alone that of the defendant.[18] A judge may comment on conflicts in the evidence but should not "inflate the conflict and . . . describe it in sarcastic or extravagant language."[19] The jury should not be told that the judge has rejected a submission of no case to answer,[20] and a summing up should not contain any comment suggesting that an acquittal might ruin a police witness or that police officers are in any special category.[21]

14–168   As a general principle, the Commission has held that the right to a fair trial will be violated if the judge's summing up to the jury is not "fair, balanced and accurate".[22] In practice, however, neither the Commission nor the Court has ever found a violation against the United Kingdom on this basis. In one unreported

---

[14] Application No. 5568/71, dec. 31.5.1975 (unpublished); 2 Dig. 742.
[15] *ibid.*
[16] See *Archbold* (2001) paras 4–394 and 7–67.
[17] *Mears v. R.* (1993) 97 Cr. App. R. 239 at 243 (P.C.); *Wood* [1996] 1 Cr. App. R. 207 (C.A.).
[18] *Iroegbu, The Times*, August 2, 1988.
[19] *Berrada* (1990) 91 Cr. App. R. 131 at 135 (C.A.).
[20] *Smith and Doe* (1986) 85 Cr. App. R. 197 (C.A.).
[21] *Culbertson* (1970) 54 Cr. App. R. 311 (C.A.); *Harris, The Times*, October 16, 1985; *Beycan* [1990] Crim. L.R. 185; *cf. Wellwood-Kerr* [1978] Crim. L.R. 760; *Keane* [1992] Crim. L.R. 306.
[22] *X v. United Kingdom* (1975) 3 D.R. 10 at 16; *cf. Mr and Mrs X v. United Kingdom* (1973) 45 C.D. 1.

decision[23] the Commission expressed the view that in order to found a violation of Article 6 the misdirection would have to be "decisive" in the evaluation of the fairness of the trial as a whole. The trial judge in that case had made a reference during his summing up to the finding of a gun at the applicant's home. No such allegation had in fact been made by the Crown during the trial, and the judge's statement was wholly unsupported by the evidence. The applicant appealed, but the Court of Appeal—whilst acknowledging the error—nevertheless dismissed the appeal. In rejecting the application, the Commission took the view that the judge's error, taken in isolation, was not sufficient to render the whole trial unfair for the purposes of Article 6. Particular weight was attached to the fact that the error had not been pointed out to the judge by counsel at the time, and to the consideration by the Court of Appeal of the effect of the error on the safety of the conviction:

"The Commission recalls its function in examining whether or not a trial has been fair within the meaning of Article 6(1) of the Convention. It is not called upon to decide whether or not the domestic courts have correctly assessed the evidence before them, but only 'whether evidence for and against the accused has been presented in such a manner, and the proceedings in general have been conducted in such a way, that he has had a fair trial' . . . The Commission must determine in the present case whether the reference by the trial judge to the existence of a gun was 'of such importance as to be decisive for the general evaluation of the trial as a whole'. However, the Commission observes that it was open to counsel to raise objections to the judge's summing up to the jury. No such objection was made, concerning the mention of a gun, although other objections on points of fact and law were made. Moreover, in the Commission's opinion, the decision of the Court of Criminal Appeal must be interpreted as a finding that, notwithstanding the reference to a gun, and in view of the weight of the evidence against the applicant, no miscarriage of justice had actually occurred. In such circumstances the Commission does not consider that the alleged reference to a gun, when considered in the context of the trial as a whole, could be said to have given rise to such prejudice against the applicant that he did not receive a fair trial."

In another early decision of the Commission[24] the trial judge had commented **14–169** during the summing up in a way which strongly suggested that he considered the evidence sufficient to prove guilt. Nevertheless, the Commission rejected the application primarily on the ground that the judge had made it clear to the jury that the inferences of fact were for them to draw, and that it was only directions of law which were binding:

"It cannot be ruled out that the presiding judge, in his summing up of the case, may have suggested the outcome of his personal overall evaluation of the question of guilt. However, the Commission finds that it was made sufficiently clear to the jurors that this particular part of the summing up did not bind them, nor did it in any way unduly influence the jurors, who deliberated privately, without the presence of professional judges."[25]

This is to be contrasted with the approach taken by the Privy Council in *Mears* **14–170** *v. R.*[26] and by the Court of Appeal in *R. v. Wood*,[27] where the repetition of the

---

[23] Application No. 10361/83; 2 Dig. Supp. 6.1.1.4.4.5.
[24] Application No 10135/85; 2 Dig. Supp. 6.1.1.4.4.5.
[25] *ibid.*
[26] (1993) 97 Cr. App. R. 239.
[27] [1996] 1 Cr. App. R. 207.

standard direction that the facts are for the jury to determine was considered insufficient to save an unfair summing up. It might also to be contrasted with the Court's decision in *Sander v. United Kingdom*[28] where a direction from the trial judge to the jury to put prejudice out of their minds and to try the case solely on the evidence was held to be insufficient to cure a risk of bias arising from the fact that racist remarks had apparently been made in the jury room.

14–171   In a case where the applicant complained that the trial judge had misdirected the jury on the burden of proof,[29] the Commission dismissed the application, noting that "the judge, in explaining that proof must be beyond reasonable doubt, also explained what was meant by a 'reasonable doubt' and told the jury that they must acquit the applicant if they had such a doubt."[30]

V. *Interpreters and Facilities for the Hard of Hearing*

14–172   Article 6(3)(e) guarantees to an accused the right "to have the free assistance of an interpreter if he cannot understand or speak the language used in court." The basic right to interpretation is adequately respected in domestic law: the Court of Appeal has held that unless an accused is able to comprehend the full implications of the charge he faces, to understand the potential defences and to instruct his lawyers, the trial is a nullity.[31]

14–173   However, there are two possible shortcomings in domestic practice in this area. First, the Court of Appeal has held that whilst the evidence must be translated if the defendant is unrepresented,[32] translation may be dispensed with if the accused is represented by counsel, if counsel expressly requests this, and if the judge considers that the defendant "substantially understands" the evidence to be given.[33] It is doubtful whether this test adequately meets the requirements of Article 6(3)(e). Certainly it would not satisfy section 14 of the Canadian Charter: the Supreme Court held in *Tran*[34] that any waiver of the right to an interpreter must be done personally by the defendant, if necessary following an enquiry by the court through an interpreter to ensure that the defendant fully understands the significance of waiver. It has further been held in New Zealand that the right to an interpreter extends to the pre-trial translation of documents in the case.[35]

14–174   Secondly, Part IV of the *Practice Direction (Costs in Criminal Proceedings)*[36] appears to permit a court, in its discretion, to direct that a person who has been convicted should pay the costs of an interpreter. Such an order would not be compatible with the clear principle in the Court's case-law that interpreters' costs are an integral part of the state's obligations to operate a fair judicial system. Under Article 6(3)(e) such costs must always be paid by the court and not by the

---

[28] *The Times*, May 12, 2000.
[29] Application No. 5768/72 (1975) 2 Dig. 388.
[30] *ibid.*
[31] *Iqbal Begum* (1991) 93 Cr. App. R. 96 (C.A.).
[32] *Lee Kun* [1916] 1 K.B. 337; see also *Kunnath v. The State* [1993] 1 W.L.R. 1315 (P.C.).
[33] [1916] 1 K.B. 337 at 343.
[34] [1994] 2 S.C.R. 951.
[35] *Alwen Industries Ltd v. Collector of Customs* [1996] 3 N.Z.L.R. 226, applying s. 24(g) of the Bill of Rights.
[36] (1991) 93 Cr. App. R. 89.

defendant, regardless of the means of the defendant or the outcome of the case. In *Luedicke, Belkacem and Koc v. Germany*[37] the Court held that Article 6(3)(e) provides "neither a conditional remission, nor a temporary exemption, nor a suspension, but a once and for all exemption or exoneration." Under the Human Rights Act, the Practice Direction must be read subject to this principle.

Defendants who are deaf and dumb were formerly treated as being "mute by visitation of God"[38] but it is now well established that they may enter a plea and be tried through an interpreter.[39] In *Stamford v. United Kingdom*,[40] the accused, who was hard of hearing, was prevented from participating effectively in the trial since the acoustics in court were inadequate and he was unable to hear the evidence properly. Despite this, the Court found that his trial had not been in breach of Article 6 since he had been represented by experienced counsel with whom he had been able to communicate, and who had defended him well. Where, however, an interpreter *is* provided, it is submitted that the costs must be borne by the Court and not by the defendant.[41]   **14–175**

VI. *Costs Following Aquittal*[42]

A refusal to order the payment of costs to an acquitted defendant will violate the presumption of innocence if the ground for the refusal reflects a suspicion that the accused is guilty. In *Minelli v. Switzerland*[43] the Commission found a violation of Article 6(2) where an acquitted defendant had been ordered to pay costs on the basis that he would "very probably" have been convicted had he not been saved by the operation of a limitation period: **14–176**

> "The mere fact of ordering certain court costs or prosecution costs against an accused when the proceedings are terminated neither by a conviction nor by an acquittal cannot in itself amount to a violation of the presumption of innocence. It is conceivable that considerations completely alien to an assessment of guilt may influence the court required to reach a decision on the apportionment of costs arising out of the proceedings. On the other hand, a problem does arise under Article 6(2) if the reasons for the Court's decision, or any other precise and conclusive evidence, show that the apportionment of these costs, as ordered, results from an appraisal of the guilt of the accused, so that the costs ordered against him may appear as a sort of penalty imposed on the grounds of suspicion."

The Court agreed, but expanded the principle to include not only an order for costs to be paid by the defendant, but any costs order which reflects an assumption of guilt, including a refusal to award defence costs: **14–177**

---

[37] (1979–80) 2 E.H.R.R. 149 at para. 40.
[38] *Pritchard* (1836) 7 C. & P. 303.
[39] *Archbold* (2001), paras 4–37 and 4–164 to 4–169.
[40] (1994) A.182–A.
[41] By analogy with the Court's decision in *Luedicke, Belkacem and Koc v. Germany* (1979–80) 2 E.H.R.R. 149.
[42] In *R. v. Canterbury Crown Court ex parte Regentford Ltd* (*The Times*, February 6, 2001) Waller L.J. held that section 29(3) of the Supreme Court Act 1981, as interpreted by the House of Lords in *Re Sampson* ([1987] 1 W.L.R. 194) that an order as to costs following a trial on indictment could not be judicially reviewed as it was a decision "relating to trial on indictment", was an interpretation that was compatible with the Convention. There was no Convention right to have decisions reviewed.
[43] (1983) 5 E.H.R.R. 554.

"[T]he presumption of innocence will be violated if, without the accused's having previously been proved guilty according to law . . . a judicial decision concerning him reflects an opinion that he is guilty. This may be so even in the absence of any formal finding; it suffices that there is some reasoning suggesting that the court regards the accused as guilty."[44]

14–178   In *Leutscher v. Netherlands*[45] the Court re-stated its position on both discontinued proceedings and rulings that a prosecution would be time-barred. A refusal to award defence costs in those circumstances:

" . . . may raise an issue under Article 6(2) if supporting reasoning, which cannot be dissociated from the operative provisions, amounts in substance to a determination of the guilt of the former accused without his previously having been proved guilty according to law and, in particular, without his having had an opportunity to exercise the rights of the defence."[46]

14–179   In England and Wales the award of costs to an acquitted defendant in the Crown Court is governed by paragraph 2.2(b) of the *Practice Direction (Costs in Criminal Proceedings)*.[47] This paragraph formerly permitted the judge to decline to award defence costs from central funds on the grounds that "there was ample evidence to support a conviction but the defendant has been acquitted on a technicality which has no merit". A number of cases against the United Kingdom involving a refusal of costs under former paragraph 2(2)(b) were declared admissible by the Commission, and resulted in friendly settlements with the Government. In *DF v. United Kingdom*,[48] for example, the applicant was charged with 17 offences of obtaining a pecuniary advantage by deception contrary to section 15(1) of the Theft Act 1968. The charges related to the purchase of pharmaceutical products with a view to circumventing the Pharmaceutical Price Scheme. The case was transferred to the Crown Court under section 4 of the Criminal Justice Act 1987. The applicant was acquitted on a submission of no case to answer, but the judge refused defence costs on the grounds that the applicant had brought the prosecution on himself. The judge added that his conduct "stinks of greed". After the case was declared admissible by the Commission, a friendly settlement was reached between the parties.

14–180   Similarly, in *Moody v. United Kingdom*[49] the applicant was acquitted of having obscene articles (magazines and video tapes) for publication for gain contrary to section 2(1) of the Obscene Publications Act 1959. The defence had argued *inter alia* that the material was not obscene. The trial judge refused to order defence costs from central funds on the grounds that the defendant had brought the prosecution on himself by "choosing to work among the material". Again, the case was declared admissible and then settled by the Government.[50] Prior to the implementation of the Human Rights Act 1998, the *Practice Direction* was

---

[44] Note, however, the subsequent decision in *Englert and Nolkenbockhoff v. Germany* (1987) A–123, discussed critically in M. Delmas-Marty (ed.), *The European Convention for the Protection of Human Rights: International Protection versus National Restrictions* (1992), pp 126–127.
[45] (1997) 24 E.H.R.R. 181.
[46] *ibid.*, para. 29, referring to *Lutz v. Germany* (1988) 10 E.H.R.R. 182, paras 59–60.
[47] (1991) 93 Cr. App. R. 89 at 90.
[48] Application No. 22401/93.
[49] Application No. 22613/93.
[50] See also *Lochrie v. United Kingdom* Application No. 22614/93 and *Cybulski v. United Kingdom* Application No. 24266/94.

amended so as to delete paragraph 2(2)(b) in order to forestall such violations in the future.[51]

However, this does not prevent a court from refusing an award of defence costs **14–181** on other grounds. In *Byrne v. United Kingdom*[52] the judge refused to make an order for costs in favour of the acquitted applicant, essentially on the ground that she had (following legal advice) remained silent when originally interviewed and had only revealed her defence at the trial. The Commission declared her application inadmissible, since the judge's conduct did not violate the presumption of innocence in Article 6(2). The judge, in refusing to award costs, had relied on that part of the Practice Direction relating to the applicant's conduct prior to trial; it could be argued that, if the applicant had disclosed her defence earlier, the prosecution might well have been dropped. However, her conduct was well within her right to remain silent (the interview was prior to the Criminal Justice and Public Order Act 1994)—indeed, she had followed legal advice in doing so—and therefore this ruling seems to lack a secure foundation. In *Condron and Condron v. United Kingdom*[53] the Court laid great emphasis on the value of legal advice and stated that it may constitute a sufficient reason for declining to answer police questions. The Commission's respones to another challenge also seems insecure. In *Fashanu v. United Kingdom*[54] the applicant was acquitted of conspiracy charges but the judge refused to make a costs order, on the ground that the applicant's silence had brought suspicion on himself. Rebutting the challenge based on Article 6(2), the Commission refused to accept;

> "that the applicant was penalised for exercising his right to silence: in the absence of a right to reimbursement of costs on acquittal, the fact that a person has to bear his or her own costs on acquittal cannot be equated to a penalty. Rather, it is an inevitable consequence of the bringing of proceedings."

This reasoning is less than fully convincing. The "inevitable consequence" point is an over-statement. The rejection of the "right to silence" argument calls for reconsideration after decisions such as *Condron* and *Averill v. United Kingdom*[55]; the leading decisions, discussed in Chapter 15 below, recognise that an innocent person may have good reason for remaining silent, even though, there are some circumstances which "clearly call for an explanation" from an accused. At the very least, decisions on the refusal of costs to acquitted defendants should reflect this distinction.

VII. *The Right to a Reasoned Ruling*

It is a requirement of a fair trial in both civil and criminal matters that a court **14–182** should give reasons for its judgment. The national courts must "indicate with sufficient clarity the grounds on which they based their judgment" so as to enable an unsuccessful litigant to exercise any right of appeal and to maintain public

---

[51] *Practice Direction (Crime: Costs in Criminal Proceedings) (No. 2), The Times*, October 6, 1999.
[52] [1998] E.H.R.L.R. 626.
[53] [2000] Crim. L.R. 677, discussed in detail, with other relevant decisions, in Chapter 15 below.
[54] (1998) 26 E.H.R.R. CD 217.
[55] [2000] Crim. L.R. 684.

confidence in the administration of justice.[56] The extent of the duty to give reasons varies according to the nature of the decision so that "the question whether a court has failed to fulfil the obligation . . . can only be determined in the light of the circumstances of the case".[57] However, the essential issues must be addressed,[58] and where a submission is clearly relevant, and potentially decisive, it should be specifically dealt with in the judgment.[59]

14–183   In the United Kingdom, no reasons are generally given either by a magistrates court or by a jury. It is obviously impossible for a jury to give a reasoned judgment, and the Court has recently held that reasons are not required from a jury[60]: "The absence of reasons in the High Court's judgment was due to the fact that the applicant's guilt was determined by a jury, something which cannot in itself be considered contrary to the Convention."[61]

14–184   The same principle cannot be applied in the magistrates court. The position of a district judge would appear to be indistinguishable for this purpose from that of any other judge. And Whilst it is true that lay justices have no legal training, they are assisted by a qualified clerk and do provide reasons when requested to do so for the purposes of an appeal by way of case stated. It is strongly arguable that the Human Rights Act, read in conjunction with Article 6, has imposed a duty on magistrates to give brief reasons for their decisions. This is consistent with the obligation under Article 5 for courts to give a reasoned ruling when remanding a defendant in custody.[62] A duty on magistrates to give reasons for their decisions appears to have been assumed in the *Practice Direction (Justices' Clerk to the Court).*[63]

---

[56] *Hadjianastassiou v. Greece* (1993) 16 E.H.R.R. 219 (para 33).
[57] *Ruiz Torija v. Spain* (1995) 19 E.H.R.R. 553 (para. 29); *Stefan v. General Medical Council* [1999] 1 W.L.R. 1293 (P.C.).
[58] *Helle v. Finland* (1998) 26 E.H.R.R. 159 (para. 60).
[59] *Ruiz Torija v. Spain* (1995) 19 E.H.R.R. 553 (para. 30) (failure of court to address limitation argument).
[60] *Saric v. Denmark* Application No. 31913/96, February 2, 1999.
[61] As to the effect of the absence of reasons for a jury's decision on the ability of the Court of Appeal to review the safety of a conviction, see *Condron and Condron v. United Kingdom* [2000] Crim. L.R. 677.
[62] See para. 13–29 above.
[63] [2001] 1 Cr.App.R. 147. There is however no duty to give a fully reasoned ruling where a magistrates court commits a defendant to the Crown Court for sentence, since there is a ample opportunity for effective representations on the appropriate penalty to be made in the subsequent proceedings; *R (Jermyn) v. Wirral Magistrates Court* (Unreported October 20, 2000).

CHAPTER 15

CRIMINAL EVIDENCE

A. The Evaluation of Evidence

In general, the *assessment* of evidence is a matter for the domestic courts, and the **15–01** European Court of Human Rights will not substitute its own view of the facts for an assessment that has been fairly reached by an impartial and independent tribunal. This is an important application of the Court's "fourth instance" doctrine,[1] under which recourse to Strasbourg is characterised as a *review* of domestic practice for compliance with the Convention, rather than an *appeal* against the national courts' decisions. Thus, the European Court of Human Rights will only interfere with a conclusion of fact where there is an indication that the domestic courts have drawn unfair or arbitrary conclusions from the evidence before them.[2] As the Commission observed in *Stewart v. United Kingdom*[3]:

> "[T]he national judge, unlike the Commission, has had the benefit of listening to the witnesses at first hand and assessing the credibility and probative value of their testimony after careful consideration. Accordingly, in the absence of any new evidence having been brought before the Commission and of any indications that the trial judge incorrectly evaluated the evidence before him, the Commission must base its examination of the Convention issues before it on the facts as established by the national courts."

In *IJL, GMR and AKP v. United Kingdom*[4] the applicants complained that there **15–02** had been improper collusion between Inspectors of the Department of Trade and Industry and police officers investigating their involvement in an alleged share support scheme, a complaint which had previously been rejected by the Court of Appeal. The Court held that "when faced with a dispute over facts it must turn in the first place to the facts as found by the domestic authorities". After referring to the Court of Appeal's conclusion on the issue, the judgment continued:

> "The Court, for its part must give due weight to this finding, reached as it was after lengthy adversarial argument and in the light of all the materials assembled by the applicants' lawyers in support of their case. On the basis of its own careful examination of these materials the Court does not consider that the Court of Appeal's assessment of the evidence or establishment of the facts can be impeached on the ground that they were manifestly unreasonable or in any other way arbitrary."

However, in an exceptional case the Court will be prepared to assess the weight **15–03** of the evidence before a national court in determining whether a trial was fair. In

---

[1] See para. 2–114 above.
[2] *Schenk v. Switzerland* (1991) 13 E.H.R.R. 242; *Edwards v. United Kingdom* (1993) 15 E.H.R.R. 417 at para. 34; *Van Mechelen v. Netherlands* (1998) 25 E.H.R.R. 647 at para. 50.
[3] (1984) 39 D.R. 162 at 168.
[4] [2001] Crim. L.R. 133.

Barbera, Messegue and Jabardo v. Spain[5] the applicants were convicted of serious terrorist offences allegedly committed on behalf of a Catalan separatist organisation. The defendants alleged that their confessions had been obtained through torture. However they were not permitted to give evidence orally to this effect; their evidence was taken by letters rogatory. The allegation of torture was rejected by the domestic courts. In finding a violation of Article 6, the Court noted that the defendants had allegedly confessed after a long period of incommunicado detention, and expressed "reservations" about the confession evidence and the manner in which it had been considered.[6] The Court concluded that "very important pieces of evidence were not adequately adduced and discussed at the trial in the applicants' presence and under the watchful eye of the public."[7]

15–04　　Over the years there have been numerous attempts, usually by unrepresented applicants, to persuade the Commission to examine the evidence which had led to a conviction. These attempts have almost all been unsuccessful. In one case[8] the applicant had been convicted of murder by a 10 to two majority verdict on visual identification by a single eyewitness. The applicant complained that his conviction on identification alone was unfair, and that an important alibi witness had not been called in his defence. The Commission appeared to take the view that visual identification evidence does call for special caution, but nevertheless rejected the application as manifestly ill-founded on the ground that the judge had adequately directed the jury on the issue:

> "The case before the court was by no means simple as is shown by the fact that the jury reached its verdict of guilty by a majority decision of 10 to 2. The crucial issue in the evidence was the identification of the applicant by one witness at the material time and place, but the judge in his summing up took trouble to explain to the jury the problems which arose thereby and the difficulties of their decision on this evidence. Furthermore, one of the relevant witnesses whom the applicant says should have been called to prove an alibi had made a statement which was in itself inconclusive as to the critical periods of time and was not even mentioned by the applicant in his own testimony before the court of first instance."

B. Rules of Admissibility

15–05　　The Convention does not lay down a comprehensive set of rules for the admissibility of evidence, which is primarily a matter for regulation through national law. The Court's function is to determine whether the proceedings in question, taken as a whole, were fair, and whether the rights of the defence under Article 6 were adequately respected.[9] Applying this approach, the Court and the Commission have considered the application of Article 6 in the context of evidence which has been obtained unlawfully or in breach of Convention rights,[10] evidence obtained by ill-treatment in custody,[11] or by powers of compulsory questioning,[12] the drawing of adverse inferences from a defendant's silence under

---

[5] (1989) 11 E.H.R.R. 360.
[6] *ibid.*, at para. 87.
[7] *ibid.*, at para. 89.
[8] Application No 6208/73 (1975, unpublished), 2 Dig. 389.
[9] *Miailhe v. France (No. 2)* (1997) 23 E.H.R.R. 491, para. 43.
[10] See para. 15–06 below.
[11] See para. 15–28 below.
[12] See para. 15–73 below.

police questioning where there are insufficient safeguards against unfairness,[13] the admission of evidence obtained by entrapment,[14] the evidence of accomplices who have been offered immunity from prosecution, or undercover agents placed in a prison to eavesdrop on conversations involving the accused,[15] the admission of a co-defendant's plea of guilty pursuant to section 74 of the Police and Criminal Evidence Act 1984, the admission of anonymous witnesses,[16] or important hearsay evidence without an opportunity to cross-examine,[17] and the refusal to call a witness central to the defence case.[18] These issues are considered in detail in the sections which follow.

C. Unlawfully Obtained Evidence

I. *The Strasbourg Caselaw*

Article 6 and Article 13, taken together, have been held to imply that there must **15–06** be an effective procedure during a criminal trial by which to challenge the admissibility of evidence which has been obtained unlawfully or in breach of the Convention.[19] Where a breach of domestic law is relied upon, the existence of the *voir dire* procedure has been held to be sufficient to comply with this procedural obligation,[20] and the same will generally be true of an application to exclude evidence under sections 76 and 78 of the Police and Criminal Evidence Act 1984. However, where it is alleged that the evidence was obtained in breach of a Convention right, these procedures will only afford an effective remedy if that breach is capable in practice of affording a ground for the exclusion of the evidence.[21]

The admission of evidence obtained in breach of Article 3 will inevitably violate **15–07** Article 6.[22] In *Austria v. Italy*[23] the Commission held that where "the accused,

---

[13] See para. 15–94 and 15–98 below.
[14] See para. 15–37 below.
[15] *X v. Federal Republic of Germany* Application No. 12127/86 (1989) 11 E.H.R.R. 84.
[16] See para. 15–126 below.
[17] *Unterpertinger v. Austria* (1991) 13 E.H.R.R. 175: see Art. 6(3)(d) at paras 15–108 to 15–110 below. As to hearsay evidence relied upon by the defence, see para. 15–131 below.
[18] See para. 15–132 below.
[19] *Schenk v. Switzerland* (1991) 13 E.H.R.R. 242, para. 47; *Khan v. United Kingdom*, 8 B.H.R.C. 310.
[20] *G v. United Kingdom* (1983) 35 D.R. 75, where the applicant's case was that the police had refused to allow him to see his solicitor until he signed a confession. The Commission held that the trial was not unfair, since he had been able to ventilate his concerns at the *voir dire* and the judge had considered them before making an adverse ruling.
[21] In *R. v. Sultan Khan* [1997] A.C. 558, the House of Lords held that the opportunity to rely on the Convention in an application under s.78 complied with the duty to provide an effective domestic remedy under Art. 13 of the Convention. The European Court of Human Rights disagreed, holding that since there was no legally enforceable right to privacy in English law prior to the enactment of the Human Rights Act 1998, s.78 was incapable of meeting the requirements of Art. 13: see paras 15–12 and 15–26 below.
[22] As to the relationship between this principle and the duty to exclude evidence obtained by oppression under s.76 of the Police and Criminal Evidence Act 1984, see para. 15–28 below.
[23] (1961) 4 Y.B. 116 at 784; 2 Digest 722. See also *Barbera, Messegue and Jabardo v. Spain* (1989) 11 E.H.R.R. 360. *Cf. Ferrantelli and Santangelo v. Italy* (1997) 23 E.H.R.R. 288, paras 49–50.

during the preliminary investigation, has been subjected to any maltreatment with the aim of extracting a confession from him", Article 6(2) will be violated "if the Court subsequently accepted as evidence any admissions extorted in this manner." As we shall see, the Court has held that the admission of evidence obtained by entrapment may violate Article 6,[24] and the same is true of evidence obtained by powers of compulsory questioning, enforceable by criminal proceedings in default.[25] However, it does not necessarily follow that the admission of evidence obtained in breach of other Convention rights, such as Article 8, will render the trial unfair. Whether or not it does so will depend on the circumstances of the case.[26]

15–08   In *Scheichelbauer v. Austria*[27] the Commission appeared to establish the basis for an exclusionary rule, when it observed that in a legal system based on respect for the individual, a suspect can legitimately demand that the law should give him suitable protection against interference with other substantive rights in the evidence-collection process. On the facts of that case, however, the Commission found no violation, emphasising that the recording of a telephone intercept was shown to be an accurate record of the conversation, and concluding that the trial as a whole was not unfair.

15–09   In *Schenk v. Switzerland*,[28] the Court adopted an altogether stricter line on the issue. The Swiss government had conceded that intercept evidence used against the applicant in a trial for attempted incitement to murder had been obtained without the requisite authority, and therefore both unlawfully in domestic law and in contravention of Article 8 of the Convention. The Court found no violation of Article 6:

> "While Article 6 of the Convention guarantees the right to a fair trial, it does not lay down any rules on the admissibility of evidence as such, which is therefore primarily a matter for regulation under national law. The Court cannot therefore exclude as a matter of principle and in the abstract that unlawfully obtained evidence of the present kind may be admissible. It has only to ascertain whether Mr Schenk's trial as a whole was fair. Like the Commission it notes first of all that the rights of the defence were not disregarded. The applicant was not unaware that the recording complained of was unlawful because it had not been ordered by a competent judge. He had the opportunity—which he took—of challenging its authenticity and opposing its use . . . The fact that his attempts were unsuccessful makes no difference . . . The Court also attaches weight to the fact that the recording of the telephone conversation was not the only evidence on which the conviction was based . . . . [The Rolle Criminal Court] carefully stated in several passages of its judgment that it relied on evidence other than the recording but which corroborated the reasons based on the recording for concluding that Mr Schenck was guilty . . . It emerges clearly from [the judgment] that the criminal

---

[24] See para. 15–37 below.
[25] See para. 15–73 below.
[26] *Schenk v. Switzerland* (1991) 13 E.H.R.R. 242, paras 46–48; *X v. Federal Republic of Germany* Application No. 12127/86 (1989) 11 E.H.R.R. 84; *Khan v. United Kingdom* [2000] Crim. L.R. 684.
[27] (1970) 14 Y.B. 902.
[28] (1991) 13 E.H.R.R. 242.

court took account of a combination of evidential elements before reaching its opinion."[29]

The Court's judgment in *Schenck* appeared to place considerable emphasis on the existence of other evidence implicating the accused.[30] However, in *Khan v. United Kingdom*[31] the Court held that the admission of evidence obtained by means of a listening device in breach of Article 8 did not render the proceedings unfair, despite the fact that the prosecution case rested entirely on the disputed tape recording. The Court held that where unlawfully obtained evidence was relied upon to secure a conviction, the compatibility of the proceedings with Article 6 would depend upon an examination of the nature of the unlawful activity alleged and, if it involved a violation of another Convention right, the nature of the violation found. The Court noted that the use of a listening device was not unlawful under domestic law since there was, at the time, no legally enforceable right to privacy in English law. The police had acted compatibly with Home Office guidelines on intrusive surveillance and the breach of Article 8 related solely to the absence of a statutory basis for the surveillance. Moreover, the incriminating statements had been made voluntarily and without inducements. Whilst the Court would attach weight to the existence of other evidence implicating the accused, the relevance of independent evidence depended on the circumstances. Where the contested evidence was compelling, and there was no challenge to its reliability, the need for supporting evidence would be correspondingly weaker. The applicant had had the opportunity to challenge both the authenticity and the admissibility of the tape recording. After it was ruled admissible he pleaded guilty. At each stage of the domestic proceedings the courts had assessed the impact of the admission of the evidence on the fairness of the proceedings and if they had concluded that its admission would have led to substantive unfairness, they would have had a discretion to exclude it. In those circumstances, the proceedings as a whole were fair.

15–10

In a strongly worded dissenting judgment, Judge Loucaides expressed the argument in favour of an exclusionary rule thus:

15–11

"This is the first case which comes before the Court where the only evidence against an accused in a criminal case which also led to his conviction, was evidence obtained in a manner contrary to Article 8 of the Convention . . . I cannot accept that a trial can be "fair", as required by Article 6, if a person's guilt for any offence is established through evidence obtained in breach of the human rights guaranteed by the Convention . . . I do not think one can speak of a "fair" trial if it is conducted in breach of the law . . . If violating Article 8 can be accepted as "fair" then I cannot see how the police can be effectively deterred from repeating their impermissible conduct . . . Breaking the law, in order to enforce it, is a contradiction in terms and an absurd proposition."

---

[29] See also *Smith v. United Kingdom* [1997] E.H.R.L.R. 277 where the Commission declared inadmissible a complaint based on the use in evidence of a conversation between the applicant and a disguised security service officer, on the ground that it did not go to the heart of the matter and as such was to be regarded as a ruse in the public interest.
[30] This is in line with the Court's decisions on the admission of hearsay evidence without an opportunity for cross-examination (see para. 15–120 *et seq.* below) and with the Court's approach to entrapment evidence (see para. 15–43 below).
[31] 8 B.H.R.C. 310.

15–12   Despite its principal finding that the proceedings did not involve a violation of
Article 6, the majority of the Court in *Khan* held that Article 13 of the Convention required an effective remedy before a national authority for the alleged
violation of Article 8. In the Court's view, the discretion to exclude evidence
under section 78 of the Police and Criminal Evidence Act 1984 was inadequate
to meet this requirement because, prior to the enactment of the Human Rights
Act 1998 there was no legally enforceable right to privacy in English law. The
national courts therefore lacked the necessary jurisdiction to rule on the substance of the applicant's Article 8 complaint, or to grant appropriate relief if the
complaint was well-founded. There had accordingly been a violation of Article
13. The implications of this finding for English law were considered by the
House of Lords in *R. v. P.*[32] On one view, the violation of Article 13 in *Khan*
could be taken to support the proposition that a breach of Article 8 should now
be remediable through the exclusion of evidence, since the Human Rights Act
has introduced a legally enforceable right to privacy in English law. This reading
of the judgment was however rejected by Lord Hobhouse, in the leading speech
in *P*. In his view, the European Court's decision in *Khan* that there had been a
violation of Article 13 confirmed the existing position in English law that the
power to exclude evidence under section 78 was concerned with the fairness of
the trial and not with providing a remedy for a breach of Article 8. If the evidence
could be admitted in a manner consistent with Article 6, then there was no basis
for its exclusion in order to afford a remedy for a breach of Article 8. The
criterion to be applied was the criterion of fairness and the Human Rights Act did
not require section 78 to be read as affording any broader remedial jurisdiction:

> "[T]he ECHR decision that any remedy for a breach of Article 8 lies outside the scope
> of the criminal trial and that Article 13 does not require a remedy for a breach of Article
> to be given within that trial shows that their Lordships [in *R. v. Sultan Khan* [1997] A.C.
> 558] were right to say that a breach of Article 8 did not require the exclusion of
> evidence. Such an exclusion, if any, would have to come about because of the
> application of Article 6 and section 78."

II. *Comparative Approaches*

15–13   The courts in New Zealand have developed an exclusionary principle where
evidence has been obtained in breach of the Bill of Rights Act.[33] In *Simpson v.
Attorney-General (Baigent's Case)*[34] Hardie Boys J. said:

> "The New Zealand Bill of Rights Act, unless it is to be no more than an empty
> statement, is a commitment by the Crown that those who in the three branches of
> government exercise its functions, powers and duties will observe the rights that the Bill
> affirms. It is, I consider, implicit in that commitment, indeed essential to its worth, that
> the Courts are not only to observe the Bill in the discharge of their own duties, but are
> able to grant appropriate and effective remedies where rights have been infringed . . . In
> the limited range of cases that have thus far come before it, this Court has been
> consistent in the view that the terms of the Covenant and the terms of the Bill of Rights

---

[32] [2001] 2 W.L.R. 463 Judgment of December 11, 2000, (HL).
[33] *Simpson v. Attorney-General* [1994] 3 N.Z.L.R. 667; *R. v. H* [1994] 2 N.Z.L.R. 143; *R. v. Goodwin*
[1993] 2 N.Z.L.R. 153 at 191–194.
[34] [1994] 3 N.Z.L.R. 667.

Act itself require a rights-centred response to infringements. That is not to exclude other objectives: to ensure compliance in the future, and to secure the wider public interest. But the primary focus has been on providing an appropriate remedy to a person whose rights have been infringed . . . Thus, the Courts have responded to breaches of [the Bill of Rights Act] by adopting a rule of *prima facie* exclusion of evidence obtained in consequence of the breach. This has certainly had the effect of securing general recognition by law enforcement authorities of the rights affirmed by those sections. And while there are doubtless those who believe that this has favoured criminals to the detriment of the public interest, it may also have advanced that interest in other ways by emphasising the importance of what is often taken for granted, and by demonstrating that the Courts will not be party to breaches, but will insist on preserving the integrity of the administration of justice."[35]

Similarly, in *Te Kira*[36] Sir Robin Cooke P. observed that: **15–14**

"In affirming certain rights and freedoms the New Zealand Bill of Rights Act does not merely repeat the old law. In so far as the rights and freedoms concerned coincide with the old law, the legislature has given them an added emphasis. It would be inconsistent with the concept of a Bill of Rights to relegate them to be matters to be given some weight in the exercise of judicial discretion."

This points the way towards a rights-centred approach to the exercise of judicial **15–15** discretion, and suggests that courts should treat the breach of a constitutional right as a strong argument for excluding the evidence thereby obtained. Thus, in *Kirifi*,[37] where the accused had been questioned at length before being informed of his right to a lawyer, it was held that the resulting admissions should have been excluded. To do otherwise, said Sir Robin Cooke, would be to treat the right as "a dead letter." However, the rule of exclusion is not absolute and the courts in New Zealand have placed increasing emphasis on "the public interest" as a competing consideration.[38] Accordingly, a number of circumstances have come to be recognised in which evidence obtained in consequence of a breach of the Bill of Rights Act may nevertheless be admitted. The courts may, for example admit evidence where there was no causal link between the breach and the obtaining of the evidence,[39] where the defendant was aware of the right but waived it,[40] where it is inevitable that the evidence would have been discovered apart from the violation of the right,[41] or where the breach was trivial or technical.[42]

In Canada, the exclusion of evidence obtained in breach of the Canadian Charter **15–16** of Rights and Freedoms 1982 is expressly provided for.[43] Section 24(1) provides

---

[35] At 702–703.
[36] [1993] 3 N.Z.L.R. 257 at 262.
[37] [1992] 2 N.Z.L.R. 8.
[38] In *Barlow* (1996) 14 C.R.N.Z. 9 at 24; see also *Grayson and Taylor* [1997] 1 N.Z.L.R. 399 at 411.
[39] *Grant* (1992) 8 C.R.N.Z. 483.
[40] *Wojcik* (1994) 11 C.R.N.Z. 463.
[41] *Butcher* [1992] 2 N.Z.L.R. 257; *cf. H* [1994] 2 N.Z.L.R. 143, where Richardson J. (at 150) argued against this exception on the ground that it "would encourage warrantless searches and seizures" and might therefore undermine the very purpose of the Bill of Rights.
[42] *E.g., Goodwin* [1993] 2 N.Z.L.R. 153, *per* Cooke P. at 171.
[43] For brief discussion, see P. Mirfield, *Silence, Confessions and Illegally Obtained Evidence* (1997), pp 365–370; for fuller treatment, see D.R. Stuart, *Charter Rights in Canadian Criminal Law* (2nd ed., 1996), Chapter 24.

that a person whose rights or freedoms have been infringed may apply to a court for a remedy. Section 24(2) provides:

> "Where, in proceedings under subsection (1) a court concludes that evidence was obtained in a manner that infringed or denied any rights or freedoms guaranteed by this Charter, the evidence shall be excluded if it is established that, having regard to all the circumstances, the admission of it in the proceedings would bring the administration of justice into disrepute."

15–17 This creates an exclusionary rule, rather than a discretion, but the operation of the rule depends on a finding that admission of the evidence would "bring the administration of justice into disrepute." This rather open-ended formulation has been refined in subsequent decisions. In *Stillman*[44] the Supreme Court held that, for these purposes, evidence could be classified either as "conscriptive" (where the accused has been compelled to incriminate himself orally or by the giving of bodily samples) or as "non-conscriptive" (where the evidence was obtained without the participation of the accused). The admission of conscriptive evidence obtained in breach of the Charter would generally be taken to render the trial unfair, unless the evidence could have been discovered by other means. So far as "non-conscriptive" evidence is concerned, at least three factors have been identified as relevant in deciding whether admission would bring the administration of justice into disrepute. First, the court should ask whether the breach of the Charter was serious (which depends on "the deliberate or non-deliberate nature of the violation by the authorities, circumstances of urgency and necessity, and other aggravating or mitigating factors"[45]). Secondly, the court should ask whether other investigatory techniques, compatible with the Charter, could have been used. Thirdly, the nature of the breach will be relevant. If the violation of the defendant's right was relatively minor compared with the seriousness of the offence, then its admission would be less likely to bring the administration of justice into disrepute.[46] The relevance of good or bad faith on the part of law enforcement officers has been narrowly circumscribed in Canada. Thus, in *Elshaw*[47] Iacobucci J. held that:

> "[T]he bad faith of the police may strengthen the case for exclusion because . . . it may tend to show a 'blatant disregard for the Charter.' However, the good faith of the police will not strengthen the case for admission to cure an unfair trial. The fact that the police thought they were acting reasonably is cold comfort to an accused if their actions result in a violation of his or her right to fair criminal process."

15–18 The United States jurisprudence on unlawfully obtained evidence has, in the past, tended towards an absolute exclusionary rule—the so-called "fruit of the poisoned tree" doctrine—although a measure of flexibility has been introduced in

---

[44] (1996) 113 C.C.C. (3d) 321.
[45] *Elshaw* [1991] 3 S.C.R. 24, *per* Iacobucci J. at 39–40.
[46] *Collins* [1987] 1 S.C.R. 265.
[47] [1991] 3 S.C.R. 24 at 43. This was a case where the accused had been questioned by an officer in the police van immediately after arrest, at which stage he made admissions. On arrival at the police station he was charged and told of his right to a lawyer, and no subsequent admissions were made. The Supreme Court held that the violation of his Charter right to a lawyer before being questioned was such as to adversely affect the fairness of the trial and bring the administration of justice into disrepute.

recent years.[48] The Fourth Amendment to the United States Constitution establishes the right not to be subjected to an unlawful search or seizure. In the landmark decision of *Mapp v. Ohio*[49] the Supreme Court declared that evidence obtained in breach of this provision should be excluded automatically from the trial. Subsequent decisions have supported this rule for its deterrent effect on the police, but have nevertheless recognised a "good faith" exception where, for example, a search warrant is invalid because of some error by the issuing authority—an error which *ex hypothesi* is unlikely to be relevant to the rationale of deterring police misconduct.[50] The other principal United States rule flows from the Fifth Amendment privilege against self-incrimination. The right to counsel, recognized in *Miranda v. Arizona*,[51] is supported by a rule of exclusion of evidence obtained in breach. Subsequent Supreme Court decisions have tempered the absolute nature of the exclusionary rule, creating a more finely calibrated approach. In *New York v. Quarles*,[52] for example, the Supreme Court held that exclusion of evidence should not follow inexorably when the police asked questions in breach of *Miranda* in a situation in which public safety was at issue.

The Supreme Court of Ireland has taken the view that, where evidence has been   **15–19**
obtained by intentional breach of a constitutional right, there is a much stronger presumption that the evidence should be excluded than where there has merely been some other unlawful act during the investigation. Thus in *The People (AG) v. O'Brien*[53] the Supreme Court held that evidence obtained in "deliberate and conscious" breach of a constitutional right was inadmissible except in "extraordinary excusing circumstances".[54] Among the decisions which followed this approach is *The People (DPP) v. Kenny*,[55] where some of the prosecution evidence had been obtained through an unlawful search which violated the defendant's right, under Article 40 of the Constitution, to the inviolability of his dwelling. Finlay C.J. held that evidence obtained through breach of a personal constitutional right "must be excluded" unless the breach was "accidental" or there were other exceptional circumstances affording an excuse. The court held that it was immaterial that the police officer was unaware that the warrant was defective.[56] However, in *People v. Balfe*[57] the Court of Criminal Appeal took a less stringent approach, and held that where the police seized evidence in innocent reliance on a defective search warrant, the evidence need not be

---

[48] For an accessible and thoughtful discussion, see P. Mirfield, *Silence, Confessions and Illegally Obtained Evidence* (1997), pp 319–339.
[49] 367 U.S. 643 (1961).
[50] See the discussion of *United States v. Leon* 468 U.S. 897 (1984) and other cases cited by Mirfield, *op. cit.*, pp 322–324.
[51] 384 U.S. 436 (1966).
[52] 467 U.S. 649 (1984), discussed by Mirfield, *op. cit.*, pp 335–336.
[53] [1965] I.R. 142.
[54] An approach based on *People v. O'Brien* has also been followed in South Africa. Thus, in *S v. Motloutsi* [1996] 1 S.A.C.R. 78, the court held that a strict approach to exclusion would be appropriate where there had been a deliberate breach of a constitutional right. In such cases the evidence should only be admitted if "extraordinary excusing circumstances" existed, such as the imminent destruction of vital evidence or the need to rescue a victim in peril, or when the evidence was obtained by "a search incidental to and contemporaneous with a lawful arrest although made without a valid search warrant."
[55] [1990] I.R.L.M. 569.
[56] *Larkin v. O'Dea* [1995] 2 I.R.L.M. 1.
[57] [1998] 4 I.R. 50.

excluded. The prevailing rationale for exclusion in Ireland is that the courts have a duty "to defend and vindicate" constitutional rights. The Irish courts have thus rejected the deterrent rationale adopted in the United States.

15–20   The rules and exceptions developed by the courts in these jurisdictions raise questions about the rationale for excluding evidence for breach of a fundamental right. One prominent rationale is often said to be the deterrence of law enforcement officers: if they know that the evidence is likely to be excluded, they will acquire greater respect for the rights of the individuals with whom they deal. This is in one sense a rights-centred rationale, in that it regards respect for rights as the goal and selects deterrence as the means to achieving it. Another prominent rationale is the protective principle, that individuals should not be disadvantaged if one of their declared rights is infringed in the investigation process. This approach aims to vindicate the declared importance of individual rights in constitutions or human rights documents. A further rationale is that it would undermine the integrity of the criminal justice system if a court were to act on evidence obtained unlawfully or through violation of a constitutional right.[58] To proclaim certain rights and then to act on evidence obtained through breaches of those rights is said to be a contradiction in terms and to undermine the rule of law.

15–21   Each of the three remedial rationales has its weaknesses,[59] and the courts in New Zealand, Canada and the United States have all begun to move in the direction of greater recognition of "the public interest" and "public safety" in recent years. However, it is important to note that in all those jurisdictions the movement amounts to the development of exceptions to what remains an accepted starting point, which is that in principle a violation of a constitutional right ought to be followed by exclusion of the resulting evidence. Where such exceptions are permitted, reliance on "the public interest", or "the interests of the wider community", generally requires careful analysis, including a discussion of whether the protection of individual rights is not itself in the interests of the community and its members.

III. *Exclusion of Evidence under the Human Rights Act 1998*

15–22   Traditionally, English law has not regarded the fact that evidence was obtained illegally as a ground for exclusion in itself.[60] The focus has always been on the effect of the evidence on the fairness of the trial. How, then, should the English courts approach the exercise of their exclusionary discretions, under section 78 of the Police and Criminal Evidence Act 1984, and at common law, under the new constitutional framework established by the Human Rights Act? Section 8 of the Act provides that where a public authority has acted in a manner which is

---

[58] This approach has been reflected in a number of English decisions on abuse of process: See *R. v. Horseferry Road Magistrates ex parte Bennett* [1994] 1 A.C. 42; *R. v. Mullen* [2000] Q.B. 520. *cf. Latif and Shahzad* [1996] 1 W.L.R. 104. As to the appropriateness of abuse of process as a remedy in these circumstances see A. Choo, *Abuse of Process and Judicial Stays of Criminal Proceedings* (1993), and A. Choo, "Halting Criminal Prosecutions: the Abuse of Process Doctrine Revisited" [1995] Crim. L.R. 864.

[59] For argument, see Mirfield, *op. cit.*, Chapter 2, and Ashworth, *The Criminal Process* (2nd ed., 1998), pp 52–55 and pp 312–315.

[60] *R. v. Sang* [1980] A.C. 402 (H.L.); *R. v. Sultan Khan* [1997] A.C. 558 (H.L.).

incompatible with a complainant's Convention rights, a court may grant any remedy, within its powers, which it considers "just and appropriate". In the context of a criminal trial, this obviously includes an order for the exclusion of evidence (as well as, in extreme circumstances, an order for the stay of criminal proceedings as an abuse of process).

In exercising the remedial jurisdiction under section 8 of the Human Rights Act, **15–23** the Strasbourg approach cannot be transplanted directly into English law. The Court and Commission have always adhered strictly to the "fourth instance" doctrine,[61] when dealing with Article 6 applications, and have been reluctant to disturb the findings of domestic courts so long as the hearing itself was procedurally fair. Consistent with the Court's general approach to the evaluation of evidence,[62] the emphasis is on ensuring that questions concerning the admissibility of unlawfully obtained evidence are addressed effectively *at the national level*. Thus, the Court has required an effective procedure within the trial for examining allegations of illegality, and for excluding evidence obtained unlawfully or in breach of Convention rights.[63] In *Khan v. United Kingdom*,[64] as we have seen, the Court found a violation of Article 13 on the ground that—prior to the Human Rights Act—there was no legally enforceable right to privacy in English law. Accordingly a breach of Article 8 was not, in itself, a sufficient basis for the exclusion of evidence under section 78, and there was therefore no effective remedy in national law. Although Article 13 is not amongst the rights specifically incorporated by section 1 of the Human Rights Act, the courts are expected to take the Convention caselaw under Article 13 into account when exercising their remedial powers under section 8 of the 1998 Act.[65] For section 8 remedial powers to be exercised conformably with the Convention, an English court must, as a minimum, have jurisdiction to rule on the alleged violation and to exclude evidence if the violation is well-founded. However, as the House of Lords emphasised in *R. v. P*,[66] the dominant consideration in the exercise of this jurisdiction remains the fairness of the proceedings, and their compatibility with Article 6. A breach of Article 8 is not sufficient, in itself, to require the exclusion of evidence. Depending on the nature of the breach it may nonetheless be an important factor in the court's determination of whether the admission of the evidence would be fair for the purposes of section 78.

English courts have to fulfil their duty under section 6 to act in a way which is **15–24** compatible with Convention rights (unless they are obliged to do otherwise by the terms of incompatible primary legislation which cannot be construed compatibly under section 3). This means that they have to apply the Convention directly to the case before them, and to afford "just and appropriate" remedies where a violation is found on the facts, rather than following the residual or supervisory approach adopted by the Strasbourg institutions. Under section 3, they also have to interpret *and give effect* to section 78 of the Police and Criminal Evidence Act in a manner which is compatible with the Convention rights "so far as it is possible to do so". The open-textured wording of section 78 is plainly capable of

---

[61] See para. 2–114 above.
[62] See paras 15–06 to 15–12 above.
[63] See para. 15–08 and para. 15–09 above.
[64] [2000] Crim. L.R. 684. See para. 15–12 above.
[65] See para. 3–46 above.
[66] [2001] 2 W.L.R. 463 Judgment of December 11, 2000, (HL). See further para. 15–12 above.

being construed in a manner which is compatible with Article 6 jurisprudence. Even before the Act came into force, Lord Nicholls had observed, in *R. v. Sultan Khan*,[67] that section 78 and Article 6 are both in effect directed towards the same question:

> "[T]he discretionary powers of the trial judge to exclude evidence march hand in hand with Article 6(1) of the European Convention on Human Rights. Both are concerned to ensure that those facing criminal charges receive a fair hearing. Accordingly, when considering the common law and statutory discretionary powers under English law, the jurisprudence on Article 6 can have a valuable role to play."

15–25   In determining whether exclusion of evidence is the "just and appropriate" remedy for a breach of Convention rights, there is thus an important distinction to be drawn between two categories of complaint. The first category concerns evidence, the admission of which would breach Article 6. This would apply, for example, to the admission of evidence obtained by ill-treatment in custody[68] or improper entrapment,[69] to the admission of statements or evidence obtained by compulsory questioning powers,[70] and to the admission of certain forms of hearsay evidence.[71] Here, the trial court retains a theoretical power under section 78 to admit the evidence, but it is a power which can, in practice, only be exercised one way. As Lord Nicholls put it in *R. v. Sultan Khan*, Article 6 and section 78 "march hand in hand". If the admission of certain evidence would result in a breach of the right to a fair trial, as interpreted in Strasbourg, then the judge, as a public authority, will be acting unlawfully within the meaning of section 6 of the Human Rights Act if he exercises his power under section 78 in favour of admitting the evidence.[72] To quote Sir John Laws, section 78 "will look less like a general discretion (which anyway it is not), and more like a means of vindicating concrete requirements of fairness".[73]

15–26   The second category concerns evidence which has been obtained in breach of a Convention right other than Article 6, such as the right to privacy in Article 8. Here, the position is more subtle, and the trial court has a genuine discretion to examine all the circumstances before ruling under section 78. In accordance with the Court's decision in *Khan v. United Kingdom*, the judge will wish to take account of the nature of the unlawful activity alleged, the gravity of the breach of Convention rights, any element of inducement or compulsion, the existence of other evidence implicating the accused, the probative weight of the disputed evidence and its reliability.[74] Breach of a Convention right is inherently more serious than breach of a rule of domestic law, for the simple reason that the right in issue has been accorded the status of a basic or fundamental right, deserving of special protection by the courts. Such a breach does not necessarily require the exclusion of evidence obtained in consequence, but the constitutional nature of

---

[67] [1997] A.C. 558 at 583.
[68] See para. 15–07 above and para. 15–28 below.
[69] See para. 15–37 below.
[70] See para. 15–73 below.
[71] See para. 15–108 below.
[72] As Kennedy L.J. accepted in *Attorney-General's Reference No. 3 of 2000* (May 17, 2001) (CA) where the admission of evidence would violate Article 6 the Court is bound to afford a remedy.
[73] *The Human Rights Act and the Criminal Justice and Regulatory Process* (Hart Publishing, 1999), p. xiv.
[74] See para. 15–10 above.

the right will weigh heavily in the balance. This approach appears consistent with the decision of the House of Lords in *R. v. P*,[75] where the appellants had argued that evidence obtained by telephone interception according to the law of another jurisdiction should be excluded under section 78 because its admission would involve a breach of Article 6. The House of Lords found no violation of Article 8 in the way the evidence had been obtained or used, and held that under both Article 6 and section 78 of PACE a defendant was entitled, not to the exclusion of the evidence, but to the opportunity to challenge its use in evidence, and to a judicial assessment of the effect of its admission upon the fairness of the proceedings.[76] This may be compared to the somewhat stronger approach of Lord Steyn, for the Privy Council, in *Allie Mohammed v. The State*.[77] In *Allie Mohammed* the appellant had unsuccessfully challenged the admissibility of a statement made to the police on the ground that he had been denied his constitutional right to consult with a solicitor in the police station. Relying on the New Zealand approach of *prima facie* exclusion of evidence obtained in breach of constitutional rights, the appellant argued that his conviction should be quashed. Lord Steyn held that where there had been a breach of the constitutional right to a fair trial it would always be right for a conviction to be quashed.[78] Where other rights were violated, the court should recognise the added value attached to breach of a constitutional right but was not bound to apply a presumption in favour of exclusion:

"On balance, their Lordships have arrived at a view that does not entirely accord with the view which has prevailed in New Zealand . . . [T]he discretion of a trial judge is neither *prima facie* exclusionary, nor *prima facie* inclusionary. It is, however, not a completely open-textured discretion . . . On the one hand the judge has to weigh the interest of the community in securing relevant evidence on the commission of serious crime so that justice can be done. On the other hand, the judge has to weigh the interest of the individual who has been exposed to an illegal invasion of his rights . . . It is a matter of fundamental importance that a right has been considered important enough . . . to be enshrined in [the] Constitution. The stamp of constitutionality on a citizen's right is not meaningless: it is clear testimony that added value is attached to the protection of the right . . . On the other hand, it is important to bear in mind the nature of a particular constitutional guarantee and the nature of a particular breach. For example, a breach of a defendant's constitutional right to a fair trial must inevitably result in the conviction being quashed. By contrast, the constitutional provision requiring a suspect to be informed of his right to consult a lawyer, although of great

---

[75] [2001] 2 W.L.R. 463 Judgment of December 11, 2000, (HL). See further para. 15–12 above.

[76] In its decision in the same case (*R. v. X, Y and Z, The Times*, May 23, 2000) the Court of Appeal observed *obiter* that a judge considering an application under section 78 should attach "considerable importance" to any breach of Article 8, but that it would remain necessary to engage in the exercise of reviewing and balancing all the circumstances of the case. In *R. v. Loveridge, Lee and Loveridge, The Times*, May 3, 2001 the defendants had been unlawfully filmed whilst in the cell area of a magistrates court. The Court of Appeal held that the filming was unlawful because it was in breach of section 41 of the Criminal Justice Act 1925 which prohibits photography in court. The Court thus found that there had been a breach of the defendant's right to private life under Article 8 as the interference had not been in accordance with the law. However the Court agreed with the trial judge that the admission of the unlawfully obtained video evidence did not affect the fairness of the trial.

[77] [1999] 2 W.L.R. 552 at 562–563.

[78] The implications of this decision for the jurisdiction of the Court of Appeal (Criminal Division) are discussed in para. 17–27 below. It is important, however, to note that the scope of the right to a fair to a fair trial under the Constitution of Trinidad and Tobago which was at issue in *Allie Mohammed* is considerably narrower than Art. 6 as interpreted in Strasbourg.

importance, is a somewhat lesser right and potential breaches can vary greatly in gravity. In such a case, not every breach will result in a confession being excluded. But their Lordships make clear that the fact that there has been a breach of a constitutional right is a cogent factor militating in favour of the exclusion of the confession. In this way the constitutional character of the infringed right is respected and accorded a high value. Nevertheless, the judge must perform a balancing exercise in the context of all the circumstances of the case."

15–27 In the controversial case of *Attorney-General's Reference No. 3 of 1999,*[79] the House of Lords found no breach of Article 8 and therefore did not have to confront these issues. In this case a DNA sample had been retained, despite the defendant's acquittal, contrary to section 64 of PACE. Although the use of that sample would have been contrary to Article 8, because it was not in accordance with the law, Lord Steyn held that it was not in breach of Article 8 to use a subsequent DNA sample (which had been matched with the wrongly retained sample, in order to identify the defendant as the perpetrator) as evidence against the defendant. Although it amounted to an interference with the defendant's right to privacy under Article 8(1), the later sample had admitted in evidence obtained in accordance with the law (because it did not breach section 64) and its admission was necessary in a democratic society for the investigation and prosecution of serious crime. The interference with the Article 8(1) right was therefore justified according to Article 8(2).

15–28 Turning finally to evidence obtained by ill-treatment, we have seen that the admission of such evidence is *a fortiori* in breach of Article 6.[80] It seems clear that the existing procedure under section 76(2) of the Police and Criminal Evidence Act, which creates a statutory test of voluntariness as a condition precedent to the admissibility of a confession, will normally satisfy the requirements of Article 6. One element in that condition precedent is that a confession which is represented to have been obtained by oppression is not to be admitted into evidence unless the prosecution proves that it was not so obtained. Section 76(8) defines oppression so as to include "torture, inhuman or degrading treatment, or the use or threat of violence (whether or not amounting to torture)".[81] This lays the foundation for a close correspondence between English law and the Convention.

D. ENTRAPMENT

I. *In English Law*

15–29 In *R. v. Sang*[82] the House of Lords held that entrapment is not a defence in English law. There is, however, ample authority that entrapment may be a ground for staying a prosecution as an abuse of process, or for excluding evidence under section 78 of the Police and Criminal Evidence Act 1984. The leading authority on the exclusion of evidence obtained by entrapment remains *R. v. Smurthwaite*

---

[79] [2001] 2 W.L.R. 56.
[80] See para. 15–07 above.
[81] See, for example, *Fulling* [1987] Q.B. 426, *Paris, Abdullahi and Miller* (1993) 97 Cr. App. R. 99.
[82] [1980] A.C. 402.

and Gill,[83] in which the Court of Appeal proposed that when a judge is considering the exercise of the section 78 discretion, six factors should be taken into account:

"(1) Was the officer acting as an agent provocateur[84] in the sense that he was enticing the defendant to commit an offence he would not otherwise have committed? (2) What was the nature of the entrapment? (3) Does the evidence consist of an admission to a completed offence, or does it consist of the actual commission of the offence? (4) How active or passive was the officer's role in obtaining the evidence? (5) Is there an unassailable record of what occurred or is it strongly corroborated? (6) Has the officer abused his role to ask questions which ought properly to have been asked as a police officer and in accordance with the PACE codes?"

Applying criteria such as these, the Court of Appeal has quashed a conviction for conspiracy to supply cannabis where the officer concerned had "persistently and vigorously pressed the appellant to supply it" and the relevant conversations were not recorded.[85]

In *R. v. Latif and Shahzad*[86] the appellants had been involved in a scheme for the   **15–30**
importation of heroin into the United Kingdom. S had approached a man (H) in Pakistan who, unknown to him, was an informer for the United States Drugs Enforcement Agency. S offered to supply drugs for importation into the United Kingdom, and subsequently delivered 20 kilogrammes of heroin to H. The drugs were physically imported by a British Customs officer, and some time later S arrived in this country. He was arrested, together with L, as he took possession of a dummy consignment. In their defence L and S argued that they had been lured into the crime by undercover officers acting as agents provocateurs. The House of Lords rejected both the argument that the proceedings should have been stayed as an abuse of process, and an alternative argument that the evidence should have been excluded under section 78. In respect of the abuse of process argument Lord Steyn said:

"Weighing countervailing considerations of policy and justice, it is for the judge in the exercise of his discretion to decide whether there has been an abuse of process which amounts to an affront to the public conscience and requires the criminal proceedings to be stayed ... The speeches in *R. v. Horseferry Road ex parte Bennett* conclusively establish that proceedings may be stayed ... not only where a fair trial is impossible, but also where it would be contrary to the public interest in the integrity of the criminal justice system that a trial should take place ... [The] judge must weigh in the balance the public interest in ensuring that persons charged with grave crimes should be tried and the competing public interest in not conveying the impression that the court will adopt the approach that the end justifies any means."

S had taken the initiative at the crucial meeting with H when the importation was   **15–31**
agreed. He was in no way vulnerable, and had been an organiser in the heroin

---

[83] [1994] 1 All E.R. 898.
[84] The 1929 Royal Commission on Police Powers and Procedures Cmnd. 3297 at 40–41 defined an agent provocateur as "a person who entices another to commit an express breach of the law which he would not otherwise have committed and then proceeds or informs against him in respect of such offences".
[85] *R. v. Lawrence and Nash* (1993, unreported), discussed in G. Robertson, "Entrapment Evidence: Manna from Heaven or Fruit of the Poisoned Tree?" [1994] Crim. L.R. 805 at 811.
[86] [1996] 1 W.L.R. 104.

trade in the past. He had indicated from the start that he was ready and willing to arrange the importation. While it was true that this particular importation would not have occurred in the way, and at the time it did without the involvement of the undercover officers, the actions of the officer were not so unworthy or shameful as to make it an affront to the public conscience to allow the prosecution to proceed. The appellants' subsequent application to Strasbourg was held by the Commission to be manifestly ill-founded.[87] The House of Lords' decision in *Latif and Shahzad* may be thought to have added two additional factors to the *Smurthwaite* criteria—the seriousness of the offence,[88] and the predisposition of the accused.[89]

15–32   Where predisposition is clearly established, the courts have been reluctant to hold that the public interest requires either a stay of proceedings or the exclusion of evidence. Thus, in *DPP v. Marshall*[90] the Divisional Court allowed a prosecution appeal against the defendant's acquittal for selling alcohol without a licence, rejecting the argument that section 78 should be used to exclude evidence obtained by police officers who had purchased liquor from his premises by pretending to be ordinary customers. Similarly, in *London Borough of Ealing v. Woolworths plc*,[91] another "test purchase" case, it was held that Trading Standards officials had not acted improperly in sending an 11-year-old boy into a shop in order to purchase an 18 category video film. By purchasing the video the boy had simply played his part in the situation which rendered the defendant culpable.

15–33   In *R. v. Christou*[92] undercover police officers opened a shop in North London purporting to buy and sell second hand jewellery, but understood to be open for the purchase of stolen goods. A number of people were prosecuted for burglary or handling in relation to goods which passed through the shop. In dismissing an appeal against conviction Lord Taylor C.J. observed that;

> "[T]he trick was not applied to the appellants: they voluntarily applied themselves to the trick. It is not every trick producing evidence against an accused which results in unfairness. There are, in criminal investigations, a number of situations in which the police adopt ruses or tricks in the public interest to obtain evidence."

15–34   In *Christou*, the ruse involved the obtaining of evidence of offences which had already been committed. There was no question of incitement as such. A more controversial decision is *Williams v. DPP*[93] in which police officers set up a "virtue-testing operation" by leaving a van load of cigarette cartons unsecured and unattended in a public street. Two members of the public who came across the van, and began to unload the cartons, were arrested. It was held that the police had done nothing to force, persuade, encourage or coerce them into doing what they had done. They had been free to decide whether or not to succumb and were

---

[87] *Shahzad v. United Kingdom* Application No. 34225/96. See also *KL v. United Kingdom* Application No. 32715/96, both reported at [1998] E.H.R.L.R. 210. See further, para. 15–44 below.
[88] As to the relevance of the seriousness of the offence under Art. 6 see para. 15–40 below.
[89] Predisposition has featured as an important factor in the Strasbourg decisions: see para. 15–42 below.
[90] [1988] 3 All E.R. 683.
[91] [1995] Crim. L.R. 58.
[92] [1992] 4 All E.R. 559.
[93] [1993] 3 All E.R. 365.

victims not of a trick, but of their own dishonesty. This was despite the fact that there was no evidence of prior involvement in offences, nor any real evidence of predisposition (beyond perhaps a predisposition to opportunist theft). Certainly there was no suggestion that the offence would have been committed but for the actions of the police.

II. *Under Article 6*

In *Ludi v. Switzerland*[94] an undercover agent posed as a potential purchaser of 2   **15–35**
kg of cocaine and the applicant had offered to sell the drugs to him. His conviction depended heavily upon tape recorded telephone conversations which had occurred during the course of the negotiations. The applicant's complaint that the investigation violated his right to privacy was rejected on the ground that he had knowingly run the risk of encountering an undercover police officer, and could not therefore invoke the protection of Article 8.[95] The Court went on to find a violation of Article 6 on the ground that there had been no opportunity to cross-examine the undercover officer in the criminal proceedings. There was, however, no suggestion in the judgment that the admission of the evidence would have violated Article 6 if the officer had been called to give oral evidence at the trial.

The approach to Article 8 adopted by the Court in *Ludi* placed great emphasis on   **15–36**
the first of the *Smurthwaite* criteria—whether the defendant was already engaged in criminal activity before he was approached. This issue was considered by the Commission in the context of Article 6 in *Radermacher and Pferrer v. Germany.*[96] The applicants had been convicted of dealing in counterfeit currency. There was no dispute that a police informer (W) and an undercover agent had played "an important and active part" during the long series of events which finally resulted in the delivery of the counterfeit notes, but there was a conflict of evidence as to the precise nature of that role. The Commission was unwilling to elaborate any general principles governing the use of undercover officers or informants, but nevertheless described the question of whether the offences had been instigated by W as "crucial" to its decision. Since there was conflicting evidence on the point, the Commission found no violation of Article 6:

> "The Commission notes that, according to the Government's . . . account of events, the police informer W has not taken the initiative to arrange a delivery of counterfeit money, but only reacted to an offer by G who visited him on 12 December 1982. Furthermore, W had not incited the second applicant to commit the offence but the second applicant had already been prepared to participate in the delivery of counterfeit money and had, together with G and on their own initiative, come to see W in order to follow up G's earlier offer . . . In the absence of any evidence to the contrary . . . the Commission accepts this version of the origin of the offences as corresponding to the truth. It follows that W cannot be regarded as the real initiator of the offences. Consequently, it is not necessary to examine further the question whether there was a violation of Article 6(1) on the ground that the offences had been brought about by the activities of an undercover agent."

---

[94] (1993) 15 E.H.R.R. 173.
[95] See also *Speckman v. United Kingdom* Application No. 27007/95 (unreported). See further para. 7–27 above.
[96] Application No. 12811/87 (unreported).

15–37 In *Teixeira de Castro v. Portugal*[97] the issue could not be so easily avoided. Two undercover police officers approached a man (S) who was suspected of small scale drug trafficking and asked him to supply them with several kilogrammes of cannabis. When he was unable to find a supplier, they said that they were interested in buying heroin. S mentioned the applicant's name as a possible supplier of heroin. S took the officers to the applicant's home and the officers told the applicant that they wished to buy 20 grams of heroin and produced a roll of banknotes. The applicant agreed and went, without the officers, to the home of another man (O). O obtained three wraps of heroin amounting to a total of 20 grams and handed them to the applicant, who took the drugs to another location where he was intending to meet the officers. On producing the heroin he was arrested, and subsequently charged.

15–38 The Commission concluded, by 30 votes to one, that the proceedings as a whole violated Article 6. In reaching this conclusion it referred to the approach adopted in the United States:

> "[T]he Commission considers that, even if it is not its task to give an opinion on the lawfulness of police provocation, it does nonetheless have a duty to ascertain whether the proceedings, considered as a whole, were fair. To this end, the Commission must consider whether the role played by the police officers was so decisive in the commission of the offence with which the applicant was charged that it affected the fairness of the proceedings in question . . . [I]t is clear . . . that an issue as to the fairness of the proceedings may arise in this type of situation. This might be the case where a criminal offence is committed and the accused convicted purely as a result of the conduct of the officers in question. The Commission notes, moreover, that the same approach is adopted by the courts of a number of member states of the Council of Europe, such as Germany, and by the Supreme Court of the United States, which held, in *Sherman v. United States* (1958) 356 U.S. 369 that evidence obtained by inciting someone to commit an offence which they would not otherwise have committed is inadmissible."

15–39 The Commission attached importance to the fact that the officers were conducting the operation without judicial supervision; that there was nothing in the evidence to "pinpoint any conduct of the applicant, prior to his arrest, which would suggest that he would have committed the offence in question even if the police officers had not provoked him"; and that the verdict of guilty was based "mainly" on the evidence of the officers concerned. The Commission continued:

> "All the foregoing circumstances lead the Commission to consider that the police officers' actions were essentially, if not exclusively, the cause of the offence being committed and the applicant being sentenced to a fairly heavy penalty. They thus incited the applicant to commit a criminal offence which he might not have committed if he had not been provoked. In the Commission's opinion, this situation irremediably affected the fairness of the proceedings."

15–40 The Court agreed, by eight votes to one. In contrast to the "public interest" test apparently adopted by the House of Lords in *Latif and Shahzad*[98] the Court held

---

[97] (1999) 28 E.H.R.R. 101.
[98] See para. 15–30 above.

that the seriousness of the offence could never justify a conviction obtained as a result of police incitement:

> "The use of undercover agents must be restricted and safeguards put in place even in cases concerning the fight against drug-trafficking. While the rise in organised crime undoubtedly requires that appropriate measures be taken, the right to a fair administration of justice nevertheless holds such a prominent place that it cannot be sacrificed for the sake of expedience. The general requirements of fairness embodied in Article 6 apply to proceedings concerning all types of criminal offence, from the most straightforward to the most complex. The public interest cannot justify the use of evidence obtained as a result of police incitement."

The Court distinguished the facts of *Teixeira* from those of *Ludi*, noting that in the latter case there was already a criminal investigation underway into the applicant's activities, the officer had been subject to judicial supervision, and his role had been limited to acting as an undercover officer, as distinct from an *agent provocateur*: **15–41**

> "In the instant case it is necessary to determine whether or not the two police officers' activity went beyond that of undercover agents. The Court notes that the Government have not contended that the officers' intervention took place as part of an anti-drug trafficking operation ordered and supervised by a judge. It does not appear either that the competent authorities had good reason to suspect that Mr Teixeira de Castro was a drug trafficker; on the contrary, he had no criminal record and no preliminary investigation concerning him had been opened. Indeed, he was not known to the police officers, who only came into contact with him through intermediaries . . . Furthermore, the drugs were not at the applicant's home; he obtained them from a third party who had in turn obtained them from another person. Nor does the [domestic court judgment] indicate that, at the time of his arrest, the applicant had more drugs in his possession than the quantity the police officers had requested thereby going beyond what he had been incited to do by the police. There is no evidence to support the government's argument that the applicant was predisposed to commit offences. The necessary inference from these circumstances is that the two police officers did not confine themselves to investigating Mr Teixeira de Castro's criminal activity in an essentially passive manner, but exercised an influence such as to incite the commission of the offence."

The Court thus attached prime importance to two linked factors: (i) the absence of evidence to suggest that the applicant was already engaged in drug trafficking, or was otherwise predisposed to commit the offence, and (ii) the undoubted fact that the officers had instigated the commission of this particular offence: **15–42**

> "[T]he Court concludes that the two police officers' actions went beyond those of undercover agents because they instigated the offence and there is nothing to suggest that without their intervention it would have been committed. That intervention and its use in the impugned criminal proceedings meant that, right from the outset, the applicant was definitively deprived of a fair trial."[99]

Since the applicant had been convicted "mainly" on the basis of the statements of the two police officers, there had been a violation of Article 6. The force of the Court's condemnation is underlined by its approach to the award of just satisfaction. It is rare for the Court to award compensation in respect of a violation of **15–43**

---

[99] *ibid.*, at paras 38–39.

Article 6 since the necessary causation is difficult to establish.[1] In *Teixeira*, however, the Court held that the applicant's detention had resulted directly from the use of evidence that was incompatible with Article 6. In those circumstances he was entitled to recover loss of earnings for the period of his sentence, and an additional sum in non-pecuniary loss to reflect the damage he had suffered and the difficulties he had faced in finding employment after his release.

15–44 *Teixeira* was distinguished by the Commission in *Shahzad v. United Kingdom*,[2] the Strasbourg proceedings in *R. v. Latif and Shahzad*.[3] The Commission held that although the particular importation in respect of which the applicants had been convicted would not have occurred without the assistance of undercover officers, the offence had been instigated by S himself, without any prompting. Moreover, S was proved to have had a history of involvement in heroin trafficking:

> "[T]he Commission notes that, as the House of Lords observed, undercover agents gave the applicant the opportunity to attempt to commit the crime of importing heroin into the United Kingdom and that the particular importation would not have taken place when and how it did without the assistance of undercover agents. However, the Commission also notes that, as accepted by the national courts, the undercover agents did not take the initiative to contact the applicant with a view to importing heroin into the United Kingdom, but only reacted to an offer by the applicant. In this respect, the applicant's case is distinguishable from *Teixeira de Castro v. Portugal*, where the Commission found a violation of Article 6(1) of the Convention because of the role played by "agents provocateurs" in bringing about that applicant's conviction. As opposed to *Teixeira de Castro v. Portugal*, in the present case, it has not been established that the undercover agents were the real initiators of the offences. The Commission also notes that, as opposed to the applicant in *Teixeira de Castro v. Portugal*, the applicant in the present case had a long-term involvement in the heroin trade and was ready and willing to commit crime even without the involvement of the undercover agents. Moreover, the testimony of the undercover agents did not form the exclusive basis of the applicant's conviction, which was also supported by other evidence such as tape and video recordings."

15–45 What then are the implications for English law? It is clear that the Convention decisions turn principally on whether the undercover officer has actively instigated an offence which would not otherwise have occurred. This active/passive distinction is a familiar part of the *Smurthwaite* criteria, but in the Convention decisions it is linked to another consideration that remains less precise—the predisposition of the accused. The emphasis on predisposition in *Teixeira de Castro* and *Shahzad* suggests that there may be a need to revisit decisions on "virtue testing operations" such as *Williams v. DPP*.[4] Whilst it may be possible to justify that decision on the basis that in placing an insecure lorry load of cigarettes in a street, the officers had not *actively* incited the offence, this seems a tenuous distinction to draw, given that the officers had gone out of their way to create the conditions in which the accused were able to commit a purely opportunistic offence which they would not otherwise have committed. On the

---

[1] See paras 1–140 to 1–146 above.
[2] Application No. 34225/96. See also *KL v. United Kingdom* Application No. 32715/96, both reported at [1998] E.H.R.L.R. 210.
[3] See para. 15–30 above.
[4] [1993] 3 All E.R. 365.

other hand, the emphasis on predisposition is entirely consistent with the "test purchase" decisions such as *DPP v. Marshall*[5] and *London Borough of Ealing v. Woolworths plc.*[6]

In *Nottingham City Council v. Amin*[7] two plain clothes police officers hailed the   **15–46**
defendant driver, and asked him to take them to a particular destination, which he did. No element of persuasion was necessary. He was prosecuted under the Town Police Clauses Act for an offence of plying for hire without a licence. Having heard submissions on *Teixeira de Castro* the stipendiary magistrate acquitted him. On a prosecution appeal by way of case stated, the decision was overturned. The Divisional Court allowed the appeal. Lord Bingham C.J. summarised the English authorities thus:

> "On the one hand it has been recognised as deeply offensive to ordinary notions of fairness if a defendant were to be convicted and punished for committing a crime which he only committed because he had been incited, instigated, persuaded, pressurised or wheedled into committing it by a law enforcement officer. On the other hand, it has been recognised that law enforcement agencies have a general duty to the public to enforce the law and it has been regarded as unobjectionable if a law enforcement officer gives a defendant an opportunity to break the law, of which the defendant freely takes advantage, in circumstances where it appears that the defendant would have behaved in the same way if the opportunity had been offered by anyone else."

As to *Teixeira de Castro*, there were a number of factors which the Court had   **15–47**
apparently regarded as significant that had no obvious parallel in English criminal procedure. No police operation could be ordered or supervised by a judge; evidence of propensity would not ordinarily be admissible before a trial court; nor would there generally be evidence as to the information or suspicion which had led the police to mount the operation in the first place. Despite the principle established in *Teixera de Castro* it was not possible to accept that the decision required the exclusion of any evidence obtained by test purchases of goods or services believed to infringe a statutory provision or regulation. The Court's conclusion had to be understood in the context of the argument before it, and the facts of the case:

> "It is true that in the present case the criminal activity alleged was much more minor. It is also true that the facts are much simpler and that they simply do not lend themselves to the construction that this defendant was in any way prevailed upon or overborne or persuaded or pressured or instigated or incited to commit the offence."

A similar reluctance to apply *Teixeira de Castro* is found in the Court of Appeal's decision in *Shannon*.[8] The accused, a television actor, had been subjected to an elaborate ploy in which he was wined and dined, and actively incited to procure cannabis and cocaine for an undercover journalist posing as an Arab sheikh. The reason for the ploy was that he was believed to be a supplier of cocaine in show business circles. Despite being referred to *Teixeira*, the Court held that the trial judge was right to admit the evidence. In the Court's view the discretion under section 78 was concerned only with the question whether the manner in which

---

[5] [1988] 3 All E.R. 683.
[6] [1995] Crim. L.R. 58.
[7] [2000] 1 W.L.R. 1080.
[8] [2001] 1 Cr.App.R. 168.

the evidence was obtained adversely affected its quality—in the sense of undermining the defendant's ability to test the evidence in adversarial proceedings. This would arise, for example, if there was no accurate record of what had been said. The Court held that section 78 should not be used to exclude evidence obtained by entrapment where "the unfairness complained of is no more than the visceral reaction that is in principle unfair as a matter of policy, or wrong as a matter of law, for a person to be prosecuted for a crime which he would not have committed without the incitement or encouragement of others." This comes close to suggesting that if the police conduct in *Teixeira* had occurred in London rather than Lisbon there would have been no remedy, although *Shannon* might be distinguished on the ground that it involved journalists rather than law enforcement officers.[9] The implications of these decisions were again considered in *Attorney-General's Reference No. 3 of 2000*.[10] The trial judge in that case had stayed a prosecution for supplying heroin in reliance on *Teixeira de Castro*. The acquitted person had been persuaded to arrange the supply of heroin to two undercover police officers who had gained his confidence over a period of time by selling him large quantities of cut price tobacco, on the pretence that it was contraband. Although he had agreed to arrange the supply of the drugs in order to return the favour, there was no suggestion that he stood to profit from the transaction, and he had said to the officers at one point that he was "not into" heroin himself. There was no evidence to suggest that he had previously supplied heroin, although he had a previous conviction for supplying cannabis. Kennedy L.J. accepted that where the admission of such evidence would amount to a breach of Article 6 the court was obliged to afford a remedy. However that was to beg the question of what Article 6 required. A court considering an application to exclude evidence under section 78 or to stay proceedings as an abuse of process would be concerned both with the propriety or impropriety of the officers' actions and with the willingness or otherwise shown by the accused. A remedy would generally be appropriate only where the actions of the officers were unworthy or shameful and the will accused had been undermined or overborne as a result. At one end of the spectrum there would usually be no basis for the court to intervene where an accused who was dealing in drugs had been offered the market price and had freely become involved in the transaction. At the other end of the scale, to dangle the offer of large sums of money in front of a person who was in desperate need of money, perhaps for his family, and who would otherwise have had no involvement in drugs might be considered sufficiently unworthy or shameful to require the court's intervention.

III. *Comparative Approaches*

15–48 The strong stand taken by the European Court against entrapment finds echoes in other jurisdictions. In the United States it is the question of predisposition that is crucial. If there is evidence that the defendant was predisposed towards the type of offence alleged, active incitement by undercover officers does not ground a defence of entrapment, whereas in the absence of predisposition it does.[11] It is to

---

[9] *cf. Hardwicke and Thwaites* [2001] Crim. L.R. 220.
[10] May 17, 2001 (CA).
[11] The leading case is *Jacobsen v. United States* 503 U.S. 540 (1992). For discussion of the American and Canadian decisions, see A. Choo, *Abuse of Process and Judicial Stays of Criminal Proceedings* (1993), Chapter 6, and P. Mirfield, *Silence, Confessions and Unlawfully Obtained Evidence* (1996), pp 199–209.

be noted that the American approach is to provide a full defence to crime, rather than the mere exclusion of evidence. In Canada, the courts have held that police incitement may be acceptable where there is objective evidence of reasonable suspicion that the defendant was involved in some connected criminal activity, but otherwise entrapment evidence should be excluded.[12] These United States and Canadian authorities tend to support the approach taken by the European Court in *Teixeira de Castro*, with its strong declaration that the defendant had been deprived of a fair trial "from the outset." This raises the question whether the discretion to exclude evidence under section 78 of the Police and Criminal Evidence Act is an appropriate response to entrapment, or whether the doctrine of abuse of process might not be more appropriate.[13]

E. Admissions Obtained by Subterfuge

The issues considered in the previous section concerned conduct by undercover **15–49** officers which is alleged to have had a causal connection with the commission of the offence. A related but discrete question is the use of undercover officers to obtain admissions to past offences. We noted above that the case of *R. v. Christou*,[14] which is often cited in the entrapment context, was not really a case of entrapment at all, since the subterfuge used (the setting up of a shop purporting to deal in stolen goods) was intended primarily as a means of gathering intelligence concerning offences of theft and handling which had already occurred. This distinction, between undercover activity before and after the commission of an offence, is also recognised in the third[15] and sixth[16] of the criteria identified in *R. v. Smurthwaite and Gill*.[17]

When this issue first arose for consideration in Strasbourg the Commission held **15–50** that it is not a breach of Article 6 to admit the evidence of an undercover agent placed in a prison to eavesdrop on conversations involving the accused, so long as the evidence was not unlawfully obtained, and there was no element of coercion or covert interrogation involved. In *X v. Federal Republic of Germany*[18] two German citizens had been arrested in Italy for drugs offences. An undercover Italian police officer was placed in their cell, posing as a remand prisoner. Not knowing that their "cellmate" could speak German the two men had a conversation in which the applicant admitted to murder. He subsequently repeated his confession to the Italian and German police, and to an Italian investigating magistrate. He was then extradited to Germany. Before the German court of trial he retracted his formal confessions, and challenged the admissibility of the cell

---

[12] *Mack* (1988) 44 C.C.C. (3d) 513.
[13] See JUSTICE, *Under Surveillance: Covert Policing and Human Rights Standards* (1998), Chapter 3.
[14] [1992] 4 All E.R. 559, see para. 15–33 above.
[15] The third criterion was whether the evidence consists of an admission to a completed offence or the actual commission of an offence.
[16] The sixth criterion was whether the officer had abused his role to ask questions which ought properly to have been asked as a police officer and in accordance with the PACE codes. This plainly relates to the possibility of obtaining a confession to a past offence by subterfuge.
[17] [1994] 1 All E.R. 898.
[18] Application No. 12127/86 (1989) 11 E.H.R.R. 84.

confession on the ground that the evidence was unlawfully obtained. The Commission rejected his complaint in these terms:

> "It is true that the use of evidence obtained unlawfully by coercive means may raise an issue as to the fairness of criminal proceedings. However, the Commission first notes that the applicant's conviction is mainly based on his initial confession which was considered to be confirmed by other circumstantial evidence . . . In addition the Commission notes that according to the Federal Constitutional Court the ruse employed by the Italian police against the applicant does not in itself constitute an unlawful method of obtaining evidence. The applicant had an interest in not talking to his accomplice about the crime in the presence of a third person. If he nevertheless freely did so it is his own responsibility that this turned against him. He has not alleged that the undercover agent in any way caused him to talk about the killing of the businessman. In these circumstances it cannot be found that the applicant's freedom of will was affected by the action of the Italian police so as to make the use of the evidence obtained from the Italian undercover agent deprive the applicant of his right to a fair trial as guaranteed by Article 6 of the Convention."

15–51 The criteria applied by the Commission to this situation broadly correspond with the third, fourth and sixth of the *Smurthwaite* criteria. There was no evidence that the officer's role was other than passive, thus supporting the conclusion that the defendant had voluntarily surrendered his right to privacy under Article 8 by speaking freely in the presence of an unknown third party.[19] The Commission referred in particular to the fact that there was no improper or unlawful conduct by the undercover officer concerned, and it seems clear that the extent of any misconduct—which roughly equates to the sixth *Smurthwaite* criterion—would be regarded as relevant under Article 6. In *Smith v. United Kingdom*,[20] MI5 officers secretly taped a telephone conversation between the defendant and an undercover security service officer. The Commission distinguished this situation from one in which the evidence has been obtained unlawfully. The conversation had been conducted with the consent of one party; it was brief; and it did not go to the heart of the matter. The Commission therefore held that it had to be regarded as a ruse in the public interest, and declared the application inadmissible.

15–52 Similar distinctions have been drawn in Canada and in New Zealand. The leading decisions of the Supreme Court of Canada distinguish between conduct which is passive (where an undercover officer simply records what is said without posing questions to the suspect),[21] and conduct which amounts to an active attempt to elicit comments or admissions about the case.[22] These decisions were followed in the New Zealand case of *Barlow*,[23] where the Court of Appeal admitted tape recordings of conversations between the defendant and a friend of his. The friend

---

[19] Although the applicant had not apparently invoked Art. 8, the Commission observed that the obtaining of the evidence and its use in the criminal proceedings did not "disclose *any* appearance of a violation of the rights and freedoms set out in the Convention". *Cf. Ludi v. Switzerland* (1993) 15 E.H.R.R. 173. For doubts as to the Court's approach to this issue in *Ludi*, where telephone eavesdropping was involved, see para. 7–28 above.

[20] [1997] E.H.R.L.R. 277.

[21] *Hebert* (1990) 57 C.C.C. (3d) 1, evidence admitted.

[22] *Broyles* [1991] 3 S.C.R. 595, evidence excluded. In *Broyles*, the person eliciting the information was a friend of the suspect, acting at the instigation of the police, but the principles are the same as for an undercover officer.

[23] (1995) 14 C.R.N.Z. 9.

had initially been telephoned by the defendant, but then contacted the police and thereafter followed police instructions, so as to avoid deliberately eliciting comments about the alleged offence.

F. ACCOMPLICES AND PARTICIPANT INFORMERS

For several years the use of participant informers was governed by the 1969 **15–53** Home Office guidelines and the 1984 guidelines of the Association of Chief Police Officers.[24] The latter made it clear that no police officer or informant should counsel, procure or incite the commission of crime. The guidelines emphasised that where police allowed an informant to participate in an offence, the informer's role was to be passive and minor, and his participation had to be absolutely necessary to enable police to frustrate and arrest the principal offenders. No undertaking was to be given which would necessitate misleading a court in subsequent criminal proceedings; the role of the participant informer was to be disclosed to the prosecution and to the defence; and payments were to be supervised by a senior officer. There was compelling evidence, however, that these guidelines were not always followed.[25] ACPO issued revised and more detailed "Codes of Practice" which came into force in January 2000, when the Home Office circular was withdrawn. The use of "covert human intelligence sources" is now subject to a statutory framework under the Regulation of Investigatory Powers Act 2000.[26]

In deciding whether to admit or exclude the evidence of a participating informant **15–54** the Court of Appeal guidelines in *R. v. Smurthwaite and Gill*[27] have considerable analogical force in English law. The English courts have long recognised that accomplice evidence is inherently vulnerable. Where the accomplice has "an obvious and powerful inducement" to implicate an accused person in order to advance his own position, the Court of Appeal has previously held that it may be necessary for the trial judge to exercise his discretion to exclude the evidence.[28] In *R. v. Pipe*[29] the prosecution had called an accomplice who had been charged for his part in the offence alleged against the accused, but against whom the proceedings had not been concluded. The Court of Appeal held that this procedure was "wholly irregular", saying:

> "It may well be . . . that in strict law [the accomplice] was a competent witness, but for years now it has been the recognised practice that an accomplice who has been charged, either jointly in the indictment with his co-accused or in the indictment though not under a joint charge shall not be called by the prosecution, except in limited circumstances. Those circumstances are set out correctly in *Archbold*, in paragraph 1297 of the current edition, where it is said that where it is proposed to call an accomplice at the trial, it is the practice (a) to omit him from the indictment or (b) take his plea of Guilty

---

[24] Home Office Circular 97/1969, "Informants who Take Part in Crime".
[25] For evidence and discussion, see JUSTICE, *Under Surveillance: Covert Policing and Human Rights Standards* (1998), pp 38–51.
[26] See paras 7–23 *et seq.* above.
[27] [1994] 1 All E.R. 898.
[28] *R. v. Pipe* (1966) 51 Cr. App. R. 17; *R. v. Turner (BJ)* (1975) 61 Cr. App. R. 67.
[29] (1966) 51 Cr. App. R. 17.

on arraignment, or before calling him either (c) to offer no evidence and permit his acquittal or (d) to enter a *nolle prosequi* . . .

This Court is quite satisfied that if this case had to go on, and the prosecution were still minded to call [the accomplice], they must have let it be known that in no event would proceedings be continued against him. In the judgment of this court it is one thing to call for the prosecution an accomplice, a witness whose evidence is suspect, and about whom the jury must be warned in the recognised way. It is quite another to call a man who is not only an accomplice, but is an accomplice against whom proceedings have been brought which have not been concluded. There is in his case an added reason for making his evidence suspect."[30]

15–55 By contrast, in *R. v. Turner (BJ)*[31] the Crown relied upon a supergrass against whom there was no realistic prospect of further prosecution. The Court of Appeal observed that where there was a very powerful inducement operating on the mind of the accomplice, the judge could secure a fair trial by exercising his discretion to exclude the evidence. On the facts however the Court of Appeal held that the admission of the evidence did not result in an unfair trial. The accomplice was no longer at risk of being prosecuted for his part in the offences, regardless of whether he chose to give evidence or not, and regardless of the nature of the evidence which he gave. The court pointed out that: "These facts distinguished this case from *Pipe*, and would have justified the judge in refusing to exercise his discretion to exclude [the accomplice's] evidence."[32]

15–56 The Court further held that the rule in *Pipe* was:

" . . . confined to a case in which an accomplice who has been charged, but not tried, is required to give evidence of his own offence in order to secure the conviction of another accused. *Pipe*, on its facts, was clearly a right decision. The same result could have been achieved by adjudging that the trial judge should have exercised his discretion to exclude [the accomplice's] evidence on the ground that there was an obvious and powerful inducement for him to ingratiate himself with the prosecution and the court and that the existence of this inducement made it desirable in the interests of justice to exclude it . . . If the inducement is very powerful, the judge may decide to exercise his discretion."[33]

15–57 When one of the defendants in *Turner* subsequently applied to the European Commission of Human Rights, alleging *inter alia* a violation of Article 6(1) arising from the admission of the accomplice's evidence, the Commission in *X v. United Kingdom*[34] established the principle that the introduction of the evidence of an accomplice who has been offered immunity may "put in question" the fairness of a trial under Article 6.[35] Whether or not it did so was to be determined by a consideration of the circumstances of the domestic proceedings as a whole. The Commission held that there was no violation of Article 6 on the facts of the case since the defence and the jury had been made fully aware of the

---

[30] *ibid.*, at 21.
[31] (1975) 61 Cr. App. R. 67.
[32] *ibid.*, at 79.
[33] *ibid.*, at 78.
[34] (1976) 7 D.R. 115.
[35] "The Commission observes in this connection that the use at the trial of evidence obtained from an accomplice by granting him an immunity from prosecution may put in question the fairness of the hearing granted to an accused person, and thus raise an issue under Article 6(1) of the Convention." *Ibid.*, at 118.

circumstances in which the evidence was obtained; the evidence had been treated with appropriate caution and subjected to accomplice warnings; and the Court of Appeal had fully evaluated the whole of the evidence in considering an appeal against conviction. The Commission observed that:

> "[T]he manner in which the evidence . . . was obtained was openly discussed with counsel for the defence and before the jury. Furthermore, the Court of Appeal examined carefully whether due account was taken of these circumstances in the assessment of the evidence and whether there was corroboration. The Commission concludes, therefore, that an examination of the trial as a whole does not disclose any appearance of a violation of Article 6(1) of the Convention."[36]

The Commission also emphasised that the immunity which had been granted did **15–58** not amount to an inducement to give testimony favourable to the Crown since the accomplice could not in any event be prosecuted:

> "As regards the complaint that the trial was not fair because S. in giving evidence was influenced by the inducements contained in the letter of . . . April 1973, from the Director of Public Prosecutions to S's solicitors, the Commission observes that:
>
> (a) At the time he gave evidence, there was no possibility of S. being prosecuted because;
>
> > (i) he had been acquitted of certain charges at the Central Criminal Court before the proceedings against the applicant were commenced at the magistrates' court,
> > (ii) if other charges were later brought against S, his statements could not have been given in evidence against him because they had been obtained from him as a result of inducements."[37]

Once again, the chief concerns of the Commission lay with the safeguards in **15–59** place and the fairness of the trial as a whole.[38] However, it is noteworthy that one element to which the Commission appeared to attach importance was that the trial judge had warned about the dangers of accomplice evidence and that the Court of Appeal had made sure that there was corroboration. Since 1994 the trial judge's *duty* to give a warning about the dangers of acting on an accomplice's evidence without corroboration has been abrogated, in favour of a *discretion* to warn (where appropriate) of the dangers of acting on unsupported evidence.[39] It is likely that most judges would give some kind of warning in cases where an accomplice has given evidence for the Crown,[40] but the absence of an adequate warning has the potential to violate the defendant's right to a fair trial under Article 6.

---

[36] *ibid.*, at 118.
[37] *ibid.*, at 118.
[38] On this, see also *MH v. United Kingdom* [1997] E.H.R.L.R. 279, where a co-defendant's guilty plea was admitted into evidence on a conspiracy charge. The judge had warned the jury but had declined to exclude the guilty plea by using the s.78 discretion. The Commission did not find the trial as a whole unfair, and declared the application inadmissible.
[39] Section 32 of the Criminal Justice and Public Order Act 1994, analysed by P. Mirfield, "'Corroboration' after the 1994 Act" [1995] Crim. L.R. 448, and D. Birch, "Corroboration: Goodbye to all that?" [1995] Crim. L.R. 524.
[40] See *Makanjuola* [1995] 1 W.L.R. 1348.

15–60 A similar point arose in *Charlene Webb v. United Kingdom*,[41] where the applicant had been charged with drugs offences in Bermuda.[42] Two prosecution witnesses (who were servicemen) had pleaded guilty before a court martial and had been sentenced for their part in the offence. They received lenient treatment in return for agreeing to co-operate with the military authorities by providing information on civilians involved. The defendant was arrested and charged on the basis of the information which the accomplices had provided. The two accomplices then entered into a further agreement with the civilian authorities that they would not be prosecuted in the civilian courts provided that (a) they agreed to give evidence for the prosecution of the applicant, (b) neither of them committed perjury in the course of giving evidence and (c) the testimony they gave was consistent with the statements that they had previously made to the Bermuda police implicating the applicant. Despite the obvious risks associated with condition (c), and its potential inconsistency with (b), the Commission declared the application inadmissible:

> "The Commission notes that [the accomplices] had been charged, convicted and sentenced by the US court martial prior to giving evidence. Further [they] were granted immunity from prosecution in the civil jurisdiction. With regard to the condition imposed on [them] that they give evidence in accordance with their statements to the Bermuda police, the Commission notes that there was also an express obligation on [them] not to commit perjury. The judge further gave a clear direction on assessing the credibility of witnesses and the dangers of convicting on uncorroborated evidence, and the Court of Appeal confirmed this. The Commission considers that in these circumstances the exercise of the judge's discretion to admit the evidence of [the accomplices] cannot be said to have rendered the trial unfair within the meaning of Article 6(1)."

15–61 Whilst this decision shows a certain reluctance to intervene in accomplice cases, it is notable that the Commission again referred to the warnings which had been given to the jury as an important safeguard for the accused. Similarly, in *Baragiola v. Switzerland*[43] the Commission emphasised the importance of careful scrutiny of accomplice evidence, but held that there was no objection in principle to allowing the prosecution to rely on the evidence of co-defendants who had already received reduced sentences for their co-operation:

> "[T]he sentences imposed on the co-defendants who had given evidence for the prosecution were considerably reduced and alleviated in other ways under the Italian legislation . . . As they ran the risk of losing the advantages they had been given if they went back on their previous statements or retracted their confessions, their statements were open to question. It was therefore necessary for the Swiss courts to adopt a critical approach in assessing the statements of the [accomplices]."

15–62 The Commission held that so long as that testimony was open to challenge and was not the only evidence, the trial was likely to be fair. However, in a case where there was evidence that police officers had spoken to the accomplice during his evidence, and another accomplice witness (who was in prison) had been allowed to read newspaper reports of the evidence given at trial before he

---

[41] (1997) 24 E.H.R.R. CD 73.
[42] The United Kingdom has made a declaration under Art. 63 of the Convention extending the application of the Convention to certain overseas territories, including Bermuda.
[43] (1993) 75 D.R. 76.

was called, the Commission considered that the fairness of the trial was called into question.[44]

G. The Privilege Against Self-Incrimination

I. *The Strasbourg Caselaw*

In *Funke v. France*[45] the Court held that the right to a fair trial in a criminal case   **15–63** includes "the right of anyone charged with a criminal offence . . . to remain silent and not to contribute to incriminating himself". Customs officers made a search of the applicant's house and, finding evidence that he had foreign bank accounts, they issued orders requiring him to produce certain details of those accounts. Failure to produce the documents was an offence, for which he was prosecuted, convicted and fined. It was submitted on his behalf that his conviction infringed his right to a fair trial under Article 6(1). He claimed that there was a right not to give evidence against oneself in the legal orders of the Contracting States, under the European Convention on Human Rights, and under the International Covenant on Civil and Political Rights (ICCPR). The French authorities had brought criminal proceedings calculated to compel M. Funke to co-operate in a future prosecution to be mounted against him.

The French Government submitted that the customs and exchange control regime   **15–64** operated in France saved taxpayers from having their affairs systematically investigated, but imposed duties in return, such as the duty to keep papers concerning their income and property, and the duty to make them available to the authorities on request. The customs, the argument continued, had not required M. Funke to confess to an offence or to provide evidence of one himself. They had merely asked him to give particulars of bank statements and cheque-books discovered during a search of his house.

The Commission held that the applicant's right to a fair trial under Article 6 had   **15–65** not been breached. It could not "choose to ignore the special character of inquiries of an economic and financial nature", which are necessary "to protect the country's vital economic interests." In this context "coercion to supply information or produce documents is not as such exceptional," and indeed it can be regarded as "a *quid pro quo* for the trust reposed by the State in every citizen, which enables it to forego the adoption of more restrictive measures of control and supervision."[46]

The Court, on the other hand, took the view that the customs officers, being   **15–66** unable or unwilling to obtain the desired evidence by alternative means, had attempted to compel the applicant himself to provide evidence of the offences he had allegedly committed. In "discovering" a right to silence in Article 6, the Court said this:

---

[44] *X v. United Kingdom* (1978, unpublished) 2 Dig. 393.
[45] (1993) 16 E.H.R.R. 297.
[46] *ibid.*, at pp 313–314.

"The special features of [French] customs law . . . cannot justify such an infringement of the right of anyone charged with a criminal offence, within the autonomous meaning of this expression in Article 6, to remain silent and not to contribute to incriminating himself. There has accordingly been a breach of Article 6(1). The foregoing conclusion makes it unnecessary for the Court to ascertain whether M. Funke's conviction also contravened the presumption of innocence in Article 6(2)."[47]

15–67 With this statement, the Court established the accused's right to remain silent as a requirement of a fair trial under Article 6. Moreover, it established that the right is one that cannot easily be brushed aside by "public interest" considerations, since the Court departed clearly from the Commission's view that any interests of the applicant must be subordinated to the importance of protecting a country's economic interests.

15–68 The operative passage of the *Funke* decision, has been described as "brief and Delphic."[48] It left several questions unanswered. It was not clear whether the right "to remain silent and not to contribute to incriminating himself" was intended to apply only in court, or also at the investigation stage. The facts of the case were distributed across the two possibilities, since the applicant was fined for the non-production of documents, but those proceedings (although criminal) were ancillary to the prosecution that the customs authorities were intending to institute. However, since the original prosecution had never been brought (the first applicant having died), the case tends to suggest that the Court regarded the right as applicable at the investigatory stage. As Sir Nicolas Bratza has pointed out, "the Court appears to have considered that the mere fact that a sanction is imposed for a refusal to produce potentially self-incriminating evidence constitutes a violation of the right to a fair hearing."[49] Further, the Court appears to have treated the right as applying not only to answers to questions but also to the compulsory production of documents or other real evidence.

15–69 A different approach to these issues is evident in the subsequent decision in *Saunders v. United Kingdom.*[50] In this case the Court considered that the admission in evidence at the applicant's trial of transcripts of interviews with Inspectors of the Department of Trade and Industry, appointed to carry out an investigation under sections 432–436 of the Companies Act 1985, violated Article 6(1) since at the time of the interrogation the applicant was under a duty to answer the inspectors' questions, which was enforceable by proceedings for contempt. The British Government argued that the principle in *Funke* was not strictly relevant because in that case the applicant was punished for refusal to incriminate himself, whereas Ernest Saunders had co-operated with the Inspectors without incurring any penalty. The response of the Commission was that anyone "who incriminates himself under threat of punishment . . . and provides evidence for use against himself at trial may be as seriously prejudiced, perhaps more so, as the applicant who incurs the punishment for refusing to incriminate himself."

---

[47] *ibid.*, at paras 44–45.
[48] By Sir Nicolas Bratza, "The Implications of the Human Rights Act 1988 for Commercial Practice" [2000] E.H.R.L.R. 1 at 10.
[49] *ibid.*, at 11.
[50] (1997) 23 E.H.R.R. 313.

The Commission did observe that "the right to silence is not expressly guaran-   **15–70**
teed by Article 6 of the Convention, and accept[ed] that the right may not be
unqualified." Nevertheless, the Commission went on:

> "[T]he privilege against self-incrimination is an important element in safeguarding an
> accused from oppression and coercion during criminal proceedings. The very basis of
> a fair trial presupposes that the accused is afforded the opportunity of defending himself
> against the charges brought against him. The position of the defence is undermined if
> the accused is under compulsion, or has been compelled to incriminate himself. . . .
> Whether a particular applicant has been subject to compulsion to incriminate himself
> and whether the use made of the incriminating material has rendered criminal proceed-
> ings unfair will depend on an assessment of each case as a whole."[51]

The Government argued that "the right to silence or the privilege against self-   **15–71**
incrimination is not absolute, and that any departure from it [was] justified . . .
having regard . . . to the special status of persons conducting affairs of public
companies, who enjoy a fiduciary position towards the public." Here again, the
Commission decisively rejected the argument: "The right to silence, to the extent
that it may be contained in the guarantees of Article 6 must apply as equally to
alleged company fraudsters as to those accused of other types of fraud, rape,
murder or terrorist offences."[52]

The Court agreed with the conclusion of the Commission, holding that the right   **15–72**
to silence and the right not to incriminate oneself are generally recognised
international standards which lie "at the heart of a notion of a fair procedure"
under Article 6. The Court continued:

> "The right not to incriminate oneself, in particular, presupposes that the prosecution in
> a criminal case seek to prove their case against the accused without resort to evidence
> obtained through methods of coercion or oppression in defiance of the will of the
> accused. In this sense the right is closely linked to the presumption of innocence
> contained in Article 6(2) of the Convention."[53]

Before the Court the Government submitted that the admission of the interviews   **15–73**
could not violate the right to self-incrimination because nothing said by the
applicant was overtly harmful to his interests. He had merely given exculpatory
answers which, if true, supported his defence. The Court held that the prohibition
on the admission of evidence obtained by compulsory questioning did not depend
on a confession of guilt:

> "[T]he right not to incriminate oneself cannot reasonably be confined to statements of
> admission of wrongdoing or to remarks which are directly incriminating. Testimony
> obtained under compulsion which appears on its face to be of a non-incriminating
> nature—such as exculpatory remarks or mere information on questions of fact—may
> later be deployed in criminal proceedings in support of the prosecution case, for
> example to contradict or cast doubt upon other statements of the accused or evidence
> given by him during the trial, or otherwise to undermine his credibility. Where the
> credibility of an accused must be addressed by a jury the use of such testimony may be

---

[51] *ibid.*, Commission, para. 70.
[52] *ibid.*, para. 71; *cf.* the similar rejection, by the Court in *Teixeira de Castro v. Portugal* (above, para.
15–37), of the proposition that an exception to the Art. 6 right should be made for drug-trafficking
investigations.
[53] *ibid.*, Court, para. 68.

especially harmful. It follows that what is of the essence in this context is the use to which evidence obtained under compulsion is [put] in the course of the criminal trial."[54]

On the facts, the Court concluded that the prosecution had used the transcripts during the trial in a manner which sought to incriminate the applicant. Accordingly their use was held to have rendered the trial unfair and in breach of Article 6.

15–74 The protection against self-incrimination as it was understood in *Saunders* appears to relate only to the admission of the evidence in the criminal proceedings. It does not, in itself, prohibit the use of compulsory questioning powers in the course of a *purely administrative* investigation.[55] The Court emphasised that the role of the DTI investigation was essentially regulatory, and was thus distinct from that of the investigation or prosecution of crime. The role of the Inspectors was; " . . . to ascertain and record facts which might subsequently be used as the basis for action by other competent authorities—prosecuting, regulatory, disciplinary or even legislative."[56] In *Abas v. Netherlands*[57] the applicant had given information to the tax authorities when required to do so. Subsequently his family home was searched, and evidence thereby obtained was used in a prosecution for fraud and tax evasion. He was convicted and sentenced to imprisonment. The Commission declared the application inadmissible, on the basis that the obligation to answer the tax inspector's questions did not infringe the right to silence (and the answers were not used in the criminal prosecution). The Commission also mentioned that compulsory powers are regarded as necessary in most countries to allow tax inspectors to carry out their functions. The Court recently considered the very point in *IJL, GMR and AKP v. United Kingdom*,[58] an application by other defendants in the first Guinness trial. The applicants argued that the proceedings before the DTI inspectors should be treated as part of the prosecution process because of collusion between the inspectors and the prosecuting authorities, and that therefore they should have been accorded the rights of persons "charged with a criminal offence" during the DTI hearings. The Court rejected this argument, and with it the view that "a legal requirement for an individual to give information demanded by an *administrative body* necessarily infringes Article 6 of the Convention."[59] The use of the evidence at the subsequent trial infringed Article 6, but the compulsory questioning did not.

15–75 A final point about the Court's judgment in *Saunders* concerns its treatment of "real evidence", as distinct from oral or testimonial evidence. After stating that the right not to incriminate oneself is closely linked to the presumption of

---

[54] *ibid.*, para. 71.
[55] The Court has recently confirmed that where compulsory questioning powers are exercised in the context of a *criminal* investigation, as distinct from an *administrative* investigation, the protection against self-incrimination bites at the investigation stage. In *Heaney and McGuinness v. Ireland*, Judgment December 21, 2000, the Court found a violation of Article 6 where two defendants who had been arrested on suspicion of terrorism (and who had refused to answer questions under caution) were subsequently prosecuted for an offence of withholding information.
[56] Para. 67.
[57] [1997] E.H.R.L.R. 418.
[58] [2001] Crim. L.R. 133.
[59] *ibid.*, para. 100.

innocence, forming part of fair procedure and contributing to the avoidance of miscarriages of justice, the Court went on:

> "The right not to incriminate oneself is primarily concerned, however, with respecting the will of an accused person to remain silent. As commonly understood in the legal systems of the Contracting Parties to the Convention and elsewhere, it does not extend to the use in criminal proceedings of material which may be obtained from the accused through the use of compulsory powers but which has an existence independent of the will of the suspect such as, *inter alia*, documents acquired pursuant to a warrant, breath, blood and urine samples, and bodily tissues for the purpose of DNA testing."[60]

This distinction seems to be a pragmatic attempt to rein back the possible **15–76** implications of the privilege against self-incrimination. It is true that the laws of many Contracting States contain provisions for the compulsory taking of blood samples and other samples, in motoring cases and for other crimes. In terms of practical law enforcement, it is difficult to resist the pressure to allow some such procedures.[61] However, the distinction has not been convincingly explained or consistently applied.[62] As we have seen,[63] the Court found a violation in *Funke* in respect of the failure to provide documents which, one would have thought, had an existence independent of the will of the accused. Notwithstanding the subsequent decision in *Saunders*, the Court has recently followed *Funke* in finding a breach of Article 6 where the applicant was fined for failing to hand over financial records to the tax authorities. In *JB v. Switzerland*[64] the Court distinguished such documents from the blood or urine samples referred to in *Saunders*, noting that the latter "had an existence independent of the person concerned and [were] not, therefore, obtained by means of coercion and in defiance of the will of that person".[65]

On the other hand, the exception for "real evidence" recognised in *Saunders* is **15–77** consistent with earlier decisions of the Commission. In a 1962 case the Commission held that a legal obligation to undergo a medical examination in the course of a criminal investigation is not, in itself, incompatible with Article 6(2).[66] And in *X v. Netherlands*[67] the Commission adopted the same approach in relation to a statutory requirement to provide an evidential breath specimen, in the context of an investigation into an offence of driving with excess alcohol. Accordingly,

---

[60] (1997) 23 E.H.R.R. 313 at para. 69.
[61] For discussion of the American authorities, see S. Easton, "Bodily Samples and the Privilege against Self-Incrimination" [1991] Crim. L.R. 18, and I. Dennis, "Instrumental Protection, Human Right or Functional Necessity? Reassessing the Privilege against Self-Incrimination" (1995) 54 Camb. L.J. 342 at 373–375.
[62] See the doubts expressed by Lord Bingham in *HM Advocate v. Brown* [2001] 2 W.L.R. 817, discussed at para. 15–89 below.
[63] See para. 15–63 above.
[64] Judgment May 3, 2001 at para. 68.
[65] *cf. Attorney-General's Reference No. 7 of 2000, The Times*, April 12, 2001, where the Court of Appeal held that documents delivered to the Official Receiver under compulsion fell within the *Saunders* exception for "real evidence" and, unlike statements made by the accused under compulsion, were outside the privilege against self-incrimination. See also the discussion of a production order under PACE in the judgment of Judge L.J. in *R. v. Central Criminal Court ex parte The Guardian, The Observer and Bright*, Judgment of July 21, 2000 (DC).
[66] *X v. Germany* (1962) 5 Y.B. 193 at 199.
[67] (1978) 16 D.R. 184.

a complaint that the applicant's prosecution for failure to provide a specimen was in breach of Article 6(2) was declared manifestly ill-founded.[68]

15–78   The Commission's ruling in *Tora Tolmos v. Spain*[69] sits uneasily with these other decisions. The applicant's car was photographed breaking the speed limit, and the police sent him a notice requiring him to state who was driving his car at that particular time and place. He contended that his conviction for the offence of failing to comply with this notice breached his privilege against self-incrimination. The Commission declared the application inadmissible, holding that a law of this kind is not necessarily incompatible with Article 6:

> " . . . the person concerned is not inevitably obliged to admit his or her own guilt or to incriminate a relative. Depending on the circumstances, they may be able to show that they had nothing to do with the offence committed by the driver, for instance by establishing that the vehicle was being used by someone whose identity is unknown to them or whom they had not authorised to use it."

15–79   In reaching this conclusion the Commission did not discuss *Funke*, which ought to have had a bearing on the reasoning adopted[70]; and in any event the *Tora Tolmos* ruling must now be read in the light of the subsequent decisions of the Court on the right to silence discussed in section H below.[71] Those decisions suggest that where there is direct compulsion, in that failure to answer a question leads to criminal liability, this destroys the "very essence" of the privilege against self-incrimination.[72]

15–80   In *Serves v. France*[73] the Court found no violation of Article 6 where the applicant was fined after refusing to take the oath as a witness. The Court, disagreeing with the Commission's ruling, drew a distinction between the solemn act of taking the oath—a necessary foundation for judicial proceedings—and any subsequent obligation to answer questions or to incriminate oneself:

> "Whilst a witness's obligation to take the oath and the penalties imposed for failure to do so involve a degree of coercion, the latter is designed to ensure that any statements made to the judge are truthful, not to force witnesses to give evidence. In other words, the fines imposed on Mr Serves did not constitute a measure such as to compel him to incriminate himself as they were imposed before such a risk ever arose."[74]

15–81   In this case the applicant had been called as a witness in the investigation of two other men involved in an alleged murder, and his argument was that the decision to call him as a witness was a subterfuge to avoid according to him his privilege against self-incrimination under French law. The Court held that the applicant was to be treated as a "person charged", for the purposes of Article 6, because a case file was still open against him; but the decision to find no violation of

---

[68] *cf. HM Advocate v. Brown* [2001] 2 W.L.R. 817.
[69] (1995) 81 D.R. 82.
[70] As suggested in the article by Sir Nicolas Bratza (above, n. 48), at 11–12.
[71] Notably the decisions in *John Murray, Condron*, and *Averill*. See also *Heaney and McGuinness v. Ireland*, Judgment December 21, 2000, discussed at para. 15–93 below.
[72] *John Murray v. United Kingdom* (1996) 22 E.H.R.R. 29, para. 49.
[73] (1999) 28 E.H.R.R. 265.
[74] *ibid*., para. 47.

Article 6 implies that he should have taken the oath but may then have chosen not to answer questions that might incriminate him.

II. *Self-Incrimination and the Human Rights Act*

After the Strasbourg decision in *Saunders*, the Court of Appeal held in *Morrisey and Staines*[75] that an English court had no power to apply a judgment of the European Court of Human Rights which would render an English statute ineffective, and that, for the same reasons, it would not be appropriate rely on such a decision to exclude evidence under section 78 of the Police and Criminal Evidence Act 1984. Now that the Human Rights Act is in force, neither of these propositions can be sustained. The practical importance of this problem is significantly reduced by section 59 and Schedule 3 to the Youth Justice and Criminal Evidence Act 1999 which amend many statutory provisions of this kind, and introduce restrictions on the use of answers obtained under compulsion. Thus, for example, section 434 of the Companies Act 1985 is amended as follows:

15–82

"In criminal proceedings in which that persons is charged with an offence to which this subsection applies—

(a) no evidence relating to the statement may be adduced, and
(b) no question relating to it may be asked,

by or on behalf of the prosecution, unless evidence relating to it is adduced, or a question relating to it is asked, in the proceedings by or on behalf of that person."

It is apparent that the amendment leaves untouched the compulsion to answer an Inspector's questions, but provides that answers may not be referred to by the prosecution in criminal proceedings.

One of the statutory provisions which has not been amended by the 1991 Act is section 71(2) of the Environmental Protection Act 1990. The House of Lords had the opportunity in *R. v. Hertfordshire County Council ex parte Green Environmental Industries Ltd*[76] to consider the relationship between that provision and the Strasbourg authorities. When clinical waste was found on an unlicensed site used by the applicants, the Council served on them a notice under section 71(2)(b), which empowers a waste regulation authority "by notice in writing served on him, [to] require any person to furnish such information specified in the notice as the authority reasonably considers it needs . . . " Failure to comply with the notice is an offence triable either way. The applicants asked for an undertaking that the information would not be used in a subsequent prosecution, but the Council declined to give one. The applicants then challenged the validity of the notice. Lord Hoffman, in the leading speech in the House of Lords, held that the notice was not in breach of Article 6 of the Convention, because the case raised the question of the duty to provide information, whereas the Strasbourg authorities were concerned with the use to which answers were put in criminal proceedings. If a prosecution had been brought, an English judge would have the opportunity to exclude the evidence under section 78 of the Police and Criminal

15–83

Evidence Act 1984; but that would not affect the validity of the statutory notice itself. Lord Hoffman based his conclusion on *Saunders v. United Kingdom*[77]:

> "The European jurisprudence under Article 6(1) is firmly anchored to the fairness of the trial and is not concerned with extrajudicial inquiries. Such impact as Article 6(1) may have is upon the use of such evidence at a criminal trial. Although it is true that the council, unlike the DTI inspectors, had power to prosecute in criminal proceedings, I do not think that the request for information under section 71(2) could be described as an adjudication . . . "[78]

15–84 When he came to consider *Funke v. France*,[79] Lord Hoffman found "obscurities" in the court's reasoning. He pointed out that Funke had not been obliged to incriminate himself in the proceedings for failure to produce the documents, since he could be convicted of that offence simply for the non-production; and no further prosecution had been brought.[80] This approach draws some support from *IJL, GMR and AKP v. United Kingdom*,[81] where the Court held that "whether or not information obtained under compulsory powers by such a body violates the right to a fair hearing must be seen from the standpoint of the use made of that information at the trial."

15–85 Lord Hoffman supported his conclusion by reference to the decision of the European Court of Justice in *Orkem v. Commission of the European Communities*.[82] By a Regulation the Commission was empowered to obtain information in relation to price-fixing activities, in order to enforce competition laws. The Court drew a distinction between questions "intended only to secure factual information . . . and the requirement of disclosure of documents", which were permissible, and questions designed to secure admissions that the company had been involved in price fixing, which were invalid as infringing the "need to safeguard the rights of the defence which the court had held to be a fundamental principle of the Community legal order."[83] Lord Hoffman noted that in *Green* all the Council's requests were for factual information. None invited any admission of wrongdoing.

15–86 The unanimous decision of the House of Lords in *Green* is therefore based on the finding that, because a request under section 71(2) of the 1990 Act "does not itself form a part, even a preliminary part, of any criminal proceedings," it does not "touch the principle which prohibits interrogation of a person charged or accused." It may be that the decision in *Ex parte Green* is best viewed as turning on the *administrative* nature of the investigation which was underway.[84] In the light of the Court's subsequent decision in *Heaney and McGuinness v. Ireland*,[85] it appears that if a person is prosecuted for an offence arising out of a failure to answer questions in a *criminal* investigation there will be a breach of Article 6.

---

[77] Above, para. 15–69.
[78] [2000] 2 W.L.R. 373 at 381–382.
[79] Above, para. 15–63.
[80] See however the discussion of *Heaney and McGuinness v. Ireland*, Judgment December 21, 2000 below at para. 15–92.
[81] [2001] Crim. L.R. 133.
[82] [1989] E.C.R. 3283.
[83] *ibid.*, at 3351, para. 52.
[84] See para. 15–74 above.
[85] Judgment December 21, 2000, see para. 15–92 below.

The connection with possible prosecution is much stronger if one considers a production order for special procedure material under the Police and Criminal Evidence Act 1984. Such an order may only be granted if there are reasonable grounds for believing that the material will be of substantial value to the investigation of a serious arrestable offence. In *R. v. Central Criminal Court ex parte The Guardian, The Observer and Bright*,[86] Judge L.J. held that a production order of this kind may breach the privilege against self-incrimination insofar as it obliges a journalist to hand over items of evidence to the police which may be incriminating.

The connection between requiring a person to furnish information and the use of   **15–87**
that information in subsequent proceedings came into sharp focus in relation to section 172(2) of the Road Traffic Act 1988. We have already seen that in *Tora Tolmos v. Spain*[87] the European Commission on Human Rights held that such a requirement is not necessarily inconsistent with the privilege against self-incrimination because it is possible to fulfil it without incriminating oneself. This issue has now been discussed by both the High Court of Justiciary and the Privy Council in *Brown v. Procurator Fiscal, Dunfermline*,[88] where the appellant was arrested for theft from a supermarket and then observed to smell of alcohol. She was asked who had been driving her car about an hour earlier and, on answering that it was her, was then breathalysed and arrested for driving with excess alcohol. At her trial she challenged this use of the power in section 172 of the Road Traffic Act 1988 on the ground that it infringed her rights under Article 6. In a lengthy and detailed judgment delivered by the Lord Justice General, the High Court of Justiciary upheld her challenge.

Whereas in *Saunders* the statements made by the applicant to the DTI inspectors   **15–88**
were taken to have been made in an *administrative* investigation before a criminal investigation was in train, in this case the power under section 172 had been used by the police as part of their criminal investigation. In response to the argument that section 172 forms a necessary part of a regulatory scheme, the Lord Justice General followed the Supreme Court of Canada in *White*[89] in holding that the privilege against self-incrimination applies where compelled self-incriminatory statements are admitted in evidence, whether part of a "regulatory" scheme or otherwise:

> "I am satisfied that the applicant was subject to compulsion to make an incriminating reply under threat of being found guilty of an offence and punished with a fine. The Crown propose to use evidence of the answer given by the appellant as a significant part of the prosecution case against her at her trial. For the reasons which I have given, the use that the Crown propose to make of the appellant's answer would offend her right not to incriminate herself, which is a constituent element of the basic principles of fair procedure inherent in Article 6(1)."

[86] [2001] 1 W.L.R. 662.
[87] Above, para. 15–78.
[88] High Court of Justiciary, February 4, 2000; [2001] 2 W.L.R. 817.
[89] [1999] 2 S.C.R. 417, *per* Iacobucci J. at 450.

15–89   The Privy Council unanimously allowed the prosecutor's appeal in *Brown v. Stott*.[90] In the leading speech Lord Bingham surveyed the Convention jurisprudence in a general fashion, and then articulated three reasons why neither section 172 itself, nor the use at a subsequent trial of evidence obtained by invoking section 172 is contrary to Article 6:

> "(1) Section 172 provides for the putting of a single, simple question ... the section does not sanction prolonged questioning about the facts alleged to give rise to criminal offences such as was understandably held to be objectionable in *Saunders*, and the penalty for declining to answer under the section is moderate and non-custodial. There is in the present case no suggestion of improper coercion or oppression ... "

This first reason appears to draw the line between permissible and improper coercion by reference to two considerations, the length of questioning and the size of the penalty for not answering.

> "(2) While the High Court was entitled to distinguish between the giving of an answer under section 172 and the provision of physical samples, and had the authority of the European Court in *Saunders* for doing so, this distinction should not in my opinion be pushed too far. It is true that the respondent's answer, whether given orally or in writing, would create new evidence which did not exist until she spoke or wrote. In contrast, it may be acknowledged that the percentage of alcohol in her breath was a fact ... "

In this passage Lord Bingham points to an obvious weakness in the *Saunders* judgment: why should compulsion to submit one's body to tests be regarded as less significant or intrusive than the compulsion to speak? The only reason advanced in *Saunders* was that all legal systems find the former to be necessary, but that is an essentially unprincipled explanation. Moreover in *Funke* the Strasbourg Court had earlier held that a requirement to produce documents was contrary to the privilege against self-incrimination. The line of authority was therefore both unstable and unconvincing.[91]

> "(3) All who own or drive motor cars know that by doing so they subject themselves to a regulatory regime ..., imposed because the possession and use of cars (like, for example, shotguns, the possession of which is very closely regulated) are recognised to have the potential to cause grave injury... If ... one asks whether section 172 represents a disproportionate legislative response to the problem of maintaining road safety, whether the balance between the interests of the community at large and the interests of the individual is struck in a manner unduly prejudicial to the individual, whether (in short) the leading of this evidence would infringe a basic human right of the respondent, I would feel bound to give negative answers."

All their Lordships recognised the force of the *Saunders* decision but felt able to distinguish it on the facts. As Lord Bingham put it, "the High Court interpreted the decision in *Saunders* as laying down a more absolute standard than I think the European Court intended." Lord Steyn made exactly the same point.

15–90   The decision of the Privy Council in *HM Advocate v. Brown* is significant both for its general approach to the issue of proportionality and its conclusion on the

---

[90] [2001] 2 W.L.R. 817. The Privy Council's decision in *Brown* was applied by the Court of Appeal in *DPP v. Wilson*, *The Times*, March 21, 2001.
[91] See para. 15–76 above.

particular point. Their Lordships emphasised that the relatively low level of coercion inherent in section 172 was insufficient to make it incompatible with Article 6. But surely in a subsequent prosecution for a substantive offence (speeding, failing to stop, dangerous driving) that failure to reply could be used as the basis for inviting the court to draw adverse inferences, relying on the reference in *Murray v. United Kingdom*[92] to "situations which clearly call for an explanation." If that is so, then the amount of indirect compulsion exerted by section 172 could be significantly greater than the Privy Council acknowledge.

The Privy Council's judgment is unsatisfactory in two respects. First, there **15-91** appears to be no reference to the House of Lords decision in *R. v. Hertfordshire County Council ex parte Green Environmental Industries*,[93] where similar issues were discussed in the Convention context. It is not clear what remains of the distinction drawn in that case between "extra-judicial inquiries" on the one hand and the admission of evidence at trial on the other, a distinction which (following the Strasbourg judgment in *IJL, GMR, and AKP v. United Kingdom*)[94] seems to have much greater support than some of the propositions in *HM Advocate v. Brown*. Indeed, it could be argued that many of the provisions for compulsory powers that were amended by section 59 and Schedule 3 of the Youth Justice and Criminal Evidence Act 1999 need not have been amended if the restrictive interpretation of *Saunders* adopted in *Brown* had been thought plausible.

Secondly, a subsequent Strasbourg decision confirms that the essentially sub- **15-92** jective approach to proportionality in *Brown* is at odds with the Convention jurisprudence. In *Heaney and McGuinness v. Ireland*[95] the applicants had been arrested on suspicion of terrorist activities. They had exercised their right to remain silent under caution during police interrogation. Section 52(1) of the Offences Against the State Act 1939 empowered the police to demand "a full account of such person's movements and actions during any specified period". Section 52(2) provided that refusal or failure to give such information was a criminal offence, punishable with up to six months imprisonment. The Court held that the applicants' prosecution for withholding information breached Article 6. In the Court's view;

> " . . . the degree of compulsion imposed on the applicants by the application of section 52 of the 1939 Act with a view to compelling them to provide information relating to charges against them under the Act, in effect destroyed the very essence of their privilege against self-incrimination and right to remain silent."

The Irish government had argued that the power was necessary to protect the community against terrorism, but the Court held that "the security and public order concerns of the government cannot justify a provision which extinguishes the very essence of the applicants' rights" as guaranteed by Article 6. The refusal of the Court to yield to public policy arguments, even in the context of alleged involvement in terrorism, provides a marked contrast to the approach of the Privy Council in *Brown*, where an arguably substantial incursion into the protection against self-incrimination was held to be a proportionate legislative response to

---

[92] (1996) 22 E.H.R.R. 29.
[93] Above, para. 15–83.
[94] Above, para. 15–74.
[95] Judgment December 21, 2000.

the problem of maintaining road safety. The *Heaney and McGuinness* judgment also prompts a fresh look at Lord Hoffman's reasoning in *Ex parte Green Environmental Industries*. Insofar as he found "obscurities" in the Court's judgment in *Funke* this was because the prosecution for failing to furnish documents was distinct from the potential prosecution in respect of which the documents were being sought.[96] The applicant had not been required to incriminate himself in the former offence, because that offence consisted simply in his failure to comply with the request. And he had not been required to incriminate himself in respect of the exchange control offences under investigation, because no criminal proceedings had ever been brought in respect of those offences. Yet this was precisely the situation confronting the Court in *Heaney and McGuinness*. Looking at the two offences together, the Court held that the protection against self-incrimination in respect of the criminal investigation into the first offence was violated by the very fact of the prosecution for the second offence.

H. ADVERSE INFERENCES FROM SILENCE

I. *The Strasbourg Caselaw*

15–93   Different considerations apply to rules permitting the drawing of adverse inferences from the silence of an accused under interrogation or at trial. The first of the important decisions is *Murray v. United Kingdom*,[97] where the Court found that the Criminal Evidence (Northern Ireland) Order 1988,[98] as applied to the facts of that case, did not constitute a violation of Article 6(1). The applicant had remained silent under police questioning and in court, and failed to account for his presence at the scene of the alleged crime. The Court emphasised that the independent evidence of guilt was strong, and that the Northern Ireland legislation incorporated a number of safeguards: in particular, the adverse inferences had been drawn by a judge sitting without a jury, and his decision was recorded in a reasoned judgment which was susceptible to scrutiny on appeal.[99]

15–94   The Court went on to hold that whether the drawing of adverse inferences is compatible with Article 6 will depend on the degree of compulsion inherent in the situation and the nature of any inferences which are drawn:

> "On the one hand, it is self-evident that it is incompatible with the immunities under consideration to base a conviction solely or mainly on the accused's silence or on a refusal to answer questions or to give evidence himself. On the other hand, the Court deems it equally obvious that these immunities cannot and should not prevent that the accused's silence, in situations which clearly call for an explanation from him, be taken into account in assessing the persuasiveness of the evidence adduced by the prosecution."[1]

15–94a   The Court in *Murray* nevertheless found a breach of Article 6 arising out of the denial of access to a solicitor in the course of police detention. Since the relevant

---

[96] See para. 15–84 above.
[97] (1996) 22 E.H.R.R. 29.
[98] S.I. 1988 No. 1987.
[99] *cf. Dermott Quinn v. United Kingdom* [1997] E.H.R.L.R. 167.
[1] *ibid.*, para. 47.

legislation permitted adverse inferences to be drawn from a failure to answer questions, access to legal advice was of "paramount importance" to ensure that the position of the detained person was not "irretrievably prejudiced". In the light of this finding, section 24 of the Youth Justice and Criminal Evidence Act 1999 was enacted so as to provide that an adverse inference cannot be drawn under section 34 of the Criminal Justice and Public Order Act 1994 in respect of a person who is at an authorised place of detention and who has not been allowed an opportunity to consult a solicitor prior to interview.

The possible problems of applying the *Murray* approach in the context of trial by   **15–95**
jury were first identified in the opinion of Nicholas Bratza Q.C., then the British member of the Commission:

> "In reaching the view that there has been no violation of the Convention, I attach considerable importance to the fact that adverse inferences under the 1988 Order are drawn by a judge sitting without a jury. Not only is a judge, by his training and legal experience, likely to be better equipped than a lay juryman to draw only such inferences as are justified from a defendant's silence but, as pointed out by the Commission, a judge in Northern Ireland gives a reasoned judgment as to the grounds on which he decides to draw inferences, and the weight he gives to such inferences in any particular case . . . The same safeguards against unfairness do not appear to me to exist in the case of a jury trial. When it is a jury which must decide, without giving reasons, what adverse inferences, if any, to draw against an accused from his silence, and what weight to attach to such inferences in arriving at a verdict, the risk of unfairness seems to me to be substantially increased, however carefully formulated a judge's direction to the jury might be."[2]

In two subsequent decisions the Court has had the opportunity to consider the   **15–96**
limits imposed by Article 6 on the drawing of adverse inferences, and in the first of those, *Condron and Condron v. United Kingdom*,[3] adverse inferences had been drawn in a jury trial. The applicants, who were heroin addicts, were certified fit to be interviewed. Their solicitor did not believe that they were fit, and advised them not to answer the questions put by the police. On appeal against conviction, the Court of Appeal accepted that the judge's direction to the jury was inadequate, but nevertheless held that the convictions were safe in the light of the other evidence in the case. The European Court of Human Rights held that the direction given to the jury had failed to strike the balance required by Article 6. In particular, the jury should have been directed, as a matter of fairness, that if there might be an innocent explanation for the applicants' silence at interview, no adverse inference should be drawn. The unfairness which resulted from such a misdirection could not be cured on appeal. Whilst it was possible, in some cases, for a defect at trial to be remedied at the appellate level, that was not the position in the instant case, since the Court of Appeal had no means of knowing whether the applicants' silence had played a significant role in the jury's decision to convict them.

The decision in *Condron* is founded on *Murray*, but goes beyond it in a number   **15–97**
of respects. The Court in *Murray* laid great emphasis on access to legal advice, and found a breach of Article 6 on this point. The Court in *Condron* held that the

---

[2] (1996) 22 E.H.R.R. 29, Commission at para. 37.
[3] [2000] Crim. L.R. 677.

same principle requires courts to have due regard to the content of any legal advice that is given:

> "The very fact that an accused is advised by his lawyer to maintain his silence must also be given appropriate weight by the domestic court. There may be good reason why such advice may be given. The applicants in the instant case state that they held their silence on the strength of their solicitor's advice that they were unfit to answer questions."[4]

15–98 The Court accepted that it was not contrary to Article 6 to leave the drawing of adverse inferences from the accused's silence to a jury, but held that the directions of the trial judge must be scrutinised carefully. In this case the trial judge failed to "reflect the balance which the Court in its *John Murray* judgment sought to strike between the right to silence and the circumstances in which an adverse inference may be drawn from silence." The trial judge drew the jury's attention to the applicants' explanation that they remained silent in reliance on legal advice, but:

> "he did so in terms which left the jury at liberty to draw an adverse inference notwithstanding that it may have been satisfied as to the plausibility of the explanation ... In the Court's opinion, as a matter of fairness, the jury should have been directed that if it had been satisfied that the applicants' silence at the police interview could not sensibly be attributed to their having no answer or none that would stand up to cross-examination they should not draw an adverse inference. Unlike the Court of Appeal, the Court considers that a direction to that effect was more than merely 'desirable'."[5]

15–99 In *Averill v. United Kingdom*[6] the applicant had been detained near the scene of a double murder. He was initially denied access to his solicitor whilst being questioned. He did not reply to questions about his movements at the time of the murder, or offer an explanation for the finding of fibres on his hair and clothing which matched fibres on clothing discarded by the gunmen. The Court found a violation of Article 6(3)(c) in the denial of access to a lawyer, but held that the drawing of inferences from the applicant's failure to answer questions was not in breach of Article 6. The trial in Northern Ireland had been by judge alone, and he had given a reasoned judgment on the drawing of inferences. In particular, he had cited the strength of the forensic evidence linking the applicant with the murders, and the failure to respond to other police questioning.

15–100 Four main points emerge from the judgment in *Averill*. First, the Court recognised that the caution administered to persons about to be questioned, under the Northern Ireland order and under the Criminal Justice and Public Order, to the effect that adverse inferences may be drawn from failure to mention facts, "discloses a level of indirect compulsion."[7] Secondly, the Court was clear in its recognition that the drawing of adverse inferences from a failure to answer police questions must be limited. The Court accepted that provisions such as those in Northern Ireland and in the Criminal Justice and Public Order Act 1994 are intended:

---

[4] *ibid.*
[5] *ibid.*, paras 61–62.
[6] [2000] Crim. L.R. 682.
[7] Judgment of June 6, 2000, para. 46.

"to prevent the hampering of police investigations by accused who take advantage of their right to silence by waiting until trial to spring exculpatory explanations, in circumstances in which the accused has no reasonable excuse for withholding an explanation. Notwithstanding these justifications, the Court considers that the extent to which adverse inferences can be drawn from an accused's failure to respond to police questioning must necessarily be limited. While it may no doubt be expected in most cases that innocent persons would be willing to co-operate with the police in explaining that they were not involved in any suspected crime, there may be reasons why in a specific case an innocent person would not be prepared to do so."[8]

Thirdly, the Court suggested that there is a range from acceptable to unacceptable **15–101** reasons for silence. Silence following a lawyer's advice will usually be accept- able, but in this case the applicant's explanation was that he had a policy of not co-operating with the police:

"the applicant did not contend at his trial that he remained silent on the strength of legal advice. His only explanation was that he did not co-operate with the Royal Ulster Constabulary for reasons of policy . . . It must also be noted that the applicant was fully apprised of the implications of remaining silent and was therefore aware of the risks which a policy-based defence could entail for him at his trial."[9]

This passage implies that the Court did not regard such a policy as a respectable reason for failing to answer police questions, despite the fact that the same explanation might equally have been expressed as an insistence on putting the prosecution to proof.

Fourthly, the *Averill* judgment develops the observation in *Murray* that there may **15–102** be circumstances which "call for an explanation". In this case it was "the presence of incriminating fibres in the applicant's hair and clothing" which was held to call for an explanation, and the Court considered that it was fair to draw adverse inferences in the absence of any explanation from the applicant when the matter was put to him. The Court points out that the finding of the fibres was put to the applicant after he had consulted his lawyer; it does not state whether, if the lawyer had advised him not to respond, the Court would have regarded the lawyer's advice as a more powerful factor than the presence of circumstances calling for an explanation. The tone of the judgment suggests not.

II. *Adverse Inferences and the Human Rights Act*

Section 36 of the Criminal Justice and Public Order Act 1994 allows the drawing **15–103** of an adverse inference from a person's failure to explain marks on his clothing or objects in his possession when arrested close to the scene of the alleged offence. Section 37 allows adverse inferences from a person's failure to explain his presence at or near the scene. In the light of the *Averill* judgment it is likely that a case falling within either of these sections will be regarded under the Human Rights Act as "calling for an explanation", and therefore as justifying an adverse inference in the absence of a plausible explanation. However, it should be noted that sections 36 and 37 do not contain an explicit requirement to consider the circumstances obtaining at the time of the failure to provide an

---

[8] *ibid.*, para. 47.
[9] *ibid.*, para. 49.

explanation, or to consider the reasonableness of the defendant's refusal to offer an explanation at that time. There is a strong argument, based on the Strasbourg judgment in *Condron*, that juries should be directed to consider these issues in deciding whether the defendants' silence could fairly be attributed to their guilt rather than to some other reason.

15–104 Section 34 permits the drawing of an adverse inference where the accused fails to mention when questioned a fact which he later relies on in his defence and which he could reasonably have been expected to mention when questioned by the police. It is fair to recall that there is a range of cases in which section 34 does not apply,[10] but where its terms do apply, as the Court of Appeal recognised in *Birchall*,[11] its application in a jury trial could lead to violations of Article 6 unless the judge's directions are carefully framed. Both *Condron* and *Averill* suggest that silence on legal advice ought not to be the basis for drawing an adverse inference, because the right to legal advice is valued so highly under the Convention. In *Betts and Hall*[12] the Court of Appeal applied the principles laid down in *Condron*, observing that it is the genuineness of the defendant's decision to remain silent that matters, not its quality. The Court held that if it was plausible that a defendant did not mention facts because he acted on legal advice then no inference could be drawn.[13] More generally, in *R. v. Francom*,[14] Lord Woolf C.J. held that in the light of *Condron*, when the Court of Appeal was considering the effect of a misdirection on the adverse inference provisions, it should assimilate the test for the safety of a conviction, with the test of fairness under Article 6. If a misdirection or non-direction rendered the proceedings unfair for the purposes of Article 6, then the conviction would also be regarded as unsafe for the purposes of section 2 of the Criminal Appeal Act.[15]

15–105 Two further issues should be considered. First, all the Strasbourg cases make it clear that adverse inferences from silence should never constitute the main basis for a conviction. This aspect of the oft-repeated phrase, "solely or mainly", is not reflected adequately in section 38(3) of the 1994 Act and needs to be emphasised. Secondly, juries should be directed, in line with *Averill*, to consider whether there are other good reasons for silence in each particular case. This forms part of the general injunction in *Condron* that courts should maintain "an appropriate balance" between the right of silence and the drawing of adverse inferences.

15–105a Another piece of recent legislation to make a statutory inroad on the "right of silence" is the Criminal Justice (Terrorism and Conspiracy) Act 1998, passed when Parliament was recalled for a single day in September 1998 following the

---

[10] See the article by D.J. Birch, "Suffering in Silence: a Cost-Benefit Analysis of section 34 of the Criminal Justice and Public Order Act 1994" [1999] Crim. L.R. 769 at 782–783.

[11] [1999] Crim. L.R. 311.

[12] Judgment February 9, 2000 (CA).

[13] The Court suggested that the jury should be directed in these terms: "If, on the other hand, you are satisfied that the true explanation for either defendant's failure is that he did not at that time have any answer to the allegations that were being put to him, or that he realised that such explanation as he had would not at that stage stand up to questioning or investigation by the police, and that the advice of the solicitor did no more than provide him with a convenient shield behind which to hide, then and only then can you draw such inferences as you consider proper from his failure".

[14] [2000] Crim. L.R. 1018.

[15] As to the relationship between fairness and safety generally see para. 17–25 below.

bombing at Omagh.[16] Section 1 of the Act amends the provision in section 2 of the Prevention of Terrorism (Temporary Provisions) Act 1989 for an offence of belonging to a proscribed organisation. Among its provisions is section 1(6), which allows courts to draw inferences from an accused's failure "to mention a fact which is material to the offence and which he could reasonably be expected to mention", but which also states that no committal for trial, submission of no case or conviction should be based solely on the inferences.[17] At the time the Government stated that it had been advised that this was ECHR-proof, and satisfied the points made by the European Court in the *Murray* decision.[18] It is true that the 1998 Act states that inferences may only be drawn if the defendant was permitted to consult a solicitor before the questioning from which adverse inferences are drawn. But, on the other hand, the 1998 Act also allows the admission in evidence of a senior police officer's opinion that the accused belongs to a proscribed organisation; and the various points just made in relation to the proper assessment of failures to answer questions remain to be taken into account. In particular, it should be made clear that no conviction or other finding should be based solely *or mainly* on adverse inferences from silence. The relevant provisions are now to be found in section 109 of the Terrorism Act 2000.

Finally, the effect of the Privy Council's decision in *HM Advocate v. Brown*[19] **15–106** must be considered. The decision that the compulsory power of enquiry under section 172 of the Road Traffic Act 1988 is compatible with Article 6 raises the further question of whether adverse inferences may be drawn from a failure to reply. If the circumstances giving rise to the section 172 enquiry, and the failure to reply, are regarded as a situation "calling for an explanation", then it seems that adverse inferences will be permissible, so long as the prosecution case does not rest "wholly or mainly" on the inferences.

III. *Comparative Approaches*

Finally, reference should be made in this context to the approach of the United **15–107** Nations Human Rights Committee in interpreting the parallel provisions of the International Covenant on Civil and Political Rights. Article 14 of the ICCPR guarantees the right to a fair trial. Article 14(3)(g) expressly provides that in the determination of any criminal charge the accused has "the right not to be compelled to testify against himself or to confess guilt."[20] In July 1995 the Human Rights Committee considered the United Kingdom's fourth periodic report under the ICCPR and addressed directly the question whether the relevant provisions of the 1988 Order and the 1994 Act conformed to the requirements of Article 14. The Committee concluded that the adverse inference rules "violate various provisions in Article 14 of the Covenant [fair trial], despite a range of

---

[16] For full analysis, see C. Campbell, "Two Steps Backwards: the Criminal Justice (Terrorism and Conspiracy) Act 1998" [1999] Crim. L.R. 941.
[17] This is a parallel provision to s.38(3) of the Criminal Justice and Public Order Act 1994. It does not however appear to prevent a conviction being based "mainly" on such an inference: see para. 15–105.
[18] (1996) 22 E.H.R.R. 29, discussed above, para. 15–93.
[19] Above, paras 15–89 *et seq.*; but *cf. Heaney and McGuinness* para. 15–92.
[20] To that extent the ICCPR mirrors exactly the protection implied into Art. 6 of the ECHR in *Funke* and *Saunders*.

safeguards built into the legislation and the rules enacted thereunder." In accord with the ICCPR approach are the laws of the United States and Canada. In the former, the landmark Supreme Court decision in *Griffin v. California*[21] established that the Fifth Amendment to the United States Constitution forbids both comments by the prosecution on the accused's silence and instructions by the court that such silence may be evidence of guilt. Similarly, it is well established under section 4(6) of the Canada Evidence Act that a trial judge may not comment on the accused's silence, and similarly the prosecution may not rely on evidence of the accused's silence either under police questioning or in court.[22] In this respect the Charter changed nothing.

I. HEARSAY, CONFRONTATION AND WITNESS STATEMENTS

I. *The general Strasbourg approach*

15–108   Article 6(3)(d) provides that everyone charged with a criminal offence has the right: "to examine or have examined witnesses against him and to obtain the attendance and examination of witnesses in his behalf under the same conditions as witnesses against him."

The term "witness" has an autonomous meaning under the Convention, which includes a person whose statements are produced as evidence before a court, even though the maker is not called to give oral evidence.[23] The opportunity to cross-examine need not be available at the trial itself, provided the witness was available for cross-examination at an earlier stage, such as a full committal.[24] In this sense Article 6(3)(d) has much in common with the "right to confrontation" under the Constitution of the United States,[25] and the European Court has occasionally referred to "the lack of any confrontation" as the reason for finding a trial unfair.[26]

15–109   The starting point of the Strasbourg interpretation of Article 6(3)(d) is that "all the evidence must in principle be produced in the presence of the accused at a public hearing with a view to adversarial argument."[27] In certain situations the admission of depositions or other witness statements for the prosecution, without the presence of the maker, may be inconsistent with the right to confrontation. However, the Court has not applied the rule inflexibly. In keeping with the general approach to Article 6, the Court will examine the reasons advanced for the non-attendance of the witness; any compensating safeguards; the opportunity,

---

[21] 380 U.S. 609 (1965).

[22] See, *e.g.*, *Chambers* [1990] 2 S.C.R. 1293.

[23] *Kostovski v. Netherlands* (1990) 12 E.H.R.R. 434; *cf. Bonisch v. Austria* (1987) 9 E.H.R.R. 191, where the Court declined to make a ruling on whether a court-appointed expert fell within the definition of a witness in Art. 6(3)(d).

[24] *Kostovski v. Netherlands* (1990) 12 E.H.R.R. 434 at para. 41.

[25] The Sixth Amendment right "to be confronted with the witnesses against him": on the parallels between this and the ECHR jurisprudence, see R. Friedman, "Thoughts from across the water on Hearsay and Confrontation" [1998] Crim. L.R. 697.

[26] *E.g.*, *Saidi v. France* (1994) 17 E.H.R.R. 251 at para. 44.

[27] *Barbera, Messegue and Jabardo v. Spain* (1989) 11 E.H.R.R. 360 at para. 78, a passage repeated in many later judgments, *e.g.*, *Ludi v. Switzerland* (1993) 15 E.H.R.R. 173 at para. 47, and *Van Mechelen v. Netherlands* (1998) 25 E.H.R.R. 647 at para. 51.

if any, which the defence has had to confront the witness at an earlier stage of the proceedings; the possibility of introducing the evidence in a manner less intrusive to the rights of the accused; whether the defence requested the attendance of the witness; and the importance of the prohibited hearsay evidence in the context of the proceedings as a whole.[28]

Four decisions illustrate the circumstances in which the Court may find a   **15–110**
violation. In *Unterpertinger v. Austria*[29] the prosecution's case was based largely on the formal statements of two witnesses who, as relatives of the defendant, were non-compellable and exercised their privilege not to give oral evidence. Their statements were read out at the trial, and the Court held that "in itself the reading out of statements in this way cannot be regarded as being inconsistent with Article 6". However, the Court added that "the use made of them as evidence must nevertheless comply with the rights of the defence, which it is the object of Article 6 to protect."[30] The applicants' inability to cross-examine the witnesses, and the court's refusal to hear evidence attacking the credibility of the witnesses, meant that the defence rights were "appreciably restricted",[31] in breach of Article 6(1) in conjunction with Article 6(3)(d). Although there was other evidence in the case, the court had clearly treated the witnesses' written statements as "proof of the truth" of their accusations, basing the conviction on their (untested) statements.[32]

A breach of Article 6 was also found in *Kostovski v. Netherlands*,[33] where the   **15–111**
conviction was based "to a decisive extent" on the statements of two anonymous witnesses who gave evidence but whom neither the defendant, nor defence counsel, nor the trial court was able to observe.[34] The right to confrontation, held the Court,

> "does not mean, however, that in order to be used as evidence statements of witnesses should always be made at a public hearing in court: to use as evidence such statements obtained at the pre-trial stage is not in itself inconsistent with paragraphs (3)(d) and (1) of Article 6, provided the right of the defence have been respected. As a rule, these rights require that an accused should be given an adequate and proper opportunity to challenge and question a witness against him, either at the time the witness was making his statement or at some later stage in the proceedings."[35]

In this case the defence had been able to submit questions, which an examining magistrate had then put to one of the two witnesses (the other was only questioned by police), but the Court held that "it cannot be said that the handicaps under which the defence laboured were counterbalanced by the procedures

---

[28] See *Unterpertinger v. Austria* (1991) 13 E.H.R.R. 175; *Kostovski v. Netherlands* (1990) 12 E.H.R.R. 434; *Windisch v. Austria* (1991) 13 E.H.R.R. 281; *Lüdi v. Switzerland* (1993) 15 E.H.R.R. 173; *Barberà, Messegué and Jabardo v. Spain* (1989) 11 E.H.R.R. 360; *Bricmont v. Belgium* (1990) 12 E.H.R.R. 217; *Delta v. France* (1993) 16 E.H.R.R. 574; *Saidi v. France* (1994) 17 E.H.R.R. 251; *Asch v. Austria* (1993) 15 E.H.R.R. 597; *Artner v. Austria* (1992) Series A No./242–A; *Isgro v. Italy* (1990) Series A No./194.
[29] (1991) 13 E.H.R.R. 175.
[30] *ibid.*, para. 31.
[31] *ibid.*, at para. 33.
[32] *ibid.*, at para. 33.
[33] (1991) 12 E.H.R.R. 434.
[34] *ibid.*, at para. 44.
[35] *ibid.*, at para. 41, citing the *Unterpertinger* judgment.

followed by the judicial authorities."[36] The Court's comments on the difficulties facing a defendant against whom witnesses testify anonymously demonstrate its belief in the value of cross-examination:

> "If the defence is unaware of the identity of the person it seeks to question, it may be deprived of the very particulars enabling it to demonstrate that he or she is prejudiced, hostile or unreliable. Testimony or other declarations inculpating an accused may well be designedly untruthful or simply erroneous and the defence will scarcely be able to bring this to light if it lacks the information permitting it to test the author's reliability or to cast doubt on his credibility. The dangers inherent in such a situation are obvious."[37]

15–112 The *Kostovski* judgment was followed in *Windisch v. Austria*,[38] where there had been no opportunity for the defence to question the two anonymous witnesses and, since the trial court had relied "to a large extent" on their written statements, the Court held that the restrictions on defence rights deprived the applicant of a fair trial.[39]

> "The collaboration of the public is undoubtedly of great importance to the police in their struggle against crime. In this connection the Court notes that the Convention does not preclude reliance, at the investigative stage, on sources such as anonymous informants. However, the subsequent use of their statements by the trial court to found a conviction is another matter. The right to a fair administration of justice holds so prominent a place in a democratic society that it cannot be sacrificed."[40]

The same conclusion was reached in *Ludi v. Switzerland*,[41] where the written statement of an undercover agent had "played a part" in the conviction, and where the anonymity of the undercover agent could and should have been preserved without denying the applicant his rights of defence.[42]

15–113 On the other side lies *Asch v. Austria*,[43] a case of alleged domestic violence in which the accused's partner had called the police, described the assault to the police officer, gone to hospital and been medically examined, but later withdrew her complaint and exercised her right (under Austrian law) not to testify. The prosecution continued with the case, and at the trial the police officer testified to what the woman had said to him at the time (on the basis of the statement he had recorded), and also told the court about the bruises he had seen and described her frightened state. The Court found no violation of Article 6 on the facts, since the defendant had not taken the opportunity to cross-examine the police officer, the defendant himself gave conflicting accounts, and there was corroborative medical evidence:

> "It would clearly have been preferable if it had been possible to hear her [the victim] in person, but the right on which she relied in order to avoid giving evidence should not

---

[36] *ibid.*, at para. 43.
[37] *ibid.*, at para. 42.
[38] (1991) 13 E.H.R.R. 281.
[39] *ibid.*, at para. 31.
[40] *ibid.*, at para. 30.
[41] (1993) 15 E.H.R.R. 173.
[42] See to similar effect: *Barbera, Messegue and Jabardo v. Spain* (1989) 11 E.H.R.R. 360; *Bricmont v. Belgium* (1990) 12 E.H.R.R. 217; *Delta v. France* (1993) 16 E.H.R.R. 574; *Saidi v. France* (1994) 17 E.H.R.R. 251.
[43] (1993) 15 E.H.R.R. 597.

be allowed to block the prosecution . . . The fact that it was impossible to question [the victim] at the hearing did not therefore, in the circumstances of the case, violate the rights of the defence."[44]

What appears from these and other decisions[45] is a complex mixture of at least   **15-114**
three major factors. First, the Court's chief concern is the fairness of the trial as a whole: the defendant's right to "confront" or cross-examine every prosecution witness is important, but not absolute. Or, to express the point differently, reliance on pre-trial witness statements is not contrary to the Convention, so long as the rights of the defence are respected.[46] Secondly, the Court's judgment on overall fairness is much affected by the significance of the written or reported statements for the prosecution case: it is fairly clear that a trial would be unfair if the conviction rested "solely or mainly" on the disputed statement, but in some decisions the test is expressed in terms more favourable to the defence. Thus in *Ludi v. Switzerland*[47] the Court thought it sufficient to render the trial unfair that the written evidence had "played a part" in the conviction.

However, this may be explained by a third factor: that the Court has regard to the   **15-115**
practical possibility of according greater recognition to defence rights than was done at the trial. In other words, there are some cases where the impracticability of producing the witness at the trial might lead the Court to adopt a more flexible approach to Article 6(3)(d) (as, for example, in *Artner v. Austria*,[48] where the witness had gone missing and was untraceable; or in *Asch v. Austria*,[49] where the witness exercised her right not to testify). But the national court should always look for alternative safeguards. As the Court put it in *Van Mechelen v. Netherlands*, "any measures restricting the rights of the defence should be strictly necessary. If a less restrictive measure can suffice then that measure should be applied."[50]

II. *Applying the Strasbourg jurisprudence to the Criminal Justice Act 1988*

Section 23 of the Criminal Justice Act 1988 provides four sets of circumstances   **15-116**
in which a witness statement (first-hand hearsay) may be admitted in the absence of its maker, and section 26 provides that a court should give leave for the admission of such evidence only if this would be in the interests of justice.[51] The four sets of circumstances are:

"(2)(a) that the person who made the statement is dead or by reason of his bodily or mental condition unfit to attend as a witness;
(b) that (i) the person who made the statement is outside the United Kingdom and (ii) it is not reasonably practicable to secure his attendance; or

---

[44] (1993) 15 E.H.R.R. 597 at para. 31.
[45] *E.g., Isgro v. Italy* (1990) A–194, *Artner v. Austria* (1992) A–242–A, and the many decisions discussed at paras 15–116 to 15–123 below. For general discussion, see C. Osborne, "Hearsay and the European Court of Human Rights" [1993] Crim. L.R. 255.
[46] See particularly *Windisch v. Austria* (1990) 13 E.H.R.R. 281 at para. 26.
[47] (1993) 15 E.H.R.R. 173.
[48] (1992) A–342.
[49] (1993) 15 E.H.R.R. 597.
[50] (1998) 25 E.H.R.R. 647 at para. 59.
[51] See generally *Archbold*, (2001), paras 9–126 to 9–142.

(c) that all reasonable steps have been taken to find the person who made the statement, but he cannot be found;

(3) (a) that the statement was made to a police officer or some other person charged with the duty of investigating offences or charging offenders; and (b) that the person who made it does not give oral evidence through fear or because he is kept out of the way."

The relevance of Strasbourg decisions to the interpretation of these provisions under the Human Rights Act is considered in the paragraphs which follow.

15–117   The first set of circumstances is where "the person who made the statement is dead or by reason of his bodily or mental condition unable to attend as a witness": section 23(2)(a). In *Bricmont v. Belgium*[52] the Court found a breach of Article 6 on the ground that there had been no opportunity for confrontation of the principal witness against the applicant,[53] who had not given oral evidence in court due to ill-health. The Court attached importance to the possibility that arrangements could have been made to enable the witness to be examined at his home, which "would have made it possible to clarify certain facts and to lead the [witness] to give further particulars of—or even withdraw—one or more of his charges."[54] Since it appeared that the courts had relied to some extent on the witness's statements, Article 6 had been breached. By way of contrast, the Court held in *Ferrantelli and Santangelo v. Italy*[55] that the evidence of a witness who had died could be admitted, despite the impossibility of confrontation. The Court concluded that the statements were "corroborated by a series of other items of evidence" and so found no violation of Article 6(3)(d).

15–118   Two subsequent decisions of the Commission considered the issue. In *MK v. Austria*[56] the trial court had admitted the statements of two witnesses, one the young victim of the alleged sexual abuse, and the other his younger sister. Both were in psychiatric care and the trial court held that requiring them to testify could lead to irreparable psychological harm. The course adopted was to appoint as a court expert a psychiatrist who interviewed the victim and then gave evidence and was cross-examined by the defence. The Commission reiterated that the Convention in principle protects the rights of victims and witnesses, as well as those of the accused. In concluding that there had been no violation of Article 6, the Commission attached importance to the ability of the defence to cross-examine the expert, and to the existence of independent evidence of guilt.

15–119   The other decision is *Trivedi v. United Kingdom*.[57] The applicant was a general practitioner who was charged with false accounting in respect of claims which he had made for night visits to a patient C. The prosecution relied on the evidence

---

[52] (1990) 12 E.H.R.R. 217.
[53] The witness in question was the Prince of Belgium. The Court considered that special procedures for taking evidence from "high-ranking persons of State" were not, in themselves, incompatible with Art. 6, provided the rights of the defence were adequately respected.
[54] (1990) 12 E.H.R.R. 217 at para. 81.
[55] (1997) 23 E.H.R.R. 288 at para. 52; *cf. Bricmont v. Belgium* (last note), where the Court found a breach where the trial court had "frequently referred" to the statements of the absent witness, and had "relied on" them (paras 83–84), even though there was other evidence.
[56] (1997) 24 E.H.R.R. CD 59.
[57] (1997) 89 A.D.R. 136.

of C that the applicant had often provided him with several prescriptions on a single visit, and had not attended on each of the occasions for which he had made claims. C was elderly and suffered from a number of illnesses. Before the trial began the prosecution served a medical report indicating that his condition had deteriorated and that he would never be able to attend to give oral evidence. Despite defence objections, the trial judge admitted two statements made by C pursuant to sections 23 and 26 of the 1988 Act. The applicant was convicted and his appeal was dismissed.

In his application to the Commission the applicant complained that the admission   **15–120** of C's witness statements violated Article 6(1) and 6(3)(d). The Commission recalled that the use of statements obtained at a pre-trial stage would not violate Article 6, provided the rights of the defence had been properly respected. Those rights meant that the defendant had to have an adequate opportunity to challenge and question the witness, either at the time when the statement was made or at a later stage of the proceedings. In the present case the Commission laid particular emphasis on the fact that the trial judge had conducted a detailed inquiry into C's condition, including his memory, at the material time. It noted that the statements were "not the only" evidence in the case to show that the applicant had claimed for visits which had not occurred. Evidence relevant to C's reliability had been admitted and the defence had had the opportunity to comment on this to the jury. Finally, the judge had specifically warned the jury in his summing up that less weight should be attached to C's evidence. For these reasons the Commission, by a majority, declared the application inadmissible.

It is particularly important not to over-emphasise the effect of this ruling. It does   **15–121** not establish that sections 23–26 are "Convention-proof". It merely demonstrates that there may be situations in which evidence may be admitted under this part of section 23 without rendering the trial as a whole unfair, and it spells out some of the conditions under which that will be so. If a key witness is claimed to be too ill to attend court, consideration should be given to arranging the confrontation at his residence, in order to respect defence rights.[58] If a key witness has died before the trial, it may be satisfactory to admit his statement in evidence so long as the rights of the defence are as well respected as they were in *Trivedi*.[59]

The second set of circumstances, in section 23(2)(b), is that the maker of the   **15–122** statement is outside the United Kingdom and it is not reasonably practicable to secure his attendance. There is a Commission ruling to the effect that, if the witness can be located, defence rights may be respected by having evidence taken by a judicial officer of the other country:

> "The Commission recalls that Art. 6(3)(d) of the Convention does not grant the accused an unlimited right to secure the appearance of witnesses in court. Its purpose is rather to ensure equality between the defence and the prosecution as regards the summoning and examining of witnesses . . . It does not exclude the possibility that witnesses

---

[58] See *Bricmont v. Belgium* (1990) 12 E.H.R.R. 217 at para. 81.
[59] See the Scottish decision in *McKenna v. HM Advocate*, 2000 J.C. 291, where the High Court of Justiciary based its judgment on *Trivedi*, and noted that Scots law's requirement of corroboration means that a conviction would rarely, in any event, be based "solely or mainly" on a statement admitted under ss.23–26. See also *Kennedy v. United Kingdom* (1999) 27 E.H.R.R. CD 266.

residing abroad whose presence at the trial cannot be enforced by the trial court are examined on commission by a court at their place of residence."[60]

15-123   Provisions for mutual assistance and mutual recognition among member states of the European Union may render this more practicable in future, and the Criminal Justice (International Co-operation) Act 1990 makes provision for the taking of statements on commission abroad. In *Radak*[61] a key witness refused to leave the United States in order to give evidence at a fraud trial in this country. The Court of Appeal explored various possibilities, such as making use of a mutual assistance treaty with the United States to set up an examination of the witness before an appointed judge, which might possibly be on a live link. Since the prosecuting authorities in England had taken no steps to avail themselves of this possibility, but had applied to have the witness's written statement admitted under section 23, the Court held that the trial judge had wrongly exercised his discretion under section 26 of the 1988 Act to admit the statement. The Court cited the above passage from *X v. Germany* and held that the Convention jurisprudence "coincides with the proper application of the [English] statute".

15-124   The third set of circumstances is where "all reasonable steps have been taken to find the person who made the statement, but . . . he cannot be found": section 23(2)(c). Two decisions of the Court are relevant here. In *Delta v. France*[62] the prosecution relied on the statements of the victim and another witness: they were summoned to attend but failed to do so, and the judge did not take any steps to have them brought before the court. On appeal the defence asked for the two witnesses to be produced, but the request was refused. The Court held that Article 6(3)(d) had been violated: the defence had never had an adequate opportunity to examine the witnesses or to test their reliability, and it was the only evidence against the applicant.[63] To be contrasted with this is *Doorson v. Netherlands*,[64] where efforts to have a particular witness brought before the court were made on three separate occasions, and when he was brought to court by force he absconded. The Court held that "in these circumstances it was open to [the Dutch court] to have regard to the statement obtained by the police, since it could consider that statement to be corroborated by other evidence before it."[65]

15-125   The fourth set of circumstances is where the maker "does not give oral evidence through fear or because he is kept out of the way," and the statement was made previously to a police officer or other investigator: section 23(3). At least four Strasbourg cases have a bearing on this. In *Windisch v. Austria*[66] the two witnesses declined to give evidence for fear of reprisals and remained anonymous, which meant that the defence could not even attack their credibility (since it did not know who they were). The Court held that this was too great a restriction on the applicant's right to a fair trial.[67] In *Saidi v. France*[68] fear of

---

[60] *X v. Germany* (1988) 10 E.H.R.R. 503: the ruling is somewhat vague on the rights of the parties to attend and to put questions directly in the foreign proceedings.
[61] [1999] 1 Cr. App. R. 187.
[62] (1993) 16 E.H.R.R. 574.
[63] *ibid.*, at para. 37.
[64] (1996) 22 E.H.R.R. 330, above, para. 15–115.
[65] *ibid.*, para. 88, referring to *Artner v. Austria* (1992), Series A–242–A at para. 22.
[66] (1990) 13 E.H.R.R. 281.
[67] See para. 15–112 above.
[68] (1994) 17 E.H.R.R. 251.

reprisals was the justification advanced for not requiring the witnesses to give oral evidence (identifying the accused) in a case of drug trafficking and involuntary homicide. Finding a violation, the Court observed that the written witness statements:

> "constituted the sole basis for the applicant's conviction . . . Yet neither at the stage of the investigation nor during the trial was the applicant able to examine or have examined the witnesses concerned. The lack of any confrontation deprived him in certain respects of a fair trial. The Court is fully aware of the undeniable difficulties of the fight against drug-trafficking—in particular with regard to obtaining and producing evidence—and of the ravages caused to society by the drug problem, but such considerations cannot justify restricting to this extent the rights of the defence . . . "[69]

This may be regarded as a strong decision, in view of the emphasis placed by the French government on the importance of protecting the safety of witnesses. But it was the absence of any corroborating evidence that weighed heavily with the Court.

In *Doorson v. Netherlands*[70] the Court accepted that the witnesses had previously **15–126** been threatened by drug dealers and declared that the interests of witnesses (for example, under Article 8) should be taken into account by trial courts.[71] The witnesses had been allowed to remain anonymous, and had been questioned by an investigating judge (in the absence of defence lawyers), their statements then being admitted at trial. The Court held that in this case there were certain "counter-balancing" procedures (the earlier judicial questioning, the opportunity for the defence to cast doubt on the reliability of the witnesses, which they did) "to compensate sufficiently for the handicaps under which the defence labours",[72] and that there was sufficient other evidence against the defendant, to justify the conclusion that there had been no violation. In *Van Mechelen v. Netherlands*,[73] the critical factors pointing towards a violation of Article 6(3)(d) were that the witnesses were police officers who should be expected to give evidence, that there had been no investigation of the risk of reprisals against the officers, that the measures taken at trial did not adequately respect defence rights, and that the convictions were based "to a decisive extent" on the identification evidence of the officers.

The distinction between *Doorson* and *Saidi* seems to turn largely on the strength **15–127** of the other evidence in the case. This may have important but novel implications for English law. Under section 26 of the 1988 Act the judge has to determine whether it would be in the interests of justice to admit the section 23 statement as evidence. The Human Rights Act requires courts to take account of the decisions of the Court, summarised above. To do this faithfully will require that the judge consider the range of factors identified in the Strasbourg decisions. In two cases where the Court of Appeal discussed the relevance of the Convention to sections 23–26, albeit prior to the coming into force of the Human Rights Act, it drew attention to the provisions in Schedule 2 to the Criminal Justice Act

---

[69] *ibid.*, at para. 44; to similar effect, *Windisch v. Austria* (1991) 13 E.H.R.R. 281 at para. 30.
[70] (1996) 22 E.H.R.R. 330.
[71] The key passage (*ibid.*, para. 70) is considered at paras 14–27 *et seq.* above.
[72] *ibid.*, para. 76.
[73] (1998) 25 E.H.R.R. 647.

1988 which provide a procedure for the credibility of an absent witness to be attacked, and to the principles in section 25 relating to the authenticity of the statement and the extent to which it supplies evidence not otherwise readily available.

15–128 Thus in *Gokal*[74] the prosecution at a fraud trial wished to introduce statements made by the defendant's brother-in-law, who was overseas and unwilling to return to this country. The statements implicated the defendant in material ways. The Court of Appeal upheld the trial judge's ruling that the statement should be admitted under sections 23–26. Ward L.J. gave brief consideration to some of the Strasbourg decisions discussed above: he stated that *Unterpertinger*[75] was distinguishable because the Austrian court had there refused to allow the defendant to attack the credibility of the absent witnesses, whereas English law would allow that; and he stated that *Kostovski*[76] was "a far cry from the facts before us" since it concerned an anonymous witness.

15–129 As we have seen, the Strasbourg decisions suggest that a conviction should not rest solely or mainly on evidence adduced under provisions such as those in the 1988 Act, even if the judge is as meticulous as the trial judges in *Gokal* and in *Trivedi*. In the latter case the European Commission was able to find that there had been other confirmatory evidence.[77] In *Gokal* the Court of Appeal made no such enquiry and no such finding. Indeed, it might be said that the wording of section 25(2)(b) points in the opposite direction: it requires the court to have regard to the extent to which "the statement appears to supply evidence which would otherwise not be readily available". Whether the facts of *Gokal* were such that the prosecution case rested mainly on the statement is difficult to say: it appears that some of the contents of the witness statement did coincide with notes written by the witness and obtained from a different source. But other decisions may now be more doubtful—for example *Dragic*,[78] where the prosecution for burglary rested on the identification of the defendant (by recognition) in a statement from a witness who was now too ill to attend court, and there was no scientific or other supporting evidence.

15–130 In *Thompson*[79] the trial judge, in a case of conspiracy to supply heroin in which the defence claimed that the prosecution witnesses were the true heroin dealers, decided to admit the statement of one witness who refused to attend court because of fear. The Court of Appeal upheld his decision, on the basis that he had taken account of all the relevant considerations. The Court added, citing *Trivedi*, that section 23–26 were not in themselves contrary to the Convention. The Court appears not to have considered whether the statement was the sole or main basis for the conviction, but Professor Birch commented that this requirement would "reduce statements admitted under the [1988] Act to the level of an inferior form of evidence which at best could be corroborative of direct testimony."[80] This is

---

[74] [1997] 2 Cr. App. R. 266.
[75] Above, para. 15–110.
[76] Above, para. 15–116.
[77] To the same effect, see *Kennedy v. United Kingdom* (1999) 27 E.H.R.R. CD 266.
[78] [1996] 2 Cr. App. R. 232.
[79] [1998] Crim. L.R. 887.
[80] In her commentary on *Thompson et al.* [1998] Crim. L.R. 887, 889; she adds that the effect of this would be "particularly unfortunate if the Act could not be invoked in circumstances where the only possible prosecution witness has been frightened out of giving evidence."

a classification to which English lawyers may have to become accustomed: it applies also, as we have seen, to the admissibility of improperly obtained evidence, to the drawing of adverse inferences from silence, and to reliance on accomplice evidence.[81] Evidence can certainly tip the balance in favour of conviction, and may indeed contribute significantly to that outcome; but there is consistent Strasbourg authority that it should not be the sole or even the main evidence supporting conviction. It does not have to be supported by *direct* testimony, since there are cases where the other evidence has been circumstantial,[82] but English courts may have to modify their approach to sections 23 and 26 to take account of this approach.

The presumption against hearsay embodied in Article 6(3)(d) is worded so as to   **15–131** apply only to witnesses who give evidence against the accused. There is no equivalent rule against the introduction of hearsay evidence by the defence. Where the admission of such evidence is permitted under national law there is nothing in Article 6 to prevent this. On the other hand, there is no obligation in Article 6 for a court to admit hearsay evidence which purports to exonerate the accused.[83]

In *Bricmont v. Belgium*[84] the Court observed that whilst the assessment of   **15–132** evidence was generally a matter for the domestic courts, there could be exceptional circumstances in which a failure to call witnesses helpful to the defence would amount to a violation of Article 6.[85] In *Vidal v. Belgium*[86] the Court found such a violation where the national courts had refused without reason to call the key witness upon whom the defence case rested. In the Court's view, the "complete silence" of the national court's judgment on this central issue was not consistent with the concept of a fair trial.

J. Admission of a Co-Defendant's Plea of Guilty

Sections 74 and 75 of Police and Criminal Evidence Act (PACE)[87] provide a   **15–133** mechanism for admitting evidence of a criminal conviction of any person other than the accused, in order to prove the commission by that person of the offence, where this "is relevant to any issue in those proceedings". The commission by another person of an offence may be relevant to an issue in the proceedings because it is an essential element of the offence with which the accused is charged[88]; or it may be relevant in order to show the purpose of a joint enterprise to which the Crown allege that the accused was a party[89]; or to show that the

---

[81] Above, paras 15–10, 15–57 and 15–94.
[82] *E.g.*, the domestic violence case of *Asch v. Austria* (1993) 15 E.H.R.R. 597, above, para. 15–119
[83] *Blastland v. United Kingdom* (1988) 10 E.H.R.R. 528; 52 D.R. 273.
[84] (1990) 12 E.H.R.R. 217.
[85] On the facts, however, the failure to call certain defence witnesses was not found to violate Art. 6.
[86] (1992) Series A No. 235–B.
[87] See generally *Archbold* (2001) para. 9–82 *et seq.*
[88] *E.g.*, proof of theft on a charge of handling; or proof of the guilt of another on a charge of assisting an offender.
[89] *Robertson and Golder* [1987] Q.B. 920.

accused was seen at the relevant time in company with a person who has admitted being involved in the commission the offence charged.[90] This provision is subject to the discretionary power of exclusion in section 78. In *R. v. Curry*[91] the Court of Appeal endorsed the views expressed in *R. v. Robertson and Golder*[92] to the effect that section 74 should be sparingly used, especially in relation to joint offences such as conspiracy and affray. Where the evidence sought to be put before the jury under section 74 expressly or by necessary inference involved the guilt of the person on trial[93] the evidence should be excluded under section 78.

15–134   The application of section 74 arose for consideration by the Commission in *MH v. United Kingdom*.[94] The applicant was charged with conspiracy to cheat the Inland Revenue in relation to the tax affairs of a company of which he was director and the second largest shareholder. The total sum involved was £85 million. His co-defendant (who was named as a co-conspirator) pleaded guilty to a substantive offence arising out of the same transaction. The judge permitted the co-defendant's plea to be proved in evidence under section 74 of PACE, and declined to exercise his discretion under section 78 to exclude it. The applicant complained that the admission of the plea denied him the opportunity to cross-examine the co-defendant and in effect reversed the burden of proof by requiring him to prove that he did not know of the fraud which the co-accused had admitted. The Commission concluded that the admission of the plea did not render the trial unfair. The judge had made it clear to the jury that the co-defendant's plea did not prove the existence of a conspiracy, and there were no grounds to criticise the judge's refusal to exercise his discretion to exclude the evidence under section 78. The defence could have called the co-defendant and could have examined him, albeit that cross-examination would only have been possible if the witness had been declared hostile. Whilst the admission of the co-defendant's plea strengthened the case against the applicant, it did not alter the burden of proof. The Commission's response here is consistent with the Strasbourg institutions' general unwillingness to review decisions on the admissibility of evidence so long as the procedures adopted seem fair as a whole.

K. CROSS-EXAMINATION OF RAPE COMPLAINANTS ON SEXUAL HISTORY

15–135   In 1975 the Heilbron Committee reviewed the law on rape and recommended restrictions on the cross-examination of complainants, on the basis that a woman's sexual experience with chosen partners does not indicate either untruthfulness or a general willingness to consent to intercourse.[95] The reform was accomplished by section 2 of the Sexual Offences (Amendment) Act 1976, but a recent subsequent Home Office report concluded that there was "overwhelming evidence that the present practice in the courts is unsatisfactory and that the existing law is not

---

[90] *Grey (Kenneth)* (1988) 88 Cr. App. R. 375 (C.A.); *Kempster* (1989) 90 Cr. App. R. 14 (C.A.).
[91] [1988] Crim. L.R. 527.
[92] [1987] Q.B. 920.
[93] As where the person concerned has pleaded guilty to conspiring *with the defendant*.
[94] [1997] E.H.R.L.R. 279.
[95] Home Office, *Report of the Advisory Group on the Law of Rape* (1975).

achieving its purpose."[96] The evidence was that judges were giving leave to cross-examine too frequently, and that strictly irrelevant evidence was being admitted, to the considerable distress of complainants. This view was strongly contested by some judges,[97] but the Government pressed ahead with legislation.

Section 41(1) of the Youth Justice and Criminal Evidence Act 1999 provides that **15–136** in proceedings for a sexual offence no evidence may be adduced or question asked by or on behalf of the accused about any sexual behaviour of the complainant without leave of the judge. The restriction thus applies to previous sexual activity of the complainant, whether it is alleged to have occurred with a third party or with the accused himself. Subsections (2) and (3), together provide that the judge may not give leave where the evidence or question is said to relate to the issue of consent, unless either (i) the sexual behaviour to which the evidence relates is alleged to have occurred "at or about the same time" as the event which is the subject of the charge (section 41(3)(b)), or (ii) the alleged past sexual behaviour of the complainant is so similar to the behaviour of the complainant at the time of the alleged offence that the similarity cannot be explained by coincidence. The rationale behind the provision is that each act of sexual intercourse requires a separate consent, and accordingly the fact that the complainant has, in the past, given her consent to sex with the accused is logically irrelevant to the issue of whether she consented on the occasion in question. There is of course a *non-sequitur* in this reasoning. As enacted, the section had two anomalous consequences. First, where the issue is not consent but the accused's erroneous belief that the complainant was consenting, the section does not apply and the evidence can be admitted. In these circumstances the judge has to direct the jury that the past sexual history is relevant to the accused's state of mind (*i.e.* his belief in consent) but not to the state of mind of the complainant (*i.e.* whether she was in fact consenting). More importantly, the section prevented evidence being adduced of a long term sexual relationship between the complainant and the accused unless there was some feature of their sexual activity which was so strikingly similar in its pattern that it could not be explained by coincidence (in effect, a similar fact principle).

The compatibility of this provision with Article 6 was considered by the House **15–137** of Lords in *R. v. A.*[98] The appellant had been denied leave to adduce evidence of previous sexual relations between himself and the complainant, which had taken place over a number of weeks before the alleged offence. Lord Steyn reviewed the Canadian jurisprudence on rape shield provisions.[99] He concluded that:

> "[T]he 1999 Act deals sensibly and fairly with questioning and evidence about the complainant's sexual experience with other men. Such matters are almost always irrelevant to the issue whether the complainant consented to sexual intercourse on the occasion alleged in the indictment, or to her credibility. To that extent the scope of the reform of the law by the 1999 Act was justified. On the other hand, the blanket

---

[96] Home Office, *Speaking Up for Justice* (1998), para. 9.64.
[97] See, *e.g.*, Judge L.J., interviewed in *The Guardian*, July 21, 1998, p. 7, and Lord Bingham C.J. in the second reading debate in the House of Lords, who stated that "no one has rights coterminous with those of the defendant because it is he alone who is at risk of being punished by the state." For further discussion, see N. Kibble, "The Sexual History Provisions" [2000] Crim. L.R. at 289–292.
[98] [2001] 2 W.L.R. 1546.
[99] Especially *R. v. Seaboyer* 83 D.L.R. (4th) 193 and *R. v. Darrach* (2000) 191 D.L.R. (4th) 539.

exclusion of prior sexual history between the complainant and the accused in section 41(1), subject to narrow categories of exception in the remainder of section 41, poses an acute problem of proportionality. As a matter of common sense, a prior sexual relationship between the complainant and the accused may, depending on the circumstances, be relevant to the issue of consent. It is a species of prospectant evidence which may throw light on the complainant's state of mind. It cannot, of course, prove that she consented on the occasion in question. Relevance and sufficiency of proof are different things. The fact that the accused a week before an alleged murder threatened to kill the deceased does not prove an intent to kill on the day in question. But it is logically relevant to that issue. After all, to be relevant the evidence need merely have some tendency in logic and common sense to advance the proposition in issue. It is true that each decision to engage in sexual activity is always made afresh. On the other hand, the mind does not usually blot out all memories. What one has engaged on in the past may influence what choice one makes on a future occasion. Accordingly, a prior relationship between a complainant and an accused may sometimes be relevant to what decision was made on a particular occasion."

15–138   A majority[1] of the House of Lords agreed that Parliament had adopted a legislative scheme which made an "excessive inroad" into the right to a fair trial. Read according to ordinary cannons of construction, it amounted to a blanket exclusion of potentially relevant evidence, subject only to narrow exceptions. This denied to the accused in a significant range of cases the right to put forward a full and complete defence. Whilst the statute had pursued desirable goals the method adopted amounted to "legislative overkill" when applied to a sexual relationship between the complainant and the accused. Applying the test of proportionality adopted in *De Freitas v. Permanent Secretary of Ministry of Agriculture, Fisheries, Lands and Housing*[2] Lord Steyn held that the reach of the section went beyond what was necessary to achieve its legitimate purpose and was therefore incompatible with Article 6.

15–139   Lord Steyn then went on to consider whether it was possible, within the meaning of section 3 of the Human Rights Act 1998,[3] to resolve the incompatibility by construction. He considered first whether the words "at or about the same time" in section 41(3)(b) could be stretched to include past sexual activity which was probative of the issue of consent but had taken place several weeks before the alleged offence. He held that these words could extend to an act which had taken place earlier the same evening, but that even with the benefit of section 3 they could not encompass events occurring days, weeks or months beforehand. Lord Steyn went on, however, to consider the exception in section 41(3)(c) for sexual behaviour which was so similar to the alleged behaviour of the complainant at the time of the offence that it could not be explained by coincidence. On ordinary cannons of construction the subsection pointed to a narrow exception resembling either the old *Boardman*[4] test for similar fact evidence or, at the very least, the test of high probative force laid down by the House of Lords in *DPP v. P.*[5] Even adopting the latter approach, the threshold test would be too high. It was therefore necessary to turn to the Human Rights Act. In His Lordship's view, it

---

[1] Lord Hope dissented, holding that the restriction was within the "discretionary area of judgment" which the courts should accord to the legislature. See further paras 2–132—2–133 above.
[2] [1999] 1 A.C. 69. See para. 2–110 above.
[3] See para. 3–31 above.
[4] [1975] A.C. 421.
[5] [1991] 2 A.C. 447.

was possible, applying section 3 to achieve a compatible construction. Section 3 required the court to "subordinate the niceties of the language of section 41(3)(c), and in particular the touchstone of coincidence, to broader considerations of relevance judged by logical and common sense criteria of time and circumstances". It was reasonable to assume that the legislature, if alerted to the problem, would not have wished to deny the accused the right to put forward a full and complete defence. It was therefore possible to read the section as subject to an implied provision that evidence or questioning which is required to ensure a fair trial under Article 6 should not be treated as inadmissible. The result would be that sometimes logically relevant sexual experiences between a complainant and accused would be admitted, although a judge would still be justified in excluding evidence of an isolated incident distant in time and circumstances. By introducing a judicial discretion, the section could be saved from a declaration of incompatibility.[6] It would have achieved a major part of its objective but its excessive reach would be attenuated in accordance with the will of Parliament as expressed in the Human Rights Act.

This decision is entirely consistent with the balance required by the Convention **15-140** caselaw. In *Baegen v. Netherlands*,[7] the applicant had not been allowed to question the complainant directly in a rape trial, although he had been offered the opportunity to put written questions (which he declined). The Commission recognised that proceedings for sexual offences "are often conceived of as an ordeal by the victim", and stated:

> "In the assessment of the question whether or not in such proceedings an accused received a fair trial, account must be taken of the right to respect for the victim's private life. Therefore, the Commission accepts that in criminal proceedings concerning sexual abuse certain measures may be taken for the purpose of protecting the victim, provided that such measures can be reconciled with an adequate and effective exercise of the rights of the defence."

L. EVIDENCE OF THE ACCUSED'S PREVIOUS CONVICTIONS

There are of course a number of circumstances in which the previous convictions **15-141** of an accused may be introduced into evidence in a criminal trial in England and Wales. This is not an area of criminal procedure in which there is any consensus between Member States of the Council of Europe. For example, a section of the Austrian Code of Criminal Procedure which provides for the accused's criminal record to be read out at the hearing has been quoted by the Court without comment.[8] It is therefore most unlikely that the admission of a defendant's previous convictions would be found in Strasbourg to violate the right to a fair hearing under Article 6. In *X v. Denmark*[9] the jury were informed of the previous convictions of the defendant during a trial on two charges of rape. The Commission held that:

---

[6] See para. 3–35 above.
[7] (1995) A.327–B.
[8] See *Asch v. Austria* (1993) 15 E.H.R.R. 597 at para. 21.
[9] (1965) 18 C.D. 44 at 45; 2 Dig 739.

"When interpreting such fundamental concepts as 'fair hearing' within the meaning of Article 6(1) and 'presumption of innocence' within the meaning of Article 6(2), the Commission finds it necessary to take into consideration the practice in different countries which are members of the Council of Europe . . . [Since it is] clear that in a number of these countries information as to previous convictions is regularly given during the trial, before a court has reached a decision as to the guilt of the accused . . . the Commission is not prepared to consider such a procedure as violating any provision of Article 6 of the Convention, not even in cases where a jury is to decide on the guilt of an accused."

This suggests that proposals made by the Law Commission and by the Government for the wider admissibility of evidence of previous misconduct are unlikely to encounter Convention problems.[10]

M. Phychiatric Evidence Relating to a Co-Defendant

15–142   In *Hardiman v. United Kingdom*[11] the Commission rejected a complaint arising out of the non-disclosure of a psychiatric report relating to a co-accused who was running a "cut-throat" defence on a murder charge. From the report of the decision it does not appear that the Commission specifically addressed the "equality of arms" problem raised by this case. In *R. v. Smith (SI)*[12] the Court of Appeal held that the prosecution could cross-examine an accused person on the contents of a psychiatric report where his account in evidence differed from his account to the psychiatrists. The Court also approved the trial judge's decision to allow the prosecution to call the psychiatrists to give evidence in rebuttal. It is difficult to see how the considerations of confidentiality and the absence of a caution, mentioned by the Commission in its decision, could be sufficient to render such reports immune from disclosure to a co-accused when they could be used by the prosecution. In this respect the *Hardiman* decision does not sit comfortably with the declaration of the Court in *Edwards v. United Kingdom* that "it is a requirement of fairness under Article 6 . . . that the prosecution authorities disclose to the defence all material evidence for or against the accused."[13]

N. Polygraph Evidence

15–143   Article 6 does not entitle the accused to insist on the introduction of polygraph evidence, where this is not permitted under domestic law. *Archbold* states as settled law the principle that "evidence produced by the administration of a mechanically or chemically or hypnotically induced test on a witness so as to show the veracity or otherwise of that witness is not admissible in English law."[14] However, the authority cited in support of that proposition, *Fennell v.*

---

[10] *cf.* Law Commission Consultation Paper No. 141, *Evidence in Criminal Proceedings: Previous Misconduct of a Defendant* (1996).
[11] [1996] E.H.R.L.R. 425. See para. 14–94 above.
[12] (1979) 69 Cr. App. R. 378.
[13] (1993) 15 E.H.R.R. 417 at para. 36, discussed in detail (with *Hardiman*) in paras 14–89 *et seq.*; for a further application of the principle of "equality of arms" to experts' reports, see *Mantovanelli v. France* (1997) 24 E.H.R.R. 370 at paras 33–36.
[14] *Archbold* (2001), para. 8–158.

Jerome Property Maintenance Ltd,[15] is concerned only with "truth drug" evidence.

In *Application No. 9696/82*[16] the applicant was convicted of murder on the basis **15–144** of circumstantial evidence. The trial judge refused his request to be examined by polygraph and the applicant alleged that this violated his right to a fair trial. The Commission rejected the application as manifestly ill-founded:

> "In the opinion of the Commission the rejection of the applicant's request to be interrogated with the use of a lie detector does not make the proceedings unfair . . . [I]t is, according to the present state of knowledge, not possible to obtain fully reliable results by the use of a lie detector. Under those circumstances the Commission considers it justified that no general right for the use of a lie detector is granted to suspected persons or to convicted persons. The authorisation of some persons to use a lie detector would inevitably influence the position of other persons who would refuse to be subjected to a lie detector. Their refusal might be interpreted as a sign of guilt."

O. EXPERT EVIDENCE

The use of "independent" or court-appointed experts in criminal proceedings can **15–145** have significant implications for the equality of arms guarantee in Article 6 if the expert expresses a firm opinion adverse to one of the parties. In *Bonisch v. Austria*[17] a court-appointed expert, who had drafted the report relied upon to institute criminal proceedings against the applicant, was afforded preferential status over an expert witness appointed by the defence. He was permitted to attend throughout the hearing, to put questions to the accused and the witnesses, and to make comments on their replies (facilities which were denied to the defence expert). In view of the fact that his evidence was adverse to the accused, the Court considered that he should have been treated as a prosecution witness. Accordingly, the failure to maintain equality of treatment violated Article 6. However, in *Brandsetter v. Austria*[18] the Court held that the mere fact that the court-appointed expert was employed by the same institute as the expert whose report had led to the commencement of the prosecution was insufficient to give rise to legitimate doubts as to his impartiality.

P. RETROSPECTIVE CHANGES IN THE LAW OF EVIDENCE

In *X v. United Kingdom*[19] the Commission held that it is not a breach of Article **15–146** 7 of the Convention for the Court of Appeal to uphold a conviction by reference to a precedent in the law of evidence decided after the applicant's conviction. Article 7 prohibits the retroactive application of criminal offences so as to penalise conduct which was not criminal at the time when the relevant act or omission occurred. It does not apply to the law of evidence.

---

[15] *The Times*, November 26, 1986.
[16] (1983, unpublished) 2 Dig. Supp. 6.1.1.4.4.5 at 6.
[17] (1987) 9 E.H.R.R. 191.
[18] (1993) 15 E.H.R.R. 378.
[19] (1976) 3 D.R. 95.

CHAPTER 16

SENTENCING AND RELATED ISSUES

In this chapter we examine the relevance of the Human Rights Act 1998 to the **16–01** sentencing process. Under section 6 of the Act judges and magistrates are obliged to exercise their sentencing discretion in conformity with Convention rights. A court will be acting unlawfully if it imposes a sentence which is incompatible with the defendant's Convention rights, unless it is required to do so by the terms of primary legislation which cannot be interpreted in any other way: a situation which is only likely to arise where the legislature has provided for a mandatory sentence.

In the pages which follow we consider the principle of proportionality in **16–02** sentencing,[1] as it arises under Article 3,[2] and in relation to offences involving the exercise of the rights conferred by Articles 8 to 11[3]; the safeguards applicable to preventive and partly preventive sentences,[4] and their application to the discretionary life sentence,[5] detention during Her Majesty's Pleasure,[6] the mandatory life sentence for murder,[7] the sentence of custody for life,[8] automatic life sentences under section 2 of the Crime (Sentences) Act 1997,[9] hospital orders with restrictions without limit of time,[10] and "longer than normal" sentences imposed under section 2(2)(b) of the Criminal Justice Act 1991.[11] We examine the principles applicable to credit for time served abroad pending extradition,[12] and at home pending appeal[13]; the principle of equal treatment in sentencing[14]; the issue of consent in the imposition of a community service order[15]; the procedure for imprisoning fine defaulters[16]; the burden of proof in confiscation proceedings[17]; the Article 6 safeguards appropriate at the sentencing stage,[18] including the issues raised by the practice of giving credit for a guilty plea[19]; and the obligation of prosecution disclosure for the purposes of sentence.[20] The

---

[1] Paras 16–03—16–04.
[2] Para. 16–05.
[3] Para. 16–12.
[4] Para. 16–21.
[5] Para. 16–23.
[6] Para. 16–27.
[7] Para. 16–30.
[8] Para. 16–34.
[9] Para. 16–36.
[10] Para. 16–38.
[11] Para. 16–39.
[12] Para. 16–41.
[13] Para. 16–43.
[14] Para. 16–44.
[15] Para. 16–52.
[16] Para. 16–53a.
[17] Para. 16–56.
[18] Para. 16–54.
[19] Para. 16–58.
[20] Para. 16–61.

chapter concludes with a consideration of the important principle of non-retrospectivity in sentencing,[21] and the impact of Article 8 on the rights of an accused with family ties in the United Kingdom who is facing a recommendation for deportation.[22]

A. CHALLENGES TO THE SEVERITY OF SENTENCES

16–03   No article of the Convention provides a specific right to question the severity of a sentence imposed following conviction for a criminal offence.[23] However, the Commission and Court have indicated that the overall length of a custodial sentence could, in principle and in appropriate circumstances, amount to inhuman punishment contrary to Article 3 of the Convention. Although the Court would undoubtedly hesitate before making such a finding,[24] it has on occasions raised doubts about the length of sentences imposed. Another possibility arises in the context of an attempt by the government to rely on the second paragraph of Articles 8 to 11 to justify an interference with the declared right: a disproportionately severe sentence would make that justification difficult to sustain. These possible avenues of challenge are discussed in turn in the paragraphs below, but it should be borne in mind that it is not only custodial sentences that might be disproportionately severe. As the New Zealand case of *Lyall v. Solicitor-General*[25] illustrates, a forfeiture order might impose a disproportionate burden on an offender, although in that case the Court of Appeal held that the forfeiture of a house following convictions for dealing in cannabis did not violate the Bill of Rights Act.

16–04   Proportionality of sentence may also be an issue where there is a legislative provision for the administrative imposition of penalty points on a driver's licence following an on-the-spot fine. Convention jurisprudence has long required that a person who is liable to such a penalty must have the right to challenge that penalty in a court.[26] In *Malige v. France*[27] the Court held that the applicant, who received an on-the-spot fine with four penalty points for grossly exceeding the speed limit, did have the opportunity to challenge this in a court. The Court was also satisfied that the sanction was sufficiently proportionate: "the legislation itself makes provision to a certain extent for the number of points deducted to vary in accordance with the seriousness of the offence committed by the accused."[28]

---

[21] Para. 16–62.
[22] Para. 16–76.
[23] *X v. United Kingdom* (1974) 1 D.R. 54 at 55 (application in respect of four-year sentence for arson).
[24] See, *e.g. Treholt v. Norway* (1991) 71 D.R. 168 at 191: "the prospects of serving a 20-year sentence [imposed for espionage] may well cause severe problems for the applicant and his family without necessarily coming within Article 3 of the Convention."
[25] [1997] 2 N.Z.L.R. 641 (Court of Appeal).
[26] *Ozturk v. Germany* (1984) 6 E.H.R.R. 409.
[27] (1999) 28 E.H.R.R. 578.
[28] *ibid.*, at para. 49.

I. *Disproportionately Severe Sentences as "Inhuman" Punishment*

Observations on the possibility of challenging the length of a punitive sentence   **16–05**
are to be found in *Weeks v. United Kingdom.*[29] The applicant (then aged 17) had
been sentenced to life imprisonment for an offence of armed robbery, by threatening the owner of a pet shop with an unloaded starting pistol and stealing 35
pence. The trial judge, in passing sentence, indicated that he had imposed a
discretionary life sentence because of the applicant's dangerousness, and not
because of the gravity of his offence. The sentence was intended to protect the
public and it was to be a matter for the Secretary of State to determine when it
was safe to release the applicant. The European Court accepted that subject to
appropriate safeguards[30] indeterminate detention of this nature could be justified
by the need to protect society. However, the Court held that if a term of life
imprisonment had been imposed for this offence on purely punitive grounds "one
could have serious doubts as to its compatibility with Article 3 of the Convention
which prohibits *inter alia* inhuman punishment."[31] This is a significant statement, even though the Court has not yet acted upon it. In *Abed Hussain v. United
Kingdom*[32] the Court expressed a similar opinion in relation to a sentence of
detention during Her Majesty's Pleasure[33] imposed on a juvenile convicted of
murder.[34] The Supreme Court of Canada has suggested that a sentence that is
"grossly disproportionate" will amount to "cruel and unusual punishment"
contrary to section 12 of the Charter, arguing that the "totality principle"
(recognised in this country in section 28 of the Criminal Justice Act 1991) ought
to operate to prevent disproportionality in the sentencing of multiple
offenders.[35]

In order to constitute a violation of Article 3, the punishment complained of   **16–06**
"must attain a minimum level of severity."[36] Thus, for example, the Court had
no difficulty in concluding that judicial corporal punishment on the Isle of Man
was in breach of Article 3.[37] Whether a custodial sentence imposed on an adult
would be found to be "inhuman or degrading punishment"[38] will depend on the
"sex, age and state of health" of the defendant.[39] In determining the standard to
be applied, some assistance can be gained from decisions of the Court and
Commission in the extradition context. The Court has held that a proposed
extradition can give rise to inhuman treatment under Article 3 where there is a
"real risk" that the sentence which is liable to be imposed in the requesting state
will be "disproportionate to the gravity of the crime committed."[40] The fact that

---

[29] (1988) 10 E.H.R.R. 293.
[30] In particular the Court held that such a sentence gives rise to a right of periodic access to a court
under Art. 5(4) to review the justification for continued detention: *ibid.*, at paras 58–59.
[31] *ibid.*, at para 47.
[32] (1996) 22 E.H.R.R. 1.
[33] Under s.53(1) of the Children and Young Persons Act 1933.
[34] (1996) 22 E.H.R.R. 1, at para. 53.
[35] *M (CA)* [1996] 1 S.C.R. 500, upholding a total sentence of 25 years for several offences which did
not carry a maximum of life imprisonment.
[36] See, *e.g. Ireland v. United Kingdom* (1979–80) 2 E.H.R.R. 25 at para. 162.
[37] *Tyrer v. United Kingdom* (1979–80) 2 E.H.R.R. 1.
[38] *X v. Germany* (1976) 6 D.R. 127, and *Treholt v. Norway*, above, n. 6.
[39] *Ireland v. United Kingdom* (1979–80) 2 E.H.R.R. 25 at para. 162; see also *Campbell and Cosans
v. United Kingdom* (1982) 4 E.H.R.R. 293 at para. 28, and *A v. United Kingdom* (1999) 27 E.H.R.R.
611 at para. 20.
[40] *Soering v. United Kingdom* (1989) 11 E.H.R.R. 439 at para. 104.

a person extradited or deported may face prosecution for a criminal offence which carries a severe sentence, or one that is more severe than would apply in other European states, is not sufficient.[41] In *Altun v. FRG*[42] the Commission held that a violation of Article 3 could arise from the risk that criminal proceedings abroad would lead to an "unjustified or disproportionate sentence,"[43] whereas the Commission subsequently held that "only in exceptional circumstances could the length of a sentence be relevant under Article 3."[44] There is some evidence that the English courts may be willing to treat gross disproportionality as contrary to Article 3: in his judgment on automatic life sentences,[45] Lord Woolf C.J. stated that a "wholly disproportionate" punishment might contravene Article 3, as well as being a "arbitrary and disproportionate" and thus in breach of Article 5. The example given was a sentence of life imprisonment imposed on a person convicted of manslaughter resulting from a simple unjustified push which gave rise to a fatal head injury.

16–07 There are two particular types of case in which English courts may need to draw upon the Convention. Inasmuch as severity and disproportionality, in the context of Article 3, turn on the "sex, age and state of health" of the offender, this raises questions about certain sentences imposed on young offenders and on mentally disordered offenders. The leading cases discussed above, *Weeks* and *Hussain*, both involved young offenders. In certain circumstances—broadly speaking, for crimes carrying a maximum sentence of 14 years or more for an adult—a court may impose on an offender aged between 10 and 18 a sentence under section 53(2) of the Children and Young Persons Act 1933, as amended. That sentence may be longer than the normal maximum for offenders under 18, which stands at two years' detention. In his guideline judgment on the subject, *Mills*,[46] Lord Bingham C.J. emphasised that custodial sentences for young offenders should be no longer than is necessary. But there are other authorities suggesting that it is proper to impose deterrent sentences on young offenders under the section 53(2) powers,[47] and this raises the possibility of a sentence whose length is based on deterrence and is disproportionate in relation to the offence itself. Such a sentence might be open to challenge under Article 3.

16–08 In *T and V v. United Kingdom*[48] the applicants argued that the sentence of detention during Her Majesty's Pleasure (HMP), imposed on a child as young as 11, amounted to a breach of Article 3. However, the Court held that there was no violation. The punitive element inherent in the "tariff" did not, of itself, give rise to a breach of Article 3. The Court recognised:

> "that Article 37 of the U.N. Convention [on the Rights of the Child] . . . provides that the detention of a child 'shall be used only as a measure of last resort and for the shortest appropriate period of time,' and that Rule 17.1(b) of the Beijing Rules

---

[41] *C v. FRG* (1986) 46 D.R. 179.
[42] (1983) 36 D.R. 209.
[43] *ibid.*, at 233.
[44] *C v. Germany* (1986) 46 D.R. 179.
[45] *Offen et al*, [2001] 1 W.L.R. 253.
[46] [1998] 2 Cr. App. R. (S) 128.
[47] See, for example, *Ford* (1976) 62 Cr. App. R. 303; *cf. Cunningham* (1993) 14 Cr. App. R. (S) 444, which prohibits exemplary sentences but upholds deterrent sentencing based on, for example, the "prevalence of the offence."
[48] (2000) 30 E.H.R.R. 121.

recommends that 'restrictions on the personal liberty of the juvenile shall . . . be limited to the possible minimum'."[49]

In this case the applicants had already been detained for six years from the age of 11, but the Court did not consider: "that in all the circumstances of the case including the applicant's age and his conditions of detention, a period of punitive detention of this length can be said to amount to inhuman or degrading treatment."[50]

Turning to mentally disordered offenders, the law provides a range of special **16–09** disposals under the Mental Health Act 1983 and other statutes. Despite section 4 of the Criminal Justice Act 1991,[51] courts find themselves sending mentally disordered offenders to prison (or, in the case of young offenders, detention) for various reasons—for example, because there is no hospital willing to offer a bed to an offender, or because an offender diagnosed as suffering from mental impairment or psychopathic disorder is regarded as "untreatable".[52] For some mentally disordered offenders, prison is likely to be such an adverse and damaging environment, even if the offender is held in the prison hospital, that it may amount to "inhuman treatment" under Article 3.[53]

In *Aerts v. Belgium*[54] the applicant, a mentally disturbed arrestee, had been **16–10** detained for nine months in the crowded psychiatric wing of a prison before transfer to a mental hospital. The European Committee for the Prevention of Torture and Inhuman or Degrading Conduct (CPT) had reported on this particular prison in 1994, concluding that "keeping mental patients for long periods in the conditions [which apply in the Lantin psychiatric annexe] carries an undeniable risk of causing their mental state to deteriorate." At the Commission's hearing on the merits, a majority held that the applicant's treatment had been in breach of Article 3:

> "By failing to take, within a reasonable time, the steps necessitated by the applicant's particular state of mental suffering caused by his extreme anxiety, the State caused him, by omission, to be treated in a manner which cannot be justified on any ground—certainly not on the ground of financial exigencies—and which, in the circumstances of the case, was 'inhuman' or, at the very least, 'degrading'."[55]

---

[49] *ibid.*, at para. 97.

[50] Taken from the judgment in *T and V v. United Kingdom, ibid.*, para. 99.

[51] In broad terms, s.4 requires courts to obtain reports before sentencing persons who appear mentally disordered, and to consider the likely effect on the offender's condition of imposing a custodial sentence.

[52] For evidence of the numbers and needs of mentally disordered persons in prison, see J. Gunn, A. Maden and M. Swinton, "Treatment Needs of Prisoners with Psychiatric Disorders" (1991) 303 *British Medical Journal* 338. For discussion of the Mental Health Act provisions and relevant case-law, see A. Ashworth, *Sentencing and Criminal Justice* (3rd ed., 2000), pp. 333–343.

[53] An application based on the effects of prison overcrowding and inadequate facilities failed in *Delazarus v. United Kingdom* (Application No. 17525/90, discussed by Harris, O'Boyle and Warbrick, *The Law of the European Convention on Human Rights* (1995), pp 70–71), but those prison conditions were in any event not specific to the applicant, who was in solitary confinement. See now *Keenan v. United Kingdom* (judgment of April 3, 2001), where the Court found a violation of Article 3 through failure adequately to supervise a prisoner who was a known suicide risk.

[54] (2000) 29 E.H.R.R. 50.

[55] *ibid.*, Commission report, para. 82.

16–11 A majority of the Court, however, held that "the living conditions on the psychiatric wing at Lantin do not seem to have had such serious effects on [the applicant's] mental health as would bring them within the scope of Article 3." The conclusion suggests that the standard of proof had not been reached:

> "Even if it is accepted that the applicant's state of anxiety, described by the psychiatric report of 10 March 1993, was caused by the conditions of detention in Lantin, and even allowing for the difficulty Mr Aerts may have had in describing how these had affected him, it has not been conclusively established that the applicant suffered treatment that could be classified as inhuman or degrading."[56]

The terms of this conclusion suggest a narrow basis for the decision, and the issue of the length of detention is much intertwined with the conditions of detention. This part of the *Aerts* decision was reached by a majority of seven to two, and the dissenting opinion argues strongly, with reference to the CPT report on conditions at Lantin prison, that the suffering caused to the applicant "by keeping him in the above-described conditions for such a long time exceeds . . . the minimum level of severity required for inhuman treatment under Article 3 of the Convention."

II. *Disproportionately Severe Sentences and Articles 8 to 11*

16–12 Where it is alleged that criminal proceedings have involved a violation of Articles 8 to 11, the severity of the sentence imposed will be highly material in determining whether the interference was "necessary in a democratic society" within the meaning of the second paragraph of each article, and to the proportionality of the measure.[57] There is ample authority from Commonwealth courts to support the view that an interference with a particular right may be held disproportionate if the severity of the sentence is not justified by the purpose it is intended to serve.[58]

16–13 Under the Convention the principle was stated in the early case of *Handyside v. United Kingdom*[59] emphasising the importance attached to the ability of citizens to exercise their freedom of expression under Article 10, and hence the Court's need to enquire "whether 'restrictions' or 'penalties' were necessary for the 'protection of morals'." This principle was reiterated by the Commission in *Arrowsmith v. United Kingdom*,[60] where one of the questions was whether the applicant's conviction for incitement to disaffection violated her right to freedom of expression. In determining whether the interference with her right was "necessary in a democratic society", the Commission stated that it:

> "must finally consider the severity of the sentence. [The Commission] is of the opinion that the sentence which the applicant finally received and served (seven months' imprisonment), although admittedly severe, was not in the circumstances so clearly out of proportion to the legitimate aims pursued that this severity in itself could render

---

[56] *ibid.*, Court, para. 66.
[57] For a fuller discussion see Chapter 8 above.
[58] *E.g. R v. Edwards Books and Art Ltd* [1986] 2 S.C.R. 713 (Supreme Court of Canada).
[59] (1979–80) 1 E.H.R.R. 737 at para. 49.
[60] (1978) 19 D.R. 5, discussed in para. 8–21 above.

unjustifiable such an interference which the Commission otherwise had held justified."[61]

This is an important statement of the need to distinguish between a sentence that is severe and one that is significantly out of proportion to the seriousness of the offence.

The question came up for decision in connection with Article 8 in *Laskey and* **16–14** *others v. United Kingdom.*[62] The applicants had been convicted of assaults arising out of consensual sadomasochistic activity involving the infliction of minor physical injuries to one another's genitals. The acts consisted of maltreatment of the genitalia (with, for example, hot wax, sandpaper, fish hooks and needles) and ritualistic beatings with either bare hands or a variety of implements, including stinging nettles, spiked belts and a cat-o'nine tails. There were instances of branding and infliction of injuries which resulted in the flow of blood and which left scarring. Laskey was sentenced to four years imprisonment for keeping a disorderly house (together with concurrent sentences for aiding and abetting assault occasioning actual bodily harm). Jaggard was sentenced to three years imprisonment for assaults occasioning actual bodily harm and unlawful wounding. Brown was sentenced to two years and nine months imprisonment for assault occasioning actual bodily harm. The defendants appealed to the Court of Appeal against conviction and sentence. Their appeals against conviction were dismissed but the Court of Appeal reduced their sentences to 18 months in the case of Laskey, six months in the case of Jaggard and three months in the case of Brown.

The Strasbourg Court considered that the prosecution itself did not amount to a **16–15** violation of Article 8 since the domestic authorities were entitled to conclude that a prosecution was necessary in a democratic society for the protection of health and/or morals (within Article 8(2)).[63] The Court then went on to consider whether the sentences imposed were disproportionate to that objective. The Court's reasoning on this point appears to suggest that the original sentences imposed by the trial judge may well have been held to be a disproportionate measure. But having regard to the reductions ordered by the Court of Appeal, the sentences did not violate Article 8:

> "[The Court] notes that in recognition of the fact that the applicants did not appreciate their actions to be criminal, reduced sentences were imposed on appeal. *In these circumstances*, bearing in mind the degree of organisation involved in the offences, the measures taken against the applicants cannot be regarded as disproportionate."[64]

This is important recognition that, even where it is held that there is sufficient justification for interfering with one of the rights in Articles 8–11, through prosecution and conviction, it is still necessary to ensure that any sentence imposed takes account of the fact that a fundamental right is being thereby restricted.

---

[61] *ibid.*, at para. 99.
[62] (1997) 24 E.H.R.R. 39.
[63] See para. 8–13 above.
[64] (1997) 24 E.H.R.R. 39 at para. 49 (emphasis added).

16–16 An argument along these lines was mounted in the Court of Appeal in *T and others*,[65] where the appellants had been sentenced for various consensual homosexual acts done in a private house but in the presence of several other men. One had received a suspended sentence, whereas the others received various community sentences, including combination orders and community service orders. Their argument was that, because their Convention rights under Article 8 were being interfered with, the trial judge was required by the Convention to show recognition of this by imposing only an absolute or a conditional discharge on each of them. The Court of Appeal rejected the argument. When this issue subsequently came before the European Court of Human Rights, on virtually identical facts, the Court held that the applicant's prosecution, conviction and sentence for consensual group homosexual activity in private was incompatible with Article 8. The applicant was awarded substantial compensation in respect of the consequences of the conviction, despite the fact that a non-custodial sentence had been imposed.[66] It seems therefore that if the case of *T and others* were to be reconsidered under the Human Rights Act, a different result would follow. Given that the prosecution and conviction of the appellants would have involved a clear violation of their rights under Article 8, it is difficult to see how the sentencing court could lawfully exercise a discretion so as to impose any significant penalty, still less a sentence of imprisonment.

16–17 The general proportionality requirement in cases engaging Articles 8–11 is supported by other Strasbourg decisions. In *Hoare v. United Kingdom*[67] the applicant was engaged in the publication and distribution of pornographic videotapes by post. The applicant was convicted of six counts of publishing obscene articles contrary to section 2(1) of the Obscene Publications Act 1959 and sentenced to 30 months imprisonment. In the Commission's view, the sole question arising under the proportionality test was whether the sentence imposed was necessary in a democratic society. Although the Commission noted that the tapes had only been sent to people who had obtained a catalogue and placed a specific order, it nevertheless considered that there was no certainty that only the intended purchasers would have access to the material. The Commission accordingly concluded that the sentence was proportionate to the aim of protecting morals, and dismissed the application as manifestly ill-founded.

16–18 In *Worm v. Austria*,[68] the Court held that it could be said to be "necessary in a democratic society" to punish a journalist for writing critical comments about a person currently being tried for serious offences. The Court went on to consider whether the sentence was "disproportionate to the legitimate aim pursued" and held that it was not: it was a substantial fine, for which the publishing company was jointly and severally liable. Similarly in *Steel v. United Kingdom*[69] the Court held that it was not a disproportionate interference with the first applicant's Article 10 rights to bind her over to keep the peace and to fine her £70. She was then imprisoned for 28 days when she declined to be bound over. A majority of the Court held that this was not a disproportionate period of

---

[65] [1999] Crim. L.R. 432.
[66] *ADT v. United Kingdom, The Times*, August 8, 2000; Judgment July 31, 2000. See para. 8–10 above.
[67] [1997] E.H.R.L.R. 678.
[68] (1998) 25 E.H.R.R. 454 at para. 57.
[69] (1999) 28 E.H.R.R. 603 at paras 106–109.

detention, taking account both of "the public interest in deterring such conduct" (*i.e.* disruptive protests against fox-hunting, held to create a risk of disorder and violence) and of the "importance in a democratic society of maintaining the rule of law and the authority of the judiciary." Four judges recorded strong dissents from this conclusion, holding that Article 10 had been violated in the case of the first applicant because the deprivation of liberty had been disproportionately long, or indeed "manifestly extreme", for "a person who, albeit in an extreme manner, jumped up and down in front of a member of the shoot to prevent him from killing a feathered friend."[70]

The decisions thus far discussed demonstrate the relevance of custodial sentences   **16–18a** to decisions about compliance with, or violation of, Articles 8 to 11. But the issue is one of proportionality generally, and there has been scrutiny of other types of penalty imposed on an offender, such as forfeiture orders.[71] Thus in *X Co v. United Kingdom*[72] the Commission declared inadmissible a complaint relating to seizure and forfeiture of magazines under the Obscene Publications Act. The applicant alleged that the forfeiture order breached Article 10 and Article 1 of the First Protocol to the Convention (the right to peaceful enjoyment of property). The Commission considered that the "protection of morals" exception in Article 10(2) was not confined to the moral standards of likely readers, but extended to the state's general interest in preventing the diffusion of immoral publications within its territory. Forfeiture was therefore in the public interest and "necessary" within the meaning of Article 10(2).

Orders for the forfeiture of allegedly obscene original works of art, on the other   **16–19** hand, require a particularly compelling justification. In *Muller v. Switzerland*[73] the applicant exhibited a series of large paintings in a public gallery, one of which included graphic depictions of sexual activity including homosexuality and bestiality. He was convicted of publishing obscene items and fined. The paintings were confiscated, but returned almost eight years later. The Court held that the conviction itself was justified for the protection of public morals and the rights of others. However, the confiscation order was different since the artist lost the opportunity of showing his work in a less sensitive location. On the facts, the Court found that the confiscation did not violate Article 10 since the applicant could have applied for the return of the painting sooner than he did.

III. *Disproportionate Penalties and European Community Law*

Finally, brief reference should be made to the possibility that a disproportionate   **16–20** sentence may be held contrary to European Community Law. In *Sofia Skanavi and Konstantin Chryssanthakopoluos*[74] the two defendants were prosecuted in

---

[70] *ibid.*, at pp 650–651.
[71] The question was also raised by the Commission in connection with the duty to register under the Sex Offenders Act 1997. In *Adamson v. United Kingdom* (1999) 28 E.H.R.R. CD 209, discussed in section H below, the Commission satisfied itself that the duty to register, which required information in breach of Art. 8, was "proportionate to the aims pursued" so as to be necessary in a democratic society for preventive purposes.
[72] (1983) 32 D.R. 231.
[73] (1991) 13 E.H.R.R. 212.
[74] [1996] E.C.R. I–929, discussed by E. Baker, "Taking European Criminal Law Seriously" [1998] Crim. L.R. 361 at pp 371–373.

Germany for driving without a valid German driving licence, an offence punishable with up to one year's imprisonment. The European Court of Justice held that, because they had valid Greek driving licences, their offences were merely administrative in nature. The prosecution breached the right to freedom of movement, especially as "Member States may not impose a penalty so disproportionate to the gravity of the infringement that this becomes an obstacle to the free movement of persons, [which] would be especially so if the penalty consisted of imprisonment."[75] Thus, where an offence and its penalty tend to restrict a right protected by European Community Law, the question of proportionality of sentence becomes an important consideration.

B. PREVENTIVE SENTENCES

16–21   All the sentences considered in section A (with the exception of the discretionary sentence of life imprisonment in *Weeks*) were punitive rather than preventive sentences, for Convention purposes; the grounds for challenging punitive sentences are relatively narrow. Where the purpose of the sentence is preventive, *i.e.* based solely or partly on some characteristic of the offender which renders him dangerous and not solely on the need to impose retribution for the offence, the main concern of the Strasbourg organs has been to ensure compliance with the Article 5(4) requirements on periodic judicial review and related safeguards. Where the sentence has a mixed punitive-preventive purpose, the punitive element must comply with the requirements for punitive sentences and the preventive element must comply with the requirements for preventive sentences. Hospital orders are an example of preventive sentences, and the position of restricted patients was analysed in *X v. United Kingdom*.[76] Discretionary sentences of life imprisonment, an example of partly preventive sentences, are discussed in paragraph I below. There has however been no great vigilance about the borderline between the purely punitive and mixed punitive-preventive sentences,[77] despite the different standards to be applied to them.

16–22   Under Article 5(4) of the Convention, everyone deprived of liberty by detention "shall be entitled to take proceedings by which the lawfulness of his detention shall be decided speedily by a court." It is not sufficient that the detention was ordered by a court following conviction, if the reason for continued detention turns on characteristics of the offender that may change over time (*e.g.* dangerousness and/or maturity), so that it can be said that "the very nature of the deprivation of liberty . . . appears to require a review of lawfulness at reasonable intervals."[78] At least six forms of sentence under English law fall to be considered here, and they are discussed in turn.

I. *Discretionary Sentences of Life Imprisonment*

16–23   One area where the Convention has been held to impose important safeguards is preventive detention on grounds of dangerousness (as for example in the post-

---

[75] [1996] E.C.R. I–929 at para. 36.
[76] (1982) 4 E.H.R.R. 188.
[77] See the Commission's ruling in *Mansell v. United Kingdom* [1997] E.H.R.L.R. 666, criticised below at para. 16–40.
[78] *Winterwerp v. Netherlands* (1979–80) 2 E.H.R.R. 387 at para. 55.

tariff phase of a discretionary life sentence or sentence of detention at Her Majesty's Pleasure). Under Article 5(4) such sentences have been held to carry a right of periodic review by a judicial tribunal and release if the offender is no longer dangerous.[79] This is because the justification for imposing such a sentence relates not to the gravity of the crime itself, but to characteristics of the offender which are "susceptible of change with the passage of time."[80] Thus, the continued detention of a discretionary life sentence prisoner beyond the expiry of the judicially imposed tariff period requires regular independent review by a judicial body.[81]

In *Thynne, Wilson and Gunnell v. United Kingdom*[82] the Court observed that: **16–24**

"[T]he discretionary life sentence has clearly developed in English law as a measure to deal with mentally unstable and dangerous offenders; numerous judicial statements have recognised the protective purpose of this form of life sentence.[83] Although the dividing line may be difficult to draw in particular cases, it seems clear that the principles underlying such sentences, unlike mandatory life sentences, have developed in the sense that they are composed of a punitive element and subsequently of a security element designed to confer on the Secretary of State the responsibility for determining when the public interest permits the prisoner's release . . . [T]he factors of mental instability and dangerousness are susceptible to change over the passage of time and new issues of lawfulness may thus arise in the course of detention. It follows that at this phase in the execution of their sentences the applicants are entitled under Article 5(4) to take proceedings to have the lawfulness of their continued detention decided by a court at reasonable intervals."[84]

As a result of the decision in *Thynne* section 34 of the Criminal Justice Act 1991   **16–25** was enacted. Section 34 introduced a procedure for Article 5(4) review of the post-tariff phase of a discretionary life sentence.[85] It also formalised the sentencing procedure so that a judge imposing a discretionary life sentence must now specify in open court the "relevant part" or tariff which is to be served to meet the requirements of retribution and deterrence.[86] The *Practice Direction (Crime: Life Sentences)*[87] makes it clear that it is only in very exceptional circumstances that a judge would be justified in not specifying a relevant part or tariff. Such circumstances would arise only where the judge considers that the offence is so serious that detention for life is justified by the gravity of the offence alone, irrespective of the risk to the public. In such a case the judge should state this in open court when passing sentence.[88] An order under section 34 is a "sentence"

---

[79] *Van Droogenbroeck v. Belgium* (1982) 4 E.H.R.R. 443 paras. 48–49.
[80] *Thynne, Wilson and Gunnell v. United Kingdom* (1991) 13 E.H.R.R. 666 at para. 70; the Supreme Court of Canada has also recognised the validity, under section 12 of the Charter (prohibition on "cruel and unusual punishment"), of indeterminate sentences for dangerous serious offenders who satisfy certain criteria: *Lyons* [1987] 2 S.C.R. 309.
[81] *Weeks v. United Kingdom* (1988) 10 E.H.R.R. 293 at para. 58; *Thynne, Wilson and Gunnell v. United Kingdom* (1991) 13 E.H.R.R. 666 at para. 76.
[82] *ibid.*
[83] The Court here referred to *R. v. Hodgson* (1967) 52 Cr. App. R. 113 (C.A.); *R. v. Wilkinson* (1983) 5 Cr. App R. (S) 105 (C.A.); *R. v. Secretary of State ex parte Bradley* [1991] 1 W.L.R. 134 (D.C.).
[84] (1991) 13 E.H.R.R. 666 at paras 73, 76.
[85] The procedure is now governed by s.28 of the Crime (Sentencing) Act 1997.
[86] Section 34(1) and (2); see generally *Archbold* (2001) paras 5.199 to 5.212.
[87] [1993] 1 W.L.R. 223.
[88] See *Practice Direction*, para. 3.

for the purposes of the Criminal Appeal Act 1968 and so may be subject to appeal.[89]

16–26 Once the tariff period has expired the applicant's case is referred automatically to the Parole Board which must hold an oral hearings before a "Discretionary Lifer Panel" (DLP), at which the applicant is legally represented and has a right to give evidence and to cross-examine. The Act provides for two year intervals between DLP hearings.[90] However in *AT v. United Kingdom*[91] the Commission held that periodic review under Article 5(4) should—on the facts of the case— have been more frequent than the two years specified in the Act. This conclusion, which was subsequently endorsed by the Committee of Ministers, was based partly on evidence that the applicant was no longer mentally ill, and partly on a recommendation from the previous DLP for an earlier review. Similarly, in *Oldham v. United Kingdom*[92] a recalled life sentence prisoner attended courses to address his problems in the first eight months after recall, but was then informed that it would be a further 16 months before the need for his continued detention could be reviewed. The Court held that, given that the applicant's condition was subject to change over time, the period of two years between reviews was not sufficiently "speedy" to comply with Article 5(4). However, that decision was confined to its own facts in *R. v. Parole Board ex parte MacNeil*,[93] where Peter Gibson L.J. held that an interval of two years between reviews by the Parole Board did not constitute a breach of Article 5(4) on the facts of the case.

II. *Detention during Her Majesty's Pleasure*

16–27 In *Abed Hussain v. United Kingdom*[94] the European Court of Human Rights held that juveniles convicted of murder and detained during Her Majesty's Pleasure under section 53(1) of the Children and Young Persons Act 1933 are entitled to the same regular periodic review by the Parole Board as discretionary life sentence prisoners:

"It is undisputed that in its statutory origins the expression 'during Her Majesty's pleasure' had a clearly preventative purpose and that—unlike sentences of life custody or life imprisonment—the word 'life' is not mentioned in the description of the sentence . . . In the case of young persons convicted of serious crimes, the corresponding sentence undoubtedly contains a punitive element and accordingly a tariff is set to reflect the requirements of retribution and deterrence. However, an indeterminate term of detention for a convicted young person, which may be as long as that person's life, can only be justified by considerations based on the need to protect the public. These considerations, centred on an assessment of the young offender's character and mental state and of his or her resulting dangerousness to society, must of necessity take into account any developments in the young offender's personality and attitude as he or she grows older . . . Against the foregoing background the Court concludes that the applicant's sentence, after the expiration of his tariff, is more comparable to a discretionary life sentence . . . The decisive ground for the applicant's continued detention was and continues to be his dangerousness to society, a characteristic susceptible to change with

---

[89] *R. v. Dalton* [1995] 2 Cr. App. R. 340 (C.A.).
[90] Section 34(5)(b).
[91] [1996] E.H.R.L.R. 92.
[92] [2000] Crim. L.R. 1011.
[93] *The Times*, April 18, 2001.
[94] (1996) 22 E.H.R.R. 1.

the passage of time. Accordingly, new issues of lawfulness may arise in the course of detention and the applicant is entitled under Article 5(4) to take proceedings to have these issues decided by a court at reasonable intervals."[95]

Parliament has given effect to this decision in section 28 of the Crime (Sentences) Act 1997, which extends to juveniles sentenced to HMP detention the same rights in the post-tariff phase of detention as those which apply to a discretionary life sentence prisoner (*i.e.* a right to periodic review by way of an oral hearing before an HMP panel of the Parole Board.)

Two aspects of the HMP procedure were challenged successfully by the appli-   **16–28**
cants in *T and V. v. United Kingdom*.[96] The Court held unanimously that the fixing of the tariff by the Home Secretary, a member of the Executive, violates the applicants' right under Article 6(1) to a "fair and public hearing . . . by an independent and impartial tribunal." The Court held that the fixing of the tariff period "amounts to a sentencing exercise,"[97] and that the Home Secretary "was clearly not independent of the executive."[98] The applicants also challenged the sentence under Article 5(4), alleging that there was no provision for periodic judicial review of the lawfulness of continued detention. Once again, the Court unanimously found a violation:

"Given that the sentence of detention during Her Majesty's Pleasure is indeterminate and that the tariff was initially set by the Home Secretary rather than the sentencing judge, it cannot be said that the supervision require by Article 5(4) was incorporated in the trial court's sentence.[99] . . . Moreover, the Home Secretary's decision setting the tariff was quashed by the House of Lords on 12 June 1997 and no new tariff has since been substituted. This failure to set a new tariff means that the applicant's entitlement to access to a tribunal for periodic review of the continuing lawfulness of his detention remains inchoate. It follows that the applicant has been deprived, since his conviction in November 1993, of the opportunity to have the lawfulness of his detention reviewed by a judicial body in accordance with Article 5(4)."[1]

The judgment in this case has already led to changes. The Home Secretary has   **16–29**
relinquished his power, and the tariff will now be set by the trial judge in the same way as for adults subject to discretionary life sentences. The Lord Chief Justice has issued a Practice Direction, which anticipates legislation to give statutory force to the new procedure, and which also sets out the various factors which judges should take into account when setting tariff periods for murder by offenders of all ages.[2]

III. *Mandatory Life Sentences for Murder*

The mandatory sentence of life imprisonment for murder was first analysed as   **16–30**
ordering lifelong punitive detention in the Myra Hindley case,[3] and this approach

---

[95] *ibid.*, at paras 53–54.
[96] (2000) 30 E.H.R.R. 121.
[97] *T and V v. United Kingdom, ibid.*, para. 111.
[98] *ibid.*, para. 114.
[99] The Court here referred to *De Wilde, Ooms and Versyp v. Belgium* (1979–80) 1 E.H.R.R. 373, para. 76, and to *Wynne v. United Kingdom* (1995) 19 E.H.R.R. 353, para. 36.
[1] *T and V v. United Kingdom*, paras 120–122.
[2] *Practice Statement (Life Sentences for Murder)* [2000] 2 Cr.App.R. 457.
[3] *X v. United Kingdom* (1975) 3 D.R. 10.

was followed in *Thynne, Wilson and Gunnell v. United Kingdom*.[4] In *Wynne v. United Kingdom*[5] the Court had to determine whether the rights accorded to those subject to discretionary life sentences in *Thynne* should be extended to those convicted of murder and sentenced to a mandatory life sentence. The applicant argued that the distinctions between the two forms of life sentence had narrowed to such an extent that it was no longer possible to distinguish between them for the purposes of Article 5(4). In particular, both sentences involved the fixing of a tariff period for retribution and deterrence before which release is impossible. Thereafter release was determined by the danger which the prisoner was considered to pose to the public. The applicant pointed to the observations of Lord Mustill in *R. v. Secretary of State for the Home Department ex parte Doody*[6]:

> "The discretionary and mandatory life sentences, having in the past grown apart, may now be converging. Nevertheless, on the statutory framework, the underlying theory and the current practice, there remains a substantial difference between them. It may be—I express no opinion—that the time is approaching when the effect of the two types of sentence should be further assimilated."[7]

16-31   The Strasbourg Court, however, considered that the essential rationale of the mandatory life sentence—namely, that the crime of murder was so serious that the offender must be considered to have forfeited his liberty to the state for life[8]—meant that early release in this context was a privilege rather than a right. Accordingly, there was no right under Article 5(4) to periodic review in the post-tariff phase of detention. Equally, it was not a requirement of Article 5 that it should be the judge (rather than the Secretary of State) who has responsibility for fixing the tariff period:

> "[T]he fact remains that the mandatory sentence belongs to a different category from the discretionary sentence in the sense that it is imposed automatically as the punishment for the offence of murder, irrespective of considerations pertaining to the dangerousness of the offender. That mandatory life prisoners do not actually spend the rest of their lives in prison,[9] and that a notional tariff period is also established in such cases . . . does not alter this essential distinction between the two types of sentence . . . Against the above background, the Court sees no reason to depart from the finding in the *Thynne, Wilson and Gunnell* case that, as regards mandatory life sentences, the guarantee of Article 5(4) was satisfied by the original trial and appeal proceedings and confers no additional right to challenge the lawfulness of continuing detention or re-detention following revocation of the life licence."[10]

16-32   The equanimity with which the Court viewed the role of the Home Secretary in setting the tariff period for offenders convicted of murder is disappointing, and may have to be revisited in the light of *T and V. v. United Kingdom*.[11] One might also dispute the conclusion that detention in the post-tariff period does not have a preventive element, which ought therefore to attract the safeguards of Article

---

[4] (1991) 13 E.H.R.R. 666.
[5] (1995) 19 E.H.R.R. 333.
[6] [1994] 1 A.C. 531.
[7] *ibid.*, at 105.
[8] For a similar conclusion, see the decision of the Supreme Court of Canada in *Arkell* [1990] 2 S.C.R. 695.
[9] These words are considered below, at para. 16–33.
[10] (1995) 19 E.H.R.R. 333 at paras. 35–36.
[11] Above, para. 16–28.

5(4). Since the *Wynne* judgment the House of Lords has adopted a distinctly stronger line on the matter, and in *R. v. Secretary of State for the Home Department, ex parte Pierson*[12] the House decided, by a majority, to allow judicial review of the Home Secretary's decision to raise the tariff period for the applicant from 15 to 20 years, on the basis that the new policy announced by the Home Secretary in 1993 was either unlawful or, at least, insufficient to authorise the increase.[13] It is therefore suggested that the *Wynne* judgment should not be regarded as the last word on the mandatory sentence for murder. However, in *R. v. Secretary of State for the Home Department ex parte Anderson*[14] a challenge to the Home Secretary's role was rejected by the Divisional Court. The Court followed the approach of *Wynne* in declaring that the sentence for murder is imprisonment for life, and that the setting of the tariff is part of the administrative arrangements for early release and not a judicial exercise to which Article 6 ought to apply.

In this connection it is relevant that the German Constitutional Court has **16–33** considered the constitutionality of the mandatory life sentence for murder under German law.[15] In its major decision in 1977 the Court held that life imprisonment does not infringe the fundamental right to human dignity guaranteed by Article 1 of the German Constitution.[16] However, the Court took seriously the argument that the psychological effects of life imprisonment could be crushing and recognised a duty on the State to provide a prison regime aimed at resocialization, in order to respect human dignity. This and other arguments in the case might be developed in relation to the notion of "inhuman punishment" under Article 3 of the Convention. In the passage from the European Court's judgment in *Wynne v. United Kingdom* (cited above),[17] the Court observed that "mandatory life prisoners do not actually spend the rest of their lives in prison", an observation that raises questions about the humanity of ordering a murderer to be detained for his whole natural life. This question has also been considered by the German Constitutional Court, albeit in the context of the German constitution's fundamental guarantee of human dignity. In its 1977 decision there was support for the conclusion that "life means life" would be inhuman, but in its 1983 decision it accepted that this would not be incompatible with the constitutional right.[18]

IV. *Custody for Life*

As we have seen the Court has so far accepted that the mandatory sentence of life **16–34** imprisonment for murder authorises lifelong retributive detention, such that early release is a matter of executive clemency. Accordingly the sentence does not

---

[12] [1998] A.C. 539.
[13] See also the decision of the Ontario Court of Appeal in *Logan* (1986) 51 C.R. (3d) 326, declaring invalid a legislative provision purporting to increase the "minimum non-parole period" for offenders already serving life imprisonment for murder. Section 11(I) of the Charter deals expressly with cases where the statutory punishment is increased between offence and the time of sentencing, stating that the offender should have the benefit of the lesser punishment.
[14] *The Times*, February 27, 2001.
[15] For discussion, see D. van Zyl Smit, "Is Life Imprisonment Constitutional? The German Experience" [1992] *Public Law* 263.
[16] *B.Verf.G.E.* 45 187 of June 21, 1977.
[17] Above, para. 16–31.
[18] *B.Verf.G.E.* 64 261 of June 28, 1983.

attract the right to Article 5(4) review and (as the authorities presently stand) the fixing of the tariff by the Home Secretary does not infringe Article 6. On the other hand, both the discretionary life sentence and the mandatory sentence of detention during Her Majesty's Pleasure for a juvenile convicted of murder have been recognised as partly preventive in character. In respect of both sentences the tariff must be judicially determined and there is a right to an oral hearing before the Parole Board in the post-tariff phase of detention. How then should the Court approach the mandatory sentence of custody for life imposed on a person aged 18 to 20 who has been convicted of murder? Is it to be assimilated to the mandatory life sentence for murder in respect of an adult, or the mandatory sentence of HMP detention in respect of a juvenile?

16–35   In *Bromfield v. United Kingdom*[19] the Commission held, in the case of a 20 year old, that:

> "Custody for life is similar to mandatory life imprisonment for murder in that, like the latter, it has an essentially punitive character and is imposed because of the inherent gravity of the offence. The Commission is unable to agree with the applicant's submission that the sentence of custody for life, as in the case of detention during Her Majesty's Pleasure, is based on considerations such as the offender's immaturity and danger to society which effectively suggest the existence of factors which may change over time thereby requiring periodic judicial review of the lawfulness of the continued detention."

In *Ryan v. United Kingdom*[20] the Commission reached the same conclusion, effectively assimilating custody for life with the mandatory life sentence for murder.

V. *Automatic Life Imprisonment under the Crime (Sentences) Act 1997*

16–36   Section 2 of the Crime (Sentences) Act 1997 (now consolidated as section 109 of the Powers of Criminal Courts (Sentencing) Act 2000) requires a court, on convicting of a "serious offence" someone who has at least one previous conviction for a "serious offence", to impose a sentence of life imprisonment unless it finds "exceptional circumstances" for not doing so. At least part of the rationale for introducing this measure was preventive, in terms of greater public protection,[21] and therefore the sentence might be placed in the mixed punitive-preventive category for Convention purposes.[22] However, where this sentence differs from the discretionary life sentence is that there need be no finding by the trial court that the offender is dangerous: the life sentence follows automatically on the second conviction for any of the "serious offences" listed. However, if the measure is to be regarded as having a significant preventive element, its imposition in each case must surely be preceded by a judicial assessment of the evidence of dangerousness. In *Offen et al,*[23] the Court of Appeal held that the automatic life sentence is undoubtedly a partly or wholly preventive sentence,

---

[19] (1998) 26 E.H.R.R. CD 138.
[20] (1999) 27 E.H.R.R. CD 204.
[21] Home Office, *Protecting the Public*, Cmnd. 3190, (1996), para. 10.11.
[22] Under ss.2 and 28 of the Crime (Sentences) Act 1997 the judge has to specify a minimum period of detention: the first appellate case on this was *Errington* [1999] Crim. L.R. 91.
[23] [2001] 1 W.L.R. 253.

and that therefore the task of the courts should be to ensure that such a sentence is only passed where there is evidence of the need for prevention. Lord Woolf, C.J., therefore held that such a sentence will not contravene Convention rights if courts apply the statutory provision so that "it did not result in offenders being sentenced to life imprisonment when they did not constitute a significant risk to the public." Thus: "If the offences were of a different kind, or if there was a long period which elapsed between the offences during which the offender had not committed other offences, that might be a very relevant indicator as to the degree of risk to the public that he constituted."

Lord Woolf held that to relate "exceptional circumstances" directly to the need **16-37** for public protection from the defendant would be in accordance with the intentions behind the automatic life sentence, as well as consistent with the Human Rights Act. It would prevent an offender from being subjected to arbitrary detention in breach of Article 5. The result is that several decisions made in the early years of the automatic life sentence, and notably the leading authority of *Kelly*,[24] are effectively overrruled.

VI. *Hospital Orders with Restrictions without Limit of Time*

Under sections 37 and 41 of the Mental Health Act 1983 a court may, on **16-38** receiving the necessary psychiatric evidence, impose a hospital order with a restriction order without limit of time. This is a purely preventive order, to be made only after certain procedural requirements have been fulfilled and where it is held necessary in order to "protect the public from serious harm from" the offender.[25] Its predecessor was considered by the Strasbourg Court in *X v. United Kingdom*[26] and found to be in breach of Article 5(4), in that release was in the hands of the Home Secretary and there was no means of testing the lawfulness of detention before a court.[27] The law was changed in the 1983 Act, and a Mental Health Review Tribunal (chaired by a judge) is now regarded as a court for this purpose and has the power to direct release without requesting the leave of the Home Secretary.[28] Section 46 of the Crime (Sentences) Act 1997 introduced a new form of order, the hospital and limitation direction, which may be added to a prison sentence (including a discretionary or automatic life sentence) in certain circumstances.[29] In *R. v. Mental Health Review Tribunal, North and East London Region and anor.*[30] the Court of Appeal issued a declaration of incompatibility holding that sections 72 and 73 of the Mental Health Act 1983 were incompatible

---

[24] [1999] 2 Cr. App. R. (S) 176; see also, *e.g., Turner* [2000] Crim. L.R. 492.
[25] *cf. Erkalo v. Netherlands* (1999) 28 E.H.R.R. 509, where the Court found a violation in respect of the Netherlands procedure, where the government had failed to make a timely application for the continuation of the applicant's detention, even though he was eligible for early release.
[26] (1982) 4 E.H.R.R. 188.
[27] See also *Gordon v. United Kingdom* (1986) 47 D.R. 36 (Commission) and 46 (Committee of Ministers).
[28] The tribunal has a duty to discharge a patient in certain circumstances: *cf.* the recent decision in *Johnson v. United Kingdom* (1999) 27 E.H.R.R. 296, finding a violation where the conditional discharge of an unrestricted patient had been ordered subject to finding a place at a hostel where he could reside, but where no hostel place was forthcoming and he remained in detention for a further three years.
[29] For further discussion, see N. Eastman and J. Peay, "Sentencing Psychopaths: is the 'Hospital and Limitation Direction' an Ill-Considered Hybrid?" [1998] Crim. L.R. 93.
[30] *The Times*, April 2, 2001.

with Article 5 since they reversed the burden of proof onto the patient to satisfy the tribunal that he was no longer suffering from a mental disorder warranting detention.

VII. *Longer than Normal Sentences*

16–39   In *Mansell v. United Kingdom*[31] an attempt was made to apply the Article 5(4) principle to "longer than normal" sentences imposed under section 2(2)(b) of the Criminal Justice Act 1991 (now consolidated as section 80 of the Powers of Criminal Courts (Sentencing) Act 2000). Under this section the Crown Court is required to impose a sentence which is longer than that commensurate with the seriousness of the offence where (a) an offender is convicted of a violent or sexual offence and (b) in the opinion of the judge it is necessary to impose a longer than normal sentence to "protect the public from serious harm from the offender". The applicant was convicted on three counts of indecent assault on men aged between 18 and 22. He had previously been convicted for indecent assault and kidnapping of an 18 year old man. In sentencing the applicant the judge stated that although a sentence of two and a half years imprisonment would normally be appropriate for an act of indecent assault, the proper sentence— having regard to the need to protect the public—was five years. The applicant was refused parole, and applied to the Commission, alleging a breach of Article 5(4). He submitted that since two and a half years of his sentence had been imposed on the grounds of dangerousness, he was entitled to the same protection during the extended portion of his sentence as a discretionary lifer in the post-tariff phase of detention. The Commission declared the application manifestly ill-founded, on the ground that there was an essential distinction between a fixed term sentence and an indeterminate sentence. There was—in the Commission's view—no question of the sentence having been imposed because of the presence of factors which "were susceptible to change with the passage of time." Rather, there was an element of "simple" punishment as well as an element of deterrence. In the Commission's view, nothing in the sentencing procedure indicated that the fixed term sentence of five years imprisonment was anything other than a sentence which was imposed as punishment for the offences committed. As such the judicial control required by Article 5(4) was incorporated in the original conviction and sentence, and Article 5(4) did not apply to the parole proceedings in which the applicant was denied an oral hearing.

16–40   This is a difficult decision. There is absolutely no doubt that the purpose of "longer than normal" sentences is partly preventive[32]: "public protection" is mentioned in the sub-section, and the duty of courts to impose such sentences is restricted to cases where "serious harm" is in prospect.[33] The proper approach for a trial judge, having decided that a case qualifies for a "longer than normal" sentence, is to consider what the normal sentence would be for the offence and then to add an "enhancement" for additional public protection. In some very serious cases, as Lord Taylor C.J. recognised in his judgment in the Court of

---

[31] [1997] E.H.R.L.R. 666.
[32] For full discussion, see A. von Hirsch and A. Ashworth, "Protective Sentencing under Section 2(2)(b): the Criteria for Dangerousness" [1996] Crim. L.R. 175.
[33] "Serious harm" is defined in s.31(3) of the Criminal Justice Act 1991.

Appeal in *Mansell*[34] itself, the proper sentence will be life imprisonment. Where that is not the case, the judge should lengthen the sentence whilst retaining some proportionality with the seriousness of the offence. This confirms that sentences imposed under this provision are partly punitive and partly preventive. The Commission was therefore wrong to conclude, as it did in *Mansell*, that there was "no question of the sentence being imposed because of the presence of factors which 'were susceptible to change with the passage of time, namely mental instability and dangerousness'."[35] However, "longer than normal" sentences are not indeterminate, unlike all the other forms of preventive sentence discussed above. The actual time served will be subject to the decision of the Parole Board, but in that respect they do not differ from all other fixed term sentences of four years and longer. The fuller kind of review being sought by the applicant is reserved for indeterminate sentences. This may have been the distinction for which the Commission was reaching, but unfortunately its actual reasoning is erroneous.

C. CUSTODIAL SENTENCES: CREDIT FOR TIME SERVED

The question of making allowance for time already served in custody has arisen, **16-41** in respect of the Convention, in two different situations—custody abroad, and custody pending appeal. First, there are persons who have already served a period in prison abroad. Section 47 of the Criminal Justice Act 1991 allows a court which is dealing with an offender who has been extradited to the United Kingdom to order that the whole or part of the time spent in foreign custody should count as a "relevant period" in computing the length of his sentence under section 67 of the Criminal Justice Act 1967.[36] Alternatively, a court can take account of the time served abroad by reducing the length of the sentence imposed rather than exercising the power under section 47.[37] Whichever procedure is followed, the matter is within the discretion of the trial judge, and the authorities establish that an offender who has deliberately prolonged his time in custody abroad should not be given credit for the full period.[38]

In *C v. United Kingdom*[39] the time spent by the applicant in custody abroad **16-42** awaiting extradition was not taken into account by the trial judge in computing the length of his prison sentence. The Commission held that this did not render the additional period of detention "arbitrary" for the purposes of Article 5. On the other hand, where detention prior to extradition from another signatory state was found by the Court to have exceeded the reasonable time guarantee in Article 5(3), the fact that the Crown Court judge who sentenced the applicant *had* taken the period into account in fixing the length of his sentence was held to be a ground for refusing to award compensation under Article 50.[40]

---

[34] (1994) 15 Cr. App. R. (S) 771 at 775.
[35] For critical discussion, see E. Fitzgerald, "The Criminal Justice Act 1991: Preventative Detention of the Dangerous Offender" [1995] 1 E.H.R.L.R. 39.
[36] As to the effect of s.67 of the 1967 Act see *Archbold* (2001) paras 5.129 *et seq.*
[37] *R. v. Vincent* [1996] 2 Cr. App. R. (S) 6.
[38] *R. v. Scalise and Rachel* (1985) 7 Cr. App. R. (S) 395; *R. v. Stone* (1988) 10 Cr. App. R. (S) 332; *R. v. Peffer* (1991) 13 Cr. App. R. (S) 150.
[39] (1985) 43 D.R. 177.
[40] *Scott v. Spain* (1997) 24 E.H.R.R. 391.

16–43   The question of time in custody in this country awaiting appeal was raised in
Monnell and Morris v. United Kingdom,[41] where the applicants complained that
the decision of the Court of Appeal, that time spent awaiting appeal should not
count towards sentence because they had both persisted in unmeritorious appeals,
breached Article 5(1)(a). The Court recognised that the Court of Appeal had
exercised its statutory power for deterrent reasons, and that this had no connection with the offences committed, but held that nonetheless the statutory power
was "an inherent part of the criminal appeal process following conviction" and
that it "pursues a legitimate aim" within Article 5(1)(a).[42] Also relevant was the
fact that in many continental systems a sentence of imprisonment does not start
to run until the appeal process has been terminated. The Court in *Monnell and
Morris* did not directly consider the inhibiting effect which this power may have
on the exercise of a right of appeal in borderline cases. In the light of the Court's
subsequent decision in *Omar v. France*,[43] it is open to serious doubt whether the
loss of time provisions[44] would be regarded as compatible with the right of
access to an appellate court if the issue were to be reconsidered today. In *Omar*
the Court held that a rule which required an appellant to surrender to custody
before he could be heard on appeal against his conviction was incompatible with
Article 6 since it imposed a disproportionate restriction on the exercise of his
right of appeal.[45] The same principle should surely apply where the court
considering the appeal has power to impose what is, in effect, an additional
prison sentence as a deterrent against appeals which turn out, on examination, to
be unmeritorious.

D. EQUAL TREATMENT IN SENTENCING

16–44   Article 14 of the Convention provides that Convention rights are to be secured
"without discrimination on any ground such as sex, race, colour, language,
religion, political or other opinion, national or social origin . . . property, birth or
other status." Article 14 must be pleaded in conjunction with another Convention
right, but it is not necessary to establish that the substantive right concerned has
been violated.[46] In order to rely on Article 14, the applicant need only establish
that his claim falls "within the ambit" of the right concerned.[47] Once this hurdle
is overcome, the applicant must then show that there has been a difference in
treatment *in the delivery* of the right as between himself and another person in a

---

[41] (1988) 10 E.H.R.R. 205, criticised in paras 17–21 to 17–22 below.
[42] *ibid.*, at para. 46.
[43] (2000) 29 E.H.R.R. 210.
[44] Under the Criminal Appeal Act 1968, s.29(1) the Court of Appeal may, if it considers that an
appeal is without merit, direct that time served between the imposition of the sentence and the
disposal of the appeal should not count towards the accused person's sentence. As to the circumstances in which such an order may be made see *Practice Direction (Crime: Sentences: Loss of Time)*
[1980] 1 W.L.R. 270.
[45] For the effect of this decision on the practice of the Court of Appeal (Criminal Division) see *R. v.
Charles, R. v. Tucker, The Times,* February 20, 2001 (the Registrar should no longer treat an
application for leave to appeal on behalf of a defendant who has absconded as ineffective).
[46] *Belgian Linguistics Case (No. 1)* (1979–80) 1 E.H.R.R. 241, and *(No. 2)* (1979–80) 1 E.H.R.R.
252.
[47] *Abdulaziz, Cabales and Balkandali v. United Kingdom* (1985) 7 E.H.R.R. 471 at para. 71; *Inze v.
Austria* (1988) 10 E.H.R.R. 394 at para. 36; *Van der Mussele v. Belgium* (1984) 6 E.H.R.R. 163 at
para. 43.

relevantly similar position. If such a difference in treatment is established then there will be a violation of Article 14 if *either* (a) the difference does not pursue a legitimate aim (in the sense that there is no "objective and reasonable justification" for it) *or* (b) there is no reasonable relationship of proportionality between the means employed and the end sought to be achieved. Thus in the *Belgian Linguistics* case the Court observed: "[A] difference in treatment in the exercise of a right laid down in the Convention must not only pursue a legitimate aim: Article 14 is likewise violated when it is clearly established that there is no reasonable relationship of proportionality between the means employed and the end sought to be realised."[48] The difference in treatment need not be on grounds analogous to race or sex. The use of the words "on any such grounds as", and the inclusion of "any other status" in the non-exhaustive list of prohibited grounds within Article 14 permits comparisons to be made on the basis of any abiding characteristic.[49] Four examples may be briefly discussed—AIDS, race, sex, and age.

The potential application of Article 14 in the sentencing context is illustrated by   **16–45** *RM v. United Kingdom.*[50] In that case the applicant, who was suffering from HIV/ AIDS had been sentenced to imprisonment for drugs offences. He sought to rely on his illness as a mitigating factor. The sentencing judge held that he was bound by the Court of Appeal decision in *R. v. Stark*[51] to ignore HIV/AIDS as a mitigating circumstance. In *Stark* the Court of Appeal had held that HIV/AIDS was a matter not for mitigation, but for the Secretary of State in exercising the power of compassionate release. *M* appealed against sentence but the Court of Appeal, again applying *Stark*, confirmed that the illness was immaterial to sentence.[52]

In his application to the Commission, *M* alleged a violation of Article 14 of the   **16–46** Convention in conjunction with Article 5. The sentencing decision clearly fell "within the ambit" of Article 5 (1)(a) which permits deprivation of liberty "after conviction by a competent court". The applicant pointed to a range of sentencing precedents which established that other debilitating fatal illnesses were regularly treated as mitigating circumstances by the domestic courts. Accordingly he submitted that there had been an unjustified difference in treatment between the sentencing of a defendant with HIV/AIDS and the sentencing of defendants with other comparable illnesses. In its response the Government argued that this difference in treatment had an objective and reasonable justification. HIV/AIDS —so the argument went—was less predictable in its outcome than the other terminal illnesses which the applicant had relied upon as comparators. The Commission accepted that Article 14 was capable of applying in conjunction with Article 5 so as to prohibit discrimination in sentencing. Nevertheless, on the facts the Commission found that the difference in treatment was justified for the reasons advanced by the Government. The Court of Appeal has subsequently reaffirmed the principle that a medical condition which may at some future date affect either life expectancy or the prison authorities' ability to treat the prisoner

---

[48] (1979–80) 1 E.H.R.R. 252 at para. 10.
[49] *Stubbings v. United Kingdom* (1997) 23 E.H.R.R. 213 at para. 70.
[50] (1994) 77A D.R. 98.
[51] (1992) 13 Cr. App. R. (S) 548.
[52] *Moore* (1993) 15 Cr. App. R. (S) 97.

satisfactorily is not a reason to alter the sentence, and should be left for the Home Office and Parole Board to deal with appropriately.[53]

16–47   In *Grice v. United Kingdom*[54] the Commission declared inadmissible an application based on alleged violations of Articles 3 and 14. The applicant's case was that his continued imprisonment amounted to "inhuman punishment", but the Commission found no evidence that the detention of an AIDS sufferer has any long term effect on his health or life expectancy. The applicant also alleged that the Home Office discriminated against him, as an AIDS sufferer, in failing to grant compassionate early release when it did so more readily for prisoners suffering from cancer or senile dementia. The Commission held that if release procedures did discriminate there would indeed be a case under Articles 5 and 14, but it found no evidence of discrimination on the facts.

16–48   The Commission has, in the past, recognised that "where a settled sentencing policy appears to affect individuals in a discriminatory fashion . . . this may raise issues under Article 5 read in conjunction with Article 14".[55] In general, however, the more insidious forms of discrimination, such as race and sex discrimination, do not manifest themselves in settled sentencing policy. Under the Human Rights Act, an individual needs to be able to demonstrate that he or she is a "victim" of a violation of the Convention.[56] In the context of sentencing discrimination, this is likely to raise almost insurmountable difficulties. Research into race and sentencing has found that offenders from an Afro-Caribbean background were, after taking account of the seriousness of their offences and their criminal records, some five per cent more likely to be sent to prison, with an even higher probability at one court and a lower probability at another.[57] These findings consist of strong statistical inferences, but they do not demonstrate discrimination in any particular case. This would of course be extremely difficult to prove, unless injudicious remarks were made at the sentencing stage.

16–49   Although the general statistical evidence suggests elements of leniency rather than greater severity in the sentencing of women,[58] there have been several findings that suggest undue severity against certain types of woman offender who, it is alleged, receive longer sentences because of their "inappropriate" lifestyle.[59] Here too, however, discrimination is likely to be difficult to prove in an individual case, although it may be easier to demonstrate that a particular sentence has a disproportionate impact where the female defendant has children. It should be recalled that the question whether a sentence is so disproportionately severe as to be an "inhuman punishment" contrary to Article 3 depends to some extent on the "sex, age and state of health" of the offender.[60] The imposition of

---

[53] *Bernard* [1997] 1 Cr. App. R. (S) 135; *cf. Green* (1992) 13 Cr. App. R. (S) 613 for an exceptional case.
[54] (1994) 77 D.R. 90.
[55] *Neilson v. United Kingdom* (1986) 49 D.R. 170.
[56] See para. 3–43 above.
[57] R. Hood, *Race and Sentencing* (1992), p.78; see also R. Hood, "Race and Sentencing—a Reply" [1995] Crim. L.R. 272.
[58] C. Hedderman and L. Gelsthorpe (eds.), *Understanding the Sentencing of Women* (Home Office, 1997).
[59] See, for example, A. Morris, "Sex and Sentencing" [1988] Crim. L.R. 163 at 166–167.
[60] *Ireland v. United Kingdom* (1979–80) 2 E.H.R.R. 25 at para. 162.

a custodial sentence on the mother of a young child (which enforces separation between the two) might be thought to raise proportionality issues in certain cases[61]; as might the imposition of a custodial sentence on a pregnant woman, which may mean that she gives birth whilst serving a prison sentence.[62]

An example of a settled policy which is arguably in breach of Articles 5 and 14 **16-50** is section 23(5) of the Children and Young Persons Act 1969. Under section 23(5), read in conjunction with the Secure Remands and Committals (Prescribed Descriptions of Children and Young Persons) Order 1999,[63] a 14 year old boy may be remanded into local authority accommodation pending trial, whereas a girl of the same age cannot be. In the absence of a clear justification for this difference of treatment, the policy would appear to be incompatible with the Convention.

Age-based arguments are most likely to arise where the offender is very young. **16-51** However, we have already noted that this was one of the unsuccessful grounds of challenge in *T and V v. United Kingdom*.[64] The Court recited the provision in Article 37 of the United Nations Convention on the Rights of the Child, to the effect that detention of a child "shall be used only as a measure of last resort and for the shortest appropriate time", and also Rule 17(1)(b) of the Beijing Rules, recommending that "restrictions on the personal liberty of the juvenile . . . shall be limited to the possible minimum." Nevertheless, the Court concluded that, taking account of all the circumstances including the fact that the two applicants were aged only 11 when sentenced, punitive detention for six years could not be said to amount to inhuman or degrading treatment.[65]

It is interesting in this context to note that in the case of *R. v. Secretary of State* **16-51a** *for the Home Department ex parte Pearson and others*[66] the High Court held that section 3(1) of the Representation of the People Act 1983, which prohibits serving prisoners from voting in parliamentary or local government elections, is not incompatible with Article 3 of the First Protocol, which provides for the holding of free elections, and ensures the "free expression of the opinion of the people in the choice of the legislature." The Court emphasised that remand prisoners and mental patients could, since February 2001, vote under the Representation of the People Act 2000 and that in relation to discretionary lifers who had not been released on licence there was no breach of the requirement in Article 14 not to discriminate in the securing of rights.

E. CONSENT TO COMMUNITY SERVICE ORDERS

Article 4(2) of the Convention declares that "no one shall be required to perform **16-52** forced or compulsory labour", and Article 4(3) lists various forms of work to

---

[61] In *Togher v. United Kingdom* [1998] E.H.R.L.R. 636 the Commission declared admissible a complaint, under Art. 3, by a young mother remanded in custody and separated from her new-born child, whom she had been breast-feeding. For broader evidence, see the report by D. Caddle and D. Crisp, *Mothers in Prison*, Home Office Research Findings No.38 (1997).
[62] See, *e.g., Scott* (1990) 12 Cr. App. R. (S) 23.
[63] S.I. 1999 No. 1265.
[64] (2000) 30 E.H.R.R. 121.
[65] *T and V v. United Kingdom, ibid.*, paras 97–99.
[66] *The Times*, April 17, 2001.

which Article 4(1) does not apply. Compulsory labour ordered by a court following conviction of an offence is not listed. When the community service order was introduced into English law in 1972, it was thought necessary to insert a requirement that the offender should consent to the order, so as to comply with Article 4(2) of the Convention. In 1995 the Government took the view that this had been an "over-cautious" interpretation,[67] and section 38 of the Crime (Sentences) Act 1997 removed the consent requirement. Does the community service order now breach the Convention in this respect? In *Van der Mussele v. Belgium*,[68] the Court held that compulsory labour would only violate Article 4(2) if it was both against the person's will and "unjust or oppressive".

16–53 It is well known that the giving of consent to a community service order was in many cases a sham, since the probable alternative sentence would be immediate custody. To that extent the 1997 amendment merely gave statutory effect to the existing reality. Article 4(3) expressly cites work carried out in prison or on conditional release as examples which fall outside the notion of compulsory labour. The Court in *Van der Mussele* emphasised that the categories set out in Article 4(3) are not to be regarded as an exhaustive list of exceptions, to be restrictively construed. Rather, they are illustrative of the limits to the concept of compulsory labour as it is understood in Article 4(1). This opens the way to analogical analysis, especially since the sentence of community service is less intrusive of individual rights than work required to be performed as part of a prison sentence. The omission of community service from Article 4(3) is best explained by the fact that it was not generally available as a sentence within Europe when the Convention was drafted. Applying the "living instrument" principle,[69] the Court would doubtless be influenced by its current availability in many European states. Given that community service is imposed as an alternative to custody, it seems most unlikely that a compulsory community service order would be found to violate Article 4.

F. PROCEEDINGS AGAINST FINE DEFAULTERS

16–53a When a fine defaulter is brought back to a magistrates' court for enforcement proceedings, it is normal for the justices' clerk or a court clerk to put questions to the offender. There is no prosecutor present, and so the clerk acts as inquisitor. When the justices consider what action to take, it is the clerk who advises them on the law. In *Corby JJ ex parte Mort*[70] the impartiality of the clerk's role in such proceedings was challenged, but the Divisional Court held that on the facts the clerk had not assumed a partisan role. The Court stated that fine enforcement proceedings are neither civil nor criminal, and that they could see no alternative to the clerk putting questions. However, the involvement of the clerk as an inquisitor, and then as adviser to the justices on the law, is potentially incompatible with Article 6. The proceedings are surely "criminal", in Convention

---

[67] Home Office, *Strengthening Punishment in the Community*, Cmnd. 2780, (1995), para. 4.20, citing the *Van der Mussele* decision (next note).
[68] (1984) 6 E.H.R.R. 163.
[69] See para. 2–18 above.
[70] (1998) 162 J.P. 310.

terms.[71] A recent Practice Direction attempts to explain and to limit the clerk's role in enforcement proceedings, and to emphasise the overriding duty of impartiality.[72]

G. SENTENCING PROCEDURE

In *X v. United Kingdom*[73] the Commission emphasised that Article 6 continues to apply at the sentencing stage.[74] Thus, the entitlements to *inter alia* legal representation and legal aid, a public hearing, equality of arms, adequate time and facilities, and free interpretation would all continue at a sentencing hearing: **16–54**

> "The Commission considers that complaints concerning proceedings on sentence, even after a plea of guilty, could raise issues under Art 6 of the Convention; so that for example a defendant should have the opportunity of being represented where the prosecution gives evidence in relation to sentence. In the opinion of the Commission, the determination of a criminal charge, within the meaning of Article 6(1) of the Convention, includes not only the determination of the guilt or innocence of the accused, but also in principle the determination of his sentence; and the expression 'everyone charged with a criminal offence' in Article 6(3) includes persons who, although already convicted, have not been sentenced. The Commission observes that questions of sentence may be closely related to questions of guilt or innocence, and that in the Criminal Procedure of many States Parties to the Convention, they cannot be separated at this stage of the proceedings."

The application of Article 6 to the sentencing stage has been accepted by the Commission and the Court, and was not regarded as a matter for dispute in the decision of the Court in *T and V v. United Kingdom*.[75] However, the concern of the Court is with the minimum procedural guarantees provided by Article 6 and its attendant jurisprudence. Thus, for example, Article 6 does not prevent a judge from taking account at the sentencing stage of matters that would not be admissible at the trial, such as the offender's previous convictions.[76]   **16–55**

Questions about the burden of proof at the sentencing stage have arisen in stark form in relation to the confiscation legislation. Provisions in the Drug Trafficking Act 1994 (and the Proceeds of Crime (Scotland) Act 1995) state that, after a person has been convicted of a drug trafficking offence, the court may make certain assumptions, "except insofar as any of them may be shown to be incorrect"in the particular offender's case. The presumption is that any property transferred to him in the six years before indictment represented the proceeds of drug trafficking, and is therefore liable to be confiscated. In *Benjafield*[77] the Court of Appeal had to deal with a challenge to the assumptions in the 1994 Act on the basis that they violate Article 6(2). Lord Woolf C.J. held that: **16–56**

---

[71] See *Benham v. United Kingdom* (1996) 22 E.H.R.R. 293; and see generally para. 4–20 above.
[72] *Practice Direction (Justices' Clerk to the Court)* [2001] 1 Cr. App. R. 147, para. 11.
[73] (1972) 2 Digest 766.
[74] This observation can not of course apply to the presumption of innocence in Art. 6(2). See para. 16–56 below.
[75] (2000) 30 E.H.R.R. 121.
[76] *Albert and le Compte v. Belgium* (1983) 5 E.H.R.R. 533.
[77] *The Times*, December 28, 2000 (CA Crim. Div.).

"The confiscation order is made in criminal proceedings. It is accepted by all parties that it is penal. It must therefore be regarded for the purposes of Article 6(1) as at least part of the determination of a criminal charge since there is no other option for which Article 6(1) provides. The fact that a defendant who does not comply with a confiscation order, which may not be based on criminal conduct proved at the trial, may be ordered to serve a substantial custodial sentence in default underlines that fact. A defendant threatened with consequences of this nature would be expected to be entitled to protection equivalent to that provided by Article 6(2) even if that paragraph did not exist, under Article 6(1)."

However, having held that the protection of Article 6(2) was relevant, Lord Woolf went on to conclude that "the interests of the public that those who have offended should not profit from their offending and should not use their criminal conduct to fund further offending," outweighed the offender's interest in not bearing a burden of proof on these matters. The Court of Appeal laid considerable emphasis on the fact that Parliament had so decreed, and that courts have a discretion not to make a confiscation order if there is a serious risk of injustice.

16–57 In *McIntosh v. HM Advocate*[78] the High Court of Justiciary had reached a different view, holding that the assumptions required by the legislation violate Article 6(2). The prosecution bears no burden of proof at all, and the statutory assumptions are "in a quite literal sense baseless," Lord Prosser held. The statute could have made them contingent on the raising of a reasonable suspicion by the prosecution, but it did not—the assumptions are automatic. On appeal to the Privy Council,[79] the prosecutor's appeal was allowed. Lord Bingham held that Article 6(2) does not apply to confiscation proceedings because the person against whom the application for an order is made is not "by virtue of that application a person charged with a criminal offence." This approach is problematic, because there is no doubt that a convicted defendant is a person charged with a criminal offence for the purpose of the other guarantees in Article 6, which are applicable both at the sentencing stage and during any appeal against conviction and sentence. A preferable approach would have been to hold that Article 6 is engaged, but that the specific guarantee in Article 6(2) cannot apply at this stage because, as Lord Hope pointed out, it states only that a person charged shall be presumed innocent "until proved guilty according to law." This leaves the difficulty that, when there has been an application for a confiscation order, there are underlying allegations that the offender has been concerned in other drug trafficking. Lord Hope answered this by arguing that confiscation proceedings are more in the nature of a civil process which does not require the court to assume criminal wrongdoing. However, their Lordships went on to hold that, even if Article 6(2) were held relevant (or, as Lord Woolf argued in *Benjafield*, Article 6(1) would imply similar protection), the drug trafficking legislation was "approved by a democratically elected Parliament and should not be at all readily rejected."

16–58 Not surprisingly, the procedure whereby a defendant may plead guilty and be sentenced without a trial or examination of the evidence has been held compatible with the right to a fair trial under Article 6. This is despite the fact that in

---

[78] Judgment of 13 October 2000.
[79] *The Times*, 8 February 2001. See also *Phillips v. United Kingdom*, judgment July 5, 2001, adopting Lord Hope's analysis of the point.

many European Countries no such procedure is available. In the later case of *X v. United Kingdom*[80] the Commission noted that:

"[U]nder English criminal procedure, if a person pleads guilty there is no trial in the usual sense; if the judge is satisfied that the accused understands the effect of his plea, his confession is recorded, and the subsequent proceedings are concerned only with the question of sentence. The Commission having examined this practice in the context of English criminal procedure, and also in other systems among those State Parties to the Convention where a similar practice is found, is satisfied that the procedure as such is not inconsistent with the requirements of Article 6(1) and (2) of the Convention. In arriving at this conclusion the Commission has had regard to the rules under which the practice operates and in particular to the safeguards which are provided to avoid the possibility of abuse."

The safeguards to which the Commission was adverting presumably include not **16–59** only the rules governing fitness to plead, equivocal pleas, and the availability of legal representation, but also the potential for a *Newton*[81] hearing—in which the burden of proof is on the prosecution—whenever a factual issue relevant to sentence is in dispute. Thus in *De Salvador Torres v. Spain*[82] the Court held that a defendant must be given due warning, to comply with Article 6(3)(a), of any circumstance to be alleged by the prosecution as constituting a factor aggravating sentence.[83] In this case the aggravating factor was that the defendant was a public official in a position of trust, which gave the court access to a higher sentence, and the Court found that he must have been well aware that that was regarded as an aggravating factor. Proper application of the extensive case-law following the *Newton* decision[84] should ensure that an offender is given the opportunity to contest any significant aggravating factor alleged by the prosecution, although sentencing principles relating to persons convicted on specimen counts were probably in breach of Article 6 of the Convention until the Court of Appeal decided the case of *Canavan, Kidd and Shaw*.[85]

In *X v. United Kingdom*[86] the trial judge observed in passing sentence that a **16–60** guilty plea would have constituted a mitigating circumstance. The applicants argued in Strasbourg that this amounted to the imposition of a heavier sentence on the grounds that they had contested the charge and accordingly that the sentence was in breach of Article 6. In rejecting the application as manifestly ill-founded the Commission observed:

"It is clear from the statements by the trial judge that he did not increase the applicants' sentence on the ground that they had affirmed their innocence throughout the trial, but rather refrained from reducing what he deemed to be the proper sentence, having regard to the gravity of the offences concerned."

---

[80] (1972) 40 C.D. 64 at 67; 2 Dig. 744.
[81] (1982) 77 Cr. App. R. 13.
[82] (1997) 23 E.H.R.R. 601.
[83] *cf.* the decision of the Supreme Court of Canada in *Lyons* [1987] 2 S.C.R. 309, to the effect that the Crown's failure to give the defendant notice that they intended to invite the sentencer to impose an extended sentence on grounds of public protection did not infringe s.7 of the Charter.
[84] See *Archbold* (2001), paras 5.10 to 5.23.
[85] [1998] 1 W.L.R. 604.
[86] (1975) 3 D.R. 10 at 16.

This is consistent with the theory behind the guilty plea discount in English law.[87] However, the compatibility of a discount for pleading guilty may depend on the extent of the inducement involved. In *Deweer v. Belgium*[88] the Court found a violation of Article 6 where the applicant had been offered the choice between paying a relatively modest fine by way of "compromise" or facing lengthy criminal proceedings. If he had chosen to contest the charge his butcher's shop would have remained closed by administrative order, thus depriving him of income. The Court held that a procedure under which an accused can waive the right to a hearing on payment of a penalty is not necessarily inconsistent with Article 6, but that such a settlement must be free from "constraint." In the present case there was such disproportionality between the fine and the consequences of contesting the proceedings that the settlement was tainted by constraint and therefore in breach of Article 6. In English cases the discount on a custodial sentence can be as much as one-third, and there may be some cases in which the effect of pleading guilty might make the difference between a custodial sentence and a community sentence. The practice of accepting a plea of guilty to a significantly less serious charge also has the capacity to exert pressure on the accused. The question arises whether a decision to plead guilty made in those circumstances is sufficiently free from "constraint." Such questions are, however, only likely to arise where the accused seeks to withdraw an apparently unequivocal plea of guilty.

16–61   In relation to mitigation of sentence, it will be recalled that the prosecution's duty of disclosure under Article 6 and the doctrine of "equality of arms" extends to the disclosure of "any material in their possession . . . which may assist the accused in exonerating himself *or in obtaining a reduction in sentence.*"[89] The recent Attorney-General's *Guidelines on the Disclosure of Information in Criminal Proceedings*[90] now recognise that the prosecution should consider disclosing any material which is relevant to sentence, such as information which might mitigate the seriousness of the offence or assist the accused to lay blame in whole or in part on a co-accused or another person.[91]

H. THE PROHIBITION ON RETROSPECTIVE PENALTIES

16–62   The second limb of Article 7(1) prohibits a court from imposing a heavier penalty than the one which was applicable at the time the offence was committed. Article 7 only prohibits an increase in the penalty for the offence, and so it is first necessary to determine what amounts to a "penalty", and then to determine when it is "heavier" than the one applicable at the time of the offence.

I. The Meaning of "Penalty"

16–63   The term "penalty" has an autonomous meaning, defined by reference to criteria analogous to those which apply to the term "criminal charge" in Article 6.[92] The

---

[87] See, for example, *Harper* [1968] 1 Q.B. 108.
[88] (1979–80) 2 E.H.R.R. 439.
[89] *Jespers v. Belgium* (1981) 27 D.R. 61, discussed in para. 14–89 above.
[90] November 29, 2000.
[91] Para. 44.
[92] *Welch v. United Kingdom* (1995) 20 E.H.R.R. 247 at paras 27–35.

domestic classification is no more than a starting point, and the Court has held that[93]:

"To render the protection offered by Article 7 effective, the Court must be free to go behind appearances and assess for itself whether a particular measure amounts in substance to a 'penalty' within the meaning of this provision . . . [T]he starting point in any assessment of a penalty is whether the measure in question is imposed following conviction for a 'criminal offence'. Other factors that may be taken into account as relevant in this connection are the nature and purpose of the measure in question; its characterisation under national law; the procedures involved in the making and implementation of the measure and its severity."

In *Welch v. United Kingdom*[94] a confiscation order was made under the Drug   **16–64**
Trafficking Offences Act 1986 in respect of an offence committed before the Act entered into force. Section 38(4) of the Act expressly gave retroactive effect to the powers of confiscation, provided the defendant had been *charged* after the Act came into force. The Government argued that the confiscation order was not a penalty but rather a preventive measure "designed to bleed the drug trafficking economy of its lifeblood." The Court held unanimously that the confiscation order was an additional penalty, and therefore in violation of Article 7(1). It noted that the measure had punitive as well as preventive and reparative aims; that the order was calculated by reference to "proceeds" rather than profits, and therefore had a reach beyond the mere restoration of the *status quo ante*; that the amount of the order could take account of the offender's culpability; and that the order was enforceable by a term of imprisonment in default.

The meaning of "penalty" does not extend to a (retrospective) increase—through   **16–65**
changes in the law governing early release—in the amount of a sentence actually served.[95] However, the House of Lords has struck down an attempt by a former Home Secretary to extend the tariff period (or "penal element") in a sentence of life imprisonment for murder from 15 to 20 years: this clearly concerned a penalty.[96]

An attempt was made to invoke Article 7 in *Ibbotson v. United Kingdom*[97] in   **16–66**
respect of the provisions for the registration of sex offenders introduced by the Sex Offenders Act 1997. The principal issue was whether the requirement to register is a "penalty" within the autonomous meaning of the term under the Convention, and the Commission ruled that it is not. It purported to follow the criteria set out by the Court in *Welch*, but whereas in that case it was held that confiscation of assets is punitive in nature, here the Commission concluded that the restrictions on sex offenders are preventive, "in the sense that the knowledge that a person has been registered with the police may dissuade him from

---

[93] *ibid.*, at paras. 27–28.
[94] (1995) 20 E.H.R.R. 247.
[95] *Hogben v. United Kingdom* (1986) 46 D.R. 231.
[96] *R. v. Secretary of State for the Home Department, ex parte Pierson* [1998] A.C. 539; see also the decision of the Ontario Court of Appeal in *Logan* (1986) 51 C.R. (3d) 326, holding invalid a statutory increase in the tariff period for persons serving life sentences for murder.
[97] (1999) 27 E.H.R.R. CD 332. See also *B v. Chief Constable of Avon and Somerset Constabulary* [2001] 1 W.L.R. 340 (considered at para. 4–35 above).

committing further offences." It was also relevant that the registration require-ment was far less "severe" than a confiscation order,[98] and that there was no provision for imprisonment in default: any proceedings for breach of the 1997 Act would have to be brought independently.

16–67   The Commission's response to the similar application in *Adamson v. United Kingdom*[99] started from the same premiss. The Commission recalled that the Sex Offenders Act is "an Act to require the notification of information to the police by persons who have committed sexual offences." The same conclusions were reached about the application of the *Welch* criteria to the requirement of notifica-tion, but in this case it was strongly argued that there was a danger of vigilante attacks on paedophiles, rendering the applicant vulnerable to further detriments. This line of argument was also pressed under Article 8: the Commission accepted that the applicant's right to respect for his private life was breached by the requirement to notify the police of changes of address, etc., but held that this was necessary in a democratic society for the protection of others from harm. The requirement to register with the police was regarded as proportionate, but the Commission added that there was "no evidence before it to suggest that the applicant is at particular risk of public humiliation or attack as a result of his obligations under the Act." This raises two questions. First, if there were compelling evidence of such a risk, would the same conclusion still be reached? Secondly, if the law were to be amended to require the police to inform local people about convicted paedophiles living in their area, would that increase the risk of vigilante action aimed specifically at a person such as the applicant in *Adamson*, and thus raise questions about compatibility with the Convention? The decision of the President of the Family Division in *Venables and Thompson v. News Group Newspapers and ors.*[1] to grant lifelong injunctions against the world protecting the new identities given to two juveniles who had been convicted of the murder of a two year old, and were due to be released, suggestst that there may indeed be a duty on the courts, under Articles 2 and 3 of the Convention, to prevent the dissemination of information which could lead to life-threatening reprisals against convicted offenders.

16–68   The definition of "penalty" arose in a different context in *Malige v. France*,[2] where the French system of justice meant that after a motoring offender had been convicted the imposition of penalty points on the driver was an administrative procedure. In domestic French law the system of penalty points is regarded as separate from the criminal law and as a "secondary penalty" of a purely administrative nature. However, the Court held that, since the docking of points was an automatic consequence of conviction, it has a sufficiently punitive and deterrent character to qualify as a penalty.

II. *Retrospectivity*

16–69   The Drug Trafficking Offences Act 1986 (DTOA), challenged successfully under Article 7 in *Welch v. United Kingdom*, was unusual in this country since its

---

[98] The Court rejected the applicant's argument that the hostility of the public towards persons on the Sex Offenders Register should be considered as part of the severity of the penalty.
[99] (1999) 28 E.H.R.R. CD 209.
[1] January 8, 2001.
[2] (1999) 28 E.H.R.R. 578.

provisions for confiscation of assets were explicitly retrospective. However, Dr Thomas has argued that nonetheless the provisions challenged in *Welch* could have been held to comply with Article 7.[3] The purpose of the prohibition on retrospective increases in sentence is to ensure that people are not punished more heavily than they contemplated when they committed the crime. Dr Thomas argues that under the pre-1986 law the offender in *Welch* could easily have been ordered to pay a sum similar to the £60,000 he was ordered to pay under the confiscation order: he could have been fined that amount, for example, and the enforcement procedure for unpaid fines would be similar to those for confiscation orders. Dr Thomas recognises that there are some counter-arguments, and leaves open the question whether an Article 7 challenge to the law relied on by the sentencing court (confiscation) can be answered by reference to a law that the court did not rely upon (fine).

Retrospective confiscation provisions identical to section 38(4) of the DTOA **16–70** have been included in subsequent confiscation legislation.[4] A challenge to the equivalent provisions in the Criminal Justice Act 1988 foundered on procedural grounds.[5] A challenge to section 38 of the DTOA was unsuccessful before the Commission in *Taylor v. United Kingdom*,[6] where confiscation orders had been made in respect of drug trafficking in 1974–79 (for which he had been convicted previously without a confiscation order being made) and further drug trafficking in 1990–93. The Commission declared the application inadmissible, on the ground that Taylor must have known when committing the 1990–93 offences that he would be liable under the DTOA for confiscation of proceeds from the 1974–79 offences, and on the ground that he had admitted "benefiting" from drug trafficking during 1974–79.

In *RC v. United Kingdom*[7] the applicant had been convicted on a charge of **16–71** conspiracy to import cannabis. The conspiracy period as laid in the indictment began long before the coming into force of the DTOA, but ended shortly afterwards. There had been a number of substantive importations in furtherance of the conspiracy. The majority of these had occurred before the relevant date but one had occurred thereafter. The evidence showed conclusively that the applicant had withdrawn from the conspiracy before it came to an end, and the prosecution accepted that he had not participated in the importation which occurred after the DTOA had come into force. Relying on the rationale behind Article 7 the applicant argued that he should have been exposed only to the range of penalties which were available at the time of his last participation in the conspiracy. It should not, in other words, have been open to the state to impose a heavier penalty by reference to the criminal acts of others committed after he had withdrawn from the conspiracy. The Commission, by a majority, ruled the complaint inadmissible, on the unconvincing basis that the relevant dates should be determined by reference to the conspiracy period laid in the indictment:

"[N]otwithstanding the specific acts in which the applicant participated, the offence in respect of which the applicant was charged and convicted was a conspiracy which

---

[3] [1996] Crim. L.R. 276–278.
[4] See, *e.g.* s.102 of the Criminal Justice Act 1988.
[5] *Foxley v. United Kingdom* 8 B.H.R.C. 571.
[6] [1998] E.H.R.L.R. 90.
[7] Unreported, April 6, 1994 (Application No. 22668/93).

existed between the dates of 1 January 1983 and 29 February 1988. The relevant provisions of the 1986 Act came into force during the subsistence of this conspiracy. The Commission finds therefore that since the conspiracy was in existence at and after the date on which the legislation came into force, it cannot be said that a heavier penalty was imposed on the applicant than the one which was applicable at the time."

16–72   The principle in *Welch*, as developed in *Taylor*, raises an interesting question concerning the application of the Human Rights Act. When *Taylor*[8] had been before the Court of Appeal, in view of the fact that section 38(4) is unambiguous, it held that under the then rules governing the relevance of the Convention it had no power to apply *Welch*. Accordingly the Court of Appeal could not overturn a retrospective confiscation order, even if it had been imposed in clear breach of Article 7.[9] However, the interpretation section of the Human Rights Act, section 3(1), requires courts to read and give effect to primary legislation in a way which is compatible with the Convention "so far as it is possible to do so." Assuming the courts are prepared to adopt the interpretative flexibility shown by the House of Lords in *R. v. A*[10] then it will be possible to read and give effect to provisions of this kind by implying into the legislation a safeguard that it is not to be enforced if this would violate Article 7. Alternatively, the higher courts will be obliged to grant a declaration of incompatibility.

16–73   We noted earlier that a change to the minimum tariff period of offenders already serving sentences of life imprisonment for murder may violate the prohibition on retrospective penalties.[11] Not only did Lords Steyn and Hope treat this as the governing principle in their speeches in *Ex parte Pierson*, but in *Ex parte McCartney*[12] Hoffman L.J. held that the imposition of a tariff on discretionary life prisoners whose offences were committed in the 1970s violated Article 7 because it took account of an increase in the tariff for terrorist offences in the 1980s.

16–74   A retrospectivity argument formed part of the challenge to automatic sentences of life imprisonment under section 2 of the Crime (Sentences) Act 1997 in *R. v. Offen and ors.*[13] This provision, discussed at para. 16–36 above, requires a court to impose a sentence of life imprisonment on the conviction for a "serious offence" of an offender who has previously been convicted of a "serious offence", unless there are "exceptional circumstances." The argument was that this effectively increases the punishment for the previous offence if, when it was committed, that offence did not have the status of a qualifying offence for the new automatic life sentence.[14] The life sentence is imposed on account of the two offences taken together, and therefore subjects the offender to a "more far-reaching detriment" than he could have contemplated when committing the first serious offence. However, the Court of Appeal held that the qualifying offences were all offences for which a discretionary life sentence had been possible, and

---

[8] [1996] 2 Cr. App. R. 64.
[9] In determining whether there has been a breach of the Convention, a court will now be obliged to take account of the distinctions drawn by the Commission in *Taylor* (above, n. 85).
[10] [2001] 2 W.L.R. 1546. See para. 3–32a and 15–37 above.
[11] See para. 16–65.
[12] *The Times*, May 25, 1994, judgment May 19, 1994.
[13] [2001] 1 W.L.R. 253.
[14] For a similar (unsuccessful) argument, see *Ibbotson v. United Kingdom* (1999) 27 E.H.R.R. CD 332.

that in all cases the court considers the previous record of the offender. Lord Woolf C.J. concluded that "the first offence and the penalty imposed for it remained the same after the coming into force of the 1997 Act; it was the penalty for the trigger offence that section 2 changed."

Article 7 is likely to have a continuing relevance largely because of the conjunc- **16–75** tion of two features of recent sentencing practice—the increasing number of prosecutions in respect of offences committed many years previously, particularly sex offences; and the rapid changes in sentencing law. Where a person is prosecuted for an offence allegedly committed several years before, it will be important for both the prosecution and the defence to acquaint themselves with relevant maximum sentences then and now. It would be contrary to Article 7 for a person convicted of an offence committed many years previously to be liable now to a higher penalty than would have been lawful at the time of the offence. This should apply not only where the maximum sentence has been increased but also where wider sentencing powers (such as the forms of extended sentence under section 44 of the Criminal Justice Act 1991 and section 58 of the Crime and Disorder Act 1998) have been introduced. The problem is rendered more pressing by the legislature's increased awareness of the non-retrospectivity principle. By ensuring that new statutory provisions only apply to offences committed after a certain date (as, for example, in the Proceeds of Crime Act 1995), Parliament also ensures that earlier sentencing provisions will remain relevant for some years to come. The Court of Appeal has however confirmed that Article 7 only applies to increases in the maximum sentence available for an offence, and not to changes in the judicial tariff. In *R. v. Alden and Wright*[15] the Court held that there was no incompatibility where a sentencer imposed a sentence higher than that which would have been imposed if the offender had been convicted soon after the commission of the offence, where the tariff had moved up in the intervening years.

I. RECOMMENDATION FOR DEPORTATION

Section 3(6) of the Immigration Act 1971 provides that a non-British citizen who **16–76** is convicted of an offence punishable with imprisonment is liable to deportation if he is recommended for deportation by the sentencing court.[16] Sections 6 and 7 of the Act provide supplementary procedural guarantees. Where a defendant has family ties in the United Kingdom, a recommendation for deportation may involve a violation of the right to family life in Article 8 of the Convention.

In *R. v. Nazari*[17] the Court of Appeal gave guidance on the exercise of the power **16–77** to recommend deportation. For present purposes the relevant passage reads:

> "The next matter [which courts should keep in mind] is the effect that an order recommending deportation will have upon others who are not before the court and who are innocent persons. This Court and all other courts would have no wish to break up families or impose hardship on innocent people."[18]

---

[15] *The Times*, February 27, 2001.
[16] See generally *Archbold* (2001), para. 5.586 *et seq.*
[17] [1980] 1 W.L.R. 1366.
[18] *ibid.*, at 95.

16–78 The effect of the Human Rights Act ought to be to harden this general guidance into a legally enforceable right. Under section 2, any court considering a recommendation will be required to have regard to the case-law of the Commission and the Court. The Court has repeatedly held that in maintaining public order Contracting States are entitled to exercise their right to control the entry and residence of aliens and to expel aliens convicted of criminal offences. However, decisions in that field which might interfere with the right to family life in Article 8(1) must be "necessary in a democratic society" to comply with Article 8(2).[19] Thus, the interference must be justified by a "pressing social need" and, in particular, it must be proportionate to the legitimate aim pursued. In *Beldjoudi v. France*[20] the applicant, an Algerian national, was a professional criminal who had been convicted of numerous criminal offences and had served a total of 10 years in prison (approximately half of his adult life). The French Government proposed his deportation to Algeria. In holding that the proposed deportation would violate Article 8, the Court emphasised that the applicant had lived in France all his life and had married a French woman. He had been educated in France and all of his close relatives had lived there for many years. He had had no contact with Algeria and did not speak Arabic. The Court held that in those circumstances the applicant's criminal record had to be balanced against the interference with his family life. The deportation would imperil his marriage and damage his relationship with his immediate family. As such, it could not be regarded as proportionate to the threat which he posed to public order in France.

16–79 By contrast, in *Boughanemi v. France*[21] the applicant was a Tunisian national convicted of living on the earnings of prostitution. He was sentenced to three years imprisonment and ordered to be deported. He had previous convictions for burglary, serious assault, and driving offences. The applicant, who was 36, had lived in France since the age of eight. His parents and 10 siblings lived in France, and he had a child by a relationship with a French woman (although he did not live with the mother). The Court accepted that the applicant's relationship with his child constituted family life despite the absence of cohabitation. Exceptional circumstances were required to break the parent/child tie so as to take the relationship outside the protection of Article 8. Nevertheless, the Court held that the proposed deportation was proportionate to the aim of the prevention of disorder or crime. The Court attached particular significance to the seriousness of the applicant's offence, and to his criminal record. It also noted that he had retained some ties with Tunisia which went beyond the mere fact of his nationality. There was no evidence to suggest that he was unable to speak Arabic. Nevertheless, *Boughanemi* must be regarded as a borderline case, if only because the Commission had concluded by the clearest of majorities that the deportation did violate Article 8.

16–80 In *Bouchelkia v. France*[22] the Court found no violation of Article 8 where an Algerian national who had lived in France since the age of two was deported following his conviction for rape. The fact that he was married to a French

---

[19] *Beldjoudi v. France* (1992) 14 E.H.R.R. 801; *Boughanemi v. France* (1996) 22 E.H.R.R. 228; *Nasri v. France* (1996) 21 E.H.R.R. 458; *Bouchelkia v. France* [1997] E.H.R.L.R. 433.
[20] (1992) 14 E.H.R.R. 801.
[21] (1996) 22 E.H.R.R. 228.
[22] [1997] E.H.R.L.R. 433.

woman with whom he had a child was held insufficient to outweigh the seriousness of his offence. The applicant had maintained real links with Algeria, where a number of close family members still lived, and was able to speak Arabic.

A further important question about the application of Article 8 is whether a **16–81** recommendation for deportation may be made solely on the basis of past offences, or whether it is necessary to show that the applicant is likely to re-offend. In practice, the two will often go hand in hand, but cases have arisen in which a recommendation has been made, despite acknowledgement that the defendant is most unlikely to commit further offences. Article 8(2) is unambiguously prospective in that it refers to the *prevention* of disorder or crime. Where it is clear that the risk of re-offending is minimal, it may be difficult to show that deportation is proportionate to this objective.

A similar issue has previously arisen in the context of European Union law. **16–82** Article 48 of the E.C. Treaty and Council Directive 64/221 restricts the power of member states of the European Union to exclude nationals of other member states who are workers, or spouses or dependants of workers. In *R. v. Bouchereau*[23] the European Court of Justice (ECJ) held that a recommendation for deportation of an E.C. national may only be made in accordance with Article 48 and Directive 64/221.

Article 48 EC provides that: "Freedom of movement . . . shall entail the right, *subject to limitations justified on grounds of public policy [or] public security . . .* (c) to move freely within the territory of the member states."[24]

This is supplemented by Article 3(2) of the Directive which provides that: "Previous criminal convictions shall not in themselves constitute grounds for [deportation]."

On its face, Article 3(2) would appear to suggest that a decision to deport an E.C. **16–83** national from one member state to another cannot be taken exclusively because he has been convicted of a criminal offence, but only where there is a risk of future offences. However, this is not how the Directive has been interpreted, either by the Courts of the United Kingdom, or by the ECJ. In *Bouchereau* the ECJ said:

> "The existence of a previous conviction can . . . only be taken into account insofar as the circumstances which gave rise to that conviction are evidence of personal conduct constituting a present threat to the requirements of public policy. Although, in general, a finding that such a threat exists implies the existence in the individual concerned of a propensity to act in the same way in the future, *it is possible that past conduct alone may constitute such a threat to the requirements of public policy.*"

The effect of this decision on United Kingdom deportations was considered in **16–84** *Al-Sabah v. Immigration Appeal Tribunal*[25] and *Olavo Marchon v. Immigration Appeal Tribunal.*[26] In *Marchon* the applicant was convicted of serious drug trafficking, but in the unusual circumstances of that case the Secretary of State was prepared formally to concede that there was no propensity for re-offending,

---

[23] [1978] Q.B. 732; [1978] 2 W.L.R. 251.
[24] Emphasis added.
[25] [1992] Imm. A.R. 223.
[26] [1993] Imm. A.R. 384.

and no likelihood of further unlawful activity of any specific kind. Nevertheless, the Court of Appeal held that the requirements of public policy fully justified his deportation:

> "It seems to me that even the hint that society was prepared to tolerate such conduct, by accepting the presence of persons who have been prepared to import large quantities of such drugs under the cloak of legitimate business would undermine the overwhelming public interest in defeating this subversive trade . . . [T]his interest of society is one which today must be taken to transcend the personal rights of residence if those rights are abused in the way that this appellant abused his rights of residence."[27]

---

[27] *Per* Beldam L.J. at 390.

CHAPTER 17

APPEALS

A. GENERAL PRINCIPLES

I. *Application of Article 6 to Appeals*

Article 6 of the Convention does not guarantee a right of appeal as a component **17–01** of the right to a fair hearing. But where domestic law provides for an appeal against conviction or sentence, whether on grounds of fact or law, then the appeal proceedings will be treated as an extension of the trial process, and accordingly will be subject to the requirements of Article 6. Thus in *Delcourt v. Belgium* the Court held:

> "A criminal conviction is not really 'determined' as long as the verdict of acquittal or conviction has not become final. Criminal proceedings form an entity and must, in the ordinary way, terminate in an enforceable decision . . . The Convention does not, it is true, compel the Contracting States to set up courts of appeal or of cassation. Nevertheless, a State which does institute such courts is required to ensure that persons amenable to the law shall enjoy before these courts the fundamental rights guaranteed in Article 6."[1]

Several subsequent decisions of the Court affirm the principle that, in applying **17–02** Article 6, "account must be taken of the entirety of the proceedings in the domestic legal order and the role of the appellate courts therein."[2] Article 6 applies not only to the determination of a substantive appeal, but also to proceedings for leave to appeal: the Court confirmed in *Monnell and Morris v. United Kingdom*[3] that "applications for leave to appeal . . . constituted part of the determination of the criminal charges."

It is safe to assume that Article 6 would also be held apply on an appeal which **17–03** has been referred to the Court of Appeal by the Criminal Cases Review Commission, despite the fact that the criminal charge has been finally "determined", and the conviction and sentence have acquired the quality of *res judicata*. In *Callaghan and others v. United Kingdom*[4] the European Commission on Human Rights held that Article 6 was applicable to a Home Secretary's reference to the Court of Appeal under section 17 of the Criminal Appeal Act 1968 (prior to its amendment). The Commission recognised that the procedure was not part of the ordinary appeals process and took place long after the criminal proceedings had finally been determined. Nevertheless:

---

[1] (1979–80) 1 E.H.R.R. 335 at para. 25.
[2] *Helmers v. Sweden* (1993) 15 E.H.R.R. 285 at para. 31; to similar effect, see, *e.g. Edwards v. United Kingdom* (1993) 15 E.H.R.R. 417, para. 34.
[3] (1988) 10 E.H.R.R. 205 at para. 54.
[4] (1989) 60 D.R. 296. *Callaghan* must be taken to have overruled the much earlier decision in *X v. Austria* (1962) 9 E.H.R.R. CD 17.

"the proceedings on the Secretary of State's reference had all the features of an appeal against conviction, and could have resulted in the applicants being found not guilty or . . . their convictions being upheld. They must therefore, in the Commission's view, be regarded as having the effect of determining, or re-determining, the charges against the applicants."

17–03a The Commission's approach was confirmed by the Court in *IJL, GMR and AKP v. United Kingdom*[5] where, in assessing a complaint that proceedings had extended beyond a reasonable time for the purposes of Article 6(1) the Court aggregated the time taken to hear and dispose of the original prosecution and appeal with the time taken to dispose of a further appeal following a reference by the Home Secretary.[6]

17–04 In addition, the Government has indicated its intention to sign, ratify and incorporate Protocol 7 to the Convention as soon as practicable. Article 2 of Protocol 7 provides:

"2(1) Everyone convicted of a criminal offence by a tribunal shall have the right to have his conviction or sentence reviewed by a higher tribunal. The exercise of this right, including the grounds on which it may be exercised, shall be governed by law.

(2) This right may be subject to exceptions in regard to offences of a minor character, as prescribed by law, or in cases in which the person concerned was tried in the first instance by the highest tribunal or was convicted following an appeal against acquittal."

17–05 The terms of Protocol 7 give rise to two practical points. First, the term "criminal offence" has the same extended definition here as the term "criminal charge" in Article 6.[7] It follows that the right of appeal in Article 2 of Protocol 7 may apply to proceedings which are not currently defined as "criminal" in domestic law. Secondly, the additional guarantees of Protocol 7 cannot be read as intended in any way to limit the applicability or the requirements of Article 6 in appellate proceedings. This is expressly confirmed in the Explanatory Report to Protocol 7, cited with approval by the Court in *Ekbatani v. Sweden*.[8]

II. *Retrospective Application of the Human Rights Act*

17–06 The extent to which the Human Rights Act 1998 has retrospective effect in criminal proceedings is considered in detail in Chapter 3 above.[9] Prior to the House of Lords decision in *Lambert*[10] the Court of Appeal had held on a number of occasions that the Act would operate retrospectively on appeal, requiring the Court to approach the safety of a conviction as if the Act had been in force at the time of the trial.[11] Lord Woolf C.J. expressed "reservations" as to whether

---

[5] [2001] Crim. L.R. 133.
[6] See para. 14–40 above.
[7] *Gradinger v. Austria*, October 23, 1995, (unreported).
[8] (1988) 13 E.H.R.R. 504 at para. 26.
[9] See paras. 3–05 to 3–09.
[10] [2001] UKHL 37, July 5, 2001.
[11] *R. v. Lambert and Ali* [2001] 2 W.L.R. 211; *R. v. Benjafield and ors.* Judgment December 21, 2000; *R. v. Kansal* Judgment May 24, 2001.

Parliament had truly intended the Act to be retrospective in criminal appeals,[12] although he accepted that this construction was supported by the speech of Lord Steyn in *Kebilene*.[13] He emphasised on more than one occasion that the Court would not ordinarily be willing to extend time to allow an appellant to appeal on Convention grounds, although in exceptional cases it might do so where there was an important point of principle involved.[14] No such filter was available where a case was referred to the Court of Appeal by the Criminal Cases Review Commission under section 9 of the Criminal Appeal Act 1995. In *R. v. Kansal*[15] Rose L.J. quashed a conviction following a reference by the CCRC "with no enthusiasm whatever". He considered that the combined effect of the CCRC reference and the retrospective effect of the 1998 Act was to "emasculate" the previous practice of the Court of Appeal, and he called for a reconsideration by Parliament or the House of Lords. This mounting judicial concern was put to rest in *Lambert* where a majority of the House of Lords held that the Act did not permit an appellant to mount a retrospective challenge on appeal to the decision of a trial court which was lawful at the time when it was made. The speeches of the majority reflect different processes of reasoning on the point. Lord Hope, in particular, held that where the challenge was directed not to an act of the trial court, but to an act of the prosecuting authority, the Act would operate retrospectively on appeal. He thus distinguished *Lambert*, which was a challenge to the way in which the judge had directed the jury on a reverse onus clause, from *Kebilene* which was a challenge to the decision of the DPP to consent to a prosecution for an offence which contained such a clause.

B. THE REQUIREMENTS OF ARTICLE 6

I. *The General Position*

The requirements of fairness will not necessarily be the same on appeal as they would be at first instance. In *Monnell and Morris v. United Kingdom*[16] the Court pointed out that the manner of application of Article 6 to appellate proceedings depends upon the special features of the proceedings involved, seen in their domestic law context, and taking account of the role and functions of the appeal court. In order to determine whether the requirements of Article 6 were met, the Court held that it was necessary to consider matters such as; **17–07**

— the significance of appellate procedure in the context of the criminal proceedings as a whole;

— the scope of the powers of the Court of Appeal; and

— the manner in which the appellant's interests were presented and protected in practice.

---

[12] *R. v. Lambert and Ali* [2001] 2 W.L.R. 211.
[13] [2000] 2 A.C. 326 at 362.
[14] In *R. v. Benjafield and ors*. Judgment December 21, 2000 Lord Woolf C.J., though granting leave, emphasised that "any legal system is entitled to impose time limits and, if reasonable, they can apply to disable an individual from alleging a breach of the Convention".
[15] Judgment May 24, 2001.
[16] (1988) 10 E.H.R.R. 205.

It follows that the guarantees of Article 6 require adaptation in the context of appeal proceedings, particularly where the appeal concerns only a point of law.

17–08   On the other hand, in *Ekbatani v. Sweden*[17] the Court held that where an appellate court is called upon to examine the facts of the case, and to make an assessment of the probative weight of evidence adduced by the prosecution, the requirements of fairness are more akin to those of a criminal trial. In view of the test under the Criminal Appeal Act, section 2, as amended—which requires the Court to allow an appeal only if it considers that the conviction is "unsafe"—there is an argument that all criminal appeals involve some consideration of the evidence.[18]

II. *The right to free legal representation and a public hearing in the presence of the accused*

17–09   As a general rule Article 6(1) and Article 6(3)(c), taken together, require a public hearing at which the accused person is entitled to be present, and to be legally represented, with legal aid if necessary. The Court has insisted in several cases that it is "of crucial importance for the fairness of the criminal justice system that the accused be adequately defended, both at first instance and on appeal".[19] The application of these general principles to appeal proceedings in the United Kingdom has been considered by the Court in three cases.

17–10   In *Monnell and Morris v. United Kingdom*[20] the Court examined the procedure whereby the Court of Appeal may determine an application for leave to appeal against conviction "on the papers", without the accused being present or represented by counsel, and without hearing oral argument on the merits of the appeal. The Court found that this procedure was compatible with Article 6, noting that on an application for leave, the Court of Appeal did not re-hear the facts of the case, and no witnesses were called, even where the grounds involved mixed questions of law and fact. The sole issue before the Court of Appeal was whether the applicant had demonstrated arguable grounds which would justify a hearing on the merits. In the Court's view, the limited nature of this issue did not, in itself, call for oral argument at a public hearing in the presence of the applicants. The Court attached importance to the fact that the prosecution were unrepresented; that the applicants had received legally aided advice on appeal from counsel; and that the applicants had had the opportunity of submitting written grounds of their own with argument in support. The Court went on:

> "Under paragraph 3(c) of Article 6, they were guaranteed the right to be given legal assistance free only so far as the interests of justice so required. The interests of justice cannot, however, be taken to require an automatic grant of legal aid whenever a convicted person, with no objective likelihood of success, wishes to appeal after having received a fair trial at first instance in accordance with Article 6. Each applicant, it is

---

[17] (1991) 13 E.H.R.R. 504.
[18] *See*, for example *R. v. Craven*, *The Times*, February 2, 2001, where the court found irregularities at trial but upheld the conviction in the light of fresh DNA evidence.
[19] *Lala v. Netherlands* (1994) 18 E.H.R.R. 586 at para. 33; *Pelladoah v. Netherlands* (1995) 19 E.H.R.R. 81 at para. 40.
[20] (1988) 10 E.H.R.R. 205.

to be noted, benefited from free legal assistance both at his trial and in being advised as to whether he had any arguable grounds of appeal. In the Court's view, the issue to be decided in relation to section 29(1) of the Criminal Appeal Act 1968 did not call, as a matter of fairness, for oral submissions on behalf of the applicants in addition to the written submissions and material already before the Court of Appeal."[21]

This decision has been criticised, and some of the Court's subsequent judgments appear to have taken a stricter line.

In *Granger v. United Kingdom*,[22] a Scottish case, the Court held that a refusal of   **17–11** legal aid for the applicant's appeal against a conviction for perjury violated Article 6. Under Scots law there was, at that time, no requirement for leave to appeal. But the decision as to whether legal aid should be granted lay with the Legal Aid Committee of the Scottish Law Society, which had to decide whether an applicant for legal aid had substantial grounds for appealing, and whether it was in the interests of justice that s/he be granted legal aid. The Committee could therefore refuse legal aid on the ground that the appeal was unmeritorious. Following an unfavourable advice from counsel, legal aid was refused. The applicant appeared at the hearing in person and read out a statement prepared by his solicitor. The Court noted that Article 6(3)(c) only guarantees a right to legal aid where the interests of justice require this. However, the interests of justice criterion must be assessed in the light of all the circumstances of the case. The applicant was serving a five year prison sentence, so that there was no doubt about the importance of what was at stake for him. The Court of Appeal had been addressed at length by the Solicitor General who appeared for the Crown. One of the issues which arose was of considerable complexity, but the applicant was not in a position to understand the prepared statement he read out. He could neither understand nor reply to the arguments against him, nor could he answer questions from the bench. It was therefore held that the proceedings had breached Article 6, irrespective of the merits of the applicant's case.

In *Maxwell v. United Kingdom*[23] and *Boner v. United Kingdom*,[24] two further   **17–12** Scottish cases, the Court unanimously found a violation of Article 6 despite concluding that the legal issues in the appeal were straightforward. Here again, legal aid had been refused on the ground that the appeal was without merit. In the light of *Granger*, the Government had introduced a new provision in Scotland which enabled the Court of Appeal to grant legal aid if, on examination, it considered that there was a point of substance in the appeal. This was held to be insufficient to meet the requirements of Article 6. The Court accepted that the legal issues were not complex, that no point of substance had arisen in the appeal, and that prosecution counsel had not been called upon to address the Court of Appeal. The Court nevertheless held that in the absence of legal representation the applicants had been unable to address the court on the issues raised in the appeal and thus had been deprived of the opportunity to defend themselves effectively.

One interpretation of these cases is that the right to be present and represented by   **17–13** counsel applies only once leave to appeal has been granted. However, the Court

---

[21] *ibid.*, at para. 67.
[22] (1990) 12 E.H.R.R. 469 at paras 42–48.
[23] (1995) 19 E.H.R.R. 97.
[24] (1995) 19 E.H.R.R. 246.

has since offered a different rationale. In *Ekbatani v. Sweden*[25] the Court suggested that the decisive consideration in *Monnell and Morris* was not that the proceedings in that case had involved applications for leave (as distinct from a full appeal) but that the appeals were concerned with questions of law alone and not with questions of fact. In *Ekbatani*, the applicant's appeal against conviction was determined on written submissions made by the prosecutor and the defence. The Court noted that the "equality of arms" principle in Article 6 had been maintained, but emphasised that this was "only one feature of the wider concept of a fair trial in criminal proceedings". The Swedish appellate court in *Ekbatani* had had the function of considering both fact and law, and "had to make a full assessment of the applicant's guilt or innocence". Accordingly, in the absence of a public and adversarial procedure, there had been a violation of Article 6.

17–14   The Court held that in order to justify a departure from the requirement of a public hearing in the presence of the accused there had to be some "special feature" of the appeal proceedings. It explained that the "underlying reason" for the finding of no violation in *Monnell and Morris* "was that the court concerned did not have the task of establishing the facts of the case, but only of interpreting the legal rules involved."[26] It is fair to say that the Court's judgment in *Monnell and Morris* does not appear to attach the same degree of importance to this aspect of the case as the Court subsequently suggested it had in *Ekbatani*, and therefore that the latter decision may betoken a change of approach. However, in *Belziuk v. Poland*[27] the Court held that the personal attendance of the accused does not necessarily take on the same significance for an appeal hearing, and Article 6 does not always entail the right to a public hearing or the right to be present in person, even when the appellate court has full jurisdiction to review the case on questions of both fact and law. Moreover, in the recent case of *Cookson v. United Kingdom*,[28] the Court dismissed an argument that the refusal of legal aid for a renewed application for leave to appeal was incompatible with Article 6.

17–15   What are the implications of these decisions for the application of the Human Rights Act? Five tentative conclusions may be suggested:

— A consideration of an application for leave on the papers by the single judge is unlikely to raise a serious issue under Article 6 since the application can be renewed to the full court.

— The dismissal of an application for leave by the full court in the non-counsel list *may* raise an issue under Article 6 in an exceptional case if the case is a complex one, or if it involves a detailed consideration of the evidence. However, it would be necessary for the applicant to persuade the Court to depart from *Monnell and Morris*, or to distinguish it by pointing to a real unfairness on the facts of the case.

— Where an oral hearing for leave is held, there *may* be an argument for the presence of the accused (despite the presumption in section 22(2) of the 1968 Act) and for the grant legal aid if the accused would otherwise be

---

[25] (1991) 13 E.H.R.R. 504 at paras 25–33.
[26] *ibid.*, para. 31.
[27] (2000) 30 E.H.R.R. 614.
[28] Inadmissibility decision, May 4, 2001, Application No. 56842/00.

unrepresented. As regards of legal aid, however, it should be noted that Article 6(3)(c) guarantees a right to legal representation and not a right to free legal aid as such. If counsel in fact appears on a *pro bono* basis on an application for leave, the requirements of Article 6(3)(c) will have been met in that case. Article 6 does not assist counsel who has appeared *pro bono* to argue that the Court is obliged to grant retrospective legal aid for the hearing.

— On a full hearing of an appeal the appellant is generally entitled to be present and to be represented on legal aid (subject to means) in cases of any seriousness.

— Where an appeal involves the consideration of fresh evidence called by either side, compliance with Article 6 will generally require the provision of safeguards akin to those required in a criminal trial.

III. *Reasons in appeal proceedings*

It is a general principle of Article 6(1) that a court (including an appellate court)   **17–16**
must give reasons for its decision. All courts must "indicate with sufficient clarity the grounds on which they based their decision."[29] The purpose of this requirement is partly to enable the unsuccessful litigant to exercise any (further) right of appeal, and partly to maintain public confidence in the administration of justice.

The practice of the Court of Appeal in this respect is fully in compliance with   **17–17**
Article 6. Reasons are given not only for the dismissal of a substantive appeal, but also for a refusal of leave. However, in those cases where the Court of Appeal has certified a point of public importance but has refused leave to appeal to the House of Lords, the position is different. It is not the usual practice of the Appellate Committee of the House of Lords to give reasons when refusing an application for leave to appeal. Similarly, it is common practice for courts of cassation in some European jurisdictions to give the briefest of reasons for refusing leave to appeal. In some instances, the Commission has regarded as acceptable reasoning which does little more than refer to the applicable provision under which the appeal was refused.[30] As the Commission has put it:

"where a supreme court refuses to accept a case on the basis that the legal grounds for such a case are not made out, very limited reasoning may satisfy the requirements of Article 6 of the Convention (see, for example, *Muller-Eberstein v. Germany*[31] concerning the Federal Constitutional Court of Germany, which rejects decisions in summary proceedings by reference to the statutory provisions governing the Federal Constitutional Court)."[32]

Although it is unlikely that the House of Lords' current practice will be sig-   **17–18**
nificantly affected by the Human Rights Act, it may, exceptionally, be arguable that reasons are required for a refusal of leave on the facts of a particular case.

---

[29] *Hadjianatassiou v. Greece* (1993) 16 E.H.R.R. 219 at para. 33.
[30] Application 9223/80 October 15, 1981 (unpublished); Application No. 9982/82 May 18, 1984 (unpublished).
[31] Application No. 29752/96, November 27, 1996 (unpublished).
[32] *Webb v. United Kingdom* (1997) 24 E.H.R.R. CD 73 at 74.

Thus the Court has held that the extent of the duty to give reasons varies according to the nature of the decision in issue and the applicable substantive law and procedure, and that "the question whether a court has failed to fulfil the obligation to state reasons . . . can only be determined in the light of the circumstances of the case."[33]

17–19 In *Webb v. United Kingdom*[34] the applicant complained that Privy Council had failed to give reasons for refusing an application for special leave to appeal against her conviction in Bermuda on drug trafficking charges. The Commission declared the application inadmissible. It noted that appeal to the Privy Council was limited to points of "great and general importance" or a "grave injustice", and held that in these circumstances very limited reasoning may satisfy the requirements of Article 6 since "it must be apparent to litigants who have been refused leave that they have failed to satisfy the Privy Council that their case involves [such a point]".

IV. *Loss of Time and other Procedural Sanctions on Appeal*

17–20 Under section 29(1) of the Criminal Appeal Act 1968 the Court of Appeal may, if it considers that an appeal is without merit, direct that time served between the imposition of the sentence and the disposal of the appeal should not count towards sentence. The circumstances in which such an order may be made are set out in a *Practice Direction.*[35]

17–21 The most surprising aspect of the Court's decision in *Monnell and Morris v. United Kingdom*[36] was its conclusion that a loss of time order made in that case, following an application for leave to appeal which had been dismissed in the non-counsel list, was compatible both with Article 5 and with Article 6. The Court recognised that the order effectively imposed an additional period of imprisonment on the applicants, and that it was ordered for reasons unconnected with the facts of the offence or with the character or antecedents of the applicants. Nevertheless, the Court held that the order for loss of time was lawful under Article 5(1)(a), as being detention after conviction by a competent court. Although it was not treated under domestic law as part of the sentence, it did form a component part of the period of detention which resulted from the applicants' conviction. The Court therefore found a sufficient connection between the conviction and the loss of time to prevent the detention from being characterised as "arbitrary". The Court reasoned that the power to make the order, which had the express policy of deterring unmeritorious appeals, was part of the domestic machinery for ensuring that criminal proceedings generally were concluded within a reasonable time, as required by Article 6(1).

17–22 Moreover, the fact that the Court of Appeal had power to (and did) make such an order was held to be insufficient to tip the balance in favour of a requirement for legal representation for the application for leave. The applicants had been given the benefit of free legal advice after conviction about the prospect of an appeal,

---

[33] *Ruiz Torija v. Spain* (1995) 19 E.H.R.R. 553 at para. 29.
[34] (1997) 24 E.H.R.R. CD 73.
[35] *Practice Direction (Crime: Sentence: Loss of Time)* [1980] 1 W.L.R. 270.
[36] (1988) 10 E.H.R.R. 205.

and that advice has been negative. The applicants were able to present written grounds of appeal to the Court, which they did. No question of inequality of arms arose, because the Crown was not represented on the appeal either. The Court concluded that "the interests of justice and fairness" were met by the applicants' ability to make written submissions, and that, despite the significant period of extra detention ordered by the Court, no oral hearing was necessary to comply with Articles 5 and 6.[37] The renewed application for leave in *Monnell and Morris* was made contrary to the advice of counsel. The fact that grounds have been settled (or even argued) by counsel is not, of itself, an absolute bar to a loss of time order, although the Court of Appeal would doubtless hesitate long and hard before making an order in such circumstances. It is certainly difficult to see how such an order could be compatible with the right to counsel or with the duty to attach "appropriate weight" to legal advice.[38] More generally, however, it is open to doubt whether this aspect of the decision in *Monnell and Morris* is consistent with the Court's subsequent decision in *Omar v. France*.[39]

Where domestic law goes further, and provides for an appeal to be disallowed in   **17–23**
response to unacceptable conduct by the would-be appellant, the Court has held that this may contravene Article 6. Thus in *Poitrimol v. France*[40] the French appellate courts had refused to allow the applicant's appeals because he had absconded to another country: his trial had been conducted *in absentia*, but the Cour de Cassation refused to allow his appeal to be heard in that way or to allow him to be legally represented at such hearings. The Court held that this denial was disproportionate, having regard to the importance of the rights of the defence. In *Omar v. France*[41] the Cour de Cassation had declared the applicants' appeal on points of law inadmissible, on the ground that they had failed to comply with warrants for their arrest, in accordance with the order made by the trial court. The Court held that to compel a person to subject himself to deprivation of liberty before an appeal on a point of law can be heard is incompatible with Article 6:

"This impairs the very essence of the right of appeal, by imposing a disproportionate burden on the appellant, thus upsetting the fair balance that must be struck between the legitimate concern to ensure that judicial decisions are enforced, on the one hand, and the right of access to the Court of Cassation and the exercise of the rights of the defence on the other."[42]

In *R. v. Charles, R. v. Tucker*[43] the Court of Appeal held that the Registrar of Criminal Appeals should no longer treat an application for leave to appeal on behalf of a defendant who has absconded as ineffective, considering the practice to be potentially incompatible with Article 6(1) in the light of the judgment in *Omar*. In *Vacher v. France*[44] the Court emphasised that it was the duty of the state to ensure that an appellant was notified of time limits and other procedural restrictions, in order to ensure his effective participation in an appeal.

---

[37] *ibid.*, paras 62–68.
[38] *Condron and Condron v. United Kingdom* (2001) 31 E.H.R.R. 1.
[39] See para. 16–43 above and para. 17–23 below.
[40] (1994) 18 E.H.R.R. 130.
[41] (2000) 29 E.H.R.R. 210.
[42] *ibid.*, para. 40.
[43] *The Times*, February 20, 2001.
[44] (1996) 24 E.H.R.R. 482.

V. *Appeals and the Reasonable Time Guarantee*

17–24   Since the Article 6 guarantee of fair trial applies to the proceedings as a whole, from arrest through to the final determination of any appeal, it follows that appeals should be heard within a reasonable time. There is authority for the proposition that this requirement applies less strictly to a constitutional court or other final court of appeal. The constitutional role of such a court justifies a more flexible approach, since it is reasonable for a final appellate court to give priority to considerations other than "the mere chronological order in which cases are entered on the list, such as the nature of a case and its importance in political and social terms."[45] Whilst this principle would undoubtedly apply to the House of Lords, the Court of Appeal is expected to operate within tighter time constraints, as appears from *Howarth v. United Kingdom*.[46] Following his conviction after a lengthy fraud trial, the applicant lodged his notice of appeal against conviction in March 1995. In April 1995 the Attorney General made a reference to the Court of Appeal for review of his sentence, a community service order. Perfected grounds of appeal were lodged in September 1995, but the Court of Appeal did not hear his appeal until March 1997, dealing with the Attorney General's reference the following day. In view of the unexplained delay of 19 months, in which there was no judicial activity, the Strasbourg Court held that the applicant's right to a hearing "within a reasonable time" had been breached, and thus that there had been a violation of Article 6(1). The time taken to deal with the Attorney General's reference (which ordered him to serve a sentence of 20 months imprisonment) was the subject of unreasonable delay; that depended on the disposal of the applicant's appeal against conviction; and that was complicated by the complexity of the fraud trial and the appeals of co-defendants. However, the Court found "no convincing reasons" for the delays.

VI. *Substituted Verdicts*

17–24a   By section 3 of the Criminal Appeal Act 1968, the Court of Appeal may, instead of allowing or dismissing an appeal, substitute a verdict of guilty of another offence provided it is an offence of which the jury could, on the indictment, have found the accused guilty. We have already seen that the availability of lesser alternative verdicts at trial has been held compatible with the right in Article 6(3)(a) to be informed promptly and in detail of the nature and cause of the accusation.[47] There is no obvious reason why the same principle should not apply on appeal, although it will obviously be important to ensure that the appellant has had an adequate opportunity to meet the allegation. In *Pélissier v. France*,[48] for example, the Court found a violation of Article 6 where a conviction for aiding and abetting an offence had been substituted on the applicant's appeal against his conviction as a principal. On the facts, the Court held that the applicant had not been given an effective opportunity to deal with what was, in effect, a new allegation. The risk of a similar violation occurring in this jurisdiction is substantially mitigated by the Court of Appeal's practice. Under section 3 the Court may only substitute a verdict where the ingredients of the lesser offence are, in

---

[45] *Sussmann v. Germany* (1998) 25 E.H.R.R. 64 at paras 55–60.
[46] [2001] Crim. L.R. 227; see also *Bunkate v. Netherlands* (1995) 19 E.H.R.R. 477.
[47] Para. 14–162 above.
[48] (2000) 30 E.H.R.R. 715.

law, subsumed within those of the offence of which the appellant was convicted: it is not sufficient that the evidence adduced at trial could have supported a conviction for a different offence in law.[49] Moreover, the section provides that the Court must, before exercising its powers, first conclude that from their verdict the jury must have been satisfied of the facts upon which the substitute verdict depends. The Court will not generally exercise its powers if the jury received an inadequate direction on the alternative charge, or if the conduct of the defence could have been materially affected if the appellant had been charged with the alternative.[50]

C. UNFAIR TRIALS AND UNSAFE CONVICTIONS

Is a conviction which has been obtained in breach of a Convention right, and **17–25** especially Article 6, for that reason alone to be regarded as "unsafe", within the meaning of section 2 of the Criminal Appeal Act 1968 as amended? The term "unsafe" must, like any other statutory provision, be read in a way which conforms with Convention rights, so far as it is possible to do so.[51] The question is thus whether and in what circumstances the fact that a trial was "unfair" for the purposes of Article 6 means that the resulting conviction must be regarded as "unsafe" within the meaning of section 2 of the 1968 Act, when that provision is read with the benefit of section 2 of the Human Rights Act 1998.

I. Reinterpreting the Criminal Appeal Act

In many European jurisdictions, there are two ways in which a defendant can **17–26** challenge his conviction: appeal (which goes to the *correctness* of the verdict) and cassation (which goes to the *legality* of the proceedings which resulted in the conviction). Under the pre-1995 formulation of section 2, it could be said that the Court of Appeal was exercising both jurisdictions simultaneously. A conviction could be quashed for misdirection or for error of law, but subject to the application of the proviso. Then the Criminal Appeal Act 1995 replaced the old phrase "unsafe or unsatisfactory" with the single word "unsafe."

The Court of Appeal initially inclined to the view that the 1995 Act had, in effect, **17–27** abolished the Court's jurisdiction to quash a conviction simply on the ground that it was procedurally defective or otherwise tainted with unfairness, and that the sole question for the Court was whether the conviction was "safe".[52] However, in subsequent decisions the Court began to move away from this stance,[53] and the

---

[49] *R. v. Cooke* [1997] Crim. L.R. 436 (CA).
[50] *R. v. Caslin* 45 Cr. App. R. 47 (CA); *R. v. Graham and ors.* [1997] 1 Cr. App. R. 302 (CA).
[51] Human Rights Act 1998, s.3. See para. 3–31 above.
[52] *R. v. Chalkley and Jefferies* [1998] 2 Cr. App. R. 79 (CA).
[53] See, for example, *Mullen* [2000] Q.B. 520, and the opinion of Lord Steyn in *Allie Mohamed v. The State* [1999] 2 W.L.R. 552 that "it is important to bear in mind the nature of the particular constitutional breach. For example, a breach of the defendant's constitutional right to a fair trial must inevitably result in a conviction being quashed."

judgment of Lord Woolf C.J. in *Togher, Doran and Parsons*[54] effectively over-rules the narrower view and restores the pre-1995 position.

17–28 Although many believed that the narrower view of the term "unsafe" was wrong as an interpretation of the 1995 Act,[55] the coming into force of the Human Rights Act 1998 and the Strasbourg decision in *Condron and Condron v. United Kingdom*[56] made it necessary for the Court of Appeal to review its approach urgently after October 2, 2000. One of the arguments for the Government in *Condron* was that the applicants had received a fair trial because, whatever errors might have been made by the trial judge, the Court of Appeal had been able to review matters and to ensure overall fairness. The response of the Strasbourg Court was this:

> "The Court must also have regard to the fact that the Court of Appeal was concerned with the safety of the applicants' conviction, not whether they had in the circumstances received a fair trial. In the Court's opinion, the question whether or not the rights of the defence guaranteed to an accused under Article 6 of the Convention were secured in any given case cannot be assimilated to a finding that his conviction was safe in the absence of any enquiry into the issue of fairness."[57]

This decision therefore recognised that, at that time, it was possible for the English Court of Appeal to uphold a conviction as safe even if it was satisfied that the trial had been unfair. The Court did not consider that this amounted to an adequate remedy for a serious misdirection concerning the adverse inferences which could be drawn from the appellants' silence at interview. The Court of Appeal had acknowledged the misdirection, but had dismissed the appeal on the ground that there was other compelling evidence of guilt. In the Court's view, this was no answer to the complaint of a breach of Article 6. In the absence of a reasoned judgment from the jury the Court of Appeal had no means of knowing how significant a role the applicants' silence had played in the jury's decision to convict them, and was therefore driven to speculate about the jury's process of reasoning.

17–28a Similar reservations about the role of the Court of Appeal were voiced in *Rowe and Davis v. United Kingdom*,[58] where the Court suggested that there was a risk of the Court of Appeal being unconsciously influenced by a jury's guilty verdict into underestimating the significance of fresh evidence. That case, it will be recalled, turned on the non-disclosure of relevant evidence on public interest immunity grounds. In *Edwards v. United Kingdom*[59] the Court had previously held that where relevant evidence was wrongly withheld at trial, its disclosure prior to an appeal, and the subsequent consideration by the Court of Appeal of its impact on the safety of the conviction was capable of curing the defect which had arisen at first instance. The government argued that the same principle should apply where there had been an *ex parte* public interest immunity hearing before the Court of Appeal. The Court disagreed;

---

[54] [2001] Crim. L.R. 124.
[55] See, *e.g.*, Sir John Smith, "The Criminal Appeal Act 1995" [1995] Crim. L.R. 920, and his note on *Chalkley and Jeffries* at [1999] Crim. L.R. 215.
[56] [2000] Crim. L.R. 677.
[57] *ibid*, at para. 65.
[58] (2000) 30 E.H.R.R. 1. See para. 14–115 above.
[59] (1992) 15 E.H.R.R. 417. See para. 14–90 *et seq.* above.

"[T]he Court does not consider that this procedure before the appeal court was sufficient to remedy the unfairness caused at the trial by the absence of any scrutiny of the withheld information by the trial judge. Unlike the latter, who saw the witnesses give their testimony and was fully versed in all the evidence and issues in the case, the judges in the Court of Appeal were dependent for their understanding of the possible relevance of the undisclosed material on transcripts of the Crown Court hearings and on the account of the issues given to them by prosecuting counsel. In addition, the first instance judge would have been in a position to monitor the need for disclosure throughout the trial, assessing the importance of the undisclosed evidence at a stage when new issues were emerging, when it might have been possible through cross-examination seriously to undermine the credibility of key witnesses and when the defence case was still open to take a number of different directions or emphases. In contrast, the Court of Appeal was obliged to carry out its appraisal *ex post facto* and may even, to a certain extent, have unconsciously been influenced by the jury's verdict of guilty into underestimating the significance of the undisclosed evidence."

The question came before the Court of Appeal in *Davis, Johnson and Rowe*.[60] **17-29** The Court of Appeal accepted that the Strasbourg Court's determination was obviously relevant, and that it would be difficult to go behind that ruling "without doing serious injury to the intent and purpose" of the Human Rights Act, but pointed out that English courts are bound only to take account of, and not strictly to follow, judgments from Strasbourg:

"We are required to review the safety of convictions resulting from a trial which the ECHR has adjudged to have been unfair. It may be the first case of its kind; it certainly will not be the last. How should we proceed? . . . We see no difficulty in giving effect to the 'right to a fair trial' when discharging our duty to consider the safety of a conviction . . . The Court is concerned with the safety of a conviction. A conviction can never be safe is there is doubt about guilt. However, the converse is not true. A conviction may be unsafe even where there is no doubt about guilt but the trial process has been 'vitiated by serious unfairness or significant legal misdirection' . . . Usually, it will be sufficient for the court to apply the test in *Stirland*[61] which, as adapted . . . might read: 'Assuming the wrong decision on law or the irregularity had not concurred and the trial had been free from legal error, would the only reasonable and proper verdict have been one of guilty?' That being so, there is no tension between section 2(1)(a) of the Criminal Appeal Act 1968 as amended and section 3(1) of the Human Rights Act 1998."

The Court went on to note that a decision of the European Court of Human Rights does not involve any express finding on the nature and quality of a breach of Article 6 or its impact on the safety of a conviction. In view of this limitation on the European Court's function, it would remain necessary for the Court of Appeal itself to assess the impact which a particular breach of Article 6 might have on the safety of a conviction:

"We are satisfied that the two questions [of fairness and safety] must be kept separate and apart. The ECHR is charged with inquiring into whether there has been a breach of a Convention right. This court is concerned with the safety of a conviction. That the first question may intrude upon the second is obvious. To what extent it does so will depend on the circumstances of the particular case. We reject therefore the contention that a finding of a breach of Article 6(1) by the ECHR leads inexorably to the quashing of a conviction. Nor do we think it helpful to deal in presumptions. The effect of any

---

[60] (2001) 1 Cr. App. R. 115.
[61] [1944] A.C. 315.

unfairness upon the safety of a conviction will vary according to its nature and degree. At one end of the spectrum [counsel] cites the example of an appropriate sentence following a plea of guilty passed by a judge who for some undisclosed reason did not constitute an impartial tribunal. At the other extreme there may be a case where a defendant is denied the opportunity to give evidence on his own behalf."

17–30 The leading decision now is that of the Court of Appeal in *Togher, Doran and Parsons*,[62] where Lord Woolf C.J. delivered the judgment. Having reviewed the varied case law since *Chalkley and Jeffries*, Lord Woolf concluded that, even if there was previously a difference of approach:

> "Now that the European Convention is part of our domestic law, it would be most unfortunate if the approach identified by the European Court of Human Rights and the approach of this Court continued to differ unless this is inevitable because of provisions contained in this country's legislation or the state of our case law. As a matter of first principles, we do not consider that either the use of the word "unsafe" in the legislation or the previous cases compel an approach which does not correspond with that of the ECHR. The requirement of fairness in the criminal process has always been a common law tenet of the greatest importance . . . Fairness in both jurisdictions is not an abstract concept. Fairness is not concerned with technicalities. If a defendant has not had a fair trial and as a result of that injustice has occurred, it would be extremely unsatisfactory if the powers of this Court were not wide enough to rectify that injustice. If, contrary to our expectations, that has not previously been the position, then it seems to us that this is a defect in our procedures which is now capable of rectification under section 3 of the Human Rights Act 1998 . . . The 1998 Act emphasises the desirability of taking a broader rather than a narrower approach as to what constitutes an unsafe conviction. In *R. v. Davis, Rowe and Johnson* this Court acknowledged that there could still be a distinction between its approach and the approach of the European Court of Human Rights. However, in the later case of *R. v. Francom*[63] this Court indicated . . . that we would expect, in the situation there being considered, that the approach of this Court, applying the test of lack of safety would produce the same result as the approach of the ECHR applying the test of lack of fairness. We would suggest that, even if there was previously a difference of approach, that since the 1998 Act came into force, the circumstances in which there will be room for a different result before this Court and before the ECHR because of unfairness based on the respective tests we employ will be rare indeed. Applying the broader approach identified by Rose L.J.,[64] we consider that if a defendant has been denied a fair trial it will almost be inevitable that the conviction will be regarded as unsafe. Certainly, if it would be right to stop a prosecution on the basis that it was an abuse of process, this court would be most unlikely to conclude that if there was a conviction despite this fact, the conviction should not be set aside."

17–31 The effect of applying the interpretative obligation in section 3 of the Human Rights Act is thus to widen the meaning given to the term "unsafe" so as to include unfairness. Circumstances that ought to have led to a stay of the prosecution for abuse of process would clearly afford a strong example of when a conviction should be quashed as unsafe. But the judgment in *Togher* leaves the possibility of a small gap between the Strasbourg test and the Court of Appeal's test.

17–32 In what circumstances might a trial be held unfair in terms of Article 6 and yet not lead to the quashing of a conviction as "unsafe"? The example suggested in

---

[62] [2001] Crim. L.R. 124.
[63] [2000] Crim. L.R. 1018.
[64] In *Mullen* [2000] Q.B. 520.

Davis, Johnson and Rowe[65] is where it is established that the machinery by which the judge was appointed failed to ensure independence or impartiality within Article 6(1). This might be because a part-time or temporary judge was either appointed by a political figure or subject to renewal procedures after a short time in office.[66] The argument is that this might be regarded merely as a technical defect, which has no bearing on the actual conduct of the proceedings and which therefore should not be allowed to undermine a conviction on the evidence. This point requires close scrutiny. The reason for the requirement of impartiality and independence in Article 6(1) is to ensure that there are no improper influences on the court of trial, whether direct or indirect. This might be the case if a part-time or temporary judge is subject to renewal according to "performance indicators" which do not focus on the fairness with which proceedings are conducted. It is far from self-evident that a breach of Article 6 on a ground of that kind is a mere technicality, and that any resulting conviction should nonetheless be upheld. Indeed, the early indications from the House of Lords point to a rather stronger line. In *Forbes*,[67] the House of Lords appeared to suggest that *any* significant breach of Article 6 ought to be sufficient to render a conviction unsafe:

> "Reference was made in argument to the right to a fair trial guaranteed by Article 6 of the ECHR. That is an absolute right. But as the Privy Council pointed out in *Brown*,[68] the subsidiary rights comprised within that Article are not absolute, and it is always necessary to consider all the facts and the whole history of the proceedings in a particular case to judge whether a defendant's right to a fair trial has been infringed or not. If on such consideration it is concluded that a defendant's right to a fair trial has been infringed, a conviction will be held to be unsafe within the meaning of section 2 of the Criminal Appeal Act 1968."

This approach was confirmed in *R. v. A*[69] where Lord Steyn observed that it was;

> " . . . well-established that the guarantee of a fair trial under Article 6 is absolute: a conviction obtained in breach of it cannot stand. The only balancing permitted is in respect of what the concept of a fair trial entails: here account may be taken of the familiar triangulation of interests of the accused, the victim and society".

Thus, the view which now seems to have taken root is that the relative importance of a particular defect in the trial may be taken into account when the Court is considering whether the proceedings, taken as a whole, were unfair. But once that threshold is crossed, the conviction is necessarily unsafe. The qualitative assessment which the Court of Appeal considered to be axiomatic in *Davis, Johnson and Rowe* is now to take place not when the Court is considering whether to quash a conviction obtained in breach of Article 6 (as the Court in *Davis* had assumed) but rather at the antecedent stage of determining whether or not such a breach has occurred. This distinction is easier to state than it is to apply, and there are instances in which the Court of Appeal has treated the two

---

[65] Para. 17–29 above.
[66] See, *e.g.*, *Starrs and Chalmers v. Procurator Fiscal, The Times*, December 17, 1999; (2000) H.R.L.R. 191; 2000 S.L.T. 42.
[67] [2001] 2 W.L.R. 1. See also *Brown v. Stott* [2001] 2 W.L.R. 817 at 825A.
[68] [2001] 2 W.L.R. 817. See para. 15–87 *et seq.* above.
[69] Judgment May 17, 2001; [2001] UKHL 25.

approaches as interchangeable. Thus, in *Williams*[70] the Court of Appeal was apparently prepared to accept that a serious non-direction on an element of an offence could result in breach of Article 6, since a resulting conviction would not have been obtained "according to law" as required by Article 6(2). Not surprisingly, the Court went on to hold that a non-direction would have to be significant before it could have this effect. In deciding this latter issue, however, the Court applied the modified *Stirland* test propounded in *Davis, Johnson and Rowe* for determining when a breach of Article 6 should render the conviction unsafe:

> "The misdirection or non-direction must be significant. If it is insignificant it cannot have any effect on the safety of a conviction. Nor do we accept that the omission of an element of an offence from the directions to the jury necessarily involves a breach of Article 6(1) or 6(2) of the Convention. If the omission is insignificant there is no breach. Convention rights are to be applied in a sensible and practical way. There is nothing formalistic about them . . . A legal misdirection or non-direction is not significant unless it is possible that, but for the error of law, the jury would have acquitted. This is no more than a restatement of the *Stirland* test, adapted by this Court in *Davis*, to take account of Article 6 of the Convention. This test applies equally to errors of law as to procedural irregularities."

Moreover, there is a limited range of cases in which the European Court has held that a fundamental defect which has occurred at trial has been *cured* by the proceedings on appeal. This may occur, as in *Edwards v. United Kingdom*,[71] where evidence undisclosed at trial has been admitted on appeal, and subjected to adversarial argument.[72] This principle was pressed into service in *Craven*[73] where a conviction was upheld despite a number of irregularities at trial. Referring directly to *Edwards* the Court held that it was entitled to have regard not only to the evidence which had been wrongly withheld at trial, but also to fresh DNA evidence which pointed strongly to the appellant's guilt. The duty of the Court was to evaluate all the evidence available to it in deciding whether a conviction was safe. In that way, the Court held that the rights of the defence under Article 6 were properly secured.

17–33 If the Court of Appeal were to find that there has been a breach of a defendant's Convention rights, but does not consider it necessary or appropriate to quash a conviction, is it able to afford any other remedy? Section 8 of the Human Rights Act enables a court to grant any remedy which is *within its existing powers* and which it considers just and appropriate. One possibility might be for the Court of Appeal to grant a remedy in damages whilst leaving the conviction intact. This would depend upon treating the Court of Appeal as a single court which sits in

---

[70] *The Times*, March 30, 2001.
[71] (1992) 15 E.H.R.R. 417.
[72] See paras 14–90 *et seq.* above. Whilst the European Court has been prepared to adopt this approach in relation to undisclosed evidence, this appears to be the exception rather than the rule. Thus, in *Findlay v. United Kingdom* (1997) 24 E.H.R.R. 221, a case involving a lack of structural independence and impartiality, the Court held that since the applicant was charged with a serious offence he was "entitled to a first instance tribunal which fully met the requirements of Article 6". See also *Condron and Condron v. United Kingdom* (2001) 31 E.H.R.R. 1, above para. 17–28 (Court of Appeal unable to remedy misdirection on adverse inference from silence); and *Rowe and Davis v. United Kingdom* (2000) 30 E.H.R.R. 1, above para. 17–28a (Court of Appeal unable to remedy unfairness arising from non-disclosure through an *ex parte* public interest immunity hearing).
[73] *The Times*, February 2, 2001.

two divisions, and which therefore already has jurisdiction to award compensation. Apart from any technical objections, there is an obvious risk that this would be seen by the public and the appellant as an unsatisfactory and inadequate remedy.

A further possibility might be to follow the approach of the South African   **17-34**
Constitutional Court, which has held that a breach of constitutional rights which has caused no prejudice to the accused can be marked by a real, as opposed to nominal, reduction in the sentence imposed.[74] This is an approach already taken in cases where the police have overstepped the mark in encouraging the commission of the offence, but their conduct is held to fall short of the level required to exclude evidence on grounds of entrapment. Mitigation of sentence may be substantial.[75]

II. *The Duty to Reopen Proceedings*

In January 2000 the Committee of Ministers adopted Recommendation No. R   **17-35**
(2000) 2 on the re-examination or reopening of certain cases at domestic level following judgments of the European Court of Human Rights. Paragraph II of the Recommendation;

> "Encourages the Contracting Parties, in particular, to examine their national legal systems with a view to ensuring that there exist adequate possibilities of re-examination of the case, including reopening of proceedings, in instances where the Court has found a violation of the Convention, especially where:
>   (i) the injured party continues to suffer very serious negative consequences because of the outcome of the domestic decision at issue, which are not adequately remedied by the just satisfaction and cannot be rectified except by re-examination or re-opening, and
> (ii) the judgment of the Court leads to the conclusion that (a) the impugned domestic decision is on the merits contrary to the Convention, or (b) the violation found is based on procedural errors or shortcomings of such gravity that a serious doubt is cast on the outcome of the domestic proceedings complained of."

The question is whether English law makes provision for such reopening. It   **17-36**
seems that this can be achieved through the Criminal Cases Review Commission considering a case and deciding to refer it to the Court of Appeal. The Recommendation falls short of imposing an absolute obligation to make such a reference, but one might expect that in all but the most exceptional case the Criminal Cases Review Commission should be expected to refer back to the Court of Appeal a case in which a violation has been found in Strasbourg.

D. DECLARATIONS OF INCOMPATIBILITY

It is inevitable that in certain cases the Court of Appeal will be confronted with   **17-37**
an appellant whose conviction is found to be incompatible with a Convention

---

[74] *Wild and anor v. Hoffert and ors* (1998) 6 B.C.L.R. 656; (1998) 2 S.A.C.R. 1 (CC).
[75] *E.g. Beaumont* (1987) 9 Cr. App. R. (S) 342; *Tonnessen* [1998] 2 Cr. App. R. (S) 328.

right as a result of primary legislation which cannot "possibly" be interpreted compatibly, under section 3 of the Human Rights Act. The Court of Appeal has power under section 4 to make a declaration of incompatibility. It has been suggested that the word "may" in section 4 will in practice be interpreted by the Court as meaning "shall". It seems unlikely that there will be many cases in which the Court would consider it appropriate to exercise its discretion against the making of a declaration where the legislation itself was found to be incompatible, and the issue was likely to arise in future cases.

17–38 There might, of course, be cases in which the incompatibility is specific to the particular facts, and is never likely to arise again. But even in that situation the Court would presumably have to determine the issue of compatibility as a precondition to the exercise of its discretion under section 4. This would, in itself, come very close to a declaration of incompatibility. One situation in which the Court might consider it unnecessary to grant a declaration would be where there was no substantial injustice to the individual and the legislation in question had since been amended or repealed so as to remove the incompatibility.

17–39 Section 5 of the Human Rights Act provides that where the Court is considering whether to make a declaration of incompatibility the Crown is entitled to notice and the relevant Minister is entitled to be joined as a party. In criminal proceedings the Crown is of course already a party. However, it is open to doubt whether the presence of prosecuting counsel meets the requirements of section 5. The object of the section is to enable the Minister responsible to make representations to the Court. The DPP is not a member of the Executive, and does not act on behalf of any government Minister. It may therefore be appropriate for the Home Office or other relevant body to be notified by the Court directly and given an opportunity to intervene, as occurred recently in *R. v. A* in the House of Lords.[76]

17–40 In those cases in which the Court of Appeal does go on to make a declaration under section 4, there is a potentially serious lacuna in the Act. This is because it is for the Minister to determine whether to make a remedial order under section 10 and Schedule 2, and if so whether to make it retrospective in effect and whether to grant any incidental relief. The Minister could in principle release an individual from custody pending the making of a remedial order, in the exercise of prerogative powers (although an arrangement under which the Executive— rather than the judiciary—decides on whether an individual should be deprived of their liberty may give rise to other Convention points).

17–41 If a remedial order is made, the Minister can remove all the consequences of the conviction, either by granting a pardon or in the exercise of the powers provided in Schedule 2 of the Act. However, a Minister cannot quash a criminal conviction. That can only be done by the Court of Appeal. Thus, if the Court of Appeal is to have power to quash the conviction in these circumstances then it would have to be able to retain jurisdiction over the appeal by adjourning the case after the declaration has been made, so as to enable the Minister to consider his/her

---

[76] See para. 15–137 above. The procedural issue is reported as *R. v. A (Joinder of Appropriate Minister)* [2001] 1 W.L.R. 789.

response. If that were possible, then the Court would also have power to grant bail in a very clear case, where the likely Ministerial response was known.

However, the terms of the Act appear to preclude this. Under section 10(1) the **17–42** Minister can only take remedial action following a declaration of incompatibility if all parties to the proceedings in which the declaration was made have abandoned any right of appeal, the time limit for appeal has expired, or any further appeal has been determined. This suggests that the Court of Appeal is *functus officio* once it has made a declaration under section 4. The unfortunate consequence is that the appellant's conviction will have to stand despite any remedial order which the Minister may make in the light of the Court's declaration. The appellant's only recourse is to petition the CCRC for a reference back to the Court of Appeal under section 9 of the Criminal Appeal Act 1995, a result which is cumbersome, expensive and unjust.

CHAPTER 18

THE RIGHTS OF VICTIMS OF CRIME

A. INTRODUCTION

The principal purpose of the Convention is the protection of the rights of **18–01**
individuals from infringement by states. However, the Court has recognised that,
if the rights declared in the Convention are to be protected effectively, certain
provisions must be read as imposing positive obligations on the state. This
chapter examines those positive obligations that protect victims (and potential
victims) of crime, and others (notably witnesses) whose rights may be infringed
during the criminal process.[1]

The chapter is divided into six parts. Part B discusses the duty on public **18–02**
authorities to take steps to protect individuals from the infringement of their
rights under Article 2 and Article 3. Part C examines the state's duty to have in
place criminal laws that prohibit certain forms of conduct which infringes
Convention rights. Part D concerns the duty to investigate alleged breaches of
Articles 2 and 3. Part E examines the related duty to bring a prosecution where
there is evidence of such a breach. In Part F there is discussion of the procedural
rights of victims and witnesses in the course of a criminal prosecution. Finally,
Part G examines the rights of victims and their families in relation to the
sentencing process.

B. OBLIGATION TO PREVENT INFRINGEMENTS OF RIGHTS UNDER ARTICLES 2 AND 3

As its starting point in the judgment in *Osman v. United Kingdom*[2] the Court **18–03**
made the following general statement:

"The Court notes that the first sentence of Article 2(1) enjoins the State not only to
refrain from the intentional and unlawful taking of life, but also to take appropriate
steps to safeguard the lives of those within its jurisdiction.[3] It is common ground that
the State's obligation in this respect extends beyond its primary duty to secure the right
to life by putting in place effective criminal law provisions to deter the commission of
offences against the person backed up by law enforcement machinery for the prevention, suppression and sanctioning of breaches of such provisions. It is thus accepted by
those appearing before the Court that Article 2 of the Convention may also imply in
certain well-defined circumstances a positive obligation on the authorities to take

---

[1] For a useful brief survey, see J. Wadham and J. Arkinstall, "Rights of victims of crime" (2000) New
L.J. 1023 and 1083.
[2] (2000) 29 E.H.R.R. 245.
[3] The Court referred here to its judgment in *LCB v. United Kingdom* (1999) 27 E.H.R.R. 212, para.
36.

preventive operational measures to protect an individual whose life is at risk from the criminal acts of another individual."[4]

18–04   This passage establishes two separate but related obligations. The positive obligation to have "effective criminal law provisions" to protect the Article 2 rights of individuals is a duty that lies on the state as a whole. That obligation extends to enforcement procedures and systems: there must be courts, police, and prosecutors and so forth. But the focus of the present discussion is the related positive obligation to take *operational* measures in order to secure the protection of Article 2 rights in circumstances where particular persons are at risk. The taking of operational measures will usually be a matter for the police, but the state is ultimately responsible for ensuring that Article 2 rights are protected.

18–05   In *Osman*, where the applicant and his family had notified the police about the threatening behaviour of a certain schoolteacher, the government argued before the Court that the obligation should not arise unless the failure of the police to perceive the risk to life amounted to gross negligence or wilful disregard of the duty to protect life. However, the Court held that the test is whether "the authorities knew or ought to have known at the time of the existence of a real and immediate risk to the life of an identified individual or individuals from the criminal acts of a third party."[5] Although there will always be difficulties in applying this to the facts,[6] this is a broader standard of liability designed to ensure greater protection for the Article 2 rights of individuals. Mere negligence rather than gross negligence is the ground for liability. Put in terms of the positive obligation, the authorities have a duty to assess the situation as they may reasonably be expected to do.

18–06   The Court acknowledged "the difficulties involved in policing modern societies, the unpredictability of human conduct and the operational choices which must be made in terms of priorities and resources," and it therefore concluded that the scope of the positive obligation must not be such as to "impose an impossible or disproportionate burden on the authorities." However, the Court again rejected the government's argument that gross negligence should be the standard of liability. It held that the test should be whether the authorities "failed to take measures within the scope of their powers which, judged reasonably, might have been expected to avoid that risk" (*i.e.* the identified risk to life). Put in terms of the positive obligation, the authorities have a duty to "do all that could be reasonably expected of them to avoid a real and immediate risk to life of which they have or ought to have knowledge."[7]

18–07   The Court made it clear that a principal reason for imposing a more demanding standard than that for which the government had contended was the fundamental nature of the right declared by Article 2. Since the right to life is in one sense the

---

[4] (2000) 29 E.H.R.R. 245 at para. 115.
[5] *ibid.*, para. 116.
[6] See also *Keenan v. United Kingdom* Judgment April 3, 2001.
[7] (1998) 29 E.H.R.R. 245 at para. 116.

most basic of all the Convention rights, it is appropriate to expect the authorities to take seriously any threats to that right, and to give some priority to preventive measures in cases where the risk of an attack on that right is foreseeable. But, as will be seen in section C below, those preventive measures must be taken with due regard to the rights of others who may be affected. This means not only the right to life of the person who is alleged to pose the threat, but also wider rights of that person and others. Police powers must be exercised "in a manner which fully respects the due process and other guarantees which legitimately place restraints on the scope of their action to investigate crime and bring offenders to justice, including the guarantees contained in Articles 5 and 8 of the Convention."[8]

This last consideration was one of several factors which led the Court to conclude   **18–08**
in the *Osman* case that there had been no violation of Article 2 in failing to prevent the incident in which the schoolteacher shot and killed the father of the boy with whom he was infatuated. Although there had been a sequence of incidents, some strange and others potentially dangerous, the Court held that there was no stage at which it could be said that the police knew or ought to have known that the lives of any members of the Osman family "were at real and immediate risk" from the schoolteacher. The police could not be criticised for failing to arrest him, since they have a duty to act in accordance with the rights of freedoms of all individuals, and the required standard of suspicion was not fulfilled.

The decision in *Osman* was followed in the context of an alleged violation of   **18–09**
Article 3 in *Z and ors v. United Kingdom.*[9] The applicants were four children who suffered appalling neglect at the hands of their parents, over a period of years. The local authority with statutory responsibility for the children were kept fully informed of the conditions, but devoted their resources to keeping them with their parents instead of removing them into care. There was no dispute that the conditions amounted to inhuman and degrading treatment. The more difficult issue was whether the state could be held responsible for the criminal acts of the parents committed in their own home. The Court held that it could:

> "Article 3 enshrines one of the most fundamental values of a democratic society. It prohibits in absolute terms torture or inhuman or degrading treatment or punishment. [The Convention] requires States to take measures designed to ensure that individuals within their jurisdiction are not subjected to torture or inhuman or degrading treatment, including such ill-treatment administered by private individuals. These measures should provide effective protection, in particular, of children and other vulnerable persons and include reasonable steps to prevent ill-treatment of which the authorities had or ought to have had knowledge . . . [The local authority] was under a statutory duty to protect the children and had a range of powers available to them, including removal from their home. The children were however only taken into emergency care, at the insistence of the mother, on 30 April 1992. Over the intervening period of four and a half years, they had been subject in their home to what the consultant child psychiatrist who examined them referred to as horrific experiences. The Criminal Injuries Compensation Board had also found that the children had been subject to appalling neglect over an extended period and suffered physical and psychological injury directly attributable to a crime of violence. The Court acknowledges the difficult and sensitive decisions facing social

---

[8] *ibid.*.
[9] Judgment May 10, 2001.

services and the important countervailing principle of respecting and preserving family life. The present case however leaves no doubt as to the failure of the system to protect these child applicants from serious, long-term neglect and abuse. Accordingly, there has been a violation of Article 3 of the Convention."

C. OBLIGATION TO HAVE IN PLACE LAWS WHICH PENALISE INFRINGEMENTS OF BASIC RIGHTS

18–10   Several decisions of the Strasbourg Court confirm that Contracting States have obligations to ensure that their domestic criminal law penalises the infringement of certain basic rights, so as to provide protection for those rights.

I. *Protection of Article 3 Rights*

18–11   Article 3 has an obvious application in the field of corporal punishment, which may amount to inhuman and degrading treatment. Two separate questions then arise. First, what degree of physical chastisement constitutes "inhuman and degrading treatment" for the purposes of Article 3? And secondly, is the state responsible for what one private individual does to another?

18–12   In the well-known decision in *Tyrer v. United Kingdom*[10] the Court held that the use of the birch as a punishment in the Isle of Man was "degrading" and therefore contravened Article 3. By contrast, in *Costello-Roberts v. United Kingdom*[11] the Court held that beating a boy three times through his shorts with a rubber-soled gym shoe did not amount to "degrading punishment", the Court referring to the absence of serious long-term physical effects. Two years earlier, in *Y v. United Kingdom*,[12] the Commission had found a violation of Article 3 in a case of caning over trousers, where the caning had left the boy with severe bruising and swelling. Neither of the last two cases derived from criminal proceedings, and both of them concerned the use of corporal punishment in schools. Indeed, several applications to Strasbourg have concerned physical discipline at schools,[13] with the Commission particularly ready to find that the treatment or punishment was degrading where it was administered by a male teacher to a teenage girl pupil.[14]

18–13   The question of the limits of Article 3 came squarely before the Court in the case of *A v. United Kingdom*,[15] where the applicant's stepfather had been acquitted of assault occasioning actual bodily harm. It was admitted that the stepfather had caned the boy (then aged nine) on several occasions, but the jury evidently did not believe that the prosecution had proved that the canings were more than "moderate and reasonable chastisement." By the time the case reached the

---

[10] (1979–80) 2 E.H.R.R. 1.
[11] (1995) 19 E.H.R.R. 112.
[12] (1994) 17 E.H.R.R. 238.
[13] See, *e.g.*, *Mrs X v. United Kingdom* (1979) 14 D.R. 205, *B and D v. United Kingdom* (1986) 49 D.R. 44, and *Family A v. United Kingdom* (1987) 52 D.R. 156.
[14] See *Mrs X and Miss Y v. United Kingdom* (1984) 36 D.R. 49, and *Warwick v. United Kingdom* (1989) 60 D.R. 5 and 22.
[15] (1999) 27 E.H.R.R. 611.

Strasbourg Court the United Kingdom government had accepted that there was a breach of Article 3. The Commission had found that "the strokes were severe enough to leave bruises which . . . were visible several days later."[16]

Turning to the issue of state responsibility, the Court held that the United **18–14** Kingdom was responsible for the violation committed by the stepfather because the criminal law afforded too great a degree of latitude to a jury. The obligation laid on states by Article 1 of the Convention, taken together with Article 3:

> "requires States to take measures designed to ensure that individuals within their jurisdiction are not subjected to torture or inhuman or degrading treatment or punishment, including such ill-treatment administered by private individuals. Children and other vulnerable individuals, in particular, are entitled to State protection, in the form of effective deterrence, against such serious breaches of personal integrity."[17]

In principle, therefore, the laws of each state must, at a minimum, be defined in such a way as to ensure that any breach of Article 3 constitutes a criminal offence.

In *A v. United Kingdom* the Court held that the breadth of the defence of **18–15** reasonable chastisement in English law is such that it "fails to provide adequate protection to children and should be amended."[18] The scope of the defence remains uncertain. One of the few cases in which it has been considered by the Court of Appeal is *Smith*,[19] where the mother of a six year old boy asked her partner to "smack" the child for disobedience and the man gave the child two strokes with his belt. He was convicted of assault occasioning actual bodily harm, the jury having rejected his defence that he did no more than inflict "moderate and reasonable chastisement". The Court of Appeal dismissed his appeal, on the basis that this was the correct test.

In what way should English law be amended? One approach would be to **18–16** criminalise all physical chastisement of children, following the laws of certain other Contracting States[20] so as to protect children against physical abuse. Another approach would be to attempt to criminalise the inhuman or degrading treatment of children without prohibiting all "smacking." The Scottish Law Commission proposed, some years ago, that it should not be a defence to any assault charge that a parent struck a child with a stick, belt or other object, or in such a way as to cause or risk causing injury or lasting pain or discomfort.[21] Like all such compromises, this leaves a considerable area of uncertainty which magistrates and jurors would have to resolve in individual cases, without parents always being able to foresee on which side of the line their conduct would be held to fall.

---

[16] *ibid.*, at 619.
[17] Para. 22.
[18] Para. 24.
[19] [1985] Crim. L.R. 42.
[20] See, *e.g.*, the Swedish law discussed by the Commission in *Seven Individuals v. Sweden* (1982) 29 D.R. 104.
[21] Scottish Law Commission, *Report on Family Law*, Scot Law Com. No. 135, (1992), pp 19–33.

II. *Protection of Article 2 Rights*

18–17   Article 2 declares everyone's right to life, but allows exceptions when depriva-tion of life "results from the use of force which is no more than absolutely necessary (a) in defence of any person from unlawful violence; (b) in order to effect a lawful arrest or to prevent the escape of a person lawfully detained; (c) in action lawfully taken for the purpose of quelling a riot or insurrection."

Justifiable Force

18–18   The scope and application of the exceptions in Article 2 were considered in the Gibraltar shooting case, *McCann and others v. United Kingdom*,[22] where the European Court differed from the Commission's finding and held (by 10 votes to nine) that the United Kingdom had violated Article 2 in the shooting by SAS soldiers of three IRA terrorist suspects. The government's argument had been that the three suspects were believed to have a radio-control detonator which would activate a car bomb, and that it was necessary to kill them to prevent the imminent detonation. In the event, neither a radio-control device nor a car bomb was found. The majority judgment began by stating that the purpose of Article 2 is to secure practical and effective protection of each individual's life, and it went on to make three significant points:

— it emphasised that a person may only be intentionally killed by the state where "absolutely necessary", a "stricter and more compelling test" than that applicable to the phrase "necessary in a democratic society" under paragraph 2 of Articles 8 to 11.

— it stated that its inquiries concerned not only the actions of the law enforcement officers but also the planning of any law enforcement opera-tion, to ascertain whether it was organised so as to "minimise, to the greatest extent possible, recourse to lethal force".

— it held that the actions of the officers should be judged on the facts that they honestly believed, for good reasons, to exist.

18–19   The Court found that the soldiers themselves had not violated Article 2 because, on the information given to them, they did have good reason for the beliefs that led them to fire the shots. However, the majority of the Court added that the immediate reaction of the soldiers, in shooting the three suspects dead, lacked "the degree of caution in the use of firearms to be expected from law enforce-ment personnel in a democratic society, even when dealing with dangerous terrorist suspects." The Court went on to hold however that the United Kingdom government had violated Article 2, through its failure to ensure that the operation was planned so as to minimise the risk of death: the killings had not been shown to be "absolutely necessary" for the "defence of any person from unlawful violence."

18–20   In the subsequent case of *Andronicou and Constantinou v. Cyprus*[23] the Court differed from the Commission's finding of a violation of Article 2 and held (by five votes to four) that there had been no breach. The case arose from a siege, in

---

[22] (1996) 21 E.H.R.R. 97.
[23] (1998) 25 E.H.R.R. 491.

which Andronicou was holding Ms Constantinou hostage. Andronicou was known to be unstable, and to have a gun, and when Ms Constantinou was heard to scream a special police unit went in. They used tear-gas and then, when Andronicou fired at them as they entered his house, they replied with several rounds of automatic fire. Andronicou was killed instantly; Ms Constantinou was wounded and died shortly afterwards. The majority of the Court accepted that it had to consider the "planning and control" of the operation, and determine whether the force used was "strictly proportionate" to the purpose, on the facts that the officers honestly believed, for good reasons, to exist. In view of the deployment of machine guns in a confined space the Court regretted that so much fire power had been used, but narrowly concluded that the use of lethal force could not be said to have exceeded what was absolutely necessary for the purpose of defending the lives of Ms Constantinou and of the officers themselves.

The application of Article 2 to the facts created great difficulty in these cases: not   **18–21**
only did the Commission and the Court take different views, but the Court's decisions were both by the narrowest of majorities and contain some powerful dissenting judgments. Moreover, the Court stated that in interpreting Article 2 it was neither determining the compatibility of a state's laws with the Convention nor determining the criminal liability of any party.[24]

However, on a direct analogy with the decision of the Court in *A v. United*   **18–22**
Kingdom,[25] it can be strongly argued that the rules of English law on self-defence and the justifiable use of force ought to be framed in such a way as to afford greater protection for the right to life of those against whom force is used under colour of justification. The Court in *McCann* considered the Gibraltar law of justifiable force, contained in Article 2 of the Gibraltar Constitution, which provides for a killing to be justified on stated grounds if the force was "reasonably justifiable". The Court observed that "the Convention standard appears on its face to be stricter", but it concluded that the difference was not so great as to justify a finding of a violation of Article 2 on this ground alone.[26] This raises the question whether the even less demanding English rules, under section 3 of the Criminal Law Act 1967 or at common law, give adequate protection to Article 2 rights.

The jurisprudence starts from the proposition that the right to life of everyone   **18–23**
(including suspected or actual offenders) should be protected so far as possible. This emphasis on the right to life is not usually to be found as the starting point in English criminal cases, where the focus is upon whether the court has been left in reasonable doubt over the justifiability of the killing. In the same vein, the term "absolutely necessary" is undoubtedly stronger than the term "necessary" as it is understood in English law. Beyond that, there are at least three issues that warrant further consideration.

First, the Strasbourg jurisprudence is most closely concerned with cases in which   **18–24**
there was a killing by law enforcement officers or other state agents. The English approach is not to differentiate between private individuals and state agents in the

---

[24] (1996) 21 E.H.R.R. 97 at paras 155 and 173.
[25] Discussed at para. 18–13 above.
[26] (1996) 21 E.H.R.R. 97 at paras 154–155.

standards of reasonableness laid down. There has been criticism of this,[27] and it seems that the Article 2 jurisprudence requires law enforcement officers to plan their operations so as to minimise the risk to life. The requirement of proper planning suggests that the ambit of criminal liability might be spread wider than the law enforcement officers who actually caused the death, and raises the possibility that commanding officers might in some circumstances be prosecuted for aiding and abetting the killing. If it could be established that there had been gross negligence on the part of senior officers which led to deaths, a prosecution for manslaughter might have a realistic prospect of resulting in conviction[28]— the Human Rights Act would not be creating a criminal offence,[29] but the Convention would be grounding the duty of the senior police officer which might then be the basis for a manslaughter conviction. This line of argument is strengthened by the decision in *Osman v. United Kingdom*.[30] More generally, one implication of section 6 of the Human Rights Act 1998, requiring public authorities to act in accordance with the Convention, is that senior law enforcement officers should train their personnel and plan their operations so as to preserve life to the maximum degree.

18–25 Secondly, the Court insisted, in both *McCann*[31] and *Andronicou*,[32] that the beliefs on which officers act should be based on "good reason." This appears to be a more demanding standard than the "honest belief" held sufficient in *Gladstone Williams*[33] and *Beckford v. R.*[34] even though the Court was mindful of the need to avoid imposing "an unrealistic burden on the state and its law enforcement officers". The purpose of the stricter standard in the Strasbourg cases is to provide greater protection of the right to life by requiring law enforcement personnel, where the situation permits it, to make efforts to verify their beliefs. If "good reason" is to be required where a defence of mistaken belief is raised in a case of this kind, the subjective test of mistake may need to be refined where the defence is based on justifiable force. On the other hand the application of Article 2 in *Andronicou* suggests that, even in respect of trained law enforcement officers, some indulgence should be granted to "heat of the moment" reactions, along the lines of *Palmer v. R.*[35]

18–26 A third cluster of points relate to the precise wording of the exceptions to Article 2. Although the killing must be "absolutely necessary" for the achievement of one of the three stated purposes, there is no requirement of proportionality on the face of Article 2: that defect in the drafting has, however, been remedied by the case law, and in *Andronicou* the Court stated that the force must be "strictly proportionate."[36] The first exception to Article 2 refers to the "defence of any

---

[27] A. Ashworth, *Principles of Criminal Law* (3rd ed., 1999), pp 137–151.
[28] *cf.* the facts of the well-known tort case of *Alcock v. Chief Constable of South Yorkshire* [1992] 1 A.C. 155, arising out of the Hillsborough football stadium disaster.
[29] Section 7(8) of the HRA 1998, discussed at 18–44 below.
[30] (2000) 29 E.H.R.R. 245.
[31] (1996) 21 E.H.R.R. 97 at para. 200.
[32] (1998) 25 E.H.R.R. 491 at para. 192.
[33] (1984) 78 Cr. App. R. 276.
[34] [1988] A.C. 130.
[35] [1971] A.C. 814.
[36] See the Commission's decision in *Stewart v. United Kingdom* (1984) 39 D.R. 162, the Court's statement in *Andronicou and Constantinou* (1998) 25 E.H.R.R. 491 at para. 171, and the statement and application of the principle in *Gulec v. Turkey* (1999) 28 E.H.R.R. 121 at para. 71.

person from unlawful violence". The reference is to "violence" rather than to "killing", suggesting that it is in conformity to the Convention to deprive a person of their life when that person is inflicting, or about to inflict, serious but non-life-threatening injury on another. The wording also leaves open the question of how imminent the "unlawful violence" must be. This was an issue before the Commission in *Kelly v. United Kingdom*,[37] where soldiers in Northern Ireland had opened fire on a stolen car containing three youths which was speeding away from a checkpoint, and one of the occupants was killed. In the civil action that followed, the Northern Ireland courts accepted that the soldiers suspected the youths of being terrorists and thought that they would continue terrorist (therefore life-threatening) activities if allowed to drive away. How far into the future might such activities take place, and does this affect the "prevention of crime" justification? These important questions were not resolved by the Commission, which pointed out that the prevention of crime is not mentioned as an exception to Article 2 and could therefore not be relied upon. But the same issue of "imminence" arises in relation to the "unlawful violence" exception in Article 2(2)(a). In *McCann* the point was not tested because it was assumed that the detonation of the alleged bomb was indeed imminent.

In rejecting the application in *Kelly*, the Commission held that the soldiers' use **18–27** of deadly force was justified according to Article 2(2)(b), as "absolutely necessary . . . in order to effect a lawful arrest." Sir John Smith has pointed out that there was no power of arrest in the circumstances of that case, and that the Commission misunderstood the position.[38] Moreover there is a fundamental question about the drafting of Article 2: how can a killing be necessary to effect an arrest, since by definition there can be no arrest if the person has been killed? Even if this point is regarded as overdone, there are other difficulties. As Trechsel has argued, what is missing from this part of Article 2 "is a reference to the relationship between the force used for the purpose of the arrest on the one hand and the reason for the arrest on the other hand."[39] The force permissible to arrest a speeding motorist, a truanting child or an illegal immigrant ought to be severely limited, as Trechsel argues.

There are also further questions about the scope of the exceptions: Article 2(2)(c) **18–28** creates an exception for cases of killing in the course of lawful action to quell a riot or insurrection (which must be "strictly proportionate", as for the other exceptions),[40] but the absence of any general "prevention of crime" exception means that killing to protect property is always a breach of the Convention. Only if the term "unlawful violence" in the Convention were to be given an artificially wide meaning could killing in imminent cases of burglary or arson be brought within the exceptions to Article 2, although there might be an argument that

---

[37] (1993) 74 D.R. 139, on which see the valuable discussion by Sir John Smith, "The right to life and the right to kill in law enforcement" (1994) N.L.J. 354.
[38] *ibid.*, at 355.
[39] S. Trechsel, "Spotlights on Article 2 ECHR, the Right to Life", in W. Benedek, H. Isak and R. Kicker (eds), *Development and Developing International and European Law* (Frankfurt, 1999), p. 685.
[40] *Stewart v. United Kingdom* (1999) 39 D.R. 162, *Gulec v. Turkey* (1999) 28 E.H.R.R. 121.

robbery (which is defined so as to require an element of force) and rape would satisfy the requirement.[41]

18–29   The Strasbourg case law is of course primarily concerned with killings by law enforcement officers. But the state's positive obligation is to ensure that the law protects the lives of citizens from unjustifiable deprivation by other individuals.[42] Although a private citizen would be unlikely to violate Article 2 rights by failing to plan an "operation" with sufficient care and respect for life,[43] a private citizen might well use force against another without "good reason" and that might lead to an acquittal under current English law whilst violating the Article 2 right of the victim. This may suggest that the relevant rules of English law require adaptation generally, and not just in their application to law enforcement officers.

Abortion

18–30   A second question arising from Article 2 is whether it protects the right to life of a foetus or unborn child and, therefore, whether the provisions of the Abortion Act 1967 are vulnerable to challenge. The 1967 Act specifies various procedures for therapeutic abortion, allowing medical termination *inter alia* if the pregnancy is in the first 24 weeks and "the continuance of the pregnancy would involve risk, greater than if the pregnancy were terminated, of injury to the physical or mental health of the pregnant woman or any existing children of her family." Questions about the impact of the Convention on abortion have not been faced directly by the Court, but there are a few decisions of the Commission which may be taken to suggest the likely approach of the Court.

18–31   In *Paton v. United Kingdom*[44] the Commission held that Article 2 does not confer on unborn children an absolute right to life, and that the abortion of a 10–week old foetus in order to prevent "injury to the physical or mental health of the pregnant woman", under the 1967 Act, did not violate Article 2. The Commission stated that, even assuming that the right to life is secured to a foetus from the beginning of pregnancy, this right is subject to an implied limitation allowing pregnancy to be terminated in order to protect the mother's life or health.[45] In a subsequent decision, *H. v. Norway*,[46] the Commission held that the abortion of a 14–week old foetus on the statutory ground that the "pregnancy, birth or care of the child may place the woman in a difficult situation in life" did not violate Article 2. In a sphere in which the laws of Contracting States vary somewhat, it is normal for the Strasbourg organs to leave a significant margin of appreciation. However, the Commission went on to state that it "will not exclude that in certain circumstances" the right to life of an unborn child might be protected.

---

[41] For comparison, see the extended notion of a "violent offence" for the purpose of s.2(2)(b) of the Criminal Justice Act 1991, as defined in s.31 of that Act, discussed in *Archbold 2001*, para. 5–6.
[42] By analogy with the Court's decision in *A v. United Kingdom* (1998) 27 E.H.R.R. 611.
[43] There may be rare cases where this is relevant: see Ashworth, "Self-Defence and the Right to Life" [1976] Camb. L.J. 282 at 292–296.
[44] (1980) 3 E.H.R.R. 408.
[45] The applicant in this case was the prospective father, and the Commission considered (and dismissed) various arguments based on Art. 8 to the effect that the prospective father's right to respect for his family life was violated if the prospective mother was allowed to have a termination without regard for his wishes.
[46] (1992) 73 D.R. 155.

There remains a theoretical possibility that the availability of therapeutic abortion   **18–32**
up to 24 weeks (under the 1967 Act) might be attacked as affording insufficient
protection to the life of the unborn child. This argument is left open by the two
decisions of the Commission discussed above, although its prospects of success
are diminished by the emphasis in the Commission's reasoning on the risk to the
mother's health and by the considerable margin of appreciation appropriate to
this issue. As Trechsel comments, the Commission avoided taking a definite
position on the application of Article 2 in this sphere, "by saying that even if a
certain protection of the foetus were to be regarded as being covered by the
guarantee, the interference was justified in the circumstances."[47] However, it is
noteworthy that the German Constitutional Court, in reviewing two successive
abortion statutes, has recognised the foetus as having a right to life that should
be granted protection under the German constitution—not an absolute right, but
one that cannot simply be subordinated to the pregnant woman's interests.[48]

Controversy has also raged on this issue in the United States since the historic   **18–33**
decision in *Roe v. Wade*,[49] where the Supreme Court struck down a Texas statute
that prohibited abortion in all cases except where the mother's life was in danger.
The rationale for the decision, much debated, was that the pregnant woman's
right to privacy was fundamental. The right was not absolute, but states could
only place limits on it for compelling reasons. The majority of the Court stated,
further, that a foetus is not a "person", for constitutional purposes, but that states
do have an interest in protecting "potential life", an interest that becomes
compelling when the foetus is viable. The decision has generated enormous
debate,[50] and subsequent decisions of the Supreme Court have diluted its effect
while stopping short of overruling it. There is now recognition that states have an
interest in protecting potential human life from the stage of conception,[51] and
there is also acceptance that states do not need to find a "compelling" reason for
restricting abortion so long as they do not impose an "undue burden on a
woman's ability" to make a decision.[52]

A different approach may be found in some of the jurisprudence of the Supreme   **18–34**
Court of Canada, interpreting Article 7 of the Canadian Charter which guarantees
an individual's "right to life, liberty and security of person." In the leading case
of *Morgentaler, Smoling and Scott v. R*,[53] the Court focussed on the bodily
security of the pregnant woman. The provisions of the Criminal Code required a
pregnant woman who wanted an abortion to submit an application to a local
"therapeutic abortion committee", resulting in delays and, in some areas, the
virtual unavailability of therapeutic abortions. The Supreme Court found that this
procedure infringed the guarantee of security of the person, in both physical and
emotional senses, by subjecting pregnant women to psychological stress. It is
highly unlikely that existing English procedures would be vulnerable on the

---

[47] Trechsel (n. 43, above), p. 672.
[48] See BVerfGe 39, 1 (1975), and BVerfGe, 203 (1993).
[49] 410 U.S. 113 (1973).
[50] See, for example, the extensive treatment in L.A. Tribe, *American Constitutional Law* (2nd ed., 1988), Chapter 15, and the same writer's monograph, *Abortion: the Clash of Absolutes* (1990).
[51] *Webster v. Reproductive Health Services* 492 U.S. 490 (1989).
[52] *Planned Parenthood v. Casey* 505 U.S. 833 (1992). For a recent survey, see D.P. Kommers and J.E. Finn, *American Constitutional Law* (1998), pp 450–454 and 460–464.
[53] (1988) 44 D.L.R. (4th) 385.

Morgentaler approach, but if restrictions on the availability of abortions under English law were contemplated, it would be necessary to reckon with the possibility of a challenge under the Convention along these lines.

Patients in a Persistant Vegetative State

18–35   In its well-known decision in *Airedale NHS Trust v. Bland*,[54] the House of Lords held that it is lawful to discontinue the life-sustaining treatment of a PVS patient if it is no longer in the patient's best interests for the treatment to continue. The discontinuance of treatment is regarded as an omission, which then raises the question whether there is a duty to continue treatment. If it is not in the patient's best interests, then no such duty exists. Is this reasoning consistent or inconsistent with the right to life declared in Article 2?

18–36   There is no Strasbourg decision on this point. The closest case is *Widmer v. Switzerland*,[55] where the applicant alleged a breach of Article 2 when hospital staff had declined to treat his father in an advanced state of Parkinson's disease, who then died. The application was dismissed by the Commission on the ground that the offence of negligent manslaughter in Swiss law was sufficient to discharge the state's positive duty to "take all reasonable steps to protect life" under Article 2. There was no need for the Swiss legislature to go further and to enact a special law penalising passive euthanasia. This ruling suggests that the "negligence" approach is sufficient, and that the question whether there should be a duty to provide life-sustaining treatment where there are unlikely to be any benefits to the patient is crucial. On euthanasia there is no uniformity among the laws of European states, and van Dijk and van Hoof comment that:

> "even in those situations where it must in reason be assumed that human life still exists, euthanasia does not *per se* conflict with the Convention. In fact, the value of the life to be protected can and must be weighed against other rights of the person in question, particularly his right, laid down in Article 3, to be protected from inhuman and degrading treatment. Whether the will of the person is decisive in such a case depends on whether the right to life is or is not to be regarded as inalienable."[56]

18–37   The matter becomes more complicated when the patient's will has not been and cannot be expressed. In *NHS Trust A v. Mrs M* and *NHS Trust B v. Mrs H*,[57] Butler-Sloss P. held that the law as formulated in *Airedale NHS Trust v. Bland* is consistent with the Article 2 rights of PVS patients and with the Article 2 obligations of the government. "An omission to provide treatment by the medical team will, in my judgment, only be incompatible with Article 2 where the circumstances are such as to impose a positive obligation on the state to take steps to prolong a patient's life."[58]

18–38   If there is agreement that further treatment will not be in the patient's best interests, there is no duty to continue and the state's obligation does not arise. This reasoning rests on the initial characterisation of the withdrawal of treatment

---

[54] [1993] A.C. 789.
[55] Application No. 20527/92, (unreported).
[56] P. van Dijk and G.J.H. van Hoof, *Theory and Practice of the European Convention on Human Rights* (3rd ed., 1999), pp 302–303.
[57] [2001] 2 W.L.R. 942.
[58] *ibid.*, para. 31.

as an omission rather than an action. In a sphere so sensitive as this, it is most unlikely that the Strasbourg Court would adopt an approach which required member states to criminalise withdrawal of treatment, euthanasia, or (probably) even mercy killings.

Other Surgical Procedures

The Court of Appeal has had to grapple with a question which has not been **18–39** before any of the Strasbourg organs, notably the application of Article 2 to the lawfulness of an operation to separate conjoined twins which is likely to result in the saving of one life and the termination of the other. In *Re A (children)(conjoined twins: surgical separation)*[59] the Court of Appeal held that the operation would be lawful, even though it would result in the death of the weaker twin. The Court did not follow the *Bland* decision[60] in characterising the operation as an omission. It accepted that the separation was an intentional act, but held that the intention was to separate the twins so as to give the stronger twin the opportunity of a long and healthy life. This would not breach Article 2 since it would not amount to depriving the weaker twin of her life "intentionally": her death would be "foreseen as an inevitable consequence" of an operation intended to save her sister, and her death would occur because "her body on its own is not and never has been viable."[61] This interpretation restricts the meaning of "intentionally" to "purposively", which Robert Walker L.J. referred to as the "natural and ordinary meaning" of the word,[62] and which is clearly narrower than the meaning adopted for English criminal law by the House of Lords in *Woollin*.[63] On the *Woollin* definition a result which is "foreseen as an inevitable consequence" is intended, and if the Court of Appeal had adopted this definition they would not have been able to reach their conclusion by this route.

III. *Protection of Article 8 Rights*

The principal thrust of Article 8(1) is to protect an individual's own private life, **18–40** and therefore an application by a person convicted of aiding and abetting the suicide of others was declared inadmissible.[64]

The concept of "private life" in Article 8 "covers the physical and moral integrity of the person, including his or her sexual life."[65] Whilst the Strasbourg Court has insisted that consensual sexual behaviour between adults in private should not be criminalised,[66] it has also recognised the importance of ensuring that the rights of vulnerable people not to be subjected to sexual abuse should be upheld.[67] Thus in *X and Y v. Netherlands*[68] the Court declared that:

> "although the object of Article 8 is essentially that of protecting the individual against arbitrary interference by the public authorities, it does not merely compel the State to

---

[59] [2000] 4 All E.R. 961.
[60] *Airedale NHS Trust v. Bland* [1993] A.C. 789.
[61] [2000] 4 All E.R. 961, *per* Robert Walker L.J. at pp 1068d and 1070e.
[62] *ibid.*, at 1068c.
[63] [1999] A.C. 92.
[64] *R v. United Kingdom* (1983) 33 D.R. 270—see *Reid* [1982] Crim. L.R. 514.
[65] *X and Y v. Netherlands* (1986) 8 E.H.R.R. 235 at para. 22.
[66] *Cf.* the discussion of decisions such as *Dudgeon* and *ADT* in Chapter 8 above.
[67] This was recognised by the Court in the *Dudgeon* judgment itself: (1982) 4 E.H.R.R.
[68] (1986) 8 E.H.R.R. 235.

abstain from such interference; in addition to this primarily negative undertaking, there may be positive obligations inherent in an effective respect for private or family life. These obligations may involve the adoption of measures designed to secure respect for private life even in the sphere of the relations of individuals between themselves."[69]

18–41   This statement has particular implications for the sexual abuse of children and the mentally handicapped: States must, in principle, provide protection from sexual molestation in these cases. The difficulty with Netherlands law, which was identified in the *X and Y* case, was that prosecutions for most sexual offences required a complaint by the victim. Where the victim was a child under 16, a parent or guardian could bring the complaint. Where the victim was aged 16 but mentally handicapped, there was no such possibility. Since in this case the victim's mental state was such that she could not make a complaint in the required form, the Netherlands courts had held that her father could not lawfully bring a complaint on her behalf when the prosecution service declined to prosecute. The Court held that "recourse to the criminal law is not necessarily the only" means of ensuring that Article 8 rights are respected, but concluded thus:

> "The Court finds that the protection afforded by the civil law in the case of wrongdoing of the kind inflicted on Miss Y is insufficient. This is a case where fundamental values and essential aspects of private life are at stake. Effective deterrence is indispensable in this area and it can only be achieved by criminal provisions; indeed, it is by such provisions that the matter is normally regulated. Moreover . . . this is in fact an area in which the Netherlands has generally opted for a system of protection based on the criminal law. The only gap, so far as the Commission and the Court have been made aware, is as regards persons in the situation of Miss Y; in such cases, this system meets a procedural obstacle which the Dutch legislature had apparently not foreseen."[70]

IV. *The Protection of other Rights*

18–42   In principle the state has the same duty to ensure the protection of other rights as it has to protect Article 8 rights. The same argument can therefore be mounted in relation to Articles 9, 10 and 11 of the Convention. Thus the State's obligation to ensure protection of the right to practise religion under Article 9 has been recognised in a number of decisions. In *Otto-Preminger-Institut v. Austria*[71] the Court held that "the manner in which religious beliefs are opposed or denied is a matter which may engage the responsibility of the State, notably its responsibility to ensure the peaceful enjoyment of the right guaranteed under Article 9 to the holders of those beliefs or doctrines." For this reason the Court held that a prosecution for blasphemy did not violate Article 10. Similar reasoning may be found in *Wingrove v. United Kingdom*[72]: Article 10(2) allows for interference with the right to freedom of expression in order to protect the rights of others, and states have a duty to protect the right to freedom of religion. However, the extent of this obligation remains uncertain. The Commission held in *Choudhury v. United Kingdom*[73] that the absence of a criminal sanction against publications which offend those of minority faiths was not a violation of Article 9.

---

[69] *ibid.*, at para. 23.
[70] *ibid.*, para. 27.
[71] (1995) 19 E.H.R.R. 34 at para. 47, citing *Kokkinakis v. Greece* (1994) 17 E.H.R.R. 397.
[72] (1997) 24 E.H.R.R. 1 at para. 48.
[73] (1991) 12 H.R.L.J. 172.

The state's positive obligation to safeguard freedom of assembly under Article 11   **18–43**
has also been recognised explicitly. In *Plattform Artze fur das Leben v. Austria*[74]
the Court acknowledged that the exercise of the right to demonstrate might cause
annoyance to other citizens, but maintained the right to demonstrate without fear
of attack:

> "In a democracy the right to counter-demonstrate cannot extend to inhibiting the right
> to demonstrate. Genuine, effective freedom of peaceful assembly cannot, therefore, be
> reduced to a mere duty on the part of the State not to interfere; a purely negative
> conception would not be compatible with the object and purpose of Article 11. Like
> Article 8, Article 11 sometimes requires positive measures to be taken, even in the
> sphere of relations between individuals, if need be."[75]

This passage has significance both for the content of the criminal law and for the
practicalities of law enforcement.[76]

V. *Section 7(8) of the Human Rights Act*

Section 7(8) of the 1998 Act states that "nothing in this Act creates a criminal   **18–44**
offence." Thus, even if an English court were to determine that the state has
failed to fulfil one of its positive obligations, the court would be unable to afford
a remedy to the victim within the context of the criminal proceedings. The
creation of a new offence to meet the requirements of the Convention would
require legislation. More contentious would be a case where an English court
finds that a particular criminal law defence is too broadly stated to provide
adequate protection for the rights of the victim. By analogy with *A v. United
Kingdom*[77] it might be argued that a common law defence such as reasonable
chastisement should be re-defined so as to ensure that the defence is not available
where the beating inflicted on a child was so serious as to amount to inhuman and
degrading treatment. This is, in effect, what the House of Lords did in *R. v. R*,[78]
when it removed the marital rape defence on the ground that it reflected an
outdated and unacceptable conception of marriage. The effect of such a ruling is
undoubtedly to enlarge the scope of the offence, but it is doubtful whether it
amounts to the *creation* of an offence for the purposes of section 7(8) of the 1998
Act. If this issue were to arise, the approach of the national courts may well be
influenced by the principles applicable under Article 7 of the Convention[79] which
have been held to allow "gradual clarification" of the elements of criminal
responsibility, providing any resulting development is consistent with the essence
of the offence, and could reasonably have been foreseen with appropriate legal
advice.[80]

---

[74] (1991) 13 E.H.R.R. 204.
[75] *ibid.*, at para. 32; note the similarity in the phrasing of the last sentence with the passage cited from
X and Y v. Netherlands at n. 74 above.
[76] See the discussion of *Redmond-Bate v. DPP* [1999] Crim. L.R. 998 in para. 8–62 above.
[77] (1998) 27 E.H.R.R. 611.
[78] [1992] A.C. 559.
[79] See Chapter 10 above.
[80] *SW and CR v. United Kingdom* (1995) 21 E.H.R.R. 363. For criticism of the test adopted in this
decision, and its potential application where defences are "narrowed", see paras 10–27 *et seq.*
above.

D. Duty to Investigate Alleged Breaches of Articles 2 and 3

18–45   The state is under a duty to have in place an effective machinery for investigating complaints of violations of Convention rights, especially Articles 2 and 3. Thus in *Ribisch v. Austria*[81] the Court held that allegations of ill-treatment in custody, amounting to torture, had not been investigated adequately. The Court stated that "its vigilance must be heightened when dealing with rights such as those set forth in Article 3 of the Convention, which prohibits in absolute terms torture and inhuman or degrading treatment or punishment, irrespective of the victim's conduct."[82] In this case it was held that the Austrian authorities had failed to conduct an investigation which offered a plausible explanation for the injuries sustained by the applicant whilst in custody. There had been a prosecution of one police officer, resulting in an acquittal, but no other inquiry.

18–46   In *Aksoy v. Turkey*[83] the applicant had been subjected to ill-treatment whilst in police custody which, the Court held, amounted to torture. The Turkish prosecutor had a duty to carry out an investigation but, despite the applicant's injuries being brought to his attention, no action was taken. The Court founded its judgment on Article 13 taken together with Article 3:

> "Given the fundamental importance of the prohibition on torture and the especially vulnerable position of torture victims, Article 13 imposes, without prejudice to any other remedy available under the domestic system, an obligation on States to carry out a thorough and effective investigation of incidents of torture."[84]

18–47   In *Aydin v. Turkey*[85] the applicant alleged, and the Court found, that she had been subjected by the security forces to rape and prolonged physical and mental violence amounting to torture. The Court adopted the same approach as in *Aksoy*, relying on Article 13 in combination with Article 3:

> "where an individual has an arguable claim that he or she has been tortured by agents of the State, the notion of an 'effective remedy' entails, in addition to the payment of compensation where appropriate, a thorough and effective investigation capable of leading to the identification and punishment of those responsible and including effective access for the complainant to the investigatory procedure."[86]

The Court found that the Turkish prosecutor had conducted an incomplete inquiry with serious shortcomings. It added that in circumstances such as this there must be provision for a sensitive medical examination of the complainant by experts "whose independence is not circumscribed by instructions given by the prosecuting authority as to the scope of the examination."[87]

18–48   The question was raised in relation to Article 2 in *McCann v. United Kingdom*,[88] where there had been an inquest into the deaths of the three victims. The

---

[81] (1995) 21 E.H.R.R. 573.
[82] *ibid.*, at para. 32.
[83] (1997) 23 E.H.R.R. 553.
[84] *ibid.*, at para. 98.
[85] (1998) 25 E.H.R.R. 251.
[86] *ibid.*, at para. 103.
[87] *ibid.*, para. 107.
[88] (1996) 21 E.H.R.R. 97, discussed in section CII above.

applicants alleged that the inquest failed to meet the required standards of thoroughness and impartiality, but the Court held otherwise. The Court relied upon Article 1 in combination with Article 2 to ground the right to an official investigation of a death caused by state officials:

> "The obligation to protect the right to life under this provision, read in conjunction with the State's general duty under Article 1 of the Convention to 'secure to everyone within their jurisdiction the rights and freedoms defined in the Convention', requires by implication that there should be some form of effective official investigation when individuals have been killed as a result of the use of force by, *inter alios*, agents of the State."[89]

It is already clear that the mechanism in English law for investigating certain **18–49** breaches of the Convention is inadequate. In two decisions the Strasbourg organs have found that the Police Complaints Authority (PCA) is not a satisfactory mechanism for dealing with alleged breaches of Article 8 and, by implication, other breaches of Convention rights. In *Khan v. United Kingdom*[90] the Court found the English system wanting in a number of respects. First, unless the allegation is one of death or serious injury (or certain other specified instances) it is for the local Chief Constable to decide whether to deal with the complaint, and then to appoint a member of his own force to carry out the investigation. Secondly, members of the PCA are appointed and remunerated by the Home Secretary, and the PCA is bound statutorily to have regard to guidance laid down by the Home Secretary. Thus the Court concluded that "the system of investigation of complaints does not meet the requisite standards of independence needed to constitute sufficient protection against the abuse of authority and thus provide an effective remedy within the meaning of Article 13."[91]

E. OBLIGATION TO PROSECUTE OR GIVE REASONS

There is no specific endorsement in the Strasbourg jurisprudence of a duty to **18–50** bring a prosecution where there is sufficient evidence (howsoever defined) of a breach of Article 2 or Article 3, but there are several statements of the Court which might be said to support that proposition. Thus in *Aydin v. Turkey*[92] the Court referred to the need for "a thorough and effective investigation *capable of leading to the identification and punishment of those responsible*". This may be thought to put the matter rather too strongly: all that can reasonably be required is a system designed to ensure that persons against whom there is sufficient evidence are prosecuted.

The issue arose before the Divisional Court in *R. v. DPP ex parte Manning and* **18–51** *Melbourne*,[93] where the CPS had decided not to bring a prosecution against a prison officer in respect of the death of a prisoner. There was evidence that the death had been caused by the way in which the prisoner had been restrained by

---

[89] *ibid.*, at para. 161.
[90] [2000] Crim. L.R. 684.
[91] Judgment of May 2, 2000, para. 47.
[92] (1998) 25 E.H.R.R. 251, para. 103; see above, n. 92 and text; see also *Selmouni v. France* (2000) 29 E.H.R.R. 403, para. 79.
[93] [2000] 3 W.L.R. 463.

the officer, in response to an incident; the jury at the inquest had returned a verdict of unlawful killing; but the CPS decided that there was not sufficient evidence to raise a realistic prospect of conviction. Lord Bingham C.J. held that such a decision ought to be supported by the disclosure of fairly full reasons:

> "Where such an inquest following a proper direction to the jury culminates in a lawful verdict of unlawful killing implicating a [certain] person . . . the ordinary expectation would naturally be that a prosecution would follow. In the absence of compelling grounds for not giving reasons, we would expect the Director to give reasons in such a case: to meet the reasonable expectations of interested parties that either a prosecution would follow or a reasonable explanation for not prosecuting be given, to vindicate the Director's decision by showing that solid grounds exist for what might otherwise appear to be a surprising or even inexplicable decision, and to meet the European Court's expectation that if a prosecution is not to follow a plausible expectation will be given."

18–52   This constitutes a significant development of two principles evident in the Strasbourg jurisprudence—the responsibility of the State for furnishing a plausible explanation of the causes of a death or injury sustained in custody, and the state's duty to provide the machinery for a "thorough and effective investigation" capable of leading to the identification of the probable offender. Although Lord Bingham's judgment is limited in its terms to cases of deaths in custody where the inquest jury subsequently returns a verdict of unlawful killing, the principle is a clear one, and it might well come to be applied in a wider range of cases.

F. RIGHTS OF VICTIMS AND WITNESSES IN CRIMINAL TRIALS

18–53   There is no provision of the Convention which sets out the procedural rights of victims of crime or witnesses. Other international conventions declare certain victims' rights, notably the United Nations Declaration of Basic Principles of Justice for Victims of Crime and Abuse of Power (1985) and the Council of Europe's Recommendations on The Position of the Victim in the Framework of Criminal Law and Procedure (1985).[94] It is possible that the Strasbourg Court will draw upon those declarations, as it has drawn on the United Nations Convention on the Rights of the Child, when interpreting Article 6. However, for the present the Court has begun to construct procedural rights for victims and witnesses out of the Convention itself. Three forms of protection seem to be emerging. First, protection of the identity of a witness who is at risk of reprisal has been recognised as a legitimate ground for implying limitations into Article 6 rights of the accused. Secondly, there are issues about the protection of witnesses from infringements of their rights by questioning during court proceedings. And thirdly, there is the question of access to the medical records of witnesses.

I. *Protecting the Identity of Witnesses*

18–54   The Court has considered on a number of occasions whether a trial can be fair if witnesses for the prosecution remain anonymous and do not give evidence in

---

[94] Recommendation R (85) 11 of the Committee of Ministers.

open court. Anonymity might be justified as protecting the witness's right to respect for private life and, more seriously, as protecting the witness from the risk of intimidation or physical attack. In *Doorson v. Netherlands*[95] the Court held that the trial was not unfair when two prosecution witnesses remained anonymous and were questioned by the judge in the presence of counsel (but not the accused), whereas in *Van Mechelen v. Netherlands*[96] the Court held that the trial was unfair when 11 police officers gave evidence for the prosecution, remained anonymous, and were questioned by the judge whilst prosecuting and defence counsel were kept in another room, with only a sound link to the judge's chambers. In both cases there was a fear that the witnesses and their families would be subjected to reprisals if their anonymity was not preserved. In the absence of an express reference in the Convention to the rights of witnesses, the Court implied the rights into Article 6:

"It is true that Article 6 does not explicitly require the interests of witnesses in general, and those of victims called upon to testify in particular, to be taken into consideration. However, their life, liberty or security of person may be at stake, as may interests coming generally within the ambit of Article 8 of the Convention . . . Contracting States should organise their criminal proceedings in such a way that those interests are not unjustifiably imperilled. Against this background, principles of fair trial also require that in appropriate cases the interests of the defence are balanced against those of witnesses or victims called upon to testify."[97]

These decisions establish the significance of the rights of all witnesses in criminal **18–55** proceedings. The rights of the defendant under Article 6 may be curtailed to some extent in order to protect the rights of witnesses, which derive from the right to security of person under Article 5 and the right to respect for private life under Article 8. However, any curtailment of a defendant's rights must be kept to a minimum: "the handicaps under which the defence labours [must] be sufficiently counterbalanced by the procedures followed by the judicial authorities".[98]

The question of informer anonymity has arisen in English law in the context of **18–56** disclosure and public interest immunity. One of the grounds on which material used to be classified as "sensitive" under the Attorney-General's 1981 guidelines was that the disclosure of a witness's identity might put him or his family in danger of assault or intimidation. In *Rowe and Davis v. United Kingdom*[99] the Strasbourg Court recognised that this could amount to a sufficient reason for withholding evidence from the defence:

"the entitlement to disclosure of relevant evidence is not an absolute right. In any criminal proceedings there may be competing interests, such as national security or the need to protect witnesses at risk of reprisals or keep secret police methods of investigation of crime, which must be weighed against the rights of the accused. In some cases it may be necessary to withhold certain evidence from the defence so as to preserve the fundamental rights of another individual or to safeguard an important public interest."[1]

---

[95] (1996) 22 E.H.R.R. 330.
[96] (1998) 25 E.H.R.R. 657.
[97] (1996) 22 E.H.R.R. 330 at para. 70.
[98] (1998) 25 E.H.R.R. 657 at para. 54.
[99] (2000) 30 E.H.R.R. 1.
[1] *ibid.*, at para. 61.

This judgment follows the approach developed in the *Doorson* and *van Mechelen* judgments. Whilst it approves the risk of intimidation or assault as a justification for withholding evidence, in principle, it also emphasises the need to ensure that the defence is not placed at a greater disadvantage than is strictly necessary to protect the rights of the witness.

II. *Protecting Witnesses' Rights during the Trial*

18–57   There may be situations in which the rights of a witness are put at risk during the course of a criminal trial. Some witnesses are vulnerable and therefore require special protection, even in ordinary circumstances. Some witnesses are liable to be questioned in a manner that may be degrading, raising the issue of their Article 3 rights. And on other occasions the nature of the questions may raise the issue of a witness's right under Article 8 to respect for private life. In the key passage in *Doorson v. Netherlands*,[2] the Court referred to Articles 5 and 8 as sources of rights for victims and other witnesses; and it is possible that Article 3 would also be invoked if the questioning of the witness was humiliating and debasing, of a certain duration and such as to produce significant adverse physical or mental effects.[3] Article 3 was the basis for the application in *M v. United Kingdom*,[4] where a complainant had been subjected to lengthy questioning about sexual details by the defendant in person in a rape trial. The application was withdrawn when the government stated its intention to introduce legislative protection.

18–58   There is increasing recognition of the rights of victims and witnesses in English law. Thus, in another case where the defendant in person had questioned the complainant in a rape case in an intimidatory and humiliating manner, Lord Bingham C.J. in the Court of Appeal stated that:

> "It is the clear duty of the trial judge to do everything he can, consistently with giving the defendant a fair trial, to minimise the trauma suffered by other participants . . . [T]he judge should, if necessary in order to save the complainant from avoidable distress, stop further questioning by the defendant or take over the questioning of the complainant himself. If the defendant seeks by his dress, bearing, manner or questions to dominate, intimidate or humiliate the complainant, or if it is reasonably apprehended that he will seek to do so, the judge should not hesitate to order the erection of a screen, in addition to controlling questioning in the way we have indicated."[5]

18–59   Parliament has now stepped in, and section 34 of the Youth Justice and Criminal Evidence Act 1999 prevents a defendant charged with a sexual offence from cross-examining the complainant in person. Section 35 extends the protection for child witnesses from cross-examination by the defendant. Sections 36 and 37 confer on the courts a power to disallow cross-examination by the defendant in person in other cases which satisfy certain criteria, and section 39 provides a procedure for the appointment of counsel to undertake cross-examination on behalf of the defence if that is necessary.

---

[2] See para. 18–54 above.
[3] See the definitions of "degrading" in *Costello-Roberts v. United Kingdom* (1995) 19 E.H.R.R. 112, para. 30, and *A v. United Kingdom* (1999) 27 E.H.R.R. 611, para. 20.
[4] Unreported (1999).
[5] *Brown (Milton Anthony)* [1998] 2 Cr. App. R. 364 at 371.

It has been suggested that to compel a defendant to have legal representation   **18–60**
infringes his rights under Article 6(3)(c), but the Strasbourg caselaw does not
support that view. In *Croissant v. Germany*[6] the applicant, himself a lawyer, was
required by German law to be represented by a court-appointed lawyer during a
trial on terrorist charges. The Court held that there was no violation of his
rights:

> "It is true that Article 6(3)(c) entitles 'everyone charged with a criminal offence' to be
> defended by counsel of his own choosing. Nevertheless, and notwithstanding the
> importance of a relationship of confidence between lawyer and client, this right cannot
> be considered to be absolute. It is necessarily subject to certain limitations where free
> legal aid is concerned and also where, as in the present case, it is for the courts to decide
> whether the interests of justice require that the accused be defended by counsel
> appointed by them. When appointing defence counsel the national courts must certainly
> have regard to the defendant's wishes; indeed, German law contemplates such a course.
> However, they can override those wishes when there are relevant and sufficient grounds
> for holding that this is necessary in the interests of justice."[7]

In addition to sections 34–39, there are other provisions in the Youth Justice and   **18–61**
Criminal Evidence Act 1999 designed to protect witnesses from unfair treatment.
Sections 16–33 provide a statutory framework for the use of screens to protect
witnesses, for clearing the court, for the use of video recorded testimony and
other measures, all of which go further than the Strasbourg Court's scattered
observations would require. Section 41 of the Act places significant constraints
on the cross-examination of complainants in sexual cases on their previous
sexual behaviour. This is a controversial measure, which makes no separate
provision for past sexual experiences which the complainant has had with the
accused, treating these in precisely the same way as it treats sexual relations with
other men. Where the issue is consent, such evidence could only be introduced
where the other sexual act occurred "at or about the same time" as the alleged
offence, or there is some similarity about the conduct which cannot be explained
on the basis of coincidence. In *R. v. A*[8] the House of Lords held that whilst this
provision pursued the legitimate object of protecting the complainant against
intrusive and irrelevant questioning it had, by extending the restrictions to past
sex with the accused, made an excessive inroad into the right to a fair trial. Read
according to orthodox cannons of construction it was incompatible with Article
6. In order to achieve compatibility Lord Steyn, with whom the majority agreed,
held that the provision should be read subject to an implied discretion on the part
of the trial judge to ensure that any relevant evidence would be admitted.

III. *Victims, Witnesses and Confidential Medical Records*

If the medical records of a witness are produced in court by the prosecution,   **18–62**
at a trial of another, it seems clear that this raises questions about the Article 8
rights of the witness. In *Z v. Finland*[9] the Court held that there will be an
interference with the right to respect for private life under Article 8 where such

---

[6] (1993) 16 E.H.R.R. 135.
[7] *ibid.*, at para. 29.
[8] [2001] 2 W.L.R. 1546. For a full discussion see para. 15–137 above.
[9] (1998) 25 E.H.R.R. 371.

evidence is adduced without the consent of the witness. However, the Court held that the prosecution may nonetheless be justified in adducing the evidence in certain circumstances. In this case the husband of the witness was being prosecuted for serious sexual offences and for attempted manslaughter, and a key issue was the stage at which he knew he was HIV positive. Both she and her husband had been treated by particular doctors. The Court recognised that the wife's right to the confidentiality of her medical records weighed "heavily in the balance", but held that the prosecution of serious crimes might well give rise to a public interest strong enough to justify the interference with her Article 8 rights. The Court found no breach of Article 8 either in the order for her medical advisers to give evidence or in the seizing of confidential documents for use by the prosecution.

18–63   However, the national court had ordered that details of the proceedings should remain confidential for only 10 years, after which the public interest in publicity should have priority. The Strasbourg Court rejected this, on the ground that it "attached insufficient weigh to the applicant's interests." The Court recalled that, on account of the use of confidential records against her wishes, "she had already been subjected to a serious interference with her right to respect for private and family life."[10] The reasons for removing the ban on publicity after only 10 years were said to be insufficient. Furthermore, the decision of the Finnish court to publish the names of those involved in the case, with the result that the witness could be identified, was a breach of her Article 8 rights without sufficient justification.

18–64   To some extent the last point is dealt with in English law by the Sexual Offences (Amendment) Act 1992, as amended by the Youth Justice and Criminal Evidence Act 1999. However, that legislation is confined to sexual offences, and the general principle in *Z v. Finland* applies irrespective of the nature of the proceedings, since the primary concern is to protect the rights of the witness under Article 8.

G. VICTIMS' RIGHTS AND THE SENTENCING PROCESS

18–65   In 1985 the Council of Europe agreed a recommendation on The Position of the Victim in the Framework of Criminal Law and Procedure. Although it declared that "the needs and interests of the victim should be taken into account to a greater degree, throughout all stages of the criminal process", it did not recommend a formal role for victims in the sentencing process. It signalled the desirability of a change of emphasis in these terms:

> "Traditionally, criminal legislation and practice have emphasised constitutional guarantees and procedural safeguards for the offender. However, another essential function of a criminal justice system is to do justice to the interests of the victim. This calls for an examination of desirable improvements in national legislation such that the system of criminal justice could take more fully into account the wrongs suffered by the victim. To this end, special account should be taken of the physical, psychological, material

---

[10] *ibid.*, at para. 112.

(such as damage to property, loss of earnings) or social (such as defamation) damage at every stage in the criminal proceedings."[11]

The emphasis of the report is on the gathering and communication of information, both information *to* the victim about the progress of the case and information *from* the victim to the police, prosecution and the court about the effects of the crime.

During 2000 the Council of the European Union continued its work on a "Draft   **18–66**
Framework Decision on the standing of victims in criminal procedure." The June 2000 draft of this document[12] sets out some 18 articles, declaring the right of victims to respect and recognition during criminal proceedings, their right to protection of their safety and privacy, and the right of victims to receive information on a range of matters. Once again, there is no requirement of a specific role for victims at the sentencing stage, but there is a clear requirement to ensure victim compensation (discussed in paragraph 18–78 below). The following draft Articles are also relevant:

— Article 3: Right to be heard and to supply evidence
  "Each Member State shall safeguard the right of victims to be heard during criminal proceedings and their right to supply evidence . . . "

— Article 6: Right to participate in proceedings and legal aid
  "Each Member State shall provide a real and appropriate role for victims in its criminal justice system and shall maximise the involvement of victims in criminal procedure to the extent allowed by its legal system . . ."

— Article 10: Penal mediation in the course of criminal proceedings
  "Each Member State shall seek to promote penal mediation where appropriate . . ."

The terms of this draft are notable in two respects. First, they constitute evidence   **18–67**
of a growing commitment to the recognition of victims' rights in Europe, which is likely to have some influence on the Strasbourg Court in its interpretation of Convention rights. Secondly, the terms of the document remain relatively flexible. Thus Article 6 merely urges the state to ensure greater victim involvement "to the extent allowed by its legal system," a form of words that allows the diversity of legal responses to be preserved. The qualification "where appropriate" in Article 10 points in the same direction. However, these concessions to national legal traditions leave the broad purposes of the Draft Framework untouched.

Thus, neither of these two European documents declares the desirability of   **18–68**
allowing a victim impact statement to be received by a court before sentence, let alone of allowing the victim to be heard on the question of sentence. They do, however, permit both developments, and the British government currently intends to introduce a scheme allowing victim statements to be made, detailing the effects of the offence, and forwarded to the prosecutor and the court.

---

[11] Council of Europe Recommendation R (85) 11, Explanatory Report, p. 15.
[12] Council of the European Union, Working Party on Cooperation on Criminal Matters, Document 9720/00 COPEN 45, June 19 and 20, 2000.

18–69 The question of victims' rights in the sentencing process has been considered in two Strasbourg cases. In *McCourt v. United Kingdom*[13] the Commission considered an application by the mother of a woman who had been murdered. She alleged a breach of Article 8 on the ground that she had been accorded no right to participate in the sentencing process, no right to be informed of the date of the murderer's release, and no right to express her views to those deciding on release. The Commission noted that it was the practice of the Home Office to accept submissions from victims' families and to place them before the Parole Board, and also the practice to inform victims' families of the impending release of a murderer. However, the Commission accepted the government's argument that it would be inappropriate to recognise any role for the victim's family in setting the tariff period for the offence, since they would lack the necessary impartiality. The Commission concluded that the application disclosed no interference with the right to respect for family life under Article 8.

18–70 In *T and V v. United Kingdom*[14] the Court took the exceptional course of allowing the parents of James Bulger to intervene in the case brought by the two juveniles convicted of his murder, and permitted the parents' legal representatives to address the Court in oral argument. The reasons of the President for taking this course are not set out in the judgment, but they may reflect a more receptive attitude towards hearing representations from victims or their families in matters relating to sentence.

18–71 A similar approach is apparent in the *Practice Statement* issued by Lord Woolf C.J. which sets out the procedure and considerations for determining the tariff period to be served by young offenders ordered to be detained during Her Majesty's Pleasure.[15] Lord Woolf states that, before making his recommendation, he will "invite written representations from the detainees' legal advisers and also from the Director of Public Prosecutions who may include representations on behalf of victims' families." Although this procedure preserves the English approach of not allowing victim statements to be submitted directly, and requiring them to be channelled through the prosecution, it gives clear recognition to the relevance of submissions by victims' families.

18–72 Although these developments will be welcomed by some, the Strasbourg Court's decision to hear submissions from the victim's family in *T and V v. United Kingdom* does not deal with the point of principle raised in *McCourt v. United Kingdom*. That point is that every person charged with a criminal offence has the right under Article 6 to a "fair and public hearing . . . by an independent and impartial tribunal." The right extends to the sentencing process, and so the question is whether the tribunal's impartiality is compromised by hearing submissions on behalf of the victim's family (or, in non-fatal cases, the victim). The obvious response to this is that the tribunal itself remains impartial, and that its decision-making is no more likely to be prejudiced by representations on behalf of the victim or victim's family than by representations on behalf of the offender. However, it is noteworthy that when the Lord Chief Justice invited representations from the victim's family before setting the tariff period for Thompson and

---

[13] (1993) 15 E.H.R.R. CD 110.
[14] (2000) 30 E.H.R.R. 121.
[15] *Practice Statement (Life Sentences for Murder)* [2000] 2 Cr. App. R. 457.

Venables, he: "invited, and received, representations from [Mr Bulger] and his family as to the impact of his son's death on them, but had not invited them to give their views on what they thought was an appropriate tariff."[16]

This approach draws strength from a line of Court of Appeal decisions in which **18–73** the Court has pointed out why paying heed to representations by victims is not a proper foundation for the administration of criminal justice. The clearest expression of this view is that of Judge L.J.:

> "We mean no disrespect to the mother and sister of the deceased, but the opinions of the victim, or the surviving members of the family, about the appropriate level of sentence do not provide any sound basis for reassessing a sentence. If the victim feels utterly merciful towards the criminal, and some do, the crime has still been committed and must be punished as it deserves. If the victim is obsessed with vengeance, which can in reality only be assuaged by a very long sentence, as also happens, the punishment cannot be made longer by the court than would otherwise be appropriate. Otherwise cases with identical features would be dealt with in widely differing ways, leading to improper and unfair disparity, and even in this particular case . . . the views of the members of the family of the deceased are not absolutely identical."[17]

This was a case in which two members of the victim's family were asking the **18–74** Court to reduce the sentence, but, as Judge L.J. recognises, the argument should be the same whether the submission is for leniency or for severity. Indeed, this is one of the principal difficulties with any acceptance that the views of the victim's family are relevant: that those views may go to one extreme or the other, and a court should not be swayed by those differing reactions, nor should offenders be liable to be sentenced on that basis.[18] The logical consequence of this argument is that the views of the victim or victim's family on sentence are irrelevant, and this points to the conclusion that those views should not be heard. To make provision for them to be heard is either to allow the introduction of irrelevant considerations or to mislead victims' families into thinking that their submissions are relevant when they are not.

Arguments of this kind will have to be confronted by the Strasbourg Court **18–75** whenever it has to give a reasoned decision on victims' rights in relation to sentencing. It will be important to distinguish between three different forms of representation from victims.

First, there are representations about the effects of the offence on the victim and **18–76** his or her life and wellbeing. The proposals for victim statements encompass this kind of representation, and they are intended to ensure that courts are more fully informed about the effects of crime. Although there may be procedural issues about victim statements which contain allegations of a more serious crime than the prosecution has alleged, such statements are generally consistent with the

---

[16] *Per* Rose L.J. in *R. v. Secretary of State for the Home Department and another ex parte Bulger, The Times*, March 7, 2001.
[17] *Nunn* [1996] 2 Cr. App. R. (S) 136 at p. 140; see also *Roche* [1999] 2 Cr. App. R. (S) 105 and *Attorney-General's Reference (No. 18 of 1993)* (1994) 15 Cr. App. R. (S) 800.
[18] The last few words of the quotation from *Nunn* also point to a practical difficulty where there are two or more victims, or where a deceased victim's family is making submissions—that there may be different views about what should be done. In *Nunn* two members of the family wanted leniency and two did not.

Convention and with the two European documents outlined above. A victim statement of this kind does not contain opinions on sentence.

18–77   Secondly, there are representations as to the length or type of sentence. It was argued above that to admit such representations may raise the issue of impartiality under Article 6, as suggested in *McCourt v. United Kingdom*, or alternatively may involve misleading victims and their families as to the significance of their representations.

18–78   Third, there are representations directed solely to issues of compensation. Victims should have a right to receive compensation from offenders who are in a position to pay, as the Draft Framework for the European Union recognises in Article 9:

> "1. Each Member State shall ensure that victims of criminal acts have the right to compensation as quickly as possible in the course of criminal proceedings, except where, in certain specific cases, national legislation provides for compensation to be awarded in another manner.
>
> 2. Each Member State shall take appropriate measures facilitating the provision of adequate compensation to victims by the offender. These measures may, for example, provide that provision of compensation by the offender to the victim is taken into account when deciding on measures concerning probation, pre-release and conditional release.
>
> 3. To the extent possible, fines paid or sums obtained from instrumentalities or from proceeds of crime recovered, as well as a proportion of any salary received by the offender during his term of imprisonment may be used primarily to compensate victims, either directly or indirectly."[19]

Insofar as victim statements themselves are directed to this purpose, they will make an important contribution to securing rights that ought to be recognised, but are not recognised, in the Convention.

18–79   Although there is a European Convention on the Compensation of Victims of Violent Crimes,[20] which the United Kingdom ratified in 1990, the European Convention on Human Rights does not contain any enforceable right to state compensation for the victims of violent crime. However, the introduction of a statutory system may be held to give rise to a "civil right", which means that Article 6 protections must be in place. It has been argued that some of the procedures of the Criminal Injuries Compensation Appeals Panel may be open to challenge under Article 6.[21]

---

[19] Above, n. 25 (para. 18–83).
[20] Cmnd. 1427, (1988).
[21] Wadham and Arkinstall (above, n.1 (para. 18–01)), p. 1084.

EUROPEAN MATERIAL

Convention for the Protection of Human Rights and Fundamental Freedoms as amended by Protocol No. 11

ROME, 4.XI.1950

The governments signatory hereto, being members of the Council of Europe,

Considering the Universal Declaration of Human Rights proclaimed by the General Assembly of the United Nations on 10th December 1948;

Considering that this Declaration aims at securing the universal and effective recognition and observance of the Rights therein declared;

Considering that the aim of the Council of Europe is the achievement of greater unity between its members and that one of the methods by which that aim is to be pursued is the maintenance and further realisation of human rights and fundamental freedoms;

Reaffirming their profound belief in those fundamental freedoms which are the foundation of justice and peace in the world and are best maintained on the one hand by an effective political democracy and on the other by a common understanding and observance of the human rights upon which they depend;

Being resolved, as the governments of European countries which are like-minded and have a common heritage of political traditions, ideals, freedom and the rule of law, to take the first steps for the collective enforcement of certain of the rights stated in the Universal Declaration,

Have agreed as follows:

Article 1—Obligation to respect human rights

The High Contracting Parties shall secure to everyone within their jurisdiction the rights and freedoms defined in Section I of this Convention.

SECTION I—RIGHTS AND FREEDOMS

Article 2—Right to life

1. Everyone's right to life shall be protected by law. No one shall be deprived of his life intentionally save in the execution of a sentence of a court following his conviction of a crime for which this penalty is provided by law.
2. Deprivation of life shall not be regarded as inflicted in contravention of this article when it results from the use of force which is no more than absolutely necessary:

    a. in defence of any person from unlawful violence;

[561]

b. in order to effect a lawful arrest or to prevent the escape of a person lawfully detained;

c. in action lawfully taken for the purpose of quelling a riot or insurrection.

Article 3—Prohibition of torture

No one shall be subjected to torture or to inhuman or degrading treatment or punishment.

Article 4—Prohibition of slavery and forced labour

1. No one shall be held in slavery or servitude.
2. No one shall be required to perform forced or compulsory labour.
3. For the purpose of this article the term "forced or compulsory labour" shall not include:

   a. any work required to be done in the ordinary course of detention imposed according to the provisions of Article 5 of this Convention or during conditional release from such detention;

   b. any service of a military character or, in case of conscientious objectors in countries where they are recognised, service exacted instead of compulsory military service;

   c. any service exacted in case of an emergency or calamity threatening the life or well-being of the community;

   d. any work or service which forms part of normal civic obligations.

Article 5—Right to liberty and security

1. Everyone has the right to liberty and security of person. No one shall be deprived of his liberty save in the following cases and in accordance with a procedure prescribed by law:

   a. the lawful detention of a person after conviction by a competent court;

   b. the lawful arrest or detention of a person for non-compliance with the lawful order of a court or in order to secure the fulfilment of any obligation prescribed by law;

   c. the lawful arrest or detention of a person effected for the purpose of bringing him before the competent legal authority on reasonable suspicion of having committed an offence or when it is reasonably considered necessary to prevent his committing an offence or fleeing after having done so;

   d. the detention of a minor by lawful order for the purpose of educational supervision or his lawful detention for the purpose of bringing him before the competent legal authority;

   e. the lawful detention of persons for the prevention of the spreading of infectious diseases, of persons of unsound mind, alcoholics or drug addicts or vagrants;

   f. the lawful arrest or detention of a person to prevent his effecting an unauthorised entry into the country or of a person against whom action is being taken with a view to deportation or extradition.

2. Everyone who is arrested shall be informed promptly, in a language which he understands, of the reasons for his arrest and of any charge against him.
3. Everyone arrested or detained in accordance with the provisions of paragraph 1.c of this article shall be brought promptly before a judge or other officer authorised by law

[562]

to exercise judicial power and shall be entitled to trial within a reasonable time or to release pending trial. Release may be conditioned by guarantees to appear for trial.

4. Everyone who is deprived of his liberty by arrest or detention shall be entitled to take proceedings by which the lawfulness of his detention shall be decided speedily by a court and his release ordered if the detention is not lawful.

5. Everyone who has been the victim of arrest or detention in contravention of the provisions of this article shall have an enforceable right to compensation.

Article 6—Right to a fair trial

1. In the determination of his civil rights and obligations or of any criminal charge against him, everyone is entitled to a fair and public hearing within a reasonable time by an independent and impartial tribunal established by law. Judgment shall be pronounced publicly but the press and public may be excluded from all or part of the trial in the interests of morals, public order or national security in a democratic society, where the interests of juveniles or the protection of the private life of the parties so require, or to the extent strictly necessary in the opinion of the court in special circumstances where publicity would prejudice the interests of justice.

2. Everyone charged with a criminal offence shall be presumed innocent until proved guilty according to law.

3. Everyone charged with a criminal offence has the following minimum rights:

   a. to be informed promptly, in a language which he understands and in detail, of the nature and cause of the accusation against him;

   b. to have adequate time and facilities for the preparation of his defence;

   c. to defend himself in person or through legal assistance of his own choosing or, if he has not sufficient means to pay for legal assistance, to be given it free when the interests of justice so require;

   d. to examine or have examined witnesses against him and to obtain the attendance and examination of witnesses on his behalf under the same conditions as witnesses against him;

   e. to have the free assistance of an interpreter if he cannot understand or speak the language used in court.

Article 7—No punishment without law

1. No one shall be held guilty of any criminal offence on account of any act or omission which did not constitute a criminal offence under national or international law at the time when it was committed. Nor shall a heavier penalty be imposed than the one that was applicable at the time the criminal offence was committed.

2. This article shall not prejudice the trial and punishment of any person for any act or omission which, at the time when it was committed, was criminal according to the general principles of law recognised by civilised nations.

Article 8—Right to respect for private and family life

1. Everyone has the right to respect for his private and family life, his home and his correspondence.

2. There shall be no interference by a public authority with the exercise of this right except such as is in accordance with the law and is necessary in a democratic society in the interests of national security, public safety or the economic well-being of the country, for the prevention of disorder or crime, for the protection of health or morals, or for the protection of the rights and freedoms of others.

Article 9—Freedom of thought, conscience and religion

1. Everyone has the right to freedom of thought, conscience and religion; this right includes freedom to change his religion or belief and freedom, either alone or in

community with others and in public or private, to manifest his religion or belief, in worship, teaching, practice and observance.

2. Freedom to manifest one's religion or beliefs shall be subject only to such limitations as are prescribed by law and are necessary in a democratic society in the interests of public safety, for the protection of public order, health or morals, or for the protection of the rights and freedoms of others.

Article 10—Freedom of expression

1. Everyone has the right to freedom of expression. This right shall include freedom to hold opinions and to receive and impart information and ideas without interference by public authority and regardless of frontiers. This article shall not prevent States from requiring the licensing of broadcasting, television or cinema enterprises.
2. The exercise of these freedoms, since it carries with it duties and responsibilities, may be subject to such formalities, conditions, restrictions or penalties as are prescribed by law and are necessary in a democratic society, in the interests of national security, territorial integrity or public safety, for the prevention of disorder or crime, for the protection of health or morals, for the protection of the reputation or rights of others, for preventing the disclosure of information received in confidence, or for maintaining the authority and impartiality of the judiciary.

Article 11—Freedom of assembly and association

1. Everyone has the right to freedom of peaceful assembly and to freedom of association with others, including the right to form and to join trade unions for the protection of his interests.
2. No restrictions shall be placed on the exercise of these rights other than such as are prescribed by law and are necessary in a democratic society in the interests of national security or public safety, for the prevention of disorder or crime, for the protection of health or morals or for the protection of the rights and freedoms of others. This article shall not prevent the imposition of lawful restrictions on the exercise of these rights by members of the armed forces, of the police or of the administration of the State.

Article 12—Right to marry

Men and women of marriageable age have the right to marry and to found a family, according to the national laws governing the exercise of this right.

Article 13—Right to an effective remedy

Everyone whose rights and freedoms as set forth in this Convention are violated shall have an effective remedy before a national authority notwithstanding that the violation has been committed by persons acting in an official capacity.

Article 14—Prohibition of discrimination

The enjoyment of the rights and freedoms set forth in this Convention shall be secured without discrimination on any ground such as sex, race, colour, language, religion, political or other opinion, national or social origin, association with a national minority, property, birth or other status.

Article 15—Derogation in time of emergency

1. In time of war or other public emergency threatening the life of the nation any High Contracting Party may take measures derogating from its obligations under this Convention to the extent strictly required by the exigencies of the situation, provided that such measures are not inconsistent with its other obligations under international law.

2. No derogation from Article 2, except in respect of deaths resulting from lawful acts of war, or from Articles 3, 4 (paragraph 1) and 7 shall be made under this provision.

3. Any High Contracting Party availing itself of this right of derogation shall keep the Secretary General of the Council of Europe fully informed of the measures which it has taken and the reasons therefor. It shall also inform the Secretary General of the Council of Europe when such measures have ceased to operate and the provisions of the Convention are again being fully executed.

Article 16—Restrictions on political activity of aliens

Nothing in Articles 10, 11 and 14 shall be regarded as preventing the High Contracting Parties from imposing restrictions on the political activity of aliens.

Article 17—Prohibition of abuse of rights

Nothing in this Convention may be interpreted as implying for any State, group or person any right to engage in any activity or perform any act aimed at the destruction of any of the rights and freedoms set forth herein or at their limitation to a greater extent than is provided for in the Convention.

Article 18—Limitation on use of restrictions on rights

The restrictions permitted under this Convention to the said rights and freedoms shall not be applied for any purpose other than those for which they have been prescribed.

SECTION II—EUROPEAN COURT OF HUMAN RIGHTS

Article 19—Establishment of the Court

To ensure the observance of the engagements undertaken by the High Contracting Parties in the Convention and the Protocols thereto, there shall be set up a European Court of Human Rights, hereinafter referred to as "the Court". It shall function on a permanent basis.

Article 20—Number of judges

The Court shall consist of a number of judges equal to that of the High Contracting Parties.

Article 21—Criteria for office

1. The judges shall be of high moral character and must either possess the qualifications required for appointment to high judicial office or be jurisconsults of recognised competence.
2. The judges shall sit on the Court in their individual capacity.
3. During their term of office the judges shall not engage in any activity which is incompatible with their independence, impartiality or with the demands of a full-time office; all questions arising from the application of this paragraph shall be decided by the Court.

Article 22—Election of judges

1. The judges shall be elected by the Parliamentary Assembly with respect to each High Contracting Party by a majority of votes cast from a list of three candidates nominated by the High Contracting Party.
2. The same procedure shall be followed to complete the Court in the event of the accession of new High Contracting Parties and in filling casual vacancies.

[565]

Article 23—Terms of office

1. The judges shall be elected for a period of six years. They may be re-elected. However, the terms of office of one-half of the judges elected at the first election shall expire at the end of three years.
2. The judges whose terms of office are to expire at the end of the initial period of three years shall be chosen by lot by the Secretary General of the Council of Europe immediately after their election.
3. In order to ensure that, as far as possible, the terms of office of one-half of the judges are renewed every three years, the Parliamentary Assembly may decide, before proceeding to any subsequent election, that the term or terms of office of one or more judges to be elected shall be for a period other than six years but not more than nine and not less than three years.
4. In cases where more than one term of office is involved and where the Parliamentary Assembly applies the preceding paragraph, the allocation of the terms of office shall be effected by a drawing of lots by the Secretary General of the Council of Europe immediately after the election.
5. A judge elected to replace a judge whose term of office has not expired shall hold office for the remainder of his predecessor's term.
6. The terms of office of judges shall expire when they reach the age of 70.
7. The judges shall hold office until replaced. They shall, however, continue to deal with such cases as they already have under consideration.

Article 24—Dismissal

No judge may be dismissed from his office unless the other judges decide by a majority of two-thirds that he has ceased to fulfil the required conditions.

Article 25—Registry and legal secretaries

The Court shall have a registry, the functions and organisation of which shall be laid down in the rules of the Court. The Court shall be assisted by legal secretaries.

Article 26—Plenary Court

The plenary Court shall:

    a. elect its President and one or two Vice-Presidents for a period of three years; they may be re-elected;

    b. set up Chambers, constituted for a fixed period of time;

    c. elect the Presidents of the Chambers of the Court; they may be re-elected;

    d. adopt the rules of the Court, and

    e. elect the Registrar and one or more Deputy Registrars.

Article 27—Committees, Chambers and Grand Chamber

1. To consider cases brought before it, the Court shall sit in committees of three judges, in Chambers of seven judges and in a Grand Chamber of seventeen judges. The Court's Chambers shall set up committees for a fixed period of time.
2. There shall sit as an *ex officio* member of the Chamber and the Grand Chamber the judge elected in respect of the State Party concerned or, if there is none or if he is unable to sit, a person of its choice who shall sit in the capacity of judge.
3. The Grand Chamber shall also include the President of the Court, the Vice-Presidents, the Presidents of the Chambers and other judges chosen in accordance with the rules of the Court. When a case is referred to the Grand Chamber under Article 43, no judge from the Chamber which rendered the judgment shall sit in the Grand Chamber, with

the exception of the President of the Chamber and the judge who sat in respect of the State Party concerned.

Article 28—Declarations of inadmissibility by committees

A committee may, by a unanimous vote, declare inadmissible or strike out of its list of cases an application submitted under Article 34 where such a decision can be taken without further examination. The decision shall be final.

Article 29—Decisions by Chambers on admissibility and merits

1. If no decision is taken under Article 28, a Chamber shall decide on the admissibility and merits of individual applications submitted under Article 34.
2. A Chamber shall decide on the admissibility and merits of inter-State applications submitted under Article 33.
3. The decision on admissibility shall be taken separately unless the Court, in exceptional cases, decides otherwise.

Article 30—Relinquishment of jurisdiction to the Grand Chamber

Where a case pending before a Chamber raises a serious question affecting the interpretation of the Convention or the protocols thereto, or where the resolution of a question before the chamber might have a result inconsistent with a judgment previously delivered by the Court, the Chamber may, at any time before it has rendered its judgment, relinquish jurisdiction in favour of the Grand Chamber, unless one of the parties to the case objects.

Article 31—Powers of the Grand Chamber

The Grand Chamber shall:

a. determine applications submitted either under Article 33 or Article 34 when a Chamber has relinquished jurisdiction under Article 30 or when the case has been referred to it under Article 43; and

b. consider requests for advisory opinions submitted under Article 47.

Article 32—Jurisdiction of the Court

1. The jurisdiction of the Court shall extend to all matters concerning the interpretation and application of the Convention and the protocols thereto which are referred to it as provided in Articles 33, 34 and 47.
2. In the event of dispute as to whether the Court has jurisdiction, the Court shall decide.

Article 33—Inter-State cases

Any High Contracting Party may refer to the Court any alleged breach of the provisions of the Convention and the protocols thereto by another High Contracting Party.

Article 34—Individual applications

Chart of Declarations under former Articles 25 and 46 of the ECHR

The Court may receive applications from any person, non-governmental organisation or group of individuals claiming to be the victim of a violation by one of the High Contracting Parties of the rights set forth in the Convention or the protocols thereto. The High Contracting Parties undertake not to hinder in any way the effective exercise of this right.

[567]

Article 35—Admissibility criteria

1. The Court may only deal with the matter after all domestic remedies have been exhausted, according to the generally recognised rules of international law, and within a period of six months from the date on which the final decision was taken.
2. The Court shall not deal with any application submitted under Article 34 that:

   a. is anonymous; or

   b. is substantially the same as a matter that has already been examined by the Court or has already been submitted to another procedure of international investigation or settlement and contains no relevant new information.

3. The Court shall declare inadmissible any individual application submitted under Article 34 which it considers incompatible with the provisions of the Convention or the protocols thereto, manifestly ill-founded, or an abuse of the right of application.
4. The Court shall reject any application which it considers inadmissible under this Article. It may do so at any stage of the proceedings.

Article 36—Third party intervention

1. In all cases before a Chamber or the Grand Chamber, a High Contracting Party one of whose nationals is an applicant shall have the right to submit written comments and to take part in hearings.
2. The President of the Court may, in the interest of proper administration of justice, invite any High Contracting Party which is not a party to the proceedings or any person concerned who is not the applicant to submit written comments or take part in hearings.

Article 37—Striking out applications

1. The Court may at any stage of the proceedings decide to strike an application out of its list of cases where the circumstances lead to the conclusion that:

   a. the applicant does not intend to pursue his application; or

   b. the matter has been resolved; or

   c. for any other reason established by the Court, it is no longer justified to continue the examination of the application.

   However, the Court shall continue the examination of the application if respect for human rights as defined in the Convention and the protocols thereto so requires.
2. The Court may decide to restore an application to its list of cases if it considered that the circumstances justify such a course.

Article 38—Examination of the case and friendly settlement proceedings

1. If the Court declares the application admissible, it shall:

   a. pursue the examination of the case, together with the representatives of the parties, and if need be, undertake an investigation, for the effective conduct of which the States concerned shall furnish all necessary facilities;

   b. place itself at the disposal of the parties concerned with a view to securing a friendly settlement of the matter on the basis of respect for human rights as defined in the Convention and the protocols thereto.

2. Proceedings conducted under paragraph 1.b shall be confidential.

[568]

Article 39—Finding of a friendly settlement

If a friendly settlement is effected, the Court shall strike the case out of its list by means of a decision which shall be confined to a brief statement of the facts and of the solution reached.

Article 40—Public hearings and access to documents

1. Hearings shall be in public unless the Court in exceptional circumstances decides otherwise.
2. Documents deposited with the Registrar shall be accessible to the public unless the President of the Court decides otherwise.

Article 41—Just satisfaction

If the Court finds that there has been a violation of the Convention or the protocols thereto, and if the internal law of the High Contracting Party concerned allows only partial reparation to be made, the Court shall, if necessary, afford just satisfaction to the injured party.

Article 42—Judgments of Chambers

Judgments of Chambers shall become final in accordance with the provisions of Article 44, paragraph 2.

Article 43—Referral to the Grand Chamber

1. Within a period of three months from the date of the judgment of the Chamber, any party to the case may, in exceptional cases, request that the case be referred to the Grand Chamber.
2. A panel of five judges of the Grand Chamber shall accept the request if the case raises a serious question affecting the interpretation or application of the Convention or the protocols thereto, or a serious issue of general importance.
3. If the panel accepts the request, the Grand Chamber shall decide the case by means of a judgment.

Article 44—Final judgments

1. The judgment of the Grand Chamber shall be final.
2. The judgment of a Chamber shall become final:

   a. when the parties declare that they will not request that the case be referred to the Grand Chamber; or

   b. three months after the date of the judgment, if reference of the case to the Grand Chamber has not been requested; or

   c. when the panel of the Grand Chamber rejects the request to refer under Article 43.

3. The final judgment shall be published.

Article 45—Reasons for judgments and decisions

1. Reasons shall be given for judgments as well as for decisions declaring applications admissible or inadmissible.
2. If a judgment does not represent, in whole or in part, the unanimous opinion of the judges, any judge shall be entitled to deliver a separate opinion.

Article 46—Binding force and execution of judgments

1. The High Contracting Parties undertake to abide by the final judgment of the Court in any case to which they are parties.

[569]

2. The final judgment of the Court shall be transmitted to the Committee of Ministers, which shall supervise its execution.

Article 47—Advisory opinions

1. The Court may, at the request of the Committee of Ministers, give advisory opinions on legal questions concerning the interpretation of the Convention and the protocols thereto.
2. Such opinions shall not deal with any question relating to the content or scope of the rights or freedoms defined in Section I of the Convention and the protocols thereto, or with any other question which the Court or the Committee of Ministers might have to consider in consequence of any such proceedings as could be instituted in accordance with the Convention.
3. Decisions of the Committee of Ministers to request an advisory opinion of the Court shall require a majority vote of the representatives entitled to sit on the Committee.

Article 48—Advisory jurisdiction of the Court

The Court shall decide whether a request for an advisory opinion submitted by the Committee of Ministers is within its competence as defined in Article 47.

Article 49—Reasons for advisory opinions

1. Reasons shall be given for advisory opinions of the Court.
2. If the advisory opinion does not represent, in whole or in part, the unanimous opinion of the judges, any judge shall be entitled to deliver a separate opinion.
3. Advisory opinions of the Court shall be communicated to the Committee of Ministers.

Article 50—Expenditure on the Court

The expenditure on the Court shall be borne by the Council of Europe.

Article 51—Privileges and immunities of judges

The judges shall be entitled, during the exercise of their functions, to the privileges and immunities provided for in Article 40 of the Statute of the Council of Europe and in the agreements made thereunder.

SECTION III—MISCELLANEOUS PROVISIONS

Article 52—Inquiries by the Secretary General

On receipt of a request from the Secretary General of the Council of Europe any High Contracting Party shall furnish an explanation of the manner in which its internal law ensures the effective implementation of any of the provisions of the Convention.

Article 53—Safeguard for existing human rights

Nothing in this Convention shall be construed as limiting or derogating from any of the human rights and fundamental freedoms which may be ensured under the laws of any High Contracting Party or under any other agreement to which it is a Party.

Article 54—Powers of the Committee of Ministers

Nothing in this Convention shall prejudice the powers conferred on the Committee of Ministers by the Statute of the Council of Europe.

Article 55—Exclusion of other means of dispute settlement

The High Contracting Parties agree that, except by special agreement, they will not avail themselves of treaties, conventions or declarations in force between them for the purpose of submitting, by way of petition, a dispute arising out of the interpretation or application of this Convention to a means of settlement other than those provided for in this Convention.

Article 56—Territorial application

1. Any State may at the time of its ratification or at any time thereafter declare by notification addressed to the Secretary General of the Council of Europe that the present Convention shall, subject to paragraph 4 of this Article, extend to all or any of the territories for whose international relations it is responsible.
2. The Convention shall extend to the territory or territories named in the notification as from the thirtieth day after the receipt of this notification by the Secretary General of the Council of Europe.
3. The provisions of this Convention shall be applied in such territories with due regard, however, to local requirements.
4. Any State which has made a declaration in accordance with paragraph 1 of this article may at any time thereafter declare on behalf of one or more of the territories to which the declaration relates that it accepts the competence of the Court to receive applications from individuals, non-governmental organisations or groups of individuals as provided by Article 34 of the Convention.

Article 57—Reservations

1. Any State may, when signing this Convention or when depositing its instrument of ratification, make a reservation in respect of any particular provision of the Convention to the extent that any law then in force in its territory is not in conformity with the provision. Reservations of a general character shall not be permitted under this article.
2. Any reservation made under this article shall contain a brief statement of the law concerned.

Article 58—Denunciation

1. A High Contracting Party may denounce the present Convention only after the expiry of five years from the date on which it became a party to it and after six months' notice contained in a notification addressed to the Secretary General of the Council of Europe, who shall inform the other High Contracting Parties.
2. Such a denunciation shall not have the effect of releasing the High Contracting Party concerned from its obligations under this Convention in respect of any act which, being capable of constituting a violation of such obligations, may have been performed by it before the date at which the denunciation became effective.
3. Any High Contracting Party which shall cease to be a member of the Council of Europe shall cease to be a Party to this Convention under the same conditions.
4. The Convention may be denounced in accordance with the provisions of the preceding paragraphs in respect of any territory to which it has been declared to extend under the terms of Article 56.

Article 59—Signature and ratification

1. This Convention shall be open to the signature of the members of the Council of Europe. It shall be ratified. Ratifications shall be deposited with the Secretary General of the Council of Europe.
2. The present Convention shall come into force after the deposit of ten instruments of ratification.

[571]

3. As regards any signatory ratifying subsequently, the Convention shall come into force at the date of the deposit of its instrument of ratification.
4. The Secretary General of the Council of Europe shall notify all the members of the Council of Europe of the entry into force of the Convention, the names of the High Contracting Parties who have ratified it, and the deposit of all instruments of ratification which may be effected subsequently.

Done at Rome this 4th day of November 1950, in English and French, both texts being equally authentic, in a single copy which shall remain deposited in the archives of the Council of Europe. The Secretary General shall transmit certified copies to each of the signatories.

Protocol No. 1 to the Convention for the Protection of Human Rights and Fundamental Freedoms, as amended by Protocol No. 11

PARIS, 20.III.1952

The governments signatory hereto, being members of the Council of Europe,

Being resolved to take steps to ensure the collective enforcement of certain rights and freedoms other than those already included in Section I of the *Convention for the Protection of Human Rights and Fundamental Freedoms* signed at Rome on 4 November 1950 (hereinafter referred to as "the Convention"),

Have agreed as follows:

Article 1—Protection of property

Every natural or legal person is entitled to the peaceful enjoyment of his possessions. No one shall be deprived of his possessions except in the public interest and subject to the conditions provided for by law and by the general principles of international law. The preceding provisions shall not, however, in any way impair the right of a State to enforce such laws as it deems necessary to control the use of property in accordance with the general interest or to secure the payment of taxes or other contributions or penalties.

Article 2—Right to education

No person shall be denied the right to education. In the exercise of any functions which it assumes in relation to education and to teaching, the State shall respect the right of parents to ensure such education and teaching in conformity with their own religious and philosophical convictions.

Article 3—Right to free elections

The High Contracting Parties undertake to hold free elections at reasonable intervals by secret ballot, under conditions which will ensure the free expression of the opinion of the people in the choice of the legislature.

Article 4—Territorial application

Any High Contracting Party may at the time of signature or ratification or at any time thereafter communicate to the Secretary General of the Council of Europe a declaration stating the extent to which it undertakes that the provisions of the present Protocol shall apply to such of the territories for the international relations of which it is responsible as are named therein.

Any High Contracting Party which has communicated a declaration in virtue of the preceding paragraph may from time to time communicate a further declaration modifying the terms of any former declaration or terminating the application of the provisions of this Protocol in respect of any territory.

A declaration made in accordance with this article shall be deemed to have been made in accordance with paragraph 1 of Article 56 of the Convention.

Article 5—Relationship to the Convention

As between the High Contracting Parties the provisions of Articles 1, 2, 3 and 4 of this Protocol shall be regarded as additional articles to the Convention and all the provisions of the Convention shall apply accordingly.

Article 6—Signature and ratification

This Protocol shall be open for signature by the members of the Council of Europe, who are the signatories of the Convention; it shall be ratified at the same time as or after the ratification of the Convention. It shall enter into force after the deposit of ten instruments of ratification. As regards any signatory ratifying subsequently, the Protocol shall enter into force at the date of the deposit of its instrument of ratification.

The instruments of ratification shall be deposited with the Secretary General of the Council of Europe, who will notify all members of the names of those who have ratified. Done at Paris on the 20th day of March 1952, in English and French, both texts being equally authentic, in a single copy which shall remain deposited in the archives of the Council of Europe. The Secretary General shall transmit certified copies to each of the signatory governments.

Protocol No. 6 to the Convention for the Protection of Human Rights and Fundamental Freedoms concerning the abolition of the death penalty, as amended by Protocol No. 11

STRASBOURG, 28.IV.1983

The member States of the Council of Europe, signatory to this Protocol to the *Convention for the Protection of Human Rights and Fundamental Freedoms*, signed at Rome on 4 November 1950 (hereinafter referred to as "the Convention"),

Considering that the evolution that has occurred in several member States of the Council of Europe expresses a general tendency in favour of abolition of the death penalty,

Have agreed as follows:

Article 1—Abolition of the death penalty

The death penalty shall be abolished. No-one shall be condemned to such penalty or executed.

Article 2—Death penalty in time of war

A State may make provision in its law for the death penalty in respect of acts committed in time of war or of imminent threat of war; such penalty shall be applied only in the instances laid down in the law and in accordance with its provisions. The State shall communicate to the Secretary General of the Council of Europe the relevant provisions of that law.

Article 3—Prohibition of derogations

No derogation from the provisions of this Protocol shall be made under Article 15 of the Convention.

[573]

Article 4—Prohibition of reservations

No reservation may be made under Article 57 of the Convention in respect of the provisions of this Protocol.

Article 5—Territorial application

1. Any State may at the time of signature or when depositing its instrument of ratification, acceptance or approval, specify the territory or territories to which this Protocol shall apply.
2. Any State may at any later date, by a declaration addressed to the Secretary General of the Council of Europe, extend the application of this Protocol to any other territory specified in the declaration. In respect of such territory the Protocol shall enter into force on the first day of the month following the date of receipt of such declaration by the Secretary General.
3. Any declaration made under the two preceding paragraphs may, in respect of any territory specified in such declaration, be withdrawn by a notification addressed to the Secretary General. The withdrawal shall become effective on the first day of the month following the date of receipt of such notification by the Secretary General.

Article 6—Relationship to the Convention

As between the States Parties the provisions of Articles 1 and 5 of this Protocol shall be regarded as additional articles to the Convention and all the provisions of the Convention shall apply accordingly.

Article 7—Signature of ratification

The Protocol shall be open for signature by the member States of the Council of Europe, signatories to the Convention. It shall be subject to ratification, acceptance or approval. A member State of the Council of Europe may not ratify, accept or approve this Protocol unless it has simultaneously or previously, ratified the Convention. Instruments of ratification, acceptance or approval shall be deposited with the Secretary General of the Council of Europe.

Article 8—Entry into force

1. This Protocol shall enter into force on the first day of the month following the date on which five member States of the Council of Europe have expressed their consent to be bound by the Protocol in accordance with the provisions of Article 7.
2. In respect of any member State which subsequently expresses its consent to be bound by it, the Protocol shall enter into force on the first day of the month following the date of the deposit of the instrument of ratification, acceptance or approval.

Article 9—Depositary functions

The Secretary General of the Council of Europe shall notify the member States of the Council of:

a. any signature;

b. the deposit of any instrument of ratification, acceptance or approval;

c. any date of entry into force of this Protocol in accordance with Articles 5 and 8;

d. any other act, notification or communication relating to this Protocol.

In witness whereof the undersigned, being duly authorised thereto, have signed this Protocol.

Done at Strasbourg, this 28th day of April 1983, in English and in French, both texts begin equally authentic, in a single copy which shall be deposited in the archives of the

Council of Europe. The Secretary General of the Council of Europe shall transmit certified copies to each member State of the Council of Europe.

Protocol No. 7 to the Convention for the Protection of Human Rights and Fundamental Freedoms, as amended by Protocol No. 11

STRASBOURG, 22.XI.1984

The member States of the Council of Europe signatory hereto,

Being resolved to take further steps to ensure the collective enforcement of certain rights and freedoms by means of the *Convention for the Protection of Human Rights and Fundamental Freedoms* signed at Rome on 4 November 1950 (hereinafter referred to as "the Convention"),

Have agreed as follows:

Article 1—Procedural safeguards relating to expulsion of aliens

1. An alien lawfully resident in the territory of a State shall not be expelled therefrom except in pursuance of a decision reached in accordance with law and shall be allowed:

   a. to submit reasons against his expulsion,

   b. to have this case reviewed, and

   c. to be represented for these purposes before the competent authority or a person or persons designated by that authority.

2. An alien may be expelled before the exercise of his rights under paragraph 1.a, b and c of this Article, when such expulsion is necessary in the interests of public order or is grounded on reasons of national security.

Article 2—Right of appeal in criminal matters

1. Everyone convicted of a criminal offence by a tribunal shall have the right to have his conviction or sentence reviewed by a higher tribunal. The exercise of this right, including the grounds on which it may be exercised, shall be governed by law.
2. This right may be subject to exceptions in regard to offences of a minor character, as prescribed by law, or in cases in which the person concerned was tried in the first instance by the highest tribunal or was convicted following an appeal against acquittal.

Article 3—Compensation for wrongful conviction

When a person has by a final decision been convicted of a criminal offence and when subsequently his conviction has been reversed, or he has been pardoned, on the ground that a new or newly discovered fact shows conclusively that there has been a miscarriage of justice, the person who has suffered punishment as a result of such conviction shall be compensated according to the law or the practice of the State concerned, unless it is proved that the non-disclosure of the unknown fact in time is wholly or partly attributable to him.

Article 4—Right not to be tried or punished twice

1. No one shall be liable to be tried or punished again in criminal proceedings under the jurisdiction of the same State for an offence for which he has already been finally

acquitted or convicted in accordance with the law and penal procedure of that State.

2. The provisions of the preceding paragraph shall not prevent the reopening of the case in accordance with the law and penal procedure of the State concerned, if there is evidence of new or newly discovered facts, or if there has been a fundamental defect in the previous proceedings, which could affect the outcome of the case.
3. No derogation from this Article shall be made under Article 15 of the Convention.

Article 5—Equality between spouses

Spouses shall enjoy equality of rights and responsibilities of a private law character between them, and in their relations with their children, as to marriage, during marriage and in the event of its dissolution. This Article shall not prevent States from taking such measures as are necessary in the interests of the children.

Article 6—Territorial application

1. Any State may at the time of signature or when depositing its instrument of ratification, acceptance or approval, specify the territory or territories to which the Protocol shall apply and state the extent to which it undertakes that the provisions of this Protocol shall apply to such territory or territories.
2. Any State may at any later date, by a declaration addressed to the Secretary General of the Council of Europe, extend the application of this Protocol to any other territory specified in the declaration. In respect of such territory the Protocol shall enter into force on the first day of the month following the expiration of a period of two months after the date of receipt by the Secretary General of such declaration.
3. Any declaration made under the two preceding paragraphs may, in respect of any territory specified in such declaration, be withdrawn or modified by a notification addressed to the Secretary General. The withdrawal or modification shall become effective on the first day of the month following the expiration of a period of two months after the date of receipt of such notification by the Secretary General.
4. A declaration made in accordance with this Article shall be deemed to have been made in accordance with paragraph 1 of Article 56 of the Convention.
5. The territory of any State to which this Protocol applies by virtue of ratification, acceptance or approval by that State, and each territory to which this Protocol is applied by virtue of a declaration by that State under this Article, may be treated as separate territories for the purpose of the reference in Article 1 to the territory of a State.
6. Any State which has made a declaration in accordance with paragraph 1 or 2 of this Article may at any time thereafter declare on behalf of one or more of the territories to which the declaration relates that it accepts the competence of the Court to receive applications from individuals, non-governmental organisations or groups of individuals as provided in Article 34 of the Convention in respect of Articles 1 to 5 of this Protocol.

Article 7—Relationship to the Convention

Chart of Declarations under former paragraph 2 of this article

As between the States Parties, the provisions of Articles 1 to 6 of this Protocol shall be regarded as additional Articles to the Convention, and all the provisions of the Convention shall apply accordingly.

Article 8—Signature and ratification

This Protocol shall be open for signature by member States of the Council of Europe which have signed the Convention. It is subject to ratification, acceptance or approval. A member State of the Council of Europe may not ratify, accept or approve this Protocol without previously or simultaneously ratifying the Convention. Instruments of ratification, acceptance or approval shall be deposited with the Secretary General of the Council of Europe.

Article 9—Entry into force

1. This Protocol shall enter into force on the first day of the month following the expiration of a period of two months after the date on which seven member States of the Council of Europe have expressed their consent to be bound by the Protocol in accordance with the provisions of Article 8.
2. In respect of any member State which subsequently expresses its consent to be bound by it, the Protocol shall enter into force on the first day of the month following the expiration of a period of two months after the date of the deposit of the instrument of ratification, acceptance or approval.

Article 10—Depositary functions

The Secretary General of the Council of Europe shall notify all the member States of the Council of Europe of:

a. any signature;

b. the deposit of any instrument of ratification, acceptance or approval;

c. any date of entry into force of this Protocol in accordance with Articles 6 and 9;

d. any other act, notification or declaration relating to this Protocol.

In witness whereof the undersigned, being duly authorised thereto, have signed this Protocol.

Done at Strasbourg, this 22nd day of November 1984, in English and French, both texts being equally authentic, in a single copy which shall be deposited in the archives of the Council of Europe. The Secretary General of the Council of Europe shall transmit certified copies to each member State of the Council of Europe.

European Court of Human Rights
Rules of Court

STRASBOURG 1999

(AS IN FORCE AT 1 NOVEMBER 1998)

CONTENTS

The European Court of Human Rights,

Having regard to the Convention for the Protection of Human Rights and Fundamental Freedoms and the Protocols thereto,

Makes the present Rules:

Rule 1

(Definitions)

For the purposes of these Rules unless the context otherwise requires:

(a) the term "Convention" means the Convention for the Protection of Human Rights and Fundamental Freedoms and the Protocols thereto;

(b) the expression "plenary Court" means the European Court of Human Rights sitting in plenary session;

(c) the expression "Grand Chamber" means the Grand Chamber of seventeen judges constituted in pursuance of Article 27 § 1 of the Convention;

(d) the term "Section" means a Chamber set up by the plenary Court for a fixed period in pursuance of Article 26(b) of the Convention and the expression "President of the Section" means the judge elected by the plenary Court in pursuance to Article 26(c) of the Convention as President of such a Section;

(e) the term "Chamber" means any Chamber of seven judges constituted in pursuance of Article 27 § 1 of the Convention and the expression "President of the Chamber" means the judge presiding over such a "Chamber";

(f) the term "Committee" means a Committee of three judges set up in pursuance of Article 27 § 1 of the Convention;

(g) the term "Court" means either the plenary Court, the Grand Chamber, a Section, a Chamber, a Committee or the panel of five judges referred to in Article 43 § 2 of the Convention;

(h) the expression "*ad hoc judge*" means any person, other than an elected judge, chosen by a Contracting Party in pursuance of Article 27 § 2 of the Convention to sit as a member of the Grand Chamber or as a member of a Chamber;

(i) the terms "judge" and "judges" mean the judges elected by the Parliamentary Assembly of the Council of Europe or *ad hoc* judges;

(j) the expression "Judge Rapporteur" means a judge appointed to carry out the tasks provided for in Rules 48 and 49;

(k) the term "Registrar" denotes the Registrar of the Court or the Registrar of a Section according to the context;

(l) the terms "party" and "parties" mean

— the applicant or respondent Contracting Parties;
— the applicant (the person, non-governmental organisation or group of individuals) that lodged a complaint under Article 34 of the Convention;

(m) the expression "third party" means any Contracting State or any person concerned who, as provided for in Article 36 §§ 1 and 2 of the Convention, has exercised its right or been invited to submit written comments or take part in a hearing;

(n) the expression "Committee of Ministers" means the Committee of Ministers of the Council of Europe;

(o) the terms "former Court" and "Commission" mean respectively the European Court and European Commission of Human Rights set up under former Article 19 of the Convention.

[581]

TITLE I
ORGANISATION AND WORKING OF THE COURT

CHAPTER I
JUDGES

Rule 2

(Calculation of term of office)

1. The duration of the term of office of an elected judge shall be calculated as from the date of election. However, when a judge is re-elected on the expiry of the term of office or is elected to replace a judge whose term of office has expired or is about to expire, the duration of the term of office shall, in either case, be calculated as from the date of such expiry.

2. In accordance with Article 23 § 5 of the Convention, a judge elected to replace a judge whose term of office has not expired shall hold office for the remainder of the predecessor's term.

3. In accordance with Article 23 § 7 of the Convention, an elected judge shall hold office until a successor has taken the oath or made the declaration provided for in Rule 3.

Rule 3

(Oath or solemn declaration)

1. Before taking up office, each elected judge shall, at the first sitting of the plenary Court at which the judge is present or, in case of need, before the President of the Court, take the following oath or make the following solemn declaration:

"I swear"—or "I solemnly declare"—"that I will exercise my functions as a judge honourably, independently and impartially and that I will keep secret all deliberations."

2. This act shall be recorded in minutes.

Rule 4

(Incompatible activities)

In accordance with Article 21 § 3 of the Convention, the judges shall not during their term of office engage in any political or administrative activity or any professional activity which is incompatible with their independence or impartiality or with the demands of a full-time office. Each judge shall declare to the President of the Court any additional activity. In the event of a disagreement between the President and the judge concerned, any question arising shall be decided by the plenary Court.

Rule 5

(Precedent)

1. Elected judges shall take precedence after the President and Vice-Presidents of the Court and the Presidents of the Sections, according to the date of their election; in the

event of re-election, even if it is not an immediate re-election, the length of time during which the judge concerned previously held office as a judge shall be taken into account.

2. Vice-Presidents of the Court elected to office on the same date shall take precedence according to the length of time they have served as judges. If the length of time they have served as judges is the same, they shall take precedence according to age. The same rule shall apply to Presidents of Sections.

3. Judges who have served the same length of time as judges shall take precedence according to age.

4. *Ad hoc* judges shall take precedence after the elected judges according to age.

Rule 6

(Resignation)

Resignation of a judge shall be notified to the President of the Court, who shall transmit it to the Secretary General of the Council of Europe. Subject to the provisions of Rules 24 § 3 *in fine* and 26 § 2, resignation shall constitute vacation of office.

Rule 7

(Dismissal from office)

No judge may be dismissed from his or her office unless the other judges, meeting in plenary session, decide by a majority of two-thirds of the elected judges in office that he or she has ceased to fulfil the required conditions. He or she must first be heard by the plenary Court. Any judge may set in motion the procedure for dismissal from office.

CHAPTER II
PRESIDENCY OF THE COURT

Rule 8

(Election of the President and Vice-Presidents of the Court and the Presidents and Vice-Presidents of the Sections)

1. The plenary Court shall elect its President, two Vice-Presidents and the Presidents of the Sections for a period of three years, provided that such period shall not exceed the duration of their terms of office as judges. They may be re-elected.

2. Each Section shall likewise elect for a renewable period of three years a Vice-President, who shall replace the President of the Section if the latter is unable to carry out his or her duties.

3. The Presidents and Vice-Presidents shall continue to hold office until the election of their successors.

4. If a President or a Vice-President ceases to be a member of the Court or resigns from office before its normal expiry, the plenary Court or the relevant Section, as the case may be, shall elect a successor for the remainder of the term of that office.

5. The election referred to in this Rule shall be by secret ballot; only the elected judges who are present shall take part. If no judge receives an absolute majority of the elected judges present, a ballot shall take place between the two judges who have received most votes. In the event of a tie, preference shall be given to the judge having precedence in accordance with Rule 5.

Rule 9

(Functions of the President of the Court)

1. The President of the Court shall direct the work and administration of the Court. The President shall represent the Court and, in particular, be responsible for its relations with the authorities of the Council of Europe.
2. The President shall preside at plenary meetings of the Court, meetings of the Grand Chamber and meetings of the panel of five judges.
3. The President shall not take part in the consideration of cases being heard by Chambers except where he or she is the judge elected in respect of a Contracting Party concerned.

Rule 10

(Functions of the Vice-Presidents of the Court)

The Vice-Presidents of the Court shall assist the President of the Court. They shall take the place of the President if the latter is unable to carry out his or her duties or the office of President is vacant, or at the request of the President. They shall also act as Presidents of Sections.

Rule 11

(Replacement of the President and the Vice-Presidents of the Court)

If the President and the Vice-Presidents of the Court are at the same time unable to carry out their duties or if their offices are at the same time vacant, the office of President of the Court shall be assumed by a President of a Section or, if none is available, by another elected judge, in accordance with the order of precedence provided for in Rule 5.

Rule 12

(Presidency of Sections and Chambers)

The Presidents of the Sections shall preside at the sittings of the Section and Chambers of which they are members. The Vice-Presidents of the Sections shall take their place if they are unable to carry out their duties or if the office of President of the Section concerned is vacant, or at the request of the President of the Section. Failing that, the judges of the Section and the Chambers shall take their place, in the order of precedence provided for in Rule 5.

Rule 13

(Inability to preside)

Judges of the Court may not preside in cases in which the Contracting Party of which they are nationals or in respect of which they were elected is a party.

[584]

Rule 14

(Balanced representation of the sexes)

In relation to the making of appointments governed by this and the following chapter of the present Rules, the Court shall pursue a policy aimed at securing a balanced representation of the sexes.

CHAPTER III
THE REGISTRY

Rule 15

(Election of the Registrar)

1. The plenary Court shall elect its Registrar. The candidates shall be of high moral character and must possess the legal, managerial and linguistic knowledge and experience necessary to carry out the functions attaching to the post.

2. The Registrar shall be elected for a term of five years and may be re-elected. The Registrar may not be dismissed from office, unless the judges, meeting in plenary session, decide by a majority of two-thirds of the elected judges in office that the person concerned has ceased to fulfil the required conditions. He or she must first be heard by the plenary Court. Any judge may set in motion the procedure for dismissal from office.

3. The elections referred to in this Rule shall be by secret ballot; only the elected judges who are present shall take part. If no candidate receives an absolute majority of the elected judges present, a ballot shall take place between the two candidates who have received most votes. In the event of a tie, preference shall be given, firstly, to the female candidate, if any, and, secondly, to the older candidate.

4. Before taking up office, the Registrar shall take the following oath or make the following solemn declaration before the plenary Court or, if need be, before the President of the Court:

"I swear"—or "I solemnly declare"—"that I will exercise loyally, discreetly and conscientiously the functions conferred upon me as Registrar of the European Court of Human Rights."

This act shall be recorded in minutes.

Rule 16

(Election of the Deputy Registrars)

1. The plenary Court shall also elect two Deputy Registrars on the conditions and in the manner and for the term prescribed in the preceeding Rule. The procedure for dismissal from office provided for in respect of the Registrar shall likewise apply. The Court shall first consult the Registrar in both these matters.

2. Before taking up office, a Deputy Registrar shall take an oath or make a solemn declaration before the plenary Court or, if need be, before the President of the Court, in terms similar to those prescribed in respect of the Registrar. This act shall be recorded in minutes.

[585]

Rule 17

(Functions of the Registrar)

1. The Registrar shall assist the Court in the performance of its functions and shall be responsible for the organisation and activities of the Registry under the authority of the President of the Court.

2. The Registrar shall have the custody of the archives of the Court and shall be the channel for all communications and notifications made by, or addressed to, the Court in connection with the cases brought or to be brought before it.

3. The Registrar shall, subject to the duty of discretion attaching to this office, reply to requests for information concerning the work of the Court, in particular to enquiries from the press.

4. General instructions drawn up by the Registrar, and approved by the President of the Court, shall regulate the working of the Registry.

Rule 18

(Organisation of the Registry)

1. The Registry shall consist of Section Registries equal to the number of Sections set up by the Court and of the departments necessary to provide the legal and administrative services requires by the Court.

2. The Section Registrar shall assist the Section in the performance of its functions and may be assisted by a Deputy Section Registrar.

3. The officials of the Registry, including the legal secretaries but not the Registrar and the Deputy Registrars, shall be appointed by the Secretary General of the Council of Europe with the agreement of the President of the Court or of the Registrar acting on the President's instructions.

CHAPTER IV
THE WORKING OF THE COURT

Rule 19

(Seat of the Court)

1. The seat of the Court shall be at the seat of the Council of Europe at Strasbourg. The Court may, however, if it considers it expedient, perform its functions elsewhere in the territories of the member States of the Council of Europe.

2. The Court may decide, at any stage of the examination of an application, that it is necessary that an investigation or any other function be carried out elsewhere by it or one or more of its members.

Rule 20

(Sessions of the plenary Court)

1. The plenary sessions of the Court shall be convened by the President of the Court whenever the performance of its functions under the Convention and under these Rules so requires. The President of the Court shall convene a plenary session if at least one-third

of the members of the Court so request, and in any event once a year to consider administrative matters.

2. The quorum of the plenary Court shall be two-thirds of the elected judges in office.

3. If there is no quorum, the President shall adjourn the sitting.

Rule 21

(Other sessions of the Court)

1. The Grand Chamber, the Chambers and the Committees shall sit full time. On a proposal by the President, however, the Court shall fix session periods each year.

2. Outside those periods the Grand Chamber and the Chambers shall be convened by their Presidents in cases of urgency.

Rule 22

(Deliberations)

1. The Court shall deliberate in private. Its deliberations shall remain secret.

2. Only the judges shall take part in the deliberations. The Registrar or the designated substitute, as well as such other officials of the Registry and interpreters whose assistance is deemed necessary, shall be present. No other person may be admitted except by special decision of the Court.

3. Before a vote is taken on any matter in the Court, the President may request the judges to state their opinions on it.

Rule 23

(Votes)

1. The decisions of the Court shall be taken by a majority of the judges present. In the event of a tie, a fresh vote shall be taken and, if there is still a tie, the President shall have a casting vote. This paragraph shall apply unless otherwise provided for in these Rules.

2. The decisions and judgments of the Grand Chamber and the Chambers shall be adopted by a majority of the sitting judges. Abstentions shall not be allowed in final votes on the admissibility and merits of cases.

3. As a general rule, votes shall be taken by a show of hands. The President may take a roll-call vote, in reverse order of precedence.

4. Any matter that is to be voted upon shall be formulated in precise terms.

CHAPTER V
THE COMPOSITION OF THE COURT

Rule 24

(Composition of the Grand Chamber)

1. The Grand Chamber shall be composed of seventeen judges and at least three substitute judges.

2. (a) The Grand Chamber shall include the President and the Vice-Presidents of the Court and the Presidents of the Sections. Any Vice-President of the Court or

President of a Section who is unable to sit as a member of the Grand Chamber shall be replaced by the Vice-President of the relevant Section.

(b) The judge elected in respect of the State Party concerned or, where appropriate, the judge designated by virtue of Rule 29 or Rule 30 shall sit as an *ex officio* member of the Grand Chamber in accordance with Article 27 §§ 2 and 3 of the Convention.

(c) In cases referred to the Grand Chamber under Article 30 of the Convention, the Grand Chamber shall also include the members of the Chamber which relinquished jurisdiction.

(d) In cases referred to the Grand Chamber under Article 43 of the Convention, the Grand Chamber shall not include any judge who participated in the original Chamber's deliberations on the admissibility or merits of the case, except the President of that Chamber and the judge who sat in respect of the State Party concerned.

(e) The judges and substitute judges who are to complete the Grand Chamber in each case referred to it shall be designated from among the remaining judges by a drawing of lots by the President of the Court in the presence of the Registrar. The modalities for the drawing of lots shall be laid down by the Plenary Court, having due regard to the need for a geographically balanced composition reflecting the different legal systems among the Contracting Parties.

3. If any judges are prevented from sitting, they shall be replaced by the substitute judges in the order in which the latter were selected under paragraph 2(e) of this Rule. Should the need arise, the President may in the course of the proceedings designate additional substitute judges in accordance with paragraph 2(e) above.

4. The judges and substitute judges designated in accordance with the above provisions shall continue to sit in the Grand Chamber for the consideration of the case until the proceedings have been completed. Even after the end of their terms of office, they shall continue to deal with the case if they have participated in the consideration of the merits.

5. (a) The panel of five judges of the Grand Chamber called upon to consider requests submitted under Article 43 of the Convention shall be composed of

— the President of the Court;
— the Presidents or, if they are prevented from sitting, the Vice-Presidents of the Sections other than the Section from which was constituted the Chamber that dealt with the case whose referral to the Grand Chamber is being sought;
— further judges designated in rotation from among the judges other than those who dealt with the case in the Chamber.

(b) No judge elected in respect of, or who is a national of, a Contracting Party concerned may be a member of the Panel.

(c) Any member of the panel unable to sit shall be replaced by another judge who did not deal with the case in the Chamber, who shall be designated in rotation."

Rule 25

(Setting up of Sections)

1. The Chambers provided for in Article 26(b) of the Convention (referred to in these Rules as "Sections") shall be set up by the plenary Court, on a proposal by its President,

[588]

for a period of three years with effect from the election of the presidential office-holders of the Court under Rule 8. There shall be at least four Sections.

2. Each judge shall be a member of a Section. The composition of the Sections shall be geographically and gender balanced and shall reflect the different legal systems among the Contracting Parties.

3. Where a judge ceases to be a member of the Court before the expiry of the period for which the Section has been constituted, the judge's place in the Section shall be taken by his or her successor as a member of the Court.

4. The President of the Court may exceptionally make modifications to the composition of the Sections if circumstances so require.

5. On a proposal by the President, the plenary Court may constitute an additional Section.

Rule 26

(Constitution of Chambers)

1. The Chambers of seven judges provided for in Article 27 § 1 of the Convention for the consideration of cases brought before the Court shall be constituted from the Sections as follows.

(a) The Chamber shall in each case include the President of the Section and the judge elected in respect of any Contracting Party concerned. If the latter judge is not a member of the Section to which the application has been assigned under Rule 51 or 52, he or she shall sit as an *ex officio* member of the Chamber in accordance with Article 27 § 2 of the Convention. Rule 29 shall apply if that judge is unable to sit or withdraws.

(b) The other members of the Chamber shall be designated by the President of the Section in rotation from among the members of the relevant Section.

(c) The members of the Section who are not so designated shall sit in the case as substitute judges.

2. Even after the end of their terms of office judges shall continue to deal with cases in which they have participated in the consideration of the merits.

Rule 27

(Committees)

1. Committees composed of three judges belonging to the same Section shall be set up under Article 27 § 1 of the Convention. After consulting the Presidents of the Sections, the President of the Court shall decide on the number of Committees to be set up.

2. The Committees shall be constituted for a period of twelve months by rotation among the members of each Section, excepting the President of the Section.

3. The judges of the Section who are not members of a Committee may be called upon to take the place of members who are unable to sit.

4. Each Committee shall be chaired by the member having precedence in the Section.

Rule 28

(Inability to sit, withdrawal or exemption)

1. Any judge who is prevented from taking part in sittings for which he has been convoked shall, as soon as possible, give notice to the President of the Chamber.

2. A judge may not take part in the consideration of any case in which he or she has a personal interest or has previously acted either as the Agent, advocate or adviser of a party or of a person having an interest in the case, or as a member of a tribunal or commission of inquiry, or in any other capacity.

3. If a judge withdraws for one of the said reasons, or for some special reason, he or she shall inform the President of the Chamber, who shall exempt the judge from sitting.

4. If the President of the Chamber considers that a reason exists for a judge to withdraw, he or she shall consult with the judge concerned; in the event of disagreement, the Chamber shall decide.

Rule 29

(*Ad hoc* judges)

1. If the judge elected in respect of a Contracting Party concerned is unable to sit in the Chamber or withdraws, the President of the Chamber shall invite that Party to indicate within thirty days whether it wishes to appoint to sit as judge either another elected judge or, as an *ad hoc* judge, any other person possessing the qualifications required by Article 21 § 1 of the Convention and, if so, to state at the same time the name of the person appointed. The same rule shall apply if the person so appointed is unable to sit or withdraws.

2. The Contracting Party concerned shall be presumed to have waived its right of appointment if it does not reply within thirty days.

3. An *ad hoc* judge shall, at the opening of the first sitting fixed for the consideration of the case after the judge has been appointed, take the oath or make the solemn declaration provided for in Rule 3. This act shall be recorded in minutes.

Rule 30

(Common interest)

1. If several applicant or respondent Contracting Parties have a common interest, the President of the Court may invite them to agree to appoint a single elected judge or *ad hoc* judge in accordance with Article 27 § 2 of the Convention. If the Parties are unable to agree, the President shall choose by lot, from among the persons proposed as judges by these Parties, the judge called upon to sit *ex officio*.

2. In the event of a dispute as to the existence of a common interest, the plenary Court shall decide.

TITLE II
PROCEDURE

CHAPTER I
GENERAL RULES

Rule 31

(Possibility of particular derogations)

The provisions of this Title shall not prevent the Court from derogating from them for the consideration of a particular case after having consulted the parties where appropriate.

Rule 32

(Practice directions)

The President of the Court may issue practice directions, notably in relation to such matters as appearance at hearings and the filing of pleadings and other documents.

Rule 33

(Public character of proceedings)

1. Hearings shall be public unless, in accordance with paragraph 2 of this Rule, the Chamber in exceptional circumstances decides otherwise, either of its own motion or at the request of a party or any other person concerned.

2. The press and the public may be excluded from all or part of a hearing in the interest of morals, public order or national security in a democratic society, where the interests of juveniles or the protection of the private life of the parties so require, or to the extent strictly necessary in the opinion of the Chamber in special circumstances where publicity would prejudice the interests of justice.

3. Following registration of an application, all documents deposited with the Registry, with the exception of those deposited within the framework of friendly-settlement negotiations as provided for in Rule 62, shall be accessible to the public unless the President of the Chamber, for the reasons set out in paragraph 2 of this Rule, decides otherwise, either of his or her own motion or at the request of a party or any other person concerned.

4. Any request for confidentiality made under paragraphs 1 or 3 of this Rule must give reasons and specify whether the hearing or the documents, as the case may be, should be inaccessible to the public in whole or in part.

Rule 34

(Use of languages)

1. The official languages of the Court shall be English and French.

2. Before the decision on the admissibility of an application is taken, all communications with and pleadings by applicants under Article 34 of the Convention or their representatives, if not in one of the Court's official languages, shall be in one of the official languages of the Contracting Parties.

3. (a) All communications with and pleadings by such applicants or their representatives in respect of a hearing, or after a case has been declared admissible, shall be in one of the Court's official languages, unless the President of the Chamber authorises the continued use of the official language of a Contracting Party.

   (b) If such leave is granted, the Registrar shall make the necessary arrangements for the oral or written translation of the applicant's observations or statements.

4. (a) All communications with and pleadings by Contracting Parties or third parties shall be in one of the Court's official languages. The President of the Chamber may authorise the use of a non-official language.

   (b) If such leave is granted, it shall be the responsibility of the requesting party to provide for and bear the costs of interpreting or translation into English or French of the oral arguments or written statements made.

5. The President of the Chamber may invite the respondent Contracting Party to provide a translation of its written submissions in the or an official language of that Party in order to facilitate the applicant's understanding of those submissions.

6. Any witness, expert or other person appearing before the Court may use his or her own language if he or she does not have sufficient knowledge of either of the two official languages. In that event the Registrar shall make the necessary arrangements for interpreting or translation.

Rule 35

(Representation of Contracting Parties)

The Contracting Parties shall be represented by Agents, who may have the assistance of advocates or advisers.

Rule 36

(Representation of applicants)

1. Persons, non-governmental organisations or groups of individuals may initially present applications under Article 34 of the Convention themselves or through a representative appointed under paragraph 4 of this Rule.

2. Following notification of the application to the respondent Contracting Party under Rule 54 § 3(b), the President of the Chamber may direct that the applicant should be represented in accordance with paragraph 4 of this Rule.

3. The applicant must be so represented at any hearing decided on by the Chamber or for the purposes of the proceedings following a decision declaring the application admissible, unless the President of the Chamber decides otherwise.

4. (a) The representative of the applicant shall be an advocate authorised to practice in any of the Contracting Parties and resident in the territory of one of them, or any other person approved by the President of the Chamber.

   (b) The President of the Chamber may, where representation would otherwise be obligatory, grant leave to the applicant to present his or her own case, subject, if necessary, to being assisted by an advocate or other approved representative.

   (c) In exceptional circumstances and at any stage of the procedure, the President of the Chamber may, where he or she considers that the circumstances or the conduct of the advocate or other person appointed under the preceding subparagraphs so warrant, direct that the latter may no longer represent or assist the applicant and that the applicant should seek alternative representation.

5. The advocate or other approved representative, or the applicant in person if he or she seeks leave to present his or her own case, must have an adequate knowledge of one of the Court's official languages. However, leave to use a non-official language may be given by the President of the Chamber under Rule 34 § 3.

Rule 37

(Communications, notifications and summonses)

1. Communications or notifications addressed to the Agents or advocates of the parties shall be deemed to have been addressed to the parties.

2. If, for any communication, notification or summonses addressed to persons other than the Agents or advocates of the parties, the Court considers it necessary to have the assistance of the Government of the State on whose territory such communication, notification or summons is to have effect, the President of the Court shall apply directly to that Government in order to obtain the necessary facilities.

3. The same rule shall apply when the Court desires to make or arrange for the making of an investigation on the spot in order to establish the facts or to procure evidence or when it orders the appearance of a person who is resident in, or will have to cross, that territory.

Rule 38

(Written pleadings)

1. No written observations or other documents may be filed after the time-limit set by the President of the Chamber or the Judge Rapporteur, as the case may be, in accordance with these Rules. No written observations or other documents filed outside that time-limit or contrary to any practice direction issued under Rule 32 shall be included in the case file unless the President of the Chamber decides otherwise.

2. For the purposes of observing the time-limit referred to in paragraph 1 of this Rule, the material date is the certified date of dispatch of the document or, if there is none, the actual date of receipt at the Registry.

Rule 39

(Interim measures)

1. The Chamber or, where appropriate, its President may, at the request of a party or of any other person concerned, or of its own motion, indicate to the parties any interim measure which it considers should be adopted in the interests of the parties or of the proper conduct of the proceedings before it.

2. Notice of these measures shall be given to the Committee of Ministers.

3. The Chamber may request information from the parties on any matter connected with the implementation of any interim measure it has indicated.

Rule 40

(Urgent notification of an application)

In any case of urgency the Registrar, with the authorisation of the President of the Chamber, may, without prejudice to the taking of any other procedural steps and by any available means, inform a Contracting Party concerned in an application of the introduction of the application and of a summary of its objects.

Rule 41

(Case priority)

The Chamber shall deal with applications in the order in which they become ready for examination. It may, however, decide to give priority to a particular application.

Rule 42

(Measures for taking evidence)

1. The Chamber may, at the request of a party or a third party, or of its own motion, obtain any evidence which it considers capable of providing clarification of the facts of the case. The Chamber may, *inter alia*, request the parties to produce documentary evidence and decide to hear as a witness or expert or in any other capacity any person whose evidence or statements seem likely to assist it in the carrying out of its tasks.

2. The Chamber may, at any time during the proceedings, depute one or more of its members or of the other judges of the Court to conduct an inquiry, carry out an investigation on the spot or take evidence in some other manner. It may appoint independent external experts to assist such a delegation.

3. The Chamber may ask any person or institution of its choice to obtain information, express an opinion or make a report on any specific point.

4. The parties shall assist the Chamber, or its delegation, in implementing any measures for taking evidence.

5. Where a report has been drawn up or some other measure taken in accordance with the preceding paragraphs at the request of an applicant or respondent Contracting Party, the costs entailed shall be borne by that Party unless the Chamber decides otherwise. In other cases the Chamber shall decide whether such costs are to be borne by the Council of Europe or awarded against the applicant or third party at whose request the report was drawn up or the other measure was taken. In all cases the costs shall be taxed by the President of the Chamber.

Rule 43

(Joinder and simultaneous examination of applications)

1. The Chamber may, either at the request of the parties or of its own motion, order the joinder of two or more applications.

2. The President of the Chamber may, after consulting the parties, order that the proceedings in applications assigned to the same Chamber be conducted simultaneously, without prejudice to the decision of the Chamber on the joinder of the applications.

Rule 44

(Striking out and restoration to the list)

1. When an applicant Contracting Party notifies the Registrar of its intention not to proceed with the case, the Chamber may strike the application out of the Court's list under Article 37 of the Convention if the other Contracting Party or Parties concerned in the case agree to such discontinuance.

2. The decision to strike out an application which has been declared admissible shall be given in the form of a judgment. The President of the Chamber shall forward that judgment, once it has become final, to the Committee of Ministers in order to allow the latter to supervise, in accordance with Article 46 § 2 of the Convention, the execution of any undertakings which may have been attached to the discontinuance, friendly settlement or solution of the matter.

3. When an application has been struck out, the costs shall be at the discretion of the Court. If an award of costs is made in a decision striking out an application which has not been declared admissible, the President of the Chamber shall forward the decision to the Committee of Ministers.

4. The Court may restore an application to its list if it considers that exceptional circumstances justify such a course.

CHAPTER II
INSTITUTION OF PROCEEDINGS

Rule 45

(Signatures)

1. Any application made under Articles 33 or 34 of the Convention shall be submitted in writing and shall be signed by the applicant or by the applicant's representative.

2. Where an application is made by a non-governmental organisation or by a group of individuals, it shall be signed by those persons competent to represent that organisation or group. The Chamber or Committee concerned shall determine any question as to whether the persons who have signed an application are competent to do so.

3. Where applicants are represented in accordance with Rule 36, a power of attorney or written authority to act shall be supplied by their representative or representatives.

Rule 46

(Contents of an inter-State application)

Any Contracting Party or Parties intending to bring a case before the Court under Article 33 of the Convention shall file with the Registry an application setting out

(a) the name of the Contracting Party against which the application is made;

(b) a statement of the facts;

(c) a statement of the alleged violation(s) of the Convention and the relevant arguments;

(d) a statement on compliance with the admissibility criteria (exhaustion of domestic remedies and the six-month rule) laid down in Article 35 § 1 of the Convention;

(e) the object of the application and a general indication of any claims for just satisfaction made under Article 41 of the Convention on behalf of the alleged injured party or parties; and

(f) the name and address of the person(s) appointed as Agent; and accompanied by

(g) copies of any relevant documents and in particular the decisions, whether judicial or not, relating to the object of the application.

Rule 47

(Contents of an individual application)

1. Any application under Article 34 of the Convention shall be made on the application form provided by the Registry, unless the President of the Section concerned decides otherwise. It shall set out

(a) the name, date of birth, nationality, sex, occupation and address of the applicant;

[595]

(b) the name, occupation and address of the representative, if any;

(c) the name of the Contracting Party or Parties against which the application is made;

(d) a succinct statement of the facts;

(e) a succinct statement of the alleged violation(s) of the Convention and the relevant arguments;

(f) a succinct statement on the applicant's compliance with the admissibility criteria (exhaustion of domestic remedies and the six-month rule) laid down in Article 35 § 1 of the Convention; and

(g) the object of the application as well as a general indication of any claims for just satisfaction which the applicant may wish to make under Article 41 of the Convention;

and be accompanied by

(h) copies of any relevant documents and in particular the decisions, whether judicial or not, relating to the object of the application.

2. Applicants shall furthermore

(a) provide information, notably the documents and decisions referred to in paragraph 1(h) of this Rule, enabling it to be shown that the admissibility criteria (exhaustion of domestic remedies and the six-month rule) laid down in Article 35 § 1 of the Convention have been satisfied; and

(b) indicate whether they have submitted their complaints to any other procedure of international investigation or settlement.

3. Applicants who do not wish their identity to be disclosed to the public shall so indicate and shall submit a statement of the reasons justifying such a departure from the normal rule of public access to information in proceedings before the Court. The President of the Chamber may authorise anonymity in exceptional and duly justified cases.

4. Failure to comply with the requirements set out in paragraphs 1 and 2 of this Rule may result in the application not being registered and examined by the Court.

5. The date of introduction of the application shall as a general rule be considered to be the date of the first communication from the applicant setting out, even summarily, the object of the application. The Court may for good cause nevertheless decide that a different date shall be considered to be the date of introduction.

6. Applicants shall keep the Court informed of any change of address and of all circumstances relevant to the application.

CHAPTER III
JUDGE RAPPORTEURS

Rule 48

(Inter-State applications)

1. Where an application is made under Article 33 of the Convention, the Chamber constituted to consider the case shall designate one or more of its judges as Judge Rapporteur(s), who shall submit a report on admissibility when the written observations of the Contracting Parties concerned have been received. Rule 49 § 4 shall, in so far as appropriate, be applicable to this report.

2. After an application made under Article 33 of the Convention has been declared admissible, the Judge Rapporteur(s) shall submit such reports, drafts and other documents as may assist the Chamber in the carrying out of its functions.

Rule 49

(Individual applications)

1. Where an application is made under Article 34 of the Convention, the President of the Section to which the case has been assigned shall designate a judge as Judge Rapporteur, who shall examine the application.

2. In their examination of applications Judge Rapporteurs

(a) may request the parties to submit, within a specified time, any factual information, documents or other material which they consider to be relevant;

(b) shall, subject to the President of the Section directing that the case be considered by a Chamber, decide whether the application is to be considered by a Committee or by a Chamber.

3. Where a case is considered by a Committee in accordance with Article 28 of the Convention, the report of the Judge Rapporteur shall contain

(a) a brief statement of the relevant facts;

(b) a brief statement of the reasons underlying the proposal to declare the application inadmissible or to strike it out of the list.

4. Where a case is considered by a Chamber pursuant to Article 29 § 1 of the Convention, the report of the Judge Rapporteur shall contain

(a) a statement of the relevant facts, including any information obtained under paragraph 2 of this Rule;

(b) an indication of the issues arising under the Convention in the application;

(c) a proposal on admissibility and on any other action to be taken, together, if need be, with a provisional opinion on the merits.

5. After an application made under Article 34 of the Convention has been declared admissible, the Judge Rapporteur shall submit such reports, drafts and other documents as may assist the Chamber in the carrying out of its functions.

Rule 50

(Grand Chamber proceedings)

Where a case has been submitted to the Grand Chamber either under Article 30 or under Article 43 of the Convention, the President of the Grand Chamber shall designate as Judge

[597]

Rapporteur(s) one or, in the case of an inter-State application, one or more of its members.

CHAPTER IV
PROCEEDINGS ON ADMISSIBILITY

INTER-STATE APPLICATIONS

Rule 51

1. When an application is made under Article 33 of the Convention, the President of the Court shall immediately give notice of the application to the respondent Contracting Party and shall assign the application to one of the Sections.

2. In accordance with Rule 26 § 1(a), the judges elected in respect of the applicant and respondent Contracting Parties shall sit as *ex officio* members of the Chamber constituted to consider the case. Rule 30 shall apply if the application has been brought by several Contracting Parties or if applications with the same object brought by several Contracting Parties are being examined jointly under Rule 43 § 2.

3. On assignment of the case to a Section, the President of the Section shall constitute the Chamber in accordance with Rule 26 § 1 and shall invite the respondent Contracting Party to submit its observations in writing on the admissibility of the application. The observations so obtained shall be communicated by the Registrar to the applicant Contracting Party, which may submit written observations in reply.

4. Before ruling on the admissibility of the application, the Chamber may decide to invite the Parties to submit further observations in writing.

5. A hearing on the admissibility shall be held if one or more of the Contracting Parties concerned so requests or if the Chamber so decides of its own motion.

6. After consulting the Parties, the President of the Chamber shall fix the written and, where appropriate, oral procedure and for that purpose shall lay down the time-limit within which any written observations are to be filed.

7. In its deliberations the Chamber shall take into consideration the report submitted by the Judge Rapporteur(s) under Rule 48 § 1.

INDIVIDUAL APPLICATIONS

Rule 52

(Assignment of applications to the Sections)

1. Any application made under Article 34 of the Convention shall be assigned to a Section by the President of the Court, who in so doing shall endeavour to ensure a fair distribution of cases between the Sections.

2. The Chamber of seven judges provided for in Article 27 § 1 of the Convention shall be constituted by the President of the Section concerned in accordance with Rule 26 § 1 once it has been decided that the application is to be considered by a Chamber.

3. Pending the constitution of a Chamber in accordance with paragraph 2 of this Rule, the President of the Section shall exercise any powers conferred on the President of the Chamber by these Rules.

Rule 53

(Procedure before a Committee)

1. In its deliberations the Committee shall take into consideration the report submitted by the Judge Rapporteur under Rule 49 § 3.

2. The Judge Rapporteur, if he or she is not a member of the Committee, may be invited to attend the deliberations of the Committee.

3. In accordance with Article 28 of the Convention, the Committee may, by a unanimous vote, declare inadmissible or strike out of the Court's list of cases an application where such a decision can be taken without further examination. This decision shall be final.

4. If no decision pursuant to paragraph 3 of this Rule is taken, the application shall be forwarded to the Chamber constituted under Rule 52 § 2 to examine the case.

Rule 54

(Procedure before a Chamber)

1. In its deliberations the Chamber shall take into consideration the report submitted by the Judge Rapporteur under Rule 49 § 4.

2. The Chamber may at once declare the application inadmissible or strike it out of the Court's list of cases.

3. Alternatively, the Chamber may decide to

(a) request the parties to submit any factual information, documents or other material which it considers to be relevant;

(b) give notice of the application to the respondent Contracting Party and invite that Party to submit written observations on the application;

(c) invite the parties to submit further observations in writing.

4. Before taking its decision on admissibility, the Chamber may decide, either at the request of the parties or of its own motion, to hold a hearing. In that event, unless the Chamber shall exceptionally decide otherwise, the parties shall be invited also to address the issues arising in relation to the merits of the application.

5. The President of the Chamber shall fix the procedure, including time-limits, in relation to any decisions taken by the Chamber under paragraphs 3 and 4 of this Rule.

INTER-STATE AND INDIVIDUAL APPLICATIONS

Rule 55

(Pleas of inadmissibility)

Any plea of inadmissibility must, in so far as its character and the circumstances permit, be raised by the respondent Contracting Party in its written or oral observations on the admissibility of the application submitted as provided in Rule 51 or 54, as the case may be.

Rule 56

(Decision of a Chamber)

1. The decision of the Chamber shall state whether it was taken unanimously or by a majority and shall be accompanied or followed by reasons.

2. The decision of the Chamber shall be communicated by the Registrar to the applicant and to the Contracting Party or Parties concerned.

Rule 57

(Language of the decision)

1. Unless the Court decides that a decision shall be given in both official languages, all decisions shall be given either in English or in French. Decisions given shall be accessible to the public.

2. Publication of such decisions in the official reports of the Court, as provided for in Rule 78, shall be in both official languages of the Court.

CHAPTER V
PROCEEDINGS AFTER THE ADMISSION OF AN APPLICATION

Rule 58

(Inter-State applications)

1. Once the Chamber has decided to admit an application made under Article 33 of the Convention, the President of the Chamber shall, after consulting the Contracting Parties concerned, lay down the time-limits for the filing of written observations on the merits and for the production of any further evidence. The President may however, with the agreement of the Contracting Parties concerned, direct that a written procedure is to be dispensed with.

2. A hearing on the merits shall be held if one or more of the Contracting Parties concerned so requests or if the Chamber so decides of its own motion. The President of the Chamber shall fix the oral procedure.

3. In its deliberations the Chamber shall take into consideration any reports, drafts and other documents submitted by the Judge Rapporteur(s) under Rule 48 § 2.

Rule 59

(Individual applications)

1. Once the Chamber has decided to admit an application made under Article 34 of the Convention, it may invite the parties to submit further evidence and written observations.

2. A hearing on the merits shall be held if the Chamber so decides of its own motion or, provided that no hearing also addressing the merits has been held at the admissibility stage under Rule 54 § 4, if one of the parties so requests. However, the Chamber may exceptionally decide that the discharging of its functions under Article 38 § 1(a) of the Convention does not require a hearing to be held.

3. The President of the Chamber shall, where appropriate, fix the written and oral procedure.

4. In its deliberations the Chamber shall take into consideration any reports, drafts and other documents submitted by the Judge Rapporteur under Rule 49 § 5.

Rule 60

(Claims for just satisfaction)

1. Any claim which the applicant Contracting Party or the applicant may wish to make for just satisfaction under Article 41 of the Convention shall, unless the President of the Chamber directs otherwise, be set out in the written observations on the merits or, if no such written observations are filed, in a special document filed no later than two months after the decision declaring the application admissible.

2. Itemised particulars of all claims made, together with the relevant supporting documents or vouchers, shall be submitted, failing which the Chamber may reject the claim in whole or in part.

3. The Chamber may, at any time during the proceedings, invite any party to submit comments on the claim for just satisfaction.

Rule 61

(Third-party intervention)

1. The decision declaring an application admissible shall be notified by the Registrar to any Contracting Party one of whose nationals is an applicant in the case, as well as to the respondent Contracting Party or Parties under Rule 56 § 2.

2. Where a Contracting Party seeks to exercise its right to submit written comments or to take part in a hearing, pursuant to Article 36 § 1 of the Convention, the President of the Chamber shall fix the procedure to be followed.

3. In accordance with Article 36 § 2 of the Convention, the President of the Chamber may, in the interests of the proper administration of justice, invite or grant leave to any Contracting State which is not a party to the proceedings, or any person concerned who is not the applicant, to submit written comments or, in exceptional cases, to take part in a hearing. Requests for leave for this purpose must be duly reasoned and submitted in one of the official languages, within a reasonable time after the fixing of the written procedure.

4. Any invitation or grant of leave referred to in paragraph 3 of this Rule shall be subject to any conditions, including time-limits, set by the President of the Chamber. Where such conditions are not complied with, the President may decide not to include the comments in the case file.

5. Written comments submitted in accordance with this Rule shall be submitted in one of the official languages, save where leave to use another language has been granted under Rule 34 § 4. They shall be transmitted by the Registrar to the parties to the case, who shall be entitled, subject to any conditions, including time-limits, set by the President of the Chamber, to file written observations in reply.

Rule 62

(Friendly settlement)

1. Once an application has been declared admissible, the Registrar, acting on the instructions or the Chamber or its President, shall enter into contact with the parties with

[601]

a view to securing a friendly settlement of the matter in accordance with Article 38 § 1 (b) of the Convention. The Chamber shall take any steps that appear appropriate to facilitate such a settlement.

2. In accordance with Article 38 § 2 of the Convention, the friendly-settlement negotiations shall be confidential and without prejudice to the parties' arguments in the contentious proceedings. No written or oral communication and no offer or concession made in the framework of the attempt to secure a friendly settlement may be referred to or relied on in the contentious proceedings.

3. If the Chamber is informed by the Registrar that the parties have agreed to a friendly settlement, it shall, after verifying that the settlement has been reached on the basis of respect for human rights as defined in the Convention and the Protocols thereto, strike the case out of the Court's list in accordance with Rule 44 § 2.

CHAPTER VI
HEARINGS

Rule 63

(Conduct of hearings)

1. The President of the Chamber shall direct hearings and shall prescribe the order in which Agents and advocates or advisers of the parties shall be called upon to speak.

2. Where a fact-finding hearing is being carried out by a delegation of the Chamber under Rule 42, the head of the delegation shall conduct the hearing and the delegation shall exercise any relevant power conferred on the Chamber by the Convention or these Rules.

Rule 64

(Failure to appear at a hearing)

Where, without showing sufficient cause, a party fails to appear, the Chamber may, provided that it is satisfied that such a course is consistent with the proper administration of justice, nonetheless proceed with the hearing.

Rule 65

(Convocation of witnesses, experts and other persons; costs of their appearance)

1. Witnesses, experts and other persons whom the Chamber or the President of the Chamber decides to hear shall be summoned by the Registrar.

2. The summons shall indicate

(a) the case in connection with which it has been issued;

(b) the object of the inquiry, expert opinion or other measure ordered by the Chamber or the President of the Chamber;

(c) any provisions for the payment of the sum due to the person summoned.

3. If the persons concerned appear at the request or on behalf of an applicant or respondent Contracting Party, the costs of their appearance shall be borne by that Party

[602]

unless the Chamber decides otherwise. In other cases, the Chamber shall decide whether such costs are to be borne by the Council of Europe or awarded against the applicant or third party at whose request the person summoned appeared. In all cases the costs shall be taxed by the President of the Chamber.

Rule 66

(Oath or solemn declaration by witnesses and experts)

1. After the establishment of the identity of the witness and before testifying, every witness shall take the following oath or make the following solemn declaration:

"I swear"—or "I solemnly declare upon my honour and conscience"—"that I shall speak the truth, the whole truth and nothing but the truth."

This act shall be recorded in minutes.

2. After the establishment of the identity of the expert and before carrying out his or her task, every expert shall take the following oath or make the following solemn declaration:

"I swear"—or "I solemnly declare"—"that I will discharge my duty as an expert honourably and conscientiously."

This act shall be recorded in minutes.

3. This oath may be taken or this declaration made before the President of the Chamber, or before a judge or any public authority nominated by the President.

Rule 67

(Objection to a witness or expert; hearing of a person for information purposes)

The Chamber shall decide in the event of any dispute arising from an objection to a witness or expert. It may hear for information purposes a person who cannot be heard as a witness.

Rule 68

(Questions put during hearings)

1. Any judge may put questions to the Agents, advocates or advisers of the parties, to the applicant, witnesses and experts, and to any other persons appearing before the Chamber.

2. The witnesses, experts and other persons referred to in Rule 42 § 1 may, subject to the control of the President of the Chamber, be examined by the Agents and advocates or advisers of the parties. In the event of an objection as to the relevance of a question put, the President of the Chamber shall decide.

Rule 69

(Failure to appear, refusal to give evidence or false evidence)

If, without good reason, a witness or any other person who has been duly summoned fails to appear or refuses to give evidence, the Registrar shall, on being so required by the

[603]

President of the Chamber, inform the Contracting Party to whose jurisdiction the witness or other person is subject. The same provisions shall apply if a witness or expert has, in the opinion of the Chamber, violated the oath or solemn declaration provided for in Rule 66.

Rule 70

(Verbatim record of hearings)

1. The Registrar shall, if the Chamber so directs, be responsible for the making of a verbatim record of a hearing. The verbatim record shall include

(a) the composition of the Chamber at the hearing;

(b) a list of those appearing before the Court, that is to say Agents, advocates and advisers of the parties and any third party taking part;

(c) the surname, forenames, description and address of each witness, expert or other person heard;

(d) the text of statements made, questions put and replies given;

(e) the text of any decision delivered during the hearing by the Chamber or the President of the Chamber.

2. If all or part of the verbatim record is in a non-official language, the Registrar shall, if the Chamber so directs, arrange for its translation into one of the official languages.

3. The representatives of the parties shall receive a copy of the verbatim record in order that they may, subject to the control of the Registrar or the President of the Chamber, make corrections, but in no case may such corrections affect the sense and bearing of what was said. The Registrar shall lay down, in accordance with the instructions of the President of the Chamber, the time-limits granted for this purpose.

4. The verbatim record, once so corrected, shall be signed by the President and the Registrar and shall then constitute certified matters of record.

CHAPTER VII
PROCEEDINGS BEFORE THE GRAND CHAMBER

Rule 71

(Applicability of procedural provisions)

Any provisions governing proceedings before the Chambers shall apply, *mutatis mutandis*, to proceedings before the Grand Chamber.

Rule 72

(Relinquishment of jurisdiction by a Chamber in favour of the Grand Chamber)

1. In accordance with Article 30 of the Convention, where a case pending before a Chamber raises a serious question affecting the interpretation of the Convention or the Protocols thereto or where the resolution of a question before it might have a result inconsistent with a judgment previously delivered by the Court, the Chamber may, at any

time before it has rendered its judgment, relinquish jurisdiction in favour of the Grand Chamber, unless one of the parties to the case has objected in accordance with paragraph 2 of this Rule. Reasons need not be given for the decision to relinquish.

2. The Registrar shall notify the parties of the Chamber's intention to relinquish jurisdiction. The parties shall have one month from the date of that notification within which to file at the Registry a duly reasoned objection. An objection which does not fulfil these conditions shall be considered invalid by the Chamber.

Rule 73

(Request by a party for referral of a case to the Grand Chamber)

1. In accordance with Article 43 of the Convention, any party to a case may exceptionally, within a period of three months from the date of delivery of the judgment of a Chamber, file in writing at the Registry a request that the case be referred to the Grand Chamber. The party shall specify in its request the serious question affecting the interpretation or application of the Convention or the Protocols thereto, or the serious issue of general importance, which in its view warrants consideration by the Grand Chamber.

2. A panel of five judges of the Grand Chamber constituted in accordance with Rule 24 § 6 shall examine the request solely on the basis of the existing case file. It shall accept the request only if it considers that the case does raise such a question or issue. Reasons need not be given for a refusal of the request.

3. If the panel accepts the request, the Grand Chamber shall decide the case by means of a judgment.

CHAPTER VIII
JUDGMENTS

Rule 74

(Contents of the judgment)

1. A judgment as referred to in Articles 42 and 44 of the Convention shall contain

(a) the names of the President and the other judges constituting the Chamber concerned, and the name of the Registrar or the Deputy Registrar;

(b) the dates on which it was adopted and delivered;

(c) a description of the parties;

(d) the names of the Agents, advocates or advisers of the parties;

(e) an account of the procedure followed;

(f) the facts of the case;

(g) a summary of the submissions of the parties;

(h) the reasons in point of law;

(i) the operative provisions;

(j) the decision, if any, in respect of costs;

(k) the number of judges constituting the majority;

(l) where appropriate, a statement as to which text is authentic.

2. Any judge who has taken part in the consideration of the case shall be entitled to annex to the judgment either a separate opinion, concurring with or dissenting from that judgment, or a bare statement of dissent.

Rule 75

(Ruling on just satisfaction)

1. Where the Chamber finds that there has been a violation of the Convention or the Protocols thereto, it shall give in the same judgment a ruling on the application of Article 41 of the Convention if that question, after being raised in accordance with Rule 60, is ready for decision; if the question is not ready for decision, the Chamber shall reserve it in whole or in part and shall fix the further procedure.

2. For the purposes of ruling on the application of Article 41 of the Convention, the Chamber shall, as far as possible, be composed of those judges who sat to consider the merits of the case. Where it is not possible to constitute the original Chamber, the President of the Court shall complete or compose the Chamber by drawing lots.

3. The Chamber may, when affording just satisfaction under Article 41 of the Convention, direct that if settlement is not made within a specified time, interest is to be payable on any sums awarded.

4. If the Court is informed that an agreement has been reached between the injured party and the Contracting Party liable, it shall verify the equitable nature of the agreement and, where it finds the agreement to be equitable, strike the case out of the list in accordance with Rule 44 § 2.

Rule 76

(Language of the judgment)

1. Unless the Court decides that a judgment shall be given in both official languages, all judgments shall be given either in English or in French. Judgments given shall be accessible to the public.

2. Publication of such judgments in the official reports of the Court, as provided for in Rule 78, shall be in both official languages of the Court.

Rule 77

(Signature, delivery and notification of the judgment)

1. Judgments shall be signed by the President of the Chamber and the Registrar.

2. The judgment may be read out at a public hearing by the President of the Chamber or by another judge delegated by him or her. The Agents and representatives of the parties shall be informed in due time of the date of the hearing. Otherwise the notification provided for in paragraph 3 of this Rule shall constitute delivery of the judgment.

3. The judgment shall be transmitted to the Committee of Ministers. The Registrar shall send certified copies to the parties, to the Secretary General of the Council of Europe, to any third party and to any other person directly concerned. The original copy, duly signed and sealed, shall be placed in the archives of the Court.

Rule 78

(Publication of judgments and other documents)

In accordance with Article 44 § 3 of the Convention, final judgment of the Court shall be published, under the responsibility of the Registrar, in an appropriate form. The Registrar shall in addition be responsible for the publication of official reports of selected judgments and decisions and of any document which the President of the Court considers it useful to publish.

Rule 79

(Request for interpretation of a judgment)

1. A party may request the interpretation of a judgment within a period of one year following the delivery of that judgment.

2. The request shall be filed with the Registry. It shall state precisely the point or points in the operative provisions of the judgment on which interpretation is required.

3. The original Chamber may decide of its own motion to refuse the request on the ground that there is no reason to warrant considering it. Where it is not possible to constitute the original Chamber, the President of the Court shall complete or compose the Chamber by drawing lots.

4. If the Chamber does not refuse the request, the Registrar shall communicate it to the other party or parties and shall invite them to submit any written comments within a time-limit laid down by the President of the Chamber. The President of the Chamber shall also fix the date of the hearing should the Chamber decide to hold one. The Chamber shall decide by means of a judgment.

Rule 80

(Request for revision of a judgment)

1. A party may, in the event of the discovery of a fact which might by its nature have a decisive influence and which, when a judgment was delivered, was unknown to the Court and could not reasonably have been known to that party, request the Court, within a period of six months after that party acquired knowledge of the fact, to revise that judgment.

2. The request shall mention the judgment of which revision is requested and shall contain the information necessary to show that the conditions laid down in paragraph 1 of this Rule have been complied with. It shall be accompanied by a copy of all supporting documents. The request and supporting documents shall be filed with the Registry.

3. The original Chamber may decide of its own motion to refuse the request on the ground that there is no reason to warrant considering it. Where it is not possible to constitute the original Chamber, the President of the Court shall complete or compose the Chamber by drawing lots.

4. If the Chamber does not refuse the request, the Registrar shall communicate it to the other party or parties and shall invite them to submit any written comments within a time-limit laid down by the President of the Chamber. The President of the Chamber shall also fix the date of the hearing should the Chamber decide to hold one. The Chamber shall decide by means of a judgment.

Rule 81

(Rectification of errors in decisions and judgments)

Without prejudice to the provisions on revision of judgments and on restoration to the list of applications, the Court may, of its own motion or at the request of a party made within one month of the delivery of a decision or a judgment, rectify clerical errors, errors in calculation or obvious mistakes.

CHAPTER IX
ADVISORY OPINIONS

Rule 82

In proceedings relating to advisory opinions the Court shall apply, in addition to the provisions of Articles 47, 48 and 49 of the Convention, the provisions which follow. It shall also apply the other provisions of these Rules to the extent to which it considers this to be appropriate.

Rule 83

The request for an advisory opinion shall be filed with the Registry. It shall state fully and precisely the question on which the opinion of the Court is sought, and also

(a) the date on which the Committee of Ministers adopted the decision referred to in Article 47 § 3 of the Convention;

(b) the names and addresses of the person or persons appointed by the Committee of Ministers to give the Court any explanations which it may require.

The request shall be accompanied by all documents likely to elucidate the question.

Rule 84

1. On receipt of a request, the Registrar shall transmit a copy of it to all members of the Court.
2. The Registrar shall inform the Contracting Parties that the Court is prepared to receive their written comments.

Rule 85

1. The President of the Court shall lay down the time-limits for filing written comments or other documents.
2. Written comments or other documents shall be filed with the Registry. The Registrar shall transmit copies of them to all the members of the Court, to the Committee of Ministers and to each of the Contracting Parties.

Rule 86

After the close of the written procedure, the President of the Court shall decide whether the Contracting Parties which have submitted written comments are to be given an opportunity to develop them at a hearing held for the purpose.

Rule 87

If the Court considers that the request for an advisory opinion is not within its consultative competence as defined in Article 47 of the Convention, it shall so declare in a reasoned decision.

Rule 88

1. Advisory opinions shall be given by a majority vote of the Grand Chamber. They shall mention the number of judges constituting the majority.
2. Any judge may, if he or she so desires, attach to the opinion of the Court either a separate opinion, concurring with or dissenting from the advisory opinion, or a bare statement of dissent.

Rule 89

The advisory opinion shall be read out in one of the two official languages by the President of the Court, or by another judge delegated by the President, at a public hearing, prior notice having been given to the Committee of Ministers and to each of the Contracting Parties.

Rule 90

The opinion, or any decision given under Rule 87, shall be signed by the President of the Court and by the Registrar. The original copy, duly signed and sealed, shall be placed in the archives of the Court. The Registrar shall send certified copies to the Committee of Ministers, to the Contracting Parties and to the Secretary General of the Council of Europe.

CHAPTER X
LEGAL AID

Rule 91

1. The President of the Chamber may, either at the request of an applicant having lodged an application under Article 34 of the Convention or of his or her own motion, grant free legal aid to the applicant in connection with the presentation of the case from the moment when observations in writing on the admissibility of that application are received from the respondent Contracting Party in accordance with Rule 54 § 3(b), or where the time-limit for their submission has expired.

2. Subject to Rule 96, where the applicant has been granted legal aid in connection with the presentation of his or her case before the Chamber, that grant shall continue in force for the purposes of his or her representation before the Grand Chamber.

Rule 92

Legal aid shall be granted only where the President of the Chamber is satisfied

(a) that it is necessary for the proper conduct of the case before the Chamber;

(b) that the applicant has insufficient means to meet all or part of the costs entailed.

Rule 93

1. In order to determine whether or not applicants have sufficient means to meet all or part of the costs entailed, they shall be required to complete a form of declaration stating their income, capital assets and any financial commitments in respect of dependants, or any other financial obligations. The declaration shall be certified by the appropriate domestic authority or authorities.

2. The Contracting Party concerned shall be requested to submit its comments in writing.

3. After receiving the information mentioned in paragraphs 1 and 2 of this Rule, the President of the Chamber shall decide whether or not to grant legal aid. The Registrar shall inform the parties accordingly.

Rule 94

1. Fees shall be payable to the advocates or other persons appointed in accordance with Rule 36 § 4. Fees may, where appropriate, be paid to more than one such representative.

2. Legal aid may be granted to cover not only representatives' fees but also travelling and subsistence expenses and other necessary expenses incurred by the applicant or appointed representative.

Rule 95

On a decision to grant legal aid, the Registrar shall fix

(a) the rate of fees to be paid in accordance with the legal-aid scales in force;

(b) the level of expenses to be paid.

Rule 96

The President of the Chamber may, if satisfied that the conditions stated in Rule 92 are no longer fulfilled, revoke or vary a grant of legal aid at any time.

TITLE III
TRANSITIONAL RULES

Rule 97

(Judges' terms of office)

The duration of the terms of office of the judges who were members of the Court at the date of the entry into force of Protocol No. 11 to the Convention shall be calculated as from that date.

Rule 98

(Presidency of the Sections)

For a period of three years from the entry into force of Protocol No. 11 to the Convention,

(a) the two Presidents of Sections who are not simultaneously Vice-Presidents of the Court and the Vice-Presidents of the Sections shall be elected for a term of office of eighteen months;

(b) the Vice-Presidents of the Sections may not be immediately re-elected.

Rule 99

(Relations between the Court and the Commission)

1. In cases brought before the Court under Article 5 §§ 4 and 5 of Protocol No. 11 to the Convention the Court may invite the Commission to delegate one or more of its members to take part in the consideration of the case before the Court.

2. In cases referred to in paragraph 1 of this Rule the Court shall take into consideration the report of the Commission adopted pursuant to former Article 31 of the Convention.

3. Unless the President of the Chamber decides otherwise, the said report shall be made available to the public through the Registrar as soon as possible after the case has been brought before the Court.

4. The remainder of the case file of the Commission, including all pleadings, in cases brought before the Court under Article 5 §§ 2 to 5 of Protocol No. 11 shall remain confidential unless the President of the Chamber decides otherwise.

5. In cases where the Commission has taken evidence but has been unable to adopt a report in accordance with former Article 31 of the Convention, the Court shall take into consideration the verbatim records, documentation and opinion of the Commission's delegations arising from such investigations.

Rule 100

(Chamber and Grand Chamber proceedings)

1. In cases referred to the Court under Article 5 § 4 of Protocol No. 11 to the Convention, a panel of the Grand Chamber constituted in accordance with Rule 24 § 6 shall determine, solely on the basis of the existing case file, whether a Chamber or the Grand Chamber is to decide the case.

[611]

2. If the case is decided by a Chamber, the judgment of the Chamber shall, in accordance with Article 5 § 4 of Protocol No. 11, be final and Rule 73 shall be inapplicable.

3. Cases transmitted to the Court under Article 5 § 5 of Protocol No. 11 shall be forwarded by the President of the Court to the Grand Chamber.

4. For each case transmitted to the Grand Chamber under Article 5 § 5 of Protocol No. 11, the Grand Chamber shall be completed by judges designated by rotation within one of the groups mentioned in Rule 24 § 3, the cases being allocated to the groups on an alternate basis.

Rule 101

(Grant of legal aid)

Subject to Rule 96, in cases brought before the Court under Article 5 §§ 2 to 5 of Protocol No. 11 to the Convention, a grant of legal aid made to an applicant in the proceedings before the Commission or the former Court shall continue in force for the purposes of his or her representation before the Court.

Rule 102

(Request for interpretation or revision of a judgment)

1. Where a party requests interpretation or revision of a judgment delivered by the former Court, the President of the Court shall assign the request to one of the Sections in accordance with the conditions laid down in Rule 51 or 52, as the case may be.

2. The President of the relevant Section shall, notwithstanding Rules 79 § 3 and 80 § 3, constitute a new Chamber to consider the request.

3. The Chamber to be constituted shall include as *ex officio* members

(a) the President of the Section;

and, whether or not they are members of the relevant Section,

(b) the judge elected in respect of any Contracting Party concerned or, if he or she is unable to sit, any judge appointed under Rule 29;

(c) any judge of the Court who was a member of the original Chamber that delivered the judgment in the former Court.

4. (a) The other members of the Chamber shall be designated by the President of the Section by means of a drawing of lots from among the members of the relevant Section.

(b) The members of the Section who are not so designated shall sit in the case as substitute judges.

TITLE IV
FINAL CLAUSES

Rule 103

(Amendment or suspension of a Rule)

1. Any Rule may be amended upon a motion made after notice where such a motion is carried at the next session of the plenary Court by a majority of all the members of the

Court. Notice of such a motion shall be delivered in writing to the Registrar at least one month before the session at which it is to be discussed. On receipt of such a notice of motion, the Registrar shall inform all members of the Court at the earliest possible moment.

2. A Rule relating to the internal working of the Court may be suspended upon a motion made without notice, provided that this decision is taken unanimously by the Chamber concerned. The suspension of a Rule shall in this case be limited in its operation to the particular purpose for which it was sought.

Rule 104

(Entry into force of the Rules)

The present Rules shall enter into force on 1 November 1998.

UNITED KINGDOM MATERIAL

Human Rights Act 1998

1998 CHAPTER 42

ARRANGEMENT OF SECTIONS

INTRODUCTION

LEGISLATION

PUBLIC AUTHORITIES

REMEDIAL ACTION

OTHER RIGHTS AND PROCEEDINGS

DEROGATIONS AND RESERVATIONS

14. Derogations.
15. Reservations.
16. Period for which designated derogations have effect.
17. Periodic review of designated reservations.

JUDGES OF THE EUROPEAN COURT OF HUMAN RIGHTS

18. Appointment to European Court of Human Rights.

PARLIAMENTARY PROCEDURE

19. Statements of compatibility.

SUPPLEMENTAL

20. Orders etc. under this Act.
21. Interpretation, etc.
22. Short title, commencement, application and extent.

SCHEDULES

An Act to give further effect to rights and freedoms guaranteed under the European Convention on Human Rights; to make provision with respect to holders of certain judicial offices who become judges of the European Court of Human Rights; and for connected purposes.

[9TH NOVEMBER 1998]

BE IT ENACTED by the Queen's most Excellent Majesty, by and with the advice and consent of the Lords Spiritual and Temporal, and Commons, in this present Parliament assembled, and by the authority of the same, as follows:

Introduction

The Convention Rights

   1.—(1) In this Act "the Convention rights" means the rights and fundamental freedoms set out in—

   (a) Articles 2 to 12 and 14 of the Convention,

[616]

(b) Articles 1 to 3 of the First Protocol, and

(c) Articles 1 and 2 of the Sixth Protocol,

as read with Articles 16 to 18 of the Convention.

(2) Those Articles are to have effect for the purposes of this Act subject to any designated derogation or reservation (as to which see sections 14 and 15).

(3) The Articles are set out in Schedule 1.

(4) The Secretary of State may by order make such amendments to this Act as he considers appropriate to reflect the effect, in relation to the United Kingdom, of a protocol.

(5) In subsection (4) "protocol" means a protocol to the Convention—

(a) which the United Kingdom has ratified; or

(b) which the United Kingdom has signed with a view to ratification.

(6) No amendment may be made by an order under subsection (4) so as to come into force before the protocol concerned is in force in relation to the United Kingdom.

Interpretation of Convention rights

2.—(1) A court or tribunal determining a question which has arisen in connection with a Convention right must take into account any—

(a) judgment, decision, declaration or advisory opinion of the European Court of Human Rights,

(b) opinion of the Commission given in a report adopted under Article 31 of the Convention,

(c) decision of the Commission in connection with Article 26 or 27(2) of the Convention, or

(d) decision of the Committee of Ministers taken under Article 46 of the Convention,

whenever made or given, so far as, in the opinion of the court or tribunal, it is relevant to the proceedings in which that question has arisen.

(2) Evidence of any judgment, decision, declaration or opinion of which account may have to be taken under this section is to be given in proceedings before any court or tribunal in such manner as may be provided by rules.

(3) In this section "rules" means rules of court or, in the case of proceedings before a tribunal, rules made for the purposes of this section—

(a) by the Lord Chancellor or the Secretary of State, in relation to any proceedings outside Scotland;

(b) by the Secretary of State, in relation to proceedings in Scotland; or

(c) by a Northern Ireland department, in relation to proceedings before a tribunal in Northern Ireland—

(i) which deals with transferred matters; and
(ii) for which no rules made under paragraph (a) are in force.

[617]

Legislation

Interpretation of legislation

3.—(1) So far as it is possible to do so, primary legislation and subordinate legislation must be read and given effect in a way which is compatible with the Convention rights.

(2) This section—

(a) applies to primary legislation and subordinate legislation whenever enacted;

(b) does not affect the validity, continuing operation or enforcement of any incompatible primary legislation; and

(c) does not affect the validity, continuing operation or enforcement of any incompatible subordinate legislation if (disregarding any possibility of revocation) primary legislation prevents removal of the incompatibility.

Declaration of incompatibility

4.—(1) Subsection (2) applies in any proceedings in which a court determines whether a provision of primary legislation is compatible with a Convention right.

(2) If the court is satisfied that the provision is incompatible with a Convention right, it may make a declaration of that incompatibility.

(3) Subsection (4) applies in any proceedings in which a court determines whether a provision of subordinate legislation, made in the exercise of a power conferred by primary legislation, is compatible with a Convention right.

(4) If the court is satisfied—

(a) that the provision is incompatible with a Convention right, and

(b) that (disregarding any possibility of revocation) the primary legislation concerned prevents removal of the incompatibility,

it may make a declaration of that incompatibility.

(5) In this section "court" means—

(a) the House of Lords;

(b) the Judicial Committee of the Privy Council;

(c) the Courts-Martial Appeal Court;

(d) in Scotland, the High Court of Justiciary sitting otherwise than as a trial court or the Court of Session;

(e) in England and Wales or Northern Ireland, the High Court or the Court of Appeal.

(6) A declaration under this section ("a declaration of incompatibility")—

(a) does not affect the validity, continuing operation or enforcement of the provision in respect of which it is given; and

(b) is not binding on the parties to the proceedings in which it is made.

Right of Crown to intervene

5.—(1) Where a court is considering whether to make a declaration of incompatibility, the Crown is entitled to notice in accordance with rules of court.

(2) In any case to which subsection (1) applies—

(a) a Minister of the Crown (or a person nominated by him),

(b) a member of the Scottish Executive,

(c) a Northern Ireland Minister,

(d) a Northern Ireland department,

is entitled, on giving notice in accordance with rules of court, to be joined as a party to the proceedings.

(3) Notice under subsection (2) may be given at any time during the proceedings.

(4) A person who has been made a party to criminal proceedings (other than in Scotland) as the result of a notice under subsection (2) may, with leave, appeal to the House of Lords against any declaration of incompatibility made in the proceedings.

(5) In subsection (4)—

"criminal proceedings" includes all proceedings before the Courts-Martial Appeal Court; and

"leave" means leave granted by the court making the declaration of incompatibility or by the House of Lords.

Public authorities

Acts of public authorities

6.—(1) It is unlawful for a public authority to act in a way which is incompatible with a Convention right.

(2) Subsection (1) does not apply to an act if—

(a) as the result of one or more provisions of primary legislation, the authority could not have acted differently; or

(b) in the case of one or more provisions of, or made under, primary legislation which cannot be read or given effect in a way which is compatible with the Convention rights, the authority was acting so as to give effect to or enforce those provisions.

(3) In this section "public authority" includes—

(a) a court or tribunal, and

(b) any person certain of whose functions are functions of a public nature,

but does not include either House of Parliament or a person exercising functions in connection with proceedings in Parliament.

(4) In subsection (3) "Parliament" does not include the House of Lords in its judicial capacity.

(5) In relation to a particular act, a person is not a public authority by virtue only of subsection (3)(b) if the nature of the act is private.

(6) "An act" includes a failure to act but does not include a failure to—

(a) introduce in, or lay before, Parliament a proposal for legislation; or

(b) make any primary legislation or remedial order.

Proceedings

7.—(1) A person who claims that a public authority has acted (or proposes to act) in a way which is made unlawful by section 6(1) may—

(a) bring proceedings against the authority under this Act in the appropriate court or tribunal, or

(b) rely on the Convention right or rights concerned in any legal proceedings,

but only if he is (or would be) a victim of the unlawful act.

(2) In subsection (1)(a) "appropriate court or tribunal" means such court or tribunal as may be determined in accordance with rules; and proceedings against an authority include a counterclaim or similar proceeding.

(3) If the proceedings are brought on an application for judicial review, the applicant is to be taken to have a sufficient interest in relation to the unlawful act only if he is, or would be, a victim of that act.

(4) If the proceedings are made by way of a petition for judicial review in Scotland, the applicant shall be taken to have title and interest to sue in relation to the unlawful act only if he is, or would be, a victim of that act.

(5) Proceedings under subsection (1)(a) must be brought before the end of—

(a) the period of one year beginning with the date on which the act complained of took place; or

(b) such longer period as the court or tribunal considers equitable having regard to all the circumstances,

but that is subject to any rule imposing a stricter time limit in relation to the procedure in question.

(6) In subsection (1)(b) "legal proceedings" includes—

(a) proceedings brought by or at the instigation of a public authority; and

(b) an appeal against the decision of a court or tribunal.

(7) For the purposes of this section, a person is a victim of an unlawful act only if he would be a victim for the purposes of Article 34 of the Convention if proceedings were brought in the European Court of Human Rights in respect of that act.

(8) Nothing in this Act creates a criminal offence.

(9) In this section "rules" means—

(a) in relation to proceedings before a court or tribunal outside Scotland, rules made by the Lord Chancellor or the Secretary of State for the purposes of this section or rules of court,

(b) in relation to proceedings before a court or tribunal in Scotland, rules made by the Secretary of State for those purposes,

(c) in relation to proceedings before a tribunal in Northern Ireland—

(i) which deals with transferred matters; and
(ii) for which no rules made under paragraph (a) are in force,

rules made by a Northern Ireland department for those purposes,

and includes provisions made by order under section 1 of the Courts and Legal Services Act 1990.

(10) In making rules, regard must be had to section 9.

(11) The Minister who has power to make rules in relation to a particular tribunal may, to the extent he considers it necessary to ensure that the tribunal can provide an appropriate remedy in relation to an act (or proposed act) of a public authority which is (or would be) unlawful as a result of section 6(1), by order add to—

(a) the relief or remedies which the tribunal may grant; or

[620]

(b) the grounds on which it may grant any of them.

(12) An order made under subsection (11) may contain such incidental, supplemental, consequential or transitional provision as the Minister making it considers appropriate.

(13) "The Minister" includes the Northern Ireland department concerned.

Judicial remedies

8.—(1) In relation to any act (or proposed act) of a public authority which the court finds is (or would be) unlawful, it may grant such relief or remedy, or make such order, within its powers as it considers just and appropriate.

(2) But damages may be awarded only by a court which has power to award damages, or to order the payment of compensation, in civil proceedings.

(3) No award of damages is to be made unless, taking account of all the circumstances of the case, including—

(a) any other relief or remedy granted, or order made, in relation to the act in question (by that or any other court), and

(b) the consequences of any decision (of that or any other court) in respect of that act,

the court is satisfied that the award is necessary to afford just satisfaction to the person in whose favour it is made.

(4) In determining—

(a) whether to award damages, or

(b) the amount of an award,

the court must take into account the principles applied by the European Court of Human Rights in relation to the award of compensation under Article 41 of the Convention.

(5) A public authority against which damages are awarded is to be treated—

(a) in Scotland, for the purposes of section 3 of the Law Reform (Miscellaneous Provisions) (Scotland) Act 1940 as if the award were made in an action of damages in which the authority has been found liable in respect of loss or damage to the person to whom the award is made;

(b) for the purposes of the Civil Liability (Contribution) Act 1978 as liable in respect of damage suffered by the person to whom the award is made.

(6) In this section—

"court" includes a tribunal;

"damages" means damages for an unlawful act of a public authority; and

"unlawful" means unlawful under section 6(1).

Judicial acts

9.—(1) Proceedings under section 7(1)(a) in respect of a judicial act may be brought only—

(a) by exercising a right of appeal;

(b) on an application (in Scotland a petition) for judicial review; or

(c) in such other forum as may be prescribed by rules.

(2) That does not affect any rule of law which prevents a court from being the subject of judicial review.

(3) In proceedings under this Act in respect of a judicial act done in good faith, damages may not be awarded otherwise than to compensate a person to the extent required by Article 5(5) of the Convention.

(4) An award of damages permitted by subsection (3) is to be made against the Crown; but no award may be made unless the appropriate person, if not a party to the proceedings, is joined.

(5) In this section—

"appropriate person" means the Minister responsible for the court concerned, or a person or government department nominated by him;

"court" includes a tribunal;

"judge" includes a member of a tribunal, a justice of the peace and a clerk or other officer entitled to exercise the jurisdiction of a court;

"judicial act" means a judicial act of a court and includes an act done on the instructions, or on behalf, of a judge; and

"rules" has the same meaning as in section 7(9).

Remedial action

Power to take remedial action

10.—(1) This section applies if—

(a) a provision of legislation has been declared under section 4 to be incompatible with a Convention right and, if an appeal lies—

    (i) all persons who may appeal have stated in writing that they do not intend to do so;

    (ii) the time for bringing an appeal has expired and no appeal has been brought within that time; or

    (iii) an appeal brought within that time has been determined or abandoned; or

(b) it appears to a Minister of the Crown or Her Majesty in Council that, having regard to a finding of the European Court of Human Rights made after the coming into force of this section in proceedings against the United Kingdom, a provision of legislation is incompatible with an obligation of the United Kingdom arising from the Convention.

(2) If a Minister of the Crown considers that there are compelling reasons for proceeding under this section, he may by order make such amendments to the legislation as he considers necessary to remove the incompatibility.

(3) If, in the case of subordinate legislation, a Minister of the Crown considers—

(a) that it is necessary to amend the primary legislation under which the subordinate legislation in question was made, in order to enable the incompatibility to be removed, and

(b) that there are compelling reasons for proceeding under this section,

he may by order make such amendments to the primary legislation as he considers necessary.

(4) This section also applies where the provision in question is in subordinate legislation and has been quashed, or declared invalid, by reason of incompatibility with a Convention right and the Minister proposes to proceed under paragraph 2(b) of Schedule 2.

[622]

(5) If the legislation is an Order in Council, the power conferred by subsection (2) or (3) is exercisable by Her Majesty in Council.

(6) In this section "legislation" does not include a Measure of the Church Assembly or of the General Synod of the Church of England.

(7) Schedule 2 makes further provision about remedial orders.

Other rights and proceedings

Safeguard for existing human rights

11.—(1) A person's reliance on a Convention right does not restrict—

(a) any other right or freedom conferred on him by or under any law having effect in any part of the United Kingdom; or

(b) his right to make any claim or bring any proceedings which he could make or bring apart from sections 7 to 9.

Freedom of expression

12.—(1) This section applies if a court is considering whether to grant any relief which, if granted, might affect the exercise of the Convention right to freedom of expression.

(2) If the person against whom the application for relief is made ("the respondent") is neither present nor represented, no such relief is to be granted unless the court is satisfied—

(a) that the applicant has taken all practicable steps to notify the respondent; or

(b) that there are compelling reasons why the respondent should not be notified.

(3) No such relief is to be granted so as to restrain publication before trial unless the court is satisfied that the applicant is likely to establish that publication should not be allowed.

(4) The court must have particular regard to the importance of the Convention right to freedom of expression and, where the proceedings relate to material which the respondent claims, or which appears to the court, to be journalistic, literary or artistic material (or to conduct connected with such material), to—

(a) the extent to which—

    (i) the material has, or is about to, become available to the public; or

    (ii) it is, or would be, in the public interest for the material to be published;

(b) any relevant privacy code.

(5) In this section—

"court" includes a tribunal; and

"relief" includes any remedy or order (other than in criminal proceedings).

Freedom of thought, conscience and religion

13.—(1) If a court's determination of any question arising under this Act might affect the exercise by a religious organisation (itself or its members collectively) of the Convention right to freedom of thought, conscience and religion, it must have particular regard to the importance of that right.

(2) In this section "court" includes a tribunal.

[623]

Derogations and reservations

Derogations

14.—(1) In this Act "designated derogation" means—

(a) the United Kingdom's derogation from Article 5(3) of the Convention; and

(b) any derogation by the United Kingdom from an Article of the Convention, or of any protocol to the Convention, which is designated for the purposes of this Act in an order made by the Secretary of State.

(2) The derogation referred to in subsection (1)(a) is set out in Part I of Schedule 3.

(3) If a designated derogation is amended or replaced it ceases to be a designated derogation.

(4) But subsection (3) does not prevent the Secretary of State from exercising his power under subsection (1)(b) to make a fresh designation order in respect of the Article concerned.

(5) The Secretary of State must by order make such amendments to Schedule 3 as he considers appropriate to reflect—

(a) any designation order; or

(b) the effect of subsection (3).

(6) A designation order may be made in anticipation of the making by the United Kingdom of a proposed derogation.

Reservations

15.—(1) In this Act "designated reservation" means—

(a) the United Kingdom's reservation to Article 2 of the First Protocol to the Convention; and

(b) any other reservation by the United Kingdom to an Article of the Convention, or of any protocol to the Convention, which is designated for the purposes of this Act in an order made by the Secretary of State.

(2) The text of the reservation referred to in subsection (1)(a) is set out in Part II of Schedule 3.

(3) If a designated reservation is withdrawn wholly or in part it ceases to be a designated reservation.

(4) But subsection (3) does not prevent the Secretary of State from exercising his power under subsection (1)(b) to make a fresh designation order in respect of the Article concerned.

(5) The Secretary of State must by order make such amendments to this Act as he considers appropriate to reflect—

(a) any designation order; or

(b) the effect of subsection (3).

Period for which designated derogations have effect

16.—(1) If it had not already been withdrawn by the United Kingdom, a designated derogation ceases to have effect for the purposes of this Act—

(a) in the case of the derogation referred to in section 14(1)(a), at the end of the period of five years beginning with the date on which section 1(2) came into force;

(b) in the case of any other derogation, at the end of the period of five years beginning with the date on which the order designating it was made.

(2) At any time before the period—

(a) fixed by subsection (1)(a) or (b), or

(b) extended by an order under this subsection,

comes to an end, the Secretary of State may by order extend it by a further period of five years.

(3) An order under section 14(1)(b) ceases to have effect at the end of the period for consideration, unless a resolution has been passed by each House approving the order.

(4) Subsection (3) does not affect—

(a) anything done in reliance on the order; or

(b) the power to make a fresh order under section 14(1)(b).

(5) In subsection (3) "period for consideration" means the period of forty days beginning with the day on which the order was made.

(6) In calculating the period for consideration, no account is to be taken of any time during which—

(a) Parliament is dissolved or prorogued; or

(b) both Houses are adjourned for more than four days.

(7) If a designated derogation is withdrawn by the United Kingdom, the Secretary of State must by order make such amendments to this Act as he considers are required to reflect that withdrawal.

Periodic review of designated reservations

17.—(1) The appropriate Minister must review the designated reservation referred to in section 15(1)(a)—

(a) before the end of the period of five years beginning with the date on which section 1(2) came into force; and

(b) if that designation is still in force, before the end of the period of five years beginning with the date on which the last report relating to it was laid under subsection (3).

(2) The appropriate Minister must review each of the other designated reservations (if any)—

(a) before the end of the period of five years beginning with the date on which the order designating the reservation first came into force; and

(b) if the designation is still in force, before the end of the period of five years beginning with the date on which the last report relating to it was laid under subsection (3).

(3) The Minister conducting a review under this section must prepare a report on the result of the review and lay a copy of it before each House of Parliament.

[625]

Judges of the European Court of Human Rights

Appointment to European Court of Human Rights

18.—(1) In this section "judicial office" means the office of—

(a) Lord Justice of Appeal, Justice of the High Court or Circuit judge, in England and Wales;

(b) judge of the Court of Session or sheriff, in Scotland;

(c) Lord Justice of Appeal, judge of the High Court or county court judge, in Northern Ireland.

(2) The holder of a judicial office may become a judge of the European Court of Human Rights ("the Court") without being required to relinquish his office.

(3) But he is not required to perform the duties of his judicial office while he is a judge of the Court.

(4) In respect of any period during which he is a judge of the Court—

(a) a Lord Justice of Appeal or Justice of the High Court is not to count as a judge of the relevant court for the purposes of section 2(1) or 4(1) of the Supreme Court Act 1981 (maximum number of judges) nor as a judge of the Supreme Court for the purposes of section 12(1) to (6) of that Act (salaries etc.);

(b) a judge of the Court of Session is not to count as a judge of that court for the purposes of section 1(1) of the Court of Session Act 1988 (maximum number of judges) or of section 9(1)(c) of the Administration of Justice Act 1973 ("the 1973 Act") (salaries etc.);

(c) a Lord Justice of Appeal or judge of the High Court in Northern Ireland is not to count as a judge of the relevant court for the purposes of section 2(1) or 3(1) of the Judicature (Northern Ireland) Act 1978 (maximum number of judges) nor as a judge of the Supreme Court of Northern Ireland for the purposes of section 9(1)(d) of the 1973 Act (salaries etc.);

(d) a Circuit judge is not to count as such for the purposes of section 18 of the Courts Act 1971 (salaries etc.);

(e) a sheriff is not to count as such for the purposes of section 14 of the Sheriff Courts (Scotland) Act 1907 (salaries etc.);

(f) a county court judge of Northern Ireland is not to count as such for the purposes of section 106 of the County Courts Act Northern Ireland) 1959 (salaries etc.).

(5) If a sheriff principal is appointed a judge of the Court, section 11(1) of the Sheriff Courts (Scotland) Act 1971 (temporary appointment of sheriff principal) applies, while he holds that appointment, as if his office is vacant.

(6) Schedule 4 makes provision about judicial pensions in relation to the holder of a judicial office who serves as a judge of the Court.

(7) The Lord Chancellor or the Secretary of State may by order make such transitional provision (including, in particular, provision for a temporary increase in the maximum number of judges) as he considers appropriate in relation to any holder of a judicial office who has completed his service as a judge of the Court.

[626]

Parliamentary procedure

Statements of compatibility

19.—(1) A Minister of the Crown in charge of a Bill in either House of Parliament must, before Second Reading of the Bill—

(a) make a statement to the effect that in his view the provisions of the Bill are compatible with the Convention rights ("a statement of compatibility"); or

(b) make a statement to the effect that although he is unable to make a statement of compatibility the government nevertheless wishes the House to proceed with the Bill.

(2) The statement must be in writing and be published in such manner as the Minister making it considers appropriate.

Supplemental

Orders etc. under this Act

20.—(1) Any power of a Minister of the Crown to make an order under this Act is exercisable by statutory instrument.

(2) The power of the Lord Chancellor or the Secretary of State to make rules (other than rules of court) under section 2(3) or 7(9) is exercisable by statutory instrument.

(3) Any statutory instrument made under section 14, 15 or 16(7) must be laid before Parliament.

(4) No order may be made by the Lord Chancellor or the Secretary of State under section 1(4), 7(11) or 16(2) unless a draft of the order has been laid before, and approved by, each House of Parliament.

(5) Any statutory instrument made under section 18(7) or Schedule 4, or to which subsection (2) applies, shall be subject to annulment in pursuance of a resolution of either House of Parliament.

(6) The power of a Northern Ireland department to make—

(a) rules under section 2(3)(c) or 7(9)(c), or

(b) an order under section 7(11),

is exercisable by statutory rule for the purposes of the Statutory Rules (Northern Ireland) Order 1979.

(7) Any rules made under section 2(3)(c) or 7(9)(c) shall be subject to negative resolution; and section 41(6) of the Interpretation Act (Northern Ireland) 1954 (meaning of "subject to negative resolution") shall apply as if the power to make the rules were conferred by an Act of the Northern Ireland Assembly.

(8) No order may be made by a Northern Ireland department under section 7(11) unless a draft of the order has been laid before, and approved by, the Northern Ireland Assembly.

Interpretation, etc.

21.—(1) In this Act—

"amend" includes repeal and apply (with or without modifications);

[627]

"the appropriate Minister" means the Minister of the Crown having charge of the appropriate authorised government department (within the meaning of the Crown Proceedings Act 1947);

"the Commission" means the European Commission of Human Rights;

"the Convention" means the Convention for the Protection of Human Rights and Fundamental Freedoms, agreed by the Council of Europe at Rome on 4th November 1950 as it has effect for the time being in relation to the United Kingdom;

"declaration of incompatibility" means a declaration under section 4;

"Minister of the Crown" has the same meaning as in the Ministers of the Crown Act 1975;

"Northern Ireland Minister" includes the First Minister and the deputy First Minister in Northern Ireland;

"primary legislation" means any—

(a) public general Act;
(b) local and personal Act;
(c) private Act;
(d) Measure of the Church Assembly;
(e) Measure of the General Synod of the Church of England;
(f) Order in Council—

    (i) made in exercise of Her Majesty's Royal Prerogative;
    (ii) made under section 38(1)(a) of the Northern Ireland Constitution Act 1973 or the corresponding provision of the Northern Ireland Act 1998; or
    (iii) amending an Act of a kind mentioned in paragraph (a), (b) or (c);

and includes an order or other instrument made under primary legislation (otherwise than by the National Assembly for Wales, a member of the Scottish Executive, a Northern Ireland Minister or a Northern Ireland department) to the extent to which it operates to bring one or more provisions of that legislation into force or amends any primary legislation;

"the First Protocol" means the protocol to the Convention agreed at Paris on 20th March 1952;

"the Sixth Protocol" means the protocol to the Convention agreed at Strasbourg on 28th April 1983;

"the Eleventh Protocol" means the protocol to the Convention (restructuring the control machinery established by the Convention) agreed at Strasbourg on 11th May 1994;

"remedial order" means an order under section 10;

"subordinate legislation" means any—

(a) Order in Council other than one—

    (i) made in exercise of Her Majesty's Royal Prerogative;
    (ii) made under section 38(1)(a) of the Northern Ireland Constitution Act 1973 or the corresponding provision of the Northern Ireland Act 1998; or
    (iii) amending an Act of a kind mentioned in the definition of primary legislation;

    (b) Act of the Scottish Parliament;

    (c) Act of the Parliament of Northern Ireland;

    (d) Measure of the Assembly established under section 1 of the Northern Ireland Assembly Act 1973;

    (e) Act of the Northern Ireland Assembly;

    (f) order, rules, regulations, scheme, warrant, byelaw or other instrument made under primary legislation (except to the extent to which it operates to bring one or more provisions of that legislation into force or amends any primary legislation);

    (g) order, rules, regulations, scheme, warrant, byelaw or other instrument made under legislation mentioned in paragraph (b), (c), (d) or (e) or made under an Order in Council applying only to Northern Ireland;

    (h) order, rules, regulations, scheme, warrant, byelaw or other instrument made by a member of the Scottish Executive, a Northern Ireland Minister or a Northern Ireland department in exercise of prerogative or other executive functions of Her Majesty which are exercisable by such a person on behalf of Her Majesty;

"transferred matters" has the same meaning as in the Northern Ireland Act 1998; and

"tribunal" means any tribunal in which legal proceedings may be brought.

(2) The references in paragraphs (b) and (c) of section 2(1) to Articles are to Articles of the Convention as they had effect immediately before the coming into force of the Eleventh Protocol.

(3) The reference in paragraph (d) of section 2(1) to Article 46 includes a reference to Articles 32 and 54 of the Convention as they had effect immediately before the coming into force of the Eleventh Protocol.

(4) The references in section 2(1) to a report or decision of the Commission or a decision of the Committee of Ministers include references to a report or decision made as provided by paragraphs 3, 4 and 6 of Article 5 of the Eleventh Protocol (transitional provisions).

(5) Any liability under the Army Act 1955, the Air Force Act 1955 or the Naval Discipline Act 1957 to suffer death for an offence is replaced by a liability to imprisonment for life or any less punishment authorised by those Acts; and those Acts shall accordingly have effect with the necessary modifications.

Short title, commencement, application and extent

22.—(1) This Act may be cited as the Human Rights Act 1998.

(2) Sections 18, 20 and 21(5) and this section come into force on the passing of this Act.

(3) The other provisions of this Act come into force on such day as the Secretary of State may by order appoint; and different days may be appointed for different purposes.

(4) Paragraph (b) of subsection (1) of section 7 applies to proceedings brought by or at the instigation of a public authority whenever the act in question took place; but otherwise that subsection does not apply to an act taking place before the coming into force of that section.

(5) This Act binds the Crown.

(6) This Act extends to Northern Ireland.

(7) Section 21(5), so far as it relates to any provision contained in the Army Act 1955, the Air Force Act 1955 or the Naval Discipline Act 1957, extends to any place to which that provision extends.

Schedules

SCHEDULE 1

THE ARTICLES

PART I

THE CONVENTION

RIGHTS AND FREEDOMS

Article 2

Right to Life
1. Everyone's right to life shall be protected by law. No one shall be deprived of his life intentionally save in the execution of a sentence of a court following his conviction of a crime for which this penalty is provided by law.
2. Deprivation of life shall not be regarded as inflicted in contravention of this Article when it results from the use of force which is no more than absolutely necessary:

   (a) in defence of any person from unlawful violence;

   (b) in order to effect a lawful arrest or to prevent the escape of a person lawfully detained;

   (c) in action lawfully taken for the purpose of quelling a riot or insurrection.

Article 3

Prohibition of Torture
No one shall be subjected to torture or to inhuman or degrading treatment or punishment.

Article 4

Prohibition of Slavery and Forced Labour
1. No one shall be held in slavery or servitude.
2. No one shall be required to perform forced or compulsory labour.
3. For the purpose of this Article the term "forced or compulsory labour" shall not include:

   (a) any work required to be done in the ordinary course of detention imposed according to the provisions of Article 5 of this Convention or during conditional release from such detention;

   (b) any service of a military character or, in case of conscientious objectors in countries where they are recognised, service exacted instead of compulsory military service;

   (c) any service exacted in case of an emergency or calamity threatening the life or well-being of the community;

   (d) any work or service which forms part of normal civic obligations.

Article 5

Right to Liberty and Security
1. Everyone has the right to liberty and security of person. No one shall be deprived of his liberty save in the following cases and in accordance with a procedure prescribed by law:

   (a) the lawful detention of a person after conviction by a competent court;

   (b) the lawful arrest or detention of a person for non-compliance with the lawful order of a court or in order to secure the fulfilment of any obligation prescribed by law;

   (c) the lawful arrest or detention of a person effected for the purpose of bringing him before the competent legal authority on reasonable suspicion of having committed an offence or when it is reasonably considered necessary to prevent his committing an offence or fleeing after having done so;

(d) the detention of a minor by lawful order for the purpose of educational supervision or his lawful detention for the purpose of bringing him before the competent legal authority;

(e) the lawful detention of persons for the prevention of the spreading of infectious diseases, of persons of unsound mind, alcoholics or drug addicts or vagrants;

(f) the lawful arrest or detention of a person to prevent his effecting an unauthorised entry into the country or of a person against whom action is being taken with a view to deportation or extradition.

2. Everyone who is arrested shall be informed promptly, in a language which he understands, of the reasons for his arrest and of any charge against him.

3. Everyone arrested or detained in accordance with the provisions of paragraph 1(c) of this Article shall be brought promptly before a judge or other officer authorised by law to exercise judicial power and shall be entitled to trial within a reasonable time or to release pending trial. Release may be conditioned by guarantees to appear for trial.

4. Everyone who is deprived of his liberty by arrest or detention shall be entitled to take proceedings by which the lawfulness of his detention shall be decided speedily by a court and his release ordered if the detention is not lawful.

5. Everyone who has been the victim of arrest or detention in contravention of the provisions of this Article shall have an enforceable right to compensation.

Article 6

Right to a Fair Trial

1. In the determination of his civil rights and obligations or of any criminal charge against him, everyone is entitled to a fair and public hearing within a reasonable time by an independent and impartial tribunal established by law. Judgment shall be pronounced publicly but the press and public may be excluded from all or part of the trial in the interest of morals, public order or national security in a democratic society, where the interests of juveniles or the protection of the private life of the parties so require, or to the extent strictly necessary in the opinion of the court in special circumstances where publicity would prejudice the interests of justice.

2. Everyone charged with a criminal offence shall be presumed innocent until proved guilty according to law.

3. Everyone charged with a criminal offence has the following minimum rights:

(a) to be informed promptly, in a language which he understands and in detail, of the nature and cause of the accusation against him;

(b) to have adequate time and facilities for the preparation of his defence;

(c) to defend himself in person or through legal assistance of his own choosing or, if he has not sufficient means to pay for legal assistance, to be given it free when the interests of justice so require;

(d) to examine or have examined witnesses against him and to obtain the attendance and examination of witnesses on his behalf under the same conditions as witnesses against him;

(e) to have the free assistance of an interpreter if he cannot understand or speak the language used in court.

Article 7

No Punishment without Law

1. No one shall be held guilty of any criminal offence on account of any act or omission which did not constitute a criminal offence under national or international law at the time when it was committed. Nor shall a heavier penalty be imposed than the one that was applicable at the time the criminal offence was committed.

2. This Article shall not prejudice the trial and punishment of any person for any act or omission which, at the time when it was committed, was criminal according to the general principles of law recognised by civilised nations.

Article 8

Right to Respect for Private and Family Life

1. Everyone has the right to respect for his private and family life, his home and his correspondence.

[631]

2. There shall be no interference by a public authority with the exercise of this right except such as is in accordance with the law and is necessary in a democratic society in the interests of national security, public safety or the economic well-being of the country, for the prevention of disorder or crime, for the protection of health or morals, or for the protection of the rights and freedoms of others.

Article 9

Freedom of Thought, Conscience and Religion

1. Everyone has the right to freedom of thought, conscience and religion; this right includes freedom to change his religion or belief and freedom, either alone or in community with others and in public and private, to manifest his religion or belief, in worship, teaching, practice and observance.

2. Freedom to manifest one's religion or beliefs shall be subject only to such limitations as are prescribed by law and are necessary in a democratic society in the interests of public safety, for the protection of public order, health or morals, or for the protection of the rights and freedoms of others.

Article 10

Freedom of Expression

1. Everyone has the right to freedom of expression. This right shall include freedom to hold opinions and to receive and impart information and ideas without interference by public authority and regardless of frontiers. This Article shall not prevent States from requiring the licensing of broadcasting, television or cinema enterprises.

2. The exercise of these freedoms, since it carries with it duties and responsibilities, may be subject to such formalities, conditions, restrictions or penalties as are prescribed by law and are necessary in a democratic society, in the interests of national security, territorial integrity or public safety, for the prevention of disorder or crime, for the protection of health or morals, for the protection of the reputation or rights of others, for preventing the disclosure of information received in confidence, or for maintaining the authority and impartiality of the judiciary.

Article 11

Freedom of Assembly and Association

1. Everyone has the right to freedom of peaceful assembly and to freedom of association with others, including the right to form and to join trade unions for the protection of his interests.

2. No restrictions shall be placed on the exercise of these rights other than such as are prescribed by law and are necessary in a democratic society in the interests of national security or public safety, for the prevention of disorder or crime, for the protection of health or morals or for the protection of the rights and freedoms of others. This Article shall not prevent the imposition of lawful restrictions on the exercise of these rights by members of the armed forces, of the police or of the administration of the State.

Article 12

Right to Marry

Men and women of marriageable age have the right to marry and to found a family, according to the national laws governing the exercise of this right.

Article 14

Prohibition of Discrimination

The enjoyment of the rights and freedoms set forth in this Convention shall be secured without discrimination on any ground such as sex, race, colour, language, religion, political or other opinion, national or social origin, association with a national minority, property, birth or other status.

Article 16

Restrictions on Political Activity of Aliens

Nothing in Articles 10, 11 and 14 shall be regarded as preventing the High Contracting Parties from imposing restrictions on the political activity of aliens.

Article 17

Prohibition of Abuse of Rights
Nothing in this Convention may be interpreted as implying for any State, group or person any right to engage in any activity or perform any act aimed at the destruction of any of the rights and freedoms set forth herein or at their limitation to a greater extent than is provided for in the Convention.

Article 18

Limitation on Use of Restrictions on Rights
The restrictions permitted under this Convention to the said rights and freedoms shall not be applied for any purpose other than those for which they have been prescribed.

PART II

THE FIRST PROTOCOL

Article 1

Protection of Property
Every natural or legal person is entitled to the peaceful enjoyment of his possessions. No one shall be deprived of his possessions except in the public interest and subject to the conditions provided for by law and by the general principles of international law.
The preceding provisions shall not, however, in any way impair the right of a State to enforce such laws as it deems necessary to control the use of property in accordance with the general interest or to secure the payment of taxes or other contributions or penalties.

Article 2

Right to Education
No person shall be denied the right to education. In the exercise of any functions which it assumes in relation to education and to teaching, the State shall respect the right of parents to ensure such education and teaching in conformity with their own religious and philosophical convictions.

Article 3

Right to Free Elections
The High Contracting Parties undertake to hold free elections at reasonable intervals by secret ballot, under conditions which will ensure the free expression of the opinion of the people in the choice of the legislature.

PART III

THE SIXTH PROTOCOL

Article 1

Abolition of the Death Penalty
The death penalty shall be abolished. No one shall be condemned to such penalty or executed.

Article 2

Death Penalty in Time of War
A State may make provision in its law for the death penalty in respect of acts committed in time of war or of imminent threat of war; such penalty shall be applied only in the instances laid down in the law and in accordance with its provisions. The State shall communicate to the Secretary General of the Council of Europe the relevant provisions of that law.

SCHEDULE 2

REMEDIAL ORDERS

Orders
1.—(1) A remedial order may—

    (a) contain such incidental, supplemental, consequential or transitional provision as the person making it considers appropriate;

[633]

(b) be made so as to have effect from a date earlier than that on which it is made;

(c) make provision for the delegation of specific functions;

(d) make different provision for different cases.

(2) The power conferred by sub-paragraph (1)(a) includes—

(a) power to amend primary legislation (including primary legislation other than that which contains the incompatible provision); and

(b) power to amend or revoke subordinate legislation (including subordinate legislation other than that which contains the incompatible provision).

(3) A remedial order may be made so as to have the same extent as the legislation which it affects.

(4) No person is to be guilty of an offence solely as a result of the retrospective effect of a remedial order.

Procedure

2. No remedial order may be made unless—

(a) a draft of the order has been approved by a resolution of each House of Parliament made after the end of the period of 60 days beginning with the day on which the draft was laid; or

(b) it is declared in the order that it appears to the person making it that, because of the urgency of the matter, it is necessary to make the order without a draft being so approved.

Orders laid in draft

3.—(1) No draft may be laid under paragraph 2(a) unless—

(a) the person proposing to make the order has laid before Parliament a document which contains a draft of the proposed order and the required information; and

(b) the period of 60 days, beginning with the day on which the document required by this sub-paragraph was laid, has ended.

(2) If representations have been made during that period, the draft laid under paragraph 2(a) must be accompanied by a statement containing—

(a) a summary of the representations; and

(b) if, as a result of the representations, the proposed order has been changed, details of the changes.

Urgent cases

4.—(1) If a remedial order ("the original order") is made without being approved in draft, the person making it must lay it before Parliament, accompanied by the required information, after it is made.

(2) If representations have been made during the period of 60 days beginning with the day on which the original order was made, the person making it must (after the end of that period) lay before Parliament a statement containing—

(a) a summary of the representations; and

(b) if, as a result of the representations, he considers it appropriate to make changes to the original order, details of the changes.

(3) If sub-paragraph (2)(b) applies, the person making the statement must—

(a) make a further remedial order replacing the original order; and

(b) lay the replacement order before Parliament.

(4) If, at the end of the period of 120 days beginning with the day on which the original order was made, a resolution has not been passed by each House approving the original or replacement order, the order ceases to have effect (but without that affecting anything previously done under either order or the power to make a fresh remedial order).

Definitions
5. In this Schedule—

"representations" means representations about a remedial order (or proposed remedial order) made to the person making (or proposing to make) it and includes any relevant Parliamentary report or resolution; and

"required information" means—

    (a) an explanation of the incompatibility which the order (or proposed order) seeks to remove, including particulars of the relevant declaration, finding or order; and

    (b) a statement of the reasons for proceeding under section 10 and for making an order in those terms.

Calculating periods
6. In calculating any period for the purposes of this Schedule, no account is to be taken of any time during which—

    (a) Parliament is dissolved or prorogued; or

    (b) both Houses are adjourned for more than four days.

SCHEDULE 3

Derogation and Reservation

Part I

Derogation

The 1988 notification

The United Kingdom Permanent Representative to the Council of Europe presents his compliments to the Secretary General of the Council, and has the honour to convey the following information in order to ensure compliance with the obligations of Her Majesty's Government in the United Kingdom under Article 15(3) of the Convention for the Protection of Human Rights and Fundamental Freedoms signed at Rome on 4 November 1950.

There have been in the United Kingdom in recent years campaigns of organised terrorism connected with the affairs of Northern Ireland which have manifested themselves in activities which have included repeated murder, attempted murder, maiming, intimidation and violent civil disturbance and in bombing and fire raising which have resulted in death, injury and widespread destruction of property. As a result, a public emergency within the meaning of Article 15(1) of the Convention exists in the United Kingdom.

The Government found it necessary in 1974 to introduce and since then, in cases concerning persons reasonably suspected of involvement in terrorism connected with the affairs of Northern Ireland, or of certain offences under the legislation, who have been detained for 48 hours, to exercise powers enabling further detention without charge, for periods of up to five days, on the authority of the Secretary of State. These powers are at present to be found in Section 12 of the Prevention of Terrorism (Temporary Provisions) Act 1984, Article 9 of the Prevention of Terrorism (Supplemental Temporary Provisions) Order 1984 and Article 10 of the Prevention of Terrorism (Supplemental Temporary Provisions) (Northern Ireland) Order 1984.

Section 12 of the Prevention of Terrorism (Temporary Provisions) Act 1984 provides for a person whom a constable has arrested on reasonable grounds of suspecting him to be guilty of an offence under Section 1, 9 or 10 of the Act, or to be or to have been involved in terrorism connected with the affairs of Northern Ireland, to be detained in right of the arrest for up to 48 hours and thereafter, where the Secretary of State extends the detention period, for up to a further five days. Section 12 substantially re-enacted Section 12 of the Prevention of Terrorism (Temporary Provisions) Act 1976 which, in turn, substantially re-enacted Section 7 of the Prevention of Terrorism (Temporary Provisions) Act 1974.

Article 10 of the Prevention of Terrorism (Supplemental Temporary Provisions) (Northern Ireland) Order 1984 (SI 1984/417) and Article 9 of the Prevention of Terrorism (Supplemental Temporary Provisions) Order 1984 (SI 1984/418) were both made under Sections 13 and 14 of and Schedule 3 to the 1984 Act and substantially re-enacted powers of detention in Orders made under the 1974 and 1976 Acts. A person who is being examined under Article 4 of either Order on his arrival in, or on seeking to leave, Northern Ireland or Great Britain for the purpose of determining whether he is or has been involved in terrorism connected with the affairs of Northern Ireland, or whether there are grounds for suspecting that he has committed an offence under Section 9 of the 1984 Act, may be detained under Article 9 or 10, as appropriate, pending the conclusion of his examination. The period of this examination may exceed 12 hours if an examining officer has reasonable grounds for suspecting him to be or to have been involved in acts of terrorism connected with the affairs of Northern Ireland.

Where such a person is detained under the said Article 9 or 10 he may be detained for up to 48 hours on the authority of an examining officer and thereafter, where the Secretary of State extends the detention period, for up to a further five days.

In its judgment of 29 November 1988 in the Case of *Brogan and Others*, the European Court of Human Rights held that there had been a violation of Article 5(3) in respect of each of the applicants, all of whom had been detained under Section 12 of the 1984 Act. The Court held that even the shortest of the four periods of detention concerned, namely four days and six hours, fell outside the constraints as to time permitted by the first part of Article 5(3). In addition, the Court held that there had been a violation of Article 5(5) in the case of each applicant.

Following this judgment, the Secretary of State for the Home Department informed Parliament on 6 December 1988 that, against the background of the terrorist campaign, and the over-riding need to bring terrorists to justice, the Government did not believe that the maximum period of detention should be reduced. He informed Parliament that the Government were examining the matter with a view to responding to the judgment. On 22 December 1988, the Secretary of State further informed Parliament that it remained the Government's wish, if it could be achieved, to find a judicial process under which extended detention might be reviewed and where appropriate authorised by a judge or other judicial officer. But a further period of reflection and consultation was necessary before the Government could bring forward a firm and final view.

Since the judgment of 29 November 1988 as well as previously, the Government have found it necessary to continue to exercise, in relation to terrorism connected with the affairs of Northern Ireland, the powers described above enabling further detention without charge for periods of up to 5 days, on the authority of the Secretary of State, to the extent strictly required by the exigencies of the situation to enable necessary enquiries and investigations properly to be completed in order to decide whether criminal proceedings should be instituted. To the extent that the exercise of these powers may be inconsistent with the obligations imposed by the Convention the Government has availed itself of the right of derogation conferred by Article 15(1) of the Convention and will continue to do so until further notice.

Dated 23 December 1988.

The 1989 notification

The United Kingdom Permanent Representative to the Council of Europe presents his compliments to the Secretary General of the Council, and has the honour to convey the following information.

In his communication to the Secretary General of 23 December 1988, reference was made to the introduction and exercise of certain powers under section 12 of the Prevention of Terrorism (Temporary Provisions) Act 1984, Article 9 of the Prevention of Terrorism (Supplemental Temporary Provisions) Order 1984 and Article 10 of the Prevention of Terrorism (Supplemental Temporary Provisions) (Northern Ireland) Order 1984.

These provisions have been replaced by section 14 of and paragraph 6 of Schedule 5 to the Prevention of Terrorism (Temporary Provisions) Act 1989, which make comparable provision. They came into force on 22 March 1989. A copy of these provisions is enclosed.

The United Kingdom Permanent Representative avails himself of this opportunity to renew to the Secretary General the assurance of his highest consideration.

23 March 1989.

PART II

RESERVATION

At the time of signing the present (First) Protocol, I declare that, in view of certain provisions of the Education Acts in the United Kingdom, the principle affirmed in the second sentence of Article 2 is accepted by the United Kingdom only so far as it is compatible with the provision of efficient instruction and training, and the avoidance of unreasonable public expenditure.

Dated 20 March 1952

Made by the United Kingdom Permanent Representative to the Council of Europe.

SCHEDULE 4

JUDICIAL PENSIONS

Duty to make orders about pensions

1.—(1) The appropriate Minister must by order make provision with respect to pensions payable to or in respect of any holder of a judicial office who serves as an ECHR judge.

(2) A pensions order must include such provision as the Minister making it considers is necessary to secure that—

(a) an ECHR judge who was, immediately before his appointment as an ECHR judge, a member of a judicial pension scheme is entitled to remain as a member of that scheme;

(b) the terms on which he remains a member of the scheme are those which would have been applicable had he not been appointed as an ECHR judge; and

(c) entitlement to benefits payable in accordance with the scheme continues to be determined as if, while serving as an ECHR judge, his salary was that which would (but for section 18(4)) have been payable to him in respect of his continuing service as the holder of his judicial office.

Contributions

2. A pensions order may, in particular, make provision—

(a) for any contributions which are payable by a person who remains a member of a scheme as a result of the order, and which would otherwise be payable by deduction from his salary, to be made otherwise than by deduction from his salary as an ECHR judge; and

(b) for such contributions to be collected in such manner as may be determined by the administrators of the scheme.

Amendments of other enactments

3. A pensions order may amend any provision of, or made under, a pensions Act in such manner and to such extent as the Minister making the order considers necessary or expedient to ensure the proper administration of any scheme to which it relates.

Definitions

4. In this Schedule—

"appropriate Minister" means—

(a) in relation to any judicial office whose jurisdiction is exercisable exclusively in relation to Scotland, the Secretary of State; and

(b) otherwise, the Lord Chancellor;

"ECHR judge" means the holder of a judicial office who is serving as a judge of the Court;

"judicial pension scheme" means a scheme established by and in accordance with a pensions Act;

"pensions Act" means—

(a) the County Courts Act (Northern Ireland) 1959;

(b) the Sheriffs' Pensions (Scotland) Act 1961;

(c) the Judicial Pensions Act 1981; or

(d) the Judicial Pensions and Retirement Act 1993; and

"pensions order" means an order made under paragraph 1.

The Criminal Appeal (Amendment) Rules 2000

S.I. 2000 No. 2036

Made	*25th July 2000*
Laid before Parliament	*27th July 2000*
Coming into force	*2nd October 2000*

We, the Crown Court Rule Committee, in exercise of the powers conferred on us by sections 84(1), 84(2) and 86 of the Supreme Court Act 1981 and section 5 of the Human Rights Act 1998, hereby makes the following Rules:

Citation and commencement

1. These Rules may be cited as the Criminal Appeal (Amendment) Rules 2000 and shall come into force on 2nd October 2000.

Amendment of Criminal Appeal Rules 1968

2. The Criminal Appeal Rules 1968 shall be amended as follows—

(a) in rule 2, after paragraph (2)(a) there shall be inserted—

"(aa) A notice of the grounds of appeal or application set out in Form 3 shall include notice—

(i) of any application to be made to the court for a declaration of incompatibility under section 4 of the Human Rights Act 1998; or

(ii) of any issue for the court to decide which may lead to the court making such a declaration.

(ab) Where the grounds of appeal or application include notice in accordance with paragraph (aa) above, a copy of the notice shall be served on the prosecutor by the appellant".

(b) after rule 14 there shall be inserted—

"Human Rights Act

14A.—(1) The court shall not consider making a declaration of incompatibility under section 4 of the Human Rights Act 1998 unless it has given written notice to the Crown.

(2) Where notice has been given to the Crown, a Minister, or other person entitled under the Human Rights Act 1998 to be joined as a party, shall be so joined on giving written notice to the court.

(3) A notice given under paragraph (1) above shall be given to—

(a) the person named in the list published under section 17(1) of the Crown Proceedings Act 1947; or

(b) in the case of doubt as to whether any and if so which of those departments is appropriate, the Treasury Solicitor.

(4) A notice given under paragraph (1) above, shall provide an outline of the issues in the case and specify—

(a) the prosecutor and appellant;

(b) the date, judge and court of the trial in the proceedings from which the appeal lies;

(c) the provision of primary legislation and the Convention right under question.

(5) Any consideration of whether a declaration of incompatibility should be made, shall be adjourned for—

(a) 21 days from the date of the notice given under paragraph (1) above; or

(b) such other period (specified in the notice), as the court shall allow in order that the relevant Minister or other person, may seek to be joined and prepare his case.

(6) Unless the court otherwise directs, the Minister or other person entitled under the Human Rights Act 1998 to be joined as a party shall, if he is to be joined, give written notice to the court and every other party.

(7) Where a Minister of the Crown has nominated a person to be joined as a party by virtue of section 5(2)(a) of the Human Rights Act 1998, a notice under paragraph (6) above shall be accompanied by a written nomination signed by or on behalf of the Minister."

(c) in rule 15 after paragraph (1)(d) there shall be inserted—

"(e) in the case of a declaration of incompatibility under section 4 of the Human Rights Act 1998, the declaration shall be served on—

(i) all of the parties to the proceedings; and
(ii) where a Minister of the Crown has not been joined as a party, the Crown (in accordance with rule 14A(3) above)."

Irvine of Lairg,
C.

Harry Woolf,
C.J.

L. Dickinson

Charles Harris

Master Mckenzie

Dated 25th July 2000

INDEX

Learning Resources
Centre